Special Edition

USING MICROSOFT®
WORD® 97

Special Edition

USING MICROSOFT®
WORD® 97

Written by Ron Person and Karen Rose

Special Edition Using Microsoft Word 97

Library of Congress Catalog No.: 96-70787

ISBN: 0-7897-0962-7

99 98 97   6 5 4 3 2 1

Interpretation of the printing code: the rightmost double-digit number is the year of the book's printing; the rightmost single-digit number, the number of the book's printing. For example, a printing code of 97-1 shows that the first printing of the book occurred in 1997.

Screen reproductions in this book were created using Collage Plus from Inner Media, Inc., Hollis, NH.

Credits

PRESIDENT
Roland Elgey

PUBLISHING DIRECTOR
David W. Solomon

EDITORIAL SERVICES DIRECTOR
Elizabeth Keaffaber

MANAGING EDITOR
Michael Cunningham

DIRECTOR OF MARKETING
Lynn E. Zingraf

TITLE MANAGER
Kathie-Jo Arnoff

ACQUISITIONS MANAGER
Elizabeth A. South

SENIOR PRODUCT DIRECTOR
Lisa D. Wagner

PRODUCT DEVELOPMENT SPECIALISTS
Bill Camarda
Dana S. Coe
Robin Drake
Carolyn Kiefer
Jan Snyder

PRODUCTION EDITORS
Rebecca M. Mounts
Thomas Hayes

EDITORS
Kate Givens
Sarah Rudy
Brian Sweany
June Waldmon
Nicholas Zafran

STRATEGIC MARKETING MANAGER
Barry Pruett

PRODUCT MARKETING MANAGER
Kris Ankney

ASSISTANT PRODUCT MARKETING MANAGERS
Karen Hagen
Christy M. Miller

TECHNICAL EDITORS
Rick Brown
Tony Schafer
Robert Hartley

MEDIA DEVELOPMENT SPECIALIST
David Garratt

TECHNICAL SPECIALIST
Nadeem Muhammed

ACQUISITIONS COORDINATOR
Tracy M. Williams

OPERATIONS COORDINATORS
Patty Brooks
Susan Gallagher

EDITORIAL ASSISTANT
Virginia Stoller

BOOK DESIGNER
Ruth Harvey

COVER DESIGNER
Dan Armstrong

PRODUCTION TEAM
Marcia Brizendine
Julie Geeting
Kay Hoskins
Tony McDonald
Nicole Ruessler
Julie Searls
Lisa Stumpf

INDEXER
Craig A. Small

Composed in *Century Old Style* and *Franklin Gothic* by Que Corporation.

About the Authors

Ron Person has written more than 20 books for Que Corporation, including the best-seller *Special Edition Using Microsoft Excel 97*. He was lead author for the best-sellers *Special Edition Using Windows 95* and *Platinum Edition Using Windows 95*. He has an M.S. in physics from The Ohio State University and an M.B.A. from Hardin-Simmons University. Ron was one of Microsoft's original Consulting Partners and Microsoft Solutions Partners. Ron Person & Co. creates and delivers online support and training materials for Microsoft applications. You can reach Ron and sample a variety of free and licensed training materials at **http://www.ronperson.com/**.

Karen Rose has written six books for Que Corporation, including *Using Microsoft Windows 3*, 2nd Edition and *Using Word for Windows 95*. Karen has taught for the University of California, Berkeley Extension, and Sonoma State University. Karen is the owner and publisher of *Little Red Book Press*, publishers of hand-bound books.

Acknowledgments

The expertise, knowledge, and production skills that go into a book like *Special Edition Using Microsoft Word 97* requires teams of talented people. A book of this size and detail can be updated only through conscientious and dedicated work from each person. To meet incredibly short deadlines, while covering Word in the depth it deserves, everyone missed weekends and worked long hours—and in some cases, all night. Thank you for your work and skill.

Que, the world's largest publisher of computer books, continues to stay ahead of the competition through the energy and skills of its people. We appreciate their grace and humor while under incredible time and quality pressure.

David Solomon, Elizabeth South, Kathie-Jo Arnoff, Rebecca Mounts, Tom Hayes, Lisa Wagner, Bill Camarda, and all the editors did a very smooth job on what, to my knowledge, has been the fastest turnaround ever of a pair of large books. The development and editing teams worked the long hours necessary to get this book through development and editing. Their contributions and long hours give the book that distinctive Que style.

Special thanks go to the software consultants, professional writers, and technical editors who helped revise *Special Edition Using Microsoft Word 97*. Their expertise and long hours of work revised this book so it would be available when Word 97 for Windows was released. However, the responsibility for errors that may have slipped through their knowledgeable watch lies solely with me. Should you find an error, please check for corrections or report book errata at the Ron Person & Co. World Wide Web site listed at the end of these acknowledgments.

I truly appreciate the long hours, overlapped schedules, and missed time with families that it took to meet these tough deadlines. My thanks to the following experts:

Carlos Quiroga made significant contributions throughout this book. He updated many chapters including those on tables, outlining, and mail merge. Carlos is the owner of Pacific Technical Documentation, a high-technology writing firm in Windsor, California. Pacific Technical Documentation has considerable experience producing customized written documentation, online help, and training systems for high-technology software, products, and services. Pacific Technical Documentation can be reached at 707-838-0918.

Elaine Marmel made room in her full schedule to do an excellent job of updating styles, columns, and page layout. Elaine has written numerous books for Que, including *Word for Windows 2 QuickStart* and *Easy Excel for Windows 95*, and was lead author for *Using SmartSuite 97, Special Edition*. Elaine is an independent technical writer in Tampa, FL. She lives in Florida, but rarely sees the sun because she works too much. She does, however, have a hobby: She sings barbershop harmony with the Toast of Tampa, 1994 International Chorus Champions of Sweet Adelines International.

Dina Pavlis put her in-depth knowledge of users to work when she updated the chapters on customizing Word and customizing menus and toolbars. Dina is an Information Systems Analyst for the Seattle law firm Perkins Coie and has worked with Word for Windows since its first beta release in 1989. Originally the training administrator for Perkins Coie, Dina is now a software developer for the firm, designing and developing applications that work hand-in-hand with Word. In addition to writing for and publishing several local Word for Windows and Windows-related newsletters, Dina has traveled around the globe to provide training and demonstrations and to speak at conferences. Dina can often be found answering questions in the Word forum on CompuServe (GO MSWORD), where she volunteers as a CompuServe Support Partner (CSP). In her spare time, Dina likes to write poetry and short stories, volunteer for nonprofit, people-oriented charities and service organizations, and take her dogs hiking. She's also an avid Australian Rules Football fan. Dina can be reached via e-mail at **71154.3165@compuserve.com**.

Pamela Palmer did a very precise job of writing about the new drawing tools and WordArt. Pamela is an independent consultant who has been working with computers for 13 years. She has contributed to Que's *Using Visual Basic 3* and is a Microsoft Certified Instructor for Visual Basic. She develops applications using Visual Basic, Visual Basic for Applications, and Word Basic, as well as delivering training and writing books and training documentation. She can be reached on CompuServe at **74170,1526**.

Sharon Podlin put her extensive knowledge to work writing a new chapter on Visual Basic for Applications. Sharon is a graduate of the University of Texas and is president of PTSI, a consulting firm specializing in the development and presentation of computer training courses. Sharon has over 15 years in the industry and has primarily worked with Fortune 100 companies including J. C. Penney, Hyatt International Hotels, and United Airlines. She actively participates in the Microsoft Certified Professional program as well as being a Microsoft Certified Trainer for a wide range of products including Microsoft SQL Server, Excel, Visual Basic for Applications, and Windows NT. She can be reached via CompuServe at **76350,1424**.

Lorry Laby contributed her experience as a Word trainer and technical writer to a number of chapters. Lorry has considerable experience as a software trainer and technical writer. Lorry teaches Word for Windows at Santa Rosa Junior College and trains municipal governments and businesses in Northern California in Word for Windows and WordPerfect.

Bob Voss, Ph. D., updated the chapter on using Word with Office applications. He has made significant contribution to the best-selling book, *Special Edition Using Microsoft Excel 97*. Bob is an independent technical writer and Microsoft Office trainer in San Rafael, California. He can be reached via CompuServe at **71630,3337**.

Visit our World Wide Web site for free tips and training on Microsoft Office

The Ron Person & Co. Web site is a community of data and people supporting Microsoft Office users. It contains free software, tips, and training to help you work better with Windows and Microsoft Office. At our Web site, you will find:

Free help files and demonstrations
Free data files used in book chapters
Free add-in software
Corporate online help systems
Courseware and training modules
Sample chapters from our books
Error corrections to our books
Profiles of book contributors
Online book ordering information
Bibliographies of recommended books
Links to major business research sites
Links to major computer and software support sites

Visit our community of Office users and consultants at:

http://www.ronperson.com

We'd Like to Hear from You!

As part of our continuing effort to produce books of the highest possible quality, Que would like to hear your comments. To stay competitive, we *really* want you, as a computer book reader and user, to let us know what you like or dislike most about this book or other Que products.

You can mail comments, ideas, or suggestions for improving future editions to the address below, or send us a fax at (317) 581-4663. For the online inclined, Macmillan Computer Publishing has a forum on CompuServe (type **GO QUEBOOKS** at any prompt) through which our staff and authors are available for questions and comments. The address of our Internet site is **http://www.mcp.com** (World Wide Web).

In addition to exploring our forum, please feel free to contact me personally to discuss your opinions of this book: I'm **74404,3307** on CompuServe and **lwagner@que. mcp.com** on the Internet.

Thanks in advance—your comments will help us to continue publishing the best books available on computer topics in today's market.

Lisa Wagner
Product Development Specialist
Que Corporation
201 W. 103rd Street
Indianapolis, Indiana 46290
USA

Contents at a Glance

Table of Contents

5   Editing a Document   131

III | Web Publishing

IV | Creating Envelopes and Mailings

V | **Mastering Special Features**

VII | Handling Large Documents

Introduction

Each new edition of Microsoft Word is easier to use.
Microsoft Word 97 is even easier to use than Word for
Windows 95, and its menus and toolbars are even more
compatible with the menus and toolbars of other applications in the Microsoft Office suite. More importantly,
Word 97 can now help you work with others in your
workplace and can communicate over corporate
intranets and the Internet.

This new capability to work in groups, work over the
Internet, and gather information could change the
nature of how we learn, how we work, and how companies are structured. The printing press was a catalyst
of the same magnitude. The break-away from a domi-
nating church, the development of independent and
scientific thought, and the rise of new constructs in
philosophy are all linked by historians and philoso-
phers to the explosion of information brought about by
the printing press. The changes we see over the next
decade may be as significant. Word 97 is designed to
help you ride this wave of change. It can even help you
write a better letter. ■

Why You Should Use this Book

 Word 97 is an important upgrade from Word 95. In addition to the important inclusion of Web browsing and publishing, Word has again become easier to use. Throughout the book, new features specific to Word 97 are marked by a New Feature icon (shown at the right of this paragraph). If you used Word before, watch for these icons so that you can quickly learn about new features. If you used a previous version of Word, you should read Chapter 1, "Word Processing Power in Word 97." It catalogs the major new features in Word 97.

If you're an experienced user of Word, this book gives you quick access to new features—both in Chapter 1, where we summarize new features, and throughout the book, with New Feature icons to help you see what's new at a glance. If you're new to Word, or if you're moving to Word 97 from an older version, this is a complete guide to using Word 97 efficiently and productively. The authors and contributors are experts in Microsoft Word and other applications in the Microsoft Office suite. They have added their tips, tricks, and troubleshooting to help you get more out of Word 97.

Why You Should Use Word

Many reasons exist for choosing Word as your word processor, including its wide array of features, accessibility, power, and capability to exchange data and graphics with other Windows applications. If you're standardizing on a word processor, Word is the preferred choice. For those of you already using one or more word processors, Word can increase productivity and decrease support costs.

Word Has Accessible Power

Word is the industry's most powerful word processor, but it also has features that make it the easiest to use and the easiest for which to get help.

Most people do not need or use advanced word processing features regularly. On most days, you want a convenient word processor that doesn't get in the way. Word toolbars, shortcut menus, and excellent online help make it one of the easiest word processors to learn. You can also customize the screen display and menus to make the program even more straightforward and easy to use. Although Word's advanced features don't get in the way, they are there to handle any type of specialized work you need, such as drawing on a document, outlining, importing, or linking to mainframe database, desktop publishing, and much more.

Even if you use a feature only occasionally, Word makes it easy to learn or remember the feature. The toolbars shown in Figure I.1, for example, enable you to click a button to choose the most frequently used commands, such as opening or saving files, inserting bulleted lists, making tables or columns, or formatting for bold with centered alignment. You can even customize the toolbar to fit your needs by adding or removing buttons for specialized commands.

FIG. I.1
Select text and click buttons on toolbars to execute many commands.

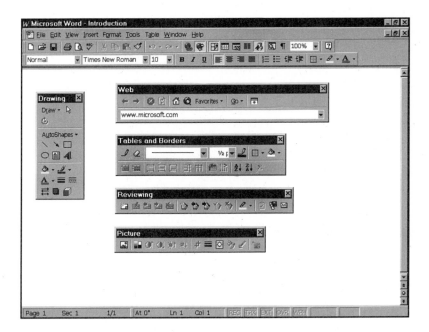

Word Works in the Windows 95 Environment

If you know any other Windows 95 application, you already know how to use Word menus and commands, choose from dialog boxes, use the Help window, and operate document windows. Another advantage of Windows is that you can easily transfer data between applications, embed graphics or text in a Word document, or link graphics or text between applications. Figure I.2 shows a Word 97 document linked to Microsoft Excel 97 charts and tables. You can easily switch between the two applications.

Word 97 is well integrated with the other applications in the Office 97 suite. For example, you can embed charts, graphics, worksheet ranges, or other objects in a Word document. When you activate those objects, Word's menus and toolbars change to the menus and toolbars necessary to edit or format the object.

FIG. 1.2

You can paste, link, or embed data from other Windows applications so that your word processor gives you the capability to integrate data from many different sources.

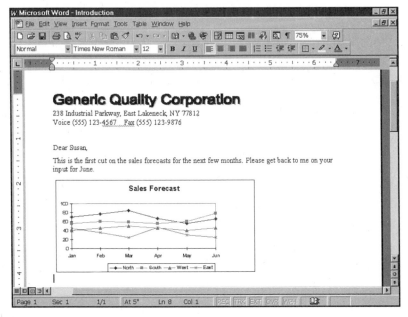

Word Helps You Work in Groups

Word makes it easier. Tracking all the changes and revisions that occur in group projects can be tough, but with Word's change tracking and comments features and the Reviewing toolbar, it is much easier to integrate ideas from your entire workgroup.

Word Publishes and Browses the Internet

Nowadays, the Internet and corporate intranets are concepts that are hard to avoid. They represent an entirely new way to publish and access information. With Word 97, instead of having to exit what you are doing to go to a browser and get on the Web, you can browse through linked Office documents or the World Wide Web right from within Word.

Word 97 also includes new Web authoring tools. You can insert simple hyperlinks into Word documents that enable you to jump between Office documents with a click—or you can use the full power of the authoring tools and create your own Web pages. You can use them as your own startup pages for your browser—or create your own Web pages for publishing on the World Wide Web.

Word Shows You Results

Word enables you to zoom from a 25 to 500 percent view of your document. If you are using the new Microsoft IntelliPoint mouse, you can zoom in or out of your document with the mouse wheel, located between the two mouse buttons. You can edit and format text or move framed objects while you are in any zoomed view. If you are using TrueType fonts, you are guaranteed to see what will print. Word has the features necessary to do most desktop publishing. Figure I.3 shows a document zoomed out to show an entire page.

FIG. I.3
Word has the desktop publishing capabilities to satisfy most business and personal needs.

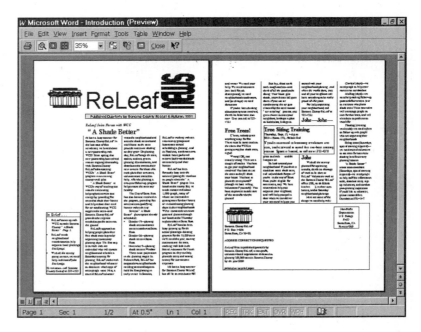

Word Reduces the Need for Technical Support

Word 97 contains the Office Assistant, an intelligent guide that monitors your work and proposes help when appropriate. There are many different personalities for Office Assistant, so make sure you find one that you like. In addition to the Office Assistant, Word has extensive help files you can use to get an overview of a procedure. To go immediately to a step-by-step guide or to use key words to search for help, choose the Help, Contents and Index command.

Word Helps WordPerfect Users

If you're moving to Word from WordPerfect, Word will translate your documents and graphics, and even give you special help to learn how to use Word. When you install

Word, or at any later time, you can turn on the capability to use WordPerfect menus and navigation keys. While the WordPerfect help system is on, you can press a WordPerfect key such as Ctrl+F8 for fonts and the WordPerfect Help dialog box, shown in Figure I.4, will appear with the appropriate WordPerfect menu. (Figure I.4 shows the highest level WordPerfect dialog box.) Use the same keystrokes you would use in WordPerfect. When you finish making menu choices, Word displays a note describing what to do, or actually makes the Word menu and dialog choices for you. As you watch it make the correct choices, you learn how to use Word.

FIG. I.4
WordPerfect users can retrieve their WordPerfect documents and get extra help with commands.

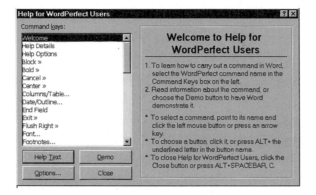

If you are a professional typist who likes a clean, clear screen to work on, you can choose View, Full Screen to remove the menu bar, status bar, scroll bars, ruler, ribbon, and toolbar so that the Word screen is clear. Pressing Esc or clicking the Full Screen button returns the screen to its original view.

Working with Word 97

Word 97 has features that fit many working environments. Even beginning and intermediate operators can customize Word to fit specific job needs. This section includes several examples of the many types of documents you can produce with Word.

Word Processing in Daily Business

Word makes repetitive work very easy. Business typists of all skills and levels will find Word's features oriented to help them in their daily business work. Some of Word's general business features are:

- Search through news and business sources on the Internet.
- Get technical support and software updates from the Internet.
- Automatically format standard types of documents with the AutoFormat command.
- Use template wizards to guide you through building brochures, newsletters, letters, and so on.
- Create forms that contain pull-down lists and check boxes to replace your office's printed forms.
- Use Print Preview or Page Layout views to see results before you print.
- Use the mail-merge capabilities that guide you through mailings and labels.
- Automatically generate envelopes.
- Use templates to hold repetitive documents, formatting styles, macros, text you want entered automatically, and shortcut keys.
- Choose the symbol for foreign languages or special characters like trademarks from a table.
- Insert tables that look like spreadsheets by clicking a toolbar button.
- Format numbered and bulleted lists by clicking a single toolbar button.
- Add toolbar buttons for the commands you use frequently.
- Include Portrait (vertical) and Landscape (horizontal) pages in the same document.
- Automatically spell check documents as you type and suggest correct spellings.

Word Processing for Legal and Medical Documents

Legal and medical documents present unique word processing requirements. Word is built to handle these specialized situations:

- Search through medical and legal abstracts on the Internet.
- Create pleadings with the Legal Pleading Wizard.
- AutoText to eliminate typing long words and repetitive phrases.
- Outliners, which are one of the best available.
- Tables of authorities and automatic cross-referencing.
- Annotations, hidden text, and revision marks.

- Numbered lines with adjustable spacing.
- Inserting graphics or pictures.
- Drawing directly on the document with drawing tools.

Word Processing for Scientific and Technical Documents

When you write scientific or technical papers, you need to include references, charts, tables, graphs, equations, table references, footnotes, and endnotes. Word 97 will help your technical documents with the following:

- Stay current with research in your field by searching the World Wide Web and FTP sites from within Word.
- An equation editor that builds equations when you click equation pieces and symbols.
- Drawing and graphing tools built into Word 97.
- The capability to insert many different types of graphics files, as well as AutoCAD files.
- Spreadsheet-like tables for data.
- Mathematics in tables.
- Embedding or linking with Excel, the leading Windows worksheet software.

Word Processing for Financial Documents

The reader's initial impression of a financial report comes when you turn the first page. Word gives you on-screen tables (similar to spreadsheets) and links to Microsoft Excel and Lotus 1-2-3 worksheets and charts. You will find the following productive features:

- Embed worksheets and Excel charts in Word documents and edit them with Excel menus and toolbars.
- Commands and structure very similar to Excel.
- The capability to operate Excel or Lotus 1-2-3 and Word simultaneously and switch between them.
- The capability to embed Excel worksheets so that they can be updated within the Word document.
- The capability to link Excel or Lotus worksheets so that changes in the original worksheet appear in the Word document.

- Row-and-column numeric tables that can include math.
- The capability to use Microsoft Query to download and link to mainframe or server data.
- Borders, shading, and underlining to enhance columnar reporting.
- Tables and charts linked to other Windows applications.

Word Processing for Graphic Artists and Advertising

Creating page layouts and advertising design once required two applications: a word processor and a desktop publishing program. Word combines both. Although Word doesn't have all the "free-form" capabilities of a publishing application like Quark XPress or Aldus PageMaker, Word 97 still gives you all the capabilities you're likely to need to create a wide variety of documents, both in electronic and print media, including:

- Web pages published with Word's Web authoring tools.
- Downloadable graphic files from Microsoft's free Web art site.
- Wide range of graphic file import filters.
- Access to the Microsoft ClipArt Gallery.
- Text wrap-around graphics.
- Movable text or graphics.
- Borders and shading.
- Parallel or snaking columns that include graphics.
- Print Preview or an editable Page Layout view that zooms 25 to 200 percent in VGA resolution.
- Compatibility with PostScript typesetting or pre-press film-generating equipment.
- Linking of body copy and graphic files into a single, larger master document.
- Drawing directly in the document.
- Automatic captions and callouts that can be tied to the graphic or position.

Word Processing for Specific Industries

Word 97 is a fully customizable word processor. Therefore, industry associations, custom software houses, and application developers can tailor Word features to fit the needs of specific vertical industries or to integrate with their own custom applications. For example, they can create custom menus, toolbars, and shortcut keys that operate existing commands or run programs written in Word's Visual Basic for Applications programming language. To aid developers, Word includes the following:

- Visual Basic for Applications, based on Visual Basic, the most widely used personal computer language in the world.
- A macro recorder and editing tools.
- Customizable toolbars, menus, and shortcut keys.
- AutoText for industry-specific terms.
- Customized templates to package documents with customized features.
- Industry-specific, personal, and foreign language dictionaries.
- Control of Word features and documents from programs written in Excel, Access, or Visual Basic.
- Integration and data exchange with other Windows applications.

How this Book Is Organized

Word 97 is a program with immense capability and a wealth of features. If approached correctly, it is straightforward and easy to learn. This book is organized to help you learn Word quickly and efficiently.

If you are familiar with Word 6 or Word 95, you should scan the table of contents for new features and look through the book for pages marked with the 97 icon that marks new features. Many Word 6 and Word 95 commands have been moved so that they are more accessible to the average user and so that Microsoft Excel and Word have a similar menu structure.

Special Edition Using Microsoft Word 97 is organized into the following parts:

- Part I: Everyday Word Processing
- Part II: Formatting Documents
- Part III: Web Publishing
- Part IV: Creating Envelopes and Mailings
- Part V: Mastering Special Features
- Part VI: Publishing with Graphics
- Part VII: Handling Large Documents
- Part VIII: Using Word with Office and Networks
- Part IX: Customizing with Word

Part I helps you learn the fundamentals of Word 97 that you will need for basic letters and other documents, and gives an overview of the new features in Word 97. Even if you are very familiar with Word 6 or Word 95, you will want to look at Chapter 1 to get an overview of Word's most powerful features and learn about the new features available in Word 97. Chapters 2 through 6 describe the basics you will need to know for opening, creating, editing, and saving documents. Chapter 7 describes proofing tools such as Word's spelling checker, thesaurus, and grammar checker. Chapter 8 closes Part I by showing you how to preview and print your document.

Part II shows you features that help format your documents. You begin by learning how to format characters in Chapter 9. Chapter 10 then describes how to format lines and paragraphs with such features as alignment, indentation, and borders. One of the most useful chapters in Part II is Chapter 11, "Using Styles for Repetitive Formats," which tells you how to take advantage of the many benefits of using styles for documents with repetitive elements such as headings, titles, and so on. Chapter 12 describes how to use multiple columns if you need to create newsletters, brochures, or scripts. Finally, Chapter 13 describes how to set overall page layout with such things as margins, page orientation, numbering, and type of paper.

In Part III, you learn about one of Word 97's most exciting new features—how to publish Web pages and browse the World Wide Web. Chapter 14 shows you how to use Word's Web publishing tools to create impressive Web pages that include hyperlinks, graphics, textured backgrounds, and much more. Chapter 15 describes how to work on Word files or Web pages from within either the Internet Explorer or Word 97.

Part IV teaches you how to automate mailing lists and bring data into Word from outside databases. In Chapter 16, you learn how to use Word's built-in database features or link Word to data files stored on disk, in a network server, or on the mainframe. Chapter 17 describes how to use that data to create form letters, envelopes, and labels. You will also learn how to use Word to send e-mail and faxes.

Part V describes the many special features that make Word the industry's most powerful word processor. Chapters 18 and 19 will teach you about tables, spreadsheet-like grids that help you organize text, lists, numbers, and even graphics. In Chapter 20, you learn how to use bullets and numbering to organize thoughts into easily-read lists. If you want your thoughts to be well-organized, read Chapter 21's discussion of Word's excellent outlining features. Other chapters such as 22 through 24 describe how to automate your documents with field codes and build forms that make data easy to enter.

If you want to use Word to create newsletters and do other desktop publishing, Part VI describes how to use Word's built-in drawing tools and how to import graphics created in drawing programs. Chapter 25 shows you how easy it is to insert pictures from other programs or from one of the clip art collections. Chapter 26 shows you how to frame text or graphics so that you can make anything moveable on-screen. With frames, you can drag items anywhere on the page and the text wraps around it. Word even comes with its own drawing tools as described in Chapter 27, so creating graphics in Word is very convenient. Chapters 28 and 29 describe two of the programs included with Word: WordArt 3.0 and Microsoft Graph 97. These programs enable you to create fancy titles and banners, or build charts like those created by a program such as Excel.

If you write contracts, build large manuals, print a book with many chapters, or work with theses or formal term papers, you should turn to Part VII. You can make the contents of your documents easier to find if you use the indexing, table of contents, and cross-referencing features described in Chapters 31 and 33. Chapter 34 shows you how to build large documents, like books, from smaller chapter-sized documents. And since all good writing involves editing and tracking changes, Word's revision features, in Chapter 32, will help you track changes and edits and see who made them.

Part VIII shows you the advantage Word has when working with other applications in the Windows environment. Chapters 35 and 36 show you how to use Word with other applications and work with groups of people over a network—two very essential tasks in the workplace. You can copy and paste, link, or embed data between Windows applications. You also learn how to work in a group of people that share documents. Chapter 36 also presents an overview of sending faxes and e-mail from within Word.

Even if you don't know how to program, Part IX shows you how to customize Word to work the way you want and look the way you prefer. If you want to customize how Word works or looks to match the way you prefer to work, look to Chapter 37. Chapter 38 describes how to customize Word's features using the Tools, Options command. In addition, it shows you how easy it is to reorganize Word's menus, add new commands to toolbars, and add shortcut keys to cut down on your work. Chapter 39 describes how to automate Word and add new features through the use of the Visual Basic for Applications, a powerful programming language.

Conventions Used in This Book

Conventions used in this book have been established to help you learn how to use the program quickly and easily. As much as possible, the conventions correspond with those used in the Word documentation.

Letters pressed to activate menus, choose commands in menus, and select options in dialog boxes are underlined: File, Open. Names of dialog boxes are written with initial capital letters, as the name appears on-screen. Messages that appear on-screen are printed in a special font: Document 1. New terms are introduced in *italic* type.

Two different types of key combinations are used with this program. For combinations joined with a comma (Alt, F), you press and release the first key and then press and release the second key. If a combination is joined with a plus sign (Alt+F), you press and hold the first key while you press the second key.

An icon is used throughout this book to mark features new to Word 97.

The code continuation character ➥ is used to indicate that a breaking code line should be typed as one line. Here's an example:

```
ToolsOptionsSave .CreateBackup = 0, .FastSaves = 1,
➥ .SummaryPrompt = 0, .GlobalDotPrompt = 0,
➥ .NativePictureFormat = 0, .EmbedFonts = 0, .FormsData = 0,
➥ .AutoSave = 0, .SaveInterval = "", .Password = "",
➥ .WritePassword = "",
➥ .RecommendReadOnly = 0
```

Even though the preceding example runs across six lines, the code continuation character tells you that the code fragment should be typed as one line. The code continuation character is your cue to continue typing a code fragment as one long line.

You find four other visual aids that help you on your Word 97 journey: **Notes, Tips, On the Web, Cautions, Troubleshooting,** and **Cross-references**.

N O T E This paragraph format indicates additional information that may help you avoid problems or that should be considered in using the described features. ▪

 T I P This paragraph format suggests easier or alternative methods of executing a procedure.

Throughout this book you will find Internet references that point you to World Wide Web addresses or online addresses where you can find additional information about topics. Internet references look like this:

ON THE WEB

For online support from Microsoft, visit the following World Wide Web site:

http://www.microsoft.com/support

CAUTION

This paragraph format warns the reader of hazardous procedures (for example, activities that delete files).

TROUBLESHOOTING

This paragraph format advises on how to find solutions to common problems. Specific problems you may encounter are shown in italic. Possible solutions appear in the paragraph(s) following the problem.

Special Edition Using Microsoft Word 97 uses cross-references to help you access related information in other parts of the book. Right-facing triangles point you to related information in other chapters. ●

Word Processing Power in Word 97

Word 97 combines ease of use with power. It also brings you to the Internet. With the new Word you can publish documents for the World Wide Web or your company intranet, as well as browse the Web using Word's Web toolbar.

Even with all its new features, Word keeps getting easier to use. Microsoft has tested Word in its usability laboratory to find ways to make Word's features more accessible to you; it has many features that really simplify some tasks that used to be arduous or impossible to perform.

This chapter catalogs some of the most important features in Word 97 that will add to your word processing power. Most of the changes and new features in Word 97 are also presented. If you are an experienced Word user, browse through this chapter to find what's new and what powerful features have been added.

Changes in Word are of two types: those that enhance existing features or make them easy to use, and new features that add to the power of Word. ■

Better Access to Features

Microsoft understands that powerful features aren't important unless you can use them. In Word 97, the features you use most often are accessible and easy to use.

▶ **See** "Getting the Tip of the Day," **p. 71**

Shortcut Menus

With pull-down menus that lead into tabbed dialog boxes, you can quickly get hundreds of options. You use some of these options and features more frequently than others, however. For this reason, Microsoft provides *shortcut menus* (see Figure 1.1). Shortcut menus appear when you click the right mouse button on text, an object, or a screen element, such as a toolbar. The shortcut menu appears (right under the pointer) depending upon which item you clicked. Although it takes a little while to remember that it is not always necessary to return to the main menu, using shortcut menus will soon become automatic for you.

▶ **See** "Saving Time with Shortcut Menus," **p. 50**

FIG. 1.1
Shortcut menus appear when you click the right mouse button on text, objects, or screen elements such as toolbars.

Tabbed Dialog Boxes

Word has so many different features and options that they can't all be available from the menu. Instead, Microsoft keeps the menus relatively short and makes hundreds of options available in dialog boxes. Within the dialog boxes, the options are grouped together into tabbed "cards" (see Figure 1.2). These "cards" are referred to as "tabs" throughout this book. You can switch between different groups of options by clicking the tab or pressing Alt and the appropriate letter to choose a different tab.

▶ **See** "Working in Dialog Boxes," **p. 57**

FIG. 1.2
With Word's tabbed dialog boxes, you have quick access to many options.

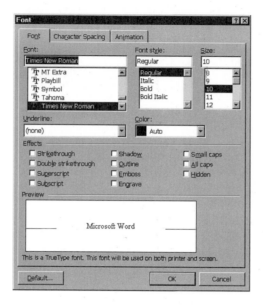

Wizards to Guide You

Wizards guide you through the process of creating special or complex documents (see Figure 1.3). To open a wizard, choose File, New, select the tab for the type of document you want to create, and select a wizard. Word comes with wizards that help you create documents such as a fax cover sheet, brochures, calendars, legal pleadings, business or personal letters, resumes, and complex tables with fancy formatting.

▶ **See** "Using Templates and Wizards for Frequently Created Documents," **p. 197**

Full Screen View

Some typists are distracted by menus, toolbars, and scroll bars. If you are such a typist, work in Word's Full Screen view. To display the full screen, just choose View, Full Screen (see Figure 1.4). Return to the previous view by pressing Esc or by clicking the Full Screen button.

▶ **See** "Controlling Your Document's Appearance On-Screen," **p. 132**

FIG. 1.3
Wizards guide you
through producing
complex documents.

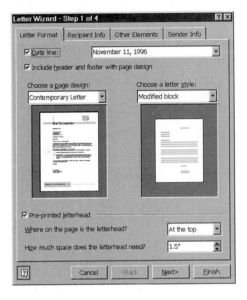

FIG. 1.4
The Full Screen view
makes your document
look like you are typing
on a white page that
fills the entire screen.

Important News About Recycling Times

Dear Recycling Times Subscriber:

We've made some important changes, and we wanted you to be the first to know.

Starting with this issue, *Recycling Times* is merging with **Planet Care 2000**. As a valued subscriber, you are entitled to one issue of **Planet Care 2000** for every issue of *Recycling Times* that remains in your subscription.

All the great ideas you've come to expect from *Recycling Times* are right here in **Planet Care 2000**, along with lots of new features and departments.

You don't have to do a thing, because we've taken care of all the subscription details. Sit back and enjoy reading your copy of **Planet Care 2000**.

We're sure that you'll be delighted, because we're continuing to bring you the most up-to-date information on recycling products and techniques. You'll also find regular columns and practical techniques developed by leaders in the field. Of course the feature articles in each issue will still be devoted to how you and your organization can make a significant impact by recycling.

If you browse Cyberspace on the World Wide Web you may be interested in looking for us at our new Web site. Our Web site contains frequently updated information about legislation, product

Automatic Corrections

With Word's AutoCorrect feature, you can type a word or abbreviation and Word will automatically replace it with the text or graphic you specified in the AutoCorrect dialog box (see Figure 1.5). This feature can make legal, medical, or other specialized typing more productive—type an abbreviation, and AutoCorrect automatically converts it to the correct word or phrase. You also can set AutoCorrect to automatically correct mistakes you frequently make, such as changing your typing of *natoin* to *nation*.

AutoCorrect in Word 97 has a large list of built-in corrections and abbreviations and will correct capitalization if you accidentally press the Caps Lock key. You can also create a list of exceptions. AutoCorrect will not make changes to words in the exception list. If you reverse a correction AutoCorrect makes, it will remember this and not make the correction again.

FIG. 1.5

You can "teach" AutoCorrect what mistakes and abbreviations you want it to recognize so that it will automatically replace the mistake or abbreviation with the text you specify.

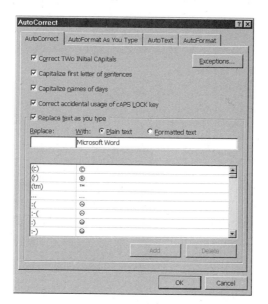

AutoFormat

The AutoFormat feature enables you to type a document and then apply a standardized set of formats to the document with a single command. Using a set of rules about what defines a heading, title, body copy, figures, tables, and so on, Word examines your document and applies styles to each element. You then can manually redefine each style or use the Style Gallery to change the overall appearance of the document.

You can apply AutoFormats as you type. For example, if you type an asterisk followed by text, Word will automatically make the text a bulleted item and add bullets to additional items in the list as you type them. Type a number before the first item in the list, and AutoFormat will create a numbered list. AutoFormat can also automatically create headings and borders, replace ordinals (1st) with superscript (1st), and replace fractions (1/2) with fraction characters (½).

Style Gallery

If you want to create a standardized appearance in your documents with more ease, use the Style Gallery (see Figure 1.6). The Style Gallery is a collection of formatting styles that are applied as a group to an entire document. You can actually see a sample of what the active document will look like as you select each different style in the gallery.

▶ **See** "Using the Style Gallery," **p. 381**

FIG. 1.6
The Style Gallery enables you to change the appearance of your entire document by changing entire collections of formatting styles.

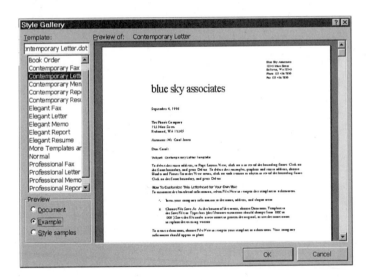

Easier Column Formatting

Newspaper or snaking columns make text more readable. They give the eye a shorter distance to travel to see part of a sentence. By choosing F̲ormat, C̲olumns, creating columns is very easy (see Figure 1.7). You can even create unevenly spaced columns of different width.

▶ **See** "Creating Columns," **p. 416**

FIG. 1.7
The Columns feature makes columns very easy to apply. You can even create unevenly spaced columns.

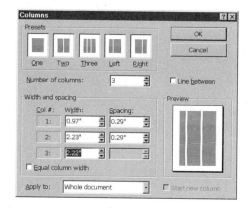

Customizable and Movable Toolbars for Quick Access to Commands

Toolbars give you quick access to commands. Word has several toolbars, which you can move and reshape on-screen (see Figure 1.8). By either choosing View, Toolbars or right-clicking a toolbar, you can display or hide a toolbar. Dragging in a toolbar's gray area moves it, while dragging an edge reshapes it.

▶ **See** "Using the Toolbars," **p. 52**

FIG. 1.8
Word's large number of movable toolbars gives you quick access to your most frequently used commands when using a mouse.

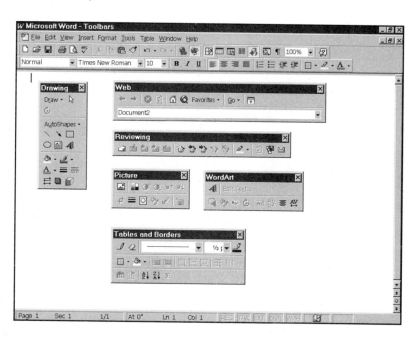

More Power

Word is one of the most powerful word processors available. With it, you have extraordinarily broad capabilities, from the ability to link to mainframe databases to the ability to publish newsletters with complex layouts.

Working with Other Windows Applications

Word has great flexibility and power when working with other Windows applications. In addition to its ability to copy and paste or link to data in other Windows applications, you can embed parts of other Office documents in your Word document. While you are working in Word, you can then activate that embedded data; the menus and toolbars that are appropriate for the data display in Word. Notice that in Figure 1.9, the Word menu and toolbar reflect the Excel chart in the document. Embedding enables you to embed Word documents in the journals, calendars, schedules, and task lists of Microsoft Outlook. Double-clicking the embedded documents make them immediately available to you without having to leave Microsoft Outlook.

▶ **See** "Embedding Data," **p. 1085**

FIG. 1.9

Word acts as a container to hold data from other Office applications.

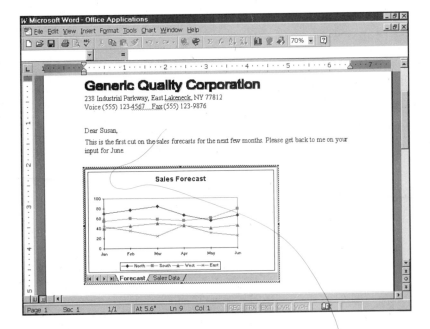

Better File Management

It doesn't take very long before you have hundreds of documents on your disk and finding a specific document becomes tedious and frustrating. Word's Open dialog box (see Figure 1.10) includes commands that let you find files and manage documents much more easily than you could in Word 6. From the Open dialog box, you can find and then open, print, move, copy, delete, and preview files.

▶ **See** "Searching for Files," **p. 124**

FIG. 1.10
Finding and managing files from within Word is much easier with the new Open dialog box.

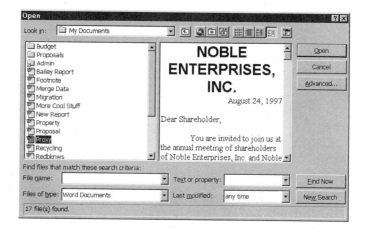

Forms That Include Pull-Down Lists, Edit Boxes, or Check Boxes

Word processors seem to lend themselves to creating forms, yet they can't manage to fill in the blanks on forms. Consequently, many businesses continue to inventory hundreds of pounds of pre-printed forms. Word helps reduce the cost of storing and printing forms with its forms feature. In a normal word processing document, you can now insert edit boxes, check boxes, and pull-down lists. You don't have to know how to program—all you have to do is make selections in a dialog box. You can save the data from the completed form in a database-acceptable format.

▶ **See** "Building Forms," **p. 755**

Improved Mail Merge

Mail merge is often looked at as a difficult task in word processing, yet it's something that many small- and medium-sized businesses do frequently. Word's Mail Merge Helper (see Figure 1.11) is a series of dialog boxes that guide you through merging data into form letters, envelopes, and labels. You can even choose the layout for the types of envelopes and labels.

▶ **See** "Merging Mailing Lists and Documents," **p. 573**

FIG. 1.11
The Mail Merge Helper guides you through the whole process of merging data with mail merge documents.

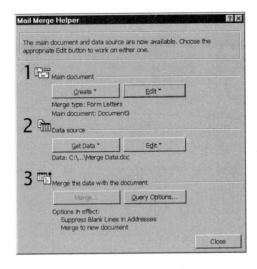

Improved Envelope and Label Printing

With Word's envelope feature, creating an envelope is as easy as typing in a document (see Figure 1.12). Select standard-sized envelopes and labels or create custom settings (see Figure 1.13).

FIG. 1.12
The Labels tab contain lists of layout definitions for most standard business labels.

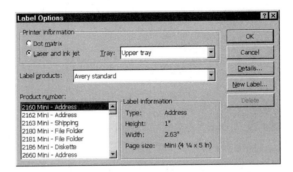

FIG. 1.13

The envelope options enable you to position addresses on envelopes of various sizes, as well as to print postal delivery bar codes automatically.

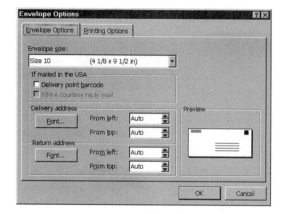

Improved Indexing and Tables of Contents or Authorities

If you work with major reports, proposals, or legal documents, you will find Word's indexing, table of contents, and table of authorities features very powerful (see Figure 1.14). You have more formatting options, and these features are easier to use than in Word 2 or Word 6. For more information on these features, turn to Chapter 31, "Creating Indexes and Tables of Contents."

FIG. 1.14

The formatting and features in Word's indexing and table generation capabilities are improved over Word 2 and Word 6.

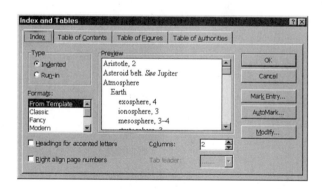

Cross-References

One of the time-consuming jobs in proposals and authoritative documents is cross-referencing tables, figures, and comments. With a little guidance, Word takes care of the job for you. You don't even have to move back and forth in a document to see what you want to cross-reference. Word keeps track of different types of content and topics and presents it to you so you can select the topic you want to cross-reference.

▶ **See** "Creating Cross-References," **p. 1029**

Callouts Attached to Objects

Anyone doing technical documentation or training materials in a word processor needs to create callouts. *Callouts* are text boxes that explain elements of a picture or drawing, as you see in Figure 1.15. Those documentation and training writers can put away their desktop publishing programs and stay in Word. Callouts in Word are easy to insert and can be formatted and attached to locations on-screen so they stay with the object they describe.

▶ **See** "Working with Callouts," **p. 914**

FIG. 1.15

With the callout feature, trainers and technical writers can create their documentation directly within Word.

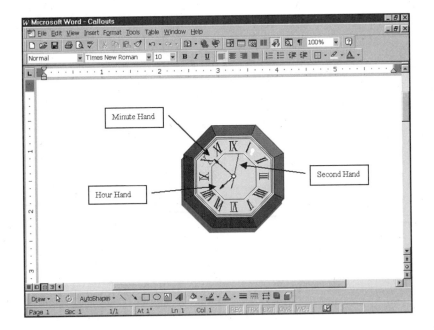

Spell It

Spell It is the ultimate spell checker. It checks your spelling as you type. When you select this option, a wavy red line will appear under any word you type that isn't in Word's dictionary. When you click the word with the right mouse button, Word displays a list of alternative spellings from which you can select the correct spelling.

Highlighter

Just as you use a highlighting pen to emphasize text in your paper documents, use Word's Highlight tool to highlight text with color on-screen. This is a great way to mark important text for yourself and others using the document online.

Find and Replace All Word Forms

An option in the Replace dialog box allows you to enter one form of a word and have Word find and replace all forms of that word. For example, if you ask Word to replace *make* with *create,* it will also replace *makes* with *creates* and *made* with *created.*

New Features in Word 97

In addition to the many outstanding features mentioned in the previous sections, Word has introduced some powerful and useful new features.

Help Assistant

Did you ever wish you had an expert sitting by your side to help you with your applications? In Office 97, Microsoft has tried to create something almost as good—the Office Assistant. The Assistant is an online help system with a personality, not an attitude. And you get to pick the personality of your assistant from a gallery that includes a friendly cat, a leering paper-clip, Albert Einstein, and a business-like Microsoft Office icon. Figure 1.16 shows the gallery from which you can choose your Assistants.

FIG. 1.16
Pick your own Office
Assistant to help you
be productive with
Word.

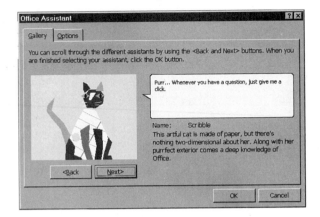

Web Publishing

Now you can use your Word skills to publish pages on the World Wide Web. Word's new
Web-authoring tools enable you to create attractive, high-quality Web pages. With the
Web Page Wizard you can start from a wide variety of sample Web pages—or with a blank
page. Create a Web page you can use as the start page for Internet Explorer 3/4—or use
Word's authoring tools to create pages for your company intranet or the World Wide Web.
Word will even save existing Word documents as Web pages. Figure 1.17 shows a Web
page created in Word.

FIG. 1.17
Convert Word to Web
documents or create
Web pages directly in
Word.

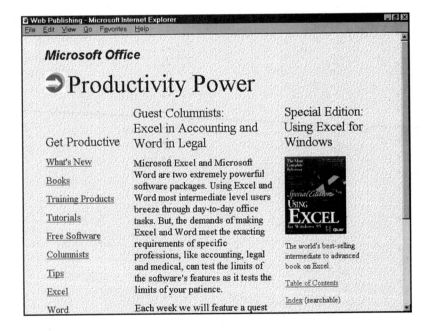

Web Browsing

You can make your own web from interconnected Office documents by putting hyperlinked words or phrases in your Word documents. Inserting hyperlinks in Word or Excel documents lets you jump between documents with a single click. If you have access to the Internet, your hyperlinks can link to Web pages. Figure 1.19 shows the new Web toolbar used to navigate through linked documents from within Word 97. You can even copy and paste text from a page in the Internet Explorer into your Word documents.

FIG. 1.18
Browse through Webs created from Office documents and pages on the World Wide Web.

Tracking Changes in Documents

As networks increase and re-engineering abounds, more people are working in teams on shared computer documents. In Word 97 you can share a document with others and keep a history of who has made changes. The new Reviewing toolbar makes it easy to accept or reject the changes made by team members.

Drawing Directly on the Document

Word's Drawing toolbar is loaded with drawing buttons that allow you to create graphics directly in Word (see Figure 1.19). You can put drawings under the text to get a watermark-like effect, within the text so the text wraps around the graphic, or over the text as an overlay. A large collection of AutoShapes enables you to draw figures using templates. A larger collection of clip art is available, as well as a link to Microsoft's clip art gallery at its World Wide Web site.

▶ **See** "Displaying and Understanding the Drawing Toolbar," **p. 894**

FIG. 1.19
With Word's drawing tools, you can draw directly in a document. You even have a choice of putting your graphics behind, with, or in front of text.

New Templates and Wizards

Word 97 contains a large collection of new templates, and many of them come in three styles: contemporary, professional, and elegant. Word's templates and wizards are organized by categories in the File New dialog box (see Figure 1.20). Additional free templates are available at Microsoft's Web site.

FIG. 1.20
Word 97 comes with many new templates and organizes the templates and wizards by categories.

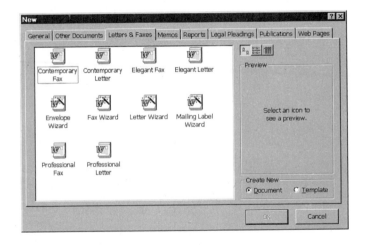

Customizable Toolbars and Menus

Word 95 had the ability to assign commands to a button on a toolbar or to a shortcut key (see Figure 1.21). You could even draw your own button faces and assign macros to buttons.

Word 97 makes it easier to put buttons and menus on toolbars. You can drag menu items or buttons directly from the Commands tab of the Customize box onto menus or toolbars.

▶ **See** "Customizing and Creating Toolbars," **p. 1141**

FIG. 1.21
You can customize existing toolbars or create your own toolbars.

Visual Basic for Applications

Visual Basic is the most widely used Windows programming language, and now all Office 97 applications use Visual Basic for Applications, based on the same programming language. Although the objects, the type of data manipulated, differ from one application to the next, the programming constructs, statements, and development environment are the same. ●

CHAPTER 2

Getting Started in Word

The basics of using Word 97 are the same for using any other Windows program. If you are familiar with another Windows application, such as Microsoft Excel, you may not need to read this "basics" chapter (or perhaps a quick scan is all you need). If you are a new Windows user, however, you will find this chapter important for two reasons: you will become comfortable navigating Word 97, and you will have a head start on the next Windows program you learn.

In this chapter, you learn how to control not only Word 97 menus and dialog boxes, but also the windows that contain Word 97 and its documents. By the time you finish this chapter, you will be able to use the mouse and the keyboard to choose commands from menus, select options from dialog boxes, access the extensive help system, and manipulate windows on-screen. Beyond these basic tasks, you should be able to organize windows so that you can access and use multiple documents at once or "clear away your desktop" so that you can concentrate on a single job. ■

Start and exit Word 97

Click the Start button or choose a document file from Windows Explorer to start Word 97. Exit by using menu commands or clicking the Close button.

Choose commands and select from dialog boxes

Some commands execute when selected from a menu, while others don't execute until you choose OK from a dialog box. Commands that are followed by an ellipsis (...) require additional information entered in a dialog box.

Operate Word 97 from the keyboard or mouse

Press Alt followed by the underlined letter to choose commands with the keyboard. Most actions, however, are significantly easier using the mouse.

Manipulate windows

Multiple applications can be run in Windows, and multiple documents can be open while you are in Word 97.

Starting and Quitting Word 97

To run Word 97, follow these steps:

1. Click the Start button in the taskbar at the bottom of the screen.

2. Move the mouse pointer over the Programs command. The Programs menu appears.

3. Click the Microsoft Word item.

Figure 2.1 shows the Programs menu with the Microsoft Word item selected.

FIG. 2.1

Start Word by selecting the Microsoft Word icon in the Programs menu.

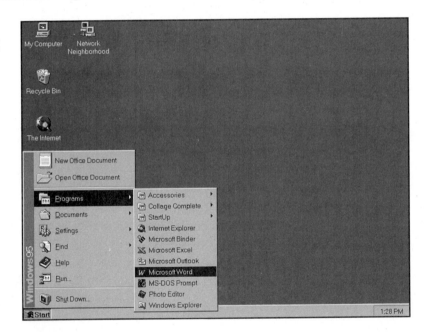

You can also start Word 97 by choosing a document file from the Windows Explorer. To start Word 97 and load the document, double-click the file name for a Word 97 document (DOC), or select the file name and press Enter. You can also start a document you have used recently by clicking the Start menu, moving the pointer over the Documents command, and then clicking the document you want loaded into Word. If Word is not running, it will start and load the document. If Word is running, it will load the document and activate Word so that it displays on top of any other windows.

Close—or "quit"—Word 97 when you are finished working for the day or when you need to free memory for other applications. To quit Word 97, follow these steps:

1. If you are using a mouse, choose <u>F</u>ile, E<u>x</u>it or click the Close button in the top-right corner. (The Close button looks like an X.)If you are using the keyboard, press the shortcut key combination Alt+F4 or choose <u>F</u>ile, E<u>x</u>it by pressing Alt, F, X.

2. If you made changes to any document, Word displays an Alert box asking whether you want to save your current work. Click the <u>Y</u>es button or press Enter to save your work, or click the <u>N</u>o button to quit without saving. The Office Assistant displays this message if it is active. To learn about the Office Assistant, see "Working with the Office Assistant" later in the chapter.

To learn how to use the mouse and keyboard for carrying out commands and other procedures, see "Understanding Windows and Word 97 Terms" later in the chapter.

ON THE WEB

For online support from Microsoft, visit the following World Wide Web site:

http://www.microsoft.com/support

You can also access Microsoft's extensive troubleshooting KnowledgeBase at the following site:

http://www.microsoft.com/kb

For tutorials, tips, and add-ins for Microsoft Office applications point your browser to:

http://www.ronperson.com

Understanding the Word 97 Screen

One advantage of Windows is the ability to run several applications and display them all on-screen simultaneously. Chapter 36, "Using Word with Office Applications," describes how to run Word 97 and other Windows applications together and transfer information among them. This capability can save you time when you transfer data into or out of Word 97, create automatically updated links from Word 97 and other Windows applications, or embed Word 97 data into other Windows application documents.

Each Windows application, like Word 97, runs in its own application window. Because some application windows can contain multiple document windows, you can work simultaneously with more than one document. Figure 2.2 shows the Word 97 application window with two document windows inside.

Table 2.1 lists and describes the parts of a Word 97 screen shown in Figure 2.2.

Part
I

Ch
2

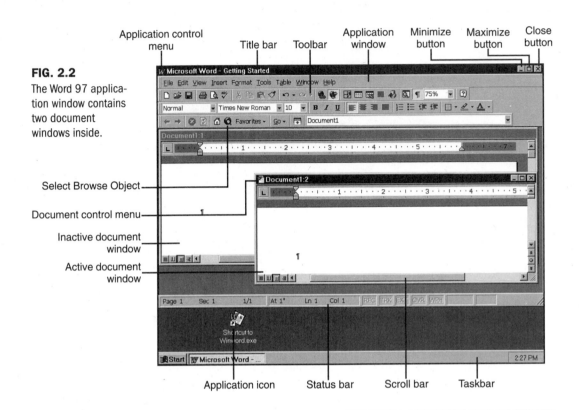

FIG. 2.2
The Word 97 application window contains two document windows inside.

Application control menu · Title bar · Toolbar · Application window · Minimize button · Maximize button · Close button

Select Browse Object

Document control menu

Inactive document window

Active document window

Application icon · Status bar · Scroll bar · Taskbar

Table 2.1   Parts of Word 97 and Windows Screens

Part	Description
Application window	The window within which Word 97 runs
Application icon	The taskbar button of a running application
Document window	The window within which documents are displayed
Application Control menu	The menu that enables you to manipulate the application window
Document Control menu	The menu that enables you to manipulate the active (top) document window
Active document window	The window that accepts entries and commands; this window is shown with a solid title bar and is normally the top window
Mouse pointer	The on-screen arrow, I-beam, or drawing button indicates the current location affected by your mouse actions

Part	Description
Inactive document window	The background window which does not accept commands other than to be activated; this window is shown with a lighter colored or patterned title bar
Insertion point	The point where text appears when you type
End of document marker	The point beyond which no text is entered
Title bar	The bar at the top of an application or document window
Menu bar	A list of menu names displayed below the title bar of an application
Toolbar	A bar containing buttons that, when chosen with the mouse pointer, produce a function or action
Minimize button	An underscore at the right of a title bar that stores an application as an application button in the taskbar at the bottom of the screen; equivalent to the application Control Minimize command
Maximize button	A box at the right of a title bar that fills available space with the document or application; equivalent to the Control Maximize command
Close button	A box at the right of a title bar that closes the window or dialog box
Restore button	A double box at the right of a title bar that restores an application or document into a sizable window; equivalent to the Control Restore command
Scroll bar	A gray horizontal and vertical bar that enables the mouse to scroll the screen; a scroll box in the bar shows the current display's position relative to the entire document
Status bar	A bar at the bottom of the screen that shows what Word 97 is prepared to do next; watch the status bar for prompts, explanations of the current command, buttons under the mouse pointer, or guidance
Indicators	These display modes of operation on the status bar, such as REC when a macro is recording, OVR for overtype mode, or EXT when the Extend mode is on

continues

Table 2.1 Continued

Part	Description
Select Browse Object	The toolbar that enables you to browse through an active document by field, endnote, footnote, comment, section, page, edits, heading, graphic, or by table; Go To and Find functions are also part of this toolbar

Figure 2.3 shows the elements within Word in more detail. The document window, Document 2, has a solid title bar, indicating that it is the active document window. You can have multiple document windows open at the same time. Most entries and commands affect only the active document window. Inactive windows are normally behind the active window and have a lighter colored or cross-hatched title bar.

FIG. 2.3
This figure shows the elements of a Word 97 program window.

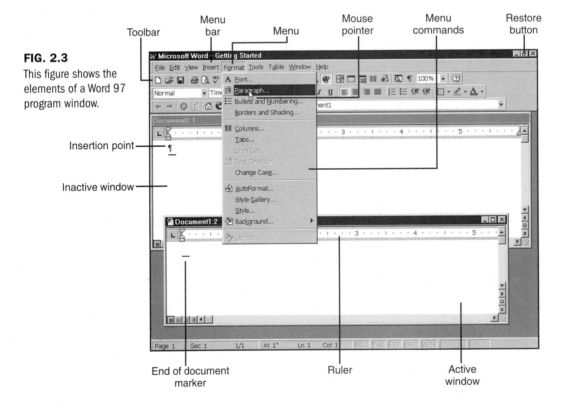

The components in a Word screen are described in Table 2.2.

Table 2.2 Parts of the Word Screen

Part	Description
Active window	The document window that accepts entries and commands. This window has a solid title bar and is normally the top window.
Inactive window	Window that contains documents that are loaded, but are not affected by commands. These windows have a lighter colored title bar and are normally behind the active window.
Menu bar	A list of menu names displayed below the title bar of an application
Menu	A drop-down list of commands
Command	A function or action chosen from a drop-down menu
Toolbar	A bar containing buttons that gives quick access to commands and features, such as the spell checker, bold, italic, edit cut and edit paste, styles, and fonts. A toolbar can be moved to different locations and reshaped to a different orientation.
Ruler	A bar containing a scale that indicates tabs, paragraph indents, and margins in the paragraph where the insertion point (cursor) is located. The ruler can be used with the mouse to format paragraphs quickly.
Mouse pointer	The on-screen pointer that shows the mouse location
Insertion point	The point where text appears when you type
End of document marker	The point beyond which no text is entered
Split box	Light gray bar at the top of the vertical scroll bar that you can drag down to split a window into two views of the same document

Part
I

Ch
2

Using the Mouse

The mouse is an optional piece of hardware that attaches to your personal computer. It enables you to move the on-screen pointer as you move the mouse with your hand. In Word, you can control the program with mouse movements or with keystrokes, but most users will find that Word is easier to learn and to use with the mouse. Some Word actions—such as drawing graphical objects—require the use of a mouse; other actions—such as moving text—are significantly easier when you use a mouse. All menu commands and many other features are all accessible through the use of the keyboard. You will find that combining mouse actions with shortcut keys is the most productive way to work.

Microsoft's IntelliPoint mouse was released coincident with the release of Office 97. This new mouse has a small wheel between the left and right mouse buttons. Rolling the wheel with your index finger enables you to scroll without using scroll bars, pan in any direction, zoom documents to different magnifications, and expand/collapse outlines or drill down or up in worksheet data.

CAUTION

The new wheel button on the IntelliPoint mouse only works if you install the IntelliPoint 2.0 or higher software for the IntelliPoint mouse. If you do not, the IntelliPoint mouse works like a normal mouse. Only programs that are designed to work with the IntelliPoint mouse take advantage of its features. Programs that use its features include:

Windows 95 Help

Windows Explorer

Internet Explorer 2.0 and greater

Products in the Office 97 Suite:

Microsoft Excel 97

Microsoft Word 97

Microsoft PowerPoint 97

Microsoft Access 97

Microsoft Bookshelf Basics

Microsoft Outlook

You can run the normal or IntelliPoint Mouse program and switch the left and right mouse button controls. This is useful if you are left-handed. To find the Mouse program, click Start, Settings, Control Panel, then double-click the Mouse icon. See your Windows documentation or *Special Edition Using Windows 95* from Que for more information about using the Control Panel functions.

The mouse pointer changes appearance depending on its location. You usually see the mouse pointer as an arrow when it's in the menus or as a vertical I-beam shape when it's placed over a text area of your document. When you use the mouse pointer for drawing graphical objects or for embedding objects on a document, its shape changes to a *crosshair* (a thin cross). Each shape signals to you what action you can perform at that location.

Table 2.3 shows and explains the different shapes of the pointer.

Table 2.3   Mouse Pointer Shapes

Pointer Appearance	Screen Location	Function
	Menu	Select commands
	Scroll bars	Scroll through document
	Objects or selected text	Move, size, or select objects
	Left edge of text	Select lines or paragraphs
	Selected text with mouse button depressed	Mouse moves selected text
	Text	Type, select, or edit text
	Window corner	Resize two sides of window
	Window edge	Resize single side of window
	Corner or side handle of selected frame or object	Resize selected picture, frame, or object picture
	Window center object edge	Move window or object
	Top of table	Select column
	Left or right edge of any cell in a table	Widen or narrow column
	Split box	Split window into two panes
	Anywhere	Get help specific to next item selected
	Help window	Select help items
	Anywhere	Wait while processing

continues

Table 2.3   Continued

Pointer Appearance	Screen Location	Function
∥	Table	Draw a table
☜	Text box	Create a text box link

Understanding Windows and Word 97 Terms

All Windows applications, including Word 97, require keyboard and mouse actions to select what is changed on-screen or to give commands. By learning the actions named in Table 2.4, you will know how to operate menus and select items within any Windows application.

Table 2.4   Windows and Word Actions

Action	Description
Select	Highlight or mark a section of text, menu name, command, dialog box option, or graphical object with the keyboard or with mouse actions.
Choose	Execute and complete a command. You may execute some commands when you select the menu command. Other commands execute when you choose OK from a dialog box.
Activate	Bring an application or document window to the foreground. When you are working with more than one application or more than one document within Word, the active window is the window you are working in.

Pointing Device Actions

Mouse and trackball techniques are simple to learn and to remember. These techniques make using Word 97 much easier. In fact, for such work as moving and copying text, scrolling through a document, and drawing and embedding objects, a mouse or trackball is nearly indispensable. Table 2.5 describes the pointing device actions that you use in carrying out Word operations.

The IntelliPoint mouse also gains special effects with different combinations of holding down the wheel button, located between the mouse buttons, and holding down keys as you roll the wheel.

▶ **See** "Selecting Text with the Mouse," **p. 156**

Table 2.5   Mouse Actions

Action	Description
Click	Place the tip of the mouse pointer or lower portion of the I-beam pointer at the desired location, and then quickly press and release the left mouse or trackball button *once*. This action chooses a menu or command, moves the insertion point, or selects a graphical object so that you can work with it; this action also places the insertion point in text boxes.
Right-click	Position the tip of the mouse pointer in the desired location on a document or toolbar, and then click the right mouse or trackball button. This action displays a menu appropriate to the item which you clicked.
Double-click	Position the tip of the mouse pointer or the lower portion of the I-beam pointer at the desired location and then quickly press the left mouse or trackball button *twice*. This action is often a shortcut for carrying out a command or opening a dialog box from the Word screen. In Word, you can select a word by double-clicking anywhere in the word.
Drag	Position the tip of the mouse pointer, center of the crosshair, or the lower portion of the I-beam on an item; then hold down the left mouse or trackball button as you move the mouse pointer. This action selects multiple items, cells (in a worksheet), or text characters, or moves graphical objects.
Roll wheel	Scroll up in a window by rolling the wheel forward. Scroll down in a window by rolling the wheel down (IntelliPoint only).
Drag wheel	Pan any direction in a window by holding down the wheel button as you move the mouse in any direction. The entire document moves in any direction (IntelliPoint only).
Ctrl+wheel roll	Zoom a document to greater or lesser magnification by holding down the Ctrl key as you roll the wheel forward or backward (IntelliPoint only).

Part
I

Ch
2

Some mouse actions have a different effect when you hold down the Shift or Ctrl key as you click, double-click, or drag with the mouse or trackball. As a general rule, holding down the Shift key as you click selects text between where your insertion point was, and the location where you Shift+click. Holding down the Ctrl button and clicking or double-clicking also has different effects, depending on what is selected when you carry out this action. You will learn about using the mouse in combination with the keyboard in the appropriate sections throughout the book.

▶ **See** "Selecting Text with the Mouse," **p. 156**

Keyboard Actions

The keyboard is most useful for entering text and numbers, performing fast operations with shortcut keys, and operating with portable or laptop computers that don't have a mouse or trackball. Don't forget, however, that the best way of operating Word 97 and other Windows applications is through the combined use of mouse and keyboard. Table 2.6 lists and describes the keyboard actions that you will use in Word 97.

Table 2.6   Keyboard Actions

Action	Description
Type	Type, but do not press the Enter key.
Enter	Press the Enter key.
Alt	Press the Alt key.
Alt, letter	Press the Alt key, release it, and then press the underlined letter or number shown. The active letters that appear underlined on-screen are underlined in this book.
Letter	Press only the underlined letter shown in the menu, command, or option.
Alt+letter	Hold down the Alt key as you press the underlined letter.
Alt, hyphen	Press the Alt key, release it, and then press the hyphen key.
Alt, spacebar	Press the Alt key, release it, and then press the spacebar.
Tab	Press the Tab key.
Esc	Press the Esc key.

Throughout this book, you see combinations of keys indicated with a plus sign (+), such as Alt+F. This combination means that you must hold down the Alt key while you press F. After pressing F, release both keys. (This book shows capital letters, as with the F, but you don't need to hold down the Shift key unless indicated.)

Keystrokes that appear separated by commas should be pressed in sequence. Alt, spacebar, for example, is accomplished by pressing and releasing Alt and then pressing the spacebar.

Part
I

Ch
2

If you have a mouse, try using both mouse actions and keystrokes to perform commands and tasks. You soon will find that the keyboard works well for some commands and features and that the mouse works well for others. A combination of mouse and keyboard usually is the most efficient. The Quick Reference card bound inside the back cover of this book shows both keyboard and mouse shortcut methods.

The keyboard also is useful for many shortcut keys. These shortcut keys are listed in the appropriate areas throughout this book.

▶ **See** "Formatting Paragraphs with Shortcut Keys," **p. 328**

The 12 function keys give you a shortcut method for choosing commands that you normally choose from a menu. Some function keys use other keys in combination. When two or more keys are listed with a plus sign, hold down the first key(s) as you press the second key.

Notice that key combinations are listed on the right side of some drop-down menus. These key combinations execute the command immediately, without going through the menu and menu item. Instead of choosing Edit, Clear, for example, you can press the Delete key.

N O T E If you are working in Word 97 and forget a function key or shortcut key combination, choose Help, Microsoft Word Help Topics, and then select the Contents tab. In the Contents tab select Reference Information, then Keyboard Guide. Click the type of keyboard shortcuts you are interested in. Remember that you can print a Help Topic window of keyboard shortcuts for later reference by clicking the Options button then clicking Print Topic. ▪

Choosing Commands

Word 97 uses the same menu-selection methods used by all Windows applications. You can control commands with the mouse, keystrokes, directional keys, or shortcut keys. You often can mix your methods of menu selection by starting with one method and finishing with another.

CAUTION

You cannot use a shortcut key while a menu is pulled down or a dialog box is displayed.

Notice that some commands in a menu may be gray. These commands are unavailable at that current point in Word operation.

Commands in the menu that are followed by an ellipsis (…) need more information from you before they execute. These commands display dialog boxes that ask you for more information.

In Word 97, you can back out of any drop-down menu or dialog box by pressing Esc. If you are using a mouse, you can back out of a menu by clicking the menu name a second time or by clicking the Cancel button in a dialog box.

Reading and Editing Document Summary Information

The Properties command makes it easy to view general, summary, statistical, or version information that relates to a Word document, an application, or a file item in the Windows Explorer. You can also add detailed information to Word documents. For example, you can add a more descriptive title, add subject, author, manager, and company name information, and even customize the information you want to view.

Figures 2.4 through 2.6 show the various types of property dialog boxes accessed using the Properties command.

FIG. 2.4

Choose File, Properties to display the Properties dialog box of an open Word document.

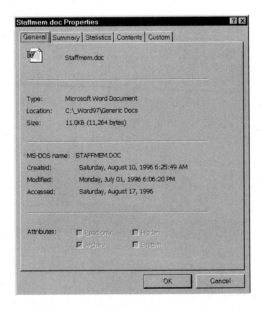

FIG. 2.5
Clicking an application icon with the right mouse button and choosing Properties displays the Properties dialog box of the selected application.

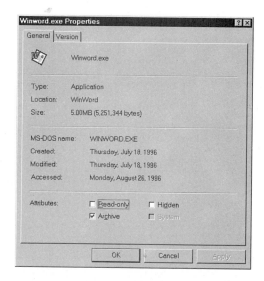

Part

I

Ch

2

FIG. 2.6
Clicking a folder item in the Windows Explorer with the right mouse button then choosing Properties displays the Properties dialog box of the selected item.

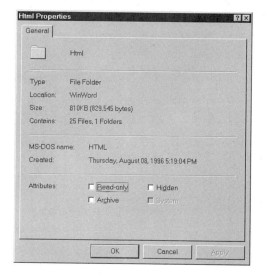

Some property dialog boxes have several options that can be selected for a customized configuration. Figure 2.7 shows the Taskbar Properties dialog box with its selectable options.

FIG. 2.7

Clicking the right mouse button between the taskbar buttons then choosing Properties displays the Taskbar Properties dialog box.

Saving Time with Shortcut Menus

You can save yourself time by using shortcut menus. Shortcut menus display the most frequently used commands that relate to the selected item or object.

To display a shortcut menu, click with the right mouse button on the item or object for which you need a shortcut menu. If you are using a keyboard, select the item and then press Shift+F10. For example, to open a shortcut menu that applies to text, select the text you want to work with, and click with the right mouse button on the text.

Shortcut menus appear under the mouse pointer or at the top left of the document window, if activated by the keyboard. Select a command by clicking it or by pressing the up- or down-arrow key and then pressing Enter. To remove a shortcut menu, click outside the menu or press the Esc key.

Figures 2.8 through 2.10 show a few shortcut menus, and the captions indicate the items with which the menus appear.

FIG. 2.8

A right mouse click on selected text displays a shortcut menu for text and the Draw Table function.

FIG. 2.9
Right-clicking on a selected object displays a shortcut menu to quickly manipulate the object.

Part

I

Ch

2

FIG. 2.10
Right-clicking on a toolbar displays a shortcut menu for other toolbars.

Choosing Commands with the Keyboard

When you are familiar with the Word 97 menus, you can perform the following steps to type commands:

1. Press Alt to select the menu bar.
2. Press the underlined letter in the menu name; for example, press F for File. The menu drops down.
3. Press the underlined letter in the command name; for example, press O for Open.

 You do not need to wait for the menu to appear when you type commands.

Hold down the Shift key as you click the File menu and you will see a helpful command, Close All. Choose Close All to close all open documents. You will be prompted to save documents that have changed.

Using Drag-and-Drop Commands

You can save a great deal of time in Word 97 when moving or copying text if you learn how to use *drag and drop*. Drag-and-drop commands are executed using the mouse and enable you to do with a simple mouse action what might require many keystroke steps.

For example, to move selected text you only need to select the text, then move the pointer into the selected text and *drag* the selection. You will see a gray insertion point indicating where the text will be inserted. Position the insertion point and let go of the mouse button to *drop* the text. If you want to make sure you can use drag-and-drop commands, choose Tools, Options and select the Edit tab. Within the Edit tab, select the Drag-and-Drop Text Editing check box.

TROUBLESHOOTING

When I try to choose a command from a menu, it is grayed out. When a menu command is grayed out, it means the command is not available at that time for some reason. For example, until you have used Edit, Copy or Edit, Cut to move text to the Clipboard, Edit, Paste will be grayed out and unavailable. You must carry out some other action before you can use a grayed out menu command.

Using the Toolbars

The toolbars in Word 97 give you quick access to frequently used commands and procedures. Buttons on toolbars can only be used with a mouse (or similar pointing device). To use a button on a toolbar, click the button that represents the command or procedure you need. You decide which toolbars are displayed and where they appear on-screen. Toolbars are always accessible because they float above document windows.

In Word 97, you can display and work with more than one toolbar at a time. Word 97 has thirteen predefined toolbars, described in the following list:

■ *Standard toolbar.* The Standard toolbar contains the buttons most frequently used during document creation, file handling, and printing.

■ *Formatting toolbar.* The Formatting toolbar contains buttons used for formatting fonts, setting alignment, applying numbering or bullets, applying format styles, and formatting borders.

- *AutoText toolbar.* The AutoText toolbar contains buttons used for assigning unique names to text or graphics that will be used frequently.

- *Control toolbox.* The Control toolbox contains buttons used to aid in the design of a user interface in Microsoft Visual Basic.

- *Database toolbar.* The Database toolbar contains buttons to help you sort lists, edit a database, add or delete columns from a database, start mail merge, and insert data from a database outside of Word 97.

- *Drawing toolbar.* The Drawing toolbar contains buttons for drawing, filling, reshaping, and grouping objects in the document.

- *Forms toolbar.* The Forms toolbar contains buttons to help you insert edit boxes, check boxes, lists, and tables. You also can change the properties of a form field and lock the form when you are finished.

- *Picture toolbar.* The Picture toolbar contains buttons for inserting, controlling the image, increasing or decreasing contrast, increasing or decreasing brightness, cropping, changing line styles, wrapping text, formatting, setting transparent color, and resetting a picture.

■ *Reviewing toolbar.* The Reviewing toolbar contains buttons for inserting and editing comments, reviewing comments and changes to a document, creating a Microsoft Outlook task, saving a document version, and sending a document to a mail recipient.

■ *Tables and Borders toolbar.* The Tables and Borders toolbar enables you to quickly draw a table and apply borders, change their thicknesses, apply shading, sort rows or columns, and insert formulas.

■ *Visual Basic toolbar.* The Visual Basic toolbar contains buttons for running and recording a macro, accessing the Visual Basic Editor, accessing the Control Toolbox, and exiting Design mode.

■ *Web toolbar.* The Web toolbar contains buttons for loading and navigating Web pages.

■ *WordArt toolbar.* The WordArt toolbar contains buttons for inserting, editing, formatting, shaping, rotating, changing letter heights, aligning text vertically, text alignment, and character spacing.

Word 97 comes with many buttons that are not on the predefined toolbars. To customize predefined toolbars, you can drag off the buttons that you do not need and drag on the buttons that you do need. This is described in Chapter 38, "Customizing the Toolbar, Menus, and Shortcut Keys."

If someone has used Word 97 before you, the predefined toolbars may be modified. Additional custom toolbars may be available to you that previous users have created or that have been created to assist you with specific tasks.

Getting Help on Buttons in the Toolbar

To see what a button does, move the mouse pointer over the button, pause, then read the name of the button in the ScreenTip that pops up.

When you need help using a button, press Shift+F1 and click the button you need help with. A Help window appears to show you how to use the tool. Click the mouse button to close the Help window.

Displaying or Hiding Toolbars

You can choose View, Toolbars or right-click a toolbar to display and hide toolbars on-screen.

To display a toolbar, follow these steps:

1. Choose View, Toolbars to display the toolbar shortcut menu shown in Figure 2.11.

FIG. 2.11
Choose View, Toolbars or the shortcut menu to view the toolbar shortcut menu.

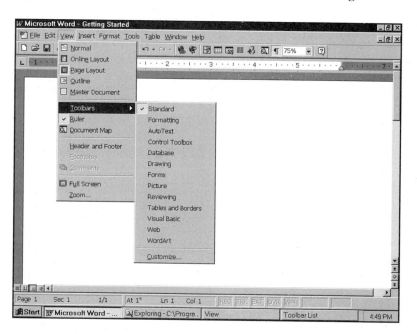

2. Select the toolbar that you want to display. Toolbars with selected check boxes will be displayed.

3. Word 97 displays the toolbar you selected. The toolbar is displayed in the last position in which it was used.

To display a toolbar if you are using a mouse and a toolbar is currently displayed, follow these steps:

1. Right-click in the toolbar to display a shortcut menu.

2. Click the name of the toolbar you want to display.

You can hide a toolbar in three ways:

■ Right-click the toolbar to display the toolbar shortcut menu. In the shortcut menu, displayed toolbars appear with a check mark. Click the name of the displayed toolbar that you want hidden.

■ If a toolbar is in a floating window, you can close it by clicking once on the window's Close button.

■ You can close a toolbar by choosing View, Toolbars. When the toolbar shortcut menu appears, clear the toolbar check box you do not want displayed, and choose OK.

Word 97 records the toolbars and their locations. When you restart Word 97, the toolbars you last used will be available to you.

Moving, Resizing, and Reshaping Toolbars and Menus

You can move and reshape toolbars and menus to fit the way you want to work. Toolbars and menus can be *docked* in a position along an edge of the window, or they can *float* free in their own window. Docked toolbars and menus are one button or word wide or high. You can reshape toolbars and menus that float in a window and drag them wherever they are most convenient to use. Figure 2.12 shows floating and docked toolbars.

To move a toolbar or menu, click the bar at the left edge or top of the toolbar or menu and drag. If you drag the toolbar or menu to an edge of the window, the toolbar or menu docks against the edge. A toolbar or menu is ready to dock when its gray outline becomes thinner.

Toolbars docked against a left or right edge may be too narrow for buttons with a drop-down list to display, such as the Style button. While docked against a left or right edge, these toolbars replace wide drop-down lists with buttons. Clicking a button displays the appropriate dialog box.

Drag on the double gray lines   Floating toolbar
to move this toolbar

FIG. 2.12
Toolbars can be
docked or float free.

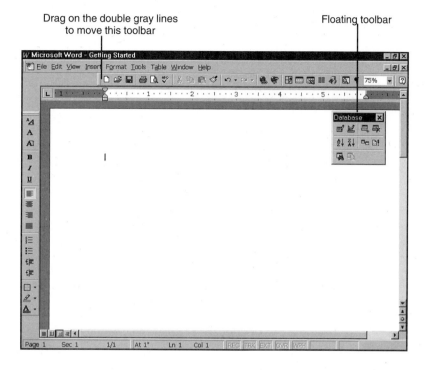

Toolbars and menus also can float free in a window. To move a floating toolbar or menu, click the gray area along one of the wide edges and drag. You can resize a floating toolbar or menu window by dragging on a border. To return the toolbar or menu to a dock, drag the title bar to an edge of the screen and then release.

 You can dock a floating toolbar by double-clicking it in the title bar.

If you use a monitor with higher than VGA resolution, the normal size of buttons may be too small for you to see easily. You can manually switch between normal buttons and larger buttons by choosing View, Toolbars, Customize, Options tab, selecting the Large Icons option, and choosing OK.

▶ **See** "Customizing and Creating Toolbars," **p. 1141**

Working in Dialog Boxes

In drop-down menus, commands that require additional information are followed by an ellipsis (...). Choosing one of these commands displays a dialog box in which you enter needed information. Format, Font, for example, displays the dialog box shown in Figure 2.13. This dialog box contains tabbed sections—the tabs showing across the top of the dialog box. Each tabbed section contains a different type of formatting.

FIG. 2.13

The Font dialog box contains tabbed sections with text boxes, check boxes, and lists.

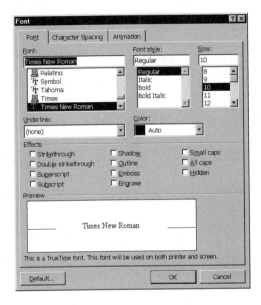

Dialog boxes contain different types of items. These items are described in more detail in the sections immediately following. The following list will help familiarize you with Word 97 dialog box items:

- *Tab.* Multiple sections of a dialog box. Only one group at a time is displayed, and each group contains related options.

- *Text box.* A box in which you can type and edit text, dates, or numbers.

- *Option button.* A button that gives you one choice from a group of options. These are sometimes called *radio buttons*.

- *Check box.* A square box that can be turned on or off.

- *List box.* A list or drop-down list that scrolls to display available alternatives.

- *Command button.* A button that completes or cancels the command; some buttons give you access to additional options.

- *Spinner box.* A box with up-and down-arrowhead buttons which increase or decrease the number in the box.

Selecting a Tab in a Dialog Box

A dialog box like the one shown in Figure 2.13 may contain more than one tab. The tabs appear within the dialog box as though they are cards within a card file—all related options are on the same card. For example, all options relating to formatting fonts are in the Font tab of the Format Font dialog box. The titles of each section appear across the top of the dialog box as though they were tabs on filing cards.

To select a tab with the mouse, click the tab title.

To select a tab by keyboard, you can do one of two things:

■ Press Alt+*letter*, where *letter* is the underlined letter in the tab's name.

■ Hold down the Ctrl key and press the Tab key until the tab title you want displayed is selected.

Selecting Option Buttons and Check Boxes

Figure 2.13 shows check boxes, which appear as squares. Figure 2.14 shows groups of option buttons that appear as circles. You can select only one option button from within a group, but you can select one or more check boxes.

FIG. 2.14
A dialog box can contain groups of option buttons.

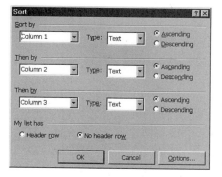

Check boxes are square boxes that you can turn on or off and use in combination with other check boxes. A check box is on when a ✓ appears in the box.

To select or clear a check box, click the check box that you want to change. From the keyboard, press Alt+*letter* where *letter* is the underlined letter in the name of the check box.

To select an option button using the mouse, click the button. To clear an option button, you must click another in the same group. A dot within the option indicates that the option is on. Remember that you can select only one button in a group, but one is always selected.

To select an option button from the keyboard, hold down the Alt key and then press the underlined letter of the option group you want. Alternatively, press Tab until an option in the group is enclosed by dashed lines. After you select the group, press the arrow keys to select the option button that you want from within the group.

 T I P Shift+Tab moves through option buttons in the reverse direction.

When you are using a keyboard and making a succession of changes in a dialog box, pressing the Tab key is probably the easiest way to move between items in the box. The active item is enclosed in a dashed border or is highlighted and contains the flashing insertion point for text editing. To change a check box that is enclosed by the dashed line, press the spacebar. To change an option button in a group enclosed by the dashed line, press the arrow keys.

Editing Text Boxes

You use text boxes to type information, such as file names and numbers, into a dialog box. You can edit the text within a text box the same way you edit text elsewhere in Word 97.

The following mouse actions are used to select multiple letters, a word, or words or formula terms:

Select	Mouse Action
Multiple letters	Drag across letters
Single word	Double-click word
Multiple words	Double-click word; hold down button, then drag over adjacent words

To select text with the keyboard, press the Alt+*letter* combination for the text box. Press the ← or → key to move the flashing insertion point and then type the text you want to insert.

Delete characters to the right of the flashing insertion point by pressing the Delete key. Delete characters to the left of the insertion point by pressing the Backspace key.

N O T E Keep in mind that the insertion point and the I-beam are not the same. The *insertion point* is where typing or deletions will take place. The *I-beam* is the mouse pointer—it moves when you move the mouse. The insertion point moves to the current I-beam location only when you click the left mouse button. ■

To select multiple characters using the keyboard so that you can delete or replace characters by typing, perform the actions listed in Table 2.7.

Part

I

Ch

2

Table 2.7 Text-Editing Actions

Mouse Action	Result
Click I-beam in text	Moves the insertion point in text (flashing cursor) to the I-beam location
Shift+click in text	Selects all text between the current insertion point and the I-beam
Drag	Selects all text over which the I-beam moves while you hold down the mouse button

Keyboard Action	Result
Left/right-arrow key	Moves the insertion point arrow key left/right one character
Shift+arrow key	Selects text as the insertion point moves left or right
Ctrl+left/right-arrow key	Moves the insertion point to the arrow key at the beginning of the preceding/next word
Shift+Ctrl+left/right-arrow key	Selects from the insertion point right-arrow key to the beginning of the preceding or next word
Home	Moves the insertion point to the beginning of the line
Shift+Home	Selects from the insertion point to the beginning of the line
End	Moves the insertion point to the end of the line
Shift+End	Selects from the insertion point to the end of the line

To insert text in a text box using the mouse, click the I-beam at the location where you want the text, and then type the text. If you use a keyboard, press the Alt+*letter* combination or the Tab key to activate the text box, and then press one of the cursor-movement keys shown in Table 2.7 to position the insertion point. Then type your text.

Text you type replaces the selected text only when you select the Typing Replaces Selection check box from the Edit tab of Tools, Options.

You can copy and paste in edit boxes within dialog boxes. This can be useful with commands such as Find or Replace. To do this, select text using the techniques described here, then press Ctrl+X to cut, Ctrl+C to copy, or Ctrl+V to paste. You can even copy and paste between dialog boxes or from a document into a dialog box.

Selecting from List Boxes

In some cases, Word 97 will give you many alternatives from which to select. The Font tab in the Font dialog box, for example, shows you lists of fonts (refer to Figure 2.13).

Some list boxes show only the current selection in what appears to be a text box. To see the entire list of alternatives, you must pull down the list. Figure 2.13, for example, shows the Underline drop-down list in the up position. Figure 2.15 shows the list dropped down to make the selection easier.

FIG. 2.15
The Underline list is a drop-down list which makes choosing a selection easy.

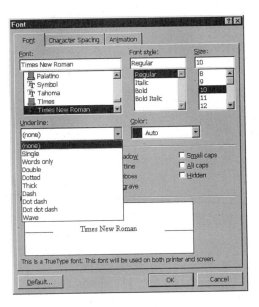

To select an item from a list box, follow these steps:

1. If the list is not displayed, click the down arrow to the side of the list or activate the list box by pressing Alt+*underlined letter.*

2. When the list is displayed, click the arrowheads in the scroll bar to scroll to the name you want. Then click the name you want to select it.

Alternatively, select the name you want by pressing the ↑ key, ↓ key, Home key, or End key.

3. Choose OK.

In most dialog boxes, you can double-click a name in a list box to select the name and choose OK in one operation. You cannot double-click a name in a drop-down list box.

Before you click a command button such as OK, make sure that the name you want to select from the list box is selected (highlighted), not just surrounded by a dashed line.

Part
I
Ch
2

Command Buttons and How to Close Dialog Boxes

Command buttons usually appear at the upper-right corner or down the right side of dialog boxes. You usually use these buttons to execute or cancel a command. With a mouse, you can click a command button to choose it.

From the keyboard, you can choose a command button in three different ways:

- If the command button contains an underlined letter, press Alt+*underlined letter.*
- If a button is bordered in bold, press Enter to choose the button. In most cases, pressing Enter will choose OK. Choose Cancel by pressing Esc.
- You can select any command button by pressing Tab until the button is bordered in bold and then pressing Enter.

Getting Help

Windows and Word 97 have Help information to guide you through new commands and procedures. Word's Help files are extensive and explain topics that range from parts of the screen to commands, dialog boxes, and business procedures.

 TIP You can print the contents of most Help windows by choosing Options, Print Topic from the Help window toolbar.

Working with the Office Assistant

 A new feature that provides tips, helps guide you to the right help information quickly, and interprets what you need before you ask for help is the Office Assistant. The Office Assistant is an on-screen, interactive program that can be customized to provide help while you work. If you don't like the personality of the Assistant or find it too intrusive, try one of the other personalities available for the Assistant. There is a wide range of personalities, including the obnoxious ClipIt—a paper clip with an attitude; a very feline cat; Albert Einstein; and a very unobtrusive Office Assistant. If you are very experienced in the Office applications and find the Assistant gets in the way too much, use the options to specify when the Assistant should appear.

▶ **See** "Customizing the Office Assistant," **p. 1131**

CAUTION

Because the Office Assistant works across all Microsoft Office applications, customizations you make while in Word will also apply while working in other Office applications, such as Excel or PowerPoint.

Opening and Customizing the Assistant   To customize the Office Assistant while working in Word, follow these steps:

1. The Office Assistant is not already running, activate it by choosing Microsoft Word Help from the Help menu, or clicking the Question Mark button on the Standard toolbar. The Office Assistant appears on-screen (see Figure 2.16).

   If you didn't install all the Assistants during the initial setup, you'll need the install disk.

   If the Office Assistant is already running, click the Office Assistant with the left mouse button to display the Office Assistant message box, as shown in Figure 2.16.

FIG. 2.16
The Office Assistant can be customized by choosing the Options button.

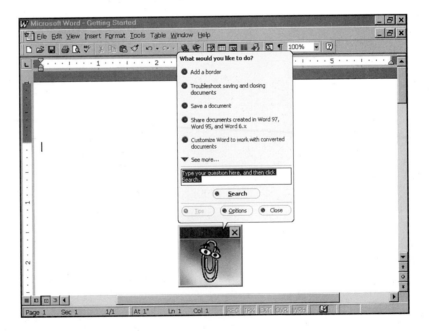

2. Choose <u>O</u>ptions to access the Office Assistant dialog box (see Figure 2.17).

FIG. 2.17

You can customize the Office Assistant to provide only the help you need.

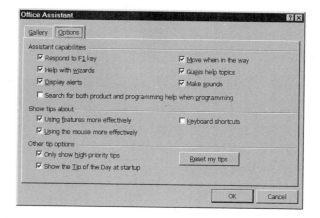

3. Change any of the following options:

Respond to F<u>1</u> Key	Select to display the Office Assistant (rather than the standard Help dialog box) when the F1 key is pressed.
Help with <u>W</u>izards	Select to have the Office Assistant provide instructions while using wizards. For more information about wizards, see Chapter 6, "Using Templates and Wizards for Frequently Created Documents."
<u>D</u>isplay Alerts	Select to have alerts displayed through the Office Assistant (when active) rather than through a standard dialog box.
Search for Both Product and Programming Help When <u>P</u>rogramming	Select to retrieve both product and programming help topics while working with Visual Basic for Applications (VBA); clear this option if you want to see only programming help topics while using VBA. For more information about VBA, see Chapter 39, "Introducing Visual Basic for Applications."

continues

continued

<u>M</u>ove When in the Way	Select to force the Office Assistant to automatically move when it is blocking dialog boxes or other screen elements; the Office Assistant will also shrink in size if it is not used within five minutes.
Gu<u>e</u>ss Help Topics	Select to display suggested Help topics based on your actions prior to asking for help.
Make <u>S</u>ounds	Select to hear sounds made by the Office Assistant.
Using <u>F</u>eatures More Effectively	Select to display tips about features you may not know and ideas on how to better utilize the features you do know.
<u>U</u>sing the Mouse More Effectively	Select to display tips about using the mouse more efficiently.
<u>K</u>eyboard Shortcuts	Select to display shortcut keys for the features you use.
Only Show <u>H</u>igh Priority Tips	Select to display only those tips that are especially important, such as tips about time-saving features.
Show the <u>T</u>ip of the Day at Startup	Select to display the Tip of the Day when Word or any other Office application starts.
<u>R</u>eset My Tips	Select to see tips you have already seen.

▶ **See** "Customizing the Office Assistant," **p. 1131**

To change the look of your assistant, follow these steps:

1. Make sure the Office Assistant is running (see the previous section for instructions).

   If you didn't install all the Assistants during the initial setup, you'll need the install disk.

2. Click the Office Assistant with the right mouse button and select <u>C</u>hoose Assistant from the shortcut menu. The Office Assistant dialog box appears with the <u>G</u>allery tab selected (see Figure 2.18).

FIG. 2.18
Use the Gallery to
select any of nine
assistants.

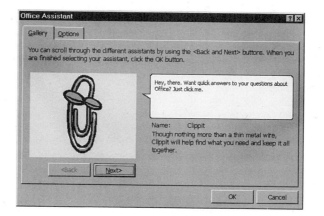

3. Use the <u>N</u>ext and <u>B</u>ack buttons to scroll through the different assistants.

T I P You can sample the animation of an assistant by right-clicking the Office Assistant and choosing <u>A</u>nimate from the shortcut menu.

4. When you find an assistant you like, choose OK.

Learning with the Assistant   The Office Assistant can help you learn while you work by providing tips, helping when using wizards, and suggesting help based on your current actions. As your knowledge increases, customize the Office Assistant, as described in the "Opening and Customizing the Assistant" section, to provide only the type of help you need.

Tips provide information while you work about how to use features and keyboard short-cuts more effectively. When a light bulb appears in the Office Assistant, click it to display the tip. If the Office Assistant is not visible, click the Office Assistant button, then click the light bulb to display the tip.

To select specific types of tips, follow these steps:

1. If the Office Assistant is not already running, activate it by choosing Microsoft Word <u>H</u>elp from the <u>H</u>elp menu or click the Office Assistant button. The Office Assistant appears on-screen (see Figure 2.16).

   If the Office Assistant is already running, click the Office Assistant with the left mouse button to display the Office Assistant message box, as shown in Figure 2.16.

2. Choose <u>O</u>ptions to access the Office Assistant dialog box (see Figure 2.17).

3. In the Show Tips About group, click the Using Features More Effectively check box to have Office Assistant display tips about how to use features more effectively.

   Click the Using the Mouse More Effectively check box to have Office Assistant display tips about how to use the mouse more effectively.

   Click the Keyboard Shortcuts check box to have Office Assistant display tips about keyboard shortcuts for the features you are currently using.

   Click the Using the Mouse More Effectively check box to have Office Assistant display tips about how to use the mouse more effectively.

4. In the Other Tip Options group, click the Only Show High Priority Tips check box to have Office Assistant display only the most important tips.

   Click the Show the Tip of the Day at Startup check box to have Office Assistant display the tip of the day each time you start up the application.

5. Click OK.

Office Assistant can provide helpful instructions while running a wizard by selecting the following options:

1. If the Office Assistant is not already running, activate it by choosing Microsoft Word Help from the Help menu or click the Office Assistant button. The Office Assistant appears on-screen (see Figure 2.16).

   If the Office Assistant is already running, click the Office Assistant with the left mouse button to display the Office Assistant message box, as shown in Figure 2.16.

2. Choose Options to access the Office Assistant dialog box (see Figure 2.17).

3. In the Assistant capabilities group, click the Help with Wizards check box.

4. Click OK.

Office Assistant can also return a list of help topics related to your current task before you need to ask for Help.

To have the Office Assistant return relevant Help topics while you work, follow these steps:

1. If the Office Assistant is not already running, activate it by choosing Microsoft Word Help from the Help menu or click the Office Assistant button. The Assistant appears on-screen (see Figure 2.16).

   If the Office Assistant is already running, click the Assistant with the left mouse button to display the Office Assistant message box, as shown in Figure 2.16.

2. Choose Options to access the Office Assistant dialog box (see Figure 2.17).

3. In the Assistant Capabilities group, click the Guess Help Topics check box.

4. Click OK.

Hiding the Assistant   You may want to hide the Office Assistant and display it only when you press F1 or click the Office Assistant button. To hide the Office Assistant, click the Close button on the Office Assistant.

Getting Help Without the Assistant   To get help in Word or a Windows application without the Office Assistant, choose Help, Contents and Index. The Help Topics dialog box is displayed as shown in Figure 2.19.

FIG. 2.19
The Help Contents window lists the topics you can get help on.

The Help Topics dialog box can also be displayed when you press F1. Follow these steps:

1. If the Office Assistant is not already running, activate it by choosing Microsoft Word Help from the Help menu or click the Office Assistant button. The Assistant appears on-screen (see Figure 2.16).

   If the Office Assistant is already running, click the Assistant with the left mouse button to display the Office Assistant message box, as shown in Figure 2.16.

2. Choose Options to access the Office Assistant dialog box (see Figure 2.17).

3. In the Assistant Capabilities group, clear the Respond to F1 key check box.

4. Click OK.

From this Help Topics dialog box, you can learn how to use Help, or you can see the contents of all Help topics. Notice that you can access or control Help information in different ways:

- You can select a topic from the list in the Contents tab.
- You can select the Index tab and select a topic.
- You can select the Find tab and search for a topic.

Command buttons are located under the title bar in a Help topic window and help you move through the Help topics. Choose a button by clicking it or by pressing Alt+*letter.* The following command buttons help you move through information:

Button	Action
Help Topics	Shows the index or contents of Help at the highest level.
Back	Returns to the preceding Help topic. With this button, you can retrace the topics you have viewed back to the initial Help Index.
Options	Displays a list of options used for adding notes, copying and printing the topic, changing the font, keeping the help dialog box open and displayed over other active windows, and changing system colors. Click an option or press the underlined letter to select the topic.

Within Word's dialog boxes, you can often get help on the dialog box contents by clicking the ? button, located at the top right of the box. When the pointer changes to a question mark, click the element of the dialog box with which you need help. A pop-up help window describes the part of the dialog box which you clicked, as shown in Figure 2.20.

FIG. 2.20
Get help in dialog boxes by clicking the question mark and then clicking an item in the box.

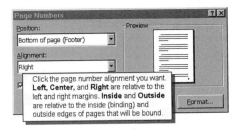

Getting the Tip of the Day

Often we get so involved with daily tasks we forget to look for ways to improve our work or to improve our skills. Word comes with a feature called Tip of the Day that is a painless way to learn a few of the many shortcuts in Word.

By selecting the Show the Tip of the Day at Startup check box of the Options tab of the Office Assistant dialog box, a tip will appear each time you start up Word 97.

Whenever you see a light bulb displayed next to the Office Assistant, click it to see a helpful tip about your current actions.

Searching for a Topic in Help

The Find tab enables you to search for specific words and phrases in Help topics. To use Find, choose Help, Contents and Index, then choose the Find tab. The dialog box shown in Figure 2.21 appears.

FIG. 2.21
The Find tab in Help is used to search for specific words or phrases.

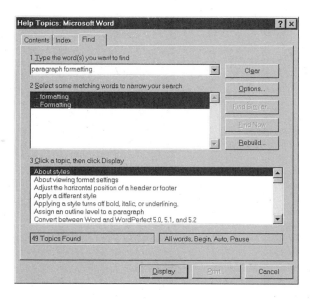

Type a word in the second drop-down list box. The top list will display matching words or phrases that you can select to narrow the search. Select a topic from the bottom list and click the Display button.

You also can click the Options button to select additional search options, or click the Find Similar button to display a list of similar topics.

The Rebuild button creates a list of every word from the help files. The list must be created before you can use Find.

The Index tab enables you to search for a specific word by typing the first few letters of the word. To use Index, choose Help, Contents and Index, then choose the Index tab. The dialog box shown in Figure 2.22 displays.

FIG. 2.22

The Index tab in Help is used to search for a specific word.

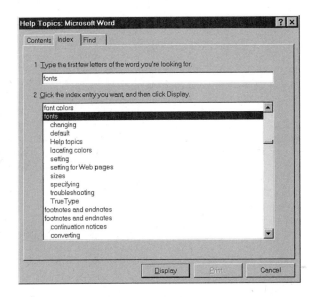

Type a few letters of the word you want to find in the first text box. The second box displays matching words and phrases that you can select to narrow the search. Select an index entry you want from the second box and click the Display button.

Jumping Between Help Topics

Hot words or *hot phrases* appear within the actual Help text. These words or phrases have a solid or dashed underline and are displayed in green, meaning that the word or phrase is linked to additional information. Words or phrases with definitions appear with a dashed underline.

To jump to the topic related to a solid underlined word, click the word or press Tab until the word is selected and press Enter.

To display the definition of a word that appears with a dashed underline, click the word or tab to the word and press Enter. Click again or press Enter to remove the definition.

Getting Help in Dialog Boxes

You can get help for any dialog box or error message that appears in Word 97. You can get help in a dialog box by clicking the ? button then clicking the specific item you want information about, or by moving the mouse pointer over the item you want information about then right-clicking the mouse (see Figure 2.23).

FIG. 2.23
The Help message appears after you click the Help button when the Font tab in the Font dialog box is active.

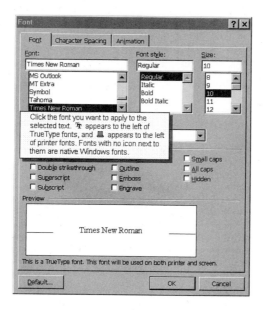

TROUBLESHOOTING

A dialog box is displaying an error message that I don't understand. Press F1. A help window appears with an explanation of the error. Read the help window and follow the recommendations to resolve the problem.

To learn what action a command performs or how a portion of the screen works, press Shift+F1 and then click that command or portion of the screen. You can also click the Help button in the Standard toolbar. Notice that the mouse pointer changes to a question mark that overlays the pointer. You can press Shift+F1 to ask a question about the item you click.

TROUBLESHOOTING

When I press Shift+F1 to display the question mark cursor so I can get context-sensitive help, a Help for WordPerfect Users dialog box appears. The Help for WordPerfect Users option is turned on, which is why you get this dialog box instead of the question mark cursor. To turn off this option, choose Tools, Options, and select the General tab. Clear the Help for WordPerfect Users option and choose OK.

Annotating, Copying, or Printing Help

You can add your own notes to tailor the Help system to your specific needs using the Annotate command. The Copy command enables you to copy the text of a help topic and then paste it into a document. You also can print the text of a help topic by choosing Print Topic.

To add notes to a help topic, click the Options button in a Help Topic window, choose Annotate, type in your notes in the Annotate dialog box, and then choose Save. Notice that a paper clip symbol appears before the text of the help topic. Clicking this symbol accesses your notes.

To copy the text of a help topic, click the Options button, and then choose Copy. The help text is now copied to the Clipboard, enabling you to paste it into a document.

To print the text of a help topic, click the Options button, choose Print Topic, set up the desired printer options, and then choose OK.

Closing the Help Window

Because Help is an actual application, you need to close its window when you are done. To remove the Help window, click the X in the top-right corner; or press Alt, spacebar, and then C for Close, or press Alt+F4.

Manipulating Windows

When you use Word 97, you can display and run more than one application in Windows or use multiple documents while you are in Word 97. Seeing that much information on your screen can be confusing unless you keep your windows organized. Just as you organize folders and papers on your desk, you can organize your Windows applications and Word 97 documents.

▶ **See** "Working with Multiple Documents," **p. 98**

You will see two types of windows on-screen:

- An application window contains an application, such as Windows Explorer, Word 97, or Excel.
- A document window contains a Word 97 document. You can open multiple document windows within the Word 97 window.

Switching Between Applications

You can work in an application or document only when its window is active. The active window has a solid title bar. In most cases, the active window is also the top window. In a few instances, however, such as during the process of linking documents together, the active window may not be on top.

If you are running Word 97 with other Windows or non-Windows applications, you can switch between application windows by activating the application whose window you want. If the taskbar is not displayed at the bottom of the screen, move the mouse pointer to the bottom of the screen. The taskbar appears, displaying the applications that are currently running. Choose an application by clicking its button in the taskbar. If you are using a keyboard or cannot find the taskbar with the mouse, press Ctrl+Esc to make it appear.

You also can cycle between applications by holding down the Alt key and pressing Tab. An application bar displays icons for each open application. Pressing the Alt+Tab key moves a selection box between icons. Release Alt and Tab when the box encloses the icon for the application you want active.

Switching Between Document Windows

Because Word 97 makes working with several documents easy, you frequently may have more than one window on-screen. Each document window may contain a different document. You can affect only the active document window, however. From within the Word 97 window, if you can see the window, you can make it active by clicking it with the mouse pointer. If you cannot see the document window, move the other document windows so that you can see it.

To switch to another window from the keyboard, choose the Window menu and then press or click the number of the document window that you want to activate. The name of each document appears in the menu. You can cycle between document windows by pressing Ctrl+F6.

Minimizing, Maximizing, and Restoring Windows

For complex jobs, you may need to work with more than one application and each application may have more than one document. Working with many applications and documents at once can become visually confusing, so Windows supplies a way for you to work with multiple windows at a time and to get unused windows out of the way but keep them quickly available.

Applications and documents use three control buttons at the top right corner of each window or title bar. When a document window fills the application, then the document's control buttons move to the right edge of the application's menu bar.

To gain more room on the desktop, you can store open applications by minimizing them so that they become small buttons in the taskbar at the bottom of the Windows desktop. To *minimize* an application, click the minimize button at the right end of the application title bar. When an application minimizes to a button on the taskbar, it is still open, but out of the way on the screen. Click the application button on the taskbar to reopen the application window.

 If you can't see the Windows taskbar, press Ctrl+Esc. The Start menu and taskbar will display.

To minimize a document window so it is out of the way but still open, click the minimize button at the right side of a document window's title bar. The minimize button looks like a small bar. If the document window fills the application window, then the document's minimize button will be at the right edge of the menu bar. A minimized document becomes a small taskbar at the bottom of the application window. Click the restore or maximize buttons on a minimized document to restore the document to a window or fill the inside of the application window.

Restore applications or documents into a window by clicking the Restore button. This button looks like overlapping windows.

Fill the Windows desktop with an application by clicking the application's maximize button. The maximize button looks like a single large square window. Maximize a document so that it fills the inside of an application window by clicking the document's maximize button.

NOTE Double-click the title bar of an application to maximize or restore it. Double-click the title bar of a document to restore it to a window. ▮

TIP Press Alt, spacebar to open the application's Control menu. Press Alt, hyphen (-) to open the document's Control menu.

Moving a Window

With multiple applications or multiple Word 97 documents on-screen, you will want to move windows for the same reason that you shuffle papers on your desk. You can move a window with the mouse or the keyboard by following these steps:

■ If you are using a mouse, activate the window that you want to move. Drag the title bar until the shadow border is where you want the window to be located. Release the mouse button to fix the window in its new location.

■ From the keyboard, select the application or document Control menu by pressing Alt, spacebar for the application Control menu or Alt, hyphen for the document Control menu. Press M to select <u>M</u>ove. A four-headed arrow appears in the title bar. Press an arrow key to move the shadowed outline of the window. Press Enter to fix the window in its new location, or press Esc to retain the original location.

Sizing a Window

You often want to see only part of an application or document window. The following steps show you how to change the size of the window by using the mouse or the keyboard.

To resize a window with the mouse, drag the window edge or corner to the location you want, then release the mouse button.

To resize a window from the keyboard, follow these steps:

1. Activate the window.
2. Press Alt, spacebar for the application Control menu or Alt, hyphen for the document Control menu.
3. Press S for <u>S</u>ize.

 TIP The Size feature is not available if the window is maximized.

4. Press the arrow key that points to the edge you want to reposition.
5. Press the arrow keys to move that edge.
6. Press Enter to fix the edge in its new location, or press Esc to cancel.

Part
I
Ch
2

Closing a Document Window

When you finish with a document, you should close the window to remove it from the screen and to free memory. If you made a change since the last time you saved the document, Word displays an Alert dialog box, shown in Figure 2.24, asking whether you want to save your work before closing. Choose Yes if you want to save your most recent changes before closing a document.

▶ **See** "Saving a Document," **p. 100**

FIG. 2.24
An Alert dialog box prompts you for a specific action.

There is an important difference between closing a document window and closing the document. If more than one window is open on a document, you can close a window without closing the file. However, if there is only one document window or if you choose File, Close, you close the file and all document windows that show that file.

To close the active document window using a mouse when more than one window is open on a document, double-click the document Control menu icon on the left side of the document's title bar (when the document is in its own window), or click the Close button on the right-end of the menu bar.

To close the active document window by keyboard when more than one window is open on a document, press Alt, hyphen to choose the document Control menu, and press C for Close.

To close the file so that all windows using a document close, follow these steps:

1. Choose File, Close.

   The window closes if no changes have been made to the document since the last save.

2. If you made changes to the document after the last save, a dialog box appears, asking you to confirm whether you want to save your changes.

   In the dialog box, click the No command button if you don't want to save the changed version of the file, or click the Yes command button to save your changes.

3. If you chose Yes and the file has not been saved before, a Save As dialog box appears. Enter a new file name and choose Save.

   ▶ **See** "Closing a Document," **p. 112**

To close all visible documents, hold down the Shift key as you choose the File menu. The Close All command will be available in place of Close. Choose Close All to close all visible documents. ●

CHAPTER 3

Creating and Saving Documents

Word processing basics begin with creating a new document, typing the text, and saving the document. You need to know how to accomplish these basic tasks before you move on to learn about the more advanced tools that Word 97 offers for working with your documents. In this chapter, you learn how to create a new document, open an existing document, and how to save your documents. You also learn how to work with more than one document at the same time. ◼

Name documents and folders

Long file names are easier to understand, but they still must adhere to a few rules.

Opening documents

Open new documents or documents based on templates and predefined documents.

Saving documents

Save documents using Word or other file formats to the hard disk, intranet, or Internet.

What You Need to Know About Creating and Saving Documents

When you are working on a document in Word, the document is stored in the memory of your computer. This memory is often referred to as *RAM*, or *random-access memory*, and it is a temporary location for the programs and documents you use when you are working with your computer. When you exit a program or turn off your computer, whatever was stored in memory vanishes. For this reason, you need a permanent storage location for your programs and files. Floppy disks and hard disks are used for this purpose. They are magnetic media, much like the cassette tapes that are used to record music, on which information from your computer can be stored for as long as you want.

When you first open Word, you are presented with a blank document. You can begin typing text into this document right away. Until you save the file, the work you do is only temporarily stored in the computer's memory. Eventually, you need to save this document onto a disk, either the hard disk in your computer or a floppy disk, using File, Save. When you first save the document, you need to give it a name, which you do in the Save As dialog box. From then on, you have the choice of saving the file with the same name, or saving it with a new name, which you can do using File, Save As.

Understanding File Names

The first time you save a new document, you must give it a name and assign it to a disk drive and folder. With previous versions of Word, you were limited to an eight-character file name, with a three-character extension. With Windows 95, you can now use longer file names. Keep these guidelines in mind when naming files:

- For the file name, you can type as many as 255 characters, including spaces.
- You can use letters A through Z (uppercase or lowercase), numbers 0 through 9, hyphens (-), underscores (_), and exclamation points (!).
- Legal characters include !, @, #, $, %, ~`, &, (,), _, -, {, and }.

 TIP   If you want a file to be listed first when sorted alphabetically, precede the file name with an underscore character. For example:

_Read me
_Read me next
Anderson sales information
Barkely statistics
Procedure manual-first draft

■ You cannot use the following characters:

   \ ? : * , " < > |

■ Word provides its own extension, DOC. You can override this default when you name your file by including a period and an extension. Using the Word default extension is better, however, because the extension helps you to identify each file's type and eases the task of opening files. (By default, Word lists only files with the DOC extension in the Open dialog box.)

Understanding Folders

You usually save files within a folder on your hard disk. Folders are a way of organizing files. Folders are analogous to the file drawers and file folders you use in your office to help you organize and locate your paper files. You can locate files more easily if you store related files together in a folder. For example, you could store all the business letters you create in Word in a folder named \BUSINESS LETTERS and all your proposals in a folder named \PROPOSAL.

Part

I

Ch

3

> **CAUTION**
>
> Don't store the files you create in the folders where your program files are stored. If you ever have to reinstall or upgrade Word, you could lose any files you stored in the program folders. Create your own folders and folders within folders for storing your files.

The first time you use File, Open or File, Save As, Word assumes that you want to open or save a document in the MY DOCUMENTS folder. Instead, you usually want to open or save a file in one of your own folders. For example, you may have a folder named C:\ LETTERS. You must tell Word where the file you want to open is located or where you want to save a file—whether that location is a different folder, a different drive on your hard disk, or a disk in drive A or B. To switch folders or drives, use the appropriate list boxes in the Open and Save As dialog boxes, as discussed in the following paragraphs.

The selected folder appears in the Look In list (see Figure 3.1). You can display this list to select another drive.

The list box includes all the subfolders in the current folder. You may see different folders in the dialog box, depending on the folders you have set up on your system. An icon that resembles a file folder represents each folder. If you want to open a file in a subfolder, you first must open the folder. You can do so by double-clicking the subfolder icon.

FIG. 3.1

You can change drives and folders in the Save As dialog box or the Open dialog box.

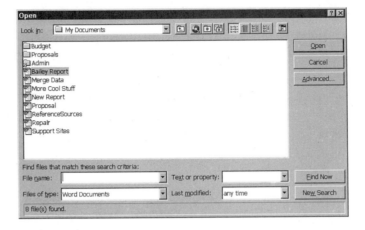

To change disk drives or folders in the Open dialog box, follow these steps:

1. Click the Look In list and select the drive you want.

2. To select a folder, double-click the folder icon. You also can use the Up One Level button to move up one level in the folder structure.

3. Select the file from the list. Or type the file name in the File Name box.

4. Choose Open.

You can use the same procedures as just described in the Save As dialog box to change drives and folders when you are saving a file.

Setting the Default Folder

When you first choose File, Open or File, Save As, you see a listing of files in the \MY DOCUMENTS folder. When you switch folders in the Open dialog box (or the Save As dialog box), that folder becomes the current folder until you close Word, and whenever you choose File, Open or File, Save As, the files in the current folder are listed.

You can change the default folder, which is the folder that appears when you first choose File, Open or File, Save As. Making the folder where you store the files that you use most often your default folder can save you some time when you open and save files.

To change the default folder, follow these steps:

1. Choose Tools, Options to display the Options dialog box.

2. Select the File Locations tab. The File Locations tab displays (see Figure 3.2).

3. Select Documents in the File Types list.

4. Click Modify to display the Modify Location dialog box.

5. Select the folder you want to use as the default from the list box or type the full path name for the folder in the Folder Name text box.

6. Choose OK and then choose Close.

FIG. 3.2

You can change the default folder for Word documents.

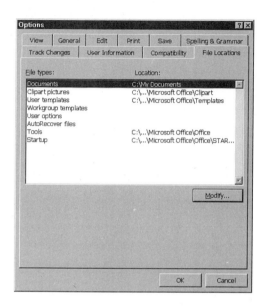

Opening an Existing Document

The great advantage to word processors is that you can use the same files repeatedly to create similar documents. You can return to the same document as many times as you want to print it, edit it, or add new material to it. Or you can open an existing document and use parts of it in a new document.

You are not restricted to opening files created by Word. When you install Word, you are given the option of installing one or more conversion files that enable you to open files created by other programs, for example, WordPerfect. Word's conversion capability enables you to view and edit a document created by another user using a different program or to convert documents you created on another word processor as you make the transition to Word.

You can speed up the process of opening a file by automatically opening Word and a document at the same time by double-clicking a file's icon in My Computer or Windows Explorer.

What You Need to Know About Opening a Document

Opening a document involves locating the document in a drive and folder and knowing what type the file is. Word, by default, lists only files that end in the extension DOC in the Open dialog box. The program also can open template files (which have the extension DOT) and files created by other programs (which have various extensions). To open a file with an extension other than DOC, you must specify the extension you want to list by choosing the file type in the Files of Type box in the Open dialog box or by typing the extension preceded by the characters *. in the File Name box and then pressing Enter.

You can use wild cards to help you locate the type of file you want. An asterisk (*) means any character or characters, and a question mark (?) means any single character. If you want to locate all files that end in the extension EXT, for example, type ***.EXT** in the File Name box. If you want to list files with any name that end in any extension, type ***.*** in the File Name box.

Opening a Document

Use File, Open to open an existing document. Switch to the drive and folder where the file is stored, and then select the file from the list of files in the Open dialog box.

To open an existing document, follow these steps:

1. Choose File, Open or press Ctrl+O or click the Open button on the Standard toolbar. The Open dialog box appears (see Figure 3.3).

FIG. 3.3

Select the file you want to open in the Open dialog box.

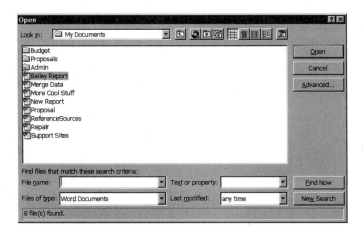

2. If necessary, select a different disk drive in the Look In drop-down list (see "Understanding Folders," earlier in this chapter).

3. If necessary, select a different folder in the list (see "Understanding Folders," earlier in this chapter).

4. If necessary, select a different file type in the Files of <u>T</u>ype box.

5. If you want to prevent changes to the original document, choose the Commands and Settings button in the dialog box toolbar and choose Op<u>e</u>n Read Only from the menu.

   This option prevents the use of <u>F</u>ile, <u>S</u>ave, which replaces the original version with the changed document. Documents opened with Read Only must be saved with <u>F</u>ile, Save <u>A</u>s and a new file name.

6. In the File <u>N</u>ame text box, type the name of the file you want to open, or select the file you want to open from the list.

7. Choose <u>O</u>pen. As a shortcut for steps 6 and 7, you can double-click the file name to open it.

To add a file or folder, select it in the Open dialog box. Then choose the Add to Favorites button. To open the file or folder, use the Look in Favorites button.

> **NOTE** You can use the Open dialog box to search for files. For example, you can find files using summary information, file information, or any string of characters that appears in the file. After you find a file, you can open, print, view, copy, or delete it. For details about the search features, see Chapter 4, "Managing Documents and Files." ■

 TIP If you want fast access to a frequently used folder or file, you can create a shortcut and keep it in the Favorites folder. You can then select the shortcut and open the folder or file without having to figure out where that file or folder is stored.

 TIP Right-click file names in the Open dialog box to see a shortcut menu with many file management commands.

▶ **See** "Searching for Files," **p. 124**

Opening Documents Containing Macros

When you attempt to open a document containing macros, the dialog box shown in Figure 3.4 appears. This dialog box offers you protection against a new breed of computer viruses that are embedded in Word documents and can infect other files on your computer when activated. Once infected, every document file you open and save can become infected. Although Excel cannot check for and remove these macro viruses, you will be

Part
I

Ch
3

warned whenever you open a document containing macros so that you can choose not to open the file or to open it but disable the macros. A macro virus can only infect other files if you run the macro containing the virus.

When the warning dialog box appears, choose Disable Macros if you are unsure of the source of the document and don't want to risk infecting your computer with a macro virus. In this case, you can either check with the author of the document to be sure that the document is clean or you can scan the file for macro viruses using one of the antivirus software applications available for Windows 95. The latest versions of the well-known antivirus applications include protection against Excel and Word macro viruses. If you disable the macros, be aware that the macros will not run and some of the custom features in the document may not work.

If you are confident that the document is safe, choose Enable Macros. Choose Do Not Open if you decide not to open the document until you can check it for macro viruses. You can turn off the check for macros by choosing Tools, Options, then select the General tab and clear the Macro Virus Protection option.

FIG. 3.4

When you open a document containing macros, you can disable the macros to protect your computer against potential macro viruses.

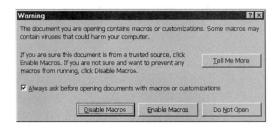

ON THE WEB

For online information on anti-virus software and up-to-date virus definition files, visit the following Web sites:

http://www.mcafee.com

http://www.symantec.com

Opening a Recently Used File

Word remembers the last several documents you have used and lists them at the bottom of the File menu. You can quickly open any of these documents by selecting it from the list.

To reopen a recently closed file, follow these steps:

1. Choose <u>F</u>ile.
2. Select the file name from the bottom of the menu by clicking the file you want to reopen or typing the number of the file you want to reopen.

N O T E   You can specify how many files appear in the list at the bottom of the <u>F</u>ile menu by choosing <u>T</u>ools, <u>O</u>ptions and selecting the General tab. Select or type the number of entries you want to appear in the list in the Entries spin box next to the <u>R</u>ecently Used File List check box and choose OK. ▦

Opening Word Documents on the Internet or Intranet

You can open Word documents from within Windows Explorer or Outlook. Opening from within Windows Explorer is a convenient way to quickly see many files and their folders—folder navigation seems faster within Explorer. To open a DOC file from the Explorer, follow these steps:

1. Open Windows Explorer.
2. In the left pane, double-click the folder containing the file you want to open.
3. In the right pane, double-click the file you want to open.

T I P   Open multiple documents at one time from the Explorer by selecting multiple files in the Windows Explorer's right pane. Use Ctrl+click and Shift+click to select multiple files. After selecting multiple files, right-click and choose Open.

To open files from within Outlook, Microsoft's personal information manager, follow these steps:

1. Click the Other group located on the Outlook bar. The Outlook bar appears at the left side of Outlook as shown in Figure 3.5.
2. Select the folder containing the file you want to open. Double-click folders to open them.
3. Double-click the file you want to open.

   For easier access to folders and files within Outlook, click the Folder List button in the Outlook toolbar. This inserts a hierarchical folder list to the right of the Outlook bar. Open and close this folder list just as you open and close folders within Explorer.

FIG. 3.5

After selecting the Other button, you can double-click documents or folders you want to open.

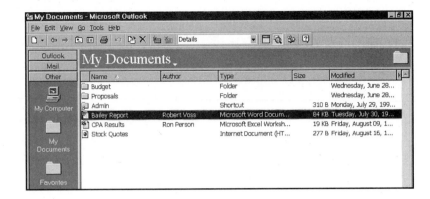

Opening an Intranet or Internet Page

Although HTML pages, also known as Web pages, are easily accessed over networks, they do not have all the formatting capabilities of Word documents. If you want people to have easy access to files and documents that contain advanced formatting, use Word documents on the Internet or company intranet.

Any Internet browser can view and print a Word document with the use of the free Word viewer add-in available from Microsoft. If you already have Word and are connected to a Web, your browser can load Word when you access a Web page. Using Word with a browser is described in "Working and Browsing in Office Applications" in Chapter 15.

You also can save or open Word documents that are stored on an FTP (File Transfer Protocol) site on the Internet or intranet. Word can use the FTP site like any other hard drive or network drive.

Before you can access an FTP site, you must add the FTP site to the list in the Save As and Open dialog boxes. To add an FTP site, see the section "Adding an FTP Site to the Open and Save As Dialog Box" in Chapter 4.

▶ **See** "Browsing Office Documents Without the Application," **p. 540**

You can open Word documents that are on either a File Transfer Protocol (FTP) site on your company's intranet site or on the Internet. An FTP site is a useful way to both load and transfer your documents, making them accessible to others on the Net.

To open a Word document on an FTP site, follow these steps:

1. Choose File, Open.

2. Scroll to the bottom of the Look In list to see available FTP sites.

3. Click the FTP site containing the file you want to open.

   Your Internet browser will activate, and you may be prompted for access information. Once connection is established, browse through the folders as you would on your own hard disk.

4. Select a file, or in the File Name text box type the file name.

5. Click Open.

Opening Non-Word Files

Word can open files created by other programs such as the Windows Notepad (or any other application that creates a text file), WordPerfect, Word for DOS, Works, and others. You use File, Open, but then you must identify the file type so that Word can convert the file into its own format. (Word proposes the file type it thinks the file should be, which is usually correct.)

To open non-Word files, follow these steps:

1. Choose File, Open, or click the Open button on the Standard toolbar.

2. Select the drive and folder containing the file you want to open.

3. Display the Files of Type drop-down list and select the type of file you want to open.

4. From the list of files, select the file you want to open.

5. Choose OK.

Opening a Document While Starting Word

From My Computer or Windows Explorer, you can start Word and open a file at the same time. This is handy if you use these tools to help you find a file and you want to immediately open the file.

To open a file from My Computer or Windows Explorer, follow these steps:

1. Display the window containing the Word document you want to open.

2. Double-click the file. Word starts and displays the document you selected.

   You can also open a document from the Office toolbar on the desktop.

TROUBLESHOOTING

When I choose File, Open and switch to the folder where my file should be stored, I don't see the file listed. If you selected to display only certain file types, you may not see the file listed. Be sure that Word Documents or All Documents is selected in the Files of Type list.

Whenever I try to open a particular document in Word, I get a dialog box asking me for a password. How can I access this document? Someone must have saved the document as a protected file. This means you must know the password that was assigned to the document to open it. Find out from others who have worked on the document what the password is.

Creating a New Document

When you first start Word (see Chapter 2, "Getting Started in Word"), you see a blank document, ready for typing (see Figure 3.6). This new document is named Document1 to indicate that the document is the first one you have created since starting the program.

FIG. 3.6

A blank document, ready for you to begin entering text.

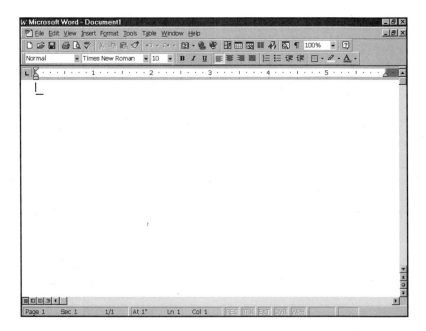

If your new document isn't the first one you have seen since starting Word, however, the document is numbered accordingly: the second new document is called Document2, the third is Document3, and so on. Even if you save and close Document1, the next new document in the current working session is numbered Document2.

You can create a new document in Word in three ways. New documents can be based on three different types of *templates*. These templates contain frequently used text, formatting styles, macros, and custom settings. The three different templates that documents can be based on are the following:

- NORMAL.DOT, which contains the default settings for standard documents.
- Custom templates that come with Word (such as Professional Fax) or that you create that contain predefined text, formatting styles, macros, and custom features necessary for a specific type of document.
- Template Wizards, which are templates combined with intelligent dialog boxes that guide you through the process of completing the document. Wizards come with Word, or they can be built by individuals familiar with Visual Basic for Applications (VBA).

The following sections describe how to open documents based on these three different templates.

Understanding Templates

When you create a new document, Word bases the new document on a template. Unless you specify otherwise, Word uses the Normal template, NORMAL.DOT, as the basis for your new document.

A *template* is a predefined set of formatting characteristics, such as type style, margin width, tab settings, and so on, and can also contain boilerplate text, such as a letterhead. Word comes with templates for creating standard business letters, memos, fax cover sheets, and many other types of documents. These templates save you the trouble of having to type standard text, such as the To, From, and Subject fields in a memo, and they help you produce documents that are formatted consistently from one to the next.

You also can create your own templates. For example, you may want to base your document on a special template you have created called Letters that includes formatting to match your company's letterhead. Unless you choose otherwise, however, Word bases new documents on the Normal template. You can think of NORMAL.DOT as the global template, which contains the settings that are used by default for new documents.

Part
I
Ch
3

Creating a New Blank Document

When you want to start writing in a blank document, you will usually use the NORMAL.DOT template as a basis for the new document. Opening a document based on NORMAL.DOT is very easy.

To start a new document, follow these steps:

1. Choose File, New or press Ctrl+N. The New dialog box appears (see Figure 3.7).

2. Choose OK.

 You also can start a new document by clicking the New button on the Standard toolbar. A new document based on the Normal template opens.

FIG. 3.7
Start a new document from the New dialog box.

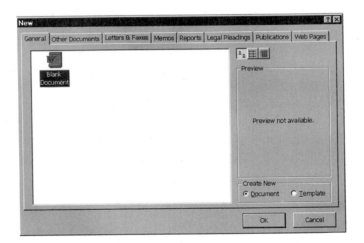

Creating a New Document from a Template

When you use File, New to open a new document, the New dialog box appears on-screen (see Figure 3.7). In the New dialog box, you see tabs for different template types. By default, the General tab is displayed, and the Normal template is selected (the template that a new document opened with the New button is based on). You will probably use the Normal template for most of your documents. However, you can choose one of the other predefined templates if you want, or you can choose a custom template that you have created. Select the tab to see the available templates. You also can preview a template to see what it contains.

T I P You can change how the available templates appear in the New dialog box using the buttons. You can select List, Details, or Large Icons as the view.

To open a new document based on a template, follow these steps:

1. Choose File, New. The New dialog box appears (refer to Figure 3.7).
2. Select the tab that contains the template you want to use or preview.
3. To see a preview of a template, select it in the list (see Figure 3.8).
4. If you want to use this template, choose OK.

FIG. 3.8
Preview a template
by selecting it.

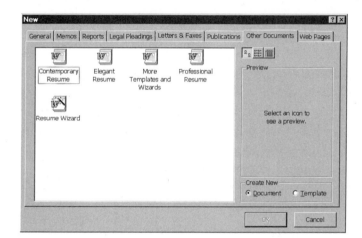

Creating a New Document with a Template Wizard

When you display some of the tabs, you will notice that some templates include "Wizard" after the name. Wizards provide on-screen guidance as you create a new document. For example, if you choose the Fax Wizard, you are guided through the entire process of creating a fax cover sheet, step-by-step. All you have to do is follow the instructions in the dialog boxes as they appear on-screen. A series of buttons along the bottom of the Wizard dialog boxes enable you to move from one dialog box to the next.

To create a new document using a wizard, follow these steps:

1. Choose File, New.
2. Select the tab that contains the type of document you want to create.
3. Select the wizard you want to use from the list. A sample appears in the Preview box.
4. Choose OK. A Wizard dialog box appears, as shown in Figure 3.9.
5. Follow the steps in the Wizard dialog box, using the buttons at the bottom of the dialog box to move from box to box.

FIG. 3.9
Wizards guide you
through the process
of creating a new
document.

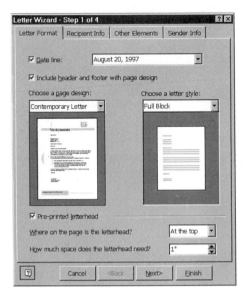

N O T E   Most of your documents will probably be based on NORMAL.DOT. If you don't like the predefined settings in the Normal template, you can modify them so that all new documents based on the Normal template use your preferred settings and you don't have to change them for each new document. For example, if you want to use different margin settings or a different font, you can change these settings in the Normal template. For more information on how to modify a template, see Chapter 6, "Setting Default Formats in the Normal Template." ▪

TROUBLESHOOTING

I opened a new document using one of the templates that comes with Word and typed in some text that I always want to appear in documents using this template. I saved the document, but when I open a new document using this template, the text I typed doesn't appear in the document. To edit a template, you must work directly with the template. Choose File, Open, switch to the TEMPLATE folder, and select Document Templates in the Files of Type box. Select the template you want to modify in the File Name list box and choose OK. Edit the template to your liking and then save it. Now, whenever you open a new document template based on this template, the changes you made will apply to the new document. See Chapter 6, "Using Templates and Wizards for Frequently Created Documents," for more information on templates.

▶ **See** "Changing a Template," **p. 210**

Working in a Document

After you open a new or existing document, you need to know how to work with that document. This section introduces some of the basic concepts and procedures you need to know to work in a document. Many of the concepts and procedures discussed in the following section will be familiar to you if you have worked with other word processors. If you have never used a word processor, you need to become familiar with these basics before you start working with a document in Word 97.

When you create a new document in Word, you see a blank typing screen (except for the helpful tools at the top, bottom, and right). A vertical bar—the insertion point—flashes at the top left. Below the insertion point is a horizontal line called the *document end mark*. When you begin typing, your characters appear on-screen to the left of the insertion point, which moves to the right as you type.

Part

I

Ch

3

If you have never typed in a word processor before, you immediately become aware of one difference from typing on a typewriter: you don't have to press the Enter key at the end of every line. You continue typing past the end of the right margin, and Word wraps sentences around to fit within the margins.

Press the Enter key only to mark the end of a paragraph or to insert a blank line. Pressing Enter inserts a paragraph mark. (Normally you don't see paragraph marks on-screen; if you want to see them, see Chapter 10, "Formatting Lines and Paragraphs.")

There are two important reasons for pressing Enter only when you want to end a paragraph. First, if you add or delete text from the paragraph, the word-wrap feature ensures that the paragraph stays intact. If you press Enter at the end of each line and then add or delete text, each line ends where you pressed Enter, whether it's at the beginning or middle of the line. Second, as you learn in Chapter 10, a paragraph is a special set of text with its own useful formatting commands, such as alignment, indents, line spacing, and tabs.

When you type text on-screen, you can use all the characters on your keyboard. Besides the normal characters you see on your keyboard, however, Word offers many special characters, including bullets, typesetting quotes, wide dashes, and many others. For details about entering these characters, see Chapter 9, "Formatting Characters and Changing Fonts."

When you type in Word Insert mode, you add text to an existing document between the existing words. In some cases, you may prefer to type in the Overtype mode so that new text types over existing text.

If you want to switch from the Insert mode to the Overtype mode, press the Insert key on your keyboard or double-click the OVR indicator in the status bar. OVR becomes dark in the status bar at the bottom of the screen. Press the Insert key a second time to return to insert mode. If your status bar isn't displayed, you don't see a screen message reminding you that you're in the Overtype mode. (To display the status bar, choose Tools, Options and select the View tab. In the Window group, select Status Bar so that a check mark appears in the check box.)

If you prefer to use the Overtype mode all the time, you can customize Word to use the overtype mode as the default (see Chapter 37, "Customizing and Optimizing Word Features").

CAUTION

Be careful when you use the Overtype mode. It is very easy to forget to return to the Insert mode and then you end up typing over text you didn't want to replace.

You can move to a location where you were previously working in your document by pressing Shift+F5. Word remembers the previous three locations of the insertion point, so you can return to any of these locations by pressing Shift+F5 until you get to the location you want. When you first open an existing document, pressing Shift+F5 returns you to where the insertion point was located when you closed the document.

TROUBLESHOOTING

Whenever I try to enter new text, the new text I enter overwrites the text that was already in my document. How can I prevent this? This happens when you are in the Overtype mode. Press the Insert key to return to the Insert mode. When you type in the insert mode, the new text is inserted after the insertion point and any existing text is moved to make room for the new text.

▶ **See** "Selecting the Correct View for Your Work," **p. 132**
▶ **See** "Moving in the Document," **p. 144**
▶ **See** "Selecting Text," **p. 156**

Working with Multiple Documents

In Word, you can work with several documents simultaneously. Each new document you create or each existing document you open resides in its own document window on your screen. (For details on the difference between the program window and document windows and moving and sizing windows, see Chapter 2, "Getting Started in Word.")

One benefit to working with multiple documents simultaneously is that you can easily copy or move text between them. This feature eases the task of creating two different versions of one basic document or borrowing from an existing document as you build a new one.

To work with multiple documents, you simply open additional new or existing documents as discussed in the previous sections. As you open successive documents, they appear in document windows that hide the previously opened documents. To work with these hidden documents, you can switch between them in this full-screen mode, or you can arrange the windows so that you can see at least a portion of each of them. Only one window can be active at a time. The window on top, with the different-colored title bar, is the active window. It displays the document in which you are working.

To arrange multiple document windows, choose <u>W</u>indow, <u>A</u>rrange All. Word reduces the size of each window so that you can see them all on-screen. You can resize or move these windows using normal Windows techniques.

To switch between full-screen document windows, follow these steps:

1. Choose <u>W</u>indow, which lists all currently open files.

2. Select the name of the file to which you want to switch.

As an alternative to using the <u>W</u>indow menu to switch between open documents, you can click the window you want to select, or use Ctrl+F6. Press Ctrl+F6 repeatedly to cycle through all open documents. This method is quickest when you have only two files open. To restore any window to its full-screen size, click the Maximize button at the top right of the window, or choose Ma<u>x</u>imize in the Control menu.

To open a second copy of the current file, the one in the active window, follow these steps:

1. Choose <u>W</u>indow, which lists all currently open files.

2. Choose <u>N</u>ew Window.

When you open multiple copies of the same file, the first file name in the title bar ends with :1, the second with :2, and so on. You can switch between these windows in the same way you switch between any document windows, but any edits you make to one are made to all, and you can save the document from any of the windows displaying that document. If you close the document choosing <u>F</u>ile, <u>C</u>lose, all copies of the document are closed. To close just one of the windows for the document, select the control menu for that window (click the control menu bar or press the Alt+Hyphen keys) and choose <u>C</u>lose. Or double-click the Control menu icon.

Part

I

Ch

3

NOTE You can open a second window and then change the way you view that document in the new window. In this way, you can have two different views of the same document. For example, you can view the document as an outline in one window and view the document normally in the second window. ▪

▶ **See** "Selecting the Correct View for Your Work," **p. 132**

Saving a Document

By now, you probably have heard the lecture advising you to save your document frequently. Saving your work stores the work as a file on disk. Until you save, your work exists only in your computer's memory. Thus, if the electricity goes off, even for a very short time, everything in your computer's memory is lost—including your work.

Saving frequently also reduces the time required for Word to store your work on disk. In effect, you save time by saving often.

After you have saved a file, you can save it again with the same name or save a new copy of the file with a different file name and storage location. You can attach summary information to the file when you save it, which makes it easier to find the file when you want to work with it again.

You can tell Word to automatically save your document at specified time intervals and to make a backup copy of your file each time you save a document. In this way, if you have forgotten to save a file and your power fails or some other problem occurs, you will at least be able to recover some of your lost work.

You can save a document created in Word in other formats so that you can transfer the document to other computers that do not have Word installed. For example, you can save a document as a WordPerfect file to give to someone who uses WordPerfect. You can also save a document as a protected file to limit access to the document and prevent anyone from altering the document unless you give them access to it.

The first time you save a document, you give it a file name and decide on what disk and in which folder you want to store it. After you have saved a file for the first time, you can save it again with the same file name or you can save it as a new file, with a different file name. This is what you would do if you wanted to save successive drafts of a document as you worked on it.

Creating Long Names for Files and Folders

Folders and files with long names can be used on older Windows and DOS systems. The *FAT (File Allocation Table)*, an area on the disk that stores file information, has been especially modified to store both old-style 8.3 file names, as well as long file names.

> **CAUTION**
>
> Beware of using MS-DOS based or previous Windows versions of file management software or file utilities with files that have long file names. These old disk and file management utilities can destroy the data on Windows 95 disks.

In Windows 95, you can have file and folder names up to 255 characters long, and the names can include spaces. This long file name is stored in an extended location in the FAT of the disk. This extended location does not hamper the normal 8.3 name also stored in the FAT.

Part
I

Ch
3

> **CAUTION**
>
> Long file names cannot use the following characters:
>
> / \ : * ? " < > |

When you use a long file name, Windows automatically creates a file name fitting the 8.3 convention. This 8.3 file name is saved in its normal location in the FAT so that older Windows and DOS systems can still use the 8.3 file name.

You can see the MS-DOS file name that will be used for a file by right-clicking the file name in the Open dialog box and choosing Properties. Click the General tab. The long file name will be at the top of the box, the MS-DOS name appears near the middle.

Some of the rules involved in converting long file names to 8.3 file names are:

- Blank spaces are deleted before truncating long file names.
- File names of eight characters or less, when spaces are removed, are left unchanged.
- File names involving multiple periods, such as PROPOSAL.HODGKINS.DOC, will use the file name to the left of the first period and the extension to the right of the last period.
- File names longer than eight characters, but having a first word that is eight characters long and is followed by a space, use the first word as the file name.

- File names that are created by truncating long file names end with ~`#, where # is a number.

- No truncated file name will duplicate a file name existing in the same directory. ~`# will be placed as the seventh and eighth characters and the # will be a number used to differentiate files with the same names.

If you use a DOS command from the command prompt, such as `dir` to list a directory containing files with long names, you see the eight-character file information, as well as the long file names. The long file name is displayed in the far right column when using the DOS `dir` command.

Creating a Folder

As the number of files you create in Word increases, you may want to come up with some system for organizing files. The easiest way is to set up folders on the hard disk that contain related files. For example, you might have a folder for letters and another for memos.

One of the new features of Word is the capability of creating a new folder right from the Save As dialog box. This feature saves you the hassle of having to first create the folder in Windows and then save the file to the new folder. You will most often use this feature when you are saving documents, although the Create New Folder button is also available in the Open dialog box.

Follow these steps to create a new folder from the Save As dialog box:

1. Choose File, Save As. You see the Save As dialog box.

2. Change to the folder where you want to place the new folder. For example, if you want to place the folder within the MY DOCUMENTS folder, change to that folder.

3. Click the Create New Folder button in the dialog box toolbar. You see the New Folder dialog box (see Figure 3.10).

4. Type the folder name. You can type as many as 255 characters, including spaces.

5. Choose the OK button.

FIG. 3.10
You can create a new folder right from the Save As dialog box.

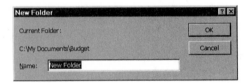

Saving Your Document

The first time you save a document, you must name it and decide where you want to store it.

To save and name a file, follow these steps:

1. Choose <u>F</u>ile, Save <u>A</u>s or press F12 or choose the Save button on the Standard toolbar (the third button from the left). The Save As dialog box appears (see Figure 3.11).

FIG. 3.11
Use the Save As dialog box to name a file and assign where you want it stored.

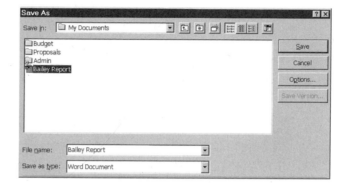

2. Type a file name in the File <u>N</u>ame box. Word will assign the extension DOC. (See the section "Saving for Other Word Processors or Applications" later in this chapter for information on saving the file as another document type.)

3. In the Save <u>I</u>n list, select the drive where you want to save your file. Use this option to save your file to a disk in drive A or B, for example, or to save the file to a different drive on your hard disk. (See "Understanding Folders," an earlier section in this chapter).

4. In the list box, select the folder where you want to save your file. (See "Understanding Folders," an earlier section in this chapter).

5. Choose OK.

6. If you have selected the option to display the Properties dialog box when you first save a file, fill in the dialog box when it appears and choose OK (see "Saving with Properties to Make Documents Easier to Find," later in this chapter). You can bypass the dialog box by choosing OK without entering any information.

You can change the default folder that is listed when you first choose <u>F</u>ile, <u>S</u>ave or File, Save <u>A</u>s. See "Setting the Default Folder," an earlier section in this chapter.

N O T E   If you are familiar with folder path names, you can save a file into another folder by typing the path name and file name in the File Name box of the Save As dialog box. To save a file named REPORTS into the CLIENTS folder on drive C, for example, type the following path name and then choose OK:

C:\CLIENTS\REPORTS ▧

Saving Files with a New Name

You can use File, Save As to save a named file with a new name, which creates a backup of your file. If you have a file called LETTER 01.DOC, for example, you can save your file a second time, giving it the name LETTER 02.DOC. You then have two versions of the same file, each with a different name. You can save the new version of your file in the same folder as the original, or in any other folder or drive.

Revising your file before saving it with a new name is a common practice. You then have the original file and the second, revised file, each with a unique name. Using this method, you can store successive drafts of a document on disk. You can always return to an earlier draft if you need to.

To save a named file with a new name, choose File, Save As, change the file name in the File Name box, change the drive or folder if you want, and then choose OK.

N O T E   You can use File, Save As to make sequential backups of important documents. The first time you save a file, name the file with a number, such as FILE01. Then each time you save the file again, rename the document with the next higher number: FILE02, FILE03, and so on. The file with the highest number is always the most recent version. When you finish the project, you can delete the files with low numbers.

Be sure to name the files FILE01 and FILE02—including the zero—so that the files stay in numerical order in dialog box lists. If you don't, FILE11 is listed before FILE3 because files are listed alphabetically and numerically. ▧

Saving Documents to an Intranet or Internet FTP Site

You can save Word documents to either a File Transfer Protocol (FTP) site on your company's intranet site or to one on the Internet. An FTP site is a useful way to both load and transfer your documents, making them accessible to others on the net.

Once you have access to an FTP site and the site displays in your Save As dialog box, you can save your Word documents to the site. To learn how to make an FTP site accessible, see "Adding an FTP Site to the Open and Save As Dialog Box" in Chapter 4.

To save to an FTP site, follow these steps:

1. Choose File, Save As.
2. Scroll to the bottom of the Look In list to see available FTP sites.
3. Click the FTP site you want to store the file in.

   Your Internet browser will activate, and you may be prompted for access information. Once connection is established, browse through the folders as you would on your own hard disk.
4. In the File Name text box, type the file name.
5. Click Save.

Saving Documents with Descriptions to Make Documents Easier to Find

Information that describes a document is called a *property*. For example, the file name, date created, and file size are all file properties for a Word document. You can also save summary information using the Properties tab. Summary information includes descriptive notes that can ease the task of organizing and finding files later, after you have created many files. You can attach summary information to your document when you first create the file, while you work on the file, or when you save the file.

To add summary information to a document, follow these steps:

1. Choose File, Properties. The Properties dialog box appears.
2. Select the Summary tab (see Figure 3.12).
3. Fill in any of the fields with descriptive text. Include as much (as many as 255 characters) or as little information as you like.
4. Choose OK.

The Statistics tab in this dialog box tells when you created the document, when the document was most recently saved, and how many pages, words, and characters the document contains. To aid you in searching for linked pages in a Web, you can also type the path used for relative hyperlinks within the document in the Hyperlink Base box.

To view the statistics for a document, follow these steps:

1. Select the Statistics tab in the Properties dialog box. The Statistics tab displays (see Figure 3.13).
2. Take note of the statistics that interest you.
3. Choose OK.

Part
I

Ch
3

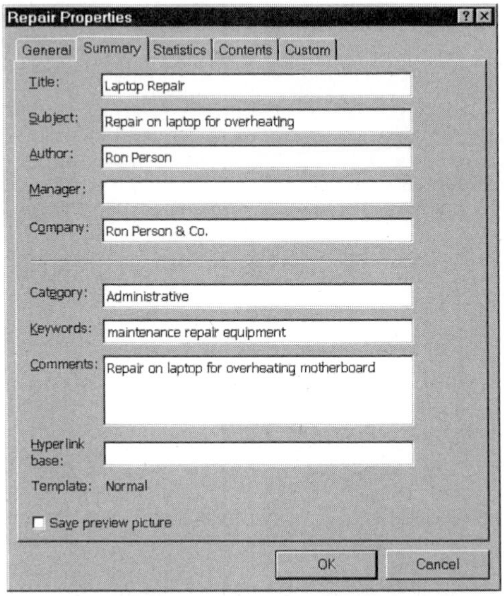

FIG. 3.12
Use the Summary tab to attach useful information to your documents.

FIG. 3.13
The Statistics tab provides detailed information on your document.

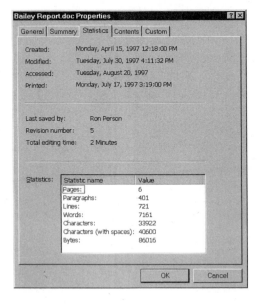

If you want to be prompted to enter summary information when you save a file, you can select an option to display the Properties dialog box whenever you choose File, Save As. Choose Tools, Options and select the Save tab. Select the Prompt for Document Properties option and choose OK. Now, whenever you first save a file, the Properties dialog box appears. If you don't want to enter summary information for that file, choose OK to bypass the dialog box.

Whichever method you choose, including summary information is a wonderful time-saver. In Chapter 4, "Managing Documents and Files," you learn how to use this information to locate misplaced files or files whose names you don't quite remember. You can include any text, as many as 255 characters, in any of the Summary fields. No naming or character restrictions exist.

Filling in the Summary tab may seem like a nuisance, but try the box before giving it up. When you learn how to use the powerful find features, you see that summary information helps you find files much more easily.

Saving Without Renaming

Every time you save a document with a unique name, you create a new file on disk—a good way to keep backups of your document. Not all files are so important, however, that you need multiple backups. In that case, you can save the document to its existing file name, replacing the current version of the file.

> **CAUTION**
>
> Remember that when you save without renaming, you erase and replace the existing file with the new file.

 To save without renaming, choose File, Save or press Shift+F12 or click the Save button on the toolbar (the third button from the left).

Saving Many Documents at Once

If you have several documents open at once, you can save them all simultaneously by using File, Save All. The Save As dialog box appears for any documents that have not been saved before.

Files you normally don't see, including glossary and macro files, also are saved when you use this command.

Automatically Saving Documents

You can tell Word to automatically save a recovery version of your document at specified intervals. Should Word fail and you have to exit without saving, the files created by AutoRecover are automatically reopened the next time Word opens. You can change the folder in which AutoRecover files are saved by following these steps:

1. Choose Tools, Options and select the File Locations tab.

2. Select AutoRecover files from the File Types list and choose Modify. The Modify Location dialog box appears.

3. Specify the drive and folder where you want AutoRecover files to be stored and choose OK. You also have the option of creating a new folder for your AutoRecover files in the Modify Location dialog box.

If you are working on a critical document where you can't afford to lose or recreate information, you will want Word to save AutoRecover files frequently. As a default, Word saves AutoRecover files every 10 minutes. To specify how frequently Word creates AutoRecover files, follow these steps:

1. Choose File, Save As, or press F12 and select Options, or choose Tools, Options and select the Save tab. The Save tab appears (see Figure 3.14).

FIG. 3.14
You can specify several save options in the Save tab.

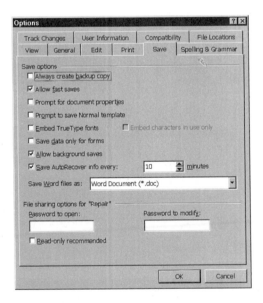

2. Select the Save AutoRecover Info Every check box.

3. Select or type the time interval, in minutes, between automatic saves in the Minutes spin box.

4. Choose OK.

As you are working in your document, Word periodically saves a recovery version of your document. A message in the status bar indicates that your file is being saved.

If a power failure or other problem causes Word to shut down while you are working on a document, and you have selected the automatic save option, you can recover everything that was entered up until the last automatic save. The next time you start Word, any files that were open when Word shut down will automatically be reopened. Any recovered file will be displayed in a window with (Recovered) next to the document name in the title bar.

Creating Automatic Backups

You can tell Word to create a backup copy of your document every time you save it. When you choose this option, Word saves the previous version of the document as a backup file and gives it the name "Backup of *filename*."

To create a backup copy of your document, follow these steps:

1. Choose File, Save As, or press F12 and select Options, or choose Tools, Options and select the Save tab. The Save tab is displayed (refer to Figure 3.14).

2. Select the Always Create Backup Copy option.

3. Choose OK.

Backup files are just another safety factor. If an original file is damaged due to a disk error or if it can't be recovered from the Recycle Bin, then you can open the backup file. The backup copy is stored in the same folder as the original document.

Saving with Fast Save

You can speed up the process of saving a file by selecting the Allow Fast Saves option. With this option selected, Word saves faster because the program saves only the changes, not the entire document. Fast saves occur only with Save, not Save As. If you have selected the Always Create Backup Copy option (see previous section), you cannot use the fast save feature because backups can be made only with full saves.

To turn on the fast saves feature, follow these steps:

1. Choose File, Save As, or press F12 and select Options, or choose Tools, Options and select the Save tab. The Save tab is displayed (refer to Figure 3.14).

2. Select the Allow Fast Saves option.

3. Choose OK.

N O T E When you select the Allow Fast Saves option to save time when saving files, the files you save take up more disk space than those created using a full save, because Word must keep the original file plus the changes. To free up disk space, choose File, Save As, choose the Options button, clear the Allow Fast Saves check box, and choose OK twice when you make your final save for the document. This will create a smaller file. ■

Part

I

Ch

3

Saving for Other Word Processors or Applications

When you save a file in Word, by default the document is saved in Word format. Word, however, enables you to save your file in many formats. You may need to save a file into another format, such as a WordPerfect format. At other times, you may need to save the file in Text (ASCII) format so that you can import the file into a different type of program.

To save your file in a non-Word format, follow these steps:

1. Choose File, Save As, or press F12.
2. In the File Name box, type the file name without an extension.
3. Select the file format from the Save as Type list box.
4. Choose OK to save your file.

Word assigns an appropriate extension to the file name.

Word displays only the types of files for which converters have been installed in the Save as Type list box. If the word processor you need doesn't appear, reinstall Word using the custom installation option. You will be given the chance to install converter files without reinstalling all of Word.

> **CAUTION**
>
> If you do not see file extensions for DOC files in the Open or Save As dialog boxes, then do not type the DOC file extension at the end of a file name. If you do, the file will end up with two extensions, for example, *filename*.DOC.DOC. File extensions are hidden or displayed for registered file types by choosing View, Options from the Explorer. Select or clear the Hide MS-DOS File Extensions option.

Saving a Document as a Protected File

If you share files or your PC with other users, you may want to prevent people from opening some files or from modifying others. To prevent users from opening a file, you can assign a Protection Password. The next time you open the file, you must type the password. Another option is to assign a Write Reservation Password, which allows anyone who knows the password to open the document and make and save changes to it. A user who does not know the password can open the file as a read-only document. They can read the document but cannot make and save changes to that document.

You can also assign the Read-Only Recommended option to a document. When a document with this option assigned is opened, a dialog box appears advising the user to open the document as a read-only document to which changes cannot be saved. However, the user does have the option of opening the document normally and saving changes to the document. For maximum protection, therefore, assign a password to the document.

You can also limit changes to a document to annotations, which are comments in a document that are viewed in a separate annotation pane, and marked revisions, which can be incorporated into the document only by a user who knows the password. See Chapter 32, "Tracking Revisions and Versions," for details on protecting a document with annotations and revisions.

If you have created a form in a Word document, you can protect the document against all changes except entries into the form fields. See Chapter 23, "Building Forms and Fill-In Dialog Boxes," for details on how to protect a form.

To assign a password to a document, follow these steps:

1. Choose File, Save As, or press F12 and select Options, or choose Tools, Options and select the Save tab to produce the Save dialog box.

2. To assign your file a password, select either Password to Open or the Password to Modify text box and type a password.

   As you type, you see only asterisks—no written record of your password exists anywhere. Your password can consist of as many as 15 characters, including letters, numbers, symbols, and spaces.

3. Choose OK. Reenter the password in the Confirm Password dialog box and choose OK.

4. Choose OK at the Save As dialog box to save the file.

> **CAUTION**
>
> When a file is password-protected, no one can open that file without the password—including you. Don't forget your password.

To change or delete a password, follow the same procedure, but delete the existing password (which still appears only as a string of asterisks) and type the new password (or not, if you want to remove the password).

To assign the Read-Only Recommended option to a document, follow these steps:

1. Choose File, Save As or press F12 and select Options, or choose Tools, Options and select the Save tab (refer to Figure 3.14).

2. Select the Read-Only Recommended option.

3. Choose OK.

Part

I

Ch

3

TROUBLESHOOTING

Periodically, Word saves the document I am working on. I find this annoying, because it distracts me when I am entering text into the document. You need to turn off the AutoSave feature in Word. Choose Tools, Options, select the Save tab, clear the Automatic Save Every option, and choose OK.

I made some changes to a document and wanted to save the document with a new name. When I clicked the Save button on the toolbar, the document was saved with the same name and I lost my original document. To save a document with a new name, you must use File, Save As to open the Save As dialog box, where you can enter a new name for the document. The Save button on the Standard toolbar opens the Save As dialog box only the first time you save a document. After that, it saves the document with the same file name you gave it when you first saved it.

▶ **See** "Protecting and Saving the Form," **p. 759**

Closing a Document

After you finish working on a document and save the file, you may want to close the document, especially if you have several documents open.

To close a document, choose File, Close. If the document is in a window, you can close it by clicking the Close button to the right of the title bar or by double-clicking the Control icon at the top left corner of the document window. When a document is maximized to full screen, the Control icon appears in the menu bar to the left of File. Be careful not to double-click the application Control icon in the top left corner of the Word window, or you will close Word.

If you have made changes since you last saved, Word asks whether you want to save your changes. Respond Yes to save them. (If you haven't named the document, the Save As dialog box appears, and you must name the file.) Respond No to discard changes. Choose Cancel to cancel the close, or choose Help to access the Word help window. ●

CHAPTER 4

Managing Documents and Files

Although word processors undoubtedly offer a tremendous advantage over the typewriter for producing written documents, one fact remains: You accumulate Word files as fast as you gathered paper files before the advent of the word processor. Word 97, however, can help you to find and manage these files, using the options in the Open dialog box.

From the Open dialog box, you can sort the files in the list and preview any file without opening it in Word. Furthermore, you can view information about a file.

You can accomplish many other file-related tasks from the Open dialog box—open, print, copy, or delete the files. The capability to work with multiple files is a powerful feature and a great time-saver. Finally, you can search for files by file name, location, author, date, summary information, or contents. ■

View files and file information

Working with just a file name, even a long file name, may leave you in doubt about the contents. You can preview a file before opening it, as well as review summary information you've typed to help you identify a document.

Manage files

Organizing files is much easier when you can duplicate, move, delete, and rename files or folders from within Word's Open or Save As dialog boxes. You can even create a new folder with the click of a button in the Save As dialog box.

Find files

As hard disk capacity gets larger and networks span further, it becomes more difficult than ever before to find the document you want. Word's Find feature enables you to quickly search for a file by name, content, or approximate modification date.

What You Need to Know About Managing Documents

The best way to keep track of files is to set up some type of folder structure and use this structure to organize your work. For example, you can set up one folder for your proposals, one for letters, and another for each project you are currently working on. By using this structure, you can place your work files in the appropriate folder.

After you have decided where to store your files, you still need to locate them when you need to work with them again. If you haven't worked with a document for a long time, you can easily forget its name or location when you want to reopen it. You can use the view features in the Open dialog box to display a document's contents or find other information about a document.

If you can't find the file you want by browsing, you can use the Open dialog box's find features to search through the files on your computer. You can search by name, date, contents, or other criteria. When you execute a search, the matching files are listed in the Open dialog box. Then, in this list, you simply find and open the file you want. You can also use the find features to group similar files together so that you can work on them all at the same time.

Viewing Documents and File Information

Even though a file might have a descriptive name, you may not be able to figure out what that file contains. If you are uncertain about a particular file, you can display additional information about it. For example, you can display a detailed view of the file, which lists the file size and date; these details might help you recognize the file. Or you can display a quick view of the document contents. Finally, you can display a document's properties.

Viewing file information and previewing files can help you manage your documents. For example, you can preview a file before you open or print it so that you know you are working with the right document. Or, you can view file information to find out which is the most recent version of a document on which you have been working.

The Open dialog box lists the files in the current folder. If you have performed a search (you learn how later in this chapter), the dialog box lists those files that match the criteria you entered. When you see the file you want in the list, you can select it to display information. To select the file, click the file name with the mouse, or press the Tab key until the *focus* (the dotted border) is in the list box. Then use the up- and down-arrow keys to select the file.

This section describes how to sort a list of files, preview a file, and view file information.

Changing the View in the Open Dialog Box

By default, files are listed by name in the Open dialog box. To change to a different view, use the buttons in the dialog box. You can select List, Details, Properties, or Preview. Figure 4.1 shows the list of files in Details view, which lists the file name, as well as other information (the size of the file and the date it was last accessed).

FIG. 4.1
Use the buttons in the Open dialog box to control how the files are listed.

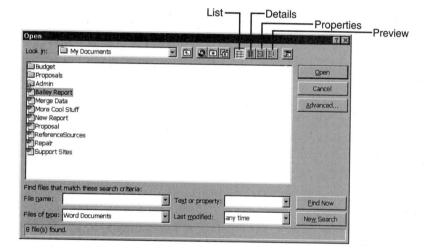

Displaying a Quick View

Among the most useful features in the Open dialog box is the capability of previewing a document. When you search for files to work with, it is helpful to view the contents of the files before opening them. In Word, there are two ways to view files from the Open dialog box. You can click Preview to see a miniature preview, or you can use the Quick View feature to open a window that shows a larger view of a file.

 You can display a preview of the selected document by clicking the Preview button in the Open dialog box. Previewing is useful if you want to quickly examine a document to make sure you are opening the correct one. Preview only enables you to see the top or first page of the document. If you want to be able to scroll through a document to see other areas, you should use Quick View.

TIP Dialog boxes that are similar to Open, such as Insert Picture, also contain a Preview button.

When you click Preview, the right side of the Open dialog box becomes a display screen showing you the top of the document, as shown in Figure 4.2. Notice that the file being previewed is a Word template.

FIG. 4.2
Preview enables you to quickly see a document before opening it.

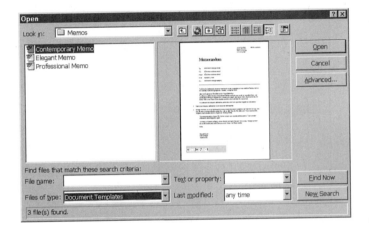

If you want to see more of a document, scroll through its pages, or open a file belonging to another application; you will want to use Quick View to do this. Quick View is a program separate from Word, yet it can run from within Word's Open dialog box. Figure 4.3 shows a Quick View window being used to view the Excel file, ACCOUNT TOTALS.XLS.

To display a quick view of a file, follow these steps:

1. In the Open dialog box, select the file you want to view.
2. Right-click the file name, and then choose Quick View. You see the contents of the document in a separate window (refer to Figure 4.3).

   If the Quick View command is not visible in the shortcut menu, Windows does not have the Quick View conversion filters necessary to view this file type.

You can view the document in two ways: full sized in a window or Page view. Full sized in a window is shown in Figure 4.3. Page view appears as the document prints to a page. Change between full window and Page view by choosing View, Page View. To change pages while in Page view, click the corner tabs at the top right corner of the pages. While in full window view, change pages using the scroll bars. You also can press Page Up and Page Down to scroll through the document.

FIG. 4.3
Use Quick View when you need to scroll through the file during preview.

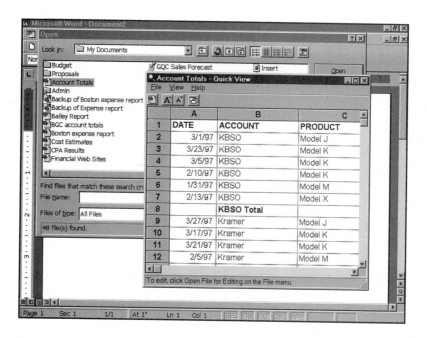

After reviewing the file, click the Close button to close the Quick View window. If, after previewing the document, you decide that you want to open the document for editing, you can either click the Open File for Editing button in the toolbar, or choose File, Open File for Editing.

Viewing File Properties

In the Open dialog box, you can use the Properties button to display a short list of some key document information (title, author, template, revision number, application, pages, words, characters, lines, and paragraphs). You can display file properties for the selected file in the Open dialog box. You can view, for example, the summary information you entered, or other file information, such as statistical data about the file. In the Properties dialog box, you can display different information by selecting the following tabs:

- *General tab*. Displays the name, type, location, size, creation, modify, and access dates, and the file attributes (see Figure 4.4).

- *Summary tab*. Displays the Summary information, including title, author name, subject, keywords, and comments you enter in the Properties dialog box.

- *Statistics tab*. Displays statistics about the file (see Figure 4.5).

Part
I

Ch
4

FIG. 4.4
Use the General tab to display general information about the selected file.

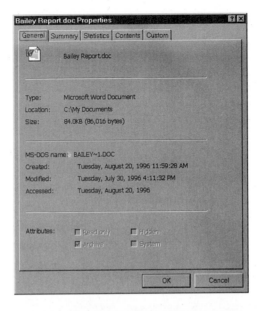

FIG. 4.5
Use the Statistics tab to display file statistics.

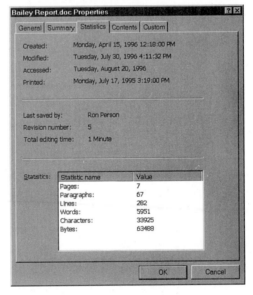

To view file properties, follow these steps:

1. In the Open dialog box, select the file you want to view.

2. Right-click the file, then select Properties from the menu that appears. Or click the Commands and Settings button, then select Properties.

3. In the Properties dialog box, select the tab you want to display. When you finish viewing the information, choose OK.

 TIP If you have already opened a document, you can view and edit properties by choosing File, Properties.

▶ **See** "Saving Documents with Descriptions to Make Documents Easier to Find," **p. 105**

Editing and Adding File Properties

If you didn't add summary information to a document when you created or saved it (refer to Chapter 3, "Creating and Saving Documents"), or if you want to edit the summary information for a file, you can do so from the Open dialog box.

To edit or add summary information, follow these steps:

1. In the Open dialog box, select the file with which you want to work.

2. Right-click the file, and then select Properties from the menu that appears. Or, click the Commands and Settings button, and then select Properties.

3. Select the Summary tab, and then fill in or edit any of the text boxes. Include as much information (up to 255 characters in each text box) or as little as you want.

4. Choose OK.

Sorting File Lists

If the list of files in a folder is long, you may want to sort the files in the list. You can sort by file name, size, file type, or date last modified.

To sort a list of files, follow these steps:

 1. In the Open dialog box, click the Commands and Settings button.

2. From the menu that appears, choose Sorting. The Sort By dialog box appears (see Figure 4.6).

3. In the Sort Files By drop-down list, select one of the following sorting options:

Option	How Files are Listed
File Name	Alphabetically by file name
Size	Numerically by file size
Files of Type	Alphabetically by file type
Last Modified	Chronologically by the date files are saved (most recent date first)

FIG. 4.6
In the Sort By dialog box, you can select how you want to sort and list files.

4. Select a sort order: Ascending or Descending.

5. Choose OK.

The files in all folders in the Open dialog box are sorted.

▶ **See** "Opening a Document," **p. 86**

▶ **See** "Saving Documents with Descriptions to MAke Documents Easier to Find," **p. 105**

Managing Files

You can accomplish many tasks with the files listed in the Open dialog box. You can open, print, copy, or delete a file or a group of selected files—all from this dialog box. Being able to select more than one file at a time from the list is a tremendous time-saver. For example, if you want to print several files at once, you can select them and issue one print command. This approach is much simpler and quicker than opening each file, one by one from within Word, and printing them separately. You can use the same approach to copy or delete groups of files. Being able to do something to several files simultaneously, as well as being able to preview the contents of a file without having to open it, makes the process of managing your files much smoother and easier.

Displaying and Selecting Files for File Management

Before you issue various commands to manage your files, you need to display the file or files you want to work with. If the files are in the same folder, you can simply change to that folder. If the files are in different folders, you can use a search to group the files together. Searching for files is covered later in this chapter in the section "Searching for Files."

When the files are displayed, you can select one or more of the files with which you want to work. To select a file with the mouse, click the name of the file you want, or press and hold down the Ctrl key while you click multiple file names (see Figure 4.7). If you want to select several sequential files, press and hold down the Shift key while you click the first and last file you want. Press and hold down the Ctrl key and click a second time to deselect any file you select by mistake.

FIG. 4.7
You can select multiple files in the file list.

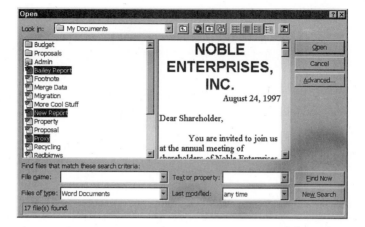

To select a file with the keyboard, press the Tab key until the focus (the dotted border) is in the file list box. Then use the up- or down-arrow key to move to the file you want to select. To select multiple files that are not contiguous, hold down the Ctrl key, use the arrow keys to move to the file you want to select, and press the space bar. To select multiple contiguous files, press the up- or down-arrow key to select the first file. Next, press and hold down the Shift key while you press the up- or down-arrow key to extend the selection.

Adding an FTP Site to the Open and Save As Dialog Box

The FTP site to which you want to save a document must be on the list of Internet sites. To add an FTP site to your Open and Save As dialog boxes, follow these steps:

1. Choose File, Open or Save As, or click Open.

2. Click the Look In or Save In list box to display the list as shown in Figure 4.8. Select the Add/Modify FTP Locations item as shown in Figure 4.9.

FIG. 4.8
You must add the Internet FTP location before you can open or save files.

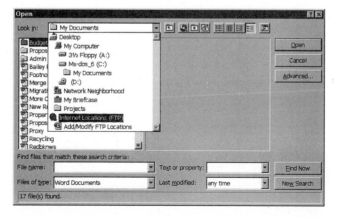

FIG. 4.9

Use the Add/Modify FTP Locations dialog box to specify the FTP site where you want access.

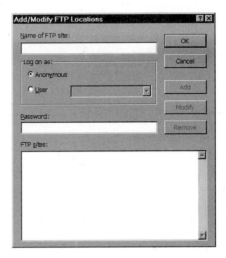

3. Type the name of the FTP site in the Name of FTP Site text box. For example, you might type **ftp.business.com**.

4. If this is an anonymous logon site, most are, then click Anonymous.

   Or, if a user password is required, click User, then type your password.

5. Click Add.

Printing Files

You can choose File, Print to print the open document. If you want to print several documents with the same printing parameters simultaneously, however, use the Open dialog box. If all the files you want to print are in the same folder, you can simply display that folder. If the files are in different folders, you can use a search criterion to find and group the files you want to print.

▶ **See** "Controlling Printing Options," **p. 274**

To print documents from the Open dialog box, follow these steps:

1. Select one or more files you want to print.

2. Click the Commands and Settings button, and then choose Print from the submenu. You also can right-click the selected files and choose Print.

3. In the Print dialog box, choose OK.

Word opens the files, prints them, and then closes them. For more information about printing, see Chapter 8, "Previewing and Printing a Document."

Copying or Moving Files

You can use the Open dialog box to copy selected files from one location to another. Similarly, you can use this dialog box to move files.

To copy files, follow these steps:

1. In the Open dialog box, select one or more files you want to copy.
2. Right-click the files, and then choose Copy in the shortcut menu that appears.
3. Use the Look In drop-down list to select the drive or folder where you want to place the copy.
4. Right-click the drive or folder, and then choose Paste.

Files with their original name and extension are copied to a new location.

If you want to copy files to a floppy disk, you can use the Send To command. Select the files to copy, and then right-click one of the files. From the shortcut menu that appears, choose Send To, and then select the disk drive.

The process of moving a file from one folder to another or one drive to another is similar to that of copying a file. To move files, follow these steps:

1. In the Open dialog box, select one or more files you want to move.
2. Right-click the files, and then choose Cut from the shortcut menu.
3. In the Look In drop-down list, select the drive or folder where you want to move the file.
4. Right-click the file list box, and then choose Paste.

 T I P Instead of creating Web pages in Word and saving them to a site one page at a time, create all the pages and their hyperlinks within a folder on your local hard disk. You can then move all the files at one time to the site by cutting and pasting them.

Deleting Files

You can also delete files you no longer need. In Windows 95, when you delete a file, that file is moved to the Recycle Bin—a holding spot for deleted files. If you make a mistake, you can open the Recycle Bin and retrieve the files you've deleted. You can also choose to empty the Recycle Bin when you want to permanently get rid of the files.

Part

I

Ch

4

The following steps show you how to delete files:

1. In the Open dialog box, select the files you want to delete.

2. Right-click the selected file(s) and choose Delete.

3. A dialog box asks you to confirm the move to the Recycle Bin. Choose Yes to delete the files; choose No if you don't want to erase them.

If you accidentally delete a file, you can retrieve it from the Recycle Bin: On the desktop, double-click the Recycle Bin, select the files you want to undelete, and choose File, Restore.

N O T E You cannot delete an open file, nor can you delete a file from which you cut or copied text during the current work session. ■

▶ **See** "Working with Multiple Documents," **p. 98**

Searching for Files

If you can't find the file you want after browsing through the drives and folders, you can click the Find Now button in the Open dialog box. Word offers powerful search capabilities that enable you to search for files by file name, location, author, and the date the files were created or last saved. Alternatively, you can use the information you entered in the Properties dialog box. You also can search for specific text that occurs in a document.

With the Find Now button, you can bring together a list of related files or find a specific file. The search can be narrow; for example, you can look for a particular file with a familiar file name. You also can search for a group of files that match whatever criteria you specify. The more you narrow the search, the fewer the files you will find.

Using Search Options in the Open Dialog Box

The bottom half of the Open dialog box contains text boxes in which you enter common search criteria. For example, you can use these text boxes to search for a file name, last modified date, file type, or text or property. You can also combine these options—for example, search for all files that start with B that were modified last week. If these options don't help you locate the file you want, you can build more complex search criteria by clicking the Advanced button. These search options are covered in the rest of this section.

After Word finds files that match the criteria you specified, it displays a list of their names in the Open dialog box. You can preview any file to make sure that it is the one you want, and then open, print, copy, or delete the file. To act on several files at once, you can select them first and then issue one of the commands that act on these files. You can select a group of files, for example, and then copy them to a disk to back them up, or print several files at once without opening the files in Word.

▶ **See** "Understanding File Names," **p. 82**

▶ **See** "Understanding Folders," **p. 83**

Searching for a File by Name

You can search for a file by name if you know its name (or at least a partial name). Follow these steps:

1. In the Open dialog box, enter the name (or partial name) of the file in the File <u>N</u>ame text box. You can use the * and ? wild cards. An asterisk (*) represents any string of characters; to search for all files that start with CH, for example, simply type **CH***. A question mark (?) represents any one character; you can search for **CHAP?.DOC** to find all files named CHAP1.DOC, CHAP2.DOC, CHAP3.DOC, and so on.

2. Change to the drive that you want to search using the Look <u>I</u>n drop-down list. Select the folder by double-clicking it in the file list. If you want to search the subfolders in the selected folder, click the Commands and Settings button and then choose Searc<u>h</u> Subfolders from the menu that appears. There should be a check mark next to this command for it to be activated. Selecting the command again turns off the check mark and the feature.

3. Click the <u>F</u>ind Now button in the dialog box. Word searches the current folder, displays the names of any matching files, and indicates the number of objects found at the bottom of the dialog box. Figure 4.10 shows a list of all files that start with B.

Part

I

Ch

4

FIG. 4.10
You can see the results of a search for all files that start with B.

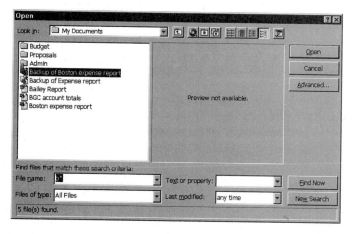

If you don't find the files you want with this search, you can clear the search results by clicking the New Search button. Then you can start again. To cancel a search in progress, click the Stop button which appears in place of the Find Now button.

Searching for Specific Files or Different File Types

By default, Word searches for Word files in the current folder, but you can search also for a specific file or different types of files. If the files are compatible with Word, you can open or print them; you can copy or delete the files you find, even if they are not compatible with Word.

To search for different file types, take these steps:

1. In the File Name text box of the Open dialog box, type the name of the file for which you want to search. If you just want to list all files of a certain type, leave the file name blank.

2. Display the Files of Type list, and select the type of file for which you want to search.

Searching by Date Modified

You can search for files based on the date you last modified the file. This feature is convenient, especially when used with other search criteria (covered in later sections). You can search for files created last week, for example, that contain the words *bank* and *letter.*

To search for files by date modified, follow these steps:

1. In the Open dialog box, enter a full or partial file name. You can also leave the file name blank, to search for all files in a certain range of dates.

2. Display the Last Modified drop-down list, and select the time interval: Yesterday, Today, Last Week, This Week, Last Month, This Month, or Any Time (the default).

Searching by File Properties or Text in the File

One of the greatest advantages to including summary information in all Word files is that you can search for files by text contained in any of the summary information fields. You can add a title to a document, for example, and then use it to search through files.

▶ **See** "Saving Documents with Descriptions to Make Documents Easier to Find," **p. 105**

To search by text or properties, follow these steps:

1. In the File <u>N</u>ame text box of the Open dialog box, enter a full or partial file name (optional). You can also leave the file name blank to search for all files with certain text or properties.

2. In the Te<u>x</u>t or Property text box, enter the text you want to search for.

 TIP Try to think of a unique word or phrase so that you limit your search. If you use a common word or phrase, the search takes longer, and the search results will include too many files.

▶ **See** "Saving Documents with Descriptions to Make Documents Easier to Find," **p. 105**

Understanding Find Fast

Word supports a new method of finding files faster. Office 97 includes a Find Fast feature that locates files faster on local drives, Windows NT Server, or Workstation drives. The new Web Find Fast, used with the Internet Explorer, searches local folders on Web servers in your company's intranet.

Find Fast creates an index of information about Office documents and other document types. You can use these indexes to perform rapid searches for documents.

Find Fast places the index at the topmost level of the drive or folder you index. The entire drive or folder is indexed. Find Fast files are hidden and use the file extensions FFL, FFX, FFO, and FFA. Normally, you will never see nor work with these files.

You use the Find Fast feature when you choose <u>F</u>ile, <u>O</u>pen, then click <u>A</u>dvanced to open the Advanced Find dialog box. All searches that use the Advanced Find dialog box employ Find Fast to increase performance when looking for documents.

Find Fast does not preclude searching for files that have not been indexed. You can still use the Advanced Find dialog box but searches take longer.

N O T E For additional information on administering Find Fast and Web Find Fast, refer to the Microsoft Office 97 Resource Kit available from Microsoft. ■

Using Advanced Search Options

By clicking the <u>A</u>dvanced button, you can narrow the list of files you are searching for. You do this by specifying additional criteria, such as the file creation or save date, author name, summary information, or specific text strings (such as a word or phrase).

Part
I
Ch
4

You can create one or more search criteria. For example, you can tell Word to find all files that contain the words *health insurance,* created by the author *Smith.* When you select A̲nd, Word must match all the criteria you enter. When you select O̲r, Word can match either set of search instructions.

When you create a set of search instructions, you enter two to three parts to build the criteria. First, you select the property you want to search. You can select from many different properties including application name, author, category, company, keyword, last printed date, contents, and more.

Second, you select the condition to match. Depending on the property, the conditions will vary. For example, if you select the last printed date, you can select these conditions: Yesterday, Today, Last Week, This Week, Last Month, This Month, Any Time, Anytime Between, On, On or Before, On or After, or In the Last.

Finally, for some conditions, you enter the value. For example, if you want to find all files printed yesterday, you don't have to enter a value. On the other hand, if you want to find all files printed on a certain date, you need to enter the date in the Val̲ue text box.

Here are some additional examples of different search instructions:

`Author ` **`includes words`** ` Annika.`

This example would list all files where the Author information includes the name *Annika.*

`Contents ` **`includes phrase`** ` book proposal.`

This example would list all files that contained the phrase *book proposal.*

`Hyperlink base ` **`includes words`** ` budget.`

This example would list all files that have a hyperlink base that includes the word budget. A *hyperlink base* is the relative path for a hyperlink to another document. Follow these steps to create a set of search instructions:

1. In the Open dialog box, click the A̲dvanced button. You see the Advanced Find dialog box (see Figure 4.11).

2. To select which folders are searched, display the Look I̲n drop-down list and select the drive. You can also type the path to search directly in this text box. To include subfolders in the search, select the Searc̲h Subfolders check box.

3. Select the type of criteria: A̲nd or O̲r.

4. Display the P̲roperty drop-down list, and select the property you want to match.

5. Display the C̲ondition drop-down list, and select how you want to make the match.

6. Enter the value to match in the Val̲ue text box.

7. To add this set of search instructions to the list, click the A̲dd to List button.

FIG. 4.11
Use the Advanced
Find dialog box to
further narrow your
search.

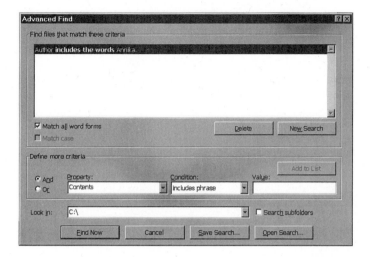

8. Follow steps 3–7 to build the next set of instructions.

9. Select Match Case to match upper- and lowercase exactly. To match word variations, select Match All Word Forms.

10. When you finish all your search criteria, click the Find Now button.

You can continue to add the criteria you want until the list is complete. The more narrow the criteria, the fewer the files found. If you want to delete a criterion, you can do so by selecting it and then clicking the Delete button. To clear all the criteria, click the New Search button.

Some combinations of criteria won't work. In this case, you'll see an error message. Review the message and then make the appropriate change. For example, you cannot search for files that start with both B and C because that search criteria doesn't make sense.

Saving Search Criteria

If you have entered a set of search criteria and want to reuse it for future searches, you can save the criteria with a name. When you want to reuse the criteria, you select the named set of criteria and then initiate a new search.

To save search criteria, follow these steps:

1. Set up the search criteria you want, as outlined in the preceding sections.

2. Click the Save Search button in the Advanced Find dialog box. The Save Search dialog box appears (see Figure 4.12).

3. In the Name for This Search text box, type a name for the search criteria.

Part

I

Ch

4

FIG. 4.12
You can name a set
of search criteria,
save it, and reuse it.

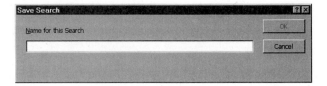

4. Choose OK.

5. To start a search with these criteria, click Find Now.

To reuse saved search criteria, follow these steps:

1. In the Advanced Find dialog box, choose Open Search.

2. From the list that appears, select the search you want to execute.

3. Choose Open.

4. Choose Find Now.

TROUBLESHOOTING

I tried a search and didn't find the file I wanted. Now the file list is blank. If you perform a search and no matching files were found, the file list is blank. To redisplay all the files that were listed before the search, clear the search instructions by clicking the New Search button.

I tried a search and didn't find the file I wanted. I'm sure the search should work. Keep in mind that you can combine criteria. Be sure that you have entered only the criteria you want to use. For example, suppose that you started by searching for a file by name and entered a file name. When you didn't find the file, you tried searching by date. You still can't find the file. Remember that both the name and date criteria will be used if they are both entered. You may need to clear—in this example—the file name criteria and use just the date.

When I choose the File, Open command, I don't see all my files listed. Keep in mind that Word remembers the last set of properties you entered. For example, if you selected to display a different file type using the Files of Type list, the next time you use the Open command, that file type will still be listed. Change the options back to what you want displayed.

ON THE WEB

For more troubleshooting and training tips, point your Internet browser to these URLs:

http://www.microsoft.com/msword

http://www.microsoft.com/kb

http://www.ronperson.com

http://www.microsoft.com/support

CHAPTER 5

Editing a Document

As you begin working with Word, you'll want to gain a solid understanding of the basics. For example, several different options exist for viewing your document: You can work very quickly in Normal view, or you can slow down and zoom in to do detailed work by choosing the Page Layout view and enlarging it up to 500 percent. You can move around in your document in many ways, using both mouse and keyboard techniques.

To begin with, you should understand one of the most important principles in working with Word: *Select, then do.* You can move and copy text and objects from one part of your document to another, from one document to another, or even from one application to another.

This chapter teaches you the important features that will help you edit a document, and many editing shortcuts have been included. ■

Control document windows and the display

Customize how your documents are displayed and design a workspace that accommodates you.

Select, edit, and delete text

You can easily select and manipulate text to transform a draft document into a final version.

Insert frequently used text

Take advantage of Word's AutoText and AutoCorrect features to speed up repetitive tasks.

Check spelling and hyphenation

Word's spelling and hyphenation tools make it easy to create smart-looking documents.

Move and copy text and graphics

Word's Clipboard and linking features allow you to copy, move, and link text within or between documents.

Controlling Your Document's Appearance On-Screen

In Word, you can display your document in the way that best fits what you need to do. As you work, you can use Normal view to see the body text as it will print, use Outline view for outline expansion or contraction, and use Page Layout view to see the entire page exactly as it will print, including columns, headers, footers, and page numbers.

You can use Master Document view to simplify the creation and reorganization of long documents and Online Layout view to make it easier to tell how your document will appear when you publish it online. Full Screen view can be set to display only your document text, excluding all other screen elements. In each of these views you can type, format, and edit. A seventh view, File, Print Preview, shows thumbnail pictures of how pages will print and enables you to make last-minute adjustments and edits before printing. The sections that follow describe the various Word views.

▶ **See** "Previewing Pages Before Printing," **p. 264**

▶ **See** "Working with the Master Document," **p. 1053**

You also can add or remove screen elements, such as scroll bars and the status bar, in many of these views. Screen elements are controlled by selections you make by choosing Tools, Options (see the section "Modifying the Screen Display" later in this chapter).

Figure 5.1 shows the screen modified to provide access to the menu bar and a maximum of typing space.

Selecting the Correct View for Your Work

The work you do will help determine the best screen view for your needs. If you are a production typist, you may desire as much on-screen typing space as possible. If, on the other hand, you are a desktop publisher and constantly use various Word tools, you will need to work in Page Layout view and have those tools easily accessible at all times. For example, you can choose the Drawing toolbar to display Word's drawing tools on-screen. You can customize the view of your document as you change tasks.

Figure 5.2 shows one type of view you can choose in Word—Master Document view.

There are three ways that you can change the view:

■ Menu commands

■ Shortcut keys

■ View buttons that are found to the left of the horizontal scroll bar

FIG. 5.1

The Word screen can be modified to display the menu bar and a maximum of typing space.

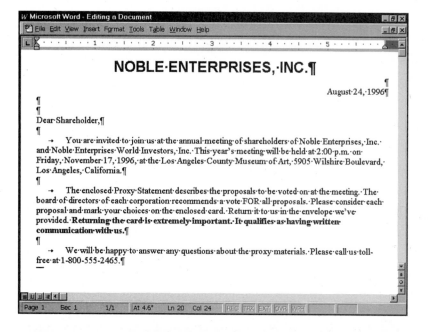

FIG. 5.2

Master Document view is used to assemble a long document from several shorter ones.

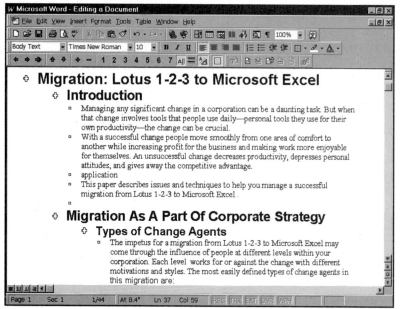

To change the view using menu commands, follow these steps:

1. Choose <u>V</u>iew. Notice that the current view is shown as selected on the View menu.

2. Choose the view you want—Normal, Online Layout, Page Layout, Outline, Master Document, or Full Screen.

To change the view, you can use the following shortcut keys or view buttons located on the horizontal scroll bar:

Shortcut key	Button	View
Alt+Ctrl+N		Normal view
		Online Layout view
Alt+Ctrl+P		Page Layout view
Alt+Ctrl+O		View Outline view
Alt+Ctrl+I		Print Preview

Editing in Normal View

Use *Normal view*, shown in Figure 5.3, for most of your typing and editing. In this view, which is the Word default view, you see character and paragraph formatting as they print. Line and page breaks, tab stops, and alignments are accurate. The area outside the text body—the area containing headers, footers, footnotes, page numbers, margin spacing, and so on—does not appear. You also cannot see the exact placement of such features as snaking columns, positioned paragraphs, or text wrapping around fixed paragraphs or objects. Images are also not shown. Because Word does not have to display and update text layouts in Normal view, editing and cursor movement will be quicker than in Page Layout view.

To display Normal view, choose View, Normal, or press Alt+Ctrl+N. The selected option appears with a bullet to the left of the option.

Editing in Full Screen View

Use *Full Screen view* when you want to maximize the typing area. Full Screen view is comparable to Normal view in its display of character and paragraph formatting, line and page breaks, tab stops, and alignments. However, the title bar, menu bar, all toolbars, the Ruler, the scroll bars, and the status bar are all removed from the screen in Full Screen view. A special Full Screen toolbar appears on-screen to indicate that Full Screen view is currently displayed. Figure 5.4 shows a document in Full Screen view with the Full Screen toolbar displayed.

FIG. 5.3

Normal view provides the fastest performance for basic typing and editing.

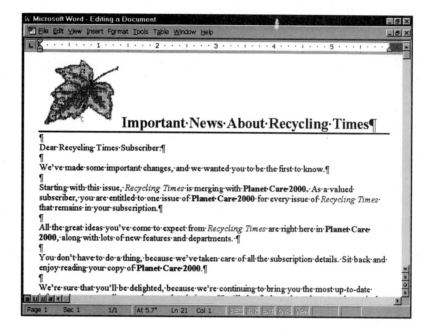

FIG. 5.4

You can use Full Screen view to maximize typing space.

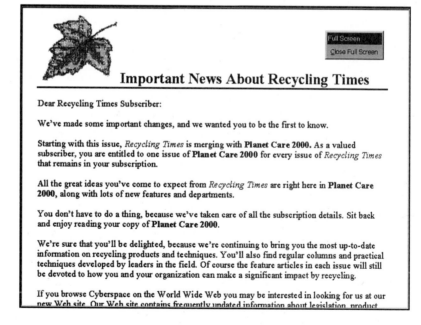

▶ **See** "Displaying or Hiding Toolbars," **p. 55**

To display the Full Screen view, choose <u>V</u>iew, F<u>u</u>ll Screen. To return to the previous view, choose <u>C</u>lose Full Screen on the Full Screen toolbar or press Esc.

N O T E You can access the menu bar in Full Screen view by positioning the mouse along the top edge of the screen. ▪

Like all toolbars, you can move the Full Screen toolbar anywhere on-screen by dragging the title bar. Position the mouse pointer in the title bar of the Full Screen toolbar, hold down the mouse button, and then drag it to a new location. Position the toolbar where you want it and release the mouse button.

If you don't want the Full Screen toolbar to appear as a floating window over your document, double-click its title bar. The button immediately moves to the top of the screen and becomes a toolbar. To refloat the Full Screen toolbar, position the mouse pointer at the left edge of the <u>C</u>lose Full Screen button and drag the toolbar down from the top edge of the screen. All toolbars and even the menu bar can be manipulated in this manner.

Editing in Page Layout View

In *Page Layout view*, your document shows each page as it will appear when printed. You can scroll outside the body copy area of the page to see such items as headers, footers, footnotes, page numbers, and margin spacing. Snaking columns and text that wraps around fixed-position objects appear as they will print. You can type and make formatting changes in Page Layout view.

To change to Page Layout view, choose <u>V</u>iew, <u>P</u>age Layout, or press Alt+Ctrl+P.

Figure 5.5 shows a document in the Page Layout view. Notice the vertical ruler along the left side of the screen. You can use it to change the top and bottom margins of the document.

▶ **See** "Setting Margins," **p. 438**

Zooming In or Out

You can choose <u>V</u>iew, <u>Z</u>oom to further hone your screen view.

To see more of your document, follow these steps:

1. Choose <u>V</u>iew, <u>Z</u>oom.
2. When the Zoom dialog box shown in Figure 5.6 appears, select the desired magnification.

The lower the magnification, the more you will see of your document on-screen.

The <u>W</u>hole Page and <u>M</u>any Pages options are only available if you are working in Page Layout view.

3. Click OK.

FIG. 5.5
Page Layout view shows how your page will appear in print.

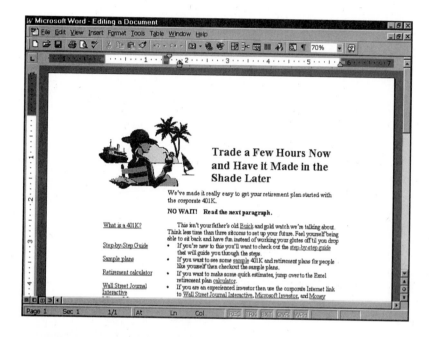

FIG. 5.6
The Zoom dialog box enables you to zoom in or out of your document.

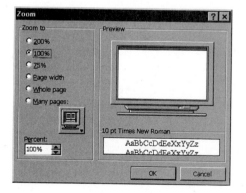

 N O T E Word 97 enables you to zoom in up to 500%. You can accomplish this by typing any number between 10 and 500 in the <u>P</u>ercent box while in the Zoom dialog box. ■

To change the screen magnification from the toolbar, you have two options:

- Click the Zoom Control's down arrow, and then select a preset percentage or document size.
- Click within the Zoom Control's text box, and then type a new percentage between 10% and 500%; press Enter.

Naturally, you can zoom in for a closer look by selecting 500% magnification. This could be useful if you work with small font sizes or if you need to precisely align objects while doing desktop publishing.

If you are working with your document in Page Layout view, you can use the Zoom feature to see the entire page at the same time, or to view several pages at once.

To see the entire page at once, follow these steps:

1. Choose View, Page Layout if you are not already in Page Layout view.
2. Choose View, Zoom.
3. Select Whole Page.
4. Click OK.

TIP You can choose Whole Page from the Zoom Control list box on the Standard toolbar to view the whole page at once when working in Page Layout view.

One screen is equal to one printed page. Figure 5.7 shows a page zoomed to Whole Page in Page Layout view. Whole Page view is available only in Page Layout view.

Use Many Pages in Page Layout view to see and edit the layout of a group of pages.

TIP You can also change the number of displayed pages by increasing or decreasing the value in the Percent box in the Zoom dialog box.

To see more than one page at a time, follow these steps:

1. Choose View, Page Layout, if you are not already in Page Layout view.
2. Choose View, Zoom.
3. Select the Many Pages option.
4. Click the monitor button. A grid appears (see Figure 5.8).

FIG. 5.7
An entire page can be displayed with the Whole Page zoom option.

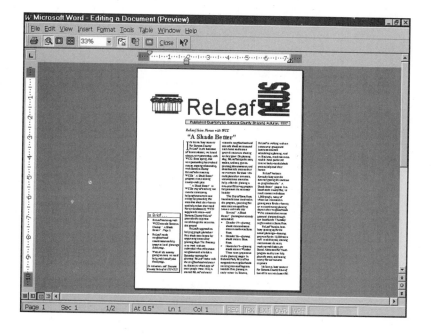

FIG. 5.8
The Many Pages zoom option enables you to see the layout of several pages at once.

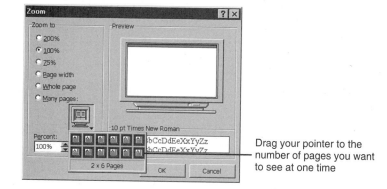

Drag your pointer to the number of pages you want to see at one time

5. Drag across the grid to indicate how many pages you want displayed.

6. Click OK.

Editing in Outline View

In *Outline view,* your document shows the levels of an outline structure. The Outline toolbar appears at the top of the screen, enabling you to easily promote and demote outline topic levels (see Figure 5.9).

▶ **See** "Organizing Content with an Outline," **p. 675**

To change to Outline view, choose <u>V</u>iew, <u>O</u>utline, or press Alt+Ctrl+O.

FIG. 5.9

Outline view shows topic levels of an outline or entire document.

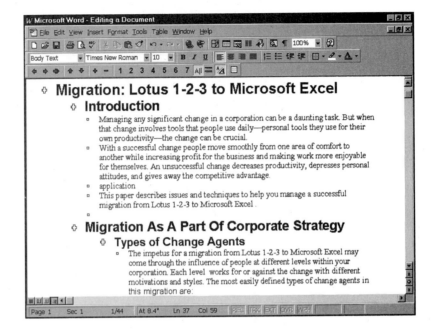

Editing in Online Layout View

Online Layout view enables you to view your document as it might appear online. The Document Map appears to the left of the screen in Online Layout view and enables you to quickly jump to any heading within your document (see Figure 5.10).

Online Layout view is useful for jumping between locations in a large document. While in Online Layout view, Word automatically detects headings and titles and displays them in the left pane. Clicking one of these headings or titles in the left pane moves the display in the right pane to that location in the document.

To work in Online Layout view, follow these steps:

1. Choose <u>V</u>iew, Onli<u>n</u>e Layout.

2. Toggle the Document Map on or off by clicking the Document Map button on the Standard toolbar.

The horizontal scroll bar at the bottom of the screen includes four buttons for changing the view. You can choose the first to switch to Normal view, the second to switch to Online Layout view, the third to switch to Page Layout view, and the fourth to switch to Outline view.

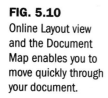

FIG. 5.10
Online Layout view
and the Document
Map enables you to
move quickly through
your document.

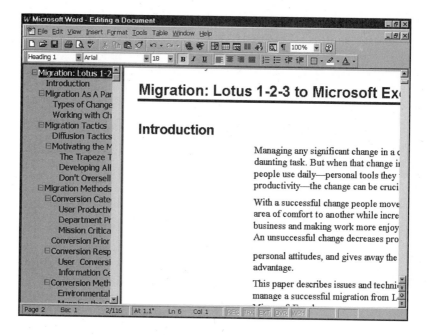

Modifying the Screen Display

By choosing Tools, Options, you can further modify the display to fit your preferences.
You can, for example, request that tab and paragraph marks be displayed as special characters, margins be displayed as dotted lines, or horizontal and vertical scroll bars be displayed. The Options dialog box presents each option on an index tab that is pulled to the
front when you click its name or index tab. The View tab contains options that change the
appearance of the screen.

To change your screen's appearance in Normal view, follow these steps:

1. Choose Tools, Options. The Options dialog box appears, as shown in Figure 5.11.
2. Select the View tab.
3. Select the appropriate options (see Table 5.1).
4. Click OK.

N O T E The View tab options in the Options dialog box will vary depending on the currently
selected view. Figure 5.11 shows the View tab of the Options dialog box while Normal
view is active. The following table lists all View options and indicates in which view the options are
available. ■

▶ **See** "Customizing and Optimizing Word Features," **p. 1115**

Part

I

Ch

5

FIG. 5.11

The View tab in the Options dialog box enables you to change the appearance of the screen.

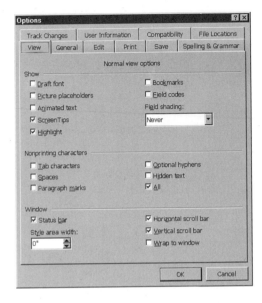

Table 5.1   View Options in the Options Dialog Box

Option	Function	View
Show Group		
Draft Font	Displays the document without formatting or graphics, to speed up editing	Normal, Outline, Master Document
Drawings	Display drawing objects	Page Layout, Online Layout
Object Anchors	Display object anchors. (If cleared, anchors will still display when Show/Hide ¶ is selected)	Page Layout, Online Layout
Text Boundaries	Display page margins and text/object boundaries as dotted lines	Page Layout, Online Layout
Picture Placeholders (Reads as Picture Placeholders in Page Layout and Online Layout)	Displays placeholders instead of the full pictures or graphics on-screen to speed up editing	All views
Animated Text	Displays text animation	All views

Option	Function	View
Show Group		
ScreenTips	Display reviewer comments, footnotes, and endnotes when activated by the mouse	All views
Highlight	Displays text highlighting	All views
Bookmarks	Display a thick I-beam or bracket symbol in the position of each bookmark	All views
Field Codes	Display field codes on-screen in place of field results	All views
Field Shading	Shades fields never, always, or when selected	All views
Nonprinting Characters Group		
Tab Characters	Display tabs as right arrows	All views
Spaces	Display spaces as dots	All views
Paragraph Marks	Display paragraph marks as ¶	All views
Optional Hyphens (Reads as Optional Hyphens in Page Layout and Online Layout)	Display optional hyphens as ¬	All views
Hidden Text	Displays hidden text	All views
All	Displays all nonprinting characters	All views
Window Group		
Status Bar	Displays the status bar	All views
Style Area Width	Controls the width for the area by the left margin where the style name is displayed. (Set to zero to turn off this display.)	Normal, Outline, Master Document

continues

Part

I

Ch

5

Table 5.1   continued

Option	Function	View
Show Group		
Vertical Ruler	Displays the vertical ruler on the left side of the screen	Page Layout
Enlarge Fonts Less Than	Controls which fonts will be enlarged for online viewing	Online Layout
Horizontal Scroll Bar	Displays the horizontal scroll bar	Normal, Outline, Master Document
Vertical Scroll Bar	Displays vertical scroll bar	Normal, Outline, Master Document
Wrap to Window	Displays the document with line breaks to fit the current window width. Warning: Selecting this option prevents text from displaying as it will print.	Normal, Outline, Master Document, Online Layout

Figures 5.12 and 5.13 show two screens of the same document in Page Layout view. Each screen has different options selected in the View tab of the Options dialog box. The screen displays were modified by choosing Tools, Options.

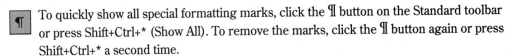

To quickly show all special formatting marks, click the ¶ button on the Standard toolbar or press Shift+Ctrl+* (Show All). To remove the marks, click the ¶ button again or press Shift+Ctrl+* a second time.

Moving in the Document

If you're familiar with word processing, you will learn to move efficiently through a Word document in no time at all. However, never stop trying to learn more, because Word provides a number of unique methods to cut your search time to the absolute minimum.

Moving and Scrolling with the Mouse

To relocate the insertion point by using the mouse, scroll so that you can see the location you want, and then click the I-beam pointer at the character location where you want the insertion point.

FIG. 5.12
A screen displaying scroll bars but no status bar; non-printing characters are also displayed.

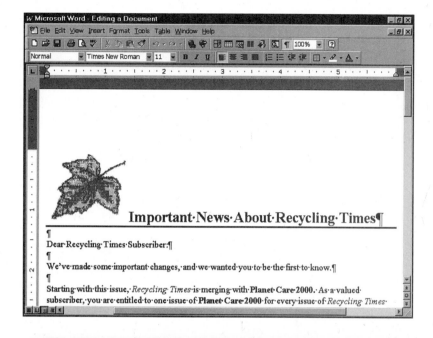

FIG. 5.13
A screen with the scroll bars, non-printing characters, vertical ruler, and status bar hidden; Picture Placeholders has also been selected to show placeholders on-screen rather than pictures.

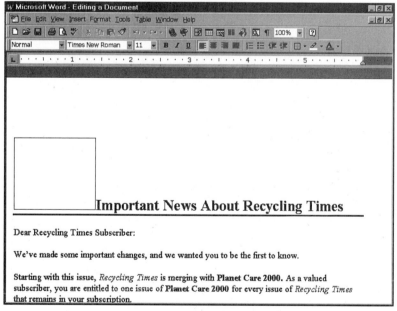

NOTE If you are using an *IntelliPoint mouse*, see the next section, "Scrolling, Panning, and Zooming with IntelliPoint Mouse," for accurate instructions. ■

Part
I
Ch
5

Using your mouse pointer in the horizontal and vertical scroll bars enables you to scroll the document easily so that a new area is displayed. Figure 5.14 shows the parts of the scroll bars, which include the scroll box and page view buttons. The location of the scroll box in the vertical scroll bar shows the screen's location relative to the entire document's length and width. Several buttons are located at the bottom of the vertical scroll bar to help you navigate more quickly. You can control the view of your document using one of five buttons located to the left of the horizontal scroll bar.

If you use a mouse, display the horizontal and vertical scroll bars so that you can scroll with the mouse. As you drag the scroll box down the vertical scroll bar, the page number will show to the side of the scroll bar. If you use the keyboard, you may want to turn off the horizontal and vertical scroll bars to display more of your document on-screen.

FIG. 5.14
The horizontal and vertical scroll bars.

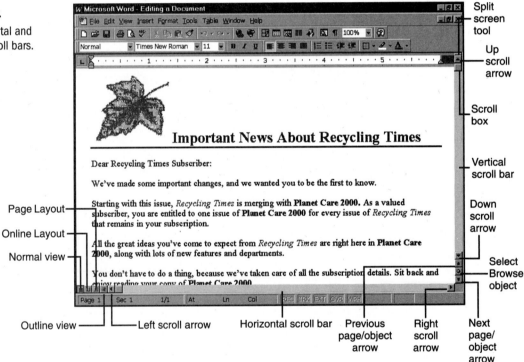

The Select Browse Object button enables you to quickly move through your document using a variety of methods (see "Browsing by Objects" in the next section of this chapter).

Table 5.2 lists the scrolling methods you can use with the mouse and the scroll bars.

Table 5.2   Scrolling Methods for Using the Mouse and the Scroll Bars

To Move	Click
One line	Up or down scroll arrow
One screen up or down	Gray area above or below the scroll box in the vertical scroll bar
One page or object	Next or Previous Page/Object buttons
Large vertical moves	Drag vertical scroll box to a new location in the vertical scroll bar
Horizontally in small increments	Right or left scroll arrow
Horizontally in relative increments	Drag horizontal scroll box to a new location in the horizontal scroll bar
Into left margin	Left scroll arrow while holding Shift (Normal view); left scroll arrow (Page Layout view)

N O T E You must click the I-beam at the new typing location when you arrive at the text you want to edit. If you scroll to a new location and leave the insertion point at the old location, your typing or editing appears at the old location. ■

Scrolling, Panning, and Zooming with IntelliPoint Mouse

The Microsoft IntelliPoint Mouse is a step beyond the normal two-button mouse. It includes a small wheel between the buttons. The wheel rolls forward and backward and depresses. The IntelliPoint mouse makes navigating in Office 97 applications even easier. In Word 97, you can use the IntelliPoint mouse to do the following:

Scroll	Roll the wheel forward to scroll up and backward to scroll down. You don't need to use the vertical scroll bars.
Pan any direction	Hold down the wheel as you drag in any direction to rapidly move the window in that direction.
Zoom document	Hold Ctrl as you roll the wheel to zoom a document to greater or lesser magnification.
Expand data	Hold Shift as you roll the wheel to expand or collapse outlines.

Part
I

Ch
5

CAUTION

The wheel button on the IntelliPoint mouse only works if you install IntelliPoint 2.0 software or later and are using applications that take advantage of the IntelliPoint mouse.

Browsing by Objects

An exciting new feature in Word 97 is the Browse Object command. This feature enables you to move, object by object, through your document. Valid objects are headings, tables, and other objects as outlined in Table 5.3 at the end of this section.

To move using the Browse Object method, follow these steps:

1. Click the Select Browse Object button on the vertical scroll bar. The Browse Object menu displays above the Select Browse Object button (see Figure 5.15).

FIG. 5.15
Use the commands on the Select Browse Object menu to browse through your documents object by object.

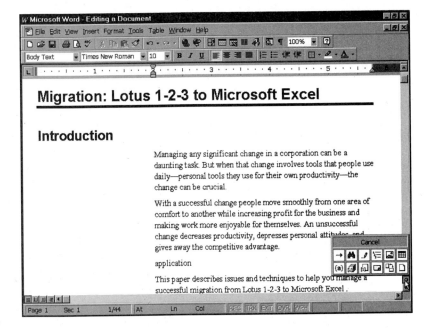

2. Click the icon representing the type of browse you want to activate. Table 5.3 lists the available icons.

   If you click the Go To or Find icon, Word will display the Find and Replace dialog box with the appropriate tab selected. Select or input the item you want to find or go to. (See "Going to a Specific Page" and "Moving to or Selecting a Bookmark" later in this chapter, and Chapter 7, "Using Find and Replace.")

   The Previous and Next Page/Object arrows turn blue to indicate the Browse Object feature has been activated (the arrows will remain black if you select the Page icon from the Browse Object menu, since Previous and Next Page are the default functions of these buttons).

Table 5.3   Icons Available on the Browse Object Menu

Icon	Browse by...
→	Go To
🔍	Find
✎	Edits
☰	Heading
🖼	Graphic
▦	Table
{a}	Field
📑	Endnote
📄	Footnote
🗌	Comment
▢	Section
🗋	Page

3. Click the Previous or Next Page/Object arrows to navigate through your document by the selected browse object.

4. To stop browsing by object and reset the Previous and Next Page/Object arrows to the Page default, click the Select Browse Object button and select the Page icon.

Moving and Scrolling with the Keyboard

The arrow keys ($\uparrow$, $\downarrow$, $\leftarrow$, and $\rightarrow$) and cursor-movement keys (Page Up, Page Down, Home, and End) move the insertion point as you would expect. Combine these keys with the Ctrl key, however, and they become powerful navigation allies. Table 5.4 shows cursor movements you can make with the keyboard.

Part

I

Ch

5

To Move	Press
Table 5.4 Moving and Scrolling with the Keyboard	
One character left	← key
One character right	→ key
One line up	↑ key
One line down	↓ key
One word to the left	Ctrl+←
One word to the right	Ctrl+→
To the end of a line	End
To the beginning of a line	Home
One paragraph up	Ctrl+↑
One paragraph down	Ctrl+↓
Up one window	Page Up key
Down one window	Page Down key
To bottom of window	Ctrl+Page Down
To top of window	Ctrl+Page Up
Up one page	Alt+Ctrl+Page Up
Down one page	Alt+Ctrl+Page Down
To end of document	Ctrl+End
To beginning of document	Ctrl+Home

Going to a Specific Page

When you need to move to a specific page number, choose Edit, Go To. (You can also use Go To to move to specific sections, lines, bookmarks, comments, footnotes, endnotes, fields, tables, graphics, equations, objects, or headings. Inserting bookmarks is covered later in this chapter. You can read about going to other locations in your document in the section "Moving the Insertion Point a Relative Distance.")

N O T E   If you are working with Background Repagination turned off, you can still use the Go To command. However, Word may need to repaginate all or part of the document to move the insertion point to the correct location. See "Repaginating a Document" later in this chapter to learn about Background Repagination. ■

TIP You can press Ctrl+G or double-click Page on the status bar to display the Go To tab of the Find and Replace dialog box.

To move to a specific page, follow these steps:

1. Choose <u>E</u>dit, <u>G</u>o To, or press Ctrl+G. The Go To tab of the Find and Replace dialog box shown in Figure 5.16 appears. (Your dialog box may appear with another option selected.)

2. Select Page in the G<u>o</u> to What list box, if it is not already selected.

3. Type a page number in the <u>E</u>nter Page Number text box.

4. Choose Go <u>T</u>o. The Go <u>T</u>o button does not appear until you type a page number in the <u>E</u>nter Page Number text box.

FIG. 5.16
The Go To dialog box enables you to move to a specific location in your document.

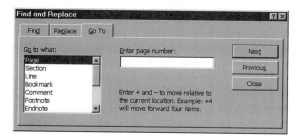

Moving with the Document Map

Another new feature in Word 97 is the *Document Map,* a vertical pane that displays to the left of your document window and helps you to move quickly and easily through long or online documents. The Document Map also keeps track of your current location in a document.

To move through your document using the Document Map, follow these steps:

1. Choose <u>V</u>iew, <u>D</u>ocument Map, or click the Document Map icon on the Standard toolbar. The Document Map is displayed on the left side of the screen (see Figure 5.17).

The Document Map command is a toggle; if the Document Map is not displayed, choosing <u>V</u>iew, <u>D</u>ocument Map will display the Document Map on the screen. If the Document Map is already displayed, choosing this command closes the Document Map display.

Part
I
Ch
5

2. Use the mouse to click the heading or text in the Document Map pane to which you want to move.

   Notice that as you scroll through your document, the highlight in the Document Map pane moves to indicate the current location of the insertion point.

   If you prefer to use the keyboard, you can use the F6, Enter combination to manipulate the Document Map pane. Press F6 to move from the document into the Document Map pane, press ↑ or ↓ to select a desired heading, and then press Enter to return to the document at the selected location.

3. Click the + or − next to any heading to collapse or expand the headings for the selected section.

   If you prefer to use the keyboard, press F6 to move to the Document Map pane, use ↑ or ↓ to select the heading you want to expand or collapse, then press Alt+Shift++ to expand the section, or press Alt+Shift+ − to collapse the section.

   You can also right-click any heading and choose to expand or collapse the section using the shortcut menu options.

4. Change the width of the Document Map pane (make it wider or narrower) to a size that works best for you. Position the mouse pointer along the right edge of the pane so the pointer changes to a resize icon, and then drag the edge of the pane left or right.

FIG. 5.17
The Document Map makes it easy to navigate through long or online documents.

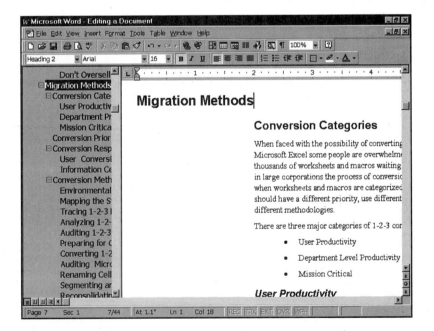

Moving the Insertion Point a Relative Distance

You can move a specified distance relative to the insertion point's current location by choosing Edit, Go To. The move can be in increments of pages, sections, lines, bookmarks, comments, footnotes, endnotes, fields, tables, graphics, equations, objects, or headings. You can even move to a location that is a certain percentage of the way through the total document. The Next and Previous buttons move the insertion point to the next or previous item you select.

To move a relative distance, follow these steps:

1. Choose Edit, Go To or press Ctrl+G to display the Go To tab of the Find and Replace dialog box.

2. Select one of the options listed in Go to What box.

3. Enter the number or other identifier you want to go to. You can also choose Next or Previous to go to the next or previous occurrence of the selected option. (These buttons appear when appropriate.) Or, as a third option, you can enter a percentage that represents the distance you would like to move through the document.

   You must have Page selected in the Go to What list box to use a percentage.

   Some of the selections in the Go to What list box will activate a drop-down list in the Enter Item text box that will enable you to select a valid item, such as a bookmark or field name.

4. Choose Go To (or Next or Previous).

5. Choose Close or press Esc to close the Find and Replace dialog box.

 TIP You can leave the Find and Replace dialog box open on your screen and click back and forth between the document and the dialog box to quickly move to and edit multiple locations.

Sections, lines, comments, footnotes, endnotes, fields, tables, graphics, and equations are numbered from the beginning of the document. To move through these items, select the item in the Go to What list box, then enter the number of the item you want to move to or select an option from the Enter Item drop-down list box, when applicable. You can use a plus sign (+) to indicate a relative number forward in the document or a minus sign (–) to indicate a relative number backward in the document. For example, 9 is the ninth footnote in the document, but +9 is the ninth footnote forward from the current position.

Table 5.5 shows some examples of how to move the insertion point to a relative location.

Table 5.5 Moving to a Relative Location

To Move Insertion Point	Type or Select
To page n	n
Forward n pages	$+n$
Backward n pages	$-n$
To section n	n
Forward n sections	$+n$
Backward n sections	$-n$
To line n	n
Forward n lines	$+n$
Backward n lines	$-n$
To bookmark	The name of the bookmark
To comment	The reviewer's name, then choose Next or Previous; or the comment number
Forward n comments	$+n$
Backward n comments	$-n$
To footnote n	n
Forward n footnotes	$+n$
Backward n footnotes	$-n$
To endnote n	n
Forward n endnotes	$+n$
Backward n endnotes	$-n$
To a field	The field name or the field number
Forward n fields	$+n$
Backward n fields	$-n$
To table n	n
Forward n tables	$+n$
Backward n tables	$-n$
To graphic n	n
Forward n graphics	$+n$

To Move Insertion Point	Type or Select
Backward *n* graphics	*-n*
To equation *n*	*n*
Forward *n* equations	*+n*
Backward *n* equations	*-n*
To an object	The object name
Heading	The heading number
n percent through document	*n*%

n is the number of units (pages, sections, lines, comments, footnotes, endnotes, fields, tables, graphics, or equations) you want to move forward or backward from the current location.

Combine move codes and their relative numbers to move to the exact location you want. When Page is selected in the Go To What list box, the following code, for example, moves the insertion point to the beginning of the third section:

```
s3
```

This command moves the insertion point to the 12th line on page 15 in the third section:

```
p15s3l12
```

Moving to Previous Locations

To return the insertion point to the last three locations where an action occurred, press Shift+F5. Each of the first three presses moves the insertion point to the immediately preceding place of action. Pressing a fourth time returns the insertion point to the location where Shift+F5 was first pressed.

Pressing Shift+F5 after opening a document returns the insertion point to the location where the last revision was made before you saved and closed the document.

TROUBLESHOOTING

Sometimes I need to move back further than the last three locations where an action occurred. How can I quickly move back and forth between multiple locations? You can insert bookmarks into your document to mark specific places that you expect to return to often. See "Marking Locations with Bookmarks" later in this chapter for information about using bookmarks.

ON THE WEB

For online support from Microsoft, visit the following World Wide Web site:

http://www.microsoft.com/support

You can also access Microsoft's extensive troubleshooting KnowledgeBase at the following site:

http://www.microsoft.com/kb

For tutorials, tips, and add-ins for Microsoft Office applications point your browser to:

http://www.ronperson.com

Selecting Text

Like all standard Windows applications, Word works on the *select, then do* principle. Whether you want to delete a word, format a phrase, or move a sentence, you must select what you want to change before choosing the command. As with other commands and features, you can use the mouse or the keyboard to select text. Many shortcuts and tips are available for selecting text quickly.

Selecting Text with the Mouse

Selecting text with the mouse is easy and convenient. You can select any amount of text, from a single character to an entire document. You also can combine mouse and keyboard selection techniques. Use whichever method or combination is effective for you.

To select a small amount of text with the mouse, follow these steps:

1. Click and hold the mouse button at the beginning of the text you want to select.

2. Drag the pointer in any direction across the text you want to select.

If the pointer touches the edge of the window as you are dragging, the window scrolls in that direction if more text exists.

To select from the current insertion point to a distant location, follow these steps:

1. Click the I-beam at the beginning of the text to relocate the insertion point.

2. Hold down the Shift key *or* press F8 (Extend Selection).

   While you are in Extend Selection mode, EXT appears on the status bar at the bottom of the screen.

3. Scroll the screen so that the end of text you want selected shows.

4. Click the I-beam at the end of the text.

5. Release the Shift key if you held it down in Step 2, or press Esc if you pressed F8 in Step 2. Esc turns off Extend Selection mode, but leaves the text selected.

N O T E As an alternative, position the insertion point where you want to start the selection, scroll until the end of the text is visible, and then hold down the Shift key while you click the I-beam where you want to end the selection. ▨

To deselect text, click the mouse anywhere in the document window.

You can select specific units of text—such as words, sentences, lines, paragraphs, or the whole document—by using one of the techniques listed in Table 5.6. Notice that clicking or dragging in the Selection bar (as shown in Figure 5.18) is a shortcut for selecting text. The *selection bar* is the blank vertical space on the left side of the Word document. Text never extends into this area. The mouse pointer points in the opposite direction (to the right) to indicate it has been properly positioned in the selection bar.

Table 5.6   Selecting Blocks of Text with the Mouse

Text to Select	Mouse Action
A word	Double-click the word
A sentence	Press Ctrl and click the sentence
A line	Click selection bar (blank margin to left of a line of text)
Multiple lines	Click selection bar and drag up or down
A paragraph	Double-click selection bar
Document	Press Ctrl and click in selection bar
Rectangular block or column (not within a table)	Click the top left of the column to be selected, and then hold Alt while you drag to select the text

Part
I
Ch
5

N O T E After selecting text with the mouse, right-click *the selection* to activate the shortcut menu. Frequently-used commands can be found on the shortcut menu. Using the shortcut menu saves time because you are not required to move the mouse across the screen or navigate through complex menus and toolbars. You can even customize the shortcut menu to contain the commands you use most often. ▨

▶ **See** "Customizing Shortcut Menus," **p. 1156**

If you frequently select the same block of text or need to select text under macro control, use a bookmark. Refer to the section "Inserting Bookmarks" later in this chapter to find out how to insert bookmarks.

▶ **See** "Introducing Visual Basic for Applications," **p. 1163**

FIG. 5.18
Use the mouse to
select text in the
selection bar.

Selecting Text with the Keyboard

If you are a touch typist, you don't need to move your fingers from the keyboard to select text. Word enables you to select varying amounts of text quickly and conveniently.

The method most convenient for selecting text is to hold down the Shift key as you move the insertion point. You can select text by using Shift in combination with any move key. Some of these key combinations are listed in Table 5.7.

N O T E A complete list of keyboard movement commands can be found in Table 5.4 in the section "Moving and Scrolling with the Keyboard" earlier in this chapter. Add Shift to any of the combinations found in Table 5.4 to select text with the keyboard. ■

Table 5.7 Selecting Text with the Shift Key

To Select	Press
A word	Shift+Ctrl+← or → key
To the beginning of a line	Shift+Home
To the end of a line	Shift+End
One line at a time	Shift+↑ or ↓ key

To select	Press
To the beginning of a document	Shift+Ctrl+Home
To the end of a document	Shift+Ctrl+End

You can select large amounts of text or an amount relative to your current location by combining the F8 (Extend Selection) key with the Ctrl+G (Go To) command and a move code as described in the following procedure.

To select large amounts of text with the keyboard, follow these steps:

1. Move the insertion point to the beginning of the text you want to select.
2. Press F8 (Extend Selection).
3. Press Ctrl+G (Go To).
4. Select the item to which you want to move, and enter the number or other identifier that represents the relative location of the end of your selection, as described earlier in the section "Moving the Insertion Point a Relative Distance."
5. Choose Go To.
6. Press Esc one time to close the Find and Replace dialog box, and then a second time to turn off Extend Selection mode.

To select the next 20 lines in your document, for example, press F8 (Extend Selection), and then Ctrl+G (Go To). Select Line in the Go to What list box and enter +20, and then choose Go To. Press Esc to close the dialog box and Esc again to turn off Extend Selection mode.

Press Ctrl+5 to select the entire document. This shortcut works only with the 5 key on the numeric keypad. Num Lock can be on or off. You can also choose Edit, Select All.

To select an entire table, place the insertion point inside the table and press Alt+5 on the numeric keypad. Num Lock must be off. You can also choose Table, Select Table. The insertion point must be inside the table for the table selection commands to work.

Another way of selecting text with the keyboard is to use the F8 (Extend Selection) key. Press F8 and then move the insertion point to select the desired amount of text.

To select from the insertion point to a distant location, follow these steps:

1. Move the insertion point to the beginning of the text you want to select.
2. Press F8 (Extend Selection).

Part

I

Ch

5

3. Press one of the keys listed in Table 5.8.

4. Press Esc to turn off Extend Selection mode.

Table 5.8   Selecting Text in Extend Selection Mode

To Select	Press
Next or previous character	← or → key
From the insertion point to a specific character	That character (for example, pressing a period would extend the selection to the next period in the document)
The end of a line	End
The beginning of a line	Home
The top of the previous screen	Page Up
The bottom of the next screen	Page Down
The beginning of a document	Ctrl+Home
The end of a document	Ctrl+End

After you turn off Extend Selection mode, you can press any arrow key to deselect the selected text.

You also can use Extend Selection mode to select specific units of text, such as a word, sentence, or paragraph. To select specific units of text, move the cursor into the text, then press F8 (Extend Selection), as indicated in this chart:

To select current...	Press F8
Word	2 times
Sentence	3 times
Paragraph	4 times
Section	5 times (if there is only one section in the document, then the entire document is selected)
Document	6 times

If the insertion point is in a field code when you press the F8 key, the field code and then the next larger block of text are selected. (Field codes are hidden codes used to automate Word processes. Reading Chapter 22, "Automating with Field Codes," will help you understand field codes.)

Press Esc to turn off Extend Selection mode when you are finished making your selection.

▶ **See** "Understanding the Basics of Fields," **p. 694**

To select a unit of text smaller than the current selection, press Shift+F8 as many times as needed to decrease the selection. You can also use one of the arrow keys to deselect portions of the selected text. (If you have already pressed Esc to turn off Extend Selection mode, then pressing an arrow key will deselect the entire selection.)

Remember to press the Esc key to turn off Extend Selection mode.

Deleting Text

Effective writing doesn't come easily, and good writers spend a great deal of time deleting text. Deleting is a simple operation in Word, but you should be aware of some nuances.

To delete text, first select it using any selection technique or shortcut, and then press the Delete or Backspace key. You can use one of the following key combinations to delete specific units of text:

To delete	Press
Characters to right of insertion point	Delete
Characters to left of insertion point	Backspace
The next word	Ctrl+Delete
The preceding word	Ctrl+Backspace

 TIP If you accidentally delete something, choose <u>E</u>dit, <u>U</u>ndo Clear to restore the deleted item. Ctrl+Z is the shortcut key to undo an action.

To make editing quick and easy with the keyboard, use the F8 or Shift key combinations to select text; then press Delete or Backspace. To delete a sentence, for example, press F8 three times and then press Delete.

 TIP If you use F8 (Extend Selection) to select text, Word automatically turns off Extend Selection mode when an editing action occurs, such as Delete or Copy. If you need to manually turn off Extend Selection mode, press Esc.

N O T E You can choose <u>E</u>dit, Re<u>p</u>lace to delete text formatted with a particular style. Choose <u>M</u>ore on the Re<u>p</u>lace tab of the Find and Replace dialog box, then choose F<u>o</u>rmat, <u>S</u>tyle. In the Find Style dialog box that appears, choose the style of the text you want to delete, and then choose OK. Leave the Fi<u>n</u>d What and Replace W<u>i</u>th boxes empty. Choose <u>F</u>ind Next. If

continues

Part
I

Ch
5

continued

the text you find is text you want to delete, choose <u>R</u>eplace. If you don't want to delete the text, choose <u>F</u>ind Next again to proceed through the document to the next text with the style you specified. Choose Close or press Esc to close the Find and Replace dialog box. ▪

▶ **See** "Finding and Replacing Formatting and Styles," **p. 234**

TROUBLESHOOTING

Why does my text change its formatting when I press the Delete or Backspace keys? Word stores paragraph formatting in the paragraph mark at the end of each paragraph. If you delete the paragraph mark of a particular paragraph, it takes on the format of the following paragraph. Choose <u>E</u>dit, <u>U</u>ndo immediately to reverse the deletion and restore the paragraph formatting. (See "Undoing Edits" later in this chapter.)

If you cannot undo the deletion for some reason, you can reformat the paragraph or copy a paragraph mark from a similar paragraph and paste it at the end of the problem paragraph.

▶ **See** "Formatting Lines and Paragraphs," **p. 321**

▶ **See** "Applying, Copying, and Removing Styles," **p. 389**

To avoid deleting a paragraph mark inadvertently, turn on paragraph marks by selecting the Show/Hide ¶ on the Standard toolbar. You can also turn on nonprinting characters by choosing <u>T</u>ools, <u>O</u>ptions, selecting the View tab, and selecting <u>A</u>ll in the Nonprinting Characters group.

Typing over Text

One helpful feature in Word enables you to replace selected text with text you type or paste from the Clipboard.

 If you accidentally type over selected text, you can undo your mistake by immediately choosing <u>E</u>dit, <u>U</u>ndo, clicking the Undo button, or pressing Ctrl+Z. (See "Undoing Edits" later in this chapter for more information about the Undo command.)

If you want to turn off this feature so selected text is not replaced, follow these steps:

1. Choose <u>T</u>ools, <u>O</u>ptions to display the Options dialog box.

2. Select the Edit tab.

3. Clear <u>T</u>yping Replaces Selection.

4. Choose OK. If you type or paste text while existing text is selected, the text is placed before the selection.

CAUTION

Typing Replaces Selection is a normal Windows standard. If you turn this feature off, others using your computer may have a difficult time. Additionally, if you install other programs that contain macros that work with Word, these applications may not function properly without this feature activated.

If you want to type over existing text as you type (rather than have text automatically inserted), select Overtype mode on the Edit tab of the Options dialog box. You can also double-click the OVR on the status bar to toggle Overtype mode on or off.

CAUTION

If you're working in Overtype mode, typing replaces selected *as well as* unselected text.

In previous versions of Word, Overtype mode could be toggled on and off via the Insert key. This was an annoying feature for many longtime Windows users who used the old Shift+Insert command to paste. A slip of the Shift key often resulted in Overtype mode being activated. To aid users, Microsoft has removed this function from the Insert key.

Hyphenating Words

Hyphenation joins words used in combination (for example, up-to-date) or splits long words so that they can break to the next line. Splitting long words with hyphens reduces the ragged appearance of your right margin or the amount of white space between words in justified text. Word has three types of hyphens: optional, regular, and nonbreaking.

Inserting Regular and Nonbreaking Hyphens

Use regular hyphens when you want to control where a hyphen is inserted or to join two words used in combination. A regular hyphen breaks a word, when necessary, so that it can wrap at the end of a line. Use a nonbreaking (or *hard*) hyphen to join words or acronyms that you do not want broken at the end of a line. (Optional hyphens break words at the end of a line.) Table 5.9 summarizes the three types of hyphens available in Word.

Part
I

Ch
5

Table 5.9 Types of Hyphens

Hyphen	Keystroke	Appearance on Screen	Function
Regular	Hyphen	-	For words that are always hyphenated and can be split at line breaks.
Optional	Ctrl+Hyphen	¬	To split words at the end of a line. Not displayed unless the word appears at the end of the line.
Nonbreaking	Shift+Ctrl+Hyphen	—	For words that are always hyphenated and that you do not want to split at the end of the line.

Inserting Optional Hyphens Throughout a Document

You may want to add hyphens to your document to enhance the layout of the text on the page. Hyphenating a document will prevent large amounts of white space from appearing within the lines of justified paragraphs or at the end of lines in left-aligned paragraphs.

▶ **See** "Formatting Lines and Paragraphs," **p. 321**

You can choose to have Word automatically insert optional hyphens throughout your document. It will identify the first word in each line and, if the word can be hyphenated, Word will insert an optional hyphen. The first part of the word is then moved to the end of the preceding line of text. Optional hyphens are printed in your document only if they are needed to break a word at the end of a line.

If you prefer to have more control over where hyphens are inserted, you can use the Manual Hyphenation option. During manual hyphenation, Word displays each instance of a proposed hyphenation and asks for your approval before inserting a hyphen.

Viewing Optional Hyphens

 You normally don't see optional hyphens unless they are used to break a word.

Optional hyphens will only appear in your document when Word actually uses them to break a word. To see all optional hyphens in your document, follow these steps:

1. Choose <u>T</u>ools, <u>O</u>ptions.
2. Select the View tab.
3. Select either <u>A</u>ll or <u>O</u>ptional hyphens in the Nonprinting characters group. (If you are in Page Layout or Online Layout view, the underlined letter for Optional Hyphens will be "y".)

   When optional hyphens are displayed, they appear as ¬ in your document text. Optional hyphens that appear in the middle of a line will *not* print. They will only print when they are at the end of a line.

   When optional hyphens are not displayed, they do not show in the middle of lines and the optional hyphens at the end of lines display as regular hyphens (-).

 T I P You can quickly display all nonprinting characters by clicking Show/Hide ¶ on the Standard toolbar, or by pressing Shift+Ctrl+*.

Customizing Hyphenation Options   You can customize the hyphenation options to control how Word hyphenates your document.

To customize hyphenation options, follow these steps:

1. Choose <u>T</u>ools, <u>L</u>anguage, <u>H</u>yphenation. The Hyphenation dialog box appears (see Figure 5.19).

Part
I
Ch
5

FIG. 5.19
The Hyphenation dialog box enables you to customize how Word hyphen- ates your document.

2. Select from among the options in the dialog box:

Option	Action
<u>A</u>utomatically Hyphenate Document	Hyphenates existing text without asking for confirmation; new and existing text is automatically hyphenated as you edit.
Hyphenate Words in <u>C</u>APS	Hyphenates words in all caps.

continues

continued

Option	Action
Hyphenation Zone	Determines the space at the right margin within which a word can be hyphenated. To increase the number of hyphenated words and decrease right-margin raggedness, lower the number in the Hyphenation Zone box. Increase the number for less hyphenation with a more ragged right margin.
Limit Consecutive Hyphens To	Sets the maximum number of consecutive lines that can end with hyphens.
Manual	Starts checking the document, and asks for confirmation of each word that appears to require hyphenation.

Inserting Optional Hyphens Automatically   To insert optional hyphens automatically, follow these steps:

1. If hidden text and nonprinting characters are displayed, press Shift+Ctrl+* or choose Tools, Options, View tab and turn off the display of hidden text and other nonprinting characters before hyphenating. Text will be hyphenated based on how your document will be printed, for example, without hidden text or nonprinting characters.

2. Choose Tools, Language, Hyphenation. The Hyphenation dialog box appears (refer to Figure 5.19, if necessary).

3. Select Automatically Hyphenate Document, and customize the remaining options as desired.

4. Choose OK. The existing text is hyphenated. New and existing text is automatically hyphenated as you edit your document.

To remove automatically inserted optional hyphens from your document, clear Automatically Hyphenate Document in the Hyphenation dialog box.

Inserting Optional Hyphens Automatically   To insert optional hyphens manually, follow these steps:

1. If hidden text and nonprinting characters are displayed, press Shift+Ctrl+* or choose Tools, Options, View tab and turn off the display of hidden text and other nonprinting characters before hyphenating. Text will be hyphenated based on how your document will print out.

   If you want to only hyphenate a portion of your document, you must select that portion first. Otherwise, Word will hyphenate the entire document.

2. Choose Tools, Language, Hyphenation. The Hyphenation dialog box appears (refer to Figure 5.19, if necessary).

3. Select among the options in the Hyphenation dialog box. Do *not* select Automatically Hyphenate Document.

4. Choose Manual. The Manual Hyphenation dialog box appears.

5. Choose Yes to accept the proposed hyphenation, use the mouse, or press ← or → to reposition where the word will break, and then choose Yes. Word automatically moves to the next suggested hyphenation.

   Choose No to refuse a suggested break and move to the next possible hyphenation.

6. Continue in this manner until Word informs you that the hyphenation is complete. Choose OK.

   If you selected text prior to starting manual hyphenation, Word notifies you when the selection has been hyphenated and give you the opportunity to continue hyphenating the remainder of the document; choose Yes to hyphenate the remaining text, or choose No to end manual hyphenation.

Removing Manually Inserted Optional Hyphens   You must use the Find and Replace dialog box to remove optional hyphens that have been manually inserted:

 You do not have to display optional hyphens to remove them.

▶ **See** "Finding and Replacing Special Characters," **p. 239**

1. Choose Edit, Replace, or press Ctrl+H, to display the Find and Replace dialog box with the Replace tab selected. Select the Replace tab if necessary.

2. Position the insertion point inside the Find What text box and choose Special. If you do not see the Special button, choose More to expand the dialog box, and then choose Special.

3. Select Optional Hyphen from the Special menu (see Figure 5.20). The search code for an optional hyphen is inserted into the Find What text box.

T I P You can type the search code for an optional hyphen directly into the Find What text box by typing ^-.

4. Leave the Replace With text box empty to replace the optional hyphens with nothing. If there is text in the Replace with text box, use the Delete key to remove it. (See "Deleting Text" earlier in this chapter for more information about using the Delete key.)

Part

I

Ch

5

FIG. 5.20
Use the Find and
Replace dialog box
to remove optional
hyphens that have
been manually
inserted.

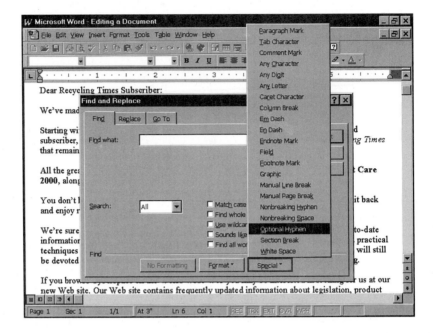

5. Choose Replace <u>A</u>ll to remove *every* optional hyphen from your document.

   To remove only selected hyphens, choose <u>F</u>ind Next, and then choose <u>R</u>eplace when you find a hyphen you want to remove.

   To remove optional hyphens from a portion of your document, select the text before opening the Find and Replace dialog box. When you choose Replace <u>A</u>ll, Word will only remove hyphens within the selected area.

6. Press Esc or choose Close to exit the Find and Replace dialog box.

Undoing Edits

The <u>U</u>ndo command reverses the most recent editing action (assuming the action can be reversed). Almost any action can be reversed. You can reverse a number of actions until a command that cannot be reversed is executed. (In earlier versions of Word, the Undo command was limited to 100 or fewer actions.) It is often a good idea to undo an action as soon as you realize you made a mistake. Continuing to work may result in an action that cannot be reversed, thus making it impossible to automatically reverse earlier actions. Also, any steps performed after the action you want to undo will also be reversed.

To undo the last action, choose <u>E</u>dit, <u>U</u>ndo, or press Ctrl+Z.

You can also use the mouse to undo the last action by clicking the Undo icon on the Standard toolbar. Undo several commands by clicking the down arrow to the right of the Undo icon; a list of actions that can be reversed will be displayed.

You can redo any command you undo by clicking the Redo icon on the Standard toolbar. Redo several reversed actions by clicking the down arrow to the right of the Redo icon and selecting from the list of actions that can be redone. You can also press Ctrl+Y or choose Edit Redo to reverse a single undone action.

If no actions can be reversed or redone, the icons on the Standard toolbar become disabled.

Inserting Frequently Used Material

The Word AutoText feature is like word processing shorthand. It saves you time by storing selected text and graphics (and their formatting) that are used repeatedly. If you have a long company name that you frequently must type in documents, for example, you can abbreviate it as AutoText and insert it with only a few keystrokes. AutoText also ensures that repetitive material is typed correctly and consistently. If you create templates for standardized documents, you should consider including AutoText entries in the templates for frequently used words, phrases, formats, or pictures. (A *template* provides a guide or pattern for creating specific types of documents.)

▶ **See** "Using Templates and Wizards for Frequently Created Documents," **p. 197**

Part

I

Ch

5

AutoText is not limited to text. It can contain pictures and graphics of digitized signatures, graphic letterheads, logos, or symbols. If you frequently use a table with special formatting, you can make it an AutoText entry.

Word 97 contains more than 40 predefined AutoText entries that are used frequently by most users. These entries include, among other things, letter closings (such as Sincerely or Best regards) and Mailing Instructions (such as Confidential and Via Airmail). To see the predefined entries, choose Insert, AutoText and scroll through the various menus for the predefined entries. Under certain conditions, the predefined entries may not be visible on the AutoText menu; "Inserting AutoText" later in this chapter discusses these conditions in detail and provides instructions for viewing all AutoText entries.

In the previous version of Word, AutoText was located on the Edit menu. AutoText can be found on the Insert menu in Word 97 and can also be accessed in the AutoCorrect dialog box (Tools, AutoCorrect).

Another new feature in Word 97 is the AutoText toolbar, which provides quick access to AutoText entries for mouse users.

Creating an AutoText Entry

You can use the AutoText command to store text or graphics as AutoText entries by choosing Insert, AutoText.

To create an AutoText entry, follow these steps:

1. Select the text, graphic, table, or combination of items that you want to add as an AutoText entry.

2. Choose Insert, AutoText, and then select New from the AutoText menu, or press Alt+F3. The Create AutoText dialog box appears (see Figure 5.21).

   Word suggests a name for your entry based on the selected text.

FIG. 5.21
Use the Create AutoText dialog box to create an AutoText entry.

3. You can change the suggested name by deleting it and typing in a logical name for this entry.

   An AutoText entry name can contain spaces and special characters such as * or %. Try to keep AutoText entry names short to minimize the number of keystrokes needed to insert them.

   If you type a name that is already in use for another entry, Word will warn you before proceeding.

4. Choose OK.

AutoText entries can be stored with the document template or with NORMAL.DOT (to make them accessible in all documents). Using the above method does not give you control over where your AutoText entry is stored (it is stored in the template that was last accessed by Word—that might be the document template *or* NORMAL.DOT).

To change the default storage location, follow these steps:

1. Choose Insert, AutoText, and then select AutoText from the AutoText menu. The AutoCorrect dialog box appears with the AutoText tab selected. A suggested name appears in the Enter AutoText Entries Here text box (see Figure 5.22).

2. Select the template you want in the Look In list box (select Normal or All Active Templates to store future entries in NORMAL.DOT), and then choose OK.

The selected template will only remain as the default until another template is selected when inserting or creating an AutoText entry.

Storing an entry in NORMAL.DOT enables you to access the entry from any document. Storing an entry in a document template other than NORMAL.DOT will enable you to access the entry *only* when working in a document based on that template.

▶ **See** "Working with Templates," **p. 198**

To control the storage location when creating an AutoText entry, follow these steps:

1. Select the text, graphic, table, or combination of items that you want to add as an AutoText entry.

2. Choose Insert, AutoText, and then select AutoText from the AutoText menu. The AutoCorrect dialog box appears with the AutoText tab selected. A suggested name appears in the Enter AutoText Entries Here text box (see Figure 5.22).

FIG. 5.22
The AutoText tab of the AutoCorrect dialog box enables you to control where AutoText entries are stored.

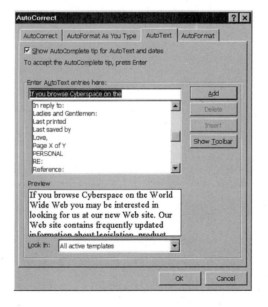

Part
I

Ch
5

3. Type a name for your entry into the Enter AutoText Entries Here text box.

4. Select the template in which you want to store this entry in the Look In list box. Choose All Active Templates or NORMAL.DOT to make this entry available in all documents. Selecting a template other than NORMAL.DOT will make this entry *only* available in documents based on that template.

▶ **See** "Opening a New Document Based on a Template," **p. 204**

5. Choose <u>A</u>dd. The entry is stored to the selected template. The AutoText entry is added and the AutoCorrect dialog box closes.

Depending on how the Word's Save options have been customized, you may or may not be prompted to save NORMAL.DOT after an AutoText entry has been added; Word may save it automatically. If you store an AutoText entry to a template other than NORMAL.DOT, Word will prompt you to save the template when you next save or close the document; at that time, you can choose to save the newly created entries or discard them.

Inserting AutoText

Once you've created an AutoText entry, it's easy to use it in your document.

To insert an AutoText entry into your text, follow these steps:

1. Position the insertion point where you want the AutoText entry to appear.

2. Type the abbreviation you gave the AutoText entry.

3. Press F3 (the Insert AutoText key).

When you press F3, Word replaces the AutoText abbreviation with the AutoText. (The AutoText abbreviation you type in your document must be at the beginning of a line or preceded by a space. Otherwise, the AutoText abbreviation will not be replaced with the AutoText.)

If you cannot remember the AutoText abbreviation, or if you want to insert one of the predefined AutoText entries, you can access a list of entries in the <u>I</u>nsert menu.

To insert an AutoText entry from the <u>I</u>nsert menu, follow these steps:

1. Position the insertion point where you want the AutoText entry to appear.

2. Choose <u>I</u>nsert, <u>A</u>utoText. The AutoText menu appears.

▶ **See** "Opening a New Document Based on a Template," **p. 204**

▶ **See** "Applying Paragraph Styles," **p. 390**

Entries listed will depend on the currently selected style or template. For example, assume you are working in a letter. If the insertion point is positioned in a paragraph that is formatted with the Body Text style, you will see different options on this menu than you will see if the insertion point is in a paragraph that is formatted with the Normal style.

The selected option in the Look In list box on the AutoText tab of the AutoCorrect dialog box will also control what is displayed on the AutoText menu. For example, if you are working in a letter and All Active Templates has been selected in the Look In list box, and if you have positioned the insertion point within the salutation of the letter (so Salutation is the active style), various salutations will be displayed. However, if the letter template is the selected template in the Look In list box, different options will appear on the AutoText menu. You can change the selection in the Look In list box by choosing Insert, AutoText. Choose AutoText to display the AutoCorrect dialog box with the AutoText tab selected. Select the option you want in the Look In list box, and then choose OK.

N O T E   To list *all* AutoText entries on the AutoText menu, hold down Shift while pressing Alt+A to access AutoText or while clicking AutoText on the insert menu. ▮

3. Select the AutoText entry from the AutoText menu. The entry is inserted.

Understanding the AutoText Toolbar

You can use the AutoText toolbar to quickly create and insert AutoText entries.

To display the AutoText toolbar on-screen, choose View, Toolbars, and choose AutoText from the Toolbars menu. Figure 5.23 shows the AutoText toolbar displayed on the screen.

You can also display the toolbar by choosing Show Toolbar from the AutoText tab in the AutoCorrect dialog box.

To create an AutoText entry using the AutoText toolbar, select the text for your entry and click New on the AutoText toolbar. Enter the name for your entry and choose OK. See "Creating an AutoText Entry" earlier in this section for more information about creating AutoText entries.

T I P   You can press Alt+N to access the New option on the AutoText toolbar.

To insert an entry using the AutoText toolbar, click "All Entries." In Figure 5.23, the AutoText toolbar menu reads `All Entries`. However, the wording of this menu may vary depending on the selected style or template. To see all AutoText entries, hold down Shift and then click the toolbar menu. Click the AutoText you want inserted.

You can display the AutoText tab of the AutoCorrect dialog box by clicking the AutoText icon on the AutoText toolbar.

Part

I

Ch

5

FIG. 5.23
The AutoText toolbar provides quick access to AutoText entries.

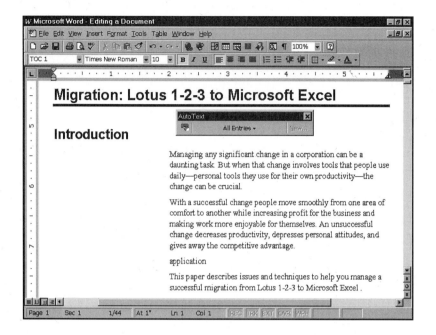

Deleting AutoText

You may want to delete an AutoText entry if you no longer use it.

To delete an AutoText entry, follow these steps:

1. Choose Insert, AutoText and choose AutoText from the AutoText menu, or click the AutoText icon on the AutoText toolbar.

2. Type the name of the AutoText entry you want to delete in the Enter AutoText Entries Here text box, or select the name from the list.

3. Choose the Delete button.

You may or may not be prompted to save NORMAL.DOT after an AutoText entry has been deleted; if you have set up Word to automatically save NORMAL.DOT, you will not be prompted. If you delete an AutoText entry from a template other than NORMAL.DOT, Word will prompt you to save the template when you next save or close the document; at that time, you can choose to save the changes you made or discard them.

Using AutoComplete

A new feature in Word 97 is the AutoComplete tip. If you select this option, Word will suggest a complete word or phrase when you type the first three or more letters of a common item, such as a date (day of the week or month) or an AutoText entry.

To turn on and use AutoComplete, follow these steps:

1. Choose Insert, AutoText and choose AutoText from the AutoText menu, or click the AutoText icon on the AutoText toolbar. The AutoCorrect dialog box appears with the AutoText tab selected.

2. Select Show AutoComplete Tip for AutoText and Dates.

3. Type a date or the beginning of an AutoText entry name into your document. A tip will appear as soon as Word recognizes the text as a date or AutoText entry.

   When you type the name of an AutoText entry that is three characters or longer, the tip will display the first several words of the entry; press Enter to insert the suggested entry. Tips are not displayed for entry names that are less than three characters.

4. Press Enter (or F3) to accept the suggested text or continue typing to ignore it.

Using the Spike

The *spike* is a special type of AutoText entry that enables you to remove selected items from different places in your document (or from different documents), collect them, and insert them into your document as a group. The term *spike* comes from the old office spikes that impaled bills and invoices until they could all be dealt with at once. Contents stored in the spike are inserted just as you would insert a regular AutoText entry. You also can empty the contents of the spike and make it available to store another collection of text and graphics.

To add text or graphics to the spike, follow these steps:

1. Select the text or graphics you want to add to the spike.

2. Press Ctrl+F3, the Spike key combination. Word cuts the selected text or graphic and adds it to the spike AutoText entry.

N O T E   Spiked selections are cut from your document, not copied. ■

TROUBLESHOOTING

Sometimes I want to copy items to the spike without deleting them from my document. How can I do this? By adding a few extra key commands, you can copy items to the spike, rather than cut them. First, select the text you want to spike. Choose Edit, Copy or press Ctrl+C to copy the selected text to the Clipboard. Next, press Ctrl+F3 to cut the information to the spike. After spiking the text, choose Edit, Paste or press Ctrl+V to paste the text from the Clipboard to your

continues

Part

I

Ch

5

continued

document. See "Moving, Copying, and Linking Text or Graphics" later in this chapter for more information about copying text.

You can reduce these three steps into one by recording a macro that will copy, spike, and paste the selected text. See Chapter 39, "Introducing Visual Basic for Applications," for information about recording macros.

---

3. Select additional items in the order you want them added to the spike and repeat step 2.

After you create a spike entry, you will see it listed as spike in the AutoText tab of the AutoCorrect dialog box.

To insert the spike's contents into your document, follow these steps:

1. Position the insertion point where you want the spike's contents to appear.

2. Press Shift+Ctrl+F3 (the Unspike key combination) to paste the spike and empty its contents. You must empty the contents of the spike if you want to add a new set of entries to the spike.

   You also can type **spike**, then press F3 (AutoText) to paste the spike and retain its contents so that you can paste them again.

   If AutoComplete is selected, you can type the first three letters **(spi)** and then press Enter to accept the AutoComplete tip.

If you want to delete the spike, but not insert the contents, you can delete spike from the AutoText list (see "Deleting AutoText" earlier in this section).

Printing AutoText Entries

▶ **See** "Using Templates as a Pattern for Documents," **p. 202**

If you do not use certain AutoText entries regularly, you may soon forget what the abbreviation in the AutoText list does. To see a more complete view of each AutoText entry, including its format, print a list of AutoText entries.

To print a list of AutoText entries, follow these steps:

1. Open a document based on the template containing the AutoText entries.

2. Choose File, Print, and select AutoText Entries from the Print What drop-down list box.

3. Choose OK.

Correcting Spelling Errors as You Type

Almost every typist has at least one or two typing mistakes that are made frequently. The Word AutoCorrect feature recognizes common typing mistakes and automatically substitutes the correct spelling for you. You also can use AutoCorrect to automatically type long words from an abbreviation. You could use AutoCorrect to automatically type the phrase **not applicable**, for example, every time you type the abbreviation **na**.

The AutoCorrect feature can also correct accidental usage of the Caps Lock key, automatically capitalize the first word of every sentence, and automatically capitalize the names of days of the week.

N O T E As you type you may see words with a wavy red underline. These words do not appear in Word's spelling dictionary. You can right-click them to display a list of suggested corrections. To learn more about automatic spell checking, see Chapter 7, "Using Editing and Proofing Tools." ■

Creating AutoCorrect Entries

You can create AutoCorrect entries in two ways:

- You can manually add entries using menu commands.
- You can add an AutoCorrect entry while you perform a spelling check.

Adding AutoCorrect Entries with Menu Commands   To add an AutoCorrect entry using the menu commands, follow these steps:

1. Choose Tools, AutoCorrect. Word displays the AutoCorrect dialog box with the AutoCorrect tab selected.

   Select the AutoCorrect tab if it is not selected.

2. In the Replace text box, type the misspelling or abbreviation that you want to have corrected automatically.

3. In the With text box, type the correct spelling of the word or phrase (see Figure 5.24).

TIP Select long phrases in the document before accessing the AutoCorrect dialog box to have Word automatically insert the selected text into the With text box.

Part

I

Ch

5

FIG. 5.24

Use the AutoCorrect dialog box to create new AutoCorrect entries and to set the AutoCorrect options.

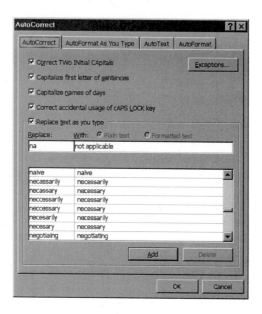

4. Choose Add to add the new entry to the list of AutoCorrect entries.

   If an AutoCorrect entry of the same name as that in the Replace text box already exists, the Add button will read Replace. Word will prompt you for confirmation before replacing the selection. Choose Yes to replace the existing entry, or No to cancel the action; you can then type a different AutoCorrect entry name in the Replace text box.

5. Choose OK.

To have AutoCorrect automatically replace the misspelling or abbreviation with the correct spelling or complete phrase, make sure to select the Replace Text as You Type option.

You cannot use the Enter key within the AutoCorrect dialog box (pressing Enter activates the OK button). If your phrase contains a paragraph return, you must select the text prior to selecting the AutoCorrect dialog box. Word will insert the phrase and the return(s) into the With text box.

AutoCorrect entries are limited to 255 characters. If you need a longer phrase, you can use AutoText along with the AutoComplete feature to create an effective shortcut (see "Using AutoComplete" in the previous section).

Adding AutoCorrect Entries During a Spelling Check
You also can add AutoCorrect entries as you perform spelling checks on your document. To add an AutoCorrect entry during a spelling check, follow these steps:

1. Choose Tools, Spelling and Grammar, to start the spelling check, if you have not already done so.

2. Choose the AutoCorrect button to add the misspelled word in the Not in Dictionary: text box and the selected spelling in the Suggestions list box to the list of AutoCorrect entries.

   You can only add entries from the Suggestions list box to AutoCorrect. If you type in a correction, it cannot be added.

   If an AutoCorrect entry of the same name as that in the Suggestions list box already exists, Word will prompt you and ask if you want to redefine the entry. Choose Yes to replace the existing entry, or No to correct the spelling in the document, but not create an AutoCorrect entry.

3. Continue the spelling check.

   ▶ **See** "Using Editing and Proofing Tools," **p. 225**

Using AutoCorrect

The AutoCorrect feature works automatically as you type, without any special actions on your part. AutoCorrect offers several options that you can change to suit your working style and preferences.

To change the AutoCorrect options, follow these steps:

1. Choose Tools, AutoCorrect. The AutoCorrect dialog box appears (refer to Figure 5.24).

2. Choose any combination of the available options. Each option is described in the following table:

Part
I

Ch
5

Option	Result	Example
Correct TWo INitial CApitals	Changes the second of two capital letters at the beginning of a word to lowercase.	"THe" becomes "The"
Capitalize First Letter of Sentences	Changes the first letter of a word beginning a sentence to uppercase.	"now is the time..." becomes "Now is the time..."
Capitalize Names of Days	Capitalizes the first letter of names of days of the week.	"monday" becomes "Monday"

continues

continued

Option	Result	Example
Correct Accidental Usage of cAPS LOCK key	Corrects the case of text accidentally typed while the Caps Lock key is on (automatically turns off the Caps Lock key after the first correction).	"wORD FOR wINDOWS" becomes "Word for Windows"
Replace Text as You Type	Replaces misspelled words with correct spellings, based on the list of entries maintained by AutoCorrect.	"teh" becomes "the"

Word performs the corrections listed in the Result column when the spacebar is pressed after a word is completed.

Creating AutoCorrect Exceptions

Sometimes you will have words that should not be capitalized, even if they appear at the beginning of a sentence. For example, you will often have abbreviations that end in periods that you do not want capitalized. You may also have exceptions for "Correct TWo INitial Capitals," such as trademarked names that may use nonstandard capitalization. To accommodate these, you can set up exceptions in the AutoCorrect Exceptions dialog box.

To set up exceptions, follow these steps:

1. Choose Tools, AutoCorrect. The AutoCorrect dialog box appears (refer to Figure 5.24).

2. Choose Exceptions. The AutoCorrect Exceptions dialog box appears (see Figure 5.25).

FIG. 5.25

Use the AutoCorrect Exceptions dialog box to keep Word from correcting certain abbreviations and spellings.

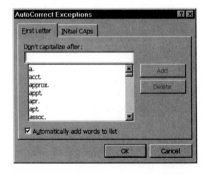

3. To prevent Word from capitalizing a first letter, select the First Letter tab.

4. Type the exception into the Don't Capitalize After text box and choose Add.

   If you want to set up an exception for initial caps, select the INitial CAps tab. Type the exception into the Don't Correct text box and choose Add.

5. Select Automatically Add Words To list if you would like Word to automatically add words to the exceptions list.

   Words are added to the exception list if you use Backspace to erase the word immediately after a correction is made by AutoCorrect, and then you retype the original word into the document.

   If you use Edit, Undo (or press Ctrl+Z), Word will restore the original word, but will *not* add it to the exceptions list.

6. When you are finished adding exceptions, choose OK.

Deleting an AutoCorrect Entry or Exception

Occasionally, you may want to remove an AutoCorrect entry because you no longer use an abbreviation or because the AutoCorrect entry conflicts with a legitimately spelled word (it doesn't always make sense to have AutoCorrect replace misspellings such as *tow* for *two*, because *tow* is actually a correctly spelled word). Likewise, you may find that you want to remove an exception from the Exceptions list.

To delete an AutoCorrect entry, follow these steps:

1. Choose Tools, AutoCorrect to display the AutoCorrect dialog box.

2. Select the entry you want to delete in the list at the bottom of the dialog box.

3. Choose the Delete button.

4. Choose OK.

When you choose Delete, Word leaves the deleted entry in the Replace and With text boxes. If you decide you would rather not delete this entry, simply choose Add to once again add this item to the list.

To delete an AutoCorrect exception, follow these steps:

1. Choose Tools, AutoCorrect to display the AutoCorrect dialog box.

2. Choose Exceptions to display the AutoCorrect Exceptions dialog box.

3. Select either the First Letter or INitial CAps tab.

4. Select the entry you want to delete in the list at the bottom of the dialog box.

5. Choose the Delete button.

6. Choose OK.

Marking Locations with Bookmarks

A *bookmark* in Word is a specific named item. The item can be a portion of the document—including text, graphics, or both—or it can simply be a specific location. Spreadsheet users will readily recognize the concept—bookmarks are similar to named ranges in a worksheet.

Use bookmarks to move quickly to a given point in a document, or to mark text or graphics for efficient moving, copying, indexing, or cross-referencing. Bookmarks also are vital when you create a macro that performs an operation on a specific portion of a document.

▶ **See** "Introducing Visual Basic for Applications," **p. 1163**

Bookmarks can be used in calculations, much as you use a range name in a spreadsheet. The bookmark represents the location of a number, rather than the number itself. The number can change, and the calculation will reflect the new result.

For example, to total an invoice, create a bookmark for each of the subtotals (job1, job2, job3, and so on). Position the insertion point where you want the total due to print. Choose Table, Formula; in the Formula text box, type an expression using the bookmark names:

> =job1+job2+job3

Choose OK. If the individual amounts change, position the cursor in the total due, press F9 to update the formula field, and the results will be updated.

▶ **See** "Using Bookmarks to Perform Calculations in Text," **p. 788**

Creating Bookmarks

When you create a bookmark, you assign a unique name to a location or item in the document.

To create a bookmark, follow these steps:

1. Position the insertion point at the location you want to name, or select the text or graphic you want named.

2. Choose Insert, Bookmark, or press Shift+Ctrl+F5. The Bookmark dialog box is displayed so that you can name a new bookmark, redefine an existing one, delete an existing one, or go to an existing bookmark (see Figure 5.26).

3. Type a new name for the bookmark in the Bookmark Name text box, or select from the list an existing name that you want to redefine.

4. Choose Add.

FIG. 5.26
The Bookmark dialog box enables you to add a name to a location or item in your document.

Bookmark names can contain up to 40 characters. A name must begin with a letter but can include numbers, letters, and underlines. Do not use spaces, punctuation marks, or other characters.

One way in which bookmarks can save you time is in selecting text or graphics that you frequently copy, move, or reformat. By naming the text or graphic with a bookmark, you can select the text or graphic no matter where you are in the document. Bookmarks are important when you construct macros in which a portion of text must always be found.

You can make bookmarks visible on-screen by choosing Tools, Options. Choose the View category by clicking the View tab. Select Bookmarks. Open and closed brackets indicate the position of each bookmark that includes text. A thick I-beam marks the position of each bookmark that is a location only.

Editing, Copying, and Moving Bookmarked Text

The text you select and mark with a bookmark can be edited, copied, or moved. If you add text to any part of a bookmarked item, the following will result:

Add Text	Result
Between any two characters	Text is added to bookmarked text within bookmark brackets.
Immediately after opening bookmark bracket	Text is added to bookmarked text.
Immediately after closing bookmark bracket text	Text is not added to bookmarked.
To the end of a marked table, add row	Row is included with same bookmark.

Part

I

Ch

5

You can copy a bookmarked item with the following results:

Copy Text	Result
Paste it into another document	Bookmark is inserted into the other document as well.
Paste it into the same document	Bookmark stays with the first item.

You can delete bookmarked text with the following results:

Delete Text	Result
Part of a bookmarked item	The remainder stays with the bookmark.
Entire bookmarked item	The bookmark is deleted with the text.
Cut text and bookmark and paste elsewhere	The text and bookmark are moved to a new location.

Moving To or Selecting a Bookmark

If you want to quickly go to a location or select items named by a bookmark, choose Insert, Bookmark. Then select the bookmark name to which you want to move, and choose Go To. Bookmark names are listed alphabetically. To list bookmark names in the order they occur in the document, choose Sort by Location in the Bookmark dialog box.

Hidden bookmarks are listed when you select the option for Hidden bookmarks. Hidden bookmarks are inserted by Word when you create a table of contents or other automatically generated reference.

▶ **See** "Using Bookmarks to Perform Calculations in Text," **p. 788**
▶ **See** "Creating Indexes and Tables of Contents," **p. 969**
▶ **See** "Creating Cross-References," **p. 1029**

You can also choose Edit, Go To, or press Ctrl+G, type in the bookmark name and press Enter, or select Bookmark in the Go to What list box and select the bookmark name from the Enter Bookmark Name box, and choose OK. (The Go To command is described earlier in more detail in "Moving in the Document.")

Deleting Bookmarks

You can remove bookmarks from a document. You might want to remove a bookmark if you no longer use it.

To delete a bookmark, follow these steps:

1. Choose Insert, Bookmark.
2. Select the name of the bookmark you want to delete.
3. Choose the Delete button.
4. Choose the Close button or press Esc. The bookmark is deleted and the previously marked text remains a part of the document.

You can undo a bookmark deletion by choosing Edit, Undo. You can remove a bookmark and its marked text by selecting all the text and pressing Backspace or Delete. If you delete only a portion of the marked text, the rest of the text along with the bookmark will remain.

Moving, Copying, and Linking Text or Graphics

With Word's Move and Copy commands, you can reorganize your thoughts to make your writing flow smoothly and logically.

Word also has the powerful capability to link text or graphics within a document or to other documents. This feature enables you to link text or graphics in one location to another location in the same document. When you change the original, the linked copy changes simultaneously.

Word incorporates *OLE*—Object Linking and Embedding. This enables you to link or embed documents and data, such as an Excel chart, into a Word document. When you want to update the Excel chart, you can double-click the chart to update it. A linked Excel chart will open Excel so you can do editing in Excel. An embedded Excel chart will replace Word's menus and toolbars with those of Excel so you can edit the chart within Word.

▶ **See** "Using Word with Office Applications," **p. 1077**

Understanding the Clipboard

A section of text or a graphic being moved or copied is kept in a temporary area of memory known as the *Clipboard*. The Clipboard holds an item while it is being moved to a new location in the same or a different document. In fact, you can even move or copy text from Word to other Windows or DOS applications.

Part

I

Ch

5

To see the contents of the Clipboard, follow these steps:

N O T E You can only view the contents of the Clipboard if the Clipboard viewer has been installed. Consult your Windows manual or online Help for information about installing the Clipboard viewer. ■

1. Click the Start button in the taskbar at the bottom of the screen.

T I P If the taskbar is currently hidden, move the pointer to the bottom of the screen and the taskbar will appear.

2. Move the mouse pointer over the <u>P</u>rograms command. The <u>P</u>rograms group is displayed.

3. Move the mouse pointer over Accessories. The Accessories group is displayed.

4. Move the mouse pointer over Clipboard Viewer and click it or press Enter.

The Clipboard displays in its own window. The Clipboard may be empty if you have not cut or copied something to it. Existing information remains in the Clipboard until you cut or copy new information.

To close the Clipboard, press Alt+F4, or click the Clipboard's Close button.

Moving Text or Graphics

You probably are familiar with the concept of moving text or graphics. A portion of text or a graphic is "cut" from the original location and then "pasted" into a new location. The existing text at the new location moves to accommodate the new arrival. You can perform move operations from the menu command, the keyboard or mouse, or the Standard toolbar.

To move text or graphics, follow these steps:

1. Select the text or graphic you want to move.

2. Choose <u>E</u>dit, Cu<u>t</u>.

You can also press Ctrl+X, or click the Cut button on the Standard toolbar. Mouse users can right-click the selected text and choose Cu<u>t</u> from the shortcut menu.

The selection is removed from the document and stored in the Clipboard.

3. Reposition the insertion point where you want the item to reappear.

4. Choose <u>E</u>dit, <u>P</u>aste.

You can also press Ctrl+V, or click the Paste button on the Standard toolbar. Mouse users can right-click the new location and choose <u>P</u>aste from the shortcut menu.

The information in the Clipboard is pasted into its new location.

If you would like to paste this information in additional locations, simply position the insertion point at the desired location and paste the information using one of the methods described in step 4. This information will remain in the Clipboard until you cut or copy new information.

If you need to accumulate and move multiple pieces of text to the same location, you will want to use the spike. The spike enables you to cut several pieces of text, move all of them to a new location, and paste them in the order they were cut. "Using the Spike," an earlier section in this chapter, describes how to use the Word AutoText feature to spike your selections.

Copying Text or Graphics

Copying text uses a process similar to moving text. The difference is that copying retains the original text and inserts a duplicate in the new location. You even can copy information from one document and paste the information into another document. You can choose the Copy command from the menu, the toolbar, or the keyboard.

To copy text or graphics to a new location, follow these steps:

1. Select the text or graphic you want copied.

2. Choose Edit, Copy.

   You can also press Ctrl+C, or click the Copy button on the Standard toolbar. Mouse users can right-click the selected text and choose Copy from the shortcut menu.

   The selection is stored in the Clipboard.

3. If you want to paste into another document, open that document now. If it is already open, make it active by choosing it from the Window menu or by clicking any portion of that document if you can see it.

4. Reposition the insertion point where you want the copy to appear.

5. Choose Edit, Paste

   You can also press Ctrl+V, or click the Paste button on the Standard toolbar. Mouse users can right-click the new location and choose Paste from the shortcut menu.

 T I P You can make repeated pastes of the same item until you cut or copy a new item to the Clipboard.

Shortcut keys for moving and copying text or graphics can save you time. Table 5.10 lists available shortcuts for moving and copying text or graphics quickly.

Part

I

Ch

5

Table 5.10 Using Shortcut Keys to Move and Copy

Keys	Function
Ctrl+X	Cuts the selected text or graphic to the Clipboard. This shortcut works the same as choosing Edit, Cut. You can paste the cut material multiple times.
Ctrl+C	Copies the selected text or graphic to the Clipboard. This shortcut works the same as Edit, Copy. You can paste the copied material multiple times.
Ctrl+V	Pastes the Clipboard's contents at the cursor's location. This shortcut works the same as Edit, Paste.
F2	Moves the selected text or graphic without using the Clipboard. To use this shortcut, select what you want to move and then press F2. The prompt Move to Where? appears in the status bar at the bottom of Word's window. Use the mouse or keyboard to move the insertion point to the new location and press Enter.
Shift+F2	Copies the selected text or graphic one time without using the Clipboard. To use this shortcut, select what you want to copy and then press Shift+F2. The prompt Copy to where? appears in the status bar at the bottom of Word's window. Move the insertion point to the new location and press Enter.
Alt+Shift+↑	Cuts the selected paragraph and pastes it above the preceding one.
Alt+Shift+↓	Cuts the selected paragraph and pastes it below the following one.

Using the Mouse to Move and Copy Items

With Word, you can move, copy, and link items within a document by using only the mouse. This feature enables you to quickly move paragraphs or sentences, copy phrases, or drag pictures to new locations.

▶ **See** "Inserting Text Boxes," **p. 859**

To move text or a graphic to a new location using the mouse, follow these steps:

1. Select the text or graphic you want to move. (If you are dragging a picture to a new location, choose View, Page Layout to change to Page Layout view before dragging.)

2. Move the mouse pointer over the selected text or graphic. The mouse pointer changes from an I-beam into a pointer over selected text or into an arrow pointer over graphics.

TROUBLESHOOTING

Why doesn't my mouse pointer change into an arrow when I drag it over selected text? You need to turn on Word's *drag-and-drop text editing* feature. To do this, choose Tools, Options and select the Edit tab by clicking on it with the mouse. Select the option for Drag-and-Drop Text Editing, and then choose OK.

3. Hold down the left mouse button and drag to where you want the text or graphic located.

   To copy the selection, rather than move it, hold down the Ctrl button before dragging the selection.

   The text pointer becomes an arrow pointer combined with a small gray box. The text insertion point appears as a grayed vertical bar. The graphic will appear as a grayed outline as it is dragged to a new location.

   If you are copying text, a small box with a plus sign will appear next to the pointer. This indicates that the current selection will be copied rather than moved.

4. Release the left mouse button to insert the selected text or graphic.

To move text or graphics quickly, select the text or graphic you want to move. Then scroll to the screen area where you want to move the text or graphic. Hold down the Ctrl key as you click the right mouse button at the target location. To copy the selection, rather than move it, hold down Shift+Ctrl, and then right-click the new location.

You also can use the right mouse button to cut, copy, and paste. When you click the right mouse button, a shortcut menu appears at the position of the insertion point (see Figure 5.27).

To move or copy text to a new location using the right mouse button, follow these steps:

1. Select the text or graphic you want to move or copy.

2. Place the pointer directly over the selected text and click the right mouse button to display the shortcut menu.

3. Choose Cut or Copy from the shortcut menu.

After a selection has been copied to the Clipboard (using any method), you can use the right mouse button menu to paste it in other locations.

Part

I

Ch

5

To paste text using the right mouse button, follow these steps:

1. Position the insertion point.

2. Click the right mouse button.

3. Choose Paste from the shortcut menu.

FIG. 5.27
A quick cut, copy, and paste menu can be displayed by clicking the right mouse button.

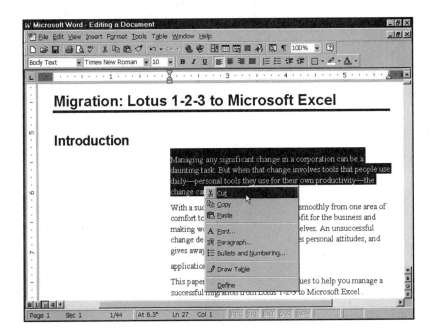

Linking Text

A special technique exists for forging a link between the source and the destination when you copy text or an object between or within documents. The *source* is the original text or graphic that you select and copy; the *destination* is the location to which you copy the text or graphic. By linking the object as you copy it, you can automatically update the destination each time you make a change to the source. For example, a CPA might maintain a library of boilerplate paragraphs to borrow from when writing individual letters to clients advising them about tax matters. If tax laws change, the CPA can change the source (boilerplate) document and, by simply selecting a command or pressing a key, update the destination document to reflect the changes.

To copy and link text or an object, follow these steps:

1. Select and copy the text or object in the source document.

2. Position the insertion point where you want to link the text or object in the destination document (the destination also can be a new location within the same document).

3. Choose Edit, Paste Special. The Paste Special dialog box appears (see Figure 5.28).

4. Choose the Paste Link option.

5. Select the type of object you want from the As list box; an explanation of an object will appear at the bottom of the Paste Special dialog box when you select the object in the As list box. (Notice that Word 97 gives you the option of inserting your link as a *Word Hyperlink*. Hyperlinks are discussed in "Inserting Hyperlinks" later in this chapter.)

6. Select the Display as Icon option if you want the linked selection to appear as an icon on-screen and in print. You can read the contents of an icon by double-clicking it.

7. Choose OK. Word inserts the linked object. This link is a field code that specifies the contents of the linked selection from the source document.

FIG. 5.28
Use the Paste Special dialog box to create links within or between documents.

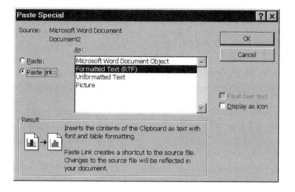

The advantage of linking text is the ease of transferring changes between the original and the linked text. Linked text actually is created by inserting a hidden field code that links the original text to the location you indicate. An example of a field code linking within the same document is as follows:

```
{LINK Word.Document.8 "C:\\My Documents\\Filename.doc" "OLE_LINK1" \a \r}
```

▶ **See** "Understanding the Basics of Fields," **p. 694**
▶ **See** "Using Word with Office Applications," **p. 1077**

In the previous Link field code, the \a switch tells Word to update this link automatically any time changes are made to the source. The \r indicates that this item is in Rich Text Format (RTF), so any formatting at the source, such as bold or italics, will appear in the destination text as well.

You can edit and format linked text just as you would normal text. When the linked text is updated, however, the destination changes to reflect the current status of the original text.

The linked text will automatically change when you change the source, but only if the \a switch appears within the field code (as mentioned earlier in this section). If you modify

Part
I
Ch
5

the linked text and later want to reset the link to reflect the source, you can update the linked text manually. To update the linked text to match the original text, position the insertion point anywhere within the linked text, and then press F9 (the Update Field key). You will see the linked text update to match the original.

You can unlink linked text from its original by positioning the insertion point anywhere within the linked text and pressing Shift+Ctrl+F9 (the Unlink Field key). This changes the link into normal text.

You can quickly jump from the linked text back to the source. This is helpful if you want to modify the original text. To do this, point to the linked text and click the right mouse button. Choose Linked Document Object from the shortcut menu, and then choose Edit Link. If the source is in a different document, Word will open that document (if it is not already open) and position the cursor at the original location. If the source document has been moved or renamed, you must edit the Link field code to reflect the new information or Word will not be able to locate the source. To edit a link field, select the linked text or link field code and choose Edit, Links. Then choose Change Source and select the source from the Change Source dialog box.

▶ **See** "Creating Hyperlinks in Word Documents," **p. 510**

▶ **See** "Linking Documents and Files," **p. 1091**

CAUTION

The Link field code, like any field, can be manually edited. If you manually change the path or file name of the source document, the link may remain broken, even if the information you type is correct. If this happens, you can restore the link by choosing Edit, Links, and then choosing Change Source from the Links dialog box.

TROUBLESHOOTING

A message appeared on my screen, saying I don't have enough memory for a large Clipboard, and asked whether I want to discard the Clipboard. What should I do? After you cut or copy information, it is stored on the Clipboard. Discarding the Clipboard clears its contents. In most cases, the Clipboard contains the information you last cut or copied. If you no longer need this material, discard the Clipboard. If you need the information, reduce memory use and recut or recopy the information.

▶ **See** "Customizing and Optimizing Word Features," **p. 1115**

Working with Multiple Windows

You can have multiple documents open at one time in Word. The number of documents you can have open at one time is limited only by the amount of memory on your system. If your documents are large and heavily formatted, you will not be able to open as many at one time.

When working with multiple documents, each document occupies its own window. You can arrange these windows within Word just as you would place pieces of paper on a desk. By choosing Window, Arrange All, you can arrange all open windows so that each has a portion of the screen.

You can also open more than one window onto the same document when you need to work on widely separated parts of the same document. And as mentioned earlier in this chapter, you can cut or copy from one document and paste into another.

Viewing Different Parts of the Same Document

If you are working with a long document, you may want to see more than one part of it at the same time. This can be useful when you need to compare or edit widely separated parts of the same document.

You can expand your view in two ways. The first method is to open a new window by choosing Window, New Window. This technique creates a second window containing the same document. If you are displaying a single document with the document window maximized, the title bar will appear as `Microsoft Word—PAKINSTR.DOC`. If you display the same document in more than one window, each document's window will show the document name followed by the window number—for example, `PAKINSTR.DOC:1` and `PAKINSTR.DOC:2`. Figure 5.29 shows two windows displaying the same document.

To close a new window, choose the window you want to close from the Window menu, or click the window to select it. Then click the close box or press Ctrl+W to close the current window. If you choose File, Close, all of the open windows for this document will close.

You also can split a window so that you can see two different areas of a document in the same window. This approach is helpful when you type lists. You can split the document's window so that the upper part shows column headings and the lower part shows the list you are typing. As you scroll the list, the headings stay in place.

FIG. 5.29
View different parts of a long document by displaying the document in two windows.

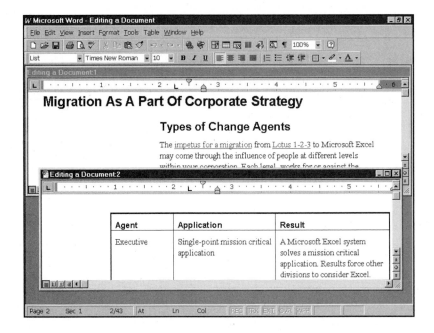

To split a window with the keyboard, choose Window, Split. Then press the ↑ or ↓ key to position the horizontal gray line where you want the split, and press Enter. Move between the two windows by pressing F6. To remove the split, choose Window, Remove Split.

To split the window with the mouse, look for the split box above the up arrow in the vertical scroll bar (refer to Figure 5.14, if necessary). Drag this split box down and release the mouse button to position the split. Move between the windows by clicking the mouse inside the window you want to activate. To remove the split, drag the split box all the way up or down, and then release the button.

Double-click the split bar to split the screen in half. Drag the split bar to reposition the split. Double-click the split bar when the window is split, and you remove the split.

Cutting and Pasting Between Documents

When you have several documents on-screen, you can move from one document window to the next in the stack by pressing Ctrl+F6 or by choosing Window and selecting the document you want active. Press Shift+Ctrl+F6 to move to the preceding document window. You also can use the mouse to move to a specific document window—just point and click. The documents do not all have to be visible to use the Ctrl+F6 method. Word will still move through each open document.

Displaying two or more documents on-screen at one time can be useful. If you have two similar contracts to prepare, for example, you can choose Edit, Copy to copy paragraphs from one contract, press Ctrl+F6 to switch to the other contract, and then paste the paragraphs in the second contract by choosing Edit, Paste.

If you have many documents open, you may want to directly activate one. To do this, choose Window. At the bottom of the menu is a list of all open documents. Select the document you want active.

Working with Pages

Before you print your document, be sure that it's paginated correctly. You don't want a page to break right below a title, for example, and you may not want certain paragraphs separated on two pages. You can let Word manage page breaks for you, or you can control them yourself.

Repaginating a Document

By default, Word repaginates whenever you make a change in your document. Word calculates how much text fits into a page and inserts a soft page break, which appears as a dotted line in Normal view or as the end of a page in Page Layout view. This feature is called *background repagination*. You can have Word repaginate for you, or you can repaginate manually with a command.

To change background repagination, follow these steps:

1. Choose Tools, Options.
2. Select the General tab.
3. Select the Background Repagination option to repaginate as you work and keep the page numbers in the status bar current.
4. Choose OK.

Word operates faster with background repagination turned off. To update page breaks if you have background repagination turned off, change to Page Layout view or Print Preview; Word repaginates the document.

> **NOTE** Word repaginates automatically whenever you print, when you choose View, Page Layout or File, Print Preview, or when you compile or update an index or table of contents. It may also partially or fully repaginate a document when choosing Edit, Go To, as described in "Going to a Specific Page" earlier in this chapter. ▪

Part

I

Ch

5

Inserting Manual Page Breaks

As you work on a document, Word breaks pages every time you fill a page with text or graphics. These breaks are automatic and known as *soft page breaks*. If background repagination is on, Word recalculates the amount of text on the page and adjusts soft page breaks as you work.

You can insert page breaks manually whenever you want to force a page break at a particular spot—at the beginning of a new section, for example. Page breaks you insert are called *hard page breaks*. A hard page break appears as a heavy dotted line with the words Page Break centered in the line. When you insert a hard page break, Word adjusts the soft page breaks that follow. Word cannot move hard page breaks; you must adjust them yourself.

Unless a page break is required at a specific location, such as at the beginning of a new chapter, it's much easier to allow Word to insert soft page breaks as you edit the document. Otherwise, you must constantly delete and reinsert your hard page breaks to accommodate for added or deleted text. You can control soft page breaks from the Line and Page Breaks tab of the Format Paragraph dialog box.

▶ **See** "Controlling Where Paragraphs and Pages Break," **p. 449**

To insert a hard page break using menu commands, follow these steps:

1. Place the insertion point where you want the page break to occur.
2. Choose Insert, Break.
3. Select the Page Break option.
4. Choose OK.

   ▶ **See** "Working with Sections in Your Document," **p. 452**

To insert a hard page break from the keyboard, press Ctrl+Enter.

To delete a hard page break, choose one of two options:

- Move the insertion point onto the dotted line created by the page break, and press the Delete key.
- Place the insertion point just past the dotted line, and press Backspace.

If you find a page break difficult to delete, choose Format, Paragraph to format the paragraph after the page break. If any of the pagination options on the Line and Page Breaks tab are selected (Page Break Before, Keep With Next, or Keep Lines Together), they may be causing a page break before the paragraph. Try clearing these options. ●

CHAPTER 6

Using Templates and Wizards for Frequently Created Documents

Templates can save you work and improve the consistency of any documents you create frequently. A template acts as a guide or pattern for documents of a specific type, such as form letters, newsletters, letters of engagement, invoices, contracts, or proposals. ■

Using predefined templates provided with Word

By using the predefined templates, you can quickly produce standardized versions of any document you produce frequently.

Sharing elements between templates

Save time by using the Organizer to transfer elements from one template to another.

Modifying existing templates and creating your own

Because predefined templates may meet *most* but not *all* of your needs, learn how to change templates and create new templates.

Setting up documents using wizards

Wizards walk you through the steps for creating different types of specialized documents.

Using add-in programs to increase Word's power

Programs from third-party vendors behave like they are part of Word and extend Word's capabilities by adding features such as menu choices or toolbars.

Working with Templates

A *template* is a file that contains the parts of a document and features used for a specific type of document. Word templates can contain text, pictures, graphs, formatting, styles, macros, AutoText, buttons on the toolbar, field codes, custom menu commands, and shortcut keys. You can put text, formatting, and settings you use repeatedly for a specific task into a template.

When you open a new document, all the contents and features of the template are transferred to the new untitled document. The original template remains unaltered on disk.

Add-ins are supplemental programs that extend the functionality of Word 97. You can purchase add-ins from software vendors. Once installed, an add-in acts as if it is a part of Word and may add a new menu command or toolbar, for example. At the end of this chapter, you learn more about add-in programs, where you can find them, and what they can do for you.

Figures 6.1, 6.2, and 6.3 show some examples of templates in use.

FIG. 6.1

Everyday blank documents are based on the Normal template, which includes font selections and other formatting settings, but no text.

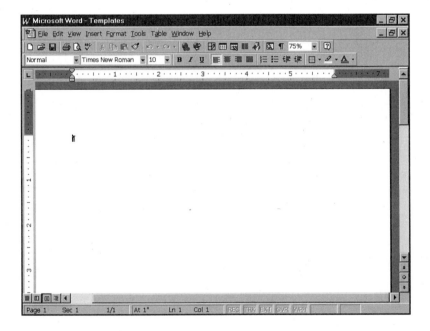

FIG. 6.2
You can base frequently used documents, such as forms, memos, and invoices, on a custom template.

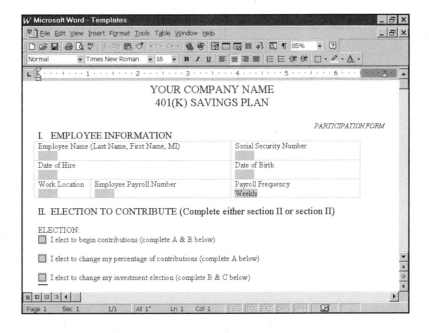

FIG. 6.3
Template wizards guide you through document creation for documents such as résumés, legal pleadings, and newsletters.

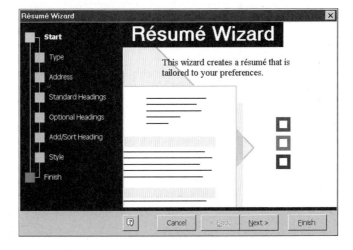

Part
I

Ch
6

You can use templates to simplify the creation of any frequently used document. You may find templates useful for these types of documents:

- Invoices, employee records, or any standardized form
- Web pages

■ Proposals and reports

■ Newsletters

■ Memos and fax sheets

Using templates to create Web pages and preprinted forms can significantly reduce your company's costs. Attaching templates to reports ensures that all reports have the same format and layout. You can build into the template special commands or macros needed to produce a report, such as integrating Excel charts, so that they are readily available. When certain phrases and names are stored in AutoText, you can more easily keep the spelling and formatting the same across documents. All table and figure formatting, tables of contents, and indexes look the same from report to report because they are created and formatted with macros and styles attached to the template.

From the Help menu in Word, you can access the World Wide Web. And, you can use Word to create Web pages. Word comes with a template to help you create a blank Web page that you can then fill in, or you can use Word's Web Page Wizard to guide you through the process of creating a Web page.

ON THE WEB

Planning a Web page and want design ideas? Check out:

http://www.microsoft.com/workshop

Many companies use templates to prepare interoffice memos and fax cover letters. The headings and document formatting are predefined and, therefore, are standardized. ASK or FILLIN fields prompt the operator for entries. The DATE and AUTHOR fields can be used to enter automatically the current date and name of the operator.

Word comes with several predesigned templates that you can use as a basis for your own business documents. You can modify the Word templates to meet your needs, or you can create your own templates from scratch.

In addition, Word provides *wizards* to automate customizing your documents. The wizard you select, such as Letter or Fax, displays a series of dialog boxes in which you make selections. Word uses your responses to design your document.

Templates remove some of the tedium that comes with typing the same text over and over. Rather than retyping a memo heading, for example, you can create or modify a template to include the repeated text. Many of the templates are automated and require only that you point, click, and type to fill out a form. Figure 6.4 shows an example of an easy-to-use memo template.

FIG. 6.4
This memo template provides on-screen instructions and requires only that you point, click, and type.

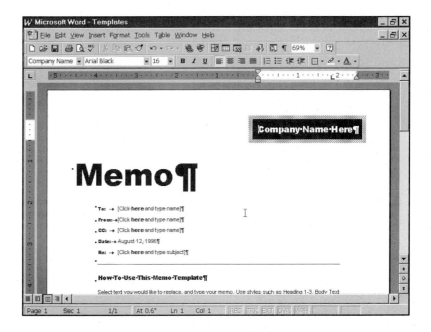

What You Need to Know About Templates

Word normally saves templates as files with the DOT file extension in the Templates subfolder under the folder that contains Word. DOT files in this subfolder appear as choices in each category of the New dialog box. This accessibility makes templates readily available regardless of which folder you are working in.

N O T E If you're using Word as part of Microsoft Office, you'll find the Templates folder located under the folder in which you installed Office. In Office 97, all of Office is installed in the Program Files folder. ■

Word normally looks to the Templates folder when it searches for the templates used in the New dialog box. The tabs that appear in the New dialog box are determined by the structure of the folder that contains the template files. Each tab corresponds to the name of a subfolder in the Templates folder. To change the folder Word uses for templates, choose Tools, Options, and select the File Locations tab. Double-click User Templates and select a new template folder.

All documents in Word are based on a template. Even the default new document is based on a template, NORMAL.DOT. The NORMAL.DOT file contains the formatting and default settings for the new document you open when you choose File, New.

Part

I

Ch

6

Styles, macros, AutoText, and other items stored in the NORMAL.DOT template are available to all documents at all times. Because the information stored in NORMAL.DOT is available to all documents all the time, they are said to be available *globally*.

Templates can contain the following:

- Body text, headers, footers, footnotes, and graphics with formatting
- Page and paper layouts
- Styles
- AutoText entries
- Bookmarks
- Macros
- Custom menus and commands
- Tools
- Shortcut keys

 Word uses a different format for its files than previous versions of Word. You can open and use templates you created in prior versions, but remember that menu commands may have moved or changed. Word may display a warning to let you know that some elements contained in those templates, such as macros, may not work properly.

When you create a document based on a template, the document opens to show the body text, graphics, and formatting contained in the template. All the styles, macros, tools, and so on that are in the template are available for use with the document.

After you create a document, you can attach the document to a different template so that you can use the features (but not the text or page formatting) found in that template. Later sections of this chapter show you how you can transfer features between templates so that a style or macro you create in one template can be copied into another.

Using Templates as a Pattern for Documents

Most people use only a few templates. The templates they use may include the NORMAL.DOT template for everyday work or one of a few custom templates for use in memos or reports. Many people use the NORMAL.DOT template to create the blank document with which they normally work. Examine the predefined templates that come with Word, because you may find one appropriate to your particular task.

Using Word's Predefined Templates

Word for Windows comes with predefined templates you can use to create many typical business documents. Many of the templates contain special tools, formatting styles, custom menus, macros, and AutoText for frequently used procedures. The template layouts fall into three categories: *contemporary*, *elegant*, and *professional*, and use similar design principles within each group. You can select a style that suits your needs. Using the templates from that group, be assured that all your documents will have a harmonious, professional appearance. Many of the templates include on-screen instructions that guide you step-by-step in creating some very sophisticated effects.

The predefined templates are organized on different tabs in the New dialog box and are described in Table 6.1.

Table 6.1 Predefined Word Templates

Category	Template
General	Normal (default document)
Other Documents	Contemporary Resumé Elegant Resumé Professional Resumé
Letters & Faxes	Contemporary Letter Elegant Letter Professional Letter Contemporary Fax Elegant Fax Professional Fax
Memos	Contemporary Memo Elegant Memo Professional Memo
Reports	Contemporary Report Elegant Report Professional Report
Publications	Newsletter
Web Pages	Blank Web Page
Office 95 Templates	Templates you created or modified in Office 95

Downloading Free Templates from the Web

Microsoft has many other templates available at the Microsoft Office Web sight on the Internet—and they're free. All you need to do is download them. To find the templates,

Part
I
Ch
6

use a computer that has an Internet connection setup. Then, open Word's Help menu and choose Microsoft on the Web. From the submenu that appears, choose Free Stuff.

ON THE WEB

Or, if you prefer to use your Web browser instead of Word, check the following Web site for free templates:

http://www.microsoft.com/msword/fs_wd.htm

Opening a New Document Based on a Template

Opening a new document is easy. To do so, follow these steps:

1. Choose File, New. The New dialog box opens to the General tab with the NORMAL.DOT template selected (see Figure 6.5).

2. Select a tab, then click the name or icon of the template you want to use. The Preview box shows a sample document for which the template is designed.

3. Choose OK.

N O T E   If you select the Blank Document icon in the New dialog box, you are actually selecting the Normal template. In this case, because the document is blank, Word doesn't offer a preview, as you can see in Figure 6.5. ▤

▶ **See** "Opening a Document," **p. 86**

T I P   To open a new document based on NORMAL.DOT using a tool, click the New button in the Standard toolbar or press Ctrl+N.

FIG. 6.5
Most documents are based on the NORMAL.DOT template.

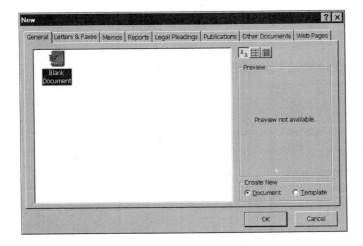

Opening a Template on Startup   You can make Word open a specific template when it starts by following these steps:

1. Open the NORMAL.DOT template.

2. With the NORMAL.DOT template active, record a macro and assign it the name **AutoExec**.

3. While the macro recorder is on, create a new document based on the template you want Word to open automatically. Then, turn off the macro recorder.

4. You can close the new document you started to create without saving it, but save the Normal template and exit from Word.

From this point on, when you start Word, it automatically opens a new document based on the template you specified. Remember, if that template contained text, you'll see that text in Document 1 *every time you start Word.*

N O T E   If you make a mistake and want Word to open the Normal template at startup, reopen the Normal template. Then, open the Macro dialog box and delete the AutoExec macro. Don't forget to save the Normal template. ▪

T I P   If Word doesn't find a Normal template, it automatically creates a new one, with the same settings Word had when you first installed it. Use this information to re-create a Normal template if yours becomes corrupted.

N O T E   If you frequently use the same templates, you can save yourself time by creating a tool or menu command that opens a new document from each of these templates. Use the macro recorder to record a macro when you open a template. Assign this macro to a button on a toolbar or to a menu command. See Chapter 38, "Customizing Toolbar, Menus, and Shortcut Keys," for more information. ▪

Opening Word 7 Templates   Templates created for Word 7 can be opened and used in Word. When you close a document based on the old template, Word automatically saves the document in Word format. If you edit and save the old template, it is saved in the Word format. The file is no longer compatible with Word 7, however. In addition, some of your macros may not convert or function properly because menu commands have changed.

Part

I

Ch

6

Using Information from Another Template

If you are working on a document and decide you want to have access to all the features in another template, you can attach that template to the document. Attaching a new template does not change the existing document text, but it does change specified settings, such as macros, AutoText, menu commands, margins, shortcut key assignments, and buttons.

To attach another template to a document, follow these steps:

1. Open the document to which you want to attach a template.

2. Choose Tools, Templates and Add-Ins. The Templates and Add-ins dialog box appears. Notice that the Document Template edit box displays the name of the template currently attached to the document (see Figure 6.6).

FIG. 6.6
Use features from other templates by attaching a different template containing those features to a document.

3. Choose the Attach button to display the Attach Template dialog box (see Figure 6.7).

FIG. 6.7
From the Attach Template dialog box, choose the template to which you want to attach the document.

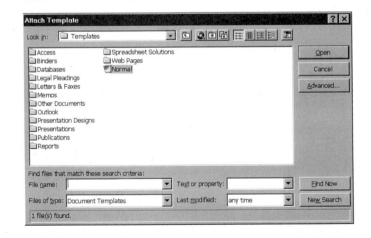

4. Double-click the folder that contains the template you want. Select the template or type the template name in the File Name box.

5. Choose Open. The Attach Template dialog box closes, and the template name you selected replaces the selection in the Document Template edit box of the Templates and Add-ins dialog box.

6. Choose OK.

For a single Word session, you can load several templates simultaneously and make the features of those templates available globally, similar to the way features in the Normal template are available globally. In the Templates and Add-Ins dialog box, choose the Add button to display the Add Template dialog box. Navigate to the folder containing the template whose features you want available. When you choose Open, Word redisplays the Templates and Add-Ins dialog box. The template you selected appears in the Global Templates and Add-ins list box—preceded by a check to indicate its features are available. The features of all selected templates that appear in this list box are available to you for the rest of the Word session. When you start your next session, the templates still appear in the list box, but they aren't selected. You can select them to make the settings available to you.

 T I P If you want the features of a particular template or several templates available *every time* you start Word, copy the template to your \WinWord\Startup folder. The Startup folder is the default folder used for startup files. If you do not have a Startup folder, choose Tools, Options and select the File Locations tab. Select the Startup folder in the File Types list, and then choose Modify to set a new folder as the startup folder.

Transferring Template Contents Using the Organizer

As you work, you may find that you need a style, macro, toolbar, or AutoText entry that is stored in another template. Or you may develop a style, macro, toolbar, or AutoText entry in one document and want to use it with other documents. After you learn how to use the Organizer, you'll be able to transfer features between templates so that they are available wherever you need them.

To copy a style, macro, toolbar, or AutoText entry from one template to another, follow these steps:

1. Open a document based on the template that contains the feature you want to copy.

2. Choose Tools, Templates and Add-Ins, then choose the Organizer button. The Organizer, shown in Figure 6.8, appears. The left side of the dialog box shows the template of the current document, and the right side of the dialog box shows the Normal template.

FIG. 6.8

Use the Organizer to transfer styles, macros, AutoText, or toolbars between templates and documents.

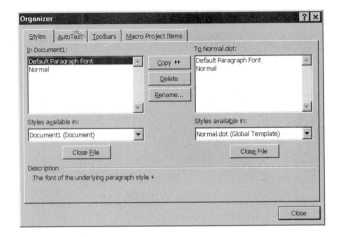

3. If you want to transfer an entry to some other template, choose the Close File button. Word then replaces Close File with an Open File button. Choose the Open File button to display the Open dialog box. Navigate to the folder containing the template you want to receive the feature. Choose Open to display the contents of that template in the right side of the Organizer dialog box.

4. Select the tab for the type of feature you want to transfer.

5. From the lists on the left, select the feature you want to copy.

6. Choose the Copy button.

7. Repeat steps 4–6 to transfer additional features, or choose Close at the bottom of the dialog box to close the Organizer.

Transferring styles, macros, AutoText, or toolbars is described in more detail in the specific chapters that discuss those features.

▶ **See** "Creating an AutoText Entry," **p. 170**

▶ **See** "Customizing and Creating Toolbars," **p. 1141**

▶ **See** "Introducing Visual Basic for Applications," **p. 1163**

Storing Summary Information About a Document

Each Word document can have summary and other information attached. This information can remind you about the source or contents of a document, when the document was created, how much time you've spent creating it, and more. You can also search for keywords, which can be very helpful if you forget a file's name or need a list of all files that have similar key words in the summary.

If you want to attach summary information to a document, choose File, Properties, and complete the Properties dialog box. When you save the document you have opened, the property information is saved with the file. You can edit the property information for the active document by choosing File, Properties.

The Properties dialog box includes the following tabs:

Tab	Description
General	Provides information about the file's location, size, and save dates.
Summary	Provides space for you to note important information about the document itself, such as who wrote it, keywords (for document searches), and comments.
Statistics	Includes information like number of pages, lines, words, and so forth.
Contents	Provides space for you to describe the document's contents.
Custom	Provides space for you to customize the information you save with the document.

TROUBLESHOOTING

The template on which my document was originally based is no longer available. What happened? It may have been erased, renamed, or moved to a different folder. You cannot use the macros, AutoText, or toolbars that were assigned to that template. You do, however, still have the styles that were in that template.

You can attach another template to the document to gain the use of the other template's features by opening the document and choosing File, Templates. Follow the description in the section "Using Information from Another Template" earlier in this chapter.

I don't see Word's predefined templates in the New dialog box. If Word's predefined templates do not appear in the New dialog box, the templates may not have been installed when you installed Word for Windows. You can rerun the installation procedure and choose to install only the templates.

I created a custom template, but it doesn't appear in the New dialog box. Templates use a DOT extension and are stored in the template folder. The folder to which Word normally looks for template files is C:\WinWord\Templates or C:\Office95\Templates. Choose Tools, Options, and select the File Locations tab. Confirm that User Templates shows the correct folder. If it does not, choose Modify and correct the folder name. Click Close.

Modifying Templates

The templates that come with Word for Windows are designed to handle many daily business transactions; however, you may need to modify the template to fit your business formats more closely or to add AutoText and styles specific to your needs. For example, you may want to use the Contemporary Fax template as your standard cover sheet, but the original form of the template doesn't contain your company's address and phone information, nor does it contain your name as the sender. You don't want to type this information each time you need to send a fax. You can edit the Contemporary Fax template to include your standardized information, change the format to fit your needs, and even include your own AutoText entries.

You can modify templates to incorporate the specific text, graphics, styles, formatting, macros, and AutoText you need for your documents. In other words, you can modify templates to fit your needs, even if the template came with Word or was given to you by another Word user.

What You Need to Know About Changing a Template

After you make changes to a template, all new documents using that template include the modifications or edits you've made to the template. Documents created from the template before it was modified, however, have access to only some of the changes to the template. For example, styles, text, graphics, page formatting, or print formatting added to the template do not transfer to existing documents. The following template changes *do* transfer to documents that were created from an earlier template:

- AutoText entries
- Macros
- Menus
- Shortcut keys
- Toolbar buttons

> **CAUTION**
>
> If you change a template and preserve the original name, the original template is replaced. To ensure that you will always have the original template available, consider using a new name for the modified template or giving the original template a new name.

Changing a Template

When you need to make just a few modifications to a template, you can easily modify the template with the method described in this section. However, if you have many changes to make to a template, it might be easier to use one of the methods described later in this chapter to create a new template from scratch or to use an existing document as the basis for the new template.

To change an existing template, follow these steps:

1. Choose File, Open, click the Open button, or press Ctrl+O. The Open dialog box appears (see Figure 6.9).

FIG. 6.9
Use the Open dialog box to select the template file you want to modify.

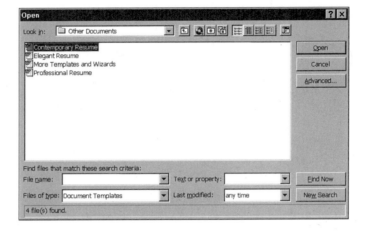

2. By using the Look In box, navigate to the Templates folder or the folder containing your template.

3. Select Document Templates (*.DOT) from the Files of Type box.

4. Select the template you want to modify and choose Open.

5. Change the template by adding or modifying text or graphics; changing formats; redefining styles or AutoText entries; or adding or changing macros, shortcut keys, or buttons.

6. Choose File, Save to save the template back to the same folder with the same name.

Part
I

Ch
6

Setting Default Formats in the Normal Template

Word for Windows bases its default settings for a new document on a template stored in the file NORMAL.DOT. All documents you create by choosing File, New and pressing Enter are based on the Normal template. Settings, such as the style, font type and size, margins, and other formats, are stored in this file.

You can change default settings for new documents in two ways. In the more powerful method, you can set new defaults for styles, AutoText, page formatting, and so on by changing the setting in the NORMAL.DOT template. If you need to change only the default for a font, style, or page layout, you can change them while editing a document using the method described later in the section "Changing Template Features from Within a Document."

If you want to change any of the default formatting or features controlled by a template, open the NORMAL.DOT template and change the appropriate format or settings. Save the NORMAL.DOT template back to the same folder with the same name.

Making Template Features Available to All Documents

If you have macros, AutoText, buttons, or styles that you want to be available to all documents, put them in the NORMAL.DOT template. However, be aware that a conflict might occur if the active document is based on a template that has styles, macros, or AutoText with the same names as those in the NORMAL.DOT template.

Whenever a conflict occurs between styles, macros, or AutoText with the same name, the template that created the document takes priority over the NORMAL.DOT template. For example, if your report is based on the ELEGANT REPORT.DOT template that contains a style named List Bullet, and the NORMAL.DOT template also contains a style named List Bullet, your document uses the List Bullet style found in ELEGANT REPORT.DOT.

Changing Template Features from Within a Document

Default settings are format settings specified when a document opens—settings such as which font and font size are used when you first begin to type. You can change default settings in two ways: you can open and modify the template that creates a type of document, or you can change some formats within a document and transfer the changes back to the template so that the changes become new defaults.

The types of changes you can transfer from a document back to its template are found in these menu choices: Format, Font; Format, Style; and File, Page Setup.

To transfer a format change from the document back to the template, follow these steps:

1. Open a new or existing document based on the template you want to change.
2. Choose Format, Font or Format, Style or File, Page Setup, depending on the type of default change you want to make.
3. Select the style or tab, if any, for the type of formatting you want to change, then select the formatting options you want to define as default settings on the template.

4. If you change the font or page setup, choose the Default button. A dialog box appears asking you to confirm the update to the template.

Or, if you change or add a style, choose the Modify button and select the Add to Template check box in the Modify Style dialog box.

5. Choose Yes or press Enter to update the document's template file with the selected default settings.

You may be able to save yourself some work when modifying a template by copying existing styles, macros, AutoText, or buttons from another template. Use the Organizer to copy template items. The Organizer is described in each chapter that deals with a feature you can transfer. The feature is covered lightly in the section "Using Information from Another Template" earlier in this chapter.

N O T E   The changes you make to default fonts, styles, or page setup affect only the current document and all new documents you subsequently create based on the current template. Old default formats remain in any existing documents. ■

 T I P   If you open a document you created before changing defaults, Word may update the document for you automatically, or you can update the document quickly by choosing Tools, Templates and Add-Ins, and placing a check in the Automatically Update Document Styles check box.

Creating a New Template

Although Word comes with many predesigned templates, you probably have many documents or forms that do not fit any of the templates. You can create a completely new template based on an existing template or document.

Creating a New Template Based on an Existing Template

You can create a template in much the same way you create any document. If you have a template that already has most of the features you want, you can save time by creating the new template based on the existing one.

To create a new template based on an existing template, follow these steps:

1. Choose File, New.
2. Choose the Template button.
3. Choose the tab that contains the template on which you want to base the new template.

Part
I

Ch
6

4. Select the template you want. Select the Normal template if you want to start with a blank template and the default settings.

5. Choose OK. Note that the title bar now displays `Template` rather than `Document` (see Figure 6.10).

6. Lay out and format the template as you would a document. Include text that will not change between documents. The template can contain text and graphics you want to appear on all documents, formatting and styles, macros, bookmarks, AutoText entries, new commands, shortcut keys, and new toolbar buttons.

FIG. 6.10

The title bar indicates that you are creating a template. This one is based on the NORMAL.DOT template.

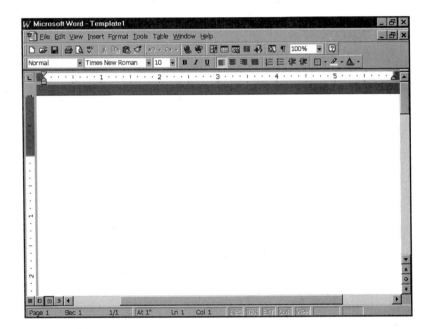

To save a template, follow these steps:

1. Choose File, Save As.

2. Select the folder in which you want to save the template. The folder you select determines the tab on which the template appears when you choose File, New.

3. Enter a name for the template in the File Name box. The extension DOT is assigned to templates.

4. Choose OK.

Creating a Template Based on an Existing Document

You already may have a document that contains most of the text, formatting, and settings you want to use in a template. Rather than re-create the document on a template, Word for Windows enables you to create a template based on the existing document.

To create a template based on an existing document, follow these steps:

1. Choose File, Open and open the document you want to use as the basis for a template.

2. Modify this document by editing text and adding graphics, styles, macros, AutoText, or buttons that you want to include in the template.

3. Choose File, Save As.

4. Select Document Template from the Save as Type pull-down list.

5. Select the folder in which you want to save the template. The folder you select determines the tab on which the template appears when you choose File, New.

6. Type the template's file name in the File Name box (see Figure 6.11). You do not have to type the DOT extension. The template file automatically is saved to the folder that contains templates.

7. Choose OK.

FIG. 6.11
If you create a particular document frequently, save it as a template.

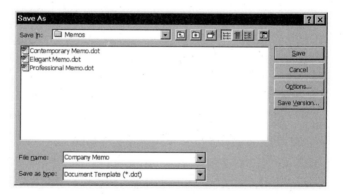

Part
I

Ch
6

> **N O T E** Templates are a key to creating forms that you use repeatedly. Word has the capability to create forms that include edit fields, drop-down lists, and check boxes. To use Word's Form Fill-in feature, you need to save forms as templates. Users can create forms easily by opening a new document based on the form template. You don't have to worry about the form being accidentally changed, because the original template stays on disk and the user works with a copy of the form. ▪

Using Wizards to Guide You

Word comes with some templates that guide you through the creation of a document. These special templates are called *wizards*. Wizards automate the process of creating a document to your specifications. For example, the Web Page Wizard walks you through the creation of a Web page. Another valuable wizard is the Newsletter Wizard. It creates multipage, multicolumn newsletters that include graphics, tables of contents, drop caps, and more.

When a wizard template opens, it displays dialog boxes, messages, and graphics that tell you how to fill in a template or complete forms. Word comes with several wizards that are very helpful.

 TIP Instead of creating documents with wizards, you can use wizards to create new templates that are based upon your choices. Use the wizard to set up a document, and then save the document as a template. See "Creating a Template Based on an Existing Document" earlier in this chapter.

Creating Documents with Wizards

Starting a wizard is like opening any other new document. Choose File, New, select the tab where the wizard you want is stored, and select the wizard template from the Template lists. Templates that contain wizards show the word wizard in their names.

Using the Letter Wizard

The Letter Wizard takes you step-by-step through the whole process of creating a letter. You can select whatever elements you want to include in the letter, such as the inside address, salutation, and closing. You can also choose the overall design for the letter, from normal to contemporary, and the style used for many of the letter elements.

To use the Letter Wizard to create a letter, follow these steps:

1. Open a new document to start a new letter or an existing document if you have already started the letter.

2. Choose Tools, Wizard to display the Letter Wizard dialog box shown in Figure 6.12.

FIG. 6.12

The Letter Wizard will take you step-by-step through the process of creating a stylish letter.

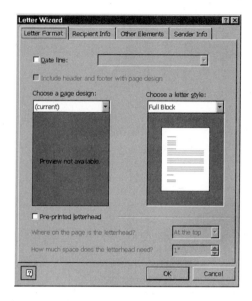

3. Make selections from among the options appearing in the Letter Format tab (see Figure 16.13). These options are discussed in the following table:

Option	Action
Date Line	Check if you want to insert the current date at the beginning of the letter. Select a style from the drop-down list.
Include Header and Footer with Page Design	Check if you want to insert a header and footer on the second and subsequent pages of the letter.
Choose a Page Design	Choose the overall look for your letter from the list of built-in designs. Preview the design in the preview box.
Choose a Letter Style	Choose from one of the letter styles. Preview the style in the preview box.
Pre-printed Letterhead	Check if you will print the letter on stock with a pre-printed letterhead.
Where on the Pages Is the Letterhead?	Specify the location of the letterhead.
How Much Space Does the Letterhead Need?	Specify, in inches, how much space the Letter Wizard needs to leave for the letterhead.

Part

I

Ch

6

4. Click the Recipient Info tab and fill in the information for the person receiving the letter (see Figure 6.13). The following options are available:

Option	Action
Click Here to Use Address Book	Click to use your Address Book to insert the name. Find the name in the Address Book and choose OK.
Recipient's Name	Type the name for the recipient in the text box. Recently used names appear in the drop-down list.
Deliver Address	Type the address of the recipient in the text box. This address that will be used for the inside address and envelope.
Salutation	Select one of the salutation options: Informal, Formal, Business, or Other. The style you select is displayed in the example box, using the recipient's name. Some example salutations appear in the drop-down list.

FIG. 6.13
Enter the information for the person receiving the letter in the Recipient Info tab.

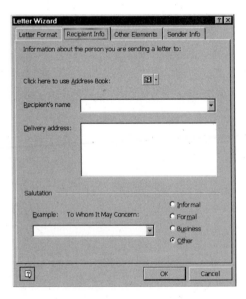

5. Click the Other Elements tab (see Figure 6.14) and select any additional items you want to include in your letter.

For each item you select in the Include area, you can type your own text or select an option from the drop-down list.

Enter the names of people who you want to send a copy of the letter to. You can type the names directly in the Cc: text box or insert them from your Address Book by clicking the Insert Address button.

FIG. 6.14

Select additional information to include in your letter in the Other Elements tab.

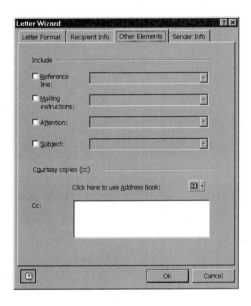

6. Click the Sender Info tab (see Figure 6.15) and enter any information you want to include regarding the sender of the letter. The options in this tab are listed below:

Option	Purpose
Click Here to Use Address Book	If you have a personal Address Book, click the Insert Address button to open it and select the sender's address from the listings.
Sender's Name	Type the name of the sender in the text box. Recently used names appear in the drop-down list.
Return Address	Type the address of the sender in the text box.
Omit	Check if the letterhead includes the sender's return address.

continues

Part

I

Ch

6

continued

Option	Purpose
Complimentary Closing	Select one of the complimentary closings from the drop-down list or type your own.
Job Title	Type the job title for the sender to include the job title below the sender's name in the complimentary closing. Recently used titles appear in the drop-down list.
Company	Type the name of the sender's company. Recently used names appear in the drop-down list.
Writer/Typist Initials	Type the initials of the writer or typist of the letter to include his or her initials at the bottom of the letter.
Enclosures	Check to include an enclosures line at the bottom of the letter. Enter the number of enclosures in the text box.

FIG. 6.15

Enter the information for the person sending the letter in the Sender Info tab.

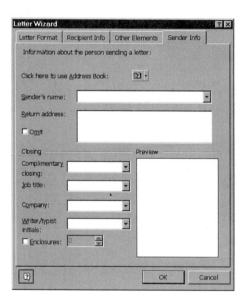

7. When you have finished entering your selections in the Letter Wizard, choose OK.

   The Letter Wizard inserts the information you entered using the design and styles you selected. The area where you will insert the text of the letter is highlighted.

8. Type the body text for the letter and save the letter.

Using Other Wizards that Come with Word

Wizards instruct you to fill in information inside dialog boxes. They use your responses to complete forms or prepare formatting. Some wizards prepare simple documents such as memos or fax cover letters (see Figure 6.16). Other wizards create more complex documents such as newsletters, legal pleadings, or Web pages. Table 6.2 lists the wizards supplied with Word. The tab on which the template is listed is included in parentheses.

FIG. 6.16
Use wizards to automate the creation of documents such as memos, newsletters, and Web pages.

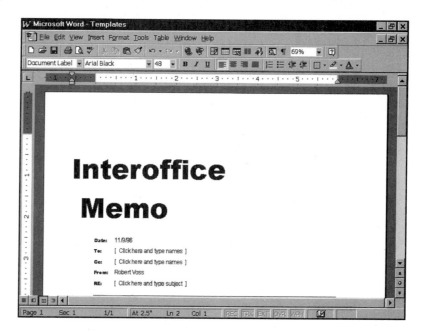

Table 6.2 Predefined Word Wizards

Wizard	Description
Fax Wizard	Helps you create customized fax cover sheets (Letters & Faxes).
Letter Wizard	Helps you create prewritten or customized letters (Letters & Faxes).

continues

Table 6.2   Continued

Wizard	Description
Envelope Wizard	Helps you create a single envelope or envelopes for a mailing list (Letters & Faxes).
Mailing Label Wizard	Helps you create a page of identical mailing labels or labels from a mailing list (Letters & Faxes).
Memo Wizard	Helps you create customized memos (Memos).
Newsletter Wizard	Helps you design and lay out a newsletter (Publications).
Pleading Wizard	Helps you create a legal pleading paper (Other Documents).
Resumé Wizard	Helps you create a customized resumé (Other Documents).
Web Page Wizard	Helps you create a Web page for the Internet.

The Envelope Wizard, Mailing Label Wizard, and Web Page Wizard are all new to Word.

ON THE WEB

Don't forget—you can find additional wizards, free of charge except for connect time, on the Microsoft Office home page. From a computer that can access the World Wide Web, open the Help menu in Word and choose Microsoft on the Web. From the submenu, choose Free Stuff.

Check the following Web site for free wizards:

http://www.microsoft.com/msword/fs_wd.htm

N O T E   Check the following Web sites for information on Web page design:

http://www.siggraph.org

http://the-tech.mit.edu/KPT

http://www.microsoft.com/workshop

http://www.w3.org/pub/WWW/Provider/Style

http://www.dsiegel.com/tips

http://www.publishersdepot.com

Adding Power and Features with Add-Ins

Add-ins are a way of extending the capabilities of Word. An add-in program is not part of Word but behaves as if it is a part of Word. An add-in program may add new menu choices to Word or add new toolbars to Word. Like a template, the add-in program remains available until you exit Word. Add-in programs for various tasks are available from a variety of third-party vendors. For specific information about using a particular add-in, consult the documentation provided with the add-in program.

ON THE WEB

Also check the following Web site for free add-ins:

http://www.microsoft.com/msword/fs_wd.htm

Loading Add-Ins

Add-in programs end with the file extension WLL. Follow the installation instructions provided with the add-in program for help in installing an add-in. To load an add-in program, follow these steps:

1. Choose Tools, Templates and Add-Ins. The Templates and Add-ins dialog box appears.

2. Choose the Add button in the Global Templates and Add-ins section. The Add Template dialog box appears.

3. Choose Word Add-ins in the Files of Type list box.

4. Select the add-in you want. If the add-in you want is not listed, change the folder or drive in the Look In box. (If you don't know the name of the add-in, consult the documentation provided with your add-in program.)

5. Choose OK. Word loads the add-in program.

You also can load add-ins automatically, every time Word starts. To load an add-in program on startup, simply copy the add-in WLL file into the Startup subfolder located in the WinWord folder. The Startup folder is the default folder used for startup files. If you do not have a Startup folder, choose Tools, Options and select the File Locations tab (see Figure 6.17). Select the Startup folder in the File Types list and then choose the Modify button to set a new folder as the Startup folder.

Part

I

Ch

6

FIG. 6.17
Modify the location of the Startup folder in the Options dialog box.

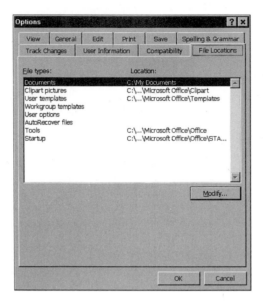

Removing Add-Ins

After an add-in is loaded, it remains available until you quit Word or explicitly remove the add-in. You may want to remove an add-in to make more system memory available.

To remove an add-in, follow these steps:

1. Choose Tools, Templates and Add-Ins. The Templates and Add-ins dialog box appears.

2. Select the add-in you want to remove in the Global Templates and Add-ins list.

3. Click the Remove button. The add-in is unloaded.

4. Choose OK.

Using Editing and Proofing Tools

By now, you're probably familiar with most of the basics of Word 97—how to create, edit, and save your documents. You can also use many tools to make entering text easier, ensure accuracy, and make sure that your document reads well.

With Word 97, you can use the Find and Replace feature to change text, formatting, special characters, and styles.

Before you print your document, you should check its spelling. Your eyes are trained to correct obvious spelling errors when you read them. However, you can still overlook a mistake when you proof a document. Use the spelling checker to catch mistakes that you missed and to correct spelling when you make an error. Use the Word 97 grammar checker to correct faulty sentence construction and style. You can use the thesaurus to find just the right word or to define a term you're unsure about.

Using Find and Replace

Use Find and Replace to search for and replace text, formatting, styles, and special characters.

Checking your spelling

Check the spelling of words in your document against words in your own custom dictionary or the dictionary in Word 97. Automatic spell checking can be turned on to check words as you type them.

Checking your grammar

Check your document for grammatical errors then correct them using suggestions provided by the grammar checker.

Using the Thesaurus

The Thesaurus provides a list of alternative terms that have the same meaning. This is useful when you think you're using a term too often.

Proofing in other languages

You can check the spelling, hyphenation, and grammar of documents written in another language by selecting the appropriate language dictionary.

Counting words

Count the number of pages, words, characters, paragraphs, and lines.

If you need to know how many words your document contains, use the Word Count feature. This feature enables you to gather information about the number of words, lines, paragraphs, and more. For example, term papers and magazine articles typically require accurate word counts.

The following two figures show a document before (see Figure 7.1) and after (see Figure 7.2) Word checked its spelling and grammar. The user also used the thesaurus to improve some of the language.

FIG. 7.1

This rough draft of a document has not been revised using Word's editing and proofing tools.

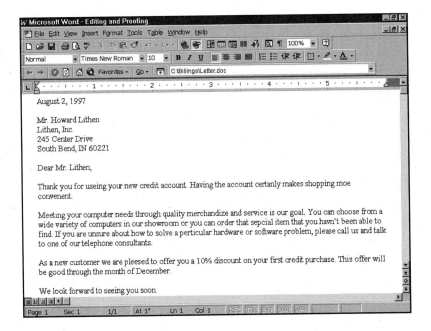

All the editing and proofing tools combine to help you hone the language of your documents. Use the tools to do the following:

- Catch typos and spelling errors.
- Make sure that your grammatical usage fits the type of document you're working on.
- Use the thesaurus to find the right replacement word. Then, choose Edit, Replace to exchange the new word for the original word.

FIG. 7.2
You can polish your writing with the editing and proofing tools.

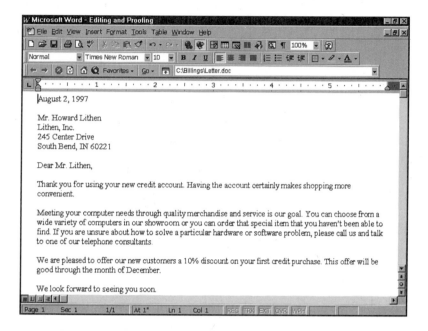

Using Find and Replace

Being able to find and replace text, formatting, styles, and special characters is an important time-saver. (This feature helps ensure that you catch every occurrence of whatever you need to find or replace.) The Edit, Find command finds and selects the text, formatting, style, or special character that you specify, enabling you to locate a certain phrase or a particular type of formatting easily. The Edit, Replace command enables you to find and replace the item in question. You can replace items selectively or globally (changing all occurrences at the same time).

Finding Text

With the Word Find feature, you can quickly locate a specific word or phrase or a special formatting character in a document that is many pages long. The text can be as brief as a single letter or as long as a sentence containing up to 255 characters. You can also search for special characters, such as tabs, page breaks, extra spaces, line numbers, footnotes, or revision marks within your document. Alternatively, you might want to search for a particular format or style.

Part

I

Ch

7

To find text (containing as many as 255 characters) or special characters, follow these steps:

1. Choose <u>E</u>dit, <u>F</u>ind, or press Ctrl+F. The Find and Replace dialog box appears with the Fin<u>d</u> tab selected (see Figure 7.3).

FIG. 7.3

Use the Find and Replace dialog box to search through your document quickly.

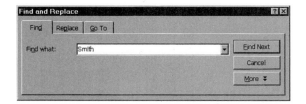

2. In the Fi<u>n</u>d What text box, type the text or special characters you want to search for. (For a list of special characters, see Table 7.2 in the section "Finding and Replacing Special Characters.")

   The text scrolls to the right if you enter more text than what will fit in the box. You can enter as many as 255 characters.

3. Choose the <u>M</u>ore button to display selectable search options (see Figure 7.4).

4. Select one or more of the following options in the Find and Replace dialog box:

Option	Effect
<u>S</u>earch	Determines the direction of the search. *Down* searches from the insertion point to the end of the document or selection. *Up* searches from the insertion point to the beginning of the document or selection. *All* searches the entire document or selection.
Matc<u>h</u> Case	Matches the text exactly as you have typed it—including capital letters. Word doesn't consider the use of small caps or all uppercase letters, but it examines the case of the letters just as you originally typed them. Do not select this option if you want to find all occurrences of the text regardless of case.

Find Whole Words Only	Finds whole words only, not parts of words. Select this option if you want to find all occurrences of the text.
Use Wildcards	Uses special search operators and expressions with which to search. See the section "Finding and Replacing Special Characters" later in this chapter.
Sounds Like	Matches words that sound alike but are spelled differently, such as *seize* and *sees*.
Find All Word Forms	Finds all forms of a word, such as *entry* and *entries*.
Format	Displays the Format options, including Font, Paragraph, Language, and Style. Depending on your selection, the dialog box displays the tab that contains the various types of formatting for each formatting option. (For more information on these options, refer to the section "Finding and Replacing Formats" later in this chapter.)
Special	Enables you to search for special codes in the text, such as paragraph marks and tab characters (see Figure 7.5). You can also type these codes. (See "Finding and Replacing Special Characters" later in this chapter.)
No Formatting	Removes any formatting codes displayed beneath the text box from a previous Find operation.

5. Choose the Find Next button to begin the search, or choose the Replace tab to display the Replace With text box.

Word finds the first occurrence of the text or special character and then moves to and selects that occurrence. The dialog box remains open so that you can immediately continue to search for other occurrences of the text or special character by choosing Find Next.

FIG. 7.4
Use the search options to find a specific word, phrase, formatting, style, or special character.

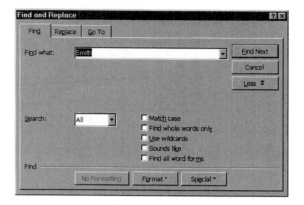

When you're finished with your search, close the Find and Replace dialog box by choosing Cancel or pressing Esc. For example, close the dialog box if you want to edit the found text.

T I P You can leave the dialog box open while editing the found text by clicking in the document window or pressing Ctrl+Tab.

After closing the Find and Replace dialog box, you can repeat the search by pressing Shift+F4. Alternatively, you can choose Edit, Find again and then choose Find Next.

If Word cannot find the text, the program displays a dialog box that indicates Word has finished searching the document. Choose OK and try again.

T I P You can display the Find and Replace dialog box by pressing Ctrl+F.

If you're unsure of how to spell the word you want to find, try using *special characters* in place of letters that you're not sure about. If you want to find *Smith*, for example, but aren't sure whether to spell it with an *i* or a *y*, search for **Sm^?th** (see Figure 7.5). You can insert the question mark by typing ^? (the caret character followed by the question mark) or by choosing Any Letter from the Special pop-up menu. Alternatively, you can search for part of a word, such as *Smi*.

FIG. 7.5

You can include special codes with search text.

 TIP If you are searching for part of a word such as Smi, make sure that the Find Whole Words Only check box in the Find and Replace dialog box is not selected.

If you want to search for or replace text in only a portion of your document, select that portion. Then follow the general instructions for finding or replacing.

Replacing Text

Besides searching for text, formatting, or special characters, you also can replace them automatically. If you finish your document and realize that *Smythe* really should have been *Smith*, you can use a simple menu command to search for every occurrence of the incorrect spelling and replace it with the correct version. Or if your typist underlined every title in a long list of books and you decide that you want to italicize book titles, you can search for every occurrence of underlining and replace it with italic.

Replacing text works much the same way as finding text. The only major difference is that, in addition to the Find What text box in the Find and Replace dialog box, the Replace tab includes a Replace With text box. In this box, you enter the text to replace the text that you find. The Find and Replace dialog box enables you to confirm each replacement. Alternatively, you can replace all occurrences of the text with a single command.

To replace text, follow these steps:

1. Choose Edit, Replace or press Ctrl+H. The Find and Replace dialog box appears (see Figure 7.6).

2. In the Find What text box, type the text that you want to replace.

3. In the Replace With text box, type the new text.

Part

I

Ch

7

FIG. 7.6

Use the Find and Replace dialog box to change one word or phrase to another throughout your document.

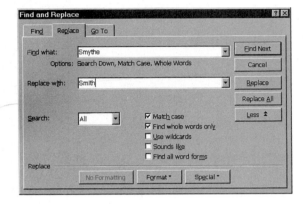

4. Select one or more options in the Find and Replace dialog box:

Option	Effect
<u>S</u>earch	Determines the direction of the search. *Down* searches from the insertion point to the end of the document or selection. *Up* searches from the insertion point to the beginning of the document or selection. *All* searches the entire document or selection.
Mat<u>ch</u> Case	Matches the text exactly as you have typed it—including capital letters. Word doesn't consider the use of small caps or all uppercase letters, but it examines the case of the letters just as you originally typed them. Do not select this option if you want to find all occurrences of the text regardless of case.
Find Whole Words Onl<u>y</u>	Finds whole words only, not parts of words. Do not select this option if you want to find all occurrences of the text.
<u>U</u>se Wildcards	Uses special search operators and expressions with which to search. See the section "Finding and Replacing Special Characters" later in this chapter.
Sounds Li<u>k</u>e	Matches words that sound alike but are spelled differently, such as *seize* and *sees*.

Find All Word Forms	Finds all forms of a word, such as *entry* and *entries*.
Format	Displays Format options, including Font, Paragraph, Language, and Style. Depending on your selection, the dialog box displays the tab that contains the various types of formatting for each formatting option. (For more information on these options, see the section "Finding and Replacing Formats" later in this chapter.)
Special	Enables you to search for special codes in the text, such as paragraph marks and tab characters (refer to Figure 7.5). You also can type these codes. See "Finding and Replacing Special Characters" later in this chapter.
No Formatting	Removes any formatting codes displayed beneath the text box from a previous Find operation (unless you want these codes to affect the current search).

5. Choose the Find Next or Replace All button.

   If you want to confirm each change, choose Find Next. When Word finds an occurrence of the text, choose the Replace button to change the text. Or choose the Find Next button again to continue the search without altering the selected occurrence.

   If you want to change all occurrences of the specified text without confirmation, choose the Replace All button.

6. Choose Cancel to return to the document.

If Word cannot find the text, you see a dialog box that indicates that Word has finished searching the document without finding the search item.

If you want to search for or replace text in only a portion of your document, select that portion. Then follow the general instructions for finding and replacing.

To cancel a Replace operation, press Esc or click the Cancel button.

Part

I

Ch

7

CAUTION

Choosing the Replace All button saves time but can be risky. You need to be absolutely certain that you want to replace *every* occurrence of a word before you use this feature. You might want to start by confirming the first few replacements. When you are sure that you want to change all remaining occurrences of the text, choose Replace All. If you choose Replace All and then realize that you made a mistake, immediately choose Edit, Undo Replace.

Unless you specify otherwise, Word applies the original formatting to the new replacement text. If you replace the boldface word *Roger* with the name *Mr. Smith* that is not bold for example, the replacement is a boldface *Mr. Smith*. To override this feature, specify formatting as part of your replacement (see this chapter's section "Finding and Replacing Formatting and Styles").

You can undo a replacement by choosing Edit, Undo Replace. If you have confirmed each replacement, Edit, Undo Replace undoes only the last replacement (however, you can choose Edit, Undo Replace repeatedly to undo replacements sequentially, starting with the last replacement). If you choose the Replace All button and make all the replacements at once, Edit, Undo Replace undoes all the replacements.

You can use the Undo button on the Standard toolbar to undo all the replacements.

 To undo all replacements using the Undo button, follow these steps:

1. Click the down arrow of the Undo button on the Standard toolbar. The box containing all the actions appears.

2. Drag to select all the Replace items listed on the Undo button's pull-down menu.

3. Release the mouse button. All the replacements revert to the original text.

If you are searching for or replacing long phrases, you can easily copy and paste the text into the Find and Replace dialog box. Highlight the text and choose Edit, Copy or press Ctrl+C to copy the text to the Clipboard. Position the insertion point in the Find What or Replace With text box. Paste the text by choosing Edit, Paste or pressing Ctrl+V.

Finding and Replacing Formatting and Styles

Finding and replacing formatting is similar to finding and replacing text. Suppose that you have a document in which you have underlined many titles, and you decide to italicize them instead. Or suppose that you have sprinkled an article with boldface phrases and decide to remove the boldface formatting. You can change the text, the formatting, or both the text and the formatting.

You can also find and replace paragraph formats, languages, and styles. For example, if your document has centered paragraphs, you can replace the centered formatting with right-aligned formatting. If you want to check the spelling in a French paragraph, you can assign a French language dictionary rather than an English (US) language dictionary. Or you can replace a style such as Heading 1 with another style, such as Heading 2.

Finding and Replacing Formats You can find and replace text (or special characters), formatting, or both. For example, you can find text and replace it with different text, as described in the preceding section, or you can find formatting and replace it with different formatting. Or you can find formatted text and replace it with different text and different formatting.

To find or replace formatting, follow these steps:

1. Choose Edit, Find or Edit, Replace. The Find and Replace dialog box appears.

2. In the Find What box, type the text that you want to locate, or leave the box empty to find only formatting.

3. Select the font, character, paragraph, language, or style formatting that you want to find or replace, as described in the following list:

   - To find a font or character formatting, choose the Format button and select Font from the menu that appears. The Find Font dialog box appears (see Figure 7.7). This dialog box looks the same as the Font dialog box that you use to format characters. Select the font or other options that you want to find. Then choose OK or press Enter.

   - To find paragraph formatting, choose the Format button and select Paragraph from the menu that appears. The Find Paragraph dialog box appears. This dialog box resembles the Paragraph dialog box that you use to format paragraphs. Select the paragraph formatting options that you want to find. Then choose OK or press Enter.

   - To find language formatting (areas of the document to which you assign a dictionary for another language), choose the Format button and select Language from the menu that appears. The Find Language dialog box displays (see Figure 7.8). Select the language assignment that you want to use in your Find and Replace operations.

   - To find style formatting, choose the Format button and select Style from the menu that appears. The Find Style dialog box appears (see Figure 7.9). Select the style that you want to find or replace. Choose OK or press Enter.

The font, paragraph, language, or style options that you select are listed beneath the Find What or Replace With text boxes.

FIG. 7.7
You can include character formatting as a Find What option or Replace With option in the Find Font dialog box.

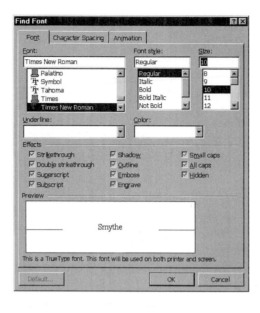

FIG. 7.8
Use the Find Language dialog box to search for or replace an area of text that has a foreign language dictionary assigned to it.

4. To replace formatting, select the Replace With text box. Then type the replacement text or leave the box empty to replace the contents of the Find What text box with formatting only.

5. To add formatting to the replacement text, choose the Format button. Then choose Font, Paragraph, Language, or Style. The Replace Font, Replace Paragraph, Replace Language, or Replace Style dialog box appears. Select the options that you want. Choose OK or press Enter.

   The formatting options that you select are listed under the Replace With text box.

6. Choose Find Next to find the next occurrence of the specified text, formatting, or both.

FIG. 7.9

In the Find Style dialog box, choose the styles that you want to find or replace.

If you're replacing formatting, choose <u>F</u>ind Next to find the next occurrence. Then choose <u>R</u>eplace, or choose Replace <u>A</u>ll to find and replace all occurrences.

7. When the <u>F</u>ind or <u>R</u>eplace operation is complete, click Cancel (or press Esc) to close the Find and Replace dialog box.

Initially, check boxes are gray and text boxes are blank on the format dialog boxes. This indicates that these fields are not involved in the <u>F</u>ind or <u>R</u>eplace operation. Clicking a check box option one time selects it—a check appears in the box. Clicking a second time clears the option. In this case, the option is still involved in the <u>F</u>ind or <u>R</u>eplace operation. However, you have specifically cleared that option, removing the format. Clicking a third time grays the option again so that it is no longer involved in the <u>F</u>ind or <u>R</u>eplace operation.

If you want to remove small caps from all occurrences of a certain word, for example, follow these steps:

1. Choose <u>E</u>dit, <u>R</u>eplace and then type the word into the Fi<u>n</u>d What text box.

2. Choose the F<u>o</u>rmat button. Then choose <u>F</u>ont.

3. Choose the S<u>m</u>all Caps option to select it. Choose OK to return to the Find and Replace dialog box. Then type the same word into the Replace W<u>i</u>th box.

4. Choose the F<u>o</u>rmat button then choose <u>F</u>ont. Select the S<u>m</u>all Caps check box twice to clear this option. If you leave this box grayed, the operation does not remove the formatting.

5. Choose OK then choose the Find Next button.

Part

I

Ch

7

The formatting selections that you make for the Fi_n_d What and the Replace W_i_th text boxes remain in effect until you change them. In other words, the selections are in effect the next time you open the Find and Replace dialog box. To remove all formatting options, select Fi_n_d What or Replace W_i_th, and then choose the No Forma_t_ting button until you end the editing session. (Each time you start Word 97, the dialog box appears with no formatting.)

You can use the shortcut keys for formatting characters and paragraphs in the Find and Replace dialog box. To specify bold formatting, for example, press Ctrl+B. To specify a font, press Ctrl+Shift+F repeatedly until the font you want is selected. See the reference card for a list of the shortcut keys.

The Find and Replace feature in Word is flexible, enabling you to replace text regardless of formatting, to replace just formatting, or to replace both text and formatting. You also can replace text with nothing (that is, delete specified text) or remove formatting. Table 7.1 outlines replacement options available when you use the Fi_n_d and R_e_place commands.

Table 7.1 Find and Replace Options

If You Replace	With	You Get
Text	Format	Old text and format, plus new format
Format or text and format	Format	Old text, new format
Text	Text and format	New text, old format, plus new format
Text	Nothing	Deleted text
Format or text and format	Nothing	Deleted text and formatting

Finding and Replacing Styles A *style* is a combination of several formatting commands. You can have a style called Title, for example, that includes the formatting commands for Times New Roman font, 24-point size, centered, underlined, and bold. A style enables you to apply all these formats with a single command. You can use the Word R_e_place command to replace a format with a style or to replace one style with another. When you replace formatting or a style with a style, all paragraphs formatted by the replacement style take on its formatting.

▶ **See** "Creating Styles," **p. 393**

The procedure to replace a format with a style, or one style with another, is identical to the procedure you use for finding and replacing formats. When you choose the F_o_rmat button and select S_t_yle in the Find and Replace dialog box, the Find Style or Replace Style dialog box displays all the defined styles (refer to Figure 7.9). When you select the style in the

Find What Style or Replace With Style list, the formatting commands that compose the selected style appear below the list.

Finding and Replacing Special Characters

Finding and replacing text in your document is handy and easy. Sometimes, however, you want to search for and replace other items. You can find and replace many special characters, including a wildcard character (?), a tab mark, a paragraph mark, section marks, a blank space, and many more. If you open a text (or ASCII) file with carriage returns at the end of every line, for example, you can replace each of those paragraph marks with a space. Alternatively, if you have a list that contains spaces rather than tabs, you can replace those spaces with tabs. Always be careful to confirm your changes at least once so that you don't inadvertently make an incorrect replacement.

You can find or replace special characters by using the Special button in the Find and Replace dialog box or by using the keyboard. Table 7.2 lists the codes that you can type from the keyboard.

Table 7.2   Codes for Special Characters

Code	Special Character
^p	Paragraph mark (¶)
^t	Tab character (→)
^a	Comment mark (Find only)
^?	Any character (Find only)
^#	Any digit (Find only)
^$	Any letter (Find only)
^^	Caret character (^)
^n	Column break
^+	Em dash (—)
^=	En dash (–)
^e	Endnote mark (Find only)
^d	Field (Find only)
^f	Footnote mark (Find only)
^g	Graphic (Find only)
^l	Manual line break

Part

I

Ch

7

continues

Table 7.2   Continued

Code	Special Character
^m	Manual page break
^~	Nonbreaking hyphen
^s	Nonbreaking space
^-	Optional hyphen
^b	Section break (Find only)
^w	White space (any space—one space, multiple spaces, tab spaces—bordered by characters) (Find only)
^c	Clipboard contents (Replace only)
^&	Find What text (Replace only)
^0*nnn*	ANSI or ASCII characters (*n* is the character number) (Replace only)

To insert special codes by choosing the Special button, follow these steps:

1. Choose Edit, Find or Edit, Replace.
2. Select the Find What or Replace With text box.
3. Choose the Special button.
4. Select the command that you want to find or replace.

To insert special codes from the keyboard, follow these steps:

1. Choose Edit, Find or Edit, Replace.
2. Type the appropriate code in the Find What or the Replace With text box. Enter the caret character (^) by pressing Shift+6.
3. Choose the No Formatting button if you do not want the formats to affect the action of the Find or Replace command.

¶ If you want to find or replace special characters, you should display nonprinting characters, such as paragraph marks and tab marks. To display nonprinting characters from the toolbar, click the Show/Hide ¶ button on the Standard toolbar.

To display nonprinting characters from the menu, follow these steps:

1. Choose Tools, Options.
2. Select the View tab.
3. Select the All check box in the Nonprinting Characters group.
4. Choose OK.

Checking Your Spelling

After you enter your text and you're fairly sure that the words are correct, check your document's spelling.

The Word spelling checker quickly pinpoints words in your document that don't match those in its or the user's dictionary, or in your own custom dictionary. When you aren't sure about a word, you can ask Word to suggest alternative spellings. The program searches its dictionary for a match and offers you a list of other spellings. It can even suggest a spelling as the most likely choice.

When automatic spell checking is turned on, Word uses a red wavy line to underline words it thinks are misspelled, which makes them easy to spot when you proofread your document. An icon of an open book with a red x also appears at the bottom-right portion of the screen indicating spelling errors exist in your document.

N O T E   The Word spelling checker also searches for several other problems: double words (*the the*), oddly capitalized words (*mY*), words that should be capitalized (*california*), and words that should be all capitals (*DOS*). You also can set additional options in the Spelling dialog box. ▩

Spell checking begins at the beginning of your document and works through your document, checking its entire contents. You can check spelling in a smaller section of text by first selecting that area (it can be as little as a single word). Then you can check the spelling as usual.

A good spelling checker gives you the confidence of knowing that your work is accurate. However, be careful. No spelling checker can tell you when you have misused words, perhaps typing *for* when you mean *four*, or *thought* when the word should be *though*. A spelling checker is an important tool but cannot replace thorough proofreading.

Checking Your Document's Spelling Automatically

Word 97 automatically underlines misspelled words with a wavy red line. Spell checking and underlining occur as you type. Automatic spell checking works only when the feature is enabled. To turn on automatic spell checking, choose Tools, Options, select the Spelling tab, and then select the Automatic Spell Checking check box. If you find that your system becomes unacceptably slow when using automatic spell checking, disable this option and use the command method of spell checking that is described in the next section.

Part

I

Ch

7

To check spelling of words with a wavy underline, follow these steps:

1. Double-click the open book icon in the status bar at the bottom of the screen to find the next underlined word in the document. Or right-click an underlined word.

   A pop-up menu appears showing a list of suggested words and additional options.

2. You have four choices for correcting the misspelled word:

   ■ Correct the word if it is misspelled.

   ■ Select a word from the list shown in the pop-up menu.

   ■ Select Ignore All to ignore all occurrences of the word in your document.

   ■ Select Add to add the word to the selected dictionary displayed in the Custom Dictionary in the Spelling dialog box.

3. Repeat this procedure for each word you want to check.

Using the Spelling Command to Check Spelling

To check spelling in your document using commands, follow these steps:

1. Select the word or section of your document that you want to check for spelling. If you select nothing, Word checks the entire document.

 2. Choose Tools, Spelling and Grammar, or click the Spelling button on the Standard toolbar. Alternatively, press F7.

   Word scrolls through your document, matching each word against the main dictionary. The program selects words that it does not recognize, and the Spelling and Grammar dialog box appears. The unrecognized word is highlighted in the text and displayed in the Not In Dictionary box (see Figure 7.10). You can move the Spelling and Grammar dialog box if it is hiding the selected word.

3. Select the correct word from the Suggestions list.

   If the Always Suggest Corrections option is turned on in the Spelling Options, and Word can suggest an alternative spelling, that suggestion appears in the Suggestions list. Other possible words appear in the Suggestions list. (For more information on using Always Suggest Corrections, see the section "Setting Spelling Options" later in this chapter.)

   If the Always Suggest Corrections option is turned off, the Suggestions list is empty. Press Alt+E to display a list of possible words, and then select the correct word from the list.

FIG. 7.10

You can choose Spelling to find misspellings and typos throughout your document.

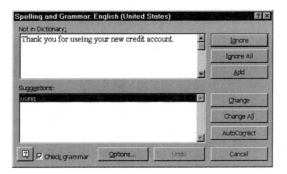

4. If the correct spelling appears in the Suggestions list, select the correct word from the Suggestions list then choose the Change button. The selected word changes to the spelling displayed in the Suggestions list. Choose Change All to change all occurrences of the misspelled word in your document.

   Alternatively, choose Ignore to leave the word as is. Choose Ignore All to ignore all future occurrences of the word in your document.

   If Word finds a word that it thinks is misspelled and you want to add that word to the dictionary, choose the Add button. The program then adds the word to the selected dictionary displayed in the Custom Dictionary box.

5. Word continues searching. Choose Cancel to discontinue the spell checking. You also can undo as many as five previous corrections by choosing the Undo command.

6. A dialog box appears when the spell checker reaches the end of the document or the selection. If you are checking a word or a selected section, a dialog box asks whether you want to check the remainder of the document. Choose Yes or No.

If you start spell checking in the middle of the document, the spell checker completes checking of the document, then returns to the beginning and continues checking to the point at which you began.

You can halt the spelling check to edit your document without closing the Spelling and Grammar dialog box. Drag the Spelling and Grammar dialog box away from the area that you want to edit. Then click in the document or press Ctrl+Tab to activate the document window. After editing your document, choose the Resume button in the Spelling and Grammar dialog box to resume spell checking where you stopped. (If you're using a keyboard rather than a mouse, press Ctrl+Tab to reactivate the Spelling and Grammar dialog box.)

Part
I

Ch
7

If none of the words in the Suggestions list are correct, you can edit the word from within the Not in Dictionary box. After you've edited the word, choose the Change button to update the document window, or choose the Undo Edit button to undo the spelling change.

You also can undo all spelling changes made during a spell check in two other ways. To undo all spelling changes from a menu command, choose Edit, Undo Spelling Change immediately after you complete the spell checking. To undo all spelling changes with the Undo button, follow these steps:

1. Click the Undo button on the Standard toolbar.

2. Drag down through all the Spelling edits.

3. Release the mouse button.

Correcting Double Words   When the Word spelling checker finds double words, the Not In Dictionary box changes to the Repeated Word box, and the repeated word is highlighted in red (see Figure 7.11).

FIG. 7.11

Word indicates double occurrences during a spelling check.

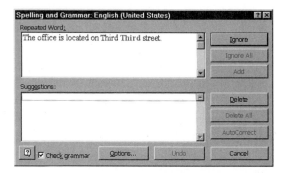

To delete the repeated word, choose the Delete button. Be sure to delete unwanted spaces.

Adding Words to a Dictionary   The spell-checking process enables you to add words to a custom dictionary. When Word selects an unrecognized word that you use often, choose the dictionary to which you want to add it. Thereafter, the spell checker will bypass the word.

To add words to a custom dictionary, select a dictionary by choosing the Options button in the Spelling and Grammar dialog box. Select a dictionary from the Custom Dictionary list in the Spelling & Grammar tab of the Options dialog box, then click the OK button. Then choose the Add button in the Options dialog box.

> **CAUTION**
>
> Be careful not to accidentally add misspelled words to the dictionary. If you want to delete a misspelled word from a dictionary, use Windows WordPad to open the dictionary and delete the word. Dictionaries are located in the Proof folder, found in the C:\Program Files\Common Files\Microsoft Shared folder.

Setting Spelling Options

The Spelling and Grammar dialog box includes the Options button. Choosing this button enables you to use a non-English dictionary or to check spelling against a custom dictionary that you create. (See the next section for information on creating a custom dictionary.) The button also enables you to select automatic spell checking.

You can set options at any time by following these steps:

1. To set options before you check spelling, choose Tools, Options. Then select the Spelling & Grammar tab.

   To set options while checking spelling, choose the Options button in the Spelling and Grammar dialog box to open the Options dialog box. The Spelling & Grammar tab for adjusting spelling options appears (see Figure 7.12).

2. Under Spelling, select among the following options:

Option	Function
Check Spelling as You Type	Automatically identifies words not found in the dictionary by placing a red wavy line under each.
Hide Spelling Errors This Document	Hides red wavy lines from beneath words not in found in the dictionary.
Always Suggest Corrections	Word will always suggest corrections. Clear this option if you don't always want suggestions (and if you want the spelling checker to work faster).
Suggest from Main Dictionary Only	Suggestions will come from the Main dictionary only, not from any open custom dictionaries.
Ignore Words in UPPERCASE	Ignores words in all uppercase letters.
Ignore Words with Numbers	Ignores words that include numbers.

Part

I

Ch

7

continues

Option	Function
Ignore Internet and File Addresses	Ignores Internet and file addresses.

3. Choose the Dictionaries button to open the Custom Dictionaries dialog box (see Figure 7.13). As many as ten custom dictionaries can be open during a spelling check. You may have many custom dictionaries available. However, Word checks spelling against only custom dictionaries that are open.

FIG. 7.12

In the Spelling & Grammar tab of the Options dialog box, you can customize a spelling check.

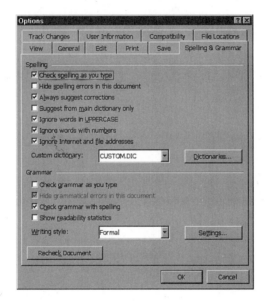

4. Choose OK.

FIG. 7.13

You can select a custom dictionary in the Custom Dictionaries dialog box.

Creating a Custom Dictionary

Each time you run the spelling checker, it compares the words in your document with those in the dictionary. The Word 97 standard dictionary contains thousands of commonly used words. However, this dictionary may not include certain words that you frequently use—for example, terms specific to your profession, your company's name, or the names of products that your firm sells. You can create custom dictionaries and specify that Word 97 consult them each time you check spelling. To learn how to open these dictionaries so that Word uses them when you check spelling, see the preceding section, "Setting Spelling Options." To learn how to add words to your custom dictionary, refer to the earlier section, "Adding Words to a Dictionary."

To create a new custom dictionary, follow these steps:

1. Choose Tools, Options. Then select the Spelling & Grammar tab.

2. Choose the Dictionaries button.

3. Choose the New button in the Custom Dictionaries dialog box. A dialog box prompts you for the name of the dictionary file.

4. In the File Name box, type a name for the new dictionary ending with the extension **DIC**. Your dictionary is stored in the C:\Program Files\Common Files\ Microsoft Shared\Proof folder. You can select another folder in which Word is to store the dictionary.

5. Choose Save.

6. To close the Custom Dictionaries dialog box, choose OK.

7. To close the Options dialog box, choose OK in the Spelling & Grammar tab.

You can remove or edit a word from a custom dictionary by selecting the dictionary in the Custom Dictionaries list in the Custom Dictionaries dialog box and then choosing the Edit button. Choose OK to close the Custom Dictionaries dialog box. Then choose OK to close the Options dialog box. The file lists all dictionary entries alphabetically. Delete the words that you no longer want or edit words that need changes. Then save the file in Text Only format (don't change the file's name or location).

The following table describes the options in the Custom Dictionaries group:

Option	Function
Edit	Makes changes to the custom dictionary that you select. You must confirm that you want to open the dictionary as a Word document. Word warns you that it will stop automatic spell checking when you edit a dictionary. You must select the Check Spelling as You Type check box to enable automatic spell checking. This check box is accessed by choosing Tools, Options, then selecting the Spelling & Grammar tab.
Add	Adds a custom dictionary from another directory or disk.
Remove	Removes a dictionary from the Custom Dictionaries list. You must select the dictionary before you can remove it.
Language	Adds language formatting to a custom dictionary. Word will use that custom dictionary only when checking the spelling of text formatted in that language. (See "Proofing in Other Languages" later in this chapter.) If you select (none), Word uses the dictionary to check spelling of text formatted in any language.

TROUBLESHOOTING

I tried to run the Spelling option, and a dialog box appeared indicating that Word 97 cannot locate that feature from the Tools menu. Many Word 97 features, such as the spelling checker, are optional during the Word 97 installation process. If a feature or command that you want to use is not installed, you can click Add/Remove Office Programs on the Office Shortcut bar menu, and then select the options you want. For example, select Proofing Tools if you want to install the spelling checker. You will need your installation CD-ROM or disks. To complete the installation process, follow the instructions that appear. If you do not use the full Office suite, follow your original installation procedure and select the Add/Remove button when the Setup dialog box appears. You will be given the opportunity to select features that are not installed.

Checking Your Grammar

While writing a document, you may be uncertain whether your sentence structure is grammatically correct. You might use the phrase *between you and I*, for example, when the grammatically correct version is *between you and me*. Use the Word grammar checker to spot grammatical errors and receive suggestions on how to correct them. The Spelling and Grammar dialog box provides several choices for making changes (see Figure 7.14).

FIG. 7.14

Use the grammar checker to flag possible errors in spelling and grammar.

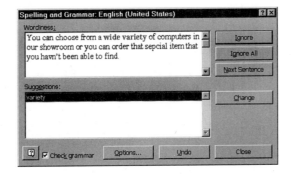

If you do not select any text before using the grammar checker, Word checks the entire document, beginning at the insertion point. If you select text, Word checks only the selection. A selection must contain at least one sentence.

By default, Word checks spelling and grammar. If you want to check only grammar, turn off the Check Grammar with Spelling option in the Spelling & Grammar tab of the Options dialog box. (To learn how to do this, see the upcoming section, "Selecting Grammar Rules.")

To check a document's grammar, follow these steps:

1. Choose Tools, Spelling and Grammar.

    The Spelling and Grammar dialog box appears when Word finds a sentence with a possible grammatical error or questionable style (refer to Figure 7.14). The grammatically questionable words appear highlighted in the upper text box.

    If Word can offer any suggestions for replacement text, it lists them in the Suggestions text box. (If the Change button is grayed, the Grammar checker cannot suggest a change.) An explanation of the error or questionable style appears just above the upper text box. For a more detailed explanation, click the question mark located in the lower left corner of the Spelling and Grammar dialog box.

2. Correct the sentence by selecting a suggestion in the Suggestions box and then choosing the Change button.

    or

    Correct the sentence by editing it in the upper text box then choosing the Change button.

    The grammar checks resumes at the insertion point.

Part

I

Ch

7

You also can choose from these Spelling and Grammar dialog box options:

Option	Function
Ignore	Ignores the questioned word or phrase.
Ignore All	Skips other similar occurrences that break the same grammar or style rule.
Undo Edit	Undoes all edits made in the upper text box.
Next Sentence	Leaves the sentence unchanged and moves to the next sentence.
Question Mark button	Provides more information about the error. A window appears describing the relevant grammar or style rule. After you read the information, click the window's X button to clear the window and return to the Spelling and Grammar dialog box.
Options	Selects different rules of grammar and style. The Spelling & Grammar Options tab that appears enables you to select an option button for the rule group that you want to observe for the remainder of the check. (See "Selecting Grammar Rules" later in this chapter.)

After reaching the end of the document, the grammar checker continues checking from the beginning. When Word finishes checking the entire document, you see a message indicating that the grammar check is completed. Choose OK to return to your document.

If you select the Show Readability Statistics option in the Options dialog box, a dialog box displays the information about the document. (The section "Testing the Readability of a Document," later in this chapter, covers readability.) Choose OK to return to your document.

Selecting Grammar Rules

You can choose the rules of style and grammar that Word uses during grammar checks. Depending on your audience, your style, and the material, you may want to follow some rules and disregard others. Choose Tools, Options and select the Spelling & Grammar tab. You can then choose among five predefined rule groups: Casual, Standard, Formal, Technical, or Custom. Table 7.3 describes these rule groups. You also can create as many as three custom rule groups or customize the predefined rule groups by selecting or clearing grammar and style options.

Table 7.3 Grammar Checker's Rule Groups

Rule Group	Rules Applied
Casual	Only those rules appropriate for informal written communication (the fewest number of rules)
Standard	Only those rules appropriate for written business communication
Formal (all rules)	All grammar and style rules except gender-specific words
Technical	Only those rules appropriate for technical communication
Custom	Rules that you apply

To customize a rule group, follow these steps:

1. Choose Tools, Options and select the Spelling & Grammar tab. If you have already started grammar checking, choose the Options button in the Spelling and Grammar dialog box. The Spelling & Grammar tab of the Options dialog box appears (see Figure 7.15).

FIG. 7.15

Use the Spelling & Grammar tab in the Options dialog box to choose the grammatical rules and styles that you want to apply to your documents.

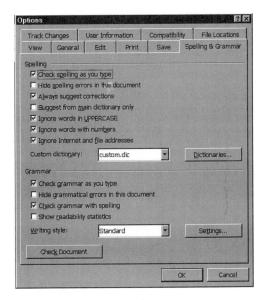

2. Select from the Writing Style list the rule group that you want to change.

3. Choose the Settings button. The Grammar Settings dialog box appears (see Figure 7.16).

FIG. 7.16

You can customize the grammatical rules that Word 97 uses to check your document.

4. If you base a custom rule group on an existing rule group, select the existing rule group from the Writing Style list.

5. Choose the Settings button and then select the check boxes for the rules that you want Word 97 to observe. Clear the check boxes for rules that you want Word to ignore.

6. Choose OK to return to the Options dialog box.

7. Choose OK to return to the document or grammar checking.

Testing the Readability of a Document

Readability statistics measure how easy your writing is to read. Writing that is easier to read communicates more clearly. *The Wall Street Journal*, for example, writes at the eighth-grade level. Hemingway wrote at the sixth-grade level. Writing need not be boring when it's readable. To make his writing interesting, Hemingway used intriguing subject matter, active writing, colorful descriptions, and variable sentence lengths.

If you choose to display readability statistics, they appear at the end of grammar checking.

To display readability statistics after you use the Spelling and Grammar command, follow these steps:

1. Choose Tools, Options.

2. Select the Spelling & Grammar tab.

3. Select the Show Readability Statistics check box.

4. Choose OK.

The Word 97 readability statistics are based on the Flesch-Kincaid index. This index assigns a reading ease score and grade level based on the average number of words per sentence and syllables per 100 words.

Using the Thesaurus

When you're not sure of a word's meaning, when you think you're using a certain term too often, or when you can't come up with the right word, take advantage of the Word 97 thesaurus. It defines selected words and offers alternative terms (synonyms). For example, Word 97 synonyms for the word *information* include *intelligence, data*, and *facts*.

The thesaurus looks up one word at a time. You can specify the word by selecting it. Otherwise, the thesaurus looks up the word that the insertion point indicates. If the insertion point is within a word, the thesaurus looks up that word. If the insertion point is outside a word, the thesaurus looks up the word preceding the insertion point.

To display a list of synonyms and definitions for a word in your document, follow these steps:

1. Select the word for which you want to locate a synonym.
2. Choose Tools, Language, Thesaurus, or press Shift+F7. The Thesaurus dialog box appears (see Figure 7.17).

FIG. 7.17
In the Thesaurus dialog box, you can find a list of meanings for almost any word you select.

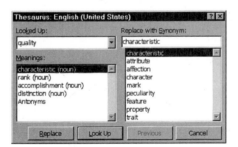

The Looked Up text box displays the selected word. The Replace with Synonym text box displays the first synonym, followed by a list of other synonyms. The word's definition appears in the Meanings box.

Part

I

Ch

7

3. You have several options:

Action	Result
Choose a synonym in the Replace with Synonym list.	The word moves into the Replace with Synonym box.
Select a different meaning from the Meanings list.	A new list of synonyms appears in the Replace With Synonym list. You can select a word from this list.
Select related words or antonyms in the Meanings list.	The Replace With Synonym list displays related words or antonyms.
Select the word from the Meanings or Replace with Synonym list, or type a word and choose Look Up.	Meanings of the new words appear.
Select the word from the Meanings or Replace with Synonym list, or type a word and choose Look Up.	Meanings of those new words appear.
Choose Previous.	The word that the thesaurus previously looked up appears.

4. Choose the Replace button to replace the selected word in the document with the word in the Replace with Synonym, Replace with Antonym, or Replace with Related Word box, or click the Cancel button.

Proofing in Other Languages

If you're reading the English language edition of this book, most of your typing is probably in this language. However, your document may contain some text in Spanish, French, or another language. You can select that text, assign to it a language other than English, and all the Word 97 proofing tools—the spell checker, hyphenation, thesaurus, and grammar checker—will use the other language dictionary that you specify to proof that text.

Before the Language command is available, you must purchase and install the appropriate language-proofing tools for the language you want to use. If you want to check the spelling of French text, for example, you must install a French dictionary. Contact Microsoft Corporation or other vendors for information on the many language-proofing tools available.

To proof text in another language, follow these steps:

1. Select the text written in another language.

2. Choose Tools, Language, Set Language to display the Language dialog box.

3. Select the language from the Mark Selected Text As list. To change the language for all the text that you proof, choose the Default button.

   You can choose (no proofing) from the list if you want the proofing tools to skip the selected text. This feature is useful for technical material that contains terms not listed in any of the standard spelling dictionaries.

4. Choose OK.

Counting Words

The Tools, Word Count command counts the number of pages, words, characters, paragraphs, and lines in a document (see Figure 7.18). You can choose to include footnotes and endnotes in the count.

FIG. 7.18
The Word Count dialog box provides statistics about a document.

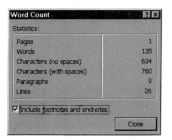

To use the word count feature for the document on-screen, follow these steps:

1. Choose Tools, Word Count. The Word Count dialog box appears. Word performs the count and displays the results.

2. Choose Include Footnotes and Endnotes if you want to include these items in the count. Word redoes the count and the new results appear.

3. Choose the Close button.

Part
I

Ch
7

Previewing and Printing a Document

Although printing with Word 97 can be as simple as opening a document, choosing a Print command, and starting the printing operation, Word gives you many additional options. You can preview one or more pages in your document and change their margins while you're in the preview, print all or part of an open document, print a draft or a final version, print hidden text and field codes, and print multiple documents without opening them. ■

Select and set up a printer

Any printer that you select and set up for use with Windows can also be used with Word 97.

View your pages before you print them

Preview your pages in Page Layout or Print Preview view. Page Layout allows you to view the page as it would print out. You also can edit a page in this view. Print Preview also allows you to view a page as it would print out but does not allow editing. However, the Preview screen's toolbar allows zooming and displaying multiple pages.

Print a document in Word

Printing in Word 97 is as simple as ever. However, many useful options have been added with this version. This chapter shows you how to make use of them.

Print documents to a file

Printing documents to a file is one method of creating an encapsulated Postscript (EPS) file that can then be printed on a Linotronic typesetting machine. This produces high-quality documents.

Selecting a Printer

Microsoft Windows is the common denominator that makes printing with Word easy. Any printer you install to use with Windows you also can use with Word.

Word prints on whichever installed printer you currently have selected as the default printer. You can find out which printer is selected by choosing File, Print and looking at the top of the Print dialog box (see Figure 8.1).

FIG. 8.1

The Print dialog box offers a variety of options.

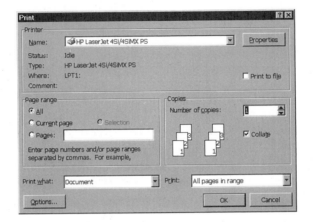

To select a printer, select the Name drop-down list in the Print dialog box. If you use only one printer, select that printer the first time you print a document with Word. After you print, your printer stays selected. If you switch between printers, you must select a printer each time you change printers.

When you select a printer, Word lists the available printers in the Name list of the Printer group (see Figure 8.2). This list includes all printers installed for use with Windows. If the printer you want to use is not on the list, you must install it in Windows. To install a printer, see the following section, "Installing a Printer in Windows."

To select a printer, follow these steps:

1. Choose File, Print. The Print dialog box appears.

2. Select a printer from the Name list in the Printer group.

3. Choose OK to print, and close the Print dialog box to return to your document.

The next time you choose File, Print, you see your selected printer listed at the top of the Print dialog box.

FIG. 8.2
Select the <u>N</u>ame drop-down list in the Print dialog box to view the installed printers.

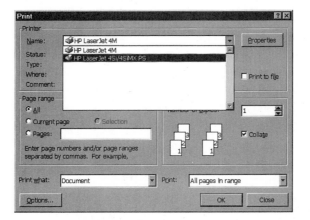

The <u>O</u>ptions button in the Print dialog box provides access to certain settings that affect the appearance of your printed document. You learn about these settings later in this chapter.

Setting Up Your Printer

Windows manages most details of setting up a printer. However, Windows leaves three tasks for you: selecting the printer you want to use in Word, installing the printers you want to use in Windows, and changing the printer setup for special printing needs.

ON THE WEB

To download the most current copies of free printer drivers, visit the following World Wide Web site:

http://www.microsoft.com/kb/softlib

In the search box, type **Printer Drivers**, and click the Go button. Lists of drivers will display that you can download and use for installation.

Installing a Printer in Windows

Selecting a printer in Word is simple—if the Print dialog box lists the printer. If your printer is not listed, Windows does not have that printer installed. You can install a printer in Windows from within Word.

To install a printer in Windows while Word is open, follow these steps:

1. Click the Start button and choose Settings, Printers to display the Printers window.

2. Double-click Add Printer to display the Add Printer Wizard.

3. Click the Next button to begin installation. Choose Local Printer if your printer is attached to your computer, or choose Network Printer if the printer is attached to a network.

4. Click the Next button.

5. From the Manufacturers list, select the printer's manufacturer.

   The list of available printers appears in the Printers list. The list of printer manufacturers and printer models appears as shown in Figure 8.3.

FIG. 8.3

Select your printer's manufacturer and model from the Add Printer Wizard.

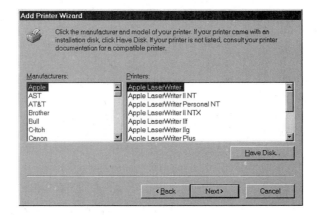

6. From the Printers list, select the printer you want to install. Then choose the Next button.

   If the Printers list does not list your printer and you have a printer driver (a file with a DRV extension) from the printer manufacturer, choose the Have Disk button. If the list doesn't include your printer and you do not have a driver, you may be able to use the driver of a compatible printer model. Otherwise, you can select Generic as the manufacturer and Generic/Text Only as the printer, but this driver does not support special fonts or graphics.

   If you clicked the Have Disk button, a dialog box prompts you to insert the disk issued by the printer manufacturer. The dialog box shows drive A as the default, but you can enter another drive letter.

7. Select the port to use with this printer from the Available Ports list, and then click the Next button (see Figure 8.4).

If you want to configure the port settings, click the Configure Port button.

If you select an LPT port as your printer port, then select the Configure Port button, select whether or not you want documents printed from MS-DOS-based programs to be spooled. You also can select whether or not you want the port state checked before printing.

8. Type a name for this printer in the Printer Name dialog box, or keep the manufacturer's name. Select the Yes option button if you want this printer to be the default printer, or choose No. Then click the Next button. Figure 8.5 shows the Printer Name dialog box.

FIG. 8.4
Configure the port you want to use with this printer.

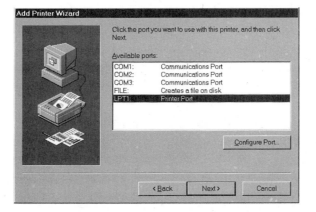

FIG. 8.5
Type a name to identify the printer you are adding.

9. A dialog box prompts you to print a test page after installing your printer. Choose Yes (recommended) or No.

10. Choose Finish. Word prompts you to insert a particular Windows 97 disk where the selected driver is located. Insert the specified disk or Windows 97 CD-ROM.

11. Choose OK. When the Copying Files dialog box appears, enter the drive and folder path that contains the new printer driver.

    If Windows does not find the driver on the disk, the dialog box reappears. Insert a different disk than the one requested and choose OK again.

N O T E   The printer driver may be on one of the other Windows installation disks. ■

You return to the Printers dialog box when the installation is complete. The Printers dialog box then lists and selects the new printer.

12. Choose File, Properties from the Printers dialog box.

13. Select the appropriate tab in the Properties dialog box (see Figure 8.6), and select the settings you use most frequently, such as printing in portrait (vertically) or landscape (horizontally), the resolution, paper source, printer memory, and font cartridges. Then choose OK.

FIG. 8.6

The Print Properties dialog box appears for an HP LaserJet printer.

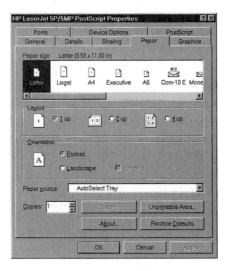

14. Close the Printers dialog box to complete the setup operation.

Using Special Print Setups

For the most part, after you install a printer in Windows, Word completes the rest of the process of setting up the printer. Because Word makes certain assumptions about such things as paper size and orientation (portrait or landscape), you usually do not have to select these options. In Chapter 13, "Formatting the Page Layout, Alignment, and

Numbering," you learn how to change the default settings. Word does enable you to choose some options from the Print dialog box, however.

To set options when printing a document, follow these steps:

1. Choose File, Print. The Print dialog box appears.
2. Select a printer from the Name drop-down list.
3. Choose the Properties button in the Print dialog box. The Properties dialog box opens. You saw an example of a Properties dialog box for the HP LaserJet printer in Figure 8.6.
4. Select the options you want. (See the section "Controlling Printing Options" later in this chapter for details on the individual options.)
5. Choose OK.
6. In the Print dialog box, choose OK.

The actual Print Setup Options dialog box you see varies depending on the printer you select in step 2.

The Properties dialog box controls options that are useful if your document contains sophisticated graphics or if you want to share the file on a network. These advanced features may be useful if you do desktop publishing with Word.

Setting Up Printer Memory and Font Cartridges

If you use a laser printer, you may have to specify which font cartridge to use and how much memory is in the printer. These settings affect the capabilities of your printer, so you should not neglect to set them. You can change many aspects of your printer setup, depending on what type of printer you have.

To set memory and select font cartridges for a laser printer, follow these steps:

1. Click the Start button and choose Settings, Printers to display the Printers window.
2. Right-click your printer and choose Properties to display the Properties dialog box.
3. Select the Device Options tab to display a tab similar to the one shown in Figure 8.7. The tab for your printer may appear different than this.
4. Choose Printer Memory, and select the amount of memory installed on your printer.
5. Select the Fonts tab.
6. In the Cartridges list, select the one or two cartridges installed in your printer. Click a cartridge once to select it, and click it again to deselect it.
7. Choose OK to return to the Printers dialog box.

FIG. 8.7
The Device Options
dialog box appears
for an HP LaserJet
printer.

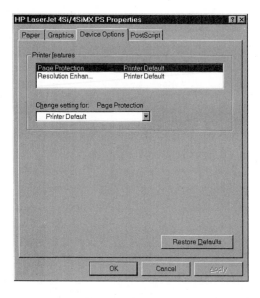

CAUTION

Before you replace and select cartridges, remember to turn off your printer. Turn your printer back on only after you finish.

N O T E   You can change certain print options (document size and paper source, for example) in the Properties dialog box. Choose File, Print, Properties. You can change other options—such as print quality and print order (along with paper source)—by choosing Tools, Options and selecting the Print tab. The Page Setup dialog box settings override the defaults and affect only the current document. The Print tab settings change the global defaults. ■

Previewing Pages Before Printing

Word offers you two alternatives for viewing your document before you print. These alternatives are the Page Layout or Print Preview view.

In Page Layout view, you can select text or graphics and enclose the selected item in a frame, and then drag the text or graphics to new locations. You can also drag page breaks to new locations.

The primary advantage of using the Print Preview view is the Preview screen's toolbar, which contains convenient buttons for zooming and displaying multiple pages.

Using Page Layout View

Different document views in Word show different perspectives on your margins. In Normal view, you don't see the margins, but you see the space between them where your text appears. In Page Layout view, you see the page as it will print, margins and all. Select this view if you want to see headers, footers, page numbers, footnotes, and anything else that appears within the margins.

 At the left of the horizontal scroll bar are three buttons offering different views of documents. (If your horizontal scroll bar is not displayed, choose Tools, Options, select the View tab, and in the Window group, select Horizontal Scroll Bar.) The Standard toolbar includes a button that displays the Print Preview view. Table 8.1 summarizes the effects of the document view icons.

Table 8.1   Effects of Document View Icons

Button	Name	Effect
=	Normal	Displays document in Normal view.
⊨	Online Layout	Displays a document in Online Layout view.
=	Page Layout	Displays document in Page Layout view.
⧦	Outline	Displays document in Outline view.
🔍	Print Preview	Displays document in Print Preview view.

To view the document in Page Layout view, follow these steps:

1. Open the document you want to preview.
2. Choose View, Page Layout (if you haven't already selected the command). Alternatively, click the Page Layout button in the horizontal scroll bar.
3. If you want, adjust the magnification by choosing View, Zoom.

 To return to Normal view, choose View, Normal or click the Normal button at the left of the horizontal scroll bar.

Using Print Preview

The other method of seeing how your document will print is to use the Print Preview view.

 To see the entire document in print preview, you first must open the document you want to preview. Then choose File, Print Preview or click the Print Preview button on the Standard toolbar. You then see a screen like that shown in Figure 8.8.

FIG. 8.8

Display a screen representation of your printed document by using the Preview screen.

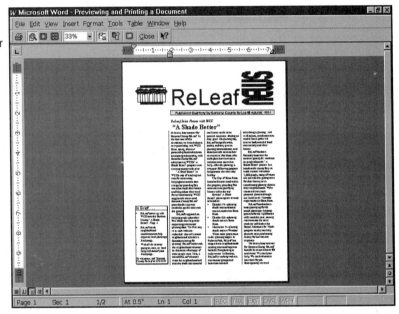

Across the top of the Preview screen is a toolbar with buttons that make it easier to work with your document in print preview. You can use the buttons on the toolbar to perform the actions listed in Table 8.2.

Table 8.2   Preview Screen Buttons

Button	Name	Effect
	Print	Prints the document using the printing options set in the Print dialog box.
	Magnifier	Toggles the mouse pointer between a magnifying glass (for examining the document) and the normal mouse pointer (for editing the document).

Part

I

Ch

8

Button	Name	Effect
One Page	One Page	Displays document in single-page view.
Multiple Pages	Multiple Pages	Displays document in multiple-page view.
41%	Zoom Control	Displays a list box of zoom magnification percentages and options.
View Ruler	View Ruler	Toggles the ruler display on and off.
Shrink to Fit	Shrink to Fit	When the last page of the document contains very little text, it tries to "shrink" the document to fit on one less page.
Toggle Full Screen View	Toggle Full Screen View	Toggles between full-screen display (which removes everything but the document and the toolbar) and normal display.
Close	Close Preview	Returns to your document.
▶?	Context-Sensitive Help	Provides context-sensitive help.

In print preview, you also have access to the normal, page layout, and outline icons at the extreme left of the horizontal scroll bar (if the bar is displayed). Clicking any of these buttons closes the preview screen and displays the document in the view mode you selected.

You can move around in the document in the Preview screen by using your keyboard's Page Up and Page Down keys and the scroll bars. When the rulers are displayed, you adjust margins in the same manner as in Page Layout view. You can also edit the document.

To edit a document in print preview, follow these steps:

1. Click the Magnifier button on the Standard toolbar. The mouse pointer changes to a magnifying lens.

2. Click the part of the document you want to edit. Word displays the document at 100 percent magnification.

3. Click the Magnifier button again to restore the normal Word mouse pointer.

4. Edit the document, revising text and repositioning margins on the page.

After you make your changes, you can reduce the document to the previous magnification by clicking the Magnifier button again and then clicking the document with the magnifying glass icon.

Printing from Print Preview   You can print all or part of your document from the Print Preview screen. To do so, you can use the Standard toolbar's Print button or the Print dialog box.

 To print using the Standard toolbar, click the Print button to print the document using the current print settings. (The Print dialog box does not appear when you click this toolbar button.)

To print using the Print dialog box, follow these steps:

1. Choose <u>F</u>ile, <u>P</u>rint.

2. Make the appropriate printing selections in the Print dialog box.

3. Choose OK.

Viewing One or Two Pages   You can view as many as 18 pages at once in 640×480 resolution—although you might not find it practical to display more than six or eight at the same time.

To view multiple pages, follow these steps:

1. Click the Standard toolbar's Multiple Pages button.

2. Move the mouse pointer over the upper-left portion of the grid that appears below the Multiple Pages button.

3. Drag the mouse pointer down and to the right until the highlighted portion of the grid reflects the number of pages you want to display. If you continue dragging, the grid expands to display additional pages to a maximum of three rows and six columns in 640×480 resolution.

4. Release the mouse button. The Preview screen now displays the arrangement of pages that the grid represented when you released the button.

 To change back to single-page view again, click the Standard toolbar's One Page button.

Cancelling or Closing the Print Preview Screen   To return to your editable document, click Close Preview from the Standard toolbar.

Printing the Current Document

The simplest way to print is to open a document and choose File, Print. By default, Word prints one copy of all pages of the currently open document on the currently selected printer without printing hidden text.

To print one copy of a document, follow these steps:

1. Open the document you want to print.
2. Choose File, Print or press Ctrl+Shift+F12. The Print dialog box appears.
3. Choose OK. The Print dialog box closes, and a printer icon in the status bar displays the process of the print job.

To cancel printing while the Print icon is displayed,

1. Press Esc.
2. When the Windows 97 printer icon appears in the taskbar, you can double-click it to open the Printers folder.
3. Select the document you want to cancel printing, and then choose Document, Cancel Printing. If the Printer icon is no longer displayed in the Windows taskbar, Word may have already sent the print job to the printer.

 You can bypass the Print dialog box and print your document quickly by clicking the Print button on the Standard toolbar. Word prints your document using settings previously selected in the Print dialog box.

Printing the Current Web Page

As you view or create World Wide Web pages in Word, you may want to print them. Use the same process you would use to print a Word document. While the HTML page (Web page) is active, choose File, Print Preview to see a preview like that shown in Figure 8.9.

Print your Web pages as you would a normal Word document using the File, Print command or the Print button on the Standard toolbar. You will find that many Web pages appear better on-screen than they do printed. If you need a higher-quality print, see if the Web page can be downloaded as a Word DOC file or an Adobe Acrobat PDF files.

FIG. 8.9
See a preview of how
the Web page will
print using Word's
File, Print Preview
command.

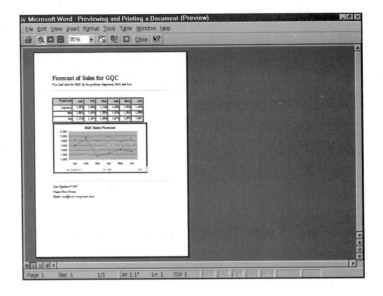

Printing Multiple Copies

With Word's Print dialog box, you can print more than one copy of your document. In fact, you can print 32,767 copies of your document (but you may want to plan a trip to Hawaii while all those copies print). By default, Word collates the copies—a handy feature for long documents.

To print multiple copies of your document, follow these steps:

1. Open the document you want to print.

2. Choose File, Print, or press Ctrl+Shift+F12. The Print dialog box appears (see Figure 8.9).

FIG. 8.10
You can print multiple
copies of your docu-
ment by changing the
number in the
Number of Copies
box of the Print
dialog box.

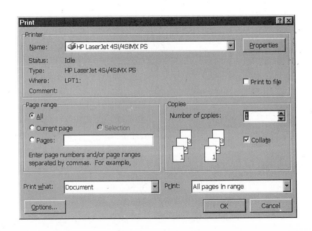

3. Select the Number of Copies box in the Print dialog box and enter the number of copies you want to print. (Alternatively, use the increment/decrement arrows to increase or decrease the specified number of copies.)

4. Choose OK.

If print time is important, you can deselect the Collate option in the bottom-right corner of the dialog box. This step enables Word to run multiple documents through the printer faster. You pay for choosing this option later, however, when you have to collate all the copies by hand.

Printing Part of a Document

Word provides two ways to print part of a document. You can select the portion of your document you want to print and then choose File, Print. You can also print by indicating specific page numbers in various way. Also, you can print on both sides of the paper even if you don't have a duplex printer. Printing a selected area is useful when you want to print a section of a larger document but don't know on which page or pages the section is located.

To print a selected area of text, follow these steps:

1. Select the text to print.

2. Choose File, Print, or press Ctrl+Shift+F12.

3. Choose the Selection option in the Page Range area of the dialog box.

4. Choose OK.

If you know exactly which pages you want to print, you can print a range of pages. Suppose you make changes to the first three pages of a long document. In that case, you might want to print from pages 1–3.

To print a specific range of pages, follow these steps:

1. Choose File, Print or press Ctrl+Shift+F12.

2. In the Pages box of the Page Range area, enter the range of pages you want to print. (For instance, to print pages 1 through 3, enter **1–3**.)

3. Choose OK.

In the Pages box, you can specify multiple page ranges (such as **1–7,8–13,14–20**) or multiple discontinuous pages (**1,2,8,13**). You can combine ranges with individual page numbers, as shown in Figure 8.11.

FIG. 8.11
Enter groups of page
ranges and selected
pages in the Pages
box of the Print
dialog box.

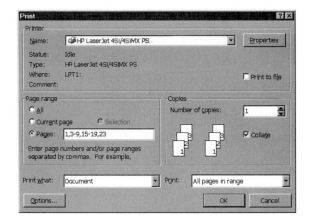

FIG. 8.11
Enter groups of page
ranges and selected
pages in the Pages
box of the Print
dialog box.

You can also print pages in a certain section. To print the second section in your document, type **s2** in the Pages box. If you want to print from page 7 in the second section to page 10 in the third section, type **p7s2–p10s3** in the Pages box.

In a long document, it's sometimes helpful to simply print the page on which you're working. To do so, follow these steps:

1. Position the insertion point on the page you want to print.
2. Choose File, Print, or press Ctrl+Shift+F12.
3. Choose Current Page.
4. Choose OK.

If you want to print on both sides of the paper and don't have a duplex printer, you should print the odd-numbered pages in one print run and the even-numbered pages in another. To print only the odd- or even-numbered pages, follow these steps:

1. Choose File, Print or press Ctrl+Shift+F12.
2. In the Print box, select the Odd Pages or Even Pages option.
3. Choose OK.

Printing Different Types of Document Information

Word documents contain associated information such as document properties, field codes, and data for forms. You can print this information with the document or separately. The first method that this section presents describes how to print the ancillary hidden information with the document. The second method describes how to print the hidden information separately.

Word enables you to include the following hidden attributes as part of your printed document:

- Document properties
- Field codes
- Comments
- Hidden text
- Drawing objects

To print hidden information with your document, follow these steps:

1. Choose Tools, Options, then select the Print tab if it is not already displayed (see Figure 8.12).

FIG. 8.12

Choose Tools, Options, and display the Print tab to specify a variety of printing options, including printing "nondisplaying" information when you print the document.

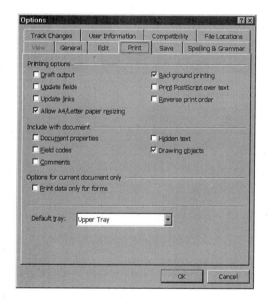

2. In the Include with Document Print options, select the options you want to print (see Table 8.3). If you choose Comments, for example, Word prints a list of the comments associated with your document. (You can use this option to display a list of the comments that a reviewer has made to your document.)

3. Choose OK.

Table 8.3   Include Associated Document Information with Document Print Options

Option	Effect
Document properties	Prints a summary of information about the document—including author, subject, print date, and number of pages, words, and characters—on separate pages at the end of the document.

continues

Part

I

Ch

8

Table 8.3   Continued

Option	Effect
Field Codes	Prints field codes rather than their results.
Comments	Prints at the end of the document a list of comments that reviewers have attached to your document, with page number headings indicating where each comment occurs.
Hidden Text	Prints any hidden text, such as table of contents entries, where text appears in document.
Drawing Objects	Prints drawing objects you created in Word.

Alternatively, you can print hidden information separately from the document itself, although you can select only one of the following items at a time:

- Document properties
- AutoText entries
- Comments
- Key assignments
- Styles

To print only a document's hidden information without printing the document, follow these steps:

1. Choose File, Print.
2. Select Print What to open the drop-down list.
3. Select one of the options from the list.
4. Choose OK.

Controlling Printing Options

Word offers you many printing options. You can print the pages in reverse order or save time by printing a draft copy (on some printers). You can print text that usually is hidden, separately or as part of your document. You can update fields as you print, or you can print on paper from a specified bin if your printer has more than one paper source.

To set printing options, follow these steps:

1. Choose Tools, Options, and select the Print tab.
2. Select the desired options.
3. Choose OK.

The following sections describe the available printing options.

Printing a Draft

Sometimes you need a quick, plain printed copy of your document. Perhaps someone else must edit the copy, or you want to take the copy home from work to review. For a quick, unadorned print, choose a draft copy. A *draft* prints quickly without formatting. Word underlines enhanced characters instead of boldfacing or italicizing them, and prints graphics as empty boxes. (The exact result of a draft print depends on your printer. For example, a Hewlett-Packard LaserJet prints formatted text but no graphics in Draft mode, but a PostScript printer does not support Draft mode.)

If you select draft printing as your default, all printing is in Draft mode until you deselect that option. Alternatively, on some printers, you can print in Draft mode only once without changing the default (this option is not available for laser printers).

To select draft as your default print-quality mode, follow these steps:

1. Choose Tools, Options. Select the Print tab.
2. In the Print tab of the Options dialog box, select the Draft Output check box.
3. Choose OK.

To print a draft copy of a document one time using a dot-matrix printer, follow these steps:

1. Choose File, Print.
2. In the Print dialog box, choose Options. The Options dialog box appears with the Print tab opened.
3. In the Printing Options area, select Draft Output.
4. Choose OK.
5. In the Print dialog box, choose OK.

Printing Pages in Reverse Order

Some printers have a collator that produces printed pages stacked in the correct order. Other printers stack pages with the last page on top. If your printer stacks with the last page on top, you might want to select the Reverse Print Order option to stack your pages in the correct order.

To print in reverse order, select the Reverse Print Order check box in the Print tab of the Options dialog box. Then choose OK.

Updating Fields

Word files can include field codes that instruct Word to insert special information into the document. A date field, for example, inserts the current date when Word prints the document. But some fields cannot be updated during the printing process. To update those fields when you print, you must choose a special option. In most cases, you want this option turned on.

To update fields when you print, select the Update Fields check box in the Print tab of the Options dialog box. Choose OK.

▶ **See** "Viewing and Printing Field Codes," **p. 698**

Updating Links

The Update Links option updates any linked information in the document before printing. To update links before you print, select the Update Links check box in the Print tab of the Options dialog box. Then choose OK.

▶ **See** "Moving, Copying, and Linking Text or Graphics," **p. 185**

Background Printing

The Background Printing option enables you to continue working in Word while you print a document. To print in the background while performing other operations in Word, select the Background Printing check box in the Print tab of the Options dialog box. Then choose OK.

Printing Form Input Data Only

If you have entered data into fields on a form, printing only the input data might make it easier to compare the data in Word to the source document. To print the input data only, select the Print Data Only for Forms check box in the Print tab of the Options dialog box. Then choose OK.

▶ **See** "Printing Forms," **p. 776**

Selecting the Paper Source

If you want to always print from a particular bin on your printer, you can change the default paper source. To do so, follow these steps:

1. Choose Tools, Options.
2. In the Print tab of the Options dialog box, choose Default Tray to open the drop-down list (see Figure 8.13).

FIG. 8.13

You can change the paper source with the Default Tray option in the Print tab.

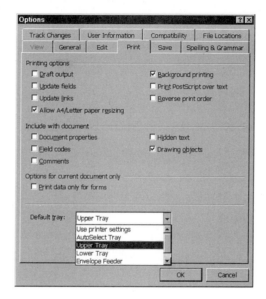

3. Select the paper source by selecting the option you want from the Default Tray list box.

You also can set the paper source for your document by choosing File, Page Setup, selecting the Paper Source tab, and selecting the First Page and Other Pages options.

▶ **See** "Selecting the Paper Source," **p. 472**

In most single-bin laser printers, you can slide your letterhead into the manual tray as far as the letterhead goes and leave your bond paper in the paper bin. After you choose OK from the Print dialog box, the printer first pulls in the letterhead and then pulls in the bond for following sheets. As a result, on printers such as the HP LaserJet Series II, III, or IV, you do not need to go through a series of steps. Just print.

Printing Multiple Unopened Documents

Occasionally, you might want to print an unopened document or several documents simultaneously. File, Print in the Windows Explorer enables you to open and print several documents at once.

To print one (or more) unopened documents, follow these steps:

1. Right-click the Start menu, and choose Explore to open the Explorer. If you prefer to use My Computer, open a window into My Computer.

2. Select the files you want to print. Click the first file; then hold down the Shift key, and click the last file to select contiguous files. Or, click the first file, then Ctrl+click other files to select non-contiguous files.

3. Move the pointer over a selected file and right-click to display the Send To shortcut menu.

4. Select the printer or fax where you want to send the files.

▶ **See** "Printing Files," **p. 122**

If you've assembled several Word documents into a master document, you can print the entire master document. You learn about master documents and related printing options in Chapter 32, "Assembling Large Documents."

Printing to a File

Someday you might need to print a Word document from a printer that doesn't have Word installed. You have two options. You can take a copy of the Word Viewer, a free subset of Word that displays and prints DOC files, or you can print the document to a printer file and take this printer file with you. The printer file you create must be made for the printer you will actually print on.

ON THE WEB

Microsoft has free Viewer applications that can display and print Word, Excel, and PowerPoint files without using the full application. To download a free copy of the Word Viewer, point your browser:

http://www.microsoft.com/msword/fs_wd.htm

Before you create a Word document that will be sent to a typesetter, check with the typesetter to learn the fonts that are compatible with their typesetting equipment. Some typesetters can suggest alternate fonts that can be substituted in the original Word document.

One use for printing to a file is when you need a Word document typeset. To create a print file for typesetting, set up Word for a PostScript printer, usually a Linotronic printer, to a file. You can then take the resulting encapsulated PostScript (EPS) file to a printer (or service bureau) to be printed on a Linotronic typesetting machine for high-quality documents. Try a test file with the printer before you get down to a deadline. In some cases, alternate settings or the original DOC file may be needed.

Another use for printing to a file is to create a file you can print on a computer that has no copy of Word. If you create the file for that model of printer, you can open an MS-DOS window and use the DOS COPY command to copy the Word file to the LPT1 printer port. The file prints even though Word is not running.

Part

I

Ch

8

To print the resulting printer file to a printer without using Word, open a DOS window by clicking Start, Programs, MS-DOS Prompt. In the DOS window use the CD, Change Directory, command to change to the folder (directory) where you saved the printer file created by Word. If your printer is connected to the LPT1 port, you will enter a command like,

```
COPY LETTER.PRN LTP1:
```

> **CAUTION**
>
> When you create a print file, Word must be set up for the specific printer that will be used to print the file. The print file contains the same codes and printer commands that would have been sent to the printer. The print file cannot be edited in Word.

To print to a file, insure that Word is setup for the printer to be used to print the file, then follow these steps:

1. Choose File, Print.
2. Select the Print to File option, and then choose OK.

   The Print to File dialog box appears.
3. Change to the folder where you want to save the printer file. In the File Name box, type the name of the file to contain the document. Then choose OK.

When you want to resume printing to your printer, deselect the Print to File option in the Print dialog box.

N O T E You can create a text file easily in Word. Just choose File, Save As; then select the Save as Type pull-down list and select one of the text file format files that Word creates. In most cases, you should choose the Text Only (*.TXT) format.

Traditionally, a printed document is the ultimate realization of what you create in word processing, and the printed hard copy is delivered physically. Increasingly, however, documents are routed electronically. Word can print a document to a file or route it to someone else in your organization or directly to a fax machine.

▶ **See** "Sending Faxes and Electronic Mail with WordMail," **p 1069**.

Formatting Documents

Formatting Characters and Changing Fonts

Characters—individual letters, numbers, punctuation marks, and symbols—are the smallest units of text you can format in a Word 97 document. You can apply formatting styles such as bold, italic, or a different font to one character or to an entire document. You can also combine character formatting options; for example, you can make a word bold and italicized. You also can use as many different types of character formatting in a document as you want. Your document's title, for example, can be in a different font or larger size, subheadings can be boldfaced, and paragraphs of text can be plain text with some italic text for occasional emphasis. ■

Format characters

Format characters using menu commands, keyboard shortcuts, or the Formatting toolbar.

Change fonts

Font types and sizes can be changed and are determined by printer and screen fonts installed on your computer.

Change languages

Change languages to enable you to share work with documents written in non-English languages.

Copy formatting

This formatting technique is a method that can save time for repetitive formatting tasks.

Format special characters

Some of the special formatting options include changing text orientation, highlighting text, making superscripts and subscripts, underlining, spacing, and adding animation characters.

Insert symbols and special fonts

Insert decorative characters, scientific symbols, or invisible characters.

Use fonts correctly

TrueType generates screen and printer fonts so that what is printed closely matches what you see on-screen.

What Is Character Formatting?

Character formatting options include fonts, sizes, boldface, italic, strikethrough, hidden text, colors, superscript and subscript, uppercase and lowercase, small caps, underlines, text orientation, and character spacing.

Word 97 also has many special characters to include in your document. You can create a list using bullets or decorative dingbats, for example, or you can include a copyright or trademark symbol. This chapter covers all the character formatting options.

Figure 9.1 shows some examples of the character formatting options available in Word.

FIG. 9.1

There are many formatting options you can apply to characters in Word.

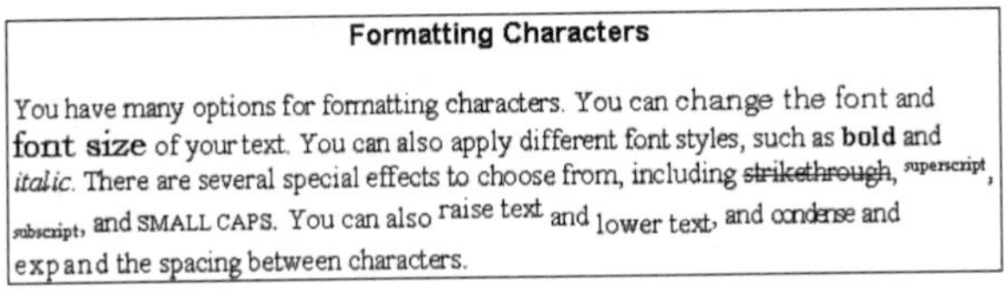

> **Formatting Characters**
>
> You have many options for formatting characters. You can change the font and **font size** of your text. You can also apply different font styles, such as **bold** and *italic*. There are several special effects to choose from, including ~~strikethrough~~, superscript, subscript, and SMALL CAPS. You can also raise text and lower text, and condense and expand the spacing between characters.

You can use character formatting to accomplish the following tasks:

- Add emphasis to text—you can boldface or enlarge important items.
- Hide notes to yourself or other readers—you can use hidden text to include notes that do not print.
- Add visual interest to text—you can change fonts to visually differentiate body text from headings.

TIP The Font list in the Formatting toolbar shows a printer icon to the left of each font available from your printer and a TT for TrueType fonts.

TROUBLESHOOTING

I don't see the formatting codes on-screen. Unlike some word processors, Word does not display formatting codes on-screen. Instead, you see the results of the formatting on-screen. The text appears as it will look in print. You can determine which formatting options have been applied by selecting the text and choosing Format, Font. The dialog box indicates those options that are currently active.

Formatting Characters

Word 97 offers no shortage of techniques for applying character formatting. If you have a mouse, you can format using tools and lists on the Standard and Formatting toolbars. If you prefer the keyboard, you can access formatting commands from the menu. You also can take advantage of many helpful mouse and keyboard shortcuts.

Whether you choose to format text before or after you type it, you must remember that most character formatting commands *toggle* on and off—you turn them on the same way that you turn them off. If you select and boldface a word and then want to remove the boldface, select the word a second time and choose the Bold command again. Toggling applies when you use buttons on the toolbars or keyboard shortcuts to apply or remove formatting. Formatting with the menu commands varies slightly.

Part
II

Ch
9

Selecting Characters to Format

You can format characters as you type or after you finish typing. To format characters as you type, choose the formatting command, type the text, and then choose the formatting command a second time to turn off the command. To format characters after you finish typing, you must remember this rule: select, then do. Select the text to format, and then choose the formatting command.

▶ **See** "Selecting Text," **p. 156**

Formatting with Menu Commands

Using a menu command is probably the most basic technique for formatting characters. Using the menu has three primary advantages: The Font dialog box displays all the character formatting commands at once; you can apply several types of character formatting simultaneously with the Font dialog box; and you can preview the results of the formatting choices you make in the Font dialog box.

To access the Font dialog box, choose Format, Font or press Ctrl+D. The Font dialog box displays three tabs: Font, Character Spacing, and Animation (see Figures 9.2, 9.3, and 9.4).

The options of each tab are described in Tables 9.1, 9.2, and 9.3. (Options marked with asterisks are detailed later in this chapter.)

FIG. 9.2

Use the Font options to change fonts, character font styles, and effects.

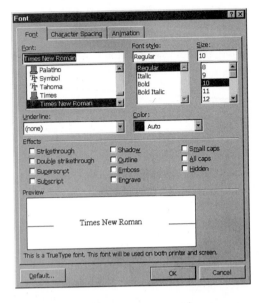

FIG. 9.3

Use the options on the Character Spacing tab to control the spacing between characters.

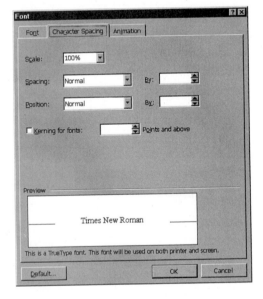

FIG. 9.4
Use the Animation
tab to add special
animation.

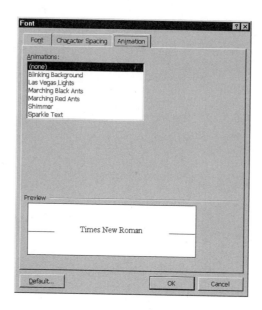

Table 9.1   The Font Tab Options

Group	Option	Description
Font*	Selection varies depending on printer	A typeface style. Common fonts include Times New Roman, Arial, and Courier.
Font Style	Regular	The basic font with no enhancements. Used for most typing.
	Italic	Oblique or slanted text: *Italic*. Often used for book or magazine names, or for emphasis. Can be combined with Bold.
	Bold	Heavy text: **Bold**. Often used for document titles or subheadings.
	Bold Italic	Bold and italic formatting combined.
Size*	8, 10, 12, and so on	Character size in points. An inch consists of 72 points (a typesetting measurement).
Underline*	None	Normal text. Used to remove underlining.
	Single	<u>Single underline</u>. The space between words is underlined.

continues

Table 9.1	continued	
Group	**Option**	**Description**
	Words only	Single <u>underline</u>. The space between words is not underlined.
	Double	<u>Double underline</u>. The space between words is double underlined.
	Dotted	Dotted underline. The space between the words is dotted underline.
	Thick	Thick underline. The space between the words is thick underlined.
	Dash	Dash <u>underline</u>. The space between the words is dashed underlined.
	Dot Dash	Dot dash underline. The space between the words is dot dash underlined.
	Dot Dot Dash	Dot dot dash underline. The space between the words is dot dot dash underlined.
	Wave	Wave underline. The space between the words is wave underlined.
Color*	Auto, Black, Red, Yellow, and so on	Changes the color of text on-screen if you have a have a color monitor. Prints in color if you have a color printer.
Effects	Strikethrough	Text crossed with a line: ~~Strikethrough~~. Often used when making revisions.
	Double Strikethrough	Text double-crossed with a line: ~~Strikethrough~~. Often used when making revisions.
	Superscript*	Text raised above the baseline.
	Subscript*	Text lowered below the baseline.
	Shadow	Text has shadow behind, under, and to the right.
	Outline	Each character's inner and outer border is displayed.
	Emboss	Text appears to be embossed.
	Engrave	Text appears to be imprinted into the page.
	Small caps	Short uppercase letters: SMALL CAPS. Used for emphasis or for graphic effect.
	All caps	All uppercase letters: ALL CAPS. Used for emphasis or for graphic effect. Harder to read than format combining uppercase and lowercase.

Group	Option	Description
	Hidden*	Text that doesn't appear or print unless you want it to. Often used for private notes or comments.
Default*	N/A	Applies selected formatting to the template attached to the document, as well as to the current document. All future documents based on this template will use the selections in the Font dialog box as the default font.
Preview	N/A	Shows a sample of text formatted with selected options.

Table 9.2 The Character Spacing Options

Group	Option	Description
Spacing*	Normal	Default spacing for the selected font.
	Expanded	Space between characters expanded to 3 points.
	Condensed	Space between characters condensed to 1.75 points.
By:*	1 pt (default), or enter your own amount	Number of points by which text is expanded or condensed. Measured in increments of tenths of a point.
Position*	Normal	Text is printed on the base line.
	Raised	Text is raised above the baseline by the increment you indicate in the By box.
	Lowered	Text is lowered below the baseline by the increment you indicate in the By box.
By:	3 pt (default), or enter your own amount	Number of points by which text is raised or lowered.
Kerning for Fonts	8 pt (default), or enter your own amount	Number of points by which specific combinations of characters are spaced. Only TrueType or Adobe Type Manager fonts can be kerned.
Default	N/A	Applies selected formatting to the template attached to the document, as well as to the current document. All future documents based on this template will use the selections in the Font dialog box as the default font.
Preview	N/A	Shows a sample of text formatted with selected options.

Table 9.3   The Animation Options

Group	Option	Description
Animations	(none)	Normal text. Used to remove animation.
	Blinking Background	Text blinks between normal and inverse video.
	Las Vegas Lights	Box around selected text changes between several patterns and colors.
	Marching Black Ants	Black dash-lined box around selected text appears to move in a clockwise rotation.
	Marching Red Ants	Red dash-lined box around selected text appears to move in a clockwise rotation.
	Shimmer	Text changes between normal and a distorted view.
	Sparkle Text	An array of small patterns of different colors randomly appear over top of text.
Preview	N/A	Shows a sample of text formatted with selected option.

To format characters using a menu command, follow these steps:

1. Select the text to format, or position the insertion point where you want formatting to begin.

2. Choose Format, Font. The Font dialog box appears (refer to Figures 9.2, 9.3, and 9.4).

3. Select the Font tab Character Spacing tab, or the Animation tab.

4. Select the formatting option or options you want.

5. Choose OK.

The Font dialog box tabs show formatting for the currently selected characters. If the selected text is bold, for example, the Bold option is selected in the Font style box on the Font tab. If, however, the selection includes various formatting options, no items in the list boxes will be selected and the check boxes will be checked and shaded, indicating that the selection includes mixed formats.

Because any formatting options you select apply to all the selected text, you can use the Font dialog box to turn on or off formatting for large areas of text, even if the text includes a variety of formatting.

TROUBLESHOOTING

Characters appear OK on-screen, but they don't print as shown. Use TrueType fonts in your documents. A selection of TrueType fonts come with Windows 95. In the Font list of the Font tab, TrueType fonts are preceded by a TT. TrueType fonts are designed to appear the same on-screen as they do in print. You are likely to have used a font on-screen that your printer cannot exactly reproduce. TrueType takes care of this problem. See "Using TrueType Fonts" later in this chapter for more information.

Formatting with Keyboard Shortcuts

You can use the keyboard to format characters in two ways. The first way is to press Alt+O, F to display the Font dialog box; you can use this dialog box to select character formatting options (as described in the preceding section). The second way to format characters with the keyboard is to use a shortcut key.

To format characters using shortcut keys, follow these steps:

1. Select the text to format, or position the insertion point where you want formatting to begin.

2. Press the appropriate key combination, described in the following table:

Format	Shortcut
Bold	Ctrl+B
Italic	Ctrl+I
Single underline	Ctrl+U
Word underline	Ctrl+Shift+W
Double underline	Ctrl+Shift+D
SMALL CAPS	Ctrl+Shift+K
ALL CAPS	Ctrl+Shift+A
Hidden text	Ctrl+Shift+H
Superscript	Ctrl+Shift+= (equal sign)
Subscript	Ctrl+= (equal sign)
Copy formatting	Ctrl+Shift+C

Format	Shortcut
Paste formatting	Ctrl+Shift+V
Remove formatting	Ctrl+spacebar
Change case of letters	Shift+F3
Font	Ctrl+Shift+F. This command activates the Font box in the Formatting toolbar. Type a new font name or use the arrow keys to highlight the desired font; press Enter to select it.
Symbol font	Ctrl+Shift+Q
Point size	Ctrl+Shift+P. This command activates the Point Size box in the Formatting toolbar. Type a new size or use the arrow keys to highlight the desired point size; press Enter to select it.
Next larger point size available for selected font	Ctrl+Shift+>
Next smaller point size available for selected font	Ctrl+Shift+<
Up one point size	Ctrl+]
Down one point size	Ctrl+[

See the following sections for more information about the preceding commands.

TROUBLESHOOTING

Character formatting appeared to be correct the last time the document was opened, but now the character formatting has changed. In some cases, formatting is missing. The currently selected printer may not be the printer that was selected during the document's original formatting. If the current printer is not capable of reproducing the fonts, sizes, or styles that you originally formatted, Windows shows you the best that the current printer can do. Correct this problem by reselecting a printer that is capable of printing the formats. Choose File, Print, and then select a new printer from the Name drop-down list.

Formatting with the Formatting Toolbar

The Formatting toolbar is a handy tool for quick character formatting (see Figure 9.5). You can change the style, font, color, or size of text, and format characters with bold, italic, or single underline. Paragraph formatting options also are included on the Formatting toolbar. For more details about paragraph formatting, refer to Chapter 10, "Formatting Lines and Paragraphs."

FIG. 9.5

You can select character formatting commands from the Formatting toolbar.

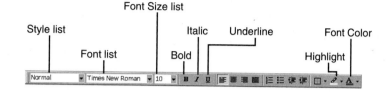

Font Size list

Style list   Italic   Underline   Font Color

Font list   Bold   Highlight

The following information provides general instructions for formatting with the Formatting toolbar; later in this section you will find more detailed instructions for using styles: bold, italic, and underline. Techniques for using the Formatting toolbar to format fonts and sizes are described in the sections "Changing Font Type" and "Changing Font Size" later in this chapter.

The Formatting toolbar first must be displayed before using it. To display the Formatting toolbar, follow this step:

Choose View, Toolbars and specify the toolbars you want to display on-screen.

To format characters using the Formatting toolbar, follow these steps:

1. Select the text to be formatted, or position the insertion point where you want formatting to begin.

2. You can choose from one of several options: select a style from the Style list, select a font from the Font list, select a select a size from the Point Size list, or select the Bold, Italic, Underline, Highlight, or Select Color button.

You can make as many of these selections as you want. For example, you can change the font and point size for the selected text and add boldfacing.

No matter how you apply formatting to text—whether you use a menu command, a shortcut, or the Formatting toolbar—the Formatting toolbar displays the formatting for that text when it is selected.

▶ **See** "Aligning Paragraphs," **p. 331**

Selecting Styles with the Formatting Toolbar   A *style* is a set of "memorized" formatting commands. Although styles apply to entire paragraphs, they often contain character formatting. Word uses the normal style to apply default formatting, but you can change the style easily.

To change the style with the mouse, follow these steps:

1. Position the insertion point inside the paragraph you want to format with a style.

2. Select a style from the Styles list box.

To change the style with a shortcut key, follow these steps:

1. Position the insertion point inside the paragraph you want to format with a style.

2. Press Ctrl+Shift+S to select the Styles list box.

3. Press the down-arrow key to drop down the list, and then press the up-arrow or down-arrow key to select the style you want.

4. Press Enter.

Even if the Formatting toolbar isn't displayed, you can apply a style by pressing Ctrl+Shift+S. The Style dialog box appears. You can select a style and then click the Apply button or press Enter. For details about creating and using styles, see Chapter 11, "Using Styles for Repetitive Formats."

▶ **See** "Creating Styles," **p. 393**

Selecting Bold, Italic, Underline, or Highlight with the Formatting Toolbar   When selected, the three-dimensional buttons on the Formatting toolbar are bright and appear pressed. Selecting a button applies (or removes) formatting to all selected text.

To apply bold, italic, or underline with the Formatting toolbar, follow these steps:

1. Select the text to be formatted, or position the insertion point where you want the formatting to begin before you enter the text.

2. Click the Bold, Italic, or Underline button to apply the formatting you want to use.

Highlighting gives you the ability to drag a highlighting marker across on-screen text. You even have the ability to choose different colors of highlighter. In the same way that you might use a real highlighter, you can use Word's highlighter to emphasize certain text. You may also want to use its different colors as a way of quickly identifying edits or comments inserted by different people.

To apply highlight with the Formatting toolbar, follow these steps:

1. Click the Highlight button so the button appears depressed. The pointer changes to a highlighting pen.

2. Drag the pointer across the text you want to highlight.

Click the Highlight button a second time or press Esc to turn off highlighting.

To change the color used for highlighting, click the down arrow on the right side of the Highlight button and drag the mouse pointer down and to the right through the displayed palette until all of the colors are displayed, position the mouse pointer over the desired color, then release the left mouse button. The Highlight color appears in the small window of the Highlight button.

Remember that these buttons toggle on and off. If you select a boldfaced word and click the Bold button, the bold formatting is removed from the selected word. If you select both a bold word and a normal word that *precedes* it and click the Bold button, both words are formatted as bold. However, if you select both a bold word and a normal word that follows it and click the Bold button, then both words are formatted as normal.

Part
II
Ch
9

TROUBLESHOOTING

There are characters in the document that were highlighted, but the highlighting color does not display. Make sure the Show Highlighting option is turned on. Choose Tools, Options; then select the View tab. Select the Highlight check box; then choose OK.

ON THE WEB

For online support from Microsoft, visit the following World Wide Web site:

http://www.microsoft.com/support

You can also access Microsoft's extensive troubleshooting KnowledgeBase at the following site:

http://www.microsoft.com/kb

For tutorials, tips, and add-ins for Microsoft Office applications point your browser to:

http://www.ronperson.com

▶ **See** "Aligning Paragraphs," **p. 331**

▶ **See** "Creating a Style by Example," **p. 394**

Changing Fonts

A *font* is a typeface style; all letters, punctuation, and other text characters of a given font have the same appearance. Three basic types of fonts exist: *serif*, with strokes at the ends of letters; *sans serif*, with no strokes; and *specialty*, such as symbols and script fonts.

Common fonts include Times Roman, a serif font; Helvetica, a sans serif font; and Zapf

FIG. 9.6

The selection of fonts available to you depends on your printer and the fonts you have purchased.

Times New Roman
Arial
Helvetica
Palatino
Bookman
ZapfChancery
Script.
Symbol: αΣψμβολ

Chancery, a script font. These and other fonts are shown in Figure 9.6.

The printer (or printers) you installed and selected determines what fonts are available for your use. An HP LaserJet, for example, may include CG Times, Univers, Courier, and Line printer. A PostScript printer usually includes Times Roman, Palatino, Bookman, New Century Schoolbook (serif fonts), Helvetica, Avant Garde (sans serif fonts), Zapf Chancery (a script font), and Zapf Dingbats (a symbol font). The selected printer determines which fonts you see listed in the Font list box. (The Font list also includes built-in Windows fonts such as the symbol fonts, Symbol and Fences.)

You can add more fonts to your printer. You can buy software fonts (which tend to print slowly) and download them to a printer, or buy font cartridges to insert into your laser printer.

Because Word and other Windows programs use printer and screen fonts, you can select screen fonts in your document that your printer cannot print. If you do, what you see on-screen isn't necessarily what you get when you print. The capability to select fonts that your printer doesn't support is handy when you want to create a document that will be printed on another printer or used by a service bureau for producing a linotype. In this case, you can select fonts that you know are supported by the other printer or service bureau, and you can see on-screen how your document will look, even though you can't obtain an accurate printout on your own printer.

To make sure that your screen displays what you will actually get when you print, follow these steps:

1. Choose Tools, Options.
2. Select the View tab.
3. Clear the Draft font check box.
4. Choose OK.

Even with the preceding procedure, lines of text may extend into the right margin, or text in a table may appear cut off at the right border of a cell. In spite of its on-screen appearance, however, text will print accurately.

Changing Font Type

You can change fonts with a menu command or from the Formatting toolbar. You can use either the mouse or the keyboard to make the change. This section includes instructions for all these methods.

 TIP You can choose <u>E</u>dit, <u>R</u>eplace (or press Ctrl+H) to search for and replace fonts (without changing the text). For details, see Chapter 7, "Using Editing and Proofing Tools."

To change the font with the mouse from the menu, follow these steps:

1. Select the text whose font you want to change, or position the insertion point where you want the new font to begin before you begin typing.
2. Choose F<u>o</u>rmat, <u>F</u>ont, press Ctrl+D, or click the right mouse button and select Font from the shortcut menu.
3. Select the Fo<u>n</u>t tab.
4. Select the font you want from the <u>F</u>ont list or type its name.
5. Choose OK.

To change the font using the Formatting toolbar, follow these steps:

1. Select the text whose font you want to change, or position the insertion point where you want the new font to begin when you begin typing.
2. Click the down arrow to the right of the Font list box, or press Ctrl+Shift+F and press the down-arrow key to display the list of fonts.
3. Select a font from the Font list box. Press Enter if you are using the keyboard.

Changing Font Size

Font sizes are measured in *points*, the traditional typesetting measuring unit. An inch consists of 72 points; thus, an inch-high letter is 72 points, and a half-inch-high letter is 36 points. Text in a book may be 10 to 12 points.

 TIP If the Formatting toolbar isn't displayed, you can change the font by pressing Ctrl+Shift+F to display the Font dialog box; then select a font or type in the font name and press Enter.

Like fonts, your printer determines what font sizes you can use. PostScript printers and HP LaserJet IV printers include scalable fonts. You can print scalable fonts from sizes as small as a barely readable 4 points to as tall as a page.

Screen fonts (fonts created without TrueType) that are included in Windows rather than in the printer don't come in all sizes, even if your printer has scalable fonts. If you change text to an odd size such as 17 points, the text looks blocklike on-screen, because Word substitutes the next closest font size for the missing screen font.

You can change font sizes in three ways: with the menu command, the Formatting toolbar, or shortcuts.

To change the font size using the menu command, follow these steps:

1. Select the text you want to resize, or position the insertion point where you want the new font size to begin when you start typing.

2. Choose Format, Font, press Ctrl+D, or click the right mouse button and select Font from the shortcut menu.

3. Select the Font tab.

4. Select the Size list.

5. Select the point size you want or type in the point size.

6. Choose OK.

The Formatting toolbar provides a quick way to change font size without using a menu command. (The Formatting toolbar must be displayed before you can use it.)

To change font size with the Formatting toolbar, follow these steps:

1. Select the text you want to resize, or position the insertion point where you want the new size to begin when you start typing.

2. Select a size from the Font Size list box by clicking the down arrow next to the font size, or press Shift+Ctrl+P and type a size or use the down-arrow key to select a size; then press Enter.

 T I P Even if the Formatting toolbar isn't displayed, you can change point size by pressing Ctrl+Shift+P to display the Font dialog box; select or type a font size and press Enter.

Another shortcut is available for increasing or decreasing point size to the next size listed in the Font Size list on the Formatting toolbar or in the Font dialog box. If sizes 9, 10, and 12 are listed, for example, you can increase 10-point text to 12 points, and you can decrease 10-point text to 9 points.

To use keyboard shortcuts to change point size, follow these steps:

1. Select the text you want to resize before you enter text, or position the insertion point where you want the new size to begin.

2. Press Ctrl+Shift+> to increase the point size, or press Ctrl+Shift+< to decrease the point size.

N O T E   You can replace a font size in your document just as you can replace text. If all of your headlines in a report are 14 points and you want to change them to 12 points, for example, you can choose <u>E</u>dit, <u>R</u>eplace to make the global change quickly (see Chapter 7, "Using Editing and Proofing Tools").

Part

II

Ch

9

Changing Languages

Microsoft has created several language (or localized) versions of Word. This enables document sharing between English and non-English speaking countries, which is especially useful given the international nature of Web and Internet communications. For example, if you receive a document written in a non-English language that requires editing, select the language from the Language dialog box to allow the use of language-specific symbols.

To change languages, follow these steps:

1. Choose <u>T</u>ools, <u>L</u>anguage, Set <u>L</u>anguage. The Language dialog box appears (see Figure 9.7).

FIG. 9.7

The Language dialog box is used to set the language in which the text is written.

2. Select the language from the <u>M</u>ark Selected Text As list.

3. Choose OK.

Notice that if you have a dictionary of the selected language, you can perform spelling and grammar checking. If not, select (no proofing) from the <u>M</u>ark Selected Text As list to skip spelling and grammar checking.

Changing the Default Character Formatting

Word uses the Normal style (contained in the Normal template) to control the default character and paragraph formatting choices for all documents. The Normal style's default type font, Times New Roman, has a default size of 10 points. If you always work with some other character formatting settings, you can apply those settings to the Normal style. Your new defaults take effect for the current document and for all future documents (but not for existing documents).

To change default character formatting, follow these steps:

1. Choose Format, Font.
2. Select the new defaults you want to use from either the Font or Character Spacing tabs.
3. Choose the Default button.
4. Click Yes to indicate that you want to change the Normal template.

If you want to immediately save these new default settings, hold the Shift key and choose File, Save All. The Save All command only appears when you hold down the Shift key as you select File.

Because you requested a change to the Normal template, when you exit Word, you see a message box asking whether you want to save changes to Word. Choose Yes.

▶ **See** "Changing a Template," **p. 210**
▶ **See** "Using Styles versus Direct Formatting," **p. 370**

Copying Formatting

If you do much repetitive character formatting, you can save some time by repeating or copying formatting between characters. You can use one of two different methods: the Edit, Repeat command and the Format Painter button.

You can choose Edit, Repeat to copy formatting immediately after you have formatted characters. The command repeats the *one* most recent edit. If you use the Font dialog box to apply several formatting choices at once, the Repeat command repeats all those choices because you made them as a single edit. But if you choose Repeat after making several formatting choices from the keyboard or with the Formatting toolbar, the command repeats only the most recent choice.

To repeat character formatting with Edit, Repeat immediately after formatting characters, follow these steps:

1. Select the new text to format.
2. Press F4, or choose Edit, Repeat.

To use this technique, you must perform it immediately after performing the edit that you want to repeat.

The Standard toolbar includes a button for copying character formatting. To copy character formatting with the Format Painter button, follow these steps:

1. Select the text whose format you want to copy.

2. Click the Format Painter button on the Standard toolbar. The mouse pointer changes to a paintbrush with an I-beam.
3. Select the text you want to change and release the mouse button. The selected text automatically takes on the new formatting when you release the mouse button.

You can copy the formatting to more than one location by double-clicking the Format Painter button in step 1, selecting the first block of text to which you want to copy the formatting, and releasing the mouse button. Then select each additional block of text to which you want to copy the formatting, and release the mouse button. When you have finished copying the formatting, click the Format Painter button again or press Esc.

If you find that the formatting you copied or added is not to your liking, you can remove all character formatting. The remaining formatting is part of the style to which the text is attached.

To remove all character formatting, follow these steps:

1. Select the text whose character formatting you want to remove.
2. Press Ctrl+spacebar.

▶ **See** "Using Paragraph Formatting Techniques," **p. 325**

Applying Special Character Formatting Options

Many formatting options are simple and straightforward: A font is a specific character set design; size is measured in points; boldfaced text is heavier than normal text. Other options, however, aren't quite so obvious, and to use them, you may need to specify some criteria that further controls the option. For example, you can specify how high you want superscript text to appear in relation to the text baseline.

All the character formatting options described in this section toggle on and off. To remove superscripting, for example, you must select the Superscripted text, choose Format, Font to access the Font dialog box, and choose Superscript again.

Changing Orientation with Text Direction

You can change text direction within a table cell, text box, or frame using either menu commands or using the Tables and Borders, Text Box, or Text Frame toolbar.

To change text direction with the menu command, follow these steps:

1. Select the text to be changed.

2. Choose Format, Text Direction. The Text Direction dialog box appears (see Figure 9.8)

FIG. 9.8
The Text Direction dialog box is used to change the text orientation within a table cell, text box, or frame.

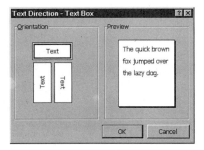

3. In the Orientation group, select the orientation you want. Notice the result in the Preview box.

4. Click OK.

To change text direction with the toolbar, follow these steps:

1. Select the text to be changed.

2. If the toolbar is not displayed, choose View, Toolbars, then select Tables and Borders or Text Box. There is no toolbar for changing text direction in a frame.

 3. Click the Change Text Direction button until text is oriented in the desired direction.

Hiding Text

At times, you may want to include in your document *hidden text*—text that disappears until you choose a command to display it. When displayed, hidden text has a dotted underline (see Figure 9.9). Hiding text doesn't affect the text formatting.

FIG. 9.9
Hidden text has a dotted underline on-screen; when printed, it has no underline.

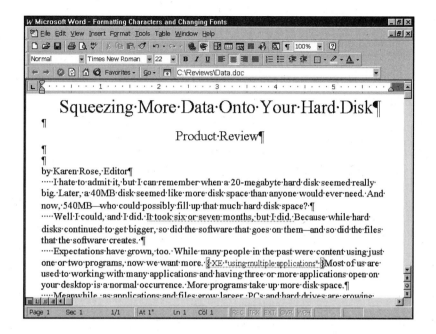

Part
II

Ch
9

You can format any text—such as notes to yourself—as hidden text. Word also uses hidden text to format table-of-contents entries, index entries (as shown in Figure 9.9), and annotations.

To hide text with the menu command, follow these steps:

1. Select the text you want to hide, or position the insertion point where you want hidden text to begin.
2. Choose Format, Font.
3. Select the Font tab.
4. Select the Hidden check box.
5. Choose OK.

To hide text with the keyboard shortcut, follow these steps:

1. Select the text you want to hide, or position the insertion point where you want hidden text to begin.
2. Press Ctrl+Shift+H.

Hide hidden text before creating indexes and tables of contents to ensure the page numbers are correct. Showing hidden text changes the page length and consequently the page numbering.

You can toggle hidden text on and off with the keyboard shortcut, as long as the text is selected. You also can display all hidden text on-screen in normal, outline, page layout, or master document views. If you intend to print hidden text, display it before you decide on final page breaks. Otherwise, page numbering and page breaks may be inaccurate.

To display hidden text, follow these steps:

1. Choose Tools, Options.
2. Select the View tab.
3. Select the Hidden Text check box (see Figure 9.10).
4. Choose OK.

FIG. 9.10

Select the Hidden text option to display hidden text on-screen.

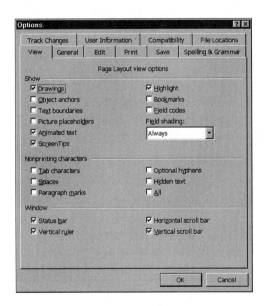

If you have not indicated that you want hidden text displayed on the Tools Options View tab, you can toggle the display of hidden text on and off with the Show/Hide ¶ button on the Standard toolbar.

To display the Standard toolbar, choose View, Toolbars, select Standard, and press Enter.

To hide and display hidden text with the Show/Hide ¶ button, click the Show/Hide button on the Standard toolbar.

You can also see hidden text by choosing File, Print Preview if you choose to print hidden text.

To print hidden text all the time, whether or not the text is displayed, follow these steps:

1. Choose Tools, Options.
2. Select the Print tab (see Figure 9.11).
3. Select the Hidden text check box.
4. Choose OK.

FIG. 9.11

Select the Hidden text option on the Tools Options Print tab to print hidden text.

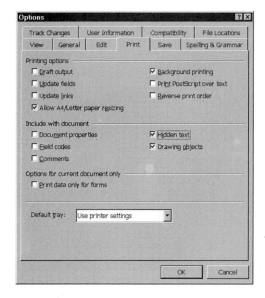

To include hidden text only when you print the current document, follow these steps:

1. Choose File, Print.
2. Click the Options button. The Tools Options Print tab appears.
3. Select the Hidden text check box.
4. Choose OK.

N O T E You can format any character as hidden text, even a page break or paragraph mark, but doing so affects the page numbering in a table of contents. For an accurate page count, remove the hidden formatting by choosing Edit, Find to locate the hidden character and remove the hidden formatting. For details about finding and replacing formatting, refer to Chapter 7, "Using Editing and Proofing Tools." ■

Highlighting Text

The Highlight feature makes it easy to highlight sections of text in up to 15 different colors, if you have a color monitor. This allows you, for example, to highlight the key points in a memo to the office staff. You also can create a color code for a documentation project: red for text that must not be changed, yellow for text that needs to be checked for accuracy, and green for text that needs further development.

To make sure that Word displays highlighted text with its highlighted color, follow these steps:

1. Choose Tools, Options.
2. Select the View tab.
3. Select the Highlight check box (see Figure 9.12).
4. Choose OK.

FIG. 9.12

Select the Highlight option on the Tools Options View tab to display highlighted text.

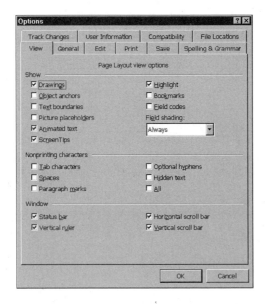

To actually highlight text, follow these steps:

1. Click the Highlight palette button that appears on the Formatting toolbar (refer to Figure 9.5). The pointer changes into a highlighting pen.
2. Drag across the text you want to highlight.

Click the Highlight button a second time or press Esc to turn off highlighting.

To change the highlighting color, follow these steps:

1. Click the down arrow to the right side of the Highlight button.
2. Position the mouse pointer over the desired color, then click the mouse button. The Highlight color appears in the small window of the Highlight button.

To remove highlighting from text, select the highlighted text and click the Highlight button.

Changing Character Colors

If you have a color monitor, you can make good use of the 16 different colors available for text in Word 97. On an office task list, for example, you can format each person's duties in a different color so that every employee can easily see who must do which job. You also can format different levels of priority as different colors: for example, red items must be done right away; blue can wait. If you have a color printer, you can print text in color.

To color text with the menu commands, follow these steps:

1. Select the text to color, or position the insertion point where you want the new color to begin.
2. Choose Format, Font.
3. Select the Font tab.
4. Select a color from the Color list.
5. Choose OK.

Auto color, also listed in the Color list, is the color you select for Window Text in the Colors section of the Control Panel. Auto color is usually black.

To color text with the Formatting toolbar, follow these steps:

1. Click the down arrow to the right side of the Font Color button.
2. Position the pointer over the color you want then click the mouse button. The color selection is displayed in the Font Color button.

After selecting the font color you want, further color changes can be made by simply selecting the text or number and clicking the Font Color button. Notice that color changes only apply to selected text.

Making Superscript and Subscript Text

Sometimes you may need to use subscripts and superscripts. You may use these features in scientific notations (for example, H_2O) or in references such as trademark or copyright symbols (for example, Microsoft®).

In calculating where superscripts and subscripts appear in relation to normal text, Word begins with the text baseline. You use the same procedure to add and remove both superscripts and subscripts.

To add or remove superscripts and subscripts, follow these steps:

1. Select the text you want to raise or lower, or position the insertion point where you want raised or lowered text to begin.
2. Choose Format, Font.
3. Select the Font tab.
4. In the Effects group, select Superscript to raise text, or select Subscript to lower text. A ✔ indicates that the feature is active.
5. Choose OK.

By default, Word raises superscript three points above the baseline and lowers subscript three points below the baseline. You can change the vertical position of superscript, subscript, or any text or graphic in the Font dialog box on the Character Spacing tab.

To change the vertical position of text, follow these steps:

1. Select the text you want to raise or lower.
2. Choose Format, Font.
3. Select the Character Spacing tab.
4. Choose Raised or Lowered from the Position box.

 TIP To superscript text by three points, select the text and press Shift+Ctrl+= (equal sign). To subscript text by three points, select the text and press Ctrl+= (equal sign).

5. In the By box, accept 3 points as the default distance to raise or lower text, click the up or down arrows to change the distance, or type a new amount.
6. Choose OK.

Underlining Text

Word 97 offers nine types of underlines:

- *Single.* Underlines words and the space between words.
- *Words only.* Underlines words but not the space between words.
- *Double.* Double-underlines words and the space between words.
- *Dotted.* Underlines with dots the words and the space between words.
- *Thick.* Underlines with a thick line the words and the space between words.
- *Dash.* Underlines with dashes the words and the space between words.
- *Dot dash.* Underlines with dot dashes the words and the space between words.
- *Dot dot dash.* Underlines with dot dot dashes the words and the space between words.
- *Wave.* Underlines with waves the words and the space between words. To add underlining from the menu command, follow these steps:

  1. Select the text you want to underline, or position the insertion point where you want underlining to begin.
  2. Choose Format, Font.
  3. Select the Font tab.
  4. In the Underline list box, select Single, Words Only, Double, Dotted, Thick, Dash, Dot Dash, Dot Dot Dash, or Wave.
  5. Choose OK.

> **TIP** To place an underline below a superscript only, select the superscript—not the surrounding text—before issuing the Underline command. Subscripted text is always underlined just below the subscripted characters.

To remove underlining with the menu command, follow these steps:

1. Select the underlined text.
2. Choose Format, Font.
3. Select the Font tab.
4. Select (none) from the Underline list box.
5. Choose OK.

To add or remove underlining with shortcut keys, follow these steps:

1. Select the text you want to underline or the text from which you want to remove underlining. Or position the insertion point where you want underlining to begin when you start typing.

2. Press one of the following shortcut keys:

Shortcut	Result
Ctrl+U	Single underline
Ctrl+Shift+W	Single underline, words only
Ctrl+Shift+D	Double underline

To use the Formatting toolbar to add or remove underlining, follow these steps:

1. Select the text you want to underline or the text from which you want to remove underlining, or position the insertion point where you want underlining to begin when you start typing.

2. Click the Underline button on the Formatting toolbar.

Adjusting Character Spacing

The normal spacing between letters in a word is right for most situations. Occasionally, however, you must fit more text on a line. Condensing the line can make the text fit. Sometimes, such as in large headlines, you also must condense the space between two individual letters to improve the headline's appearance. This process is known as *kerning*. The change in spacing is determined by the font design and the particular pair of letters being kerned.

In other instances, you may want to increase the space between letters to fill out a line or to create a special effect. Expanding makes text wider. For examples of condensed and expanded text, see Figure 9.13.

FIG. 9.13
Use condensed and expanded text to change the spacing between characters.

By default, Word expands and condenses the spacing between characters by three points. You can change the distance in increments of 0.1 of a point. You need this level of precision for kerning.

In the Font dialog box's Character Spacing tab, watch the Preview box to see how your text looks after condensing or expanding.

To condense or expand the space between characters, follow these steps:

1. Select the text you want to condense or expand, or position the insertion point where you want condensed or expanded text to begin when you start typing.
2. Choose Format, Font.
3. Select the Character Spacing tab.
4. In the Spacing box, select Expanded or Condensed.
5. In the By box, accept the default, click the up or down arrows to increase or decrease the amount, or type a new amount.
6. Choose OK.

N O T E If you select the Kerning for Fonts option in the Character Spacing tab of the Font dialog box, Word automatically adjusts the kerning for TrueType or Adobe Type Manager fonts. You can specify the point size at and above which you want automatic kerning to be applied in the Points and above box. ▓

To return expanded or condensed text to normal, follow these steps:

1. Select the text you want to return to normal, or position the insertion point where you want normal text to begin.
2. Choose Format, Font.
3. Select the Character Spacing tab.
4. In the Spacing box, select Normal.
5. Choose OK.

Switching Character Case

You can use a Word shortcut to change letters from uppercase to lowercase, or vice versa (the result depends on the case of selected text).

To change the letter case from the menu command, follow these steps:

1. Select the text whose case you want to change, or position the insertion point in or to the left of the word whose case you want to change.
2. Choose Format, Change Case. The Change Case box appears (see Figure 9.14).

FIG. 9.14
Choose Format, Change Case to alter letter case quickly.

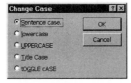

3. Select a case-change option from the following:

Option	Result
Sentence case	First character of the sentence to uppercase, all other characters to lowercase
lowercase	All lowercase
UPPERCASE	All uppercase
Title Case	First character of each word to uppercase, all other characters to lowercase
tOGGLE cASE	Switches uppercase to lowercase and lowercase to uppercase

4. Choose OK.

To change the letter case from the keyboard, follow these steps:

1. Select the text whose case you want to change, or position the insertion point in or to the left of the word whose case you want to change.

2. Press Shift+F3 to change the case. You can toggle among three options: all upper-case, all lowercase, or first character uppercase. Continue to press Shift+F3 until the case appears as you want it.

N O T E The terms *uppercase* and *lowercase* come from the days when type was set by hand from individual letters molded from lead. The capital letters were stored in the upper case above where the typesetters assembled their text, and noncapital letters were stored in the lower case. ▨

Starting Paragraphs with a Drop Cap

You can add visual interest to a paragraph by starting it with a *drop cap*, a large capital letter or first word that is set into a paragraph. The top of the drop cap or word aligns with the top of the first line of the paragraph. Succeeding lines are indented to allow space for the dropped text. Drop caps usually mark the beginnings of key sections or major parts of a document.

If you select a different font for the drop cap, choose one that blends with the rest of the paragraph. Sans serif initial letters should be used with sans serif paragraphs; serif drop caps go well with paragraphs in serif fonts. Alternatively, you may combine an elegant script or cursive drop cap with a paragraph in a serif font. Figures 9.15 and 9.16 illustrate some uses of drop caps.

FIG. 9.15
A drop cap can use the same font as the body text.

When you select a drop cap format, Word places the selected text in a frame. The rest of the paragraph wraps beside the frame.

N O T E To increase horizontal spacing between the drop cap and the body text, follow these steps. Select the drop cap. A frame will show around the drop cap when it is selected. Next choose Format, Frame. In the Frame dialog box that displays, increase the Horizontal Distance From Text to approximately 0.1". You may want to experiment with this distance. Choose OK. ▨

To create large dropped capital letters, follow these steps:

1. Select the first letter, word, or segment of the paragraph you want to format as a dropped cap.

2. Choose Format, Drop Cap. The Drop Cap dialog box appears (see Figure 9.17).

FIG. 9.16
A drop cap can use a decorative font to enhance the text.

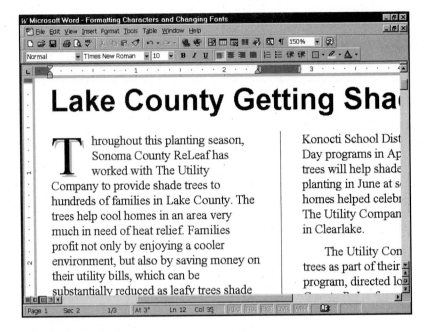

FIG. 9.17
You can design drop caps by choosing Format, Drop Cap.

3. Select <u>D</u>ropped or In <u>M</u>argin in the Position group to place the drop cap as follows:

Option	Result
<u>D</u>ropped	Dropped flush with the left margin, inside the main text area
In <u>M</u>argin	Dropped in the left margin

4. Select a font from the <u>F</u>ont box.

5. In the <u>L</u>ines to Drop text box, type or select the number of lines you want the capital to drop into the paragraph. The default is 3.

6. In the Distance from Text text box, type or select the distance you want between the drop cap and the paragraph text.

7. Choose OK.

   If you are in normal view, Word asks whether you want to switch to page layout view to see the dropped cap as it will appear in print.

   Click the Yes button to switch to page layout view.

To remove dropped capital letters, follow these steps:

1. Select the first letter, word, or segment of the paragraph from which you want to remove the drop cap.

2. Choose Format, Drop Cap.

3. Select the None option from the Position group.

4. Choose OK.

▶ **See** "Working with Frames," **p. 890**

The drop cap text is inserted into a frame and can be resized and repositioned.

Inserting Special Characters and Symbols

You can include many special characters in your document. Symbol fonts such as Symbol and Zapf Dingbats, for example, contain *dingbats* (decorative characters such as bullets, stars, and flowers) and scientific symbols. You can use foreign language characters such as umlauts (¨) and tildes (˜), or ANSI characters such as bullets (•) and *em dashes* (—), wide hyphens used in punctuation. You can also use invisible characters such as discretionary hyphens (which appear only when needed) and nonbreaking spaces (which prevent two words from separating at the end of a line).

Two techniques give you access to special characters. You can use the Symbol dialog box, which shows a keyboard of special characters to choose from, or you can use a series of special keystrokes.

Using the Symbol Dialog Box

The Symbol dialog box, shown in Figure 9.18, gives you access to symbol fonts and ANSI characters. A symbol font, Symbol, is included with Word. Other symbol fonts may be built into your printer; for example, most PostScript printers include Zapf Dingbats. ANSI characters are the regular character set that you see on your keyboard, plus another hundred or so characters that include a copyright symbol, a registered trademark symbol, and many foreign language symbols.

FIG. 9.18

You can insert symbols from the Symbol dialog box.

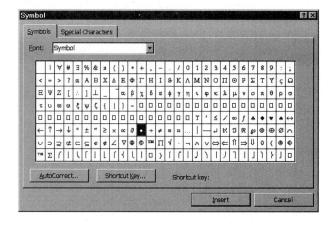

To insert symbols from the Symbol dialog box, follow these steps:

1. Position the insertion point where you want the symbol to appear.

2. Choose Insert, Symbol.

   The Symbol dialog box appears.

3. From the Font list box, select the font for which you want to see symbols. (Select Normal Text to see ANSI characters.)

4. Click a symbol to select it or to see it enlarged, or press Tab until the highlighted symbol in the box is selected (surrounded by a dotted outline), and then press the arrow keys to move the selection to the symbol you want.

5. Click the Insert button.

6. Insert more characters by repeating steps 3 through 5.

7. Choose the Close button.

Be sure to scan through all the interesting and useful symbols available in the Symbol and the Normal Text fonts.

Inserted symbols are actually field codes embedded in your document. This arrangement prevents you from accidentally selecting your symbol and changing it to a different font. Changing a symbol's font can change the symbol into a letter; for example, if you format text as Zapf Dingbats to include square bullets in your document, and then change the bullets to Times Roman, the bullet turns into n.

To delete an inserted symbol, you can position the insertion point to the right of the symbol and press Backspace. You can also follow these steps:

1. Select the symbol you want to delete.

2. Press the Delete key.

Customizing the Symbol Dialog Box

You may insert certain symbols, such as the copyright or trademark symbols, frequently in your work. You can customize the Symbol dialog box by adding shortcut keys. You then can use the shortcut keys to insert symbols directly from the keyboard.

To add shortcut keys to the Symbol dialog box, follow these steps:

1. Choose Insert, Symbol.

2. Click the symbol for which you want to add a shortcut key.

3. Click the Shortcut Key button. The Customize Keyboard dialog box, shown in Figure 9.19, appears. The symbol you have selected is displayed in the Symbol box.

Part
II
Ch
9

FIG. 9.19
You can add shortcut keys to symbols in the Customize Keyboard dialog box.

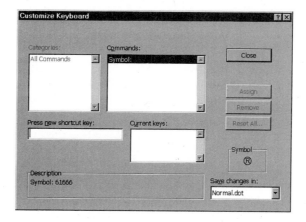

4. Press the shortcut key combination you want to assign to the symbol. The shortcut you choose appears in the Press New Shortcut Key box. You can choose from any of the following key combinations:

Key Combination	Comments
Ctrl+ any letter or single digit	Most are previously assigned by Word
Ctrl+Shift+ any letter or single digit	Many are previously assigned by Word
Alt+ any letter or single digit	Most are not assigned
Alt+Shift+ any letter or single digit	Most are not assigned

5. Click the Assign button.

6. Click the Close button.

7. Repeat steps 2 through 6 for any additional symbols you want to assign a shortcut key.

8. Click the Close button.

Inserting Special Characters from the Keyboard

You can insert special characters from the keyboard in two ways: by using shortcut keys you assign in the Symbol dialog box (see the preceding section) or by using the ANSI character numbers. You must know the ANSI character numbers for the corresponding character or symbols you want.

To insert ANSI characters from the keyboard, follow these steps:

1. Position the insertion point where you want the symbol to appear.

2. Press Num Lock on the numeric keypad (so that numbers appear when you type).

3. Hold down the Alt key and, on the numeric keypad, type **0** (zero) followed by the ANSI code for the symbol you want. To type the fraction $1/4$, for example, press Alt+**0188** on the numeric keypad.

▶ **See** "Hyphenating Words," **p. 163**

▶ **See** "Customizing the Toolbars, Menus, and Shortcut Keys," **p. 1139**

If you have a symbol font such as Zapf Dingbats, or if you want to use a special character from the Symbol font, you can type and format the corresponding character with the Zapf Dingbats or Symbol font. To type a solid square (■), for example, you can type and format the letter n as Zapf Dingbats.

Using TrueType Fonts

Most applications that run in Windows 95 use TrueType fonts. A type of built-in font-generation software, *TrueType* generates screen and printer fonts so that what you see on-screen is almost exactly the same as what prints, whether you have a laser or a dot-matrix printer.

When you choose Format, Font and select the Font tab, the fonts available with your printer appear in the Font list with printer icons next to them. TrueType fonts are listed with a TT icon next to them (see Figure 9.20). After you select a new font from the Font list, read the description of the font below the Preview box. The information in this box describes the type of font you have selected and how it affects printing.

FIG. 9.20

Printer fonts appear
with a printer icon and
a description of their
behavior.

Printer font
icon

TrueType
icon

Font
description

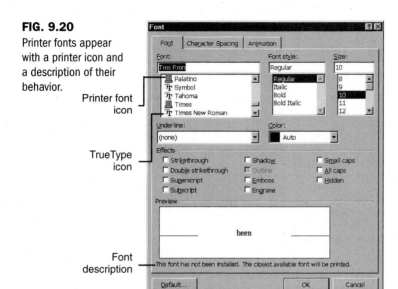

You also can use screen fonts that don't match any font in your printer. Because the
printer has no matching font, however, Windows selects a similar type and size of font
when you print. In some cases, the printer font may be similar to the screen font; in others, it may be very different. Screen fonts that don't match a printer font appear in the
Font list without an icon.

TrueType fonts give you a wide range of sizes and styles, and you can purchase additional
typefaces designed for TrueType. The disadvantage of using TrueType fonts is that the
generation time needed to create the screen fonts and download the characters slows
system performance slightly. This slowing is only noticeable, however, on older
systems. ●

CHAPTER 10

Formatting Lines and Paragraphs

In writing, a paragraph is a series of sentences linked together to convey a single thought or idea, or to describe a single image. In Word 97, the definition of a paragraph is less lyrical: A *paragraph* is any amount of text—or no text at all—that ends when you press Enter. A paragraph may be the title of a story, an item in a list, a blank line between other paragraphs, or a series of sentences linked together to convey a single thought or idea.

The paragraph mark that ends a paragraph is normally hidden from view, but it stores all the paragraph formatting for the paragraph that it ends. Paragraph formatting includes such things as centering or aligning, shading and bordering, hanging indents, and more. When you delete the paragraph mark at the end of a paragraph, the paragraph takes on the paragraph formatting of the next paragraph mark in the document.

Aligning paragraphs

Paragraphs can be left-aligned, centered, right-aligned, or justified using menu commands, the formatting toolbar, or with keyboard shortcuts.

Setting tabs and indents

Tab stops are set prior to using them. Tab styles can be selected including left, centered, right, decimal, or bar. Unlike margins, which apply to an entire document, you can change indents for specific paragraphs.

Numbering lines

Add line numbers to sections of a document or to the entire document.

Adjusting line and paragraph spacing

Space between lines and paragraphs can be adjusted to your needs.

Adding shading and borders to paragraphs

Shading and borders can be added to paragraphs to enhance the look of your document.

Whatever its contents, a paragraph, once selected, can be formatted in a variety of ways. The Word paragraph formatting options cover a wide range of features that enable you to communicate your thoughts visually, as well as through your choice of words.

Paragraph formatting is useful in many ways, including

- Centering headings
- Creating hanging indents for numbered and bulleted lists
- Aligning columns of text using the Tab command ■

Understanding Paragraph Formats

In Word, a paragraph is also a formatting unit. Just as you format individual characters with character formatting options, such as bold and italic, you can format paragraphs with paragraph, tab, and border formatting options, such as the following:

- *Alignment.* Line up the text of a paragraph to the left, center, right, or both margins.
- *Indents.* Indent the left edge, right edge, or first line of a paragraph.
- *Tabs.* Create columns of text that line up perfectly and can be adjusted easily.
- *Spacing.* Add spaces between lines and paragraphs.
- *Lines, borders, and shading.* Add graphic interest to paragraphs with lines next to paragraphs, borders surrounding paragraphs, and shading to fill a border.

New paragraphs formed when you press Enter carry over the formatting from the previous paragraph. After you format a paragraph, you can continue that format into subsequent paragraphs simply by pressing Enter (see Figures 10.1 and 10.2).

Paragraph formatting affects the entire paragraph and is stored in the paragraph mark that ends each paragraph. If you delete the paragraph mark between paragraphs, the text preceding the mark becomes part of the following paragraph. What was the second paragraph takes on the formatting of the first paragraph, as shown in Figures 10.3 and 10.4.

ON THE WEB

For online support from Microsoft, visit the following World Wide Web site:

http://www.microsoft.com/support

You can also access Microsoft's extensive troubleshooting KnowledgeBase at the following site:

http://www.microsoft.com/kb

For tutorials, tips, and add-ins for Microsoft Office applications point your browser to:

http://www.ronperson.com

FIG. 10.1

The formatting is specified in the first paragraph of this document.

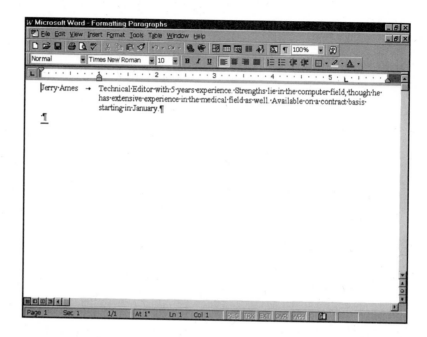

FIG. 10.2

When you press Enter, the paragraph formatting is carried forward to the new paragraph. Paragraph formatting is stored in the paragraph marks, shown in this figure.

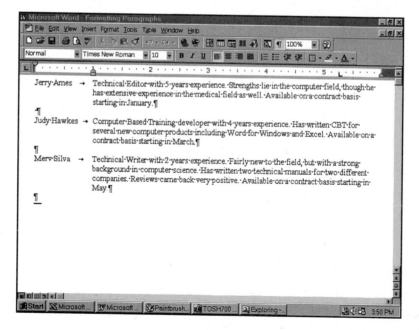

Part
II

Ch
10

FIG. 10.3

Display paragraph marks to avoid accidentally including them with selected text.

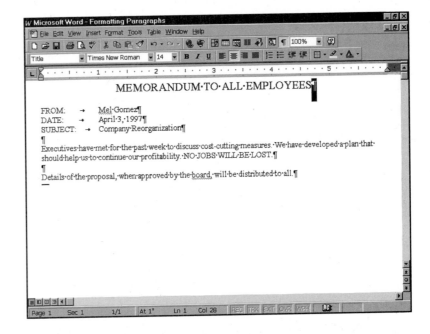

FIG. 10.4

Delete the paragraph mark between paragraphs and the following paragraph takes on the format and style of the first.

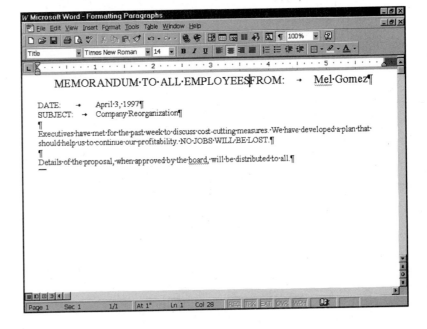

Displaying Paragraph Marks

When paragraph marks are hidden, you don't see them at the end of a paragraph. You can display paragraph marks, however (refer to Figure 10.4). If you expect to do much text editing, you should display paragraph marks to avoid accidentally deleting one of them and thereby losing your paragraph formatting.

To display paragraph marks from the menu, follow these steps:

1. Choose Tools, Options.
2. Select the View tab.
3. Choose Paragraph Marks under Nonprinting characters.

¶ To display paragraph marks from the keyboard, press Ctrl+Shift+8.

To display paragraph marks from the Standard toolbar, click the Show/Hide ¶ button on the Standard toolbar.

> **N O T E** If you turn on paragraph marks by choosing Tools, Options, then selecting the Paragraph Marks check box, you can turn on and off the display of tabs and spaces only by clicking the Show/Hide ¶ button. Paragraph marks remain on. ▪

Part
II

Ch
10

Using Paragraph Formatting Techniques

Every new document you create based on the default Normal template is controlled by the Normal style. The Normal style formats paragraphs as left-aligned and single-spaced, with left-aligned tab stops every half inch. If you usually choose different paragraph formatting selections, change the Normal style to reflect your preferences.

▶ **See** "Applying Paragraph Styles," **p. 390**

You can format a paragraph at two times: before you begin typing and after you finish typing. To format after typing, you must select the paragraph or paragraphs you want to format. If you are formatting only one paragraph instead of selecting the entire paragraph, you can position the insertion point anywhere inside the paragraph before making your formatting selections. Paragraph formatting commands apply to the entire paragraph.

▶ **See** "Selecting Text," **p. 156**

Word offers several alternative techniques for formatting paragraphs:

- ▪ Choose Format, Paragraph to select many formatting options at once and to get the widest possible range of paragraph formatting options.

■ Select the Formatting toolbar to access paragraph formatting commands individually.

■ Use the ruler to set tabs and indents quickly.

With keyboard shortcuts, you can format as you type. Figures 10.5 and 10.6 show examples of selecting and formatting text from the Formatting toolbar.

FIG. 10.5

Select the paragraphs you want to format.

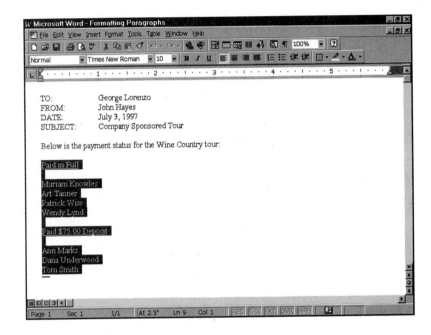

Formatting Paragraphs with Menu Commands

 You also can access the Paragraph dialog box by clicking the right mouse button and choosing Paragraph from the shortcut menu.

The Paragraph dialog box offers the greatest number of options for formatting paragraphs and shows a sample of how the formatting you choose affects your paragraph in the Preview box (see Figure 10.7). You can choose the Indents and Spacing tab to change indentation, spacing, and alignment, or you can choose the Line and Page Breaks tab to change pagination and suppress line numbers and hyphenation. Because the Paragraph dialog box provides quick access to the Tabs dialog box, you also can do quite a bit of formatting at once by choosing Format, Paragraph. See Chapter 13, "Formatting the Page Layout, Alignment, and Numbering," for more details on pagination.

FIG. 10.6
Click the button for the formatting you want. The Center button is selected in this example, and the selected text is centered.

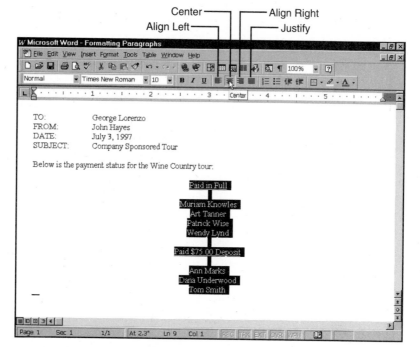

FIG. 10.7
Use the Paragraph dialog box to change the formatting of the selected text or the paragraph that contains the insertion point.

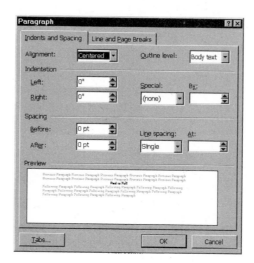

Specific instructions on using the Paragraph dialog box for setting indentation, spacing, and pagination options appear throughout this chapter.

Part
II

Ch
10

Formatting Paragraphs with Shortcut Keys

You can choose from several shortcut keys for quick formatting changes, which you can make directly from the keyboard. To use a shortcut key for formatting, first select the paragraph or paragraphs you want to change or place the insertion point in the paragraph you want to change, then choose one of the following commands:

To Do This	Press
Left-align text	Ctrl+L
Center text	Ctrl+E
Right-align text	Ctrl+R
Justify text	Ctrl+J
Indent from left margin	Ctrl+M
Create a hanging indent out one tab stop	Ctrl+T
Reduce a hanging indent by one tab stop	Ctrl+Shift+T
Single-space text	Ctrl+1
Change to 1.5 line spacing	Ctrl+5
Double-space text	Ctrl+2
Add 12 points of space before a paragraph	Ctrl+0 (zero)
Remove space before a paragraph	Ctrl+Shift+0 (zero)
Remove paragraph formatting that isn't part of the paragraph's assigned style	Ctrl+Q
Restore default formatting (from the Normal style)	Ctrl+Shift+N

Formatting Paragraphs with the Formatting Toolbar

The Word Formatting toolbar, shown in Figure 10.8, provides a quick way to choose certain paragraph formatting options using the mouse. Default paragraph formatting buttons on the Formatting toolbar include buttons for creating numbered lists and bulleted lists, indenting and unindenting, and controlling a paragraph's alignment. You also can access a special toolbar for creating lines and borders in your document.

 TIP Displaying toolbars is optional but useful if you do a lot of formatting. If you want more tyoing space on-screen, however, remove the toolbar by placing the mouse pointer between buttons or list boxes, clicking the right mouse button, then clicking the name of the toolbar in the drop-down list.

FIG. 10.8
You can change the format of selected paragraphs from the Formatting toolbar.

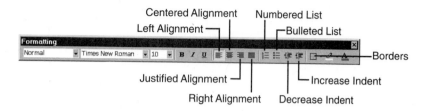

To use the Formatting toolbar for alignment, follow these steps:

1. Select the paragraph or paragraphs you want to align, or place the insertion point in the paragraph you want to align.

2. Choose the appropriate alignment button: Left, Center, Right, or Justify (both margins aligned).

N O T E You can add any button to the toolbar to either fill in blank spaces on the toolbar or replace existing buttons. ■

▶ **See** "Assigning a Command or Macro to a Toolbar Button," **p. 1149**

Formatting Paragraphs with the Ruler

The *ruler*, shown in Figure 10.9, is useful for quickly setting paragraph indentations and tabs with a click of the mouse. By default, tabs are left-aligned; if you want a different tab style, you must select that style and then position the tab on the ruler.

FIG. 10.9
The ruler provides quick access to some formatting options.

Displaying the ruler, like the toolbar, is also optional. To display or remove the ruler, choose <u>V</u>iew, <u>R</u>uler. The Ruler command has a check mark to its left when displayed. Choose the command again to remove the ruler.

T I P Displaying the ruler can speed up formatting if you have a mouse; however, removing the ruler gives you more room on-screen.

▶ **See** "Controlling Your Document's Appearance On-Screen," **p. 132**

The sections "Setting Tabs" and "Setting Indents," later in this chapter, discuss using ruler options.

Part
II

Ch
10

Duplicating Formats

The easiest way to duplicate paragraph formatting is to carry the formatting forward as you type. As you arrive at the end of the current paragraph and press Enter, the current paragraph ends and a new one begins—using the same formatting as the preceding paragraph. If, however, you use the mouse or arrow keys to move out of the current paragraph, you move into a different paragraph, which may have different formatting.

Another way to duplicate formatting is to choose Edit, Repeat, or press F4. Remember that the Repeat command duplicates only your most recent action. The command works best when you format with the Paragraph, Tabs, or Borders dialog box, making multiple formatting choices at once.

To duplicate paragraph formatting using a mouse, follow these steps:

1. Select the text containing the formatting you want to duplicate.

2. Click the Format Painter button in the Standard toolbar. The pointer changes to a combination insertion point and paintbrush.

3. Drag across the text you want formatted.

When you release the mouse button, the text over which you dragged changes to the copied format.

To duplicate paragraph formatting from the keyboard, follow these steps:

1. Select the paragraph whose format you want to copy.

2. Press Ctrl+Shift+C.

3. Select the paragraph(s) whose format you want to change.

4. Press Ctrl+Shift+V.

Probably the most powerful way to duplicate paragraph formatting is to use styles. A *style* is a set of formatting commands that you can apply all at once and can change globally later. Styles are easy to use and create—especially when you use the "styles by example" technique. Styles are explained in detail in Chapter 11, "Using Styles for Repetitive Formats."

If you deleted a paragraph mark and you need to reapply the previous formatting, reformat it or copy a paragraph mark from a paragraph that has the formatting you want to apply, and paste it at the end of the problem paragraph.

 TIP To avoid deleting a paragraph mark inadvertently, turn on paragraph marks by clicking the paragraph mark button at the right end of the Standard toolbar. Or turn on paragraph marks by choosing Tools, Options and selecting the Paragraph Marks option in the View tab.

TROUBLESHOOTING

I set up formatting in a paragraph and then moved to the next paragraph, but the formatting didn't carry over. You must press the Enter key at the end of the paragraph whose formatting you want to carry over to a new paragraph. If there is already a paragraph mark following the formatted paragraph and you use the mouse or arrow keys to move into this paragraph, the new paragraph will not necessarily have the same formatting as the previous paragraph.

Aligning Paragraphs

Part

II

Ch

10

Paragraph alignment refers to how the left and right edges of a paragraph line up (see Figure 10.10). *Left-aligned* paragraphs line up on the left edge but are ragged on the right (the Word default). Left-aligned text is commonly used in informal letters or in the body text in a book, such as this book. *Right-aligned* paragraphs line up on the right edge but are ragged on the left. Right-aligned text can be used in headers and footers in a document—for example, page numbering—or when you are creating a list and want the items in the right column to line up along the right margin. *Centered* paragraphs are ragged on both edges and centered between the margins. Centered paragraphs are most often used for headings. *Justified* paragraphs are aligned on both edges and are often used in formal business letters and in text that appears in columns, as in a newsletter.

FIG. 10.10

You can choose from four styles of alignment: left, centered, right, and justified.

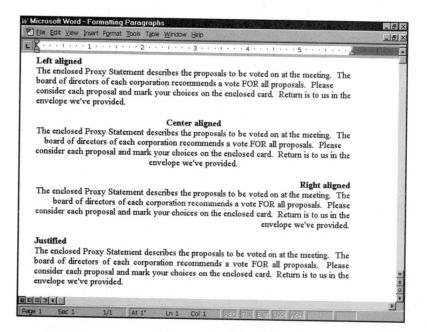

Paragraphs are aligned to the margins if no indentations are set for them. If paragraphs are indented, they align to the indentation.

You can set paragraph alignment while you're typing or editing your document. If you set alignment as you type, the alignment carries forward when you press Enter (as do all paragraph formatting selections). If you set alignment later, your setting applies only to the selected paragraph or paragraphs.

Aligning with Menu Commands

You can choose Format, Paragraph to set alignment with a mouse or your keyboard.

 T I P To justify the last line of a paragraph, end the line with a soft return, Shift+Enter, rather than Enter.

To set alignment using the menu command, follow these steps:

1. Select the paragraph or paragraphs to align, or position the insertion point where you want the new alignment to begin.
2. Choose Format, Paragraph. The Paragraph dialog box appears.
3. Select the Alignment option from the Indents and Spacing tab.
4. Select Left, Centered, Right, or Justified from the Alignment pull-down list, as shown in Figure 10.11.
5. Click OK.

FIG. 10.11
You can choose paragraph alignment from the Alignment list box in the Paragraph dialog box.

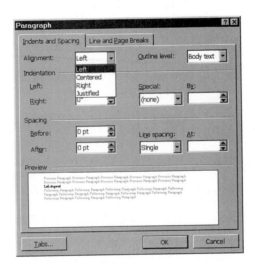

> **N O T E** You can choose formatting commands from the shortcut menu. Select the text you want to format, click the right mouse button, and choose Paragraph. The Paragraph dialog box appears. ■

Aligning with the Formatting Toolbar

If you have a mouse, a quicker way to set alignment is to display the Formatting toolbar and click the appropriate alignment button. If the Formatting toolbar isn't displayed, choose <u>V</u>iew, <u>T</u>oolbars, and specify the toolbar(s) you want to display.

 ▶ **See** "Using the Toolbars," **p. 52**

  To align paragraphs with the Formatting toolbar, follow these steps:

1. Select the paragraph or paragraphs to align, or position the insertion point where you want the new alignment to begin.
2. Click the Align Left, Center, Align Right, or Justify Alignment button.

Aligning with Keyboard Shortcuts

One of the quickest ways to align selected paragraphs is to use keyboard shortcuts. With this technique, you also can save screen space by not displaying the Formatting toolbar.

To align paragraphs using keyboard shortcuts, follow these steps:

1. Select the paragraph or paragraphs to align, or position the insertion point where you want the new alignment to begin.
2. Press the appropriate Ctrl+key combination:

Paragraph Alignment	Shortcut
Left	Ctrl+L
Centered	Ctrl+E
Right	Ctrl+R
Justified	Ctrl+J

 TROUBLESHOOTING

When I insert a page break immediately after a justified paragraph, Word justifies the words in the last line of the paragraph, resulting in very wide spacing between the words. This problem occurs because the insertion point is located at the end of the justified paragraph when you insert the page break. Be sure to press Enter at the end of the paragraph before you insert the page break.

Setting Tabs

Working with tabs is a two-part process. First, you must set the tab stops, or you must plan to use the Word default left-aligned tab stops at every 0.5". Setting the tab stops includes selecting the type of tab—left, centered, right, decimal, or bar—and specifying where the tab stops must appear. The second step in using tabs is to press the Tab key as you type your document to move the insertion point forward to the next tab stop. You also have three leader style options including dotted, dashed, or solid.

A wonderful advantage to working with tabs is that after the tabs are in your document, you can move or change the tab stops, and the selected text moves or realigns with the stops.

You can set tabs in one of two ways. You can use the Tabs dialog box, which gives you precise control over where each tab is to appear and enables you to customize tabs by adding tab leaders. Alternatively, you can use the ruler to select a tab style and then to set the tab's position using the mouse.

 TIP   When you work with a table or list made up of tabs, displaying the tab characters in your document is helpful. The tab characters appear as right-pointing arrows.

 To display the tab characters from the Standard toolbar, click the Show/Hide ¶ button at the right end of the Standard toolbar. To display the tab characters using menu commands, follow these steps:

1. Choose Tools, Options.
2. Select the View tab.
3. Select the Tab Characters option from the Nonprinting characters group.

You must understand that, like all paragraph formatting options, tabs belong to paragraphs. If you set tab stops as you type text and then press Enter, the tab settings are carried forward to the next paragraph. If you add tabs later, however, they apply only to the paragraph or paragraphs selected when you set the tab stops.

Figure 10.12 shows how each of the different tab styles affects the text to which they're applied; Figure 10.13 shows the three different tab leader styles.

Although tabs are useful for lists, menus, tables of contents, and anything requiring tab leaders, a table sometimes works better for lists. A table contains *cells* formed by rows and columns, and it is the best choice when you have many columns or when the text in each cell varies in length.

FIG. 10.12
You can select from five tab styles: left, centered, right, decimal, or bar. This example includes bar tabs set between and around the other tab styles.

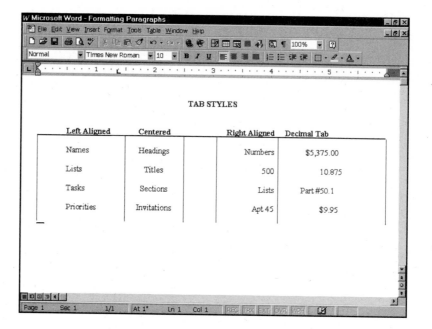

FIG. 10.13
Use any of the three leader styles to "lead" the eye to tabbed text.

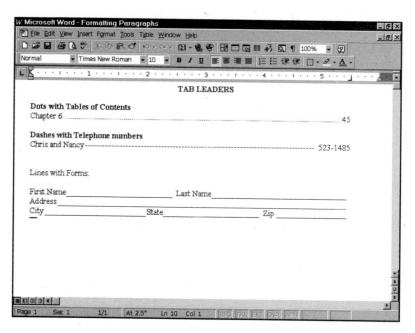

▶ **See** "Creating Tables," **p. 608**
▶ **See** "Formatting a Table," **p. 637**

Part
II

Ch
10

Using the Tabs Dialog Box

Using the Tabs dialog box to set tabs has several advantages. You can set each tab's position precisely by typing in decimal numbers, and you can add dotted, dashed, or underlined tab leaders. (A *tab leader* "leads" up to tabbed text on the left side; refer to Figure 10.13.) With a mouse or a keyboard, you can quickly clear existing tabs and change the default tab settings for the rest of your document. You can even reformat existing tabs.

To set tabs using the menu command, follow these steps:

1. Select the paragraph or paragraphs for which you want to set tabs, or position the insertion point where you want the tab settings to begin.

2. Choose Format, Tabs. The Tabs dialog box appears, as shown in Figure 10.14.

FIG. 10.14

You can set tabs at precise locations and include leaders from the Tabs dialog box.

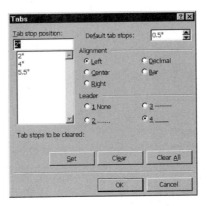

3. Using decimal numbers, type the position of the tab stop you want to set in the Tab Stop Position box.

4. From the Alignment group, select the tab style you want: Left, Center, Right, Decimal, or Bar.

5. In the Leader group, select the tab leader style you want (if any): 1 for no leader, 2 for a dotted leader, 3 for a dashed leader, or 4 for an underlined leader.

6. Click the Set button to set the tab stop.

7. Repeat steps 3 through 6 to set additional tab stops.

8. Click OK.

The Tab Stop Position list box displays your tab stops after you set them. You can reformat existing tab stops by following the same general procedure for setting tabs.

To reformat existing tab stops, follow these steps:

1. Select the tab to reformat in the Tab Stop Position list box.
2. Select the new formatting options for the selected tab stop in the Alignment and Leader groups.
3. Click Set.

You can access the Tabs dialog box through the Paragraph dialog box. Choose Format, Paragraph or click the right mouse button and choose Paragraph in the shortcut menu; then click the Tabs button. Alternatively, you can double-click any tab set on the ruler to display the Tabs dialog box.

Clearing Tabs

After you set tabs, you can *clear* (remove) them individually or as a group. The following technique works whether you set the tabs through the Tabs dialog box or use the ruler (see "Using the Ruler to Set Tabs," later in this chapter).

To clear tab stops with the menu command, follow these steps:

1. Select the paragraph or paragraphs from which you want to clear tabs, or position the insertion point where you want to begin working with the new tab settings.
2. Choose Format, Tabs.
3. Click the Clear All button to clear all the tabs.

   You can also select the tab from the Tab Stop Position list box and click the Clear button to clear one tab. Repeat this process to clear additional tab stops.
4. Click OK.

As you clear tab stops with the Clear button in Step 3, the tab stops are listed in the Tab Stops to Be Cleared area at the bottom of the Tabs dialog box.

Using the Ruler to Set Tabs

If you have a mouse, you can use the ruler to set, move, and remove left, center, right, or decimal tabs quickly. (Bar tabs are not available from the ruler.) This task involves two steps: selecting the tab style by clicking the Tab Alignment button on the ruler, and then setting the tabs where you want them on the ruler.

The ruler displays Word's default tab stops (set every 0.5", unless you change the interval) as tiny vertical lines along the bottom of the ruler. When you set your own tab stops, all default tab stops to the left are removed from the ruler (see Figure 10.15).

FIG. 10.15

This ruler shows the symbols for the various kinds of tabs.

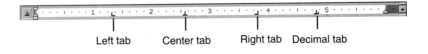

Left tab   Center tab   Right tab Decimal tab

 T I P To display the ruler, choose <u>V</u>iew, <u>R</u>uler.

▶ **See** "Controlling Your Document's Appearance On-Screen," **p. 132**

To set tabs using the ruler, follow these steps:

1. Select the paragraph or paragraphs for which you want to set tabs, or position the insertion point where you want the new tab settings to begin.

2. Click the Tab Alignment button at the far left of the ruler until the symbol for the tab style you want to use is selected: Left, Centered, Right, or Decimal. (Refer to Figure 10.12 to see how each Tab Alignment style looks on-screen.)

3. Position the pointer just below the tick mark on the ruler where you want the tab stop to appear. Click the left mouse button to place the tab stop on the ruler.

Repeat steps 2 and 3 to add various kinds of tab stops to the ruler, or just step 3 to add more tab stops of the same style.

The tab stop appears as a marker in the same style as the tab style you selected from the ruler. If you don't get the tab marker in just the right place on the ruler, position the mouse pointer on the marker, hold down the left mouse button to select the marker, and drag the tab marker to the correct position.

To use the ruler to change a tab stop's alignment or to add a leader, double-click the tab stop to display the Tabs dialog box. Select the tab stop you want to change in the <u>T</u>ab Stop Position list box and make whatever changes you want and click OK.

To use the mouse to quickly remove a tab from the ruler, follow these steps:

1. Drag the tab off the ruler onto the document.

2. Release the mouse button.

Resetting the Default Tab Stops

If you do not set custom tabs, Word has preset tabs every 0.5". When you set a custom tab, all preset tabs to the left of the custom tab are cleared. You can use the Tabs dialog box to change the default tab stop interval if you routinely use the preset tabs and do not like the default tab setting. Any custom tab stops you may have set for existing paragraphs are not affected.

To change the default tab stops, follow these steps:

1. Choose Format, Tabs.
2. In the Default Tab Stops text box, type in a new default tab interval or click the up or down arrow to change the number in the box.
3. Click OK.

Setting Default Tabs

Default tabs are set every 0.5". If you find that you are changing them frequently, you can change the default tab settings in NORMAL.DOT, the template on which most documents are based. You first need to retrieve NORMAL.DOT, then change the tabs, and finally save the template.

▶ **See** "Setting Default Formats in the Normal Template," **p. 211**

To retrieve NORMAL.DOT, follow these steps:

1. Choose File, Open.
2. Open the OFFICE folder.
3. Open the TEMPLATE folder.
4. Click the down arrow of Files of Type and choose Document Templates (*.DOT).
5. Choose NORMAL.
6. Click Open.

If you have never made any changes to the default settings in NORMAL.DOT, NORMAL.DOT will not appear in the TEMPLATE folder. If this is the case, you can create NORMAL.DOT, which can then be modified as described. To create NORMAL.DOT, open a new document, choose Format, Font, and then click the Default button. When asked if you want to change the default font, choose Yes. Because you didn't actually select a new font, you haven't really changed the default font. The idea is to trick Word into thinking you made a change in the default settings, so it will create a NORMAL.DOT file. Choose File, Save All. Click Cancel when the Save As dialog box appears, because you don't need to save the blank document. Word then automatically saves NORMAL.DOT, and NORMAL.DOT appears in the TEMPLATE folder, as described earlier.

To change the default tabs, follow these steps:

1. Choose Format, Tabs.
2. Change the setting in the Default Tab Stops text box to the interval you prefer.
3. Click OK.

To save and exit NORMAL.DOT, follow these steps:

1. Choose File, Close. You are asked whether you want to save the changes.

2. Click Yes to save the changes you have made.

The next time you create a document using NORMAL.DOT, the default tab settings will match the changes you've made to the template.

TROUBLESHOOTING

When I tried to adjust the column in a table created with tabs by dragging the tab stop on the ruler, only one row in the table changed. Tab settings are a paragraph characteristic and are stored in the paragraph mark at the end of a paragraph. To adjust the columns in a table, you must select all of the rows (paragraphs) in the table and then drag the tab stops on the ruler.

When I select the rows in a table created with tabs, some of the tab stops are grayed on the ruler. When you select a group of paragraphs that don't all have exactly the same tab settings, the tab stops that are not common to all of the paragraphs will appear in gray. You can drag a tab stop to a new setting, and it will then be applied to all of the paragraphs in the selection. This is a good way to synchronize the tab stops in a group of paragraphs if you accidentally change a tab setting in just one of the paragraphs.

Setting Indents

A document's margins are determined by selections made in the File Page Setup dialog box. Margins apply to the entire document or to sections within the document. But individual paragraphs or groups of paragraphs can be indented from those margins and therefore appear to have their own margin settings.

Although only two side margins (left and right) are available, you can indent a paragraph in many ways, as shown in Figure 10.16. You can indent from the left, right, or both margins. You can indent just the first line of a paragraph, a technique that often substitutes for pressing Tab at the beginning of each new paragraph. You can create a *hanging indent*, which "hangs" the first line of a paragraph to the left of the rest of the paragraph; hanging indents often are used for bulleted or numbered lists. You also can create *nested indents—*indentations within indentations.

Several techniques exist for creating indents. You can use the Paragraph dialog box and enter the amount of indent for the selected paragraph or paragraphs. You can use the ruler, dragging indent icons left and right. You can use a button on the toolbar to indent or unindent paragraphs quickly or to create lists with a hanging indent. You also can use keyboard shortcuts.

FIG. 10.16
You can use various levels of indenting to achieve various effects.

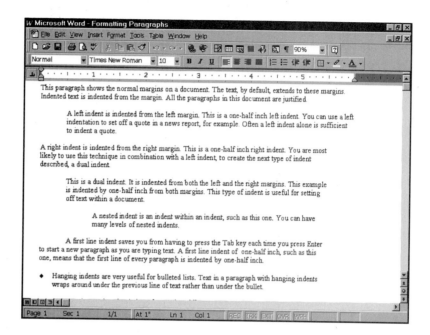

Whichever technique you use, indenting is stored in the paragraph mark and is carried forward when you press Enter at the end of a paragraph. Alternatively, you can return to a paragraph later and format the text with an indent.

N O T E   Note that numbered and bulleted lists are a special type of indented list.

▶ **See** "Creating Bulleted Lists," **p. 651**
▶ **See** "Creating Numbered Lists," **p. 659**

Using the Paragraph Command to Set Indents

You can use the Paragraph dialog box to precisely set any type of indent. The Indentation list in the Paragraph dialog box lists three options: Left, Right, and Special, as shown in Figure 10.17.

FIG. 10.17

Use the Indents and Spacing tab to change paragraph indentation.

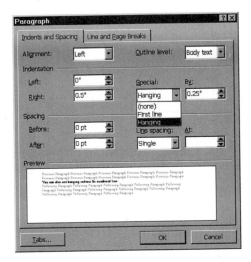

The indentation options give the following results:

Option	Result
Left	Indents selected paragraph or paragraphs from the left margin. If the number is positive, the paragraph is indented inside the left margin; if the number is negative, the paragraph is indented outside the left margin (sometimes termed *outdenting*).
Right	Indents selected paragraph or paragraphs from the right margin. If the number is positive, the paragraph is indented inside the right margin; if the number is negative, the paragraph is indented outside the right margin.
Special	Indents the first line or lines of selected paragraph or paragraphs from left indent (or margin, if no indent is made). Click the down arrow to select either First Line or Hanging. First Line indents inside the left indent. Hanging Indent indents outside the left indent. The default indent is 0.5". Change the indent by typing a new number or by using the up or down arrow to change the number.

To set indentations using the Paragraph dialog box, follow these steps:

1. Select the paragraph or paragraphs to indent, or position the insertion point where you want the new indentation to begin.

2. Choose Format, Paragraph. The Paragraph dialog box opens.

3. Select the Indents and Spacing tab.

4. Type or select a value in the L̲eft or R̲ight Indentation text box. You also can select First Line or Hanging from the S̲pecial list box and type or select a value in the By̲ text box. Or, you can preview the effects of the choices you make in the Preview box.

5. Click OK.

You can create indents in measurements other than decimal inches. To create a 6-point indent, for example, type **6 pt** in either indentation box. (An inch consists of 72 points.) To create an indent of 2 centimeters, type **2 cm**; to create an indent of 1 pica, type **1 pi** (six picas per inch; 12 points per pica).

Creating a Hanging Indent

A hanging indent is used for items such as bulleted and numbered lists, glossary items, and bibliographic entries (see Figure 10.18).

FIG. 10.18

Hanging indents can be used for creating bulleted and numbered lists and bibliographic entries.

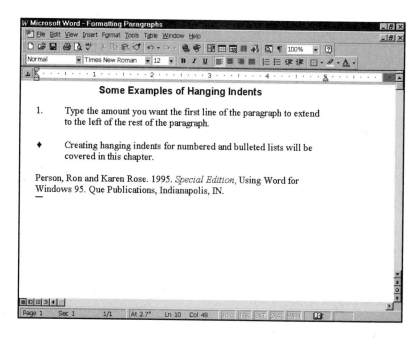

To create a hanging indent, follow these steps:

1. Choose F̲ormat, P̲aragraph.

2. Select the S̲pecial box by clicking its down arrow.

3. Choose Hanging.

4. Type the amount you want the first line of the paragraph to extend to the left of the rest of the paragraph.

5. Click OK.

To use a hanging indent, type a number or bullet at the left margin, press Tab to advance to the left indent, and then begin typing the text of the paragraph. When text reaches the end of the line, the paragraph wraps around to the left indent, not the left margin. This technique is useful for numbered and bulleted lists. (You can create hanging indents for numbered and bulleted lists automatically with the toolbar or the Bullets and Numbering dialog box.) See Chapter 20, "Creating Bulleted or Numbered Lists," for further information.

> **N O T E**   Symbol fonts such as Symbol and Zapf Dingbats are full of interesting characters you
> can use as bullets in a list. ▪

▶ **See** "Inserting Special Characters and Symbols," **p. 315**

Using the Ruler or Formatting Toolbar to Set Indents

With the ruler, you easily can create indents of any kind. With the Formatting toolbar, you can indent a selected paragraph to the next available tab stop.

The ruler contains triangular markers, called *indent markers*, at the left and right margins. You can drag them left and right on the ruler to set indents. The top triangle at the left margin represents the first-line indent. The bottom triangle represents the left indent. Both the top and bottom triangles move independently. You use the square below the bottom triangle to move both the first-line and left paragraph indents at once. The triangle at the right margin represents the paragraph's right indent. Figure 10.19 shows the indent markers on the ruler.

FIG. 10.19
Use the indent markers to set left and right indentations.

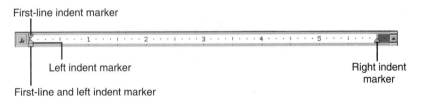

First-line indent marker

Left indent marker

First-line and left indent marker

Right indent marker

Left and right indents are measured from the left and right margins, respectively. First-line indents are measured relative to the left indent. In Figures 10.20, 10.21, and 10.22, you can see that the position of the indent markers reflects the indentation settings for the selected paragraph.

FIG. 10.20
The First-Line, Left, and Right Indent markers are set even with the left and right margins.

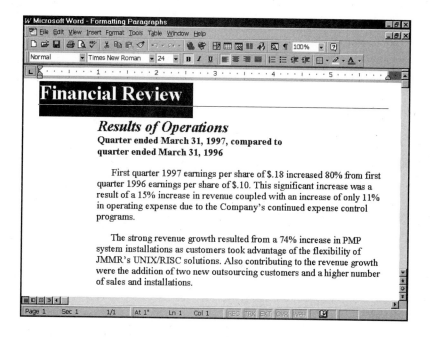

FIG. 10.21
The First-Line and Left Indent markers are set at 1.0", and the Right Indent marker has been moved to 6".

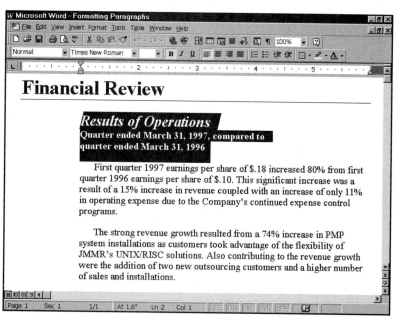

TIP To set indents with the ruler, display the ruler by choosing View, Ruler.

FIG. 10.22

The First-Line Indent marker is set to .25" from the Left Indent marker to create a first-line indentation.

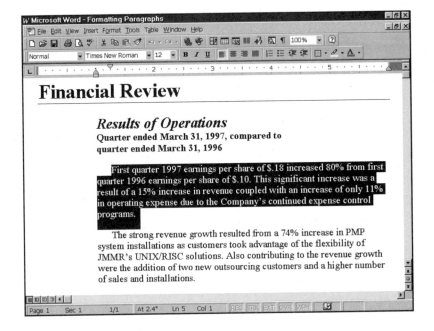

To set indentations with the ruler, follow these steps:

1. Select the paragraph or paragraphs to indent, or position the insertion point where you want the new indentation to begin.

2. To set a left indent, drag the square below the left indent marker to the ruler position where you want the indentation. (Notice that the top triangle moves also.)

   To set a right indent, drag the right indent marker to the position where you want the indentation.

   To set a first-line indent, drag the first-line indent marker to the position where you want the first-line indentation.

   To set a hanging indent with the first line at the left margin, drag the left indent marker to a new position on the ruler.

N O T E While in Normal view, when you drag the left or first-line indent to the left of the left margin, the ruler automatically scrolls to the left. If you want to scroll on the ruler into the left margin without moving the indent markers, however, hold down the Shift key while you click the left scroll arrow in the horizontal scroll bar. ■

The Formatting toolbar includes two buttons for indenting a selected paragraph to the next tab stop: the Increase Indent and Decrease Indent buttons. Increase Indent is used to indent to the next tab stop. Decrease Indent is used to decrease the indent to the previous tab stop. You use these buttons to create left indents only—not first-line or hanging indents—and to indent to tab stops already set in the current paragraph(s). To use this technique, be sure the Formatting toolbar is displayed by choosing View, Toolbars.

To indent or unindent paragraphs using the Formatting toolbar, follow these steps:

1. Select the paragraph or paragraphs to indent, or position the insertion point where you want the new indentation to begin.

2. To indent the paragraph, click the Increase Indent button.

   To unindent the paragraph, click the Decrease Indent button.

You can click the Increase Indent button as many times as you want to continue moving the left indentation to the right. The Increase Indent button, therefore, is an easy way to create nested paragraphs, which are like indents within indents (refer to Figure 10.16).

Part
II

Ch
10

Using Keyboard Shortcuts to Set Indents

If you're a touch typist, you might appreciate being able to create indents by using keyboard shortcuts. Just as when you use the Formatting toolbar to create indents, keyboard shortcuts rely on existing tab settings to determine the position of indents. If you haven't changed Word default tab stops, for example—and therefore they still are set every 0.5"—using the shortcut keys to create a hanging indent leaves the first line of the paragraph at the margin but moves the left edge for the remaining lines of the paragraph to one-half inch.

To set indents by using keyboard shortcuts, follow these steps:

1. Select the paragraph or paragraphs to indent, or position the insertion point where you want the new indentation to begin.

2. Use one of the following keyboard shortcuts to indent your text:

Shortcut	Indentation Type
Ctrl+M	Moves the left indent to the next tab stop
Ctrl+Shift+M	Moves the left indent to the preceding tab stop (but not beyond the left margin)
Ctrl+T	Creates a hanging indent
Ctrl+Shift+T	Removes an existing hanging indent

N O T E Just as you use shortcuts to format a paragraph, you can use a shortcut to remove formatting. Select a paragraph and press Ctrl+space bar to remove all character formatting and return a paragraph to only the formatting specified by the paragraph's style. ■

Setting Default Indents

One of the most commonly used letter-writing styles is modified-block style, with indented paragraphs. If you find that you are frequently changing indentations to indent paragraphs, for example, you can change the default indentation settings in NORMAL.DOT, the template on which most documents are based. You first need to retrieve NORMAL.DOT, then change the indentation, and finally save the template.

Refer to "Setting Default Tabs" earlier in this chapter for information about changing default indentation settings in NORMAL.DOT.

Numbering Lines

Line numbers are useful in preparing manuscripts or legal documents, for reference, or if you simply need to know how many lines of text are on a page, in a poem, or in a document. You can choose the starting number for line numbering, the distance between numbers and text, the interval at which line numbers appear, and whether line numbering restarts with every new page or section or continues throughout your section. You can suppress line numbering for a specific paragraph or paragraphs.

Adding Line Numbers

You can add line numbers to sections of a document or to the entire document if it isn't formatted into sections. For information about formatting a document in sections, see Chapter 13, "Formatting the Page Layout, Alignment, and Numbering."

To number lines, follow these steps:

1. Position the insertion point inside the section in which you want line numbers, or anywhere in the document to number a document that hasn't been split into sections. To number an entire document that has been divided into sections, select the entire document.
2. Choose File, Page Setup. The Page Setup dialog box appears.
3. Select the Layout tab.
4. Click Line Numbers.

5. Select the Add Line Numbering option (see Figure 10.23). Change the following default line numbering settings if you want:

FIG. 10.23
Choose line numbering options from the Line Numbers dialog box.

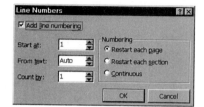

Option	Description	Then Type
Start At	Starting line number	A new starting number in the box, or click the up or down arrow to increase or decrease the starting number. (By default, line numbering begins with 1.)
From Text	Distance between line numbers and text	A distance in the box or click the up or down arrow to increase or decrease the distance by tenths of an inch. (The Auto option places line numbers .25" to the left of single-column text or .13" to the left of newspaper-style columns.) If the margin or the space between columns is too small, line numbers do not print.
Count By	Interval between printed line numbers (all lines are numbered but only those numbers specified here print)	An interval in a box, or click the up or down arrow to increase or decrease the interval.

6. Select an option from the Numbering group to establish when line numbers restart at the first number (but only those numbers specified here print):

Option	Restart Point
Restart Each Page	Beginning of each new page
Restart Each Section	Beginning of each new section
Continuous	None; number lines continuously through document

Part
II

Ch
10

7. Click OK twice.

You cannot see line numbering in Normal view. To see line numbers, choose View, Page Layout, or File, Print Preview. You also can print your document.

▶ **See** "Controlling Your Document's Appearance On-Screen," **p. 132**

N O T E You can change the formatting of line numbers by redefining the Line Number style. Refer to Chapter 11, "Using Styles for Repetitive Formats," for information about redefining styles. ■

Removing or Suppressing Line Numbers

You can remove line numbers entirely. Also, you have the chance to suppress line numbers by selecting the Suppress Line Numbers option in the Paragraph dialog box. This option clears line numbering from selected paragraphs or the paragraph containing the insertion point. (This option doesn't suppress line numbers applied in creating a numbered list, described in Chapter 20, "Creating Bulleted or Numbered Lists.")

To remove line numbers, follow these steps:

1. Position the insertion point in the section from which you want to remove line numbers, or select the entire document if it's formatted into more than one section.

2. Choose File, Page Setup.

3. Select the Layout tab.

4. Click the Line Numbers button.

5. Choose Add Line Numbering to remove the check mark.

6. Click OK or press Enter twice to return to the document.

To suppress line numbers, follow these steps:

1. Select the paragraphs for which you want to suppress line numbering.

2. Choose Format, Paragraph.

3. Select the Line and Page Breaks tab.

4. Click the Suppress Line Numbers option.

5. Click OK.

▶ **See** "Creating Numbered Lists," **p. 659**

Adjusting Line and Paragraph Spacing

Like all word processing and typesetting programs, Word spaces lines of text far enough apart so that lines don't crash into each other. If something large is on the line, such as a graphic or an oversized character or word, Word leaves extra space.

You're not limited to using Word automatic spacing, however. You can add extra space between lines and paragraphs.

N O T E   Using styles is an excellent way to ensure that adjustments made to line and paragraph spacing are consistent throughout your document. If your document's format includes subheadings preceded by extra space, for example, create a style for your subheadings that includes the extra space, and apply the style to each subheading. For details about using styles, see Chapter 11, "Using Styles for Repetitive Formats." ▨

Part

II

Ch

10

Adjusting Paragraph Spacing

You can adjust paragraph spacing by adding extra lines before or after the selected paragraphs. After you press Enter, Word skips the specified amount of space before starting the next paragraph. This technique is useful when your document's format requires extra spacing between paragraphs, before new sections, or around graphics. Adding extra spacing before or after paragraphs is like pressing Enter a second time each time you finish typing a paragraph (see Figure 10.24).

The Preview section of the Paragraph dialog box shows the effect of your selected spacing.

N O T E   When you're printing, if you format a paragraph to include extra space before and the paragraph appears at the top of a new page, Word ignores the extra space so that the top margins of your document always remain even. ▨

To adjust paragraph spacing, follow these steps:

1. Select the paragraph or paragraphs to add spacing before or after, or position the insertion point where you want the new spacing to begin.
2. Choose Format, Paragraph.
3. Select the Indents and Spacing tab.
4. To add line spacing before the selected paragraph or paragraphs, type a number in the Spacing Before text box or click the up or down arrow to increase or decrease the spacing amount in increments of half a line (see Figure 10.25).

FIG. 10.24
Use paragraph spacing to add extra spacing around headings and paragraphs.

10 points of space before 14 points of space after

0 points of space before 0 points of space after

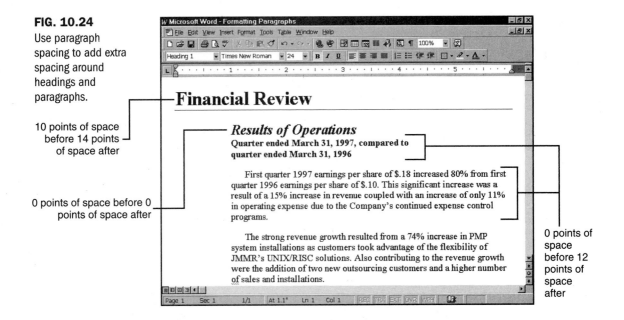

0 points of space before 12 points of space after

FIG. 10.25
Use the Paragraph Indents and Spacing tab to set paragraph spacing options.

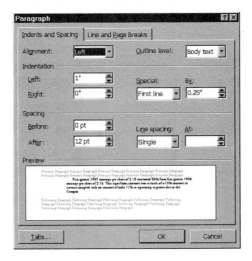

5. To add line spacing after the selected paragraph or paragraphs, type a number in the Spacing Aft̲er text box or click the up or down arrow to increase or decrease the spacing amount in increments of half a line.

You can use measurements other than decimal inches to specify spacing. To add six-point spacing, for example, type **6 pt** in the B̲efore or Aft̲er box. To add spacing of two centimeters, type **2 cm**, and to add spacing of one pica, type **1 pi**.

6. Click OK.

Adjusting Line Spacing

Typesetters and desktop publishers call the spacing between lines in a document *leading* (pronounced "ledding"). Typesetters have great control over precisely how much space appears between lines. They know that long lines need more spacing so that the eye doesn't lose its place in moving from the right margin back to the left. They know that font styles with small letters require less spacing between lines than fonts with big letters.

Word gives you a typesetter's control over spacing between lines in your document. The feature begins with automatic spacing and enables you to increase spacing, reduce spacing, or permit extra spacing for a large character or superscript on the line.

Spacing is measured by lines. Normal text has single spacing of one line, but if you request spacing of .5, you get half-line spacing. Lines formatted this way are *condensed*. If you request spacing of 1.5, the paragraph has an extra half line of space between lines of text (see Figure 10.26).

FIG. 10.26

The line spacing is set at 1.5 to put more space between the lines of the selected text.

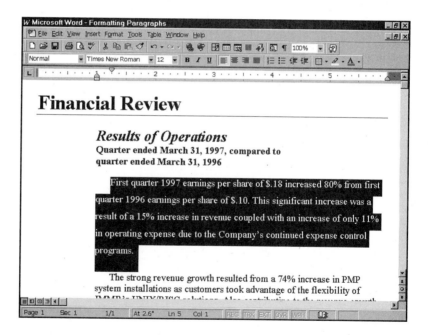

You can be very specific about line spacing. If your page design requires 10-point type with 12 points of leading, for example, type **12 pt** in the At box on the Indents and Spacing tab in the Paragraph dialog box. Word automatically changes the Line Spacing setting to Multiple and inserts a comparable number in inches.

N O T E You can include line spacing with styles so that when you press Enter to end a paragraph, the exact spacing is inserted automatically for each style of text you type, whether it's a heading that requires 14 points of space before the next line of text or body text that requires only 12 points of space between lines. ▣

▶ **See** "Applying, Copying, and Removing Styles," **p. 389**

To adjust spacing between lines using the menu commands, follow these steps:

1. Select the paragraph(s) to space, or position the insertion point where you want the new spacing to begin.

2. Choose F̲ormat, P̲aragraph to open the Paragraph dialog box.

3. Select the I̲ndents and Spacing tab.

4. Choose one of the following options in the Li̲ne Spacing box:

Option	Description
Single	Single-line spacing. Line height automatically adjusts to accommodate the size of the font and any graphics or formulas that have been inserted into a line.
1.5 Lines	Line-and-a-half spacing. Puts an extra half line between lines.
Double	Double-spacing. Puts an extra full line between lines.
At Least	At least the amount of spacing you specify in the A̲t text box. Word adds extra spacing, if necessary, for tall characters, big graphics, or super/subscript.
Exactly	The exact amount of spacing you specify in the A̲t text box. All lines are exactly the same height, regardless of the size of the characters in the line. Word doesn't add extra spacing for anything. Some text may be cut off if enough space isn't available. Increase the amount of spacing if characters are cut off.
Multiple	Multiples of single-line spacing, such as triple (3) or quadruple (4)

5. If you want to specify your own line spacing, type the spacing amount in the A̲t text box (with decimal numbers, such as **1.25** for an extra quarter-line of space between lines) or click the up or down arrow to increase or decrease the amount.

   You can choose a spacing amount in the A̲t text box without first choosing from the Li̲ne Spacing list box. Word assumes that you want at least this spacing and provides extra spacing if needed for large characters, superscript, and so on.

6. Click OK.

If you want to return to single-line spacing, select the paragraph or paragraphs, choose Format, Paragraph, and then choose Single Line Spacing.

You can change line spacing to single, 1.5, or double from the keyboard. You can also add or remove 12 points of space before a paragraph.

To adjust spacing between lines from the keyboard, follow these steps:

1. Select the paragraph or paragraphs, or place the insertion point in the paragraph in which you want to change the spacing.

2. Press one of the following key combinations:

Press	To Do This
Ctrl+1	Single-space text
Ctrl+5	1.5 line space text
Ctrl+2	Double-space text
Ctrl+0 (zero)	Add 12 points of space before a paragraph
Ctrl+Shift+0 (zero)	Remove any space before a paragraph

Inserting a Line Break

▶ **See** "Changing Styles," **p. 393**

When you type a paragraph formatted by a style that is automatically followed by a different style and then press Enter, the next paragraph is formatted with the next style. Sometimes, however, you may not be ready to change to the next style. If you have a two-line subheading, for example, you may want to press Enter after the first line and still be in the subheading style, rather than switch to the next style. In this case, you want to insert a line break, or *soft return,* rather than a new paragraph. To end a line without inserting a paragraph mark, press Shift+Enter.

Pressing Shift+Enter breaks a line without breaking the paragraph. After you finish typing your two-line subheading, press Enter in the usual way to end the paragraph and begin the following paragraph with the next style.

¶ If you click the Show/Hide ¶ button to display paragraph marks, you see that the line end marks at the ends of lines where you pressed Shift+Enter look like left-facing arrows rather than paragraph marks (see Figure 10.27).

FIG. 10.27
Press Shift+Enter to create a new line without creating a new paragraph. Line end marks display as left-facing arrows rather than paragraph marks.

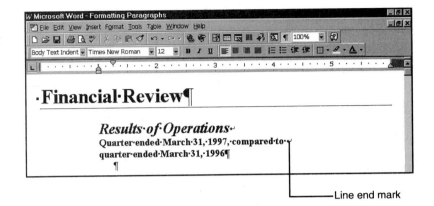

Line end mark

Shading and Bordering Paragraphs

For a finishing touch, you can add paragraph borders and shading to your document. A *border* may be a box surrounding a paragraph (or paragraphs) on all sides or a line that sets a paragraph off on one or more sides. A border can include *shading*, which fills a paragraph with a pattern. Boxes and lines can be solid black and shading can be gray, or, if you have a color monitor, they can be more colorful than a rainbow.

Borders are particularly useful in setting special paragraphs apart from the rest of your text for emphasis (see Figure 10.28) or for wonderful graphic effects. If you use Word for desktop publishing, you may find boxes, lines, and shading to be helpful.

N O T E   Creating colored lines, boxes, and shading is easy if you have a color monitor. If you have a color printer, you also can print colored lines, boxes, and shading. Service bureaus in many cities offer color printing for a per-page fee. If you want to print your document with colored lines, boxes, and shading, use your own printer to proof the pages and then take a floppy disk containing your file to the service bureau to have the final pages printed in color. Before you go to the service bureau, check to see if they have Word. You may need to reformat your document slightly for their printer. ▪

Borders, like all forms of paragraph formatting, belong to the paragraphs to which they are applied. They are carried forward when you press Enter at the end of a paragraph. Thus, if a group of paragraphs is formatted with a box around them and you press Enter at the end of the last paragraph, your new paragraph falls within the box. To create a new paragraph outside the border, move the insertion point outside the border before you press Enter. If you're at the end of the document and have nowhere to go outside of the border, create a new paragraph and remove the border.

FIG. 10.28
Borders, lines, and
shading can set
paragraphs apart.

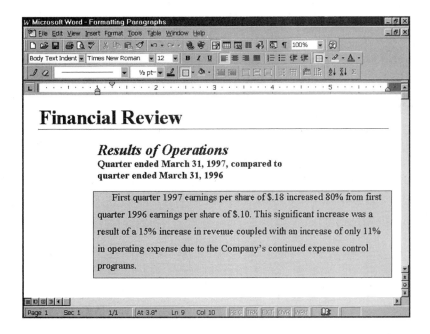

Part

II

Ch

10

T I P To change the color of the text inside a border, choose F<u>o</u>rmat, <u>F</u>ont. See Chapter 9, "Formatting
Characters and Changing Fonts," for more information.

TROUBLESHOOTING

The text changes its formatting when you press the Delete or Backspace key. Word stores
paragraph formatting in the paragraph mark at the end of each paragraph. If you delete the
paragraph mark of a particular paragraph, it takes on the format of the following paragraph.
Choose <u>E</u>dit, <u>U</u>ndo immediately to reverse the deletion and restore the paragraph formatting.

N O T E Sometimes the screen display inaccurately shows text extending beyond borders or
shading. This situation results from screen fonts and screen resolutions that differ from
the printer's fonts and resolution. Your printed text formats within the border or shading. ■

Enclosing Paragraphs in Boxes and Lines

A box fully surrounds a paragraph or selected group of paragraphs. Two types of preset
boxes are available: box and shadow. A line appears on one or more sides of a paragraph
or selected paragraphs, or may appear between selected paragraphs. You have 11 line
styles to choose from and can use any line style to create a line, a box, or a shadowed box.

You use the Borders and Shading dialog box to create boxes, lines, and shadows. Choose Format, Borders and Shading to access the dialog box. In the dialog box, you can choose either the Borders tab, Page Border tab, or Shading tab. The Borders tab shown in Figure 10.29 offers the following choices:

Borders Option	Effect
None	No box. Use this option to remove an existing box. (This option is used often with the Shading options to create a shaded box with no border.)
Box	A box with identical lines on all four sides.
Shadow	A box with a drop shadow on the bottom right corner.
3-D	A "picture frame" box. You must select an asymmetric line style such as thin-thick, thick-thin, embossed, or engraved lines for this function to work.
Custom	Custom design borders on one or more sides of the selected paragraph(s) using Preview buttons.
Preview	A line on one or more sides of the selected paragraph(s). Dotted lines at the corners and sides of the sample indicate where the lines appear; when they are selected, arrows point to these dotted lines. The sample displays each border as added (see Figure 10.30).
From Text	(Select the Options button.) The distance between the line or box and the text, measured in points. Because 72 points make up an inch, select 9 points for a .125" distance or 18 points for a .25" distance.
Style	A line or box in the selected line style. Options listed show exact point size and a sample display.
Color	A line or box in the selected color. Sixteen colors and gray shades are available. If you select the Auto option, the default color for text is used. This is usually black, but can be changed in the Windows Control Panel.
Width	A line or box in the selected width. Sixteen colors and gray shades are available. Options listed show exact point size and a sample display.

Apply to

Apply border and shade formatting to selected paragraphs or to selected text.

FIG. 10.29
The Borders tab in the Borders and Shading dialog box offers options for adding lines to any and all sides of a paragraph.

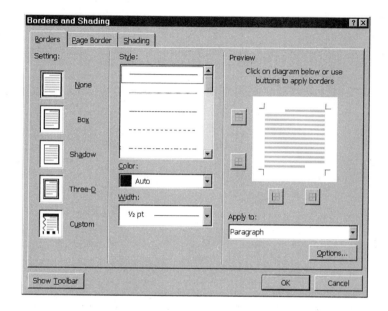

Part
II

Ch
10

FIG. 10.30
The sample box in the Borders tab shows you which line is currently selected and gives you a preview of the lines you have inserted.

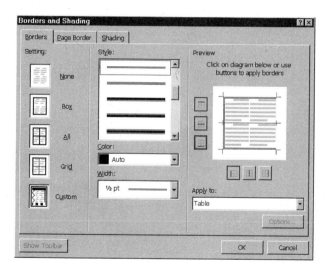

You also can use the Tables and Borders toolbar to add borders and shading to selected paragraphs (see Figures 10.31 and 10.32). Display the Tables and Borders toolbar by choosing View, Toolbars, or by clicking the Borders button on the Formatting toolbar.

FIG. 10.31
You can add borders and shading from the Tables and Borders toolbar.

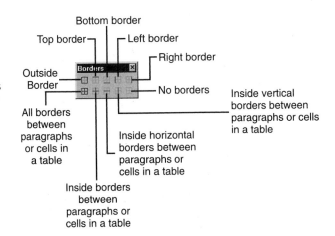

FIG. 10.32
The Tables and Borders toolbar can be torn off and placed with the other displayed toolbars, or it can be left to float in the document window.

To create a box or line from the menu command, follow these steps:

1. Select the paragraph or paragraphs for which you want to create a box or line.

   If you create a box for more than one paragraph, the box encloses the paragraphs as a group, with no borders between them.

To Add a Box or Line to	Select
A paragraph, including paragraphs inside a table cell or frame	The paragraph
A table cell	The entire cell, including the end-of-cell marker
A frame	The frame

2. Choose F<u>o</u>rmat, <u>B</u>orders and Shading. The Borders and Shading dialog box appears.

3. Select the <u>B</u>orders tab.

4. To create a box, choose Bo<u>x</u>, Sh<u>a</u>dow, or 3-<u>D</u> from the Setting group.

   To create a line using the mouse, do the following:

Click the side of the paragraph where you want the line in the Preview group or click the preview button corresponding to the line you want. The preview buttons appear depressed when a line is selected. If a style has already been selected from the Style group, a line with that style will be inserted. You can continue inserting using this approach. If multiple paragraphs are selected, you can create a line between them by clicking the horizontal line between paragraphs in the Preview box.

Choosing the line style before you create borders ensures that borders take on the appearance of the selected line style

5. To set the spacing between a box and the text, select the Options button and specify a distance in the From Text group then click OK.

6. To apply color to all your boxes and lines, choose a color from the Color list.

7. Click OK.

To create a box or line from the Tables and Borders toolbar, follow these steps:

1. Display the Tables and Borders toolbar by choosing View, Toolbars and specifying the Tables and Borders toolbar.

2. Select the paragraph or paragraphs for which you want to create a box or line.

 TIP If you create a box for more than one paragraph, the box encloses the paragraphs as a group with no borders between them.

To Add a Box or Line to	Select
A paragraph, including paragraphs inside a table	The paragraph cell or frame
A table cell	The entire cell, including the end-of-cell marker
A frame	The frame

3. Select the Line Style list box by clicking the down arrow, and choose a line style.

4. Select the Line Weight list box by clicking the down arrow, and choose a line weight.

5. Select the Border list box by clicking the down arrow, and choose the border you want to add by clicking one of the following buttons:

Choose This Button	To Do This
	Add a box border
	Add a border along the top

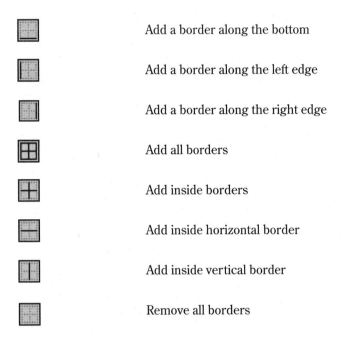

Add a border along the bottom

Add a border along the left edge

Add a border along the right edge

Add all borders

Add inside borders

Add inside horizontal border

Add inside vertical border

Remove all borders

6. Choose shading or a pattern from the Shading list box, if you want shading or a pattern added.

The width of a paragraph border (box or line) is determined by the paragraph indent. (If no indent exists, width is determined by the page margins.) If you want a paragraph's border (or line) to be narrower than the margins, indent the paragraph (see Figures 10.33 and 10.34).

FIG. 10.33

With indents set to the left and right margins, borders extend the full width of the page.

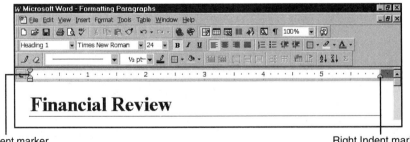

Left Indent marker

Right Indent marker

If you select and box several paragraphs that have different indents, each paragraph appears in its own separate box (instead of all appearing together in one box). To make paragraphs with different indents appear within a single box, you must create a table and put each paragraph in a row by itself and then select the table and format the outside border of the table (see Chapter 18, "Creating and Editing Tables").

FIG. 10.34

To create a shorter border, move in the Left and Right Indent markers.

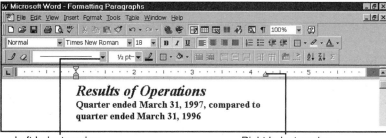

Left Indent marker   Right Indent marker

When paragraphs extend exactly to the margins of your page (as they always do if you don't indent the paragraphs), borders extend slightly outside the margins. If you want borders to fall within or exactly on the margins, you must indent the paragraph. To make borders fall on the margins, indent the paragraph by the width of the border.

For example, if the border is the double 1.5-point line, the line width totals 4.5 points including the space between the double lines, indent the paragraph by 4.5 points. Type **4.5 pt** in the Left and Right indentation boxes in the Paragraph dialog box.

N O T E   If you format groups of paragraphs to have lines between them, those lines apply to blank spaces between paragraphs if you create those blank spaces by pressing Enter an extra time. To avoid extra lines between paragraphs, use the Spacing After option in the Paragraph dialog box to add blank space between paragraphs. (See "Adjusting Line and Paragraph Spacing" earlier in this chapter.)

You can remove borders all at once or line by line. Changing the line style of existing borders is essentially the same process.

To remove or change a box or line from the menu command, follow these steps:

1. Select the paragraph or paragraphs for which you want to remove or change boxes or lines.

2. Choose Format, Borders and Shading.

3. Select the Borders tab.

4. Select the None option in the Setting group to remove all borders.

5. Select the line you want to change and choose a different option from the Style box. You also can select a different line color from the Color list box.

6. Select Box, Shadow, 3-D, or Custom to change the Setting border style.

7. Click OK.

To remove or change a line or box from the Tables and Borders toolbar, follow these steps:

1. Select the paragraph or paragraphs for which you want to remove or change boxes or lines.

2. Click the Borders button on the Formatting toolbar to display the Tables and Borders toolbar.

3. Click the No Border button to remove all borders.

4. Choose a new line style.

5. Click the button(s) for the box(es) or border(s) you want to add.

> **TIP** Before you concoct patterns that you hope to use behind text, be sure to test whether the text is readable with that pattern behind it.

Shading Paragraphs

Paragraphs can be shaded, as well as bordered. Shading comes in various percentages of black or the selected color, and in patterns (see Figure 10.35). Percentages of black appear as grays of various intensities. For each shade or pattern, you can select a foreground or background color. *Shades* create a blended effect: A foreground of yellow and a background of blue creates the effect of green.

FIG. 10.35

The Shading tab from the Borders and Shading dialog box offers options for adding varying degrees of shading and/or color to a paragraph.

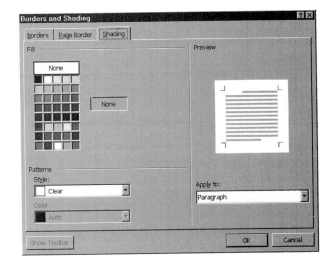

But in *patterns*, the effect is more dramatic: in a Lt Grid pattern, for example, the yellow foreground forms a light grid pattern over a blue background. With some experimentation, you can create eye-catching results that can add visual impact to documents used for presentations or overhead transparencies. Colors are converted to shades of gray or patterns on a black-and-white printer.

You can use shading with borders so that a paragraph is surrounded by a line and filled with shading, or you can use shading alone so that no border goes around the shaded paragraph. Watch the Preview box on the Shading tab to see the effect of the patterns and colors you select. To add shading, choose the Shading tab in the Borders and Shading dialog box. You have the following options:

Shading Option	Effect
Fill	A background color for the selected shading pattern. Auto selects the best color, usually white. Select from 16 colors, including black and white.
None	No shading in selected paragraph(s).
Custom	Shading in the selected custom shading. Options are shown in Shading.
Style	Shading in the selected custom darkness or pattern. Options include increasing degrees of shading and various patterns. Clear applies the selected background color; Solid applies the selected foreground color.
Color	A foreground color for the selected shading pattern. Auto selects the best color, usually black. You can select from 16 colors, including black and white.

To shade paragraphs with the menu command, follow these steps:

1. Select the paragraph or paragraphs you want to shade:

To Shade	Select
A paragraph	The paragraph including paragraphs inside a table cell or frame
A table cell	The entire cell, including the end-of-cell marker
A frame	The frame

2. Choose Format, Borders and Shading.

Part
II

Ch
10

TIP If you want borders around your selected paragraph, select the Borders tab and choose border options.

3. Select the Shading tab.

4. Select the Style pattern you want. Options include Clear (uses the background color), Solid (uses the foreground color), percentages, and striped and checkered patterns such as Dk Horizontal (for dark horizontal stripes) and Lt Grid (for a grid made of light cross-hatching).

TIP Percentage patterns consist of foreground and background colors. The result appears in the Preview box. For best results in creating colors, however, look first for the color you want in the Color list.

5. Select a color from the Color list to color a percentage pattern or a pattern foreground.

6. Select a color from the Fill list to color a percentage pattern or a pattern background.

7. Click OK.

To shade paragraphs using the Tables and Borders toolbar, follow these steps:

1. Select the paragraph or paragraphs you want to shade:

To Shade	Select
A paragraph	The paragraph including paragraphs inside a table cell or frame
A table cell	The entire cell, including the end-of-cell marker
A frame	The frame

2. Click the Borders button on the Formatting toolbar to display the Tables and Borders toolbar.

3. Choose the shading or pattern you want from the Shading Color box.

 To remove shading using the menu command, follow these steps:

1. Select the paragraph or paragraphs from which you want to remove shading.
2. Choose Format, Borders and Shading.

3. Click the Shading button.
4. Choose None from the Fill group.
5. Click OK.

To remove shading with the Tables and Borders toolbar, follow these steps:

1. Select the paragraph or paragraphs from which you want to remove shading.
2. Click the Borders button on the Formatting toolbar to display the Tables and Borders toolbar.

3. Choose the Clear setting from the Shading box.

Part

II

Ch

10

Using Styles for Repetitive Formats

What gives your document style? For the most part, *style* is the appearance of your document: the arrangement of text on pages, the shape of the paragraphs, the characteristics of the letters, and the use of lines and borders to give your document emphasis. All these elements of style are formatting choices you make while working with Word.

Style involves more than just appearance, however. Style is also readability and consistency. When your document's style is appropriate to its content and is consistent from one section to the next, the reader's job of gleaning information from your text becomes much easier.

Word offers you tools designed to make the task of developing and maintaining your document's style much easier. Appropriately, these tools are called *styles*. In Word 97, a style is a set of formatting instructions you save with a name in order to use them again and again. All text formatted with the same style has exactly the same formatting. If you make a formatting change to a style, all the text formatted with that style will reformat to match the new formatting. ■

Automatically format a document

Using the AutoFormat command, Word will apply styles and let you review and approve the changes.

Use Word standard styles

Word comes with a series of styles you can use as a foundation to format your document, or redefine them, as needed.

Create your own styles

You can build your own styles to match your formatting needs.

Changing formatting

Modify a document's appearance by switching from one style to another, by adding or removing formatting characteristics to a particular style.

Manage styles

Copy, redefine, or delete styles.

Using Styles versus Direct Formatting

You can create and apply two types of styles: character styles and paragraph styles. *Character styles* include any of the options available from the Font dialog box, such as bold, italic, and small caps. Character styles store only character formatting, and apply to selected text or to the word containing the insertion point. *Paragraph styles* include character and paragraph formatting, tab settings, paragraph positioning, borders and shading, and language used for spell checking. Paragraph styles can store both character and paragraph formatting, and apply to selected paragraphs or the paragraph containing the insertion point.

You can type a plain business letter and then apply a set of styles automatically with the AutoFormat command on the Format menu to give it a professional appearance. Word applies styles to common text elements, such as bulleted and numbered lists and headings. In addition, Word makes small improvements, such as changing straight quotation marks (") to curved typesetting quotation marks, often called "smart quotes" (" "). You can review and undo the changes Word has made and make further changes of your own.

You can also choose from among many available style groups to change the document format automatically to the style you want. The Style Gallery command displays your document in other styles and lets you select from among them the one you most like.

See Figures 11.1 and 11.2 for an example of how automatic formatting can quickly change your document's appearance with styles.

FIG. 11.1

You can choose between different families of styles. This letter uses the Contemporary Letter template.

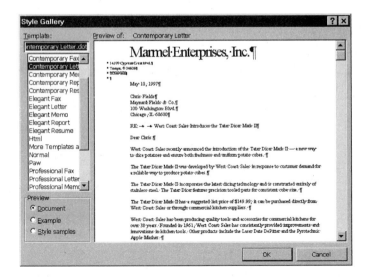

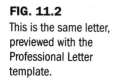

FIG. 11.2
This is the same letter, previewed with the Professional Letter template.

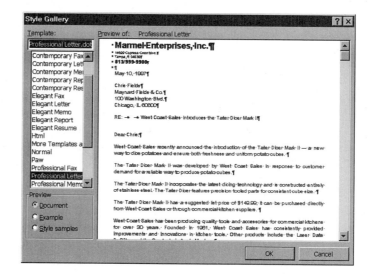

Instead of directly formatting each word, phrase, paragraph, or page individually, using styles offers several benefits:

- *Saves time.* You can format one word or paragraph the way you like it and copy that formatting to other words or paragraphs. The AutoFormat command applies styles automatically, quickly formatting a simple document into a professional-appearing document.

- *Preserves consistency.* By using styles to format your document, you can be sure that each selected item or paragraph looks the same as others of its type.

- *Reduces the effort required to change your document's appearance.* By changing a style, you also change all the selected text or paragraphs associated with that style. For example, you can easily change styles used in a proposal or marketing letter to see which gives the appearance you want. Literature produced by committee can be changed as quickly as the committee changes members.

Choosing a Formatting Method

You're always using at least one style when you work with Word. The *Normal style*, built into Word, gives your document its default formatting choices. If you have the Formatting toolbar displayed when you start a new document, you can see the Normal style in the Style Preview box, already selected (see Figure 11.3). The Normal style's formatting selections are basic: they include a font and font size (12-point MS Serif, 10-point Times New Roman, or a different font, depending on your printer), left alignment, and single-line spacing. Word also makes other styles available for items like page numbers, headers,

Part
II

Ch
11

and footers. You learn how to change the Normal style in the section "Redefining Standard Styles" later in this chapter.

N O T E Style information for a paragraph, such as alignment, is stored in the paragraph mark at the end of each paragraph. If you delete a paragraph mark, that paragraph assumes the style of the next paragraph. If the next paragraph has a different style, you will see formatting change.

¶ Be aware when deleting paragraph marks. Because of the danger in losing a paragraph's formatting, some Word users prefer to work with paragraph marks showing. You can display paragraph marks in your document by clicking the Show/Hide Paragraph button in the Standard toolbar. When displayed, paragraph marks appear like a reversed bold P, (¶), at the end of each paragraph. ▪

FIG. 11.3

The Normal style is displayed in the Formatting toolbar when you start a new document.

The list of styles from which you can select depends on the *template* you select when you create a document. The default template is Normal. In addition to the Normal style, a template may contain styles for indenting, tables of contents, titles, headings, lists, envelopes, and many more. You can use the styles built into a template as they come, you can modify them, or you can create your own styles.

▶ **See** "Using Templates as a Pattern for Documents," **p. 202**

Except for the Normal template, which is designed for general use, each template's styles have been designed to suit one particular application, such as a memo, a fax cover sheet, or a résumé. The Normal style in one template may be 10-point Times New Roman, while in another template it may be 12-point Century Schoolbook. Changing the template may change the formatting of the style. Word provides a Style Gallery in which you can preview the effects of changing a template and its resultant changes to the styles you use. The Style Gallery is covered later in this chapter, in the section "Using the Style Gallery."

You can apply and change styles in three ways. Each method has advantages and disadvantages, as described in the following paragraphs.

▪ *Method 1.* The fastest formatting method is formatting automatically with Format, AutoFormat.

Advantage: The formatting is done automatically without having to select styles.

Disadvantage: You have less control over the selection of styles, although you can manually override any style selections.

■ *Method 2.* The method that allows you the greatest control over the format of the text is manually formatting by creating, selecting, and/or modifying those styles available in the template on which your document is based.

Advantages: You can make your document appear any way you choose by creating and selecting suitable styles.

Styles you create can be based on existing styles and/or followed by other styles. For example, you can follow a heading style with a body text style, automatically incorporating consistent spacing and other formatting.

Disadvantage: You have to create and/or select a style for each element of your document.

■ *Method 3.* The third formatting method is selecting a new template with Format, Style Gallery.

Advantage: You can preview your document as it will appear based on each of many other templates, and then select and apply that template. For example, you can choose from three different letter styles.

Disadvantage: You have less control over the selection of styles, although you can manually override any style selections.

The following sections describe in detail each method of formatting.

Formatting a Document Automatically

Imagine that you quickly dash off an important business letter, paying no special attention to the letter's formatting. Then with a click of the mouse, the letter suddenly takes the shape of the formal business letter you had in mind. The Format, AutoFormat command gives you that power.

When you choose Format, AutoFormat, Word goes through your document paragraph by paragraph, applying appropriate styles. If you've included a list of items, each preceded with an asterisk, for example, Word reformats the list, replacing asterisks with bullets and adding the bulleted list style. If you've only formatted some of the text, AutoFormat completes the job. AutoFormat ensures that the formatting is consistent throughout the document and also improves the appearance. The styles Word applies come from the template that is currently attached to the document. See Figures 11.4 and 11.5 for an example of a document that has been formatted with AutoFormat.

Part II

Ch 11

FIG. 11.4
You can type letters, documents, and memos without worrying about formatting.

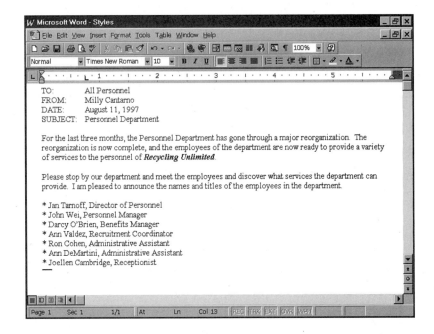

FIG. 11.5
The AutoFormat command uses its rules to apply formats, such as bullets, to your documents.

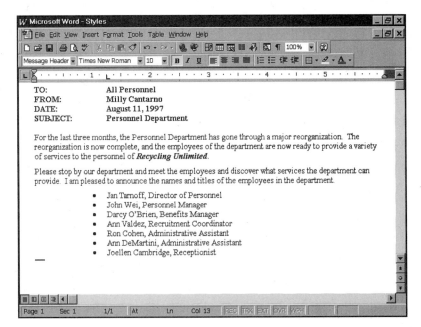

After the text has been formatted with AutoFormat, you can polish the document's appearance by manually applying styles or formatting to any elements of the document. You can also choose a new template from the Style Gallery to change the overall design of the document. Each of these topics is covered later in this chapter, in the sections "Using the Style Gallery" and "Applying, Copying, and Removing Styles."

TROUBLESHOOTING

As I type, Word automatically inserts bullets, changes my tabbed lists to tables, indents lines, or starts automatically numbering lists. It's driving me crazy. How do I turn it off? Word is attempting to help you by automatically formatting as you type. But you're right, it can be very annoying when you don't want its help. There are two ways to handle this feature. If you want automatic formatting most of the time, but just not for this one instance, then backspace over the automatic formatting and retype it as you want it. Word will "learn" that you want it that way and leave it. If you want to turn portions of AutoFormatting off then, choose Format, AutoFormat. When the AutoFormat dialog box displays click Options. Select the AutoFormat as You Type tab from the AutoCorrect dialog box. Clear options for AutoFormatting that you do not want.

Applying Styles with AutoFormat

AutoFormat analyzes the document in the active window and applies a style to each paragraph that is currently formatted with either the Normal or Body Text style. The styles AutoFormat applies are designed to format common writing elements such as quotations, bulleted lists, headings, and more. AutoFormat applies styles and makes corrections as described in the following list:

- Uses its formatting rules to find and format such items as headings, body text, lists, superscript and subscript, addresses, and letter closings.
- Removes extra paragraph marks.
- Replaces straight quotation marks (") and apostrophes (') with typesetting quotation marks (" ") and apostrophes (' ').
- Replaces "(c)," "(R)," and "(TM)" with copyright ©, registered trademark ®, and trademark ™ symbols.
- Replaces asterisks, hyphens, or other characters used to list items with a bullet character (■).
- Replaces horizontal spaces inserted with the Tab key or the space bar with indents.

To format text automatically with the menu command, follow these steps:

1. Select the text you want to format. If you want to format the entire document, position the insertion point anywhere in the document.
2. Choose Format, AutoFormat. The AutoFormat dialog box appears (see Figure 11.6).

FIG. 11.6

You can automatically format a document by choosing Format, AutoFormat.

You can determine which changes AutoFormat makes by clicking the Options button in the AutoFormat dialog box or by changing the settings in the AutoFormat tab of the Options dialog box. See the section "Setting AutoFormat Options," later in this chapter, for more information.

3. Select AutoFormat Now to format the document and not review formatting changes.

or

Select AutoFormat and Review Each Change to accept or reject formatting after this procedure is complete.

To improve AutoFormat's accuracy when selecting formats, open the list box and choose the type of document you are formatting: General document, Letter, or Email.

4. Choose OK to begin formatting. Word reviews the text and selects styles from the current template.

5. When AutoFormat is finished, the document will have the new format. If you selected the AutoFormat and Review option then another dialog box appears, and you have four choices (see Figure 11.7):

- Choose Accept All to accept all the changes.
- Choose Reject All to reject all the changes.
- Choose Review Changes to examine changes one by one, accepting or rejecting individual changes. See "Reviewing Format Changes" in this section for more information.
- Choose Style Gallery to apply styles from another template. See "Using the Style Gallery" later in this chapter for more information.

If you don't like the result of the AutoFormatting, you can undo the formatting changes you've made.

FIG. 11.7

When AutoFormat is complete, you can choose to accept or reject all changes, to review the changes, or to change templates in the Style Gallery.

 To undo all changes after accepting them, click the down-arrow button next to the Undo button on the Standard toolbar and undo AutoFormat Begin.

> **CAUTION**
>
> You may have noticed, in the AutoFormat dialog box, the AutoFormat now option. If you choose this option, Word doesn't prompt you to review the changes it makes—you simply see them on-screen. If you don't like what you see, click the Undo button.

T I P You can automatically format tables with AutoFormat on the Table menu.

▶ **See** "Formatting a Table with Table AutoFormat," **p. 638**

Part
II

Ch
11

Reviewing Format Changes

After a document has been automatically formatted, you may want to review the changes and possibly make some alterations. You can choose the Review Changes button in the AutoFormat dialog box to review the changes one by one (refer to Figure 11.7). As you review each change, you can accept or reject it. You can also scroll through the document and select specific changes for review.

Word indicates changes to text and formatting with temporary revision marks and color. With paragraph marks displayed, Word highlights the extra paragraph marks it deleted and also those to which a style was applied.

 To display paragraph marks, click the Show/Hide ¶ button on the Standard toolbar.

You can also review the document with the revision marks hidden. To hide revision marks, choose the Hide Marks button in the Review AutoFormat Changes dialog box.

Table 11.1 describes Word's revision marks.

Table 11.1 AutoFormat Revision Marks

Visual Change	Meaning
Blue paragraph mark (¶)	Applied a style to that paragraph
Red paragraph mark (¶)	Deleted that paragraph mark
Strikethrough character (–) (indicated in red)	Deleted text or spaces
Underline (_) (indicated in blue)	Added the underlined characters
Vertical bar in the left margin	Changed the text or formatting in that line of text

To review changes made by AutoFormat, follow these steps:

1. After Word completes the AutoFormat, choose the Review Changes button. The Review AutoFormat Changes dialog box appears (see Figure 11.8).

FIG. 11.8

Use options in the Review AutoFormat Changes dialog box to reject or accept the changes made by AutoFormat.

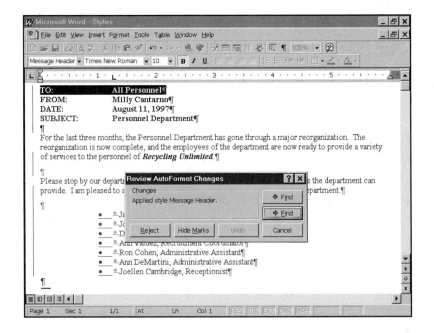

2. Choose from among the following options to target the change(s) you want to review:

   To see text under the dialog box, drag the box by its title bar to a new location.

   To see the entire document, use the vertical scroll bar in the document window to scroll through the document.

To see changes one by one, use the Find buttons in the Review AutoFormat Changes dialog box.

To see the effect of another style, select the text and then select another style from the Style Preview box on the Formatting toolbar.

3. Choose from among the following options to alter the selected change:

To undo the displayed change, choose Reject.

To undo the last rejected change, choose Undo.

To view the document with all remaining changes and revision marks turned off, choose Hide Marks.

4. Click the Cancel button to accept all remaining changes. Any text for which you rejected changes returns to its original appearance, but Word applies all remaining changes. The AutoFormat dialog box is displayed again.

5. Choose Accept All to accept all changes.

Or, you can choose Reject All to reject all changes.

You can even choose Style Gallery to select a different AutoFormat style.

> **T I P** AutoFormat can format a document with styles you've designed if you redefine the built-in styles. See "Getting the Most from AutoFormat" and "Creating Styles" later in this chapter.

Setting AutoFormat Options

You can change the rules that Word follows each time it performs an AutoFormat. You can choose whether to apply styles to headings and lists, for example.

To change the AutoFormat formatting rules, follow these steps:

1. Choose Format, AutoFormat and select the Options button to display the AutoCorrect dialog box. Then, choose the Auto Format tab (see Figure 11.9).

2. Select from the Apply group the document parts to which you want Word to apply styles (selected options are marked with a ✓).

3. Select from the Replace group the characters or symbols you want Word to replace (selected options are marked with a ✓).

4. Click OK.

The options for AutoFormat As You Type now appear on their own tab in the AutoCorrect dialog box. Choose Format, AutoFormat, and then select AutoFormat As You Type.

FIG. 11.9
Specify the settings you want to control the changes Word makes during an AutoFormat.

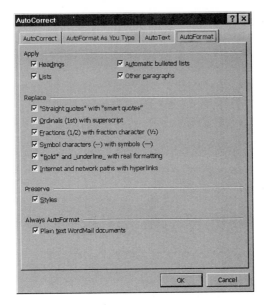

 T I P To speed up the formatting process, have Word automatically format as you type. Set the options for this type of automatic formatting on the AutoFormat As You Type tab in the AutoCorrect dialog box. This tab contains three sections: Apply As You Type, Replace As You Type, and Automatically As You Type.

Getting the Most from AutoFormat

Any formatting you have applied using commands on the Format menu helps Word determine which styles to apply during AutoFormat. For example, styles previously applied can be preserved or changed, depending on the settings you establish on the AutoFormat tab (see the preceding section). In addition, the following tips will help you maximize the results you get from the AutoFormat command.

- *Use a larger font for level 1 headings than you use for subordinate level headings.* Higher heading style levels are applied to larger point sizes.

- *Clear all the check boxes on the AutoFormat tab, choose OK, and then do an AutoFormat.* Extra hard returns will be removed from files, such as those you've converted from another file format.

- *Type (c), (R), or (TM).* Word converts this text to the appropriate ©, ®, or ™ symbol.

■ *Redefine built-in styles.* Word assigns styles, such as heading styles, formatted as you
   want them.

▶ **See** "Checking Your Grammar," **p. 248**

Using the Style Gallery

Each document you create is based on a template. When you create a new document, the
styles that are part of the template you select are copied into that document. Each template contains a set of standard styles, most of which are available with all Word's
templates. Styles in one template may differ from those in another. For example, Heading
1 in the Normal template uses Arial 14-point, whereas in the Professional Fax template,
Heading 1 is Arial MT Black 11-point. You can use Format, Style Gallery to preview and
then change the appearance of a document by switching the style definitions to those of
another template.

You can choose from any of the document templates that appear in the New dialog box
when you start a new document. You'll find templates in the following categories: fax
cover sheet, legal pleading, letter, memo, report, resume, newsletter, and Web page—and,
of course, any existing templates from Word 7. Many of Word's templates fit into one of
three families:

■ Contemporary

■ Professional

■ Elegant

▶ **See** "Using Word's Predefined Templates," **p. 203**

Starting in Word 7, you'll find a template name preceded by its family name; for example,
the fax template in the Contemporary style family is named CONTEMPORARY FAX.DOT.
In Word 6, each template name was followed by a number to indicate the family into which
it fit, but the long file names feature of Windows 95 lets Microsoft eliminate the use of this
coding system.

To preview and change styles in the Style Gallery, follow these steps:

1. Display in the active window the document whose styles you want to change.

2. Choose Format, Style Gallery. The Style Gallery dialog box appears (see Figure
   11.10).

3. Select one of the following in the Preview group:

   Select Document to see the active document formatted with the styles from the
   template you select.

Part
II

Ch
11

FIG. 11.10

Use the Style Gallery to preview your document with styles from other templates.

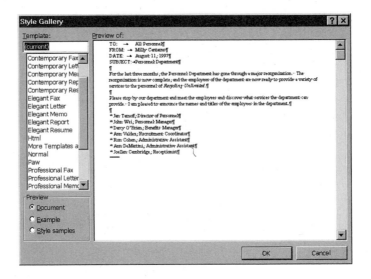

Select Example to see sample text formatted with the styles from the template you select.

Select Style Samples to see a list of styles available in the selected template including text samples of each style.

4. Select the Template you want to preview. Continue to preview other templates by selecting them.

5. Choose OK to accept the selected template. Word copies the styles from the template you selected to the active document.

   Or, choose Cancel to return to your document with its original template intact.

   ▶ **See** "Creating Documents with Wizards," **p. 216**

When you change the styles in the Style Gallery, you are copying the style formatting from the new template into the active document. You aren't replacing the template; you're replacing the style definitions in the current document only. For example, the original Body Text style of Times New Roman 10-point may be replaced by Times New Roman 12-point. In addition, any styles that exist in the new template and not in the one attached to the document are added to the document. Any styles that are unique to the document aren't affected by the change.

▶ **See** "Modifying Templates," **p. 210**

Using Word Standard Styles

Word includes a great number of *standard*, or *built-in styles*. You already are familiar with the Normal style, which Word uses to apply default formatting to all new documents based on the default Normal template. Other standard styles include those that provide formatting for outline headings, headers, footers, page numbers, line numbers, index entries, table of contents entries, comments, and footnotes.

What You Need to Know About Standard Styles

In a new document, you see the styles Heading 1, Heading 2, Heading 3, Normal, and Default Paragraph Font listed in the Formatting toolbar's Style Preview box. Word applies these styles automatically when you use the AutoFormat feature, and you can apply these styles to selected paragraphs yourself. You are likely to apply some standard styles automatically by creating headers, footers, index entries, and so on. After you use these styles in your document, their names appear in the Formatting toolbar's Style Preview box.

Many standard styles do more than just format text. When you use the automatic heading styles (Heading 1 through Heading 9), for example, you later can collect these headings into a table of contents. Or, if you insert table of contents entries (formatted with the styles TOC 1 through TOC 9), you later can collect these entries as a table of contents. Similarly, if you insert index or footnote entries into your document, Word collects them where you have specified they are to appear in your document.

Part

II

Ch

11

▶ **See** "Formatting an Index," **p. 977**

▶ **See** "Creating a Table of Contents Using Any Style," **p. 990**

▶ **See** "Formatting Cross-References," **p. 1032**

▶ **See** "Formatting Captions," **p. 1040**

To apply standard styles from the menu command, follow these steps:

1. Position the insertion point where you want the new style to begin or select the text or paragraph(s) you want formatted in the new style. (To format a single paragraph, you can position the insertion point anywhere in the paragraph.)

2. Choose F̲ormat, S̲tyle. The Style dialog box opens (see Figure 11.11).

3. Choose All Styles in the L̲ist drop-down list. All styles are displayed in the S̲tyles list.

4. Select a style from the S̲tyles list and choose the A̲pply button.

To apply standard styles from the Formatting toolbar, follow these steps:

1. Position the insertion point where you want the new style to begin or select the text or paragraph(s) you want formatted in the new style. (To format a single paragraph, you can position the insertion point anywhere in the paragraph.)

FIG. 11.11

Select any of the standard styles from the Style dialog box.

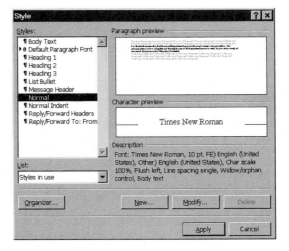

2. Click the down arrow next to the Style Preview box in the Formatting toolbar. Each style in the list appears formatted using the attributes it will apply to your document (see Figure 11.12).

Styles appear in the Style Preview box using the formatting they will apply to your document. The gray box at the right edge of the line shows you the font size of the style. You can tell the style's alignment by the four horizontal lines that appear in the same gray box. And, the symbol in the gray box (either a or ¶) identifies the type of style—character or paragraph.

FIG. 11.12

When you display styles from the Formatting Toolbar, you'll see them using the formatting they will apply to your document.

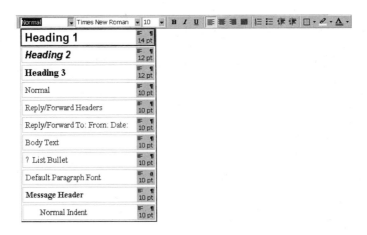

3. Click the style you want to apply.

N O T E The Style Preview box in the Formatting toolbar shows the style at the position of the insertion point or of the selected text. If the text selection includes text formatted with more than one style, the Style Preview box is blank. ▪

Table 11.1 describes some of the Word standard styles.

Table 11.1 Word Standard Styles

Standard Style or Style Family	Style Type	Default formatting	How applied
Normal (used by default to format all new text)	Paragraph	10- or 12-point serif font (varies with printer), left-aligned, single line spacing, widow/orphan control	Applied to all text automatically in document that is based on the Normal template
Normal Indent (indents paragraphs)	Paragraph	Normal + 1/2-inch left indent	Manually
Heading 1 through Heading 9 (formats outline headings)	Paragraph	Formatting ranges from large and bold (Heading 1) to small and italic	Outline view
Comment Reference (creates hidden comment references)	Character	Normal + 8 point Font	Insert, Comment
Comment Text (formats comment text)	Paragraph	Normal	Typing annotation text in the comment pane
Caption (formats figure captions)	Paragraph	Normal + bold	Insert, Caption
Footer (formats footers)	Paragraph	Normal + 3-inch centered tab, 6-inch right tab	View, Header and Footer
Footnote Reference (formats footnote references)	Character	Default Paragraph Font	Insert, Footnote
Endnote Reference (formats endnote references)	Character	Default Paragraph Font	Insert, Footnote
Footnote text (formats footnote text)	Paragraph	Normal	Typing footnote text

Part

II

Ch

11

continues

Table 11.1 Continued

Standard Style or Style Family	Style Type	Default formatting	How applied
Endnote text (formats endnote text)	Paragraph	Normal	Typing endnote text
Header (formats headers)	Paragraph	Normal + 3-inch centered tab, 6-inch right tab	View, Header and Footer command
Index 1 through Index 9 (formats index entries)	Paragraph	Varies with selection of index formats	Insert, Index and Tables, Index tab
Index Heading (formats optional heading separators in index)	Paragraph	Varies with selection of index formats	Insert, Index and Tables, Index tab
Line Number (formats line numbers)	Character	Normal	File, Page Setup Layout tab, Line Numbers
Page Number	Character	Normal	Insert, Page Numbers
TOC 1 through TOC 9 (formats table of contents entries)	Paragraph	Varies with selection of Table of Contents formats	Insert, Index and Tables, Table of Contents tab

Notice that the formatting for many standard styles is based on the Normal style. In other words, many styles include all the formatting contained in the Normal style plus additional formatting choices. The header and footer styles, for example, are Normal style plus tab settings.

N O T E If you change the Normal style, any other style based on the Normal style also changes. If you change the Normal style to double spacing, for example, headers, footers, index entries, and all other styles based on Normal also will include double spacing. If the other style includes its own definition for line spacing, then that definition takes precedence over the Normal line spacing. ▪

 T I P You can redefine a standard style except the Default Paragraph Font, but you cannot delete a standard style.

Redefining Standard Styles

Standard styles come with predefined formatting, but you can easily redefine them. Suppose that you want to use the standard heading styles (Heading 1 through Heading 9) to format your document because you can use the Outline view to apply these styles and because you want to collect the headings later as a table of contents. Unfortunately, you don't like the default formatting choices Word has made for the heading styles. Redefine the styles, using either the styles-by-example techniques, or by using Format, Style; both methods are described later in this chapter.

Displaying Styles with the Style Area

If you're working with styles extensively, you can display the style area on your screen to list each paragraph's style name in the left margin (see Figure 11.13).

FIG. 11.13
Use the Style Area to display the names of the styles currently in use.

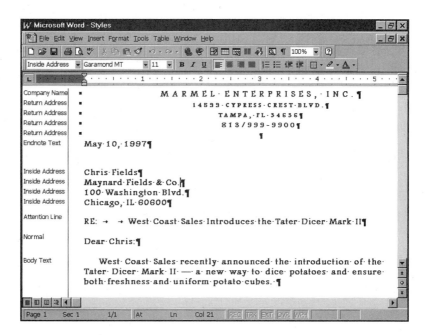

Part

II

Ch

11

Using the style area, you can see at a glance which style is applied to each paragraph. With your mouse, you also can use the style area to quickly access the Style dialog box.

To apply and redefine styles quickly, double-click the style name in the style area to display the Style dialog box. From there, you can apply, create, or redefine a style.

The width of the style area varies. When you first display the style area, you set its width. After it's displayed, however, you can change its width by using a mouse to drag the line separating the style area from the text to the left or right. You can close the style area entirely by dragging the arrow all the way to the left edge of the screen, or by resetting the style area width to zero.

To display or remove the style area, follow these steps:

1. Choose Tools, Options.

2. Select the View tab. The View dialog box lists all the view settings you can modify.

3. Type the style area width you want in decimal inches in the Style Area Width box.

    Or, click the up or down arrows at the right end of the Style Area Width spin box to increase or decrease the style area width by tenths of an inch.

    Or, type **0** (zero) to remove the style area from the screen.

4. Choose OK.

 By single-clicking the style name in the style area, you quickly can select an entire paragraph.

 If you frequently display the style area, record a simple macro that turns on the style area. (You can even edit your macro so that it toggles the style area on and off.) Chapter 39, "Recording and Modifying VBA Modules," explains how to create macros.

Overriding Styles with Manual Formatting

Although you can do most of your formatting with styles, at times you will need to override the formatting in a style you have already applied. You may want to do something simple, like making one word in a paragraph bold, or maybe something more substantial, like italicizing a whole paragraph. You can modify the formatting in a paragraph without changing the style.

Be aware, however, of the effect your formatting will have on the paragraph if you later reapply the style. Reapplying the style may cancel some of the manual formatting changes you have made. Manual formatting works with styles as follows:

- If the reapplied style contains formatting choices in the same category as those you have applied manually, the style's choices override the manual formatting. If you have manually applied double line spacing, but the style specifies single line spacing, for example, then the double line spacing is canceled when you apply the style.

- If the reapplied style contains formatting choices unrelated to the formatting you have applied manually, the style won't affect manual formatting. If you add a border to a paragraph and then reapply a style that doesn't specify borders, for example, the border will remain.

- Some character formatting choices toggle on and off—you select bold to turn it on and select it again to turn it off. If you apply a style containing bold to a paragraph with one or two words that are bold, for example, then all of the paragraph will be bold except the one or two words that you manually formatted as bold (the style toggles them off). On the other hand, if you make a whole paragraph bold, then reapply a style that contains bold, Word leaves the paragraph bold rather than toggling off the bold.

- If you want to remove all manually applied character formatting from a word formatted with a style, move the insertion point into the word that was manually formatted, then press Ctrl+space bar.

- If you want to remove all manually applied paragraph formatting from a paragraph formatted with a style, place the insertion point anywhere in that paragraph and press Ctrl+Q.

Applying, Copying, and Removing Styles

Part
II
Ch
11

The power of styles becomes apparent when you use them to apply consistent formatting to paragraph after paragraph in your document. You can apply styles to text as you type or to selected text by choosing a style from a menu command, from the Formatting toolbar, or with a keyboard shortcut. You will mostly use the Formatting toolbar.

By default, the Formatting toolbar appears when you start Word. If you don't see it, you can display the Formatting toolbar by following these steps:

1. Choose View, Toolbars.
2. Select Formatting from the Toolbars list. A ✓ appears in the check box to indicate that it is selected.

Resolving Conflicts Between Paragraph and Character Style

When you first begin to work with styles, you may not realize that there are two types of styles—paragraph and character. It is important to understand how these two styles interact. Because characters are within paragraphs, applying a paragraph style to a paragraph can change the appearance of the characters with a character style.

NOTE Remember that paragraph styles can include both paragraph-level formatting commands and character-level formatting. Character styles include only

continues

continued

character-level formatting commands. Any paragraph style you apply to text formats the entire paragraph (or the group of selected paragraphs). If a paragraph style includes character formatting, it too is applied to the entire paragraph. If you apply a character style, such as bold, to text in a paragraph, and then apply a paragraph style that includes bold, the text you bold-faced with the character style appears normal, rather than bold, because the paragraph style toggles off bold. ■

Applying Paragraph Styles

To apply a paragraph style to a single paragraph, the insertion point must first be positioned anywhere in that paragraph. You can apply a paragraph style to a group of paragraphs by first selecting those paragraphs, or at least part of each paragraph (see Figure 11.14).

FIG. 11.14
All of these paragraphs will change with a new style selection because at least part of each paragraph has been selected.

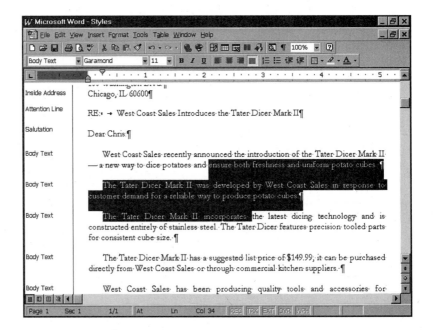

Applying Character Styles

To apply a character style, you must first select the text to which you want to apply the character style. The formatting of the new style will be added to those formats already in effect on the selected text. For example, a character style that adds bold and italic doesn't change the font or point size or other formatting applied by the paragraph style in use.

To apply a style from the menu, follow these steps:

1. Position the insertion point inside the paragraph, or select text in the paragraph(s) you want to format with a style.

2. Choose Format, Style. The Style dialog box appears.

3. Click the down arrow to the right of the List box and select one of the following options:

   Select the Styles in Use option to list standard styles and those you've created or modified for the current document.

   Select the All Styles option to list all styles available in the document.

   Select the User-Defined Styles option to list non-standard styles that you have created for the document

4. Select the style you want from the Styles list box. Paragraph styles are preceded by the paragraph symbol; character styles are preceded by the a symbol. The Paragraph Preview and Character Preview boxes provide a sample of how the style appears.

5. Choose Apply.

To apply a style from the Formatting toolbar, follow these steps:

1. Position the insertion point inside the paragraph, or select text in the paragraph(s) you want to format with a style.

In Word 97, you can distinguish a character style from a paragraph style by the symbol that appears in the same box where you see the style's point size.

2. Click the down arrow at the right side of the Style Preview box in the Formatting toolbar to display a list of available styles. In the box at the right that identifies the font size for the style, you'll see the ¶ symbol for paragraph styles and the a symbol for character styles (see Figure 11.15).

3. Select the style you want to apply to the paragraph(s) or selected text (scroll the list if necessary).

TIP The styles listed in the Style Preview box are only a partial list of what's available. To see the entire list, hold down the Shift key while you click the down arrow next to the Style Preview box.

To apply a style from the keyboard, follow these steps:

1. Position the insertion point inside the paragraph, or select text in the paragraph(s) you want to format with a style.

FIG. 11.15

You can distinguish paragraph styles from character styles by looking for the symbols in the box that displays the style's font size.

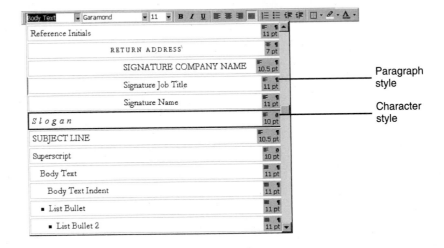

Paragraph style

Character style

2. Press any of the following key combinations:

Press This	To Apply This Style
Ctrl+Alt+1	Heading 1
Ctrl+Alt+2	Heading 2
Ctrl+Alt+3	Heading 3
Ctrl+Shift+L	List Bullet (bulleted list style)
Ctrl+Shift+N	Normal
Ctrl+Shift+S	Activates the Style Preview box on the Formatting toolbar; choose the style you want from the list

When you press Ctrl+Shift+S, Word selects the currently displayed style in the Style Preview box in the Formatting toolbar. To select another, either type a different name in the Style Preview box, or use the arrow keys to highlight another style and then press Enter. If you type the name of a style that doesn't exist, you will create a style based on the example of the selected paragraph or paragraphs, rather than applying a style.

You can assign shortcut keys to other styles, as well. See "Creating Style Shortcut Keys" later in this chapter.

Copying Styles

You can apply the same style several times consecutively. Apply the style the first time, then select the additional text you want to format with that style, and press F4 or Ctrl+Y. Continue the procedure to apply the style in other locations. This method works for both paragraph styles and character styles.

You also can use the Format Painter button on the Standard toolbar to copy character styles to paragraphs or selected text, one or several times.

To copy character styles with the Format Painter button, follow these steps:

1. Select the text or paragraph mark (¶) that has the formatting you want to copy.

2. Click the Format Painter button on the Standard toolbar.

3. Select the text you want to format with the character style. The new character style is applied to the selected text.

To copy character styles multiple times with the Format Painter button, repeat the steps above but double-click in step 2. To turn off the copy process, click the Format Painter button again.

> **TIP** If there are a lot of instances where you want to replace one style with another, then use Word's Edit, Replace command to replace all or selectively replace one style with another.

▶ **See** " Finding and Replacing Formatting and Styles," **p. 234**

Removing Character Styles

You can remove a character style and reapply the default character formatting, which will match the character formats defined for the selected paragraph style.

To remove a character style, place the insertion point in the word or select the text formatted with the character style you want to remove, and press Ctrl+spacebar.

Creating Styles

The process of using styles of your own involves two steps. First, you create the style, specifying formatting choices like paragraph indentations, line spacing, font, and font size. Then you apply that style—along with all your formatting choices—to other characters or paragraphs in your document.

You can create paragraph styles in two ways: by example (using the Formatting toolbar or a keyboard shortcut) or by menu command. Creating a style by example is a good method for a beginner to use; because creating a style by example is so easy, many advanced users also prefer this technique. Alternatively, using a menu command gives you more options, including creating character styles, and isn't difficult when you understand the concept of styles. (See "Creating Styles with a Menu Command" later in this chapter.)

Part
II

Ch
11

N O T E   Styles are saved with the document or template in which you create them. You can
share styles with other documents, however. (Refer to the section "Copying Styles
Between Documents" later in this chapter.) ▪

Naming the New Style

A new style name must be unique. If you try to create a new style with an existing name,
you apply the existing style to your paragraph instead of creating a new style. If that happens, choose Edit, Undo and try again. Be aware that Word includes quite a few built-in
styles (like Normal and Heading 1 through Heading 9); don't create new styles using the
names of these built-in styles. For a list of built-in styles, refer to the section "Using Word
Standard Styles" earlier in this chapter.

As you're naming your style, remember these rules:

- A style name can contain as many as 253 characters. Try, however, to use simple,
  memorable style names.

- The name can contain spaces, commas, and aliases. An *alias* is an optional, shorter
  name (see "Giving a Style a New Name or Alias" later in this chapter).

- Style names are case-sensitive—you can use uppercase and lowercase letters.

- Illegal characters include backslash (\), braces ({ or }), and semicolon (;).

Choose a style name that makes sense to you so that you will remember it later and use it
consistently in other documents. If you frequently use small caps in your documents, for
example, create a style called Small Caps and use it to quickly format text.

Creating a Style by Example

To create a style by example, you format a paragraph the way you want it, and then create
a style based on the formatting contained in that paragraph. If your example paragraph
contains left and right indents and a border, those formatting choices will also be part of
your style. As you format your first paragraph (the one you will use as an example to create a style), remember that although paragraph styles are paragraph-level formatting
commands, they also can contain character formatting. The character-level formatting is
defined by the font, size, and other character formats of the first character of the selected
text.

To create a style by example, follow these steps:

1. Choose View, Toolbars and select the Formatting toolbar (if it isn't already displayed).

2. Format your example paragraph.

   You can include character or paragraph formatting, borders and shading, frames and positioning, tabs, and a language for spell checking.

3. With the insertion point still in your example paragraph, select the entire name of the existing style in the Formatting toolbar's Style Preview box, or press Ctrl+Shift+S to select the name of the style in the Style Preview box (see Figure 11.16).

FIG. 11.16
Select the current style name in the Formatting toolbar's Style Preview box.

4. Type the name of the style you want to create (see Figure 11.17).

FIG. 11.17
Type the new style name to create a style by example.

5. Press Enter to create the style.

After you create your style, look in the Formatting toolbar's Style Preview box. You see your new style name displayed, indicating that its formatting choices control the appearance of your example paragraph.

You also can use a menu command to create a style by example. You might do this, for example, if you want to use a formatted paragraph as the basis for a style, but you also want to add additional formatting choices to the style.

To create a style by example using the menu command, follow these steps:

1. Format the paragraph you want to use as an example for your style, and leave the insertion point inside the paragraph.

2. Choose Format, Style and choose the New button. (See "Creating a Style with a Menu Command" for details on using this dialog box.)

3. In the Name box, type the name of your new style.

4. Choose Format and make additional formatting choices, if necessary.

5. Choose OK to return to the Style dialog box.

6. Choose Close.

Creating a Style with a Menu Command

If you want to create styles before you use them, rather than creating them by example, use Format, Style. Using this command, you name a style, define its formatting characteristics, and select options such as whether to base the style on another style, whether to follow it with another style, and whether to add the style to the current template. You can also import and export styles to and from other documents and templates. Also, using this method, you can create both types of styles: paragraph and character.

When you create a style by using the menu command, you have the option to apply the style to the currently selected paragraph or simply to add it to the list of styles you created for your document (or for your template).

All new styles you create are based on the style of the currently selected paragraph in your document. In the next section, you learn how you can base your new style on any other style.

 TIP If you plan to use your styles over and over in the same type of document, as in a monthly newsletter, create them in a new template.

▶ **See** "Creating a New Template," **p. 213**

 TIP If you want to print a list of a document's styles (along with a description of each style), choose File, Print, select Styles in the Print What box, and then choose OK.

To create a style from the menu command, follow these steps:

1. Choose Format, Style. The Style dialog box appears.

   Notice that the preview boxes display both the paragraph and character formatting of the currently selected paragraph. The Description box indicates the precise characteristics of the formatting.

2. Click the New button. The New Style dialog box appears (see Figure 11.18).

3. In the Name box, type the name of your new style. Use a unique, brief, and easy-to-recall name. Refer to "Naming the New Style," earlier in this chapter, for style naming rules.

4. In the Style Type box, select Character to create a character style, or Paragraph to create a paragraph style.

5. Click the Format button to display the list of format options and select the one you want (if you want to include bold formatting as part of your style, for example, select Font to display the Font dialog box, then select the Bold option from the Font Style group):

FIG. 11.18

You can create styles in the New Style dialog box.

Select This	To Select These Formatting options
Font	Font, style (bold, italic, underline), size, color, super/subscript, and character spacing
Paragraph	Paragraph alignment, spacing, indentation, and line spacing (not available for character styles)
Tabs	Tab stop position, alignment, and leaders, or clear tabs (not available for character styles)
Border	Border location, style, color, and paragraph shading (not available for character styles)
Language	The language that the spell checker, thesaurus, and grammar checker should use for the current paragraph
Frame	Text wrapping, frame size or position, or remove frame (not available for character styles)
Numbering	Bulleted and Numbered paragraphs in various styles (not available for character styles)

Repeat this step to include as much formatting as you want.

6. Choose OK.

   To create additional styles, you can repeat steps 2 through 5 before closing the dialog box.

7. To apply your new style to the currently selected paragraph, choose Apply.

   Or, to exit the Style dialog box without applying the style to any paragraph, choose Close.

Part
II

Ch
11

CAUTION

When you type the name of your new style in step 2, be sure that it is a unique name. If you type the name of an existing style and then make formatting choices, you will redefine the existing style. Any text formatted with the existing style then takes on this redefined formatting.

As part of the process of creating a style, you can assign shortcut keys to make the style easy to apply. See the later section "Creating Style Shortcut Keys."

Creating a Style Based on an Existing Style

You may need a group of styles that are similar to each other but have slight variations. For example, you may need a Table Body style for the contents of a table, and you also may need a Table Heading style and a Table Last Row style. Using the following technique, you can create a "family" of styles based on one foundation style.

To base one style on another style, follow these steps:

1. Choose Format, Style.
2. Choose New.
3. Choose Name and type the name of your new style.
4. Specify the name of the style on which you want to base your style in the Based On box. To display a list of styles, click the down arrow to the right of the Based On box.

   When you select a style name, you see the name of the style plus any formatting attributes from the selected paragraph in the Description box. Your new style automatically is based on that existing style, unless you specify a different style.
5. Choose any of the Format button options to add formatting options to your style.
6. Choose OK to return to the Style dialog box.
7. Choose Close.

   Or, choose Apply if you want to apply your new style to the currently selected paragraph.

   ▶ **See** "Creating a New Template," **p. 213**

Creating Style Shortcut Keys

A fast way to apply a style is with a shortcut key, which you can assign as part of the process of creating or redefining a style. The shortcut keys usually include pressing the Alt key plus a letter that you designate. You could assign the shortcut Alt+S, for example, to a style called Sub. You can use other key combinations if you want, but they may conflict with shortcut keys preassigned to Word built-in functions. (Word uses Ctrl+Shift+S, for example, to enable you to create or apply a style quickly, so you wouldn't want to assign Ctrl+Shift+S to your style Sub.)

To create shortcut keys for styles, follow these steps:

1. Choose Format, Style.
2. From the Styles list, highlight the style for which you want to create shortcut keys.
3. Click the Modify button.
4. Click the Shortcut Key button. The Customize Keyboard dialog box opens (see Figure 11.19).

FIG. 11.19

You can assign shortcut keys to styles with the Customize Keyboard dialog box.

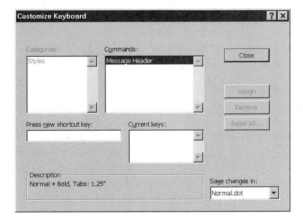

Part

II

Ch

11

5. Select the Press New Shortcut Key text box, and press the shortcut key combination you want to use. You can use the letters A through Z, the numbers 0 through 9, Insert, and Delete, combined with Ctrl, Alt, and Shift.

If the shortcut key combination you selected is already in use, Word displays the message Currently Assigned To and the command or function to which the shortcut key is assigned. If the shortcut key isn't assigned, the Currently Assigned To message line displays [unassigned].

T I P To try another combination, press the Backspace key to delete the combination you initially selected.

6. Click the Assign button.
7. Click the Close button to return to the Modify Style dialog box.

8. Choose OK to return to the Style dialog box.

9. Choose Close.

To remove a shortcut key, follow these steps:

1. Choose Format, Style.

2. From the Styles list, highlight the style for which you want to remove the shortcut key.

3. Click the Modify button.

4. Click the Shortcut Key button.

5. Select the shortcut key you want to remove in the Current Keys box.

6. Click the Remove button.

7. Click Close to return to the Modify Style dialog box.

8. Choose OK to return to the Style dialog box.

9. Choose Close.

To apply a style with a shortcut key you have assigned, follow these steps:

1. Select the paragraph (or paragraphs) to which you want to apply the style.

2. Press the key combination you assigned to the style. (If your shortcut is Alt+C, for example, hold down Alt while you press C.)

Following One Style with the Next Style

One of the most useful style options is the ability to follow one style with another. Suppose that you're editing a complex document with many subheadings, all formatted with styles. You want the text following each subheading to be formatted with the Normal style. You would save considerable time and effort if you didn't have to manually apply the Normal style to the paragraph following each subheading. Setting one style to follow another saves you that time and effort. If you tell Word that the Normal style should follow the subheading style, then, when you finish typing a subheading and press Enter, Word automatically applies the Normal style to the next paragraph.

 T I P   You can add styles to a menu or toolbar. See Chapter 38, "Customizing the Toolbar, Menus, and Shortcut Keys."

By default, Word follows each style with that same style so that when you press Enter, the style carries forward. In many cases, that's what you want. When you finish typing a paragraph formatted with the Normal style, typically you want the next paragraph also to be formatted with the Normal style.

To follow one style with another style, follow these steps:

1. Choose Format, Style.
2. Click the New button to create a new style. The New Style dialog box appears.

   Or, highlight an existing style from the list and click Modify. The Modify Style dialog box appears.
3. Select from the Style for Following Paragraph list box the style that you want to follow the current style. To display a list of styles, click the down arrow to the right of the Style for Following Paragraph box.

   If you select no style, your style will be followed by itself.
4. Choose OK to return to the Style dialog box.
5. Choose Close.

Copying Styles Between Documents

Every document you create includes styles—even if it's only the Normal style and Word's other standard styles. Each document's group of styles is provided by its template—either the Normal template, one of the other templates provided with Word, or a custom template you create.

Part

II

Ch

11

In its simplest sense, using a template is the basic way you can share styles among documents. You create a template that contains certain styles you need, and then base your documents on that template. You may, for example, have a template called Letters that contains styles for formatting letters to be printed on your company's letterhead. If you regularly produce several different types of documents, you may create a template for each of them.

▶ **See** "Creating a New Template," **p. 213**

At some point, however, you may want to use the styles from one document or template in a different document or template. You can do that by copying styles from one document or template to another. For example, you might create a template that includes styles for a sales letter that you frequently write. You notice a co-worker's letter that includes a nice style. Using the following technique, you can copy the style you want from your co-worker's template to your sales letter template.

You can copy styles to or from any document or template. If you copy an identically named style, it replaces the one in the document or template you're copying to (you will be asked to confirm the replacement); new styles are added to the document or template to which you're copying.

To copy styles from a document or template, follow these steps:

1. Choose Format, Style.

2. Click the Organizer button. The Organizer dialog box appears.

   The In box on the left displays a list of the styles in the currently open document or template. The To box on the right displays a list of the styles of the NORMAL.DOT template.

3. Select Close File (below the appropriate list) to close the current document style list or the Normal template style list. When you close either the current document or the Normal template, the Close File button changes to an Open File button and you can open a different document or template.

4. Select Open File (below the appropriate list) to open a different document or template to copy its styles. The Open dialog box appears; select the document you want to use. If you want to select a template, open the Files of Type in the Open dialog box to choose Document Templates (*.dot). If necessary, change folders or drives. When you find the document or template you want to open, choose the Open button to return to the Organizer dialog box.

5. Select the styles you want to copy from the In or To lists. The Copy button arrows change direction to indicate the direction the styles will be copied.

   You can select a contiguous group of styles by clicking the first one you want to copy, then holding down Shift while you click the last one you want to copy. To select noncontiguous styles, hold down Ctrl while you click each one.

6. Choose Copy.

7. Choose Close.

Another way to merge a *single* style into a document is to copy into your document a paragraph formatted with a different style from another document. Be careful, though. Copying styles into your document this way doesn't override existing styles, as does copying styles through the Organizer dialog box. If you copy a paragraph formatted with a style called First Item, for example, and your existing document also contains a style called First Item, the new paragraph will take on the formatting of the existing First Item style.

T I P
You can avoid copying the style along with the paragraph into the new document by *not* including the paragraph mark with the text you're copying.

Other commands for inserting text into a document, such as AutoText, Paste, and Paste Special, also can bring in new styles. You can copy in as many as 50 paragraphs that contain unique style names—if you copy in more than 50, Word merges in the document's entire style sheet.

Changing Styles

You can change any style, including standard styles. This capability makes it easy to adapt to the changing tasks you have to do. For example, suppose you defined a style for closing signatures and your company develops a new format. You don't need to define a new style; you can simply redefine the style you previously created. All you need to do is continue working like you did before; the new style definition takes care of the changes.

There are many ways to change a style. To name just a few, you can redefine the style to incorporate new or different characteristics, or you can delete or rename the style. To make assigning styles easier, provide an alias for a style. The following sections discuss these and other techniques for changing styles.

> **CAUTION**
>
> Make sure you save the template containing the styles you have modified. If you do not save the template, your changes will not be available next time you use the template.

Deleting a Style

At some point, you may decide you no longer need a style. You can delete it, and all text associated with the deleted style will revert to the Normal style. The list of styles will become shorter, making it easier to look through the Styles list. You cannot delete built-in styles.

To delete a style, follow these steps:

1. Choose Format, Style.
2. Select the style you want to delete from the Styles list.

   If you have selected a paragraph containing the style you want to delete, the style already will be selected in the Styles list box.
3. Click the Delete button. You see a message asking whether you want to delete the style.
4. Choose Yes.

You also can delete several styles at once. Choose the Organizer button in the Style dialog box. Select the styles you want to delete and click the Delete button.

 TIP You can select a group of contiguous files by clicking the first one, and then holding down Shift while you click the last one. To select noncontiguous files, hold down Ctrl while you click each one.

Part

II

Ch

11

N O T E   You can choose Edit, Replace to delete text that has been formatted with a particular style. In the Find box, click the More button. Then, click the Format button and choose Style. Word displays the Find Style dialog box. Choose the name of the style whose text you want to delete from the Find What Style list and choose OK to return to the Find and Replace dialog box. Leave the Replace With box empty. Click the Find Next button. If the text you find is text you want to delete, click the Replace button. If you don't want to delete the text, proceed through the document with the Find Next button to the next item. Choose Close when you are finished deleting text. ▪

Giving a Style a New Name or Alias

You can rename a style, which doesn't affect the associated text, but changes the style name throughout your document. You can choose to rename a style for two purposes: to give it a new name or to add an optional name, or alias. An *alias* is a shorter name or abbreviation that you can type quickly in the Style Preview box in the Formatting toolbar. For example, if you're using the Heading 1 style frequently, and applying it from the keyboard, you can give the style an alias of h1. Then to apply the Heading 1 style you press Ctrl+Shift+S, type **h1** (rather than the full name), and press Enter.

Standard styles cannot be renamed, but you can add an alias to them. Also, you cannot use a standard style name as an alias for another style.

To rename a style or add an alias, follow these steps:

1. Choose Format, Style.
2. In the Styles list, highlight the style you want to change.
3. Click the Modify button. The Modify Style dialog box appears.
4. Type the new name in the Name text box. To include an alias, type a comma after the new name and then type the alias.

   Or, to add an alias, type a comma after the current style name, and then type the alias.
5. Choose OK to return to the Style dialog box.
6. Choose Close.

Redefining a Style

When you *redefine* a style, all the text formatted with that style updates to reflect the changes you have made. Suppose that you finish a 35-page report with many subheadings formatted with a style called Subhead which includes 18-point, bold, Helvetica, centered text. Now your company's publications committee decides subheadings should be smaller and underlined. Just redefine the style Subhead to reflect the new formatting, and all the subheadings in your text will change.

It is as easy to modify a style by example as it is to create a style by example.

To redefine a style by example, follow these steps:

1. Choose View, Toolbars and select the Formatting toolbar if it isn't currently displayed.

2. Reformat the paragraph you will use as an example for the redefined style.

3. Select the paragraph (or some portion of the paragraph).

4. In the Formatting toolbar, select the current style name, or just position the insertion point to its right.

   Or, press Ctrl+Shift+S and select or type the name of the style you want to redefine.

5. Press Enter. The Modify Style dialog box appears (see Figure 11.20). You have the following options:

   Choose Update the Style to Reflect Recent Changes? to change the formatting of the current style to match the formatting of the selected text.

   Choose Reapply the Formatting of the Style to the Selection? to reapply the formatting of the style to the selected text.

   If you want Word to change style definitions to match current selections *without displaying this dialog box,* place a check in the Automatically Update The Style From Now On check box. If you decide later that you don't want automatic updating, open the Style dialog box, click Modify, and then clear the Automatically Update check box.

FIG. 11.20
The Modify Style
dialog box appears
when you redefine a
style by example.

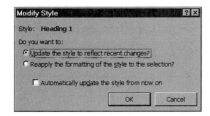

6. Choose OK or press Enter to redefine the style.

The Format, Style command gives you the greatest flexibility for changing a style. You can make a change and add that change to the template on which you based the document. That way, each time you use the template in the future, the particular style will reflect the change.

To redefine a style using the menu command, follow these steps:

1. Choose Format, Style.

2. From the Styles list, select the style you want to redefine. If the style isn't included in the list, select a different option from the List drop-down list.

3. Click the Modify button. The Modify Style dialog box appears (see Figure 11.21).

FIG. 11.21

You can change a style's formatting in the Modify Style dialog box.

Select this check box to add your changes to the document template

4. Click the Format button and select any formatting options you want to add to your style. Remove any other options as needed.

5. Select the Add to Template check box to make the change in the document's template, as well as in the document.

6. Select the Automatically Update check box if you want Word to automatically redefine this style in the future based on any manual formatting you apply to any paragraph formatted with this style.

7. Choose OK to return to the Style dialog box.

   Repeat steps 2 through 6 if you want to redefine additional styles.

8. Choose Close.

Changing the Normal Style

Each time you begin a new document based on the Normal template, Word uses the Normal style to determine the font, font size, line spacing, and other formats. If you find that you are always changing the font, the point size, or some other aspect of the Normal style, you can change its default format settings.

Changing the formats defined for the Normal style in your document affects only the current document. Modify the style and update the template to apply the change to future documents. Existing documents are not changed unless you specifically have Word update their styles. See "Updating Styles" later in this chapter.

Remember that any change you make to the Normal style will be reflected in all styles that are based on that style, which includes most styles.

To change the default settings for the Normal style with the menu command, follow these steps:

1. Choose File, New and double-click the Blank Document template.

    The Style Preview box on the Formatting toolbar should show Normal. In a new document based on the Normal template, the first paragraph will automatically use the Normal style.

2. Choose Format, Style and choose Modify. The Normal style should be selected in the Name box. If it isn't, type **Normal**.

3. Make the changes you want to the style, using the Format options.

4. When you return to the Modify Style dialog box, select the Add to Template check box.

5. Choose OK to return to the Style dialog box.

6. Choose Close.

To change the default settings for the Normal style by example, follow these steps:

1. Choose File, Open and select a document that is based on the Normal template.

2. Select text or position the insertion point in a paragraph that is formatted with the Normal style.

3. Select commands on the Format menu, from the Formatting toolbar, or with shortcut keys to make formatting changes you want applied to most documents. For example, you might want to indent the first line of each paragraph by .5".

4. Click the Style Preview box in the Formatting toolbar and press Enter. Word asks whether you want to redefine the style using the selection as an example.

5. Choose OK.

6. Choose Format, Style. The Style dialog box opens with the Normal style selected in the Styles list. Select Normal if it isn't selected.

7. Click Modify, select the Add to Template check box, and choose OK.

8. Choose Close.

Choose Format, Font to make changes to the default font of the Normal style. In the Font dialog box, make the changes you want and then click the Default button. Word displays a dialog box indicating that the changes you made will affect all new documents based on the Normal template. Choose Yes.

Updating Styles

If you create a group of documents, each based on the same template, you'll want to make sure that any change to a style is reflected in each of the documents. For example, if you're writing a book with each chapter in a separate file, you want any changes to headers, footers, and headings to be copied to each of the document files. Another example is familiar to anyone working in a large corporation where styles are set and then reset by a committee. At the beginning of a project, the committee might decide on a template containing styles for formatting each document. Because all documents are based on the same template, they contain identical formatting, which preserves consistency. Later, the committee issues major design changes. Those design changes must now be incorporated throughout all the other documents that were based on the original templates. To insure that a document updates to match changes in the template, use the Automatically Update Document Styles command.

 If you want to copy just a few styles from one template to another, see the previous section in this chapter titled, "Copying Styles Between Documents."

When you select the Automatically Update Document Styles command, Word copies the attached template's styles to the document each time you open it. The Update feature follows these rules:

- A style in the template that has the same name as a style in the document overrides the document style. The formatting from the template's style replaces the formatting from the document's style.
- Styles not found in the document are copied from the template to the document.
- Styles found in the document, but not in the template, are left unchanged.

Make sure that you use identically named styles in each of the documents. Otherwise, Word will not properly update the styles.

To update a document's styles each time you open it, follow these steps:

1. Place the insertion point anywhere in the file whose styles you want to update automatically.

N O T E Prior to Word 97, this command was the Templates command and appeared on the File menu. ▪

2. Choose Tools, Templates and Add-Ins. The Templates and Add-ins dialog box appears (see Figure 11.22). The template attached to the current document is named in the Document Template box.

FIG. 11.22

Select Automatically Update Document Styles, and each time you open the document its styles will be updated from the attached template.

3. Select the Automatically Update Document Styles check box.

4. Choose OK.

Changing the Base of a Style

Unless you specify otherwise, a new style is based on the style of the currently selected paragraph. Often, that's the Normal style. You have the option, however, to base any style on any other style. When you do, any changes you make to the base style carry through to all styles based on that style. If you change Normal, those changes are reflected in any style based on the Normal style.

This often can be to your advantage. Suppose that you work in a legal office and you regularly type certain court documents that must always be double-spaced, in a certain font and size, and have specific margins. To help automate this task, you can create a template with the correct margins, and then modify the template's Normal style to include the correct font and size and double-spacing. You then can create additional styles based on that redefined Normal style, and they too will use the specified font and size and be double-spaced.

Keep in mind that Word's standard styles are based on the Normal style, and if you alter the Normal style, your alterations will apply to all the standard styles as well.

If you don't want to alter your Normal style, you can create a base style in your document and use it as the basis for additional styles. By changing that base style, you can make extensive changes throughout a document.

To base one style on another style, follow these steps:

1. Choose F̲ormat, S̲tyle.

2. From the S̲tyles list, select a style whose base style you want to change.

3. Click the M̲odify button. The Modify Style dialog box appears.

4. Specify the name of the style on which you want to base your style in the B̲ased On box. To display a list of styles, click the down arrow to the right of the B̲ased On box.

   If you want the selected style to remain unaffected by changes to any other style, select (no style) from the top of the list in the B̲ased On box.

   When you select a style name, you see the name of the style plus any formatting attributes from the selected style in the Description box. Your new style automatically is based on that existing style, unless you specify a different style.

5. Select any of the F̲ormat button options to add additional formatting options to your style.

6. Choose OK to return to the Style dialog box.

7. Choose Close.

   Or, choose A̲pply if you want to apply your new style to the currently selected paragraph.

TROUBLESHOOTING

I attached the wrong template to my document and updated the styles. Now, all the styles in my document look wrong. What can I do? If you have not made changes to the document, a safe approach is to close the document without saving it, then reopen and attach the correct template. If you don't want to close the document without saving, then repeat the process using the correct template or the original template. Attach either the original template or the correct template to your document and again update styles. The styles in your document should return to their original appearance or to the appearance of the styles in the correct template.

Checking Formats

Formatting can be applied from a style or manually from the Format menu commands. You can quickly determine how formatting was applied to any text with the Help button on the Standard toolbar.

To determine how formatting was added, follow these steps:

1. Press Shift+F1 or open the Help menu and choose What's This?. The pointer changes to an arrow with a question mark attached.

2. Click the text you want to check. A formatting box appears, showing paragraph and font formatting (see Figure 11.23). You can continue to click other locations to see the formatting of other text.

3. Press Esc to turn off the Help feature.

FIG. 11.23

Use the What's This? Help feature to quickly check the formatting of any text.

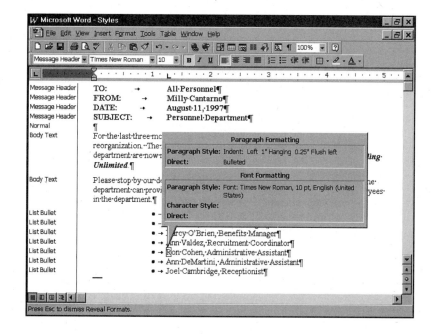

Part
II

Ch
11

Working with Columns

Sometimes what you have to say isn't best said in line after line of margin-to-margin text. Often you can help keep your reader interested and make your prose look a little more inviting by dividing the text into columns. Research has shown that text of newspaper column width is much faster to read. Columns not only make information more attractive, but also more readable.

In Word 97, you can create two types of columns: the *snaking columns* of text you see in newspapers, magazines, and newsletters; and the *parallel columns* of text and numbers you see in lists and tables. Tables (which consist of columns and rows of text, numbers, or dates) work well for parallel columns or for data that you want to keep aligned. This chapter discusses snaking columns (sometimes called *newspaper columns*) in which the text wraps continuously from the bottom of one column to the top of the next column. To learn more about parallel columns, refer to Chapter 18, "Creating and Editing Tables." ■

Creating a Newsletter the Easy Way

If you've been using Word 6 or 7, you know about wizards. If you read Chapter 6, "Using Templates and Wizards for Frequently Created Documents," you know about wizards. In Word 7, Microsoft introduced the Newsletter Wizard, which makes creating a truly professional-looking newsletter a breeze (see Figure 12.1).

To select the Newsletter Wizard, follow these steps:

1. Choose File, New. You'll see the General tab of the New dialog box.
2. Click the Publications tab. Word displays the available templates and wizards that relate to producing publications (see Figure 12.2).
3. Click the Newsletter Wizard, and choose OK. Word displays the Newsletter Wizard (see Figure 12.3). Click Next to move to the Style & Color step in the Newsletter Wizard

To design your newsletter with the Newsletter Wizard, follow these steps:

1. Choose the style of newsletter you want to create—Classic or Modern. As you click each of the option buttons, the Preview box changes to show you examples.
2. Click the Next button. In the second Newsletter Wizard dialog box, choose the number of columns you want for your newsletter: One, Two, Three, or Four. If you click each option button, you'll see the changes in the layout.
3. Click the Next button. In the third Newsletter Wizard dialog box, type the name of your newsletter. You can edit the name later.
4. Click the Next button. In the fourth Newsletter Wizard dialog box, type the number of pages you want for your newsletter. Again, you can change this later.
5. Click the Next button. In the fifth Newsletter Wizard dialog box, select the options you want to include in your newsletter: Table of Contents, Fancy First Letters, Date, Volume, and Issue.
6. Click the Next button.
7. Click the Finish button. Word displays a skeleton newsletter like the one shown in Figure 12.4, shown in Print Preview mode.

▶ **See** "Using Wizards to Guide You," **p. 216**

FIG. 12.1
Use the Newsletter Wizard to easily create a newsletter designed to your specifications.

Published Quarterly by Sonoma County ReLeaf § Autumn, 1997

ReLeaf Joins Forces with WCG

"A Shade Better"

It's been a busy summer for Sonoma County ReLeaf. In the last issue of this newsletter, we hinted about a new partnership with WCG. Since spring, that new partnership has evolved into an ongoing relationship, with Sonoma County ReLeaf administering WCG's "A Shade Better" program in an exciting county-wide pilot.

"A Shade Better" is WCG's way of reaching out into the community, helpinghomeowners save energy by providing free trees that shade their homes and help reduce their need for air conditioning. WCG supplies the trees—and Sonoma County ReLeaf provides the expertise needed to get the trees into the ground.

ReLeaf's approach to helping people plant their free shade trees begins by organizing community planting days. The first step is to work with one individual who will contact neighbors and schedule a Saturday morning for planting. ReLeaf works with the neighborhood volunteer to determine which type of trees people want. Next, a trained ReLeaf volunteer

visits the neighborhood and sites the shade trees around each home so the trees provide maximum shading as they grow. On planting day, ReLeaf brings the trees, stakes, and ties, gives a planting demonstration, and distributes the trees to their new owners. For those who can't plant their own trees, volunteers are trained to help. After the planting, a two-year follow-up program helps ensure the trees stay healthy.

The City of Santa Rosa has also become involved in the program, providing free street trees to qualifying homes within the city.

Several "A Shade Better" plantings are already scheduled:

October 19—planting shade trees and street trees in northwest Santa Rosa.

October 26—planting shade trees in Santa Rosa.

November 9—planting shade trees in Windsor.

Three more projects are in the planning stages. In Rohnert Park, ReLeaf has targeted two neighborhoods needing trees and hopes to hold the first planting in early winter. In Sonoma,

ReLeaf is working with ten community groups and businesses toward scheduling a planting. And in Petaluma, residents in two mobile home parks will receive badly-needed shade trees to help cool their homes.

ReLeaf has been furiously busy over the summer getting the word out to people about the "A Shade Better" project. In a booth at the county fair, we made contact with about 1,000 people, many of whom are interested in getting trees for their homes, or in coordinating planting days in their neighborhoods. We've contacted even more potential planters through our booth at the Thursday night market in Santa Rosa.

ReLeaf has also been busy gearing up for the actual plantings—locating growers for the 15,000 trees we'll need this year; training interns to site the trees; working with kids in the Social Advocates for Youth program so they can help plant the trees; and raising money for our non-tree expenses.

~ It's been a busy summer for Sonoma County ReLeaf, but it'll be an even busier fall

In Brief . . .

ReLeaf teams up with WCG to make Sonoma County "A Shade Better." *Page 1.*

ReLeaf needs neighborhood coordinators to help organize local plantings. *Back page.*

With all the activity going on now, we need help with lots of jobs. *Back page.*

To volunteer, call Sonoma County ReLeaf at 323-4321

FIG. 12.2
In the New dialog box, you see templates and wizards available for several different categories of documents.

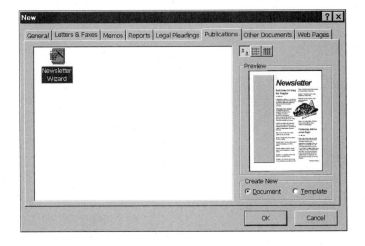

FIG. 12.3
In the second dialog box of the Newsletter Wizard, choose the style of newsletter you want to create.

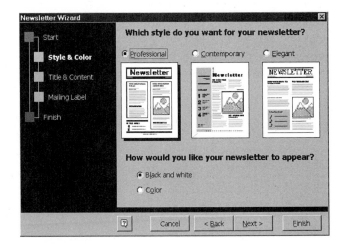

Creating Columns

If you need to work with columns and you're *not* creating a newsletter, Word's column features help you in your task. You can create columns of equal or unequal width. You also can include a vertical line between columns. You can include different numbers or styles of columns in different sections of your document. Newsletters, for example, often have two or more sections. The first section contains a large one-column banner, and the remaining text is divided into multiple columns.

FIG. 12.4
The Newsletter Wizard produces a skeleton document like this one, into which you type your information.

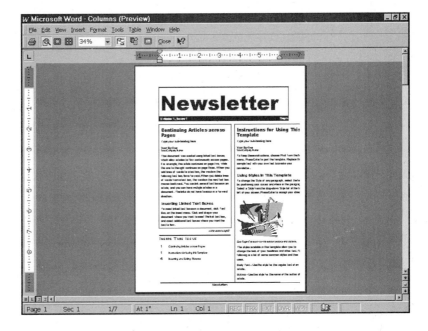

On a page with left and right margins of one inch each, you can include up to 13 columns in portrait orientation or 18 columns in landscape orientation. You can also include different numbers or styles of columns in different parts of your document, as long as you divide your document into sections. You learn more about sections later in this chapter.

▶ **See** "Determining Paper Size and Orientation," **p. 471**

CAUTION

From a readability standpoint, including too many columns on the page can make your document difficult to read. As a rule of thumb, try to include no more than three columns on a portrait-oriented sheet of paper, or five columns on a landscape-oriented sheet of paper.

Word gives you two methods of creating columns: choosing F<u>o</u>rmat, <u>C</u>olumns and clicking the Columns button on the Standard toolbar. In Normal view, you see columns in their correct width, but not side by side; only in Page Layout or Print Preview views do you see columns side by side.

Calculating the Number and Length of Columns

Word determines how many columns you can have on a page based on three factors: page width, margin widths, and size and spacing of your columns. On a wide landscape-oriented page, for example, you have more room for columns than on a narrower portrait-oriented page. Similarly, if your margins are narrow, there's more room for text on the page, and thus you can have more columns. If columns are narrow, you can fit more of them on a page than if they are wide. But remember, more isn't necessarily better; too many columns on a page can make reading difficult.

In Word, columns must be at least half an inch (.5") wide. If you try to fit too many on a page, Word displays a message reading `Column widths cannot be less than 0.5"`. You might see this message if you change your margins, for example, making them wider so that there is less room on the page for columns. If you see the message, change either your page layout or the number, width, or spacing of your columns.

Columns are the length of the current section or of the current page if there are no sections.

Understanding Sections

A new document based on the default Normal template is a single section with a one-column format. *Sections* are divisions within a document that can be formatted independently. If you want different numbers or styles of columns in different parts of your document, you must divide it into sections. In Figure 12.5, although you see three columns, the document contains only one section. Notice that the document title appears in the first column. Figure 12.6 shows a document divided into two sections. The upper section shows the title as a single column, whereas the lower section shows the body copy in three columns. Figure 12.7 shows a document with three sections; one column for the title, two columns for the upper text, and three columns for the lower text.

▶ **See** "Working with Sections in Your Document," **p. 452**

With columns, there are three ways you can insert section breaks:

- Choose F<u>o</u>rmat, <u>C</u>olumns to create columns and specify that columns apply not to the whole document, but to "this point forward" in your document; Word adds a section break before the insertion point.

- Select the text that you want to appear in different columns before you create or change the columns; a section break is added before and after the selected text (or just after the selected text if it falls at the beginning of a document).

- Choose <u>I</u>nsert, <u>B</u>reak to display the Break dialog box (see Figure 12.8).

Using the Break dialog box, you can specify that sections run continuously so that you can have a different number of columns on the same page, or you can specify that each section start on a new page or on the next even-numbered or odd-numbered page.

In Normal view, section breaks appear in your document as a double-dotted line containing the words `Section Break`.

FIG. 12.5

This document has only a single section so that when you format in columns, the entire document changes.

Declaration of Independence

When in the Course of human events, it becomes necessary for one people to dissolve the political bands which have connected them with another, and to assume among the powers of the earth, the separate and equal station to which the Laws of Nature and of Nature's God entitle them, a decent respect to the opinions of mankind requires that they should declare the causes which impel them to separation.

We hold these truths to be self-evident, that all men are created equal, that they are endowed by their Creator with certain Unalienable Rights,that among these are life, Liberty and the pursuit of Happiness. That to secure these rights, governments are instituted among Men, deriving their just powers from the consent of the governed,

That whenever any form of Government becomes destructive of these ends, it is the right of the People to alter or to abolish it and to institute a new Government, laying its foundation on such principles and organizing its power in such form, as to them shall seem most likely to affect their Safety and Happiness. Prudence, indeed, will dictate that Governments long established should not be changed for light and transient

causes; and accordingly all experience has shown, that mankind is more disposed to suffer, which evils are sufferable, than to right themselves by abolishing the forms to which they are accustomed. But when a long train of abuses and usurpations, pursuing invariably the same Object evinces a design to reduce them under absolute Despotism, it is their right, it is their duty, to throw off such Government, and to provide new Guards for their future security.

Such has been the patient sufferance of these colonies; and such is now the necessity which constrains them to alter their former Systems of Government. The history of the present King of Great Britain is a history of repeated injuries and usurpations, all having in direct object the establishment of an absolute Tyranny over these States. To prove this, let Facts be submitted to a candid world.

He has refused his Assent to Laws, the most wholesome and necessary for the public good.

He has forbidden his Governors to pass Laws of immediate and pressing importance, unless suspended in their operation until his assent should be obtained; and when so suspended, he has utterly neglected to attend to them. He has refused to pass other Laws for the

accommodation of large districts of people unless those people would relinquish the right of Representation in the Legislature, a right inestimable to them and formidable to tyrants only.

He has called together legislative bodies at places unusual, uncomfortable, and distant from the depository of their public Records, for the sole purpose of fatiguing them into compliance with his measures.

He has dissolved Representative Houses repeatedly, for the opposing with manly firmness his invasions on the rights of the people.

He has refused for a long time, after such dissolutions, to cause others to be elected; whereby the Legislative powers, incapable of annihilation, have returned to the people at large for their exercises; the state remaining in the mean time exposed to all the dangers of invasion from without, and confusions within.

He has endeavored to prevent the population of these states, for that purpose obstructing the Laws of Naturalization of Foreigners, from gaining permission to pass, other than to encourage their migrations hither, and raised the conditions of new Appropriations of lands.

Part
II

Ch
12

FIG. 12.6

This document has two sections—the title, formatted in one column, and body copy formatted in three.

Declaration of Independence

When in the Course of human events, it becomes necessary for one people to dissolve the political bands which have connected them with another, and to assume among the powers of the earth, the separate and equal station to which the Laws of Nature and of Nature's God entitle them, a decent respect to the opinions of mankind requires that they should declare the causes which impel them to separation.

We hold these truths to be self-evident, that all men are created equal, that they are endowed by their Creator with certain Unalienable Rights,that among these are life, Liberty and the pursuit of Happiness. That to secure these rights, governments are instituted among Men, deriving their just powers from the consent of the governed,

That whenever any form of Government becomes destructive of these ends, it is the right of the People to alter or to abolish it and to institute a new Government, laying its foundation on such principles and organizing its power in such form, as to them shall seem most likely to affect their Safety and Happiness. Prudence, indeed, will dictate that Governments long established should not be changed for light and transient causes; and accordingly all

experience has shown, that mankind is more disposed to suffer, which evils are sufferable, than to right themselves by abolishing the forms to which they are accustomed. But when a long train of abuses and usurpations, pursuing invariably the same Object evinces a design to reduce them under absolute Despotism, it is their right, it is their duty, to throw off such Government, and to provide new Guards for their future security.

Such has been the patient sufferance of these colonies; and such is now the necessity which constrains them to alter their former Systems of Government. The history of the present King of Great Britain is a history of repeated injuries and usurpations, all having in direct object the establishment of an absolute Tyranny over these States. To prove this, let Facts be submitted to a candid world.

He has refused his Assent to Laws, the most wholesome and necessary for the public good.

He has forbidden his Governors to pass Laws of immediate and pressing importance, unless suspended in their operation until his assent should be obtained; and when so suspended, he has utterly neglected to attend to

them. He has refused to pass other Laws for the accommodation of large districts of people unless those people would relinquish the right of Representation in the Legislature, a right inestimable to them and formidable to tyrants only.

He has called together legislative bodies at places unusual, uncomfortable, and distant from the depository of their public Records, for the sole purpose of fatiguing them into compliance with his measures.

He has dissolved Representative Houses repeatedly, for the opposing with manly firmness his invasions on the rights of the people.

He has refused for a long time, after such dissolutions, to cause others to be elected; whereby the Legislative powers, incapable of annihilation, have returned to the people at large for their exercises; the state remaining in the mean time exposed to all the dangers of invasion from without, and confusions within.

He has endeavored to prevent the population of these states, for that purpose obstructing the Laws of Naturalization of Foreigners, from gaining permission to pass, other than to encourage their migrations

FIG. 12.7

This document has three sections, each formatted in a different number of columns.

Declaration of Independence

When in the Course of human events, it becomes necessary for one people to dissolve the political bands which have connected them with another, and to assume among the powers of the earth, the separate and equal station to which the Laws of Nature and of Nature's God entitle them, a decent respect to the opinions of mankind requires that they should declare the causes which impel them to separation.

We hold these truths to be self-evident, that all men are created equal, that they are endowed by their Creator with certain Unalienable Rights,that among these are life, Liberty and the pursuit of Happiness. That to secure these rights, governments are instituted among Men, deriving their just powers from the consent of the governed,

That whenever any form of Government becomes destructive of these ends, it is the right of the People to alter or to abolish it and to institute a new Government, laying its foundation on such principles and organizing its power in such form, as to them shall seem most likely to affect their Safety and Happiness. Prudence, indeed, will dictate that Governments long established should not be changed for light and transient causes; and accordingly all experience has shown, that mankind is more disposed to suffer, which evils are sufferable, than to right themselves by abolishing the forms to which they are accustomed. But when a long train of abuses and usurpations, pursuing invariably the same Object evinces a design to reduce them under absolute Despotism, it is their right, it is their duty, to throw off such Government, and to provide new Guards for their future security.

Such has been the patient sufferance of these colonies; and such is now the necessity which constrains them to alter their former Systems of Government. The history of the present King of Great Britain is a history of repeated injuries and usurpations, all having in direct object the establishment of an absolute Tyranny over these States. To prove this, let Facts be submitted to a candid world.

He has refused his Assent to Laws, the most wholesome and necessary for the public good.

He has forbidden his Governors to pass Laws of immediate and pressing importance, unless suspended in their operation until his assent should be obtained; and

when so suspended, he has utterly neglected to attend to them. He has refused to pass other Laws for the accommodation of large districts of people unless those people would relinquish the right of Representation in the Legislature, a right inestimable to them and formidable to tyrants only.

He has called together legislative bodies at places unusual, uncomfortable, and distant from the depository of their public Records, for the sole purpose of fatiguing them into compliance with his measures.

He has dissolved Representative Houses repeatedly, for the opposing with manly firmness his

invasions on the rights of the people.

He has refused for a long time, after such dissolutions, to cause others to be elected; whereby the Legislative powers, incapable of annihilation, have returned to the people at large for their exercises; the state remaining in the mean time exposed to all the dangers of invasion from without, and confusions within.

He has endeavored to prevent the population of these states, for that purpose obstructing the Laws of Naturalization of Foreigners, from gaining permission to pass, other than to encourage their migrations hither, and raised the conditions of new Appropriations of lands.

FIG. 12.8
You can insert section breaks using the Insert, Break command.

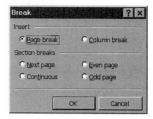

 TIP All column formatting is stored in the section break mark at the end of a section. If you delete this mark, that section takes on the column formatting and section formatting of the section after it.

Formatting Columns

When formatting your document into columns, remember the following tips:

- ■ If you want to format the entire document into columns, and your document has only one section, position the insertion point anywhere in your document.

- ■ If you want to format only one section into columns and you've already divided your document into sections, position the insertion point inside the section you want formatted into columns. (Columns apply to multiple sections if multiple sections are selected.)

- ■ If you want columns to start at a certain point in your document and you haven't divided your document into sections, position the insertion point where you want columns to start. You can apply columns from that point forward. Word inserts a section break at the insertion point.

- ■ If you want to format selected text into columns and you haven't divided your document into sections, select the text that you want in columns. Word inserts a section break before and after the selected text.

 TIP If you don't like the number of columns you've created or don't like their widths, choose Edit, Undo Columns to return to your original number of columns.

Creating Columns of Equal Width

The width of the columns in your document depends on the number of columns you choose, your margins, and the amount of space you set between columns. For example, if you have one-inch left and right margins on a standard 8 1/2-inch paper width, and you divide your text into three columns with one-quarter inch between them, you get three two-inch-wide columns.

Remember that only in Page Layout view (or Print Preview) will you see your columns side by side.

To create equal-width columns with the menu or with the Columns button, follow these steps:

1. Specify which part of your document you want divided into columns (see "Formatting Columns" earlier in this chapter).

 2. On the Standard toolbar, click the Columns button to display the column drop-down box. Drag right to select the number of columns you want (up to six). Figure 12.9 shows the Columns button drop-down box with three columns selected.

FIG. 12.9

The quickest way to format your document with columns is to use the Columns button on the Standard toolbar.

You also can choose Format, Columns. The Columns dialog box appears (see Figure 12.10).

3. In the Presets group, select One, Two, or Three columns. You also can select Number of Columns, and type or select the number of columns you want. If you want columns to start at the insertion point, click the Apply To drop-down list arrow and select This Point Forward from the list. Choose OK.

Part

II

Ch

12

FIG. 12.10

Use presets to quickly format your text into columns, or select the number of columns you want.

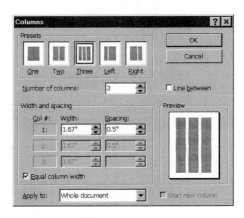

Creating Columns of Unequal Width

Although you can easily format your document with columns by clicking the Columns button, you can use more options when you use the Columns dialog box. You can define your own columns, or you can choose preset columns. *Preset columns* include a wide and a narrow column (the wide column is twice as wide as the narrow column). Preset columns make a good starting point for defining your own columns. Using them ensures that your columns are a consistent width.

When you create columns by choosing Format, Columns, you can specify whether columns apply to the whole document, the current section(s), the insertion point forward, or the selected text (if text is selected). (See "Formatting Columns," earlier in this chapter.) By choosing Format, Column, you also can specify how wide you want your columns and how much space you want between them.

To create columns of unequal width, follow these steps:

1. Select the text you want to format into multiple columns, or position the insertion point inside the section you want to format or at the point where you want a new number of columns to begin.

2. Choose Format, Columns. The Columns dialog box appears (see Figure 12.11).

FIG. 12.11
To create columns of unequal width, use presets or define your own columns.

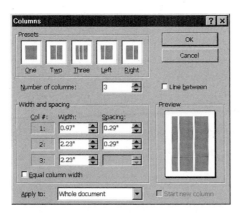

3. Optionally, from the Presets group, select Left if you want a narrow column on the left, or Right if you want a narrow column on the right.

4. Select Number of Columns, and type or select the number of columns you want. Look at the Preview box to see how your columns will appear.

5. Clear the Equal Column Width check box if it is selected.

6. If you want to define the width or spacing for individual columns, place the insertion point in the Width or Spacing box for the column you want to change. The dialog box has space for only three column numbers; click or press the down arrow to display additional column numbers.

7. Type or select the width you want for the selected column.

   You can also type or select the spacing you want to the right of the selected column (there is no space to the right of the rightmost column).

8. From the Apply To drop-down list, select the amount of text you want to format. The options shown in the Apply To list change depending on whether text is selected or whether your document contains multiple sections. Usually Word correctly guesses where you want to apply your columns, based on the location of the insertion point.

   ■ The Selected Sections option appears only when multiple sections are selected. It formats the sections you selected with columns.

   ■ The Selected Text option appears only when text is selected. This option formats the text you selected with columns. It also puts a section break before and after the selection.

   ■ The This Point Forward option appears only when no text is selected. This option formats with columns from the insertion point forward. It puts a section break at the location of the insertion point.

   ■ The This Section option appears only when the insertion point is inside one of multiple sections. This option formats with columns the section containing the insertion point.

   ■ The Whole Document option formats the entire document with columns.

9. Choose OK.

Typing and Editing Text in Columns

Typing, editing, and formatting text in columns follows all the same rules and takes advantage of the same shortcuts for typing, selecting, and editing any other text. The following two tips will help you as you move around in and select columnar text:

▶ **See** " Selecting Text," **p. 156**

■ To move from one column to the top of the next column on the current page using the keyboard, press Alt+down-arrow key. To move to the top of the previous column, press Alt+up-arrow key.

■ In a single-column document, the selection bar, an invisible column you use to select text, is normally positioned at the left margin of a page. When you move the mouse pointer into this area, the mouse pointer turns into an arrow you can use to select lines and paragraphs. In a multi-column document, you'll find a selection bar at the left margin of each column in Page Layout view.

TROUBLESHOOTING

My text seems narrower than the columns. This condition may appear if the text is indented. Use the ruler or choose Format, Paragraph to eliminate or change the indentation settings for selected text. Also check the margin settings within each column.

Adding a Line Between Columns

Adding a vertical line between columns can add interest to your page. Lines are the length of the longest column in the section. You can see lines in the Page Layout view or in Print Preview.

To add lines between columns, follow these steps:

1. Click in the section containing columns where you want vertical lines.
2. Choose Format, Columns.
3. In the Columns dialog box, check the Line Between check box.
4. Choose OK.

To remove lines between columns, remove the check from the Line Between check box in the Columns dialog box. You can also add vertical lines on your page by choosing Format, Borders and Shading. If you do, and you also add lines between columns, you may see two lines between columns. For columns, the Line Between option is a better choice than Format, Borders and Shading because it creates lines of uniform length in the section, even if one column of text is shorter than the others.

Viewing Columns

Word enables you to view a document in several ways. Views include Normal, Outline, Page Layout, Master Document, and Print Preview. Depending on which view you use, columns appear differently on-screen.

▶ **See** "Controlling Your Document's Appearance On-Screen," **p. 132**

Normal view is faster for text entry but does not display columns side by side as they will appear when printed. The text appears in the same width as the column, but in one continuous column. In Online Layout, Outline, and Master Document views, columns also appear in one continuous column. Page Layout view displays columns side by side, with vertical lines between columns if you've selected that option. Section and column breaks appear only when you've displayed paragraph marks. Print Preview gives an overview of the page as it will appear when printed. In Normal, Page Layout, and Print Preview views, you can change column width using the ruler, and in all views, you can display the Column dialog box to edit columns.

>   You can switch between Normal, Online Layout, Page Layout, and Outline views using the four icons that appear at the left edge of the horizontal scroll bar.

`100%` When you are editing a document, you may need to view a particular section up close. At other times, you may need an overview of the entire page. When you work in Page Layout view, the Zoom Control box on the Standard toolbar includes three choices that enable you to magnify or reduce the size of the display:

- *Whole Page*. Shows you a miniature view of the whole page. The view you see is very similar to Print Preview.
- *Page Width*. Shows you the full width of the page.
- *Two Pages*. Lays out your document so that you can see a miniature view of two pages simultaneously.

The Zoom Control box also has, on its drop-down list, several percentages at which you can view your page. You can also select magnification by choosing View, Zoom.

▶ **See** "Controlling Your Document's Appearance On-Screen," **p. 132**

Part
II

Ch
12

Changing Columns

Once you format your document with columns, you can change the columns in many ways:

- You can change the number of columns, or switch between equal- and unequal-width columns.
- You can change the width of columns or the spacing between them.
- You can force text to move to the top of the next column, and you can force a column to start on a new page.
- You can balance columns on a page so that they are as close to the same length as possible.

You can make some changes to columns using the ruler; for example, you can change their width or the spacing between them. Other changes are made using the Columns dialog box.

T I P You can quickly display the Columns dialog box by double-clicking the gray area between columns on the horizontal ruler.

Before you change columns, make sure you select the text you want to change, and be sure, in the Columns dialog box, to apply the changes where you want them (use the Apply To list). Follow these rules for selecting text and applying the changes:

- If you want to change columns for the entire document and your document has only one section, position the insertion point anywhere in your document. In the Apply To list of the Columns dialog box, choose Whole Document.

- If you want to change columns in only one section and you've already divided your document into sections, position the insertion point inside the section you want to change. In the Apply To list of the Columns dialog box, choose This Section.

- If you want columns to start at a certain point in your document and you haven't divided your document into sections, position the insertion point where you want columns to start. In the Apply To list of the Columns dialog box, choose This Point Forward.

- If you want to change columns in only part of your document and you haven't divided your document into sections, select the text that you want in columns. In the Apply To list of the Columns dialog box, choose Selected Text.

- If you want to change columns in multiple existing sections, select the sections. In the Apply To list of the Columns dialog box, choose Selected Sections.

Most of the time, Word understands where you want to apply changes by where you've positioned the insertion point, and you don't need to make a selection in the Apply To list.

Because you can format text in columns in the same way you can format text that is not in columns, you may create some unexpected results. If your column is too narrow, for example, you may find yourself with a vertical strip of text that isn't very readable. Try widening the column, lessening the space between the columns, reducing the number of columns, or reducing the size of the text.

Changing the Number of Columns

You can change the number of columns using either the ruler or the Columns dialog box. You can also change between equal- and unequal-width columns. If you want to change from equal-width to unequal-width columns, you must use the Columns dialog box, but you can change from unequal-width to equal-width columns using the ruler.

To change the number of equal-width columns, or to change from unequal-width to equal-width columns, follow these steps:

1. Position the insertion point or select the text where you want changes to apply.

2. On the Standard toolbar, click the Columns button and select the number of columns you want from the drop-down box (drag right in the box to display up to seven columns).

   You also can choose Format, Columns to display the Columns dialog box. From the Presets group, select One, Two, or Three. Or select Number of Columns, and type or select the number of columns you want. If you are changing from unequal-width to equal-width columns, select the Equal Column Width check box. Choose OK.

To change the number of unequal-width columns, or to change from equal-width to unequal-width columns, follow these steps:

1. Position the insertion point or select the text where you want changes to apply.

2. Choose Format, Columns to display the Columns dialog box. If you want two preset columns of unequal width, select Left or Right from the Presets group. Or, select Number of Columns, and type or select the number of columns you want.

3. If you're changing from equal-width to unequal-width columns, clear the check from the Equal Column Width check box.

4. Choose OK.

Changing the Width of Columns and the Spacing Between Columns

When you first create columns, Word determines their width based on your margins and the number of columns you want. You can change the width of all or some columns.

You can also change the spacing between columns. By default, columns have a half inch (.5") of spacing between them, but you may want to decrease or increase this distance. You may want to decrease the distance if you have many columns, because the greater number of columns you have, the narrower they are, and the less space you need between them. You may want to increase the distance with fewer columns, as you might in a three-column brochure printed sideways on the page, for example.

You can change the width of columns or the space between columns in two ways: using the ruler or using the Columns dialog box. Using the ruler, you drag column margin markers to change the width and spacing at the same time.

If your columns are currently equal-width and you want to change them to unequal-width, you must use the Columns dialog box.

To change the width of columns or the space between columns using the ruler, follow these steps:

1. Make sure the ruler is displayed; if it is not, choose Yiew, Ruler.

2. Position the insertion point inside the section containing the columns you want to change.

3. The gray areas in the horizontal ruler indicate the spaces between columns. Move the mouse pointer into one of these gray areas. Choose any gray area if your columns are all the same width; choose the gray area above the space you want to change if your columns are different widths. After you slide the mouse pointer into a gray area, the pointer will turn into a two-headed arrow, and you'll see a text tip on-screen. What you see in the text tip depends on whether your columns are all the same width or whether they are different widths:

   - If your columns are all the same width, you won't see any text tip when you slide the mouse pointer into the middle of the gray area, but the text tip will display either Right Margin or Left Margin as you slide the mouse pointer over the left or right edge of the gray area (see Figure 12.12).

   - When your columns are different widths, the middle of the gray area contains a grid-like icon. You'll see the same text tip (Right Margin or Left Margin) if you move the mouse pointer over the right or left edge of the gray area; in the center of the gray area, however, you'll see Move Column in the text tip (see Figure 12.13).

4. Hold down the mouse button and drag the edge of the gray area away from the center to widen the space between columns, or drag it toward the center to lessen the space between columns. If columns are different widths, you can drag either side of the gray area to change the spacing in either direction.

N O T E   When dragging the unequal columns marker, remember that it functions two ways, depending upon how you drag it:

Dragging the *edge* of the marker changes the *widths* of unequal columns.

Dragging the *grid-like icon* to move the column changes the *space between* unequal columns.

T I P   If columns are all the same width, changing the spacing for one changes the spacing for them all. If columns are different widths, changing the spacing for one affects only that column.

FIG. 12.12
Using the ruler, you can change the width of columns and the spacing between them. If your columns are all the same width, changing one changes them all identically.

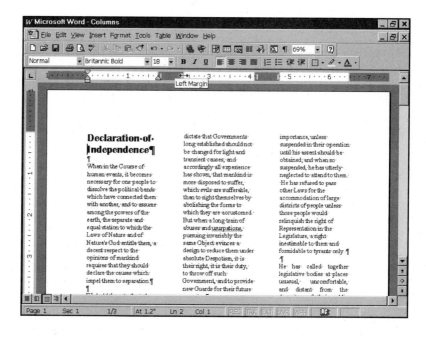

FIG. 12.13
When columns are of unequal widths, or if they were created using the Columns button, the gray area of the ruler contains a grid-like icon.

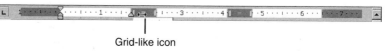

Grid-like icon

To change the width of columns or the space between columns using the Columns dialog box, or to change columns of equal width into columns of unequal width, follow these steps:

1. Position the insertion point inside the section containing the columns you want to change.

2. Choose Format, Columns.

3. If you are changing equal-width columns to unequal-width columns, remove the check from the Equal Column Width check box.

TIP If your columns are all the same width, change the width of column 1 only; all the rest use the same measurements.

4. In the Width and Spacing group, place the insertion point in the Width box of the column you want to change and type or select the width you want for your column or columns. Word then automatically recalculates the dimensions of the remaining columns to fit within the margins of the page.

5. In the Width and Spacing group, place the insertion point in the Spacing box of the column you want to change and type or select the spacing you want between your columns.

6. Choose OK.

Removing Columns

If your document is formatted into columns, you can remove them easily using either the Columns button or the Columns dialog box.

To remove columns, follow these steps:

1. Position the insertion point or select text where you want to remove columns.

2. Use the Columns button to select one column.

   You also can choose Format, Columns. From the Presets group, select One. Choose OK.

Starting a New Column

When Word creates columns, it automatically breaks the columns to fit on the page. Sometimes, the column may break inappropriately. On a three-column page, for example, column 2 may end with a heading that should be at the top of column 3. By inserting a column break directly before the heading, you shift the heading to the top of the next column, keeping the heading and its following text together.

If you want a column to start on a new page, you can insert a page break.

To insert a column break, press Ctrl+Shift+Enter or follow these steps:

1. Position the insertion point at the beginning of the line where you want the new column to start.

2. Choose Insert, Break. The Break dialog box appears (see Figure 12.14).

3. Select the Column Break option.

4. Choose OK.

To insert a page break, press Ctrl+Enter or repeat the steps above, choosing Page Break in step 3.

FIG. 12.14
Inserting a column break causes text to move to the top of the next column.

Balancing Column Lengths

On pages where the text in columns continues to the next page, Word automatically balances (lines up) the last line of text at the bottom of each column. But when columnar text runs out on a page, you may be left with two full-length columns and a third column that's only partially filled. You can balance column lengths so that the bottom of all the columns are within one line of each other. Figures 12.15 and 12.16 show unbalanced and balanced columns.

To balance the length of multiple columns, follow these steps:

1. Position the insertion point at the end of the text in the last column of the section you want to balance.

2. Choose Insert, Break.

3. Select the Continuous option in the Section Breaks group.

4. Choose OK.

TROUBLESHOOTING

I have several columns and I want to change their width and spacing, but in the Columns dialog box I can select only column 1. Your columns are currently of equal width. Clear the Equal Column Width check box if you want to make them different widths.

Product lists, date schedules, and the dialogue for plays all appear to use columns, but it's impossible to keep related items lined up across the columns. Adding or editing in one column changes the position of items in following columns. Use Word's table feature to create scripts for plays, procedural steps, duty rosters, product catalogs, and so on. Tables are grids of rows and columns. Information within a cell in a table will stay adjacent or parallel to other information in the same row, even when you add lines in the cell. Cells can contain entire paragraphs, math calculations, field codes, and even pictures. Tables are described in detail in Chapter 18, "Creating and Editing Tables."

Part
II

Ch
12

FIG. 12.15
These columns have
not been balanced.

ReLeaf Plants and Trees Throughout the State

Lorem ipsum dolor sit amet, consectetuer adipiscing elit, sed diam nonummy nibh euismod tincidunt ut laoreet dolore magna aliquam erat volutpat. Ut wisi enim ad minim veniam, quis nostrud exerci tation ullamcorper suscipit lobortis nisl ut aliquip ex ea commodo consequat. Duis autem vel eum iriure dolor in hendrerit in vulputate velit esse molestie consequat, vel illum dolore eu feugiat nulla facilisis at vero eros et accumsan et iusto odio dignissim qui blandit praesent luptatum zzril delenit augue duis dolore te feugait nulla facilisi.

Lorem ipsum dolor sit amet, consectetuer adipiscing elit, sed diam nonummy nibh euismod tincidunt ut laoreet dolore magna aliquam erat volutpat.

Lorem ipsum dolor sit amet, consectetuer adipiscing elit, sed diam nonummy nibh euismod tincidunt ut laoreet dolore magna aliquam erat volutpat. Duis autem vel eum iriure dolor in hendrerit in vulputate velit esse molestie consequat, vel illum dolore eu feugiat nulla facilisis at vero eros et accumsan et iusto odio dignissim qui blandit praesent luptatum zzril delenit augue duis dolore te feugait nulla facilisi.

Lorem ipsum dolor sit amet, consectetuer adipiscing elit, sed diam nonummy nibh euismod tincidunt ut laoreet dolore magna aliquam erat

volutpat. Ut wisi enim ad minim veniam, quis nostrud exerci tation ullamcorper suscipit lobortis nisl ut aliquip ex ea commodo consequat.

Lorem ipsum dolor sit amet, consectetuer adipiscing elit, sed diam nonummy nibh euismod tincidunt ut laoreet dolore magna aliquam erat volutpat. Duis autem vel eum iriure dolor in hendrerit in vulputate velit esse molestie consequat, vel illum dolore eu feugiat nulla facilisis at vero eros et accumsan et iusto odio dignissim qui blandit praesent luptatum zzril delenit augue duis dolore te feugait nulla facilisi.

Lorem ipsum dolor sit amet, consectetuer adipiscing elit, sed diam nonummy nibh euismod tincidunt ut laoreet dolore magna aliquam erat volutpat. Ut wisi enim ad minim veniam, quis nostrud exerci tation ullamcorper suscipit lobortis nisl ut aliquip ex ea commodo consequat. Duis autem vel eum iriure dolor in hendrerit in vulputate velit esse molestie consequat, vel illum dolore eu feugiat nulla facilisis at vero eros et accumsan et iusto odio dignissim qui blandit praesent luptatum zzril delenit augue duis dolore te feugait nulla facilisi.

Lorem ipsum dolor sit amet, consectetuer adipiscing elit, sed diam nonummy nibh euismod tincidunt ut laoreet dolore magna aliquam erat

volutpat. Ut wisi enim ad minim veniam, quis nostrud exerci tation ullamcorper suscipit lobortis nisl ut aliquip ex ea commodo consequat.

Lorem ipsum dolor sit amet, consectetuer adipiscing elit, sed diam nonummy nibh euismod tincidunt ut laoreet dolore magna aliquam erat volutpat. Duis autem vel eum iriure dolor in hendrerit in vulputate velit esse molestie consequat, vel illum dolore eu feugiat nulla facilisis at vero eros et accumsan et iusto odio dignissim qui blandit praesent luptatum zzril delenit augue duis dolore te feugait nulla facilisi.

FIG. 12.16
You can balance columns by adding a section break at the end of your document.

ReLeaf Plants and Trees Throughout the State

Lorem ipsum dolor sit amet, consectetuer adipiscing elit, sed diam nonummy nibh euismod tincidunt ut laoreet dolore magna aliquam erat volutpat. Ut wisi enim ad minim veniam, quis nostrud exerci tation ullamcorper suscipit lobortis nisl ut aliquip ex ea commodo consequat. Duis autem vel eum iriure dolor in hendrerit in vulputate velit esse molestie consequat, vel illum dolore eu feugiat nulla facilisis at vero eros et accumsan et iusto odio dignissim qui blandit praesent luptatum zzril delenit augue duis dolore te feugait nulla facilisi.

Lorem ipsum dolor sit amet, consectetuer adipiscing elit, sed diam nonummy nibh euismod tincidunt ut laoreet dolore magna aliquam erat volutpat.

Lorem ipsum dolor sit amet, consectetuer adipiscing elit, sed diam nonummy nibh euismod tincidunt ut laoreet dolore magna aliquam erat volutpat. Duis autem vel eum iriure dolor in hendrerit in vulputate velit esse molestie consequat, vel illum dolore eu feugiat nulla facilisis at vero eros et accumsan et iusto odio dignissim qui blandit praesent luptatum

zzril delenit augue duis dolore te feugait nulla facilisi.

Lorem ipsum dolor sit amet, consectetuer adipiscing elit, sed diam nonummy nibh euismod tincidunt ut laoreet dolore magna aliquam erat volutpat. Ut wisi enim ad minim veniam, quis nostrud exerci tation ullamcorper suscipit lobortis nisl ut aliquip ex ea commodo consequat.

Lorem ipsum dolor sit amet, consectetuer adipiscing elit, sed diam nonummy nibh euismod tincidunt ut laoreet dolore magna aliquam erat volutpat. Duis autem vel eum iriure dolor in hendrerit in vulputate velit esse molestie consequat, vel illum dolore eu feugiat nulla facilisis at vero eros et accumsan et iusto odio dignissim qui blandit praesent luptatum zzril delenit augue duis dolore te feugait nulla facilisi.

Lorem ipsum dolor sit amet, consectetuer adipiscing elit, sed diam nonummy nibh euismod tincidunt ut laoreet dolore magna aliquam erat volutpat. Ut wisi enim ad minim veniam, quis nostrud exerci tation ullamcorper suscipit lobortis nisl ut

aliquip ex ea commodo consequat. Duis autem vel eum iriure dolor in hendrerit in vulputate velit esse molestie consequat, vel illum dolore eu feugiat nulla facilisis at vero eros et accumsan et iusto odio dignissim qui blandit praesent luptatum zzril delenit augue duis dolore te feugait nulla facilisi.

Lorem ipsum dolor sit amet, consectetuer adipiscing elit, sed diam nonummy nibh euismod tincidunt ut laoreet dolore magna aliquam erat volutpat. Ut wisi enim ad minim veniam, quis nostrud exerci tation ullamcorper suscipit lobortis nisl ut aliquip ex ea commodo consequat.

Lorem ipsum dolor sit amet, consectetuer adipiscing elit, sed diam nonummy nibh euismod tincidunt ut laoreet dolore magna aliquam erat volutpat. Duis autem vel eum iriure dolor in hendrerit in vulputate velit esse molestie consequat, vel illum dolore eu feugiat nulla facilisis at vero eros et accumsan et iusto odio dignissim qui blandit praesent luptatum zzril delenit augue duis dolore te feugait nulla facilisi.

Part
II

Ch
12

CHAPTER 13

Formatting the Page Layout, Alignment, and Numbering

Of the four levels of formatting—page, section, paragraph, and character—page layout is the broadest. Page layout often encompasses formatting choices that affect the entire document—for most documents, page layout choices such as margins and page size do apply to the whole document. In a change from tradition, however, Word 97 also enables you to apply page-level formatting to portions of the document known as sections.

Page layout options include margins, vertical alignment on the page, page and paragraph breaks, section breaks, page numbers, headers and footers, paper size and orientation, and the paper source. By default, many page setup options, such as margins, headers and footers, and page numbers, apply to the entire document. Alternatively, you can apply these options to a designated section of text or from the position of the insertion point forward in your document.

Set margins

In Word, you can set margins for the entire document or, using sections, you can set different margins for different parts of the document.

Control text flow

Avoid breaking paragraphs and pages at inopportune places.

Use sections to support different formats within one documents

If you need portions of the document formatted in two columns while others are formatted into three columns, divide your document into sections.

Create headers and footers

To place repeating information at the top or bottom of every page, use headers and footers.

Paginate your document

You can insert or remove page numbers and control page number appearance.

You can include an envelope and a letter in a single document, for example, by specifying different margins, paper size, paper orientation, and paper source for the first page of the document—the envelope—than you specify for the remaining pages—the letter. Or you can create different headers and footers for different parts of a long document. Being able to divide your document into sections and specify where page layout options apply gives you great flexibility in designing your document. ■

Setting Margins

Margins are the borders on all four sides of a page, within which the text of your document is confined. Margins aren't necessarily blank, however; they may contain headers, footers, page numbers, footnotes, or even text and graphics.

Word default margins are 1 inch at the top and bottom and 1.25 inches on the left and right. You can change the margins for the entire document or for parts of the document (if you divide the document into sections). See Figure 13.1. If you use different margin settings regularly, you can modify the Normal template so that they become the new defaults.

▶ **See** "Setting Default Formats in the Normal Template," **p. 211**

Different views in Word show different perspectives on your margins. In Normal and Online Layout view, you don't see the margins, but you see the space between them, where your text appears. In Page Layout view, you see the page as it will print, margins and all. Select that view if you want to see headers, footers, page numbers, footnotes, and anything else that appears within the margins.

 To select a view, choose <u>V</u>iew, <u>N</u>ormal; <u>V</u>iew, Onlin<u>e</u> Layout; or <u>V</u>iew, <u>P</u>age Layout; you can also click the appropriate icon at the left edge of the horizontal scroll bar.

 You can change the margins in your document in two ways. First, you can make selections from the Page Setup dialog box. When you set margins this way, you control margin settings precisely. A second technique for setting margins is to use the ruler. Using this technique, you can see how margin settings affect the appearance of your page.

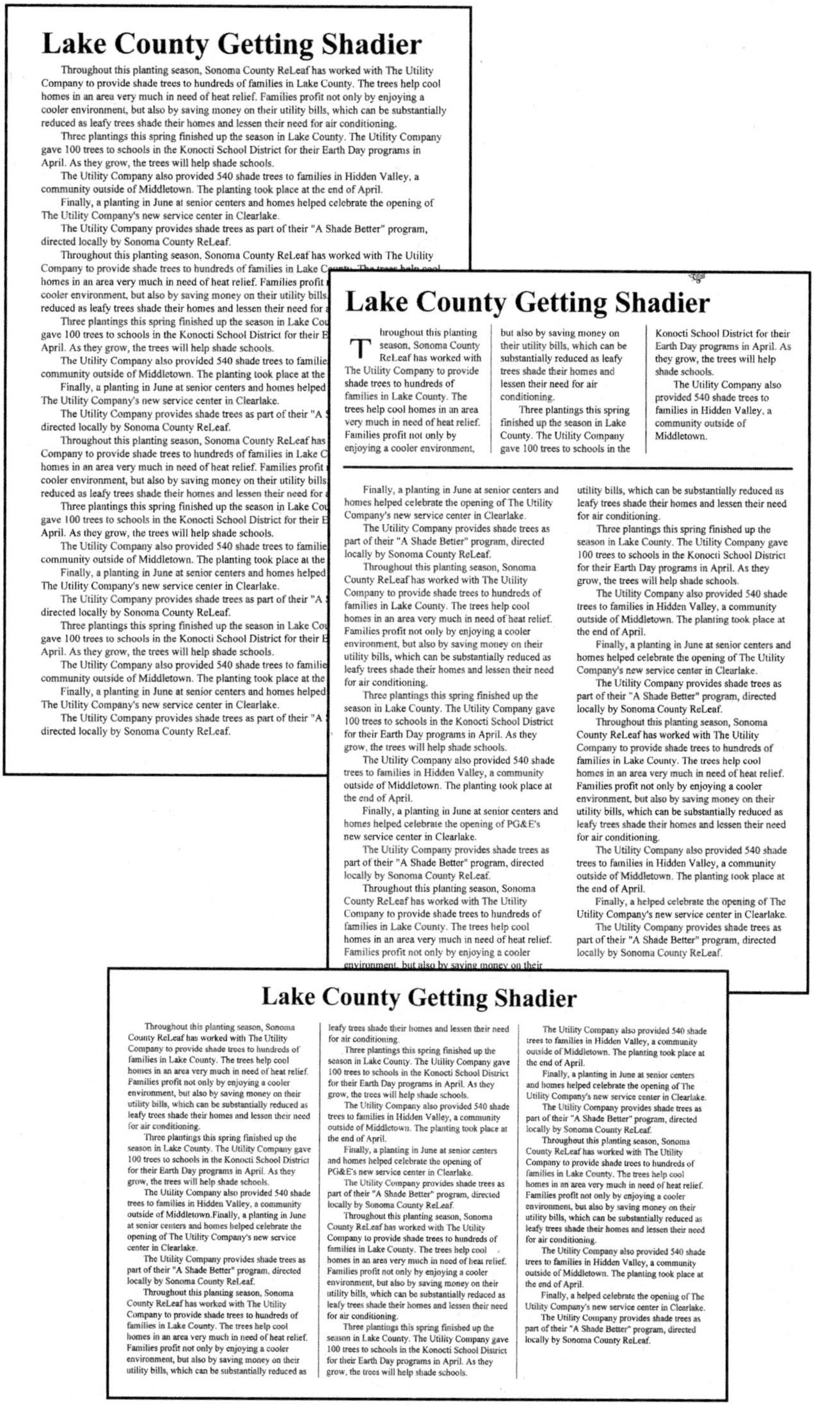

FIG. 13.1

You can set margins however you want.

Lake County Getting Shadier

Throughout this planting season, Sonoma County ReLeaf has worked with The Utility Company to provide shade trees to hundreds of families in Lake County. The trees help cool homes in an area very much in need of heat relief. Families profit not only by enjoying a cooler environment, but also by saving money on their utility bills, which can be substantially reduced as leafy trees shade their homes and lessen their need for air conditioning.

Three plantings this spring finished up the season in Lake County. The Utility Company gave 100 trees to schools in the Konocti School District for their Earth Day programs in April. As they grow, the trees will help shade schools.

The Utility Company also provided 540 shade trees to families in Hidden Valley, a community outside of Middletown. The planting took place at the end of April.

Finally, a planting in June at senior centers and homes helped celebrate the opening of The Utility Company's new service center in Clearlake.

The Utility Company provides shade trees as part of their "A Shade Better" program, directed locally by Sonoma County ReLeaf.

(The preceding article text repeats throughout the three sample documents shown in the figure.)

Lake County Getting Shadier

Throughout this planting season, Sonoma County ReLeaf has worked with The Utility Company to provide shade trees to hundreds of families in Lake County. The trees help cool homes in an area very much in need of heat relief. Families profit not only by enjoying a cooler environment, but also by saving money on their utility bills, which can be substantially reduced as leafy trees shade their homes and lessen their need for air conditioning.

Three plantings this spring finished up the season in Lake County. The Utility Company gave 100 trees to schools in the Konocti School District for their Earth Day programs in April. As they grow, the trees will help shade schools.

The Utility Company also provided 540 shade trees to families in Hidden Valley, a community outside of Middletown.

Finally, a planting in June at senior centers and homes helped celebrate the opening of The Utility Company's new service center in Clearlake.

The Utility Company provides shade trees as part of their "A Shade Better" program, directed locally by Sonoma County ReLeaf.

Lake County Getting Shadier

Throughout this planting season, Sonoma County ReLeaf has worked with The Utility Company to provide shade trees to hundreds of families in Lake County. The trees help cool homes in an area very much in need of heat relief. Families profit not only by enjoying a cooler environment, but also by saving money on their utility bills, which can be substantially reduced as leafy trees shade their homes and lessen their need for air conditioning.

Three plantings this spring finished up the season in Lake County. The Utility Company gave 100 trees to schools in the Konocti School District for their Earth Day programs in April. As they grow, the trees will help shade schools.

The Utility Company also provided 540 shade trees to families in Hidden Valley, a community outside of Middletown. The planting took place at the end of April.

Finally, a planting in June at senior centers and homes helped celebrate the opening of PG&E's new service center in Clearlake.

The Utility Company provides shade trees as part of their "A Shade Better" program, directed locally by Sonoma County ReLeaf.

Part

II

Ch

13

Setting Margins with a Precise Measurement

Using the Page Setup command to set margins gives you the greatest number of options. You can set the margins to precise measurements, establish facing pages and gutters for binding (discussed later in this chapter), set varying margins for different sections of your document, and apply your margin settings to the Normal template so that they become the new default settings.

To apply margin settings to your entire document, you can locate the insertion point anywhere in the document when you set your margins. If you want to apply margins to only one part of your document, however, you must do one of three things:

- To apply margins to a selected portion of your text, select that text before you set the margins. If you apply margins to selected text, Word automatically inserts section breaks before and after the selected text.

- To apply margins to existing sections, first place the insertion point in the section, or select those sections whose margins you want to change.

- To apply margins from a specific point forward in your document, position the insertion point where you want the new margins to start and then specify that the margins apply to the text from This Point Forward. If you apply margins from the insertion point forward, Word inserts a section break at the insertion point.

Setting different margins for different parts of your document is covered in a later section in this chapter, "Working with Sections in Your Document."

To set measured margins, follow these steps:

1. Position the insertion point inside the section for which you want to set margins. (The margins apply to the entire document unless the document has multiple sections.) Or select the text for which you want to set margins.

2. Choose File, Page Setup. In the Page Setup dialog box, select the Margins tab (see Figure 13.2).

3. Choose your margin settings. Your options include Top, Bottom, Left, Right, and Gutter. Gutter controls extra spacing on pages for binding (see the section "Creating Facing Pages and Gutters"). For each setting, type the amount of the margin or use the spinner (or press the up- or down-arrow key) to increase or decrease the margin setting by tenths of an inch.

4. Choose OK.

FIG. 13.2

Set precisely measured margins using the Page Setup dialog box.

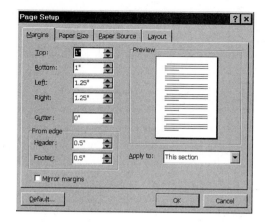

N O T E As you select your margin settings, notice that the Preview box in the Page Setup dialog box shows you how a typical page will look.

Margins usually are measured in decimal inches, unless you change your default measurement system by using Tools, Options (General tab). You can create margins in a different measurement system by typing in amounts such as **36 pt** for 36 points (72 points equal one inch), **3 cm** for 3 centimeters, or **9 pi** for 9 picas (6 picas equal an inch). If you use the inch measurement system, the next time you open the Page Layout dialog box you see that your measurements have been converted back to the equivalent in inches.

▶ **See** "Customizing Commonly Used Features," **p. 1116**

Setting Different Margins for Different Parts of Your Document   To vary the margin settings in different parts of your document, you must divide the document into sections. You can create sections with unique margins in several ways. You can insert section breaks manually and then format the text between the breaks, or before or after a break, with different margin settings. Alternatively, you can select text and choose File, Page Setup to apply margins to only the selected text or from the insertion point forward in your document. When necessary, Word inserts section breaks.

The Apply To list in the Page Setup dialog box, which determines where margins are applied, changes depending on two factors:

- Whether your document is divided into sections
- Whether you've selected text before choosing File, Page Setup

Word tries to apply your margin settings logically; for example, if your document is divided into sections, and the insertion point is inside one of those sections when you set margins, then, in the Apply To list, Word proposes applying those margin settings to This Section. You can select a different option in the list, however.

Part

II

Ch

13

You learn more about creating sections later in this chapter in the section "Working with Sections in Your Document."

To set different margins for specific parts of your document, follow these steps:

1. Position the insertion point inside the section or sections for which you want to set margins.

    You can also select the text for which you want to set margins.

    Or, you can position the insertion point where you want new margins to begin in your document.

2. Choose File, Page Setup, and in the Page Setup dialog box, select the Margins tab.

3. Type or select Top, Bottom, Left, and Right margin amounts.

4. From the Apply To list, select the section to which you want to apply margins (choices on the list vary depending on the amount of text currently selected):

Option	Applies Margins to	When
This Section	Current section (No section break is inserted)	Insertion point is located within a section
Selected Sections	Multiple sections (No section breaks are inserted)	At least part of more than one section is selected
This Point Forward	Insertion point (Inserts new-page section break at insertion point)	Insertion point is where you want new margin to start
Selected Text	Selected text (Inserts new page section breaks at beginning and end of text)	Text is selected
Whole Document	Entire document (No section breaks inserted)	Insertion point is anywhere

5. Choose OK.

TIP If you include sections with different margins in your document, remember that you delete the section (and thus lose its margins) if you delete the section break. If you accidentally delete a section break, choose Edit, Undo.

Creating Facing Pages and Gutters *Facing pages* in a document are the left and right pages of a double-sided document, as in a book or magazine. You can set up your document for facing pages by selecting the Mirror Margins check box in the Page Setup dialog box (see Figure 13.3). When you do, you no longer have left and right margins; instead, you have inside and outside margins. Facing pages are ideal when you plan to print your document on both sides of the paper and want wider margins on the inside than on the outside edges.

FIG. 13.3
When you select Mirror Margins, you create facing pages with inside and outside margins, rather than left and right margins.

Check this box to format margins for facing pages

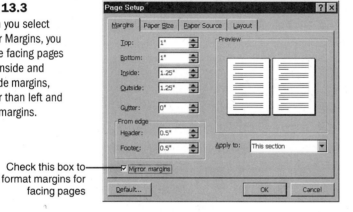

With facing pages, you can have different headers and footers on each page and can position page numbers on opposite sides of the facing pages. In a newsletter footer, for example, you may want to position page numbers below the outside margins and the date below the inside margins.

Like margins, facing pages apply to sections. You can insert section breaks before you select facing pages, or you can create sections as part of the process. (For details, see "Setting Different Margins for Different Parts of Your Document" earlier in this chapter.)

To create facing pages, follow these steps:

1. Position the insertion point or select the text where you want facing pages.
2. Choose File, Page Setup and select the Margins tab.
3. Select the Mirror Margins check box.
4. Choose OK.

Part
II

Ch
13

Adding Extra Margin Space in Gutters Whether you're working with normal pages that have left and right margins or facing pages that have inside and outside (mirror) margins, you can add a *gutter* to leave extra space for binding. A gutter on normal pages adds space at the left edge of the page; a gutter on facing pages adds space at the inside edges of each page. To leave an extra half-inch for binding, for example, include a gutter of 0.5". A gutter doesn't change your document's margins, but it does reduce the printing area.

Like margins, gutters apply to sections. You can insert section breaks before you select gutters, or you can create sections as part of the process. (For details, see "Setting Different Margins for Different Parts of Your Document" earlier in this chapter.)

To set a gutter, follow these steps:

1. Position the insertion point or select the text where you want a gutter.

2. Choose File, Page Setup and select the Margins tab.

3. Select Gutter and type or select the amount by which you want to increase the left margin (if you have left and right margins) or the inside margin (if you select mirror margins so that you have inside and outside margins). The Preview box shows a shaded area where the gutter appears (see Figure 13.4).

4. Choose OK.

FIG. 13.4

Gutters appear as a shaded area in the Preview box

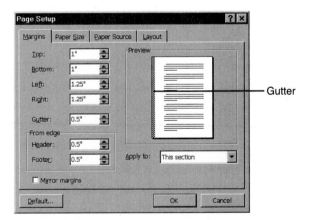

Setting Margins Visually

A quick way to set margins for your document or for a section in your document is to click the ruler.

You must display a ruler to set margins with a mouse. In Page Layout or Print Preview view, Word has two rulers:

- A horizontal ruler, which appears at the top of your document and can be used to set left and right (or inside and outside) margins

- A vertical ruler, which appears at the left side of your document and can be used to set top and bottom margins (see Figure 13.5)

TIP Only the horizontal ruler is available in Normal view.

On each ruler is a gray area and a white area. The gray area indicates the margins; the white area indicates the space between the margins. The line where the gray and the white areas connect is the *margin boundary*. You can drag the margin boundaries on either ruler to change the margins for the currently selected section or sections. To make the left margin smaller, for example, you can drag the left margin boundary toward the left edge of the page.

The ruler doesn't insert any section breaks into your document; it sets the margins for the entire document or for the section containing the insertion point. If you want to use the ruler to create margins for multiple sections in your document, insert section breaks before you begin. Then you can select the sections and use the ruler to change their margins.

FIG. 13.5
You can set left and right (or inside and outside) margins with the horizontal ruler, and you can set top and bottom margins with the vertical ruler.

Margin boundaries —

Horizontal ruler —

Vertical ruler —

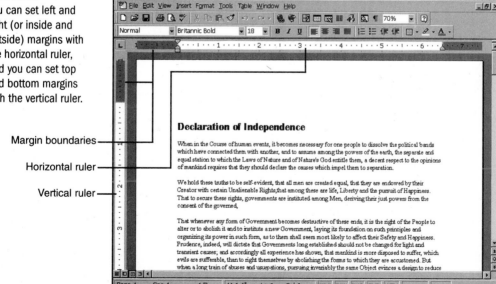

Part
II

Ch
13

T I P Choose File, Page Setup if you want to change margins in the Outline, Online Layout, or Master Document view.

If you want to change the margins for just one or a few paragraphs, use indents instead of the ruler. Use the ruler to change margins only when you want to change margins for the entire document or for a large section.

▶ **See** "Setting Indents," **p. 340**

To change margins with a ruler, follow these steps:

1. If the ruler is not displayed, choose View, Ruler.

2. Switch to Page Layout view by clicking the appropriate icon at the left edge of the horizontal scroll bar or by choosing View, Page Layout.

N O T E If you don't see the vertical ruler in Page Layout view, choose Tools, Options, then select the View tab, and in the Window group select the Vertical Ruler option. In Print Preview view, click the Ruler button to display rulers. ▪

3. Position the mouse pointer between the indent markers of the margin boundary that you want to change. When the arrow turns into a two-headed arrow and the text tip (telling which margin you're changing) appears, you can drag the boundary (see Figure 13.6).

two-headed arrow

FIG. 13.6

When you see a two-headed arrow and a text tip, you are ready to drag the margin boundary.

CAUTION

Be sure you're pointing at the margin boundaries on the ruler. If you see the one-headed mouse arrow instead of the two-headed arrow, you're pointing to something other than the margin boundary— probably an indent marker. At the left margin boundary, for example, if you haven't set indents for your document, it's easy to point at the indent markers because they are right on top of the margin boundary. Watch the text tip to be sure you're pointing at the margin boundary.

4. Drag the margin boundary toward the edge of the page to make the margin smaller or toward the center of the page to make the margin wider. A dotted line on your document shows you where the new margin will appear (see Figure 13.7).

TIP You can hold down the Alt key as you drag a margin boundary to see margin measurements in the ruler.

If you change your mind about dragging a margin, you can cancel your change by pressing Esc before you release the mouse button, or by choosing Edit, Undo Formatting, or by clicking the Undo button after you release the mouse button.

FIG. 13.7

You can drag margin boundaries to make your margins narrower or wider.

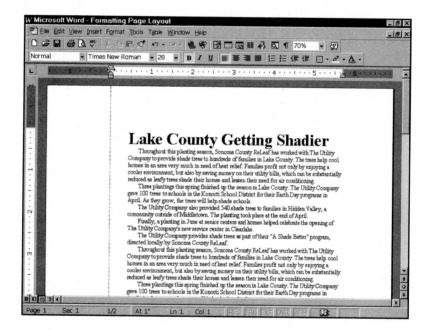

N O T E If your document has facing pages (mirror margins), display multiple pages in Print Preview view so that you can see the effect of any change you make to the inside margins. If you change the inside margin on one page, all pages in the section reflect that change. ■

Aligning Text Vertically

Text is normally aligned to the top margin in your document. But you may want to align it differently—in the center of the page or justified on the page (see Figure 13.8). When you justify text, the paragraphs (not the lines within paragraphs) on the page are spread evenly between the top and bottom margins.

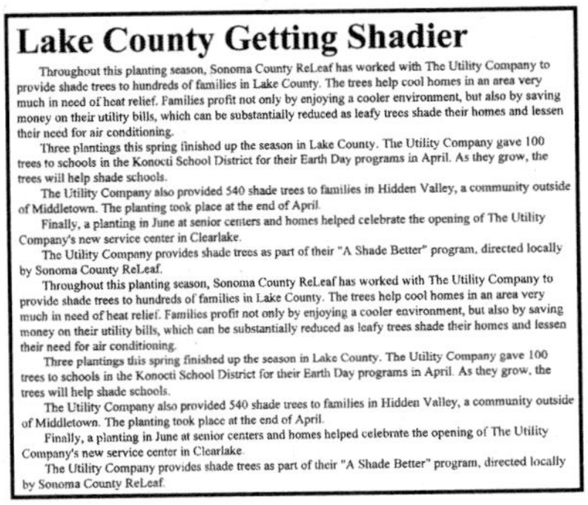

FIG. 13.8

You can align text in the center of the page or justified.

Text alignment applies to sections (you learn more about sections in "Working with Sections in Your Document," later in this chapter). If you haven't divided your document into sections, it applies to the entire document. If text fills each page, changing its vertical alignment does not make much difference; reserve this technique for pages that are not full or for sections that are less than a page in length.

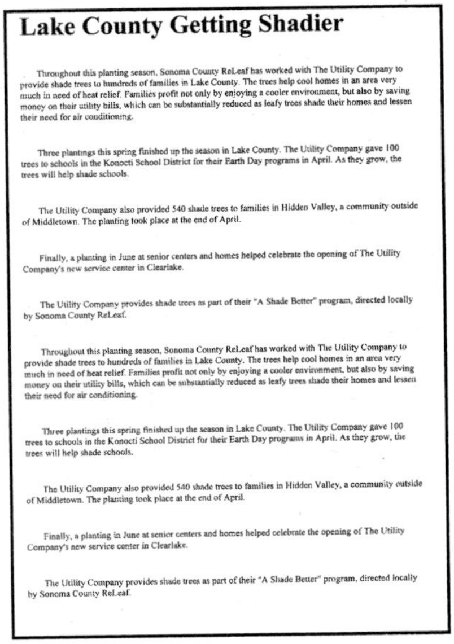

To vertically align text on the page, follow these steps:

1. Position the insertion point inside the section where you want to align text.
2. Choose File, Page Setup. The Page Setup dialog box appears.
3. Select the Layout tab.
4. In the Vertical Alignment list, select Center to center text on the page.

You can also select Justify to spread paragraphs between the top and bottom margins on the page.

Or, you can select Top to align text to the top margin.

5. Choose OK.

Controlling Where Paragraphs and Pages Break

As you type your document, Word automatically breaks text at the bottom margin of each page. Text continues on the next page, unless you specify otherwise. Word determines how much text appears on a page based on many factors, including margins, type size, paragraph specifications, and the size of footnotes. Displaying hidden text and field codes also can affect page breaks—hide them to see accurately how your pages will break.

You have many ways to control how text breaks on a page. You can specify that paragraphs stay together, for example, or with other paragraphs. You can specify at which line a page will break.

Controlling Paragraph Breaks

By default, paragraphs break at the bottom margin of a page and continue at the top margin of the next page. Many times you might want to prevent paragraphs from breaking arbitrarily at the bottom of the page. You may want to keep a heading paragraph together with the paragraph that follows it, for example. Or you may want certain paragraphs not to break at all. You may want to avoid widows and orphans, single lines of text that appear at the top or bottom of the page.

Regardless of how you format paragraphs to control paragraph breaks, hard page breaks that you insert manually take precedence. If you format a paragraph to stay together on a page but insert a hard page break inside the paragraph, for example, the paragraph always breaks at the line containing the hard page break. You must remove the hard page break if you want the paragraph to stay together (see the next section).

To control paragraph breaks, follow these steps:

1. Position the insertion point inside the paragraph you want to affect.

2. Choose Format, Paragraph. The Paragraph dialog box appears. Select the Line and Page Breaks tab (see Figure 13.9).

Part

II

Ch

13

FIG. 13.9

In the Paragraph dialog box, you can control how paragraphs break—or don't break—at the bottom of a page.

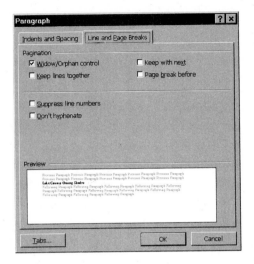

3. Select the following options you want from the Pagination group:

Select this option	To get this result
Widow/Orphan Control	Prevents single lines in selected paragraphs from appearing alone at the top or bottom of a page.
Keep Lines Together	Prevents a page break inside a selected paragraph. Moves the paragraph to the next page if there's not room on the current page for all of it.
Keep with Next	Ensures that the selected paragraph always appears on the same page as the next paragraph. Moves the paragraph to the next page if there's not room on the current page for it and the next paragraph.
Page Break Before	Starts the selected paragraph at the top of the next page. Inserts a page break before selected paragraph.

4. Choose OK.

A nonprinting square selection handle appears in the left margin next to any paragraph for which you've selected a pagination option. If text breaks on the page in a way you don't like, look for these squares to see whether the page break is caused by a pagination option. If it is, you can remove it by following the preceding steps and clearing the offending pagination option.

Inserting Page Breaks

Word inserts soft page breaks at the end of every page and adjusts them as necessary when you edit, add, or remove text. If you want to force a page to break at a particular place in your document, you can insert a hard page break. Word always starts text following a hard page break at the top of the next page.

In Normal view, a soft page break appears as a dotted line; in Page Layout or Print Preview view, you see the page as it will print. In Outline and Online Layout views, you don't see soft page breaks. Hard page breaks appear in the Normal and Outline views as a dotted line containing the words Page Break; they appear this way in the Page Layout and Master Document views when you display nonprinting characters. In Online Layout view, hard page breaks appear as excessive space between paragraphs.

> **N O T E** Hard page breaks take priority over paragraph pagination options. ▪

After you insert a hard page break, you can delete it, move it, copy it, or paste it.

You can insert a hard page break by using a command or a keyboard shortcut. You also can insert a page break by inserting a section break that begins on the next page, or on the next odd- or even-numbered page; see "Working with Sections in Your Document" later in this chapter. To insert a hard page break, follow these steps:

1. Position the insertion point at the beginning of the text that you want to start on a new page.
2. Choose Insert, Break. The Break dialog box appears (see Figure 13.10).
3. Select Page Break.
4. Choose OK.

FIG. 13.10
In the Break dialog box, you can insert a hard page break by selecting the Page Break option.

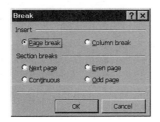

> **T I P** To insert a hard page break using a keyboard shortcut, press Ctrl+Enter.

Working with Sections in Your Document

Initially, in word processing programs, many formatting choices—margins, columns, headers and footers, line numbers, page numbers, and footnotes—applied to the entire document. Later, users' needs grew to require different settings for different parts of the document; Word uses *sections* as its way to divide your document into parts that you can format differently. Each section is like a document within a document.

Sections are especially important in creating two types of documents: those with chapters and those that fall into the desktop publishing category. Sections are useful for chapters because you can force a section to start on a right-facing page (as most chapters do) and can change headers, footers, page numbers, line numbering, and so on for each chapter. Sections also are indispensable for desktop publishing, where you often need to vary the number of columns on a single page.

▶ **See** "Creating Columns," **p. 416**

▶ **See** "Changing Columns," **p. 427**

▶ **See** "Working with Subdocuments within the Master Document," **p. 1056**

Dividing a Document into Sections

By default, a document contains only a single section. Section breaks divide your document into sections. The breaks appear as double-dotted lines containing the words Section Break in Normal view (the type of section break will appear in parentheses). You'll see section breaks in Page Layout view if all nonprinting characters are displayed (see Figure 13.11). (You can display nonprinting characters by choosing Tools, Options, selecting the View tab, and then selecting All.) The dotted lines do not print.

A *section break* marks the point in your document where new formatting begins. In a newsletter, for example, a section break often follows the title, so that a multiple-column format can begin. The text following the section break, along with its new formatting, can begin in your document immediately, on the next page, or on the next even-numbered or odd-numbered page. You determine where the new section formatting begins when you insert the section break.

To insert a section break, follow these steps:

1. Position the insertion point where you want the section break.
2. Choose Insert, Break. The Break dialog box appears (refer to Figure 13.10).

FIG. 13.11
Section breaks appear as a double-dotted line in Normal view and in Page Layout view when all nonprinting characters are displayed.

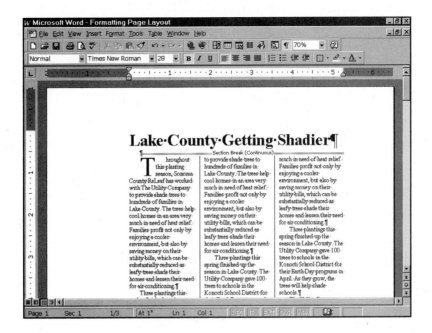

3. Select from the following Section Breaks options:

Option	Section starts
Next Page	Top of the next page in document
Continuous	Insertion point (causing no apparent break in the document)
Even Page	Next even-numbered page in the document (generally a left-facing page)
Odd Page	Next odd-numbered page in the document (generally a right-facing page)

4. Choose OK.

Use the Next Page section break when you want the new section to begin on the next page. Use the Continuous section break when you want the new section to begin at the insertion point; for example, when you create a newsletter that has different-width columns on the same page (such as a full-width title followed by a three-column story). Another use for the Continuous section break is to balance columns on a page: Insert a Continuous section break at the end of a document that is divided into columns but that doesn't fill the last column of the last page.

Part

II

Ch

13

Use the Odd Page section break for chapters when you want them to start always on a right-facing page (assuming page numbering in your document starts with page 1 on a right-facing page). Use the Even Page section break to start a section on the next even-numbered page; on facing page layouts with mirror margins, even-numbered pages usually are on the left side of the layout.

Word inserts section breaks for you on some occasions. When you format a document for columns and specify that the columns take effect from This Point Forward, Word inserts a continuous section break at the insertion point. When you select text and format it for columns, Word inserts continuous section breaks both before and after the selected text. The same rule holds true when you make many page setup selections.

▶ **See** "Creating Columns," **p. 416**

Removing Section Breaks

In the same way that paragraph marks store paragraph formatting, section break marks store section formatting. Although you can remove a section break easily, remember that when you do, you also remove all section formatting for the section that precedes the deleted break. The preceding section merges with the following section and takes on its formatting characteristics. If you accidentally delete a section break marker, immediately choose Edit, Undo to retrieve the marker.

 To remove a section break, position the insertion point on the section break and press the Delete key. As alternatives, you can position the insertion point just after the section break marker and press Backspace; you can select the section break and click the Cut button or choose Edit, Cut.

To remove all the section breaks in your document, follow these steps:

1. Choose Edit, Replace and choose More.
2. With the insertion point in the Find What box, open the Special list and choose Section Break.
3. Make sure that the Replace With box contains no text, and choose Replace All.

Copying Section Formatting

The section break stores section formatting. You can duplicate (or apply) section formatting quickly by selecting, copying, and then pasting the section break elsewhere. After you paste the section break, the preceding text takes on the formatting of the copied section break.

Another way to duplicate section formatting is to copy and store a section break as AutoText. That way, the break becomes available in all new documents and can be applied quickly and easily.

A final way to duplicate section formatting is to include the formatting in a template—even the Normal template. Remember that by default, a new document includes only one section. That section carries certain default formatting characteristics: one column, a half-inch space between columns (if columns are selected), and no line numbers. If you always format sections differently, modify the Normal template or create a new template that includes your own custom section formatting selections.

▶ **See** "Creating a New Template," **p. 213**

▶ **See** "Changing a Template," **p. 210**

Changing the Section Break Type

If you insert a continuous section break and want to change it to a new page section break, you must delete the existing section break and insert a new one. If you want to make this change without removing the previous section's formatting, insert the new section break so that it appears after the old one and then delete the old page break. The section will then take on the formatting contained in the next section break, which is the new break you added.

Finding Section Breaks

If you want to find section breaks, choose Edit, Find. Next, choose More, select Special, and then select Section Break. Choose Find Next to find the next section break. You can find section breaks this way even if they are not displayed.

You can choose Edit, Replace to find a section break and replace it with something else, but you cannot replace something with a section break. Use this technique if you want to remove all the section breaks in your document: simply replace section breaks with nothing.

▶ **See** "Using Find and Replace," **p. 227**

Part
II

Ch
13

Creating Headers and Footers

Headers and footers contain information repeated at the top or bottom of the pages of a document. The simplest header or footer may contain only a chapter title and page number. More elaborate headers or footers may contain a company logo (or other graphic), the author's name, the time and date the file was saved or printed, and any other information that may be needed.

You can format headers and footers like any other part of the document, but you usually position them within a page's top and bottom margins, although Word enables you to position them anywhere on the page.

Word also gives you the option of having a different header or footer on the first page of a document or section. You also can have different headers and footers on even and odd pages. This feature is useful for chapter headers in books and manuscripts. Each section of a document—a chapter, for example—can have its own headers and footers.

When you create and edit headers and footers, Word switches you to Page Layout view and displays headers and footers at the top or bottom of the page, just as they appear when you print your document.

Adding Headers and Footers

When you add headers and footers, Word switches you to Page Layout view, activates a pane where you can create your header, displays a special Header and Footer toolbar, and dims the text of your document so that you can't edit it (see Figure 13.12).

FIG. 13.12
You create headers and footers in a special pane.

You create your header or footer inside the pane, and you can edit and format it the same way you do any text. After you finish creating the header or footer, close the Header and Footer toolbar. You can move the Header and Footer toolbar by dragging it to a different position on the page.

You can include text or graphics, or both, in a header or footer. If you want, you can insert autotext entries, page numbers, date and time, fields, symbols, cross-references, files, frames, pictures, objects, or a database. Or you can draw a picture using buttons on the Drawing toolbar.

Buttons on the toolbar aid you in creating your header or footer (see Figure 13.13). If the status bar is visible at the bottom of your screen, you can display a message explaining each button by pausing the mouse pointer over the button.

FIG. 13.13
Create a header or footer using the buttons in the Header and Footer toolbar.

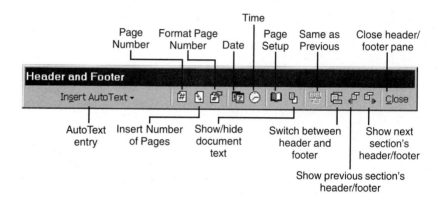

In Page Layout view, your document appears grayed when you're creating or editing headers or footers; headers and footers appear grayed when you're working on your document. To see both your document and its headers and footers, choose File, Print Preview.

To add a header or footer to your document, follow these steps:

1. Choose View, Header and Footer.

2. Type and format the text of your header. Click the Page Number, Number of Pages, Date, and/or Time buttons to quickly add those elements to your header.

3. Click the Switch Between button to display the footer, and type and format just as you did the header (see step 2). Alternatively, use the scroll bars or press Page Up or Page Down to scroll to the footer.

4. Choose Close or double-click your document to close the header or footer pane and return to your document.

Another way to include an automatic date or time in a header or footer is to insert a date or time field by choosing Insert, Field. Using this command, you can select among different formatting options for your date or time.

▶ **See** "Formatting Date-Time Results," **p. 713**

If your header or footer is larger than your margin, Word adjusts the margins of your document to make room. If you don't want Word to adjust your margins, make your header or footer smaller or move it closer to the edge of the page (see "Positioning Headers and Footers," later in this chapter). If you want text to overlap a header or footer (as you might if the header or footer is a graphic that is to appear behind text), type a minus sign (–) in front of your margin measurement. If your header is four inches high, for example, and you want a top margin of one inch, and you want the text to overlap the header, type **–1**" as your top margin. You can use this technique to create a "watermark" that appears behind the text on every page of your document.

Varying Headers and Footers Within a Single Document

Each section in a document can have unique headers and footers. This setup is helpful if you format each chapter in a book as a separate section. Or you can create different headers and footers on odd and even pages. You also can have a different header or footer on the first page of a document. If your document has facing pages and mirror margins, for example, you might want a right-aligned header on odd-numbered pages (which appear on the right side of a facing-page layout) and a left-aligned header on even-numbered pages (which appear on the left). In a newsletter, you might want no header on the first page.

Changing Headers and Footers for Specific Sections   When you first create headers and footers, Word applies them to all the sections in your document. That way, all the headers and footers in your document are the same. Similarly, if you divide into sections a document with existing headers or footers, the headers and footers are the same in all sections.

If you want a different header or footer in a section, you must go to that section and unlink the existing header or footer; then you must create the new header or footer. The new header or footer applies to the current section and to all following sections. Later, if you decide you want your new header or footer to be the same as the previous header or footer, you can relink it.

If you want different headers and footers in different sections of your document, you first must divide your document into sections. To learn how, see "Working with Sections in your Document" earlier in this chapter.

To change the header or footer in one section of your document, follow these steps:

1. Position the insertion point inside the section where you want to change the header or footer.

2. Choose <u>V</u>iew, <u>H</u>eader and Footer. Word selects the header for the section in which you're located. If you want to change the footer for that section, click the Switch Between button instead.

3. To unlink the header or footer, click the Same as Previous button. The Same as Previous line disappears from the top right of the header or footer editing pane.

4. Create the new header or footer.

5. Choose the <u>C</u>lose button or double-click your document to close the Header and Footer toolbar.

You also can click the Show Next button to change the header or footer in the following section.

The new header or footer applies to the current section and to all following sections.

As an alternative to steps 1 and 2, you can choose <u>V</u>iew, <u>H</u>eader and Footer from within any section to activate headers and footers. Then click the Switch Between button to jump between headers and footers, or click the Show Next or Show Previous buttons to activate headers or footers in a different section.

To relink a different header or footer to the previous header or footer, follow these steps:

1. Position the insertion point inside the section containing the header or footer you want to relink.

2. Choose <u>V</u>iew, <u>H</u>eader and Footer. Word selects the header for the section in which you're located. If you want to change the footer for that section, click the Switch Between button.

3. To relink the header or footer, click the Same as Previous button. Word displays a message box asking whether you want to delete the header/footer and connect to the header/footer in the previous section.

Part

II

Ch

13

4. Choose <u>Y</u>es.

5. Choose <u>C</u>lose, or double-click your document to close the Header and Footer toolbar.

By relinking the header or footer to the previous header or footer, you change not only the current header or footer, but also those in all the following sections.

CAUTION

If you change one header or footer without unlinking it, all the headers and footers in all the sections change.

Creating Special First-Page and Odd/Even Page Headers and Footers   Many documents have a different header or footer on the first page—or have no header or footer on the first page. In Word, first-page headers and footers apply to sections, not to the whole document. That way, you can have a different header or footer at the beginning of each section in a document that is divided into sections.

Sometimes you want different headers and footers for the odd- and even-numbered pages in your document. In a document with facing pages (mirror margins), odd-numbered pages appear on the right side and even-numbered pages appear on the left side. You might want left-aligned headers on even-numbered pages and right-aligned headers on odd-numbered pages so that headers always appear on the outside edges of your document.

To specify special headers and footers for first pages or odd and even pages in your document, follow these steps:

1. Choose <u>V</u>iew, <u>H</u>eader and Footer.

2. Click the Show Previous or Show Next button to locate the section in which you want a different first-page header or footer.

3. Click the Page Setup button (or choose <u>F</u>ile, Page Set<u>u</u>p) to display the Page Setup dialog box.

4. Select the Layout tab.

5. In the Headers and Footers group, select Different <u>F</u>irst Page to create specific first page headers or footers, and then choose OK. The header or footer editing pane for the section you're in is titled `First Page Header` or `First Page Footer`.

Or, in the Headers and Footers group, select Different O̲dd and Even and choose OK. Word re-titles the header or footer editing box for the section you're in to `Even Page Header`, `Even Page Footer`, `Odd Page Header`, or `Odd Page Footer`.

6. If you want no header or footer, leave the header or footer editing area blank. If you want a different header or footer on the first page or odd/even pages of the section, create it now.

7. Choose C̲lose or double-click your document.

To remove first-page headers and footers from a section or document, follow these steps:

1. Position the insertion point anywhere inside a document containing only one section.

   You can also position the insertion point inside the section for which you want to remove first-page headers and footers.

2. Choose F̲ile, Page Set̲up.

3. Select the L̲ayout tab.

4. Clear the Different F̲irst Page check box in the Headers and Footers group.

5. Choose OK.

Positioning Headers and Footers

By default, headers and footers appear one-half inch from the top or bottom edge of the document page. You can change that distance in the Header and Footer view.

To specify a header's or footer's distance from the edge of the paper, follow these steps:

1. Choose V̲iew, H̲eader and Footer.

 2. Click the Show Previous or Show Next button to locate the section containing the header or footer you want to affect.

 3. Click the Page Setup button (or choose F̲ile, Page Set̲up) to display the Page Setup dialog box.

4. Select the M̲argins tab.

5. In the From Edge group, select H̲eader and type or select the distance that you want your header from the top edge of the page.

Or, select Footer and type or select the distance that you want your footer from the bottom edge of the page.

6. Choose OK to close the Page Setup dialog box.

7. Choose Close or double-click your document to return to it.

 T I P   Remember that most printers have a quarter-inch nonprinting edge on all sides.

Formatting Headers and Footers

Anything you can do to or in regular text, you can do to a header or footer. You can change the font, reduce or enlarge the size of the text, insert graphics, draw pictures, include a table, add a line or box, or add shading. You also can add tabs, change the alignment or indents, or change line or paragraph spacing. Use any of Word's formatting techniques to make headers and footers look distinct from the text in your document.

▶ **See** "Formatting Characters," **p. 285**

▶ **See** "Changing Fonts," **p. 295**

▶ **See** "Shading and Bordering Paragraphs," **p. 356**

You can use most of the commands in the Insert, Format, Tools, and Table menus to format headers and footers. You can use the ruler to set tabs and indents.

Editing Headers and Footers

In Normal view, you can't see headers or footers. In Page Layout view, you can see headers and footers, but they appear dimmed. In any view, you must activate a header or footer to edit it. You can activate a header or footer using the same command you used to create it, or in Page Layout view, you can double-click a header or footer to activate it. After it is activated, you edit the header or footer using the same commands you used to create it.

If your document contains only one section, then the headers and footers are the same throughout your document, and you can edit headers and footers with the insertion point anywhere within the document. If your document contains multiple sections with different headers and footers, you must locate the header or footer you want to edit. You can do that two ways:

    ■ Activate headers and footers and then use the Show Previous and Show Next buttons on the Header and Footer toolbar to move between sections.

■ First locate the header or footer you want to edit and then activate it.

To edit headers and footers, follow these steps:

1. Choose <u>V</u>iew, <u>H</u>eader and Footer. Word activates the header for the section containing the insertion point. Or, in Page Layout view, double-click the header or footer you want to edit.

2. To edit a footer rather than a header, click the Switch Between button or press Page Down to scroll to the bottom of the page.

3. To locate a header or footer in a different section of your document, click the Show Previous or the Show Next button.

4. After you locate the header or footer you want to edit, make the changes you want.

5. Choose <u>C</u>lose or double-click the document.

You can delete a header or footer by activating it, selecting all the text or objects contained in the header or footer, pressing Delete, and then choosing <u>C</u>lose.

Hiding the Text Layer

Normally, the text layer appears dimmed while you're working on headers and footers. If you want to hide it altogether, you can click a special button on the Header and Footer toolbar. Text is only hidden while you're working on the header or footer.

To hide or display the text layer, follow these steps:

1. Activate headers and footers by choosing <u>V</u>iew, <u>H</u>eader and Footer or by double-clicking an existing header or footer in Page Layout view.

2. Click the Hide/Show Document Text button. The text (grayed already), disappears from your screen. Click the button a second time to display the text.

3. Choose <u>C</u>lose or double-click your document to return to it.

Working with Page Numbers

Long documents are easier to read and reference when the pages are numbered. In Word, you can insert a page number quickly, and Word formats it as a header or footer for you. That way, you can use all the techniques for working with headers and footers to work with page numbers. See "Creating Headers and Footers" earlier in this chapter.

Inserting Page Numbers

Page numbers can appear at the top or bottom of the page and can be aligned to the center or either side of the page. When you insert a page number, Word includes a PAGE field and frames the page number. Because of the field, Word can update the page number even if you move the page to another portion of the document. Because of the frame, you can move the page number anywhere within the header or footer.

▶ **See** "Inserting Field Codes," **p. 700**

 Another way to include page numbers is to insert them as part of creating a header or footer, by clicking the Page Numbers button on the Header and Footer toolbar. This technique is the best if you want to include text with your page number.

To insert page numbers, follow these steps:

1. Choose Insert, Page Numbers. The Page Numbers dialog box appears (see Figure 13.14).

FIG. 13.14
Using the Page Numbers dialog box, you can include page numbers at the top or bottom of the page, in any alignment. You can choose whether to show them on the first page of your document.

2. In the Position list, select Bottom of Page (Footer) to position your page number at the bottom of the page in a footer or choose Top of Page (Header) to position your page number at the top of the page in a header.

3. In the Alignment list, select Left, Center, Right, Inside, or Outside to line up your page number to the center or one side of the page.

4. Select Show Number on First Page if you want a page number to appear on the first page of your document. Clear this check box to prevent the page number from appearing on the first page.

5. Choose OK.

To reposition page numbers, choose Insert, Page Numbers and choose a different option from the Alignment list. Alternatively, in Page Layout view, double-click the page number to activate the Header or Footer editing pane. Select the page number and drag it to a new position (or select the frame and reposition it by choosing Format, Frame and making selections from the Frame dialog box). Then choose Close.

Removing Page Numbers

Because page numbers appear within headers or footers, to remove them you must activate the header or footer, select the page number, and delete it.

To remove page numbers, follow these steps:

1. In Page Layout view, double-click the page number.

   You can also choose View, Header and Footer and click the Switch Between, Show Next, or Show Previous button to locate the page number.

2. Select the page number.
3. Press Delete.
4. Choose Close or double-click your document.

Formatting Page Numbers

You can format your page numbers in a variety of ways. They can appear as numbers, uppercase or lowercase letters, or uppercase or lowercase Roman numerals.

You can include chapter numbers if your document's chapter numbers are formatted with Word default heading styles (Heading 1 through Heading 9) and if you've formatted the headings by choosing Format, Bullets and Numbering and making a selection from the Outline Numbered tab. If you include chapter numbers, you can separate them from the page numbers with a hyphen, a period, a colon, or a — (a wide hyphen).

▶ **See** "Creating Numbered Headings," **p. 670**

You can format page numbers at the same time that you insert them, or you can format them later. To format page numbers, follow these steps:

1. If you're creating new page numbers, choose Insert, Page Numbers. Make selections from the Position and Alignment lists.

Part

II

Ch

13

If you want to format existing page numbers for a single section, you can also position the insertion point inside that section and choose Insert, Page Numbers.

2. Click the Format button. The Page Number Format dialog box displays (see Figure 13.15).

FIG. 13.15
You can format your page numbers as you create them or after you've already created them.

3. In the Number Format list, select the style you want your numbers to be.

4. Select Include Chapter Number if you want to include a chapter number before your page number. In the Chapter Starts with Style drop-down list, choose the style (Heading 1 through Heading 9) that you use for chapter numbers in your document.

5. If you want a separator between the chapter number and page number, make a selection from the Use Separator list.

6. Choose OK.

Numbering Different Sections in a Document

Even if your document contains more than a single section, page numbering applies by default to your entire document, and numbers are continuous throughout the document. You can start page numbering at the number you specify in any section, however. You may want page numbering to restart at "1" for each section, for example.

To create page numbering by section, follow these steps:

1. If necessary, divide your document into sections by inserting section breaks.

2. Position the insertion point inside the section for which you want unique page numbering.

3. Unlink the header or footer from previous headers or footers (see the section "Varying Headers and Footers within a Single Document," earlier in this chapter).

4. Choose Insert, Page Numbers, and then choose Format.

5. In the Page Numbering group, select Start <u>A</u>t and type or select the starting page number for the current section.

6. Choose OK to return to the Page Numbers dialog box; choose OK again to return to your document.

If headers and footers containing page numbers are unlinked from previous sections but you want page numbering to be continuous from section to section, repeat the steps above, choosing <u>C</u>ontinue from the Previous Section in the Page Numbering Group. Finally, choose OK.

▶ **See** "Creating Numbered Headings," **p. 670**

Repaginating in the Background

By default, Word automatically calculates page breaks as you work on your document. In the Normal, Outline, Or Master Document view, you can turn off background pagination, but in Online Layout, Page Layout or Print Preview views, you cannot. You may see a slight performance improvement if you turn off background repagination.

Word always repaginates when you print your document, switch to Online Layout, Page Layout or Print Preview view, or compile an index or table of contents.

To turn off background repagination, follow these steps:

1. Choose <u>V</u>iew, and then choose either <u>N</u>ormal, <u>O</u>utline, or <u>M</u>aster Document.

Click the appropriate button on the horizontal scroll bar to switch to Normal or Outline view.

2. Choose <u>T</u>ools, <u>O</u>ptions, and select the General Tab.
3. Clear the <u>B</u>ackground Repagination check box.
4. Choose OK.

Inserting a Date and Time

In Word, there are several ways to insert the date and time automatically. You can use a command to insert the current date and time as frozen—that is, the date and time do not change—or you can insert them as a field that you can update to reflect the current date and time. You can choose among many different date and time formats. Or you can include a date and time field in a header or footer. These fields also update to reflect the current date or time.

Part
II

Ch
13

▶ **See** "Understanding the Basics of Fields," **p. 694**

▶ **See** "Inserting Field Codes," **p. 700**

 T I P   To update a date or time field, select the field and press the F9 key. Date and time fields automatically update whenever you open or print a document if you set your options accordingly.

To insert a date or time, follow these steps:

1. Position the insertion point where you want the date or time to appear. You can insert the date or time in your document or in a header or footer.

2. Choose Insert, Date and Time. The Date and Time dialog box appears (see Figure 13.16).

FIG. 13.16

Choose Insert, Date and Time to insert a date or time.

3. Choose the date and time format you want from the Available Formats list.

4. If you want the date and time to update to reflect the current date and time, select Update Automatically (Insert as Field).

5. Choose OK.

Inserting Line Numbers

If a document is used for reference, it is helpful to readers if the lines are numbered. You can number lines in text that a class shares or in legal briefs, for example.

You can number some or all of the lines in a document. If your document contains no section breaks, line numbers apply to the entire document. If your document contains sections, line numbers apply to the currently selected section. If you select text before you assign line numbers, Word places page section breaks before and after the selected text, isolating it on a page (or pages) by itself. If you want to apply line numbers to an entire document that contains multiple sections, select the entire document before you apply the line numbers.

Word offers many options for controlling how line numbers appear. Numbers can start at 1 or some other number, and they can appear on each line or on only some lines. They can be continuous, or they can restart at each section or page. You can control the distance between text and the line numbers. You also can suppress line numbers for selected paragraphs.

Line numbers appear in the left margin of your page or to the left of text in columns.

To add and format line numbers, follow these steps:

1. Position the insertion point inside the section containing lines you want to number. (Position the insertion point anywhere inside a document that is not divided into sections.)

   You can also select the text whose lines you want to number.

   Or, you can select the entire document if it is divided into sections and you want line numbering for all the sections.

2. Choose File, Page Setup. The Page Setup dialog box appears.

3. Select the Layout tab.

4. Choose Line Numbers. The Line Numbers dialog box appears (see Figure 13.17).

FIG. 13.17
Using the Line Numbers dialog box, you can number the lines of your text for easy reference.

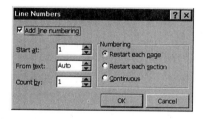

5. Select Add Line Numbering.

6. Make changes to any of the following:

   - Select Start At and type or select the starting line number.
   - Select From Text and type the distance between the line numbers and text. (Be sure your margins are wide enough to accommodate this distance.)
   - Select Count By and type or select the increment by which you want lines to be numbered. Select 3, for example, if you want every third line numbered.

7. In the Numbering group, select any of the following:

   - Select Restart Each Page for numbering to start over on each page.
   - Select Restart Each Section to start over in each section.
   - Select Continuous if you want line numbers continuous throughout the document.

Part
II

Ch
13

8. Choose OK.

Choose OK again to close the Page Setup dialog box and return to your document, where you can see the line numbers (see Figure 13.18).

FIG. 13.18

This document is divided into two sections, so that the title line isn't numbered.

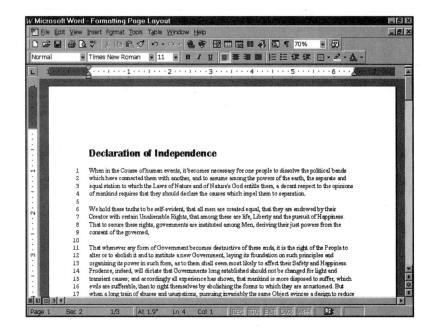

To remove line numbers, follow these steps:

1. Follow steps 1–4 above.

2. Clear the check from the Add Line Numbering check box.

3. Choose OK. Choose OK again to close the Page Setup dialog box.

To suppress line numbers, follow these steps:

1. Select the paragraphs where you don't want line numbers to appear.

2. Choose Format, Paragraph. The Paragraph dialog box appears.

3. Select the Lines and Page Breaks tab.

4. Select Suppress Line Numbers.

5. Choose OK.

Determining Paper Size and Orientation

You can change the paper size or orientation for your entire document or for part of your document. You may select a different paper size to create something smaller than usual, such as an invitation. You can select landscape (horizontal) orientation rather than the usual portrait (vertical) orientation to create a brochure or envelope.

Word offers several predefined paper sizes, including letter and legal. If none of these sizes suits your needs, you can select a custom size instead and enter your own measurements.

Paper size and orientation settings apply to the current section, just like margin settings. If you haven't divided your document into sections, your settings apply to the whole document, unless you choose to apply them to the currently selected text or from the insertion point forward in your document. If you apply settings to selected text, Word inserts a new-page section break before and after the selection. If you apply settings to the insertion point forward, Word inserts a new-page section break at the insertion point's current position.

 T I P When you're changing paper size and orientation, you can insert a new-page section break to isolate the new section on a separate sheet of paper.

To set paper size and orientation, follow these steps:

1. Select the text or section where you want to set paper size and orientation.

2. Choose File, Page Setup; in the Page Setup dialog box, select the Paper Size tab (see Figure 13.19).

FIG. 13.19
You can select a preset or custom paper size, and you can choose the paper orientation—portrait (vertical) or land-scape (horizontal).

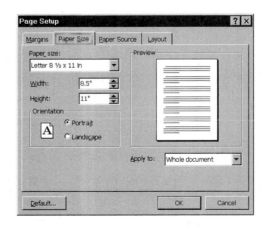

3. From the Paper Size list, select a predefined paper size.

   In the Width and Height boxes, you can also type or select the width and height of your custom paper size.

4. For a vertical page, select Portrait from the Orientation group.

   Or, for a horizontal page, select Landscape from the Orientation group.

5. From the Apply To list, select the section to which you want to apply paper size and orientation settings. (For more information about the Apply To list, see "Setting Different Margins for Different Parts of Your Document" earlier in this chapter.)

6. Choose OK.

Note that if you create custom-size paper, the paper measurements you type are usually in inches, unless you change the default measurement system by choosing Tools, Options and then selecting the General tab. You can override the default inches by typing your measurement using text that describes a different measurement system. To set a paper width of 36 picas, for example, type **36 pi**; to set a paper height of 24 centimeters, type **24 cm**.

CAUTION

If you set width and height for the page size, be sure your printer can handle the paper size you specify. Some laser printers don't handle custom paper sizes well. Consult your printer manual for more information.

Selecting the Paper Source

In Word, you not only can alter margins, paper size, and paper orientation for your document or for a section of your document, but you also can specify where your printer finds the paper.

Many printers have different options for storing paper. Most laser printers, for example, have a default paper tray and a manual feed. You can specify that one section of your document be printed from the manual feed, whereas the rest of the document be printed from paper in the default paper tray. Some printers have two paper trays; you can specify that one section, such as the first page of a letter, be printed on letterhead in the first tray, whereas the remaining pages be printed on plain paper from the second tray.

As you can do with all page setup options, you can insert section breaks before you select paper source, or Word can insert section breaks for you.

To select a paper source for your document, follow these steps:

1. Position the insertion point inside the section for which you want to set the paper source. (The change applies to the entire document unless the document has multiple sections.)

   You can also select the section for which you want to set the paper source.

   Or, position the insertion point where you want the new paper source to begin in your document.

2. Choose File, Page Setup. In the Page Setup dialog box, select the Paper Source tab (see Figure 13.20).

FIG. 13.20
Using the Page Setup dialog box, you can print different sections of your document on paper from different sources.

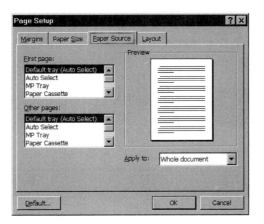

3. From the First Page list, select the paper source for the first page of your document.

4. From the Other Pages list, select the paper source for the remaining pages of your document.

5. From the <u>A</u>pply To list, select the section to which you want to apply paper source settings (the list displays different options, depending on how much text is selected in the document):

Option	Applies margins to	When
This Section	Current section (No section break is inserted)	Insertion point is located within a section
Selected Sections	Multiple sections (No section breaks are inserted)	At least part of more than one section is selected
This Point Forward	Insertion point (Inserts new page section break at insertion point)	Insertion point is where you want new margin to start
Selected Text	Selected text (Inserts new page section breaks at the beginning and end of text)	Text is selected
Whole Document	Entire document (No break inserted)	Insertion point is anywhere

6. Choose OK.

When you print a document with various paper sizes, orientations, or sources, your printer may pause at the end of each page and wait for you to indicate that it should continue. In some cases, you may need only to access the Print Manager and click Resume. In other cases, you may need to press a button on the printer. Newer laser printers work well with varying paper sizes and orientations, but if you experience difficulties, check your printer manual.

▶ **See** "Selecting the Paper Source," **p. 276**

If you want to apply your paper source selections to the Normal template so that they become the default settings, choose the <u>D</u>efault button before you choose OK.

 TIP Be sure that you have installed the correct printer driver for your printer in Windows so that Word knows which paper trays your printer has available. Refer to your Windows book or printer manual for details.

Changing Page Setup Defaults

All new documents are based on a template, and unless you choose a different template, Word bases new documents on the Normal template, which contains default page setup choices. Because these default choices may not be exactly what you want, Word gives you the chance to change them by applying your own page setup options to the Normal template and, thus, use your own page setup choices as defaults. You can change the default margins, for example, if you always print on paper that requires different margin settings than those supplied by the Normal template. You can change the paper size if you normally use paper different from standard letter size.

▶ **See** "Setting Default Formats in the Normal Template," **p. 211**

You can change defaults for any option in the Page Setup dialog box. Then each new document you create based on the Normal template has your new defaults. (Your current document—or the text or section you've selected—also uses your new settings.)

To change the default page setup settings, follow these steps:

1. Choose File, Page Setup.
2. On each tab in the Page Setup dialog box, make the page setup selections you want.
3. Click the Default button on any of the tabs. A dialog box asks you to confirm that all new documents based on the Normal template are affected by the change.
4. Choose OK.

Part

II

Ch

13

Web Publishing

CHAPTER 14

Publishing to a Web

Some experts forecast that the *Internet* and corporate *intranets* will make as great a change in business and society as the personal computer. These networks are changing the speed and pattern of communication. Webs of interlinked pages on the Internet and intranets enable people with little computer knowledge to move quickly between related information no matter where the information is located and no matter what type of computer they are using. ■

Convert Word documents into Web pages

Choosing File, Save As HTML converts Word documents into HTML pages, one of the easiest Web conversions available.

Create hyperlinks in documents

Hyperlink from text in a Word document to other Office documents and Web pages.

Work with Office documents on FTP sites

Save Office documents to or open documents stored in Internet FTP sites, just as if the FTP site were part of your local network.

Create your own Web of hyperlinked Office files

Link together Word, Excel, PowerPoint, and HTML documents in a small Web.

Distribute free Excel, Word, and PowerPoint viewers

People without Microsoft Office can view Office files using Microsoft's free viewers.

TIP Intranets are proprietary networks that operate within a company or organization. They use the same browsers and communication software as is used on the Internet. Some intranets allow users access to the Internet through secure gateways, called *firewalls*.

With Office 97's capability to create HTML pages you can create your own pages for the Internet, your corporate intranet, or your own office network. Through hyperlinks between Office documents you can create Webs that do not even need networks. As part of the Office 97 Suite, Word 97 can convert Word documents to Web pages or create new Web pages that include background patterns, graphics, formatted fonts, music, video, and hyperlinks. Microsoft has also created free viewers that enable people who don't have Excel, Word, or PowerPoint to view Office documents that are on the Web.

Word's Web page authoring tools make it easy to create new Web pages or enhance existing Web pages with data, tables or charts. Figure 14.1 shows a Web page created with Word's Web authoring tools.

FIG. 14.1
With Word's authoring tools you can create complete Web pages containing the most widely used HTML elements.

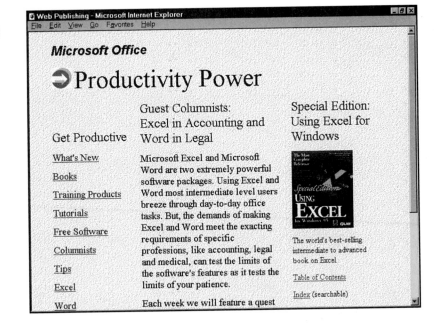

 ON THE WEB

http://www.microsoft.com/FrontPage To create complex Webs and pages, use a Web editor such as Microsoft FrontPage 97. It is a desktop publishing program for Web creation and management. It will help you create Web pages as well as manage Webs that include Office documents and HTML pages. Microsoft FrontPage 97 menus and toolbars are very similar to

Word. Its add-in "bots" enable even novices to include features such as full-text searching, data capture, and chat boxes. FrontPage 97 includes the capability to use ActiveX and Java components and link to databases.

What Are Web Pages?

A Web page is a simple text document. When opened inside Web *browser* software such as Netscape Navigator or Internet Explorer, that simple text document displays text, graphics and hyperlinks to other documents. Clicking a hyperlink takes the user to another document on the Internet or company intranet.

The Internet and intranets are networks that make information easily accessible, even between different types of computers with different capabilities. Instead of having to use arcane networking commands, you can view pages of information by typing in a simple address for a page. This address is known as a *Uniform Resource Locator (URL)*. A URL for a location on the World Wide Web might look like:

http://www.mcp.com

http://www.ronperson.com

http://www.microsoft.com

If you do not specify a specific file after the URL, then a default page for the Web site opens.

As you jump between pages using hyperlinks you create a path or history of all the pages you have viewed. Web browsers have navigation buttons in their toolbars that let you move forward or backward through the pages you have visited. At any time, on any page you can click a hyperlink to go off the "path" you've already viewed.

A Web page includes any or all of the following elements:

- Text
- Text formatting codes
- Headings, levels 1 through 6
- Lists: bulleted, numbered, or glossary
- Tables
- Divider lines, called horizontal rules
- Graphics, sounds, animations
- Hyperlinks to large sound, video, and animation files

Part

III

Ch

14

- Hyperlinks to other locations in the same document, other documents, or other locations on the Web
- Interactive form fields such as check boxes, text edit fields, and drop-down lists

Publishing with Word's Web Page Authoring Tools

Microsoft's Web page authoring tools in Word enable you to use your Word skills to develop fully functional Web pages. You don't need to know how to write *Hypertext Markup Language (HTML)* the code used to create Web pages. With many of the same commands you use in Word you can insert and format text, graphics, and hyperlinks to create your own Web pages.

Web page authoring tools are not available when you work in a Word document. They become available only when an HTML document is active. You can open an existing HTML document, open a new blank HTML document, or use the Web Page Wizard to guide you through the process of creating a Web page.

The Web pages you create in Word are saved as HTML files. They appear on your disk with the HTM file extension.

 TIP
If you already have documents in Word that you want to use as Web pages, you can copy and paste text from the Word document into a Web page, insert a file into a Web page by choosing Insert, File, or save a Web page as a Web (HTML) page.

 TROUBLESHOOTING

The Web Pages tab does not appear in the New dialog box when I choose File, New. If you choose File, New and do not see a Web Pages tab in the New dialog box, you need to install Word's Web page authoring tools. To install them run Setup as though you were going to install Word. Choose to do a Custom installation and select the Web Page Authoring (HTML) option. This will install the Web page authoring tools without reinstalling all of Office.

Toolbars and commands for authoring Web pages do not appear. Web page authoring tools only appear when the active document is an HTML document. You can either open an existing HTML document or choose File, New, select the Web Pages tab, and then choose either the Blank Web Page template or Web Page Wizard.

ON THE WEB

For online support from Microsoft, visit the following World Wide Web site:

http://www.microsoft.com/support

You can also access Microsoft's extensive troubleshooting KnowledgeBase at the following site:

http://www.microsoft.com/kb

For tutorials, tips, and add-ins for Microsoft Office applications point your browser to:

http://www.ronperson.com

Tips on Creating Web Pages

While creating a Web page is easy, creating an attractive, easy-to-read page takes thought and work. The communication style and layouts for publishing Web pages are different than they are for publishing to print. There are many sources on the Web that discuss design tools, aesthetics, and techniques. Here are a few tips to help you get started:

- Structure the content in smaller bites than you would for print. Try to make pages no more than one or two screens high.

- Write headings for major topics and format them with HTML heading styles so that readers can use Word's document map as well as visually browse through a document more quickly.

- Tables are excellent for presenting data in HTML just as they are in Word documents. The majority of current generation browsers support tables.

- All Internet Web pages and most corporate intranet pages should have their appearance tested on different browsers. While all browsers display the basic content of a page, they handle formatting differently.

- Use small graphics that are less than 30K in size. Large graphics take a long time to download. If you must display a large chart or other graphic, consider inserting a hyperlink to a page containing the large graphic so only interested viewers endure the longer wait.

To learn more about design principles on the Web, a good place to look is to the Web itself. The following Web sites discuss Web design and refer to Web sites that are very good or very bad examples of Web design. For more information, point your browsers to:

Part
III

Ch
14

ON THE WEB

Topic	URL	Description
Mecklermedia Corporation	**http://www.meck-lermedia.com**	Comprehensive source for information and articles on Internet/intranet. Publishers of magazines and conferences.
MS Internet/ Intranet developers authors workshop	**http://www.micro-soft.com/workshop**	Excellent source of software and white papers on authoring, editing, designing, programming, administering, and planning and production. Links to Microsoft's Web gallery.
SunSoft Engr, Jakob Nielsen	**http://www.sun.com:80/sun-on-net uidesign**	Interface design of Sun's internal Web page
Design issues	**http://www.sig-graph.org**	Site for international graphics organization
ActiveX controls	**http://enet.ca/ Softoholic/ocx-server**	List of links to Web pages and demos using ActiveX
Microsoft Best-of-Best	**http://www.micro-soft.com/powered/ bestofbest.htm**	Microsoft's survey of best sites
Design tips	**http://the-tech. mit.edu/KPT**	Design tips
Style guidelines	**http://www.w3.org/ pub/WWW/Provider/ Style**	Style guidelines
Style guidelines	**http://www.dsiegel. com/tips**	Style guidelines

Opening a New Web Page

If you are creating a simple Web page that fits a predefined category, or if you are new to Web publishing, you may want to use the Web Page Wizard to help you get started. But when you want to let your creativity fly, start with a blank document and see what you can do with Word's Web authoring tools.

To open a new blank Web page and make Web authoring tools accessible, follow these steps:

1. Choose File, New to display the New dialog box, then select the Web Pages tab shown in Figure 14.2.

FIG. 14.2
Select Blank Web Page to open a new document and access the Web authoring tools.

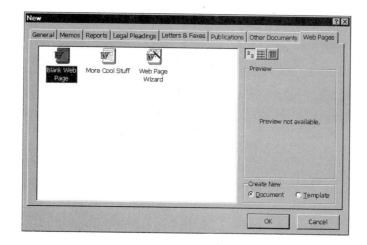

2. Select the Blank Web Page icon and choose OK.

A blank document opens. Notice that if you choose File, Save As, the Save as Type lists this document as an HTML document, not a Word DOC document. If you look through the menus, you will find that some Word menu items have disappeared and Web publishing menu items have appeared.

NOTE Word menus and menu items are available when a Word DOC document is active. Web authoring menus and menu items are available when an HTML document is active. Switching between documents automatically changes the menus and menu items to be appropriate for the active document. ▪

You can use all the Web authoring tools described in following sections to enhance this document. When you save it as an HTML document, it will become a Web page in a file with the extension HTM.

Creating a Web Page with the Web Page Wizard

When you are new to Web authoring, or if the Web page you want to create fits within one of Word's predefined categories, you can use the Web Page Wizard to save yourself work and produce pages with a uniform appearance.

Part
III

Ch
14

To create a Web page using the Web Page Wizard, follow these steps:

1. Choose File, New to display the New dialog box, then select the Web Pages tab shown in Figure 14.2.

2. Select the Web Page Wizard icon and choose OK. The Web Page Wizard dialog box appears as shown in Figure 14.3.

FIG. 14.3
The Web Page Wizard begins by asking you the type of page you want to create.

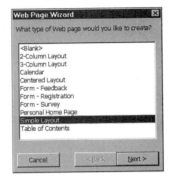

3. Select the type of Web page you want to create and preview the page behind the dialog box. Choose Next.

   Figure 14.4 shows that selecting the Calendar item displays the Calendar template behind the dialog box. Click Next when you find the type of page you want to create.

FIG. 14.4
Preview the type of page you select by watching the document behind the Web Page Wizard dialog box.

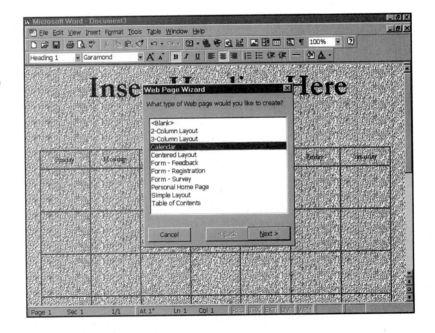

4. Select the style of Web page from the dialog box in Figure 14.5, then choose <u>F</u>inish.

Figure 14.5 shows how the Personal Home Page selection appears with the Community style. (The Personal Home Page is useful as your starting page for your Web browser.) Each style is unique and gives a different impression.

FIG. 14.5
Preview the appearance of different formatting styles.

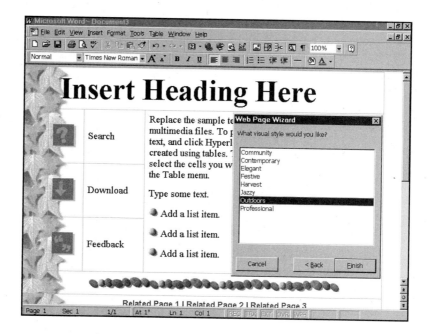

5. Choose <u>F</u>ile, Save <u>A</u>s and give the file a name to save the HTML page. If you want to preserve this file as a template for other HTML pages, select Document Template from the Save as <u>T</u>ype list before saving.

Once you choose <u>F</u>inish, the Web Page Wizard disappears, leaving you with an HTML document and the Web authoring tools. At this point you can type in your own text, reformat, insert files, add multimedia links, insert graphics, and of course create hyperlinks.

Using Word's Web Page Authoring Tools

Word's Web page authoring tools give you all the tools needed to create attractive Web pages. Your pages can be displayed with virtually all Internet browsers if you only use basic features such as formatting, graphics, and hyperlinks. Major browsers like Microsoft Internet Explorer and Netscape Navigator will also be able to display special features such as tables and scrolling text.

Viewing Your Web Page   As you work in Word, the screen displays an image close to how it will appear in Internet Explorer. However, different browsers may display the page differently: You should test your Web page against all the browsers used in your company and the major browsers used on the Internet.

To open an HTML file you have already created, double-click the HTM file and the file will open in the browser currently registered for HTM files. To see an approximation of how the HTML file appears in a browser as you are working in Word, choose File, Web Page Preview.

> **CAUTION**
>
> The view you see in Word's Web Page Preview only approximates how the page will appear in a browser. If you are creating Web pages that involve more than simple text, graphics, and tables, you should develop the page through an iterative process of working in Word and viewing on the browsers most widely used by your target audience.

Inserting Background Patterns   At any time you can change the background pattern that displays behind your Web page. Although there are many beautiful patterns and textures available, have mercy on the readers eyes. What might look pleasing as a graphic background could prevent people from even attempting to read text.

To change the Web page background, follow these steps:

1. Choose Format, Background to display the background palette shown in Figure 14.6.

FIG. 14.6
The first background palette shows plain colors, but patterns and fill effects are available.

2. Select a color by clicking it.

   or

   Select More Colors to display the palette shown in Figure 14.7. Select the Standard tab to choose a color or select the Custom tab to blend your own color. Choose OK.

   or

   Select Fill Effects to display the textured and marbled background shown in Figure 14.8. Choose OK.

FIG. 14.7
Choose from a wide variety of colors or blend you own custom color.

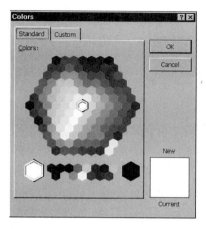

FIG. 14.8
Textured or marbled backgrounds look elegant.

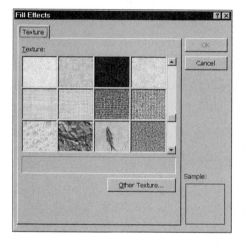

 TIP Go to **http://www.microsoft.com/gallery** to enter Microsoft's gallery of free image and background files you can download. To download a file, right-click the graphic in your Web browser, then choose Save Picture As. Specify the folder where you want the file stored. Insert these files in your own pages or use them as Web page backgrounds.

If you want to use a picture file as the background for your Web page, choose Format, Background, Fill Effect. Click the Other Texture button. Select the GIF, JPG, or WMF file you want as a background, then choose OK twice. Only small files, on the order of 1K, can be used as backgrounds. If you installed Office 97, look in the CLIPART\ BACKGROUNDS folder for background files.

Formatting the Color of Body Text and Hypertext At any time in your document you can change the color of all body text. It's also easy to change the color of hyperlinks.

Part
III

Ch
14

Hyperlinks have two colors that can be changed: the color before a link has been used, and the color after a link has been used. Two colors are used so it's easy to tell which links the reader has previously used.

TIP Many designers recommend that you leave hypertext colors at their default settings because people are used to seeing and reacting to the default colors.

To change the color of body text or hyperlinks, follow these steps:

1. Choose Format, Text Colors to display Document Text Colors dialog box shown in Figure 14.9.

FIG. 14.9
Change the color of
body text or hyperlinks
at any time.

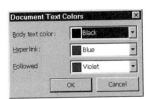

2. Select a color from one or more of the following:

Body Text Color	Changes the color of text that has not been formatted with the Format, Font command
Hyperlink	Changes the color of hyperlink text that has not been used for a jump this session
Followed	Changes the color of hyperlink text that has been used for a jump this session

3. Choose OK.

Formatting Selected Text   Currently, HTML does not enable you to specify the exact font and size for text as it will appear in all browsers. Instead, you specify a type of font appearance, which the browser displays according to its own capabilities and user preferences. Microsoft and other industry leaders are developing TrueType fonts for use by Web browsers as well as cascading style sheets, which will make it easier for an author to specify exactly how text will appear.

ON THE WEB

Download free TrueType fonts for Web pages, learn about Cascading Style Sheets, and learn about typography on the Web by pointing your browser to

http://www.microsoft.com/truetype

To format a font on a Web page, follow these steps:

1. Select the text and choose Format, Font to display the Font dialog box shown in Figure 14.10.

FIG. 14.10
Font formats are more limited in HTML pages than in Word documents.

2. Select the font options you want applied, then choose OK.

Although the Font dialog box enables you to choose from a font and size that the browser displays, your finished Web page may use a different font and size. Most browsers currently do not specify exact fonts or type sizes, instead they use a family of fonts, such as san serif, and type sizes relative to the other type sizes on the page. If you are unsure how your font formatting will appear, choose File, Web Page Preview to see the page in your browser. If you expect the page to be viewed by browsers such as Netscape or Mosaic, then you should open the page in those browsers and examine the appearance.

Tricks for Creating Custom Font Colors   Word's Web page authoring tools only have sixteen colors available for fonts and tables. If you want to add more colors, format the text with one of the sixteen colors, then modify the color by going into the HTML source code and replacing the color code with a color code you prefer.

 TIP   The book and CD-ROM, *Designing Web Graphics*, described in the section "Inserting Graphics" in this chapter, contains time-saving lists of color codes and palettes.

To find a color code you want to use for your fonts, you will open a blank document, change its background color to what you want, and then see what the color code is for the background. You can then use that color code to color other page elements such as the font color.

To find the code for the color you want, open a blank Web document. Choose Format, Background, More Colors. Select a color from the Standard or Custom tab and choose OK. If this is the color you want for your font, choose View, HTML Source. This displays the HTML source code for the colored Web page. Look for the HTML tag <BODY BGCOLOR="*hexnumber*">. For example, a hot pink background has the code,

```
<BODY BGCOLOR="#ff0066">
```

Part
III

Ch
14

The number in quotes is a hexadecimal number that includes some letters. Write down the number you see or select it and choose Edit, Copy. Exit the source code by clicking the Exit HTML Source button or by choosing View, Exit HTML Source.

Activate the Web page with the fonts you want to color and follow these steps:

1. Select the text you want to have the special color and format it with any color from the Font dialog box.

2. Choose View, HTML Source to display the HTML tags that compose your Web page.

3. Find the text you formatted in step 1. It should be preceded by a <FONT> tag. Within that <FONT> tag will be the COLOR parameter. Select the hexadecimal number after COLOR= and paste in or type the number you copied from the <BODY BGCOLOR> tag.

4. Choose View, Exit HTML Source. You will be asked if you want to save your change. Choose Yes.

   The font will appear in the new color.

If you do a lot of Web pages using Word, you may want to create an HTML document that contains lines of different color fonts. You can use this document as a palette to keep your favorite exotic colors. Make sure each line of text you format contains different words, perhaps the color description, so that you can tell the text apart even when you are look-ing at black-and-white HTML code.

> **CAUTION**
>
> Just because you can create thousands of text colors doesn't mean you should. Consider how easy the text will be to read against the different background colors and patterns you might use.

Inserting Scrolling Text   If you really want to grab someone's attention, use scrolling text. It appears like a marquee of text traveling across the page. Be careful that you don't overuse it and make your Web look like a Las Vegas nightmare. Different browsers and different versions handle special features such as scrolling text in different ways. Test how this affect appears in your reader's browsers.

To make text scroll across your Web page, follow these steps:

1. Move the insertion point to its own line. The scrolling text must appear on its own line in the page.

2. Choose Insert, Scrolling Text and select the Scrolling Text Options tab to display the Scrolling Text dialog box shown in Figure 14.11.

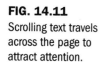

FIG. 14.11
Scrolling text travels
across the page to
attract attention.

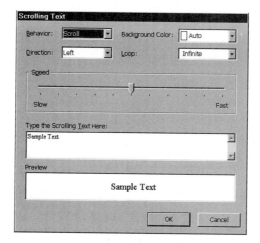

3. Type the text you want as moving text into the Type the Scrolling Text Here box.

4. Select the type of action from the Behavior box. Scroll moves the text across the screen then wraps it around in a continuous loop. Slide moves the text across the screen once and stops. Alternate bounces the text between screen edges.

5. Select Right or Left from the Direction box and select a color from the Background Color box. If you choose Scroll as the behavior you can select the number of times to scroll from the Loop box.

6. Select the Size and Speed tab shown in Figure 14.11, which selects the speed and size of the box through which the text moves. You can also specify how close body text appears next to the box containing the scrolling text.

7. Choose OK.

To reformat scrolling text click the box containing the scrolling text, then choose Format, Scrolling Text.

Inserting Horizontal Lines   Make on-screen text easier to read and absorb by breaking it into chunks. These nuggets of information should be more condensed than the long passages of text we are used to in printed material. If you need to express detail and depth you can do it with hyperlinks to lengthier explanations. One way to visually break your documents into discrete chunks is to use horizontal rules or lines to as demarcations between chunks of different information.

 TIP   The horizontal lines inserted by Word are actually graphic files with centered alignment. You can insert any GIF or JPEG graphic in the center of the page using this command.

Part
III

Ch
14

The horizontal lines used in Word's authoring tools are graphic files. To insert horizontal lines, follow these steps:

1. Move the insertion point where you want the horizontal line. If you put it within text, the text will be broken into two sections, above and below the line.

2. Choose Insert, Horizontal Line to display the Horizontal Line dialog box shown in Figure 14.12.

FIG. 14.12
A wide variety of horizontal lines are available for separating sections of your page.

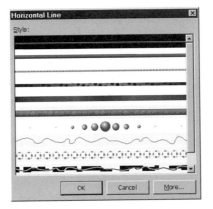

3. Select one of the lines from the Style box, then choose OK.

    or

    Choose More. Select from the Insert Picture dialog box a graphic file that you want used as a line. If you installed Microsoft Office 97, look in the CLIPART\LINES folder. Choose Insert.

Formatting Lines with Bullets and Numbers   Web pages can have bulleted or numbered lists similar to those in Word. However, Web pages have a greater variety of bullets than Word because they use graphic images as a bullet. Bullets and numbers are applied in front of the first line of each paragraph.

If by accident you format a line on a Web page twice with the bullets command, the line will have two bullets. To delete the bullet you do not want, select that bullet, then press the Del key.

To format paragraphs with bullets, follow these steps:

1. Select the paragraphs to be preceded by a bullet.

2. Choose Format, Bullets and Numbering, then select the Bulleted tab to display the Bullets and Numbering dialog box shown in Figure 14.13.

FIG. 14.13
Bullets precede the
first line of each
paragraph.

3. Select the type of bullet you want and click OK.

or

Click More to display the Insert Picture dialog box. The dialog opens with images in the CLIPART\BULLETS folder listed. Select an image or change to another folder and select an image, then choose Insert.

The numbering feature precedes the first line of each paragraph with numbers of different format. With the command you can also remove numbering, restart numbering, or continue the numbers from an adjacent list. To apply numbering or change existing numbering, follow these steps:

1. Select the lines or paragraphs.

2. Choose Format, Bullets and Numbering, then select the Numbered tab to display the Bullets and Numbering dialog box shown in Figure 14.14.

FIG. 14.14
Numbering precedes
the first line of each
selected paragraph.

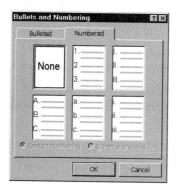

3. Select one of the following options.

| None | Removes numbering from selected paragraphs. |
| Numbered examples | Inserts a number of the format shown in front of the first line of selected paragraphs. |

<u>R</u>estart Numbering	Starts the numbering from 1 even if the selection is adjacent to an existing list.
<u>C</u>ontinue Previous List	Continues the numbering from the adjacent list.

4. Click OK.

Typing Hyperlinks to Web or Local Files

One very quick way to create a hyperlink in an HTML document is to type it directly into the document. If Word recognizes what you type as a valid URL, then it will convert your typed URL into a hyperlink. For example, the following lines will be recognized and turned into hyperlinks:

http://www.mcp.com

www.mcp.com

ftp://ftp.microsoft.com

ftp.microsoft.com

file://C:\business

Once you have typed the hyperlink, you may want to replace it with more readable and understandable text. To do this, select the hyperlink by dragging across it or by right-clicking it and choosing <u>H</u>yperlink, <u>S</u>elect Hyperlink. Once it is selected, type the text you want displayed. For example, you might want to replace,

www.wsj.com

with

Wall Street Journal Interactive

Edit the hyperlink by right-clicking it and choosing <u>H</u>yperlink, Edit <u>H</u>yperlink. The Edit Hyperlink dialog box is described in the section "Inserting Hyperlinks to Web or Local Files."

Inserting Hyperlinks

Another method of creating a hyperlink in the Web page is with the <u>I</u>nsert, Hyperl<u>i</u>nk command. If you are unfamiliar with the path name to a local or networked file, this method enables you to use a Link to File dialog box to find the file to which you want to link. You also can link to a specific named location in an Office document or HTML page. For detailed instructions on inserting a hyperlink using the Insert menu, see "Inserting Hyperlinks to Web or Local Files" later in this chapter.

To create a graphical hyperlink, see the following section "Creating Hyperlinked Graphics."

Inserting Graphics   Visually attractive Web pages are both a boon and bane. They make a page more enjoyable and appealing, yet the size of the graphics slow down the time it takes to load a graphic. There is both an art and a science in the use of graphics on a Web page. The art is in creating a visual layout that is appealing yet doesn't take too long to load. The science is in knowing how to create graphics that load quickly. There are special techniques you can use to make graphics of the same size load many times faster. For tips on design and how to create graphics that work well in Web pages, read these four books:

Title, Author, Publisher, ISBN	Description
Designing Business Clement Mok $60 Adobe Press ISBN 1-56830-282-7	A visually gorgeous book that fills your mind with ideas and then sets your neurons on fire with the desire to make changes. Don't read this late at night, be alert. It's about the use of design at the leading edge of technology. CD-ROM of interactive prototypes and projects.
Creating Killer Web Sites David Siegel $45 Hayden Books ISBN 1-56830-289-4	This book shows specific examples of great Web site design and how Web page design has evolved. David Siegel is one of the Web's design Gods. Pay attention to the leading edge. Check out his Web site.
Designing Web Graphics Lynda Weinman $50 New Riders ISBN 1-56205-532-1	In addition to teaching step-by-step graphics techniques, Lynda does a great job of showing you how to optimize graphics for speed. CD-ROM with lots of demo software.
Creating Your Own Web Graphics with Paint Shop Pro Andy Shafran Dick Oliver $34.99 Que ISBN 0-7897-0912-0	Have you seen impressive buttons and banners on a Web page and wondered how they were drawn? This book shows step-by-step drawing techniques for great Web graphics with Paint Shop Pro.

Part
III

Ch
14

Web pages use graphic files in the GIF or JPEG format. You can insert graphic files in other image formats that are recognized by Word such as PCX and BMP. When you save the HTML page, Word will convert the graphics that are not GIF or JPEG into GIF format. If Word does not convert your graphic files, rerun the Office 97 or Word 97 installation and install the HTML and graphic converters.

CAUTION

Inserting a large image and then resizing it in Word to a smaller dimension will not make the Web page load faster because the full image must still be downloaded. You can use a simple graphics editor such as Microsoft Photo Editor to crop an image. If you want to create high-performance images that load quicker while preserving color and resolution refer to the book *Designing Web Graphics* listed earlier in this section.

Changing a Web page in Word and then viewing it with your browser may not display the changes you have made. The browser may display the same Web page that you last viewed in the browser. This is because most browsers *cache* or save a few of their most recent pages. This improves speed but means that you may not see changes that have occurred. To see changes you have made, click the Refresh button.

To insert a graphic into your Web page, follow these steps:

1. Move the insertion point to where you want the image or picture.
2. Choose Insert, Picture.
3. Select Clip Art to display the Clip Gallery shown in Figure 14.15 or select From File to display the Insert Picture dialog box shown in Figure 14.16.

   Inserting from the Clip Gallery and from the Insert Picture dialog box are described in detail in Chapter 25, "Inserting Pictures."
4. Select the image you want inserted, then choose Insert.

Save graphics that you see in Internet Explorer by right-clicking the graphic, then choosing Save Picture As. Specify the file name and where you want the picture saved, then click OK. Please, do not violate copyright and trademark laws.

FIG. 14.15
Select from an
organized collection of
images and pictures
in the Clip Gallery.

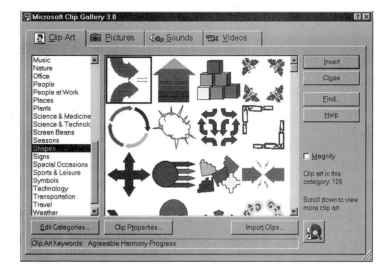

FIG. 14.16
Select files of images
from the Insert Picture
dialog box.

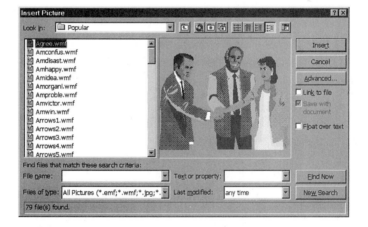

Creating Hyperlinked Graphics   As you browse the Web, it doesn't take long to notice that many of the graphics are hyperlinked to other Web sites or documents. You can hyperlink your graphics just as easily as you created text hyperlinks. To hyperlink a graphic to a Web page or document, follow these steps:

1. Insert the graphic.
2. Select the graphic by clicking it.

Part
III

Ch
14

3. Choose Insert, Hyperlink to display the Insert Hyperlink dialog box.

4. Complete the Insert Hyperlink dialog box as described in "Inserting Hyperlinks to Web or Local Files."

Edit a hyperlinked graphic by right-clicking the graphic and choosing Insert, Hyperlink, Edit Hyperlink. Make changes in the Edit Hyperlink dialog box.

Creating Alternative Text for Graphics and Hyperlinked Graphics You may want to create alternative text that displays when graphics or hyperlinked graphics cannot display. Some browsers display only text, and a high percentage of people browse the Web with the graphics turned off on their browser so they get higher-performance. For both of these types of viewers, you should create text alternatives that display when graphics and hyperlinked graphics do not display.

To create a text alternative for a graphic or hyperlinked graphics, follow these steps:

1. Select a non-hyperlinked graphic by clicking on it. Select a hyperlinked graphic by right-clicking on the hyperlinked graphic, then choose Hyperlink, Select Hyperlink.

 2. Choose Format, Picture or click Format Picture on the Picture toolbar to display the Picture dialog box. Select the Settings tab as shown in Figure 14.17.

3. Type in the Text box the text you want to appear when the graphic does not display.

4. Choose OK.

FIG. 14.17
Picture placeholders are known as alternative text on HTML pages.

Downloading Web Art from the Internet If you have access to the Internet, you can download free images for your Web page. To download images choose Insert, Picture, Browse Web Art Page. If you are asked if you would like to access the Internet to browse Microsoft's Web site, click Yes. The Web toolbar will appear, and your Internet browser will access Microsoft's Web Art Page.

Figure 14.18 shows one incarnation of the Microsoft Web Art Page. Follow the directions on the Web page to view and download art.

FIG. 14.18

Retrieve free graphics for your Web pages from Microsoft's Web Art Page.

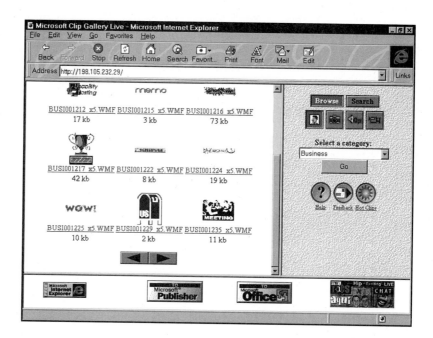

ON THE WEB

Look for additional clip art designed specifically for the Web at Microsoft's Internet developer Web sites. One valuable Web URL that contains many images, icons, backgrounds, sounds, fonts, and more for Web designers is:

http://www.microsoft.com/gallery

Another method of accessing additional clip art over the Web is to click the Connect to Web button located at the lower right corner of the Microsoft Clip Gallery dialog box.

Inserting and Formatting Tables   People who use Word love its table feature. You can continue to use Word's tables when creating your Web pages. Tables are an excellent way of displaying lists of related data. The "*information chunking*" technique that has become common on the Web fits well into a table format. While the current versions of most Web browsers can display tables, none display snaking newspaper columns. These are the multi-column layouts you might use for newsletters. If you need that type of a format however, you can fake it with the use of two- or three-column tables that have one row per

Web page. That row is as tall as the text in the column. It is up to you to cut and paste text to balance the text between columns.

Notice though that few Web pages use multiple text columns because this is hard to read. Most pages, like the Wall Street Journal Interactive or many of Microsoft's pages, use a three-column format, where the center column is reading text and the outer columns are hyperlinks.

If you have a large table of numbers or calculations in Excel that need to be ported into a Web page, don't retype them, either copy and paste them into the Web page or use Excel's Internet Assistant. To save graphics or ranges as a Web page, choose File, Save as HTML. Excel's Internet Assistant will also insert graphics or ranges into existing Web pages.

To draw or insert tables, use the same table drawing command and tools you would use in a Word document. These tools are described in depth in Chapter 18, "Creating and Editing Tables" and Chapter 19, "Modifying Tables."

Format tables

Table, Cell Properties

Table, Borders

Change formatting for the entire table with Table Properties. If you want to specify how text wraps around a table or format the text's background and the space between table columns, follow these steps:

1. Select a cell within the table.

2. Choose Table, Table Properties to display the Table Properties dialog box shown in Figure 14.19.

FIG. 14.19
Select formatting for
the entire table.

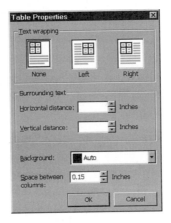

3. Click one of the table and text alignment options in Text Wrapping.

4. Enter a distance in inches in Horizontal or Vertical Distance to specify how closely text comes to the table.

5. Format the inside of the table by selecting a color from Background and specify the distance between text in cells by entering an amount in Space Between Columns.

6. Choose OK.

Change the properties within individual cells with Cell Properties. If you want to specify how text aligns in cells, its color, and a dimension for cells, follow these steps:

1. Select the cells in the table you want to format.

2. Choose Table, Cell Properties to display the Cell Properties dialog box shown in Figure 14.20.

FIG. 14.20

Select formatting for a cell within the table.

3. Select how you want cell contents to align vertical from the Vertical Alignment group.

4. Format the cell background color and dimensions with the Background, Width, and Height boxes.

5. Choose OK.

Format borders around the table by following these steps:

1. Select inside the table.

2. Choose Table, Borders to display the Table Borders dialog box shown in Figure 14.21.

3. Select Presets Grid to put borders around cells in the table. Select None to remove borders.

4. Select the border width from the Border Width box.

5. Choose OK.

Part

III

Ch

14

FIG. 14.21
Put borders around
the entire table.

Creating Forms with Controls   As you browse the Web, you will come across forms with check boxes, lists, text areas, and so on. These forms are used to send information back to the site that hosts the Web page. That information can then be used to customize the information you see to meet your needs or it can be used to customize the information you see to meet what the host wants you to see.

> **N O T E**   Form controls on a Word document do not convert to HTML form controls when you save the Word document as an HTML document. ■

Using Word's Web page authoring tools, you can create Web forms like the one shown in Figure 14.22. To use the forms as a way of gathering information however, you will need to use the forms with a Web site that has CGI scripts for forms. CGI stands for Common Gateway Interface—the programs on the Web server that add intelligence to Web pages. A CGI script will gather the information from a form and compile it into a database or return the data to you via e-mail.

 T I P   You don't have to hire a cadre of programmers and get into the expense and complexity of CGI scripts if you want to have forms on your Web. Microsoft's FrontPage 97—a Web design and management application—includes Web authoring and Web management, forms creation, and stores the data from forms in common database formats. It also manages Webs you create involving Office documents. If you want to be on the World Wide Web, you can create a Web with FrontPage and host it with all FrontPage capabilities on many Web providers.

 T I P   If you will be placing a lot of controls in a form, display the Control Toolbox toolbar for quick access to the form controls.

To insert form controls in your page, follow these steps:

1. Move the insertion point where you want the control to appear.

2. Choose Insert, Forms.

3. Select one of the following types of controls.

The control will appear in the form. If it is the first control in the form, you will see horizontal lines marking the Top of Form and Bottom of Form. Form controls must be between these lines.

Check Box	On or off selection
Option Button	Only one selected within a named group
Dropdown Box	Display a list from a drop-down list
List Box	Display a visible list
Text Box	Enter text in an edit box
Text Area	Enter text in a scrollable text area
Submit	A predefined button that sends the current form control choices to the host Web site
Image Submit	A custom button from a graphic image that sends the current form control choices to the host Web site
Reset	A button that clears the forms settings
Hidden	Hide text
Password	Enter text without displaying the characters

FIG. 14.22
Word can create Web pages that accept data entry.

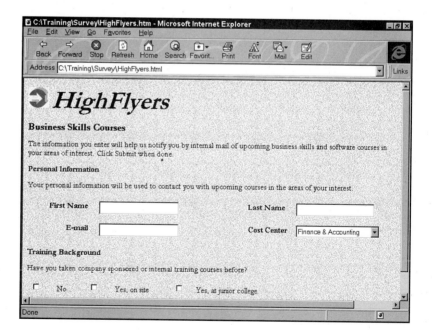

Part
III

Ch
14

4. Double-click the control to display the Properties dialog box where you set how the control will work. A Properties dialog box displays a table of settings for the control.

Settings in the Properties dialog box specify how the control will act and what its default contents will be. For example, check boxes are On when the Checked property is True and Off when it is False.

5. Close the Property sheet by clicking the Close button in the top left corner.

Copying Your Web Page to Another Location

After you create your Web page or pages, you will probably want to copy them to a Web server. If you included graphics in the Web page, you will need to copy the GIF and JPEG files for those graphics as well as the HTML files themselves.

Using the Windows Explorer, go to the folder where you saved the Web pages and graphics. Look for files with an HTM, GIF, and JPG extensions. One of these should be the HTML file you created. Look in the same folder for files with a GIF and JPG extensions that you inserted as graphics. Graphic files that Word converted from other formats will appear with a generic file name such as IMAGE1.GIF, IMAGE12.JPG, and so forth. When you copy the HTM file, you must copy the GIF and JPG files it uses or the graphics will not display.

Understanding the HTML Behind a Web Page

Word's Web authoring tools make it much easier to create Web pages than trying to write HTML code by hand. However, you may still need to know what HTML code looks like. You may want to go directly into the HTML source code and make a correction or add a special feature, such as a link to a RealAudio sound file, that Word is not capable of creating.

Web pages are written in the *HyperText Markup Language (HTML)*. HTML is made up of *elements*; each element contains a *tag* defining what kind of element it is. Most elements also contain text that defines what the element represents. In Figure 14.23, the sample HTML page as displayed by the Internet Explorer is shown at the top; the same page shown as HTML code is shown at the bottom.

Unlike traditional desktop publishing, the user's Internet browser—not the author—controls how the document is actually displayed. The document that looks just right in your 640 × 480 Internet Explorer window may look awful to users of other browsers.

 TIP   Right-click a Web page in Internet Explorer and choose <u>V</u>iew Source to view the HTML source.

FIG. 14.23
The Web page
displays with graphics
and formatting, but
the HTML source code
is text.

```
C:\Training\Survey\HighFlyers.htm - Microsoft Internet Explorer
File  Edit  View  Go  Favorites  Help
 ⇦      ⇨      ⊗      🖹      🏠      🔍      🖻▾      🖨      🗛      🗒▾      🖾
Back  Forward  Stop  Refresh  Home  Search  Favorit..  Print  Font   Mail    Edit
Address  C:\Training\Survey\HighFlyers.html                                    ▼   Links

  ➡ HighFlyers

  Business Skills Courses

  The information you enter will help us notify you by internal mail of upcoming business skills and software courses in
  your areas of interest. Click Submit when done.

  Personal Information

  Your personal information will be used to contact you with upcoming courses in the areas of your interest.

      First Name    [                ]        Last Name    [                ]

          E-mail    [                ]        Cost Center   [Finance & Accounting ▼]

  Training Background

  Have you taken company sponsored or internal training courses before?

      ☐    No        ☐    Yes, on site        ☐    Yes, at junior college

Done
```

```
HighFlyers - Notepad
File  Edit  Search  Help
<HTML>
<HEAD>
<META HTTP-EQUIV="Content-Type" CONTENT="text/html; charset=windows-1252">
<META NAME="Generator" CONTENT="Microsoft Word 97">
<META NAME="Template" CONTENT="C:\PROGRAM FILES\MICROSOFT OFFICE\OFFICE\HTML.D
</HEAD>
<BODY LINK="#0000ff" ULINK="#800080" BACKGROUND="Image11.jpg">

<P><IMG SRC="Arrow.gif" WIDTH=42 HEIGHT=41><B><I><FONT FACE="Garamond" SIZE=7>
</I></FONT><FONT FACE="Garamond" SIZE=4><P>Business Skills Courses</P>
</B></FONT><FONT FACE="Garamond"><P>The information you enter will help us not
<B><P>Personal Information</P>
</B><P>Your personal information will be used to contact you with upcoming cou
<FORM></FONT>
<TABLE CELLSPACING=0 BORDER=0 CELLPADDING=9 WIDTH=862>
<TR><TD WIDTH="16%" VALIGN="TOP" HEIGHT=17>
<P ALIGN="RIGHT"><B><FONT FACE="Garamond">First Name</B> </FONT></TD>
<TD WIDTH="31%" VALIGN="TOP" HEIGHT=17>
<FONT FACE="Garamond"><P>
<INPUT TYPE="TEXT" WIDTH="38">
</FONT></TD>
<TD WIDTH="16%" VALIGN="TOP" HEIGHT=17>
<B><FONT FACE="Garamond"><P ALIGN="RIGHT">Last Name </B></FONT></TD>
<TD WIDTH="37%" VALIGN="TOP" HEIGHT=17>
<FONT FACE="Garamond"><P>
<INPUT TYPE="TEXT" WIDTH="46">
</FONT></TD>
```

Part
III

Ch
14

Pages you view on the Web are intended to be well-formatted, well-presented displays. Because the page creator cannot know what type of computer or terminal the reader will use, the creator cannot use text with specific formatting information, such as fonts and point sizes to produce these documents. To assure that everyone sees documents with approximately the same formatting, codes are inserted into a document that describe how the document should be formatted, where hyperlinks are and where they are connected to, and which graphics should be displayed. This method of inserting formatting codes in the document allows the viewer's browser to create the best display it can on the viewer's terminal or computer. These text codes that are inserted compose the *Hypertext Markup Language, HTML*. The text codes, known as *tags*, are automatically inserted by Word's Web publishing tools as you create your Web pages.

How HTML Documents Are Structured   Like those nested Russian dolls, elements can contain other elements, and they can be nested several layers deep. HTML documents contain as a minimum head and body elements. Each of those elements can, in turn, enclose others.

The head element usually contains a *title* element, and it may also contain comments, author information, copyright notices, or special tags that help indexers and search engines use the contents of the document more effectively.

The body element holds the actual body and content of the document. For typical documents, most of the body element is text, with tags placed at the end of each paragraph. You can also use tags for displaying numbered or bulleted lists, horizontal rules, embedded images, and hyperlinks to other documents.

Understanding Some HTML Tags   All HTML tags are enclosed in angle brackets (<>). Some elements contain two matching tags, with text or hypertext in between. For example, to define a title as part of your document's <head> element, you would put this HTML into your document:

```
<title>A Simple WWW Page</title>
```

The first tag signals the start of the title element, while the same tag, prefixed with a slash (/), tells the browser that it has reached the end of the element. Some tags do not require matching tags, such as <li>, which denotes an item in a list.

The elements most often used in HTML body elements fall into three basic categories: logical styles, physical styles, and content elements.

Understanding Logical Styles   Logical styles tell the browser how the document is structured. The HTML system of nesting elements gives the browser some information; but authors can use the logical style elements to break text into paragraphs, lists, block quotes, and so on. Like styles in Word, you can use logical styles in your documents and know that they will be properly displayed by the browser.

Table 14.1 lists some common logical styles you can use to build your document, along with examples for each one.

Table 14.1   Logical Style Elements

Style Tag	What It Does	Sample
<p>	Ends paragraph	This is a very short paragraph.<p>
 	Inserts line break	First line Second line
<Hx>...</Hx>	Section heading	<H1>HTML Is Easy</H1>
...	Emphasis on text	Use this instead of bold text.
...	Stronger emphasis on text	THIS really gets the point across!
<code>...</code>	Displays HTML tags without acting on them	The <code><p></code> tab can be handy.
<quote>...</quote>	Displays a block of quoted text	<quote>No man is an island. </quote>
<pre>...</pre>	Displays text and leaves white space intact	<pre>E x t r a spaces are OK here.</pre>

Understanding Physical Styles   In ordinary printed documents, **bold**, *italic*, and underlined text all have their special uses. Web pages are the same way; you may want to distinguish the name of a book, a key word, or a foreign-language phrase from your body text. Table 14.2 shows a list of some common physical styles you can use in HTML documents, along with simple examples.

Part
III

Ch
14

Table 14.2 Physical Style Elements

Style Tag	What It Does	Sample
...	Bold text	Bold text stands out.
<i>...</i>	Italic text	<i>Belle</i> is French for "pretty."
<u>...</u>	Underlined text	<u>Don't</u> confuse underlined text with a hyperlink!
_{...}	Subscript text	Water's chemical formula is H₂O.
^{...}	Superscript text	Writing "x²" is the same as writing "x*x."
<tt>...</tt>	Typewriter text	This tag's <tt>seldom</tt> seen.

Understanding Hyperlinks The key element that makes the Web different from plain documents is hyperlinking. Each link points to an *anchor*, or destination for the link. Most anchors are implied; when you specify a page as the target of the link, it is assumed that you want that entire page to be an anchor.

The basic element for hyperlinks is <a href="*URL*">*text description*</a>. In this case, the "a" stands for "anchor," and "href" is a hypertext reference. If you wanted a hyperlink to the file "TRAVEL/EXPENSES.HTM" on your company intranet, you would use a hyperlink in a Web page, like this:

```
<a href="TRAVEL/EXPENSES.HTM">Expense information</a>
```

The text in the middle of the link appears as a link on the browser's screen. This link points to a file named "EXPENSES.HTM" in the folder "TRAVEL".

You also could include a link to Macmillan Computer Publishing's Web page so that people visiting your page could find out about Windows 95 books. Notice that this link contains a full URL instead of the name of a local document, and the link will appear within a text phrase.

```
The <a href="http://www.mcp.com">Macmillan Publishing</a> home page has
information on Macmillan's books.<p>
```

Creating Hyperlinks in Word Documents

Hyperlinks are one of the reasons the Web is so attractive. Combined with a Web browser, such as Internet Explorer, hyperlinks make it very easy for the reader of a document to click a phrase or graphic in one document and jump to a related document. It is up to you as the author to insert hyperlinks in your documents that take the reader to related documents or Web pages.

Hyperlinks in Word documents can be between different types of Office documents as well as to Internet or intranet sites. Clicking a hyperlink to an Office document will open the document in its appropriate application. Clicking a hyperlink to an Internet or intranet site will start your Internet browser and access the site.

The Web of linked documents and sites you create can be a simple personal Web of documents you use frequently, or it can be a complex Web of documents involving files on local computers and networks as well as sites on the Internet.

Some of the ways individuals and companies are using hyperlinked documents are:

■ A simple Web involving hyperlinks between Word documents, Excel worksheets, and PowerPoint slides that help you switch between documents you update frequently.

■ A Web of hyperlinked Word documents that compose a company's personnel manual. Different documents related to personnel management, rating, and hiring are all accessible from other linked documents.

■ An intranet for traveling salespeople that contains proposals and product specifications in Word documents. A client's shipping and manufacturing information is accessible through Web pages linked to ODBC database files. All users who access this Web use Windows 95 laptops.

Moving with a Hyperlink

To make a jump using a hyperlink, move the pointer over the text or graphic that is the hyperlink. The pointer changes to a pointing hand. Pause, and the path name or URL will display as a ScreenTip. Click to jump to the hyperlink's destination.

If the hyperlink is to another Office document, that document's application will open and activate. The Web toolbar (see Figure 14.24) will display over the document. To return to your original document, click on the Back navigation arrow. This returns you to the original document. While in the original document, you can click the Forward navigation arrow on the Web toolbar to move forward to the linked document. Chapter 15, "Browsing and Retrieving from a Web," goes into detail on how to use the Web toolbar to navigate between linked documents.

FIG. 14.24
Use the navigation buttons on the Web toolbar to move between linked documents.

Backward

Forward

Part

III

Ch

14

TROUBLESHOOTING

Clicking a hyperlink causes an error. The two most probable causes of hyperlink errors are that the path name or URL to the document is incorrect or that there is a problem in network communication.

To check the path name or URL to a document or site, right-click the hyperlink and choose Hyperlink, Edit Hyperlink. In the Edit Hyperlink dialog box check that the path name, file name or URL are still valid.

The other probable cause is network or communication problems. Did you see or hear your modem working correctly? If not, check the modem by trying another type of modem communication. Did the normal sign-on screens for your network connection appear? If not, check with your network administrator or attempt to access the Internet by directly using a browser. If you were trying to make an Internet connection, the Web site's server you attempted to connect to may be overloaded. You may need to try that Web site again at a later time.

Pasting Hyperlinks to Office Documents

In your work you may deal with documents created in different Microsoft Office applications. By adding hyperlinks to your documents you can move between them with a single click. Figure 14.25 shows a Word document with hyperlinks to related Word and Excel documents. Clicking one of these hyperlinks opens the linked document in its native application. The text in cells containing a hyperlink appears underlined and in color.

To create a link in a Word document to a specific location in another document created by an Office application, such as Excel, follow these steps:

1. Open the Word document and the document to be linked. Both documents should be saved in the folder in which you expect them to remain.

2. Activate the document you want linked and select the text or item in the document you want linked. The text or item you select at this point will be what appears in the linked document's window after you click on the hyperlink.

3. Choose Edit, Copy or right-click the selection and choose Copy.

4. Activate the Word document and select where you want the hyperlink.

5. Choose Edit, Paste as Hyperlink.

6. Click a location away from the hypertext link.

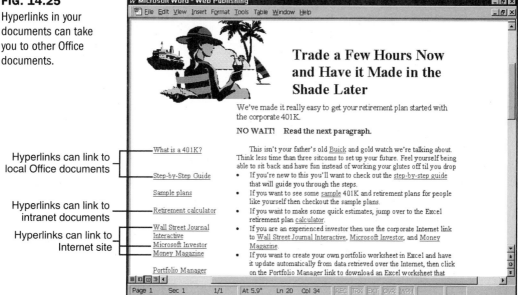

Hyperlinks can link to
local Office documents

Hyperlinks can link to
intranet documents

Hyperlinks can link to
Internet site

The text or worksheet cells you pasted as a hyperlink appears in the Word document. For example, if you copied and pasted a paragraph on safety training from the online personnel manuals, then that entire paragraph will appear as hyperlinked text. If you copied and pasted a range of Excel cells, then you will see a table of those cells as the hyperlink. Clicking anywhere in that hyperlinked paragraph or table opens the source document from which the hyperlinked data was copied.

One problem with this approach is that it is rare that an entire paragraph, sentence, or worksheet range from one document will fit in the context of another document. Usually you will only want a word or phrase as the hyperlink. You can retain the hyperlink and replace the lengthy text or worksheet range by following these steps:

1. Select the hyperlink by dragging across it or by right-clicking it and choosing
    Hyperlink, Select Hyperlink.

    If you have pasted an Excel range as the hyperlink, then use the right-click method
    to make sure the hyperlink is correctly selected.

2. Type the word or phrase that you want to appear as the hyperlink.

3. Click outside the hyperlink.

The word or phrase you type in step 2 will appear as a colored, underlined hyperlink. You can check or modify this hyperlink by right-clicking the hyperlink and choosing Hyperlink, Edit Hyperlink.

Inserting Hyperlinks to Web or Local Files

Another method of creating hyperlinks enables you to hyperlink to local files or Internet sites. To use this method you need to know or be able to browse to the file's path or Internet URL.

To insert a hyperlink, follow these steps:

1. Select the cell where you want the link to appear.

 2. Choose Insert, Hyperlink or click the Insert Hyperlink button in the Standard toolbar. The Insert Hyperlink dialog box displays as shown in Figure 14.26.

FIG. 14.26
Your hyperlink can contain a specific location in a document as well as specifying the path and file name of a document or site.

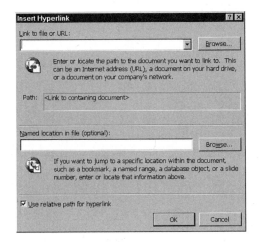

3. In the Link to File or URL box, type the path and file name or URL to the file or Web site to which you want to link.

Enter the path name or URL like these examples,

Local document	C:\MYFILES*FILENAME.DOC*
Local program	C:\MYPROGRAMS*PROGRAMNAME.EXE*
Intranet	**HTTP://COMPANY/SALES/QUARTER.XLS**
	or
	HTTP://COMPANY/SALES/QUARTER.HTM
Internet	**HTTP://WWW.COMPANY.COM**
	or
	FTP://FTP.COMPANY.COM

If you do not know the path or URL, click Browse. Use the Link to File dialog box to find the file.

To find an Internet site, select it from the bottom of the Look In list in the Link to File dialog box. If no FTP or HTTP sites appear in the list, refer to "Adding an FTP Site to the Open and Save As Dialog Box," in Chapter 4 to learn how to make FTP and HTTP sites appear in the Look In list.

4. In the Named Location in File box, type the named location in the file.

   Some examples of named locations are named ranges in Excel, bookmarks in Word documents, database objects in Access, or slide numbers in PowerPoint presentations. HTML documents can also have named locations. When you view the HTML source code for a Web page, look for the NAME attribute within an anchor.

   For example, if you are linking to an Excel worksheet containing named ranges, click the Browse button to display the Open Worksheet dialog box shown in Figure 14.27. From that dialog box, you have a choice of selecting the entire workbook, a worksheet, or a range as the link.

FIG. 14.27
Select a document's file or an Internet site from the Link to File dialog box.

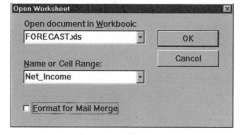

5. Select the Use Relative Path for Hyperlink option if you want to be able to move all the linked files and their directories to a new location.

6. Choose OK.

 TIP If you build Webs that must be moved to new locations, remember to select the Use Relative Path for Hyperlink option. This enables you to move all the files and their folder structures to a new drive or under a new folder.

 TROUBLESHOOTING

After creating my hyperlinks, some of the files and URLs have changed. Must the links be completely recreated? You can edit your hyperlink's path, file name, URL, and document location. To edit a hyperlink, right-click the link and choose Hyperlink, Edit Hyperlink. The Edit Hyperlink dialog box will appear showing the hyperlink's current properties. Change them so they are correct.

Part
III

Ch
14

Linking to a Named Location in a Document

In this section, you will learn how to insert a hyperlink that will jump from one document location to another.

Hyperlinks that jump within or between documents work by jumping to text or locations that have been marked with a bookmark. If you do not know how to create bookmarks, see "Marking Locations with Bookmarks" in Chapter 5.

To create a hyperlink that will jump to a specific location in a Word document, follow these steps:

1. Use Insert, Bookmark to insert a bookmark at the hyperlink destination in the target document. See "Marking Locations with Bookmarks" in Chapter 5 if you need help inserting a bookmark.

2. Activate the document that will contain the hyperlink and select the text that will contain the hyperlink.

3. Choose Insert, Hyperlink, or click Insert Hyperlink on the Standard toolbar. The Insert Hyperlink dialog box appears (see Figure 14.26).

TIP You can press Ctrl+K to quickly access the Hyperlink dialog box.

4. Enter the path and name of the destination document into the Link to File or URL text box. If you do not know the exact name or location, choose Browse and select the file from the Link to File dialog box.

   If you are jumping to another location within the same document, leave this text box blank.

5. Enter the bookmark name into the Named Location in File text box. Choose Browse to display a list of bookmark names for the current document, or for the document listed in the Link to File or URL text box.

   Entering a named location is optional if you are linking to another file. If you leave this option blank, Word will simply open the document without moving to a specific location.

6. Select or clear the Use Relative Path for Hyperlink option. Normally, you should leave this selected.

7. Choose OK.

   The hyperlink appears in blue. Click the hyperlink to move to the destination information.

To edit or remove a hyperlink, right-click the hyperlink and choose Hyperlink, Edit Hyperlink to display the Edit Hyperlink dialog box. Make any necessary changes in the Edit Hyperlink dialog box. If you want to remove the hyperlink, choose Remove Link at the bottom of the Edit Hyperlink dialog box.

Starting Programs and Non-Office Documents with Hyperlinks

You can do more than just open other Office documents or Web sites with hyperlinks. You can create a hyperlink to programs or non-Office documents that will start the program or open the document. If Windows 95 has a program associated with a document type, then you can open that document by clicking a hyperlink to the document. You can start programs by creating a hyperlink to a program file. To do this, just enter a path to the document in the Link to File or URL box. For example, if you use the URL

C:\WINDOWS\DIALER.EXE

where Windows 95 is installed in the Windows directory on your C drive, then you will have a hyperlink that starts the Dialer program.

Some of the ways you can use hyperlinks to non-Office programs and documents are to run batch files, start communication programs, run backup programs, start agents, unzip compressed files, and so forth.

Changing the Appearance of Hyperlinks

When you insert a hyperlink and you have not selected text, the URL or path to the hyperlink appears in your document. In most cases it won't be attractive, friendly, or informative. It's better to type a text phrase that will appear as the hyperlinked text.

To enter your own text over a hyperlink, select the hyperlink by right-clicking it, then choosing Hyperlink, Select Hyperlink. Type the word or phrase that you want displayed as the hyperlink. This word or phrase will appear as underlined, colored text indicating that it is hyperlinked. If you move the mouse pointer over the text, you will see the hyperlink still exists. ●

CHAPTER 15

Browsing and Retrieving from a Web

In the last few years, we have witnessed a shift in information publishing that may have as great a consequence as the invention of the printing press. The printing press did more than just break the medieval church's hold on information: It heralded a new age of thinking that enabled people to question authority and turn to a quest for knowledge. The cause of our new shift in information publishing is the development of the Internet, the World Wide Web, and the visual browsers that make it easy to gather information.

The World Wide Web links together the many resources existing on the Internet. When you use the World Wide Web, you jump among locations (thousands of computer hosts), system applications, and information formats (files and documents). The ease of navigating between documents and the ability to read documents using any computer system has pushed Web technology into corporations. Corporations are rapidly developing their own *intranets* to publish proprietary information for their employees and business affiliates.

Explore the World Wide Web

Use Internet Explorer to explore the information, technical support, free files, training, and more that reside on the World Wide Web. Copy information from Web pages into Word.

Create a Web from Office documents on your local disk or network

Use Word's Web toolbar and hyperlinks in Office documents to create a Web linking Word, Excel, PowerPoint, and Web documents on your local hard disk, corporate network, or World Wide Web.

Work and move seamlessly between Office documents and Web pages

Open and edit Office documents within the Internet Explorer even as you browse the Web or your local intranet.

Microsoft responded to the incredible growth rate of the Internet and the World Wide Web by rapidly developing Internet Explorer 3. From within Internet Explorer 3, you can browse the Internet and work on Word and Excel documents. The toolbars and menus of Internet Explorer 3 change to match the document type within the browser. Use Internet Explorer 3 to work on Excel 95 and Word 95 documents, as well as Excel 97 and Word 97 documents.

Microsoft also incorporated Web page publishing and browsing tools within Office 97. You can create Web pages that include hyperlinks, data, tables, and charts in Excel 97 work-sheets. Using Word 97, you can develop impressive Web pages, incorporating textured backgrounds, graphics, hyperlinks, and more.

In Office 97 and Windows 95, two advances in technology have combined to create a new model for work with computers. One is that information can be located anywhere—on your local hard disk, on the company network, or on the global Internet. The other is that people don't really work with applications: They work with documents and the information in those documents.

As a result of advances in Office 97, you can take two different approaches to positioning yourself in your work.

- Working primarily within an Office application, with occasional excursions to the Internet or company intranet to gather a Web page or document. Figure 15.1 shows Word after clicking Help, Microsoft on the Web, Microsoft Office Home Page, which opens Internet Explorer 3 and loads the Microsoft Office Home Page on the Web.

- Working primarily within the Internet Explorer; using it as a single vessel within which you can view and edit any document you retrieve from your local hard disk, company network, or the Internet. Figure 15.2 shows Internet Explorer 3 after browsing to a Word document on the Web. Notice that Internet Explorer displays the menus and toolbars for the document.

Eventually, Office and the Internet Explorer will evolve into a single universal viewer and editor. This capability is expected in Internet Explorer 4.0. From Internet Explorer 4.0 you will retrieve, view, and edit information from around the world. ■

TIP There is a lot of free information and software directly available from Microsoft's Web site. To get there quickly, choose Help, Microsoft on the Web, then select one of the sites. Some of the Web sites available from this Help menu are:

Free Stuff	Online Support
Product News	Microsoft Office Home Page
Frequently Asked Questions	Search the Web

FIG. 15.1

Clicking a hyperlink in an Office document or the Help menu opens Internet Explorer 3 and loads the Web page.

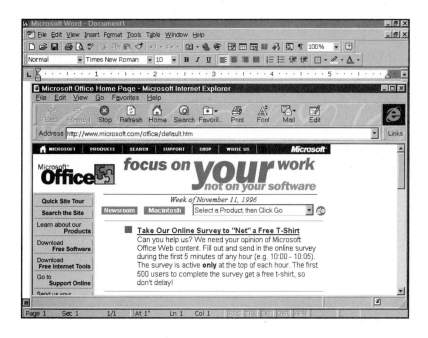

FIG. 15.2

Clicking a hyperlink to an Office document while in Internet Explorer 3 opens the document in the Internet Explorer and displays Word's menus and toolbars.

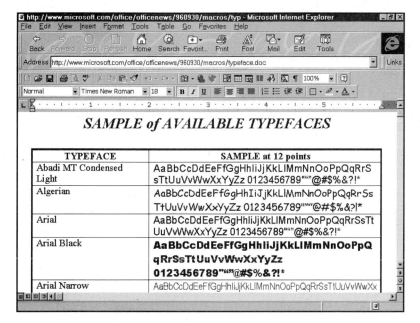

Understanding the World Wide Web and Browsers

Designed by researchers at CERN in Geneva, Switzerland, the World Wide Web is a collection of hypertext documents served from computers throughout the world. Web documents, or *pages,* can contain pictures, text, sounds, movies, and links to other documents. Web pages can—and usually do—contain links to documents on other computers. The name "Web" comes from the interlinked nature of the pages. The entire Web resides on a global computer network known as the Internet.

Using a *Web browser*—the software that navigates between and displays Web pages—you can retrieve Web pages or documents in three ways: You can manually type an *URL*, or *Uniform Resource Locator*, into the address box and let the browser retrieve the page; you can click a text or graphic hyperlink that retrieves a page; or you can click a link that has been saved in a history or list of favorite places.

Internet Explorer is Microsoft's Web browser. Internet Explorer 3 and later have been designed to work closely with Excel 97 and Word 97. Figure 15.3 shows Internet Explorer's main window and the Microsoft home page. Internet Explorer was originally distributed as part of Microsoft's Plus! Pack CD-ROM for Windows 95. If you purchase a new computer with Windows 95 installed, the Internet Explorer is probably preinstalled as well. Microsoft offers the most current version of Internet Explorer as a free download from their Internet site. If you are already accustomed to another browser, you will find the Internet Explorer comfortably familiar, yet it has received higher ratings than Netscape 3.0 in magazine reviews.

The Web toolbar, new to Word 97, enables you to stay within Word as you navigate between Word, Excel, PowerPoint, and HTML (Web) documents linked by hyperlinks. By inserting hyperlinks in your Office 97 documents, you can create your own Webs of linked documents. You don't need to use an Internet browser to jump between those documents; just click a hyperlink to one of your own documents, open the Web toolbar, and navigate.

▶ **See** "Working and Browsing in Word," **p. 537**

N O T E   This book is about Word 97, so it only begins to describe all the capabilities of the Internet and World Wide Web. For more coverage, check out *Special Edition Using the Internet, Second Edition; Special Edition Using the World Wide Web with Mosaic; Using FTP; Using Netscape; Easy World Wide Web with Netscape; Using USENET Newsgroups; Web Publishing with Word for Windows;* or any of the other Que books about the Internet and its parts. ▪

FIG. 15.3
Internet Explorer
works closely with
Office 97 applica-
tions.

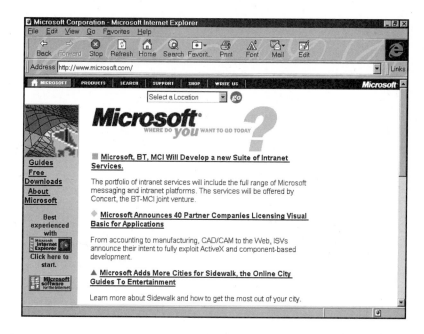

ON THE WEB

Visit the Macmillan Computer Publishing Web page for book lists, descriptions, and sample
chapters. Enter the URL

http://www.mcp.com

For Microsoft Office tips, training, and add-ins, as well as errata for the books *Special Edition
Using Windows 95, Platinum Edition Using Windows 95, Special Edition Using Microsoft Word 97,*
and *Special Edition Using Microsoft Excel 97,* please point your browser to

http://www.ronperson.com

Installing the Internet Explorer

The Internet Explorer comes on added value CD-ROMs available from Microsoft, preinstalled on many Windows computers, or can be downloaded for free from the Microsoft
Web site. If you have The Microsoft Network or Internet Explorer preinstalled on your
computer, you will see an icon on your Windows desktop. Double-click this icon to install
MSN or the Internet Explorer. The Microsoft Network is Microsoft's service that connects you to the Internet. There is a monthly subscription fee for its use. Internet access is
also available through local Internet Providers (IPs) throughout the United States. You
can use the Internet Explorer with any Internet Provider.

You also can get the Internet Explorer through added value CD-ROMs, like the ValuPak, available from Microsoft or by accessing Microsoft's Web site (**www.microsoft.com**) with any Web browser and downloading the most current version of Internet Explorer. When you download the most current version, you are given the choices of opening or saving the downloaded file. If you are using an older version of Internet Explorer and you want to immediately upgrade, choose that you want to open the upgrade. If you are using a browser other than Internet Explorer, or you want to upgrade at a later time, choose to save the upgrade to a file.

ON THE WEB

Many free Internet Explorer enhancements, Office add-ins, technical support, and hardware drivers are available at the Microsoft Web site. Point your browser to

http://www.microsoft.com/msdownload

For Windows, Internet Explorer, and Office tips and training, point your browser to

http://www.ronperson.com

Understanding World Wide Web URLs

Uniform Resource Locators (URLs) specify the location of resources on the Internet that are part of the World Wide Web. You use URLs with Internet Explorer to identify where to retrieve information from the Internet. URLs are also used within World Wide Web documents to link to other resources. Figure 15.4 illustrates an URL. The first part of an URL defines the Internet protocol used to get the resource. Use a colon to separate the protocol from the remainder of the URL. Notice that there are *two forward slashes* after the colon. The protocols used by most URLs are listed below.

Specifier	Protocol
ftp	File Transfer Protocol. The protocol used to transfer files.
http	Hypertext Transport Protocol. The protocol used on the World Wide Web.

In Figure 15.4, the protocol being used is `http`, which indicates that this resource is retrieved using the Hypertext Transport Protocol. The rest of the URL includes the Internet domain name (`www.somename.ext`) and the path to the document on the host. Some URLs end with a specific page name, such as CATALOG.HTML. If a specific page is not used in the URL, then the browser loads the default page at that location, which is usually INDEX.HTML.

FIG. 15.4
URLs serve as addresses to resources on the World Wide Web.

Paths to specific files, directories, or programs at the Web site follow the Web's domain name. Finally, arguments or parameters to server programs may be passed at the end of the URL. Consider the following examples of URLs:

- **http://www.somename.com/index.html**

  This http: URL identifies a document named index.html on the www.somename.com server, using the Hypertext Transport Protocol. Internet Explorer retrieves the document and displays it in the window.

- **http://www.someone.com/support**

  This URL ends with a slash, indicating that there is no file name that follows. When a directory is specified with no document, an HTTP server usually returns a default file or a listing of the files in the directory, depending on how the HTTP server is configured.

- **ftp://ftp.someone.com/help/FAQ**

  Notice that this URL does not end in a slash. The last word will be interpreted as a file name. This ftp: URL identifies a file named FAQ in the help directory on the ftp.someone.com anonymous-ftp server. Note that no user name and password are supplied. In this case, the ftp connection is established using the user name anonymous, and your e-mail address as the password.

- **file:c:\htdocs\default.htm**

  To reference local files, as opposed to those on the network, use a file: URL. Notice this file: URL uses backslashes as you are used to seeing in Windows and DOS path names. When you drag and drop a file onto Internet Explorer, the document appears with a file: URL. In general, URLs always use forward slashes, but Internet Explorer allows backslashes as well.

Working and Browsing in the Internet Explorer

If you find yourself doing a lot of browsing through Web sites and documents, as well as working on documents, you may want to do most of your work in Internet Explorer 3. While you are in the Internet Explorer, you can still open, view, and edit with Office application's normal menus and toolbars.

The advantages to using Internet Explorer are:

- ■ Access to files using the same procedures and appearance.

- ■ Work orients around the document rather than around the application containing the document.

- ■ Opening Office documents and Web pages uses the same procedures regardless of whether they are on a local hard drive, intranet, or Internet.

- ■ All documents and Web pages can be displayed in the same window, with the menus and toolbars changing to reflect the active document.

- ■ Moving forward or backward along the path of hyperlinks becomes easy.

The disadvantage to working in Internet Explorer 3 is that documents off the hyperlink path are not as readily available; you must use File, Open to open them. In addition, only one document window is open at a time. While you can easily use the Favorites list or History to jump to a previous document, it still must be reopened.

While you are working in Internet Explorer 3, you open documents by choosing File, Open to display the Open dialog box. Then click Browse and select the file you want opened. To open Office documents, you will need to select All Files from the Files of Type list in the Open dialog box.

> **CAUTION**
>
> When you are working on an Office document from within Internet Explorer 3, don't think you've lost your document or worksheet if you look for Word or Excel on the taskbar and don't see it. Remember that you were working within Internet Explorer 3.0. Click the Internet Explorer button on the taskbar.

Understanding the Internet Explorer

Internet browsers are simple to use and controls are very similar between browsers from different vendors. If you have used another Internet browser, you will quickly understand how to use Internet Explorer.

Figure 15.5 shows the Internet Explorer displaying a startup page for The Microsoft Network. Your browser may display the startup page for your Internet Provider or a custom startup page.

Table 15.1 describes the buttons on the Internet Explorer 3 toolbar.

FIG. 15.5
It takes only a few
buttons to navigate
the World Wide Web.

Table 15.1	Buttons on the Internet Explorer 3 Toolbar
Back	Displays the previous Web page or document in the history of hyperlink jumps
Forward	Displays the next Web page or document in the history of hyperlink jumps
Stop	Stops the current Web page or document from opening or refreshing
Refresh	Reloads the current Web page or document
Home	Displays the startup page
Search	Displays the search page where you can enter keyword for a search
Favorite	Displays a list of favorite Web pages or documents
Print	Prints the current Web page or document
Font	Cycles the display through a series of predefined font sizes
Address	Entry and edit area for the URL
Address list	Click to display the most recently opened sites
Links	Buttons linked to specific Web pages

T I P To display or remove the toolbar, choose View, Toolbar. To display or remove the Links bar, double-click the word Links. Move the toolbars or address bar by dragging them by the bar at the left or top edge of each bar.

Starting the Browser

You can start Internet Explorer 3 in three different ways. You can start it independently of Word as a separate program, start it by clicking a hyperlink in a Word document that links to a Web site, or start it from Word's Web toolbar. Internet Explorer 3 starts automatically if you are in a Word document and click a hyperlink to a Web URL. To start Internet Explorer 3 independently, double-click The Internet icon on the desktop or click Start, Programs, Internet Explorer.

 Start Internet Explorer from within Word 97 by clicking the Web toolbar icon in the Standard toolbar. The Web toolbar displays, as shown in Figure 15.6.

FIG. 15.6
Word's Web toolbar enables you to navigate between linked Office documents and start the Internet Explorer.

When you start the Internet Explorer, it displays a startup page similar to the one in Figure 15.5. There are several ways to open a page. The most common way is also the simplest: just click a hyperlink to jump to the linked page. Hyperlinks are usually shown as underlined and colored text. Another way to jump to any Web page or Office document is to use the Open dialog box (see Figure 15.7). When you type in an URL address or file path name, the Internet Explorer opens the document you requested.

FIG. 15.7
The Open dialog box enables you to jump directly to any site on the Internet, or to load Web pages or documents stored on your hard disk or intranet.

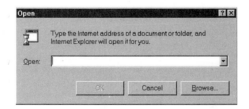

To go to any page whose URL you know or to any Office document whose path and file name you know, follow these steps:

1. Choose File, Open.

 TIP A quick way to start the Internet Explorer and enter an URL is to click the Start menu and choose Run to display the Run dialog box, then enter an URL in the command line.

2. Type in the address or select a previously used page from the list.

 TIP To find files on your hard disk or intranet, choose the Browse button.

3. Click OK.

There are several other ways to go to Web pages. You can:

- Type an address into the Address bar and press Enter.
- Select a previously visited page or Web site from the Address list.

 TIP Right-click a picture or background texture in Internet Explorer to save the picture to your disk, copy it to the Clipboard, or set it as your desktop wallpaper. You can also drag images from a Web page to the My Computer window or the Explorer to copy them onto your disk, or into Exchange to mail them.

The most recent GIF files (Web graphic files) used by the Internet Explorer are stored in the WINDOWS\TEMPORARY INTERNET FILES folder.

- At any time, you can jump back to your start page (the initial page loaded when you launch the Internet Explorer) by clicking the Home icon or choosing Go, Start Page.
- Jump directly to a Favorite Web page or document by choosing Favorites, then selecting the site you want to visit. Save the active page as a favorite by choosing Favorites, Add to Favorites.

Navigating Among Web Pages and Documents

Find your way between Web sites by typing in a new URL in the Address box and pressing Enter; by clicking a hyperlink to another Web site; by selecting from the Favorites list; or by clicking the Search button and searching for Web sites that meet criteria you set.

Once you are in a Web site, the easiest way to navigate within it and related information is to click the hyperlinks. To move forward or backward along the trail of pages you have seen, click the Back or Forward buttons on the toolbar. Table 15.1 describes the buttons on the toolbars and their uses.

Stopping or Refreshing a Web Page   Many popular servers on the Internet are slow. Why? Because they're popular! You may find that some sites impose too long of a wait. To stop loading a page, click the Stop button.

When you stop loading a page, you might change your mind and want to reload it. You might also need to reload pages that did not completely load. To reload a page, click the Refresh button on the toolbar, or select View, Refresh. The Internet Explorer reloads and redisplays the page you are on.

Keeping a Historical List of Web Pages and Documents   Internet Explorer keeps a historical list of the Web pages and Office documents you have most recently opened in Internet Explorer. To see or use this list, choose Go, Open History Folder. Figure 15.8 shows this list. To open a page or document, double-click it. To copy or delete it, right-click the name and choose a menu item.

FIG. 15.8
Instead of clicking the Back button numerous times, use the History list to quickly jump to a previous page.

Tracking Favorite Web Pages and Documents

You probably have some favorite Web pages or documents that you visit frequently. The Internet Explorer supplies two easy ways to keep track of your favorite sites: the Create Shortcut command and the Favorites list.

Create a shortcut to the currently displayed page if you want to easily return to the Web page from an icon on your desktop. To create a shortcut, follow these steps:

TIP Right-click an URL in a list and choose Copy. Select the desktop and choose Paste Shortcut to create a shortcut on your desktop.

1. Display the Web page or document for which you want a shortcut.

2. Right-click the document and choose Create Shortcut.

The shortcut will be placed on your desktop. Double-click it to open the document to which it is linked. You can drag it into Office documents, e-mails, and so on.

Windows keeps your Favorite shortcuts in the WINDOWS\FAVORITES folder. To add a page to your Favorites list, follow these steps:

1. Display the Web page or document.

2. Add the page to your Favorites list by choosing Favorites, Add to Favorites.

3. In the Add to Favorites dialog box, type an easily recognized name you want displayed in the list. If you want to place the favorite icon in a folder under the Favorites list, choose Create In and select or create a folder.

4. Choose OK.

 TIP Drag text from a Web page into any application that accepts text, such as Word or Excel.

Searching for Information on the World Wide Web

When you are comfortable with the Internet Explorer, you can travel to servers around the world with just a few clicks. There are more than 100,000 Web servers available, with millions of files. Finding what you need can be impossible if you don't know where to start. Internet Explorer makes it easy for you to get started.

To search for Web documents with Internet Explorer, click the Search button or choose Go, Search the Web. Internet Explorer displays your search page, where you can type key words and ask for links to related documents. Some Web search sites are faster than others, while others serve to index different sets of documents. To change the search page you use, see "Changing Your Search Page," later in this chapter.

If you find your searches return too many links, create a narrower search by searching for words or phrases. Enclose the words in quotes so they are searched for as a phrase and not for every occurrence of the word. For example, "venture capital" will return fewer links than *venture capital*.

 TIP To do a quick search from Internet Explorer, type **GO** in the Address box followed by a space, then your search word or words, then press Enter. Yahoo! will then do a search with the words you entered.

Here are the addresses of some excellent Web search sites that you can use to find what you are looking for:

■ **http://www.altavista.digital.com**

Digital Equipment Corporation sponsors a fast and thorough search engine, which includes timely updates of UseNet News articles. They invite you to search their databases and see if you can find a long-lost friend online!

■ **http://www.yahoo.com**

Yahoo! started as a project at Stanford University, but has quickly become such a popular site that it has spun off as a separate server. Yahoo! offers a comprehensive list of Web pages, organized into categories like law, entertainment, and business. Yahoo! stands for "Yet Another Hierarchically Organized Oracle."

■ **http://www.infoseek.com**

InfoSeek offers a reliable search service that indexes Web pages, articles from computer periodicals, wire-service news articles, and several other sources. Although it is a commercial service, the rates are quite reasonable, and it offers free trials.

Working on Office Documents in Internet Explorer

If you do a lot of work on your company's intranet or on the Internet, you may just want to stay in Internet Explorer while you work on Word 97 or Excel 97 documents. While in Internet Explorer 3 or Internet Explorer 4, you can browse across the network or through your local files, as well as read and edit Office documents.

Figure 15.9 shows a local Word document that has been opened in Internet Explorer 3. Word's menus and toolbars appear within the Internet Explorer shell so you have access to all of Word's features.

Some World Wide Web sites have links to normal Word documents, as well as the more customary HTML Web pages. When you click a link to a Word document, the Word document opens in the Internet Explorer and Word's menus and toolbars add to the Internet Explorer shell. Figure 15.2 showed an example of a Word document opened from Microsoft's Web site.

ON THE WEB

Computers that do not have Word 95 or Word 97 can open, read, and print Word documents from a Web site if they install Microsoft's free Word Viewer software. This software is available from

http://www.microsoft.com/msword

FIG. 15.9

Internet Explorer 3 and 4 display Word's menus and toolbars so you can work on Word documents from within Internet Explorer.

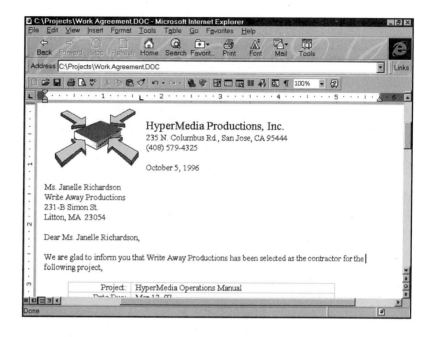

To open a local Word document from within the Internet Explorer, follow these steps:

1. Choose File, Open to display the Open dialog box.
2. Click Browse to open the Open dialog box.
3. Select All Files from the Files of Type list.
4. Select the file from your local drive or network.
5. Choose Open. Click OK.

Don't be confused if you are working on a Word document in Internet Explorer and Word at the same time. You can switch between the applications, but the document in Internet Explorer will not be in Word. Don't think you've lost the document, it's just open in the other application.

If you are interested in opening, editing, and saving Word documents from an FTP site on your company's intranet or the Internet, read the section "Saving Documents to an Intranet or Internet FTP Site" in Chapter 3.

Customizing Web Page and Document Appearance

You can control settings used for displaying Web pages with the Appearances page of the Options dialog box. To open this dialog box, choose View, Options. Here, you can change how hyperlinks are drawn, whether pictures are displayed, the text and background color for pages, and more. Figure 15.10 shows the Options dialog box when the General page is selected.

FIG. 15.10
The General page gives you control over how Web pages and links appear on your screen.

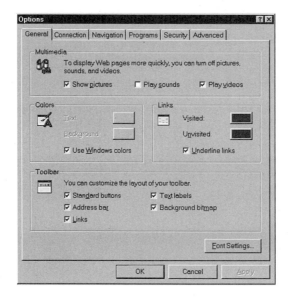

Changing Your Startup Page   The Navigation tab of the Options dialog box enables you to specify which Web page loads when you launch the Internet Explorer. You can specify a file on your local hard disk, on a shared disk (with a UNC path), or on a Web page.

T I P Start Internet Explorer quickly and display a start page with the links you want by creating your own start page with the Web Page Wizard in Word 97. You could create a start page for your company or division containing the most frequently used Internet and local hyperlinks.

To change the start page, follow these steps:

1. Display the page you want as a start page.
2. Choose View, Options and select the Navigation tab, as shown in Figure 15.11.
3. Choose the Use Current button.

Changing URL Appearance   Web addresses, or URLs, can be arbitrarily long, and many of them contain confusing query characters or computer-generated indexing markers. If you prefer, you can turn off the display of page addresses, or you can make the Internet Explorer show a shortened, simpler form of the URL for each page. To display shorter, more friendly URLs, display the Options dialog box, select the Advanced tab, then select the Show Friendly URLs option. Choose OK.

FIG. 15.11
Set your start page to
any location you want.

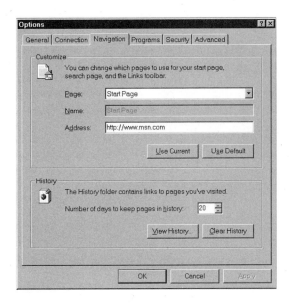

Selecting Font Appearance   Standard HTML lets Web page authors specify a font size. If the author uses *relative* font sizes, you can control the size displayed. Enlarge or reduce the font size by clicking the Font button on the toolbar. Control which fonts are displayed by choosing View, Options, selecting the General tab, and selecting a font for proportional and fixed-width text.

Changing Hyperlink Text Appearance   Internet Explorer lets you control how hyperlinks are displayed. Some users prefer their links underlined, while others like them to appear as plain text. You can set your preference using the Underline Shortcuts option found on the General tab of the Options dialog box.

Internet Explorer also lets you choose what colors to use when drawing links. To change those colors, choose one of these options:

- Click the Visited Links button to bring up the Color dialog box. Choose a color from the selected palette, or mix a custom color, then choose OK. Internet Explorer uses that color to indicate links to pages you have already visited.

- Click the Unvisited Links button to bring up the Color dialog box. Choose a color from the selected palette, or mix a custom color, then choose OK. Internet Explorer uses that color to indicate links to pages you have not yet seen.

Controlling Graphics, Sound, and Video   Text transmits very quickly. When the Web is slow, you may want to get the text information without the graphics, sound, or video. To turn graphics, sound, or video on or off, choose View, Options, select the General tab and select or clear the Show Pictures, Play Sounds, or Play Videos option.

Improving the Internet Explorer's Performance

Adjust your advanced settings using the Advanced tab in the Options dialog box (choose View, Options), as shown in Figure 15.12.

FIG. 15.12
Adjust the disk space used by the Internet Explorer cache in the Advanced tab.

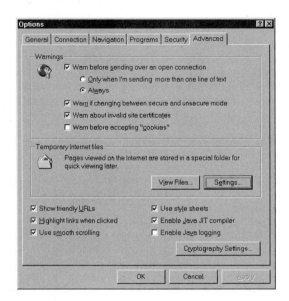

Adjusting the History List Size
Internet Explorer saves a shortcut for each Web page you visit. To adjust the number of remembered pages in your History list, choose the Navigation tab from the Options dialog box, then use the Number of Days to Keep Pages in History spin box to set how many pages are stored.

Managing How Web Pages Are Stored to Disk
Internet Explorer stores Web pages on your hard disk to increase performance when you return to those pages. Internet Explorer can automatically check for updates to the stored pages when you restart the Internet Explorer, return to a page, or only when you refresh them. However, this technique can consume lots of your hard disk if you are not careful. To set how Internet Explorer stores and manages Web pages on disk, display the Options dialog box, select the Advanced tab and choose the Settings button for Temporary Internet Files. Change the settings as you want for frequency of updates and more or less storage space.

TROUBLESHOOTING

When I navigate to Web sites that update frequently, the documents look the same as when I last read them. Why? It is possible you are actually viewing documents that Internet Explorer found in its temporary Internet file storage area, instead of the latest version available from the

Web. To force Internet Explorer to retrieve the latest version of the active document, click the Refresh button. See the previous section, "Managing How Web Pages Are Stored on Disk," to learn about the options that control temporary storage.

Working and Browsing in Word

Whether you are connected to the Internet or work on a stand-alone computer, Word's ability to navigate between linked Office 97 documents, intranet pages, and Internet pages opens new vistas.

If you work without a corporate intranet or Internet connection, you can still create a Web of Word and Office documents linked together by hyperlinks. Such a Web enables you and others to quickly jump between related documents. For example, you can create pages of product, service, and ordering information in Word and Excel documents. Link these documents by inserting hyperlinks as described in Chapter 14.

Working in a Web of Office documents might follow a scenario like the following. As you look at a table of contents for a product catalog, you click a hyperlink for the product you're interested in. This takes you to a Word document giving a product overview and picture. Clicking a hyperlink in the overview document opens pages of in-depth technical and service descriptions. A single-click on the Back button in the Web toolbar returns the display to the product overview. A click on a different hyperlink in the overview opens an Excel worksheet that is an order entry form. All of this can be done without an intranet server.

> **CAUTION**
>
> If you plan on building a Web containing more than a few documents, consider how you will manage and maintain the myriad of links and document changes. Building an extensive Web out of Office documents can be difficult to maintain.
>
> Programs such as Microsoft FrontPage are designed to build and manage small or large Webs composed of Office 97 and HTML documents. Web development software contains management tools to show you invalid hyperlinks, missing Web pages, missing graphics, and so on. Microsoft FrontPage comes with its own personal Web server software for small intranets. Free Web server extensions are available so that non-Microsoft Web servers can support the enhanced capabilities of Microsoft FrontPage on corporate intranets or on the Internet.

If your work occasionally involves connecting to the Internet or corporate intranet, Word's Web navigating abilities will save you time. When most of your work is within Word and you occasionally need to take a hyperlink jump to another Office document, or if you need to jump to a Web page on the Internet, then you will probably want to do most of your work in Word and use the Web toolbar to navigate between documents.

The Web toolbar gives you the same capabilities as the toolbar in Internet Explorer 3. Its buttons enable you to navigate forward or backward through the paths of hyperlinks in Web pages or Office documents. The Address list and Favorites button quickly display Office documents or Web pages you want. The Web toolbar includes an Address bar in which you can type path names to files or URLs for Web pages.

The advantages to staying within your application rather than working on documents within Internet Explorer are:

- Work orients around the primary application. You can leave your document to get information and then come back to the same document.

- Files on local hard drives and networks may be easier to find.

- Multiple documents can be loaded at the same time in the application.

Internet Explorer 4 makes it even easier to stay within Word while making occasional trips out to a Web page. With Internet Explorer 4, you stay within Word and browse the Web. The Web pages appear directly within the Word application as though they are Word documents. This means you won't have to switch between Word and Internet Explorer if you are working on a Word document and browsing the Web.

Understanding the Office Web Toolbar

Use the Web toolbar in Word to control Web navigation from your application. The buttons on the Web toolbar (see Table 15.2) produce the same results as the related buttons on the Internet Explorer 3 toolbar described in Table 15.1. Figure 15.13 shows the Web toolbar and its buttons.

FIG. 15.13
Many Web toolbar buttons are the same as on the Internet Explorer.

Table 15.2	Buttons on the Web Toolbar
Back	Displays the previous Web page or document in the history of hyperlink jumps
Forward	Displays the next Web page or document in the history of hyperlink jumps

Stop	Stops the current Web page or document from opening or refreshing
Refresh Current Page	Reloads the current Web page or document
Start Page	Displays the startup page
Search the Web	Displays the search page where you can enter a keyword for a search
Favorites menu	Displays a list of favorite Web pages or documents
Go menu	Menu items for navigating, and setting the start and search pages
Show Only Web Toolbar	Toggles between showing and hiding all toolbars except the Web toolbar in the application
Address	The URL entry area
Address List	The list from which you can pick previous URLs

Starting the Browser

Start the Web browser while you are in an Office document by following these steps:

1. Click the Web Toolbar button or choose View, Toolbars, Web.

2. Use one of the following methods of retrieving a document or Web page:

   - Click Start Page to open the start page.
   - Click Search the Web to open the Web search page.
   - Enter an URL by typing it in the Address box and press Enter.
   - Select a previous URL from the Address list and press Enter.
   - Click Favorites and select from the favorites list.
   - Click Go, Open History Folder and double-click a shortcut in the History dialog box.

Navigating Among Web Pages and Documents

Display the Web toolbar whenever you are moving between linked Word or Office documents. The Web toolbar enables you to move forward or backward through the hyperlink history or jump to any point within the history of hyperlinks.

When you find yourself frequently using the same documents, you can save time by storing the Office document or URL to a Web page on the Favorites list. To get to the document later, just click Favorites and the document you want to retrieve.

The Web of linked documents you move between may consist of Word, Excel, PowerPoint, and HTML (Web) documents. As you move between these documents with the Web toolbar, notice how the application menus and toolbars change to reflect the active document. Only when you jump to a Web page does the Internet Explorer 3 appear. Internet Explorer 3 is unable to display Web pages within Word's application window. To return to Word from Internet Explorer 3, just click the Back button in Internet Explorer 3.

Internet Explorer 4 can display Web pages within the Word's application window. If you have Internet Explorer 4 installed, then you can be in Word and use the Web toolbar to access a Web page. The Web page will appear within Word's application window.

Browsing Office Documents Without the Application

Don't let the absence of an Office application prevent you or others from browsing or viewing Office documents. Microsoft's free Office Viewers are designed to let anyone view or print most Office documents. The viewer can open a document like a normal application, as well as be used to view Office documents you browse.

Viewers are small applications that enable you to view or print an Office application file, but not to edit the file. Viewers are associated with a file type just like other Windows applications, so you can start the viewer and load a file, or let Internet Explorer load a document as you browse.

Viewers are available for Excel, Word, and PowerPoint. You can download viewers for free from each product's page on the Microsoft Web site.

ON THE WEB

The appropriate Web page from which to access viewers for different Microsoft Office applications is

http://www.microsoft.com/msdownload

CAUTION

There are different versions of viewers that correspond to the different application versions. Make sure the viewer you download or send to others is the viewer that works with the documents you are distributing.

CHAPTER 16

Creating and Managing Data for Mail Merge

Word 97 does more than just publish text. Think of it as a report writer or publisher of database information as well. Word has the ability to retrieve, store, and manipulate rows of information such as names and addresses, billing information, invoice data, product catalog information, and so on. Some of the tasks that are commonly relegated to database report applications can be accomplished with Word, and Word can give you a more free-form, publishing-oriented result. For example, you can use data stored or linked into Word to create:

■ *Form letters* using name and address information. Other information can be merged into the form letters such as amounts owed, product information, or notes.

■ *Envelopes* to go with the form letters. Envelopes can be printed in sorted ZIP code order and include POSTNET and FIM bar codes to save you money.

Create a new data document in Word

Use a table created in Word as your data source.

Retrieve an existing data file into Word, or link a Word document to data located in an external database

Shared office data created using Outlook or Schedule+ can be retrieved and used as the data source. Also, link to data created using Microsoft Access, Microsoft Excel, dBASE, Paradox, and so on.

Manage data through updating, sorting, finding, editing, and deleting

Perform a number of management tasks on your data source including finding and editing records, reorganizing data in columns, or merging two data source files.

- *Mailing labels* that even include logos, graphics, POSTNET, and FIM bar codes.

- *Product catalogs* that include graphics and a more professionally published appearance than what is normally produced from a database report.

- *Sales report data* in a more free-form layout. Word can publish data using features such as newspaper columns and integrated graphics that are not available in worksheets such as Excel or from database report writers. ■

Understanding the Different Methods of Storing Data

There are three sources of data Word can use for a mail merge: a Word document, an external file, and shared office data.

A Word document can consist of a table containing rows and columns of information, as shown in Figure 16.1. You can also use a tab- or comma-delimited Word document as your data source. Tables are much easier to read and edit than tab- or comma-delimited documents, so you may want to convert a tab- or comma-delimited document into a table. To do this, choose Table, Convert Text to Table. Select how the text is separated, for example by Tabs or Commas. Word will estimate how many columns to use, but you can change this in the Number of Columns box. Choose OK.

An external file can be a file imported from another application, or a database file that was created using Microsoft Access, Microsoft Excel, dBASE, Paradox, and so on. You can also use data from popular database applications if you have installed the appropriate ODBC driver. For more information about database files, see the upcoming section, "Inserting a Database from a File."

Shared office data refers to address books created in the Personal Address Book that is part of Word or in the address books available in other Microsoft applications such as Outlook, Schedule+, the Postoffice Address List, and lists for Microsoft Network.

ON THE WEB

For online support from Microsoft, visit the following World Wide Web site:

http://www.microsoft.com/support

You can also access Microsoft's extensive troubleshooting KnowledgeBase at the following site:

http://www.microsoft.com/kb

For tutorials, tips, and add-ins for Microsoft Office applications point your browser to:

http://www.ronperson.com

FIG. 16.1
A data source can be as simple as a table in Word containing rows and columns of information.

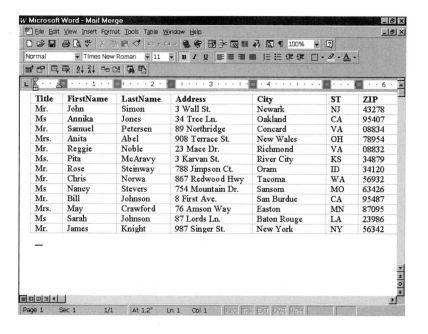

Title	FirstName	LastName	Address	City	ST	ZIP
Mr.	John	Simon	3 Wall St.	Newark	NJ	43278
Ms	Annika	Jones	34 Tree Ln.	Oakland	CA	95407
Mr.	Samuel	Petersen	89 Northridge	Concard	VA	08834
Mrs.	Anita	Abel	908 Terrace St.	New Wales	OH	78954
Mr.	Reggie	Noble	23 Mace Dr.	Richmond	VA	08832
Ms.	Pita	McAravy	3 Karvan St.	River City	KS	34879
Mr.	Rose	Steinway	788 Jimpson Ct.	Oram	ID	34120
Mr.	Chris	Norwa	867 Redwood Hwy	Tacoma	WA	56932
Ms	Nancy	Stevers	754 Mountain Dr.	Sansom	MO	63426
Mr.	Bill	Johnson	8 First Ave.	San Burdue	CA	95487
Mrs.	May	Crawford	76 Amson Way	Easton	MN	87095
Ms	Sarah	Johnson	87 Lords Ln.	Baton Rouge	LA	23986
Mr.	James	Knight	987 Singer St.	New York	NY	56342

Part

IV

Ch

16

Managing Names and Addresses with Address Books

Managing a list of names and addresses is a simple task if you use an address book application such as the one in Outlook or Schedule+ Personal Address Book. After you have entered names and addresses, you can perform a number of tasks on the information. For example, you can edit, insert, delete, search, and sort the information.

Word 97 allows you to specify the address book in Outlook or Schedule+ as the data source for a mail merge. Because many companies and individuals use Outlook or Schedule+ to manage personal schedules, meeting rooms, and resources, it makes sense to use Outlook or Schedule+ as your address book for names and contacts used by everyone in your workgroup. Names and contact information for your personal use can be stored in the Personal Address Book, described in the section, "Using Addresses from the Personal Address Book."

Don't think that you have to enter a zillion names, addresses, and phone numbers manually, especially if you are targeting a set of people or businesses you can define by geographic region, demographic profile, or business profile. There are many sources for computer lists. In the following table, some of the more popular World Wide Web locations for name and address information are:

Web Site Name	URL	Description
BigBook	**http://www. bigbook.com**	Searchable business phone directories
BigYellow	**http://s10. bigyellow.com**	Searchable business phone directories along with addresses and ZIP codes
Internet 800 Directory	**http://inter800. com**	Search businesses for 800 numbers
Switchboard	**http://www.switch board.com**	Search for businesses or people
United States Postal Service	**http://www.usps.gov**	Searchable index for ZIP+4 and lots of postal information.

Using Addresses from the Outlook Address Book

Microsoft Outlook is a personal information manager that manages e-mail, appointments, contacts, tasks, documents, and files on your hard disk. Outlook combines e-mail, phone support, group scheduling, public folders, forms, and the Internet capability to increase productivity.

If you did a Typical install of Microsoft Office 97 Suite, then you have Outlook installed. Outlook is easier to use and more robust than Schedule+. Outlook and Schedule+ are not compatible on the same network.

To use data from the Microsoft Outlook Address Book, follow these steps:

1. Choose Tools, Mail Merge. The Mail Merge Helper dialog box appears.

2. Choose Create and then select Form Letters.

3. Click the New Main Document button. This opens a blank document and returns you to the Mail Merge Helper. The Get Data button is now available.

4. Click the Get Data button. Click the Use Address Book item. The Use Address Book dialog box appears, as shown in Figure 16.2.

5. Select Outlook Address Book from the list, then click OK.

   You may be prompted to select the user profile you want to use from the Choose Profile dialog box, then click OK.

   If you do not have merge fields in your main document, Word displays a message requesting you to choose the Edit Main Document button and insert merge fields into your document.

FIG. 16.2

Select data for use in a mail merge from the Outlook Address Book, Personal Address Book, or from Schedule+ Contacts.

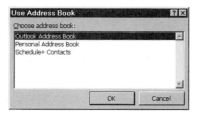

To add new data to the existing data, perform these steps:

1. Choose Tools, Mail Merge. The Mail Merge Helper dialog box appears.

2. Click the Edit button next to the Get Data button. Then select the data to edit. The Data Form dialog box appears, as shown in Figure 16.3.

FIG. 16.3

Add new data or edit existing data in the Data Form dialog box.

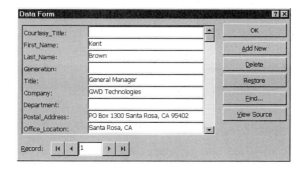

3. Click the Add New button, fill in the text boxes as appropriate, then click OK.

To edit existing data, perform these steps:

1. Choose Tools, Mail Merge. The Mail Merge Helper dialog box appears.

2. Click the Edit button next to the Get Data button. Then select the data to edit. The Data Form dialog box appears, as shown in Figure 16.3.

3. Click the Record arrow buttons to display the first, previous, next, or last record until you find the record you want to edit.

You also can click the Find button to search for the record you want to edit. Figure 16.4 is an example of the Find in Field dialog box that appears after clicking the Find button.

4. Type the appropriate information in the Find What text box. For example, if you have a last name data field in your data records, find the record to edit by typing the last name.

5. Select the appropriate merge field name from the In Field list. Make sure that the field name you select corresponds to the information you typed in the Find What text box.

6. Click the Find First button. The data record appears in the Data Form dialog box.

7. Click the Close button in the Find in Field dialog box.

8. Click the Restore button to revert to the original information.

FIG. 16.4

Use the Find in Field dialog box to find a record.

Entering Addresses in Microsoft Schedule+

Microsoft Schedule+ is a useful scheduling program that you can use for your personal schedules and contact management, or that you can share in your workgroup. It even includes tips and a wizard on how to be more productive. If you work in a corporate network that uses Schedule+, you may be using Schedule+ to maintain your e-mail, calendar, and address books. Although Outlook comes with Microsoft Office 97 Suite, it does not work in a mixed environment with Schedule+.

To enter information into the Schedule+ address book, follow these steps:

1. Click the Start button in the taskbar, then click Programs, Microsoft Schedule+.

> **TIP** If the taskbar is currently hidden, move the pointer to the bottom of the screen and the taskbar will appear, or press Ctrl+Esc.

2. If you are prompted, type your User Name and logon password in the Schedule+ Logon dialog box, and then choose OK. Schedule+ will display.

3. Click the Contacts tab to view the list of contacts to make changes or add new contacts. Figure 16.5 shows an example of a new Schedule+ Address Book.

4. In the edit boxes on the right side, type information you want stored in the Schedule+ Address Book.

The contact information you enter in the Schedule+ Address Book will be accessible in Word.

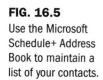

FIG. 16.5
Use the Microsoft
Schedule+ Address
Book to maintain a
list of your contacts.

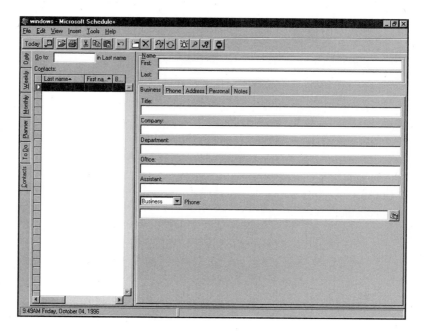

Creating Your Own Data Sources

The Mail Merge Helper allows you the flexibility to create your own data sources from a wide range of applications. You can create a data source from a Word document, spreadsheet application, database file, or some other external application. The obvious benefit to you is that you can create your data source in a familiar application and then use the data to create multiple documents in Word.

Managing Data

Word dialog boxes and the Mail Merge Helper refer to the object containing data as the *data source*. The data source can be in a wide variety of common PC formats, such as Word documents, Excel worksheets, or dBASE-compatible database files. The data source can be on your PC, or reside on another computer to which Word is linked via a network. You can also use data from a large database application, such as Oracle or SQL Server. Word can retrieve just the part of the database it needs from these larger databases.

Information stored in the data source is normally laid out in a table format of rows and columns. Each row of information is known as a *record*. If the data source contains the names and addresses of clients, a record contains an individual's name, address, and specific client information. In this case, one record of information is like a card in a card file. Each row in a data source ends with a paragraph mark.

Information is arranged within records by column. These columns are known as *fields*. Each field, or column, contains one specific type of information. For example, the name and address data source might need one field for state and another for ZIP code. A *delimiter* separates each field of data. Delimiters that Word understands are commas, tabs, or separate cells in a table. If a record contains more than 31 fields, then Word cannot use a table; it uses tabs or commas instead.

Data sources need a row of titles at the top that are known as *field names*. The field names should describe the contents of that field in the data source. You refer to these field names when you are searching for or limiting the data used from the data source. Field names are also used to indicate where information goes when it is taken from the data source and placed into the merge document such as a form letter or label.

Field names have specific requirements. They must be no longer than 40 characters, start with a letter, and cannot contain a space. Rather than use a space in a field name, you may want to use an underscore character.

 TIP Without spaces between words, a multiple word field name can be difficult to read. To solve this, just capitalize the first letter of each word (for example, **FieldName**).

A Look at the Database Toolbar

Word includes a toolbar specifically designed to help you manage tables, databases, and data sources. The Database toolbar displays by selecting <u>V</u>iew, <u>T</u>oolbars, and selecting Database from the list. Here's what the Database toolbar looks like:

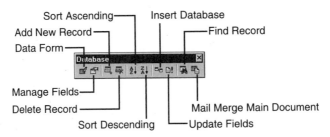

▶ **See** "Selecting a Data Source," **p. 576**

The different buttons in the Database toolbar are as follows:

Icon	Name	Description
	Data Form	Displays the Data Form, which makes adding, editing, and finding information easier in the database
	Manage Fields	Makes it easy to add, remove, or rename fields (columns) in a database
	Add New Record	Adds a new record at the current insertion point in a table or database
	Delete Record	Removes a record at the current insertion point in a table or database
	Sort Ascending	Sorts the table or database in ascending order on the current field
	Sort Descending	Sorts the table or database in descending order on the current field
	Insert Database	Displays the Database dialog box so that you can insert a file containing a database
	Update Fields	Updates fields and links in the document. Updates databases linked to files
	Find Record	Displays the Find in Field dialog box to help you search a database
	Mail Merge	Opens the Main Document attached to the current data source

Inserting a Database from a File

Small lists can be managed in a word processor; however, if you have lists or databases larger than a few hundred records, you will want to use a database application such as Microsoft Access in which to store, edit, and retrieve your data. Word makes it easy to store data in many different types of databases and then bring that data into a Word document so that it can be used as a data source for mail merge.

For Word to import or access a database file, it must have the appropriate file converters or Open Database Connectivity (ODBC) drivers installed. Installing converters and drivers can be done after Word has been initially installed. To install converters and drivers, rerun the Office or Word Setup program.

Database files that Word can convert and insert include the following:

Microsoft Word	Microsoft FoxPro
Microsoft Access	Word for Mac 3.x, 4.x, and 5.x
Microsoft Excel	Word for MS-DOS 3.0–6.0
dBASE	WordPerfect 5.x for MS-DOS or Windows
Paradox	Lotus 1-2-3 2.x and 3.x

When you insert a database, you can choose to insert the data or insert a field code, which creates a link to the database file. Inserted data acts just as though it was typed in the document. Inserting a field code enables you to quickly update the database, because it has a link to the file on disk. If the data in the file changes, you can easily update the list.

To insert a database that is in a file on disk, follow these steps:

1. Position the insertion point in the document where you want the database.

2. If the Database toolbar is not displayed, choose <u>V</u>iew, <u>T</u>oolbars, and click Database.

3. Click the Insert Database icon in the Database toolbar. The Database dialog box is displayed in Figure 16.6.

FIG. 16.6

Use the Database dialog box to insert all or part of a database that is in a file from Word or another application.

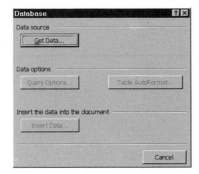

4. Click the <u>G</u>et Data button to display the Open Data Source dialog box, shown in Figure 16.7.

5. Select or type the name of the file in the File <u>N</u>ame drop-down list. Choose OK.

If it is possible to select part of the data source, such as a range on a spreadsheet, a dialog box like the one in Figure 16.8 appears. In this example, the Excel spreadsheet named CONTACTS contains a named range, TopTen. Select the range or query that defines the data you want, then choose OK to return to the Database dialog box.

FIG. 16.7

From the Open Data Source dialog box, you can open the file containing your merge data.

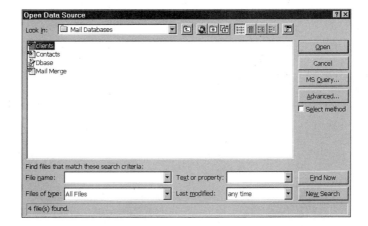

FIG. 16.8

You can insert a portion of some database files.

6. Click the Query Options button from the Database dialog box if you want the data you insert to meet certain criteria.

7. Select Table AutoFormat if you want to be guided through custom formatting of the table.

8. Click the Insert Data button to display the Insert Data dialog box, shown in Figure 16.9.

9. If you want to limit the number of records inserted, select From and To and enter the starting and ending record numbers.

10. If you want to create a link from your database to the database file on disk, select the Insert Data as Field check box.

11. Choose OK.

FIG. 16.9
From the Insert Data dialog box, you can select the amount of data you want and whether the database should be linked to the file on disk.

If you did not select the Insert Data as Field check box, the data is inserted as if it were typed. If the check box was selected, a link is created between the document and the database file. This link is created with a field code. You can update this field code by highlighting it and pressing F9. You can unlink the field code so that the database becomes fixed text by selecting the table and pressing Shift+Ctrl+F9.

Creating Your Mail Merge Data

The data source you use in Word can come from an existing Word document, be created in Word, or be linked into Word from another application.

If the amount of data you need to store is not extensive and you do not need to share the information with other users, the easiest way for you to store and manage your data is in a Word document. You can create a data source in a Word document either manually or with the guidance of the Mail Merge Helper.

Creating a Data Source Manually   You can manually create a data source document by typing data into a document. The fields of data must be separated into the cells of a table, or separated by tabs or commas. The field names in the first row of the data source document must fit the rules for field names:

- Names must start with a letter.
- Names must not contain a space. Use an underscore if you need to separate words.
- Names must not be longer than 40 characters.
- Names must be unique. You cannot have two field names spelled the same.

You must save the document containing your data source to disk before you can use it. Try to save the document with a file name that will not change frequently. If the file name of the data source changes, you must reconnect the mail merge document to use the data source.

Figure 16.1 illustrated an example of a table that is used as a data source for a mail merge document. Each field (column) in the table contained a type of information and each record (row) contained a group of information about a client. The information in this document could also have been separated by commas or by tabs.

Figure 16.10 shows the same information, written as a data source with the data separated by tabs. If you decide to use commas or tabs to separate data, use one or the other throughout the data source—do not mix them in the same document. End each record (row) with a paragraph mark if it is a comma or tab-delimited record. See the upcoming section "Managing Information in the Data Source."

FIG. 16.10

You can manually create data source documents by typing data into tables or by typing each record in a row and separating the fields with commas or tabs.

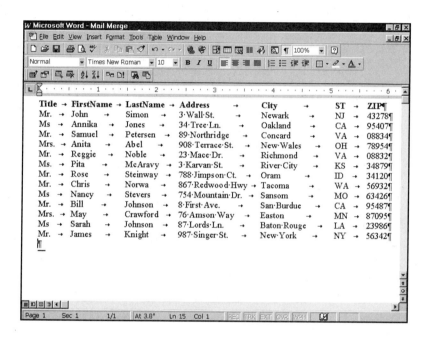

After you have created your data source document, save it and remember its name and folder. When you run a mail merge, the Mail Merge Helper asks you to select the file name of the data source.

▶ **See** "Merging Mailing Lists and Documents," **p. 573**

If you create a comma-delimited data source and some of your data contains commas, Word may be confused as to the fields in which data belongs. To solve this problem, enclose any data that contains commas within quotation marks (" ") when you use commas to separate fields of data. The quotation marks around a piece of data tell Word that any comma within the quotation marks is part of the data. Because of the problems that can occur with comma-delimited data, you may find it easier to work with tables. However, if your data files contain hundreds or thousands of lines, tables may not be practical.

Using the Mail Merge Helper to Create a New Data Source   If you want to be guided through the process of creating a data source document, use the Mail Merge Helper. The Mail Merge Helper is a series of dialog boxes that present options for creating some of the most commonly used field names. After you have created the field names, the Mail

Merge Helper gives you a chance to enter data into the new data source. A later section of this chapter, "Finding or Editing Records with the Data Form," describes a convenient way to add more records or find and edit existing records.

The following process helps you create a data source document with the Mail Merge Helper. The Mail Merge Helper assumes you are creating a form letter and the source document at the same time. Because most people create one or the other and then return later to merge the two, the following steps show you how to create only the source document.

To create a new data source with the Mail Merge Helper, follow these steps:

1. Choose Tools, Mail Merge. The Mail Merge Helper dialog box appears.

2. Choose Create and then select Form Letters.

3. Click the New Main Document button. This opens a blank document and returns you to the Mail Merge Helper. The Get Data button is now available.

 TIP The blank document that opened would normally be used to create a new form letter, but you need it open only to appease the Mail Merge Helper while you create a new data source.

4. Click the Get Data button, then select Create Data Source from the list (see Figure 16.11). The Create Data Source dialog box appears, as shown in Figure 16.12.

FIG. 16.11

Choosing Tools, Mail Merge displays the Mail Merge Helper. The Mail Merge Helper guides you through the process of creating data sources, creating main documents, and merging the data and document.

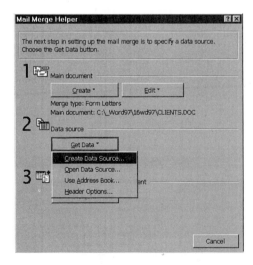

5. In the Create Data Source dialog box, add or remove field names for the columns in your data source. When the Create Data Source dialog box first appears, it shows in the Field Names in Header Row list the most frequently used field names for mail

merge. Field names appear left to right across the first row of the data source in the order they are listed in the Field Names in Header Row list. Edit the field names in the list using the following steps:

- Add a new field name to the list by typing the name in the Field Name edit box and clicking Add Field Name. The name is added to the end of the list.

FIG. 16.12
The Create Data Source dialog box gives you the opportunity to accept, add, or remove field names that are used to name each column in the data source.

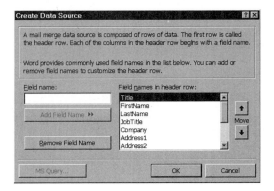

 TIP Field names must be 40 characters or less and start with a letter. Spaces are not allowed.

- Delete a field name from the list by selecting the name in the Field Names in Header Row list, and then click Remove Field Name.
- Move a field name up or down in the list by selecting the name and then clicking the up or down arrows.

6. Choose OK. The Save As dialog box appears.

7. Type a file name in the File Name edit box. Change to the folder in which you expect to keep the data source.

8. Choose OK to close the Save As dialog box. A dialog box appears warning you that the data source you created contains no data.

9. Click Edit Data Source to display the Data Form dialog box where you can add records to your new data source (see Figure 16.13).

10. Enter data in the Data Form. Press Tab or Enter to move to the next field of data. Click Add New to add another record. The Data Form is described in detail later in this chapter in "Finding or Editing Records in the Data Form."

11. When you are finished entering data and want to save the data source, click the View Source button. When the data source document appears, choose File, Save.

If you do not save the data source document, you will be given a chance to save it when you attempt to close the blank document you opened in step 3.

FIG. 16.13

Use the Data Form to add new data to your new data source. You can bring up the Data Form at any time to find or edit data in a data source.

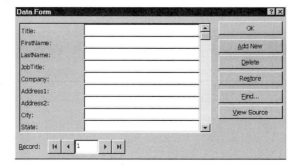

  T I P View more of a wide data source by choosing View, Zoom to fit more fields on the screen.

▶ **See** "Creating Tables," **p. 608**

 You can see the paragraph mark that ends a row of comma-delimited data if you click the Show/Hide ¶ button on the Standard toolbar.

Your data source document looks like a table if it has 31 or fewer field names. If it has more than 31 field names, data is separated by commas, and records end with a paragraph mark. The field names will be in the first row and data in following rows.

Working with an Existing Data Source   You can work with data sources that already exist, even if they aren't Word documents. The data may have come from a worksheet, database, or corporate mainframe.

You may want to work with an existing data source to edit its contents or to build a new main document that contains merge fields. For example, if you want to create a new form letter using a data source you already have, follow this procedure:

1. Choose Tools, Mail Merge.
2. Click the Main Document Create button, then select the type of main document you want to create: Form Letters, Mailing Labels, Envelopes, or Catalog. From the dialog box that appears, choose either Active Window or New Main Document to attach the data source to the existing active document or to open a new document.
3. Click Get Data, and then choose Open Data Source from the pull-down list. The Open Data Source dialog box appears.
4. Change to the folder containing the data source, and then select or type the file name of the data source in the File Name box. Choose OK.
5. Click the Set Up Main Document or Edit Main Document button.

The data source is open but does not appear in a window. If you want to edit the data in the data source, refer to the section later in this chapter, "Finding or Editing Records with the Data Form."

You can use the data source documents you used in previous versions of Word with the Mail Merge Helper in Word 97. Make sure that Word has the converters installed to convert the old document into Word format. After you have resaved the document, you can treat it the same as any data source.

Using Data from Another Application   Word can use the data from other applications as a data source. Your main documents in Word can link to data in other applications such as Access or Excel. The document can read directly from databases such as Access, Paradox, FoxPro, or dBASE through the use of Open Database Connectivity (ODBC) drivers. You also can import and convert data from any files for which you have a converter.

Using the Mail Merge Helper with a Non-Word Data Source   To work with a non-Word data source, follow these steps:

1. Open a main document.
2. Choose Tools, Mail Merge.
3. Choose Main Document Create, and then select the type of main document you want to create: Form Letters, Mailing Labels, Envelopes, or Catalog. From the Help dialog box that appears, choose either Active Window or New Main Document to attach the data source to the existing active document or to open a new document.
4. Choose Get Data, and then select Open Data Source from the drop-down list.
5. Change to the folder containing the data source, and then select or type the file name of the data source in the File Name box. Choose OK.

   Or, if you open an Excel worksheet, you are given an opportunity to specify a range name within the worksheet that describes the data you want to bring in. If you open an Access file, you can open an Access query file and only the data that satisfies that query will be loaded.

   You can also choose MS Query to open Microsoft Query so you can connect to and query an external data source. Microsoft Query is a separate Microsoft application that comes with Excel or Office. When you are finished in Microsoft Query, choose File, Return Data to Microsoft Word.

6. If the active document is not a main document that contains merge fields, Word displays a Mail Merge Helper dialog box. Click the Edit Main Document button.

Part
IV

Ch
16

Managing Information in the Data Source

You can manage the data in your data source just as though you had a small database program built into Word. You can find or edit records using the Data Form. You can also reorganize the columns in a data source or merge together two data source files.

TIP   When you don't know which field (column) contains the data you need to find, select the entire database and search with Edit, Find.

Finding or Editing Records with the Data Form   The information in your data source is of little value unless it is accurate. Word includes features to help you keep your data source up-to-date.

To quickly find data when the data source is in the active document, follow these steps:

1. Click within a data source.

2. Click the Find Record button on the Database toolbar to display the Find in Field dialog box shown in Figure 16.14.

FIG. 16.14
You can find records that contain information in the field name you select.

3. Select from the In Field list the field name of the column you want to search.

4. Type in the Find What box what you are searching for under the field name.

5. Click Find First.

6. Examine the record found or click the Find Next button to continue.

To find and edit information when a data source is in the active document, follow these steps:

1. Click within a data source.

   The database may have fields in table columns, tab-separated or comma-separated. A main document does not have to be opened or attached. It must have valid data source field names.

2. Click the Data Form button on the Database toolbar.

3. Begin at step 3 in the next procedure to find or edit data using the Data Form.

To find data within the data source when the main document is active, follow these steps:

1. Open a main document that uses your data source.

2. Click the Data Form button in the Database toolbar or choose Tools, Mail Merge, and then click the Edit button and select the data source. The Data Form dialog box appears.

3. Move to the first record in the data source if you want to begin the search from the first data record.

4. Click Find.

5. Select from the In Field list the field name of the column you want to search.

6. Type in the Find What box what you are searching for under the field name.

7. Choose Find First.

Part
IV

Ch
16

When the first record satisfying your request is found, the Find First button changes to a Find Next button. Select this button to find any further occurrences of what you are searching for. A message notifies you when you have reached the last record in the database.

When you find a record you want to edit, choose Close in the Find in Field dialog box and edit the record in the Data Form.

TIP You can delete a record by displaying it in the Data Form and then clicking Delete.

If you delete or edit a record incorrectly, immediately choose Restore to return the record to its original condition. After you move to a new record when editing, you cannot restore previous edits. If the data form is too restrictive (for example, fields contain data that is too long), you can edit the contents of the table directly, as if it was any other Word table.

Sorting a Data Source   Sorting a data source can be useful for a couple of reasons. If you are printing a large volume of mail merge envelopes or labels, you can get a discount on postage if ZIP codes are in sorted order. Another reason for sorting is to create printed lists that will be searched manually.

To quickly sort a data source, follow these steps:

1. Click in the data source in the field (column) that you want to sort.

2. Click the Ascending Sort or Descending Sort button on the Database toolbar.

If you have more complex sorts and your data is in a table, or can be converted to a table, choose Table, Sort.

Renaming, Inserting, or Removing Fields from a Data Source   When you need to change your information, you will probably have to add or remove fields (columns) from your data source. For example, you might want to add a field that includes a customer's automatic reorder date, or you might want to delete an old, unnecessary field such as a Client Priority number.

To add or remove a field in a data source, follow these steps:

1. Save your current data source under a new name. Save this file as a backup in case you make mistakes and need to return to an original copy.

2. Open the data source document and display it in the active window.

 3. Click the Manage Fields button in the Database toolbar to display the Manage Fields dialog box, shown in Figure 16.15.

FIG. 16.15

Use the Manage Fields dialog box to add or remove new fields (columns) in the Data Source as your information needs change.

4. If you want to add, remove, or rename a field, follow these steps:

   To add a field, type the new name in the Field Name edit box, then choose the Add button.

   To remove a field name and its corresponding data, select the name from the Field Names in Header Row list, then click the Remove button. Choose Yes to confirm that you want to remove the field and data.

   To rename a field name, click the Rename button, then type your name in the New Field Name edit box that appears. Choose OK.

5. When you have finished making changes to your data source, choose OK.

Inserting or Removing Records from a Data Source   It seems that the amount of information demanded only seems to grow; however, sometimes you might need to delete a record from your data source. With Word, you can easily insert or delete records.

T I P If records to be deleted have common data, sort the field containing that data so that you can delete multiple records at one time.

To insert a new blank record at the bottom of the data source, you can use the Data Form as described earlier in this chapter. Alternatively, you can follow these steps:

1. Open and activate the data source document.

 2. Click the Add New Record button on the Database toolbar.

To delete a record from the data source, follow these steps:

1. Open and activate the data source document.

2. Click in the record (row) that you want to delete. Select down through many records if you want to delete multiple records.

 3. Click the Delete Record button on the Database toolbar. You are not asked to confirm that you want to delete.

If you decide you have accidentally deleted the wrong record, immediately choose <u>E</u>dit, <u>U</u>ndo.

Scrolling Through the Data Form   You can browse through records in the data source using the buttons at the bottom of the Data Form. Clicking the left or right button moves the records one at a time. Clicking the left end or right end button (VCR end controls, |< and >|) moves to the beginning or end of the data record.

If you do not have a mouse, you can move to a specific record by pressing Alt+R and typing the numeric position of the record you want to see. When you press Enter, the insertion point moves out of the Record Number box and into the first field. ●

Part
IV

Ch
16

CHAPTER 17

Mastering Envelopes, Mail Merge, and Form Letters

Successful businesses know that staying in touch with their clients and customers is crucial to the success of the business. Staying in touch with many people can be difficult, however, unless you learn how to create personalized form letters and envelopes with Word 97.

To make single letters easier to produce, Word has automated the process of printing an envelope. The envelope printing feature uses the address from a document to print an envelope with or without a return address. The envelope can be printed separately or attached to the document with which it is associated. This feature is covered in the first section of this chapter.

Form letters broadcast information, yet add a personal touch to your work. Even if you generate only a few form letters each day, this feature allows you to automate repetitive parts of your business and gives you time to improve the creative end of your work. You can also generate invoices, appointment reminders, and so on. Learning how to create form letters is challenging, but working through the process will pay great dividends.

Insert an individual's name and address in a letter

Insert an address from the Personal Address Book, Schedule+, or Outlook.

Print envelopes and include their bar code or FIM code

Print envelopes by themselves, attached to a document, or as part of a mass mailing.

Use the Mail Merge Helper to create a main document and a data source and to control the data merging of documents

The Mail Merge Helper manages the entire mail-merge process in three easy steps.

Perform mail merge with documents such as letterheads, envelopes, and mailing labels

Specify different top margins for the first page of a form letter to allow for a letterhead page, merge envelopes or envelopes and documents at the same time, and create custom mailing labels.

Insert field codes that prompt you to enter a personal note in each mail-merge document

FILLIN is a special Word field that prompts the user to enter a personalized message to the recipient during the merge operation.

You can create two types of form letters with Word: those that are filled in manually and those that are filled in from computer-generated lists. In this chapter, you learn to create an automated form letter that prompts you for information the document needs for creating an invoice. You learn also how to fill in the blanks in a form letter by merging a mailing list with the main document. Finally, you learn advanced Word techniques for document automation, including a form letter that combines manual fill-in with merging of information. ■

Inserting a Name and Address from the Address Book

 You can use Address Books and lists of contacts to manage the names and addresses of people you write to frequently. After you enter the names, addresses, and e-mail information about people, you can retrieve the information by clicking the Insert Address button in the Standard toolbar, then selecting to use names and addresses from an address book or a contact list. You also can paste a person's address into your document by clicking their name.

If the Insert Address button (it looks like an opened address book) is not displayed in the Standard toolbar, choose View, Toolbars, Customize, select Insert from the Categories list, select Address Book from the Commands list, and drag the Address Book icon onto the Standard toolbar.

▶ **See** "Managing Names and Addresses with Address Books," **p. 545**

Before you can use the Address Book on a network or with the Address Book in Outlook or Schedule+, you must gain access to the network and Outlook or Schedule+. If your computer is on a network and you use Outlook or Schedule+, you need to follow these steps:

1. Position the insertion point in the document where you want to paste a person's address.

2. Click the Insert Address button in the Standard toolbar. If you are prompted, select an Exchange profile. The Select Name dialog box apprears as shown in Figure 17.1.

3. Select the Show Names From The list and select the address book or contact list containing the address you want to insert into your document.

FIG. 17.1
The Select Name dialog box gives you access to the address books or contact lists available in Windows.

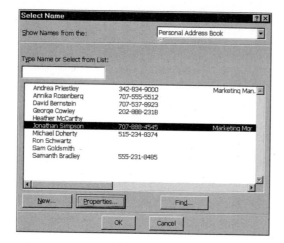

If you have installed Windows 95 and Office 97, the following address books are available:

Address Book	Description
Outlook Address Book	A name, address, and information list stored in Outlook and shared with others on your network.
Outlook Contact List	A name, address, and information list stored in Outlook and shared with others on your network.
Schedule+ Contact List	A name, address, and information list stored in Schedule+ and shared with others on your network.
Personal Address Book	A name, address, and information list used for sending e-mail and faxes from Word through Microsoft Exchange.
Postoffice Address List	A name, address, and e-mail address list used for sending e-mail messages from Word through your local network.
The Microsoft Network	A name, address, and e-mail address list used for sending e-mail messages from Word over the Microsoft Network.

4. Type the name you want into the Type Name or Select From List edit box, or click the name in the list.

5. Choose OK to insert that person's name and address into your Word document.

If you have used the address book before, a shortcut list will be available. Using this shortcut list is a very quick and convenient way to insert names and addresses. To quickly insert a name and address you have used before, follow these steps:

1. Click the drop-down arrow to the right of the Insert Address button to display the list shown in Figure 17.2.

FIG. 17.2

Use the drop-down list to the right of the Insert Address button to insert names and addresses quickly.

2. Click the name whose name and address you want to insert.

Printing an Envelope

Word offers an easy and quick solution to a common word processing problem: printing envelopes. Word can print envelopes by themselves, attached to a document, or as part of a mass mailing.

To test the envelope feature, create a short letter like the one shown in Figure 17.3.

To create an envelope, follow these steps:

1. Select the address in the letter.

   If the address is a contiguous block of three to five short lines near the beginning of the letter, you do not have to select it. Word automatically finds the address.

2. Choose Tools, Envelopes and Labels. Word displays the Envelopes and Labels dialog box (see Figure 17.4).

3. Select the Envelopes tab if it is not already active.

4. Edit the Delivery Address information if necessary. To insert line feeds (line breaks without a carriage return), press Shift+Enter.

5. Edit the <u>R</u>eturn Address information if necessary. If you do not want to print the return address (you may be working with preprinted envelopes, for example), select the O<u>m</u>it check box.

6. Click the <u>O</u>ptions button to display the Envelopes Options dialog box if you need to select an envelope size (see Figure 17.5); then make your selection from the Envelope <u>S</u>ize drop-down list.

FIG. 17.3
This figure shows a sample business letter.

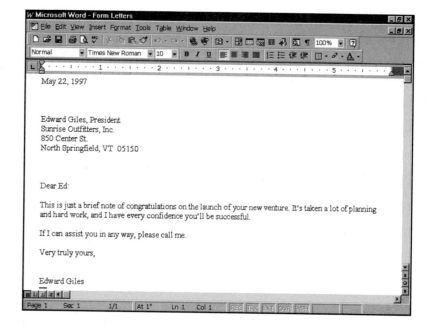

FIG. 17.4
Word will find the address in most letters and display it automatically in the Envelopes and Labels dialog box.

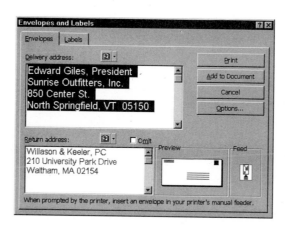

N O T E   The Delivery Address and Return Address options enable you to customize the fonts and positions of the addresses. You can read about the postal mailing areas later in this section.

FIG. 17.5

Click the Options button in the Envelopes and Labels dialog box to display the Envelope Options dialog box.

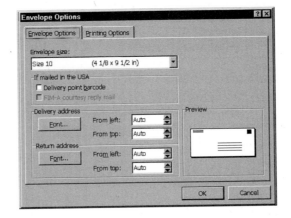

7. Choose OK when you're finished with your selections.

8. Load envelope(s) into your printer's feeder as indicated in the Feed area in the Envelopes and Labels dialog box.

9. Click the Print button to print an envelope immediately.

    You can also click the Add to Document button to add the envelope as a landscape-oriented section before the first page of your document (see Figure 17.6).

You can change the default Return Address information. Choose Tools, Options; then select User Information tab. In the Mailing Address text box, add or edit the return address. This address becomes the default return address until you change it.

When you click the Print button, many laser printers can immediately print the envelope from the envelope bin. If you do not have an envelope feeder or envelope bin, insert the envelope—narrow side in—in the form-feed guides on top of the primary paper tray. The envelope prints first, followed by the document.

To reposition the Delivery Address area, change to Page Layout view and move the mouse pointer to the striped border until a four-headed arrow appears. Then drag the entire box containing the Delivery Address to a new position (see Figure 17.7).

FIG. 17.6
The Add to Document button inserts a landscape envelope before the first page of your document.

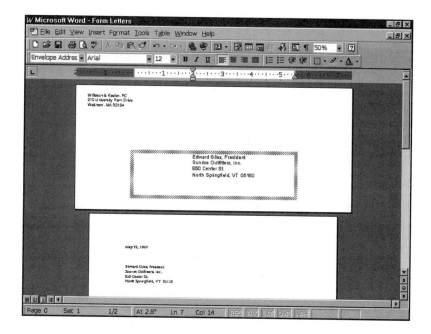

FIG. 17.7
You can drag the address area to a new position in the envelope section.

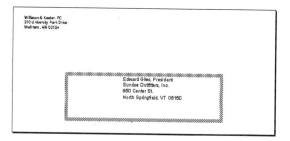

TROUBLESHOOTING

My address isn't printing properly on the envelopes. If you have trouble printing an envelope with the envelope layout or with envelope and paper feeding, examine the printer driver. Choose File, Print, and look in the Name text box of the Print dialog box to see which printer driver is selected. Make sure you have the correct driver. Check with your printer manufacturer or Microsoft for a more current version of the Windows printer driver program if you continue to have problems. Install a new printer driver by clicking Start, Settings, Printers, then double-clicking the Add Printer icon. Follow the Add Printer Wizard to install a printer driver.

Printing an Envelope with Bar Codes or FIM Codes

Word provides a way to print machine-readable codes on envelopes so that the U.S. Postal Service can process the envelopes by machine. These codes can be used as long as they are sent to addresses within the U.S., thus saving time and money.

You can print *POSTNET* codes (bar code equivalents of U.S. ZIP codes) and *facing identification marks*, or *FIMs* (vertical lines that indicate the address side of the envelope).

To print POSTNET bar codes and FIMs on envelope(s) attached to the current document, follow these steps:

1. Choose Tools, Envelopes and Labels.

2. Click the Options button in the Envelopes tab of the Envelopes and Labels dialog box. Word displays the Envelope Options dialog box (see Figure 17.8).

FIG. 17.8

Set envelope printing options in the Envelope Options dialog box.

Checking these options adds bar codes and FIMs to your envelopes

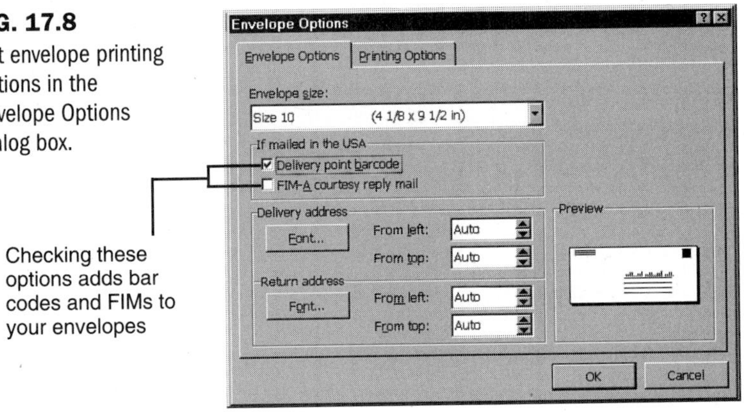

3. Select the Delivery Point Bar Code check box to print POSTNET bar codes.

4. Select the FIM-A Courtesy Reply Mail check box to print FIMs.

5. Choose OK.

Customizing Envelopes with Text and Graphics

You can easily add a graphic—such as a company logo—to your envelopes, whether the graphic consists of formatted text or actual graphics.

To set up envelopes to print your logo, follow these steps:

1. Enter your logo text and graphics in a document.

2. Put the logo in a frame.

▶ **See** "Inserting Pictures into a Document," **p. 813**

3. Choose Insert, AutoText, New.
4. Type the name **EnvelopeExtra** in the Please Name Your AutoText Entry text box.
5. Click OK.

Merging Mailing Lists and Documents

One of the most powerful and time-saving features available in any word processor is mail merge. *Mail merge* enables you to create multiple letters or envelopes by merging together a list of names and addresses with letters, envelopes, or address labels. Mail merge can also be used for such tasks as filling in administrative forms and creating invoices from accounting files. Whenever you keep a list or get a list from other programs and you need to put information into a Word document, you should consider using mail merge.

The time you save by using mail merge can be tremendous. Instead of typing or modifying tens or hundreds of documents, Word can make all the documents for you. All you need to do is keep your list (names, addresses, and so on) up-to-date and create a form letter in which to insert the data. In fact, you can even make each document pause during mail merge so that you can enter personalized information.

Understanding the Mail Merge Components: Data Sources and Main Documents

You need two documents to create form letters or mailing labels. One document, called the *data source*, contains a precisely laid-out set of data, such as names and addresses. The other document, the *main document*, acts as a form that receives the data. Most forms that receive data are form letters or multicolumn tables for mailing labels.

Although most people would use the term *form letter* to describe a Word main document, a main document can take the form of a mailing list, catalog, mailing labels, or letters.

The main document is like a normal document except that it contains MERGEFIELD field codes that specify the placement of merged data. In a typical form letter, for example, the main document is a form letter in which the names and addresses are inserted, and the data source is the list of those names and addresses.

The data source document must be organized in a very specific way, or the merge process will generate errors. The first row of the data source must be one row of field names. Below the row of names are rows of data. Each row of data is a *record*, and each piece of data

Part
IV

Ch
17

in the row, such as a last name, is a *field*. The row of names in the first row of the documents is the *header record*. Each name in the first row is a *field name*. Each field can be referenced by the name for that field in the heading.

▶ **See** "Managing Data," **p. 549**

When you merge the documents, Word replaces the merge fields with the appropriate text from the data source. At merge time, you can choose to display the result as a new document on-screen or to print it directly to the current printer.

Understanding Word's Mail Merge Helper

Word Mail Merge Helper guides you through the three stages of creating a form letter, catalog, or other merged document:

- Creating or identifying the main document
- Creating or identifying the data source
- Merging the data source and main document

To start the Mail Merge Helper, follow these steps:

1. Open the document you want to use as the main document. (If the main document doesn't exist, create a new document.)

2. Choose Tools, Mail Merge.

The Mail Merge Helper dialog box guides you through the three stages of creating a merged document (see Figure 17.9). Notice that the dialog box contains a lot of empty space; this space will fill up with useful information about the merge documents as you proceed.

FIG. 17.9

The Mail Merge Helper dialog box is the central dialog box from which you complete the three stages of form-letter production.

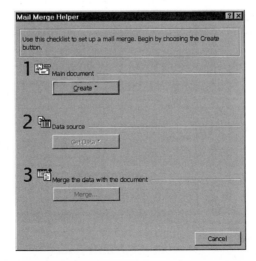

The Mail Merge Helper is designed to be flexible; you can start setting up the merge at virtually any stage in the document-creation process. At appropriate points, Word requires you to make decisions or reminds you to go back and complete some necessary steps.

You'll see many dialog boxes resembling the one in Figure 17.10. Although this dialog box does not have a name, you might think of it as the "decision" dialog box.

Sometimes the decision box offers a choice between creating a new document or changing the type of the active document. Consider carefully before changing the document type; generally, you'll want to preserve the existing document in its current form.

FIG. 17.10
At different points in the merge process, Word asks whether you want to create a new, blank document or use an existing one.

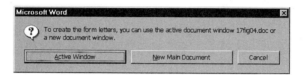

If you fail to complete a required portion of one of the three stages in the merge process, you see a dialog box like the one shown in Figure 17.11. This type of dialog box essentially forces you to add detail to incomplete documents before going through with the merge. You see this dialog box only if the Mail Merge Helper detects that you have missed a step or incorrectly entered a response.

FIG. 17.11
Word's Mail Merge Helper forces you to create complete documents before it will let you begin merging.

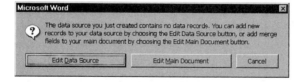

The following sections describe how to proceed through the three stages of creating mail-merge documents. The Mail Merge Helper coordinates the mail-merge documents and the merging process. When you click a button in the Mail Merge Helper, Word displays a series of windows that help you complete the part of the merge process that corresponds to the button.

Selecting the Main Document

You can use any existing document as a main document. Simply open that document before starting the Mail Merge Helper. If you need to create the main document, however, you have the following options:

1. Start Word and be sure you're in a new document.
2. Choose File, New.
3. Make sure that the Document button is selected.
4. Select the tab that contains the template you want to use.
5. Select the template you want to use.
6. Choose OK.

It's not necessary to enter any text in the document right now; you can come back to that later.

To create a main document for a form letter, follow these steps:

1. Choose Tools, Mail Merge.
2. Click the Create button under the Main document heading of the Mail Merge Helper dialog box.
3. Choose Form Letters. Word displays a decision dialog box asking what you want to use to create the form letter.
4. Click the Active Window button to use the active document as the main document. Or click the New Main Document button to open a new document that uses the Normal document template.

Word returns you to the Mail Merge Helper dialog box, which now displays the type of merge and the name and path of the main document under the Main Document heading.

This process illustrates the Mail Merge Helper's flexibility; if you realize in step 4 that you don't want to use the active document, you don't have to start over again.

Selecting a Data Source

Attaching the data source to the main document does three things:

- Shows Word the file name and path where the data will be located
- Attaches a Mail Merge toolbar with merge tools to the top of the main document
- Enables Word to read the field names used in the data source so you can include those field names in your main document

▶ **See** "Managing Data," **p. 549**

If you do not yet have a source for the data that will be merged, read Chapter 16 and create a data source before proceeding. An overview of creating a new data source is presented in the section "Creating a New Data Source" later in this chapter.

Specifying an Address Book as the Data Source   If you have created a list of contacts in a Personal Address Book, Outlook Address Book, or in the Schedule+ Address Book, you already have a data source that you can use for a mail merge by following these steps:

1. Click the Get Data button under the Data Source heading.

2. Choose Use Address Book. Word displays the Use Address Book dialog box, shown in Figure 17.12.

FIG. 17.12

You can select one of the address books available to Word for use in mail merge.

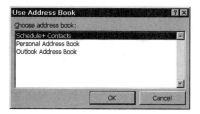

3. Select an address book from the Choose Address Book list, and then choose OK.

The next step depends on whether your main document was complete when you started the merge process. If you have not yet inserted any merge fields in your main document, Word displays the dialog box shown in Figure 17.13.

FIG. 17.13

After attaching the data source, the Mail Merge Helper detects that your main document does not have any merge fields.

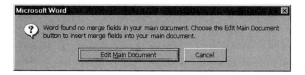

To go directly to the main document to add the merge fields, choose Edit Main Document. For instructions on inserting the merge fields in your main document, refer to the section "Edit the Main Document" in this chapter.

Specifying an Existing File as the Data Source   You can use a data source that you have already created for the mail merge. In the Mail Merge Helper dialog box, you can click the Get Data button to give you access to different sources of data. If you want to use data that is in a file or document, choose the Open Data Source item from the list.

To specify an existing file as a data source, follow these steps:

1. Click the Get Data button under the Data Source heading.

2. Choose Open Data Source. Word displays the Open Data Source dialog box, shown in Figure 17.14.

Part

IV

Ch

17

FIG. 17.14
Use the Open Data
Source dialog box to
access a data source
in Word or many other
formats.

3. Select the data source from the File Name list. Word can read many different data
source formats. Choose from the Files of Type list to see other formats. Choose OK
after selecting the file.

You can also choose the MS Query button if Microsoft Query is available on your
computer. Use Microsoft Query to access specific data in a non-Word database.

N O T E Use Microsoft Query to retrieve data meeting specific criteria. The data may be on your
computer, network, SQL server, or many types of mainframe databases. Microsoft
Query is available as a separate application and comes with Microsoft Excel. ▪

Word automatically converts non-Word files for which it has converters.

Creating a New Data Source

If you did not have a data source that contained your lists of names or database of information to be merged, you need to create one. You also can create a data source in a Word
document while you are in the Mail Merge Helper.

▶ **See** "Managing Mail Merge Data," **p. 549**

▶ **See** "Creating Your Own Data Sources," **p. 549**

The Mail Merge Helper guides you through the process of creating a data source in a
Word document. It follows a set of rules that you can learn if you want to create a data
source document manually. The data source is a grid of rows and columns. The first row
in the data source must contain the field names. These names label each column's contents. Only one row of field names can be at the top of the data source. Field names cannot

contain blanks and cannot start with a number (although you can include a number in the field name). If you need to use a two-part field name, use an underscore rather than a space. You may want to put words together and capitalize a word's leading letter, such as RegionManager. Each field name must be unique.

You can create a new data source within a Word document by using the Create Data Source command. Follow these steps:

1. Click the <u>G</u>et Data button under the Data Source heading in the Mail Merge Helper.

N O T E This button is available only if you attached a main document by clicking the Create button from the Main Document stage. If you want to create a data source and wait to create a main document, just attach a blank document as the main document. ▓

2. Choose <u>C</u>reate Data Source. Word displays the Create Data Source dialog box (see Figure 17.15).

   The Field Names in Header Row list box contains names traditionally used for fields in mailing lists. The names in the list box comprise a default list of field names.

FIG. 17.15
The Create Data Source dialog box guides you through creating a data source. It even presents the most commonly used headings for mail-merge data sources.

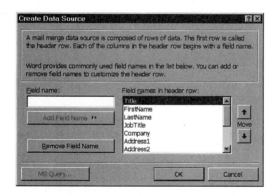

3. Edit the list of names in the Field <u>N</u>ames in Header Row list box, as described here:

   - If you see any field names you won't use in your main document, select the name from the Field <u>N</u>ames in Header Row box, and then choose the <u>R</u>emove Field Name button. Word removes the name from the list.

   - To add a field name, type it in the <u>F</u>ield Name box and then choose <u>A</u>dd Field Name.

   - When you are satisfied with your list, choose OK.

   - To change the sequence of names (reposition them), select a field name, and then click the up-or down-arrow labeled Move. The top-to-bottom sequence you see in this list box determines the right-to-left sequence of the fields in the data source.

Part
IV

Ch
17

4. Word displays the Save As dialog box. In the File Name text box, enter a name for the data source document and choose Save.

5. Word displays a decision dialog box asking what you want to do next. To enter data in the data source, click the Edit Data Source button. To edit the Main document so that you can insert the merge fields to create a main document, click the Edit Main Document button.

If you click Edit Main Document, Word displays the main document as a normal Word document with one exception—the Mail Merge toolbar is now displayed below the toolbar(s) and above the ruler (see Figure 17.16). With the main document on-screen, you can create a main document in which the data will be inserted.

FIG. 17.16
Use the Mail Merge toolbar to insert merge fields as you create the main document.

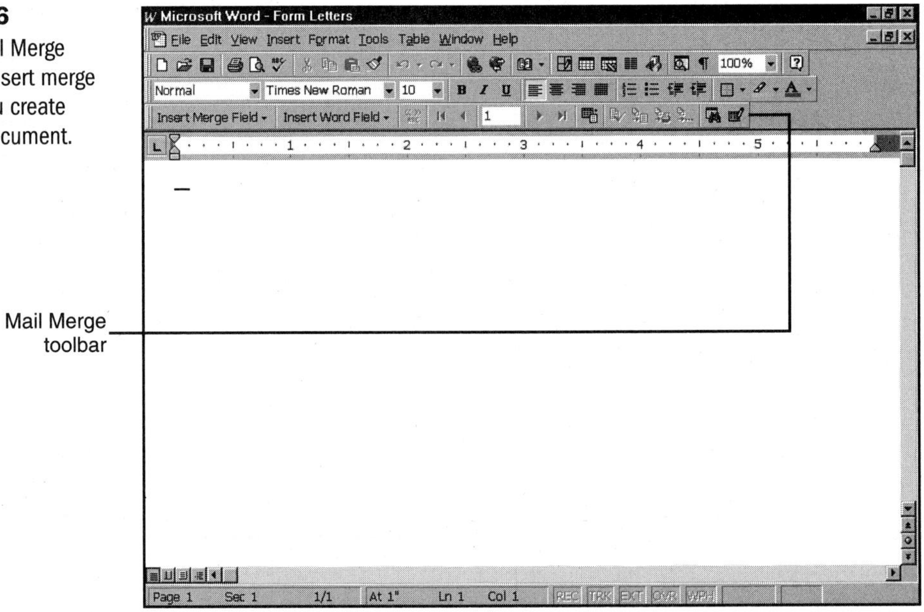

Mail Merge toolbar

Merging Data into the Main Document

When you are satisfied with your main document, you can merge it with the data by choosing one of three merge buttons in the Mail Merge toolbar. Table 17.1 shows how these buttons work.

Table 17.1 Effects of Merge Buttons in the Mail Merge Toolbar

Button	Effect
	Creates the merged document and places it in a new Word document.
	Creates the merged document and prints it on the currently selected printer.
	Displays the Merge dialog box, which provides a wide range of options for record selection and other operations (see the next section for details).

Figure 17.17 shows the merged document. The Form Letters1 document contains the full text of the merged document, with each of the individually addressed letters contained in a section. This document contains no field codes; you can treat it as you would any typed document. Each section break (represented by a double dashed line) starts a new page, so printing the document produces individual letters. Naturally, if you want to make changes to individual letters, you can edit them in the usual manner.

Part
IV
Ch
17

FIG. 17.17

Merging a form letter to a document can create a long document containing all the individual letters.

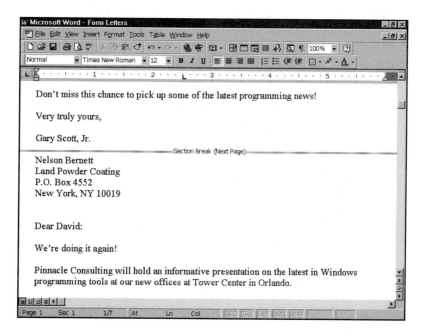

If you merge a large number of records, merge to the printer so that you do not exceed memory limits. You may want to merge a few records to a new document before printing. This enables you to see whether the merge is working correctly.

Merging Selected Records   Often you will not want to merge an entire data source into a letter. You may want to merge 20 letters at a time, or limit the merged data to specific ZIP codes or job titles. Or you may want to merge one or two letters as a text before running a large merge job.

To control the data that's merged into your main document, follow these steps:

1. Prepare your data source and save it.

2. Open your main document. When it opens, the Mail Merge toolbar also appears.

   If Word cannot find the data source for the main document, it displays a dialog box that you can use to open the correct data source.

3. Choose Tools, Mail Merge to display the Mail Merge Helper, as shown in Figure 17.18.

FIG. 17.18

A Mail Merge Helper that is ready to merge data shows both main document and data source types and locations.

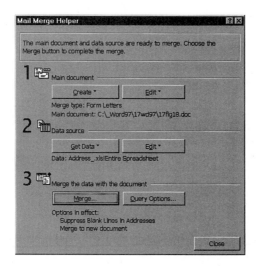

In Figure 17.18, you can see that a properly completed Mail Merge Helper displays the type and location of the main document, as well as the data source for that main document and where the data source is located.

4. Click the Merge button to begin the merge process. The Merge dialog box shown in Figure 17.19 appears.

5. Select the Merge To list and select one of the following types of merges:

Merge To:	Effect
Printer	Produces a printed result.

New Document	Produces a new document containing all resulting merged documents.
Electronic mail	Produces merged documents for electronic mailing.

6. Select the number of records to be merged from the Records to Be Merged group:

Merged Records	Effect
All	Merges all records.
From/To	Limits the range of data according to the record (row) numbers in the data source.

7. Select from the When Merging Records group how blank lines will be handled: Don't Print Blank Lines When Data Fields Are Empty, or Print Blank Lines When Data Fields Are Empty.

8. Choose Merge.

Part
IV

Ch
17

FIG. 17.19
Select how you want Word to perform the merge from the Merge dialog box.

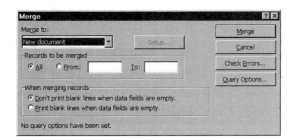

Creating Mailing Labels

If you are sending many documents, mailing labels can save you lots of time. With Word, you can easily update your mailing lists and print labels on demand.

You can design a form that prints multiple labels on a page in much the same way you create a form letter. If you've designed main documents for mailing labels in a previous version of Word, you can continue to use those documents to print mailing labels. But if you need to create a new label form, Word makes the task quite easy.

Creating a Mailing Label Main Document   The Labels tab of the Envelopes and Labels dialog box automates the process of creating mailing labels. The following example assumes that you have already created a form-letter main document.

To create mailing labels for an existing form letter, follow these steps:

1. Choose Tools, Mail Merge. (You do not need to activate the main document for the form letter.)

2. Click the Create button under the Main Document heading of the Mail Merge Helper dialog box.

3. Select Mailing Labels.

4. Click Active Window if it appears in the Decision dialog box. Otherwise, click New Main Document.

5. Click the Get Data button under the Data Source heading.

6. Select Open Data Source or Use Address Book.

7. Select the appropriate data source.

8. Click Set Up Main Document if Word displays a dialog box.

9. Select a label format from the Label Options dialog box. Label formats are explained in the following section.

Specifying Label Size and Type   The Label Options dialog box (see Figure 17.20) contains specifications for dozens of commercial preprinted label products. You'll probably be able to select the label format you want from this dialog box by following these steps:

FIG. 17.20

Select a label format from the Label Options dialog box.

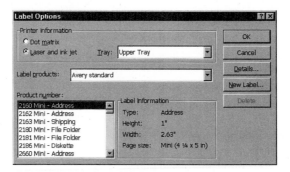

1. Select the appropriate label group from the Label Products drop-down list:

Label Products	Comments
Avery standard	Avery U.S. products
Avery A4 and A5 sizes	Avery A4 and A5 size products
MACO standard	MACO standard products
Other	Products from other manufacturers

2. Select your type of label from the Product Number drop-down list. If you are not using labels from any of the commercial products available in this dialog box, use

the product number for the same size label. If none of the label formats produce the result you want, you will have to edit the label specifications, as explained in "Creating Custom Mailing Labels" later in this section.

3. If you're not sure which label type is correct, use the arrow keys to browse through the list so that you can view in the Label Information area the label and page dimensions for each type.

4. If you want to view more details about the selected label type, click the Details button. Word displays a dialog box similar to the one in Figure 17.21. Choose OK to return to the Label Options dialog box. To learn how to create a custom mailing label size, see "Creating Custom Mailing Labels" later in this section.

FIG. 17.21
In this dialog box, you can preview any available label type and set custom sizes.

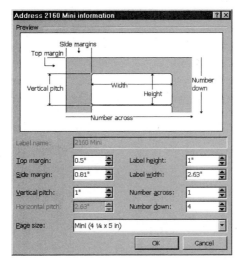

5. Choose OK when you are satisfied with all your selections. Word displays the Create Labels dialog box (see Figure 17.22).

6. Insert the appropriate merge fields in the Sample label box and choose OK. Word then displays the Mail Merge Helper.

7. Click the Merge button to display the Merge dialog box.

8. Select the options you want and then proceed with error checking, query definition, and merging. When you are finished, click the Merge button.

Word creates a new document containing a table formatted for the type of labels you selected. You can merge the labels to a new document or print them in the usual manner.

FIG. 17.22
Use the Create Labels
dialog box to build a
label by inserting
merge field codes.

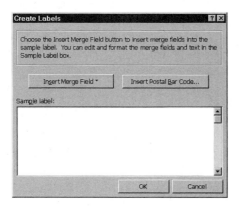

Printing Labels for a Single Address   Naturally, not all your letters will be form letters.
In the Labels tab of the Envelopes and Labels dialog box, you can print a single mailing
label or several labels containing the same address.

To print one or more mailing labels for a single document, follow these steps:

1. Activate the main document for the form letter.

2. Choose Tools, Envelopes and Labels.

3. Select the Labels tab in the Envelopes and Labels dialog box.

4. Examine the fields displayed in the Address box for accuracy. Or, if you want to print
   return address labels, select Use Return Address.

5. Print a single address label by selecting Single Label and specifying the location of
   the label where you want to print. For single-wide, continuous-feed labels for dot-
   matrix printers, use the defaults (Row 1, Column 1). For labels on cut sheets for
   laser printers, you will usually have to specify the location of the next available blank
   label on the page, as shown in Figure 17.23.

FIG. 17.23
In the Print area of the
Envelopes and Labels
dialog box, you can
choose to print a
single label. In this
example, the address
prints on the label in
the first column of the
first row of the label
sheet.

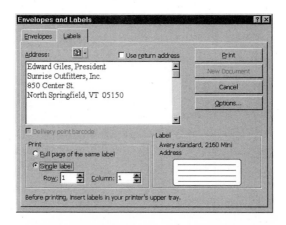

6. Click the Options button and make any necessary changes in the Label Options dialog box. Then choose OK.

7. Make sure that the label paper is loaded in the printer; then click Print to print the labels.

Creating Custom Mailing Labels   You can design your own labels if you can't find the right size in the Label Options dialog box.

To change the label format to a nonstandard size when creating a mailing label document, follow these steps:

1. Select a label format that is similar to the format you want from the Label Options dialog box.

2. Click the Details button. Word displays the Label Preview dialog box.

   The Preview window contains a representation of the current label format. In the bottom portion of the dialog box, enter your custom label specifications. (The annotations in the Preview window illustrate the effects of the specifications.) Enter a new value for any of the measurements (or change the amount by clicking the attached arrow buttons) and watch the Preview window reflect the change.

   If you change the specifications in a way that makes it impossible to fit the specified number of labels on a page, Word displays a message.

3. Choose OK when you are satisfied with all your selections.

4. Click OK in the dialog box that appears to confirm that you want to override the existing custom label specifications. In the Label Options dialog box, Word updates the information in the Label Information box.

5. Choose OK to accept the changes.

Word displays the Create Labels dialog box, where you can proceed with label creation, merging, and printing.

> **CAUTION**
>
> Do not use labels with adhesive backing in laser printers. Laser printers operate at high temperatures, which can melt and separate labels, creating a mess in your printer. Suppliers such as Avery manufacture a complete line of labels of different sizes and shapes made especially for laser printers.

Suppressing Blank Lines in Addresses   Most business mailings include fields for information such as title, suite number, mail station, and so on. If some information is missing, however, blank lines can show up in your addresses or labels, producing an unfinished, unprofessional appearance. You can make sure that blank lines are skipped by

Part
IV

Ch
17

selecting the <u>D</u>on't Print Blank Lines When Data Fields Are Empty option in the Merge dialog box that appears after you choose the <u>M</u>erge button from the Mail Merge Helper. Blank lines involving a MERGEFIELD are skipped if they end with a paragraph mark (¶). Lines ending with a linefeed (Shift+Enter) are not skipped.

Modifying Your Mail Merge

Get in the habit of testing small mail-merge runs before printing a large mail merge involving tens or hundreds of documents. In most cases, you will want to modify your main document, merge fields, or other information. This section contains tips on how to modify mail-merge documents.

Checking for Errors   Browsing through the merged document is a good way to spot problems with the merge, but when the data source contains many records, you might want a higher level of assurance. You can check the entire data source for errors by clicking an error-checking button in the Mail Merge toolbar.

 When you click the Check for Errors button, Word reads your data source and checks for errors such as field names that do not meet the rules for bookmarks. Word checks also to ensure that the number of field names and the number of fields in each record (or row) are the same. Word warns you if it cannot find the data source or if the source contains blank records.

To check the main document and data source for errors, follow these steps:

 1. Click the Check for Errors button in the Mail Merge toolbar. The Checking and Reporting Errors dialog box appears (see Figure 17.24).

FIG. 17.24
Select the appropriate error-reporting option in the Checking and Reporting Errors dialog box.

 TIP   Choose the Help button for more information specific to the problem.

2. Select the error-reporting option you want. The first option simulates the merge, and the second and third complete it. The second option displays messages as errors occur, and the third option puts them in a new document. If you expect some errors, consider simulating the merge first.

3. If you choose to report errors as they occur, the first dialog box displayed might contain an error message, like the one in Figure 17.25. Choose OK to clear the dialog box (or boxes) and proceed accordingly.

FIG. 17.25

This error message appears when Word cannot find a field name in the data source that corresponds to a merge field in the main document.

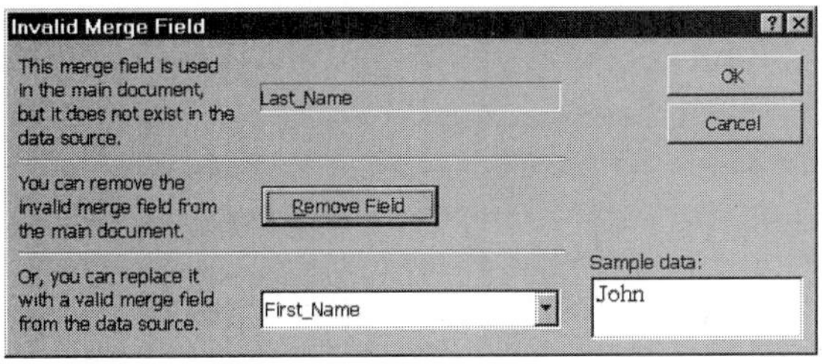

The Invalid Merge Field dialog box assists you in correcting the problem in the merge document. Click the Remove Field button to remove the offending field from the main document. If the field mismatch is the result of a typographical error in the main document, you can correct the error by selecting the valid field name from the list box at the bottom of the dialog box. When you select a field name from this list, the corresponding value from the data source is displayed in the Sample Data box.

The following guidelines can prevent errors that commonly cause problems:

- Field names must not have spaces. Use an underscore rather than a space.
- Field names must not start with a number but can have a number in them.
- Field names must be in one row at the top of the data source.
- Field names must be unique (no duplicates).
- Each field (column) of data must have a field name.
- The number of fields in each record must match the number of field names.

N O T E If the records in the data source are not in a table and if commas, tabs, or cells are missing, the number of fields in a record may not match the number of fields in the heading.

Merging to Letterhead The first page of a form letter is usually on letterhead paper and needs a top margin different from that of the following pages. To compensate for the difference in top margins in your normal documents and form letters, use a different header for the first page.

To create a first-page only header on the active document, follow these steps:

1. Choose Yiew, Header and Footer.

2. Click the Page Setup button in the Header and Footer toolbar to display the Page Setup dialog box.

3. Select the Layout tab if it is not already selected.

4. Select the Different First Page check box.

5. Choose OK.

In the header-editing box that appears at the top of the document, enter the letterhead text. This header is for the first page; the following pages begin body copy underneath the top margin set by the document format.

If your printer has double paper bins—like the HP LaserJet Series IIID, IIISi, and 4Si—you can pull letterhead paper from the letterhead bin. If your printer has only one bin, you can stack alternating letterhead and bond in the tray or feed letterhead into the manual feed tray. If you push the letterhead far enough into the manual feed at the appropriate time, the LaserJet pulls from the manual feed before pulling from the bin.

TIP The HP LaserJet accepts paper from the manual feed before pulling from the bin if the printer has the default menu settings.

Merging Envelopes   With the Mail Merge Helper, you can create mail-merge envelopes or a document that merges mail-merge envelopes and documents at the same time.

To create mail-merge envelopes, create a data source and main document, as described in the section "Creating a Form Letter" earlier in this chapter. Attach the data source to the main document. Be sure that the top of the main document contains a three-to-five-line address composed of MERGEFIELD codes. If you are not mailing a main document, create a blank letter with the MERGEFIELD codes in an address block. The automatic envelope maker uses this document as a basis for its MERGEFIELD address information.

To set up a program for creating a mass-mailing envelope based on your main document, follow these steps:

1. Activate the main document.

2. Choose Tools, Mail Merge.

T I P If the Mail Merge toolbar is displayed, you can click the Mail Merge Helper dialog box button.

3. Click the Create button under the Main Document heading of the Mail Merge Helper dialog box.

4. Select Envelopes.

   Word displays a decision dialog box. The options offered depend on the condition of the active document when you began the procedure.

5. Click Active Window if it appears in the dialog box. Otherwise, click New Main Document.

   Word displays the Mail Merge Helper dialog box (see Figure 17.26). The information under Main Document reflects the merge type (Envelopes) and new document name.

Part

IV

Ch

17

FIG. 17.26

The Mail Merge Helper dialog box changes to reflect the fact that you're creating a new main document.

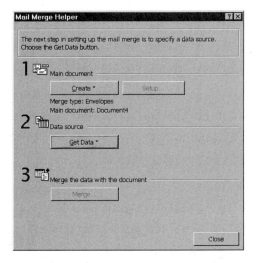

To finish creating the mass-mailing envelope, follow these steps:

1. Under Data Source, click the Get Data button.

2. Click Open Data Source.

3. Select the data source from the File Name list, and then choose Open. If necessary, browse through the folders in the usual manner. Word then displays the dialog box shown in Figure 17.27.

FIG. 17.27
Word displays this
dialog when it needs
to set up your main
document.

You can also click Use Address Book. Select Schedule+ Contacts, Personal Address
Book, or Outlook Address Book, and then choose OK.

4. Click Set Up Main Document.

5. Change any settings in the Envelope Options and Printing Options tabs in the
    Envelope Options dialog box and then choose OK. Word displays the Envelope
    Address dialog box (see Figure 17.28).

FIG. 17.28
Use the Envelope
Address dialog box to
insert the field codes
that will insert data
into the address area
of an envelope.

6. Insert the merge fields for names and addresses, adding any necessary spaces and
    punctuation. You select these fields in the same way as when you created the form
    letter earlier in this chapter—by clicking the Insert Merge Field button and select-
    ing the field names from the drop-down list.

    You can click the Insert Postal Bar Code button to print POSTNET codes on the
    envelopes. The Insert Postal Bar Code dialog box prompts you for the name of the
    field containing the postal code.

    Choose OK when you finish entering fields. Word returns you to the Mail Merge
    Helper dialog box.

7. In the Mail Merge Helper, click Merge. Your document looks something like that
    shown in Figure 17.29.

FIG. 17.29

You can create envelopes for mass mailings that use the merge fields you created for the related form-letter document. The envelopes can also include graphics and logos.

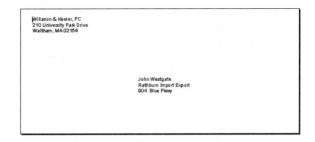

Willason & Keeler, PC
210 University Park Drive
Waltham, MA 02154

John Westgate
Rathburn Import Export
904 Blue Pkwy

8. Select the <u>M</u>erge To list and select one of the following types of merges:

   Select the number of records to be merged from the Records to Be Merged group.

   Select from the When Merging Records group how blank lines will be handled:

   - <u>D</u>on't Print Blank Lines When Data Fields are Empty.
   - <u>P</u>rint Blank Lines When Data Fields Are Empty.

9. Choose <u>M</u>erge.

The envelope is now a new document—separate and distinct from the main document. You should save the envelope main document for later use.

You might ask why steps 5–7 were necessary; that is, why doesn't Word assume that you want to attach the envelope main document to the same data source that's attached to the form letter? Actually, the reason is that your envelope main document rarely changes— unless you change envelope sizes. By contrast, you are likely to generate a variety of form letters, which are saved under different document names. By forcing you to create a "stand-alone" envelope, Word relieves you from having to go through the many steps just described for each envelope you create.

Editing the Main Document   After the data source is attached to the main document, you can edit the document by using normal typing and formatting features. Whether you start with an existing document containing body copy or a new blank document, you must enter MERGEFIELD codes to tell Word where to insert specific data from the data source. Once the data source is attached, you can use the Insert Merge Field button in the Mail Merge toolbar to insert these codes.

To insert merge fields in the main document, follow these steps:

1. Place the insertion point where you want the first merged data to appear.

2. Click the Insert Merge Field button from the Mail Merge toolbar that appears under the Formatting toolbar. This displays a list of the fields in your data source.

3. Select the field name from the Print Merge Fields list.

4. Choose OK or press Enter.

5. Move the insertion point to the next location where you want to insert data.

> **TIP** Make sure to leave a space before or after the merge field just as you would leave a space before or after a word you type.

6. Continue inserting all the merge fields necessary for the form letter. Don't forget, however, to insert needed space—for example, spaces between merge fields for city, state, and ZIP code.

To add ordinary word fields, such as Date, to main documents, you can choose Insert, Field. You can insert certain Word fields that are directly related to the mail merge—such as Ask, Fill-In, and Next Record—by clicking the Insert Word Field button and selecting the field from the drop-down list. You learn how to do this later in the chapter.

You can delete unwanted fields from main documents in the same way you delete text in any other Word document.

 You can get a sneak preview of the merged document by clicking the View Merged Data button in the Mail Merge toolbar. With View Merged Data off, your completed main document resembles the document at the top in Figure 17.31. After you click the View Merged Data button, the document appears as shown at the bottom of that figure.

By default, the main document displays the data from the first record in the data source. You can use the VCR-type control icons in the Mail Merge toolbar to browse through the entire merged document. The controls move backward and forward through records in the data source in the same way VCR controls move through a videotape.

The top screen in Figure 17.30 shows documents with the Field Codes option cleared (found in the View tab of the Options dialog box). When field codes are displayed, the document looks like that in Figure 17.31.

FIG. 17.30
When the document displays the field names (top), click the View Merged Data button to display the data merged from the data source (bottom).

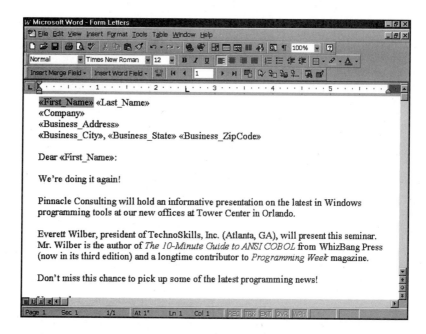

Part

IV

Ch

17

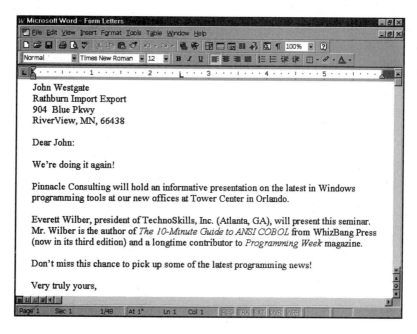

FIG. 17.31

When the Field Codes option is turned on, the document shows the MERGEFIELD field codes.

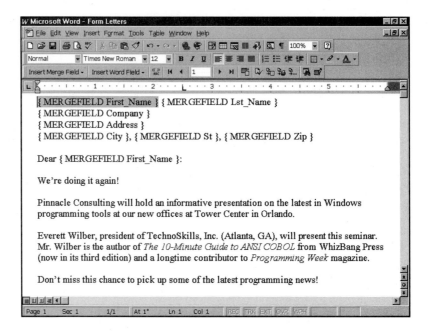

Selecting Specific Records to Merge   Word enables you to select the records you want to merge. You can build *rules* that limit which data is merged. The rules form English statements specifying the data you want to merge. You can use this feature if you are doing a targeted mailing to a particular area (selected by ZIP code). For example, the statement "ZIP code is equal to 49217" results in Word merging only those records with that ZIP code.

To select specific records for merging, follow these steps:

1. Activate the main document.

2. Click the Merge dialog box button from the Mail Merge toolbar or choose Tools, Mail Merge. Click the Merge button to display the Merge dialog box (refer to Figure 17.19).

3. Click the Query Options button in the Merge dialog box to display the Query Options list, shown in Figure 17.32.

4. Select the first field you want to limit in the Field drop-down list.

5. The phrase Equal to appears in the Comparison list. If you want something other than an exact match, select the type of comparison (such as Less than or Greater than) you want to make.

FIG. 17.32

You can use the Query Options dialog box to control the selection of records.

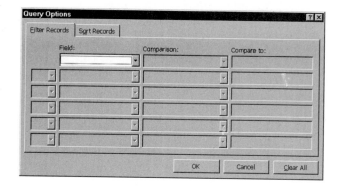

6. Type the numeric value or text you want compared to the field in the Compare To text box. Figure 17.33 shows an example that merges only those records in which the last name begins with a *P* or a letter following *P* in the alphabet.

FIG. 17.33

To select an alphabetic or numeric range of records, enter the field name, comparison phrase, and comparison value. This rule merges records with last names beginning with P through Z.

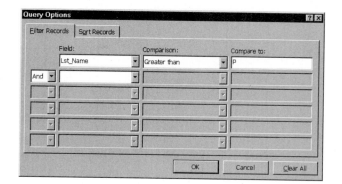

7. After you make an entry in the Compare To box, the word And appears in the leftmost drop-down list in the next row. Select the And or Or option in this box to add another selection rule. If you want to merge only those records that meet both conditions, select And. To merge all records that meet either condition, select Or.

8. To add another rule, repeat steps 4–7.

9. To sort the resulting merged records on any of the selected fields, select the Sort Records tab (see Figure 17.34). You can sort by up to three key fields. Select (or enter) the name of the primary sort field in the Sort By drop-down list box. Enter secondary or tertiary keys, if used, in the Then By and Then By boxes, respectively. You can select the sort order with the option buttons to the right of the list boxes.

Part

IV

Ch

17

FIG. 17.34

Select the Sort Records tab to sort records in a merged document.

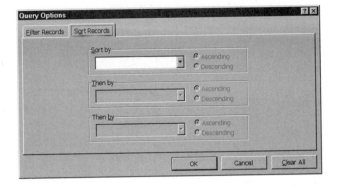

10. Complete the merge by choosing OK. When the merge is complete, click Cancel from the Mail Merge Helper.

If you make a mistake, you can revise any entry or selection at any time. To start over again, click the Clear All button in the Filter Records tab of the Query Options dialog box.

When you build rules, a complete English statement is built that specifies how data from the data source is selected for merging. Figure 17.35, for example, illustrates a rule that would be useful for mailing to a list of contributors. If the data source contains fields for amount pledged (Pledged) and amount contributed (Paid), this rule selects everyone who pledged $200 or more and paid less than $50.

FIG. 17.35

A completed dialog box selects donors who have yet to fulfill their pledges.

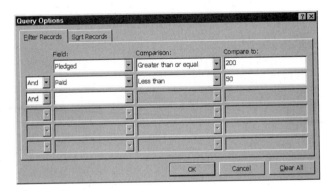

Here are some tips for building rules:

■ Text is compared in the same way as numbers. For example, B is less than C.

■ Select ranges using And. A numeric range, for example, may be ZIP is Greater than 95400 and ZIP is Less than 95600.

- A text range may be as follows: `State is Greater than or Equal to CA` and `State is Less than or Equal to NY`.
- Select individual names or numbers with Or. A numeric selection, for example, may be as follows: `ZIP is Equal to 95409` or `ZIP is Equal to 95412`.
- A text selection may be as follows: `Title is Equal to President` or `Title is Equal to Manager`.

 To personally select which records merge, create an extra field (column) with a field name such as **Selection** in your data document. In that column, enter **1** in the row of each record you want to merge. Use the Record Selection dialog box to specify that you want only records with 1 in the Selection field to merge.

Part
IV

Ch
17

Changing the Data Source Your Main Document Is Attached to   You may have one form letter that you use with different mailing lists. In that case, you will want to attach your main document to other data sources. You can use the same procedure that you do for attaching the original data source.

To attach a main document to a different data source, follow these steps:

1. Choose Tools, Mail Merge.
2. Click the Get Data button.
3. Click Open Data Source or Use Address Book if the data source is to be an existing file.

   Choose Create Data Source or Use Address Book to create a new data source.
4. Select or create the data source file, as appropriate.

> **CAUTION**
>
> Quite often, field headers in the new data source do not match the field codes in the main document. You should always check for errors immediately after you attach a main document to a new data source.

Using One Main Document with Different Data Sources and Field Names   If you use a database program to maintain your mailing lists, you will appreciate this section. Your database program may generate data sources that do not have a *header record*, the top row that contains field names. Instead of opening what may be a huge data source and adding a top row of field names, you can attach a header file. This technique also enables you to use many data sources without having to change the MERGEFIELD in a main document. A *header file* contains a top row of field names, which are used with the data source. The header file can contain a single row of names or be an existing data source with the correct field names. The header file must have the same number of field names as there are fields in the data source.

To create a separate header file, follow these steps:

1. Be sure that the main document is the active document.

2. Choose Tools, Mail Merge.

3. Click the Get Data button.

4. Select Header Options. Word displays the Header Options dialog box.

5. Click Create. Word displays the Create Header Source dialog box (see Figure 17.36).

6. Edit the list of field names as you did earlier in the chapter when you created a data source. To remove the selected field name, click Remove Field Name. To add a field name, enter it in the Field Name box and click Add Field Name. When you are satisfied with your list, choose OK. The Save Data Source dialog box appears.

FIG. 17.36

The Create Header Source dialog box works much like the Create Data Source dialog box.

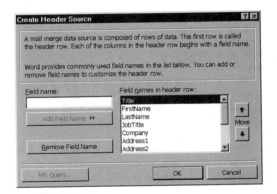

7. Enter a file name for the header source in the File Name box in the Save Data Source dialog box; then choose OK.

Word displays the Mail Merge Helper dialog box, updated for the new header source. The header source you created is attached immediately to the active main document. You still must attach a data source to the main document. The data source itself should not contain a header record because Word will merge the row of names as it would a data record.

N O T E To print with separate header and data sources, be sure that you attach the header and data sources in the Mail Merge Helper dialog box before you choose the Merge button. ▪

Putting Custom Entries in Mail Merge Documents

Having worked through all the basics of merging documents, you are now ready for a few of the most powerful features of Word. One of these features eliminates blank lines in mail-merge addresses and labels—a feature that gives your labels a more professional appearance. You also learn how to use a main document with different data sources without having to re-create field names. The secret is to use a header file that shows the field names. Another important power feature is making merge documents pause and ask for a customized entry.

Inserting Word Fields in a Main Document   You can insert certain Word fields from the Mail Merge toolbar. Suppose that you want Word to insert one of two different personalized messages in your form letter, depending on whether a condition was satisfied.

To insert an IF field in a main document, follow these steps:

| Insert Word Field ▾ |

1. Click the Insert Word Field button to display a subset of Word fields.
2. Select If…Then…Else. Word displays the dialog box shown in Figure 17.37. Enter your comparison criteria and the two conditional texts you want in the letter; then choose OK.

   If you then display field codes in the document (by choosing Tools, Options and clicking Field Codes), the IF field will look something like the one in Figure 17.38.

Requesting User Input During a Mail Merge   Word can automate and personalize your written communication at the same time, but for truly personal form letters, you can put FILLIN fields in form letters so that you can type custom phrases into each mail-merge letter.

FIG. 17.37

Using the Insert Word Field button to insert an IF field displays a helpful dialog box.

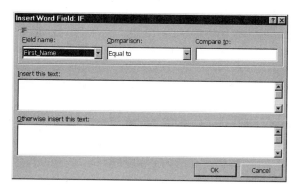

Part

IV

Ch

17

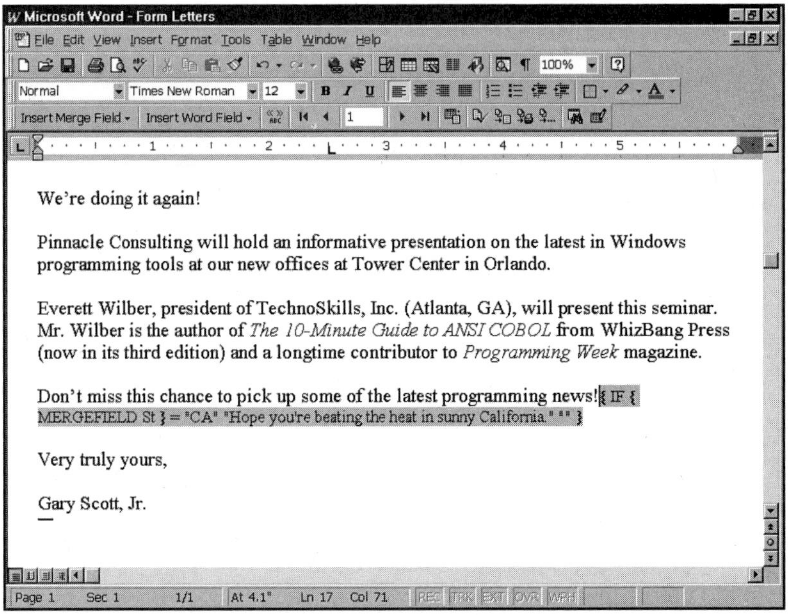
Microsoft Word - Form Letters
We're doing it again!
Pinnacle Consulting will hold an informative presentation on the latest in Windows programming tools at our new offices at Tower Center in Orlando.
Everett Wilber, president of TechnoSkills, Inc. (Atlanta, GA), will present this seminar. Mr. Wilber is the author of The 10-Minute Guide to ANSI COBOL from WhizBang Press (now in its third edition) and a longtime contributor to Programming Week magazine.
Don't miss this chance to pick up some of the latest programming news! { IF { MERGEFIELD St } = "CA" "Hope you're beating the heat in sunny California." "" }
Very truly yours,
Gary Scott, Jr.

FIG. 17.38
The IF field shown in this letter will add a personal touch to recipients with a California address.

FILLIN is a Word field (as opposed to a merge field) that can automate document creation. You learn about fields in depth in Chapter 22, "Automating with Field Codes." The following example illustrates how Word fields can be useful in form letters.

Figure 17.39 shows a main document with a FILLIN field in the second paragraph of the body text. During the merge operation, this field displays a dialog box that prompts the user to enter a personalized message to the recipient. The \d switch and the text that follows tell Word to display `Go Blue against the Wildcats in the Silicon Bowl!` as a default response.

To enter the FILLIN field in your document, insert or type the following field code where you want the results to appear:

```
{fillin \d "Go Blue against the Wildcats in the Silicon Bowl!" }
```

Naturally, you can type the FILLIN field code in the document (remember to press Ctrl+F9 to create the field characters {}), or you can insert it by choosing Insert, Field.

To personalize the letter, you need to know to whom you are sending it. To display in the fill-in dialog box the name of the person being addressed, type a prompt in quotes; then in the quotes, use the Insert Merge Field button to insert a MERGEFIELD of the person's name. The field should look like the following:

FIG. 17.39

Use the FILLIN field when you want to prompt the user to type information in merged letters.

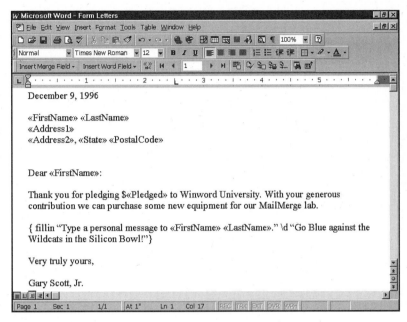

```
{fillin  "Type a personal message to
➥{mergefield Firstname}   {mergefield Lastname}"
➥\d  "Go Blue against the Wildcats in the Silicon Bowl!" }
```

Notice that the MERGEFIELD code is inside the quotes that enclose the prompt.

▶ **See** "Understanding the Basics of Fields," **p. 694**

Mastering Special Features

CHAPTER 18

Creating and Editing Tables

Word 97 has a very powerful table feature that provides an excellent way of working with columns or tabular data and for simplifying many other tasks. You can use tables to show lists of data, personnel rosters, financial information, scripts, and procedural steps. Tables can even include pasted illustrations that explain steps in a list, display side-by-side text and graphics, or present sideheads beside text in a document.

In many cases, tables provide an easier and more flexible solution to problems that you might have solved in the past by using tabs. The commands available for working with tables simplify the job of arranging and formatting tables of information. ■

Understanding tables

A table is a grid of tables and rows, much like a spreadsheet in Microsoft Excel.

Creating tables

Tables can be created anywhere in a document and can span multiple pages. Tables can be sized and positioned on a page and can have captions and headings.

Editing tables

You can edit the contents of any cell, move or copy cells, insert cells, rows, and columns, and adjust row heights and column widths.

Understanding Tables

If you have worked with a spreadsheet application such as Microsoft Excel or Lotus 1-2-3, you may find working with tables similar to working with a spreadsheet. A *table* is simply a grid of columns and rows. The intersection of a column and a row is a rectangular or square box called a *cell*. Each cell is independent and can be sized or formatted. Figure 18.1 shows an example of a table of data that was created and formatted by using the table feature.

FIG. 18.1
Producing tables with a professional look is simple in Word.

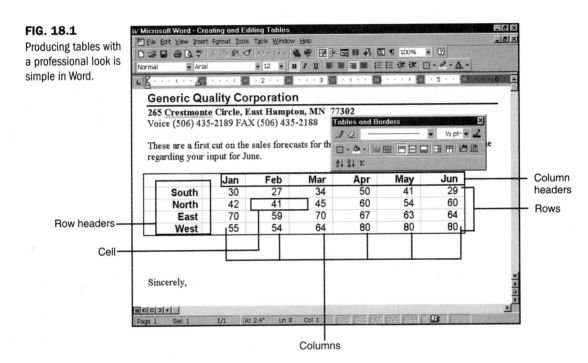

You can insert text, numbers, pictures, or formulas into a cell. If you enter text in a cell, the text wraps to the next line according to the width of the cell. If you adjust the width of the cell or column, the text adjusts to the new width. You can enter or edit text in any cell of the table. A table enables you to present text in columns and align paragraphs or graphics. Figure 18.2 shows text in a table.

Creating Tables

You can insert a table anywhere in a document. A table can span more than one page, and you can frame a table, resize it, and position it on the page. You can attach a caption to a table and designate headings for the table so that if the table splits between pages, Word automatically repeats the headings at the top of the table.

FIG. 18.2
You can use tables to create headings to the left of the body text in your documents.

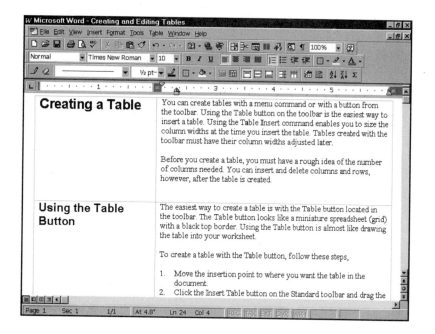

You can create tables by choosing Table, Insert Table or Draw Table from the pull-down menus, or you can click the Insert Table button on the Standard toolbar. Often, the Insert Table button is the easiest way to create a table because it takes fewer keystrokes. When you click the Insert Table button, Word sets the width of the columns automatically, so you might have to adjust the widths later. When you use the menu command, you can determine the width of the columns when you insert the table.

If the information that you want to include in a table already appears in your document as text, you can convert the text to a table.

▶ **See** "Converting Text to a Table," **p. 645**

TIP Before you create a table, it's helpful to have a general idea of the number of columns that you need. You can insert and delete columns and rows, however, after you create the table.

Drawing a Table

The Table, Draw Table command is used to draw a table anywhere within a document. Draw the outer border of the table first. Then draw lines for the cells and columns wherever you want them to be. This makes creating complex tables into a simple task.

Part
V

Ch
18

To draw a table, follow these steps:

1. Position the cursor on the line in your document where you want to insert the table.

2. Choose Table, Draw Table. The Tables and Borders dialog box appears, as shown in Figure 18.3.

   Notice that the pointer changes to a pencil.

FIG. 18.3
Drawing complex tables is a simple task using the Table, Draw Table command.

3. Drag the outline of the table until it is the size you want it to be. You can either drag the pointer downward to the left or right, or upward to the left or right.

4. Position the pointer within the table where you want to draw your first row or column line.

5. Drag the dotted line until it stretches where you want it to go. If the line does not stretch far enough, it will not be drawn.

   For a description on how to use the functions shown in the Table and Borders dialog box, see "Using the Table Toolbar" later in this chapter.

6. When you have finished creating your table, close the Tables and Borders dialog box.

Creating a Table with the Table Wizard

The Table Wizard easily formats tables of any size. The Table Wizard guides you through the table-creation process by displaying a series of boxes that graphically present the most common choices made for preformatted tables. The Table Wizard also makes it easy to handle special situations, such as repeating column headings at the top of pages when a table is longer than a single page. The Table Wizard also formats the headings and table content, and finishes by going directly into AutoFormat, which guides you through the table-formatting process.

Inserting a Table with a Command

Choose Table, Insert Table if you want to specify the width of the columns in the table at the same time you insert the table.

To insert a table in a document, follow these steps:

1. Position the insertion point where you want the top-left corner of the table.

2. Choose Table, Insert Table. The Insert Table dialog box appears, as shown in Figure 18.4.

FIG. 18.4
You can insert a table
by using the Insert
Table dialog box.

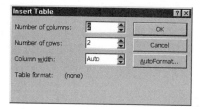

3. Select or type the number of columns that you want in the Number of Columns text box.

4. If you know how many rows you need, select or type the number of rows in the Number of Rows text box.

 TIP If you are unsure how many columns or rows you need, don't worry. You easily can add rows and columns to the end of a table or in the middle of the table.

5. If you know how wide you want all columns, adjust the Column Width box.

   You easily can change column widths if you are unsure of the column width or if you later want to adjust the table.

6. Click the Wizard button to be guided through the creation of a table.

7. Click the AutoFormat button to apply predefined formats to the table when Word creates it.

8. Click OK.

Word inserts the table in your document. The table may be visible or invisible depending on whether you have turned on table gridlines (see "Displaying or Hiding Gridlines and End Marks" later in this chapter). The insertion point appears in the first cell.

Using the Insert Table Button

 The easiest way to create a table is by using the Insert Table button on the Standard toolbar. Using the Insert Table button is almost like drawing the table into your document.

To create a table using the Insert Table button, follow these steps:

1. Move the insertion point to where you want to insert the table in the document.

2. Click the Insert Table button on the Standard toolbar and drag the mouse pointer within the grid down, to the right, or down and to the right.

   When you click the button, a grid of rows and columns that looks like a miniature table appears. As long as you continue to hold down the mouse button, you can move the pointer within the grid to select the size of the table that you want to insert. If you move the pointer beyond the right or lower borders, the grid expands. Figure 18.5 shows the Insert Table button expanded and a table size selected.

3. Release the mouse button when the selected grid is the size you want your table to be.

FIG. 18.5

The Insert Table button enables you to draw your table the size that you want.

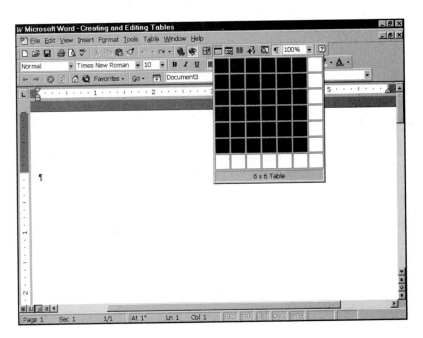

If you have already begun the selection process with the Insert Table button and then decide that you do not want to insert a table, continue to hold down the mouse button and drag the pointer until it is outside the grid and to the left; then release the button. You also can drag up until the pointer is over the button and then release the button.

N O T E   You can store tables, like text, as an AutoText entry. If you use the same type of table repeatedly, you can save considerable time by storing the table as an AutoText entry, then typing the AutoText name in the document where you want it inserted.

To store a table as an AutoText entry, select the entire table and choose Insert, AutoText. Type a name for the entry in the Please Name Your AutoText Entry box, and click OK. To later insert the AutoText entry, type the AutoText Entry name and press F3. ▪

▶ **See** "Editing a Document," **p. 131**

Using the Tables and Borders Toolbar

The Tables and Borders toolbar provides a fast way to create a new table or edit an existing one. Select from a variety of line styles, line weights, border colors, and shading. You also can merge and split cells, align text within a cell or cells, distribute rows and columns evenly, change text rotation within a cell or cells, sort in ascending or descending order, and calculate and display the sum of the values in table cells above or to the left of the cell containing the insertion point.

 Choose the Tables and Borders button. The Tables and Borders toolbar appears (see Figure 18.6).

FIG. 18.6
Use the Tables and Borders toolbar to create and edit tables.

Table 18.1 shows the Tables and Borders toolbar functions.

Table 18.1   Tables and Borders Toolbar Functions

Icon	Function
	Selects the Draw Table function for freehand table creation.
	Selects an eraser used to erase borders. Simply drag the eraser over the line you want to erase.
	Selects the line style of border.
	Selects the line weight of border.
	Selects the border color from a color palette.
	Selects the shading from a palette.

continues

Table 18.1 continued

Icon	Function
	Merges two or more cells.
	Splits a cell.
	Aligns text along the top of the selected cell or cells.
	Aligns text in the center of the selected cell or cells.
	Aligns text along the bottom of the selected cell or cells.
	Distributes selected rows evenly (makes them the same height).
	Distributes selected columns evenly (makes them the same width).
	Selects a predefined table format.
	Changes the text direction.
	Sorts in ascending order.
	Sorts in descending order.
	Calculates and displays the sum of the values in table cells above or to the left of the cell containing the insertion point.

Displaying or Hiding Gridlines and End Marks

 TIP You can add a custom button that toggles gridlines on or off to any toolbar. See Chapter 38, "Customizing the Toolbar, Menus, and Shortcut Keys," to learn about custom buttons.

Table gridlines can show you the outline of your cells and table. Such outlines can make working in tables easier. The end-of-cell mark indicates where the contents of a cell end, and the end-of-row mark indicates the end of the row. Figure 18.7 shows a table in which the gridlines and end marks are turned off. Figure 18.8 shows the same table with the gridlines and end marks turned on. As you can see, these lines and marks make it easier to read a table. The gridlines do not print.

FIG. 18.7
In this table, gridlines and end marks are turned off.

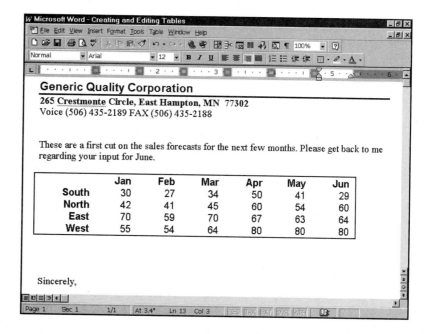

FIG. 18.8
This table is easier to read and edit because gridlines are turned on.

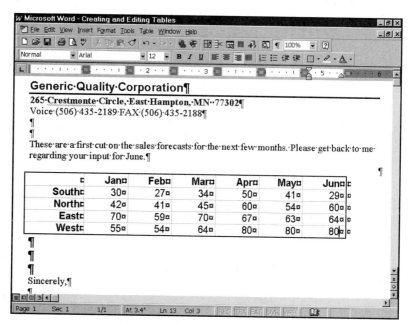

If you want gridlines on or off, choose <u>T</u>able, Show Grid<u>l</u>ines. This command toggles gridlines on or off. The icon to the left of the menu command is selected if gridlines are turned on and the command changes to Hide Grid<u>l</u>ines. To turn end marks on or off quickly, press Shift+Ctrl+8, or click the Show/Hide ¶ button in the Standard toolbar.

Typing and Moving in a Table

When you create a new table, the insertion point flashes in the first cell—the cell at the upper-left corner of the table. To insert text or numbers in the cell, just start typing.

As you enter text into a cell, characters will automatically wrap to the next line in the cell as needed. In a Word table, the entire row of cells expands downward to accommodate the text. The same thing happens if you press Enter in a cell. The insertion point moves to the next line down, and the row becomes taller. Each cell acts like a miniature word processing page.

To move forward through the cells in the table, press Tab. Press Shift+Tab to move backward through the cells. When you press Tab to move to a cell, you select any text in the cell. To move with the mouse, click the cell at the point where you want the insertion point to appear.

If you reach the table's last (lower-right) cell and press Tab, you create a new row of cells at the end of the table and move the insertion point into the first cell of that row. To leave the table, you must press an arrow key or use the mouse to move the insertion point outside the table.

Arrow keys also help you move around in a table. Table 18.2 summarizes these keyboard movements and includes several other handy shortcuts to help you move around in a table.

Table 18.2 Shortcut Keys Used to Move in a Table

Key(s)	Function
Tab	Moves the insertion point right one cell; inserts a new row when pressed in the bottom-right cell.
Shift+Tab	Moves the insertion point left one cell.
Arrow key	Moves the insertion point character by character through a cell and into the next cell when the insertion point reaches the end of the current cell.

Key(s)	Function
Alt+Home	Moves the insertion point to the first cell in the row.
Alt+End	Moves the insertion point to the last cell in the row.
Alt+Page Up	Moves the insertion point to the top cell in the column.
Alt+Page Down	Moves the insertion point to the bottom cell in the column.

Using Indents and Tabs in a Cell

Just like regular text paragraphs, cells can contain indents. You can format these indents using the same techniques that you use to format a paragraph. Use the ruler or choose Format, Paragraph.

To change the indent or first-line indent within a cell using Format, Paragraph, follow these steps:

1. Select the cell.

2. Choose Format, Paragraph.

3. Set indents in the Paragraph dialog box's Indentation group. Then choose OK.

To change the indent or first-line indent within a cell using the ruler, follow these steps:

1. Select the cell.

2. Click the right mouse button in the selected cell and select Paragraph.

3. Drag the indent and first-line indent markers to the desired position of the new indentation.

▶ **See** "Setting Indents," **p. 340**

Pressing Tab moves you from one cell to the next in a table. Pressing Shift+Tab moves you to the previous cell. You also can set tabs within a cell. Select the cells in which you want tabs, and set the tab stops in the usual way—using the ruler or choosing Format, Tabs. To move the insertion point to the tab stop within the cell, however, press Ctrl+Tab rather than just Tab.

▶ **See** "Setting Tabs," **p. 334**

Part

V

Ch

18

Attaching Captions to Tables

You can add a caption to a table to identify it, to enable you to cross-reference the table, or to create a list of tables in your document. When you insert a caption, Word uses the SEQ field code to number the table. If you insert a new table before or after an existing table, Word automatically updates the numbering for all the tables.

▶ **See** "Automating with Field Codes," **p. 693**

To attach a caption to a table, follow these steps:

1. Select the entire table by moving the insertion point anywhere in the table and choosing Table, Select Table.

2. Display the Caption dialog box by choosing Insert, Caption (see Figure 18.9).

FIG. 18.9

You can attach a caption to a table in the Caption dialog box.

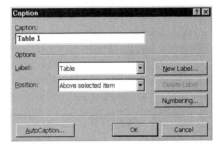

3. Select Table in the Label list if it isn't already selected.

4. Type text after the caption label in the Caption text box, if you want.

5. Select the position for the label in the Position list.

6. Choose OK.

A caption for the table then appears at the position that you specified (see Figure 18.10). If Word displays the SEQ field code rather than the table number, choose Tools, Options, select the View tab, and clear the Field Codes option. Then choose OK.

▶ **See** "Adding Cross-References and Captions," **p. 1025**

FIG. 18.10
A caption is shown above the table.

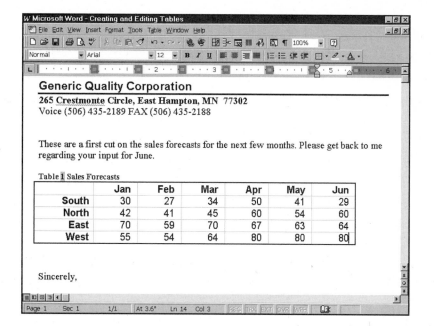

Editing Tables

After you create and fill your table, you probably will have to make changes to the table. You might need to move or copy cells, or insert new cells, rows, or columns to make room for additional text or graphics. Often you must adjust row heights and column widths. In the following sections, you learn how to perform all these tasks.

You can edit the contents within a cell using the same techniques that you use to edit text or graphics in a document. You can delete characters using the Backspace and Delete keys, and move around in the text using the mouse or the arrow keys. To edit the cells, rows, and columns in a table, you use different techniques, which the following sections describe.

By using the shortcut menus, you can quickly access many of the commands that you learn about in the following sections. To use the shortcut menus, point to a cell or selection that you have made in a table, and click the right mouse button. A list of commands that you can use to edit or format the selection appears. Use the mouse to select the appropriate command.

Selecting and Editing Cells

Before you use the table editing commands, you must select the correct cells, rows, or columns for whatever changes you are making to the table. You have two ways to select the contents of a table:

■ By character, for which you use Word's usual character-selection techniques

■ By cell, for which Word offers special techniques

When you select the entire cell (or cells), the entire cell appears darkened (see Figure 18.11). Word enables you to select an entire row, an entire column, or the entire table easily.

FIG. 18.11

A cell appears darkened when you select it.

	Jan	Feb	Mar	Apr	May	Jun
South	30	27	34	50	41	29
North	42	41	45	60	54	60
East	70	59	70	67	63	64
West	55	54	64	80	80	80

Selecting by Menu   You can select rows, columns, or the entire table by using commands from the menu.

To select cells, rows, or columns, follow these steps:

1. Move the insertion point into the cell that contains the row or column you want to select. To select a table, you can select any cell in that table.

2. Choose Table. Then choose Select Row, Select Column, or Select Table.

Selecting Cells with the Mouse   You also can use a mouse to select a cell's contents. Just drag across characters or double-click words in the usual way.

As you can do with the keyboard, you can use the mouse to extend the selection beyond the cell: as soon as the selection reaches the border of a cell, you begin selecting entire cells rather than characters. In addition, you can use special selection bars with the mouse. When you move the I-beam into a selection bar, the pointer changes to an arrow. You can use the mouse to select a cell, row, or column, depending on where you click the mouse pointer.

Table 18.3 summarizes the mouse selection techniques.

Table 18.3   Using the Mouse to Select Items in a Table

Item to Select	Mouse Action
Characters	Drag across characters.
Cell	Click the cell selection area in the left inside edge of the cell.
Group of cells	Select the first cell or characters; then drag to the last cell or Shift+click the last cell.
Horizontal row	Click the selection area to the left of the table; drag down for multiple rows.
Vertical column	Click the top line of the column; drag to either side for multiple columns. (When positioned correctly, the pointer appears as a solid black down arrow.)
Table	Click the selection area to the left of the top row and drag down to select all rows or Shift+click to the left of the last row.

TROUBLESHOOTING

When I try to drag and drop cells I have selected, it doesn't work. The mouse pointer doesn't change to an arrow when I point to the selected cells. When the drag-and-drop feature is turned off, the mouse pointer does not change to an arrow when you point to a selection, and you cannot drag the selection to a new location. To turn on drag and drop, choose Tools, Options; select the Edit tab; select the Drag-and-Drop text editing option, and then click OK.

Selecting Cells with the Keyboard   Word provides several other keyboard techniques for selecting cells and groups of cells. Table 18.4 lists these methods.

Table 18.4   Using Shortcut Keys to Select Cells

Key(s)	Selects
Tab	The next cell
Shift+Tab	The previous cell
Shift+arrow key	Character by character in the current cell and then the entire adjacent cell
F8+up or down arrow	The current cell and the cell above or below (press Esc to end the selection)
F8+left or right arrow	Text in the current cell (character by character) and then all adjacent cells (press Esc to end the selection)
Alt+5 (on the numeric keypad)	An entire table

When you select with an arrow key, you first select each character in the cell. As soon as you go beyond the border of the cell, however, you begin selecting entire cells. If you change arrow directions, you select groups of adjacent cells. If you press Shift+right arrow or F8+right arrow to select three adjacent cells in a row and then press the down-arrow key once, for example, you extend the selection to include the entire contents of the three cells below the original three.

Moving and Copying Cells

Unless you do everything perfectly the first time, you might have to reorganize data in your tables. Word gives you all the flexibility of moving and copying in a table that you have with text.

Using the Mouse to Drag and Drop Cells, Rows, and Columns   The mouse shortcuts that work with text in body copy also work on cell contents, cells, or an entire table.

To move or copy the characters in a cell or one or more cells and their cellular structure, follow these steps:

1. Select the characters, cells, rows, or columns you want to move or copy.

2. Move the mouse pointer over the selected characters until it changes from an I-beam to an arrow pointed upward and to the left, as shown in Figure 18.12. (The pointer might remain an arrow if you don't move it from the selected area.)

FIG. 18.12
Use the pointer to drag cells, rows, or columns.

	Jan	Feb	Mar	Apr	May	Jun
South	30	27	34	50	41	29
North	42	41	45	60	54	60
East	70	59	70	67	63	64
West	55	54	64	80	80	80

3. To move, hold down the left mouse button. To copy, hold down Ctrl and then the left mouse button. Notice the message in the status bar: Move to where? or Copy to where?

4. Position the grayed insertion point at the location where you want the moved or copied characters or cells to appear. Position the pointer over the top-left cell at the place where you want a range of cells to appear. The insertion point appears gray and displays a gray box at its bottom end.

5. Release the mouse button.

If you include the end-of-cell mark in your selection, the formatting for your selected cell or cells is moved or copied to the destination, along with the cell contents.

Using Cut, Copy, and Paste   Choosing Edit and then Cut, Copy, or Paste works much the same way in a table as with text outside a table. These commands enable you to move or copy cells within a table or copy a table to another location. You can cut and copy a single cell, multiple cells, or an entire table.

If you select only the text, number, or picture within a cell, you copy or cut only what you have selected, just as you do in a document's body copy. But if you select the entire cell or multiple cells, you copy the cell boundaries as well.

If you select an entire cell, the Copy command copies the entire cell to the Clipboard. The Cut command moves the entire contents of the cell to the Clipboard. The cell's boundaries remain in the table. When you paste cells from the Clipboard, the cell containing the insertion point receives the first cell on the Clipboard. The contents of the cells on the Clipboard replace the table's original cells, as shown in Figures 18.13 and 18.14.

FIG. 18.13
You can copy selected cells.

	Jan	Feb	Mar	Apr	
South	30	27	34	50	
North	42	41	45	60	
East	70	59	70	67	
West	55	54	64	80	

FIG. 18.14
The same cells are pasted into a blank area.

	Jan	Feb	Mar	Apr	Apr
South	30	27	34	50	50
North	42	41	45	60	60
East	70	59	70	67	67
West	55	54	64	80	80

When you copy cells, the Paste command becomes Paste Cells, and the command pastes the cells as cells in a table. If you copy an entire row or column, the command becomes Paste Rows or Paste Columns, respectively. When you paste cells into an area not formatted as a table, they arrive as a table. When you paste a group of cells into an existing table, the table expands, if necessary, to accommodate the new cells.

You also can paste text from outside a table into a single cell in a table. Just copy or cut the text, move the insertion point inside a cell, and choose Edit, Paste.

To move or copy cells, follow these steps:

1. Select the cells, rows, or columns that you want to move or copy.

2. To move the cells, choose Edit, Cut, press Ctrl+X, or click the Cut button on the Standard toolbar.

   To copy the cells, choose Edit, Copy, press Ctrl+C, or click the Standard toolbar's Copy button.

3. Select an area in the table to which you're moving the cells that match the shape and size of the area that you selected in Step 1.

TIP Word warns you if the shape and size of the copied cells do not match the shape and size of the cells into which you're pasting.

4. Choose Edit, Paste Cells, press Ctrl+V, or click the Paste button on the Standard toolbar.

Using the Outliner   The Word Outline view provides another option for reorganizing rows, columns, and cells. Switching to Outline view enables you to move an entire row of selected cells by dragging the selection to the location where you want the data to appear.

To move a row of cells using Outline view, follow these steps:

1. Choose View, Outline. A small box, called a *body text symbol*, appears to the left of each row (see Figure 18.15).

FIG. 18.15
To move a row, drag its body text symbol up or down.

This is the body text symbol

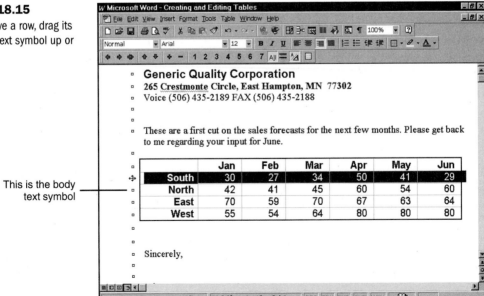

2. Select the row by clicking the body text symbol.

3. Select the up or down arrows in the outline bar or drag the body text symbol up or down to move the selected row to the desired location.

NOTE A shortcut for moving table rows up or down is to select the entire row and then press Shift+Alt+up or down arrow. You do not have to be in Outline view for this shortcut to work, nor does the document need an outline. ■

Changing the Column Width

When Word first creates a table, the columns are sized equally to fill the area between the right and left margins. You can change column or cell widths in three ways:

■ Drag the right cell border of the column in the table

■ Drag the column marker on the ruler

■ Choose Table, Cell Height and Width

Dragging Cell Borders or Using the Ruler   To change the width of a column with the mouse, position the pointer on the column's right border. The pointer changes to a vertical double bar when you position it properly. (The pointer changes even if the gridlines are turned off.) Figure 18.16 shows the shape of the pointer when it is positioned correctly to drag a cell border.

Drag this column marker to the desired column width and release the mouse button. If you have selected either the entire column or nothing in the column, the entire column adjusts to the new width. If you select cells within the column, only the selected cells adjust to the new width.

You can affect the other columns and the overall table width differently by pressing different keys as you drag the border. To see the width measurements of the columns displayed on the ruler, hold down the Alt key as you drag the border. Table 18.5 indicates the different ways that you can adjust the columns.

**Part
V

Ch
18**

Table 18.5   Changing Column Widths with the Mouse

Action	Result
Drag the border without holding down any keys	Resizes all columns to the right in proportion to their original width.
Drag the border while holding down Shift	Changes only the width of the column to the left; does not change the table width.

Table 18.5   Continued

Drag the border while holding down Ctrl	Adjusts all columns to the right equally; does not change the table width.
Drag the border down Ctrl+Shift	Leaves columns to the right unchanged; adjusts the table proportionally.
Double-click the border	Adjusts the column width to fit the widest content.

FIG. 18.16

Drag the border of a cell or selected column to change its width.

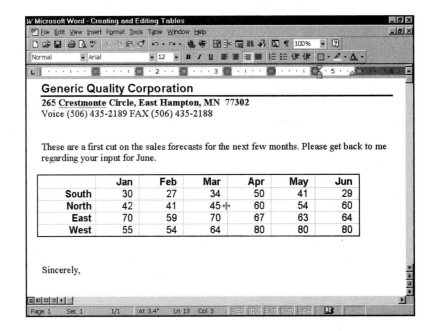

You can also use the table markers on the ruler to change column widths. Dragging the table markers has the same result as dragging the column borders, as discussed in the preceding paragraphs. If the ruler is not turned on, choose View, Ruler.

Using the Column Width Command   Choosing Table, Cell Height and Width is useful when you want to change the width of multiple columns with a single command or if you want to define the width of columns by specific amounts. The command also enables you to change the distance between columns.

T I P   To change the width of an entire column rather than just a cell in a column, be sure to select the entire column first.

To change the column width by choosing T<u>a</u>ble, Cell Height and <u>W</u>idth, follow these steps:

1. Select the columns or cells whose width you want to change.

2. Choose T<u>a</u>ble, Cell Height and <u>W</u>idth, and select the Column tab in the Cell Height and Width dialog box. The Column tab is displayed (see Figure 18.17).

FIG. 18.17
You can set the width of any number of columns at one time in the Cell Height and Width dialog box.

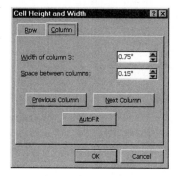

3. Select or type a number in the <u>W</u>idth of Column X text box, where X is the column number.

4. If you want to adjust other columns, click the <u>P</u>revious Column or <u>N</u>ext Column buttons to keep the dialog box open, and move to the next column. The Width of Columns label changes to tell you which row you are formatting.

5. Choose OK.

Using the AutoFit Command   You can have Word automatically adjust the width of a column in a table to accommodate the width of the column's longest line of text. One advantage to using AutoFit to adjust the columns in a table is that you ensure the columns are as wide as (but no wider than) they have to be to accommodate the table's data. This feature helps you optimize the use of space on a page.

To AutoFit the column width, follow these steps:

1. Select the columns that you want to AutoFit.

   If you do not select the entire column, only the selected cells are AutoFit.

2. Choose T<u>a</u>ble, Cell Height and <u>W</u>idth, and select the <u>C</u>olumn tab in the Cell Height and Width dialog box.

3. Click the <u>A</u>utoFit button.

Word then automatically adjusts the column, closes the dialog box, and returns you to the document.

Part
V

Ch
18

Changing Column Spacing

The Cell Height and Width dialog box also enables you to control the amount of space between columns. When you first create a table, the columns that you choose for the table are the same size and span the distance between page margins. Included in the column width is a default column-spacing setting of 0.15".

To change the spacing between columns, follow these steps:

1. Select the columns you want to adjust. Select a row if you want to adjust all columns in the table.
2. Choose Table, Cell Height and Width and select the Column tab.
3. Select or type a number in the Space Between Columns text box.

   The space that you set in this box is divided by the left and right margins within the cell—just as if the cell were a small page and you were entering the combined value for the left and right margins.
4. Click OK.

The column spacing affects the cell's usable column width. If a column width is 2 inches and the column spacing is set to 0.50 inch, for example, the column width available for text and graphics is 1.5 inches.

Changing Row Height and Position

When you first create a table, each row has the same height. However, the text and amount of paragraph spacing that you add changes the row's height. The Cell Height and Width dialog box enables you to specify how far Word indents a row from the left margin, the row's height, and the row's alignment between margins. You also use the vertical ruler to change the row's height.

Changing Row Height   You can change the height of the rows in a table by using either the Cell Height and Width dialog box or the vertical ruler. If you want to change several rows at the same time to the same height, using the menu command is easier.

To set row height using the Cell Height and Width dialog box, follow these steps:

1. Select the rows whose height you want to adjust.
2. Choose Table, Cell Height and Width, and select the Row tab in the Cell Height and Width dialog box (see Figure 18.18).

FIG. 18.18
You can control the
height and indenta-
tion of rows in a
table.

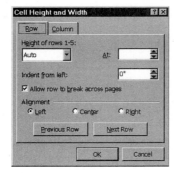

3. Select the He̲ight of Row option. The following are the available options:

Option	Result
Auto	Automatically adjusts row height to the size of the text or graphic.
At least	Sets the minimum row height. Automatically adjusts the row if text or graphics exceed this minimum.
Exactly	Sets a fixed row height. When printed or displayed on-screen, cuts off text or graphics that exceed the fixed height.

4. If you choose At Least or Exactly in step 3, type or select the row height in points in the A̲t box.

   You can also specify the height in lines (**li**) or inches (**"**) by including the abbreviation after the numeric value in the A̲t box.

5. Clear the Allow Row to B̲reak Across Pages option to keep the selected row from splitting at a page break.

   When this option is selected, if the text or graphic in a cell in the row cannot fit on the current page, Word splits the row and continues it on the next page.

6. Click the P̲revious Row or N̲ext Row button if you want to format other rows. The He̲ight of Row label changes to tell you which row you are formatting.

7. Click OK.

To set row height with the vertical ruler, follow these steps:

1. If you are not in Page Layout view, choose V̲iew, P̲age Layout.

   Every row in a table has a corresponding horizontal marker in the vertical ruler (see Figure 18.19). You can adjust the height of a row by dragging its marker.

Part
V

Ch
18

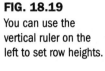

FIG. 18.19
You can use the vertical ruler on the left to set row heights.

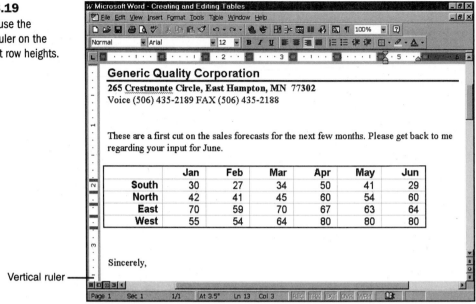

Vertical ruler

2. Drag the marker to set the height of the row that you want to change.

   If you drag the marker without pressing any keys, you set the row height to at least whatever the new measurement is. The row height automatically adjusts if the text or graphics exceed this minimum setting. If you hold down Ctrl as you drag the marker, you set the row height to exactly the new measurement. When displayed on-screen or printed, text or graphics that exceed the fixed height are cut off.

Changing Row Spacing   A little extra spacing between rows can make your table easier to read. You can adjust the amount of space between rows by choosing Format, Paragraph.

To add space between rows, follow these steps:

1. Select the rows to which you want to add spacing.

2. Choose Format, Paragraph, and select the Indents and Spacing tab in the Paragraph dialog box.

3. Type or select a spacing in the Spacing Before or the Spacing After boxes. You can use lines (**li**) or point (**pt**) measurements by typing the number and space and then the abbreviation.

4. Click OK.

Aligning and Indenting Rows With Word, you can control a table's position by changing the alignment of rows. You also can indent selected rows to align with other text in your document. Row alignment and indentation does not affect the alignment of text within the cells.

To align rows between page margins, follow these steps:

1. Select the rows that you want to align.
2. Choose Table, Cell Height and Width, and select the Row tab in the Cell Height and Width dialog box (see Figure 18.20).
3. Select Left, Center, or Right alignment.
4. Click OK.

The Cell Height and Width dialog box also enables you to indent selected rows. When you indent a row, the entire row shifts right by the amount that you specify, just as though you were indenting a paragraph.

To indent a row, follow these steps:

1. Select the row or rows that you want to indent.
2. Choose Table, Cell Height and Width, and select the Row tab in the Cell Height and Width dialog box.
3. Type or select in the Indent From Left box the amount of indentation that you want.
4. Click OK.

Adding or Deleting Cells, Rows, or Columns

Word enables you to change a table's structure by adding and deleting cells, rows, and columns. You can add or delete one or many cells, rows, or columns by using a single command. The Table menu changes its Insert and Delete commands depending on what you have selected.

If a cell is selected, the Table menu displays the Insert Cells and Delete Cells commands. If a column is selected, the Table menu displays the Insert Columns and Delete Columns commands. If a row is selected, the menu displays Insert Rows and Delete Rows.

Adding or Deleting Cells You can add or delete individual cells if you don't want to add or delete entire rows or columns. Word shifts the other cells in the table to accommodate the added or deleted cells.

To add cells to or delete cells from an existing table, follow these steps:

1. Select the cells that you want to delete or position the cursor where you want to add cells.

2. Choose Table, Insert Cells, or Table, Delete Cells. The Insert Cells or Delete Cells dialog box appears, depending on which command you chose (see Figures 18.20 and 18.21).

FIG. 18.20
The Insert Cells dialog box appears if you are inserting cells.

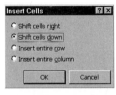

FIG. 18.21
The Delete Cells dialog box appears if you are deleting cells.

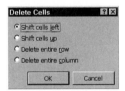

3. Choose the appropriate option button that corresponds to shifting the existing cells to the position that you want. You also have the option of inserting or deleting an entire column or row.

   Choosing Insert Cells inserts blank cells at the location of the selected cells and shifts the selected cells either down or right.

   Choosing Delete Cells deletes the selected cells and shifts adjacent cells either up or left to fill the vacancy.

4. Choose OK.

If you want to delete cell contents without deleting the actual cell, select the cell contents that you want to delete and press Delete or Backspace.

Adding or Deleting Rows and Columns   You can insert and delete columns and rows from a table using the same commands that you use to insert or delete cells. You can add columns and rows to the end of the table or insert them within the table.

To insert a new row at the end of the table, move the insertion point to the last position in the last cell and press Tab.

To insert or delete rows in the middle of an existing table, follow these steps:

1. Select the row or rows where you want to insert or delete.

   When you insert a row, Word shifts the selected row down and inserts a blank row (see Figure 18.22). When you delete a row, Word deletes the selected row and shifts up lower rows.

FIG. 18.22

An inserted row shifts the selected row down.

	Jan	Feb	Mar	Apr	May	Jun
South	30	27	34	50	41	29
North	42	41	45	60	54	60
East	70	59	70	67	63	64
West	55	54	64	80	80	80

2. Choose Table, Insert Rows, or Table, Delete Rows.

   If you are inserting a row or rows, you can click the Insert Table button on the Standard toolbar instead of choosing Table, Insert Rows.

   N O T E Word inserts the number of rows you have selected. For example, if you have selected six rows and choose Table, Insert Rows, Word inserts six rows. ■

To insert or delete one or more columns within a table, follow these steps:

1. Select one or more columns where you want to insert or delete columns.

   If you are inserting a column or columns, you can click the Insert Table button on the Standard toolbar instead of choosing Table, Insert Columns.

2. Choose Table and then Insert Columns or Delete Columns.

   When you insert columns, the selected columns shift right to make room for the inserted blank columns. When you're deleting, Word removes the selected columns and shifts columns to the right and then leftward to fill the gap.

If you insert a column, the table looks like the one shown in Figure 18.23. If you delete a column, the table looks like the one shown in Figure 18.24.

FIG. 18.23

Inserting a column shifts existing columns to the right.

	Jan	Feb	Mar	Apr		May	Jun
South	30	27	34	50		41	29
North	42	41	45	60		54	60
East	70	59	70	67		63	64
West	55	54	64	80		80	80

FIG. 18.24

Deleting a column shifts existing columns to the left to fill the gap.

	Jan	Feb	Mar	Apr	Jun
South	30	27	34	50	29
North	42	41	45	60	60
East	70	59	70	67	64
West	55	54	64	80	80

Inserting a column as the last column requires a different procedure. To insert a column to the right of a table, follow these steps:

1. Position the insertion point at the end of a table row outside the table, which places it in front of an end-of-row mark.

   If gridlines and end marks are not displayed on-screen, see the section "Displaying or Hiding Gridlines and End Marks" earlier in this chapter.

2. Choose Table, Select Column.

3. Choose Table, Insert Columns, or click the Insert Table button on the Standard toolbar.

To insert additional columns to the right of the table, choose Edit, Repeat, or press F4.

N O T E If you want to insert multiple columns quickly at the right edge of the table, select from the existing table as many columns as you want to insert. (Dragging across with the right mouse button is a quick way to select these columns.) Choose Edit, Copy. Move the insertion point to the end of the first row of the table, and choose Edit, Paste. To clear them, reselect these new columns and press Delete. ▪

TROUBLESHOOTING

When I try to insert rows or columns in a table, the Insert Rows and Insert Columns commands do not appear in the Table menu. If the Table menu doesn't display the Insert or Delete commands for rows or columns, you have selected only cells. You must select the rows or columns with which you want to work so that Word knows which Insert or Delete command to add to the menu.

▶ **See** "Moving, Copying, and Linking Text or Graphics," **p. 185**

CHAPTER 19

Modifying Tables

Tables are one of the easiest yet most productive features in Word 97. They are a feature that everyone seems to find useful. After creating your tables, however, you might find that you want to do some formatting or creative manipulation with them. This chapter explains how. ■

Merge and split cells

Merge cells to allow text or a figure to span across multiple cells. Cells that have been merged can also be split to return them to their original condition.

Format tables

Text within cells can be edited using the same features for editing body text. In addition, you can add borders and shading to selected cells or to the entire table.

Number rows and columns

Add numbering across rows, down columns, or just to the first column in a table.

Split a table into two tables

Splitting a table allows you to insert text or a heading between rows in a table.

Convert a table to text, or text to a table

A table can be converted to text with cell contents separated by commas, tabs, or a single character. Cell contents can also be converted into one or more paragraphs. Word also makes it easy to convert text into a table.

Merging and Splitting Cells and Creating Table Headings

Sometimes, you want text or a figure to span the width of multiple cells. A *heading* is an example of text that you might want to stretch across several columns. Word enables you to merge multiple cells in a row into a single cell. Merging cells converts their contents to paragraphs within a single cell.

Merging Cells

You can only merge cells horizontally. Selecting cells in more than one row results in the selected cells in each row being merged horizontally.

To merge multiple cells in a row into a single cell, follow these steps:

1. Select the cells that you want to merge (see Figure 19.1).

FIG. 19.1
Select the cells that you want to merge in the table.

		Sales Forecast					
		Jan	Feb	Mar	Apr	May	Jun
South	30	27	34	50	41	29
North	42	41	45	60	54	60
East	70	59	70	67	63	64
West	55	54	64	80	80	80

2. Choose Table, Merge Cells.

   The selected cells condense into a single cell (see Figure 19.2). You might have to reformat the contents so that the cell aligns correctly.

FIG. 19.2
Merge cells to put text such as titles into a single, wider cell.

		Sales Forecast					
		Jan	Feb	Mar	Apr	May	Jun
South	30	27	34	50	41	29
North	42	41	45	60	54	60
East	70	59	70	67	63	64
West	55	54	64	80	80	80

Creating Table Headings

To create table headings, follow these steps:

1. Select the first row and any following rows that you want to use as table headings.

2. Choose Table, Headings.

This command designates the selected rows of a table to be a table heading. However, the selected rows must include the first row of the table in order to be designated as a table heading. Table headings are repeated on subsequent pages if the table spans more than one page.

Splitting Cells

After you have merged cells, you can return them to their original condition. The text in the merged cells is divided among the split cells by paragraph marks. The first paragraph is placed in the first cell, the second paragraph in the second cell, and so on.

To split merged cells, follow these steps:

1. Select a cell that was previously merged.
2. Choose Table, Split Cells.

Text that consists of a single paragraph is inserted into a single cell. If the text consists of multiple paragraphs, each paragraph is inserted into its own cell.

Formatting a Table

You can format the text and cells in a table to produce attractive and professional-looking tables. You can format text and paragraphs just as you do in the body text of your document. To make a table more attractive and more readable, you can add borders and shading around the entire table or to selected cells. You also can draw gridlines within the table. To enhance the appearance or make important data stand out, you can use colored borders or shaded or colored backgrounds. In addition, 40 different shades and patterns are available for black-and-white laser printers—an important feature when you want your document to make a good impression.

Part
V

Ch
19

You can format the contents in the table's cells by using the same procedures that you use to format regular text. To change the font, font size, and font style, choose Format, Font. To adjust the spacing and indentation of cell contents, choose Format, Paragraph. Remember that you can use the shortcut menus to access these formatting commands. Click the right button after you select the cells, columns, or rows that you want to format, and then choose from the shortcut menu the formatting command that you want to use.

▶ **See** "Using Paragraph Formatting Techniques," **p. 325**

To add borders, shading, and color to a table, choose Format, Borders and Shading. You also can add the Tables and Borders toolbar to the screen to access the border and shading options with a mouse click.

▶ **See** "Shading and Bordering Paragraphs," **p. 356**

 T I P To add the Tables and Borders toolbar to your screen, click an existing toolbar with the right mouse button, and choose Tables and Borders from the menu. Repeat these steps to remove the toolbar.

Formatting a Table with Table AutoFormat

 Formatting a table to achieve a professional appearance could take you longer than creating and filling the table—unless you use Table AutoFormat. This feature automatically applies predesigned collections of formatting to the table that you select. The formatting includes borders, shading, fonts, colors, and AutoFit column widths. If you are familiar with Excel's time-saving AutoFormat command, you already know about this feature's usefulness.

To format a table using Table AutoFormat, follow these steps:

1. Move the insertion point inside the table.

2. Choose Table, Table AutoFormat to display the Table AutoFormat dialog box shown in Figure 19.3.

FIG. 19.3

Apply collections of predefined formats by using the Table AutoFormat dialog box.

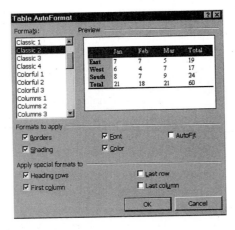

3. Select from the Formats list a predefined format. The Preview box displays an example of the format that you select.

4. If you do not want to lose existing formats in the table, clear the appropriate check box in the Formats to Apply group: Borders, Shading, Font, Color, and AutoFit. The Preview box changes as you select or clear formats.

5. If you want to apply only selected portions of the AutoFormat to your table, select from the Apply Special Formats To group the parts of the table that you want to format: Heading Rows, First Column, Last Row, and Last Column.

6. Choose OK.

Selecting Border Formats

With Word, adding borders to a table is easy. You can add borders to individual cells, rows, and columns, or to the entire table. Figure 19.4 shows a table formatted with multiple border styles.

FIG. 19.4
You can format a table with multiple border styles.

	Jan	Feb	Mar	Apr	Jun	May
South	30	27	34	50	29	41
North	42	41	45	60	60	54
East	70	59	70	67	64	63
West	55	54	64	80	80	80

To add borders to all or selected parts of your table, follow these steps:

1. Select the entire table or the cells that you want to shade or border.

2. Choose Format, Borders and Shading, and select the Borders tab in the Borders and Shading dialog box. The Borders tab appears (see Figure 19.5).

Part
V

Ch
19

FIG. 19.5
Add borders to your table by using the Borders and Shading dialog box.

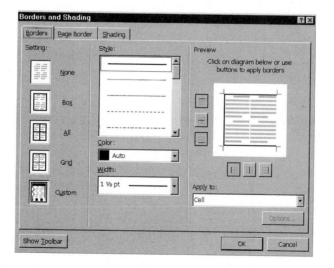

3. Select the line type from the Style box.

4. Select a line color from the Color list.

5. Select the line weight from the <u>W</u>idth list.

6. Select one of the border patterns in the Setting group: <u>N</u>one, Bo<u>x</u>, <u>A</u>ll, or <u>G</u>rid.

7. Choose OK.

If you want to specify custom combinations of border types, weights, and colors, you can select which lines are affected by the St<u>y</u>le and <u>C</u>olor selections that you make in the Bo<u>r</u>der group.

To specify custom combinations, follow these steps:

1. Select the line type and weight from the St<u>y</u>le and <u>W</u>idth options as described in the preceding steps.

2. Select the line color from the <u>C</u>olor list.

3. Select from the Preview group the line or edge that you want to change. Figure 19.6 shows the border buttons in the Preview group that select the lines to change according to the formatting selections.

FIG. 19.6

You can select any combination of individual edges or the interior gridlines to be formatted with borders.

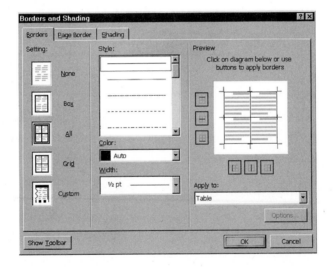

Using the mouse, click the line type shown in the St<u>y</u>le box. Click the buttons in the Preview group that correspond to the lines that you want to change.

Using the keyboard, press Alt+N to move the focus to the Setting group. Press the up- or down-arrow keys to cycle through combinations of selected lines. Stop on the combination that you want. Press Alt+Y to change the line St<u>y</u>le, Alt+C to change the line <u>C</u>olor, and Alt+W to change the line <u>W</u>idth options until you get the right combination.

4. Watch the sample in the Preview group to see the result of your choices. If you do not like the sample's appearance, choose None from the Presets group and return to step 1.

5. Choose OK.

N O T E The preceding steps show you how to add borders to an entire table or individual cells in a table. You also can add borders to the paragraphs in a cell. Click the Show/Hide button on the Standard toolbar to display paragraph marks, select the paragraph mark for the paragraph to which you want to add borders, and choose Format, Borders, and Shading. You might have to insert a paragraph mark after the text by pressing Enter. ▪

Selecting Shading and Colors

You can enhance a table or selected cells with *shading*. Shading draws attention to a particular section of a table. You also can use it to create reserved areas on office forms.

The selections that you make in the Borders and Shading dialog box can affect the currently selected paragraph, cell or cells, or the entire table.

To add shading to a table, follow these steps:

1. Choose Format, Borders and Shading, and select the Shading tab in the Borders and Shading dialog box. The Shading page appears (see Figure 19.7).

FIG. 19.7
You can add shading and color to a table by using the Shading options.

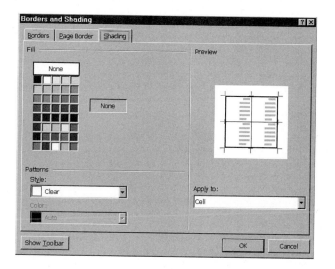

Part V
Ch 19

2. In the Fill group, select None to remove shading, or select a shade from the palette.

3. If you choose a shade, select the pattern or percentage of shading from the Style list. Many shades are available.

4. Select a color from the Color list. Select Auto or Black if you are printing to a black-and-white printer.

5. Check the Preview box to see the pattern that you have created. If you like the pattern that you see, choose OK; otherwise, return to step 2 and make other selections.

NOTE   When you apply shading, Word shades the background of selected cells. You can control the type of shading by setting the shading percentage. If you want lighter shading, choose a lower shading percentage. A higher percentage applies darker shading.

In the Borders and Shading dialog box, experiment with the options by clicking the Shading tab to find the shading pattern that looks best.

Your printer's resolution controls shading patterns. The higher the resolution—measured in *dots per inch* (*dpi*)—the finer the shading. The resolution at which your printer prints graphics and shading is an option within the Properties dialog box. To access this dialog box, choose File, Print, click the Properties button, and then select the Graphics tab. For more information about this dialog box, access Online help by clicking ?, then clicking the area of interest.

Numbering Rows and Columns

TIP   If you frequently use the same collection of formats on a table, learn about styles in Chapter 11, "Using Styles for Repetitive Formats."

To add numbers to the cells and rows in a table, you can click the Numbering button on the Formatting toolbar or choose Format, Bullets and Numbering. You can add numbers to just the first column in the table, or you can add numbers across rows or down columns in as many cells in the table as you want.

Adding Numbers with the Numbering Button

The quickest way to add numbering to a table is to use the Numbering button on the Formatting toolbar. When you use this method, however, you are limited to the numbering style currently selected in the Bullets and Numbering dialog box.

To add numbers to a table using the Numbering button, follow these steps:

1. Select the cells, rows, or columns that you want to number. In most cases, you want a number in the first cell of each row, so select the first column.

2. Click the Numbering button on the Formatting toolbar.

3. Choose OK.

Adding Numbering with the Menu

You can choose Format, Bullets and Numbering to add numbers to a table. When you use this method, you can select from a variety of numbering styles in the Bullets and Numbering dialog box.

To add numbers using the menu, follow these steps:

1. Select the cells, rows, or columns that you want to number.

2. Choose Format, Bullets and Numbering, and select the Numbered tab in the Bullets and Numbering dialog box. The Numbered page appears (see Figure 19.8).

FIG. 19.8
You can select from several numbering styles in the Numbered page of the Bullets and Numbering dialog box.

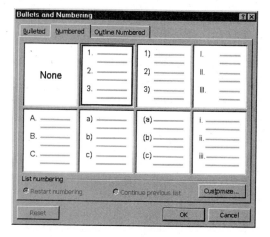

3. Select one of the numbering styles.

4. To modify the predefined style, click the Customize button, and make selections in the Customize Numbered List dialog box to change the format of the numbering.

5. Choose OK.

▶ **See** "Creating Bulleted or Numbered Lists," **p. 649**

Splitting a Table

Occasionally, you might want to insert a paragraph or heading between rows in a table. If you start a table at the top of a document and later decide that you need to insert some text before the table, you can do it easily.

To insert text above the table or between rows, follow these steps:

1. Position the insertion point in the row below where you want to insert the text. If you want to enter text above the table, position the insertion point in the first row of the table.

2. Choose Table, Split Table, or press Ctrl+Shift+Enter. A paragraph mark formatted with the Normal style is inserted above the row.

Sorting Tables

Tables often are created to arrange data in columns and rows. You can sort a table that is a database of names and addresses first by the last name, for example, and then within that sort, by the first name. You can sort text, numbers, and dates in either ascending or descending order.

To sort a table, follow these steps:

1. Select the entire table to include all the rows in the sort or select only the rows that you want to sort.

2. Choose Table, Sort. The Sort dialog box appears (see Figure 19.9).

FIG. 19.9
You can sort a table by up to three columns using the Sort dialog box.

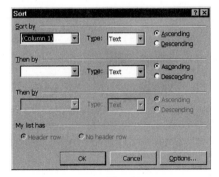

3. Select the first column that you want to sort by in the Sort By list.

4. Select either Text, Number, or Date from the Type list.

5. Select either the Ascending or Descending option.

6. Repeat steps 3 through 5 if you want to sort by additional columns in your table. Make your selections from the Then By lists.

7. If your table has headings that you don't want to include in the search, select the Header Row option in the My List Has group.

8. To make the sort case-sensitive, click the Options button, select the Case Sensitive option, and choose OK.

9. Choose OK.

 TIP Edit, Undo Sort reverses the Sort command if you use it immediately after you sort. You might want to save your document before sorting so that you can return to it if it is sorted incorrectly.

Converting a Table to Text

You can convert a table's cell contents to text separated by commas, tabs, or another single character, or you can convert each cell's contents into one or more paragraphs.

To convert a table to text, follow these steps:

1. Select the rows of the table that you want to convert to text, or select the entire table.

2. Choose Table, Convert Table to Text. The Convert Table to Text dialog box appears.

3. Select a Separate Text With option from the dialog box. You can separate each cell's contents by Paragraph Marks, Tabs, Commas, or Other (Other can be any single character).

4. Choose OK.

Converting Text to a Table

When you copy data from another application or convert a word processing file that does not have tables, your data might be in tabbed columns. To make the data easier to work with, convert the data to Word tables.

Part
V
Ch
19

To convert text to a table, follow these steps:

1. Select the lines of text or paragraphs that you want to convert to a table.

2. Choose Table, Convert Text to Table. The Convert Text to Table dialog box appears (see Figure 19.10). You also can click the Insert Table button on the Standard toolbar.

FIG. 19.10

Use the Convert Text to Table dialog box to separate text at the character that you specify.

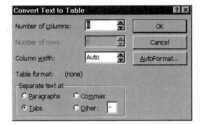

Based on the selected text, Word proposes the number of columns and rows, the width of the columns, and the separator character to use to delineate columns from the text. You can change these settings to suit your own needs.

3. Type or select the number of columns in the Number of Columns box to specify a different number of columns.

4. Type or select the number of rows in the Number of Rows box to specify a different number of rows.

5. Type or select an exact column width in the Column Width box if you don't want to use the automatic settings.

6. Select a different separator character if the default character is incorrect.

Choose one of the following options from the dialog box's Separate Text At group:

Option	Result
Paragraphs	Each paragraph is placed in its own cell.
Tabs	A tab character separates information in a cell. Word converts each paragraph and each line ending in a hard line break (created by pressing Shift+Enter) into a row. The number of columns is determined by the greatest number of tab characters in the paragraphs or lines.
Commas	A comma separates information in a cell. Word for Windows converts each paragraph and each line ending in a hard line break into a row. The number of columns is determined by the greatest number of commas in the paragraphs or lines.

Option	Result
Other	Some other character separates information in a cell. Word converts each paragraph and each line ending in a hard line break into a row. The number of columns is determined by the greatest number of the specified characters in the paragraphs or lines.

7. Choose OK.

Calculating Math Results in a Table

You can perform calculations in a table just as you do in a spreadsheet. In a Word table, you can add, subtract, multiply, and divide numbers, and you also can perform several other types of calculations, such as averaging and finding minimum and maximum values.

To perform a calculation in a table, you must position the insertion point in the cell where you want the calculation's result to appear. If text or numbers are already in that cell, you should delete them.

N O T E When you choose Table, Formula to add a group of cells, Word assumes that you want to add the cells immediately above or to the left of the cell and inserts either ABOVE or LEFT in the parentheses of the SUM function in the Formula dialog box. If you want to perform other types of calculations, you must replace the SUM function with another function and specify the cells that you want to use in the calculation.

You specify a cell by using the cell address, which consists of the row and column designation for that cell. The first cell in the upper-left corner of a table, for example, is designated as A1, where A is the column and 1 is the row. You can designate a range of cells by typing the addresses for the first and last cells in the range separated by a colon.

When you perform a calculation in a cell, a field code is inserted. The field includes the function name—for example, SUM—and the cells on which the calculation is being performed. To see the field code, choose Tools, Options, and select the View tab. Select the Field Codes option, and choose OK. Word displays the field code rather than the result.

Part

V

Ch

19

TIP A shortcut for toggling between a field code and its result is to locate the insertion point within the code and press Shift+F9. If the numbers in the calculation change, you can update the results of the calculation by selecting the cell in which the results appear and pressing F9, the Field Update key.

CHAPTER 20

Creating Bulleted or Numbered Lists

Create and customize bulleted, numbered, and outline lists

Select from seven bulleted shapes, seven standard numbered formats, and seven standard outline numbered formats. Bullets, numbers, and outlines can be customized.

Create and customize numbered or bulleted headings

Technical and legal documents often require headings to be bulleted or numbered according to paragraph and indentation levels. Paragraph text or headings can be bulleted or numbered.

Remove bulleting and numbering from lists and headings

Bulleting and numbering can be easily removed using menu commands or the Formatting toolbar.

A bulleted or numbered list is a special type of list formatted with a *hanging indent*. (A hanging indent occurs when a paragraph's first line goes all the way to the left margin, but all other lines in the paragraph are indented. Chapter 10, "Formatting Lines and Paragraphs," describes hanging indents and other paragraph formatting.) Bulleted lists have a bullet at the left margin; numbered lists have a number and are numbered sequentially. Many writers use bulleted lists to distinguish a series of important items or points from the rest of the text in a document, such as a summary of product features in a sales letter or a list of conclusions reached in a research project. Writers often use numbered lists for step-by-step instructions (as in this book), outlines, or other types of lists in which the specific order of the information is important.

Word 97 provides flexible, easy-to-use methods for creating bulleted or numbered lists with a variety of standardized numbering or bullet formats. You can vary the size of the hanging indent or the space between the numbers or bullets and the following text. You can also create your own custom numbering formats for numbered lists, or you can select characters from any of your installed fonts to use as a bullet in a bulleted list. Word even provides an easy way to remove bullets or numbering (see Figure 20.1).

You can type the text for the bulleted or numbered list and then apply the list formatting to the text; alternatively, you can place the insertion point in a blank line, apply the bulleted or numbered list format to that line, and then type the list. Either way, after you select a bulleted or numbered list format, Word sets a 1/4-inch hanging indent and adds the bullets or numbers in front of each paragraph in the selected text, or adds them to each new paragraph that you type.

FIG. 20.1

An example of the types of bulleted and numbered lists that you can create.

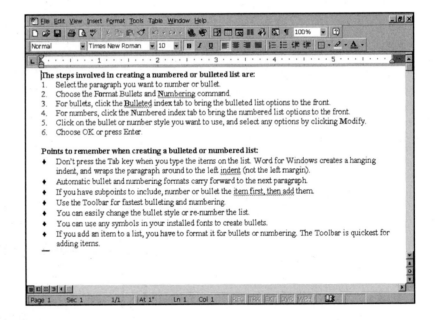

Like paragraph margin and indent formatting, the bulleted or numbered list format carries forward from paragraph to paragraph. Each time that you press Enter to begin a new paragraph, Word adds to the list a new bulleted or numbered paragraph. You can add another bulleted or numbered item anywhere in a list by placing the insertion point where you want to add the new item and then pressing Enter to begin a new paragraph. Word automatically adds a bullet or number sequentially to the beginning of the new paragraph and formats the paragraph with a hanging indent to match the other paragraphs in the bulleted or numbered list. You can also use the AutoFormat feature described in Chapter 11, "Using Styles for Repetitive Formats," to create numbered or bulleted lists automatically. ■

Creating Bulleted Lists

Word offers seven standard bullet shapes: round, diamond (solid or four small diamonds forming larger diamond), box (solid or hollow), arrow, and check. If you want to use a heart, pointing hand, or some other symbol as your bullet, Word enables you to select the character for the bullet from any of your installed fonts.

▶ **See** "Formatting Characters and Changing Fonts," **p. 283**

You can create a bulleted list in two ways: with menu commands or with a toolbar short-cut. As usual, you have many more options when you use menu commands.

Creating Bulleted Lists with Menu Commands

To create a bulleted list with menu commands, follow these steps:

1. Type the list at the left margin (without pressing Tab to indent the text) and then select it, or place the insertion point on a blank line.

2. Choose Format, Bullets and Numbering. The Bullets and Numbering dialog box appears (see Figure 20.2).

FIG. 20.2
Use the Bullets and Numbering dialog box to select the bullet and indent style options for a bulleted list.

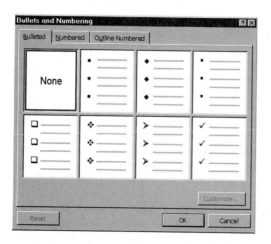

Part

V

Ch

20

3. ˙ Click the Bulleted tab to display the bulleted list options, if they are not already displayed.

4. Select the bulleted list format that you want from the predefined choices by clicking it with the mouse or using the arrow keys.

   Later in this chapter, the section "Customizing Bulleted Lists" describes how to use the Customize button to customize a bulleted list's formatting.

5. Click OK. Word formats the current line or selected text as a bulleted list.

If you have not yet typed the bulleted list, type it now. Each time that you begin a new paragraph, Word formats the paragraph as part of the bulleted list. To end the bulleted list, see "Ending the Bulleted List" later in this chapter.

N O T E   You can open the Bullets and Numbering dialog box by placing the pointer over the selected text and then clicking the right mouse button. A context-sensitive menu appears to the right of the insertion point. Choose Bullets and Numbering to display the Bullets and Numbering dialog box. ▪

If you want to replace an existing bulleted list with new bullets or change any of the bulleted list's other formatting properties, select the list, and then follow the instructions in the section "Customizing Bulleted Lists" later in this chapter. If you want to replace bullets with numbers, see the section "Creating Numbered Lists" later in this chapter for instructions on creating a numbered list. Word does not ask you to confirm that you want to replace bullets with numbers. If you inadvertently change a bulleted list to a numbered list, use the Edit, Undo Number Default command.

To add bulleted items anywhere in a bulleted list, position the insertion point where you want to add the new bulleted item, and press Enter to add a new paragraph to the list. Word automatically formats the new paragraph as part of the bulleted list.

Creating Bulleted Lists with the Toolbar

 With the Formatting toolbar, you can easily set up a bulleted list by clicking the Bullets button (near the right side of the Formatting toolbar). When you create a bulleted list with the Bullets button, Word uses the bulleted list formatting options selected most recently in the Bullets and Numbering dialog box.

To create a bulleted list with the toolbar, follow these steps:

1. Choose View, Toolbars and select Formatting, if the Formatting toolbar is not already displayed.

2. Type the list at the left margin and select it, or place the text insertion point in a blank line.

3. Choose the Bullets button on the Formatting toolbar. Word formats the current line or selected text as a bulleted list.

If you have not yet typed the bulleted list, type it now. Word formats each new paragraph as part of the bulleted list. The next section explains how to end the bulleted list.

By default, Word uses a small, round bullet and a 1/4-inch hanging indent to format lists that you create with the Formatting toolbar's Bullets button. If you recently selected different options in the Bullets and Numbering dialog box, however, Word uses those selections instead.

Ending the Bulleted List

If you apply bulleted list formatting to a blank line and then type the list, Word continues formatting each new paragraph you type as part of the bulleted list, until you end the bulleted list.

To end a bulleted list, follow these steps:

1. Press Enter to add a bulleted, blank line to the end of the bulleted list.
2. Move the pointer over the blank line and click the right mouse button. Word moves the insertion point to that line and displays a context-sensitive menu to the right of the insertion point.
3. Choose Bullets and <u>N</u>umbering. The Bullets and Numbering dialog box appears.
4. Double-click the None selection to end the bulleted list. Word removes the bullet and hanging indent from the blank line, ending the bulleted list.

Adding Subordinate Paragraphs to a Bulleted List

Sometimes you cannot adequately or gracefully discuss the topic of a bulleted list item within a single paragraph. Usually, if you require more than one paragraph to describe a single topic in a bulleted list, you want only the first paragraph for that topic to have a bullet. The remaining subordinate paragraphs for that topic do not need bullets, although they must have the same hanging indent as the list's bulleted paragraphs.

Whether you are changing an existing bulleted paragraph to a subordinate paragraph or typing the bulleted list as you go along, you can change a bulleted paragraph into a subordinate paragraph by using either a context-sensitive shortcut menu or the Formatting toolbar.

Part
V

Ch
20

Adding a Subordinate Paragraph with the Menu   To change a bulleted list item to a subordinate paragraph, follow these steps:

1. Select the bulleted list items from which you want to remove the bullets.
2. Move the pointer over the selected text, and click the right mouse button. Word moves the insertion point to that line and displays a context-sensitive menu to the right of the insertion point.
3. Choose Bullets and Numbering. The Bullets and Numbering dialog box appears.
4. Double-click the None selection. Word removes the bullet from the selected paragraphs.
5. Choose the Increase Indent button from the Formatting toolbar.

If you added a subordinate paragraph at the end of a bulleted list and you want to add another bulleted list item after the subordinate paragraph, choose the Bullets button from the Formatting toolbar to resume the bulleted list format.

Adding a Subordinate Paragraph with the Toolbar   To use the Formatting toolbar to change a bulleted list item to a subordinate paragraph in the list, follow these steps:

1. Select the bulleted list items from which you want to remove the bullets.

2. Choose the Bullets button from the Formatting toolbar. Word removes the bullet from the selected paragraphs.
3. Choose the Increase Indent button from the Formatting toolbar.

Use the Bullets button to resume formatting the bulleted list on the next line.

Customizing Bulleted Lists

To customize an existing bulleted list or to make your own specifications for the formatting of a new bulleted list, choose the Customize button from the Bullets and Numbering dialog box. Customize enables you to choose a character from any of your installed fonts to use as a bullet, to specify the bullet's point size and color, and to choose from a list of special effects. You can also specify the size of the hanging indent, how much space appears between the bullet character and the text in the bulleted item.

The only way to customize a bulleted list format is to use menu commands; no toolbar shortcut exists. If your custom bulleted list format is the most recently applied format, however, the Bullets button on the Formatting toolbar applies your custom format.

To create a custom bulleted list format, follow these steps:

1. Select the bulleted list that you want to customize.

2. Choose Format, Bullets and Numbering. The Bullets and Numbering dialog box appears.

3. Choose the Bulleted tab to display the bulleted list options, if that tab is not already up front.

4. Choose the Customize button. The Customize Bulleted List dialog box appears (see Figure 20.3).

FIG. 20.3

The Customize Bulleted List dialog box enables you to select custom bullet characters, colors, and point sizes for the bullet, and to choose the bullet character's alignment with the text.

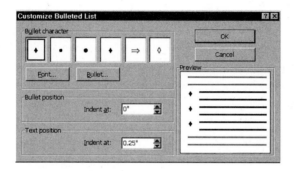

5. In the Bullet Character group, select the character that you want to use as a bullet by clicking it or by using the arrow keys.

The section "Selecting Custom Bullet Character Effects" describes how to use the Font button to select custom bullet character effects.

The section "Selecting a Custom Bullet Character" describes how to use the Bullet button to select a custom bullet character.

6. Choose any of the following options:

Option	Function
Bullet Position	Choose the bullet's alignment within the space used for the indent. Word offers you the choice of left-aligned, right-aligned, centered, or justified.
Text Position	Type or select a number to set the distance in the bulleted paragraph between the bullet and the text.

7. Click OK. The Customize Bulleted List dialog box closes, and you are returned immediately to the document.

Part

V

Ch

20

CAUTION

If you customize or reformat an existing bulleted list that contains subordinate (unbulleted) paragraphs, Word adds bullets to the subordinate paragraphs.

Selecting Custom Bullet Character Effects   Word enables you to customize a selected bullet character by adding a special effect, changing character spacing, or by animating the bullet character.

To select custom font effects, follow these steps:

1. Choose the Font button in the Customize Bulleted List dialog box. Word displays the Font dialog box (see Figure 20.4).

FIG. 20.4

The Font dialog box enables you to choose a different font and add special effects.

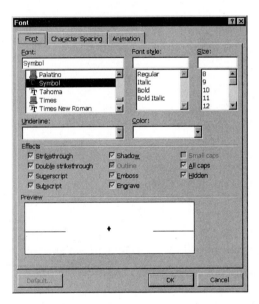

2. Choose any of the following options:

Option	Function
Font	Choose the bullet's font from any of your installed fonts.
Font Style	Choose from Regular, Italic, Bold, or Bold Italic font styles. Notice that the items listed in the Font style list may vary depending on the styles available for the particular font.
Size	Choose the font size.

Underline	Underline the bullet character. Choose from Single, Words only, Double, Dotted, Thick, Dash, Dot Dash, Dot Dot Dash, or Wave.
Color	Choose the bullet's color. Select Auto to have Word for Windows automatically select the color.
Effects	Enhance the bullet by choosing a special effect. Choose from Strikethrough, Double Strikethrough, Superscript, Subscript, Shadow, Outline, Emboss, Engrave, All Caps, or Hidden.

3. Click OK. Word closes the Font dialog box and displays your bullet character in the Bullet character and Preview group of the Customize Bulleted List dialog box.

To select custom character spacing, follow these steps:

1. Choose the Character Spacing tab in the Font dialog box (see Figure 20.5).

FIG. 20.5

The Character Spacing tab enables you to change the bullet's scale, spacing, position, and kerning.

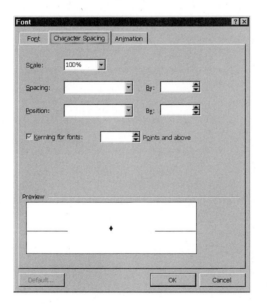

Part

V

Ch

20

2. Choose any of the following options:

Option	Function
Scale	Stretches or compresses text horizontally by the percentage you choose.
Spacing	Choose Normal, Expanded, or Condensed spacing between characters and specify the amount.

Option	Function
Position	Raises or lowers bullet character by the amount you specify.
Kerning for Fonts	Adjusts kerning automatically for the font size specified and larger.

3. Click OK. Word closes the Font dialog box and displays your bullet character in the Bullet character and Preview group of the Customize Bulleted List dialog box.

To select animation, follow these steps:

1. Choose the Animation tab in the Font dialog box (see Figure 20.6).

FIG. 20.6

The Animation tab enables you to add predefined animated text effects.

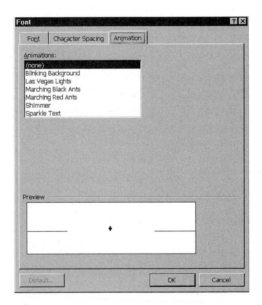

2. Choose an animated text effect from the Animations list box. Choose from Blinking Background, Las Vegas Lights, Marching Black Ants, Marching Red Ants, Shimmer, or Sparkle Text.

3. Click OK. Word closes the Font dialog box and displays your bullet character in the Bullet character and Preview group of the Customize Bulleted List dialog box.

Animated text effects are useful for on-line documentation.

Selecting a Custom Bullet Character   Word enables you to select any character from any of your installed fonts to use as the bullet character in a bulleted list.

To select a custom bullet character, follow these steps:

1. Choose the <u>B</u>ullet button in the Customize Bulleted List dialog box. Word displays the Symbol dialog box (see Figure 20.7).

FIG. 20.7

The Symbol dialog box enables you to choose a bullet character from any installed font.

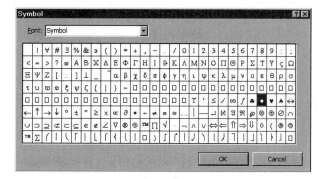

2. Select from the <u>F</u>ont list box the font that the Symbol dialog box displays. Select the bullet character that you want from the Symbol dialog box by clicking the character or by using the arrow keys.

3. Select from the Su<u>b</u>set list box the character subset you want to jump to in the symbol grid. The subset list is unavailable if the currently selected font does not contain subcategories.

4. Click OK. Word closes the Symbol dialog box and displays your selected bullet character in the B<u>u</u>llet character and Preview group of the Customize Bulleted List dialog box.

 TIP A modified bullet character is not applied to any new lists you create.

Creating Numbered Lists

▶ **See** "Formatting a Document Automatically," **p. 373**

Numbered lists are much like bulleted lists. The main difference is that a numbered list is numbered sequentially instead of bulleted. If you add a paragraph in the middle of a numbered list or rearrange the order of paragraphs in a numbered list, Word automatically renumbers all the paragraphs in the list so that they retain their sequential numbering.

Word offers six standard numbering formats and enables you to customize them. Word also offers a special type of numbered list, called an *outline numbered list*. In an outline numbered list, you can number each successive indentation level in the list. Later in this chapter, the section "Creating Outline Lists" describes outline numbered lists.

Part
V

Ch
20

You can create a numbered list in two ways: with menu commands or with a toolbar short-cut. As usual, the menu commands offer you many more options.

Creating Numbered Lists with Menu Commands

To create a numbered list with menu commands, follow these steps:

1. Type your list and then select it (don't use the Tab key to indent the items on your list). Or, place the text insertion point on a blank line.

2. Choose Format, Bullets and Numbering. The Bullets and Numbering dialog box appears (refer to Figure 20.2).

3. Choose the Numbered tab to display the numbered list options if they are not already displayed (see Figure 20.8).

FIG. 20.8

Use the Bullets and Numbering dialog box to select the num-bered list format.

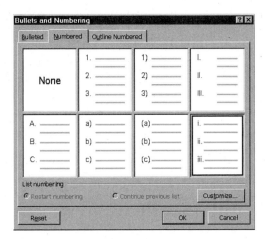

4. Select from the predefined choices the numbering style that you want. Your choices include Arabic numbers, Roman numerals, and letters with either periods or parentheses to separate the numbers from the list text.

   The section "Customizing Numbered Lists" describes how to use the Customize button to customize a numbered list.

5. Click OK. Word formats the selected text or line as a numbered list.

If you have not yet typed the numbered list, type it now. Each time that you begin a new paragraph, Word formats the paragraph as part of the numbered list. The section "Ending the Numbered List," later in this chapter, describes how to end the numbered list.

TIP You can open the Bullets and Numbering dialog box by placing the pointer over the selected text and clicking the right mouse button. A context-sensitive menu appears to the right of the insertion point; choose Bullets and Numbering to display the Bullets and Numbering dialog box.

If you want to replace an existing numbered list with new numbers or change any of the other formatting properties of the numbered list, select the list and then follow the instructions in the section "Customizing Numbered Lists," later in this chapter. If you want to replace numbers with bullets, select the list and see the previous section "Creating Bulleted Lists" for instructions on creating a bulleted list. Word does not ask you to confirm whether you want to replace numbers with bullets. If you inadvertently convert a numbered list to a bulleted list, choose Edit, Undo Bullet Default immediately after the conversion.

To add numbered items anywhere in a numbered list, position the insertion point where you want to add the numbered item, and simply press Enter to add a new paragraph to the list. Word automatically formats the new paragraph as part of the numbered list and re-numbers the list's paragraphs so that all the numbers remain sequential.

Creating Numbered Lists with the Toolbar

 A quicker way to number a list is to use the Numbering button on the Formatting toolbar. The Numbering button appears near the right side of the Formatting toolbar. When you create a numbered list with the Numbering button, Word uses the numbered list formatting options selected most recently in the Bullets and Numbering dialog box. You can change the numbered list formatting options by choosing Format, Bullets and Numbering.

To create a numbered list with the toolbar, follow these steps:

1. Choose View, Toolbars, and select Formatting. Word displays the Formatting toolbar, if it is not already displayed.
2. At the left margin, type the list and then select it, or place the text insertion point on a blank line.
 3. Click the Numbering button on the Formatting toolbar. Word formats the current line or selected text as a numbered list.

If you have not yet typed the numbered list, type it now. Word formats each new paragraph as part of the numbered list. The next section, "Ending the Numbered List," explains how to end the numbered list.

Part
V

Ch
20

By default, Word uses Arabic numbers and a 1/4-inch hanging indent to format lists with the Formatting toolbar's Numbering button. If you recently selected different options in the Bullets and Numbering dialog box, however, Word uses those selections instead.

Ending the Numbered List

As with bulleted lists, if you apply numbered list formatting to a blank line and then type the list, Word continues formatting each new paragraph that you type as part of the numbered list, until you end the numbered list.

To end a numbered list, follow these steps:

1. Press Enter to add a numbered, blank line to the end of the numbered list.
2. Move the pointer over the blank line, and click the right mouse button. Word moves the insertion point to that line and displays a context-sensitive menu to the right of the insertion point.
3. Choose Bullets and Numbering. The Bullets and Numbering dialog box appears.
4. Double-click the None selection to end the numbered list. Word removes the number and hanging indent from the blank line, ending the numbered list.

Adding Subordinate Paragraphs to a Numbered List

As with bulleted lists, sometimes the topic of a numbered list item requires more than one paragraph. And, as with bulleted lists, you probably want to number only the first of several paragraphs for the same numbered list item.

You can change a numbered paragraph into a subordinate paragraph by using either a context-sensitive shortcut menu or the Formatting toolbar.

Adding a Subordinate Paragraph with the Menu   To use the shortcut menu to change a numbered list item to a subordinate paragraph, follow these steps:

1. Select the numbered list items from which you want to remove the numbers.
2. Move the pointer over the selected text, and click the right mouse button. Word moves the insertion point to that line and displays a context-sensitive menu to the right of the insertion point.
3. Choose Bullets and Numbering. The Bullets and Numbering dialog box appears.
4. Double-click the None selection. Word removes the number from the selected paragraphs.
5. Choose the Increase Indent button from the Formatting toolbar.

If you add a subordinate paragraph at the end of a numbered list and then want to add another numbered list item after the subordinate paragraph, choose the Numbering button from the Formatting toolbar to resume the numbered list format.

Adding a Subordinate Paragraph with the Toolbar   To use the toolbar to change a numbered list item to a subordinate paragraph in the list, follow these steps:

1. Select the numbered list items from which you want to remove the numbers.

2. Choose the Numbering button from the Formatting toolbar. Word removes the number from the selected paragraphs.

3. Choose the Increase Indent button from the Formatting toolbar.

Customizing Numbered Lists

To customize an existing numbered list or to make your own specifications for the number format, choose the Customize button from the Bullets and Numbering dialog box. Customize enables you to specify the text that comes before and after the number, to specify the numbering style, and to choose the font for the numbers. In addition, you can specify the size of the hanging indent, how much space appears between the bullet character and the text in the bulleted item, and whether the number is right-, left-, or center-aligned within the indent space.

The only way to customize a numbered list format is with the menu commands; no toolbar shortcut exists for altering the format of a numbered list. If your custom numbered-list format is the most recently specified format, however, the Formatting toolbar's Numbering button applies your custom format.

To create a custom numbered-list format, follow these steps:

1. Select the numbered list whose format you want to customize.

2. Choose Format, Bullets and Numbering. The Bullets and Numbering dialog box appears (refer to Figure 20.2).

3. Click the Numbered tab to display the numbered list options, if they are not already displayed.

4. Choose the Customize button. The Customize Numbered List dialog box appears (see Figure 20.9).

Part
V

Ch
20

FIG. 20.9

Use the Customize Numbered List dialog box to select the format of the number, starting number of the list, the number style, and the number's alignment.

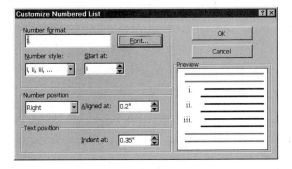

5. Choose any combination of the following numbered list options:

Option	Function
Number Format	Select the Font button to choose from fonts installed on your computer, font attributes, point size, spacing, and add special formatting effects. You can also type text in the edit box to further customize the appearance of the numbering.
Number Style	Select the numbering style that you want. Available choices include Arabic numerals, upper- and lowercase Roman numerals, upper- and lowercase alphabet letters, and word series (1st, One, and First). You can also choose no numbers at all.
Start At	Type the starting number for your list. (If you're creating a series of lists, the starting number can be a number other than 1.)
Number Position	Select the alignment of the number within the space used for the indent. Word offers you the choice of left-aligned, right-aligned, or centered.
Aligned At	Type a number to set the size of the hanging indent.
Text Position	Type a number to set the amount of space between the number and the text in the numbered paragraph.

6. Click OK in the Customize Numbered List dialog box.

CAUTION

If you customize or reformat an existing numbered list that contains subordinate (unnumbered) paragraphs, Word adds numbers to the subordinate paragraphs.

Creating Outline Lists

Outline lists are similar to numbered and bulleted lists, but number or bullet each paragraph in the list according to its indentation level. In outline lists, you can mix numbered and bulleted paragraphs based on indentation level.

▶ **See** "Formatting a Document Automatically," **p. 373**

▶ **See** "Formatting Characters," **p. 285**

You can create outline lists with as many as nine levels. You might use an outline list format if you want your list to have numbered items that contain indented, bulleted subparagraphs. Many types of technical or legal documents require that you sequentially number each paragraph and indentation level. You can also use outline lists to create outlines of various types.

Don't confuse outline lists, however, with the outline view and outlining features described in Chapter 21, "Organizing Content with an Outline," or with the heading numbering discussed later in this chapter. In the outline view and heading numbering, only paragraphs that have one of the nine heading styles are numbered. In an outline list, only paragraphs that have a body text style (such as Normal) can be part of the list.

You can create an outline list only by using the menu commands; no toolbar shortcut exists. Although you can customize the numbering formats for the various indentation levels of an outline list, you cannot use more than one outline list format in the same document.

To create an outline list, follow these steps:

1. Type and select your list. Use paragraph indenting to indent text by choosing Format, Paragraph; don't use the Tab key. Alternatively, place the text insertion point on a blank line.

2. Choose Format, Bullets and Numbering. The Bullets and Numbering dialog box appears.

3. Click the Outline Numbered tab to display the multilevel list options, if the options are not already displayed (see Figure 20.10).

4. Select from the predefined choices the outline numbering style that you want. Your choices include combinations of numbered and lettered paragraphs, and technical and legal numbering styles.

   The section "Customizing Outline Lists," describes how to use the Customize button to customize an outline numbered list.

Part

V

Ch

20

FIG. 20.10

Use the Bullets and Numbering dialog box to select the outline list format that you want.

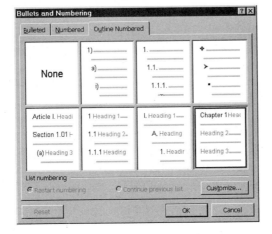

5. Click OK. Word formats the selected text or line as an outline list.

If you have not yet typed the outline list, type it now. Each time that you begin a new paragraph, Word formats the paragraph as part of the outline list and applies the appropriate numbering for that level of indentation. Use the Formatting toolbar's Increase Indent and Decrease Indent buttons (or the shortcuts Shift+Alt+right arrow and Shift+Alt+left arrow) to set the indentation level of each paragraph in the list. Word automatically adjusts the numbering to accommodate the paragraph's new level of indentation.

Ending an outline list is the same as ending a regular numbered list. For more detailed information, follow the instructions given in the previous section, "Ending a Numbered List." You can also add unnumbered subordinate paragraphs to an outline list the same way that you would for a numbered list.

Making Changes to an Outline List

If you want to replace an existing outline list with new numbers or change any of the other formatting properties of the outline list, select the list and follow the instructions in the next section, "Customizing Outline Lists." If you want to replace an outline list with a numbered or bulleted list, select the list and see the previous sections "Creating a Bulleted List" or "Creating a Numbered List" for instructions on creating a bulleted or numbered list. Word does not ask you to confirm whether you want to replace an outline list with a bulleted or numbered list format. If you inadvertently convert an outline list, choose Edit, Undo immediately after the conversion.

To add a new item to the outline list at any indentation level, position the insertion point where you want to add the item, and press Enter to add a new paragraph to the list. Choose Format, Paragraph to indent the paragraph to the desired level. Word automatically formats the new paragraph as part of the outline list and renumbers the paragraphs in the list so that all the numbers remain sequential.

Customizing Outline Lists

Customizing an outline list format is similar to customizing a numbered or bulleted list. To customize an outline list format, you can only use the menu commands.

To create a custom outline list format, follow these steps:

1. Select the outline list for which you want to customize the format.

2. Choose Format, Bullets and Numbering. The Bullets and Numbering dialog box appears (refer to Figure 20.8).

3. Click the Outline Numbered tab to display the outline list options, if they are not already displayed.

4. Choose the Customize button. The Customize Outline Numbered List dialog box appears (see Figure 20.11).

FIG. 20.11
Use the Customize Outline Numbered List dialog box to customize the numbering or bullet styles, alignment, and indentation levels of an outline list.

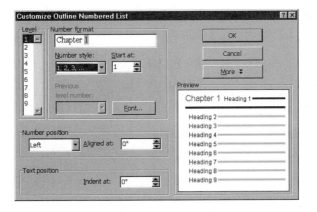

Part
V

Ch

20

5. Choose the More button to display more options (see Figure 20.12).

6. Use the Level list box to select the indentation level for which you want to adjust the formatting. You must customize each indentation level separately.

FIG. 20.12

The dialog box expands to show more options if you click More in step 5.

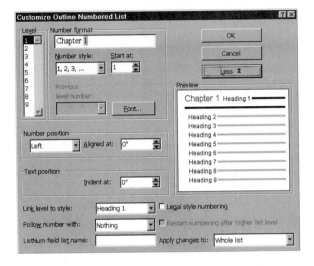

7. For each indentation level that you customize, set the following options in any combination:

Option	Function
Number Format	Select the Font button to choose any special font or font attributes (such as bold, italic, and underline), set the point size, spacing, or add special effects and animation for the numbers or bullets used at this indentation level.
Number Style	Select the numbering or bullet style that you want. Available choices include a combination of the numbering choices available for numbered lists and the bullet choices available for bulleted lists, or no number or bullet at all.
Start At	Type the starting number for paragraphs at the selected level of indentation.
Number Position	Select the alignment of the number or bullet within the space used for the indent. Word offers you the choice of left-aligned, right-aligned, or centered.
Aligned At	Type a number to set the size of the hanging indent.

Option	Function
Text Position	Type a number to set the amount of space between the number or bullet and the text in the numbered paragraph.
Link Level To Style	Link the currently selected level to a specific style.
Follow Number With	Select a Tab character or Space to follow each number or bullet at this indentation level.
ListNum Field List Name	Use this field if you want more than one number on a single line.
Legal Style Numbering	Select this check box to use legal style numbering.
Restart Numbering After Higher List Level	Select this check box to restart numbering when this list level follows a higher list level.

8. Click OK in the Customize Outline Numbered List dialog box.

Splitting a Numbered or Bulleted List

You might occasionally want to divide a long numbered or bulleted list into two or more smaller lists. To split a list, follow these steps:

1. Place the insertion point at the place where you want to divide the list.

2. Press Enter to insert a blank line.

3. Remove the bullet or numbering from the blank line by placing the insertion point on the blank line, choosing Format, Bullets and Numbering.

4. Place the insertion point on the bulleted or numbered item following the blank line then select the Restart numbering option.

   If you want to rejoin the lists, choose Format, Bullets and Numbering, then select the Continue previous list option.

If you split a numbered or outline list, Word renumbers the list so that both lists start with the starting number (specified in the Customize Numbered List dialog box) and are numbered sequentially.

Part
V

Ch
20

Removing Bullets or Numbering

You can remove bullets or numbering from a list by using either a menu command or the Formatting toolbar's Numbering and Bullets buttons.

To remove bulleted, numbered, or outline list formatting by using a menu command, follow these steps:

1. Select the list from which you want to remove bullets or numbering.

2. Choose Format, Bullets and Numbering.

3. Double-click the None selection.

To remove list formatting by using the toolbar, do one of the following:

■ To remove list formatting from a bulleted list, select the list and click the Bullets button on the Formatting toolbar.

■ To remove list formatting from a numbered or outline list, select the list, and click the Numbering button on the Formatting toolbar.

Creating Numbered Headings

When you number headings, Word looks for different heading styles to determine how to number each heading paragraph. Paragraphs formatted with the heading 1 style, for example, are numbered with the first outline level (I., II., III.); paragraphs with the heading 2 style are numbered with the second level (A., B., C.), and so on. Word provides seven predefined outline numbering formats for these different levels and enables you to establish your own custom numbering formats.

▶ **See** "Numbering an Outline," **p. 688**

Only paragraphs with a heading style are numbered. You can apply heading styles by promoting or demoting the paragraphs in the outline view or by applying the appropriate heading styles. When you delete or rearrange numbered headings, Word automatically renumbers them. You can have only one heading numbering format in your document, although you can set the heading numbering so that numbering starts over at the beginning of each new document section. You can also choose to have headings appear with bullets rather than numbers.

To number headings, follow these steps:

1. Choose Format, Bullets and Numbering. The Bullets and Numbering dialog box appears (see Figure 20.13).

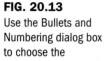

FIG. 20.13
Use the Bullets and Numbering dialog box to choose the numbering or bulleting style for headings.

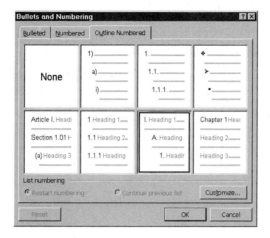

2. Select the Outline Numbered tab.

3. Select from the predefined choices the heading numbering style that you want.

   The next section, "Customizing Numbered Headings," describes how to use the Customize button to customize heading numbering.

4. Click OK.

Word applies your selected numbering format to all paragraphs in your document with a heading style.

Customizing Numbered Headings

To specify your own heading number format, use the Customize option from the Bullets and Numbering dialog box.

The only way to customize heading numbering is with the menu commands; no toolbar shortcut exists.

To create a custom heading number format, follow these steps:

1. Choose Format, Bullets and Numbering. The Bullets and Numbering dialog box appears (refer to Figure 20.13).

2. Choose the Outline Numbered tab.

3. Select a numbering style.

4. Choose the Customize button, then choose the More button. The Customize Outline Numbered List dialog box appears (see Figure 20.14).

Part
V

Ch
20

FIG. 20.14

By selecting options in the Customize Outline Numbered List dialog box, you can vary the appearance of your heading number formats.

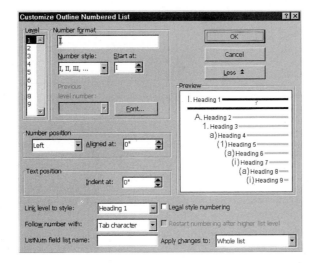

5. In the Level list box, select the heading level for which you want to adjust the formatting. You must customize each heading level separately.

6. Choose or set any of the following options, in any combination:

Option	Function
Number Format	Select the Font button to choose any special font or font attributes (such as bold, italic, and underline); set the point size, spacing, or add special effects and animation for the numbers or bullets used at this indentation level.
Number Style	Select the numbering or bullet style that you want. Available choices include a combination of the numbering choices available for numbered lists and the bullet choices available for bulleted lists, or no number or bullet at all.
Start At	Type the starting number for paragraphs at the selected level of indentation.
Number Position	Select the alignment of the number or bullet within the space used for the indent. Word offers you the choice of left-aligned, right-aligned, or centered.
Aligned At	Type a number to set the size of the hanging indent.

Option	Function
Text Position	Type a number to set the amount of space between the number or bullet and the text in the numbered paragraph.
Link Level To Style	Link the currently selected level to a specific style.
Follow Number With	Select a Tab character or Space to follow each number or bullet at this indentation level.
ListNum Field List Name	Use this field if you want more than one number on a single line.
Legal Style Numbering	Select this check box to use legal style numbering.
Restart Numbering After Higher List Level	Select this check box to restart numbering when this list level follows a higher list level.
Apply Changes To	Select whether to apply changes to the Whole list, from This point forward, to Selected text, or to the Current Paragraph.

6. Click OK to close the Customize Outline Numbered List dialog box.

Removing Heading Numbers

▶ **See** "Formatting Characters," **p. 285**

▶ **See** "Creating an Outline," **p. 679**

You can remove heading numbering by using either a menu command or the Formatting toolbar's Numbering and Bullets buttons.

To remove heading numbers by using a menu command, follow these steps:

1. Select the heading from which you want to remove numbering.

2. Choose Format, Bullets and Numbering.

3. Double-click the None selection.

 To remove heading numbers by using the toolbar, select the heading and click the Numbering button on the Formatting toolbar. ●

Part

V

Ch

20

CHAPTER 21

Organizing Content with an Outline

Create and work with an outline

Learn how to create an outline and use the outline commands to promote and demote headings, and collapse and expand the levels visible in the outline.

Reorganize your document easily by using an outline

You can easily reorganize an outline by selecting a heading and moving it, along with its subordinate headings and body text.

Use outline headings to create tables of contents

The headings in an outline can be used to create a table of contents using the Insert Index and Tables command.

Many writers feel comfortable organizing their thoughts and even their schedules with outlines. If you're in that group of organized people, you are going to enjoy working with the Word 97 outlining feature. In Word 97, an *outline* is a special view of your document that consists of formatted headings and body text. Nine possible outline heading levels are available. Each heading level can have one level of body text. Assigning each heading level a different formatting style enables you and the reader to discern your document's organization quickly.

Having an outline for your document is useful in many ways. For example, an outline can help you organize your thoughts as you compose a new document. At a glance, you can quickly see an overview of your document that shows only the headings. Later, an outline can help you reorganize and edit your document. By "collapsing" parts of your document so that only the headings show, you can easily move an entire section—heading, subheadings, and any associated body text. But Word for Windows has some other not-so-obvious uses for outlines: you can easily number the parts of a document, change heading-level formatting (each heading level has its own specific style), and use headings to generate tables of contents and other lists.

This chapter helps you maintain your documents and manage changes made within a workgroup. ■

Viewing an Outline

 To view an outline, choose <u>V</u>iew, <u>O</u>utline, or click the Outline View button at the left of the horizontal scroll bar. Figure 21.1 shows the first page of a document in the normal editing view, and Figure 21.2 shows the same document in Outline view with headings displayed. Figure 21.3 shows the document in an expanded outline view, with text and subheadings displayed.

FIG. 21.1
A document in normal view that does not show outline headings.

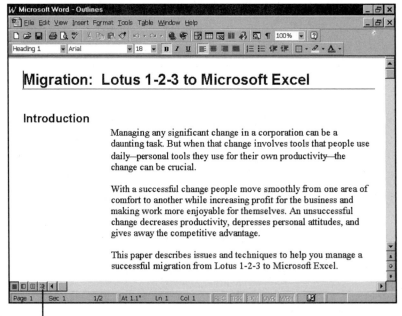

Outline view button

FIG. 21.2
The Outline view shows an overview of contents (headings only).

Outline toolbar ⏤

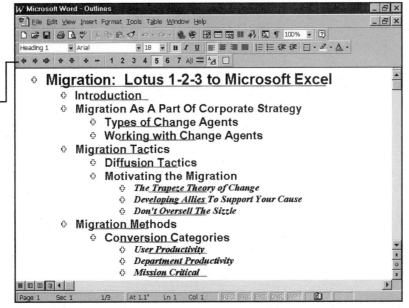

FIG. 21.3
The Outline view showing detailed contents by expanding the outline.

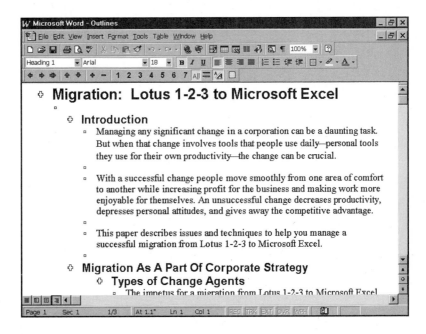

As you can see, Outline view looks different than the normal editing view in several ways. First, the *Outline toolbar* replaces the ruler. Second, Word indents the formatted headings and body text paragraphs to different levels. Third, a + or – icon appears to the left of each heading and paragraph. A plus sign (+) means that subordinate headings (those at a level lower than the heading being examined) or paragraphs of body text are associated with the heading. A minus sign (–) indicates that no headings or paragraphs are beneath the heading.

When you are in Outline view, you have the option of viewing headings at different levels or of viewing the entire document, including all body text. By viewing only the headings of a large document, you can see an overview of your document. You can also see where you have missed or misplaced topics. See the section "Collapsing and Expanding an Outline" later in this chapter to learn how to change the view of an outline.

The Outline toolbar includes buttons you can use to assign heading levels to text, promote or demote headings, and hide or display headings. Table 21.1 summarizes the functions of the Outline toolbar's buttons.

Table 21.1   The Functions of the Outline Toolbar's Buttons

Icon	Button	Function
⬅	Promote	Promotes the heading by one level, and promotes body text to the heading level of the preceding heading.
➡	Demote	Demotes the heading by one level, and demotes body text to the heading level below the preceding heading.
⏩	Demote to Body Text	Demotes the heading to body text.
⬆	Move Up	Moves the selected paragraphs before the first visible paragraph that precedes selected paragraphs.
⬇	Move Down	Moves the selected paragraphs after the first visible paragraph that follows selected paragraphs.
✛	Expand	Expands the first heading level below the currently selected heading; repeated clicks expand through additional heading levels until the body expands.
–	Collapse	Collapses body text into headings and then collapses lowest heading levels into higher heading levels.

Icon	Button	Function
1	Show Heading 1	Displays all headings and text through the lowest level number that you click.
2	Show Heading 2	
3	Show Heading 3	
4	Show Heading 4	
5	Show Heading 5	
6	Show Heading 6	
7	Show Heading 7	
All	Show All Headings	Displays all text if some is collapsed, and displays only headings if all text is already expanded.
═	Show First Line Only	Toggles between displaying all the body text or only the first line of each paragraph.
ᴬ⁄A	Show Formatting	Toggles between displaying the outline with or without full character formatting.
▣	Master Document View	Changes to Master Document view or back to simple Outline view. If Master Document view is selected, the Master Document toolbar appears.

The following sections teach you how to use these buttons to create and reorganize your outline.

▶ **See** "Creating a New Master Document," **p. 1047**

Creating an Outline

Creating an outline does two things: it organizes your work by heading, subheading, and body text, and applies formatting to each heading level. Styles define the formatting applied to each heading level. The style Heading 1 formats the first level of heading, Heading 2 formats the second level, and so on, through Heading 9. The Normal style formats body text. Word has predefined the Heading and Normal styles; however, you can redefine any of those styles by choosing Format, Style.

Word provides two ways to create an outline. The first method is to select the Outline view and then use the Outline toolbar's buttons to assign heading levels to your text (while creating or after creating the document). This chapter describes this method. The second method is to work in Normal view (or Draft or Page Layout view) of your document and assign appropriate styles, such as Heading 1 or Heading 2, to the headings in the document. To learn how to apply styles to text, see Chapter 11, "Using Styles for Repetitive Formats."

To create an outline in a new or existing document, follow these steps:

1. Choose View, Outline.

2. Type a heading or select the text that you want to convert to a heading. Select the heading by moving the insertion point anywhere within the heading's text, or by clicking to the left of the heading (but not clicking the + or − icon).

   If you're creating an outline from scratch (in a new file), Word applies the level 1 heading (Heading 1) as you begin typing.

3. Assign the appropriate heading level by clicking one of the following icons on the Outline toolbar, by clicking the Outline toolbar's arrow buttons with the mouse, or by pressing one of the following shortcut keys:

Icon	Mouse Action	Shortcut Key	Result
◀	Click the left-arrow button	Press Alt+Shift+ left arrow	Promotes the heading one level
▶	Click the right-arrow button	Press Alt+Shift+ right arrow	Demotes the heading one level
▶▶	Click the double-arrow button		Demotes the heading to body text
▲ ▼	Click the up- or down-arrow	Press Alt+Shift+ up- or down-arrow	Move line up or down

4. Press Enter to end the heading (or body text) and start a new heading (or paragraph) at the same level.

NOTE As you work in your document in Normal or Page Layout view, you might reach text that should be a heading in the outline. You can stay in Normal or Page Layout view and create this heading. One way is to format the paragraph with a heading style. Another method is to move the insertion point into the text you want to make into a heading and press Alt+Shift+←. The paragraph containing the insertion point is formatted to the same heading level as the preceding outline heading in the document. Press Alt+Shift+← or Alt+Shift+→ to adjust the heading to the level that you want. ▪

Formatting Your Outline

When you create an outline, you actually apply styles to the headings in your document. The styles determine your document's formatting. Unless you redefine Heading 1 for your document, for example, the style applies the Arial font in 14-point size, boldface, with extra space before and after the heading.

If you want to format your document's headings differently than the predefined heading styles, you must redefine the heading styles. If you want to format your outline's Level 1 headings differently, for example, you must redefine the Heading 1 style.

▶ **See** "Redefining Standard Styles," **p. 387**

Promoting and Demoting Headings

When you *promote* a heading, you raise its level in the outline. You can promote a Heading 3 to a Heading 2, for example, to make the indent smaller. *Demoting* does just the opposite. When you promote and demote headings, Word for Windows assigns the appropriate heading style for that level.

Using the Mouse to Promote or Demote Headings

You can use the mouse to promote or demote headings in two ways. One method uses the buttons in the Outline toolbar. By using this technique, you promote or demote only the selected heading. In the other method, you drag the heading's + or – icon left or right until the heading is at the level that you want; with this technique, you promote or demote the heading and all subordinate text.

If you want to use the mouse to promote or demote only the selected headings or text, follow these steps:

1. Choose <u>V</u>iew, <u>O</u>utline (if you haven't already).

2. Select the paragraphs to promote or demote.

Part

V

Ch

21

3. To promote the heading, click the Promote button (the left-arrow button) on the Outline toolbar.

To demote the heading, click the Demote button (the right-arrow button) on the Outline toolbar.

To convert the heading to body text, click the Demote to Body Text button (a double-arrow button) on the Outline toolbar.

Word for Windows treats headings independently, and thus does not promote or demote associated subheadings along with the headings. Body text, however, always remains associated with its heading. The preceding mouse method is useful for changing only the selected heading level while leaving subordinate text or levels alone.

To promote or demote a heading and have all subordinate headings and text change at once, follow these steps:

1. Choose View, Outline.

2. Move the mouse pointer over the + or – icon that appears to the left of the heading that you want to promote or demote (the pointer becomes a four-headed arrow). Click and hold down the mouse button.

3. Drag the icon to the left to promote the heading and its subordinate subheadings and body text, or drag the icon to the right to demote them. (Drag to the right edge of the outline to demote a heading to body text.)

As you drag a heading to a new level, the mouse pointer becomes a two-headed arrow, and a gray vertical line appears as you drag across each of the heading levels. When you have aligned the gray vertical line with the new heading level that you want—that is, you have aligned the line with other headings at the level that you want—release the mouse button.

Using Keyboard Shortcuts to Promote or Demote Headings

You can also use keyboard shortcuts to promote and demote individual headings (and body text). You need not be in Outline view to use this method; any view works.

To use shortcut keys to promote or demote a heading or portion of body text, follow these steps:

1. Select the headings or body text to promote or demote.

2. To promote one level, press Alt+Shift+←.

   To demote one level, press Alt+Shift+→.

This method affects only the selected headings and text; Word for Windows does not promote or demote associated subheadings along with the selected headings.

Whichever method you use, when you return to the normal editing view and display the ruler, you see that Word has applied the appropriate heading styles to your outline headings. (You can return to normal editing view by choosing View, Normal; View, Page Layout; or click the Normal View or Page Layout View icons on the horizontal scroll bar.)

Collapsing and Expanding an Outline

A *collapsed* outline shows the headings down to only a specific level. When you *expand* an outline to a specific level, you see all headings down to that level, as well as body text. You can collapse an outline all the way down so that only Level 1 headings show, or you can expand the outline all the way so that all headings and body text show. You also can expand the outline to show all headings and only the first line of each paragraph of body text.

Collapsing and expanding your outline can help you to write and edit. By collapsing your outline, you can see an overview of your entire document and can move around quickly in the outline. To move to a particular section, just collapse to the level of the heading to which you want to move, select the heading, and then expand the outline. You can also use shortcuts to move entire headings and all their subordinate headings and text to new locations in the outline.

To collapse or expand the entire outline, use the numeric buttons on the Outline toolbar. Click the lowest level that you want to display in your outline. If you want to show levels 1, 2, and 3 but no lower levels, for example, click the Show Heading 3 button.

To display all levels, including body text, click the Outline toolbar's All button. To display all heading levels but no body text, first click the All button to display all levels and body text (if not already displayed), and click All again to collapse the body text, leaving only the headings for all levels displayed. Clicking one of the Show Heading number buttons on the Outline toolbar collapses or expands your entire outline uniformly. Figure 21.4 shows the outline presented in Figure 21.2 with only two levels of headings displayed.

Using the Mouse to Collapse or Expand Headings

You can use the mouse and the Expand (+) and Collapse (–) buttons on the Outline toolbar, as well as the + and – icons in the outline, to collapse or expand headings selectively.

Part

V

Ch

21

Here are the methods that you use:

- Collapse headings and body text into the selected heading by clicking the Collapse (–) button on the Outline toolbar.

- Expand contents of selected headings by clicking the Expand (+) button on the Outline toolbar.

- Expand or contract a heading's contents by double-clicking the + icon to the left of the heading in Outline view.

FIG. 21.4
Collapsing an outline to display only the higher levels of headings.

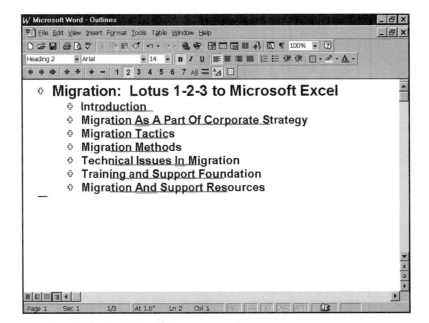

Using the IntelliPoint Mouse to Collapse or Expand Headings

Microsoft's IntelliPoint mouse uses the wheel button located between the left and right mouse buttons to collapse or expand outline headings. This makes it very easy to roll your finger over the wheel and "dial" the level of detail you want to see in an outline.

To collapse or expand an outline with the IntelliPoint mouse, follow these steps:

1. Switch into Outline view by choosing View, Outline.

2. Click the heading level you want to collapse or expand.

3. Hold down the Shift key as you roll the mouse wheel forward to expand the heading's contents and backward to collapse the heading's content.

4. Release the wheel.

TROUBLESHOOTING

When I click the mouse wheel, something unexpected happens—like Help or the Explorer displaying. The mouse wheel can be customized to produce different results. When it has been customized, then its normal behavior for outlines is unavailable. To set the mouse wheel back to its default behavior, click Start, Settings, Control Panel. When the Control Panel window appears, double-click the mouse application to display the Mouse Properties dialog box. Select the Mouse tab. Select Default from the Button Assignment list, then choose OK.

Using Keyboard Shortcuts to Collapse or Expand Headings

If you don't have a mouse or if you work faster using the keyboard, you can collapse and expand your outline by using shortcut keys. Table 21.2 lists the shortcut keys available. Before using a shortcut key, you must select the heading or text that you want to collapse or expand.

Table 21.2   Using Shortcut Keys to Collapse and Expand Headings

Shortcut Key	Description
Alt+Shift+ - (hyphen)	Collapses all body text below the heading. Pressing again collapses the heading's lowest level, and repeated presses collapse additional levels.
Alt+Shift++ (+ sign)	Expands the selected heading's next lower level. Repeated presses expand additional levels and, after expanding all headings, the body text.

Fitting More of the Outline into the Window

One of the great benefits of using an outline view of your document is that you get an overview of your document's organization. As you work with an outline to organize a document, you might want to view more of the outline than usually fits into the display window. To enable you to do so, Word for Windows provides two methods that you can use separately or in combination.

If you expand all or some headings to display subordinate body text, you might find that parts of the outline are pushed out of the display window. To view more of the outline, you can display the first line of each body text paragraph only, instead of the entire paragraph.

Part

V

Ch

21

You can also display the outline view without the full character formatting for each heading style. Because the character formatting for many of the heading styles usually uses boldface text and fairly large point sizes, each heading takes up a lot of room on the screen. If you omit the character formatting, the headings take less space.

Displaying an outline without character formatting affects the display in Outline view only; it does not make any permanent changes in the heading styles or their formatting. Figure 21.5 shows the same outline as in Figure 21.2, but without the full character formatting. Notice that you can now see much more of the outline.

FIG. 21.5

By displaying the outline without character formatting in the headings, you can fit more of the outline in the window.

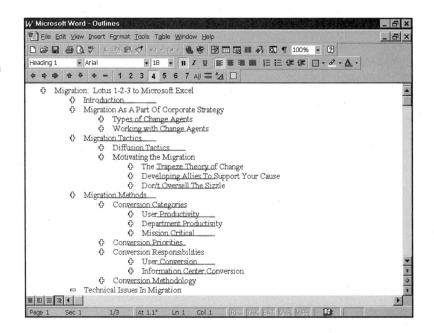

You can use the mouse and the Outline toolbar to fit more of the outline into the display window. Use either of the following methods:

 ■ To show only the first line of expanded body text paragraphs, click the Show First Line Only button on the Outline toolbar. If the body text paragraphs are already showing only the first line, clicking this button causes Word for Windows to display the entire paragraph.

 ■ To display the headings without full character formatting, click the Show Formatting button on the Outline toolbar. If the headings are already shown without character formatting, clicking this button causes Word to redisplay the formatting.

If you prefer to use the keyboard, you can fit more of the outline into the display window by using shortcut keys. Table 21.3 lists the shortcut keys available.

Table 21.3 Using Shortcut Keys to See More of the Outline

Shortcut Key	Description
/ (the slash key on numeric keypad)	Shows or hides character formatting for headings.
Alt+Shift+L	Shows only first line of each paragraph of expanded body text. Pressing this key combination a second time displays all text.

Reorganizing an Outline

By using Word's selection techniques, you can select outline headings in any of the normal ways. Outline view, however, offers a shortcut for selecting that can be a real time-saver. When you select an outline heading by clicking its icon in Outline view, you select the heading and its subordinate headings and body text.

Even if you don't use an outline to organize your thoughts before you begin writing, you can use an outline later to reorganize your document quickly. After you click a heading's + or – icon, you can move all the subordinate headings and text as a unit. (If you select only the words in an expanded heading, you move only the heading.)

N O T E   If you select the paragraph mark for a heading, Word automatically selects the entire heading. If you are editing the text in a heading and inadvertently select the paragraph mark, you could accidentally delete a heading and everything underneath it. If you are paying attention, you'll notice that the entire heading is highlighted if you select the paragraph mark. If this is not what you intended, start your selection again before editing. ■

You can move selected headings (along with associated subheadings and body text) by using the mouse or the keyboard. To move a selected heading upward (toward the first page) or downward (toward the last page), use any of these methods:

- ■ Press Alt+Shift+up or down arrow.
- ■ Drag the heading's icon up or down.
- ■ Click the Move Up or Move Down button on the Outline toolbar.

Part
V

Ch
21

By selecting multiple headings and paragraphs, you can move them as a unit. Hold down Shift as you click adjacent headings and paragraphs to select them together.

Numbering an Outline

If you need numbered outlines for legal documents, bids, or proposals, you can have Word add the numbers for you.

To number your outline (from any view), choose F<u>o</u>rmat, Bullets and <u>N</u>umbering. You can then select the type of numbering method. Figure 21.6 shows some of the numbering options available. Figure 21.7 shows an outline that uses the legal numbering style.

▶ **See** "Creating Numbered Lists," **p. 659**

To apply heading numbering quickly, click with the right mouse button on any heading and select Bullets and <u>N</u>umbering from the shortcut menu that appears.

FIG. 21.6

Using the Bullets and <u>N</u>umbering option to renumber outlines.

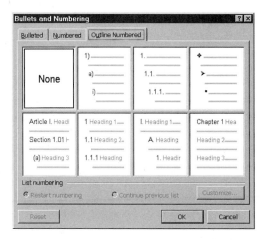

FIG. 21.7
Automatic numbering makes legal and proposal documents easy to construct.

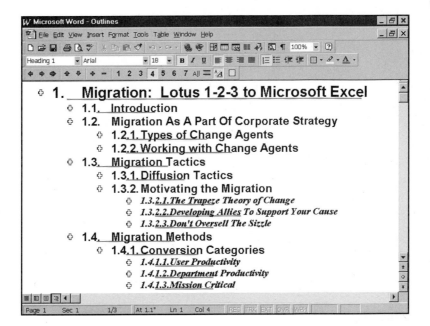

Using Outline Headings for a Table of Contents

If you need a table of contents, Word can build one from the outline. Word constructs tables of contents by accumulating outline headings and their page numbers.

To create a table of contents from outlining, choose Insert, Index and Tables. Chapter 31, "Creating Indexes and Tables of Contents," goes into detail on how to use the Indexes and Tables dialog box, shown in Figure 21.8, which you can use to create a table of contents like that shown in Figure 21.9.

To create a table of contents, follow these steps:

1. Position the insertion point where you want the table of contents to appear.

2. Choose Insert, Index and Tables.

3. Select the Table of Contents tab.

4. Select the options that you want.

5. Choose OK.

To view the table of contents as it is shown in Figure 21.8, choose View, Normal.

Part
V

Ch
21

FIG. 21.8

In the Index and Tables dialog box, you can create a table of contents.

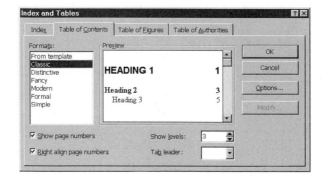

FIG. 21.9

The finished table of contents, consisting of outline headings and document page numbers.

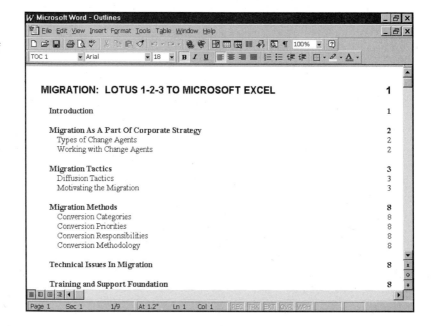

Replacing Outline Headings

You format outline headings with styles—specifically, Word built-in styles Heading 1 through Heading 9. Because you can search for and replace styles in Word, you can globally change outline headings.

▶ **See** "Using Find and Replace," **p. 227**

Using Custom Styles to Create an Outline

If you formatted a document with custom styles and want to convert the document to an outline, you can replace the custom styles with outline styles.

Suppose, for example, that you formatted your document with custom heading styles called *title*, *heading*, and *subheading*. Choose Edit, Replace. With the insertion point in Find What text box, choose More, Format, select Style, select the style title, and then choose OK. Then in the Replace With text box, choose Format, select Style, select style Heading 1, and then choose OK. (Type no text in either text box.) In the Find and Replace dialog box, choose Replace All to replace all title styles with Heading 1 styles. Do the same for all other headings and subheadings in your document. Then you can view your document as an outline.

Globally Replacing Outline Headings

In your document, you might want to promote or demote heading levels globally. For example, you might want to change all Level 3 headings to Level 4 headings. To do so, replace Heading 3 styles with Heading 4 styles (see the general instructions in the previous section, "Using Custom Styles to Create an Outline").

Removing Text from Within an Outline

You can remove all text from within an outline if the text is formatted with a style. You might want to remove all the text from an outline, for example, so that you can save just the headers. To remove the text instead of replacing the style (or styles) that formats the text with another style, replace the style with nothing. To remove text in an outline formatted with Word's default styles, for example, replace the style Normal with nothing. You might want to save the document first, because you can't undo this procedure. For details, see the general instructions in the previous section "Using Custom Styles to Create an Outline."

TIP If you want to copy just your outline without any associated text into another document, create a table of contents, as described earlier in this chapter. Select the table of contents, press Ctrl+Shift+F9 to convert it to text, and then copy and paste it into the other document.

Part
V

Ch
21

Printing an Outline

You can print your document as displayed in Outline view. To print the outline, choose View, Outline, display the levels of headings and body text that you want to print, and then choose File, Print or press Ctrl+P. ●

CHAPTER 22

Automating with Field Codes

Fields are a necessary, but often invisible, part of such features as a table of contents, an index, or a table of authorities. Fields also perform such simple tasks as inserting the date or displaying a data-entry box. They also display the text edit box, check box, and drop-down list used in forms. The value you gain from using fields comes from the repetitive work they can automate for you. ■

Use fields to automate repetitive work

Fields operate in the background to automatically insert information such as dates or numbers.

View fields

While you work in Word, you can view either field codes or the results of the field.

Insert fields

In many cases, Word inserts fields for you, or you can insert fields whenever you choose.

Edit and format fields

Move quickly between fields, edit or delete fields, and format the appearance of field results.

Update fields

As field information changes, you can update the fields to reflect those changes; alternatively, you can lock fields to preserve the results you currently see.

Understanding the Basics of Fields

Fields are hidden codes you type into a document or insert by using commands from the Insert menu. You normally see the results of fields, such as dates, page numbers, text linked to other documents, or mail-merge data. You can also see the field code for an individual field or for all fields in a document.

If you have used worksheet functions in Microsoft Excel or Lotus 1-2-3, you are familiar with the concept of fields. Fields are similar to functions. Most worksheet functions are mathematically and financially oriented; Word fields are oriented toward words, document processing, and mail-merge functions.

Figures 22.1 and 22.2 show two views of the same document. Figure 22.1 shows the field codes in the document; Figure 22.2 shows a document after the fields it contains have been updated. As you can see, the field codes create an automated document that you can update repeatedly. Toggle between displaying field codes and field results in the document by pressing Alt+F9 for the whole document or Shift+F9 for the selected area.

FIG. 22.1
Fields appear as codes in this document.

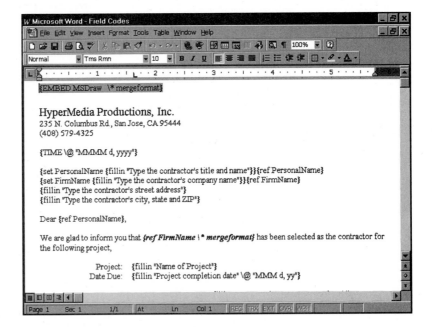

In Word 97, fields are generally updated to produce a new result when you print, print merge, or select and then manually update the fields. You can update fields individually or throughout the entire document.

FIG. 22.2
When the field results are displayed, the document looks as though it was typed.

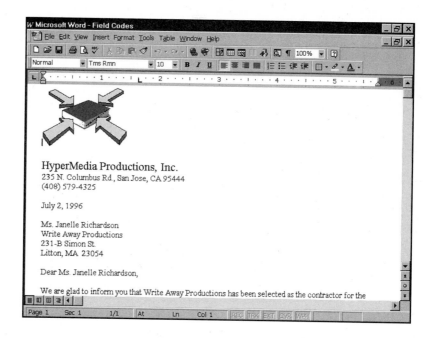

Many of the other features described in this book use fields, although you may not have been aware of them. In Chapter 13, "Formatting the Page Layout, Alignment, and Numbering," for example, the dates and page numbers in headers and footers are created with fields; in Chapter 31, "Creating Indexes and Tables of Contents," the indexes and tables of contents are created with fields. Fields are used in Chapter 17, "Mastering Envelopes, Mail Merge, and Form Letters" and Chapter 34, "Assembling Large Documents" to create mail-merge letters, build online forms, and assemble large documents.

More than 70 types of field codes are available. With these field codes, you can do the following:

- Build tables of contents, tables of authorities, and indexes
- Build mailing lists, labels, and form letters
- Prompt operators for information used repeatedly in a document
- Insert dates, times, or document summary information
- Link Word documents or data in other Windows applications with the current Word document
- Update cross-referenced page numbers automatically
- Calculate math results
- Number lists

- Enable operators to jump between related words or contents
- Start macros

 TIP For a full list of field codes and descriptions, choose <u>H</u>elp, <u>C</u>ontents and Index, open the Reference Information book, and then select Field Types and Switches.

Examining the Types of Fields

Fields can change your documents in a number of ways. Three types of Word fields are available: result fields, action fields, and marker fields.

- *Result fields* produce a result in your document by inserting information. This information may be obtained from the computer or document, as in the {author} and {date} fields. Other fields, such as {fillin}, display a dialog box that requests information from the operator and then inserts the information into the document.

- *Action fields* do something to the document but don't insert visible text. The action is performed either when you update the field, as in the {ask} field, or when you click the field, as in the {gotobutton} and {macrobutton} fields. The {ask} field, for example, displays a dialog box and prompts you to enter information. But instead of displaying the information, Word stores it in a bookmark you designate.

- *Marker fields* produce neither results nor actions. A marker field simply marks a location in the document so that you can find the location when you build such things as indexes and tables of contents. The index entry {xe} and table of contents entry {tc} fields are marker fields.

Understanding the Parts of Fields

Fields contain three parts: field characters, field code, and switches. A field that displays the current date in a format such as September 12, 1996, may look like the following:

```
{DATE \@ "MMMM d, yyyy" \* MERGEFORMAT}
```

where the braces ({ and }) are field characters, DATE is the field code, and \@ "MMMM d, yyyy" * MERGEFORMAT is the switch.

- *Field characters* define the beginning and end of a field. Although they look like braces, { and }, you cannot type the field characters. You create them by pressing Ctrl+F9 or by choosing a menu command that creates a field.

- *Field code* defines the type of action the field performs. The field code follows the first field character, {, and must be a field code (see "A Reference List of Field Codes" later in this chapter), an equal sign (=), or a bookmark name.

■ *Field switches* customize the action of some fields.

Some field codes also use *arguments*. Arguments are numbers or text used to control a field's action or results. If an argument contains more than one word, the argument usually must be enclosed in quotation marks (" "). (Exceptions are described in each field's description.) You can use the {ask} field, for example, to prompt the operator for text to be assigned to the bookmark First_Name, as follows:

```
{ask First_Name "Enter the first name."}
```

Note that the text arguments must be enclosed in quotation marks. If a field result, such as a Fillin dialog box, shows only the first word of the text you typed, you have probably forgotten to enclose the rest of the argument in quotation marks. Word uses the first word of the argument but doesn't see the rest unless it is in quotation marks.

The following table briefly describes arguments and their functions:

Argument	Function
Bookmark	In a field, is the same as a bookmark you assign to text. It names a location or selection of text. Fields use bookmarks to take action on the text or object in the document having that bookmark name. Fields also can store information in a bookmark or use the page number or sequence value of a bookmark's location.
Identifier	Distinguishes between different parts of the same document. You may use the letter F as an identifier of figures, for example, and the letter P as an identifier of pictures.
Text	Includes words or graphics used by the field. If you are entering a text argument with more than one word, you need to enclose all the text argument in quotation marks.
Switch	Toggles field results on or off. Switches include a backslash (\)followed by the switch letter. Switches can be specific to a field or can be general and used by different fields. A field can contain as many as 10 field-specific switches and 10 general switches. Field-specific switches are described in "A Reference List of Field Codes," later in this chapter.

Field Code Shortcut Keys

Table 22.1 lists shortcut keys that can make your work with fields quicker and easier. These shortcut keys and their equivalent commands are described in the appropriate sections throughout this chapter.

Table 22.1   Field Shortcut Keys

Key Combination	Function
F9	Updates fields in the selection.
Shift+F9	Toggles the selected field codes between the code and result.
Ctrl+F9	Inserts field characters, { }, to manually type field.
Ctrl+Shift+F9	Unlink—permanently replaces a field with its last result.
Alt+Shift+F9	Equivalent to double-clicking selected {gotobutton} and {macrobutton} fields.
F11	Go to next field.
Shift+F11	Go to previous field.
Ctrl+F11	Locks field to prevent updates; field remains.
Ctrl+Shift+F11	Unlocks field to permit updates.
Alt+Shift+D	Inserts {date} field.
Alt+Shift+P	Inserts {page} field.

Viewing and Printing Field Codes

Fields can appear in two ways: as a field code or as the field result. Field results display as though they were typed. You normally don't see the field codes when you work on a document, but if they return text, you see that text after the fields has been updated. If the fields have not been updated, you see the fields' previous results.

Some fields produce no visible result. Instead, they produce an action that affects other field codes. The fields that do not produce results include {ask}, {data}, {nextif}, {next}, {print}, {rd}, {set}, {skipif}, {ta}, {tc}, and {xe}.

Displaying Field Codes

You may need to see field codes on-screen so that you can review, delete, or edit them. You can display the field codes throughout the entire document or for an individual field.

To display field codes on-screen throughout the entire document, follow these steps:

1. Choose Tools, Options.
2. Select the View tab.
3. Select the Field Codes check box.

 Pressing Alt+F9 displays all field codes, and pressing Alt+F9 a second time redisplays field results.

To display an individual field code, follow these steps:

1. Move the insertion point within the field code or its result.
2. Press Shift+F9, or click the right mouse button and choose Toggle Field Codes from the shortcut menu.

These commands switch the display between showing field codes or the result. Your document probably will change its word wrap when you reveal or hide field codes. This change occurs because of the differences in length between the field codes and their results.

 A fast way to switch all the fields in a selected area between displaying field codes or their results is to select the area containing the fields and press Shift+F9. Press Shift+F9 again to redisplay field results.

A few field codes do not display. The {xe} (index entry), {tc} (table of contents entry), and {rd} (referenced document) field codes are formatted automatically as hidden text.

To see codes that display as hidden text when you display field codes, follow these steps:

1. Choose Tools, Options.
2. Select the View tab, and then select the Hidden Text check box.
3. Choose OK.

Most fields do not update automatically to show you the most current result. You must update fields manually or by using a macro. When you load a document that contains fields, each field shows its previous result. This feature enables you to load a document, such as a contract or form letter, and update only the items you want changed.

N O T E Some fields, such as the DATE field, do update automatically, unless you specify otherwise. ▤

Displaying Field Results as Shaded

Field results—whether they are text, dates, or numbers—appear on-screen just as though they were entered normally. If you are working on forms or documents and want to see which items are fields, you can shade the field results at certain times so that they stand out.

To shade field results, follow these steps:

1. Choose Tools, Options.
2. Select the View tab.
3. Select from the Field Shading drop-down list the time when you want field results shaded: Never, Always, or When Selected.
4. Choose OK.

Printing Field Codes

You probably should keep a printed copy of your documents and macros. These copies are a help if you ever lose the file or if someone else takes over your operation.

To print a copy of the document so that you can see the field codes, follow these steps:

1. Choose File, Print.
2. Click the Options button from the Print dialog box.
3. Select the Field Codes check box under the Include with Document group.
4. Choose OK to return to the Print dialog box, and then print your document.

Remember to clear the Field Codes check box when you want to print just the document (without visible field codes).

Inserting Field Codes

You can enter fields in a number of ways. Several commands enter field codes at the insertion point's position. Some of the commands that insert field codes include the following:

Edit, Paste Special, Paste Link

Insert, Page Numbers

Insert, Comment

Insert, Date and Time if you also check the Update Automatically check box

Insert, Field

Insert, Form Field

Insert, Caption

Insert, Cross-reference

Insert, Index and Tables

Another way to insert field codes into a document is to enter field codes directly into a document by pressing Ctrl+F9 to insert the field characters, { }, and then type between the field characters.

To insert field codes with the Insert, Field command, follow these steps:

1. Position the insertion point in the document at the location where you want the field result.

2. Choose Insert, Field.

   Figure 22.3 shows the Field dialog box, from which you can select field codes and instructions.

FIG. 22.3

The Field dialog box inserts fields and enables you to select appropriate switches to change format or actions.

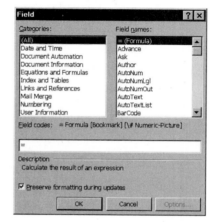

3. Select the type of field you want from the Categories list, or select All.

4. Select a field code from the Field Names list.

5. If the field code requires a bookmark, type in the bookmark. Specify bookmarks as described in the next section.

6. Select a switch to modify the field by choosing the Options button, when it is not dimmed. Select switches as described in the following text; then choose OK in the Field Options dialog box.

7. Select Preserve Formatting During Updates if you want manual formatting of the field results to remain when the field updates.

8. Choose OK.

When you choose OK, some fields update immediately. When you insert the {fillin} field, for example, Word displays the Fillin dialog box that prompts you for an entry.

Inserting Field Code Switches or Bookmarks

Some field codes have mandatory or optional switches. Some codes also require a book-mark—a named location in the document. You can find out what a field code needs and what is mandatory in two ways: look for a short prompt in the Field dialog box, or select Help for a full explanation. You can also turn to the section "A Reference List of Field Codes," later in this chapter.

In the Field dialog box, shown in Figure 22.3, look to the right of the Field Codes label in the lower third of the dialog box. You'll see a short prompt that shows what you can put in the field code that is selected in the Field Names list.

To insert switches or bookmarks into a field code, follow these steps:

1. Follow the steps in the preceding procedure, and select a field from the Field Names list.

2. If you use a field code that requires a bookmark, type in the bookmark name. You don't need to create the bookmark before you insert the field, but the field won't display results accurately until you create the bookmark.

3. To select a switch for the field, click the Options button. The Field Options dialog box appears.

4. Select the Field Specific Switches tab (see Figure 22.4).

FIG. 22.4

After you click Options, you can read a description of the available switches and choose the one you want from a list.

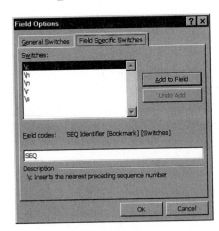

NOTE You also may see other tabs that contain other formatting information for the field. ■

5. Select a switch from the Switches list, and check the switch Description at the bottom of the dialog box. Choose Add to Field if you want to add the switch. Continue to add more switches, if necessary.

6. Choose OK in the Field Options dialog box.

7. Choose OK in the Field dialog box.

The field code you have built is then inserted into your document at the location of the insertion point.

Inserting Field Codes Manually

After you are familiar with the field code syntax, you can manually enter the field codes quickly. However, because you are not prompted with lists of correct switches, it's easier to make mistakes this way.

To enter a field code manually, follow these steps:

1. Position the insertion point in the document at the location where you want the field action or result.

2. Press Ctrl+F9.

   Even if fields are not displayed currently, Word shows the field characters you have just inserted. The insertion point appears between two field characters, { }.

3. Enter the field name followed by a space; then type the switches. If the field references a path name, be sure to type two backslashes instead of a single backslash to separate folders.

4. Update the field code by pressing F9.

Incorrect syntax in the field code causes a beep when you press F9 to see the results. Select the field and press Shift+F9 to see the field code and switches.

Another method of manually entering fields is to position the insertion point where you want the field, type the field code, arguments, and switches, select them, and then press Ctrl+F9. Word encloses the selection in field characters, { and }. This method works well when you need to nest fields inside other fields (see "Creating Complex Fields by Nesting" later in this chapter).

N O T E Remember that although the field characters appear to be braces, they are not. Fields do not work if you type brace characters. You can create a matching set of field characters only by pressing Ctrl+F9 or using a command to insert the field characters and field code. ■

Moving Between Fields

You can find fields in two ways: use a shortcut key to find the next field, or choose Ed̲it, F̲ind to find a specific field code.

To move to and select the next field after the insertion point, press F11 (Next Field). To move to and select the field preceding the insertion point, press Shift+F11 (Previous Field).

 T I P   If your keyboard does not have an F11 key, press Alt+F1. To move to the preceding field, press Alt+Shift+F1.

N O T E   The F11 and Shift+F11 shortcuts do not find the {xe} (index entry), {tc} (table of contents entry), or {rd} (referenced document) fields. You can find these fields by first displaying hidden text (by choosing T̲ools, O̲ptions), selecting the View tab, and then selecting the Hidden Text check box. After the codes are visible, you can choose Ed̲it, F̲ind. ▧

To find a specific field code, follow these steps:

1. Display field codes and hidden text. You can quickly display field codes by pressing Alt+F9. You can display both from the View tab of the Options dialog box (Choose T̲ools, O̲ptions).

2. Choose Ed̲it, F̲ind from the menu bar.

3. In the Fi̲nd What text box, type the field code you want to find, such as **fillin**. Do not type the field characters.

4. Click the F̲ind Next button.

5. If you want to edit the field, choose Cancel or press Esc.

6. Press Shift+F4 to find the next field of the same type. The insertion point moves to the next field of the type you requested.

 T I P   You can edit fields while the Find dialog box is open. Simply click once in your document to refocus Word on the document. When you want to use the Find dialog box again, click F̲ind Next.

Editing Fields

You can edit field codes or their results manually. This approach is useful for correcting the results of a field or for changing the information or switches in a field code after it has been created. By editing simple fields, you can change them into larger, nested fields containing multiple parts, which you then can use to accomplish complex tasks.

To edit a field code, follow these steps:

1. Display field codes by pressing Alt+F9 or use the View tab of the Options dialog box (choose <u>T</u>ools, <u>O</u>ptions).

 TIP

You also can select the text that encloses the field, and press Shift+F9 to display the fields.

2. Move the insertion point inside the field.

3. Edit the field as you edit text. Make sure that you preserve the correct syntax of the parts within the field. You cannot edit the field characters, { }.

To see the results of your editing, select the field and press F9 (Update Field).

TROUBLESHOOTING

I edited the results of fields on-screen and then when I printed, the fields updated and what I edited is lost. How can I keep a field from updating when I print? You can change the results of a field by editing the results on-screen as if you were editing normal text. If you edit the results, however, you do not want the field code to update when it prints. To make sure that the field code does not update, choose <u>F</u>ile, <u>P</u>rint, click the <u>O</u>ptions button, and make sure that the <u>U</u>pdate Fields check box is not selected.

N O T E Some fields, such as {include}, {dde}, and {ddeauto}, use DOS path names (folder names). When you type path names in fields, you must use double backslashes (\\) wherever the path name normally has a single backslash (\). Keep this fact in mind if you have to change the folder names used in a field. Always use a backslash before any quotation mark (") in a string that's enclosed in quotation marks. For example, the field

```
{fillin "Who wrote \"Brahms' Lullaby\""}
```

places quotation marks around the phrase Brahms' Lullaby when it appears in the prompt of a Fillin dialog box. ▮

Creating Complex Fields by Nesting

When you *nest* fields, you put one or more fields inside another field. This technique enables you to use the result of one field to change the actions of another. You can nest the {fillin} field inside the {set} field, for example, so that the typed entry in the {fillin} field can be stored by the {set} field in a bookmark. Then the text in the bookmark can be redisplayed at other locations with the {ref} field, as in the following example:

```
{set Name {fillin "Type the name"}}
```

This method is used in the letter shown in Figures 22.1 and 22.2.

To nest a field inside another field, follow these steps:

1. Display the field codes, if they are not already displayed, by pressing Alt+F9 or by choosing Tools, Options, selecting the View tab, and selecting the Field Codes check box.

2. Insert the first field into the document, using the method you normally use.

3. Position the insertion point inside the existing field at the point where you want the nested field.

4. Insert the nested field by following the Insert Field procedure for this code, or by pressing Ctrl+F9 and typing the field code and its arguments and switches between the field code characters, { }.

5. Return to step 3 and insert additional field codes, if necessary.

6. Select the field and press F9 (Update Field) to check the results.

 TIP Another quick way to update a field is to right-click the field and select Update Field.

Deleting Fields

Delete a field by selecting it and pressing Delete or Backspace. A quick way to select and delete fields is to press F11 (Next Field) until the appropriate field is selected, and then press Delete.

 TIP If you select fields manually by dragging across them, you need to drag across only the field character, { }, at either end of the field to select the entire field code.

Formatting Field Results

You can format the results of field codes in two ways:

- Using the techniques you use to format any other text or graphics.
- Inserting formatting switches in a field code.

Formatting the result of a field code is the same as formatting any item in a document. You select what you want to format and then choose a command. The next time the field code updates, however, it may lose the formatting you have applied. This situation can occur if the formatting you apply is different from the formatting contained in the switch in the field code.

Switches enable you to format the results of a field and take priority over manual formatting when the field code updates. When the field updates, the formatting specified by the switch applies itself again to the field code result. You can insert switches in a field code by selecting them from the Field Options dialog box, as described in "Inserting Field Code Switches or Bookmarks" earlier in this chapter. And you can add or change a switch by editing an existing field code.

Table 22.2 lists the four general switches you can use with most fields.

Table 22.2   General Switches for Formatting Fields

Switch	Syntax	Effect
*	{field-type * switchtype}	Formats the text result with case conversion, number conversion, or character formatting.
\#	{field-type \# numericpicture}	Formats the numeric result to match a "picture" showing the pattern of numeric format.
\@	{field-type \@ date-timepicture}	Formats the date or time result to match a "picture" showing the pattern of date-time format.
\!	{field-type \!}	Locks a field's results.

The following fields' results cannot be formatted with general switches:

{autonum}	{rd}	{formtext}
{formcheckbox}	{ta}	{listnum}
{embed}	{eq}	{autonumlgl}
{gotobutton}	{tc}	{macrobutton}
{autonumout}	{xe}	{formdropdown}

Formatting Numbers, Dates, and Text Case

In the following sections, the {fillin} field is used to illustrate how each * switch works. The {fillin} field displays a dialog box in which you can type sample text or numbers and see how the switch affects what you type.

 TIP   Always use a single space to separate the switches from the field code.

To duplicate the examples, press Ctrl+F9, type **fillin**, press the spacebar, and then type the switch type and switch. To update the field and see the results, select the field and press F9. Remember that you can switch quickly between viewing the field codes and their results by pressing Shift+F9.

Preserving Manual Formats

Two of the most valuable switches, * charformat and * mergeformat, enable you to retain formats you have applied to a field result. Without the use of these switches, your manual formatting of a field's result is removed when the field updates.

Switch Type	Effect
* charformat	Formats the field result the same as the format of the first character of the field code, the character after {. This format takes precedence over other formatting. Formatting the **f** in the {fillin} field as boldface, for example, produces a boldface field result.
* mergeformat	Preserves your manual formatting of a field's result. Character and paragraph formatting you apply to a field result are preserved after the field updates. The updated field results are reformatted on a word-by-word basis, using the original formatting as a template. If the updated results have more words than the originally formatted result, the extra words use the format of the first character after the opening field character, {. If the previous field result was not formatted, mergeformat acts like charformat.

The following example applies to the field result, the character format(s) you apply to the first letter in the field name FILLIN:

```
{fillin "Type a sample result" \* charformat}
```

Formatting remains even after the field is updated.

The following example formats the results of the field with character or paragraph formatting:

```
{fillin "Type a sample result" \* MERGEFORMAT}
```

After the field updates, the * mergeformat field preserves formatting applied previously. For example, if you manually apply bold to a field result, when you update the field Word retains the bold formatting. Formats are reapplied according to word-by-word locations. If the updated field contains words in a different order, the formatting may not coincide with the updated position of words. So, for example, if the field result includes the title of a book in italics, and when you update the field result more words are added before the book title, those words may appear in italics instead of just the book title.

Converting Uppercase and Lowercase Text   The following switches change the capitalization of the field's results:

Switch	Result
* Upper	Converts characters in the field results to all uppercase.
* Lower	Converts characters in the field results to all lowercase.
* FirstCap	Converts the first letter of the first word in the field result to a capital; converts other letters to lowercase.
* Caps	Converts the first letter of each word in the field result to a capital; converts other letters to lowercase.

The following example uses a capitalization switch:

```
{fillin "Type a sample result" \* Upper}
```

Formatting Numeric Results   The following switches change the way a numeric result appears:

Switch	Result
* Arabic	Uses Arabic cardinal numbers such as 1, 2, 3, and so on. If the field code is {page}, the switch overrides the page-number formatting set by the Edit Header/Footer dialog box.
* Ordinal	Converts a numeric field result to an ordinal Arabic number. When used with the {page} field, it produces page numbers such as 18th.
* Roman	Converts a numeric field result to Roman numerals, such as XV or xviii. Type the switch as * **Roman** for uppercase Roman numerals, or * **roman** for lowercase Roman numerals.
*Alphabetic	Converts a numeric field result to its alphabetical equivalent (changing the number 5 to the letter *e*, for example). Type the switch as * **Alphabetic** for uppercase letters, or * **alphabetic** for lowercase letters.

The following example uses a numeric switch:

```
{fillin "Type a number" \* Ordinal}
```

Formatting Numbers as Text   The following switches convert numeric results to a text equivalent. This process is useful for calculated numeric results that appear in documents—a check or invoice amount, for example. Use the capitalization switches described earlier in this chapter in "Converting Uppercase and Lowercase Text" to change the capitalization of a number as text.

Switch	Result
* Cardtext	Converts a numeric field result to text, with the first letter in uppercase (changing the number 35 to Thirty Five, for example).
* Ordtext	Converts a numeric field result to ordinal text (changing the number 35 to Thirty Fifth, for example).
* Hex	Converts a numeric field result to a hexadecimal number.
* Dollartext	Converts a numeric field result to a text and fractional dollar amount. For example, 53.67 becomes Fifty three and 67/100.

The following example uses switches to format text:

```
{fillin "Type a number" \* Cardtext \* Upper}
```

Formatting with Custom Numeric Formats

You can format numeric field results so that they appear in the numeric format you want. You can, for example, define your own custom formats that round results to the desired precision, display only significant numbers, include text, or have different formats for positive, negative, and zero results.

To format numeric results, you create a numeric picture. The switch for a numeric picture is \#. A *numeric picture* is a pattern that follows the switch and is composed of symbols that define placeholders, commas, and signs.

To format numeric fields with character formatting, such as boldface and italic, format the numeric picture. Formatting the negative portion of a numeric picture in italic, for example, produces italic formatting of negative results.

The examples use a fill-in data-entry box that enables you to type any number or text into a data-entry box. To duplicate one of the examples, use the Insert, Field command to display the Field dialog box. Select the FILLIN field, and then type the \# switch and the numeric picture following fillin in the Field Codes edit box. Leave a single space between the field name, the switch, and the numeric picture. The result should be similar to the following:

```
{fillin \# $#,##0.00}
```

To update the field so that a dialog box asks for your entry, select the field and press F9. To toggle the display between field results and field codes, press Shift+F9.

You can use the following characters to generate numeric pictures:

```
0   #   x   .   ,   -   +
```

You also can specify formatting variations for positive, negative, and zero results and can include text, sequence names, and other symbols and characters in a numeric picture. The following sections describe how to use these characters in numeric pictures.

Positive, Negative, and Zero Formatting Variations   You can specify three numeric pictures that Word can use, depending on the sign of the field's result. The three numeric pictures must be separated by semicolons (;). If the field result is positive, Word uses the numeric picture to the left of the first semicolon. If the result is negative, Word uses the numeric picture between the two semicolons. And if the result is 0, Word uses the numeric picture to the right of the second semicolon.

The numeric picture does not have to be enclosed in quotation marks if it contains only numeric formatting. If the numeric picture contains text or space characters, you must enclose the entire numeric picture in quotation marks. For example, the numeric pictures in this field

```
{fillin \# #,##0.00;(#,##0.00);0}
```

produce 4,350.78 when the field result is 4350.776; (4,350.78) when the result is -4350.776; and 0 when the result is 0.

N O T E   The right parenthesis,), accompanying a negative number can cause positive and negative numbers to misalign. If this problem occurs, align the numbers by using a decimal tab, or insert a space in the positive format to the right of the last zero. ■

The 0 Placeholder   Put a 0 in a numeric picture wherever you want a 0 to display when a number is missing. The field {fillin \# 0.00}, for example, produces the following results:

Number	Result
.646	0.65
250.4	250.40

Most currency formats use two zeros (00) to the right of the decimal.

The # Placeholder   The # character is a digit placeholder used when you do not want leading or trailing 0s (zeros) in results. The field {fillin \# #.00}, for example, produces the following results:

Number	Result
0.6	.60
250.4	250.40

The x Placeholder   The x character is a digit placeholder that *truncates*, or cuts off, numbers that extend beyond the x position. For example,

    {fillin \# #.#x}

produces .24 when the numeric result is .236.

The Decimal Point   Use the decimal point along with other numeric picture characters to specify the decimal location in a string of digits. Change the character used as the decimal separator by changing the Decimal Symbol on the Currency tab of the Regional Settings Properties dialog box. You can access this Windows 95 dialog box by clicking Start Settings, Control Panel, and then double-clicking the Regional Settings icon.

The Thousands Separator   Use the thousands separator (usually a comma) along with # or 0 numeric picture characters to specify the location of the thousands separator in a result. Change the character used as the thousands separator by changing the Digits Grouping Symbol on the Currency tab of the Regional Settings Properties dialog box. You can access this dialog box by opening the Start list, highlighting Settings, clicking the Control Panel, and then double-clicking the Regional Settings icon.

The Minus Sign (–)   Used in a numeric picture, this character (–) displays a minus sign if the result is negative and a blank space if the number is positive or 0.

The Plus Sign (+)   Used in a numeric picture, this character displays a plus sign (+) if the result is positive, a minus sign (–) if the result is negative, and a space if the result is 0.

Text   Use text formatting in a numeric picture to include measurements or messages along with the numeric result. Enclose text and the numeric picture in quotation marks (" "). The text displays in the field result in the same location as it appears in the numeric picture. For example, the numeric picture

    {fillin \# "Amount owed is $#,##0.00"}

produces Amount owed is $4,500.80 when the user types **4500.8** in the Fill-in dialog box.

If the text string contains a character that Word might interpret as an operator or as field information, enclose that character in apostrophes (' '). In the following example, the dashes on either side of the zero, - 0 -, normally do not display for the 0 result. But by enclosing the entire numeric picture in double quotation marks and the numeric picture for - 0 - in apostrophes, as in the following example, you can tell Word to display - 0 - for zero results:

    {fillin \# "0.0;(0.0);'- 0 -'"}

If you use text in a numeric picture that includes positive, negative, and zero format variations, enclose the entire pattern in quotation marks, as in the following line:

```
{fillin \# "0.0;(0.0);Enter a non-zero number"}
```

If the text itself contains quotation marks, precede those quotation marks with a backslash (\), as follows:

```
{fillin "Who wrote \"Brahm's Lullaby\"?"}
```

Other Characters   When you use symbols and characters in the numeric picture, they appear in the result. This feature is useful when you need to format a numeric result to include dollar signs, percent symbols, and international currency. A simple example is the use of the dollar sign, as in

```
{fillin \# $#,##0;($#,##0)}
```

or the percent sign, as in

```
{fillin \# #0%}
```

To enter ANSI characters such as the cent, pound, Yen, and section symbols, turn on the numeric keypad (press Num Lock) and hold down the Alt key as you type the appropriate four-number ANSI code. The character appears when you release the Alt key. Do not leave a space between the character entered and the numeric picture.

 T I P   ANSI characters and their codes are usually listed in the back of printer manuals.

N O T E   You also can add symbols in fields using the Insert, Symbol command. Simply position the insertion point at the location in the field where you want the symbol to appear, choose Insert, Symbol, find the symbol you want to insert and choose Insert. ■

Formatting Date-Time Results

You can format date and time field results so that they appear in standard or custom formats. To format date-time results, you create a date-time picture. The switch for a date-time picture is \@. A *date-time picture* is a pattern composed of characters that define date and time formats such as month, day, and hour. As it did with number formats, Word uses the pattern as a sample format. For example, the following field and pattern:

```
{DATE \@ "MMMM d, yyyy"}
```

displays the computer's current date in the format

```
December 24, 1995
```

To format date-time pictures with character formatting such as boldface and italic, format the first letter of each portion of the date-time picture. In the preceding example, you can format the first M in boldface and italic to make the entire month boldface and italic but leave the day and year as they were.

You can use the following characters to generate date-time pictures:

M   d   D   y   Y   h   H   m   am   pm   AM   PM

You also can include text, sequence names, and other characters and symbols in a date-time picture. The following sections describe how to use these characters in date-time pictures.

The Month Placeholder   Uppercase M is the month placeholder (lowercase m designates minutes). The four formats are as follows:

M	1 through 12
MM	01 through 12
MMM	Jan through Dec
MMMM	January through December

The Day Placeholder   Uppercase or lowercase d is the day placeholder. The four formats are as follows:

d or D	1 through 31
dd or DD	01 through 31
ddd or DDD	Mon through Sun
dddd or DDDD	Monday through Sunday

The Year Placeholder   Uppercase or lowercase y is the year placeholder. The two formats are as follows:

yy or YY	00 through 99
yyyy or YYYY	1900 through 2040

The Hour Placeholder   Uppercase or lowercase h is the hour placeholder. Lowercase designates the 12-hour clock. Uppercase designates the international 24-hour clock. The four formats are as follows:

h	1 through 12
hh	01 through 12
H	1 through 24
HH	01 through 24

The Minute Placeholder   Lowercase m is the minute placeholder. (Uppercase M designates months.) The two formats are as follows:

m	0 through 59
mm	00 through 59

Morning and Afternoon Indicators   You use uppercase or lowercase AM and PM with h or hh 12-hour clock formats to designate morning or afternoon. You can select characters other than AM/am and PM/pm by using the Control Panel to change settings in the International icon. The four formats are as follows:

\@ h AM/PM	8AM and 6PM
\@ h am/pm	8am and 6pm
\@ h A/P	8A and 6P
\@ h a/p	8a and 6p

Text Characters   Use text formatting in date-time pictures to include measurements or messages with the results. Enclose text in apostrophes (') and enclose the entire phrase (text and the date-time picture) in quotation marks (" "). If the text includes characters that Word can interpret as field information characters, such as a minus (-) or zero (0), enclose those characters in apostrophes (' '). The text displays the field result in the same location it appears in the date-time picture. For example, the following field and date-time picture

```
{DATE \@ "'Job complete at' HH:mm"}
```

displays a result such as Job complete at 12:45.

Other Characters   You can use the colon (:), hyphen (-), and comma (,) in the date-time picture. These characters display in the result in the same position in which they are used in the date-time picture. The date-time picture \@ "HH:mm" displays 23:15, for example, and the date-time picture \@ "MMM d, yy" displays Jun 15, 92.

Updating, Unlinking, or Locking Fields

As you learned earlier in the chapter, many field codes update automatically. You can update some codes manually, however. In some cases, you don't want field codes to update; for example, you may have a letter that begins with an automatic date field. You do not want the date on a completed letter to change the next time you open the letter.

Another instance in which you want to control updating is when you have data from an application such as Microsoft Excel linked into your Word document. You probably do not want the link refreshed each time you update the document—you may not know at that time whether the data in the source Excel worksheet is correct. Using the methods described in the following sections, you can update the document without updating the Excel data, and then return later to update just the Excel data.

Updating Fields

Updating a field produces a new result or action from the field—perhaps a change in text, numbers, or graphics. Some fields may not produce a visible change but instead affect the results in other fields.

Different fields update at different times. Fields such as {date} update when the document opens or when updated by command. Fields such as {Next} take effect only during print merge. Fields such as {Fill-in} update when you select the field and press F9 (Update Field). Other fields may update during printing, print merge, or repagination.

To update a field manually, select the field or place the insertion point anywhere in the field and press F9 (Update Field). Press F11 (Next Field) or Shift+F11 (Previous Field) to move to and select fields. Update a field with the mouse by right-clicking the field result and choosing Update Field. Display the field code by right-clicking the result and choosing Toggle Field Code.

If Word beeps when you attempt to update a field, the field is locked, there is a syntax error in the field code, or that field code does not update—as happens, for example, with the fields that generate equations on-screen.

If you want to update only part of a document, select only the portions of the document you want to update, and press F9. To update fields in a table, select the portion of the table you want to update (using any table-selection method), and then press F9.

To update an entire document, select the entire document, either by pressing Ctrl+A, or by pressing Ctrl and clicking the selection bar (the blank area to the left of the document), or by choosing Edit, Select All. Press F9 to update fields.

The following list shows fields unaffected by F9 (Update Field). Fields with an asterisk update automatically.

Field	Use
*{AutoNum}	Automatic numbers with Arabic (1, 2, 3, and so on) format.
*{AutoNumLgl}	Automatic numbers with legal (1.1.1 and so on) format.
*{AutoNumOut}	Automatic numbers with outline format.
{gotobutton}	On-screen buttons that jump to a location when double-clicked.

Field	Use
{macrobutton}	On-screen buttons that run a macro when double-clicked.
{Print}	To send information to the printer.

Undoing or Stopping Updates

You can undo field updates if you choose Edit, Undo Update Fields (or press Alt+Backspace or Ctrl+Z) immediately after updating one or more fields. This capability gives you a chance to make changes throughout a document, see how they affect the document, and then remove the changes if necessary.

 The status bar displays the percentage of updates completed.

If you are updating a document and want to stop the updates, press Esc. This method is handy if you have selected the entire document and realize that you do not want to update all fields.

Locking Fields to Prevent Updates

When you want to prevent a field from changing, you can lock it. Locking fields is useful if you want to archive a file that will not change, to prevent accidental changes, or to prevent updating a link to a file that no longer exists. Word does not update a locked field. If you attempt to update a locked field, you hear a beep and see in the status bar a warning that an attempt was made to update a locked field.

To prevent a particular field from being updated while those around it are updated, lock the field. Select the field or place the insertion point in the field and then press Ctrl+F11 (Lock Field). To unlock the field, press Shift+Ctrl+F11 (Unlock Field).

Locking a field is different from unlinking a field with Shift+Ctrl+F9. Unlinked fields replace the field code with the results. You are unable to return to a usable field code.

Unlinking Fields

You may want to unlink fields to convert them to their fixed results. Unlinking fields removes the field code and freezes the result at its current value by converting it to text. You may want to unlink field codes that link pictures, charts, and text into your document before you pass the document to someone else. If you do not want to pass all the linked documents, as well as your Word document, you should unlink the linked field codes before you give another user the document.

To unlink a field, place the insertion point in the field code or select the field code and press Ctrl+Shift+F9 (Unlink Field).

Getting Help on Field Codes

Word has more than 60 field codes that enable you to automate many of the features in documents you work in repetitively. Although most field codes are not difficult to use, much information is required about switches, bookmarks, and so on.

To get general or specific help about field codes, open the Help menu system. Choose Help, Contents and Index. Next, from the Customizing Microsoft Word section, select Fields. Select a topic and choose Display. If you need help about a specific field code, choose Help, Contents and Index, select Reference Information, and then select Field Types and Switches. You will see a list of fields (in alphabetical order). Select the one you need information about.

A Reference List of Field Codes

Exploring all the power and possibilities available with field codes is beyond the scope of this book. The following list shows some of the more frequently used field codes and their functions:

Function	Field Code
Date, Time, Summary Info	`date`, `time`, `author`, `createdate`
Index	`xe`, `index`
Forms	`formtext`, `formcheckbox`, `formdropdown`
Linking, embedding	`embed`, `includepicture`, `includetext`, `link`, `dde`, `ddeauto`, `hyperlink`, `autotextlist`
Mathematical calculations	`eq`
Mail merge	`data`, `mergerec`, `mergefield`, `next`, `nextif`, `ref`
Numbering	`autonum`, `autonumlgl`, `autonumout`, `seq`, `listnum`
Page numbering	`page`, `numpages`
Prompting	`ask`, `fillin`
Reference figures, objects, or locations	`pageref`, `ref`, `xe`
Symbol	`symbol`
Table of Contents	`tc`, `toc`

New fields in Word include the ListNum field, the AutoTextList field, and the Hyperlink field.

In the following sections, the syntax of each field code shows whether the code contains switches. Remember that a *switch* alters the behavior or format of a field code in some manner. A field may use multiple switches. Included in some field code descriptions is an explanation of the specific switches used in that field code.

The syntax also shows whether the field code uses arguments such as bookmarks or prompts. A *bookmark* is a name assigned to a selection or insertion point location. A bookmark also can be a name used to store information for future use by a field code. A *prompt* is a text message that appears on-screen when the field code updates. The prompt must be enclosed in quotation marks (" ").

Finally, the syntax also specifies the order in which you must enter information between field characters. Italicized words are information used by the field code. Optional information is enclosed in square brackets.

{advance}

Syntax:

```
{advance [switches]}
```

Offsets text that follows with a line to the left, right, up, or down, or to a specific horizontal or vertical position. Before using this field, try adjusting text placement using the Paragraph dialog box, the Tabs dialog box, or with a frame. Switches you use with this field can cause text to overlap; if this field moves text to the previous or next page or beyond the print margins, that text won't print.

Switch	Result
\d	Specifies the number of points down to move text.
\l	Specifies the number of points to the left to move text.
\r	Specifies the number of points to the right to move text.
\u	Specifies the number of points up to move text.
\x	Specifies the number of points from the left margin to move text.
\y	Specifies the number of points to move text vertically in relation to the current line position.

To see the effects of this field, use Page Layout view.

{ask}

Syntax:

```
{ask bookmark "prompt" [switches]}
```

Displays a dialog box that asks the user to enter text. Word assigns that text to the bookmark, which then can be used throughout the document to repeat the typed text. The following field code, for example, displays a dialog box asking the operator to enter the first name; Word stores the typed information in the bookmark named Firstname so that it can be used by other fields in the document:

```
{ask Firstname "Enter the first name"}
```

If you type **Mary** in response to the dialog box, you can repeat Mary throughout the document by using the field code {ref Firstname}.

Switch	Result
\o	Requests a response to the dialog box only at the beginning of the first document during a print merge.
\d	Defines default text for the dialog box. If no default exists, the last entry is repeated. Use \d"" if you want nothing as the default.

Updates during printing merge. You cannot use {ask} fields in footnotes, headers, footers, annotations, or macros.

If you want a dialog box for data entry, which you can update by pressing the F9 key, see the {fillin} field code.

{author}

Syntax:

```
{author ["new_name"]}
```

Inserts or replaces the author's name as it appears in the document's File, Properties, Summary tab.

The new name can be up to 255 characters long.

Updates when you press F9 or when you print.

{autonum}

Syntax:

```
{autonum}
```

Displays an Arabic number (1, 2, 3, and so on) when inserted at the beginning of a paragraph or outline level. Numbers display in the document in sequence, and update as other {autonum} paragraphs are inserted or deleted. Choose F*o*rmat, Bullets and <u>N</u>umbering to insert these fields more easily.

{autonumlgl}

Syntax:

```
{autonumlgl}
```

Displays a number, using legal numbering (1.2.1) format, when inserted at the beginning of a paragraph formatted with a heading style. See also {autonum}.

{autonumout}

Syntax:

```
{autonumout}
```

Displays a number, using outline number (I, A, 1, a, and so on) format, when inserted at the beginning of a paragraph formatted with a heading style. See also {autonum}.

{autotext}

Syntax:

```
{autotext AutoTextEntry}
```

The AutoTextEntry is the name in <u>I</u>nsert, <u>A</u>utoText under which text or an object is stored. As a result of updating this field, the latest definition is stored in AutoText.

{autotextlist}

Syntax:

```
{autotextlist "literal text" \s [StyleName] \t ["TipText"]}
```

Creates a drop-down list based on the AutoText entries stored in the active template. The list can vary, based on the styles applied to the AutoText entries. For literal text, type what you want the user to see before displaying the drop-down list box. If the phrase contains spaces, enclose it in quotation marks. For StyleName, specify the name of the style of the AutoText entries that you want to appear in the list—use a paragraph style or a character style. Again, if the StyleName contains spaces, enclose it in quotation marks. For TipText, type the text you want to appear as the user passes the insertion point over the field, enclosing the text in quotes if the phrase contains spaces.

To display the AutoText list, place the insertion point in the field or select the field and press the right mouse button.

Switch	Result
\s	Specifies that the link should not be added to the history list of links to which the user has jumped.
\t	Specifies a particular location, such as a bookmark or a named range in the document to which this hyperlink will jump.

{barcode}

Syntax:

```
{barcode \u "address_info" or bookmark \b [switches]}
```

Field codes: BarCode field

Inserts a postal bar code. The BARCODE field can insert either a POSTNET delivery-point bar code or a Facing Identification Mark, or FIM. You may find it easier to insert postal bar codes with the Envelopes and Labels command (Tools menu). If you use the Envelopes and Labels dialog box, Word will insert a {barcode} field. For "address_info", supply a delivery address and ZIP Code. When followed by the \b switch, a bookmark can replace address_info.

Switch	Result
\b	Specifies that a bookmark contains the address and ZIP code information.
\f	Specifies that one of two Facing Identification Marks (FIM) should be inserted: "A" inserts a courtesy reply mark; "C" inserts a business reply mark.
\u	Identifies the bar code as a United States postal address.

{comments}

Syntax:

```
{comments ["new_comments"]}
```

Inserts or replaces comments from the File, Properties. Updates when you press F9 or when you print or print merge.

{compare}

Syntax:

```
{compare first_expression operator second_expression}
```

Compares two values and displays either 1 (if the comparison is true) or 0 (zero) (if the comparison is false).

Use `first_expression` and `second_expression` as the values to compare. Expressions can be bookmark names, strings of text, numbers, nested fields that return a value, or mathematical formulas. If an expression contains spaces, enclose the expression in quotation marks.

Insert a space both before and after the operator. You can use the following operators:

=	Equal to
<>	Not equal to
>	Greater than
<	Less than
>=	Greater than or equal to
<=	Less than or equal to

If the operator is = or <>, `second_expression` can contain a question mark (?) to represent any single character or an asterisk (*) to represent any string of characters. The expression must be enclosed in quotation marks so that it is compared as a character string. If you use an asterisk in `second_expression`, the portion of `first_expression` that corresponds to the asterisk, plus any remaining characters in `second_expression`, cannot exceed 128 characters.

Suppose you're preparing a mail merge, and you want to select specific records based on the addressee's ZIP code. If any value in the PostalCode data field is within the range 33600–33699, the following COMPARE field returns the value "1".

```
{ COMPARE " { MERGEFIELD PostalCode } " = "336*" }
```

{createdate}

Syntax:

```
{createdate}
```

Inserts the date the document was created, as shown on the File, Properties, Summary tab. Formats according to the system's default format.

Updates when you press F9, when you choose File, Print Merge, or when you choose File, Print the first time (in a header or footer).

{database}

Syntax:

```
{database [switches]}
```

Used to insert data from an external database.

Switch	Result
\b	Identifies the attributes of the format set by the \l switch to apply to the table.
\c	Specifies the instructions that ODBC uses to make the connection to the database.
\d	Specifies the path and filename of the database.
\f	Specifies the starting data record for Word to use to insert data.
\h	Inserts field names from the database in the first row of the resulting table.
\l	Specifies a format from the Table AutoFormat dialog box to apply to the result of a database query.
\o	Inserts data at the beginning of a merge.
\s	Specifies the SQL instructions that query the database.
\t	Specifies the last data record in the database to insert in the table.

{date}

Syntax:

```
{date ["date_format_picture"]}
```

Inserts the current date or time.

Updates when you select this field and press F9 or print. Formats with the date-time picture-switches listed in the "Formatting Date-Time Results" section, earlier in this chapter.

{docproperty}

Syntax:

```
{docproperty "Name"}
```

Inserts the selected document information that is currently stored in the Properties dialog box (File, Properties). "Name" represents the property you want to display. To easily select a property, choose Insert, Field, and in the Field dialog box, choose Options.

For example, if the Manager field in the Document Properties dialog box contains the name Elaine Marmel, inserting

```
Contact: { DOCPROPERTY Manager }
```

in your document tells Word to display Contact: Elaine Marmel. This field updates when you press F9 or print the document.

{docvariable}

Syntax:

```
{docvariable "name"}
```

Each document has a series of variables that can be added and referenced by the Visual Basic for Applications programming language. This field inserts the string assigned to "name", the document variable, providing a way to display the contents of the document variables. For more information about document variables, see "Document Variables" in Visual Basic for Applications Help.

{edittime}

Syntax:

```
{edittime}
```

Inserts the number of minutes the document has been edited since its creation, as shown on the File, Properties, Statistics tab.

Updates when you press F9 or when you merge a mail document.

{=}

Syntax:

```
{= formula}
```

Displays the result of a mathematical calculation, such as

```
{ = Sales - Cost}
```

Expressions can use bookmarks to define the locations of numbers or can use row and column locations in document tables. Calculations on bookmarks can use common arithmetic operators, such as + (plus) and * (multiply). Calculations on row and column contents in a table use functions such as Average, Count, Sum, and Product.

▶ **See** "Creating Bookmarks," **p. 182**

▶ **See** "Performing Calculations in a Table," **p. 790**

Updates when you press F9 or print merged documents. If the expression is in the header or footer, it is updated when you print.

Following are examples of expression fields:

Field Code	Result
{= Sales - Cost}	Subtracts the value in Cost from the value in Sales.

Field Code	**Result**
`{= if (Sales > 450,Sales*.1,Sales*.05)}`	Tests whether the value in `Sales` is greater than 450; if it is, the result is the `Sales` value multiplied by .1; if not, the result is the sales value multiplied by .05.
`{= if (Sales > 450,Sales*.1,Sales*.05)*2}`	Multiplies the result of the `if` statement by two.

N O T E If you need to create a large mathematical expression, build it in pieces within the field characters. As you complete each *integral unit* (one that can calculate by itself), select the entire field and press F9 to see whether the result is correct. Select the completed expression, and press Ctrl+F9 to enclose that expression in another set of field characters. This method enables you to find errors in construction as you go, instead of trying to find problems in a large, completed expression.

You can lose a bookmark used in calculations by carelessly deleting a character. If you delete a value as well as the spaces that enclosed the value, you may have deleted the bookmark. In this case the formula no longer works because the bookmark no longer exists. You can re-create the bookmark to restore the formula. If you are in doubt about whether a bookmark still exists, open the Bookmark dialog box (Insert, Bookmark) and select the bookmark. See whether the correct value is selected in the document. If the bookmark is a name in which data is stored, rather than a document location, you may not be able to go to the bookmark.

Use the following math operators with bookmarks only:

Operation	**Operator**
Add	+
Subtract	–
Multiply	*
Divide	/
Exponentiate	^
Less than	<
Less than or equal to	<=
Greater than	>
Greater than or equal to	>=

Operation	Operator
Parenthetical	( )
Absolute value	Abs
Integer	Int
Sign	Sign
Test for error	Define
Modulus (remainder)	Mod
Round	Round
And	And
Or	Or
Not	Not

When you refer to a cell in a table, use the A1 format, in which rows are numbered, starting with 1 and going down. Columns are labeled with letters, beginning with A at the leftmost. If the expression is in the same table as the cells, only the A1 reference in brackets, [ ], is necessary.

You should use the functions and operators in the following table for any math calculations within a table. Functions can result in 1 for TRUE or 0 for FALSE.

▶ **See** "Performing Calculations in a Table," **p. 790**

Function	Name/Examples	Type/Result
Abs	Absolute value {= Abs -4}	Operator Results in 4.
And	Logical And {= And (Sales>500,Cost<300}	Operator Returns 1 if both arguments are true; 0 if either argument is false (maximum of two arguments).
Average	Averages arguments {= Average (Budget[R1C1:R1C2])}	Reduction function Averages the content of cells in row 1, column 1 and row 1, column 2 from the table named Budget.

Function	**Name/Examples**	**Type/Result**
Count	Counts arguments {= Count (Budget[C1])}	Reduction function Counts the number of numeric items in the cells of column 1 in the table Budget. Empty cells and text count as zero.
Defined	Checks for errors {Defined (Sales)}	Operator Results in 1 if Sales bookmark exists and expression evaluates without error; otherwise, results in 0.
Int	Results in integer {= Int (Sales)}	Operator Deletes decimal fraction of an argument. To round numbers, use the Round operator.
Max	Returns largest argument {= Max (Budget[R1C1:R2C2])}	Reduction function Returns the maximum value in the table named Budget within the range R1C1 to R2C2.
Min	Returns smallest argument {= Min (Budget[R1C1:R2C2])}	Reduction function Returns the maximum value in the table named Budget within the range R1C1 to R2C2.

Function	Name/Examples	Type/Result
Mod	Returns remainder `{= Mod (500,23.6)}`	Operator Returns the *modulus* (in the example, the remainder of 500 divided by 23.6).
Not	Reverses logical value `{= Not (Test)}`	Operator Returns 1 if the Test is 0 or if condition in Test is false; returns 0 if the Test is not zero or if condition in Test is true.
Or	Logical Or `{=Or (Sales$mt500,Cost$lt300)}`	Operator Returns 1 if either condition is true; returns 0 if either condition is false.
	`{= Product (Budget[R1C1:R2C1],2)}`	Returns the product of values in the range R1C1 to R2C1 of the table Budget and the number 2.
Round	Rounds value to specified digits `{= Round (SalesTotal,2)}`	Operator Returns the value of SalesTotal rounded to two decimal places.
Sign	Tests for sign of arguments `{= Sign (Profit)}`	Operator Returns 1 if Profit is positive, 0 if Profit is zero, or −1 if Profit is negative.

Function	Name/Examples	Type/Result
Sum	Totals arguments `{= Sum(Budget[R1C1:R2C1])}`	Reduction function Returns the sum of values in the range R1C1 to R2C1 of the table Budget.

{eq}

Syntax:

```
{eq [switches]}
```

Produces a mathematical equation. You'll probably find it easier to use the Equation Editor to create equations, but you can use the EQ field if you have not installed Equation Editor or if you want to write inline equations. An EQ field cannot be unlinked. If you double-click an EQ field, Word converts the field to an embedded Equation Editor object. Switches specify how to build the equation with the elements enclosed in parentheses. You can modify a switch by using the appropriate switch options.

Notes:

- To use a comma, open parenthesis, or backslash character in a resulting equation, place a backslash before the expression.

- Some switches require a list of elements separated by commas or semicolons. If the decimal symbol for your system is a period, use commas as the separators. If the decimal symbol for your system is a comma, use semicolons. See the Number tab in the Regional Settings Properties dialog box in the Windows Control Panel to identify the decimal symbol for your system.

Switch	Result
`\a( )`	Draws a two-dimensional array.
`\b( )`	Brackets a single element.
`\d( )`	Moves the next character to the left or right the specified number of points.
`\f(,)`	Creates a fraction.
`\i(,,)`	Creates an integral, using the specified symbol or default symbol and three elements.
`\l( )`	Groups values in a list, which can then be used as a single element.
`\o( )`	Prints each successive element on top of the previous one.

Switch	Result
\r(,)	Draws a radical sign (), using one or two elements.
\s()	Positions elements as superscripts or subscripts.
\x()	Draws a border around an element.

{filename}

Syntax:

```
{filename}
```

Displays the file name shown on the File, Properties, Summary tab.

Updates when you press F9, when you choose mail merge documents, or (in the header or footer) when you choose File, Print.

{filesize}

Syntax:

```
{filesize [switches]}
```

Inserts the size of the document, in bytes, using information from the Statistics tab in the Document Properties dialog box (File, Properties).

Switch	Result
\k	Displays the result in kilobytes (K), rounded to the nearest whole number.
\m	Displays the result in megabytes (MB), rounded to the nearest whole number.

For a 3,248,156-byte document, Word would display 3248K if you entered the filesize field:

```
{ filesize \k }K
```

For the same size document, Word would display 3MB if you entered the filesize field:

```
{filesize \m }MB
```

{fillin}

Syntax:

```
{fillin ["prompt"] switch}
```

Produces a dialog box, like the one shown in Figure 22.5, that displays a generic data-entry box. You can type a response in the dialog box. The result appears at the field location or can be used by other fields in which {fillin} is nested. Enclose the prompt and default text in quotation marks.

FIG. 22.5

Fillin fields display a data-entry dialog box in which a message prompts the user to type a correct entry.

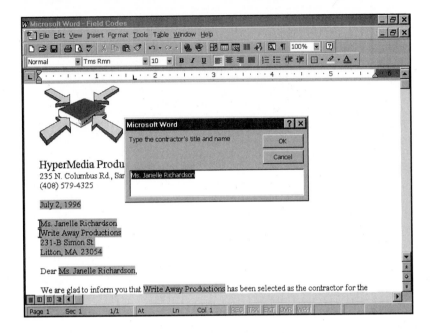

Updates when you press F9 or when you mail merge. Updates once in header or footer when you choose File, Print.

Switch	Result
\d	Default text follows the switch. The default text appears in the dialog box and is used if no entry is made. Enclose the default text in quotation marks. Use **\d ""** if you do not want any text to appear in the dialog box.
\o	Prompts at the beginning of a merge for bookmark text.

In the following example, MegaCorp appears as default text:

```
{fillin "Type your company." \d "MegaCorp" \* mergeformat}
```

{gotobutton}

Syntax:

```
{gotobutton destination button_text}
```

Produces a button in the document at the field's location. Double-clicking this button (or selecting the field by pressing F11 and then pressing Alt+Shift+F9) moves the insertion point to the destination. Use any destination you would when you're using F5 (Go To). destination can be any location where Edit, Go To will accept.

Create a button to surround the `button_text` by putting the field into a single-celled table or into a paragraph, and then formatting it to have a border. The `button_text` appears in the button. Do not enclose `button_text` in quotation marks.

{hyperlink}

Syntax:

```
{hyperlink "filename" [switches]}
```

Opens and jumps to the specified file name, which can be an Internet address, a document on your hard drive, or a document anywhere in your network. You also can use a wizard to help you create this field by pressing Ctrl+K or choosing Insert Hyperlink.

Switch	Result
\h	Specifies that the link should not be added to the history list of links to which the user has jumped.
\l	Specifies a particular location, such as a bookmark or a named range in the document to which this hyperlink will jump.
\m	Specifies that the link is an HTML 2.0 image map.
\n	Use this switch to make the hyperlink open a new window by default.

{if}

Syntax:

```
{if expr1 oper expr2 if_true_text if_false_text}
```

Use this field when you want Word to change a field action or result that depends on some value or text in the document. The `{if}` field uses the operator `oper` to compare the value of `expr1` to `exper2`.

`expr1` and `expr2` can be bookmarks of selected text, bookmarks assigned to store text, or R1C1 cell addresses from a table. `oper` is a mathematical operator separated from the `expr1` and `expr2` arguments by spaces. The following operators can be used:

=	equal
>	greater than
>=	greater than or equal to
<	less than
<=	less than or equal to
<>	not equal to

The statement you supply for `if_true_text` appears when the result of `expr1 oper expr2` is true. Similarly, the statement you supply for `if_false_text` appears when the result is false. If the statement is text, enclose it in quotation marks. Consider the following example:

```
{if daysdue >= 30 "As a reminder, your account is more than thirty days
overdue." "Thank you for your business."}
```

If the `daysdue` bookmark contains 12 when the field is updated, the field results in Thank you for your business. If the `daysdue` bookmark contains 45 when the field is updated, the field results in As a reminder, your account is more than thirty days overdue.

Updates when you press F9 or when you mail merge. In a header or footer, updates when you choose File, Print. See also `{nextif}` and `{skipif}`.

{includepicture}

Syntax:

```
{includepicture filename [\c converter]}
```

Inserts the contents of the `filename` into your document. Use **\c converter** to specify a converter file if the included file must be translated before being imported. You insert the `{includepicture}` field by choosing Insert, Picture.

Switch	Result
\c	Specifies the converter file to be used for files Word does not convert automatically. The appropriate converter file must have been installed in Word.
\d	Specifies that graphic data *not* be stored with the document, reducing the file size.

{includetext}

Syntax:

```
{includetext filename [bookmark] [\c converter]}
```

Inserts the contents of the `filename` at the location `bookmark`. Use **\c converter** to specify a converter file if the included file must be translated before being imported. See Chapter 34, "Assembling Large Documents," for more information.

Switch	Result
\!	Prevents fields in the included file from being updated.
\c	Specifies the converter file to be used for files Word does not convert automatically. The appropriate converter file must have been installed in Word.

{index}

Syntax:

```
{index [switches]}
```

Accumulates all the text and page numbers from the {xe} (index entry) fields or from outline headings, and then builds an index. Insert this field by choosing Insert, Index And Tables. See also {xe}.

You use switches to specify the range of the indexes, the separator characters, the entry's page number formatting, and more as follows:

Switch	Result
\a	Includes accented characters in their own index entries.
\b	Specifies the amount of text indexed.
\c	Creates multicolumn indexes.
\d	Specifies the separator character between a sequence number and a page number.
\e	Specifies the separator character between the index entry and page number.
\f	Creates indexes using xe fields of a specified type.
\g	Specifies the page range separator.
\h	Specifies heading letter formats used to separate alphabetical groups.
\l	Specifies the page number separator.
\p	Specifies the alphabetical range of the index.
\r	Puts sublevel indexes on the same level.
\s	Includes the sequence number with page number.

{info}

Syntax:

```
{[info] type ["new_value"]}
```

Results in information from the File, Properties, Summary tab, according to the type you use. Available types include the following:

author	numpages
comments	numwords
createdate	printdate

edittime	revnum
filename	savedate
filesize	subject
keywords	template
lastsavedby	title
numchars	

Updates when you press F9, when you print merge, or (in the header or footer), when you choose File, Print.

{keywords}

Syntax:

```
{keywords ["new_key_words"]}
```

Inserts or replaces the key words from the File, Properties, Summary tab.

Updates when you press F9, when you print merge, or (in the header or footer), when you choose File, Print.

{lastsavedby}

Syntax:

```
{lastsavedby}
```

Inserts the name of the last person to save the document, shown in the File, Properties, Statistics tab.

Updates when you press F9, when you print merge, or (in the header or footer), when you choose File, Print.

{link}

Syntax:

```
{link class_name "file_name" [place_reference] [switches]}
```

Links the contents of a file into the Word document. The link is created by choosing Edit, Paste Special with the Paste Link option. This field updates when you press F9. If the linked file cannot be updated, the results remain unchanged.

Use the following switches to modify the link:

Switch	Result
\a	Updates link when source data change.
\b	Inserts a Windows bitmap.

Switch	Result
\d	Does not store graphic data with file (smaller file size).
\p	Inserts linked data as a picture.
\r	Inserts linked data as an RTF file (with converted formatting).
\t	Inserts linked data as text.

{listnum}

Syntax:

```
{listnum "Name" [switches]}
```

Inserts a set of numbers anywhere in a paragraph. To type a list similar to the first phrase, use the list fields you see in the second phrase:

```
John asked 1) Mary, 2) Betty, and 3) Veronica to the dance, but nobody
accepted.
```

```
John asked {LISTNUM} Mary, {LISTNUM} Betty, and {LISTNUM} Veronica to the
dance, but nobody accepted.
```

Use the Name argument if you need to use more than one set of numbered items in the document, and each set must be independent of the others. You can include LISTNUM fields into text that is already numbered using, for example, a simple or outline numbered list. The LISTNUM fields will override typical numbering that might appear.

Switch	Result
\l	Specifies the number level in the list, overriding the default behavior of the field.
\s	Specifies the starting value for the field.

{macrobutton}

Syntax:

```
{macrobutton macroname instruction_text}
```

Displays the instruction_text. The macro specified by macroname runs when you double-click instruction_text or select it and press Alt+Shift+F9. Create a button to surround the text by putting the field into a single-celled table or into a paragraph, and then formatting it to have a border. The instruction_text must fit on one line. Do not enclose instruction_text in quotation marks.

{mergefield}

Syntax:

```
{mergefield field_name}
```

Inserted when you choose <u>T</u>ools, Mail Me<u>r</u>ge. Defines the field of data used at this location from the source file during a merge.

If you need to change the field name specified in a merge field, edit the field name only.

{mergerec}

Syntax:

```
{mergerec}
```

Inserts the number of the current print-merge record.

{mergeseq}

Syntax:

```
{mergeseq}
```

Inserts the number of the current print-merge sequence.

{next}

Syntax:

```
{next}
```

No result appears, but the field instructs Word to use the next record in the data file. {next} is used in mailing label templates, for example, to increment the mailing list from one record (label) to the next.

{nextif}

Syntax:

```
{nextif expr1 oper expr2}
```

{nextif} acts like a combination of the {if} and {next} fields. You can use {nextif} to specify a condition that data file records must satisfy before you use them for mail merge or form letters. No result appears.

{noteref}

Syntax:

```
{noteref bookmark [switches]}
```

Inserts a footnote or endnote reference mark you've marked with a bookmark. This field enables you to make multiple references to the same note or to cross-reference footnotes or endnotes. If you modify the sequence of footnotes or endnotes, the new result of the {noteref} field reflects the new numbering. Bookmark is the name of the bookmark that refers to the footnote or endnote reference mark. `Bookmark` must refer to the reference mark in the document text, not in the footnote or endnote pane. If the `Bookmark` doesn't exist, you must create it.

Switch	Result
\f	Inserts the reference mark with the same character formatting as the Footnote Reference style or the Endnote Reference style.
\h	Inserts a hyperlink to the footnote.
\p	Inserts the relative position of the footnote or endnote. If the `noteref` field appears before the bookmark in the document, the field evaluates to "below". If the `noteref` field appears after the bookmark in the document, the field evaluates to "above". If the `noteref` field appears in the bookmark in the document, Word returns an error.

Suppose the following text and field appear in a footnote of a document, and you create the bookmark "Wells" to mark the reference for footnote 3.

`"This process is discussed in Wells' new book (see note {NOTEREF Wells})."` When you update the field, Word displays the footnote number, and your text appears like this:

`"This process is discussed in Wells' new book (see note 3)."`

{numchars}

Syntax:

`{numchars}`

Inserts the number of characters in the document, as shown on the File, Properties, Summary tab.

Updates when you press F9 or when you print merge. In a header or footer, updates when you choose File, Print.

{numpages}

Syntax:

`{numpages}`

Inserts the number of pages the document contained when it was last printed or updated. The number comes from the File, Properties, Summary tab. See also `{page}`.

Updates when you press F9 or when you print merge. In a header or footer, updates when you choose File, Print.

{numwords}

Syntax:

```
{numwords}
```

Inserts the number of words in the document, as shown in the File, Properties, Summary tab.

Updates when you press F9 or when you print merge. In a header or footer, updates when you choose File, Print.

{page}

Syntax:

```
{page \* format_switch]}
```

Inserts the page number for the page on which the field code is located. Use numeric picture or format switches to format the number.

Updates when you press F9 or when you print merge. In a header or footer, updates when you choose File, Print.

{pageref}

Syntax:

```
{pageref bookmark \* format_switch}
```

Results in the page number on which bookmark is located. This field produces a cross-reference page number that updates itself.

Updates when you select it and press F9, or when you choose File, Print.

{print}

Syntax:

```
{print ""printer_instructions"}
```

Sends the printer_instructions text string directly to the printer, without translation. You use this field to send printer control codes to a printer or to send PostScript programs to a PostScript printer.

{printdate}

Syntax:

```
{printdate [\@ Date_time-picture switch]}
```

Inserts the date on which the document was last printed, shown on the File, Properties, Statistics tab. The default date format comes from the Date tab of the Regional Properties dialog box that you access through the Control Panel. For other date formats, use a date-time picture, as described in the "Formatting Date-Time Results" section, earlier in this chapter.

{private}

Syntax:

```
{private}
```

Word inserts a private field when converting file formats to store data for documents converted from other file formats. The private field contains data needed for converting a document back to its original file format.

A private field is formatted as hidden text and doesn't affect the document layout in Word. To hide a private field, choose Tools, Options and clear the Hidden text check box on the View tab.

{quote}

Syntax:

```
{quote "literal_text"}
```

Inserts the literal_text in the document. Updates when you select the field and press F9, or when you print merge. Enclose the literal_text in quotation marks.

{rd}

Syntax:

```
{rd filename}
```

{rd} helps you create a table of contents or index for large documents that cross multiple files. No result appears.

{ref}

Syntax:

```
{[ref] bookmark [switches]}
```

Results in the contents of the bookmark, which specifies a selection of text. The formatting of the bookmark displays as in the original.

Switch	Result
\f	Includes and increments footnote, endnote, or comment numbers.
\h	Creates a hyperlink to the marked paragraph.
\n	Inserts the paragraph number from the marked paragraph as it appears in the document.

Switch	Result
\p	Inserts the relative position of the marked paragraph.
\r	Inserts the paragraph number of the marked paragraph in relative context.
\t	Suppresses all non-delimiter characters.
\w	Inserts the paragraph number of the marked paragraph in full context.

Updates when you press F9 or when you print merge. In the header or footer, updates when you choose File, Print.

{revnum}

Syntax:

```
{revnum}
```

Inserts the number of times the document has been revised, as shown in the File, Properties, Summary tab. This number changes when the document is saved.

Updates when you select the field and press F9, or when you print merge. In the header or footer, updates when you choose File, Print.

{savedate}

Syntax:

```
{savedate}
```

Inserts the date the document was last saved, as shown on the File, Properties, Summary tab. To change formats, use a date-time picture, as described in "Formatting Date-Time Results," earlier in this chapter.

Updates when you select the field and press F9, or when you print merge. In the header or footer, updates when you choose File, Print.

{section}

Syntax:

```
{section}
```

Inserts the current section's number.

Updates when you select the field and press F9, or when you print merge. In the header or footer, updates when you choose File, Print.

{sectionpages}

Syntax:

```
{sectionpages}
```

Inserts the total number of pages in a section. When using this field, you should restart page numbering from 1 in each section after the first section.

For example, to print page numbers using the format "Page 1 of 18" at the bottom of each page of a document you've divided into sections, insert the following fields and text in the footer:

```
Page {page} of {sectionpages}
```

{seq}

Syntax:

```
{seq seq_id [bookmark] [switches]}
```

Inserts a number to create a numbered sequence of items. Use this field for numbering figures, illustrations, tables, and so on. seq_id specifies the name of the sequence, such as Figure. bookmark specifies a cross-reference to the sequence number of a bookmarked item. If you insert the following field wherever you need a figure number

```
{ref chap}.{seq figure_num}
```

the field produces an automatically numbered sequence of chapter number, period, and figure number—if the chapter number is 5 and this is the 12th figure you've inserted in the chapter, the result of the field would be 5.12. You must define the bookmark chap at the beginning of the document, and it must contain the number of the chapter. figure_num tracks only a specific sequence of items.

Updates the entire sequence when you select the entire document and press F9. Unlink (fix as values) the figure numbers by selecting them and pressing Shift+Ctrl+F9.

Switch	Result
\c	Inserts the sequence number of the nearest preceding item in a numbered sequence.
\h	Hides the field result—used in cross-references.
\n	Inserts the next sequence number If no switch is used, Word defaults to \n.
\r	Resets the sequence number as specified. The following field restarts the sequence numbering to 1 when it reaches 10, for example: {seq figurenum \r 10}.
\s	Resets the sequence number using the heading level specified by this switch.

{set}

Syntax:

```
{set bookmark "text"}
```

Use this field to assign new text (data) to a bookmark. You then can use the bookmark in multiple locations to repeat that text. No result appears when you use the set field. See also {ref}.

You cannot use {set} in comments, footnotes, headers, or footers.

Updates when you select the field and press F9, or when you print merge.

{skipif}

Syntax:

```
{skipif expr1 oper expr2}
```

You use this command in print merge to skip merging records that meet specified conditions. No result displays.

Updates when you print merge.

{styleref}

Syntax:

```
{styleref "style_id" [switch]}
```

Displays the text of the nearest paragraph containing the specified style, style_id. This field is useful for accumulating headings and topics that contain a specific style; for example, to create a dictionary-like heading.

Switch	Result
\l	Instructs Word to search from the bottom, rather than the top, of the current page.
\n	Inserts the paragraph number from the referenced paragraph as it appears in the document.
\p	Inserts the relative position of the referenced paragraph.
\r	Inserts the paragraph number of the referenced paragraph in relative context.
\t	Suppresses all non-delimiter characters.
\w	Inserts the paragraph number of the referenced paragraph in full context.

{subject}

Syntax:

```
{subject ["new_subject"]}
```

Inserts or replaces the subject in the File, Properties, Statistics tab.

Updates when you select the field and press F9, or when you print merge.

{symbol}

Syntax:

```
{symbol character [switches]}
```

Inserts a symbol character. Inserted by choosing Insert, Symbol.

Switch	Result
\f	Font set used, `{symbol 169 \f "courier new bold"}`
\h	Inserts the symbol without affecting the paragraph's line spacing.
\s	Font size used, `{symbol 169 \f Helv \s 12}`
\u	Treats the symbol as a Unicode character.

{ta}

Syntax:

```
{ta [switches]}
```

Defines the text and page number for a table of authorities entry. The TA field is formatted as hidden text and displays no result in the document. To view this field, display hidden text in the document.

Switch	Result
\b	Applies bold formatting to the page number for the entry. If the Table Of Authorities style for the entry already has bold formatting, the \b switch removes it.
\c category	Specifies the entry category, which is a number that corresponds to the order of categories in the Category box in the Mark Citation dialog box. The number determines how citations are grouped in tables of authorities.
\i	Makes the entry's page number italic. The switch removes the italic formatting if the Table Of Authorities style for the entry is italic.

Switch	Result
\l "long"	Defines the long citation for the entry in the table of authorities. This citation is from the Long Citation box in the Mark Citation dialog box (Index And Tables command, Insert menu). Enclose the long citation in quotation marks.
\r Bookmark	Inserts as the entry's page number the range of pages marked by the specified bookmark. The field { TA \l "Hotels Corporation v. Herder Assoc. 483 F.2d 247 (3d Cir. 1990)" \r hotelsvherder } displays the entry's page number in the format "20–25" in the table of authorities.
\s "short"	Defines the abbreviated form of the entry; this citation is from the Short Citation box in the Mark Citation dialog box (Index And Tables command, Insert menu). Enclose the short citation in quotation marks.

{tc}

Syntax:

```
{tc ""text"" [switch] [table_id]}
```

No result displays. {tc} marks the page and associates a text entry for later use in building a table of contents. See also {toc}.

text is the text that should appear in the table of contents.

table_id is a single letter used to identify a distinct table. This letter should follow the \f switch, with one space between the switch and the table_id letter.

Switch	Result
\f	Defines this {tc} as belonging to the table indicated by the table_id. This switch enables you to accumulate tables of contents for different topics.
\l	Specifies the level number for the table entry. The default is 1.
\n	Suppresses the page number for the entry.

{template}

Syntax:

```
{template [switches]}
```

Inserts the name of the document's template, as shown on the File, Properties, Summary tab.

Updates when you select the field and press F9, or when you print merge. In the header or footer, updates when you choose File, Print.

Switch	Result
\p	Adds the path to the file name.

{time}

Syntax:

```
{time [time_format_picture]}
```

Results in the time or date when the field was updated. Reformat by using a time_format_picture, as described in "Formatting Date-Time Results" earlier in this chapter.

Updates when you select the field and press F9, or when you choose File, Print.

{title}

Syntax:

```
{title ["new_title"]}
```

Inserts or replaces the document title, shown in the File, Properties, Summary tab.

Updates when you select the field and press F9, or when you print merge. In the header or footer, updates when you choose File, Print.

{toa}

Syntax:

```
{toa [switches]}
```

Builds and inserts a table of authorities. The TOA field collects entries marked by TA (Table of Authorities) fields. To insert a TOA field, use the Index And Tables command (Insert menu).

Switch	Result
\c category	Specifies the category of entries to collect in a table of authorities. A \c switch is required for each TOA field.
\b bookmark	Collects entries only from the portion of the document marked by the specified bookmark.
\e "separators"	Specifies the characters (up to five) that separate a table of authorities entry and its page number. Enclose the characters in quotation marks. A tab stop with leader dots is used if no \e switch is specified.

Switch	Result
\f	Removes the formatting of the entry text in the document from the entry in the table of authorities.
\g "separators"	Specifies the characters (up to five) that separate a range of pages. Enclose the characters in quotation marks. An en dash (–) is used if you omit the \g switch.
\h	Includes the category heading for the entries in a table of authorities.
\l	Specifies the characters (up to five) that separate multiple page references. Enclose the characters in quotation marks. If you omit the \l switch, Word uses a comma and a space (,).
\p	Replaces five or more different page references to the same authority with "passim".
\s identifier	Includes a number, such as a case number or section number, before the page number. The item must be numbered with a SEQ field, and the identifier must match the identifier in the SEQ field.
\d "separator"	Used with the \s switch, specifies the characters (up to five) that separate the sequence numbers and page numbers. Enclose the characters in quotation marks. A hyphen (-) is used if no \d switch is specified.

{toc}

Syntax:

```
{toc [switches]}
```

Shows a table of contents built by accumulating the text and page numbers of {tc} fields throughout the document.

Switch	Result
\a	Builds a table of figures with no labels or numbers.
\b	Builds a table of contents for the area of the document defined by the bookmark, as in {toc \b firstpart}.
\c	Use **SEQ** as a table identifier.
\d	Defines a sequence separator number.
\f	Builds a table of contents from {tc} fields with specific table identifiers.

\l	Controls the entry levels used in the table of contents.
\n	Builds a table of contents without page numbers.
\o	Builds a table of contents from the outline headings. The following field builds a table of contents from the outline by using heading levels 1, 2, and 3: {toc \o 1-3}
\p	Defines the separator between a table entry and its page number.
\s	Uses a sequence type to identify the sequence used in the table of contents.
\t	Builds a table of contents using non-standard style names.
\w	Preserves tab characters in table entries.
\x	Preserves newline characters in table entries.

{useraddress}

Syntax:

```
useraddress ["newaddress"]}
```

Inserts the user name and address from the Mailing Address box on the User Info tab in the Options dialog box (choose Tools, Options and click the User Info tab).

Use "newaddress " to insert an address you specify instead of the address on the User Info tab. Enclose "newaddress" in quotation marks. You can use ENTER or SHIFT+ENTER to break the address lines or type the address on one line. NewAddress doesn't change the contents of the User Info tab.

{userinitials}

Syntax:

```
{userinitials ["newinitials"]}
```

Inserts the user initials from the Initials box on the User Info tab in the Options dialog box (choose Tools, Options and click the User Info tab).

Use "newinitials" to insert the initials you specify instead of the initials on the User Info tab. Using "newinitials" doesn't change the contents of the User Info tab.

{username}

Syntax:

```
{username ["newname"]}
```

Inserts the user initials from the Name box on the User Info tab in the Options dialog box (choose Tools, Options and click the User Info tab).

Use "newname" to insert the name you specify instead of the name on the User Info tab. Using "newname" doesn't change the contents of the User Info tab.

{xe}

Syntax:

```
{xe "index_text" [switch]}
```

No result appears. Specifies the text and associated page number used to generate an index. You generate the index by choosing the Insert, Index and Tables command.

▶ **See** "Creating Indexes," **p. 970**

Switch	Result
\b	Toggles the page numbers for boldface.
\f	Specifies the type. Indexes can be built on this specific type of XE.
\i	Toggles the page numbers for italic.
\r	Specifies a range of pages to be indexed.
\t	Specifies the use of text in place of page numbers.

CHAPTER 23

Building Forms and Fill-In Dialog Boxes

Printed forms

Create printed forms (from a blank Word template) that duplicate the appearance of your on-screen Word forms.

On-screen data entry forms

Build on-screen forms in Word that display fill-in edit boxes, pull-down lists, and check boxes. Protect these forms so users can fill in the data, but not change a form.

Request data needed to complete a document

Create fields in any Word documents that request data once from the user, but then repeat the data as needed throughout the document.

Automate the control of forms

Create a simple program that controls your forms when the form document opens.

In the past, one office task that word processors were not able to do well was fill in forms. Typewriters were always needed to fill in a form. Storage rooms and filing cabinets took up space just to keep months' worth of inventory of forms that, in some cases, were so seldom used they were obsolete before they ever left the shelf.

Word's new forms features are a big step in the direction of being able to do away with preprinted forms. By using Word's desktop publishing features, many companies are now designing forms that they save as *templates* and print on demand. The cost savings over printing large volumes of forms can be huge.

Word also includes—in addition to its capability to produce a high-quality form on demand—features that make the task of filling in forms easy to do. By using Word's form fields, you can put edit boxes, check boxes, and pull-down lists directly into your documents. The use of {fill in} and {ask} fields enables a document to pop up dialog boxes that ask for input. ■

Understanding Form Basics

A *form* is a special kind of protected document that includes fields where people can type information. Any document that includes form fields is a form. A *form field* is a location on-screen where you can do one of three things—enter text, toggle a check box on or off, or select from a drop-down list.

Tables provide the structure for many forms, because a table's cells are an ideal framework for a form's labels and information fields. You can type labels in some cells, and insert form fields in others. Tables also make adding shading and borders to forms an easy job. You can place a dark border around a selected group of cells in a table, for example, while including no border at all around other cells. With the gridlines turned off, a table doesn't have to look like a table at all, and thus makes the ideal framework for a form.

A form can be based on any type of document. A real estate contract, for example, may include several pages of descriptive paragraphs containing form fields in which you insert information. The text in the paragraphs doesn't change—you insert information in the form fields only.

You can include three types of form fields in a form: text, check box, and drop-down. You can customize each of these field types in many ways. You can format a text field, for example, to accept only dates and to print dates as January 1, 1997, as 1/1/97, or in another format. Figures 23.1, 23.2, and 23.3 show examples of three forms that can be created using Word.

You can use forms in a variety of ways to save time, effort, and money. You can create your own commonly used business forms such as sales invoices, order sheets, personnel records, calendars, and boilerplate contracts. You can print a copy of your blank form and have it reproduced in quantity, using color if you want, then print only the information contained in your form onto your preprinted forms—the information will be positioned correctly.

You also can automate forms that don't need to be printed at all. Distribute form templates, rather than paper forms, to people in your company. You can make forms easy to use by including helpful on-screen messages and automatic macros.

You can include calculations in forms—adding up the prices of items in a sales invoice form, for example, to show a total invoice amount. And you can add form fields to documents other than forms. When the fields are shaded, people can easily see where they should insert necessary information.

FIG. 23.1

An example of an order/delivery form.

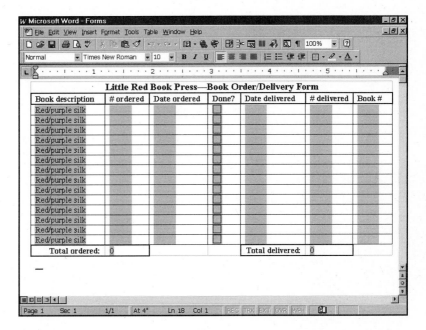

FIG. 23.2

An example of an invoice form.

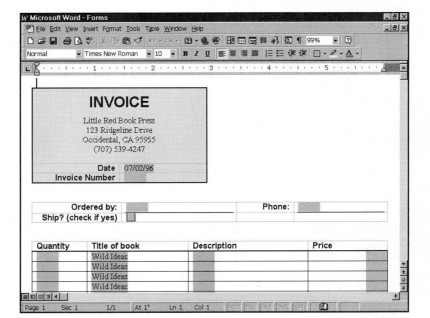

Part

V

Ch

23

FIG. 23.3

An example of an installment note form.

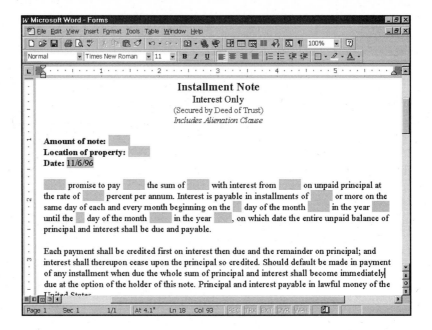

The most useful forms are based on templates, which can be used over and over again. When someone fills in such a form, he or she fills in a copy—the original does not change. (You can, of course, create a form as a document instead of a template if you plan to use the form only once.) When someone creates a new document based on your form template, he or she can type information only in the fields you designated when you created and protected the form.

> **CAUTION**
>
> Unless you add password protection, someone using the form can unprotect it and make changes not only to the fields but also to other parts of the form. In the section "Protecting and Unprotecting a Form with a Password" found later in this chapter, you learn how to provide maximum protection for form templates.

You can create forms by selecting the location where you want to place a form field, such as a check box, then clicking the Check Box Form Field tool on the Forms toolbar. The Forms toolbar contains a number of tools useful for creating forms (see Figure 23.4).

You can display the Forms toolbar by choosing View, Toolbars and selecting Forms from the Toolbars list. Alternatively, you can click with the right mouse button on any toolbar, and select Forms from the list of toolbars that appears.

FIG. 23.4
The Forms toolbar
includes tools to
help you build and
customize forms.

ON THE WEB

For online support from Microsoft, visit the following World Wide Web site:

http://www.microsoft.com/support

You can also access Microsoft's extensive troubleshooting KnowledgeBase at the following site:

http://www.microsoft.com/kb

For tutorials, tips, and add-ins for Microsoft Office applications, point your browser to:

http://www.ronperson.com

Building Forms

Building a simple form is a three-part process. First, you create a new template and build the *form structure*—the framework for the form—and add labels, formatting, shading, and borders, and anything else that won't change when users fill in the form. Next, you insert form fields where you want to type information when you fill in the form. Finally, you protect and save the form.

Creating and Saving the Form Structure

Before you begin designing a form on your computer, sketching it out on paper may be helpful, particularly if you're using a table as the structure for the form. By sketching out the form, you'll know how many rows and columns you need in your table, and you'll know where to type labels and where to insert form fields. Even if you change the form as you go, it's easier to start with a plan.

Before entering form controls, you will want to create the body or structure of your form. It may contain text, tables, graphics, columns, and of course, formatting.

To create and save the form structure using a new template as a base for your form, follow these steps:

1. Choose File, New. The New dialog box appears.
2. Select the template you want as a base from the New dialog box. In most cases, you can use the Blank Document found on the General tab.

3. Choose OK.

4. Establish the form structure in one of these ways:

Insert a table by choosing Table, Insert Table, or by clicking the Tables and Borders button or the Insert Table button on the Standard toolbar. Type labels and any other text that will not change in the form. Format the table with lines, borders, and shading.

Create a form based on paragraphs by inserting form fields where you need them as you type the text of your document. Read the next section, "Adding Form Fields," to learn how to insert form fields.

At the top of your document, insert the table or type the text that will contain form fields. Select, frame, and position this portion of your document. Then type the remainder of the form, which includes text that will not change when you fill in the form.

5. Choose File, Save As to save the template. Type the template's name in the Save As box, then choose OK. Leave your template open so that you can add the form fields.

> **TIP**
>
> If you create a new form using a document as a base for the form, you can still save it as a template. Save it again by choosing File, Save As. Select Document Template (*.DOT) in the Save As Type drop-down list.

Templates normally are saved in the TEMPLATE folder under the folder containing Word. If Microsoft Office is installed, then templates are stored in the PROGRAM FILES\MICROSOFT OFFICE\TEMPLATES folder.

▶ **See** "Understanding Templates," **p. 93**

▶ **See** "Creating Tables," **p. 608**

Adding Form Fields

After you've established the structure for your form—whether it's a table or a paragraph—you can add the form fields. Form fields enable the user to enter data. As mentioned earlier, the three types of form fields are text, check box, and drop-down. You can add form fields to your template by using a menu command or by clicking buttons on the Forms toolbar.

To add form fields to your document by using the Forms toolbar, follow these steps:

1. Display the Forms toolbar by right-clicking a toolbar and choosing Forms or by choosing the View, Toolbars, Forms command. The Forms toolbar appears (see Figure 23.4).

▶ **See** "Using the Toolbars," **p. 52**

2. Position the insertion point where you want a form field.

3. Click one of the form field tools displayed at the left side of the Forms toolbar:

abl To insert a text field, click the Text button.

☑ To insert a check box, click the Check Box button.

▦ To insert a drop-down list, click the Drop-Down button. (Notice that a drop-down list is empty until you customize it by adding items to the list; see the later section, "Customizing Drop-Down Form Fields.")

A form field appears in your document.

4. Repeat steps 2 and 3 to add additional form fields to your document.

 Notice that the Forms toolbar contains a Shading Options button. If you select this tool, form fields appear as shaded rectangles on your screen (see Figure 23.5). If you don't select this tool, text fields appear with no shading or border, check box fields appear with a square outline, and drop-down fields appear with a rectangular outline (see Figure 23.6).

FIG. 23.5
Form fields appear shaded when you click the Shading Options button on the Forms toolbar.

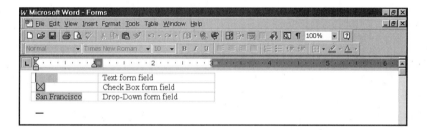

FIG. 23.6
If you don't click the Shading Options button, text form fields don't appear at all, and check box and drop-down form fields are outlined.

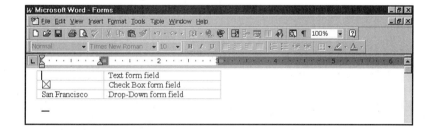

The preceding steps insert text boxes, check boxes, or lists, but you cannot use these form fields until you protect the document or template, as described in the next section.

TIP If you're creating a form that contains many of the same form fields, save time by copying one or more existing form fields and pasting them into a new location.

Part
V
Ch
23

N O T E Refer to the "Customizing Form Fields" section later in the chapter to learn how to customize each form field you add to your document. For example, you can customize a text field so that the current date automatically appears; you can customize a drop-down field to add items to the drop-down list. ■

Inserting Floating Text Boxes in a Form

One way in which you can enhance a form is by adding a box of floating text. You can position a text box anywhere you want on the page (see Figure 23.7). This way, you can separate the portion of a document that contains fields in which you must insert information from other parts of the document where the text may not change.

FIG. 23.7
By framing selected text that includes form fields, you can create a form like this.

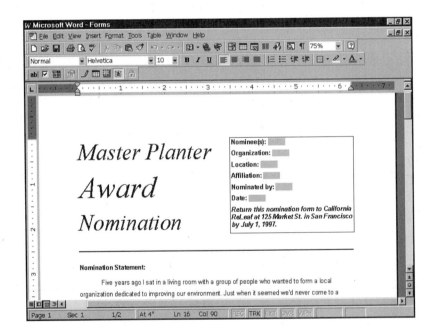

To create a text box in your form, follow these steps:

1. Click the Text Box tool on the Forms toolbar.
2. Drag across the form where you want to create the text box.
3. Type the text you need into the text box.
4. Move the selection point to the location in the text box where you want a form field, and click the appropriate tool on the Forms toolbar.

Protecting and Saving the Form

Until you protect a document containing form fields, you can edit any part of it, text or form fields. However, after the document is protected, you can fill in a form field, but you can't edit the document.

A protected form is different from an unprotected form in several ways. For example, you cannot edit the document—you can only insert a response into a form field. You can't select the entire document, and you can't use most commands, including formatting commands. Tables are fixed, and fields with formulas display results, rather than the formulas.

Part

V

Ch

23

TIP Even if you don't want form fields shaded in your final on-screen form, use shading while you create your form to make the fields easy to see and edit.

You can easily unprotect a document when you want to edit it—unless someone has protected it with a password. To learn how to use password protection, refer to the upcoming section, "Protecting and Unprotecting a Form with a Password." To learn how to protect only part of a form, see the later section "Protecting Part of a Form."

If you started your form in a template, Word automatically saves it as a template (using the extension DOT) and proposes saving it in the TEMPLATE subfolder, where it *must* remain in order for Word to find it when you create a new document. To use your form as a template that appears when you choose File, New, don't change the file extension. (You can, however, specify that all templates be stored in a different subfolder by choosing Tools, Options, selecting the File Locations tab, and modifying the User Templates item.)

To protect and save your form, follow these steps:

1. Choose Tools, Protect Document. The Protect Document dialog box appears (see Figure 23.8).

FIG. 23.8
After you protect a document, you can't edit it.

2. Select Forms, and choose OK.
3. Choose File, Save As (see Figure 23.9.) Type a name in the File Name text box, and make sure that Document Template (*.dot) is selected in the Save as Type list, and

that the TEMPLATES subfolder in the MICROSOFT OFFICE folder is selected in the folders list. The TEMPLATES folder is located under the WINWORD folder if you do not have Office 97.

4. Choose OK to save the file as a template.

FIG. 23.9

Be sure to save your form as a template.

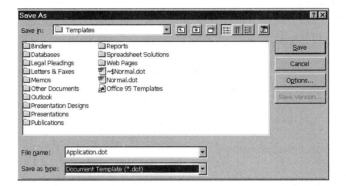

 TIP Someone may have changed the names of your MICROSOFT OFFICE folder and TEMPLATES subfolder; accept these changed names if they appear as the defaults.

To unprotect your form, choose Tools, Unprotect Document.

If your form is protected with a password, you must enter the password in order to unprotect the form. See the upcoming section, "Protecting and Unprotecting a Form with a Password."

 To protect or unprotect your form using the Forms toolbar, click the Protect Form button on the Forms toolbar. When the button appears pressed, the form is protected; when the button appears raised, the form is unprotected.

Word has two ways of saving forms. You can save the complete form, including fields, labels, and the information you enter in the form. Or you can save just the information you entered in a form, so that you can use this data with another program. See the section "Saving an On-Screen Form," later in this chapter, for details on the second method.

 TIP When you give someone an on-screen form to use, be sure to give that person the template; this is a file with the extension DOT. Tell the person to copy the template into the TEMPLATES subfolder under the MICROSOFT OFFICE folder.

▶ **See** "Using Templates as a Pattern for Documents," **p. 202**
▶ **See** "Creating Tables," **p. 608**

Using On-Screen Forms

The great advantage to forms is that you can't edit them—instead, you open a blank copy of the form (thus preserving the original), and then move from field to field, filling in information as necessary.

The three types of form fields (text, check box, and drop-down) not only look different; you also use a distinct approach with each type (see Figure 23.10).

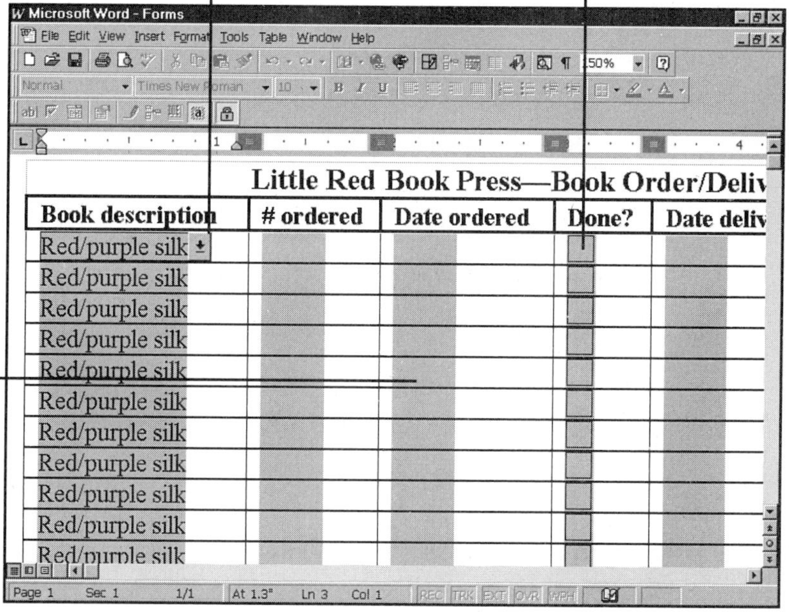

Part

V

Ch

23

FIG. 23.10
Click the arrow or press Alt+down arrow to display the items in a drop-down list.

Clicking this arrow displays
the items in a drop-down list

Select or clear a check box
by pressing the space bar

Respond to a text field
by typing text or a
number

You can customize your form in several ways. For example, you can customize a text field to hold only dates and to format the date you enter in a certain way. Any type of field may have a help message attached so that when you enter the field or press F1, instructions for using the field appear in the status bar. In some fields, a particular response may cause some action in another part of the form; for example, a positive response to a check box field may activate another field later in the form. Be alert to what happens on-screen as you fill in your form.

To open a blank form, follow these steps:

1. Choose File, New. The New dialog box appears (see Figure 23.11).

FIG. 23.11

Open a form by choosing File, New.

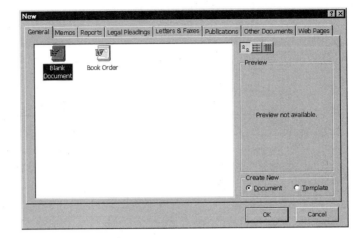

2. Click the appropriate tab and select your form.

3. Choose OK. An unnamed copy of the form appears on-screen, with the first field in the form highlighted.

If your form isn't based on a template, you can still use it by opening it as a regular file. Choose File, Open, locate and select your form, and choose OK. Save it with a new name to preserve the original.

▶ **See** "Creating and Saving Documents," **p. 81**

Filling in an On-Screen Form

When you open a new, protected form, the first field is selected (highlighted).

To fill in the fields in a form, follow these steps:

1. Respond to the selected field using one of the following methods.

   - In a text field, type the requested text or number.

   - Check boxes toggle on and off. Press the spacebar once to place a mark in an empty check box; press the spacebar a second time to remove a mark from the box. (Check boxes may contain a mark by default; if so, press the space bar once to remove the mark, and press the space bar a second time to replace the mark.)

   - In a drop-down field, click the arrow to display a list of selections, then click the item you want to select. Or, with the keyboard, press Alt+down arrow to display the list, and press the down- or up-arrow keys to select an item from the list.

You can use the up- and down-arrow keys to move between fields in a form, except while a drop-down list is displayed.

2. Press Tab or Enter to accept your entry. One of two things happens:

- If your entry is acceptable, Word selects the next field.
- If your entry is unacceptable, Word displays an error message and returns you to the current field so that you can make a correct entry. You might get an error message, for example, when you type text in a text field that's formatted to hold a number.

3. Continue filling in fields until you complete the form.

 Watch the status bar for messages that may help you fill each field in a form. You can also try pressing F1 to get help for a particular field when that field is selected.

If you make a mistake and want to return to a previous field, hold down the Shift key while you press the Tab or Enter key until you reach that field. To move to the next field without making an entry, just press Tab or Enter. You can also move between fields by pressing the up- or down-arrow keys, and you can move to the beginning or end of your form by pressing Ctrl+Home or Ctrl+End.

To edit an entry in a field you've already left, use the mouse or arrow keys to position the insertion point next to the text you want to edit; press Backspace to delete characters, or type the characters you want to insert.

If you want to insert a Tab character in a field, without moving to the next field, hold down the Ctrl key as you press Tab.

 Always watch the way Word interprets your response to a field. For example, if a text field is formatted to include numbers formatted with no decimal places, and you respond by spelling out a number (four, for example), Word interprets your response as 0 (zero) because it's expecting numbers, not letters. Return to the field and type the correct response.

If the form isn't protected, the first field isn't highlighted when you open the form, and you can't move between fields by pressing Tab or Enter. To fill in an unprotected form, use Word's normal techniques for moving the insertion point from field to field. Or better yet, protect the form by choosing Tools, Protect Document, and selecting the Forms option.

▶ **See** "Using Templates as a Pattern for Documents," **p. 202**

▶ **See** "Typing and Moving in a Table," **p. 616**

Saving an On-Screen Form

Because most on-screen forms are based on templates, they do not have names when you open them. You must save and name the form once it is filled in. (If a form is not based on a template, use the following steps to save your form with a unique name. In this way, you preserve the original for future use.)

To save a form, follow these steps:

1. Choose File, Save As. The Save As dialog box appears.

2. Type a name in the File Name box, and select the folder for the form from the list of folders.

3. Choose OK.

TROUBLESHOOTING

I opened a new form and the first field isn't selected. The form isn't protected. To fill it in, protect it by choosing Tools, Protect Document. (It may be a good idea to open the form template and protect it, so that the next time you open the form, it's protected.)

Customizing Form Fields

There are many ways you can customize form fields to make your forms more informative, more automated, and easier to use. Automatic date and time fields, for example, insert the current date or time into your form. Default entries suggest a likely response to a field. Help messages give users hints on how to fill in a particular field. Controls prevent certain types of errors. Formulas calculate results in a field. Macros run when users enter or exit a particular field.

You can also apply most types of formatting to form fields. For example, you can make a form field boldface so that the response stands out. Or you can apply a border to a form field to add boxes in a form that isn't based on a table.

You can customize form fields by editing selected fields. To edit form fields after you've inserted them, the document must be unprotected.

To customize a form field after you have inserted it, follow these steps:

1. Unprotect your document, if it's protected, by choosing Tools, Unprotect Document or by clicking the Protect Form button on the Forms toolbar.

2. Double-click the form field you want to customize or click the form field, then click the Form Field Options button on the Form toolbar. This displays the Form Field Options property sheet for that field.

   Or, click the form field you want to customize with the right mouse button to display the shortcut menu. Select Properties.

T I P If you use a form field repeatedly in a form, duplicate it by placing it in AutoText.

▶ **See** "Creating an AutoText Entry," **p. 170**
▶ **See** "A Reference List of Field Codes," **p. 718**

3. Select the properties you want this field to have, and choose OK.

Customizing Text Form Fields

Text fields are probably the most customizable of the three form field types. You can customize them by type (regular, number, date, or calculation, for example), by default text, by the size of the field, by the maximum number of characters in the response, or by the format of the response. As with all form field types, you can also customize text fields by adding macros (see the later section "Adding Macros to a Form"), by adding Help text (see the section "Adding Help to a Form"), by renaming the bookmark (see "Naming and Finding Fields in a Form"), or by disabling the field for entry (see "Disabling Form Fields").

 T I P Specifying a field size is particularly important when you are using preprinted forms.

To specify the restrictions on a text form field, follow these steps:

1. Open the Text Form Field Options property sheet (see Figure 23.12).

FIG. 23.12
Text form fields have numerous customizing options.

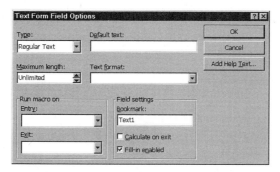

2. Select from the following types of options (see the upcoming tables for details about the Type and Format options):

Part
V
Ch
23

Option	Description
Type (see Table 23.1)	Select from six types of text entries: Regular Text, Number, Date, Current Date, Current Time, and Calculation.
Default Text	Type the text that you want to appear as the default entry in this field. Users can change the entry.
Maximum Length	Type or select "Unlimited" or the number of characters or numbers you want the field to accept (up to 255).
Text Format	Select from various types of text, numeric, and date formats, depending on what you've selected in the Type option (see Table 23.2).

3. Choose OK.

You will often use two or more of these options together. For example, if you select Number as the Type, then you might choose `0.00` as the Format so that a numeric response appears in two decimal places.

Table 23.1 Type Options for Text Form Field Options Property Sheet

Select This Option:	When Users Should Respond by Typing:
Regular Text	Text. Word formats the text according to your selection in the Text Format list.
Number	A number. Word formats the number according to your selection in the Number Format list, and displays an error message if user types text.
Date	A date. Word formats the date according to your selection in the Date Format list. Word displays an error message (A valid date is required) if user types text or a number not recognizable as a date, and returns user to the current field for an appropriate response. (Almost any response resembling a date will work, however.)
Current Date	No user response allowed. Word enters the current date (and updates the date when the document is opened).
Current Time	No user response allowed. Word enters the current time (and updates the time when the document is opened).

Select This Option:	When Users Should Respond by Typing:
Calculation	No user response allowed. Enter a formula when inserting or editing this field. Word applies your formula, and prints the result of the calculation in this field. For example, you can insert a simple SUM formula to add up the numbers in a column if your form is based on a table. (Word updates the result when the document is opened.)

▶ **See** "Creating and Editing Tables," **p. 607**

▶ **See** "Automating with Field Codes," **p. 693**

Table 23.2   Text Format Options for Text Form Field Options

Type Option	Text Format Option	What Entry Looks Like
Regular Text	Uppercase	ALL CAPITAL LETTERS
	Lowercase	all lowercase letters
	First Capital	First letter of first word is capitalized
	Title Case	First Letter Of Each Word Is Capitalized
Number	0	123456
	0.00	123456.00
	#,##0	123,456
	#,##0.00	123,456.00
	$#,##0.00;($#,##0.00)	$123,456.00
	0%	10%
	0.00%	10.00%
Date	M/d/yy	1/1/95
	dddd, MMMM dd, yyyy	Sunday, 3 January,1995
	d MMMM, yyyy	3 January, 1995
	MMMM d, yyyy	January 3, 1995
	d-MMM-yy	3-Jan-95
	MMMM, yy	Jan, 95
	MM/dd/yy h:mm AM/PM	01/03/95 2:15 PM
	MM/dd/yy h:mm:ss AM/PM	01/03/95 2:15:58 PM
	h:mm AM/PM	2:15 PM
	h:mm:ss AM/PM	2:15:58 PM
	H:mm	2:15
	H:mm:ss	2:15:58
Current Date	Same as Date	Same as Date
Current Time	h:mm AM/PM	3:30 PM
	h:mm:ss AM/PM	3:30:00 PM
	H:mm	15:30
	H:mm:ss	15:30:00
Calculation	Same as Number	Same as Number

Part

V

Ch

23

Customizing Check Box Form Fields

You can customize check box fields, which require the user to make a simple "yes or no" response, by determining size and by choosing whether they will be checked or unchecked by default. As with all form field types, you can also customize check box fields by adding macros (see the later section, "Adding Macros to a Form"), by adding Help text (see the "Adding Help to a Form" section), by renaming the bookmark (see "Naming and Finding Fields in a Form"), or by disabling the field for entry (see "Disabling Form Fields").

To customize a check box field, follow these steps:

1. Open the Check Box Form Field Options property sheet (see Figure 23.13).

FIG. 23.13

You can make a check box exactly the size you want, and you can specify whether it's checked or unchecked by default.

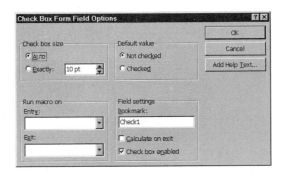

2. Determine the check box size by selecting the appropriate option:

   - Select Auto to make the check box the same size as the text around it.
   - Select Exactly to make the check box a specific size. Click the up or down arrow or press the up- or down-arrow key to increase or decrease the box size. Or type the size you want; for example, type **12 pt** for a 12-point box, **.25"** for a quarter-inch box, **1 pi** for a 1-pica box, or **1 cm** for a 1-centimeter box. (When you next open the dialog box, the measurement is converted to an equivalent value in points.)

3. Determine the Default Value by selecting one of the following options:

   - If you select Not Checked, the check box will be empty by default (a negative response). The user must press the spacebar to check the box.
   - If you select Checked, the check box will have a mark in it by default (a positive response). The user must press the spacebar to deselect the box.

4. Choose OK.

Customizing Drop-Down Form Fields

A drop-down list gives users a list of up to 25 items to choose from. It helps ensure that the user's response to a field is valid, because the list contains only valid responses. It also helps users to fill in the form, because they don't have to guess what kind of response the field requires.

You will most likely customize a drop-down form field as you insert it, because there's nothing in the list until you add items. You may want to add items to the list later, remove some items, or rearrange the items. You can do this by editing the drop-down field.

To add items to the list in a drop-down field, follow these steps:

1. Open the Drop-Down Form Field Options property sheet (see Figure 23.14).
2. In the <u>D</u>rop-Down Item box, type the item you want to add to the list.
3. Click <u>A</u>dd.
4. Repeat steps 2 and 3 to add more items to the list.
5. Choose OK.

To remove items from a drop-down list field, follow these steps:

1. Select the drop-down field and open the Drop-Down Form Field Options property sheet.

Part

V

Ch

23

FIG. 23.14

You can add items to a drop-down list, remove items from it, or rearrange the items in the list.

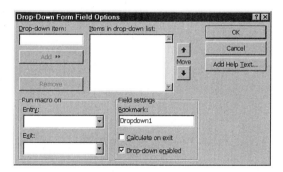

2. In the <u>I</u>tems in Drop-Down List: select the item you want to remove.
3. Click the <u>R</u>emove button.
4. Repeat steps 2 and 3 to remove more items.
5. Choose OK.

To rearrange items in a drop-down list field, follow these steps:

1. Select the drop-down field and open the Drop-Down Form Field Options property sheet.

2. In the Items in Drop-Down List, select the item you want to move.

3. Move the item up by clicking the Move up arrow, or move it down by clicking the Move down arrow. (With the keyboard, press the up or down arrow to select the item you want to move, press Tab to select the Move up or Move down arrow, and then press the space bar to move the selected item up or down.)

4. Repeat steps 2 and 3 to move more items.

5. Choose OK.

Formatting Form Fields

Users can't format entries in a protected form when they're filling in the form. But when you're creating a form, you can apply font and paragraph formatting, as well as many other formatting options, to fields. Responses will then appear in that formatting.

 You must insert a form field before you can format it. Remember, the document must be unprotected.

To format a form field, first select the form field you want to format. Then use one of the following methods to apply formatting:

- Choose the formatting command you want to use from the Format menu, and select the formatting options you want to apply.
- Click a formatting option on a toolbar.
- Press formatting shortcut keys.
- Click the selected field with the right mouse button to display the shortcut menu, and select Font, Paragraph, or Bullets and Numbering. Then select the formatting options you want to apply.
  ▶ **See** "Formatting Characters and Changing Fonts," **p. 283**

Disabling Form Fields

In most forms, you want users to respond to each field. But sometimes you'll want to disable a field, so that users cannot respond. You may want to include a default entry in disabled fields.

To disable a form field, follow these steps:

1. Unprotect the document, if necessary.

2. Select the field you want to disable, and display the Form Field Options property sheet.

3. Clear the appropriate option: Fill-in E̲nabled (for text fields), Check Box E̲nabled (for check box fields), or Drop-Down E̲nabled (for drop-down fields).

4. Choose OK.

Naming and Finding Fields in a Form

Each form field you insert in a document has a name: its *bookmark*. You can use this bookmark to help you find a field quickly. By default, Word numbers the fields you insert, calling them Text1, Check7, Dropdown13, and so forth. You can name a form field whatever you want (subject to bookmark naming rules, however). To name a form field, follow these steps:

1. Unprotect the document, if necessary.

2. Select the field and display the Form Field Options property sheet.

3. In the Field Settings group, select the B̲ookmark text box and type the name. Use only letters and numbers with no spaces.

4. Choose OK.

To find a named form field, follow these steps:

1. Unprotect the document.

2. Choose E̲dit, G̲o To.

3. Select Bookmark from the G̲o to What list, then type the name you want to find in the E̲nter Bookmark Name box, or select it from the list.

4. Click the G̲o To button. Word displays the field, but doesn't close the dialog box. Go to another field, or choose Close to close the dialog box.

Adding Help to a Form

By adding help messages, you can make it much easier for users to respond correctly to a field in your form. When the field is selected in your form, help messages can appear in the status bar at the bottom of the screen, or as a message box displayed when the user presses the F1 key.

 TIP The document must be protected in order for your help message to appear; if it isn't protected, pressing F1 displays Word help.

You can type your own text for a help message, or use an existing AutoText entry. For example, you may have an AutoText entry that reads Press F1 for Help, which you include as a status bar help message in each field for which you've included F1 help (see Figure 23.15).

FIG. 23.15

Help can appear in the status bar if you use the Status Bar tab.

To add help to a form field, follow these steps:

1. Display the Form Field Options property sheet for the field to which you want to add help.

2. Click the Add Help Text button.

3. Select the Status Bar tab to add a line of help in the status bar, or select the Help Key (F1) tab to add help that appears as a message box when the user presses F1 (see Figure 23.16).

 T I P   If you add F1 help to a field, also include a status bar message reading `Press F1 for help` so that users know where to find help.

FIG. 23.16

Help can appear as a message box when the user presses F1 if you use the Help Key (F1) tab.

4. To add your own help message, select the Type Your Own option and type your message (up to 255 characters).

   Or, to use the text of an AutoText entry as help, select the AutoText Entry option, and select the AutoText entry you want to use from the list.

5. Choose OK.

6. Choose OK again to close the Form Field Options property sheet and return to your document.

If you're including status line help messages, be aware that even if your form is protected, users can turn off the status line. Also be aware that users have no way of knowing whether F1 help is attached to a field (though a message in the status line can help, if the status line is displayed).

N O T E Help users fill in your form, or give them some instructions about what to do with the form when they're finished with it, by including a helpful message as part of a Visual Basic for Applications procedure that runs when the template opens. ■

Adding Macros to a Form

Macros can automate your forms in many ways. They can activate or deactivate fields, depending on the user's response to an earlier field. They can update fields that contain calculations. They can also cause Word to skip over unneeded fields.

▶ **See** " Automating with Visual Basic for Applications," **p. 1165**

To use a macro in a form, you must create the macro before you apply it to a particular field in the form. Macros run at one of two times: when the user enters the field or when the user leaves the field.

When you record or write macros for your form, be aware that macros use bookmarks to locate particular fields, and make sure that your form contains no duplicate bookmark names. You can find out the automatic bookmark name of any field, or give the field a new bookmark name, by selecting the field, displaying the Form Field Options property sheet, and then looking at the Bookmark text box (for details, see the "Naming and Finding Fields in a Form" section, earlier in this chapter).

To make your macros useful, attach them to the template your form is based on. You can do this most easily as you create the macro, or you can attach a macro to your template by choosing Tools, Templates and Add-Ins, clicking the Organizer button, and then selecting the Macro Project Items tab.

Before you can assign macros to a field, the document must be unprotected. And remember, before you can assign a macro to a form field, you must create the macro.

To assign a macro to a form field, follow these steps:

1. Select the field to which you want to apply a macro, and display the Form Field Options property sheet.

2. If you want the macro to run when the user moves the insertion point into the field, select the Entry list in the Run Macro On group, and select the macro you want from the list.

    Or, if you want the macro to run when the user moves the insertion point out of the field, select the Exit list in the Run Macro On group, and select the macro you want from the list.

3. Choose OK.

If no macros appear in either the Entry or Exit list, no macros are available for your form's template. You must either create a macro, or attach it to your template.

Protecting and Unprotecting a Form with a Password

If you don't want users to change your form, protect it with a password. In this way, anyone who attempts to unprotect the form must supply the password (including you—don't forget your password).

To password-protect a document, follow these steps:

1. Choose Tools, Protect Document. The Protect Document dialog box appears (see Figure 23.17).

FIG. 23.17
Type your password in the Password box to protect your form.

2. Select the Forms option.

3. Select the Password box, and type your password. Choose OK. The Confirm Password dialog box appears (see Figure 23.18).

FIG. 23.18
To confirm your password, you must retype it exactly as you typed it the first time.

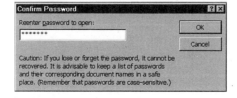

4. In the Reenter Password to Open Box, retype your password. Spelling, spacing, and capitalization must match exactly. Choose OK. (If you don't retype the password exactly as you originally typed it, you get an error message. Choose OK and try again.)

5. Choose OK to return to your document.

To unprotect a password-protected document, follow these steps:

1. Choose Tools, Unprotect Document, or click the Protect Form button on the Forms toolbar. If the document is password protected, the Unprotect Document dialog box appears (see Figure 23.19).

FIG. 23.19
To unprotect a password-protected document, you must enter the password exactly as you typed it originally.

2. Type the password exactly as you originally typed it in the Password box. Spelling, spacing, and capitalization must match exactly.

3. Choose OK. If you typed the password correctly, your document will be unprotected. If you typed the password incorrectly, Word displays a message that the password is incorrect, and you must choose OK to return to your document, which remains protected.

Protecting Part of a Form

If your form is divided into sections, you can protect parts of it, while leaving other parts unprotected. To create sections in a document, use the Insert, Break command to insert a section break between the protected and unprotected sections of your document. You can include password protection for the protected sections.

▶ **See** "Working with Sections in Your Document," **p. 452**

To protect or unprotect part of a form, follow these steps:

1. Choose Tools, Protect Document. The Protect Document dialog box appears.

2. Select the Forms option.

3. Click the Sections button to display the Section Protection dialog box (see Figure 23.20).

FIG. 23.20

You can protect part of a document if it's divided into sections.

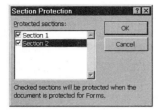

4. In the Protected Sections list, select each section you want protected, so that it appears with a mark in the box. Clear each section you want unprotected by clicking the check box to remove the check mark.

5. Choose OK to return to the Protect Document dialog box. (If you want to protect the sections with a password, do so now. For details, see the earlier section, "Protecting and Unprotecting a Form with a Password.")

6. Choose OK to return to the document.

Converting Existing Forms

The forms you want to create may already exist on paper or in another program's format. Sometimes the easiest way to convert a form is to simply retype it, but at other times you may want to use existing data.

If you have an existing printed form, you may be able to scan it using a scanner or personal scanner and convert the scanned image into text. Once it is a text document you can use Word's formatting, column, and desktop publishing features to make it organized and efficient to use.

▶ **See** "Inserting Pictures into a Document," **p. 813**

Although you can't import form fields from a document created by another program into a Word document, you can import text. If a form exists in another program, import the text, format it as you need it, and add the form fields. You can change text to a table by selecting the text and choosing Table, Convert Text to Table. To learn about tables, see Chapter 18, "Creating and Editing Tables."

Printing Forms

There are three ways you might want to print a form. You might want to print it exactly as it appears on-screen, including the labels, any graphics, and the data in the fields.

You might want to print the data onto preprinted forms only. Or you might want to print the labels and graphics only, to create a preprinted form.

Printing the Filled-In Form

To print the entire form, including everything that appears on your screen, use Word's usual printing commands. Use this method to print forms that you've already filled in.

To print the entire form, follow these steps:

1. Fill in the form, or open a filled-in form.
2. Choose File, Print.
3. Select the printing options you want from the Print dialog box, and choose OK.

To learn more about printing options, refer to Chapter 8, "Previewing and Printing a Document."

Printing Form Data Only

Print only data when you're using preprinted forms. Because you use the same form template to print the blank form as you use when you print only the data, the form data will line up correctly with the fields. Printing from laser jet printers onto preprinted forms can be tricky because print alignment, known as *registration*, on the paper can vary by as much as 1/8 of an inch.

To print only data onto a preprinted form, follow these steps:

1. Insert the preprinted form into your printer.
2. Choose Tools, Options.
3. Select the Print tab (see Figure 23.21).
4. Select Print Data Only for Forms from the Options for Current Document Only group, and choose OK.
5. Choose File, Print, select printing options, and choose OK.

Notice that this procedure ensures that each time you print this form, you will print data only. Repeat the procedure, clearing the Print Data Only for Forms option in step 4, if you want to print the entire form.

Printing a Blank Form

To make your own preprinted form, print the form only, without the data.

FIG. 23.21
Choose Tools, Options, click the Print tab, and set option to print form data only.

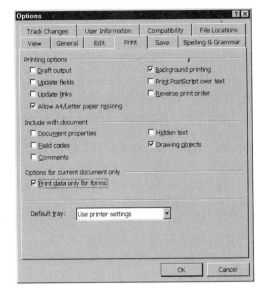

To print a blank form, follow these steps:

1. Choose File, New, select the form you want to print from the New dialog box, and choose OK.

2. Without filling in the form, print it by choosing File, Print, selecting printing options, and choosing OK.

 Remember that fields in a form appear shaded if the Shading Options button is selected in the Forms toolbar. This shading does not appear when you print your forms. If you want shading to appear on a printed form, use Format, Borders and Shading.

TROUBLESHOOTING

When I print the form data, it doesn't line up with the form fields on the preprinted form.
Be sure you're using the same form to print your data as you used to create the preprinted form. Registration, how each sheet lines up in a printer, is usually not accurate in most desktop printers. This variance may make it impossible to align forms that have narrow tolerances.

▶ **See** "Printing the Current Document," **p. 269**

Saving Data Only

You may want to use the data you collect in your forms with another program, such as a database. To do that, save only the data, and import the data into the other program.

Word saves a copy of the data as a Text Only document (with the extension TXT), creating a comma-delimited document containing only the responses in your fields.

Many applications can read the data stored in comma-delimited files. Microsoft Excel, for example, can open and automatically separate each piece of data into a worksheet cell if the file uses the file extension CSV (comma separated values).

To save data only from your form, follow these steps:

1. Choose Tools, Options.
2. Select the Save tab.
3. In the Save Options group, select the Save Data Only for Forms option.
4. Choose OK.
5. Choose File, Save As to save and name your data file.

Building Forms with Fill-In Dialog Boxes

With {fillin} fields, you can design a form letter so that you need to enter a data item (such as a name) only once—no matter how many times it appears in the letter. This feature is extremely useful for filling out invoices, contracts, proposals, or business forms in which the majority of the body copy remains unchanged. {fillin} fields are useful also when you need to insert personal phrases in mass mailings. Figure 23.22 shows a document you can create to demonstrate how {fillin} fields work. This document automatically sets the current date, then requests the customer's name. It then displays a fill-in box for each item in the table.

First you should create a new template for form letters.

To create a new template, follow these steps:

1. Choose File, New. The New dialog box appears (see Figure 23.23).
2. Select the Template option in the Create New group.

   The Blank Document icon should already be selected. If you want to base this fill-in template on an existing document, select that document's icon.
3. Choose OK.
4. Modify the template to include any body text, graphics, tables, and so on that you want in the form letter. Format the template's page layout to account for letterhead, if necessary.

Keep the template open and on-screen so that you can add {fillin} fields as described in the next section.

FIG. 23.22

Field codes can enter data or display dialog boxes that prompt users to enter data that can be used repeatedly through the document.

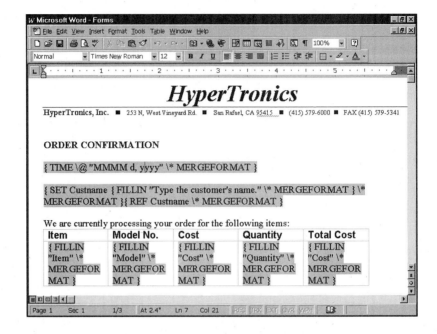

FIG. 23.23

By using a template to create a form, you prevent users from accidentally changing the original.

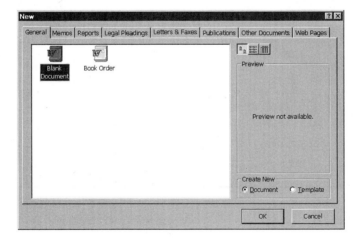

Creating *{fillin}* Fields

To set up your template to prompt the user to enter key information, use {fillin} fields. Figure 23.24 shows a dialog box prompt generated by a {fillin} field.

To insert the {fillin} field code in a document, move the insertion point to where you want the operator's input to appear. Choose Insert, Field. Make sure that [All] is selected in the categories list, then select Fill-in from the Field Names list. In the Field Codes text box, move the insertion point past FILLIN, type the text you want displayed to the user—enclosing it in quotation marks—and choose OK.

FIG. 23.24
The {fillin} field is an easy way to ask users to enter data in a dialog box. You don't need to create a macro to display the dialog box.

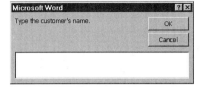

Alternatively, you can type the {fillin} field into the template. To do this, move the insertion point to where you want the results to appear, then press Ctrl+F9, the Insert Field key. Position the insertion point between the field characters, and type the following field type and instructions:

fillin "Type the customer address."

 T I P Enclose prompts of more than one word in quotation marks (" "). If you don't enclose a phrase in quotation marks, Word uses only the first word.

Displaying Fillin Dialog Boxes from the Form

To display the dialog box requesting the customer's name, and to update the {fillin} field, follow these steps:

1. Select the field character at either end of the fillin code to select the {fillin} field.
2. Press F9. The Fillin dialog box appears.
3. Type a customer address in the box. To start a new line in the box, press Enter. Choose OK to complete the box and insert your entry in the document.

 T I P To update {fillin} fields throughout an entire document, select the entire document by pressing Ctrl+A, then press F9 (Update).

The entry you typed into the Fillin dialog box appears in the document in the same location as the field code. Text following the inserted entry is pushed down or right, just as if you had manually typed text in the location.

To switch between displaying fields and their results, press Alt+F9, or display the Options dialog box (by choosing Tools, Options) and click the Field Codes check box in the View tab.

Reusing *{fillin}* Field Results Later in the Form

If you use field codes in form letters, you can request an input from the operator once, but have that information appear in multiple locations. To reuse an entry from one {fillin} box in other locations in a form letter, you must use the following three field codes:

- {set bookmark data} assigns data to a bookmark, which stores information so that it can be reused later. In the next example, because the data argument for {set} is a {fillin} field, the operator's entry in response to the [fillin] field is stored in the bookmark name Custname. If the data is explicit text that doesn't change, such as Montana, you must enclose it in quotation marks. Don't include a space in the bookmark name.

- {fillin [prompt]} displays an input box in which the operator can enter data. The brackets ([]) indicate that the prompt to the user is optional. If the prompt to the user is more than one word, enclose the words in quotes.

- {ref bookmark} displays the contents of a bookmark at the field location. You enter this field to repeat a bookmark's contents in other locations within the document. To use {ref bookmark}, the bookmark must have a stored entry from a previous location in the document. Use the {set} field to store data into a bookmark.

Figure 23.25 shows a field code that requests the customer's name and stores it in the Custname bookmark. The {fillin} field requests the name. The {set} field sets Custname equal to the {fillin} entry. The {ref} field displays the entry stored in Custname. You can use {ref} throughout the letter, following the {set} field, even though the data was entered only once.

FIG. 23.25

The combination of {fillin}, {set}, and {ref} field codes enables the user to fill in one dialog box and have the data used throughout a document.

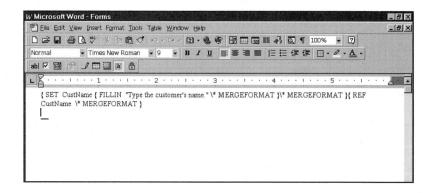

In Figure 23.25, the {fillin} field data was entered into a dialog box. The {set} field code then stores the entry in the bookmark Custname. The data stored in Custname can be redisplayed anywhere in the document with {ref custname}. The {ref} field code references the data stored in that bookmark. You can reuse {ref *bookmark*} as many times as you want in the document. Using the switches described in Chapter 22, "Automating with Field Codes," you can format the information that {ref} returns.

TIP You can make up your own single words to use as bookmarks.

TIP Word can guide you through the correct syntax for creating field codes if you use the Insert, Field command. Chapter 22 describes how to insert fields with this command.

As you may recall, *nested* fields are one field code inside another field code. In the previous CUSTNAME example, a {fillin} field is nested inside a {ref} field. The result of the {fillin} is used to supply one of the arguments required by the {ref} field. To build the nested field in Figure 23.25 from the inside out, follow these steps:

1. Position the insertion point where you need to insert the entry.
2. Press Ctrl+F9, the Insert Field key.
3. Between the field characters, type **FILLIN**, a space, then a prompt to the operator (enclosed in quotation marks), such as **"Type the customer's name."**
4. Select the field you just typed. To select field characters and field contents, select a field character at one end or the other to select the entire field.
5. Press Ctrl+F9 to enclose the selection in field characters.

   This step *nests* the first field entirely inside another set of field characters.
   The insertion point moves to directly follow the first field character.
6. Directly after the first field character, type **SET**, a space, and then the appropriate bookmark, such as **Custname**. Leave a space after the bookmark, but don't leave spaces in the name.

This new nested field requests a name and stores it in the bookmark, but the entry doesn't appear on-screen. To see the field's result, you must update the field.

To update both of these new fields and see the customer's name requested and displayed, follow these steps:

1. Select the entire line (or lines) containing both fields.
2. Press F9 (Update Fields).

   A dialog box appears, requesting the customer's name (refer to Figure 23.24).
3. Type the entry as requested.
4. Choose OK.

The {set} field stores in the bookmark the name you entered in the {fillin} field. The {ref *bookmark*} field displays the contents of a bookmark in the letter. You can enter a {ref *bookmark*} field in multiple locations in the document, wherever you need the name repeated. In Figure 23.26, the Custname bookmark is repeated at the last line on the screen. The new contents of {ref *bookmark*} don't appear, however, until each {ref *bookmark*} field is updated.

FIG. 23.26

Reuse data by repeating the {ref bookmark} combination wherever you want the data displayed. {ref} only displays the new data when it is selected and updated.

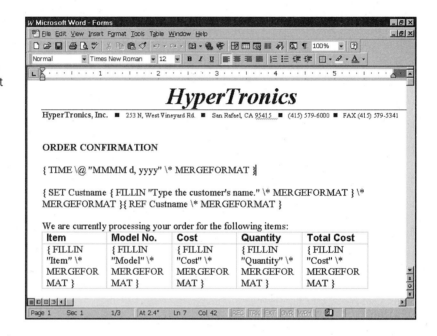

After you enter all the field codes, choose File, Save As, and choose OK to save the template.

The switch * MERGEFORMAT, used in the {REF bookmark * MERGEFORMAT} field, ensures that the formatting you applied to the field name in the document doesn't change when the field is updated. The format of field results matches the format you apply to the letter r in ref.

The inclusion of the * MERGEFORMAT switch is controlled by the Preserve Formatting During Updates option in the Field dialog box. For more information, see Chapter 22, "Automating with Field Codes."

Saving and Naming the Template

This document must be saved as a template because you opened it as one. To save your template, choose File, Save As. In the File Name text box, type an eight-letter name to describe your form. Notice that you cannot change many of the text or list boxes. Choose OK. Word saves the template and adds the extension DOT. When you save a new template, give it a name that reflects the type of document it creates.

Updating Fields in a Form

To test the fields you entered, update them. This action will display new values, or enable you to enter new ones.

To enter data in the {fillin} fields and update the {ref} fields, follow these steps:

1. Choose File, New, and select a template containing {fillin} fields. Choose OK.
2. Move the insertion point to the top of the document, then press F11 to select the next field. (Press Shift+F11 to select the preceding field, or select the entire document by pressing Ctrl+A or by choosing Edit, Select All to select all fields.)
3. Press F9 to update the selected field or, if the entire document is selected, to update each field in turn, from the beginning to the end of the document.
4. Type the data requested, and choose OK.

 T I P | To preserve the previous entry, select Cancel; nothing is produced if no previous entry existed.

If an error appears at a field's location, display the field codes in the document. Check for correct spelling and spacing. Use one space between field types, instructions, and switches.

Creating a Macro to Update Fields Automatically

Because this type of fill-in form is designed for repetitive use, you can have Word automatically prompt the user for the information as soon as the document is opened. You can

FIG. 23.27
You can record a macro that automatically updates field codes when a document or template opens.

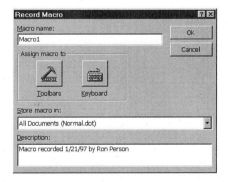

do this with an automatic macro that updates all fields in the document when the document opens. With the fill-in template as the active document, follow these steps:

1. Choose Tools, Macro, Record New Macro. The Macro dialog box appears (see Figure 23.27).

2. Type **AutoNew** in the Macro Name box.

3. In the Store Macro In list, select the name of the template. The macro will be available only to this template or to documents that originate from this template.

4. Enter a description, such as **Automatically updates all fields**, in the Description box.

5. Choose OK.

The Stop Recording toolbar appears, and the REC indicator is highlighted in the status bar, indicating that the recorder is on. Follow these steps to record a process that updates all fields in the document:

1. Press Ctrl+A to select the entire document.

2. Press F9. A prompt generated by the first {fillin} field appears.

3. Click the Cancel button for each {fillin} prompt.

4. Press Ctrl+Home to return the insertion point to the top of the document.

5. Click Stop in the Stop Recording toolbar.

Choose File, Save to save the macro and close the template.

To test the macro, follow these steps:

1. Choose File, New.

2. Select the template.

3. Choose OK.

When you open the document, the AutoNew macro runs the update macro. Enter a response to each dialog box, or choose Cancel. If the macro doesn't run correctly, record it again. If you record the macro again, using the same name (AutoNew), Word asks whether you want to replace the previous recording. Choose Yes. ●

CHAPTER 24

Working with Math and Equations

Have you ever wanted to perform calculations on the numbers in a Word table you created, and have the results automatically updated if the figures in the table change, much as you would in a spreadsheet? Or perhaps you would like to perform a calculation on numbers scattered throughout a document, without searching for each number and then performing the math yourself. Word 97 simplifies these tasks.

If you are a scientist or engineer, you may have wanted an easy way to enter equations and formulas in a polished document, instead of having to draw them by hand. Word 97 simplifies all these tasks with its built-in Equation Editor. With the Equation Editor, you can insert mathematical symbols and operators, such as integrals and fractions. You can also control the size, placement, and formatting of the different elements in an equation. ■

Perform calculations in a table

Enter a formula in a table using data from individual or a range of table cells.

Perform calculations on numbers occurring within text

Use bookmark names and fields to perform calculations using numbers that are throughout a document.

Create an equation

Templates and symbol palettes make it easy to create equations with proper positioning and spacing.

Format an equation

You can change spacing, font, font size, and adjust positioning and alignment of any element in an equation.

Work with matrices

Select from predefined matrix or vector sizes using the Matrix template palette.

View, edit, and print equations

You can select between three equation magnifications to aid in editing an equation. Editing is performed using the Equation Editor. You can also print your equations on certain printers.

Choosing Word's Math Functions or a Spreadsheet

Word has its own basic math and table features. If you have both Word and a Windows worksheet, such as Microsoft Excel or Lotus 1-2-3, you should learn the advantages and disadvantages of both.

You may want to use Word's built-in math capabilities under the following conditions:

- When problems involve simple math, such as totals or averages
- When numbers are arranged in rows and columns in a table
- When numbers are distributed throughout a document and the math result depends on those numbers
- When results do not need to be linked to or updated in other documents

You may want to do math in a worksheet and then paste, link, or embed the results into Word under these conditions:

- When problems involve complex math operations unavailable in Word
- When problems involve worksheet analysis, such as database analysis or trends forecasting
- When numbers are arranged in different cell locations throughout a table, rather than in simple rows and columns
- When one worksheet can be updated, with the result of that worksheet then updating multiple linked Word documents

  ▶ **See** "Using Word with Office Applications," **p. 1077**
  ▶ **See** "Transferring Data with Copy and Paste," **p. 1082**
  ▶ **See** "Linking Documents and Files," **p. 1091**

Using Bookmarks to Perform Calculations in Text

To perform calculations on numbers scattered throughout a document, and to allow the results of a calculation to be updated if any of the numbers change, you need to use bookmark names and fields. *Bookmarks* are used to name a location. You must use two steps to perform math on numbers placed throughout a document:

■ Mark the location of numbers in the text by assigning bookmark names to them.

■ Enter a field code that calculates the mathematical result.

To create the bookmarks that will contain numbers used in the calculations, follow these steps:

1. Create your document and type numbers where you want them. Save your document.

2. Select in the document a number you want to use in a calculation.

3. Choose Insert, Bookmark to display the Bookmark dialog box.

4. Type a name in the Bookmark Name edit box. Use a descriptive name, such as Profit, Expense, or Budget, that starts with a letter and has no spaces.

5. Click the Add button. Square brackets surrounding the selected number indicate the bookmark.

6. Repeat the process, starting with step 4, until you have assigned a bookmark to each number used in calculations.

   ▶ **See** "Marking Locations with Bookmarks," **p. 182**

N O T E   Be careful when you delete or change a number entered at a bookmark location, because you may delete the bookmark. If you accidentally delete the bookmark, a math field that uses that bookmark will produce an error. To prevent yourself from deleting bookmarks, edit the numbers in bookmarks only while the screen is set so that you can see bookmark end symbols. To view bookmark end symbols, choose Tools, Options, and select the View tab. Select the Bookmarks check box, then choose OK. ■

To insert the math function or formula that calculates by using the numbers you have just identified with bookmarks, follow these steps:

1. Position the insertion point where you want the calculation result to appear, and choose Insert, Field. Word displays the Field dialog box (see Fig-ure 24.1).

2. Select Equations and Formulas from the Categories list, and select = (Formula) from the Field Names list.

3. In the Field Codes text box, type the mathematical expression for calculating the desired result, using bookmark names and mathematical operators.

   Type a formula, using the bookmarks and math operators as you would expect to write a formula:

   =(Revenue-Cost)*0.8

FIG. 24.1
Enter a calculation formula in the Field dialog box.

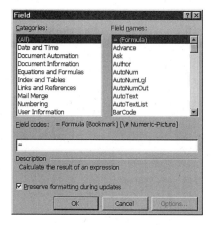

You can use any of the functions or mathematical operators listed under the entry for the {=} field in Chapter 22, "Automating with Field Codes."

4. Following the mathematical formula, add any formatting instructions.

5. Choose OK.

The results of the calculation in the field are displayed, unless you have set Word for Windows to display field codes by choosing Tools, Options, in which case the field code and formula are displayed. To turn the field code display on or off, select the field (or the field's result) and press Shift+F9. To update the field, select the field and press F9.

▶ **See** "Editing Fields," **p. 704**

▶ **See** "Formatting Field Results," **p. 706**

Performing Calculations in a Table

To perform a calculation in a table, you use table references, math operators, and special functions to create a field expression for calculating the desired result. *Functions* are built-in mathematical formulas that perform operations such as Sum and Average.

Specifying Table Cells in a Formula

As you enter a formula in a field in a table, you refer to individual cells or ranges of cells in the table by using column and row coordinates. The columns of a table are lettered A, B, C, and so on; the rows of a table are numbered 1, 2, 3, and so on, just as they are in a spreadsheet. To refer to an individual cell in a table, specify first the column letter, followed by the row number. To refer to the cell in the second column of the third row of a table, for example, you use the coordinates B3.

N O T E   Unlike the cell coordinates in Excel, the cell coordinates in Word are always absolute; you do not need to use the dollar sign ($) notation used by Excel. However, be aware that if you copy a formula from one cell in a Word table to another cell, the cell references in the formula do not adjust, as they do in Excel when you use relative cell references. ▪

You can specify ranges of cells in a table by using two cell coordinates separated by a colon (:). To specify the first three cells in column C of a table, for example, you use the coordinates C1:C3. You can specify an entire column or row by using a range without starting or ending cells. The coordinates B:B specify all the cells in the second column of a table, and the coordinates 2:2 specify all the cells in the second row of a table. This second form of cell coordinates is useful if you expect to add or remove rows or columns from a table in which you use all the cells in your calculation.

N O T E   Formulas in tables do not automatically update themselves to reflect inserted or deleted rows or columns, as they do in Microsoft Excel or Lotus 1-2-3. If you insert or delete a row or column, and your formula uses specific cell references, you must edit the formula to include the new cells. ▪

Part

V

Ch

24

Entering a Formula in a Table

Many calculations that need to be made in a document are in the form of a table. To enter a formula in a table, follow these steps:

1. Position the insertion point in the cell where you want the result to appear.

2. Choose Table, Formula. Word displays the Formula dialog box (see Figure 24.2).

FIG. 24.2

Use the Formula dialog box to enter a formula in a table.

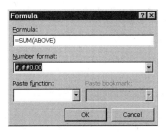

Word analyzes the table and automatically proposes an expression and enters it in the Formula text box. If Word cannot determine what formulas are appropriate, it leaves the Formula text box empty.

3. Type any additions to the suggested expression in the Formula text box, or delete the suggested expression and type your own, using any combination of reduction functions, cell references, bookmarks, and mathematical operators (+ - / *).

   ▶ **See** "A Reference List of Field Codes," **p. 718**

4. If you are writing your own formula, select the Paste Function list box to see a list of available functions. As you select the function from the Paste Function list box, it is pasted in the Formula text box.

   ▶ **See** "Automating with Field Codes," **p. 693**

   To sum a column of numbers, for example, the formula expression might look like this:

   ```
   { =SUM(D2:D10) }
   ```

5. If you want your formula expression to include numbers referenced by bookmarks, you can select the bookmark names from the Paste Bookmark list box to paste them in the Formula text box.

6. To format the formula expression's results, select a format from the Number Format list box.

7. Choose OK.

   ▶ **See** "Creating Tables," **p. 608**
   ▶ **See** "Editing Tables," **p. 619**

The results of the calculation in the field are displayed, unless you have set Word to display field codes by choosing Tools, Options, in which case the field code and formula itself are displayed. To turn the field code display on or off, select the field (or the field's result) and press Shift+F9. To update the field, select the field and press F9.

Recalculating Formulas

Formula fields, whether you enter them in a table or elsewhere in your document, do not update automatically, as do some other types of fields. You must update formula fields manually using one of the following methods:

- Place the insertion point in the field (or its result) and press Alt+Shift+U or F9 to update the field.

- Move the pointer over the field (or its result) and click the right mouse button. Choose Update Field from the context-sensitive menu.

- To update all the fields in the document, select the entire document by choosing Edit, Select All or Ctrl+A. Then press F9 to update the fields.

What You Need to Know About Displaying Formulas and Equations

Word comes with an Equation Editor that enables you to easily create publishable equations in a document. You insert as an object an equation created with the Equation Editor in your document, just as you can insert pictures, graphs, and spreadsheet tables (see Figure 24.3). To edit the equation, you must reopen the Equation Editor; you cannot edit the equation from within Word. You can, however, position and resize an equation from within a Word document, as with any object.

FIG. 24.3
You can insert an equation in a document by using the Equation Editor.

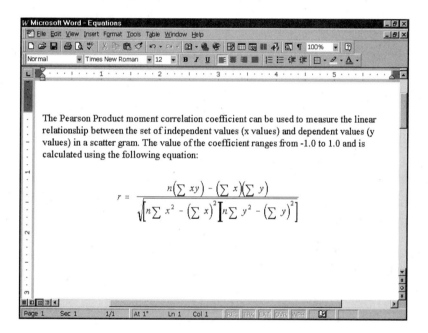

The Pearson Product moment correlation coefficient can be used to measure the linear relationship between the set of independent values (x values) and dependent values (y values) in a scatter gram. The value of the coefficient ranges from -1.0 to 1.0 and is calculated using the following equation:

$$r = \frac{n\left(\sum xy\right) - \left(\sum x\right)\left(\sum y\right)}{\sqrt{\left[n\sum x^2 - \left(\sum x\right)^2\right]\left[n\sum y^2 - \left(\sum y\right)^2\right]}}$$

N O T E If you did not choose to install the Equation Editor when you set up Word, it will not appear in the list of object types. You must run the Setup program again to install the Equation Editor. You do not have to reinstall the entire program; just tell the Setup program to install only the Equation Editor.

When you first open the Equation Editor, you are presented with a screen containing a single slot (see Figure 24.4). Slots define the different components of an equation. If you are entering a fraction, for example, one slot is available for the numerator, and another slot is available for the denominator.

The Equation Editor has several tools that simplify the task of creating an equation. The toolbar consists of buttons that open the symbol and template palettes. To access these palettes, you simply click the button to open the palette you want. In the first row of the toolbar are several palettes for entering symbols, including math operators, Greek symbols, arrows, and so on. The template palettes, displayed in the second row of the toolbar, contain collections of ready-made templates that enable you to create the different components in an equation. For example, the second template from the left in the second row of buttons contains a collection of templates for entering fractions and roots (see Figure 24.5).

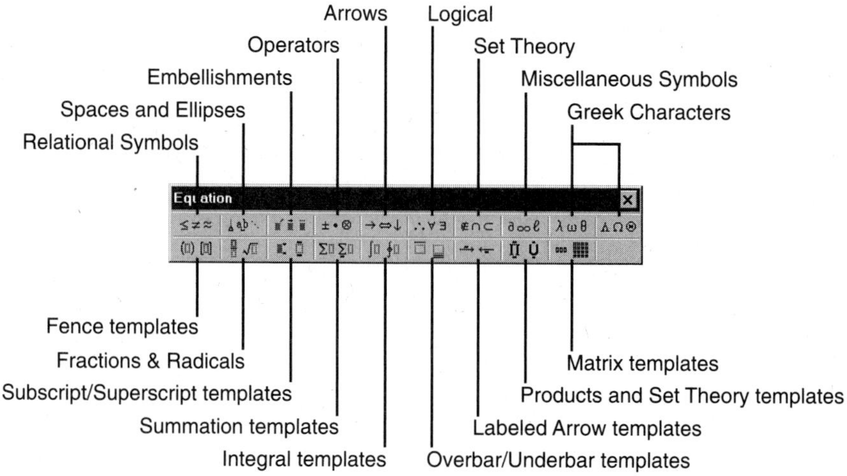

FIG. 24.4
The Equation Editor window has menu commands and palettes to help you build your equations.

FIG. 24.5
The Equation Editor contains a template palette that has been opened.

Building an Equation

The process of constructing an equation consists largely of using the template and symbol palettes and the keyboard to assemble the equation, piece by piece. Text and symbols are entered in slots, which are either separate from or part of a template. Text or symbols are entered in the slot that contains the insertion point. You can use the mouse, or the arrow and Tab keys, to move the insertion point from one slot to another.

The templates take care of most of the positioning and spacing required in equation building. Other commands are available to fine-tune spacing and alignment of the equation's components. Commands are available for controlling the font type and font size of the elements in an equation, as well.

Notice in Figure 24.6 the slot near the end of the equation into which characters have yet to be inserted.

Part

V

Ch

24

FIG. 24.6
The Equation Editor shows a partially completed equation.

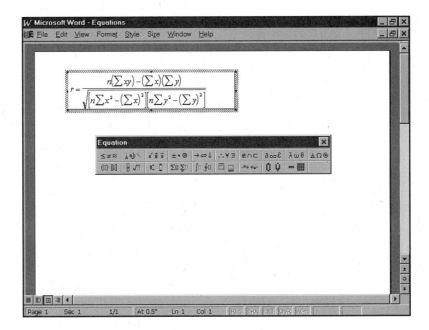

Inserting an Equation

You can choose Insert, Object to open the Equation Editor and to create an equation at the current insertion-point position.

To insert an equation in a document, follow these steps:

1. Position the insertion point where you want to insert the equation you will create.

2. Choose Insert, Object, and select the Create New tab.

3. Select Microsoft Equation 3.0 from the Object type list box, and choose OK. When you choose OK, the Equation Editor opens (refer to Figure 24.4).

4. Create the equation in the Equation Editor. (See the following sections for detailed instructions on creating an equation.)

5. Click outside the Equation box to return to the document. The Equation Editor is closed. To return to the Equation Editor, double-click the equation you want to edit.

Typing in the Equation Editor

Typing in the Equation Editor is similar to typing in a Word document, although there are some important differences. Whenever you type in the Equation Editor, text is entered in the slot containing the insertion point. As with a Word document, you can use the Backspace and Delete keys to delete characters.

Unless you use the Text style from the Style menu, the space bar has no effect. The Equation Editor takes care of the spacing in an equation. When you type an equal sign, for example, the Equation Editor adds spacing before and after it. If you press the Enter key, a new line begins.

If you want to type regular text, choose the Text style from the Style menu. Then you can enter text as you normally would. Choose Math style from the Style menu to return to the Math style—the style you normally work with when creating an equation.

Selecting Items in an Equation

You might need to select an item in an equation (to change the point size or reposition the item, for example). To select characters in a slot, use the mouse to drag across characters. To select an entire equation, choose Edit, Select All.

To select *embedded* items (items not contained in a slot), such as *character embellishments* (carets, tildes, prime signs, and so on) or integral signs, press and hold down the Ctrl key. When the mouse pointer changes to a vertical arrow, point to the embedded item and click to select it.

Entering Nested Equation Templates

Complex equations involve templates nested within templates. The result is an equation involving many templates, each nested within the slot of a larger template. An example of nested templates is the square root nested within the denominator of the equation shown in Figure 24.6.

To enter a template within an existing equation, follow these steps:

1. Place the insertion point where you want to insert the template.
2. Use the mouse to choose a template from one of the template palettes. The template is inserted immediately to the right of the insertion point.

   Or, you can use one of the shortcut keys listed in Table 24.1 to insert the template.

3. Type text or enter symbols in each slot in the template. The insertion point must be positioned in the slot before you begin entering text or symbols.

Table 24.1 lists the shortcut keys for inserting templates. To use these shortcuts, press Ctrl+T and then press the shortcut key. You can insert the items marked with an asterisk by pressing just the Ctrl key and the shortcut key—you do not have to press T first.

Table 24.1   Shortcut Keys for Inserting Templates

Template	Description	Shortcut Key
	Parentheses	(or)
	Brackets*	[or]
	Braces*	{ or }
	Absolute Value	|
	Fraction*	F
	Slash Fraction*	/
	Superscript (high)*	H
	Subscript (low)*	L
	Joint sub-/superscript*	J
	Root*	R
	Nth Root	N
	Summation	S
	Product	P
	Integral*	I

continues

Table 24.1 Continued

Template	Description	Shortcut Key
	Matrix (353)	M
	Underscript (limit)	U

Entering Symbols

Many fields of mathematics, science, and medicine use symbols to represent concepts or physical structures. To insert a symbol in a slot, follow these steps:

1. Position the insertion point in the slot where you want to insert the symbol.
2. Select the symbol you want from one of the symbol templates.

Table 24.2 lists the shortcut keys for inserting symbols. To use these shortcuts, press Ctrl+S and then the shortcut key.

Table 24.2 Shortcut Keys for Inserting Symbols

Symbol	Description	Shortcut Key
∞	Infinity	|
$\rightarrow$	Arrow	A
∂	Derivative (partial)	D
$\leq$	Less than or equal to	<
$\geq$	Greater than or equal to	>
$\times$	Times	T
$\in$	Element of	E
$\notin$	Not an element of	Shift+E

Symbol	Description	Shortcut Key
⊂	Contained in	C
⊄	Not contained in	Shift+C

Adding Embellishments

The Equation Editor has several embellishments—such as prime signs, arrows, tildes, and dots—that you can add to characters or symbols.

To add an embellishment, follow these steps:

1. Position the insertion point to the right of the character you want to embellish.

2. Choose the embellishment icon from the embellishment palette (third button from the left in the top row of buttons).

   Or, you can use one of the shortcut keys listed in Table 24.3 to add an embellishment.

Part

V

Ch

24

Table 24.3 Shortcut Keys for Inserting Embellishments

Icon	Description	Shortcut Keys
	Overbar	Ctrl+Shift+-
	Tilde	Ctrl+~ (Ctrl+" on some keyboards)
	Arrow (vector)	Ctrl+Alt+-
	Single prime	Ctrl+Alt+'
	Double prime	Ctrl+" (Ctrl+~ on some keyboards)
	Single dot	Ctrl+Alt+.

Formatting an Equation

After you create an equation, you can format it to appear exactly as you want. You can work on the spacing of the elements in the equation, adjust the positioning and alignment within the equation, and change the font and font size for any element.

Controlling Spacing

You can modify several spacing parameters by choosing Format, Spacing (line spacing, or row and column spacing in matrices are examples).

To modify the spacing setting used by the Equation Editor, follow these steps:

1. Choose Format, Spacing. A dialog box appears that displays a list of dimensions you can scroll through (see Figure 24.7).

FIG. 24.7
In the Spacing dialog box, you can control the spacing used by the Equation Editor.

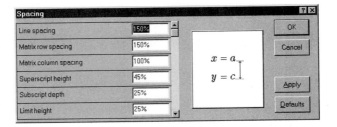

2. Select the text box next to the dimension you want to modify. Use the scroll bar to move through the list of dimensions.

3. Type a new measurement.

   The default unit of measure is points. You can specify other units by typing the appropriate abbreviation from the following list:

Unit of Measure	Abbreviation
Inches	in
Centimeters	cm
Millimeters	mm
Points	pt
Picas	pi

4. Choose Apply or OK.

Choosing <u>A</u>pply applies the modified dimension to the current equation and leaves the dialog box open, so that you can continue modifications. Choosing OK applies any modifications and closes the dialog box.

In practice, you probably should specify the spacing dimensions as a percentage of the point size given for Full size type, which is set in the Sizes dialog box. The advantage to this approach is that if you change the type size, you don't have to redefine your spacing dimensions; spacing will always be proportional to the type size.

Although the Equation Editor manages the spacing between elements in an equation, you can insert spaces manually by using four spacing symbols. These symbols are located in the second symbol palette from the left in the top row. You can also access these symbols with shortcut keys. A list of the spacing symbols and shortcut keys is shown in Table 24.4.

Table 24.4   Shortcut Keys for Inserting Spaces

Icon	Function	Shortcut Keys
a̶b̶	Zero space	Shift+space bar
a̶b̶	One point space	Ctrl+Alt+space bar
a̶b̶	Thin space	Ctrl+space bar
a̶b̶	Thick space (two thin spaces)	Ctrl+Shift+space bar

To delete a space, press the Delete or Backspace key, as you would with text.

Positioning and Aligning Equations

You can adjust the positioning of any selected item by using the Nudge commands. First select the item (refer to the "Selecting Items in an Equation" section earlier in this chapter). Then use one of the following keystrokes to move the item, one pixel at a time:

Keystrokes	Function
Ctrl+left-arrow key	Moves item left one pixel
Ctrl+right-arrow key	Moves item right one pixel
Ctrl+down-arrow key	Moves item down one pixel
Ctrl+up-arrow key	Moves item up one pixel

The Equation Editor enables you to align horizontally one or more lines of single or multiple equations, using either the Format menu or the alignment symbol. You can align lines to the left, center, or right; or you can align lines around equal signs, decimal points, or alignment symbols. To align a group of equations, simply choose one of the alignment commands from the Format menu. To align lines in an equation, position the insertion point within the lines; then choose one of the alignment commands.

To insert an alignment symbol, position the insertion point and choose from the Spaces palette (second button in the top row of buttons) the alignment symbol at the far left of the top row of symbols. The alignment symbols are used as a reference point around which one or more lines of single or multiple equations are aligned. They override the Format commands.

Selecting Fonts

Usually, when you work in the Equation Editor, you will use the Math style from the Style menu. When you use the Math style, the Equation Editor automatically recognizes standard functions and applies to them the Function style (typeface and character formatting, for example). The Variable style is applied otherwise. If the Equation Editor fails to recognize a function, you can select it and apply the Function style manually.

To define the font and character attributes for a style, follow these steps:

1. Choose Style, Define.
2. Select the style you want to define.
3. Select the font from the list of available fonts.
4. Select the Bold or Italic boxes if you want bold or italic.
5. Choose OK.

You use the Text style to type regular text. Selecting this style applies the Text style to the text you type, and enables you to use the space bar to enter spaces as normal. With the other styles, spacing is handled automatically by the Equation Editor.

Select the Other style when you want to select a font and character format that is not one of the standard styles. Selecting the Other style opens a dialog box in which you can choose a font and character format for characters that are selected or about to be entered.

Selecting Font Sizes

The Equation Editor provides not only several predefined font styles, but also certain predefined font sizes. The Full size is the choice you normally work with when you are building equations. You also have selections for subscripts, sub-subscripts, symbols, and subsymbols. You can use the Other size option for those cases in which you want to specify a size not defined by one of these standard sizes.

To apply a font size to an equation, follow these steps:

1. Select the characters whose point size you want to modify.

2. Choose the Size menu and select a size. If no defined size matches your needs, choose Size, Other and specify a size in the Other Size dialog box. Or, choose Size, Define to modify the default settings for each size in the Size menu.

To apply a size, select one from the Size menu; then type the characters you want the size applied to. Alternatively, you can select the characters after they have been typed, and then choose a size.

Working with Matrices

The Matrix template palette includes several vectors and matrices of predefined sizes. You can also select one of the template symbols in the bottom row of the palette to open a Matrix dialog box. In this box, you can specify the dimensions of the matrix or vector, and also control several other matrix characteristics.

To insert a matrix template, click the Matrix Template button (the last button on the right in the bottom row). Then click the template you want. The templates in the first three rows of the palette insert matrices and vectors of fixed dimensions directly in the equation. Selecting a template from the last row of icons opens the Matrix dialog box (see Figure 24.8), where you can specify the dimensions of the matrix and make several other selections, including alignment, column widths and row heights, and the type of partition lines you will use. To control the spacing between rows and columns, use the Spacing dialog box that is displayed when you choose Format, Spacing.

FIG. 24.8
You can specify the dimensions of a matrix in the Matrix dialog box.

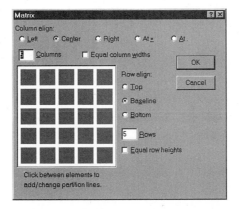

Press Tab to move from left to right through the matrix, one element at a time, or Shift+Tab to move right to left. You can also use the arrow keys to move from element to element in a matrix.

To format an existing matrix, select the entire matrix and then choose Format, Matrix. Make your selections from the dialog box, and choose OK.

N O T E   To create a determinant, you can nest a matrix within absolute value bars. Insert the absolute value bar template first, and with the insertion point inside the absolute value bars, insert a matrix template. ■

Viewing Equations

You can choose from three predefined magnifications of the equation in the Equation Editor window. Alternatively, you can choose View, Zoom to set a custom magnification for viewing your equation. To change the view, choose View. To display the equation at the actual size you want it to appear in the document and on the printed page, select 100%. To set a custom magnification, choose View, Zoom, and select the Custom option in the Zoom dialog box. Next, enter the magnification you want in the Custom text box; then choose OK.

Editing an Equation

To edit an equation, you must return to the Equation Editor. To open the Equation Editor, follow these steps:

1. Double-click the equation you want to edit.

    Or, select the equation and choose Edit, Equation Object, Edit.

2. Make your editing changes.

3. Click outside the Equation Editor to return to your document.

Printing Equations

Printing equations is easy with the TrueType fonts provided with Windows 95. In addition to the TrueType fonts that come with Windows 95, you will need the TrueType font MT Extra, which is installed when you install Equation Editor. TrueType fonts are scalable fonts used for both the screen display and the printed page, so what you see on the screen will closely match what is produced by your printer. With TrueType fonts, you can print your equations on virtually any type of printer. You don't have to worry about what fonts are built into your printer.

CAUTION

If you see boxes on screen instead of equations, choose Tools, Options, then click the View tab. Clear the Picture Placeholders check box.

▶ **See** "Setting Up Your Printer," **p. 259**

Publishing with Graphics

CHAPTER 25

Inserting Pictures

With Word 97, you can illustrate your ideas by using pictures that come from sources outside Word, such as drawing programs, scanners, and clip art collections. If a picture is worth a thousand words, think how much typing you can save! Even if your picture is worth somewhat less than a thousand words, illustrating your document with graphics can make your pages more appealing—which means that readers pay more attention to your words.

Pictures that you insert in your Word documents come from many sources. Some may come from an external drawing or painting program, which you can use to create illustrations ranging from the simple to the sophisticated. Some—including photographs—come from scanners that digitize artwork for use in a computer. Some pictures come from clip art packages that provide ready-to-use artwork. Office 97 itself includes many clip art images that you can use in Word.

Copy and insert previously created pictures into your document

Include pictures in your document that you've created in another program, or that you've purchased in a clip art collection.

Edit, size, crop, and move pictures

Alter the appearance of your picture, change its size, or move it to another location in your document.

Add fills and borders to pictures

You can add a border in any of many colors or styles to any picture, and can fill some with colors and patterns.

Hide pictures so you can work faster with text

Large picture files can slow down your work, but hiding pictures when you don't need to see them speeds you up again.

Scan pictures directly into your Word document

You don't even have to leave Word to scan an image.

Manage clip art with the Clip Gallery

The Clip Gallery is a visual organizer for your clip art—and it's a big help if you own lots of clip art.

These pictures come from a source outside of Word. In addition, you can use these pictures in many programs besides Word, which is the feature that distinguishes them from the graphic objects you create using Word's built-in drawing tools: WordArt, AutoShapes, Chart, and the Drawing toolbar. (You can learn about each of these built-in programs in Chapter 27, "Drawing with Word's Drawing Tools," Chapter 28, "Inserting Text with Special Effects," and Chapter 29, "Graphing Data"). You can use one of these built-in graphic programs to create a graphic that exists only as a part of your Word document.

Programs you use to create pictures often are more powerful than the simple built-in programs that come with Word. Word gives you the flexibility to include a range of graphics and pictures in your documents—from simple drawings that you create yourself without leaving Word to sophisticated pictures that you can make with a powerful stand-alone program. ■

ON THE WEB

For online support from Microsoft, visit the following World Wide Web site:

http://www.microsoft.com/support

You can also access Microsoft's extensive troubleshooting KnowledgeBase at the following site:

http://www.microsoft.com/kb

For tutorials, tips, and add-ins for Microsoft Office applications point your browser to:

http://www.ronperson.com

Getting Ready to Insert Pictures

Word is compatible with many of the most frequently used graphics programs and scanner formats. For some formats, you don't need a special import filter. For others you do need a filter, and you must install these filters when you set up Word or Office or rerun the Word or Office Setup program to install them later. From the Options list, select Converters and Filters.

To import pictures into a document, Word uses special *import filters*. One filter is required for each type of file you want to import. If you selected the Complete Setup option when you installed Word, all the graphics import filters were put into your system. If you selected a Custom installation, you might not have installed all the filters. To see which filters are installed (and consequently which types of graphics you are able to import), read the contents of the Files of Type list in the Insert Picture dialog box. This dialog box appears when you choose Insert, Picture, From File.

You can import pictures created with any of the following programs or in any of the formats listed:

Program Format	File Extension
Formats that don't require filters	
Windows Metafile	WMF
Enhanced Windows Metafile	EMF
JPEG Filter	JPG
Portable Network Graphics	PNG
Windows Bitmap	BMP
Formats that do require filters	
PC Paintbrush	PCX
Tagged Image Format	TIF
Encapsulated PostScript	EPS
Computer Graphics Metafile	CGM
WordPerfect Graphics	WPG
Micrografx Designer	DRW
Micrografx Draw	DRW
Targa	TGA
AutoCAD Format 2-D	DXF
CorelDRAW!	CDR
Macintosh PICT	PCT
GIF	GIF
Kodak PhotoCD	PCD

Part

VI

Ch

25

Your favorite graphic program might not be listed. However, many programs easily export graphics (or even part of a graphic) from the native format to a commonly used format. If your program isn't on the preceding list, see whether it can save graphics in one of the formats in the list, so that you can use them in Word.

Inserting and Copying Your Own Pictures into Your Document

You can insert a picture into the text of your document, a text box, or a table. Inserting a picture directly into your text is the simplest way to illustrate your document. You can work with inserted pictures in many ways; for example, you can group them together, wrap text around them, or layer them above or below text and other graphics.

Other techniques, however, sometimes offer advantages. Inserting a picture in one cell of a table enables you to position the picture adjacent to text in the next cell. Inserting a picture in a text box enables you to group the picture with text inside a common border.

Note that if you insert a picture while you're in Normal viewing mode, Word switches you to the Page Layout view. You can't see pictures in your document in Normal view.

▶ **See** "Selecting the Correct View for Your Work," **p. 132**

You can use one of three methods to insert a picture in your document:

- You can insert pictures by choosing Insert, Picture, From File or by clicking the Insert Picture button on the Picture toolbar. This command asks you to locate the file and then inserts the picture from disk. If you use this method, you don't even need to own the program used to create the picture.

- You can open the program used to create the picture and copy the picture into the Windows Clipboard. Then you can paste the picture into your Word document.

- You can insert picture objects by using Insert, Object to open a graphics program from within Word. You can use this command to insert a picture that you can edit later using the program that created it.

 TIP You can automatically include a numbered caption with each picture you insert by choosing Insert, Caption, AutoCaption. For more about captions, see Chapter 33, "Adding Cross-References and Captions."

 TIP Use the Insert Picture dialog box when you want to insert pictures that you won't want to edit later.

 TIP To quickly insert a picture, position the insertion point where you want it and double-click the picture's file name in the Insert Picture dialog box.

Inserting Pictures into a Document

Although you can insert a picture in your document without ever opening the program used to create the picture, you must first locate the picture file.

Word offers many tools for helping you find a file. You can find files that match a certain name, file type, or property, or files that were modified recently.

▶ **See** " Searching for Files," **p. 124**

You can insert a picture with or without a link to the program used to create the picture. By linking to the graphics program, you might be able to reduce the size of your document (see the upcoming section, "Minimizing File Size through Linking").

▶ **See** "Moving, Copying, and Linking Text or Graphics," **p. 185**

To insert a picture, follow these steps:

1. Position the insertion point where you want to insert the picture.

2. Choose Insert, Picture, From File, or click the Insert Picture button on the Picture toolbar.

   The Insert Picture dialog box appears (see Figure 25.1).

FIG. 25.1
Use the Insert Picture dialog box to locate a picture you want to insert. The preview box shows the selected picture.

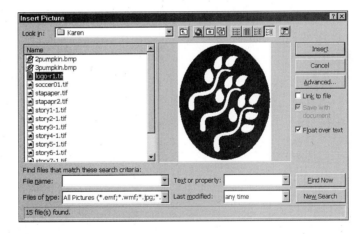

3. Locate your picture file. Use the Look In list to find the folder in which the file is stored and, if necessary, use the matching criteria at the bottom of the dialog box to search for your file.

4. Select the picture file you want to insert from the Name list. Click the Preview button if you want to see a miniature version of your picture.

5. Choose Insert.

   ▶ **See** "Searching for Files," **p. 124**

When you insert a picture in your Word document, it falls into place at the location of the insertion point and is anchored to its paragraph. The picture stays with that paragraph as you edit surrounding text. You can move the picture by dragging it with the mouse; for details, see the later section, "Working with Pictures."

If you want to embed your picture in the text (so that it is included in the text like a character), rather than allow it to be free floating, clear the Float Over Text option in the Insert Picture dialog box. An embedded picture moves with surrounding text and can even accept paragraph formatting (such as alignment, which you could use to center the picture on the page).

Performing Advanced Picture File Searches   If you're having a hard time locating the picture you want to insert, Word can help you find it. In the Insert Picture dialog box (refer to Figure 25.1), choose Advanced to display the Advanced Find dialog box. Select from the many options to find files matching naming criteria, properties such as the application name or the picture's author, or location.

▶ **See** "Searching for Files," **p. 124**

NOTE If you cannot insert a picture because it's in a format Word doesn't recognize, try opening the picture in Windows Paint or some other graphics program. Then save the picture in a format Word does recognize, such as BMP.

▶ **See** "Formatting Lines and Paragraphs," **p. 321**

Minimizing File Size Through Linking   When you insert a picture in your document, Word usually includes all the information in the picture file, as well as a representation of the picture. Each time you open your document, you see the picture. However, this method can make your Word file quite large: the file size is increased by the file size of the picture (which can be very large).

▶ **See** " Moving, Copying, and Linking Text or Graphics," **p. 185**

Another way to insert a picture is to link the picture to its picture file, but not store a copy of the picture in your Word file. Each time you open your document, Word refers to the original file to draw a representation of the picture. This method has the advantage of minimizing your file size, as Word does not store a copy of the picture in your document.

Minimizing file size in this way is helpful if your graphics files are very large or if you're using the same graphic file over and over in different documents (like a logo in your stationery). However, if the file is not available, Word cannot display or print the picture—when you open the Word file, a message box warns you that Word cannot open the picture file. Use this method for minimizing file size only when you are sure Word will be able to locate the picture file.

To minimize file size through linking, follow these steps:

1. Position the insertion point where you want the picture to appear. Then choose Insert, Picture, From File and select the picture you want to insert.

2. In the Insert Picture dialog box, select the Link to File option (at the far right of the dialog box, under the Advanced command button). Then clear the Save with Document option.

3. Choose Insert.

If you move the original picture file, you must update the link by selecting the picture and choosing Edit, Links, Change Source. (You also can use this command to save the picture in the document.) For more information, refer to Chapter 36, "Using Word with Office Applications."

If you give someone a Word file containing a picture that is linked to the file, be sure to give them a copy of the picture file as well. Have them choose Edit, Links, Change Source to identify the picture file's location on their hard disk.

Another way to minimize file size is to save picture files in a format that creates smaller files, when that is an option. PCX, BMP, and WMF files are usually smaller than EPS or TIF files, for example. You can also minimize document file size by using black-and-white pictures, rather than color, especially if you'll print in black and white anyway.

Copying Pictures into Your Document

Sometimes the easiest way to get a picture you created with a graphics program into Word is to use the Clipboard to copy the picture. You can even link the picture to the original file when you paste it into Word; in this way, you can update the picture if you later make changes to the original.

▶ **See** "Moving, Copying, and Linking Text or Graphics," **p. 185**

▶ **See** "Embedding Data," **p. 1085**

To copy a picture into your document, follow these steps:

1. Start your graphics or charting program. Then open the file containing the picture you want to copy into your Word document.

2. Select the picture or chart.

3. Choose Edit, Copy.

4. Switch to your Word document.

5. Position the insertion point where you want to insert the picture.

6. Choose Edit, Paste.

Or, choose <u>E</u>dit, Paste <u>S</u>pecial to link the picture to the original file. Select Paste <u>L</u>ink from the Paste Special dialog box. In the <u>A</u>s list, select the format for your picture (formats vary depending on what type of picture you copied). Select the <u>D</u>isplay as Icon option if you want to display an icon, rather than the picture, in your text. (You can double-click the icon to display and edit the picture.)

7. Click OK.

 Images and pictures you see on Web pages can be copied to a file or to the Windows Clipboard. Right-click an image, then choose <u>C</u>opy to copy to the Clipboard or <u>S</u>ave Picture As to display a Save As dialog box. Choose P<u>r</u>operties to see the size and type of file. Insert files and paste Clipboard copies into your documents. Not all images are free for the taking. Do not violate trademark, copyright, and registration laws.

When you paste in a picture with a link, you get some choices. If you paste the picture as an *object*, you can edit it later. If you paste the picture as a *picture*, it might take up less space. To get an idea of the best way to paste in your picture, read the Result box at the bottom of the Paste Special dialog box as you select each of the different formats in the <u>A</u>s list.

For more information about how to work with links, refer to Chapter 36, "Using Word with Office Applications."

Inserting Picture Objects in Your Document

A *picture object* is a picture in your Word document that you can edit. You edit the picture by double-clicking it to display the program used to create the picture, if the program is available. All the data that creates a picture object is contained within the Word document—it is not linked to a file outside the document.

▶ **See** " Inserting Text with Special Effects," **p. 921**

▶ **See** " Choosing to Paste, Link, or Embed Data," **p. 1079**

You can insert many types of picture objects in your document. If Adobe Illustrator or another OLE-based graphics program is installed on your computer, you can insert an Illustrator object. If Microsoft Excel is installed, you can embed an Excel chart as an object. You can insert an equation, graph, picture, or WordArt image as objects, and you can insert a Microsoft Word Picture object.

You can insert new or existing picture objects. If you insert new picture objects, Word displays the graphics program you've chosen, and you must draw the picture.

For example, if you choose to insert a new Illustrator picture object, Word starts Illustrator and presents you with a blank drawing screen. You draw the picture, and then you choose a command to return to your Word document with the picture.

If you insert existing picture objects, the existing picture appears in your document. Whether you insert new or existing picture objects, you always can double-click one of these objects to display the program used to create the picture. Then you can edit the picture. Alternatively, you can use a command to edit the picture.

To insert a new picture object, follow these steps:

1. Position the insertion point where you want to insert the picture object.

2. Choose Insert, Object. The Object dialog box appears (see Figure 25.2).

FIG. 25.2

When you insert a new picture object, Word displays the program you use to create it.

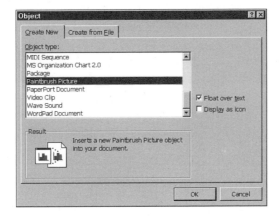

3. Select the Create New tab.

4. Select the type of picture object you want to insert from the Object Type list. For example, to insert a Microsoft Word picture, select Microsoft Word Picture from the list.

   Select the Display as Icon check box if you want to display an icon rather than the picture. Icons can be used if a picture will take too much room in a document. The icon displays on-screen or when printed. You can double-click the icon to see its contents.

5. Choose OK. A rectangular selection appears in your document, and tools from the program you'll use to create the object appear at the edges of the screen.

   For example, if you chose Paintbrush Picture, the screen shown in Figure 25.3 appears. Notice the Drawing tools at the left edge of the screen and the color palette at the bottom.

Part

VI

Ch

25

FIG. 25.3
You can insert or
draw a picture using
Microsoft Paint.

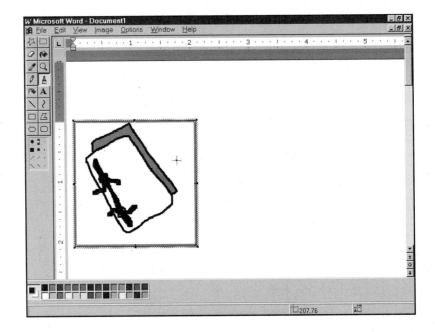

6. Create the picture.

7. Return to your Word document by clicking your Word document page, outside
the object work area.

To insert an existing picture object, follow these steps:

1. Position the insertion point where you want to insert the picture object.

2. Choose Insert, Object. The Object dialog box appears (see Figure 25.4).

FIG. 25.4
You can insert an
existing picture object
and edit it later.

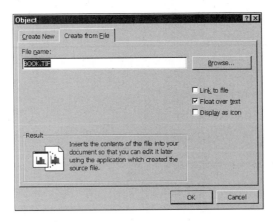

3. Select the Create from File tab.

4. Type the path and file name of the picture you want to insert in the File Name box. Locate the file, if necessary, by selecting Browse.

5. Select Link to File if you want the picture in your Word document to update when you change the original picture.

6. Select Display as Icon if you want to display an icon rather than the picture.

7. Click OK.

Read the message in the Result box at the bottom of the Object dialog box to see the results that the currently selected options have produced in your document.

▶ **See** "Searching for Files," **p. 124**

T I P   Choose Insert, Object when you want to insert pictures that you can edit later.

Inserting Clip Art in Your Document

Part

VI

Ch

25

Clip art is one of the most economical tools you can use to illustrate a document professionally, and with Word, using clip art is easy. Microsoft Office includes a good collection of more than 1,000 clip art images on disk, and if you're on the Internet, you can download even more. In addition, Word includes a clip art gallery that organizes your clip art into categories and shows you a miniature picture of each piece so you can choose it visually, rather than guessing what a picture looks like by its file name. Word's clip art gallery works equally well with Microsoft clip art and with non-Microsoft clip art packages.

Microsoft Clip Gallery not only manages your clip art, letting you organize, preview, and insert clip art pictures but also is the tool you use in Word to organize and insert sound clips and video clips. The gallery automatically accesses Microsoft clip art that is stored on your Office CD when the CD is in its drive. Other clip art must be added to the gallery—even if the clip art is already on your hard disk—if you want to use the gallery to preview and insert it. If you want to have access to the clip art on your Office CD even when the CD is not in its drive, you must copy the clip art to your hard drive and add it to the gallery.

Many World Wide Web sites contain free graphics, images, and photographs. Stock image companies display on the Web catalogs of the images and photographs they have for sale. To see two sites that have clip art, point your browser to:

Web Site	URL	Description
Microsoft's Gallery	**http://www.microsoft.com/gallery**	Gallery of free images, photos, and multimedia for use in Word and Web pages.
Publisher's Depot	**http://www.publishersdepot.com**	Desktop publishing software distributor that sells digitized photos, illustrations, and images.

Inserting Clip Art Pictures

Microsoft Clip Gallery is not like a folder that stores files; rather, it is like a pointer that tells Word where to find your clip art files. It organizes your clip art into categories to help you manage them and displays a miniature picture of each clip art image that you can view to select the best picture for your document. If you attempt to insert clip art but find none in the gallery, go to the next section, "Adding Clip Art to the Gallery," to learn how to add your clip art to the gallery.

The gallery dialog box includes two tabs that show different types of clip art. One tab, Clip Art, shows object-based images, some of which you can ungroup and modify using color tools on the Drawing toolbar; the other tab, Pictures, shows bitmap images, some of which you can modify using image, contrast, and brightness tools on the Picture toolbar.

Also included in the Clip Gallery dialog box are two tabs, Sounds and Videos, that display audio and video clips you can include in your documents.

To insert a clip art picture into your document, follow these steps:

1. Position the insertion point where you want the clip art.
2. Choose Insert, Picture, Clip Art to display the Microsoft Clip Gallery dialog box, shown in Figure 25.5.
3. Select the Clip Art or the Pictures tab to locate the clip art you want to insert.
4. Scroll through the Categories list and select the category that contains the clip art you want to insert.
5. Click the clip art image you want to insert. If necessary, scroll the viewing screen to see all the art included in the category you selected.

If you're having trouble locating the image you want, choose Find. In the Find Clip dialog box, type a description of what you're looking for in the Keywords list or type a partial file name in the File Name containing list or select a file type in the Clip Type list. Then choose Find Now. The gallery finds images that match your criteria and displays them in a category called Results of Last Find.

Choose Magnify if you want to see a magnified view the selected image, along with its file name.

6. Choose Insert.

Alternatively, you can insert an image by double-clicking it in the gallery.

FIG. 25.5
The Microsoft Clip Gallery organizes, previews, and inserts clip art.

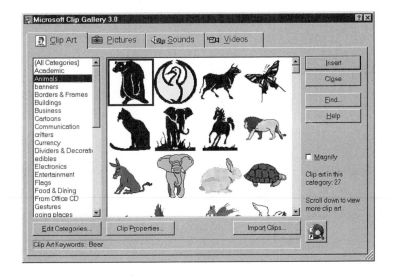

Creating and Changing Clip Art Categories

The clip art that comes free with Microsoft Office is organized by category for you. Other clip art is not. You can easily create categories or modify existing categories. You should try to create categories, if you need them, before adding new clip art to the gallery, especially when you're adding a whole new package of clip art to the gallery.

To create or change a clip art gallery category, follow these steps:

1. Choose Insert, Picture, Clip Art to display the Microsoft Clip Gallery dialog box.

2. Choose the tab where you want to add a clip art category: Clip Art or Pictures.

3. Choose Edit Categories to display the Edit Category List dialog box, shown in Figure 25.6. Then do one of the following:

Select <u>N</u>ew Category to add a category. Then type the new category name and choose OK.

Select the category you want to delete and choose <u>D</u>elete Category.

Select the category you want to rename, choose <u>R</u>ename Category, type the new category name, and choose OK.

4. Choose Close. Choose Cl<u>o</u>se again if you want to close the gallery.

FIG. 25.6
You can easily add or edit a clip art category.

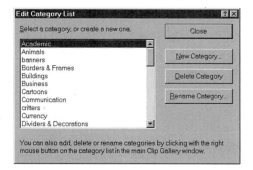

Adding Clip Art to the Gallery

Although Microsoft Clip Gallery automatically recognizes Microsoft Office clip art, you must add other clip art to the gallery in order for the gallery to recognize it. Clip art might include packages of clip art that you purchase, or it might be art you've drawn yourself using graphics software. Keep in mind that the gallery must always be able to find the clip art files if it is to display them; see the upcoming section, "Relocating Clip Art Files," to learn what to do if you've moved a file.

To add clip art to the gallery, follow these steps:

1. Choose <u>I</u>nsert, Picture, Clip Art to open the Microsoft Clip Gallery dialog box.

2. Choose Impor<u>t</u> Clips to display the Add Clip Art to the Clip Gallery dialog box, shown in Figure 25.7.

3. Locate and select the clip art you want to add to the gallery. You can add one at a time or many at once.

4. Choose <u>O</u>pen to display the Clip Properties dialog box, shown in Figure 25.8. Notice the preview of the image at the top of the dialog box.

5. Type any key words you want associated with this clip art in the <u>K</u>eywords box. (You can search for clip art using these keywords.)

6. Select the categories in the Categories list where you want your clip art. Clear categories where you don't want it. (Clip art can go into as many categories as you want.) If you don't have a category for your clip art, choose <u>N</u>ew Category, type the new category name, and choose OK.

If you're adding many clip art files to the gallery at once and they're all going into the same category or categories, choose <u>A</u>dd All Clips to the Selected Categories.

If you're adding many clips at once but they're going to different categories, then don't choose <u>A</u>dd All Clips to the Selected Categories; you see in the next step how you can choose categories for each file individually.

7. Choose OK. If you selected multiple clip art files to add all at once but didn't select the <u>A</u>dd All Clips to the Selected Categories option, then the Clip Properties dialog box reappears for each clip and gives you the option to change categories, or even to choose <u>S</u>kip This Clip to bypass this particular clip.

FIG. 25.7

Select the clip art files you want to add to the gallery.

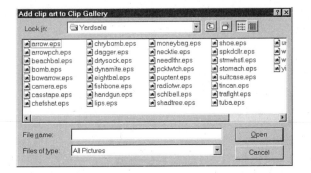

FIG. 25.8

Enter keywords and select categories for the clip art you add to the gallery. You can later search for clip art using keywords.

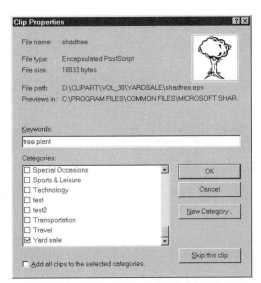

Changing Keywords and Categories

Categories help you organize clip art and are especially helpful if you have a lot of clip art. Keywords help you find clip art by using a descriptive word. If you want to change the category a piece of clip art is in, or add or change its keywords, you change its properties. (You can't change properties for the Microsoft Office clip art.)

To change a clip's keywords or category, follow these steps:

1. Select the clip art from the Microsoft Clip Gallery whose keywords or category you want to change.

2. Choose Clip Properties to display the Clip Properties dialog box (refer to Figure 25.8).

3. Type in the Keywords box any new key words by which you'd like to be able to search for this piece of clip art, or edit existing words. You can separate the words any way you want or even not separate them.

4. Select from the Categories list the category or categories where you want to store this clip art or clear any categories where you don't want to store it.

5. Click OK.

Downloading Clip Art from the Internet

If you have access to the Internet, you can add to your clip art collection by downloading images from Microsoft. The Clip Gallery includes a tool to help you acquire the files and add them to the Clip Gallery. (You must have an Internet connection and browser.)

▶ **See** "Understanding the Word Wide Web and Browsers," **p. 522**

To download clip art files from the Internet, follow these steps:

1. Choose Insert, Picture, Clip Art to display the Microsoft Clip Gallery.

2. Click the Connect to Web for Additional Clips button, which looks like a globe, at the bottom right of the dialog box. Then choose OK to continue.

3. Choose Accept when the Microsoft Clip Gallery Live screen, shown in Figure 25.9, appears.

4. Click the button that describes the type of clips you want to download: clip art, pictures, sound, or video. Click the leftmost button to download clip art.

FIG. 25.9
The Microsoft Clip Gallery Live is a source on the Internet for clip art, pictures, video clips, and sound clips.

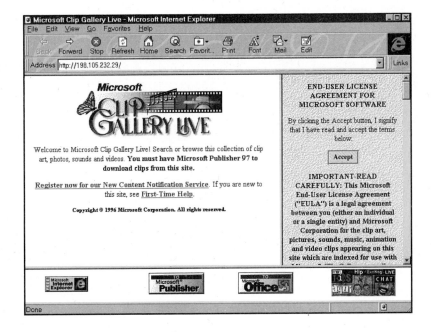

5. Define your search criteria by doing one of two things:

   Click Browse and select a clip art category or,

   Click Search and enter keywords.

6. Click Go to perform the search. The Gallery returns the results of the search on the left side of the screen, as shown in Figure 25.10.

7. Scroll through the images displayed on the screen to decide which image(s) to download. To download an image, click the file name under the preview picture. Your browser returns two options for downloading the image.

8. Choose Open it to install the image in the Microsoft Clip Gallery.

   Or, choose Save It to Disk to copy the file onto your disk. Enter a name and path for the file.

9. Exit your browser.

FIG. 25.10
The Gallery displays images that match your search criteria; you can download them to your Word gallery.

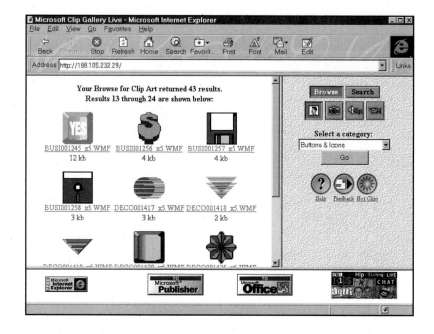

Relocating Clip Art Files

If you move a clip art file or remove the disk from where Microsoft Clip Gallery expects to find it, then the Gallery cannot find the file and you cannot use the Gallery to insert the clip art into your document. If you try to insert a moved clip art file, you'll get a message saying, Word can't find the file. Choose OK to go on.

The Cannot Insert Picture box recommends that you remove the clip from the Gallery. Choose Remove Preview to remove a single clip art preview or choose Update All to remove all previews whose files have moved.

If you move a clip art file, but still want to use it in the Gallery, first remove it from the Gallery to omit incorrect references to its old location and then import it again.

▶ **See** "Managing Files," **p. 120**

Scanning Pictures

If a scanner is attached to your computer, you can use Word to scan images directly into your document. Word uses a program that comes with Microsoft Office, called Microsoft Photo Editor, to manage the scanning process (although your own scanning software performs the actual scan). Photo Editor also is a powerful picture editing program that lets you manipulate scanned (and other) images in many artistic ways.

Scanning with Photo Editor is a two-part process. When you begin the scan, Photo Editor starts your scanner software, which performs the scan. Then, rather than creating a separate graphic file, your scanner transmits the image into Photo Editor, where you can edit it. When you close Photo Editor, the scanned image becomes part of your Word document (although the File, Save As command also allows you to save the image as a separate file). By contrast, when you scan an image with separate scanning software, most people create a separate graphic file for the scanned image. You can import those files into many programs, including Word.

Photo Editor, shown in Figure 25.11, has many tools you can use to manipulate your scanned images. These tools exist in menus on the Photo Editor menu bar, and in the editing buttons on Photo Editor's Standard toolbar. You can edit scanned images immediately after scanning, or later, by double-clicking a scanned image to restart Photo Editor.

FIG. 25.11
Photo Editor is a powerful image editing program which you can use to scan and manipulate pictures.

Using Microsoft Photo Editor to Scan an Image

You can scan an image using Photo Editor from within Word in one of three ways:

- The most direct is to choose Insert, Picture, From Scanner, which starts both Photo Editor and your scanner software, and performs the scan.

- A less direct way is to choose Insert, Object, select Photo Editor from the Object Type list on the Create New tab, and then select Scanner from the New dialog box that appears.

■ A final method is to choose Insert, Object, and select Microsoft Photo Editor Scan from the Object Type list on the Create New tab.

All three methods do the same job, but because the first is the quickest, that's what this section describes.

Before you use Word to scan an image, be sure your scanner is turned on and the image you want to scan is in the scanner. You may need to turn on your scanner before you turn on your computer in order for your computer to recognize your scanner.

To scan an image, follow these steps:

1. Choose Insert, Picture, From Scanner. Photo Editor starts, and your scanner software starts.

2. Use your scanner software to complete the scan. The final scanned image appears in the Photo Editor window.

3. Use Photo Editor to edit the scanned image as necessary. (The next section, "Manipulating an Image with Photo Editor," describes how to use Photo Editor's editing tools.)

4. Choose File, Exit and Return to Document to close Photo Editor and return to your Word document, where your scanned image appears. Or click the Word document outside the Photo Editor window to return to Word.

The resolution and file type of your scanned image affect how it behaves in Word. The higher the resolution you choose in your scanner software when performing the scan, the larger the file in Word (and the slower it performs when you edit it). Choose the right resolution for the job—if your image will only appear on your computer screen, choose screen resolution. If you'll print it on a 300 dot per inch laser printer, choose a resolution of 300 dpi.

Image type is also important. As explained in the next section, "Manipulating an Image with Photo Editor," you can't use many of Photo Editors tools with black-and-white images; grayscale or color may be better if you want to edit the image.

 T I P If you plan to choose Photo Editor's File, Save As command to save a scanned image as a separate file to use in another program, be sure to save your image in the appropriate file format. For example, if you'll be using a scanned photo in a Web page, you should probably save it in JPEG format. To learn about creating Web pages with Word, see Chapter 14, "Publishing to a Web."

Manipulating an Image with Photo Editor

To edit a scanned image with Photo Editor, double-click the image. Photo Editor starts, and you can use its many tools to manipulate your image.

 TIP You can use Photo Editor to edit other images besides those you've scanned. Choose Tools, Options, Edit, and in the Picture Editor list, select Microsoft Photo Editor. Then when you double-click imported pictures of a format Photo Editor can import, Photo Editor starts. You can use it to edit the image.

You may find that some editing tools are unavailable to use. This is because your file type may not permit some types of editing. Images scanned as black-and-white line drawings, for example, can't take advantage of many tools and effects. If you want to use those tools and effects, you must convert your image to a grayscale or color image. One way to convert an image is to do so when you scan it, using your scanner software. Another way is to choose File, Properties and select a different Image Type. Unavailable editing commands, when you select them, will offer to convert your image to a format they can use.

Selecting the Editing Range   Many of Photo Editor's commands and tools apply either to the entire image, or to a selected portion of the image. For example, if there's no selection when you choose the special effect "Sharpen," then the entire image is sharpened, but if there is a selection, then only the selection is sharpened.

To select part of an image, follow these steps:

1. Click the Select button on the Photo Editor's Standard toolbar.
2. Move the pointer over the image. The pointer does not change shape.
3. Drag the pointer to define a rectangular selection area.

In Photo Editor, a selected area is defined by a marquis-like animated border that has selection handles on each corner and side. You can resize the selection by dragging any handle, and you can drag the selection to another location.

Using Photo Editor's Editing Commands   Photo Editor has three menus containing commands useful for editing an image: File, Edit, and View. Each of the commands is described in the following table. For greater detail about any command, refer to the Help file (described in the later section, "Getting Help").

Menu	Command	Result
File	New	Displays the Blank Picture dialog box; use it to determine image type, resolution, size, and background color of a new, blank image.
	Open	Displays the Open dialog box; use it to open a graphic file into a blank window or into a new window if the current window is not blank.
	Close	Close an image if more than one is open, or close Photo Editor if only one image is open.
	Update	Update the image in your document without closing Photo Editor.
	Save As	Allows you to save the scanned image as a stand-alone file in any of many formats.
	Revert	Reverts image to last saved version.
	Scan Image	Scans an image and places it in a new window inside Photo Editor.
	Select Scanner Source	Allows you to select the scanner software you want Photo Editor to use.
	Print	Allows you to print your image.
	Send	Allows you to send the image via e-mail.
	Properties	Allows you to change properties including image type, resolution, and transparency.
	Exit or Exit and Return to Document	Exits the open window, or exits Photo Editor.
Edit	Undo	Undoes last edit.
	Redo	Redoes last edit.
	Cut	Removes selection, or removes image, to Clipboard.
	Copy	Copies selection, or copies image, to Clipboard.
	Paste	Paste contents of Clipboard in Photo Editor window.

Menu	Command	Result
	Paste as <u>N</u>ew Image	Pastes the contents of the Clipboard into a new Photo Editor window.
	<u>S</u>elect All	Selects the entire image. (Press Esc to cancel the selection.)
<u>V</u>iew	<u>T</u>oolbar	Displays/hides the Photo Editor toolbar.
	<u>R</u>uler	Displays/hides vertical and horizontal rulers.
	<u>S</u>tatus Bar	Displays/hides status bar.
	Measurement <u>U</u>nits	Allows you to select <u>C</u>m (centimeters), <u>I</u>nches, or <u>P</u>ixels as the measurement unit for rulers and dialog boxes.

Using Photo Editor's Toolbar   Photo Editor's Standard toolbar, shown in Figure 25.12, contains familiar editing tools (and a scanning tool) along the top, and image editing tools on the bottom. Table 25.1 describes the scanning tool and each of the image editing tools.

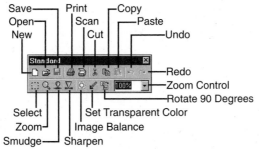

FIG. 25.12
Photo Editor's toolbar offers many image editing tools.

Save — Print — Copy
Open — Scan — Paste
New — Cut — Undo
— Redo
— Zoom Control
— Rotate 90 Degrees
Select — Set Transparent Color
Zoom — Image Balance
Smudge — Sharpen

Table 25.1   Image Editing Tools

Icon	Tool	Effect and How to Use the Tool
	Scan	Scans an image and places it in a new Photo Editor window.
	Select	Allows you to drag to select an area of your image.
	Zoom	Zooms in to the place in the image where you click. Press Shift while you click to zoom back out.

continues

Table 25.1   Continued

Icon	Tool	Effect and How to Use the Tool
	Smudge	Gives you a finger-shaped tool you can use to blend colors. Right-click the tool to display the Smudge Brush options box which you can use to change brush attributes. Drag the Smudge tool over the area of your image you want to smudge.
	Sharpen	Gives you a finger-shaped tool you can use to increase the contrast in an area. Right-click the tool to display the Sharpen Brush dialog box which you can use to change brush attributes. Drag the Sharpen tool over the area of your image you want to sharpen.
	Image Balance	Displays the Balance dialog box, which you can use to increase or decrease brightness, contrast, and gamma levels (background contrast) of your image. (This is the same dialog box you get when you choose Image, Balance; for details, see the next section, "Using Photo Editor's Image Control Commands.")
	Set Transparent Color	Gives you a tool you can use to change a color to transparent. When you click your image with the tool, the Change Color to Transparent dialog box appears, which you can use to do three things: define the color you want to change, expand the range of color that changes to transparent, and select a degree of transparency. Transparent areas appear checkered on the screen. You can use the tool as many times as you want, adding to the transparent areas of your image.
	Rotate	Rotates your image 90 degrees clockwise.
100%	Zoom Control	Lists zoom percentages, from 10 to 1600 percent.

Using Photo Editor's Image Control Commands   Two menus, Image and Effects, allow you to manipulate the scanned image's appearance. The Image menu includes commands you may already be familiar with if you've worked with graphics, including cropping, resizing, and rotating. It also gives commands for adjusting lighting in your image—useful if you're working with photographs.

Remember that if you choose an effect that you don't like, you can choose Edit, Undo to undo the most recent edit, or File, Revert to revert to the last saved version of your image.

Cropping means cutting away a picture's edges—usually to remove what's unimportant in a picture and focus on what's interesting. Photo Editor gives you many interesting cropping options.

To crop a picture, follow these steps:

1. Choose Image, Crop. The Crop dialog box appears offering these option groups:
   - *Mat Margins*. Entering mat margins adds the amount you specify around the edges of the cropped image, to allow for matting.
   - *Units*. Select the unit of measure for this dialog box.
   - *Crop Margins*. Select the distance you want cut away from each edge of your picture. Choose whether the shape is to be Rectangle or Oval.
   - *Corners*. Select the size and style of the corners (for rectangle shapes only).

2. Select the options you want.

3. Choose OK.

 TIP You can crop to just the part of the image you want to keep by first selecting the part of the image you want, and then choosing the Crop command. Photo Editor removes everything outside the selection area.

Resizing means changing the size of an image. You may want to both crop and resize an image, to focus on the most important part of an image, and then enlarge or reduce it. Note that you may lose some image quality when you resize a photograph; if you need to make it smaller, first try cropping.

To resize an image, follow these steps:

1. Choose Image, Resize. The Resize dialog box appears.

2. Select Width and Height, and use the spinner boxes to alter the image width or height either by an amount or a percentage. When you change one, the other changes to keep the image in proportion unless you select the Allow Distortion option.

3. Select Allow Distortion if you want to change either the width or height alone, causing the image to be distorted.

4. Select Smooth to help compensate for quality loss when resizing photos or other complex images.

5. Select Units if you want to change the unit of measure in this dialog box.

6. Click OK.

Part
VI

Ch
25

To quickly crop and resize, select the portion of the image you want to keep and then choose the Resize command. Photo Editor resizes the portion of the image inside the selection and discards the portion of the image outside the selection.

To rotate, transpose, invert, or mirror an image, follow these steps:

1. Choose Image, Rotate. The Rotate dialog box appears with these options:

   - *Rotate Left or Rotate Right.* Rotates 90 degrees left or right.
   - *Transpose.* Flips the image vertically (upside down) and horizontally.
   - *Invert.* Flips the image vertically (upside down).
   - *Mirror.* Flips the image horizontally.
   - *By Degree.* Lets you specify rotation by increments of a single degree. Option buttons indicate whether to rotate counterclockwise or clockwise.

2. Select the option you want, and watch the Image group to see how it affects your picture.

3. Click OK.

Balance means the amount of light and dark in a picture. With Photo Editor, you can change the balance of brightness (the amount of light), contrast (the amount of gray), and gamma (the amount of contrast in just the dark areas of the picture). You can adjust any of these characteristics for all colors, or (in a color image) for red, green, or blue.

To change the balance of an image, follow these steps:

1. Choose Image, Balance. The Balance dialog box appears.

2. Use the Brightness, Contrast, and Gamma sliders to adjust your image. Sliding to the right means greater brightness, contrast, or gamma; to the left means less. Your image changes as you move the sliders, so you can see the effect of your selections before you close the dialog box.

3. If you want to adjust the balance for only a single color (red, green, or blue), select that color from the list of color options.

4. Click OK.

If you want Photo Editor to balance your image automatically, choose Image, Autobalance.

Using Photo Editor's Special Effects Commands   The Effects menu contains 14 commands for applying special artistic effects to your image. These commands change the overall appearance of your image; for example, applying the effect Chalk and Charcoal changes a photograph into what looks like a chalk or charcoal drawing. If you want to change just part of your image, select that part first.

Two groups of commands are on the Effects menu. The first six commands listed have simple dialog boxes with only a few options. The next eight have more complicated dialog boxes that include preview screens.

Figure 25.13 shows the Chalk and Charcoal dialog box, which is representative of these more complex dialog boxes. At the top left is a Preview screen, which shows your entire image. Included within the preview is a movable square, which identifies the area displayed in the Before and After windows to the right. You can move the preview square by dragging it, and thus change the preview area. You must click Preview to update the After window.

FIG. 25.13
The bottom eight commands in the Effects menu all have a dialog box similar to this one.

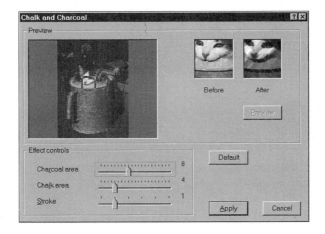

The best way to see how the effects commands work is to experiment with them. Remember, you can choose Edit, Undo if you don't like the result of a choice you make.

To use the special effects commands, select the command, choose your options (watching the preview box if there is one), and then choose OK or Apply. The following table lists the commands and their general effects:

Effects Menu Command	Result
Sharpen	Increases image sharpness by heightening the difference between the edges of adjoining colors.
Soften	Blurs the difference between edges of adjoining colors.
Negative	Inverses colors or shades to create a negative image.

continues

continued

Effects Menu Command	Result
Despeckle	Removes speckles; sensitivity refers to the amount of change needed to define an area as a speck.
Posterize	Reduces the number of colors or shades of gray to create an abstract image.
Edge	Outlines the edges of an image.
Chalk and Charcoal	Makes an image look like chalk or charcoal.
Emboss	Makes an image look raised.
Graphic Pen	Renders a pen and ink drawing.
Notepaper	Creates a raised white image on a gray background.
Watercolor	Renders a watercolor painting.
Stained Glass	Creates bordered polygons of color that suggest a stained glass window.
Stamp	Creates a picture in simple black-and-white shapes; you could use it for a stamp.
Texturizer	Applies textures such as canvas, so the image looks like it's painted on a surface.

Getting Help   Photo Editor has its own Help file you can use to learn more about any of the program's features. Use it the same way you use Word Help files. Another source of help is in many of Photo Editor's dialog boxes. Click the question mark in the title bar, then click with the resulting question arrow on the feature you want to learn more about. For more about Help, see Chapter 2, "Getting Started in Word."

Working with Pictures

After you insert a picture in your document, you can manipulate it in many ways. You can select and move it, and you can group it with other pictures, with text, or with other objects. You can ungroup pictures that are composed of a group of objects—including some clip art. You can layer pictures in front of or behind text, pictures, and other objects.

Selecting Pictures

Before you change a picture, you must select it. When a picture is selected, it has square selection handles on all four corners and sides—eight in all. You must select a picture before you revise it in any way or before you move, group, or layer it.

To select a picture, simply click it. If you're working with layers, you can use a special tool on the Drawing toolbar to select pictures that are layered behind text or another object; see the later section, "Layering Pictures with Text and Other Objects," for details.

Clicking an inserted picture selects it. Double-clicking a picture often has a very different effect. If it's a picture object, double-clicking will bring up the program used to create the picture; if it's clip art, double-clicking will display the Microsoft Clip Gallery dialog box, which you can use to replace the picture.

▶ **See** "Using the Mouse," **p. 41**

▶ **See** "Aligning Paragraphs," **p. 331**

Moving, Positioning, or Copying a Picture

Inserted pictures move easily and freely in a Word document. By simply dragging a picture with a mouse, you can move it anywhere.

To move a picture, follow these steps:

1. Position the insertion point over the picture so that it turns into a pointer arrow over a four-headed arrow.
2. Drag the picture where you want it (see Figure 25.14).

You can also use a command to position a picture in a precise location on the page. The position is horizontally and vertically relative to some edge on your page. Objects are always positioned relative to the left margin, the left edge of a column, the top of the page, or the beginning of a paragraph.

To position a picture precisely, follow these steps:

1. Click the picture to select it.
2. Choose Format, Object or Format, Picture to display the Format dialog box.
3. Select the Position tab, shown in Figure 25.15.
4. Select Horizontal and enter a distance; then select From and select Margin, Page, or Column. The picture will be positioned that distance from the left margin, page edge, or column edge.

Part
VI

Ch

25

FIG. 25.14

You can drag a picture to move it.

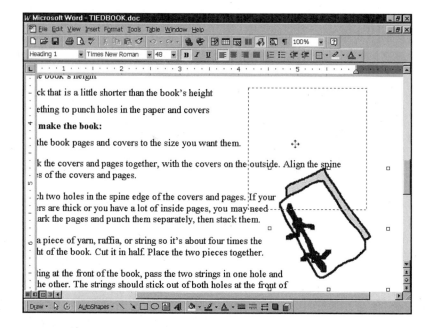

FIG. 25.15

You can choose Format, Object, Position or Format, Picture, Position to position a picture precisely.

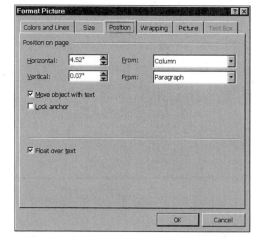

5. Select <u>V</u>ertical and enter a distance; then select F<u>r</u>om and select Margin, Page, or Paragraph. The picture will be positioned that distance from the top margin, the top of the page, or the beginning of the paragraph.

6. Click OK.

Usually pictures float over the top of text (or can be layered below it; see the upcoming section, "Layering Pictures with Text and Other Objects"). When pictures float in this way, you can move them freely on the page. But there may be times when you want an inserted picture to behave like a text character. Inserted this way, you can move the picture like a text character; you can select it like a text character; you can apply paragraph formatting like a text character. You might want a non-floating picture, for example, to serve as a small icon that moves with the characters adjacent to it.

To position a picture so that it behaves like text (to anchor it), follow these steps:

1. Select the picture by clicking it.
2. Choose Format, Object, Position or Format, Picture, Position.
3. Clear the Float Over Text option.
4. Click OK.

TIP
If you can't move or position a picture, the picture may have been inserted with the Float Over Text option cleared. To float the picture so you can move or position it in your document, choose Format, Object, Position or Format, Picture, Position and then select the Float Over Text option.

By default, a picture moves along with the text where you inserted it because it is anchored to that text. For example, if you insert it in the third paragraph on a page and then add text above the third paragraph, the picture moves forward along with the paragraph. If you don't want the picture to move with the text, you can override that default.

If you move an anchored picture to another page, the anchor moves with it. You can prevent the picture from moving to another page by locking its anchor.

To change a picture's anchors, follow these steps:

1. Select the picture and choose Format, Object, Position or Format, Picture, Position.
2. Select Move Object with Text to anchor a picture to the paragraph where you insert it; clear this option if you don't want it to move as you edit text.

   Or, select Lock Anchor if you want to keep a picture on the page where it's currently positioned; clear this option to allow the picture to move to another page.
3. Click OK.

   ▶ **See** "Moving, Positioning, or Copying a Picture," **p. 837**
   ▶ **See** "Wrapping Text Around a Picture," **p. 852**
   ▶ **See** "Working with Frames," **p. 890**

Part
VI

Ch
25

You can use a command to move or copy a picture. And here's a trick for copying a picture (or any other object) using the mouse—hold down the Ctrl key on your keyboard while you drag the object with the mouse.

To move or copy a picture using a command, follow these steps:

1. Select the picture.

2. Choose <u>E</u>dit, Cu<u>t</u> (Ctrl+X or Shift+Delete) to move a picture, or <u>E</u>dit, <u>C</u>opy (Ctrl+C or Ctrl+Insert) to copy it.

3. Move the insertion point to the place where you want to move the picture. Then choose <u>E</u>dit, <u>P</u>aste (Ctrl+V or Shift+Insert).

Grouping and Ungrouping Pictures

Grouping pictures allows you to move them as a unit and to apply formatting to all the pictures in a group simultaneously. You can group pictures with other pictures or with other objects. For example, you can group a picture with its caption to keep the picture and its caption together.

When you apply formatting to objects in a group, the formatting applies to each individual object. For example, a line border applied to a group appears around the edges of each of the objects in the group, not around the group as a whole. If you want a border or other formatting to apply to the group as a whole, try inserting the objects together in a text or picture box.

▶ **See** " Grouping Text and Graphics in a Text Box," **p. 885**

To group pictures, follow these steps:

1. Select each of the pictures you want to include in the group by holding the Shift key while you click on each picture. Each picture should show selection handles.

2. Click one of the selected objects with the right mouse button to display the shortcut menu, shown in Figure 25.16.

3. Choose <u>G</u>rouping, <u>G</u>roup. Once grouped, the pictures share a single set of selection handles.

FIG. 25.16
When you group pictures (or other objects), they function as a single unit.

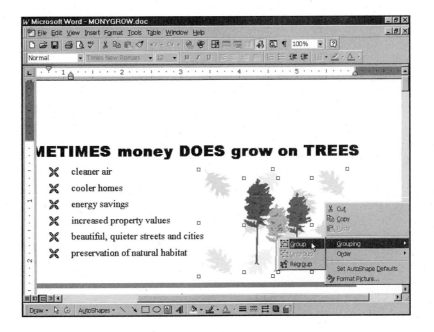

Ungrouping a group releases the individual components. Often you can ungroup inserted clip art; if so, you may be able to use individual components in the clip art or modify individual parts of it.

To ungroup pictures or other objects, follow these steps:

1. Click the group with the right mouse button to display the shortcut menu.

2. Choose Grouping, Ungroup.

To regroup a previously grouped collection of objects, you need to select only one of the objects and choose Grouping, Regroup. The objects are regrouped, but not moved—they are grouped in the position they are in when you choose the Regroup command, not in the position they were in the first time you grouped them.

Layering Pictures with Text and Other Objects

Pictures and other Word objects usually are placed in a layer that floats over the top of text. (If you want a picture to be embedded in the text, rather than floating over it, see the earlier section, "Moving, Positioning, or Copying a Picture.") You can layer pictures so that they appear behind text or behind other pictures and objects. You can move a selected object one layer behind or in front of another object, or all the way behind or to the front of several other objects. The Drawing toolbar has a tool to help you select an object that's layered behind text.

Note that you can't layer a picture behind text if you've selected a text wrapping option for the picture. If you can't layer your picture, select the picture and make sure no wrapping is selected. For more information, see the section, "Wrapping Text Around a Picture."

▶ **See** "Rearranging Drawing Objects," **p. 917**

To layer a picture behind or in front of text or another object, follow these steps:

1. Click the picture with the right mouse button to display the shortcut menu.

2. Choose Order and then choose one of the following commands:

Select This Option	To Have This Effect
Bring to Front	Bring to the front of a stack of pictures or objects.
Send to Back	Send to the back of a stack of pictures or objects.
Bring Forward	Bring forward by a single picture or object.
Send Backward	Send backward by a single picture or object.
Bring in Front of Text	Brings a picture in front of text.
Send Behind Text	Sends a picture box behind text.

Be sure to use the Bring in Front of Text and Send Behind Text commands when you want to layer an object with text.

To select a picture that's layered behind text, do the following:

1. Display the Drawing toolbar.

2. Choose the Select Objects tool.

3. Position the Select Objects pointer over the picture and click to select it.

4. Click the Select Objects tool to deselect it when you're finished.

Displaying and Hiding Pictures

Pictures use up a lot of your computer's memory (and disk space). Thus they can slow you down when you're working, especially if your document contains several pictures. Hiding pictures is a good way to save time when you don't need to see them. You might display the pictures only while you're inserting and formatting them. Then you can hide them while you work on the text in your document.

To hide pictures, follow these steps:

1. Choose Tools, Options and select the View tab.
2. Clear the Drawings option in the Show group.
3. Click OK.

To display hidden pictures, follow these steps:

1. Choose Tools, Options and select the View tab.
2. Select Drawings in the Show group.
3. Click OK.

Formatting Pictures

Word gives you many ways to format pictures. You can size and crop them; add a border around them; add a fill color to some pictures; place a shadow behind them; or you can wrap text around pictures. Three important tools help you perform all these formatting feats: the Picture toolbar (shown in Figure 25.17), the Format command, and the Drawing toolbar.

In the upcoming section, "Modifying Pictures," you learn how to can modify the appearance of pictures in other ways, such as by altering a picture's brightness.

▶ **See** "Formatting Text Boxes," **p. 868**

Part

VI

Ch

25

FIG. 25.17
The Picture toolbar has many tools that help you work with pictures.

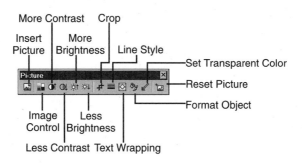

You may have to experiment with your picture to find out the ways in which you can change it. Pictures come in one of two formats: bitmap and object. A bitmap picture is like a painting; it is a single layer of varying colors and shapes. An object-oriented picture, on the other hand, is made up of objects which can be moved, layered, grouped, reshaped, and colored. You can change bitmap pictures by altering their brightness and contrast, but you can't change their fill color. You can change the fill color of an object, but you can't alter its brightness or contrast. You can add borders to any picture, size it, crop it, or wrap text around it.

TIP A quick way to display the Format dialog box is by clicking a picture (or its border, if it's framed) with the right mouse button to display the shortcut menu and then selecting the Format Object or Format Picture command.

Resizing and Cropping Pictures

After you insert a picture in your document, you can scale the picture to a smaller or larger size. You also can size it to the exact dimensions you want, or crop away parts of the picture you don't want to use. Resizing is useful when you need a picture to be a certain size in your document. Cropping helps when you want to zoom in on the most important part of the picture.

You can change the dimensions of a picture in three ways:

- Scale the picture larger or smaller by a percentage (proportionally or nonproportionally)
- Size the picture to an exact width and height
- Crop away part of the picture

You can make any of these changes with the mouse or keyboard commands.

Resizing and Cropping with the Mouse   Using the mouse to scale, size, or crop a picture is a visual process: It enables you to see how your changes look while you're making them. If you use the mouse to change a picture and you later want to see what its dimensions are, select the picture. Then choose Format, Object, Size or Format, Picture, Size. The entries in the Size and Scale groups tell you the picture's current dimensions.

To change a picture, you select it and drag the selection handles that appear on the sides and corners of the picture. After you select the picture and move the mouse pointer over the selection handles, the pointer changes shape: It turns into a two-headed arrow if you're resizing the picture (left side of Figure 25.18) or a cropping tool if you're cropping the picture (right side of Figure 25.18).

FIG. 25.18
You can resize the picture by dragging its handles (left); crop the picture by selecting the Crop tool from the Picture toolbar and then dragging a handle (right).

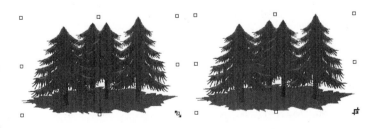

Each of the eight selection handles surrounding a selected picture has a specific purpose. The corner handles enable you to scale or crop from two sides. When you use a corner handle to resize a picture, the picture remains proportional. The side handles enable scaling and cropping from just one side. When you use a side handle to resize, the picture's proportions change. Whenever you drag a handle, the opposite handle stays anchored to its current position.

When you resize a picture by dragging a handle toward the center of the picture, you make the picture smaller. When you crop a picture by dragging toward the center, you cut away part of the picture. When you drag the handle away to resize a picture, you make the picture larger. If you're cropping, you add a blank border after you pass the picture's original edges. Figure 25.19 shows an original picture (on the left) that has been sized smaller (top right example) and cropped (bottom right example).

FIG. 25.19
The original picture (left) becomes smaller or larger when you resize it (top right). Some of it is cut away when you crop it (bottom right).

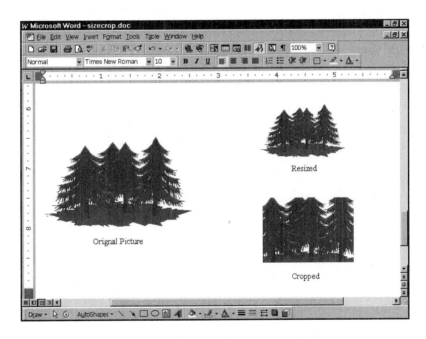

Part
VI

Ch
25

As you drag the handles to resize or crop the picture, you see a dotted-line box that represents the picture's new size and shape. When you release the mouse button, the picture snaps to fit inside the box.

To resize a picture with the mouse, follow these steps:

1. Select the picture.

2. Move the mouse pointer over a selection handle until it turns into a two-headed arrow.

3. Drag a corner handle to scale the picture proportionally or drag a side handle to scale a picture nonproportionally, distorting it.

4. Release the mouse button when the picture is the size you want.

To crop a picture, follow these steps:

1. Select the picture.

2. Select the Crop tool on the Picture toolbar.

3. Drag any selection handle.

4. Release the mouse button when the picture is cropped the way you want it.

Resizing and Cropping with the Format Dialog Box   You can use the Format dialog box to scale, size, or crop a picture. The Format dialog box includes boxes in which you can adjust measurements. Each box has up and down arrows to its right. Click the up arrow to increase the measurement; click the down arrow to decrease it.

Note that the command to format some pictures is Format, Object, while for others it is Format, Picture. The resulting dialog box uses the same name.

TIP   If you want to use a different measurement system in the Format dialog box—for example, points instead of inches—choose Tools, Options, General, and select the system you want in the Measurement Units list.

To size or scale a picture with the Format dialog box, follow these steps:

1. Select the picture.

2. Choose Format, Object, Size or Format, Picture, Size; or click with the right mouse button on the picture and select Format Object or Format Picture, Size.

   The Format dialog box appears (see Figure 25.20).

3. If you want to make your picture an exact size, use the Size and Rotate group (even though you can't rotate a picture). Enter the dimensions for your picture in the Height and Width boxes.

   If you want your picture to be exactly 3 inches high, for example, type **3** in the Height box; if you want the picture to be 2 inches wide, type **2** in the Width box.

4. If you want to scale your picture by a percentage, use the Scale group. In the Height or Width box (or both), enter the percentage by which you want to scale the picture.

   If you want to scale the picture to half its original height, for example, type **50** (for 50 percent) in the Height box. To double its height, type **200** (for 200 percent) in the Height box.

If you want to scale proportionally (so that the height and widths change to the same percent), select the Lock Aspect Ratio option. Then you need enter only one value for either height or width to scale the picture.

If you want to scale the picture from its original size, rather than from whatever size you've already scaled it to, select the Relative to Original Picture Size option.

5. Click OK.

FIG. 25.20

You can crop, scale, and size a picture to specific dimensions in the Format dialog box.

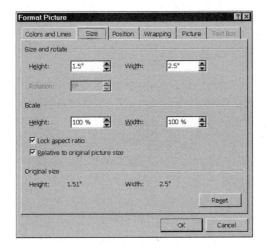

To crop a picture, follow these steps:

1. Select the picture.

2. Choose Format, Object, Picture or Format, Picture, Picture; or click with the right mouse button on the picture and select Format, Object or Format, Picture, Picture. The Picture tab in the Format dialog box is shown in Figure 25.21.

3. Enter cropping amounts in the Crop From group, using the Left, Right, Top, and Bottom list boxes.

   To crop 1/2 inch off the bottom of the picture, for example, type **.5** in the Bottom box. To crop 1/4 inch off the right side, type **.25** in the Right box.

   You can crop by a negative number; in this way, the picture box grows to be larger than the picture.

4. Click OK.

Part

VI

Ch

25

FIG. 25.21

You can use the Format dialog box to crop a picture precisely.

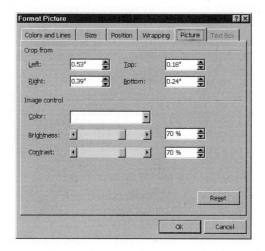

Resetting the Picture to its Original Dimensions   You easily can reset your picture to its original dimensions (even if you changed it with the mouse rather than the Format dialog box). Follow these steps:

1. Select the picture.

2. Choose Format, Object or Format, Picture. Select the Size tab to reset the picture's size; select the Picture tab to undo cropping.

3. Choose the Reset button.

 Alternatively, you can reset a picture by selecting it and clicking the Reset Picture button on the Picture toolbar.

Adding Lines, Fills, and Color

Unless a border is part of your original composition, pictures arrive in your document with no lines around their edges. You easily can add a line border around a picture, in any of many line styles and colors. (Whenever you choose a line for a picture, it borders the picture on all four sides.) For some pictures, you can add fill color. Some clip art, for example, can be ungrouped into individual components, and you can change the fill in each piece.

One tool to help you border and color a picture is the Colors and Lines tab in the Format dialog box. Another tool is the Drawing toolbar, which contains tools for quickly changing fill and line color, and style, and for adding a shadow or 3-D effect. You can access the Format dialog box by command, by using the Format button on the Picture toolbar, or by clicking with the right mouse button on the picture and choosing Format Object or Format Picture in the shortcut menu. Display the Drawing toolbar by choosing View, Toolbars, Drawing.

In addition to plain colors, you can also fill and border objects with a variety of textures and patterns. Those options are explained in depth in Chapter 26, "Inserting Text Boxes," in the section, "Creating Custom Colors and Effects."

▶ **See** "Creating Custom Colors and Effects," **p. 874**

Keep in mind that if you can't change the fill of a picture that looks like an object (for which you should be able to change the fill), you may need to first ungroup the picture and then alter the fill for each individual component. You may need to use this method with clip art included on the Microsoft Office CD.

To add and change colors, borders, shadows, and 3-D settings using the Drawing toolbar, follow these steps:

1. Select the picture. Ungroup it if necessary and select the individual component you want to change.

2. Select one of the following options:

Select This Button	And Do This	For This Result
Fill Color	Select the fill color you want from the palette or select More Fill colors for more color options, or select Fill Effects to fill a shape with a gradient, texture, pattern, or picture.	Add a fill color or fill effect to an object-type picture.
Line Color	Select the line color you want from the palette or select More Line colors for more color options or select Pattern Fill to fill a line with a pattern.	Add a colored border around the edge of a picture.
Line Style	Select the line width you want.	Change the width of the line around the border of a picture. (Or change the drawing lines of an ungrouped object.)

continues

continued

Select This Button	And Do This	For This Result
Dash Style	Select the dashed line style you want.	Add a dashed line around a picture. (Or change the drawing lines of an ungrouped object.)
Shadow	Select the shadow style you want from the palette or select Shadow Settings to display the Shadow Settings toolbar to modify the shadow.	Add a shadowed border to a picture.
3-D	Select the 3-D style you want from the palette or select 3-D Settings to display the 3D Settings toolbar to modify the third dimension.	Add a 3-D effect to a picture. (3-D effects are only available for object-oriented pictures, not bitmaps.)

To add and change colors and lines using a command, follow these steps:

1. Select the picture.

2. Choose Format, Object or Format Picture; click the Format button on the Picture toolbar; or click with the right mouse button on the object and choose Format Object or Format Picture from the shortcut menu.

3. Choose the Colors and Lines tab, shown in Figure 25.22.

FIG 25.22
You can use the Format dialog box to choose colors and lines.

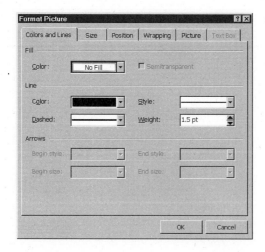

4. In the Fill group, choose Color and select a fill color. Select More Colors to choose from a wider range of colors or choose Fill Effects to select a gradient, texture, pattern, or picture fill.

   Select Semi-Transparent to lighten the shade of the color you've chosen.

5. In the Line group, choose Color and select a color or select More Colors to choose from a wider selection of colors or select Patterned Lines to choose a line pattern.

6. Select a dash style from the Dashed list if you want a dashed line.

7. Choose Style and select a line width or style. Line width, called *weight*, is measured in points. A *point* is about 1/72 of an inch; a .25 pt line is very thin, like a hairline; while a 4 pt line is fairly heavy. (This option is not available for ungrouped objects.)

8. Choose Weight and enter the line weight, measured in points, to change the width of a line.

9. Click OK.

Removing Lines, Fills, and Color

If you want to remove a line, fill, or color, select the picture and follow the same steps as for adding lines, fills, and colors. To remove a fill, select No Fill; to remove a line, select No Line; to remove a shadow, select No Shadow; to remove a 3-D effect, select No 3-D.

Coloring Bitmap Pictures

You can use a tool on the Picture toolbar to make pictures transparent. This option offers some interesting possibilities for bitmap images, for which you can't alter the fill color: You can layer a transparent bitmap picture over a block of color to change the picture, or some part of it, to the color of the block.

To color a bitmap picture, follow these steps:

1. Select the bitmap picture.

2. Choose the Set Transparent Color button on the Picture toolbar.

3. Click the portion of the picture that you want to make transparent with the Transparent Color pointer.

4. Choose the Rectangle tool on the Drawing toolbar, and use it to draw a rectangle over the picture.

5. Choose a fill color for the rectangle.

6. Layer the colored rectangle behind your picture. The part of the picture that you made transparent changes to the color of the rectangle.

You can change the part of the picture that you want transparent by selecting the Transparent Color button and clicking a different part of your picture.

It might be helpful to group the color rectangle and your transparent picture if you want to move or size them as a unit.

Wrapping Text Around a Picture

Being able to wrap text around pictures opens up a world of design possibilities. You can place a picture anywhere in your document—even in a margin—and wrap text around it in many different ways. You can specify how far from the text the picture will be. And pictures have an extra wrapping option not shared by other objects: the ability to edit the wrap points, available through the Picture toolbar. Consequently, you can shape the text in any way you want around the picture.

To wrap text around a picture using a command (or to remove text wrapping), follow these steps:

1. Select the picture.

2. Choose Format, Object or Format, Picture or click the Format button on the Picture toolbar, or click with the right mouse button on the object and choose Format Object or Format Picture from the shortcut menu.

3. Choose the Wrapping tab, shown in Figure 25.23.

FIG. 25.23
You can use the Format dialog box to wrap text around a picture.

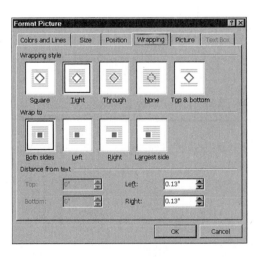

4. In the Wrapping Style group, select the style of text wrap you want. Look at the icons to see the effect of each option. The Square option wraps text around all four

sides of a picture in a square shape; the Tight option wraps the text so that it conforms to the shape of the picture.

Select None to remove text wrapping.

5. In the Wrap To group, select an option for wrapping to both sides or to one side. Look at the icons to see the effect of each option.

6. In the Distance From Text group, select each of the sides listed and enter how far you want the text from that side. Notice that if you choose a Tight wrapping style, the Top and Bottom options are unavailable.

7. Click OK. Figure 25.24 shows text wrapped.

   ▶ **See** "Wrapping Text Around a Text Box," **p. 882**

   ▶ **See** "Controlling Text Wrap Around Your Drawing Objects," **p. 919**

TIP You can choose a text-wrapping style quickly and close the Format dialog box by double-clicking the wrapping style you want.

FIG. 25.24
You can create interesting design effects by wrapping text around a picture.

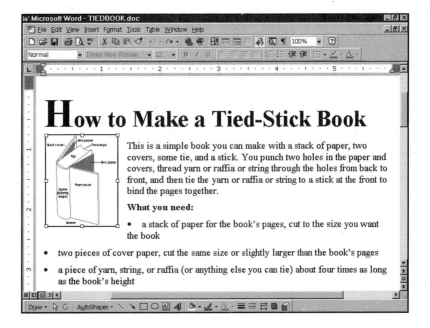

Part
VI

Ch
25

To select or remove text wrapping using the Picture toolbar, follow these steps:

1. Select the picture.

2. Choose the Text Wrapping button on the Picture toolbar. A list of wrapping styles appears.

3. Choose the wrapping style you want. Choose No Wrapping to remove text wrapping.

Being able to edit wrapping points allows you to shape the text wrap exactly as you want it. *Tight Wrapping* style uses the same number of wrapping points as any other type of wrap: eight. But when you edit the wrapping points, you get any number of wrapping points (depending on the complexity of your picture) that you can drag anywhere.

To edit the wrapping points, follow these steps:

1. Select the picture.

2. Choose the Text Wrapping button on the Picture toolbar.

3. Choose <u>E</u>dit Wrap Points. The picture is surrounded by an irregular wrap shape containing any number of wrap points.

4. Drag any of the wrap points to move the point and thus alter the shape of the text wrap. A special pointer that looks like a small four-sided star lets you know you're in position to drag a wrap point.

5. Click and drag anywhere on the dashed wrapping border when you see the wrap crosshair (a crosshair with a small square at the center) to add wrap points.

6. Click anywhere in the document to deselect the picture and hide the wrap points.

The next time you select the picture, you'll see the usual eight selection handles, though the edited wrapping points are still in place and visible if you choose the <u>E</u>dit Wrap Points command again.

Modifying Pictures

Some of the pictures you include in a Word document are like photographs—they may be scanned photographs or bitmap pictures created with a range of colors and shades. You can modify these pictures in many ways using tools on the Picture toolbar. You can use the Image Control button to change the image type, or you can increase or decrease the contrast and brightness in the picture.

To change the image type, follow these steps:

1. Select the picture.

2. Choose the Image Control button on the Picture toolbar. Select one of these options:

- <u>A</u>utomatic is the picture's native type. A color photograph appears in color, for example.

- <u>G</u>rayscale converts a picture to a continuous-tone image made of different shades of gray. It is like a black-and-white photograph rendered as a "halftone" in preparation for offset printing. This option is good for printing color pictures on a black-ink printer.

- Black & White converts a color or grayscale picture to black and white, like a line drawing.
- Watermark changes the picture to a light gray image which you can layer behind text.

To change the contrast or brightness in a picture, follow these steps:

1. Select the picture.
2. Click on one of the following buttons on the Picture toolbar. You can click repeatedly to increase the effect; watch your picture to see how it changes.

The More Contrast button heightens the differences between the dark and light areas of a picture, moving it closer to black and white. Increasing the contrast usually makes a picture look more dramatic.

The Less Contrast button reduces the differences between the dark and light areas, making the picture grayer and more monochromatic. Reducing the contrast makes a picture softer.

The More Brightness button adds light to all areas of the picture, making it brighter.

The Less Brightness button removes light from all areas of the picture, making it darker.

Another way you can alter a picture's color, brightness, and contrast is through the Format dialog box. Using the command has the same effect as using the tools on the Picture toolbar.

To adjust color, brightness, and contrast with a command, follow these steps:

1. Select the picture.
2. Choose Format, Object, Picture or Format, Picture, Picture (see Figure 25.25).
3. In the Image control group, do the following:

Select this	And do this	To get this result
Color	Select Automatic, Gray scale, Black & white, or Watermark.	Change the picture type.
Brightness	Move the slider left to make the picture darker or right to make it brighter. Or select a percent: a lower number is darker; a higher number is brighter.	Darken or brighten the picture.

Part

VI

Ch

25

| Contrast | Move the slider left for less contrast or right for more contrast. Or select a percent: a lower number has less contrast; a higher number has more contrast. | Adjust the picture's contrast. Less contrast is a grayer picture; greater contrast is more black and white. |

You can click the Reset button to reset the picture to its original appearance.

FIG. 25.25
You can use the Format dialog box to adjust color, brightness, and contrast.

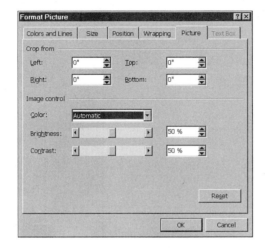

Editing and Converting Pictures

To edit a picture using the program in which it was created, you must have that program installed on your computer and the picture must have been inserted as an object. If not, when you attempt to edit the picture, Word places it in a Microsoft Word Picture window where you can edit it. The editing capabilities of Microsoft Word Picture, however, may not be as extensive as those of the original program.

▶ **See** "Embedding Data," **p. 1085**

To edit picture objects, follow these steps:

1. Double-click the picture to edit.

   Or, select the picture and choose either Edit, Picture or Edit, Picture Object. (The name of the command depends on the type of picture you've selected.)

   Either the program used to create the picture or Microsoft Word Picture appears on your screen.

2. Make your changes to the picture. In Microsoft Word Picture, you can replace the picture or enhance it by using tools on the Drawing toolbar.

3. Choose File, Update and then File, Exit in some programs, such as CorelDRAW!; in other programs, such as Excel, simply click your document.

   Or, choose the Close Picture button to close Microsoft Word Picture and return to your document.

Note that if you choose Edit, Picture to edit a picture with Microsoft Word Picture, Word converts the picture to an object. The next time you select the same picture for editing, Edit, Picture Object appears instead.

Converting Picture Objects

You can convert a picture object from its original format to a different format. For example, you might want to convert a picture created in Adobe Illustrator to a picture that can be edited by Microsoft Word Picture. You might do this, for example, if you do not own Illustrator, but you want to use Microsoft Word Picture to modify the picture.

An alternative method preserves your picture in its original format. You simply specify that the picture be activated in a different format, but not converted.

To convert an inserted picture or picture object, follow these steps:

1. Select the picture you want to convert.

2. Choose Edit, Picture Object. (The name of the object varies, depending on the program used to create it.)

3. Select Convert from the submenu. The Convert dialog box appears; the current format of your picture is displayed as Current Type near the top of the dialog box.

4. Select Convert To. Then select the format to which you want to convert your picture or picture object.

   Select Display as Icon if you want to display your converted picture as an icon.

5. Click OK.

To activate a picture in a different format without converting it, follow these steps:

1. Select the picture you want to activate in a different format.

2. Choose Edit, Picture Object.

3. Select Convert from the submenu.

4. Select Activate As. Then select the format in which you want to activate your picture or picture object.

5. Click OK.

Part
VI

Ch
25

CHAPTER 26

Inserting Text Boxes

Word 97 has many features that make your pages more graphically interesting—drawings, clip art, inserted pictures, column formatting, lines, colors, and much more. Text boxes, however, take your document a step beyond traditional word processing and into the world of page layout. Text boxes allow you to do two important things: Separate a block of text from its surrounding text so that it functions like a graphic element on the page, and link blocks of text within a document.

Text boxes move freely on the page, just like all objects and pictures inserted in a Word document. You can easily drag them anywhere in your document using a mouse, or position them precisely with a command. You can wrap text around them if you want, and format them with an almost limitless selection of colors and shapes. Even the text inside a text box is liberated from traditional constraints—you can rotate and color it, as well as apply common text formatting. And finally, text boxes serve as containers that can hold much more than text. For example, include a picture and text within a text box to create a captioned illustration that moves as a unit on the page. Or, create a blank text

Create text boxes and type text inside them

Draw a box of any size or shape, anywhere in your document, and type text inside it.

Format both the text box and the text within it

Add a line or shadow around the border of a text box, fill it with a color or pattern, and format the text however you want.

Group text and pictures together in a text box

You can insert both pictures and text in a text box so they function as a unit in your document.

Layer text and pictures for a transparent effect

You can position text boxes in front of or behind text, text boxes, or other objects on the page.

Wrap text around a text box

The text in your document wraps around the text in a text box.

Link text from one text box to another

You can continue text from one text box to another—a great way to create the columns of text in a newsletter, for example. This powerful feature is similar to the way desktop publishing programs create blocks of linked text.

box, bordered or not, to leave a space in your document where you can add handmade art after printing.

Text boxes existed in previous versions of Word, but in this version they are greatly expanded, and have taken on many of the characteristics that were previously found in frames, such as text wrapping and free positioning on the page. For this reason, you can't create frames in Word, although they do occasionally appear, such as when you create drop caps or certain text annotations. A section at the end of this chapter, "Working with Frames," describes frames.

Using text boxes, you can accomplish the following:

- Position a block of text wherever you want it on the page, even in a margin.
- Group text and other objects so that you can position them as a unit anywhere in your document.
- Link blocks of text that appear in different parts of the document.
- Wrap text around a block of text or grouped objects.
- Rotate text within a block.
- Add a border or shadow around text or grouped objects, or add a fill color to a block of text.
- Create a three-dimensional shape for a block of text, with or without border and fill colors.
- Layer text and pictures for a transparent effect.
- Leave a blank space—with or without a border—where you can paste in noncomputer graphics after you print your document.

By positioning a text box on the page, you free the text box contents from its surrounding text. Text boxes are a critical tool in helping you use Word to design a pleasing, professional, and creative page layout. ■

Creating Text Boxes

Text boxes are easy to create in one of two ways. You can choose a command, or click the Text Box button on the Drawing toolbar. Either way, if no text is selected, you get a crosshair that you can use with a mouse to draw a text box of any size. The insertion point flashes at the top of the text box, and you can type the text you want inside the text box (or you can insert a picture or object). If text is selected when you choose the Text Box command or click the Text Box button, then Word automatically creates a text box which contains the selected text. You can easily edit the text or change the text box.

To see a text box on your screen, you must be in the Page Layout (or Online Layout) view. You can choose that view before you start; however, Word will choose the Page Layout view for you any time you choose the Insert Text Box command or click the Text Box button.

 If you want to use the Text Box button to create text boxes, you must display the Drawing toolbar. Do this by choosing View, Toolbars and selecting Drawing, or by clicking the Drawing button on the Standard toolbar.

To create an empty text box, follow these steps:

1. Choose Insert, Text Box.

   or

   Click the Text Box tool on the Drawing toolbar.

2. Drag the crosshair to draw a text box the size you want. A newly created text box is shown in Figure 26.1.

An insertion point appears at the top of the new text box. Add text by simply typing. The text in your text box uses the same paragraph formatting as the surrounding text.

To add text to an existing text box, position the insertion point inside the text box; see the upcoming section, "Adding and Editing Text in Text Boxes," for details. The Text Box toolbar also appears when you draw a new text box; learn more about this toolbar, which helps you link text boxes, in the later section, "Linking Text Between Text Boxes."

A text box you draw will not automatically resize to accommodate the text you type—if you type more than it can hold, the extra text will be hidden. To resize a text box simply drag one of its side or corner handles. See the upcoming section, "Sizing, Shaping, and Rotating Text Boxes," to learn more about resizing text boxes.

Existing text on the page does not wrap around a text box you draw using the crosshair. To wrap text, see the upcoming section, "Wrapping Text Around a Text Box."

To create a text box containing selected text, follow these steps:

1. Select the text you want in the text box.

2. Choose Insert, Text Box.

   or

   Click the Text Box tool on the Drawing toolbar.

A text box created this way is a standard size—about two inches by two inches. Resize it by dragging a side or corner handle; see the upcoming section, "Sizing, Shaping, and Rotating Text Boxes," for more details about sizing text boxes.

Part
VI
Ch
26

FIG. 26.1
You can create a new text box of any size.

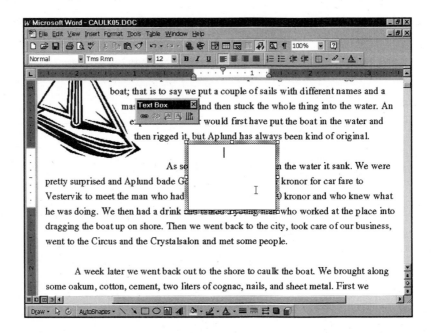

Existing text in your document automatically wraps around text boxes created this way.

> **CAUTION**
> Adding text to a text box by first selecting it *moves* the text from your document into the text box—it does not duplicate the text.

ON THE WEB

For online support from Microsoft, visit the following World Wide Web site:

http://www.microsoft.com/support

You can also access Microsoft's extensive troubleshooting KnowledgeBase at the following site:

http://www.microsoft.com/kb

For tutorials, tips, and add-ins for Microsoft Office applications, point your browser to:

http://www.ronperson.com

Adding and Editing Text in Text Boxes

A new, blank text box contains an insertion point flashing at the top (whether the insertion point is aligned left, right, or center depends on your previous text alignment selection). You can add text by typing or by pasting text in.

The text box will not enlarge automatically if you type more text than the box can hold. To enlarge or reduce it, or to change its shape, drag a selection handle. For more details, see the upcoming section "Sizing, Shaping, and Rotating Text Boxes."

You can also add text to an existing text box, or edit text in an existing text box.

To add text to a text box, or to edit text in a text box, follow these steps:

1. Position the insertion point where you want to add or edit text.

2. Type text or edit existing text.

   or

   Choose Edit, Paste (Ctrl+V) to insert text into the text box that you've previously cut or copied into the Clipboard.

Removing Text Boxes

To remove a text box, select it by clicking it and press the Delete key. Both the text box and its contents are removed from your document.

To remove a text box without removing its contents, convert it to a frame and remove the frame. See the later section, "Working with Frames," for details.

Sizing, Shaping, and Rotating Text Boxes

Part VI

Ch 26

You can easily change the size or shape of a text box, although the shape will always be some variation on a rectangle. (You can, however, create a three-dimensional text box; see the later section in this chapter, "Adding a Text Box Shadow or Third Dimension.") If you want a nonrectangular container for text, see "Understanding AutoShapes" in Chapter 27. You can also rotate a text box in increments of degrees.

The easiest way to size or reshape a text box is to drag a selection handle. The most precise way is to use a menu command.

To change the size or shape of a text box using a mouse, follow these steps:

1. Select the text box by clicking it. Selection handles appear on each side and corner—eight in all.

2. Position the mouse pointer over the selection handle on the side or corner you want to adjust. A side handle moves one side in or out; a corner handle moves a corner in or out. The pointer turns to a double-ended arrow that indicates the direction in which you can move the selection handle.

3. Drag the selection handle outward to expand the text box; drag the handle inward to make the text box smaller. Figure 26.2 shows a text box being expanded.

FIG. 26.2

Drag selection handles
to resize or reshape a
text box.

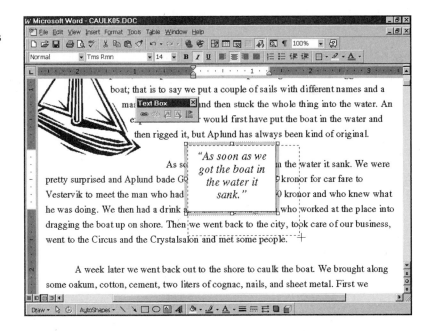

When you size a text box using a menu command, you can specify exact measurements for it. Or, you can reduce or enlarge it by a percentage.

Rotating a text box is a process similar to sizing or shaping a text box. When you enter a rotation amount, the text box rotates in a clockwise direction.

To size, shape, or rotate a text box using a command, follow these steps:

1. Select the text box by clicking it.

2. Choose Format, Text Box, or click the border of the text box with the right mouse button and choose Format Text Box.

   The Format Text Box dialog box appears.

3. Select the Size tab, shown in Figure 26.3.

4. For a measured size, select Height and Width in the Size and Rotate group and enter the measurements you want.

   For example, select Height, 2 inches for a text box that is two inches tall.

   or

For a percentage size, select Height and Width in the Scale group and enter the percentages you want. If you want both dimensions to change identically, select the Lock Aspect Ratio option.

For example, select Height, 50% to reduce the text box to half its height (or, if you selected Lock Aspect Ratio, to reduce the text box to half its height and width).

5. To rotate the text box, select Rotation in the Size and Rotate group and enter the clockwise rotation you want in degrees.

   For example, select a rotation of 90 degrees to tilt the text box a quarter-turn clockwise.

6. Choose OK.

FIG. 26.3
Use the Size tab on the Format Text dialog box to resize or reshape a text box.

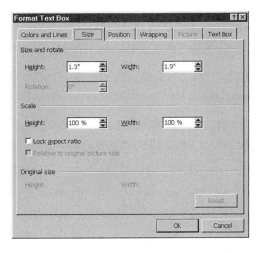

T I P If you want to use a different Unit of measurement in your dialog boxes, choose Tools, Options, General. In the Measurement Units list, select the unit of measurement you prefer: Inches, Centimeters, Points, or Picas.

To use the mouse to rotate a text box, follow these steps:

1. Display the Drawing toolbar by choosing View, Toolbars and selecting Drawing, or by clicking the Drawing Toolbar button on the Standard toolbar.

2. Select the text box you want to rotate.

3. Select the Free Rotate button on the Drawing toolbar. A rotation icon appears.

4. Position the rotation icon over one of the corner selection handles on your text box.

5. Drag the selected corner to rotate the text box.

Rotating a text box does not rotate the text within it; see the later section, "Character Formatting Inside Text Boxes," to find out how to rotate text in a text box.

Moving and Positioning Text Boxes

It's easy to move a text box anywhere in your document—either a short distance or many pages away. As with sizing or shaping a text box, you can use either the mouse or a command to move a text box. The mouse is quick, but a command is more precise.

To move a text box using a mouse, follow these steps:

1. Select the text box by clicking it. Selection handles and a shaded border appear.
2. Position the mouse pointer over the shaded border, not on a selection handle. The pointer turns into a four-headed arrow. (If you see a two-headed arrow, that means you're on a selection handle; move to a shaded area.)
3. Hold down the left mouse button and drag the text box to a new location as shown in Figure 26.4.

FIG. 26.4

You can move a text box by dragging it by the selection border.

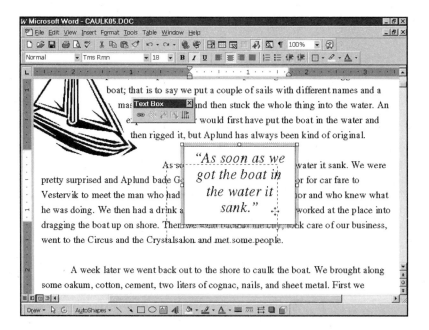

If you want to move a text box to an exact spot on the page—to the middle of the page, or to the left edge of a column, for example—you can use a command. Using the Position command, you always position an object such as a text box relative to some fixed part of the page, like the top or bottom edge of the page, or to a paragraph or margin.

Text boxes, like all objects (such as inserted pictures and clip art, drawings, and WordArt images) are anchored to text, even though they can be positioned anywhere on the page. For example, if you create a text box using text selected from a paragraph, the text box is anchored to that paragraph; if you draw a text box, it is anchored to the top of the nearest paragraph. If you move a text box to another page, the anchor moves with it. But if you lock the anchor, you prevent the text box from moving to another page.

To move or position a text box using a command, follow these steps:

1. Select the text box you want to relocate by clicking it.

2. Choose Format, Text Box, or click the border of the text box with the right mouse button and choose Format Text Box.

   The Format Text Box dialog box, shown in Figure 26.5, appears.

3. Select the Position tab.

FIG. 26.5

You can move or position a text box precisely by using a command.

Part

VI

Ch

26

4. Select Horizontal, and select the distance you want the text box to be positioned from the left edge. Select From and select Column, Margin, or Page—whichever you want the text box positioned relative to.

   For example, if you want the text box positioned one inch from the left margin, select Horizontal, 1 inch, and From, Margin.

5. Select Vertical, and select the distance you want the text box to be positioned from the top. Select From, and select Margin, Page, or Paragraph, whichever you want the text box positioned relative to.

For example, if you want the text box positioned four inches from the top of the page, select Vertical, 4 inches, and From, Page.

6. If you want the text box to move along with the text it's anchored to when you move the text, select Move Object with Text. Clear this box if you want the text box to re-anchor itself to the nearest remaining text when you move the text it's anchored to.

7. If you want the text box to always stay on the page where you created it, select Lock Anchor.

8. Choose OK.

You can see which paragraph a text box is anchored to by choosing Tools, Options to display the Options dialog box, selecting the View tab, and choosing the Object Anchors option. Anchors appear in the left margin of your document in Page Layout view. You can change the paragraph to which a text box (or any object) is anchored by simply dragging the anchor.

Duplicating Text Boxes and Moving Them Long Distances

You can easily duplicate text boxes by using Word's Copy and Paste commands. You can move a text box a long distance (several pages away, for example) by using the Cut and Paste commands. When you use the Cut and Copy commands, text boxes keep all the formatting you've applied.

To duplicate or move a text box, follow these steps:

1. Select the text box by clicking it.

 2. To duplicate it, choose Edit, Copy.

   or

    To move it, choose Edit, Cut.

3. Position the insertion point where you want the duplicated or moved text box.

 4. Choose Edit, Paste.

Formatting Text Boxes

There are two approaches to changing the appearance of a text box: You can format the text inside the box, and you can format the box itself. Formatting one does not alter the other—for example, changing the color of the text inside a text box, the color behind the text, and the color of the text box border requires three separate steps.

You can format text boxes in one of three ways—using a menu command, using the text box pop-up menu, or using tools on the Drawing toolbar. To format text inside a text box, you use the same menu commands, tools, and shortcuts you use to format any other text.

 TIP You can double-click a text box border to quickly display the Format Text Box dialog box. Using this dialog box is an efficient way to apply several different types of formatting at once.

Character Formatting Inside Text Boxes

Character formatting inside a text box works the same way as it does in any other place in your document. You don't even have to select the text box before you select the text to format it; just select the text as usual. See Chapter 9, "Formatting Characters and Changing Fonts," to learn how to format text.

Paragraph formatting in a text box is also the same as anywhere else in your document; see Chapter 10, "Formatting Lines and Paragraphs," for details. If you have the ruler displayed, you'll see that a selected text box has its own margin, indentation, and tab markers in a highlighted area. You can easily use this space on the ruler to format paragraphs within a text box. (To display the ruler, choose View, Ruler.)

There are two special ways you can affect the appearance of characters within a text box: by altering their internal margins (the distance between the text and the edges of the text box), and by rotating the text.

To rotate text inside a text box, follow these steps:

1. Click the text box to select it.
2. Choose Format, Text Direction to display the Text Direction dialog box, shown in Figure 26.6.

FIG. 26.6
You can rotate the text inside a text box forward (clockwise) or backward (counter-clockwise) by 90 degrees.

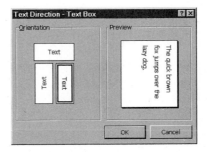

Part
VI
Ch
26

3. In the Orientation group, select the orientation you want by clicking it.
4. Choose OK.

You can quickly rotate the text in a text box by clicking the Change Text Direction button on the Text Box toolbar. For details about the Text Box toolbar, see the later section, "Linking Text Between Text Boxes."

T I P To rotate text *and* the text box, follow the above steps and then display the Format Text Box dialog box, select the Size tab, and in the Rotation spinner box select 90 degrees to rotate the text box forward by a quarter turn, or -90 degrees to rotate it backward a quarter turn. See the section "Sizing, Shaping, and Rotating Text Boxes" for details about rotating a text box.

To set the internal margins for a text box, follow these steps:

1. Select the text box.

2. Click the text box border with the right mouse button and choose Format Text Box.

   or

   Choose Format, Text Box.

3. In the Format Text Box dialog box, select the Text Box tab, shown in Figure 26.7.

4. In the Left, Right, Top, and Bottom spinner boxes, select the distance you want the text inside the text box to be from the text box.

5. Choose OK.

FIG. 26.7
Internal margins
measure the distance
between text inside a
text box and the edge
of the text box.

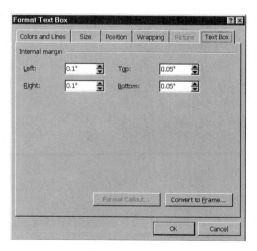

Choosing Colors and Borders

You can change the color of text in a text box, and you can change the color and style of a text box border. You can change the color and pattern of a text box fill. You can use commands or the Drawing toolbar, shown in Figure 26.8, to change colors, borders, and fills.

To display the Drawing toolbar, choose View, Toolbars, Drawing, or click the Drawing Toolbar button on the Standard toolbar.

FIG. 26.8
The Drawing toolbar has many tools you can use to help you format text boxes.

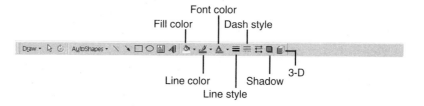

Changing the Color of Text   To change the color of text in a text box, use the same command you use to change color for any text, or use the Font Color button on the Drawing toolbar.

To change text color using a command, follow these steps:

1. Select the text whose color you want to change (if you want to change the color of all the text in a text box, you need only select the text box).
2. Choose Format, Font to display the Font dialog box.
3. Select the Font tab.
4. In the Color list, select the color you want your text to be.
5. Choose OK.

To change text color using a button, follow these steps:

1. Display the Drawing toolbar.
2. Select the text whose color you want to change.

3. Click the down arrow to the right of the Font Color button to display color choices, as shown in Figure 26.9.
4. Click the color you want.

FIG. 26.9
The Font Color palette on the Drawing toolbar lets you quickly define the color of the text in a text box.

Part
VI

Ch
26

Changing Line Color and Style, and Removing Lines   You can quickly change the color of a line or its style. Line style options include the width of a line, which is measured in points. A point is 1/72nd of an inch; therefore, a 1/4-point line is quite thin, whereas a 6-point line is heavy. Creating a custom color or choosing a pattern is a little more work; see the upcoming section "Creating Custom Colors and Effects."

To change the line color or style for a text box by using a button on the Drawing toolbar, follow these steps:

1. Select the text box.

2. On the Drawing toolbar, click the down arrow to the right of the Line Color button to display the line colors palette, as shown in Figure 26.10. Click the color you want. Click No Line to remove a line.

FIG. 26.10
The Line Color palette on the Drawing toolbar lets you quickly define line color.

or

On the Drawing toolbar, click the Line Style button to display a selection of line styles (see Figure 26.11) and select the style you want.

FIG. 26.11
The Line Style palette on the Drawing toolbar gives you line style choices.

or

Click the Dash Style button on the Drawing toolbar and select the dashed line style you want. Figure 26.12 shows the Dash Style palette.

FIG. 26.12

The Dash Style palette on the Drawing toolbar gives you dashed line style options.

To change line color and style with a command, or to remove a line, follow these steps:

1. Select the text box.

2. Display the Format Text Box dialog box either by choosing F̲ormat, Text B̲ox or by clicking with the right arrow on the text box border and choosing Format Text B̲ox from the drop-down menu.

3. Select the Colors and Lines tab (see Figure 26.13).

4. In the Line group, select the C̲olor list and click the color you want. Click No Line to remove a line.

5. In the Line group, select S̲tyle and click the line weight or style you want.

   or

   In the Line group, select W̲eight and enter a custom line weight.

6. If you want a dashed line, select the D̲ashed list in the Line group and click the dashed style you want.

7. Choose OK.

FIG. 26.13

You can use the Colors and Lines tab to quickly change the fill or line color for a text box.

Format Text Box	? X

Colors and Lines	Size	Position	Wrapping	Picture	Text Box

Fill

Color: [ ] ☐ Semi̲transparent

Line

Color: [■]   S̲tyle: [ ]

D̲ashed: [ ]   W̲eight: [0.75 pt ▲▼]

Arrows

Begin style: [ ]   End style: [ ]

Begin size: [ ]   End size: [ ]

OK   Cancel

Part

VI

Ch

26

Changing or Removing Fill Color   You can quickly select a fill color for a text box using a command or Drawing toolbar button. Creating a custom color or choosing a pattern is a little more work; see the upcoming section "Creating Custom Colors and Effects."

To select (or remove) a text box fill color using a command, follow these steps:

1. Select the text box.
2. Display the Format Text Box dialog box either by choosing Format, Text Box or by clicking with the right arrow on the text box border and choosing Format Text Box from the drop-down menu.
3. Select the Colors and Lines tab (refer to Figure 26.13).
4. In the Fill group, select the Color list to display the color options.
5. Click the fill color you want, or click No Fill to remove a fill color.
6. If you want a lighter shade of the color you've selected, select the Semi-Transparent option.
7. Choose OK.

To change or remove text box fill color using the Fill Color button on the Drawing toolbar, follow these steps:

1. Display the Drawing toolbar.
2. Select the text box.

3. Click the down arrow to the right of the Fill Color button on the Drawing toolbar to display the Fill Colors palette, as shown in Figure 26.14.
4. Click the fill color you want, or click No Fill to remove a fill.

FIG. 26.14

The Fill Color palette on the Drawing toolbar gives you color choices for filling text boxes.

Creating Custom Colors and Effects   Custom colors and effects offer you a very wide range of options for decorating text boxes. You can choose from a wider range of preset colors than is offered in the Format Text Box dialog box or the fill colors palette, or you can blend your own colors for a fill or a line. You can choose among a large selection of patterns for lines and fills, selecting both foreground and background colors. Additional options for fills include gradient fills (in which the fill fades from one color to another), textured fills, and fills created from your own pictures.

To select a custom color for a line or fill, follow these steps:

1. Select the text box.

2. Display the Colors dialog box (see Figure 26.15) by one of these methods:

 For a custom fill color using a toolbar button, click the down arrow to the right of the Fill Color button on the Drawing toolbar and select <u>M</u>ore Fill Colors.

or

For a custom fill color using a menu command, display the Format Text Box dialog box by choosing F<u>o</u>rmat, Text B<u>o</u>x or by clicking with the right mouse button on the text box and choosing Format Text Box. Then in the Fill group, select <u>C</u>olor, and select <u>M</u>ore Colors.

FIG. 26.15
The Standard tab on the Colors dialog box gives you a wide range of standard colors to choose from.

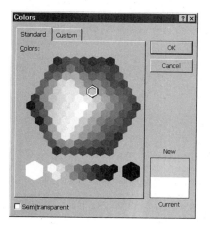

 For a custom line color using a toolbar button, click the down arrow to the right of the Line Color button on the Drawing toolbar and choose <u>M</u>ore Line Colors.

or

For a custom line color using a menu command, display the Format Text Box dialog box by choosing F<u>o</u>rmat, Text B<u>o</u>x or by clicking with the right mouse button on the text box and choosing Format Text B<u>o</u>x. Then in the Line group, select C<u>o</u>lor, and select <u>M</u>ore Colors.

3. If you want a preset range of color options, select the Standard tab (see Figure 26.15) and click the color you want. Select the Semi-Transparent option for a lighter shade of the color. Then choose OK.

4. If you want to precisely define a color, select the Custom tab (see Figure 26.16). Blend your color in one of two ways:

In the <u>C</u>olors palette, click the color you want. Then use the slidebar to the right to determine the shade of the color. To do that, click the shade you want or slide the pointer up or down. For example, you can choose a hue of purple by clicking on purple in the palette, then you can choose how light or dark that purple is by using the slidebar.

or

Use one of the two color blending systems provided on the bottom of the dialog box. Hue (color), Sat (saturation, or amount of color), and Lum (luminosity, or amount of light) define colors by color and light. Red, Green, and Blue are the standard ingredients from which color on a computer (or television) screen are blended (you may have seen the familiar acronym "RGB").

5. Select the Semitransparent option to create a lighter shade of the color you've selected.

6. Choose OK.

FIG. 26.16

Use the Custom tab on the Colors dialog box to create your own colors.

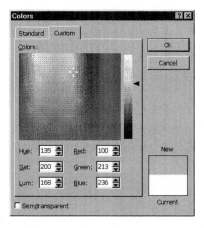

There are four types of fill effects to choose from: gradient, texture, pattern, and picture. To select any of them, you first must display the Fill Effects dialog box.

To select the Fill Effects dialog box, follow these steps:

1. Select the text box.

2. Display the Fill Effects dialog box by one of these methods:

For a custom fill effect using a toolbar button, click the down arrow to the right of the Fill Color button on the Drawing toolbar and select Fill Effects.

or

For a custom fill effect using a menu command, display the Format Text Box dialog box by choosing Format, Text Box or by clicking with the right mouse button on the text box and choosing Format Text Box. Then in the Fill group, select Color, and select Fill Effects.

To create a gradient fill for a text box, follow these steps:

1. Select the Gradient tab in the Fill Effects dialog box (see Figure 26.17).

2. In the Colors group, select from among these options (and watch the Sample box at the bottom right to see the effects of your choices):

   Select One color to fade from dark to light using only one color. In the Color 1 list, select the color you want. In the Dark slidebar, move the slider from left to right to select a dark or light blend from your color to black, white, or gray.

   Select Two colors to fade from one color to another. Then select colors from the Color 1 and Color 2 lists.

   Select Preset to select among preset gradient blends. Then from the Preset colors list, select an option.

3. From the Shading styles group, select among the options that control the direction of the gradient blend.

4. From the Variants group, select one of the four variations on the shading style you've selected.

5. Choose OK twice to close the Fill Effects and Format Text Box dialog boxes.

FIG. 26.17
A gradient fill fades from one color to another.

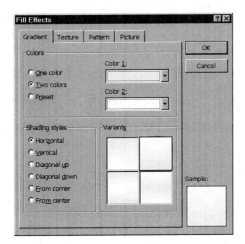

To add a texture to your text box, follow these steps:

1. Select the Texture tab in the Fill Effects dialog box (see Figure 26.18).

2. In the Texture group, select one of the 24 predefined textures listed.

   or

Select <u>O</u>ther Texture to display the Select Texture dialog box. Use this dialog box to locate your own texture file and then choose OK.

▶ **See** "Searching for Files," **p. 124**

3. Choose OK twice to close the Fill Effects and Format Text Box dialog boxes.

FIG. 26.18

You can add a texture from Word's collection, or create or purchase your own textured fills.

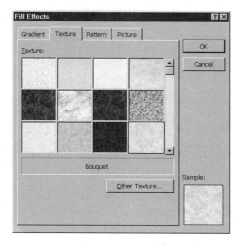

To place a pattern in your text box, follow these steps:

1. Select the Pattern tab in the Fill Effects dialog box (see Figure 26.19).
2. From the <u>F</u>oreground list, select the color you want for the pattern foreground.
3. From the <u>B</u>ackground list, select the color for the pattern background.

FIG. 26.19

You can choose foreground and background colors for any of Word's patterns.

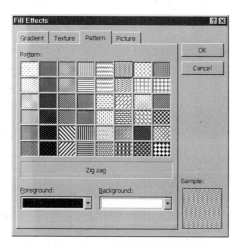

4. In the Pattern group, select the pattern you want. (No patterns appear until you've chosen a color.)

5. Choose OK twice to close the Fill Effects and Format Text Box dialog boxes.

To insert a picture in your text box, follow these steps:

1. Select the Picture tab in the Fill Effects dialog box (see Figure 26.20).

2. Choose Select Picture to display the Select Picture dialog box. Use this dialog to locate the picture you want to insert, and choose OK. You can view the picture in the Picture tab.

3. Choose OK twice to close the Fill Effects and Format Text Box dialog boxes.

FIG. 26.20
You can place a picture in a text box.

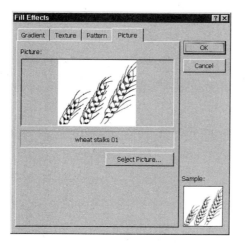

For a custom line pattern, follow these steps:

1. Select the text box.

2. Display the Fill Effects dialog box by one of these methods:

 For a custom line pattern using a toolbar button, click the down arrow to the right of the Line Color button on the Drawing toolbar and choose Pattern Fill.

or

For a custom line pattern using a menu command, display the Format Text Box dialog box by choosing Format, Text Box or by clicking with the right mouse button on the text box and choosing Format Text Box. Select the Colors and Lines tab, and then in the Line group, select Color, Patterned Lines.

3. Select the Pattern tab in the Fill Effects dialog box.

Part

VI

Ch

26

4. From the Foreground list, select the color you want for the pattern foreground.

5. From the Background list, select the color for the pattern background.

6. In the Pattern group, select the pattern you want. Patterns appear only after you select colors.

7. Choose OK twice to close the Fill Effects and Format Text Box dialog boxes.

Adding a Text Box Shadow or Third Dimension

The Drawing toolbar gives you two special effects you can use to make your text boxes more artistic: shadows and cube-like 3-D effects. The shadow and 3-D tools each include special toolbars that provide tools for special effects. For shadows, you can choose the style and direction of the shadow, as well as the shadow color; you can nudge the shadow up, down, left, or right. 3-D options include direction of tilt, the depth and direction of the third dimension, lighting, surface type, and color. The best way to see how each of these tools work is to experiment with them. You can leave your text box selected with the toolbar displayed and watch how each click of a tool affects the appearance of your text box.

Before you create a shadow or third dimension, display the Drawing toolbar.

To create, alter, or remove a text box shadow, follow these steps:

1. Select the text box.

2. Click the Shadow button on the Drawing toolbar to display the shadows palette, as shown in Figure 26.21.

FIG. 26.21
The Shadows palette on the Drawing toolbar suggests many shadow options.

3. Select the shadow style you want (select No Shadow to remove a shadow).

   or

   After you've selected a shadow style, select Shadow Settings to display the Shadow Settings toolbar (see Figure 26.22). Use the buttons on this toolbar to turn the shadow off or on (left button), to nudge the shadow (center four buttons), or to change the color of the shadow (right button). If you want a custom color, display the shadow color palette and select <u>M</u>ore Shadow Colors; for details about how to use this dialog box, see "Creating Custom Colors and Effects."

FIG. 26.22

The Shadow Settings toolbar lets you refine your text box shadows.

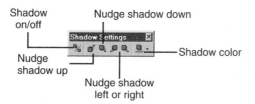

Shadow on/off

Nudge shadow down

Nudge shadow up

Nudge shadow left or right

Shadow color

To create, alter, or remove a 3-D effect, follow these steps:

1. Select the text box.

2. Click the 3-D tool on the Drawing toolbar to display the 3-D palette, as shown in Figure 26.23.

3. Select a 3-D style (select No 3-D to remove a 3-D effect).

FIG. 26.23

The 3-D palette on the Drawing toolbar lets you select from a range of 3-D effects.

or

After you've selected a 3-D style, select 3-D Settings to display the 3-D Settings toolbar, as shown in Figure 26.24. Use the buttons on this toolbar to turn the 3-D off or on (left button); to tilt the cube down, up, left or right; to alter its depth, direction, lighting, or surface; or to change its color. Five of these tools—Depth, Direction, Lighting, Surface, and 3-D Color—have palettes of their own; experiment to see how they change your text box. If you want a custom color, display the 3-D color palette and select <u>M</u>ore 3-D Colors; for details about how to use this dialog box, see the previous section "Creating Custom Colors and Effects."

FIG. 26.24

Experiment with the 3-D toolbar to see how these options change 3-D effects.

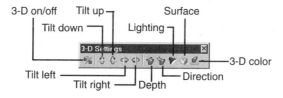

3-D on/off

Tilt up

Tilt down

Surface

Lighting

Tilt left

Tilt right

Depth

Direction

3-D color

Designing Pages with Text Boxes

In the past, word processing and desktop publishing programs differed in the way they treated text on the page. Word processors placed text from top to bottom; desktop publishing programs treated text more like graphical blocks that you could move around on the page and embellish with lines, shading, color, and more. With Word, you get both. Regular text still flows from the top of the page to the bottom, but text boxes are free to move anywhere, often with the other text on the page flowing around them. It is text boxes that make Word a workable alternative to a traditional desktop publishing program.

If you're designing publications like newsletters, magazines, or books, consider using text boxes, rather than columns, as the framework for your design. In effect, that's what a desktop publishing program does. The difference is that many desktop publishing programs create the text boxes automatically, while Word does not. For example, you might want to create a three-column newsletter in Word. Each column can be a borderless text box. You can use the rulers to size your text boxes accurately, and you can use Word's text box linking feature, discussed in the next section, "Linking Text Between Text Boxes," to link the text between text boxes. In some cases this may be easier than using Word's column feature, particularly if you want the freedom to easily move, size, and shape your text as you design your pages.

Wrapping Text Around a Text Box

One of the handiest features of a text box is that you can wrap the other text on the page around it. Use this feature to create "pull quotes," to set text in a margin or between columns, or to create blocks of text that stand apart from the rest of your document.

To wrap text around a text box, you first create the text box, then format it for text wrapping. Word offers several options for how the text wraps.

In one instance, text automatically wraps around a text box. When you first select text, and then choose a command or click a button to create a text box, Word creates a text box that contains the selected text (removing it from the place where you selected it) and wraps surrounding text around it.

To wrap text around a text box, follow these steps:

1. Select the text box.

2. Display the Format Text Box dialog box using one of these techniques: choose Format, Text Box; click the border with the right mouse button and choose Format Text Box; or double-click the border with the left mouse button.

3. Select the Wrapping tab (see Figure 26.25).

FIG. 26.25

There are many styles of text wrapping to choose from.

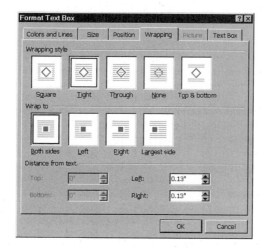

4. In the Wrapping Style group, select an option. The icons illustrate the effect each option will have. Square, for example, wraps the text around the text box in a rectangular fashion, whereas Tight wraps the text to conform with the shape of the text box.

5. In the Wrap To group, select an option for which side of the page you want text to wrap to. The icons illustrate the result of each option.

6. In the Distance From Text group, select the distance you want the text box to be from the text to its Top, Bottom, Left, and Right.

7. Choose OK. Figure 26.26 shows "Tight" text wrapping.

 TIP Double-click any of the Wrapping style or Wrap to icons to quickly select that option and return to your document.

Part
VI

Ch
26

FIG. 26.26

You can create many interesting effects by wrapping text around a text box.

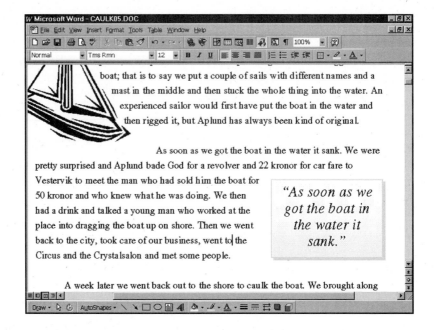

Layering Text Boxes

You can position text boxes in front of or behind text, other text boxes, or drawing objects. By default, they appear on the top of existing text and other text boxes when you first create them.

To layer text boxes on the page, follow these steps:

1. Select the text box you want to layer.

2. Use the right mouse button to click the text box border to display the text box shortcut menu, as shown in Figure 26.27.

3. Choose O_r_der and select one of the following options:

Select this option	For this effect
Bring to Fron_t_	Bring to the front of a stack of objects
Send to Bac_k_	Send to the back of a stack of objects
Bring _F_orward	Bring forward by a single object
Send _B_ackward	Send backward by a single object
Bring in F_r_ont of Text	Brings a text box in front of text
Send Be_h_ind Text	Sends a text box behind text

FIG. 26.27
You can layer text boxes above or below other objects on the page.

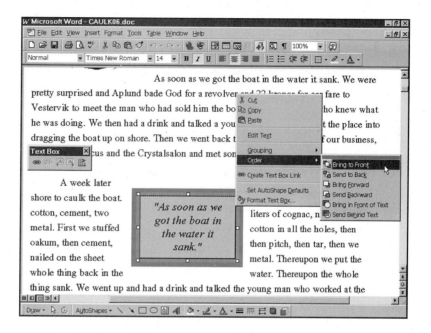

 Selecting a Text Box that Is Layered Behind Text The Select Objects button on the Drawing toolbar helps you select a text box which is layered behind text or another text box. To use it, click the Select Objects button and move the resulting arrow into your document; as you move it over a text box or other object, a four-cornered arrow appears at its tip. Click to select the text box. Click the Select Objects button a second time to return to your normal insertion point.

Part
VI

Ch
26

Grouping Text and Graphics in a Text Box

Text boxes aren't limited to containing only text. When you create a text box and see the flashing insertion point, you can insert a picture or other object. You can add text inside the text box as well, in effect grouping the picture with the text. The two then move as a unit on the page.

Though you can also group individual text boxes, there are a few advantages to including an object in your text box. For example, when you add line and fill formatting to grouped text boxes, these options are applied to each individual text box. But if you place text and objects inside a single text box, you can include a single border that goes around both.

Grouping and Ungrouping Text Boxes

You can group text boxes and other objects together so that they function in many ways as a single object. For example, you can group a picture with a text box containing its caption. A group shares a single set of selection handles.

You can move and size grouped objects as a unit, and format them as a unit if they are like objects (fill color applied to two grouped text boxes, for example, applies to both boxes). You can wrap text around them as a unit, and apply many drawing and object commands, like rotating and layering. You can, however, also format text boxes individually even when they are grouped, simply by the way you select them. To select the group, click its border when you see the arrow plus a four-headed arrow. To select one object, click it when you see an arrow.

To group text boxes and other objects, follow these steps:

1. Select the text boxes or other objects you want to group by holding down the Shift key and clicking each object individually.

2. Use the right mouse button to click on one of the selected text boxes and display the text box shortcut menu, as shown in Figure 26.28.

3. Choose <u>G</u>roup.

FIG. 26.28
By grouping text boxes you keep them together.

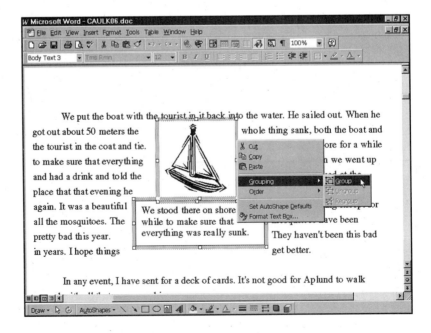

You can ungroup a group in the same way you grouped it: Select the group, click Draw on the Drawing toolbar, and choose Ungroup.

 TIP You can find commands for grouping and ungrouping text boxes in the Draw menu on the Drawing toolbar.

 Lines applied to grouped objects don't enclose the group, but rather each single object. If you want a line around a group of objects, draw it using the Rectangle tool on the Drawing toolbar and include it in the group.

Blank Text Boxes for Handmade Art

If you plan to add handmade artwork to your document after you print it, create a blank text box, with or without a lined border, to leave a space for it. You can wrap text around the empty space, and paste in your art on the printed page.

Linking Text Between Text Boxes

When you want text to flow continuously from one part of your document to the next, even if those parts are not adjacent or on the same page, you can use linked text boxes. When you link text boxes, text inserted in one automatically flows into the next. Conversely, when you remove text from one, text flows in from linked text boxes to fill the empty space. Linking text boxes is an excellent way to design publications like newsletters and magazines, especially when text may need to "jump" from one part of the publication to another.

You can link as many text boxes as you want to create what Word calls a "story," and you can have as many stories as you want in a document. You can't link text boxes between documents.

You can tell whether a text box is linked to another text box by selecting it and displaying the Text Box toolbar: If an icon for breaking a link or moving between linked text boxes is highlighted, then you know the text box is linked to another. To see which text box it's linked to, use the Previous Text Box and Next Text Box buttons.

 TIP You can delete a linked text box without deleting any text in the story: select the text box and press the Delete key.

Part
VI

Ch
26

Creating Links Between Text Boxes

To create linked text boxes, you must use the Text Box toolbar, which is available only when your document contains text boxes. When you open a new document and create text boxes, the Text Box toolbar appears automatically. If you close it, then you must open it by choosing View, Toolbars, Text Box.

Text boxes you link to existing text boxes must be empty.

To create linked text boxes, follow these steps:

1. Create all the text boxes in your linked series by choosing Insert, Text Box or clicking the Text Box button on the Drawing toolbar, and then drawing the text boxes.

2. If the Text Box toolbar, shown in Figure 26.29, did not appear, then choose View, Toolbars, Text Box while a text box is selected.

3. Select the first text box in your linked series by clicking it.

FIG. 26.29

Use the Text Box toolbar to create links between text boxes.

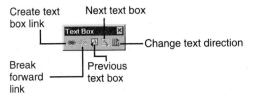

4. Click the Create Text Box Link button on the Text Box toolbar. When you move the pointer into your document, it turns into a pitcher icon, shown in Figure 26.30.

5. Move the pitcher icon over the *empty* text box you want to link to the first text box. The icon changes to a pouring pitcher, shown in Figure 26.31.

6. Click the pouring pitcher icon on the text box you want to link.

7. To link more text boxes, select the most recently linked text box and repeat steps 4, 5, and 6.

8. To add text, select the first text box in the linked series and begin typing. As each text box fills, text flows into the next linked box.

 TIP If you click the Create Text Box Link button and then change your mind about creating the link, press the Escape key to remove the pitcher icon and stop the linking process.

FIG. 26.30

The pitcher icon lets you know you're about to create a text box link.

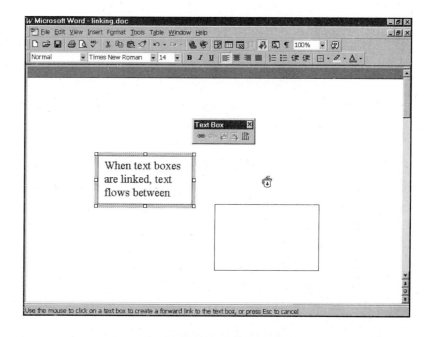

FIG. 26.31

The pouring pitcher icon indicates a text box which is eligible for linking.

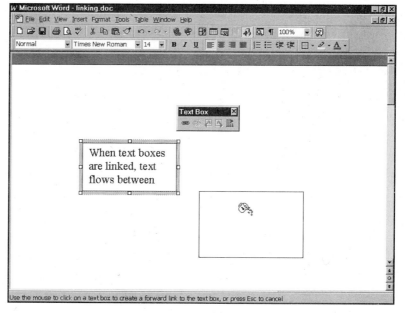

Part
VI

Ch
26

Breaking Text Box Links

If you want to unlink a text box from a linked series, break the forward link. For example, if you want to unlink text box number three, you must do so from text box number two.

To unlink a text box from a series, follow these steps:

1. Click the text box linked ahead of the one you want to unlink.
2. Click the Break Forward Link button on the Text Box toolbar (refer to Figure 26.29).

Moving Between Linked Text Boxes

You can easily move between linked text boxes simply by selecting one text box or another, or by pressing the left-or right-arrow key to move the insertion point from one linked text box to another. You can also use special tools on the Text Box toolbar—these are especially useful if your linked text boxes are not adjacent to one another or on the same page.

To move between linked text boxes, follow these steps:

1. Select the text box from which you want to move.
2. Click the Previous Text Box button on the Text Box toolbar to select the previous text box in the linked series (refer to Figure 26.29).

   or

   Click the Next Text Box button on the Text Box toolbar to select the next text box in the linked series (refer to Figure 26.29).

Notice that moving between text boxes in this way does not move the insertion point between text boxes, as does pressing an arrow key.

Working with Frames

Earlier versions of Word included a feature called "frames" rather than text boxes. They are similar to text boxes, but lack some of the advantages of text boxes. They do occasionally still appear in Word documents, however. Drop caps arrive formatted as frames, for example, as do certain text annotations, such as footnotes, endnotes, and comments. And there is one instance when you might want to convert a text box to a frame—when you want to remove a text box and its formatting without removing its contents.

To remove a text box without removing its contents, follow these steps:

1. Select the text box by clicking it.

2. Choose F_ormat, Text B_ox to display the Format Text Box dialog box.

3. Select the Text Box tab, and then select the Convert to F_rame button. Click OK if a warning box appears (you'll lose the text box and its formatting, but not the text formatting).

4. Select the frame by clicking on it, choose F_ormat, Fra_me, and select the _Remove Frame button in the Frame dialog box.

Notice that you can't convert a text box to a frame if the text box is linked to other text boxes. ●

CHAPTER 27

Drawing with Word's Drawing Tools

On the average desktop, your document will have to compete with many others to be read. Graphic elements can make your document stand out and assist you with communicating your ideas. Word has always provided easy access to graphics, but Word 97 makes the task of creating your own graphics much easier.

Chapter 25, "Inserting Pictures," focused on inserting pictures from an external graphics source such as a stand-alone graphics program or Microsoft's Clip Gallery 3.0; Chapter 26, "Inserting Text Boxes," focused on inserting text boxes, and Chapter 28, "Inserting Text with Special Effects," focuses on using WordArt to create special effects with text. This chapter will focus on adding your own custom graphics using the Drawing toolbar.

Word 97 offers a significantly enhanced set of drawing tools. You can create simple objects like lines and simple shapes or take advantage of the AutoShapes which offers some additional shape styles. ■

Displaying and using the drawing toolbar

To add customized graphics to your document, you will display the Drawing toolbar to select and use the drawing tools.

Using AutoShapes

If you need a more complex shape, the new AutoShape feature will enable you to select from a collection of shapes.

Including text, pictures, and callouts

You can add text to your drawing or incorporate pictures and clip art using the text box tool and the Insert Picture features. Word also provides a special AutoShape category for annotating your drawing or your text.

Understanding the freehand tools

In addition to the shapes, you also have the Curve, FreeForm, and Scribble tools. These enable you to create your own custom shapes.

Managing your drawing

Once you have added your shapes to your document, you may want to treat more than one shape as a group. You can also move your drawing below or above your text.

What You Need to Know About Drawing

When you decide to add graphics to your document, you will be working directly on the page. You are not restricted by your page margins or by where your text is placed. To create a drawing, you will use the Drawing toolbar to select a tool and then use it to draw the shape on your document.

When you first create the drawing object or shape, it will appear on top of any text. You do not have to worry about disturbing the text. Your document exists in three layers. There is the text layer and a layer above and below the text. When you create a drawing shape, it is in the layer above the text. After it is created, you can move the drawing to one of the other layers if desired.

In addition to the layers of the document, you will also create layers in your drawing. To create a drawing, you will combine shapes by placing them around, as well as on top of one another. You will be able to move, resize, and adjust their order as you build your drawing. You will also be able to work with the individual shapes or with the shapes as a group.

As you build your drawing, you will try out different ideas and experiment. If you find the results do not match your expectations, do not forget the Undo command. You can try out an idea and if it doesn't work, select Edit, Undo, click the Undo toolbar button, or press Ctrl+Z. This will enable you to try out several ideas without being concerned with ruining your drawing.

You may also consider creating your drawing in a new document to minimize the visual clutter as you create a new drawing. You can create a new document, then use the Drawing tools to create a new drawing, and when it is completed, you can select the entire drawing and copy it to the Clipboard. You can then paste the drawing wherever you want it.

Displaying and Understanding the Drawing Toolbar

To use Word's drawing tools, you must display the Drawing toolbar and be in the Page Layout view. Word 97 has an enhanced drawing feature and automatically switches to Page Layout view for you. It has an expanded set of drawing tools, as well as additional tools to assist you with manipulating your shapes.

Displaying the Drawing Toolbar

 You can display the Drawing toolbar by choosing View, Toolbars, and selecting Drawing from the list. Or, you can click the Drawing button on the Standard toolbar. Or you can right-click on the gray area of any toolbar and select Drawing from the list.

Unlike the Standard and Formatting toolbars, the Drawing toolbar attaches to the bottom of the window by default (see Figure 27.1). If desired, you can move it to another location.

FIG. 27.1
The Drawing toolbar will be used to add graphics to your document.

Introducing the Drawing Tools

The Drawing toolbar has been redesigned to support Word's enhanced drawing capabilities. Each button on the Drawing toolbar performs a specific function or opens a palette. Some will not be available unless a shape is selected. Browse through the buttons and their descriptions in Table 27.1 to get an idea of what you can do with the Drawing toolbar; then refer to later sections in this chapter to learn how to use each tool.

Table 27.1   Drawing Buttons

Icon	Name	Function
Draw ▾	Draw menu	This menu has many shape management commands including grouping, ordering, grid, nudging, aligning, distributing, rotating, flipping, editing points, changing shape, and setting AutoShape defaults.
☐	Select Object	Draws a selection box around an object or group of objects.
☼	Free Rotate	Activates free rotation for objects. The sizing handles will change into the rotation handles to enable you to rotate an object.
AutoShapes ▾	AutoShapes	This menu has categories of shapes that can be used to create your drawing.

continues

Part
VI

Ch
27

Table 27.1 Continued

Icon	Name	Function
	Line	Draws straight lines. Lines are vertical, horizontal, or at a 15-, 30-, 45-, 60-, 75-, or 90-degree angle if you hold Shift as you draw.
	Arrow	Draws lines with arrowheads. The Shift key will cause the same effect as it did with the Line.
	Rectangle	Draws rectangles or squares when you hold Shift as you draw.
	Ellipse	Draws ellipses or circles when you hold Shift as you draw.
	Text Box	Draws a text box into which you can type text, draw, or insert a picture created in another program.
	WordArt	Creates text with special effects. For additional information, please refer to Chapter 28, "Inserting Text with Special Effects."
	Fill Color	Fills a selected shape with color, or sets the default fill color if no shape is selected.
	Line Color	Colors a selected line (or the line around a selected shape), or sets the default line color if no line is selected.
	Font Color	Colors the text for a selected object or sets the default font color if no text object is selected.
	Line Style	Changes the line width of a line or shape outline, or sets the default if no line is selected.
	Dash Style	Changes the dash style, or sets the default if no line is selected.
	Arrow Style	Changes the arrow style, or sets the default if no line is selected.
	Shadow	Adds a shadow style for the selected object or sets the default if no object is selected.
	3-D	Adds a 3-D effect for the selected object or sets the default if no object is selected.

N O T E If you insert or draw invisible objects (such as empty rectangle, or other shapes with no fill or line), or if you lose objects that become layered behind other objects, use the Selection tool to draw a section box around the area where you've lost the object. All objects inside the selection box will be selected, and you can see their square selection handles, even if they're invisible or behind another object. ■

N O T E With Word 97, many of the buttons that were available in previous releases have been removed from the Drawing toolbar. They have been moved to the Draw menu. If you prefer to see those buttons, they can be added to the toolbar. For instructions for customizing a toolbar, please refer to Chapter 38, "Customizing the Toolbar, Menus, and Shortcut Keys." ■

Using the Drawing Tools

When you want to add drawings to your document, you will build your drawing a shape at a time. Whether you are drawing on paper or in your document, a little preparation will save you some time in the long run. If you were going to draw on paper, you would set out your materials and prepare your workspace. The same can be accomplished for your document.

Although you are working on the page rather than in a paragraph, your shape will be attached to the nearest paragraph by default. This is referred to as the *object anchor*. Object anchors are not visible by default, but you can view them by setting your view options. You can select Tools, Options. Object anchors can be selected from the View tab.

▶ **See** "Customizing the Workspace and Display," **p. 1126**

Before you begin, it is a good idea to move your insertion point to a paragraph close to where you would like the drawing object to be. After the object is placed on the page, you can change what paragraph it is anchored to—or if it is anchored to one at all.

You may also want to consider adjusting your Zoom setting. If you want to draw a graphic that fills the page, it may be easier to work with it if your Zoom setting is at Whole Page. You can adjust your Zoom setting by selecting View, Zoom, Whole Page.

Once the setup is to your liking, you are ready to begin drawing. The general procedure for creating a shape is:

1. Select a shape from the Drawing toolbar.
2. Draw the shape on the document.
3. Make any adjustments to its location and size.
4. Format its appearance.

Part
VI
Ch
27

Creating a Shape

To create a shape on your page, the first step is to select a line or shape tool from the Drawing toolbar. If you need more than one shape of a particular type, you can double-click the selected tool. It will stay selected until you select another tool. You could select a line, arrow, rectangle, oval, or any shape from the AutoShapes menu.

Once you have selected your shape, move your mouse pointer onto the page to where you would like to begin drawing your shape. As you move over the page, the mouse pointer will change into a crosshair to indicate the starting coordinates for the shape (see Figure 27.2).

When you have positioned the crosshair where you want to begin creating your shape, hold down the left mouse button as you drag the crosshair to draw. When you release the mouse button, Word will complete the shape. If you just click in your document, you will get a shape with its default dimensions.

Every shape will be surrounded by eight sizing handles, except for lines and arrows, which have only two. The sizing handles for those shapes that do not have straight borders will still form a rectangle. Using the Curve, FreeForm, and Scribble tools will produce different results. These are discussed later in the "Understanding Freehand Drawing Tools" section.

N O T E   If you hold down Shift while drawing your line, it will force a straight line at one of the nearest specified angles, your rectangle into a square, and the oval into a circle placing the corner of the shape at where you began to draw. The Ctrl key does the same thing, only centering the shape around the point where you began drawing.

The sizing handles indicate which shape is currently selected. In Figure 27.2, the five objects at the right are selected. This was done with the Select Object tool.

As you draw the shape on the page, do not worry about getting it exactly right. You can move it to a new location, resize it, delete it, and format it if it isn't right.

Moving a Shape

One of the most common problems when creating a shape is to place it in the wrong place. If this happens, you do not need to start over. You can simply move the shape with the mouse or use the Format Object dialog box to change its position.

To move a shape with the mouse, you must select the Select Objects tool from the Drawing toolbar and select the shape. If you want one shape, you can simply click the shape. If you want a group of shapes, you will need to click the first one and Shift+click the other shapes. An alternative would be to place your mouse pointer next to the shapes without being on any one shape and hold the left mouse button down while dragging the mouse pointer to surround the shapes in a selection rectangle. When all of the shapes are surrounded, release the mouse button.

FIG. 27.2

The crosshair mouse pointer is used as you draw an object and completed objects with their sizing handles.

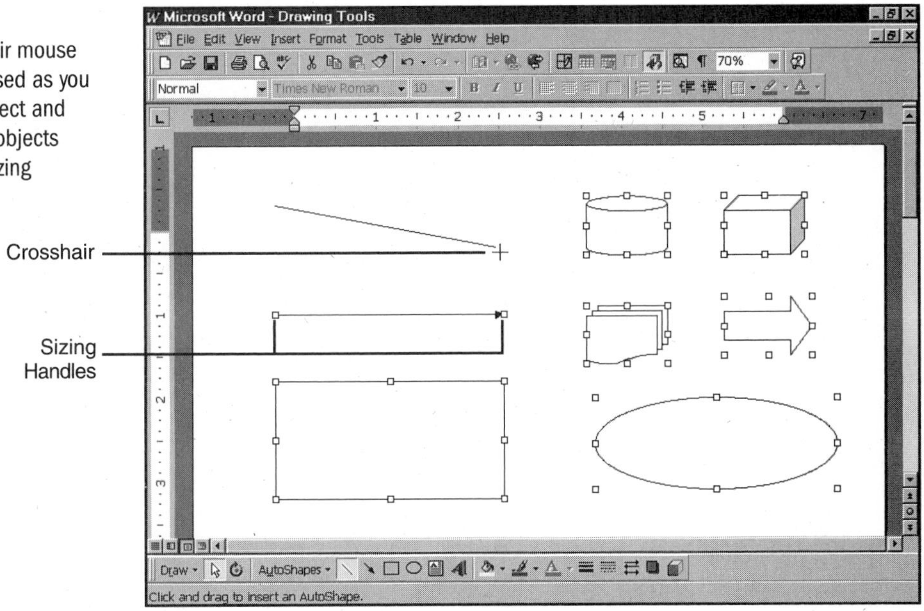

Once the shape or shapes are selected, you can point inside the shape and move the mouse pointer to a new location while holding down the left mouse button. The mouse pointer will change as you are moving the object. It will turn into the move pointer (see Figure 27.3).

Placing shapes with a mouse accurately takes some practice. If you are not comfortable about placing your shapes with the mouse, you can use the Format AutoShape dialog box. It enables you to specify the position in inches or your default measurement type. To move a shape using the Format AutoShape dialog box, you still need to have the shape selected. You will point to the shape and click with the right mouse button. Select Format AutoShape from the shortcut menu. This will open the Format AutoShape dialog box (see Figure 27.4).

One of these tabs is the Position tab. This enables you to move the shape without dragging it to a new location. You can specify the following options as shown in Table 27.2.

Part

VI

Ch

27

FIG. 27.3
When a shape is moved, the mouse pointer will change to the move pointer.

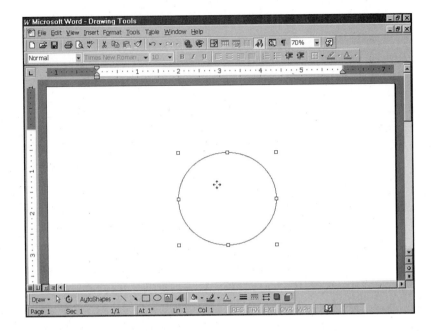

FIG. 27.4
The Format AutoShape dialog box can be used to set the Colors and Lines, Size, Position, Wrapping, Picture, and Text Box for the drawing shapes.

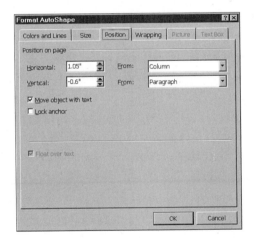

Table 27.2 The Position Tab Options for Selected Shapes Only

Selection	Application
Horizontal	Selects distance from left edge of margin, page, or column.
Vertical	Selects distance from top edge of margin, page, or paragraph.

Selection	Application
Move Object with Text	Indicates whether the shape will move when the paragraph it is anchored to moves.
Lock Anchor	Anchors objects to the paragraph in which they were drawn.
Float over Text	Indicates whether the shape will float above its paragraph anchor. It is only available when the object is in the above text layer.

N O T E Positioning an object using the Page option removes the anchor between object and paragraph. This enables you to have your text flow as more text is added and subtracted while leaving the graphic in the same place. When you choose this approach, the object can be anywhere on the page regardless of your margins or paragraphs. If you are using this approach, you need to be aware of your printer's limitations. Most printers have what is called a *hard margin* where the printer grips the paper. If you place your object beyond the edges of where the printer can print, you will lose part of your graphic. ■

Sizing a Shape

When you create shapes, it can also be a challenge to make them the correct size. If you draw a shape that is the wrong size, you can easily resize it, using a technique similar to how you've already learned to move shapes. You select the shape you want to resize. You place your mouse pointer on top of one of the sizing handles. The mouse pointer will change into the sizing pointer (see Figure 27.5). If you choose one of the shape's side handles, you will resize horizontally or vertically. If you choose one the corner handles, you resize both simultaneously.

 T I P If you hold down the Shift key or the Ctrl key, the proportions of the shape will be maintained. The Shift key will lock the position of the shape using the border opposite the sizing handle used to size the shape. The Ctrl key will size the shape from its center point. With the Ctrl key, you need to be more careful. With some shapes, you will lose some definition as you size it smaller and closer to the center point.

If you want to resize the shape to an exact measurement type, you can use the Format AutoShape dialog box. To resize a shape using the Format AutoShape dialog box, you still need to have the shape selected. Point to the shape and click with the right mouse button. Select Format AutoShape from the menu. This will open the Format AutoShape dialog box. Next, select the Size tab. You can then specify the following options as shown in Table 27.3.

FIG. 27.5
The resizing mouse
pointer positioned
on a corner handle.

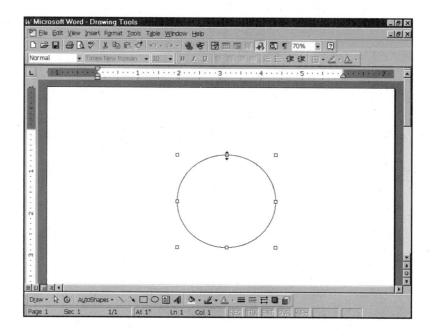

Table 27.3   The Size Tab Options for Selected Shapes Only

Selection	Application
Size and Rotate Group	
Height	Selects height of a drawing object.
Width	Selects width of a drawing object.
Rotation	Selects the number of degrees to rotate a drawing object.
Scale Group	
Height	Selects the Height scale percentage for a drawing object.
Width	Selects the Width scale percentage for a drawing object.

Deleting a Shape

If you create a shape that doesn't meet your needs, you can eliminate it easily. To remove
a shape, select it and press the Delete key. If you delete a shape by mistake, you can always use the Undo command to get it back.

Formatting Your Shapes

Once the shape is placed in your document, you can use the formatting options to make it stand out. You can change the color of the shape's outline, as well as the type of line used. You can add arrowheads to the end of lines. You can add color and a pattern to the inside of closed shapes. You can create shadows and 3-D effects. You can even change an object's perspective by rotating or flipping it.

Changing the Line Style, Dash Style, and Arrows

When you first create a shape, it has a solid black border. If it is a line, it also has plain ends. These can all be modified with the Drawing toolbar or by using the Colors and Lines tab in the Format AutoShape dialog box.

To apply formatting, select the object or objects to be formatted. You select the appropriate tool from the Drawing toolbar or click the object with the right mouse button. Select Format AutoShapes from the menu and select the Colors and Lines tab.

 The Line Style button opens the Line Style palette (see Figure 27.6). This palette can be used to select a line width and line style from those shown. The last choice on the palette is More Lines. This will open the Format AutoShapes dialog box. Although the dialog box doesn't offer any more styles, it does allow you to enter the exact width of the line you want.

 The Dash Style button opens the Dash Style palette. It can be used to change the appearance of the pattern of the border you want (see Figure 27.6). You can choose from solid, dash, dot, and so on.

 The Arrow Style button opens the Arrow palette. This palette can be used to change the appearance of the ends of lines (see Figure 27.6). You can select from no arrows, left arrows, right arrows, and so on, for your line style. This palette's selections will be disabled if the shape is not a line. The last choice is More Arrows. This will open the Format AutoShapes dialog box. The Arrows group offers greater flexibility in designing your line ends. You can select the beginning and ending of the lines independently, as well as control the size of the arrows.

Changing the Line Color, Fill Color, Pattern, and Font Color

In addition to the line style, dash style, and arrow style, you can also apply color and patterns to your drawing objects. You can change the line color, add a fill color or pattern to the inside of closed objects, or change the font color of text inside drawing objects. This formatting can be added using the Drawing toolbar or by using the Colors and Lines tab in the Format AutoShape dialog box.

Part
VI
Ch
27

FIG. 27.6

The Line Style, Dash Style, and Arrow Style palettes can be used to adjust a line or shape's appearance.

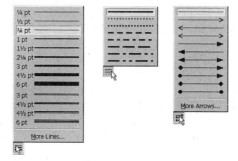

The process for applying this formatting is the same as with the line, dash, and arrow styles. Select the object or objects to be formatted. Select the appropriate tool from the Drawing toolbar or click the object with the right mouse button. Select Format AutoShapes from the menu and select the Colors and Lines tab.

 The Fill Color button will apply the selected color or the arrow to the right of the button will open the Fill Color palette. It can be used to add color or texture to your drawing objects excluding lines and arrows.

 TIP Unlike the line, dash, and arrow style palettes, you can remove the Fill Color palette from the toolbar to allow it to float over your document as you work.

To remove or tear off the palette from the toolbar, select the button that displays the palette. At the top of the palette, you will see a thin title bar. Point to that thin title bar and drag it onto the document. It will now be a floating palette (see Figure 27.7).

You can select any color that is shown in the palette or you can select More Fill Colors to access the Colors dialog box. The Colors dialog box allows you to select from a larger palette of colors or create a custom color (see Figure 27.7). To create a custom color, select the Custom tab and use the standard Custom Color palette.

FIG. 27.7

The Fill Color palette can be used to select a background color for an object, or you can select from the Colors dialog box.

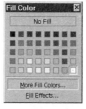

You can also add Fill Effects or patterns to the background of a drawing object. This feature has been enhanced from Word 95. When you select Fill Effects from the Fill Color palette, the Fill Effects dialog box opens. This dialog box provides 48 pattern options—

nearly twice as many as previous versions of Word. For example, you can select a solid diamond pattern (see Figure 27.8), and there are also three new fill types.

You can select the Gradient tab to select Gradient Colors and specify the gradient style. You can specify the color choices to use for the gradient; you can select a style and then select a variation for the gradient. For example, you could select a one color gradient from the center for a circle (see Figure 27.8).

If you want to use a texture instead of a gradient, you can add textures to your drawing object, by selecting a texture from those available on the Textures tab. There are 24 built-in textures, or you can add your own textures. For example, you could use the paper bag texture (see Figure 27.8). The last fill type is to add a picture as a fill. You can select any object and place a picture inside of the shape.

FIG. 27.8

There are many new fill patterns for the inside of closed shapes in Word 97.

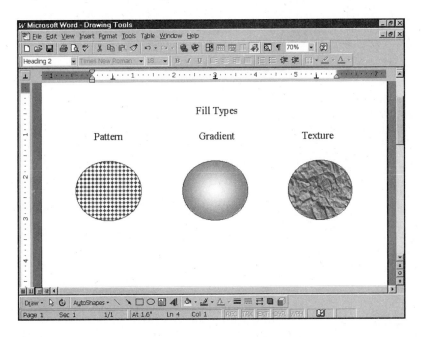

Another formatting button on the Drawing toolbar is the Font Color button. This will enable you to change the text inside any of the Drawing objects. These formatting options are covered later in this chapter in "Inserting Text and Pictures in a Drawing."

Adding Shadows and 3-D Effects

In addition to formatting the object's style and color, you can also add depth to your drawing by adding a shadow or a 3-D effect. A shadow can make a drawing object appear to lift off the page, and a 3-D effect can add dimension.

Part
VI

Ch
27

If you are using many drawing objects or you are adding a drawing with text around it, you may want to add dimension by lifting it off of the page. One option is to add a shadow. Word 95 had the shadow functionality, but Word 97 has several enhancements. Any object can now have a shadow. Originally, the shadow was a black-drop shadow placed to the right. Word 97 has added the ability to control the shadow style and direction with the Shadow button on the Drawing toolbar.

You select a shadow style from the palette. You can leave that style as is, or you can select the Shadow button and then select Shadow Settings to display the Shadow Settings toolbar (see Figure 27.9). It has buttons to allow you to turn the Shadow on and off. You also have the Nudge Shadow buttons left, right, up, and down. You can also change the shadow color.

FIG. 27.9

The Shadow Settings toolbar can be used to modify the direction, depth, and color of a drawing object's shadow.

Another option to add depth to your object is to add 3-D effects. The 3-D button on the Drawing toolbar allows you to adjust the 3-D style for your object. There are twenty preset styles to choose from, and you can also select 3-D Settings to access the 3D Settings toolbar for even more control (see Figure 27.10).

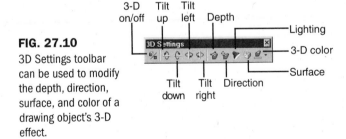

FIG. 27.10

3D Settings toolbar can be used to modify the depth, direction, surface, and color of a drawing object's 3-D effect.

The 3D Settings toolbar can be used to adjust the 3-D effect for a drawing object. You can turn the 3-D effect on or off. You can tilt the shape up, down, left, or right to control its perspective in your document. You can add depth or change the direction of the 3-D effect. You can change the lighting source or the surface type to add additional effect. You can also change the color of the 3-D effect.

Rotating and Flipping Shapes

In addition to the placement of shadows and the type of 3-D effect added to an object, you can also adjust its placement and position. The Draw option has a Rotate or Flip submenu. You can use Free Rotate (which is also on the Drawing toolbar as a separate button) or you can rotate the object left or right by 90 degrees at a time. You can also Flip the object horizontally or vertically to reverse the position of a shape. This can be very helpful especially when you want a mirror image. You can create a duplicate of the object using the Clipboard and then flip it.

To use the Rotate Left, Rotate Right, Flip Horizontal, or Flip Vertical, you will need to select the object and then select the appropriate option from the Draw, Rotate or Flip menu. These options rotate or flip your object an exact number of degrees. If you need more flexibility than that, use the Free Rotate option.

Select your object, and click the Free Rotate button on the Drawing toolbar. The object's sizing handles will change into the rotation handles, and when your mouse is over one of the handles, it will change into the rotation pointer (see Figure 27.11). To rotate the object, hold down the left mouse button and begin dragging the handle to a new position. The object will begin rotating. When the shape is in the correct position, release the mouse button.

FIG. 27.11
The Rotation pointer can be used to rotate a drawing object with greater precision than the Rotate Left and Rotate Right commands.

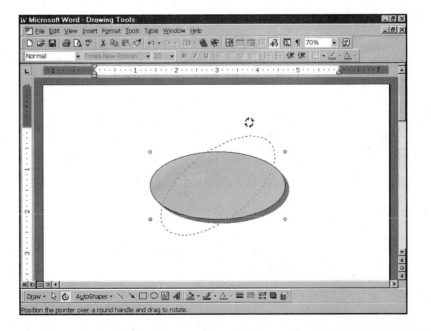

Part
VI

Ch
27

This is not as precise as Rotate Left and Rotate Right. You may have to attempt this several times to get it exactly the way you want it. If you rotate it too far and you cannot get it back where you want it, try Undo and start over with the rotation.

 TIP If you are rotating many objects, you may want to consider removing or tearing off this submenu. It will turn into the Rotate/Flip toolbar.

Using the Placement Tools

If you are creating more than one shape to create your drawing, you will likely be moving objects around in the document. There are several drawing features that will make this task much easier. There is an invisible grid to help you line up shapes. You also have two new features. You can now align a group of shapes, as well as distribute them across the page to create even white space in between them.

Using the Grid

As you draw objects, Word can help you place them precisely, using an invisible grid. When you turn on Word's Snap to Grid feature, your objects will attach themselves to the nearest intersection of grid lines. Moreover, you can specify exactly how coarse or fine to make the grid.

To set up the Grid options, use the Snap to Grid dialog box (see Figure 27.12). To access this dialog box, select D̲raw, Gri̲d from the Drawing toolbar. The S̲nap to Grid check box indicates whether you want to take advantage of this feature. This feature is turned on by default. You also need to enter the amount of Hori̲zontal spacing in between the horizontal grid lines and the amount of V̲ertical spacing in between the vertical grid lines.

 TIP If you need to place an object on the document but not align it with the grid, you can override grid placement by holding down your Alt key as you draw or move the object.

FIG. 27.12
The Snap to Grid dialog box can be used to adjust the grid settings, helping you align your objects as you create them.

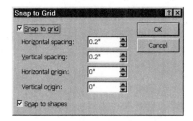

You can also enter a new Horizontal Origin or Vertical Origin. This would limit the invisible grid to a certain area of the page. For example, you could have the horizontal origin set to 3" and the vertical set to 4". This would begin the grid 3 inches from the left edge of the page and 4 inches from the top excluding margins. The last option is to Snap to Shapes. This option extends the grid feature. When you are creating more complex drawings, you will layer drawing objects. This feature turns on the alignment to the grid even if the object being drawn is on top of another object.

 TIP The grid spacing starts at .1 inches. It is best to keep the spacing as small as possible for the greatest precision when placing objects in your document.

Aligning and Distributing Objects

 Another new feature is the capability to align multiple objects relative to each other or to the page. If you are creating several shapes that need to line up, you are not looking to align to a particular position on the grid. Often, you want to line up several objects based on the position of one of them or relative to the page. You might also want to equally distribute the objects within a given area. The Draw, Align, or Distribute submenu is designed to assist you with these tasks.

When you create objects, you take advantage of the grid to place them on a given intersection. Figure 27.13 shows three squares with different fills. These squares are all aligned to the grid with the Snap to Grid option turned on, but they do not line up together. Each of these aligns with a different grid intersection.

To align all three objects relative to each other, click Draw, Align or Distribute on the Draw toolbar. Make sure the Relative To Page menu item is clear so objects will align with each other rather than aligning with the page.

If you were to select all three squares and click Draw, Align or Distribute, Align Top, all three objects would align all the squares with the object having the highest top. Click Draw, Align or Distribute, Distribute Horizontally to create even white space between objects. This keeps the left edge of the first shape and the right edge of the last shape in place and moves the middle square to evenly distribute the space (see Figure 27.14).

 TIP You can distribute shapes relative to the page margins by turning on the Relative To Page option on the Draw, Align or Distribute submenu.

Part
VI

Ch
27

FIG. 27.13
The objects are aligned to the grid, but not to one another.

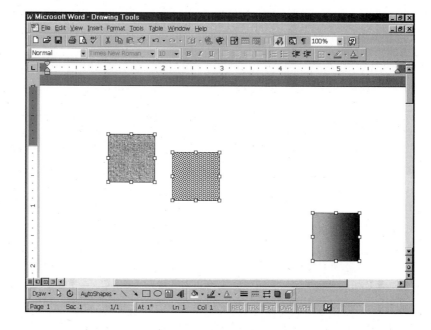

FIG. 27.14
The objects are aligned to the top border of the first object, and there is an equal amount of white space in between the objects.

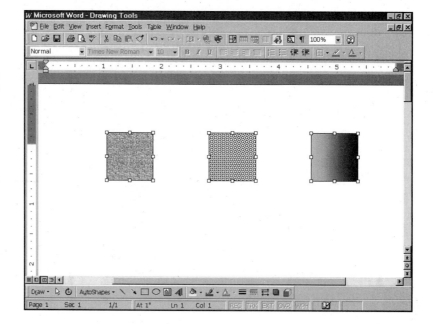

Understanding AutoShapes

The Draw feature is designed to allow you to add visual effects to your documents to draw attention to important points or make it stand out from other documents, but you do not have to be a graphics artist to take advantage of these tools. In Word 97, the number of built-in shapes has increased dramatically, so you may rarely need to create an object from scratch.

The AutoShapes button opens a menu with six categories of built-in shapes. These six categories open up tool palettes to enable you to select an object. These submenus can be removed or torn off from the menu like many of the other palettes as shown in Figure 27.15.

These categories offer a variety of shapes to work with to create visual impact. The Lines category offers a selection of lines and arrows, as well as the freehand tools discussed later in "Understanding the Freehand Tools." The Basic Shapes category has the shapes used most often, like rectangles and ovals, as well as some of the most common symbols.

FIG. 27.15
The AutoShapes menu items can be removed from the menu into individual toolbars.

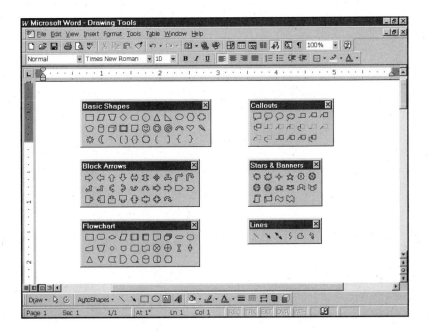

The Block Arrows category gives you a selection of directional arrows to add emphasis. The Flowchart category has some of the traditional flowchart symbols for graphing processes. Stars and Banners has some symbols that could be helpful in creating graphic headings, as well as interesting bullets. The last category is Callouts. These can be used to annotate your text or drawing. (See "Working with Callouts.")

Part
VI

Ch
27

You work with AutoShapes like you would any of the shapes on the toolbar. You select the tool you want, point to where you want to begin, and drag it to the desired size. Many of the shapes have another type of handle that increases the number of shapes available. Some of the shapes will have Adjustment handles like the diamond on the left of the first star in Figure 27.16. These enable you to reconfigure the shape to meet your needs. For example, the 16 Point Star has a handle to enable you to determine the sharpness of the points of the star. To use the Adjustment handles, you point to the handle and drag it to a new location. Each shape has limits on how far you can adjust it, but it does give you many variations on a shape.

FIG. 27.16
Use the Adjustment handle to change the angle of the points on AutoShape stars.

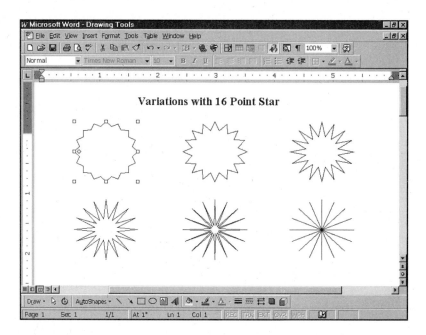

Including Text and Pictures in a Drawing

Creating shapes is only part of creating drawings with Word. You can also combine text and pictures with your drawing.

Adding Text to Your Drawing

Adding text to your drawing can be done several different ways. You can use the text box tool, as covered in Chapter 26, "Inserting Text Boxes." You can use WordArt to create text effects as described in Chapter 28, "Inserting Text with Special Effects." Or you can use the text attribute of many of the shapes.

To add text to one of the shapes, first create the shape. Next, right-click the shape to open its shortcut menu. One of the choices is Add Text (see Figure 27.17). When Add Text is selected, an insertion point appears in the shape. You can begin typing your text in the shape. You can format the text in a shape like you can in a text box.

FIG. 27.17
The Add Text option lets you add to text to many of the shapes.

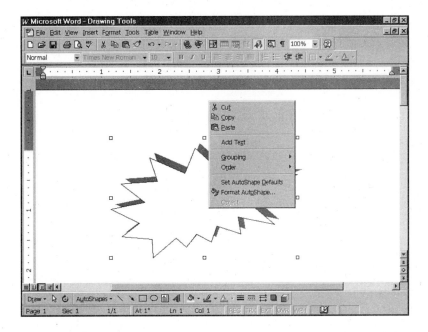

You can also set the internal margins Left, Right, Top, and Bottom settings with the Format AutoShape dialog box. To access this dialog box, right-click the border of the shape, select Format AutoShape, and then select the Text Box tab. To get the correct shortcut menu, you have to click the border because if you click with the right mouse button inside of the shape, you will get the pop-up menu for the text.

N O T E When you are using the text attribute for a shape, the text will not rotate when you rotate the shape. You may want to consider using the WordArt feature discussed in Chapter 28. With WordArt, you create a WordArt object on top of the shape and rotate it to match the rotation of the shape. ▪

Using Pictures in Your Drawing

In addition to adding text, you can add pictures to your document and add custom elements with the Drawing tools. In Chapter 25, "Inserting Pictures," the process for integrating clip art and other graphic formats was outlined. If you find a picture that you want to use, but want to add some custom elements, you can do so easily with the drawing toolbars.

Figure 27.18 shows an example of clip art, as well as the same clip art with some added drawing objects. The clip art looks unfinished because the stems of the flowers are hanging in midair. When combined with two trapezoids and one of the ribbon banners, it looks more finished and complete.

FIG. 27.18
The Drawing objects can be used to give a picture a finished look.

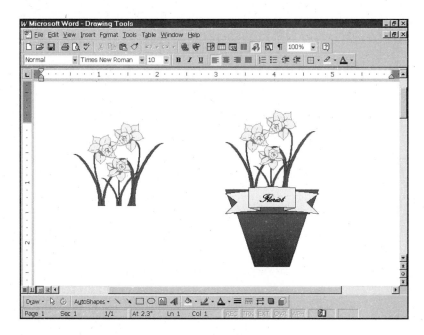

Working with Callouts

Callouts can also give your document a more polished look. Often, when you include a picture in a document, the picture needs some explanation or annotation. This is often done with blocks of text with lines pointing to specific areas of the picture. Instead of having to use a text box with the line tool, you can simply use a callout.

A callout is a text box with a line already attached. You can select from a variety of styles from the AutoShapes menu. You create a callout like any other shape, but you may spend more time with the Adjustment handles, which enable you to adjust the position of either the callout text box or the end of the line extending from the callout (see Figure 27.19).

When you draw the callout, you will need to adjust its position and its line direction to point to a particular item. Use the adjustment handle on the end of the line to drag the line so that it ends at the item you want to annotate. A second adjustment handle, located where the line meets the text box, can be used to adjust the position of the text box. This can also be accomplished by dragging from the border of the text box.

FIG. 27.19
Callouts can provide annotations for pictures, drawings, tables, and text.

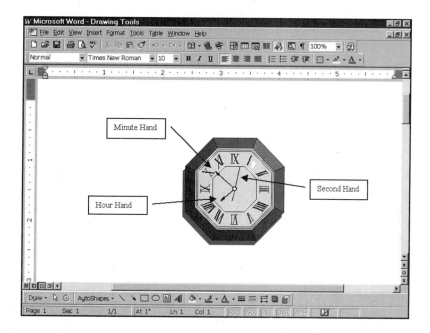

If you point to the callout line and begin dragging, it will move both the box and the line. You will need to be careful that the line still points to the correct area of the picture or text when you move it using the border.

Understanding the Freehand Drawing Tools

All of the shapes available with AutoShapes are designed to save you time, but sometimes there's no alternative but to create the shapes in a drawing from scratch. For example, you may need shapes that are highly irregular. The Lines category provides three tools to enable you to create your own freehand drawings. There are the Curve, the FreeForm, and the Scribble tools.

Creating a Freehand Shape

The Curve tool enables you to click a beginning point for the curve and then move and click where you want the next point of the curve. You can add as many points as you want. When you have as many points as needed, double-click to end the line. Word will construct a curve using those points.

Part
VI

Ch
27

The FreeForm tool is used like the Curve. You can click to begin and then move to a new point where you want to lock the line and click to create a straight line between those two points. You can click as many points as needed. When you are finished you can double-click the last point. If you want a closed shape, you can click with the right mouse button on the shape and select Close Curve from the menu. If you have a closed shape and you want to open it up, you can also do that with the menu. If you drag the mouse while creating the shape, it acts like the Scribble tool.

The Scribble tool is the one to use if you want an object that looks like it was drawn with a pen or pencil. It doesn't use the click-each-point method. You must hold down the mouse the entire time you are drawing your object.

Editing Your Freehand Shape

All of these tools will take some practice, but do not let one problem stop you from using one of your drawings. All of these tools enable you to edit specific points of the shape. If you click the object with the right mouse button and select Edit Points, you will be able to work with specific segments of your shape. The Edit Points mode will plot the points of your drawing to enable you to modify them (see Figure 27.20).

FIG. 27.20
The Edit Points mode plots the points and enables you to modify each segment separately.

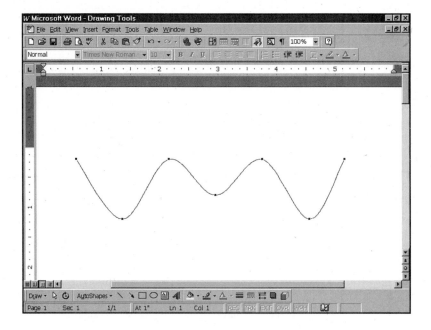

You can point to one point and drag it to a new location. You can create loops. You can also work with a special shortcut menu. When you have selected Edit Points, the shortcut menu will change to give you editing options. You can fix many freehand problems by adding points, straightening segments, curving segments, deleting segments, closing a curve, or exiting edit points mode. It will still take some practice with these tools to get the expected results.

Managing Your Drawing

As you create your drawing, you will be working with many objects. There are some tools that can assist you with managing them. You can use the Clipboard to duplicate objects. You can group objects to be treated as one unit to make them easier to move, size, format, and duplicate. You can also place your drawing on a layer of your choice and determine how the text will flow around the drawing.

Duplicating Drawing Objects

There are times that you want to create several objects that have the same size and formatting. Rather than creating several objects and having to size and format them individually or select them and format them all at once, you can take advantage of the Clipboard. You can create one object and copy it to the Clipboard and then paste as many copies as needed (see Figure 27.21).

 TIP You can also create a duplicate by holding down the Ctrl key while dragging a shape.

Rearranging Drawing Objects

To rearrange your drawing objects, you can use the Draw button. You can select the object that you want to move behind or in front of other objects and select Draw, Order. You can then select Bring to Front, Send to Back, Bring Forward, Send Backward to adjust its order in the stack.

FIG. 27.21

Save time creating complex duplicate objects by pasting from the Clipboard or dragging the object while holding the Ctrl key.

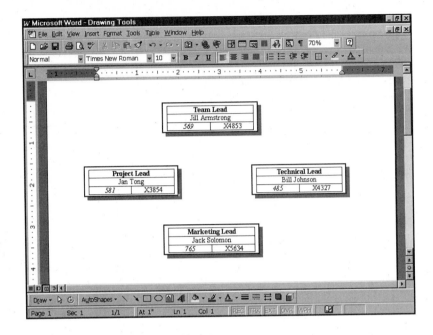

Grouping, Ungrouping, and Regrouping Objects

In creating a drawing, you may often want to format or edit many objects at once. Instead of having to select each object over again every time you want to make a change in all of them, you can group them so they all behave as if they were part of the same object. When you have your shapes arranged the way you want them, you can select all of the shapes that need to be treated as one drawing and select Draw, Group. When you group objects, their individual handles will disappear and the entire group will have eight sizing handles.

When you group objects, there will be times when you need to make a change to an individual shape in a group. You can always use the Ungrouping option. If you need to change one shape of a group, you can select the grouped object. Then you can select Draw, Ungroup. Each shape will have its own set of sizing handles. You can select the shape and make any necessary changes.

The Regroup option can be used to regroup objects that have been grouped and ungrouped. With the object selected, select Draw, Regroup. All of the objects that were previously grouped will revert back to being part of that group. If you add an object, you will need to reselect the group and select Draw Group.

Moving Drawings Below or Above the Text

There are times that your graphic may be used as a background for your text. You can take advantage of the layers of your document. When you create your drawing, it is placed in the layer above the text. There is also the layer with the text and one behind it. You can select your drawing objects and place them behind the text by selecting Draw, Order, Send Behind Text (see Figure 27.22). You can also bring it back in front by selecting Draw, Order, Bring In Front of Text.

FIG. 27.22
The shapes are behind the text.

Controlling Text Wrap Around Your Drawing Objects

If you do not want your drawing to be on top of or behind your text, you will need to determine how the text will wrap around the drawing. The way text wraps around your drawing has changed in Word 97. In the past, you had to put your drawing inside of a frame to have it in the text layer. That restriction has been eliminated. For every drawing object, you can use the Format AutoShape dialog box to control text wrapping. To use it:

1. Select the drawing object or objects.
2. Point to the selected object or objects and right-click.
3. Select Format AutoShape.
4. Select the Wrapping tab, where you can specify how your text will wrap around (or through) your graphic.

Part
VI

Ch
27

The way that text can wrap around graphic elements has been improved. You can now select a Wrapping Style which includes a new Tight style to fit around the edges of the drawing objects rather than form a box around the graphic (see Figure 27.23). You can also select a side to Wrap To and how much distance you want between the text and graphic. With these wrapping improvements, you have greater control over the layout of your page.

FIG. 27.23

The paragraph text wraps around the arrow rather than forming a rectangle around the arrow.

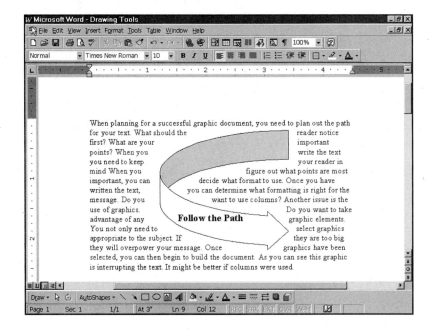

CHAPTER 28

Inserting Text with Special Effects

You see examples of words used as graphics every day: pull quotes in magazines lighten a page of text and attract attention to important points; logos turn words into symbols that you recognize without even reading; decorated words embellish the mastheads in newsletters; and special text effects add interest to advertisements.

With WordArt, you can turn ordinary words into graphics. You can pour text into a shape, flip or stretch letters, condense or expand letter spacing, rotate or angle words, or add shading, colors, borders, or shadows to text. By combining your text with WordArt effects and other graphic tools, you can create hundreds of interesting designs.

You can use WordArt with a mouse or your keyboard—either way, you can create great graphics.

Figure 28.1 shows some examples of finished WordArt objects. ■

Add a WordArt object

When you want to add special effects with WordArt, you will have to add a WordArt object and enter the text to be used.

Apply text treatments such as fonts, styles, and sizes

Once the object is in place in your document, you can work with different attributes to change the look of the text for the object.

Apply special effects such as rotation, slanting, shaping, and arcing

You can also work with the object's position to adjust the effect.

Apply colors, borders, and shading

You can change the color of the letters, its 3-D effect, as well as add special borders and fill the letters with interesting patterns and shading.

Apply typographic aids such as aligning and adjusting character spacing

One way to change the look of text is to adjust the amount of space between characters, as well as the alignment of your text.

FIG. 28.1
WordArt can create
many different graphic
effects.

FIG. 28.1
WordArt can create
many different graphic
effects.

What You Need to Know About WordArt

WordArt used to be an OLE-based, add-in program. With Word 97, WordArt has become more closely integrated into the Office package as part of the drawing tools. You can add and edit WordArt objects easily with the new WordArt toolbar. WordArt offers many new styles and formatting options for your text.

Creating a WordArt Object

The process of creating WordArt for your document has changed with Word 97. In the past, you were required to insert a WordArt object and work with it separately. Follow these steps to create a WordArt object:

1. Select the WordArt button from the Drawing or WordArt toolbar or choose Insert, Picture, WordArt. The WordArt Gallery opens.

2. Select a WordArt style (see Figure 28.2) and select OK.

3. Enter your text, make any font or attribute setting changes for the WordArt object, and select OK (see Figure 28.3).

FIG. 28.2
The WordArt Gallery allows you to select from some template styles for your WordArt object.

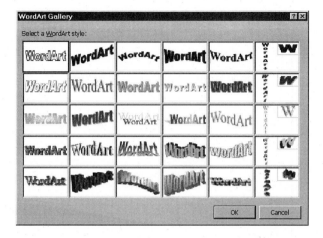

FIG. 28.3
The WordArt Text dialog box is where you enter the text that you want to enhance.

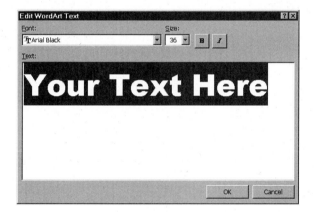

At this point, the WordArt object is placed in your document at the position of your insertion point. You can then treat it like any other drawing object or picture. It behaves the same as other drawing objects. You insert it at the insertion point, and the object moves with the text that surrounds it. You can use many of the drawing format choices to modify the original design. There is also the special WordArt toolbar with some additional formatting features.

▶ **See** "Inserting Pictures into a Document," **p. 813**
▶ **See** "Using the Drawing Tools," **p. 897**
▶ **See** "Managing Your Drawing," **p. 917**

Because WordArt graphics are based on text, you also have access to most text formatting tools, like fonts. Windows comes with some fonts, such as Arial and Times New Roman. Your printer may contain other fonts, and you can purchase additional fonts to install on your computer. Any font installed on your computer is available for use in WordArt.

Part
VI

Ch
28

> **CAUTION**
>
> WordArt will not recognize Postscript fonts.

▶ **See** "Formatting Characters and Changing Fonts," **p. 283**

Understanding WordArt's Commands, Lists, and Buttons

Once the WordArt object is created, you can modify its special effects. WordArt's special effects are available through commands in the Word menus and through lists and buttons on the WordArt toolbar. Table 28.1 describes the unique commands and buttons contained in WordArt. WordArt's commands and buttons are described in detail later in this chapter, in the "Adding Special Effects" section.

Table 28.1   WordArt Commands and Buttons

Menu Command	List or Button	Description
Insert, Picture, WordArt		Opens the WordArt Gallery to WordArt and begins the process of inserting a WordArt object.
	Edit Text...	Opens the Edit WordArt Text dialog box to edit the text for the WordArt object.
		Opens the WordArt Gallery for an existing WordArt object for modifications.
Format, WordArt		Opens the Format WordArt dialog box to set up the WordArt options.
	Abc	Opens up a palette to select the WordArt Shape.
		Activates the Free Rotate function. It changes the mouse pointer into the rotate pointer and changes the sizing handles for the object into the rotate handles.
	Aa	Stretches the lowercase letter's height to match that of the uppercase letter's.
	Ab b	Toggles the text between a horizontal and vertical arrangement.
		Opens the WordArt alignment menu.
	AV	Opens the WordArt Character spacing menu.

Adding Special Effects

When you add a special effect to a WordArt image, the image changes immediately, and you instantly see the result of each effect you choose. You can experiment with different effects and get quick feedback about how they look. If you decide you do not like an effect, you can use Undo or select another special effect.

You can add many different types of special effects to create a WordArt image. You can combine the effects to develop a look of your own. All the effects apply to the text rather than to the border or background of the text. Figure 28.4 shows just a few of the special effects you can achieve with WordArt.

FIG. 28.4
You can create many special effects with WordArt.

What You Need to Know About WordArt Effects

The effects you apply in WordArt apply to all the text in the dialog box. You cannot apply an effect to just a few of the letters in the dialog box.

 TIP If you need to differentiate formatting for a text phrase, you can use more than one WordArt object and place them next to one another.

Choosing some of the commands or buttons displays a dialog box from which you make selections. To remove the effect, choose the same command or button and select a

Part
VI

Ch
28

different option. The WordArt toolbar has most of the functions needed to customize the look of your WordArt object.

Editing the Text

 The second button on the WordArt toolbar is the Edit Text button. You can change the text of the object at any time without disturbing your formatting. To change the text, select the WordArt object and select the Edit Text button from the toolbar. The Edit WordArt Text dialog box opens (refer to Figure 28.3). You can change the font, size, and font style as well as change the text.

The restrictions of the WordArt object are that it cannot exceed the size of a page, and it starts as a 2-inch wide rectangle, but can resize to hold your text. You can add any text and punctuation. It can also accept a carriage return to break it into multiple lines. In fact, several of the styles expect carriage returns like the Button (Pour) shape of the "Shapes and Patterns" example in Figure 28.4.

Selecting a WordArt Style from the Gallery

With WordArt in Office 97, the first step is to select a style from the WordArt Gallery. There are some built-in formats for your WordArt objects. This is always the starting point. You may not find the one that is exactly right for your situation, but try to select the one that will require the least amount of modifications.

 Keep in mind that if you select something in the Gallery, you do not have to make modifications to it if it turns out the results were not even close to your expectations. Select the WordArt Gallery button from the WordArt toolbar and select another style.

Once you have an acceptable style from the gallery, you can start to customize it. You can change the text, its options, its shape, rotation, letter contrast, and arrangement, as well as alignment and character spacing.

Formatting the WordArt Object

 The Format WordArt button on the toolbar opens the Format WordArt dialog box, which is identical to the Format AutoShape dialog box except that only some of the options are available. You have access to the Colors and Lines, Size, Position, and Wrapping tabs.

▶ **See** "Formatting Your Shapes," **p. 903**

The Colors and Lines tab allows you to modify the fill color of the letters of the WordArt object. You can select a color from the drop-down list; your choices are identical to the Fill Color palette for all other objects. You can fill with a color on the palette or select More Colors to create one of your own. You could also select Fill Effects to add a gradient, texture, pattern, or picture fill. You can also change the color, style, and weight of the letter borders.

The Size tab allows you to change the height, width, and rotation of the object. You can also control its scale and aspect ratio to determine its proportion. The Position tab controls the placement of the WordArt object in relation to the document, and the Wrapping tab controls how normal text will wrap around the WordArt object.

Shaping the Text

By applying one special WordArt effect—pouring your text into a shape—you can create an interesting sign or logo. WordArt's toolbar includes a Shapes list that displays a grid of different shapes (see Figure 28.5). When you select one of these shapes, the text in the Enter Your Text Here dialog box "pours" into that shape.

Some shapes produce different results, depending on the number of lines of text you are shaping. The circle shape, for example, turns a single line of text into a circle, but turns multiple lines of text into concentric circles. The button shape turns three lines into a button, but turns a single line into an arch. Experiment to get the result you want.

FIG. 28.5
By selecting one of these shapes, you can create an interesting sign or logo.

Adding Additional Text Formatting

The remaining five buttons on the WordArt toolbar adjust the letter height and direction of the text as well as change alignment and spacing. They give you some alternatives to regular text formatting.

 The first button is the Free Rotate button. This duplicates the Free Rotate button on the Drawing toolbar. This allows you use one of the rotation handles and change the direction of the object.

 The second button allows you to adjust the character height of the WordArt object. Most fonts' lowercase letters are approximately 50 percent the height of the uppercase letters. You may want to try to change the effect by using the WordArt Same Letter Heights. Regardless of whether text is upper or lowercase, each letter will be the same height (see Figure 28.6). If you decide you do not like the effect, you can change it. To remove the effect, select the WordArt Same Letter Height button again.

Part
VI

Ch
28

FIG. 28.6
WordArt Same Letter Height can be used to modify the top border of the shape.

The third button is the WordArt Vertical Text button. This button takes text and arranges it vertically (see Figure 28.7). If this effect doesn't appeal to you, it can also be removed by selecting the button again.

FIG. 28.7
The WordArt Vertical Text button will take the text and arrange it vertically.

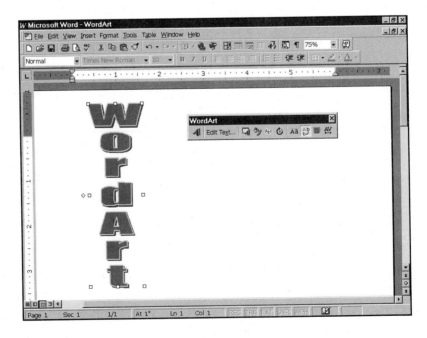

The next button is the WordArt Alignment button. It controls the alignment of the text inside of the object. You can align the text using Left Align, Center, Right Align, Word Justify, Letter Justify, and Stretch Justify. Each style in the Gallery has a default alignment.

 The last button is WordArt Character Spacing. It controls the amount of white space in between the letters. This functions like the Format Paragraph function for regular text. When you select it, a menu pops up to allow you to determine how close together the letters will be.

Using the Draw Toolbar

When the WordArt object is created, it can be treated like any other drawing object. You can take advantage of the functions available on the Drawing toolbar. For example, you can flip, rotate, copy, paste, nudge, and order WordArt with the Draw button on the Drawing toolbar. For additional information on the functions of the Drawing toolbar, refer to Chapter 27, "Drawing with Word's Drawing Tools." ●

CHAPTER 29

Graphing Data

With Microsoft Graph, you can create informative and impressive charts for your Word documents. You can turn an overwhelming table of numbers into a chart that shows important trends and changes. You can relegate the detailed numeric table to a location where it doesn't slow down communication. Microsoft Graph is not just a small charting "applet;" it is the same charting application used by Microsoft Excel, the most capable Windows spreadsheet/graphics program.

Microsoft Graph is a separate program that embeds charts and their data into Windows applications such as Microsoft Word.

Charts embedded into a Word 97 document contain both the chart and the data that creates the chart. You cannot save the chart or data separately. ■

Create charts

Word supports a number of methods for getting the data used to create a chart. Once the data is created, select a chart type or custom-design a chart type.

Edit charts

You can replace or edit existing data, insert and delete rows and columns, and include or exclude data.

Add items, such as legends and titles, to a chart

You can add titles, axes, gridlines, legends, data labels, and the data table to a chart.

Change the chart type

You can use the two or more subtypes that each standard chart type contains. You can also select from a list of custom built-in chart types or define your own.

Change the size of a chart

You can change the size of a chart by moving the black handles that appear around the chart after selecting it.

Format datasheets

You can select different number and date formats to use in your datasheets.

Creating a Chart

Charts are created from data on the worksheet or data entered into a *datasheet*, which is a spreadsheet-like view of the data displayed in rows and columns in its own window. Figure 29.1 shows a Word document with a chart from Microsoft Graph.

FIG. 29.1

You can use a chart to enhance a Word document.

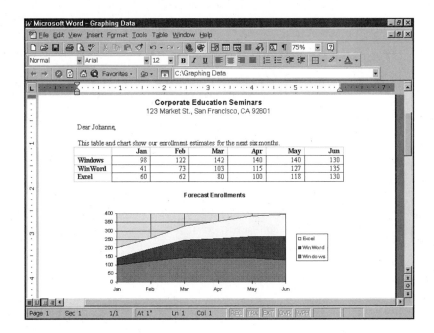

Microsoft Graph enables you to create 14 standard chart types in Word, using any of several methods. The custom chart types in Word 97 give you additional selections. Text and numbers can be entered into the datasheet in any of the following ways:

- Selected from a table in the Word document
- Typed into Microsoft Graph
- Copied in from any Windows document
- Imported from an Excel, Lotus 1-2-3, or text file
- Read in from an existing Excel chart

There are two equally valid ways of starting Microsoft Graph. To start Microsoft Graph, follow these steps:

1. If you want to enter only a chart in the document and keep the data in a Microsoft

Graph datasheet, then position the insertion point where you want the chart to appear in your document.

or

If you want to create a chart from a table of data on the worksheet, position the insertion point in the table, then select the table by choosing Table, Select Table.

2. Choose Insert, Picture, Chart.

   or

   Choose Insert, Object, and select the Create New tab in the Object dialog box. Select Microsoft Graph 97 from the list in the Object Type list box.

3. Choose OK.

   Microsoft Graph opens in the active document window, with default data in the datasheet and chart (see Figure 29.2). The chart reflects the data in the sample datasheet. The Microsoft Graph Standard and Formatting toolbars display.

FIG. 29.2
When Microsoft Graph is open, the Word toolbars disappear and the Microsoft Graph Standard and Formatting toolbars appear.

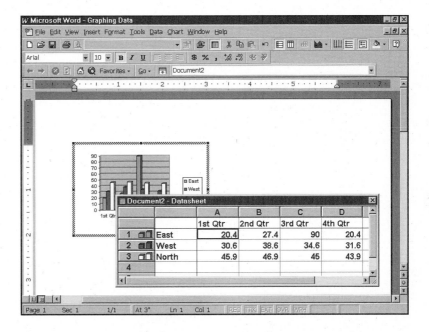

NOTE You can add the Insert Chart button to the toolbar with Tools, Customize. A chart cannot be active to do the following procedure. Select the Commands tab from the Customize dialog box. Then select Insert from the Categories box. Click Chart in the Commands list, and drag it onto the toolbar. Click Close. Click the Insert Chart button on the toolbar to start Microsoft Graph.

You can change the data in the Microsoft Graph datasheet in many ways. Select and change the data in the datasheet to change the chart. You can also add or remove chart items, such as legends, arrows, and titles, or change the appearance or position of selected chart items or data in the sheet.

When you are finished making changes, click outside the border surrounding the chart to return to your document. Microsoft Graph closes and the Word toolbar reappears.

Using the Microsoft Graph Datasheet

Microsoft Graph can plot data that is in a table in the document or from data that is on a Microsoft Graph datasheet. The Microsoft Graph datasheet does not show in the document.

Microsoft Graph plots data points as *markers* in the chart. Markers appear as lines, bars, columns, data points in X-Y charts, or slices in a pie chart. With the Microsoft Graph default settings, a row of data points appears in a chart as a *series* of markers; a series of values appears in the chart connected by a line, or as bars or columns of the same color. In Figure 29.3, for example, the row labeled East corresponds to one line in the 3-D line chart.

FIG. 29.3

By default, each row of data translates to a series of data points in the chart.

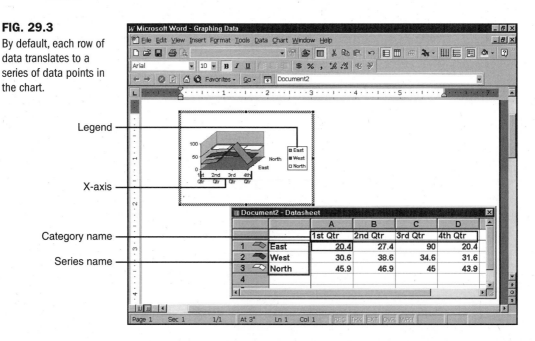

In this default orientation, known as Series in Rows, the text in the first row of the datasheet becomes the *category names* that appear below the *category (X) axis*

(the horizontal axis). The text in the left column becomes the *series names*, which Microsoft Graph uses as labels for the legend. (The *legend* is the box that labels the colors or patterns used by each series of markers.) If you change orientation and want to return to the default orientation, choose Data, Series In Rows.

If your data uses the reverse orientation on the datasheet, so that each data series goes down a column, you must choose Data, Series In Columns. When you use that command, Microsoft Graph takes the category names (x-axis labels) from the left column of the datasheet and the series names (legend labels) from the top row (see Figure 29.4).

FIG. 29.4

A data series can show column orientation.

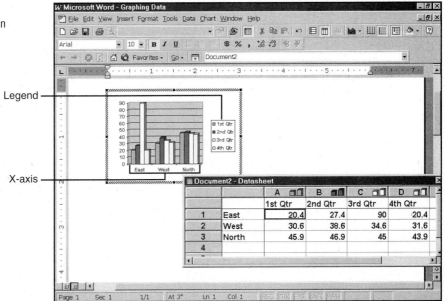

When you create a Microsoft Graph chart, be sure that you have text for each series name (legend labels), text for each category label (x-axis), and a number for each data point.

Creating Charts from Data in a Document   You can create a chart from a series of text and numbers organized in a table or aligned on tabs in Word.

Data can be in a Word table or separated by tabs. Tables are the easiest to use and edit. If you use tabs to work with data, make your work easier by using right tabs to separate data and setting all tab stops so that data aligns. Figure 29.5 shows a Word document with the data and labels separated by right-aligned tabs.

Copying Data into the Microsoft Graph Datasheet   To copy data from a Word document or Excel worksheet for use in a chart, follow these steps:

FIG. 29.5
In most cases you will find tables easier to use, but you can use data separated by tabs to create a chart.

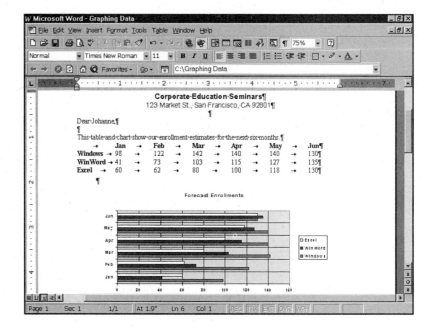

1. Select the tab-separated data, cells in a table, or range of Excel cells.

2. Choose Edit, Copy.

3. Position the insertion point where you want the chart to appear; choose Insert, Object. Select Microsoft Graph 97 from the list and then choose OK.

4. Activate the datasheet and erase all existing data by selecting it and choosing Edit, Clear, All or by pressing the Delete key.

 TIP You can select the entire datasheet by clicking the Select All button located at the top-left intersection of the column and row headings.

5. Ensure that the top-left cell in the datasheet is selected and then choose Edit, Paste.

   The data is pasted into the datasheet, and the chart updates.

6. Format, modify, or size the chart and datasheet as necessary.

7. Click outside the chart to return to the document.

   The chart is inserted into the Word document at the insertion point.

Importing Worksheet or Text Data You may want to use data from an ASCII text file or data that you have in an Excel or Lotus 1-2-3 worksheet for a chart. You can save time by importing this data directly into the Microsoft Graph datasheet.

To import data into the datasheet, follow these steps:

1. Start Microsoft Graph.

2. Choose Edit, Import File or click the Import File button. Find and select the file from which you want to import data from the Import File dialog box, then click the Open button. The Import Data Options dialog box appears (see Figure 29.6).

FIG. 29.6
The Import Data
Options dialog box.

3. Specify Entire File or Range to indicate a range, such as A12:D36, or a range name in the Import group. (Refer to your spreadsheet program for information on naming a range.) Select Overwrite Existing Cells if you want to overwrite all existing cells.

4. Choose OK.

To import data from a worksheet, you must have the worksheet converter files loaded. If they are not loaded, run the Word or Microsoft Office Setup program. Select the options to install the converters you choose without reinstalling all of Word. You must use your original Word or Microsoft Office installation disk to load the converters.

Importing a Microsoft Excel Chart   With Excel, you can create mathematical models that generate charts, and you can link the charts to Word documents. If you change the Excel worksheet that contains your mathematical model, you change the chart. These changes are reflected in the Word document.

▶ **See** "Linking Documents and Files," **p. 1091**

Importing an Excel chart into Microsoft Graph to embed the chart into the Word document has other advantages. Because embedded charts keep the data with the chart, another person can update the chart without using Excel or the original Excel worksheet. Links are not broken if the source worksheet or chart in Excel is renamed or moved to a different folder.

▶ **See** " Embedding Data," **p. 1085**

To import an Excel chart sheet into a Word document and the chart's related data, follow these steps:

1. Position the insertion point where you want the chart to appear in the document; start Microsoft Graph 97.

2. Choose Edit, Import File. The Import File dialog box appears.

3. Select the drive, folder, and file name of the Excel file and then choose Open. The Import Data Options dialog box appears (see Figure 29.6).

4. Select the chart sheet containing the chart from the Select Sheet from Workbook list.

5. Choose OK.

The chart opens in Microsoft Graph, and the associated data appears in the datasheet. Data series that were in rows in Excel are in columns in the Microsoft Graph datasheet, but the chart is correct.

Entering Data to Create Overlay Charts

Overlay charts overlay one two-dimensional chart type with another. (You cannot overlay 3-D chart types.) By overlaying chart types, you can emphasize the relationships among different types of data or data with widely different scales.

To overlay a chart with one data series over a chart of other data series, select the data series you want as a different chart type. For example, in a column chart, click one of the columns in the series you want to overlay. Choose Chart, Chart Type. Select the type of chart you want for this data series, then choose OK.

TIP

While you are in the Chart Type dialog box, you can click and hold on the Press and Hold to View Sample button to see a preview of how your overlay charts will appear.

To add a secondary axis for that data series, select the series in the chart and choose Format, Selected Data Series. Select the Axis tab, then select the Secondary axis option, and choose OK. The secondary axis can be formatted separately from the primary axis, so, for example, you can adjust the scale on this axis to match the data it represents.

TROUBLESHOOTING

Sometimes the Selected Data Series does not show on the Format menu. Make sure you have selected the data series and not the chart area, axis, or some other chart element. The data series are the columns, bars, pie wedges, and so forth.

The Axis tab appears in the Format Data Series dialog box, but the options are grayed. The axis tab only appears when you select a data series that can have a secondary axis. For example, a secondary axis is not used by a pie chart.

Editing the Datasheet

Working in the datasheet is similar to working in a Word table or an Excel worksheet. You can edit cellular data directly in a cell or in an editing box.

Selecting Data

To move and select cells in the datasheet, you use many of the same techniques used in Excel. If you are using a mouse, you can use the scroll bars to scroll to any location on the datasheet. You can select parts of the datasheet by using the following methods:

- To select a cell, click it.
- To select multiple cells, drag the mouse across them.
- To select a row or column, click its header.
- To select multiple rows or columns, drag across the headers.
- To select all cells in the datasheet, click in the blank rectangle at the top-left corner where row and column headings intersect.

 T I P Select the entire worksheet contents and press Delete to erase the entire worksheet.

If you are using the keyboard, use the keys shown in the following tables to move the insertion point, or to select cells and their contents:

To Move	Press
A cell	Arrow key in the direction to move
To first cell in row	Home
To last cell in row	End
To top-left data cell	Ctrl+Home
To lower-right data cell	Ctrl+End
A screen up/down	Page Up/Down

To Select	Press
A cell	Arrow key to cell you want
A range (rectangle) of cells	Shift+arrow key or F8 (enters Extend mode). Arrow key, and then F8 (exits Extend mode).
A row	Shift+spacebar

continues

(continued)

To Select	Press
A column	Ctrl+spacebar
The datasheet	Shift+Ctrl+spacebar, or Ctrl+A
Undo selection	Shift+Backspace

Replacing or Editing Existing Data

The easiest way to replace the contents of a cell is to select the cell by moving to it or by clicking it, and then typing directly over the cell's contents. When you press Enter or select a different cell, the change takes effect.

To edit the contents of a cell, select the cell by moving to it or by clicking it. Press F2 (the Edit key) or double-click the cell. You can edit the cell's contents as you would edit text in a document. After you finish editing, press Enter.

Inserting or Deleting Rows and Columns

Microsoft Graph can expand a chart to include data or text you add in rows or columns outside the originally charted data. If you add rows or columns of data and leave blank rows or columns, Microsoft Graph does not include the blank rows or columns as part of the chart.

To insert rows or columns in the datasheet, select the rows or columns you want to insert and then choose Insert, Cells. Rows or columns are inserted, depending on what you selected. To delete rows or columns, select what you want to delete and choose Edit, Delete. The shortcut keys for inserting and deleting are Ctrl++ (plus) and Ctrl+– (minus), respectively. (Use the plus and minus keys on the numeric keypad only.) If you do not select an entire row or column, a dialog box appears and asks you to select whether you want to affect the rows or columns that pass through the selected cells.

Including and Excluding Data from a Chart

When you add data or text to the datasheet, Microsoft Graph immediately redraws the chart, even if the data you've added is not adjacent to other data in the table. This redrawing is inconvenient if you want to add a row or column of data to the table, but not include the data in the chart.

To include or exclude a row or column with the mouse, double-click the row or column heading. The double-click toggles the row or column between being included and being excluded. Excluded rows or columns are grayed.

To include or exclude a row or column with the keyboard, select the entire row or column and then choose Data, Include Row/Col or choose Data, Exclude Row/Col.

Changing Data by Moving a Graph Marker

Microsoft Graph enables you to move column, bar, lines, or X-Y markers on 2-D charts. As you move the data point, the corresponding data changes in the datasheet—a convenient feature for smoothing a curve so that it matches real-life experience or for "fudging" numbers so that they fit the results you want.

To change values on the datasheet by moving markers on the chart, follow these steps:

1. Open the worksheet and chart. Activate the chart. The chart must be a two-dimensional column, bar, or line chart.

2. Click the column, bar, or line marker you want to change one time to select the data series; then click it a second time to select the data point. A black handle appears on the marker.

3. Drag the black handle to the new height. When you drag the black handle, a tick mark on the vertical axis moves, showing you the value of the new location.

4. Release the mouse when the marker is at the location you want.

The corresponding data in the datasheet changes.

▶ **See** "Selecting Text," **p. 156**

▶ **See** "Moving, Copying, and Linking Text or Graphics," **p. 185**

Changing the Chart Type

When Microsoft Graph first opens, the chart it displays is a 3-D column chart. Many different chart types are available. You select the chart type appropriate for the data you want to graph.

 TIP You can change the default chart that Microsoft Graph first displays by selecting a chart type from the Chart Type dialog box, then clicking the Set As Default Chart button.

Try to choose the appropriate chart type before you begin customizing. To change the chart type after you customize, follow the procedure described in the "Customizing an Existing Chart Type" section, later in this chapter.

Selecting the Original Chart Type

When you build charts, you can use any of the predefined chart formats. The easiest way to create charts is to select the predefined chart that most closely resembles the type of chart you want. Then you can customize the predefined chart until it fits your needs.

To use a predefined chart, follow these steps:

1. Choose Chart, Chart Type. The Chart Type dialog box appears (see Figure 29.7).

FIG. 29.7
To select the chart type you want from the Chart Type dialog box, double-click an example.

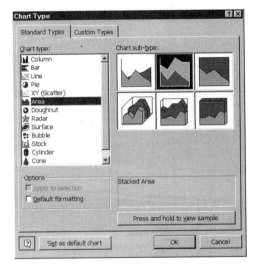

2. Select the type of chart from the Chart Type list.

3. Click a chart type from the Chart Sub-Type samples.

4. Choose the Custom Types tab to see custom chart types. You can design your own chart types and view them here by clicking the User-defined selection. The Built-in selection displays a list of custom chart types (see Figure 29.8).

5. Choose OK.

Customizing an Existing Chart Type

You can save yourself work by deciding on the type of chart you want before you customize it. Use the Chart, Chart Type command or click the Chart Type button to try different types of charts; then customize the one you decide to use. If you change the chart type after you customize a chart, you may lose some of your custom selections.

FIG. 29.8
The Custom Types tab displays built-in custom-designed and user-defined chart types.

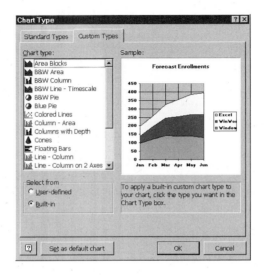

To customize a chart type, follow these steps:

1. Activate the chart and choose Chart, Chart Type or click the Chart Type button. The Chart Type dialog box appears.

2. Select a chart type from the Chart Type group and then select the subtype from the Chart Sub-Type group.

3. Click OK.

4. Choose Chart, Chart Options to display the Chart Options dialog box (see Figure 29.9). The options available are appropriate for the type of chart that is active. They include titles, axes, gridlines, legend, data labels, and data table, which displays the data table with the chart.

FIG. 29.9
Use the Chart Options dialog box to change titles, axes, gridlines, legends, data labels, and whether or not to display the data table with the chart.

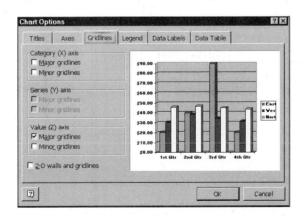

5. Choose OK.

6. Choose Chart, Add Trendline to display the Add Trendline dialog box. Add a linear, logarithmic, polynomial, power, exponential, or moving average trend line to a data series. The Add Trendline option is only available with certain types of charts (for example, an XY (Scatter) chart).

Formatting the Datasheet

The proper formatting of your datasheet is important for reasons other than ensuring the ease and accuracy of data entry. The format of dates and numbers in the datasheet controls the format of dates and numbers in the chart.

 In Microsoft Graph, the datasheet disappears when you are editing the chart. To display to datasheet, choose View, Datasheet; or click the View Datasheet button.

Adjusting Column Widths in the Datasheet

Depending on the number format of a cell, when a number is too large to fit in a cell, the cell may fill with # signs. To adjust column width with the mouse, move the pointer over the line separating the column headings until the pointer changes to a two-headed arrow. Drag the column separator line to the column width you want and release the mouse button.

To adjust column width with the keyboard, select cells in the columns you want to adjust and then choose Format, Column Width. The Column Width dialog box appears. Type a number representing the width of the column and then choose OK.

You can return column widths to their standard setting by choosing the Use Standard Width check box in the Column Width dialog box. Choose Best Fit to set the column to the minimum width required to display the current cell contents. You must change it again later if you change the cell contents.

 TIP   Double-click the right border of the column heading to set the column to the minimum width required to display the widest entry in the column.

Formatting Numbers and Dates

Microsoft Graph 97 has many predefined numeric and date formats. You can choose from these formats to format the datasheet and chart or to create your own custom formats.

You can enter a date such as **12-24-97** as a label for a category axis. You can then format the cell with a different date format (such as **d-mmm** so that the date appears as 24-Dec).

To format data cells, follow these steps:

1. Select the data cell or range you want to format. You can select entire rows or columns at one time.
2. Choose Format, Number to display the Format Number dialog box.
3. Select the type of numeric format you want from the Category list.
4. Select type of formatting you want from the options on the right side of the dialog box. These options change depending upon the numeric format type you select from the Category list. Watch the Sample area at the top of the dialog box to preview how the data will appear.
5. Choose OK.

The following table gives examples of the different formats:

Format	Entry	Result
#,###	9999.00	9,999
#,###.00	9999.5	9,999.50
$#,###	9000.65	$9,001
0.00 ;(0.00)	5.6	5.60
0.00 ;(0.00)	-9.834	(9.83)
mmm	12	Dec
dd	6	06
yy	1991	91
hh:mm AM/PM	6:12	06:12 AM

You can also use the Currency Style, Percent Style, Comma Style, Increase Decimal, and Decrease Decimal icons to format numbers.

Adding Items to a Chart

You can make your Microsoft Graph 97 charts more informative and easier to read by adding items such as titles, legends, and arrows.

Adding elements to an existing Microsoft Graph 97 chart in a Word document is easy. With a mouse, click the chart. After the chart is selected, choose Edit, Chart Object, Edit.

Microsoft Graph opens and loads the chart, after which you can use any of the procedures described in this chapter to modify your chart or data. If the datasheet is not open, choose View, Datasheet or click the View Datasheet button.

When you select an item that you've added to your chart—a title, for example—black handles appear around the item and you can move or resize it.

Adding Titles and Data Values

You can use the Chart Options menu to add or delete most items to or from a chart. To add a title or data label to a fixed location on a chart, for example, follow these steps:

1. Choose Chart, Chart Options. The Chart Options dialog box appears (see Figure 29.10).

FIG. 29.10
The Chart Options dialog box allows you to choose from several different kinds of titles.

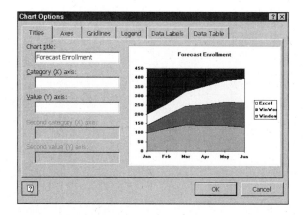

2. Type a title in the Chart Title text box to add a title to the chart.

3. Type a title in the Category (X) axis text box to add a title to the X axis.

4. Type a title in the Value (Y) axis text box to add a title to the Y axis.

5. Type a title in the Second category (X) axis text box to add a title to the X axis of the second category.

6. Type a title in the Second value (Y) axis text box to add a title to the Y axis of the second value.

7. Choose OK.

8. Type the title text you want to use while that default title is selected. Press Tab to move to a second line. Edit using normal editing keys.

9. Click OK.

To remove fixed text, select the text and then press the Delete key or choose Edit, Clear, All.

To attach numbers or labels that move with the data point in a bar, column, or line chart, follow these steps:

1. Choose Chart, Chart Options then select the Data Labels tab.
2. Select the Show Value or Show Label option. If you are working with a pie chart, the Show Percent and Show Label And Percent options are available.
3. Choose OK.

To delete data point values or labels, select them and press Delete, or choose Chart, Chart Options; then select the Data Labels tab and select None.

Adding Floating Text

You can use *floating text* to add comment boxes or to create boxes for embellishing or covering parts of a chart.

To add floating text, make sure that no other text is selected and then type the text. You don't have to choose a command; just type and then press Esc. Your text appears in a floating box. To move or resize the box, click it to display the black handles. Then resize the box or drag it by grabbing the hatch border that surrounds it to a new location. You can also select some or all of the text and format it.

To use the keyboard to select text for formatting, hold down the Shift key while you press the arrow keys until the text is highlighted in reverse video. You cannot use the keyboard to move floating text.

To edit the text in a floating text box, click the text to select it and then click where you want the insertion point. If you are using the keyboard, you must retype the text. To delete a floating text box, select the text and then press the Delete key.

Adding Legends, Arrows, Gridlines, Trendlines, and Error Bars

 To add a legend, choose Chart, Chart Options; then select the Legend tab or click the Legend button. To move a legend, select it, choose Format, Selected Legend, and select the Placement tab. Choose an option in the Type group and choose OK. Or drag the legend to a new location and release it.

To change the labels in the legend, change the series labels in the datasheet.

To add arrows to your charts, choose View, Toolbars, select the Drawing toolbar, and choose OK (see Figure 29.11). Use the Arrow tool to place an arrow in your chart. Arrows have black handles at either end so that you can resize them. To move an arrow, drag with the pointer on the arrow's shaft.

FIG. 29.11

Choose View, Toolbars to display any or all of the toolbars available in Microsoft Graph 97.

 To add gridlines to a chart, choose Chart, Chart Options; then select the Gridlines tab. The Gridlines check boxes select major and minor vertical (Y) and horizontal (X) gridlines. To delete gridlines, clear the check boxes for the gridlines you don't want. You can also click the Category Axis Gridlines and Value Axis Gridlines buttons on the Standard toolbar.

To add axes, choose Chart, Chart Options; then select the Axes tab. In the Axes tab, you control whether an axis is visible. A check mark in the box indicates that the axis will display.

Trendlines indicate direction in a data series. With Microsoft Graph 97, you can add trendlines to data series in area, bar, column, line, and XY (Scatter) chart groups. (Check Microsoft Graph's Help for information about the types of trendlines from which you can select, and how to do it.) You can add a trendline by choosing Chart, Add Trendline.

Formatting the Chart and Chart Items

After you select a predefined chart format and add chart items, you can customize your chart. You can change the colors, patterns, and borders of chart items; the type and color of the fonts; the position and size of some chart items. In addition, you can add lines, arrows, titles, legends, and floating text. By selecting an axis and then a format command, you can change the scale and the appearance of tick marks and labels. You also can rotate 3-D charts and create picture charts, in which pictures or patterns take the place of columns, bars, lines, or backgrounds.

Customize charts by selecting an item in the chart and then by choosing a format command, as described in the following steps:

1. Select the chart item you want to customize by clicking it or by pressing an arrow key until the chart item is selected.

2. Choose the Format menu and a formatting command to format the item. A dialog box appears that provides choices for the type of formatting you want to apply or change.

3. Select the changes you want to make from the dialog box.

4. Choose OK.

As a shortcut, you can double-click any chart item—such as an arrow, bar, or chart background—to produce that item's Format dialog box. You can choose from several tabs, which vary depending on the item you selected. Each tab contains many options for formatting each item on a chart.

Sizing Your Chart

Charts look best in Word if you resize them in Microsoft Graph. Resizing the chart in Word changes the size, maintains proper text placement, readjusts the scale, and so on.

Change the size of the chart as you would change the size of any window. You can drag its borders or corners with the mouse. Make the chart's window the size you want the chart to be when you paste it into the Word document.

Changing Patterns and Colors

 To add patterns or colors to an item, select the item, choose Format, and the command for that item at the top of the menu; then select the colors, patterns, shading, and line widths you want for the item. Double-click an item to display the item's Format dialog box or click the Fill Color button in the Standard toolbar. You can also press Ctrl+1 to open the Format dialog box for the selected item.

To return to the default colors, patterns, and borders, select the chart items you want to change, right-click the items, and choose the appropriate Format command; then select the Automatic option for the specific item in the Format dialog box.

Formatting Fonts and Text

Every datasheet is formatted with a single font, size, and style. You can use a different font, size, or style, however, for each text item in the chart.

To change an item's font, size, or style, select the item and then choose Format, Font. Select a font, size, or style. Double-click the item and then choose the Font tab. The Font tab of the Format dialog box looks like other Font dialog boxes in Word. It enables you to select from three types of character backgrounds:

- Automatic applies an opaque background if the color beneath the text matches the text color; otherwise, it applies a transparent background.
- Transparent makes the area behind the chart text transparent.
- Opaque applies a solid color behind the chart text.

To rotate or align text, such as the text on an axis, double-click the axis to display the Format Axis dialog box. Click the Alignment tab, select the text orientation you want, and choose OK.

Formatting Axes

Microsoft Graph automatically scales and labels the axes, but you can select any axis and change its patterns, scale, font, number format, or alignment.

To format an axis, follow these steps:

1. Double-click the axis you want to format.

   Or select the axis you want to format and choose Format, Selected Axis. The Format Axis dialog box appears.

2. Select the tab(s) you want and make changes.

3. Click OK.

Rotating 3-D Charts

You can rotate the angle of your 3-D chart to display the chart's best view. To rotate a 3-D chart, follow these steps:

1. Choose Chart, 3-D View. The 3-D View dialog box appears (see Figure 29.12).

FIG. 29.12
Changing the values of Elevation and Rotation in the 3-D View dialog box affects the wire frame sample chart.

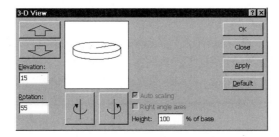

2. Change the Elevation or Rotation by clicking the large up and down arrows or by typing values into the text Elevation or Rotation boxes.

3. When the wire frame sample is oriented so that you can see the view of the chart as you want it to be, choose OK.

The Apply button enables you to apply the new orientation to the chart and keep the dialog box open—a helpful feature when you want to experiment. Click the Default button to return to the original orientation.

▶ **See** "Formatting Characters," **p. 285**

▶ **See** "Sizing, Shaping, and Rotating Text Boxes," **p. 863**

▶ **See** "Moving and Positioning Text Boxes," **p. 866**

Exiting or Updating Graphs

As soon as you click outside the chart, Microsoft Graph closes and you return to your document window. You cannot save the chart and data separately—they must be saved as embedded objects in the Word document.

To update or modify the chart, double-click it to restart Microsoft Graph. ●

Handling Large Documents

CHAPTER 30

Inserting Footnotes and Endnotes

Footnotes and endnotes have long been a staple of academic treatises—supplying additional information about a topic in the text or providing a reference. Footnotes and endnotes save you from having to clutter the text of your document with every piece of information you have. Instead, you can include parenthetical or reference information as a footnote or endnote listing. Because each note is referenced in the text, finding this extra information when you need it is easy. ■

The difference between footnotes and endnotes

Footnotes appear at the bottom of the page on which their reference marks appear; endnotes appear at the end of a section or chapter.

How to insert a footnote or endnote

Use Insert, Footnote or Insert, Endnote to insert a footnote or endnote.

How to manage footnotes or endnotes with the capability to find, delete, copy, or move them

You can manage footnotes or endnotes by working with the reference mark.

How to convert a footnote to an endnote, and an endnote to a footnote

Convert footnotes and endnotes using the Convert button in the Note Options dialog box.

How to apply custom formats, numbering, and positioning to footnotes or endnotes

Customize the separator, add a continuation notice for notes that continue on the next page, print footnotes directly beneath document text, and change the numbering scheme for notes.

What You Need to Know About Inserting Footnotes and Endnotes

Inserting, editing, and formatting footnotes and endnotes is easy in Word. Basically, a footnote consists of two parts: a footnote reference in the text (usually a superscripted number after the text), and the footnote at the bottom of the page, isolated from the body text by a separator line. An endnote is similar, except that the entry for an endnote appears at the end of the section or document, set apart from the text by a separator.

The process of creating footnotes and endnotes involves two basic steps:

1. Insert the note reference to mark the location in the document where a footnote or endnote is referred to. The note reference is usually a number.

2. After Word inserts the note reference, type the note entry (customizing the separator if you prefer). The note entry is the text information that appears in the footnote or endnote.

Several options are available for specifying where footnotes and endnotes appear, the type of separator line that is used, and the style of numbering used for the reference numbers. Figure 30.1 shows examples of footnotes being placed in a document.

FIG. 30.1
You can add footnotes to a document to provide additional information or to indicate references.

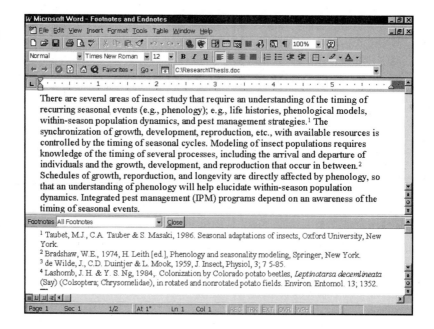

Inserting Footnotes and Endnotes

When you insert a footnote or endnote, Word inserts a reference mark in the text at the current insertion point. The reference mark is usually a sequential number that identifies the note you are adding. You are then given the opportunity to type the text to which the reference mark refers.

If you are in Normal view, a pane opens at the bottom of the window. In that pane, you can type either a footnote or an endnote, depending on the type of note you selected. If you are in Page Layout view, Word moves the insertion point to the bottom of the page for footnotes, or to the end of the document for endnotes. Entering footnotes and endnotes becomes as visual and as easy as if you were manually writing in a notebook. But Word automatically adjusts the page lengths, because footnotes fill up the page. Endnotes at the end of the document are continually pushed to the last page as your document gets longer.

Part
VII
Ch
30

N O T E Footnotes usually make a document more difficult to read because they clutter the bottom of each page. However, many academic institutions require footnotes in their papers. Endnotes are more frequently used in scholarly publications because they do not interfere with reading, but they do make the research accessible for those who need more information. ▪

To create a footnote or endnote, follow these steps:

1. Position the insertion point after the text where you want to insert a reference mark.

   Word inserts the reference mark at the insertion point, unless you have selected text, in which case it positions the mark after the selection.

2. Choose Insert, Footnote. The Footnote and Endnote dialog box appears (see Figure 30.2).

FIG. 30.2
In the Footnote and Endnote dialog box, you choose the type of note and how it should be numbered.

3. Select either the Footnote or the Endnote option.

4. Accept the default AutoNumber to have Word number your footnotes. For custom reference marks, see "Changing the Appearance of Reference Marks" later in this chapter.

5. Choose OK. Word displays the note pane (Normal view) or the bottom margin (Page Layout view) so that you can type your footnote.

6. Type the text of your footnote or endnote.

   If you're in the Normal view of your document, you type in a special note pane, which appears when you choose OK in step 5. At this point, the screen is divided into two parts: the text of your document on top showing the note reference, and the note pane below showing the note entry (see Figure 30.3).

FIG. 30.3
The note pane is at the bottom of the screen when you work in Normal view.

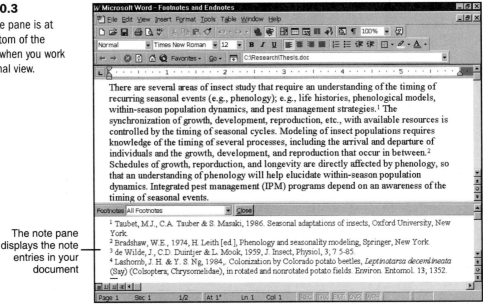

The note pane displays the note entries in your document

If you're in the Page Layout view of your document, you don't see the note pane. Instead, you type the note directly on the page (see Figure 30.4). If you are entering a footnote, you type at the bottom of the page. If you are entering an endnote, you type at the end of the document.

7. If you are in Normal view, leave the note pane visible and press F6 or click the document to move back to the document window. You can also click the document to move the insertion point. Or close the note pane by choosing the Close button or View, Footnotes (which is turned on when you insert a footnote).

FIG. 30.4
You type footnotes directly on the bottom of the page when in Page Layout view.

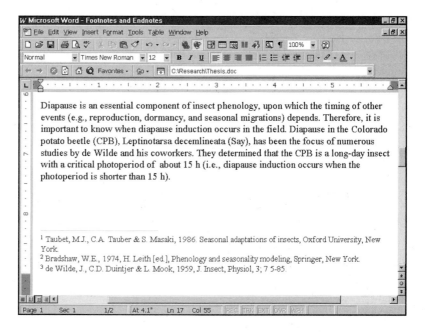

Or, if you are in Page Layout view, you can use Shift+F5 (the Go Back key) to return to where you inserted the reference. You can use the mouse to click at any location in the document.

T I P

Insert a footnote with Alt+Ctrl+F. Insert an endnote with Alt+Ctrl+E.

ON THE WEB

For information on currently recommended styles for referencing World Wide Web URLs, point your browser to:

http://falcon.eku.edu/honors/beyond-mla

http://www.cas.usf.edu/english/walker/mla.html

Inserting Multiple References to a Single Note

You can insert multiple references to the same footnote or endnote. For example, you can refer to the same footnote text several times in a document without having to repeat the footnote text.

To insert an additional reference to a note that has already been inserted in your document, follow these steps:

1. Position the insertion point where you want to insert the reference mark, and choose Insert, Cross-Reference.

2. Select either Footnote or Endnote from the Reference Type list box; then select either Footnote Number or Endnote Number from the Insert Reference To list box.

3. Select the footnote or endnote you want to refer to in the For Which Footnote or For Which Endnote list box.

4. Clear the Insert as Hyperlink check box.

5. Choose the Insert button and then click Close.

6. Select the reference mark you just inserted and choose either Footnote Reference or Endnote Reference from the Style drop-down list on the Formatting toolbar to apply the correct formatting to the reference mark.

N O T E You can insert a cross-reference to another note within the text for a note, using the procedure just described.

▶ **See** "Adding Cross-References and Captions," **p. 1025**

Changing the Appearance of Reference Marks

In the preceding procedure, it is assumed that footnotes and endnotes use the default numbering scheme. You set default numbering by selecting the AutoNumber option when creating a footnote or endnote. Footnotes are automatically numbered using Arabic numerals (1, 2, 3, and so on), and endnotes are numbered using Roman numerals (i, ii, iii, and so on). With this option selected, footnotes are renumbered when additional footnotes are added, deleted, moved, or copied.

You can create footnotes or endnotes with a custom reference mark. To use a custom reference mark when you create the note, select the Custom Mark option from the Footnote and Endnote dialog box.

In the Custom Mark text box, you can type up to 10 characters, such as asterisks or daggers; or you can choose the Symbol button and select a symbol from the Symbol dialog box. Custom reference marks are not automatically updated, but custom reference marks don't interfere with any automatically numbered footnote references already in your document.

To change an existing reference mark, follow these steps:

1. Select the mark.

2. Choose Insert, Footnote.

3. Type a new mark in the Custom Mark text box.

4. Choose OK. Word displays the footnote pane (in Normal view, choose <u>C</u>lose to close it) or the bottom margin (in Page Layout view, press Shift+F5 to return to your document).

Editing and Viewing Footnotes and Endnotes

Research papers, theses, and technical documents are rarely completed in a single pass. They usually require multiple rewrites and, after review, usually require additional footnotes or endnotes. To make changes, you need to know how to view and edit existing footnotes and endnotes.

Viewing Footnotes and Endnotes

If you choose to leave the note pane open, it will scroll along with the document to display the notes that correspond to the note references displayed in the text.

Word offers some handy shortcuts for viewing existing notes. If you have a mouse and are in Page Layout view, you can open the note pane by double-clicking any note reference in your document, and you can close the pane and move back to the note reference by double-clicking the reference mark for any note entry in the note pane. You can also open the note pane by holding down the Shift key while you drag the split bar down. (The *split bar* is the narrow gray button above the up arrow in the right scroll bar.) Close the pane by dragging the split bar back up or by double-clicking the split bar.

Once you have opened the note pane, you can switch between viewing footnotes and endnotes by selecting either All Endnotes or All Footnotes from the drop-down list at the top of the pane.

You also can choose <u>V</u>iew, <u>F</u>ootnotes to view footnotes and endnotes. When you are in Normal view, choosing this command will open the note pane. When you are in Page Layout view, a dialog box appears if your document has both footnotes and endnotes, giving you a choice to view either the footnote or endnote area.

Formatting and Editing Footnotes and Endnotes

Footnote and endnote text can be formatted and edited just like any other text. You can use the ruler, toolbars, and menu commands for formatting notes. The default point size is 10 points for the note text and eight points for the reference mark.

TIP Use shortcut menus displayed with the right mouse button to quickly format in the note pane.

▶ **See** "Formatting a Document Automatically," **p. 373**

To change the formatting of all your footnotes by redefining the Footnote and Endnote Reference and Footnote and Endnote Text styles, follow these steps:

1. Choose Format, Style, and select the style you want to change from the Styles list.

2. Choose Modify, and then choose the appropriate command from the Format submenu.

3. Make the desired formatting changes in the dialog box that is displayed and choose OK. Repeat these steps for any other formatting changes you want to make.

4. Choose OK, and then choose Apply.

   ▶ **See** "Using Word Standard Styles," **p. 383**

Finding Footnotes

If you are in Page Layout view, you can double-click the number to the left of a footnote or endnote reference to return to where you inserted the reference. You can return to the note associated with a reference by double-clicking the reference mark. This method enables you to quickly move back and forth between the document and the note while in Page Layout view. You can edit notes in Page Layout view just like any other text; simply scroll to the note and make the desired changes.

To locate notes, follow these steps:

1. Choose Edit, Go To, or press F5 to display the Find and Replace dialog box.

2. Select either Footnote or Endnote in the Go to What list box, and then enter the number of the note you want to find in the Enter Footnote Number text box.

3. Choose the Next button.

To find the next or previous note, leave the text box blank and click either Next or Previous. Choose Close to close the Go To dialog box.

▶ **See** "Using Find and Replace," **p. 227**

You can also choose Edit, Find to locate notes. Choose Edit, Find, position the insertion point in the Find What text box, select More, and click Special. Select either Endnote Mark or Footnote Mark from the list and click Find Next repeatedly until you find the note you are looking for. Choose Cancel to close the Find and Replace dialog box.

Deleting, Copying, and Moving a Footnote or Endnote

To delete, copy, or move a footnote or endnote, work with the reference mark—not the actual note text. If you delete, copy, or move the actual note text, the reference mark is left in place where it was originally inserted. When you delete, copy, or move a reference mark, Word automatically renumbers all numbered notes.

Part **VII**

Ch **30**

To delete a footnote or endnote, you must select the reference mark for the footnote and press Delete or Backspace. Deleting the note's text leaves the reference mark in the text.

If you want to remove all the footnotes or endnotes in a document, choose Edit, Replace, More, and click Special. Select Endnote Mark or Footnote Mark from the list, clear any contents in the Replace With text box, and choose Replace All. Choose Close to close the Find and Replace dialog box.

> **CAUTION**
>
> Be careful when deleting text that contains footnotes or endnotes. If you select and delete text that contains a footnote marker, you also delete the footnote or endnote.

To copy or move a note by choosing either Edit, Copy or Edit, Cut, follow these steps:

1. Select the reference mark for the note you want to move.

 2. If you want to copy the note, choose Edit, Copy. You can also click the Copy button in the Standard toolbar.

 If you want to move the note, choose Edit, Cut. You can also click the Cut button in the Standard toolbar.

3. Position the insertion point at the new position where you want the note reference.

 4. Choose Edit, Paste. You can also click the Paste button in the Standard toolbar.

To copy or move a note with the mouse, follow these steps:

1. Select the reference mark for the note you want to move.

▶ **See** "Moving, Copying, and Linking Text or Graphics," **p. 185**

2. To move the note, drag the selected note reference to the new location and release the mouse button.

To copy the note reference, hold down the Ctrl key and drag and drop the note reference to the location you want to copy it to.

Converting Footnotes and Endnotes

So you've worked and slaved to get an article written for the *Arabian Rain Forest Review*, and it's finally complete. After waiting for three weeks, you get a letter stating that if you resubmit the article by tomorrow, it will be published. But you used footnotes, and they want you to redo your article with endnotes. Because you typed it with Word, you don't have a problem; you can convert existing footnotes to endnotes, or endnotes to footnotes. You can convert all the notes in a document or individual notes.

To convert all notes, follow these steps:

1. Choose Insert, Footnote.

2. Click the Options button to display the Note Options dialog box; then click the Convert button.

3. Select one of the options in the Convert Notes dialog box (see Figure 30.5).

FIG. 30.5

Use the Convert Notes dialog box to convert footnotes to endnotes, or endnotes to footnotes.

4. Choose OK to close the Convert Notes dialog box, choose OK to close the Note Options dialog box, and then click the Close button to close the Footnote and Endnote dialog box.

To convert individual notes, follow these steps:

1. Choose View, Normal if you are not already in Normal view.

2. Choose View, Footnotes.

3. Select All Footnotes or All Endnotes in the view drop-down list at the top of the note pane.

4. Select the note you want to convert in the note pane.

5. Click the right mouse button to display the shortcut menu.

6. Choose either Convert to Footnote or Convert to Endnote.

Customizing Note Settings

You can override the default note settings to suit your particular needs in several ways. You can customize the separator—the line that separates notes from the document text and from each other if they continue across more than one page. You also can add a continuation notice specifying that a note continues on the next page.

By default, footnotes appear on the bottom of the page on which their reference marks appear. If you want, you can specify that footnotes are printed directly beneath the document text if the text on a page does not extend to the bottom. Endnotes normally appear at the end of the document. You can specify that they instead appear at the end of each section in a document.

Finally, you can change the numbering scheme for notes. You can change the starting number for notes, or choose to have note numbering restart on each page or at the beginning of each section, rather than having the notes numbered sequentially from the beginning of the document. You can also change the number format used for footnotes and endnotes.

Part

VII

Ch

30

> **NOTE** Word's footnote style is not necessarily the acceptable style for academic institutions. Many universities use Turabian (the author of a manual) as a standard for theses and dissertations. Turabian indents the first line of footnotes and double-spaces between footnotes, for example. You may need to edit the footnote reference and text styles. ■

Customizing Note Separators

Footnotes and endnotes are separated from the text in a document by a *separator*. When a footnote continues from one page to the next, Word inserts a *continuation separator* line between the document text and the continued footnote.

To customize separators, follow these steps:

1. Choose View, Normal if you are not already in Normal view.
2. Choose View, Footnotes.
3. Select either All Footnotes or All Endnotes from the view drop-down list at the top of the pane.
4. To edit the separator line, select Footnote Separator or Endnote Separator from the view drop-down list.

   The default is a two-inch line. You can keep the line, delete it, or add characters before or after the line. You can change the characters that are used as the separator or use graphics characters if you want.

5. To edit the continuation separator line, select Footnote Continuation Separator or Endnote Continuation Separator from the view list.

   The Continuation Separator is the separator between the document text and the remainder of a note that continues across more than one page. Word proposes a margin-to-margin line. You can edit this line the same way as the separator line.

6. Choose the Close button or press Alt+Shift+C to close the note pane.

To reset the default settings for the note separators, follow steps 1 through 5 in the preceding procedure, choose the Reset button and choose Close.

A *continuation notice* is text that explains that footnotes or endnotes continue on the next page. You can add a continuation notice in the note pane.

To add a continuation notice, follow these steps:

1. Choose View, Normal if you are not already in Normal view.

2. Choose View, Footnotes.

3. Select either All Footnotes or All Endnotes from the view drop-down list at the top of the pane.

4. Select either Footnote Continuation Notice or Endnote Continuation Notice from the view drop-down list.

5. Type the text you want to use for the continuation notice.

6. Choose the Close button or press Alt+Shift+C to close the note pane.

To view the text, switch to page layout view. You can only edit the continuation text in the note pane. To reset the default settings for the continuation notice, follow steps 1 through 4 in the preceding procedure, choose the Reset button, and then choose Close.

Placing Footnotes

You can specify where the footnotes or endnotes you create are to appear in your document. Traditionally, footnotes appear at the bottom of the page. Word places them at the bottom margin, below the footnote separator. You can change the placement so that footnotes appear immediately below the text in a document.

Endnotes normally appear at the end of a document. You can choose to have endnotes appear at the end of each section in a document, provided that the document is divided into sections.

To change the position of footnotes, follow these steps:

1. Choose Insert, Footnote.

2. Choose the Options button. The Note Options dialog box appears (see Figure 30.6).

FIG. 30.6
Select the position of notes in the Note Options dialog box.

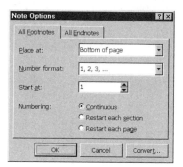

3. Select either the All Footnotes or All Endnotes tab.

4. Select one of the following options from the Place At drop-down list:

Option	Function
Bottom of Page	Places footnotes at the bottom margin of the page on which the footnote references appear (the default setting).
Beneath Text	Prints footnotes after the last line of text. This style is handy when the text is much shorter than a page.
End of Section	Prints the endnotes at the end of the section.
End of Document	Prints endnotes at the end of the document.

5. Choose OK and then choose the Close button.

Figure 30.4, shown earlier in this chapter, shows a document with the footnotes placed at the bottom of the page, just below the document text. Figure 30.7 shows the same document with the endnotes collected at the end of the document.

If you specify endnotes to appear at the end of each section, you can choose to print the endnotes at the end of the current section, or you can save them for a later section. Place the insertion point in the section in which you want to suppress the endnotes. Choose File, Page Setup, and select the Layout tab. Select Suppress Endnotes to save endnotes for the next section, or clear Suppress Endnotes to include the endnotes with the current section.

▶ **See** "Working with Sections in Your Document," **p. 452**

FIG. 30.7
A document in Page Layout view shows endnotes collected at the end of the document.

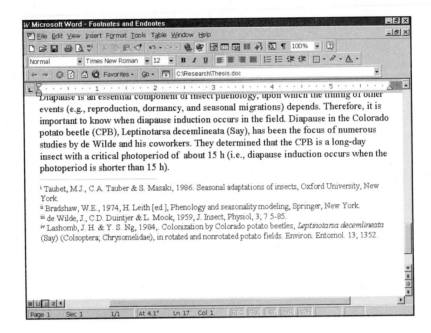

Customizing Numbering

You can change how you number your footnotes. To customize the numbering of footnotes, follow these steps:

1. Choose Insert, Footnote.

2. Choose the Options button. The Note Options dialog box appears.

3. Select either the All Footnotes or All Endnotes tab.

4. To change the starting number, type a new number in the Start At text box, or scroll the spin box arrows to select a new number.

5. Select one of the following Numbering options:

Option	Result
Continuous	Numbering is continuous from beginning to end of document.
Restart Each Section	Numbering is restarted in each section of the document.
Restart Each Page	Numbering is restarted on each page of the document (available only for footnotes).

6. Choose OK and then choose OK in the Footnote and Endnote dialog box.

Creating Indexes and Tables of Contents

This chapter shows you how to build references for documents, to make them easy for people to use. Imagine trying to locate a specific topic in a long reference book with no table of contents, trying to get information from a long technical document without a good index, or trying to remember where you saw a useful chart or table in a book with no list of figures. Word 97 is equipped with powerful tools for creating these reference aids. ■

Create, format, and edit index entries

Word 97 makes it easy to create simple as well as complex indexes containing multiple-level entries and cross-references.

Use a concordance file to automatically create index entries

You can use a concordance file to quickly and easily create index entries in long documents.

Create and format a table of contents

Word's table of contents generator maintains simplicity while providing you with powerful tools that let you include text as well as headings in a table of contents.

Create and format a table of authorities

Legal users will benefit from Word's easy-to-use table of authorities feature.

Create tables based on figures, captions, and other items

Among other things, you can create tables of figures, graphs, and equations so readers can easily locate these items in your documents.

Creating Indexes

An index, such as the one found at the end of this book, lists topics covered in a book or document and provides the page numbers where you can find the topics. Without an index, your readers will have difficulty locating information in a long document or in one that is filled with references.

In Word, creating an index involves two steps:

- You must identify each entry you want indexed.
- You must collect these entries into an index.

Word has the capability to create simple indexes, such as the following:

```
Printing, 5, 12, 25
Publishing, 37, 54, 68
```

Word also can create indexes that use subentries so that specific topics are easier to locate:

```
Printing
        Envelopes, 37, 39
        Merge, 43-45
```

If you need more in-depth or complex indexing, Word is capable of creating indexes that include different characters such as separators, unique formatting, and multiple levels of subentries:

```
Printing
        Envelopes: 37, 39-42
        Mail Merge
                Data document: 54-62
                Main document: 50-55, 67, 72
        Summary info, See Properties
```

Creating Index Entries

Identifying an entry, such as a word, to be included in your index can be as simple as selecting the word and choosing a command. As an alternative, you can position the insertion point where you want the entry referenced, choose a command, and type the word to index. This second method gives you the flexibility to decide how the topic will appear in the index.

N O T E   When creating index entries, you should select the entire word or phrase to be indexed. Remember that you can select entire words by double-clicking the word or by moving to the beginning of the word and pressing Shift+Ctrl+right arrow.

To create an index entry in your document, follow these steps:

1. Select the word or words to index, or position the insertion point where you want the entry.

2. Choose Insert, Index and Tables. Word displays the Index and Tables dialog box.

3. Select the Index tab to display the indexing options, if they are not already displayed (see Figure 31.1).

FIG. 31.1
Use the Index and Tables dialog box to create index entries and compile indexes.

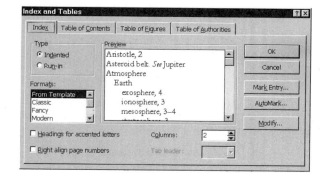

4. Choose the Mark Entry button. Word displays the Mark Index Entry dialog box.

   The Mark Index Entry dialog box includes the selected word or words (see Figure 31.2). If no word or words are selected, type the index entry.

FIG. 31.2
Create an index entry in the Mark Index Entry dialog box.

N O T E If the selected text contains a colon (:), Word prefaces the colon with a backslash (\ ). If you type text that contains a colon, you must preface the colon with a backslash yourself. As you learn in "Creating Multiple-Level Index Entries," later in this chapter, the colon has a special meaning in an index entry. The backslash character tells Word to ignore the colon's special meaning and instead to include the colon in the index entry text.

Part
VII

Ch
31

T I P You can also open the Mark Index Entry dialog box by pressing Alt+Shift+X.

5. In the Main Entry text box, make no change if the index entry looks the way you want it; or type and edit the index entry as you want it to appear in the index.

6. Select among the index entry options:

   Select Cross-reference to create a cross-reference index entry. Cross-reference index entries are described later in the section "Creating Cross-Reference Index Entries."

   Select Current Page to have the index entry refer to the current page only.

   Select Page Range, and type or select the name of a bookmark from the drop-down list if you want the index entry to refer to the range of pages spanned by the bookmark. (See this chapter's "Including a Range of Pages" section.)

   ▶ **See** "Marking Locations with Bookmarks," **p. 182**

7. Select among the Page Number Format options:

   Select Bold to print the index page numbers for this entry in boldface text.

   Select Italic to print the index page numbers for this entry in italic text.

8. Choose Mark to mark only this entry for inclusion in the index.

   Or, choose Mark All to have Word search the entire document and mark all index entries that match the text in the Main Entry text box for inclusion in the index. Mark All is available only if you have preselected text in the document and if you have chosen the Current Page option.

   The Mark Index Entry dialog box remains open after you mark the index entry, whether you choose Mark or Mark All. To create additional index entries, scroll your document and select additional text, or move the insertion point to where you want the next index entry and type the entry directly into the Main Entry text box, repeating steps 5 through 8.

   N O T E If the Mark Index Entry dialog box is covering your text, you can move the box by dragging the dialog box's title bar.

9. Choose Close to close the Mark Index Entry dialog box.

Repeat these steps for every index entry in your document.

N O T E To add character formatting to the index entry—formatting that will be evident in the compiled index—you select text in the Main Entry or Subentry text boxes, and use the character-formatting shortcut keys. If you want the main index entry to be in bold, for example, select all the text in the Main Entry text box and press Ctrl+B to apply bold character formatting. When the index is compiled, this entry appears in bold. ▪

▶ **See** "Formatting Characters," **p. 285**

Including a Range of Pages

As you create an index, you probably will want to reference a range of pages for an index entry, as in the following example:

```
Desktop Publishing, 51-75
```

To do this, you must first select the range of pages and assign a bookmark to the selection. Then, when you insert the index entry, you select the bookmark name from the Bookmark list box (part of the Page Range option) to indicate the range of pages for the entry.

▶ **See** "Marking Locations with Bookmarks," **p. 182**

You need to use a range name to mark the span of pages (rather than an actual number of pages), because editing, insertions, and deletions may move the topic so that it spans different pages than those whose numbers are typed. When using a bookmark, Word calculates the new location of the bookmark so that the index will be up-to-date.

To reference a range of pages, first create the bookmark by following these steps:

1. Select the pages you want to reference in the index entry.

2. Choose Insert, Bookmark.

T I P You can press Shift+Ctrl+F5 to open the Bookmark dialog box.

3. Type a name of up to 40 characters in the Bookmark Name text box.

4. Choose Add.

Now create the index entry, and use the bookmark to describe the page range involved in the reference by following these steps:

1. Position the insertion point where you want to insert the index entry, or select the text you want to index.

2. Choose Insert, Index and Tables.

3. Select the Index tab to display the Index options, if necessary.

4. Choose the Mark Entry button.

5. In the Main Entry text box, make no change if the index entry looks the way you want, or type an index entry.

6. Select Page Range, and type the bookmark name in the Bookmark text box or select it from the drop-down list.

7. Select other options as necessary.

8. Choose Mark to create the index entry (Mark All is not available when working with page ranges because you need to mark only one of the entries within the specified page range). The Mark Index Entry dialog box remains open.

9. Choose Close to close the Mark Index Entry dialog box.

N O T E You can also select text and set bookmarks after you open the Mark Index Entry dialog box. Open the Mark Index Entry dialog box, and then use the usual procedure to set a bookmark; the Mark Index Entry dialog box stays open.

Customizing Index Entries

When you select the Mark Entry option of the Index and Tables dialog box, enter index text, and choose Mark or Mark All, you actually are entering a hidden field code that looks like {XE} into the document at a point directly after the insertion point or the selected text. These field codes are a powerful feature that can help you automate Word and customize the results of some commands, such as Insert, Index and Tables.

To see the hidden text of the field codes inserted by the Mark Entry option, choose Tools, Options, and then select the View tab. Select Hidden Text from the Nonprinting Characters group, and choose OK. The hidden text in the index field is now displayed at all times. Clear this check box when you want to hide the {XE} field text.

T I P You can also display hidden text in {XE} fields by clicking the Show/Hide ¶ button on the Standard toolbar or by pressing Shift+Ctrl+*.

Some examples of field codes for index entries are as follows:

Field Code	Result in Index
{XE "Printing"}	Printing, 56
{XE "Printing" \r "PagesEnv"}	Printing, 72–80
{XE "Printing" \b \i}	Printing, *56*

You can modify and edit these codes to give them more capabilities or formatting than is built into Mark Index Entry dialog box. The "Formatting an Index" section, later in this chapter, covers formatting in detail.

N O T E Index entries appear in the compiled index capitalized exactly as they are in the {XE} fields. If your document contains index entries for the words *computer* and *Computer*, Word creates a separate entry in the finished index for each word. If you want only one entry for both words, you must edit the text in the {XE} field to have the same capitalization. ▪

Assembling a Simple Index

After you create an entry for each index entry or subentry you want collected into an index, you can compile the index. Follow these steps to create your index:

1. Position the insertion point in your document where you would like the index to appear.

   If you are creating an index for a master document, choose <u>V</u>iew, <u>M</u>aster Document to switch to Master Document view, and make sure that the insertion point is not in a subdocument.

2. Turn off the display of hidden text and field codes so that the document will be repaginated properly as the index is created.

N O T E If you turn off all nonprinting characters, but hidden text is still displayed, then you also must turn off the Hidden Text option in the Options dialog box. Choose <u>T</u>ools, <u>O</u>ptions and select the View tab. Clear the Hidden Text check box and choose OK. ▪

3. Choose <u>I</u>nsert, In<u>d</u>ex and Tables.

4. Select the Inde<u>x</u> tab to display the index options, if they are not already displayed (see Figure 31.3).

FIG. 31.3
You can compile an index with the Index and Tables dialog box.

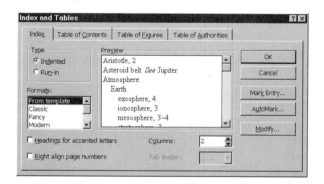

5. Choose from two types of indexes: indented or run-in. Select Indented to indent
    subentries under major entries in the index, as in the following example:

    ```
    Printing
            Envelopes, 56
    ```

    Select Run-in to include subentries on the same line as their major entries, with
    words wrapping to the next line if necessary, as in the following example:

    ```
    Printing: Envelopes, 56
    ```

6. Select among seven formats for the index in the Formats list box; a sample of the
    format you select is shown in the Preview box.

    If you select From Template, the Modify button is enabled. Choose Modify to adjust
    the style of the text used in the index. Word displays a standard Style dialog box,
    except that style editing is limited to the Index styles 1 through 9.

    ▶ **See** "Changing Styles," **p. 403**

7. Select Headings For Accented Letters if you would like words beginning with
    accented letters to be sorted under a separate heading (for example, words begin-
    ning with À would sort under a different heading than words beginning with A).

8. Set the number of columns you want for the index in the Columns spin box.

9. Select Right Align Page Numbers to have page numbers appear right aligned.

    If Right Align Page Numbers is selected, the Tab Leader list box is enabled.

10. Select a leader style (none, dots, dashes, or a solid line) in the Tab Leader list box, if
    applicable.

11. Choose OK. Word repaginates the document and compiles the index. Figure 31.4
    shows a sample index.

When you use choose Insert, Index and Tables to compile an index, you are actually inserting a hidden field code, {INDEX}. Chapter 22, "Automating with Field Codes," describes field codes in detail. The following example shows the field code for the index
shown in Figure 31.4:

```
{INDEX \h "A" \c "2" }
```

To view the index field code, place the insertion point in the index and press Shift+F9.
Press Shift+F9 while the insertion point is in the field to again view the index text.

TIP   You can right-click the index with the mouse and choose Toggle Field Codes from the shortcut
menu to display the index field code. To display the index text, right-click the index field code and
again choose Toggle Field Codes.

▶ **See** "A Reference List of Field Codes," **p. 718**

FIG. 31.4
This figure shows a sample index.

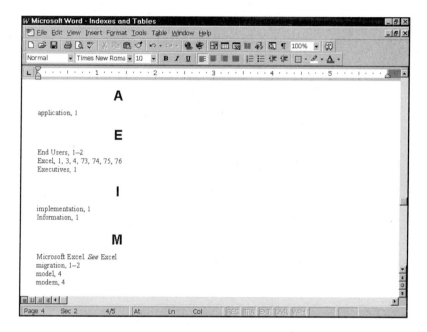

Part
VII

Ch

31

The index will not have index headings that separate the index entries (such as separating the A's from the B's) if you choose From Template in the Formats list. Formats list is located on the Index tab in the Index and Tables dialog box. If you want to include a heading in an index with a custom style, you must manually add the \h switch to the {INDEX} field code. In the preceding index field code example, the "A" after the \h indicates that the index heading should contain the letter of the alphabet for the index entries below that heading. To edit the index field code, place the insertion point in the index and press Shift+F9 to display the field code, then edit the text in the field code as you would any other text. To display the index with the new heading, follow the instructions for updating indexes, later in this chapter.

Formatting an Index

You can change the appearance of an index by formatting the index and the individual index entries.

Formatting an Index Using Styles   The easiest and fastest way to change the character and paragraph formatting of an index is to use styles. Word supplies automatic styles for index entries: Index Heading, Index 1, and so on, through Index 9. *Index Heading* is the style Word uses to format the letters at the beginning of each section of an index. In Figure 31.4, the Index Heading style has been changed to Arial font and a larger point size. To redefine a style, choose Format, Style.

▶ **See** "Redefining a Style," **p. 404**

CAUTION

If you make changes to an index style, you will lose those changes each time you replace the index. This is because Word resets the index styles each time an index is replaced. You can avoid this by using the Update Field command (rather than the Index and Tables dialog box) to update an index when you have made changes to your document. To do this, place the insertion point anywhere in the index and press the F9 (Update Field) key or right-click the index with the mouse and choose Update Field from the shortcut menu.

N O T E You can access several formatting options for indexes by using switches in the {INDEX} field. For example, you can use the \h switch to specify which characters are used to separate index headings. Or with the \e switch, you can change the characters used to separate the index text from the page numbers (the default is a comma followed by a space). To add these switches, place the insertion point within the index, and press Shift+F9 to display the {INDEX} field (or choose Tools, Options; select the View tab, and select the Field Codes check box). Next, type the desired switches. ▪

▶ **See** "Inserting Field Code Switches or Bookmarks," **p. 702**

Formatting an Index Directly   You can also format your index directly, using the Format menu commands, Formatting toolbar, and the ruler. If you update your index, however, you will lose all direct formatting changes. For this reason, you should redefine the styles for your index to make formatting changes.

Formatting Index Entries   You can also apply character formatting to individual index entries by directly formatting the text in the {XE} index entry field. Any character formatting you apply to text in the index entry field is applied to that index entry as Word compiles the index. The character formatting in the index entry field is applied in addition to any formatting dictated by the index style. Character formatting applied directly to text in the {XE} field remains unchanged when you update or replace the index.

You can apply character formatting to individual index entries in two ways:

- You can format the text in the Mark Index Entry dialog box as you create the index entry.
- You can edit the index entry field itself.

To format the text as you create the index entry, select text in either the Main Entry or Subentry text boxes, and use the character formatting shortcut keys. To make an entry appear in italics, for example, select the text in the Main Entry text box, and then press Ctrl+I.

▶ **See** "Formatting with Keyboard Shortcuts," **p. 291**

¶ To edit the {XE} index field itself, click the Show/Hide ¶ button on the Standard toolbar so that hidden text and nonprinting characters, such as tabs and paragraph marks, are displayed, or choose Tools, Options, and then select Hidden Text on the View tab to display hidden text. Select all or part of the text in the {XE} field, and use the Formatting toolbar or Format, Font to apply character formatting as you would with any other text.

N O T E If you chose Insert, Page Numbers to have Word display chapter numbers with page numbers (for example, 4–27), the chapter numbers are also shown with the page numbers in your index. ■

Updating or Replacing an Index

If you later add index entries to your document and want to update your index, move the insertion point within the {INDEX} field code (or the text that results from the code), and then press F9 (the Update Field command). Word updates the index, adding any new index entries and updating the page numbers for all index entries. Any formatting changes that you made to the index by redefining index styles or formatting individual index entries is kept; any formatting that you performed directly on the index text is lost.

Occasionally, you may want to completely replace an index, especially if you have made extensive changes in a document, or if you want to completely change the appearance of the index. To replace an index, place the insertion point within the {INDEX} field code (or the text that results from the code), and then choose Insert, Index and Tables as you would for compiling a new index. After you choose OK to begin compiling the index, Word asks if you want to replace the existing index. If you choose OK, Word compiles a new index, replacing the existing index. If you choose Cancel, Word still compiles a new index, but adds another {INDEX} field to the document.

CAUTION

If you choose Insert, Index and Tables to replace an index or to compile more than one index, Word resets all the index styles (Index heading and Index 1 through 9) to have the characteristics of the index format you choose in the Index and Tables dialog box. If you want to keep any changes you have made to the index styles, press the F9 (Update Field) key to update an index instead of replacing it.

Deleting an Index

To delete an index, select the index and press Delete. You can select the entire index quickly by clicking the mouse button in the left margin over the section break at either end of the index. To quickly select and delete an entire index using the keyboard, place the insertion point on either section break, press F8, press the down-arrow key once to select the index, and press Delete.

Another alternative is to choose <u>T</u>ools, <u>O</u>ptions, and then select F<u>i</u>eld Codes on the View tab to display field codes (or right-click with the mouse to toggle the field code), select the {INDEX} code, and press Delete.

Locking an Index or Fixing an Index as Text

An index is actually created with a hidden field code, {INDEX}. As long as the field code is there, you can quickly update the index by selecting the code and pressing F9.

There may be times when you will want to lock an index so other users cannot modify it. This is especially helpful when you have applied formatting directly to the index text and do not want it accidentally updated by another user. You can do this by locking the index field code. To do this, place the insertion point anywhere within the index or the index field code and press Ctrl+F11. This will prevent the field from being updated; however, the index can still be replaced via the Index and Tables dialog box. To unlock the index field code so updating can occur, place the insertion point anywhere within the index or the index field code and press Shift+Ctrl+F11.

▶ **See** "Updating, Unlinking, or Locking Fields," **p. 715**

CAUTION

Word gives no indication that a field has been locked except to sound an audible beep when a user attempts to update a locked field. If users are unfamiliar with this feature, they may fail to realize the index has not been updated, or they may delete and reinsert the index out of frustration when Word refuses to update it.

In some cases, you may want to change the field code to its text result so that the index cannot be changed or updated. You may want to fix the field code so that you can reformat the index without losing formatting if someone selects the document and presses F9 to update other fields, or so that you can save the document to another word processing format while preserving the index.

To fix the index field code so that it changes to text, place the insertion point anywhere within the index or the index field code. Then press Shift+Ctrl+F9, the Unlink Field command.

N O T E   You cannot change an unlinked field back into a field code; however, you can choose
Edit, Undo to undo the Unlink Field command. If you want to reinsert an index field
code, but can no longer undo the change, you must delete the text and reinsert the index via the
Index and Tables dialog box. ▪

Creating Multiple-Level Index Entries

If you have ever looked up a topic in an index and found the topic listed with a dozen or so
page numbers, you know the value of a multiple-level index. When you expect to have
several occurrences of a topic, you can help your reader by using categories and subcategories to divide the topic into more specific references. In Word, these entries are called
multiple-level index entries, and they're easy to create.

The following is an example of the difference between a regular and a multiple-level index:

Index Type	Result
Regular	Computers, 1, 6, 17, 25, 33–37, 54
Multiple-level	Computers
	hard disk drives, 6
	modems, 17
	processor types, 33–37, 54
	software, 1, 25

To create a multiple-level index entry, follow these steps:

1. Position the insertion point where you want the index entry, or select the text you
   want indexed.
2. Choose Insert, Index and Tables.
3. Select the Index tab to display the index options, if necessary (refer to Figure 31.3).
4. Choose Mark Entry. Word displays the Mark Index Entry dialog box (refer to
   Figure 31.2).
5. In the Main Entry text box, type the name of the main category, or edit the selected
   text until the main category item appears how you want it.
6. Type the name of the subcategory in the Subentry text box.

   If you want to create sub-subentries, separate each subentry level in the Subentry
   text box with a colon (:). (See the example immediately following these steps.)

7. Select other options as needed, and choose <u>M</u>ark.

   The Mark Index Entry dialog box remains open so that you can scroll through your document and create additional index entries. Repeat steps 5 through 7 for each index entry with a subentry.

8. Choose Close when you are finished creating index entries.

Follow this procedure for each index entry and subentry. To create the following multiple-level index entry, for example, you would type **Computers** in the Main <u>E</u>ntry text box, and **Hard disk drives** in the <u>S</u>ubentry text box (refer to step 6):

```
Computers
        Hard disk drives, 54, 65
```

You also can create sub-subentries, as in the following example:

```
Computers
        Hard disk drives
                Maintenance, 54
                Performance, 65
        Processors, 102
```

All the preceding sub-subentries were made with **Computers** in the Main <u>E</u>ntry text box and the following text in the <u>S</u>ubentry text box:

```
Hard disk drives:Maintenance
Hard disk drives:Performance
Processors
```

Notice how each subentry level is separated from the previous level by a colon (:). You can have up to six levels of subentries. The index entry fields for these entries would look like this:

```
{XE "Computers:Hard disk drives:Maintenance" }
{XE "Computers:Hard disk drives:Performance" }
{XE "Computers:Processors" }
```

> **CAUTION**
>
> Word will allow you to add more than six levels of subentries when marking an index entry. However, only the first six entries will be used when the index is compiled.

Marking Index Entries for Symbols

Sometimes you may want to index symbols or other special characters.

To create an index entry for a symbol, follow these steps:

1. Select the symbol in your document that you want to index.

2. Choose Insert, Index and Tables. Select the Index tab, if necessary, and then choose Mark Entry. The Mark Index Entry dialog box appears with the selected symbol in the Main Entry text box.

3. Press the right-arrow key or use the mouse to position the insertion point immediately following the symbol in the Main Entry text box.

4. Type a semicolon followed by the number sign (;#) to the right of the symbol.

   Symbols are automatically placed at the beginning of the index. If you choose an index format that includes index headings, the symbols will appear beneath the # heading at the top of the index. You may want to delete the # heading in the final index or replace it with a more meaningful heading such as *Symbols* or *Special Characters*.

N O T E To create index entries for symbols that have been inserted using Insert, Symbol (for example, the 🄢 symbol), create the index entry with any symbol or character typed in from the keyboard, then view the {XE} field code and replace the unwanted symbol with the desired symbol from the Symbol dialog box. ▨

   ▶ **See** "Inserting Special Characters and Symbols," **p. 315**

5. Choose Mark or Mark All. Continue to mark entries as necessary.

6. When you are finished, choose Close to close the Index and Tables dialog box.

Creating Cross-Reference Index Entries

You can choose Insert, Index and Tables to create cross-reference indexes. A *cross-reference* index gives the reader information such as the following:

```
Modem, see Computers.
```

To create a cross-reference index entry, follow these steps:

1. Select the word or words to index, or position the insertion point where you want the entry placed in your document.

2. Choose Insert, Index and Tables. Word displays the Index and Tables dialog box.

3. Select the Index tab to display the indexing options, if necessary.

4. Choose the Mark Entry button. Word displays the Mark Index Entry dialog box.

   The Mark Index Entry dialog box includes the selected word or words (refer to Figure 31.2). If no word or words are selected, type the index entry in the Main Entry text box.

5. Make no change if the index entry and subentry look the way you want; or type and edit the index entry and subentry as you want them to appear in the index.

6. Select Cross-reference, and type the cross-reference topic after the "See" in the Cross-reference text box. If you want the cross-reference to appear in a different format, press the formatting key command before typing in the cross-reference. For example, if you would like the entire cross-reference italicized, press Ctrl+I to turn on italics and then type the cross-reference.

▶ **See** "Formatting Characters," **p. 285**

7. Select among the other options as needed; choose Mark to mark this word in the document. The Mark All button will be disabled because you can only use this feature when page numbers are to be inserted along with an entry; there is no reason to mark all entries when cross-referencing to another entry in the index.

   The Mark Index Entry dialog box remains open so that you can scroll through your document and create additional index entries. Repeat steps 5 through 7 for each index entry.

8. Choose Close when you are finished creating index entries.

Repeat these steps for each index entry. As with all other index entries, Word inserts an {XE} field code each time you mark an index entry. If you view the cross-reference index field, you will notice that it includes a special switch—\t—to create the cross-reference entry. The text preceding the \t switch is the index entry, and the text that follows the \t switch is the cross-reference text. The following line shows a cross-reference index field:

```
{XE "Graphics" \t "See Desktop Publishing" }
```

The preceding index entry field produces the following entry in the compiled index:

```
Graphics. See Desktop Publishing
```

Automatically Creating Index Entries

If you have a large number of index entries to create or you want to standardize the capitalization of your index entries, you can have Word create index entries for you. To automatically create index entries, you must first create a concordance file containing the words or phrases you want to index and their corresponding entries and subentries. After you create the concordance file, you can select the AutoMark option in the Index and Tables dialog box to automatically mark the index entries. You can add index entries to your document automatically or manually, in any combination.

Creating a Concordance File   The *concordance file* is a Word document containing a single, two-column table, and no text outside the table. The first column of the table contains the words and phrases you want to index, and the second column of the table contains the entry and subentry that should appear in the index for the indexed word or phrase.

▶ **See** "Creating Tables," **p. 608**

▶ **See** "Adding or Deleting Cells, Rows, or Columns," **p. 631**

To create a concordance file, follow these steps:

1. Choose File, New, or click the New button to create a new document file.

2. Choose Table, Insert Table, and then choose OK. Word inserts a two-column table into the document. You can also click the Insert Table button to create a two-column table.

3. In the first column of the table, type the word or words you want to index.

4. In the second column of the table, type the text you want to appear in the index for each entry.

   To create an index subentry, separate each subentry level with a colon, as described earlier in this chapter for multi-level indexes. You cannot use a concordance file to create cross-reference index entries.

5. Perform steps 3 and 4 for each word or phrase you want to index, adding additional rows to the table, as necessary (see Figure 31.5). See Chapter 18, "Creating and Editing Tables," for more information about tables.

   If a word needs to be indexed under more than one heading, you must create an entry in the concordance file for each heading as shown in Figure 31.5.

   The concordance file is case-sensitive. You must include both uppercase and lowercase entries if you want them to be included in the index (see Figure 31.5).

   You may find it helpful to sort your table in the order of the words being indexed so you can easily determine if a word has already been added to the concordance file (see Figure 31.5).

   ▶ **See** " Sorting Tables," **p. 644**

6. Save and close the concordance file.

Creating Index Entries from a Concordance File   To create index entries from the concordance file, follow these steps:

1. Turn off the display of hidden text, if necessary. Click the Show/Hide ¶ button on the Standard toolbar, or choose Tools, Options, select the View tab, and then clear Hidden Text.

2. Choose Insert, Index and Tables.

3. Select the Index tab to display the index options, if necessary.

4. Choose the AutoMark button. Word displays the Open Index AutoMark File dialog box, which operates like the standard Open dialog box.

Part

VII

Ch

31

FIG. 31.5

You can use a concordance file to automatically insert index entries.

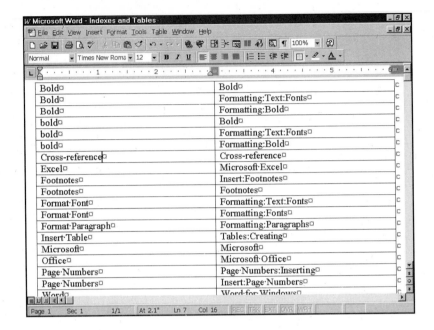

5. Select the appropriate drive or folder, and then select the concordance file you want to use.

   If the concordance file you want is not listed, use the Files of Type list box to change the files displayed in the file list, or try another drive or folder.

6. Choose Open.

   Word searches through your document and inserts an index entry at every location where a word or phrase matches a word or phrase in the first column of the table in the concordance file.

After inserting the index entries, create the index as described in "Assembling a Simple Index" earlier in this chapter. If you later make changes in the concordance file, choose Insert, Index and Tables, AutoMark again. Word adds any new index entries to reflect additions in the concordance file.

CAUTION

Word will not update existing index entries when you choose AutoMark. For example, if you specify "Formatting:Bold" in your concordance file for every occurrence of the word "Bold" and later change this entry in the concordance file to read "Formatting:Bold Text," Word will insert a new index entry reading {XE "Formatting:Bold Text"} for each occurrence of the word "Bold" within your

---

document. However, it will not remove or change the existing {XE "Formatting:Bold"} entries. Use Edit, Replace to locate and remove unwanted field codes (see Chapter 7, "Using Editing and Proofing Tools," for information on finding and replacing field codes).

Creating Tables of Contents

A table lists selected items included in your document, along with their page numbers. Building a table of contents at the beginning of a document is probably the most common use of this feature. You also can create tables of figures, photos, tables, or other items. Figure 31.6 shows one of the types of tables of contents you can create.

FIG. 31.6
Word can create tables of contents in many formats and for different items.

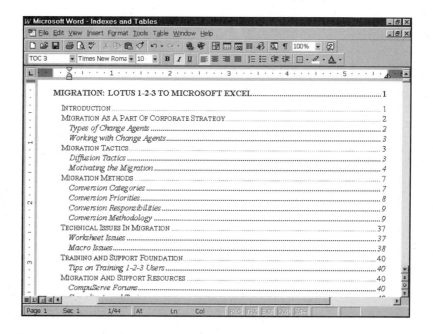

You have two ways to create a table of contents: by using heading styles, or by using special table of contents entry fields. The easiest way to create a table of contents is to collect heading styles.

▶ **See** "Applying Paragraph Styles," **p. 390**

Creating a Table of Contents Using Outline Headings

If you know you want a table of contents, you may want to format your document headings by using the built-in heading styles, Heading 1, Heading 2, and so on. When you compile a table of contents, Word recognizes these heading styles and uses the text with those styles to create the table of contents. Word provides nine heading levels, Heading 1 through Heading 9. You choose which heading levels to use when you create a table of contents.

The heading styles used to create tables of contents or lists are the same heading styles used automatically when you create an outline. If you prefer to work with Word's Outliner, you may want to outline your document before or as you write, and then use the outline headings to create your table of contents. Chapter 21, "Organizing Content with an Outline," describes how to create and use outlines.

Before you can create a table of contents, you must apply heading styles to each heading you want to include in the table of contents. (To create tables of figures or other tables, see "Creating Special-Purpose Tables" later in this chapter.) To apply heading styles, move the insertion point into the text and then use one of the following methods, which are listed in order of complexity, beginning with the easiest:

- Select the desired heading style from the style list box on the Formatting toolbar.
- Press Alt+Shift+left arrow or Alt+Shift+right arrow to change a paragraph into a heading style and move it to a higher or lower style.
- Choose Format, Style, select the desired heading style from the Styles list box, and choose Apply.

You can apply heading styles as you type the headings, using either the mouse or keyboard methods.

 T I P You can use keyboard shortcuts to quickly apply Heading 1 through Heading 3 styles. To do this, press Ctrl+Alt+1 to apply Heading 1, Ctrl+Alt+2 to apply Heading 2, and Ctrl+Alt+3 to apply Heading 3.

To create a table of contents from headings formatted with heading styles, follow these steps:

1. Position the insertion point where you want the table of contents to appear in your document.

   If you are creating a table of contents for a master document, choose View, Master Document to switch to Master Document view, and make sure that the insertion point is not in a subdocument.

2. Turn off the display of hidden text and field codes so the document will be repaginated properly as the table of contents is created (see "Assembling a Simple Index" earlier in this chapter for instructions on how to turn off the display of hidden text and field codes).

3. Choose Insert, Index and Tables.

4. Select the Table of Contents tab to display the table of contents options, if necessary (see Figure 31.7).

FIG. 31.7

Create a table of contents with the Index and Tables dialog box.

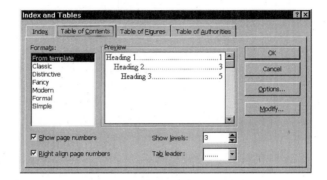

5. Select among seven Formats for the table of contents; a sample of the format you select is shown in the Preview box.

   If you select From Template, the Modify button is enabled. Choose Modify to adjust the style of the text used in the table of contents. Word displays the standard Style dialog box, except style editing is limited to TOC styles 1 through 9. The TOC styles are used for each of the heading styles; TOC1 for Heading 1, and so on.

6. Select Show Page Numbers to turn the display of page numbers on or off.

7. In the Show Levels spin box, set the number of heading levels you want to show in the table of contents.

8. Use the Right Align Page Numbers check box to turn the right alignment of page numbers on or off.

   If Right Align Page Numbers is selected, the Tab Leader list box is enabled.

9. Select the leader style (none, dots, dashes, or a solid line) in the Tab Leader list box, if applicable.

10. Choose OK. Word repaginates the document and compiles the table of contents.

▶ **See** "Changing Styles," **p. 403**

Figure 31.6, shown earlier, shows a table of contents built from heading styles.

When you choose Insert, Index and Tables to create a table of contents, you are inserting a hidden field code, {TOC}. Field codes are described in detail in Chapter 22, "Automating with Field Codes." The following example shows the field code for the table of contents

Part
VII

Ch
31

shown in Figure 31.6. To view the table of contents field code, place the insertion point in the table of contents and press Shift+F9. Press Shift+F9 while the insertion point is in the field code to view again the table of contents text.

```
{TOC \O "1-9" }
```

T I P You can use the mouse to toggle between the table of contents and the {TOC} field. Right-click the table of contents or the field code and choose Toggle Field Codes from the shortcut menu.

In the {TOC \O "1-9"} table of contents field, the \O switch tells Word to create the table of contents from outline headings; the numbers enclosed in quotation marks after the switch indicate the range of heading levels to include in the table of contents.

N O T E Create a table of contents early in your work and use it to navigate through your document. If you put the table of contents at the end of the document, you can press Ctrl+End to go to the end of the document, check the table of contents to identify the page number you want, and then choose Edit, Go To (or press F5) to quickly go to that page. ■

Creating a Table of Contents Using Any Style

You may want to create a table of contents or some other table for a document that does not contain heading styles, or you may want to include references to items that have a style other than one of the heading styles. You can create a table of contents based on any styles used in the document.

▶ **See** "Creating Styles," **p. 393**

To create a table of contents that includes entries based on styles in addition to (or instead of) the built-in heading styles, follow these steps:

1. Turn off the display of hidden text and field codes so that the document will be repaginated properly as the table of contents is created.

2. Position the insertion point where you want the table of contents to appear in your document.

   If you are creating a table of contents for a master document, choose View, Master Document to switch to Master Document view, and make sure that the insertion point is not in a subdocument.

3. Choose Insert, Index and Tables.

4. Select the Table of Contents tab to display the table of contents options, if necessary (refer to Figure 31.7).

5. Choose Options. The Table of Contents Options dialog box appears (see Figure 31.8).

FIG. 31.8

The Table of Contents Options dialog box enables you to choose which items will be included in a table of contents.

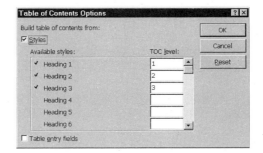

6. To create a table of contents that contains *only* entries compiled from certain styles, select the Styles check box and clear the check box for Table Entry Fields.

   Or, to create a table of contents that contains entries compiled from headings or other styles *as well as* from table entry fields, select Styles and Table Entry Fields. (See "Marking Table of Contents Entries" in the following section for more information about Table Entry fields.)

7. For every style in the Available Styles list that you want included in the table of contents, type the table of contents level for that style in the corresponding TOC Level text box. You can use levels 1 through 9.

   If you don't want a style included in the table of contents, make sure the TOC Level text box for that style is empty.

8. Choose OK to accept the options you set, or choose Cancel to exit the dialog box without saving your changes.

   If you have saved changes that you later want to reset, you can choose Reset to return all TOC levels back to their original settings. Reset will also clear the Table Entry Fields check box.

   Word closes the Table of Contents Options dialog box when you choose OK or Cancel.

9. Set additional options in the Index and Tables dialog box, as desired.

10. Choose OK to compile the table of contents. Word closes the Index and Tables dialog box and creates the table of contents.

N O T E   Word will display `Error! no table of contents entries found.` if none of the selected styles from the Table of Contents Options dialog box are found in the document.

Creating a Table of Contents Using Any Text

You may want to include references to items that don't have heading or other styles. In those cases, you can insert a table of contents entry field {TC}, along with a descriptive entry, at the beginning of each appropriate section in your document (or in the location to be referenced in the table of contents). Word then can collect these fields and descriptions into the table of contents.

A *field* is a hidden code enclosed in special characters that look like braces ({}). Fields are used to automate features of Word. Field codes were used earlier in this chapter for indexes. For more information on fields, see Chapter 22, "Automating with Field Codes."

Marking Table of Contents Entries   To insert table of contents entry fields into your document, follow these steps:

1. Position the insertion point where you want the table of contents entry.
2. Choose Insert, Field.
3. Select Index and Tables in the Categories list box.
4. Select TC in the Field Names list.
5. Position the insertion point in the Field Codes text box, leaving one space after the TC entry.
6. Type an opening quotation mark ("), type the text of the table of contents entry, and type a closing quotation mark (").

    To create the first entry in the table of contents shown in Figure 31.6, for example, type the following in the Field Codes text box (the \l switch is explained in step 7):

    TC "MIGRATION: LOTUS 1-2-3 TO MICROSOFT EXCEL" \l 1

> **N O T E**   You can save time and keystrokes, and avoid typos, by copying the text in your document that will appear in the table of contents entry field (select the text and press Ctrl+C to copy). Then, position the insertion point in the Field Codes text box of the Field dialog box and press Ctrl+V to paste the copied text into the text box. ▪

7. Type a space, a backslash, and the letter **l** (as shown in the entry line).
8. Type a space and then type the number for the level at which you want this entry to appear in the finished table of contents. You can specify a level of 1 through 9.
9. Choose Options to add additional switches to the TC entry; otherwise, skip to step 11.

    ▶ **See** "Inserting Field Codes," **p. 700**

10. Select the desired switch in the Switches list box, choose Add to Field to add the switch to the TC field, and then type any additional text needed for the switch in the Field Codes text box.

Choose Undo Add to remove a switch added with the Add to Field button or select the switch in the Field Codes text box and press the Delete key.

11. Choose OK to close the Field Options dialog box.

12. Choose OK to insert the table of contents entry field and close the Field dialog box.

Repeat these steps for each table of contents entry you want. The field codes you insert will not be visible in your document unless you have turned on the Hidden Text option on the View tab of Tools, Options. You can also click the Show/Hide ¶ button or press Shift+Ctrl+* to toggle on and off the display of hidden text.

N O T E You can bypass the Insert Field command by using the Insert Field key combination, Ctrl+F9. Position the insertion point where you want the table of contents entry field, press Ctrl+F9 (a pair of field characters will appear), and type

TC "text" switches

where *text* is the text you want to appear in the table of contents and *switches* is the \l switch and level number, followed by any of the optional field code switches you want to use.

You can also copy an existing {TC} field, and then paste it into your document, changing the "text" portion of the field to the appropriate text, see "Editing Table of Contents Entries" in the following section.

If you have several {TC} fields to insert, you might consider creating an AutoText entry; see the section "Creating an AutoText Entry," in Chapter 5, for information on how to create and use AutoText entries. ▪

Editing Table of Contents Entries You can edit a table of contents entry as you would any other text in your document. Any character formatting that you apply to the text in the table of contents entry will also appear in the finished table of contents. To display the table of contents entry text, use the Show/Hide ¶ button on the Standard toolbar to display the hidden text, or choose Tools, Options, View to turn on the display of Hidden Text.

Creating a Table of Contents Using Table of Contents Entry Fields To collect {TC} field codes into a table of contents, follow these steps:

1. Turn off the display of hidden text and field codes so that the document will be repaginated properly as the table of contents is created.

2. Position the insertion point where you want the table of contents to appear in your document.

Part
VII

Ch
31

3. Choose Insert, Index and Tables.

4. Select the Table of Contents tab to display the table of contents options, if they are not already displayed (refer to Figure 31.7).

5. Choose Options. The Table of Contents Options dialog box appears (refer to Figure 31.8).

6. To create a table of contents that contains *only* entries compiled from table of contents entry fields, clear the Styles check box and select the check box for Table Entry Fields.

   Or, to create a table of contents that contains entries compiled from heading or other styles *as well as* from table entry fields, select both the Styles and Table Entry Fields check boxes.

 T I P Creating a table of contents based on styles is described earlier in this chapter.

7. Choose OK to accept the options you set. Word closes the Table of Contents Options dialog box.

8. Set additional options in the Index and Tables dialog box, as desired.

9. Choose OK to compile the table of contents. Word closes the Index and Tables dialog box and creates the table of contents.

TROUBLESHOOTING

Table of contents entries created from any text don't appear in the compiled table of contents. Table of contents entries you created from any text (by creating a {TC} field) are included in the compiled table of contents only if you select the Table Entry Fields check box in the Table of Contents Options dialog box, or if the \f switch is in the {TOC} field. To correct this problem, do one of the following:

- Replace the table of contents by following the instructions in the section "Replacing a Table of Contents or Other Table," later in this chapter. Make sure that you choose the Options button and then select the Table Entry Fields check box in the Table of Contents Options dialog box.

- Manually edit the {TOC} field, adding the \f switch to the field, and then update the table of contents as described in the section "Updating, Replacing, or Deleting Tables of Contents and Other Document Tables," later in this chapter.

The page numbers for entries in the table of contents are incorrect. If you make extensive changes to a document, the pagination of your document may change, so that the page numbers in a table of contents no longer match the actual page numbers of a heading or table of contents entry field. If you compile a table of contents while hidden text is displayed, your document may not paginate correctly. To correct the page numbers in your table of contents, update the table of contents as described in the section "Updating, Replacing, or Deleting Tables of Contents and Other Document Tables," later in this chapter.

Creating Special-Purpose Tables

With Word, you can create not only tables of contents, but also tables of figures, photos, charts, equations, tables, or any other items. These tables usually appear in a document after the table of contents.

You can create tables of figures or other special-purpose tables in two ways:

- By compiling the special purpose tables based on text style
- By manually inserting the table entries into the document
  - ▶ **See** "A Reference List of Field Codes," **p. 718**

Using Styles to Create Special-Purpose Tables

The easiest way to assemble tables of figures or other special-purpose tables is to use the Figure Caption, Equation, and other styles built into Word. If you choose Insert, Caption to create all your figure captions, for example, you can easily build a table of figures.

▶ **See** "Creating Captions," **p. 1032**

To create a table of figures, equations, or tables based on one of Word's caption styles, follow these steps:

1. Position the insertion point where you want the table of figures to appear in your document.

   If you are creating a table of figures for a master document, choose View, Master Document to switch to Master Document view, and make sure that the insertion point is not in a subdocument.

2. Turn off the display of hidden text and field codes so that the document will be repaginated properly as the table of figures is created.

3. Choose Insert, Index and Tables.

4. Select the Table of Figures tab to display the table of figures options, if necessary (see Figure 31.9).

Part
VII

Ch
31

FIG. 31.9
Create a table of figures with the Index and Tables dialog box.

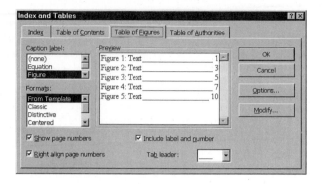

5. Select the appropriate caption in the Caption <u>L</u>abel list.

6. Select one of six Forma<u>t</u>s for the table; a sample of the format you select is shown in the Pre<u>v</u>iew box.

   If you select From Template, the <u>M</u>odify button is enabled. Choose <u>M</u>odify to adjust the style of the text used in the table of figures. A standard Style dialog box appears.

   Choose Cancel or Close when you have finished in the Style dialog box.

   ▶ **See** "Changing Styles," **p. 403**

7. Select <u>S</u>how Page Numbers to turn the display of page numbers on or off.

8. Use the <u>R</u>ight Align Page Numbers check box to turn the right alignment of page numbers on or off.

   If <u>R</u>ight Align Page Numbers is selected, the Ta<u>b</u> Leader list box is enabled.

9. Select a leader style (none, dots, dashes, or a solid line) in the Ta<u>b</u> Leader list box, if applicable.

10. Choose <u>O</u>ptions if you want to change the style on which the table of figures is based (otherwise, skip to step 12). The Table of Figures Options dialog box appears (see Figure 31.10).

FIG. 31.10
The Table of Figures Options dialog box enables you to choose how the table of figures is built.

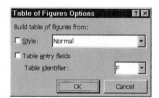

11. To create a table of figures that contains *only* entries compiled from a selected style, select the <u>S</u>tyle check box, and then select the style in the list box. Also, clear the Table <u>E</u>ntry Fields check box if it is selected.

Or, to create a table of figures that contains entries compiled from the selected style *as well as* from table entry fields, select both Styles and Table Entry Fields. Next, select the text style in the Style list box, and select the table identifier in the Table Identifier list box.

Creating a table of figures based on table entries and table identifiers is described in the next section of this chapter.

12. Choose OK. Word repaginates the document and compiles the table of figures.

When you choose Insert, Index and Tables to create a table of figures, you are actually inserting the same {TOC} hidden field code used to create a table of contents. A table of figures is really just a special variety of table of contents. The following is an example of the field code for a table of figures:

```
{TOC \c "Figure" }
```

In this example, the \c switch tells Word to create the table by using the text in paragraphs marked with {SEQ} fields, the text enclosed in quotation marks after the switch indicates which items to group together in the same table. {SEQ} fields are the hidden codes inserted by choosing Insert, Caption. If you choose Insert, Caption to insert a figure caption, for example, the following code is inserted into the document:

```
{SEQ Figure \* ARABIC }
```

▶ **See** "Inserting Field Codes," **p. 700**

▶ **See** "Creating Captions," **p. 1032**

Using Any Text to Create Special-Purpose Tables

Another way to collect special tables is to use field codes instead of (or in addition to) styles. These field codes do the following three things:

■ They mark the spot in the text you want to reference by page number.

■ They include the text you want to appear in the table.

■ They include an identifier that defines into which table they should be accumulated.

You can type these field codes directly into a document or choose Insert, Field to insert them. The field codes you insert look similar to the following:

```
{TC "Automated publishing" \f p}
```

In the previous command, TC is the field code, "Automated publishing" is the text that appears in the table, and the \f switch indicates that the table will be built from fields. The p is an identifier that associates this entry with other entries marked with the same identifier. This entry will be accumulated in a table with other field codes that have the p identifier.

The letters you use are up to you. The code for tables, for example, could be simply t. Following are some examples of how you might group items in different tables:

Item	Field Code Identifier
Charts	c
Figures	f
Lists	l
Pictures	p
Tables	t

To insert field codes that mark what will be included in tables, follow these steps:

1. Position the insertion point on the page you want referenced in the table.

2. Choose Insert, Field.

3. Select Index and Tables in the Categories list box.

4. Select TC in the Field Names list box.

5. Position the insertion point in the Field Codes text box, leaving one space after the TC entry.

6. Type an opening quotation mark ("), type the text of the table entry, and type a closing quotation mark (").

7. Press the spacebar once, and type \f, (the f indicates that the table is being built from fields).

8. Press the spacebar to insert a space, and then type a single-character list identifier, such as **g**, for graphs. Use the same single-letter character for all items to be accumulated in the same table.

9. Choose Options to add additional switches to the TC entry. Choose OK to close the Field Options dialog box.

   ▶ **See** "A Reference List of Field Codes," **p. 718**

10. Choose OK to insert the table entry and close the Field dialog box.

Repeat these steps for each entry you want. The field codes you insert do not appear in your document unless you turn on the Hidden Text option on the View tab after choosing Tools, Options. Your TC field code should look similar to the following:

```
{TC "Graph Showing Learning Retention" \f g}
```

Another, and often quicker, way to enter the field code is to position the insertion point in the document, press Ctrl+F9 to insert the field code braces, {}, and then type the code and text inside the braces.

To create a table that accumulates all the items belonging to a single identifier, such as f for figures or g for graphs, follow these steps:

1. Turn off the display of hidden text and field codes so that the document repaginates using only the text that will print.

2. Position the insertion point where you want the table to appear.

3. Choose Insert, Index and Tables.

4. Select the Table of Figures tab to display the table of figures options, if the options are not already displayed (refer to Figure 31.9).

5. Choose Options. Word displays the Table of Figures Options dialog box (refer to Figure 31.10).

6. To create a table that contains *only* entries compiled from table entry fields, select the Table Entry Fields check box and clear the Style check box.

   Or, to create a table that contains entries compiled from a selected style *as well as* from table entry fields, select both the Style and Table Entry Fields check boxes.

   (Creating tables based on styles is described earlier in this chapter.)

7. Select the table identifier in the Table Identifier list box, (for example, g for graphs). You must also select a style from the Style list box if you selected the Style check box.

8. Choose OK to accept the options you set. Word closes the Table of Figures Options dialog box.

9. Set additional options in the Index and Tables dialog box, as desired.

10. Choose OK to compile the table. Word closes the Index and Tables dialog box and creates the table.

    ▶ **See** "A Reference List of Field Codes," **p. 718**

If you display the resulting field code, it should appear similar to the following:

```
{TOC \f G \c}
```

The preceding {TOC} field produces a table from any TC fields that contain the G identifier. By using different list identifiers, you can include multiple tables for different entries in a document (for example, charts, graphs, lists, and so on).

Creating a Table of Authorities

If you work with legal documents, you are familiar with tables of authorities. A *table of authorities* lists where citations occur in a legal brief; the citations can be references to cases, statutes, treatises, constitutional provisions, and so on.

To create a table of authorities, you first create the citation entries in your document, and then compile the table of authorities.

Creating Citation Entries

To create citation entries in your document, follow these steps:

1. Select the citation text, or position the insertion point where you want the entry.

2. Choose Insert, Index and Tables. The Index and Tables dialog box appears.

3. Select the Table of Authorities tab to display the table of authorities options, if necessary (see Figure 31.11).

FIG. 31.11
Create a table of authorities using the Index and Tables dialog box.

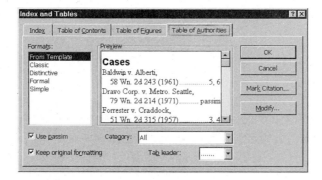

4. Choose Mark Citation. Word displays the Mark Citation dialog box.

   The Mark Citation dialog box includes the selected citation in both the Selected Text box and the Short Citation text box (see Figure 31.12). If no citation is selected, type the citation entry.

 You can also open the Mark Citation dialog box by pressing Alt+Shift+I.

FIG. 31.12
Create a citation entry in the Mark Citation dialog box.

5. In the Selected Text box, edit the text so that the long form of the citation entry looks the way you want it to appear in the table of authorities.

   You can use any of the character-formatting shortcut keys (such as Ctrl+B) to apply formatting to the text in the Selected Text box, and press Enter to add line breaks to the text.

6. Select the citation category in the Category list box (see "Customizing Citation Categories" later in this chapter for information about creating your categories).

7. Edit the text in the Short Citation text box so that it matches the short citation form you use in your document. Because Word searches for and marks short citations in your document by matching the text in the Short Citation text box, be sure that capitalization, punctuation, and abbreviations are the same.

8. Choose Mark to mark only this entry for inclusion in the table of authorities.

   You can also choose Mark All to have Word mark the current citation and then search the entire document and mark all long and short citations that match your entries in the Mark Citation dialog box.

Part
VII

Ch
31

N O T E If you mark only one citation now and want to mark additional citations later (after they have been added), you can select the original long citation, press Alt+Shift+I to display the Mark Citation dialog box, and then choose Mark All. ▪

   The Mark Citation dialog box remains open after marking the citation, whether you choose Mark or Mark All.

9. To create additional citation entries, scroll your document and select additional text, repeating steps 5 through 8.

   You can also choose Next Citation to have Word search your document for common abbreviations used in legal citations ("in re," "v.," "Ibid., or "Sess."), and then repeat steps 5 through 8.

10. Choose Close to close the Mark Citation dialog box.

Repeat these steps for every citation entry in your document.

Editing and Deleting Citation Entries

After you create a citation entry, you cannot edit it by choosing Insert, Index and Tables. Instead, you must edit the text in the hidden field code that is inserted in the document directly after the selected text whenever you create a citation entry in the Mark Citation dialog box.

To see the hidden text of the field codes inserted by the Mark Citation option, choose Tools, Options, and then select the View tab. Select Hidden Text from the Nonprinting Characters group, and choose OK. The hidden text in the index field is now displayed at all times. Clear this check box when you want to hide the {TA} field codes.

 TIP You can also display hidden text in {TA} fields by clicking the Show/Hide ¶ button on the Standard toolbar, or by pressing Shift+Ctrl+*.

Edit and format the hidden text in the citation entry field the same way you would any other text in your document.

To delete a citation entry, simply delete the hidden code from the document. Use Edit, Replace to delete multiple entries quickly (see the section "Finding and Replacing Special Characters," in Chapter 7, for information about finding and replacing field codes).

Assembling a Table of Authorities

After you create an entry for each citation you want collected into the table of authorities, you can compile the table. Follow these steps to create your table of authorities:

1. Position the insertion point where you want the table.

   If you are creating a table of authorities for a master document, choose View, Master Document to switch to Master Document view, and make sure that the insertion point is not in a subdocument.

2. Turn off the display of hidden text and field codes so that the document will be repaginated properly as the table of authorities is created.

3. Choose Insert, Index and Tables.

4. Select the Table of Authorities tab to display the table of authorities options, if necessary.

5. Select among five Formats for the table of authorities; a sample of the format you select is shown in the Preview box.

   If you select From Template, the Modify button is enabled. Choose Modify to adjust the style of the text used in the table of authorities. Word displays a standard Style dialog box. (Refer to Chapter 11, "Using Styles for Repetitive Formats," for more information about editing styles.)

   Choose Close to close the Style dialog box and return to the Index and Tables dialog box.

6. Select the Use Passim check box to substitute the term *passim* whenever a citation has five or more different page numbers.

7. Select the Keep Original Formatting check box to retain the character formatting of long citations in the table of authorities.

8. Select the tab leader style (none, dots, dashes, or a solid line) you want to use for the page numbers in the Tab Leader drop-down list box.

9. In the Category list box, select the category for this table of authorities. The All selection includes all the other categories in a single table.

10. Choose OK. Word repaginates the document and compiles the table of authorities.

When you choose Insert, Index and Tables to compile a table of authorities, you are inserting the {TOA} hidden field code. To view the {TOA} field code, place the insertion point in the table of authorities and press Shift+F9. The following is an example of a typical field code for a table of authorities.

```
{TOA \h \c "1" \p}
```

Customizing Citation Categories

You can change Word's predefined citation categories, or add your own categories.

To customize the citation categories, follow these steps:

1. Choose Insert, Index and Tables. The Index and Tables dialog box appears.

2. Select the Table of Authorities tab to display the table of authorities options, if necessary.

3. Choose Mark Citation. The Mark Citation dialog box appears.

4. Choose Category. The Edit Category dialog box appears (see Figure 31.13).

FIG. 31.13

Create customized citation categories in the Edit Category dialog box.

5. In the Category list box, select the category you want to change.

    Word permits up to 16 categories, and predefines only the first seven. The remaining categories in the Category list box are simply numbered 8 through 16.

6. Type the new category name in the Replace With text box.

7. Choose Replace to change the category name.

Part
VII

Ch
31

8. Repeat steps 5 through 7 for each category you want to customize.

9. Choose OK to close the Edit Category dialog box.

Updating, Replacing, or Deleting Tables of Contents and Other Document Tables

You can easily update, replace, or delete any table of contents, table of figures, table of authorities, or other tables you create by choosing Insert, Index and Tables.

Updating Document Tables

As you add text to or delete it from a document, you also add or delete various table entries. If you add new headings to a document, additional figures, or other items, you will need to update the various tables in your document.

To update any table of contents or other table, follow these steps:

1. Place the insertion point in the table or table field code.

2. Turn off the display of hidden text, so that the document will paginate correctly as the table is updated.

 T I P   Mouse users can right-click the table and choose Update Field from the shortcut menu.

3. Press F9, the Update Field key. Word displays a dialog box similar to the one shown in Figure 31.14 (the exact title of the dialog box depends on the type of table you are updating).

FIG. 31.14
Word asks you how extensive the table update should be.

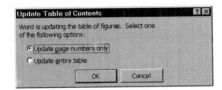

N O T E   If you are updating a table of authorities, Word will automatically update the entire table and will *not* display the Update Table dialog box as shown in Figure 31.14. ▪

4. Select Update Page Numbers Only if you have only added text to or deleted it from the document, without adding or deleting table entries.

Select Update Entire Table if you have added or deleted table entries in the document.

5. Choose OK.

If you choose to update the entire table, any formatting you applied to the table by editing the styles used by the table will remain unchanged. If you formatted the table directly, then updating page numbers leaves that formatting in place, but updating the entire table causes the formatting to be replaced by the style formatting.

Tables that have been unlinked so that their text is fixed cannot be updated; instead, you must reinsert the table if you want an updated version.

Replacing Document Tables

Occasionally, you may want to completely replace a table of contents or other table, especially if you have made extensive changes in a document, or if you want to completely change the appearance of the table. To replace a table of contents or other table, place the insertion point in the table or table field code and then choose Insert, Index and Tables as you would for compiling a new table of contents, table of figures, or table of authorities. After you choose OK to begin assembling the table, Word asks if you want to replace the existing table. Choose Yes to replace the selected table; Word compiles a new table, replacing the selected one. Choose Cancel if you do not want to replace the selected table.

Inserting Additional Document Tables

There may be times when you will want to insert a second table of the same type into your document. For example, you may want to have a different table of contents for different sections of your document (see "Limiting Tables of Contents and Other Tables" later in this chapter). If you want to add an additional table to your document, then position your cursor *outside* of the existing table and choose Insert, Index and Tables. Follow the instructions provided earlier in this chapter to insert the desired type of table. Choose OK and Word asks if you want to replace the selected (existing) table. If you choose No, then Word compiles a new table using an additional table field ({TOC} or {TOA}). If you do want to replace the existing table, choose Yes when you are prompted.

Deleting Document Tables

To delete any table of contents, table of figures, or table of authorities, just select the table and press Delete, or choose Tools, Options to turn on the view of field codes, and then delete the table field.

Limiting Tables of Contents and Other Tables

If you need to create a table of contents or other table for part of a document, you need to modify the field codes with switches. To modify the field codes, choose Tools, Options, select the View tab, and then select Field Codes so that you can see the {TOC} or {TOA} field codes. Type the switches inside the field code braces, as shown in the following table. After modifying the field code, you must update the entire table as described in the preceding section of this chapter.

Switch	Argument	Use
\b	bookmarkname	{TOC \o \b NewIdeas} The table of contents that is built is only for the area named NewIdeas.
\o	"1-4"	{TOC \o "1-4"} The table of contents is built from a limited selection of heading styles, Heading 1 through Heading 4.

▶ **See** "Marking Locations with Bookmarks," **p. 182**

▶ **See** "Editing Fields," **p. 704**

▶ **See** "A Reference List of Field Codes," **p. 718**

▶ **See** "Inserting Tables of Contents, Indexes, and Cross-References," **p. 1058**

Formatting Tables of Contents and Other Tables

If you format a table of contents, table of figures, or other table by using the format commands or the Formatting toolbar and ruler, that formatting will be lost if you update the entire table (updating page numbers only does not affect formatting). You can use two methods to format tables of contents, tables of figures, or other tables so that formatting is not lost when tables are updated.

■ Apply formatting to the table by editing the styles used by the table.

■ Use switches that are inserted in the TOC or TOA field to add or preserve formatting.

The following two sections explain these methods in detail.

Formatting with Styles

Each level in a table of contents has a specific style—TOC1, TOC2, and so on. By redefining these styles, you can change the format of the table of contents, and that new format will still be used when you update the table of contents. For a table of figures or authorities, you change the formatting of the Table of Figures and Table of Authorities styles.

▶ **See** "Redefining a Style," **p. 404**

> **CAUTION**
>
> If you make changes to a table style, you will lose those changes if you choose one of the predefined formats (any format except From Template) from the Formats list box when you insert the table. This is because Word resets the table styles each time a table is replaced. You can avoid this by using the Update Field command (rather than the Index and Tables dialog box) to update a table when you have made changes to your document. To do this, place the insertion point anywhere in the table and press the F9 (Update Field) key or right-click the table with the mouse and choose Update Field from the shortcut menu.

Part VII

Ch

31

This method of changing styles is useful if you want to format one level of the table of contents differently from other levels. For example, you might want the first level of the table, TOC1, to be in bold 12-point Times Roman without tab leaders (dots or dashes before the page number), and all other levels to use the Normal font with tab leaders.

Word's original TOC (Table of Contents) styles are based on the Normal style, with added indents, so that your table of contents will resemble the rest of your document. To redefine the TOC, Table of Figures, or Table of Authorities styles, choose Format Style, and use the Styles list to select the style you want to redefine (such as TOC1 for the first level of table of contents entries). Next, choose Modify to open the Modify Style dialog box, which gives you options for redefining styles.

Choose Format and select the font, border, and other formatting options for the style you want to change. After making the formatting changes to the style, choose OK; Word applies the changes in style to all text in your document that uses that style. When the original Style dialog box reappears, continue to redefine styles, or choose Close.

Formatting with Field Code Switches

The second method of formatting a table of contents or figures so that formatting is preserved when you update the table employs switches you include with the TOC field code. You can use many switches to format the entire table of contents or figures.

▶ **See** "Inserting Field Codes," **p. 700**

To make changes, first display the field code by choosing Tools, Options, selecting the View tab, and then selecting the Field Codes check box. Add your switch(es) inside the field code braces to tell Word how you want the table formatted after it updates. For example, if the TOC field code appears as

```
{TOC \f G \* charformat}
```

the entire table of graphs uses the formatting applied to the first letter of TOC. In this case, the bold and italic on the letter T apply to the entire table. The * charformat switch applies the formatting of the first character in the field code to the entire result.

Some useful switches are listed in the following table:

Switch	Argument	Use
*	charformat	{TOC \o * charformat} Applies the formatting of the first character in the field code to the entire field result. For example, changes the fonts of the entire table of contents.
*	upper	{TOC \f t * upper} Changes all characters in the table of contents to uppercase.
*	lower	{TOC \f g * lower} Changes all characters in the table of contents to lowercase.
*	firstcap	{TOC \o * firstcap} Changes all characters to a title-case format; words such as "and" or "of" are placed in lowercase while other words are initial-capped.

▶ **See** "Editing Fields," **p. 704**

▶ **See** "A Reference List of Field Codes," **p. 718**

After making changes in the TOC field, you must select the field and press F9 (Update Field) to see the results of the changes. ●

CHAPTER 32

Tracking Revisions and Versions

Because you don't work in a vacuum, Word 97 is ready to work with other people, too—right on your computer screen. Using the Track Changes and Comments features, you can eliminate errors and time spent transferring changes from paper to computer. Soon after you start using these features, you may wonder how you ever did without them.

Whether you work in a group or alone, the Track Changes feature can keep track of changes made to a document. Each piece of added or deleted text is marked with the date, time, and reviewer's name. In effect, the Track Changes feature creates an automatic history of the review process. Even if an edited document did not have the Track Changes feature turned on, you can create revision marks by comparing the document to the original.

Word lets you use comments just as you would jot notes in the margin, without worrying about these comments accidentally appearing in a final draft. Comments enable you and other reviewers to include comments and questions in a special window, marked by the reviewer's initials and attached to the text being commented on. ■

Track changes and edits so that they are easy to see and can be accepted or rejected

Revision bars appear in the margin showing the location of changes. You can then accept or reject the changes.

Roll forward or back through versions of the document

Manage document changes by versions. Be able to see how a document evolves through its different versions. Delete changes made in a version.

Compare two documents to see what has changed

Two documents with different names or different locations can be compared. Revision marks are added to the current document when a difference between the two is encountered.

Comment a document with remarks or notes that do not print with the main document

Inserting comments in a document is a convenient way of attaching notes to specific parts of a document.

Using the Track Changes Feature

Revising a document is often a job shared by several people. For example, several cowork-ers might work together to produce an annual report, or more than one editor might re-view a book. If a revised document has no marks, it can be hard to find everything that was changed or who did the changes. Revision marks show where the document has been changed and by whom, allowing the originator to accept or reject any of the changes.

Adding revision marks is simple. Before someone makes revisions, turn on the Track Changes feature. Revisions to the document are then marked automatically as the reviewer makes changes (see Figure 32.1).

FIG. 32.1
With Track Changes turned on, you can see exactly what additions and deletions a reviewer has made. The TRK indicator in the status bar tells you that revision marking is on.

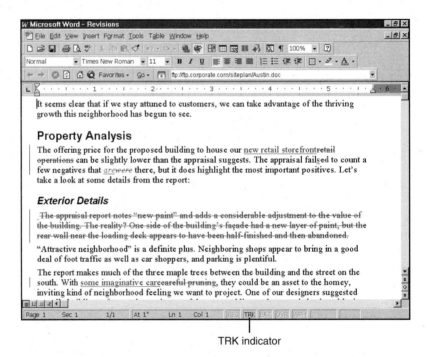

TRK indicator

When you view revision marks, you get a general idea of how much is changed in your document, as well as the details of specific words and letters that were edited. You can also hide revision marks to see exactly what the document would look like if you accepted the changes.

Tracking Changes

When Track Changes is turned on, vertical revision bars appear in the margin next to any lines where text has been inserted or deleted. Revision marks indicate the actual text that has changed—inserted text is underlined, and deleted text has strikethrough formatting. The section "Customizing Revision Marks" later in this chapter tells how you can change these marks.

Before you turn on Track Changes, you should save a copy of the original document. This can help later if incorrect revisions are accepted and you need an original for comparison.

To mark revisions in the active document using menu commands, follow these steps:

1. Choose Tools, Track Changes, Highlight Changes. The Highlight Changes dialog box appears (see Figure 32.2). You turn on the Track Changes feature in the Highlight Changes dialog box.

FIG. 32.2
Mark revisions for working on paper or on screen.

 TIP Double-clicking the TRK indicator in the status bar, shown in Figure 32.1, is a shortcut to display the Highlight Changes dialog box.

2. Select the Track Changes While Editing check box.

3. If you do not want to be distracted by revision marks while editing a document, clear the Highlight Changes On Screen check box.

4. Choose OK.

To turn off revision marking, double-click TRK in the status bar, or choose Tools, Track Changes, Highlight Changes, and clear the Track Changes While Editing check box.

To mark revisions in the active document using the Reviewing toolbar, follow these steps:

1. Choose View, Toolbars, then select Reviewing to display the Reviewing toolbar.

 2. Click the Track Changes icon. Simply click the Track Changes icon again to turn off revision marking.

The Toolbar approach is much faster—you can turn Track Changes on and off with one click.

While Track Changes feature is turned on, any text inserted in the document or deleted from it is marked. If you move a selection of text, two sets of marks appear: the text you moved appears as deleted (strikethrough) text in its original location and as inserted text in its new location. If you delete text marked as inserted, the text simply disappears. Only original text appears in strikethrough format when you delete it.

N O T E You can turn on revision marking for all documents at once, if they are based on the NORMAL.DOT template. Open the NORMAL.DOT template, choose Tools, Track Changes, Highlight Changes, select the Track Changes While Editing check box, and save the template. You can also clear the Highlight Changes On Screen and Highlight Changes in Printed Document check boxes to hide revision marks until you actually review the revisions.

Showing Changes

When a document comes back from your reviewers or you return to a document after editing it yourself, you can look over the changes. If revision marks are not visible in the document, choose Tools, Track Changes, Highlight Changes and select the Highlight Changes On Screen check box.

The document now appears with revision bars in the margin, marking where text has been inserted or deleted. If multiple reviewers made revisions, each reviewer's changes appear in a different color. If you want to continue tracking changes but without seeing revision marks, choose Tools, Track Changes, Highlight Changes, and clear the Highlight Changes On Screen check box.

By default, Word prints documents with revision marks showing. To print a document without revision marks, choose Tools, Track Changes, Highlight Changes, and clear Highlight Changes in Printed Document.

N O T E If you customize your user information, you can keep track of your own editing sessions separately. For each session you want to distinguish, choose Tools, Options, select the User Information tab, and change the Name text box. For example, start with First Draft, then use Style Review for another editing session, and then use Final Draft. Each set of revisions appears in its own color, and the Accept or Reject Changes dialog box shows those names. Also, each time you move your mouse pointer over revised text, Word displays who revised it and when. Be sure to restore your original name later, because other Word features use this information.

Accepting or Rejecting All Changes

Word makes using or discarding changes easy. To incorporate all the changes marked in the document, choose Tools, Track Changes, Accept or Reject Changes, and Accept All. When prompted to accept the revisions, answer Yes and choose Close. All the deleted text disappears, the inserted text is incorporated into the document, and revision bars are removed. Rejecting all changes means restoring your document to its contents before it was reviewed. To reject all revisions, choose Tools, Track Changes, Accept or Reject

Changes, and Reject All. When prompted to reject all revisions, answer Yes and choose Close. Inserted text disappears, deleted text is restored, and revision bars are removed.

You can undo these commands. As a safety measure, save your file with a new name before you accept or reject all revisions. You then have a copy of original and revised drafts for later reference or comparison. Remember that any *formatting* changes made by reviewers remain, whether you accept or reject revisions.

Accepting or Rejecting Individual Changes

You'll probably want to use some but not all of the changes made to your document. You can look through the document, jumping directly from change to change, and choose whether to accept or reject each change.

To accept or reject individual changes using menu commands, follow these steps:

1. Choose Tools, Track Changes, Accept or Reject Changes. The Accept or Reject Changes dialog box appears (see Figure 32.3).

   In the Accept or Reject Changes dialog box, you can review all revision marks and see which reviewer made a revision and when.

FIG. 32.3

The Accept or Reject Changes dialog box helps you move through your document to examine the revisions.

2. Click one of the Find buttons to find either the next or the previous change in the document and to show which reviewer made the change and when.

3. Select the Changes with Highlighting check box to view original text and high-lighted changes.

4. Select the Changes Without Highlighting check box to view only the changes without highlighting.

5. Select the Original check box to view the original text without changes.

6. Click the Accept button to keep the change, or the Reject button to discard it.

7. If you change your mind, click the Undo Last button to restore the most recent revision that you accepted or rejected.

8. Click one of the Find buttons to locate the next revision.

While the Accept or Reject Changes dialog box is on-screen, you can click anywhere in the document to edit the text, or you can select another change to display information about it.

To accept or reject individual changes using the Reviewing toolbar, follow these steps:

1. Choose View, Toolbars, then select Reviewing to display the Reviewing toolbar.

2. Click the Accept Change icon to accept the change.

3. Click the Reject Change icon to reject the change.

4. Click the Next Change icon to find the next change.

5. Click the Previous Change icon to find the previous change.

Customizing Revision Marks

Usually, revision bars in the margins appear black, the revision mark for inserted text is an underline, deleted text has a line through it, and changes made by up to eight reviewers are marked in different colors that Word assigns automatically. (If you have more than eight reviewers, Word reuses the earlier colors.) You can customize each of these marks to your liking. For example, you can mark deleted text as a subdued color, such as light gray, and inserted text as green.

To customize revision marks, follow these steps:

1. Choose Tools, Options, and select the Track Changes tab. You can also choose Tools, Track Changes, Highlight Changes, and then click the Options button to display the tab shown in Figure 32.4.

2. Select styles from the Mark list boxes under Inserted Text, Deleted Text, Changed Formatting, and Changed Lines.

3. If you do not need color to distinguish reviewers, select a color from the Color list boxes under Inserted Text and Deleted Text.

4. Choose OK.

If you select By Author under Color in the Inserted Text and Deleted Text sections, each reviewer's changes appear in a different color for up to eight reviewers. The Changed Lines options specify the appearance of the revision bars in the margins of your document. The Changed Formatting options specify the appearance of the revised text.

FIG. 32.4
As you customize revision marks in the Track Changes tab of the Options dialog box, you can preview the appearance of changed text in a document.

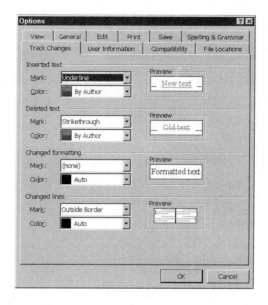

Protecting Documents for Changes

Protecting a document for changes ensures that changes are being tracked. If a reviewer turns off the Track Changes feature in your document, you could have a good deal of extra work finding where revisions are and who made them. For increased security, you can add a password so that only you can unprotect the document.

When a document is protected for changes, Word tracks all changes and does not allow revision marks to be removed by accepting or rejecting them. Reviewers can add comments as well as revise the document directly. For more information, see the section "Using Comments" later in this chapter.

To protect a document for revisions, follow these steps:

1. Choose Tools, Protect Document. The Protect Document dialog box appears (see Figure 32.5).

FIG. 32.5
Use the Protect Document dialog box to ensure that your document is not changed without your knowledge.

Part VII

Ch 32

2. Select the Tracked Changes option.

3. If you want to keep other users from unprotecting the document, type a password in the Password text box.

4. Choose OK. If you entered a password, Word prompts you to reenter the password for confirmation.

5. Reenter the password and choose OK.

CAUTION

It's easy to forget passwords. If you don't remember the password you use, you will have access to the file, but will not have the ability to accept or reject revisions. You might want to jot down the name of the document and the password you assign to it for future reference.

To unprotect a document, choose Tools, Unprotect Document. While the document is protected for changes, any changes made to the document will be tracked until it is unprotected, and you cannot choose to accept or reject any revisions. If you defined a password, you must enter it before the document can be unprotected. If you are using the routing feature of Word, you can protect the document when you add a routing slip.

Merging Changes and Comments

Several different reviewers may have worked on separate copies of a document instead of routing the same copy. If so, filtering through all the revision marks and comments in multiple files can be tedious. To make the work easier, you can combine all the changes into the original document and see them together. To do so, you need the original document and any revised documents from it.

To merge revisions and annotations, follow these steps:

1. Open one of the revised documents.

2. Choose Tools, Merge Documents. The Select File to Merge Into Current Document dialog box appears.

3. Select the original unrevised document and click Open.

4. Repeat these steps for each revised version of the document that you want to merge into the original.

Word merges the revision marks and comments into the original document, where you can see and evaluate them in one place.

TROUBLESHOOTING

I don't have any revision marks in my document. You can see revision marks only if revision marking was turned on while the document was being edited. Choose Tools, Track Changes, Accept or Reject Changes, and then click the Find button. If no revision marks are found, you can add them by comparing your document with the original version of the file. See the section "Comparing Documents" later in this chapter.

I see a revision bar in the margin but no revision marks. There may be revision marks inside hidden text, field codes, or comments. To see these, choose Tools, Options, select the View tab, and then select the Field Codes and Hidden Text check boxes.

I need to see the reviewer name and time information in the Accept or Reject Changes dialog box. Information about each change appears only after you find the change. Choose one of the Find buttons to search for changes.

I can't turn off the option for tracking changes. If the document is protected for revisions, the Track Changes While Editing check box is grayed. To turn off this option, choose Tools, Unprotect Document, asking the document's author for the password if necessary.

Opening, Saving, and Deleting Versions

The File, Versions feature allows a single writer or group of writers to save multiple versions of the same document. By adding detailed comments about each version, you keep a historical record of changes made to a document.

Multiple versions are saved under a single file name. When you open a file having multiple versions, the latest version is opened first. Once opened, you then can open a previous version by clicking the Open button in the Versions dialog box, delete a version, create a new version, or read comments associated with a version.

To open a version of a document, follow these steps:

1. Choose File, Versions. The Versions dialog box appears as shown in Figure 32.6.

2. Highlight the version to open by using the mouse or arrow keys, then click the Open button.

To save a new version or delete an existing version of a document, follow these steps:

1. Choose File, Versions. The Versions dialog box appears as shown in Figure 32.6.

2. If you want to save a version, click the Save Now button then add related comments in the Save Version dialog box. Then click OK.

FIG. 32.6

The Versions dialog box shows related information about each version of a document.

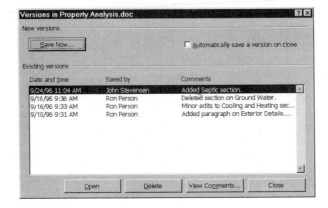

3. If you want to delete a version, highlight the version to delete using the mouse or arrow keys, then click the Delete button.

   Click the View Comments button to display the comments related to the highlighted version.

You can save a new version each time you close the document by selecting the Automatically Save A Version On Close check box in the Versions dialog box. In this way, you can avoid overwriting changes that others have made by keeping each user's edits in separate versions.

If you open a version of a document and then save it, the version is saved under a new file name. The new file name includes the version date to aid in tracking versions. You then can open a version directly instead of through the Versions dialog box. Saving a version in this manner removes from the new file the ability to see other versions.

Comparing Documents

You can pinpoint revisions by comparing the current document to an earlier version. When you compare two documents, Word applies revision marks to your current document wherever it differs from the earlier version. The two documents you're comparing must have different names or locations on the disk.

To compare two versions of a document, follow these steps:

1. Open the document where you want the revision marks added.

2. Choose Tools, Track Changes, Compare Documents. The Select File to Compare With Current Document dialog box appears.

3. Select a file to which you want to compare the current file.

4. Click <u>O</u>pen. Word will flag all differences between the two documents, but display them using the formatting settings you've established in the Track Changes tab.

You can select or reject any of the changes by using the following options in the Accept or Reject Changes dialog box:

Choose This	To Do This
<u>A</u>ccept or Reject Changes	Display each revision mark so that you can accept, reject, or ignore it. The Accept or Reject Changes dialog box provides these options.
<u>A</u>ccept All	Leave the selection unchanged and remove the revision marks.
Re<u>j</u>ect All	Reverse all changes and remove revision marks.

Using Comments

The Track Changes feature is useful for tracking editing changes in a document, whereas Comments are best for attaching comments to a document. Because Comments are linked to specific parts of a document, they are just like notes scribbled in the white space—except that Comments are more convenient.

You may have had the experience of printing a final copy of a document and then noticing a note to yourself that you forgot to delete. The Comment feature takes care of that prob-lem by keeping comments separate from the rest of your text; they aren't printed unless you specifically decide to print them. Comments are the ideal place to store questions and notes to yourself or to an author whose work you're reviewing.

Inserting Comments

When you insert a comment, Word marks the location in the document and opens the Comments pane. Here you can type your comments and even format them.

To insert a comment using menu commands, follow these steps:

1. Select the word or passage you want to comment on, or position the insertion point in the text.

2. Choose <u>I</u>nsert, Co<u>m</u>ment, or press Alt+Ctrl+M to insert a comment mark and open the Comments pane (see Figure 32.7).

3. Type your comment in the Comments pane. You can use font and paragraph formatting just as you normally would.

FIG. 32.7

The Comments pane shows the reviewer's initials and the text of the annotation. In the main document, the comment is high-lighted in yellow.

Insert Sound Object button

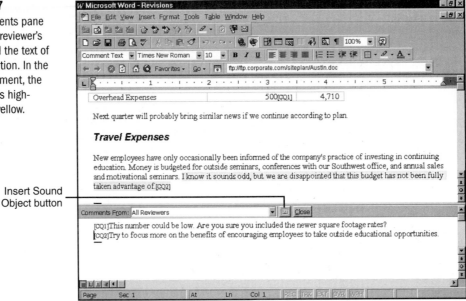

To insert a comment using the Reviewing toolbar, follow these steps:

1. Choose View, Toolbars, then select Reviewing to display the Reviewing toolbar.

2. Click the Insert Comment icon.

3. Type your comment in the Comments pane. You can use font and paragraph formatting just as you normally would.

The comment mark contains the reviewer's initials and a number—for example, [CQ1]. Comments are numbered in sequence. In the Comments pane, a corresponding mark precedes the comment text.

To close the Comments pane, click the Close button or double-click any comment mark in the pane.

Adding Audible Comments

The Insert Sound Object feature enables you to add sound annotations, providing your computer has a sound card and microphone installed. You can record an annotation, or use a prerecorded sound file, and insert it in the appropriate location in your document.

To insert a sound annotation, follow these steps:

1. Select the word or passage to which you want to add sound, or position the insertion point at the end of the text.

2. Choose Insert, Comment, or press Alt+Ctrl+M to insert a comment mark and open the Comments pane.

3. If you want to include text with the voice comment, type your comment in the Comments pane. You can use font and paragraph formatting just as you normally would.

4. Position the insertion point at the end of the comment text, then click the Tape icon in the Comments pane. The Sound Object dialog box appears. It uses VCR-like controls.

5. Click the Record button, the red circle, and speak your message into the computer's microphone.

6. Click the Stop button (next to the record function) when you complete your comment.

7. Click File, Exit and Return to Document.

A speaker icon appears in the Comments pane. Double-clicking the Speaker icon will play the voice comment you recorded. To edit the sound object, right-click it, then choose Wave Sound Object, Edit. To delete it, click it once, then press Delete.

To close the Comments pane, click the Close button or double-click any comment mark in the pane.

> **N O T E**   Sound files can get very large. To create them, you must have a sound card and microphone. The person reviewing your file must have a PC with a sound card and speakers if they want to playback the recording. ■

Finding and Viewing Comments

There are several ways to display comment marks in a document. When the Comments pane is open, comment marks always appear. Because comment marks are formatted as hidden text, they appear also when hidden text is showing (when you choose Tools, Option, View and select Hidden Text from the Nonprinting characters group). Finally, you can show comment marks by clicking the Show/Hide ¶ button on the Standard toolbar.

To find a specific comment mark using menu commands, follow these steps:

1. Choose View, Comments. The Comments pane appears.

2. Choose Edit, Go To to display the Find and Replace dialog box. In the Go To tab, you can go to a particular reviewer's next comment or type the number of a comment (see Figure 32.8).

3. Select Comment from the Go To What list box.

FIG. 32.8

The Go To tab includes a Comment option which lets you go directly to the comment you choose.

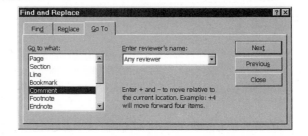

4. If you want to find a specific reviewer's comments, type or select the person's name in the Enter Reviewer's Name box.

5. If you want to find a specific comment, type a number in the Enter Reviewer's Name text box. For example, type **3** for the third comment or **+2** for the second comment after the current selection.

6. Click the Next or Previous button. The Next button changes to Go To if you type a number rather than select a reviewer's name.

To find a specific comment mark using the Reviewing toolbar, follow these steps:

1. Choose View, Toolbars, then select Reviewing to display the Reviewing toolbar.

 2. Click the Next Comment icon to find the next comment.

3. Click the Previous Comment icon to find the previous comment.

N O T E If you don't need to specify the reviewer, you can find comments quickly by choosing Edit, Find and then selecting Comment Mark from the Special pull-down list. The Comments pane appears automatically when a comment is found. (This pane does not appear when you choose Go To.) ▓

When you select a comment in the Comments pane, Word highlights the corresponding document text. This is why it's most useful to select the text in question when you insert comments, rather than simply positioning the cursor in a specific location. You can adjust the size of the Comments pane by dragging the split box—the short, gray button between the vertical scroll bars of the document and Comments panes.

Including or Deleting Comments

A comment often consists of comments or questions about the selected text. If the comment contains suggested text, however, you can easily move the text into your document. Simply select the text in the Comments pane and drag it into your document. Similarly, you can copy the text by holding down the Ctrl key while dragging. (If you cannot drag the text, choose <u>T</u>ools, <u>O</u>ptions, select the Edit tab, and then choose the <u>D</u>rag-and-Drop text editing check box.)

 Comments also can be deleted using the Delete Comment icon in the Reviewing toolbar.

> **N O T E** You can easily remove all comments at once. Choose <u>E</u>dit, R<u>e</u>place, choose Comment
> Mark in the Special pull-down list, or type **^a** in the Fi<u>n</u>d What text box, leave the
> Replace W<u>i</u>th text box empty, and click the Replace <u>A</u>ll button. ■

If several reviewers added comments to separate copies of an original document, you can merge all the comments into the original document for convenient evaluation. To merge comments, see the section "Merging Changes and Comments" earlier in this chapter.

Protecting Documents for Comments Only

At times, you might want reviewers to comment on your document but not to change it directly. You can allow comments (but no revisions) by protecting your document for comments.

To protect a document for comments, follow these steps:

1. Choose <u>T</u>ools, <u>P</u>rotect Document, and select the <u>C</u>omments option.
2. If you want to keep others from unprotecting the document, type a password in the <u>P</u>assword text box.
3. Click OK. If you entered a password, Word prompts you to reenter the password for confirmation.
4. Reenter the password and click OK.

No changes except comments can be made to the document until it is unprotected, and menu commands that could make changes are unavailable. When anyone tries to edit the document, a beep warns the user that the document is protected. A message appears in the status bar saying, `This command is not available because the document is locked for edit`.

To unprotect a document, click <u>T</u>ools, <u>U</u>nprotect Document. If you defined a password, you must enter it and click OK before the document can be unprotected.

Printing Comments

To get a printed copy of a commented document, you can either print just the comments or print them at the end of the document.

To print comments only, follow these steps:

1. Choose <u>F</u>ile, <u>P</u>rint.

2. Select Comments from the Print <u>W</u>hat drop-down list box.

3. Click OK.

Word prints the contents of the Comments pane, adding the page number where each comment mark occurs in the document.

To print a document with comments, follow these steps:

1. Click the <u>O</u>ptions button in the Print dialog box.

2. Select the <u>C</u>omments check box, which automatically selects the Hidden Text check box, and choose OK.

3. Select <u>D</u>ocument from the Print <u>W</u>hat list box.

4. Click OK.

Because comment marks in a document are formatted as hidden text, all hidden text is printed. The comments are printed at the end of the document, along with the page number of the accompanying comment mark.

▶ **See** "Controlling Printing Options," **p. 274**

TROUBLESHOOTING

When I try to delete a comment, the comment mark doesn't go away. To delete a comment, select the comment mark in the document text and press Backspace or Delete. You must select a comment mark first, before pressing Backspace or Delete, because it is a special nontext character.

I don't remember deleting a comment, but now it's gone. Why? If you delete the text surrounding a comment mark in the middle of a document, the mark is deleted, even if the mark is not visible.

How do I change the initials in a comment mark? The initials are taken from the User Information tab of the Options dialog box. If you change your initials there, future comments will contain the new initials.

CHAPTER 33

Adding Cross-References and Captions

Cross-references and captions greatly simplify the job of creating complex or illustrated documents. *Cross-references* refer to text or objects in some other part of your document, or in another document. *Captions* label and number illustrations and tables in your document. You can update cross-references and captions automatically, so that when you insert them you can be sure they remain accurate—no matter how many insertions, deletions, and other editing changes you make throughout the document. ■

Cross-reference headings, bookmarks, and page numbers

Make your documents easier to read while adhering to professional publishing standards with cross-references within the current document or related documents.

Add hyperlinks to a document

Create hyperlinks as part of the cross-reference so that readers can jump to the reference source.

Label pictures, tables, and other illustrations

Create labels that automatically format, align with, and stay next to the object they label.

Add captions automatically when you insert objects

Caption numbers used in text will automatically renumber themselves when moved.

Understanding Cross-References and Captions

Cross-references and captions simplify your job when you create a document, and they also make your reader's job easier. Cross-references give readers quick access to related information in other parts of your document; captions provide consistent and accurate labeling for the illustrations and tables that augment text.

Figures 33.1 and 33.2 show examples of a cross-reference and a caption.

FIG. 33.1

Both the section title and the page number are cross-references. If either changes, the text on this page reflects that change.

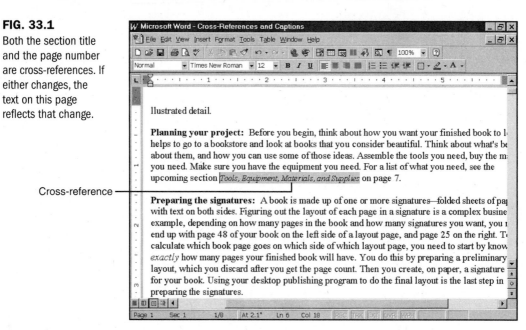

Because cross-references and captions are fields, Word can update them automatically whenever you print the document. (*Fields* are hidden text that perform special functions, such as linking parts of a document together.) Alternatively, you can update fields yourself by selecting them and pressing F9. If you have included page numbers in cross-references throughout your document, for example, and you subsequently add text (so that page numbers change), the cross-references update to show the new page numbers. Or if you include automatically numbered captions for figures and then add more figures, Word renumbers existing figures.

FIG. 33.2
Word numbers
captions automatically.

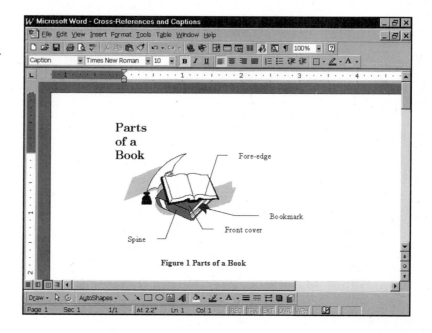

CAUTION

Word 97 does not automatically update fields in your document when you print unless you choose Tools, Options, select the Print tab, and select the Update Fields option.

In a cross-reference, the entire text (except any text you type yourself) is a *field result*. In a caption, however, only the chapter and caption number are fields. For example, in a caption reading *Figure 1*, the word *Figure* is not a field result, but the number *1* is.

▶ **See** "Understanding the Basics of Fields," **p. 694**

As a rule, you see the results of fields in your document; they look like text (see Figure 33.3). If you choose Tools, Options, however, and on the View tab, select Field Codes in the Show group, you see a code inside braces—the field code—instead of text (see Figure 33.4). Clear this option to see the result of your field, rather than the code.

FIG. 33.3

The cross-reference field code results in text that can be formatted or edited.

Field Result —

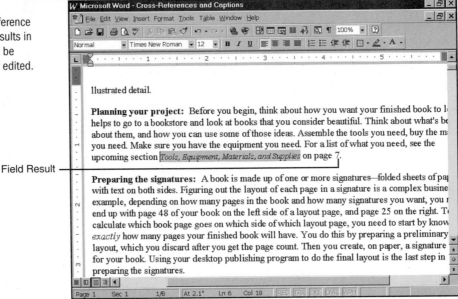

FIG. 33.4

You can choose Tools, Options, the View tab, and the Field Codes option to display field codes.

Field codes appear within braces

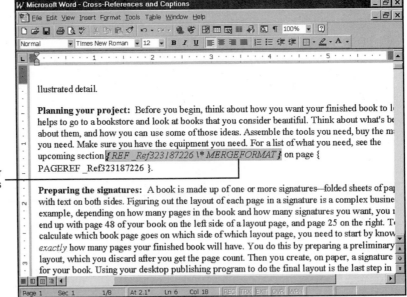

Creating Cross-References

A cross-reference refers the reader to information in another part of your document (or another document that is part of the same master document). You have the option of including a wide variety of information in your cross-references, depending on the contents of the text or other material you are cross-referencing. If the content or location of the information changes, Word automatically updates the cross-reference to reflect those changes.

Your cross-reference can display several types of information, including headings formatted with Word's built-in heading styles (Heading 1 through Heading 9), page numbers that correspond to cross-referenced text, footnotes and endnotes, captions, and bookmarks. When you apply a cross-reference in your document, Word finds the referenced information and inserts that information at the cross-reference. If you cross-reference a heading, for example, Word inserts the text of that heading at the location of the cross-reference. If you cross-reference text elsewhere in the document, Word displays the page number where that text occurs.

Cross-references generally contain two types of text: text that you type, and the cross-reference information that Word inserts. You may type, for example, the words **For more information see page** and then insert a cross-reference to a page number.

You can include multiple references within a single cross-reference in your document. For example, you may want your cross-reference to read: "For more information see X on page Y," with Word filling in both a heading title and a page number.

Adding Text and Hyperlink Cross-References

Because cross-references contain two kinds of text—the text you type and the cross-reference itself—creating a cross-reference is a two-part process. You type the introductory text and then insert the cross-reference. In many cases, you insert two cross-references—one for a title and one for a page number. Word leaves the Cross-Reference dialog box open so that you can insert as many cross-references as you need. When you use the Cross-Reference dialog box, you make three choices for each cross-reference you insert. This process involves narrowing down your options. First, you select the general category of your cross-reference; for example, you might select Heading if your cross-reference is based on one of Word's built-in heading styles (Heading 1 through Heading 9). You next select what characteristic of that heading you want to reference: the heading text, the page number where that heading appears, or the heading number (if you have included heading numbering). Finally, you select the specific heading you want to reference—the Cross-Reference For Which Heading box lists all the headings. Each reference type (Heading, Bookmark, Footnote, and so on) has specific options.

Two more cross-reference options, hyperlinks and above/below, extend the functionality of cross-references. If you select the Insert as Hyperlink option in the Cross-Reference dialog box, you can click the reference to jump to the cross-referenced item. For example, if you create a hyperlinked table of contents, you can jump from any contents heading to that topic in the body of the document. When you position the insertion point over the hyperlinked text, a tip box displays the name of the document you've referenced.

The Above/Below option is available when you reference numbered items. When you select Include Above/Below in the Cross-Reference dialog box, Word automatically inserts the word "above" or "below" in the cross-reference, depending on the position of the cross-referenced item. For example, if you are referring to a figure that is located after the cross-reference, the cross-reference reads, "Figure 1 below."

▶ **See** "Inserting Hyperlinks to Web or Local Files," **p. 514**

CAUTION

Before you can insert a cross-reference, you must mark the item you want to reference. You can use a heading style, bookmark, footnote, endnote, or caption to mark a location. If you have not marked locations in one of these ways, the lists in the Cross-reference dialog box will not display items for you to cross-reference.

To add a cross-reference, follow these steps:

1. Type the introductory text preceding the cross-reference. For example, type **"See the following page."** Leave the insertion point where you want the cross-reference to appear.

2. Choose Insert, Cross-reference. The Cross-reference dialog box appears (see Figure 33.5).

FIG. 33.5

The Cross-Reference dialog box stays open while you complete your cross-reference.

3. In the Reference Type list, select the type of item you want to reference.

   For example, select Heading if you want to cross-reference to a title or subtitle formatted with a heading style.

4. In the Insert Reference To list, select the information about the item that you want to reference.

   The list varies, according to which reference type you have selected. For example, if you had selected Heading as the Reference type, you could reference the heading's text title, the page number of the heading, or the heading number.

   If you are working in a document that contains numbered paragraphs (as in a legal document), you can select Numbered Item as the Reference Type. Your choices in the Insert Reference To List include Paragraph Number, Paragraph Number (No Context), and Paragraph Number (Full Context). Select *Paragraph Number* to include a relative reference, where shared numbering is not repeated in the reference. For example, a reference to 1.(a)(ii) from 1.(a)(i) refers to (ii) since they both share 1(a). Select *Paragraph Number (No Context)* to include only the last level of numbering in a series, such as a reference to 1.(a)(i) appears as (i), regardless of whether numbering is shared. Select *Paragraph Number (Full Context)* to include the full reference number, regardless of whether any numbering is shared. A reference to 1.(a)(ii) appears anywhere in the document as 1.(a)(ii).

5. In the For Which Numbered Item list box, select the specific item you want to reference.

   Word lists all the items of the selected type that it finds in your document. If you had selected Heading as the Reference type, you would see a list of all headings in the document.

6. Select Insert As Hyperlink to add an on-screen hyperlink from the reference to the cross-referenced item in the document. If the item you are cross-referencing is located in another document, both documents must be part of the same master document.

7. Select Include Above/Below when you are referencing a numbered item if you want Word to add the words "above" or "below" to references.

8. Click Insert to insert the cross-reference.

9. If you want to add additional text in your document before closing the Cross-Reference dialog box, click in your document and type the text. Then you can repeat steps 3 through 6 to insert an additional cross-reference. Choose Close when you are finished. (Close appears after you insert a cross-reference.)

Part

VII

Ch

33

Cross-Referencing Another Document

To include a cross-reference to another document, both documents must be part of a master document. *Master documents* are used to create a large document from many smaller subdocuments. To insert a cross-reference, choose <u>V</u>iew, <u>M</u>aster Document, and in Master Document view, insert cross-references in the usual way (see the earlier section, "Adding Cross-References"). When you are in Master Document view, the Cross-reference dialog box lists all the headings, bookmarks, and so on that are contained in the documents linked to this master document.

Updating Cross-References

You can update cross-references and captions by simply selecting them and pressing the F9 key. To update all the cross-references in your document, select the entire document and press F9. Cross-references update automatically when you print your document.

 TIP You can include a cross-reference in a header or footer. You may want to include a cross-reference, for example, which displays the title of a chapter inside a header.

▶ **See** "Marking Locations with Bookmarks," **p. 182**
▶ **See** "Creating Numbered Headings," **p. 670**
▶ **See** "Understanding the Basics of Fields," **p. 694**

Formatting Cross-References

In your document, a cross-reference looks like text (even though it is a field result), and you can edit it like text. When the insertion point is inside a cross-reference field, the entire cross-reference is highlighted. The field is selected, but the text is not. Within the highlighted field, however, you can select text and edit it using any of Word's usual editing techniques. When you cross-reference a heading, for example, you may want it to appear in italic. After you insert the cross-reference, select the text in the usual way and apply italic using a command or shortcut. For more information about selecting fields, see the section "Editing and Deleting Cross-References and Captions," later in this chapter.

Creating Captions

Captions help readers reference the illustrations you include in your document. In Word, a caption includes a label, a number, and (optionally) a chapter number. A caption may read, for example, `Figure 7` or `Table II-ii`. You can type additional text after the label and number.

When you create a caption, you can select from a list of preexisting labels such as `Figure` or `Table`, or you can create your own labels. You can select from a list of predefined numbering styles, such as `1 2 3`, `A B C`, or `I II III`. You can place a caption above or below your illustration.

You can include captions in your document in one of two ways. You can instruct Word to include a caption each time you insert a particular type of object; for example, you may want a caption for each picture you insert. Or you can select an object and create a caption for it manually.

Captions update automatically when you insert additional captions in your document. The first caption you insert, for example, may read `Figure 1` and the second `Figure 2`. If you insert a new caption between Figure 1 and Figure 2, the new caption is numbered `Figure 2` and the previous Figure 2 becomes `Figure 3`.

Word formats captions with the Caption style. The style that follows Caption is Normal; therefore, when you press Enter after inserting a caption, Word automatically sets the next paragraph's style to Normal. You can change the formatting of the Caption style by using Format, Style, or by defining a new Caption style by example. For details, see Chapter 11, "Using Styles for Repetitive Formats."

Captions work well with cross-references. You can create a cross-reference to any type of caption. If the caption number or label changes, you can update the cross-reference to reflect that change. (For information about updating, see the earlier section, "Creating Cross-References.")

Inserting Captions Manually

You can insert captions manually for figures, tables, objects, and even text. Use this technique when the illustrations are already inserted in your document, or when you include various types of illustrations (pictures and tables, for example), and you want them to have a consistent labeling and numbering scheme.

A caption always includes a label and number, but you also can add text to further explain your illustrations. For example, you may want a caption to read `Table 1 Summary of Annual Sales`. For each type of label you include, Word creates a separate numbering sequence. If you already have inserted Figure 1 and Figure 2, for example, and then insert a caption with the label `Table`, the caption reads `Table 1` rather than `Table 3`.

To insert a caption manually, follow these steps:

1. Select the object for which you want a caption.

2. Choose Insert, Caption.

   The Caption dialog box appears (see Figure 33.6).

FIG. 33.6

Captions include labels and numbers, and you can add additional text as well. In this example, Figure is the label and 1 is the number.

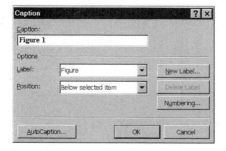

3. With the insertion point after the proposed label and number in the Caption text box, type any additional text you want in your caption.

4. You can select a different label from the Label list box. Word numbers each type of label separately.

5. You can select a different location for your caption—above or below the selected item—from the Position list box. Figure 33.7 shows a caption placed below an illustration.

FIG. 33.7

Word inserts the caption above or below the selected item.

6. Choose OK.

When you return to your document after inserting a caption, the insertion point flashes at the end of the caption. The caption is formatted with the Caption style. Press Enter to start a new paragraph formatted with the Normal style.

N O T E Because captions are formatted with a style, be sure to put them on a line by themselves; otherwise the entire paragraph where you insert the caption is formatted with Caption style.

Figure captions, unlike the other caption types, are placed in a text box beneath the figure (the Caption style is applied, however). You can manipulate them like any other text box. You can, for example, drag the caption to the right of the figure as you would any text box.

▶ **See** "Moving and Positioning Text Boxes," **p. 866**

Inserting Captions Automatically

If you plan to insert many illustrations of a certain type in your document, you can specify that Word include a caption for each one. If you intend to illustrate your document with many pictures, for example, you can have Word include a caption for each picture. You determine what label Word uses in the captions.

You can include automatic captions for as many different types of document elements, such as pictures or tables, as you want. The captions either can share a label (and thus share a numbering scheme), or captions for each type of object can have a unique label and a separate sequence of numbers. If you want to add explanatory text after an automatic caption, position the insertion point at the end of the caption and type the text.

Activate automatic captions before you begin inserting your illustrations. If you insert automatic captions after you have inserted some of your illustrations, select the existing illustrations and add their captions manually (see the earlier section, "Inserting Captions Manually," for information on this procedure). If the manually and automatically inserted captions use the same label, Word updates the caption numbers to keep them sequential.

To include automatic captions, follow these steps:

1. Choose Insert, Caption.
2. Click the AutoCaption button.

   The AutoCaption dialog box appears (see Figure 33.8).

3. In the Add caption when inserting list, select the type of document element for which you want Word to add automatic captions. Select several types of elements if you want them all to have the same label and numbering scheme.

4. Select Options for the type of object you selected. From Use Label, select the type of label for the object; from Position, select Above Item or Below Item.

   To create a unique label, choose New Label (for details, see the next section, "Creating New Caption Labels"). To change the numbering style or include chapter numbers, choose Numbering (see the "Changing Caption Numbering" later in this section).

FIG. 33.8
You can use automatic captions for many types of document elements.

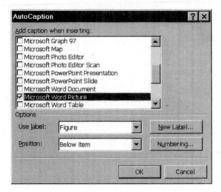

5. Repeat steps 3 and 4 to add automatic captions for additional types of document elements. By first selecting the element (step 3) and then selecting options (step 4), you can create a separate label and numbering scheme for each type of element for which you insert automatic captions.

6. Choose OK.

Creating New Caption Labels

You can create a new caption label at any of three times when working in your document: when you insert the caption manually, when you insert automatic captions, or after you have inserted your captions.

When you create a new label, Word adds it to the list of existing labels; the new label is available the next time you create a caption.

N O T E You can't drag across an existing label in the Caption box to select it; to change a label, you must choose Insert, Caption, and then select a caption from the Label list or create a new one by choosing New Label. ▪

To create a new label for a manual caption, follow these steps:

1. Select the object for which you want a caption and choose Insert, Caption.

2. Choose New Label. The New Label dialog box opens (see Figure 33.9).

3. In the Label text box, type the text of the label you want. Choose OK to close the New Label dialog box.

4. Choose OK to close the Caption dialog box.

FIG. 33.9
Create your own label
by typing it in the
Label box.

Your new label appears in the Caption list box of the Caption dialog box, as shown in
Figure 33.10.

FIG. 33.10
Your new label
appears in the
Caption box.

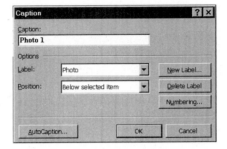

To create new labels for automatic captions, follow these steps:

1. Choose Insert, Caption.
2. Click AutoCaption to display the AutoCaption dialog box (refer to Figure 33.8).
3. From the Add Caption When Inserting list box, select the object type for which you
   want automatic captions.
4. Click New Label.
5. In the Label box, type the text of the label. Choose OK to exit the New Label
   dialog box.
6. Choose OK.

Changing Caption Labels

You can change the labels for captions you already have inserted in your document. When
you change the label for an existing caption, all captions with that label-type change. If you
change Figure to Table, for example, all the captions labeled as Figure change to Table.

To change labels for existing captions, follow these steps:

1. Select a caption with the label type you want to change. If you want to change all
   captions with the label Figure to the label Table, for example, select one *Figure*
   caption.
2. Choose Insert, Caption.

Part
VII

Ch
33

3. Select a different label from the Label list, or choose New Label and create a new label.

4. Choose OK.

Deleting a Caption Label

When you create new caption labels, they are added to the list of existing labels. You can delete these new labels from the list, but you can't delete Word's built-in labels (like Figure and Table). To delete the label, choose Insert, Caption, select the label from the Label list, click Delete Label, and then choose Close.

If you delete the label from an existing caption, the caption number remains, and the numbering scheme for that label type is unchanged. To learn about editing captions, see the section "Editing and Deleting Cross-References and Captions" later in this chapter.

Changing Caption Numbering

You can change the caption numbering style for manual or automatic captions when you insert the captions. Alternatively, you can change the numbering style for existing captions in your document. When you change the caption numbering style, the change affects all captions with the same label type as the caption you changed.

To change caption numbering when you insert captions, follow these steps:

1. For manual captions, select the object for which you want to insert a caption and choose Insert, Caption. In the Caption dialog box, click Numbering.

   For automatic captions, choose Insert, Caption. In the Caption dialog box, click AutoCaption. Select the type of object for which you want automatic captions, then choose Numbering.

   The Caption Numbering dialog box appears (see Figure 33.11).

FIG. 33.11
You can change the format of the caption number, and you can include chapter numbers in your captions.

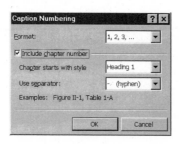

2. To change the style of the numbers, select an option from the Format drop-down list. For example, select 1, 2, 3; or a, b, c; or A, B, C; or i, ii, iii; or I, II, III.

3. Choose OK to return to the previous dialog box.

4. Choose OK to return to your document.

To change caption numbering style for existing captions, follow these steps:

1. Select a caption of the label-type whose numbering style you want to change. For example, if you want to change all the "Figure 1-*x*" captions to "Figure A-*z*" captions, select a single "Figure 1" caption.

2. Choose Insert, Caption.

3. In the Caption dialog box, click Numbering.

4. Select a different numbering style from the Format list.

5. Choose OK to return to the Caption dialog box.

6. Choose Close to return to your document.

All captions using the same label-type reflect your new numbering style.

TIP You also can change numbering by selecting a captioned object, rather than a caption. If you use this technique, close the Caption dialog box by choosing Close in step 4 rather than OK. If you choose OK, you add an extra caption.

Including Chapter Numbers in a Caption

In a caption, you can include the current chapter number, if you format your chapters with one of Word's built-in heading styles (Heading 1 through Heading 9), and if you have selected a heading numbering style. A caption with a chapter number may read, for example, Figure 1A or Table II:ii.

This technique works well with a document containing several chapters. In a document containing only one chapter, all the chapter numbers would obviously be the same.

To include chapter numbers in your captions, follow these steps:

1. Format all chapter titles and subheadings with built-in heading styles: Heading 1 through Heading 9. Be sure to format the title of each chapter as Heading 1.

2. Choose Format, Bullets and Numbering, and click the Outline Numbered tab. Select a heading numbering style or choose Customize to create your own. (Refer to Chapter 13, "Formatting the Page Layout, Alignment, and Numbering," for more information on numbering.) Choose OK.

3. For manual captions, select the object for which you want to insert a caption and choose Insert, Caption. In the Caption dialog box, choose Numbering.

Part

VII

Ch

33

For automatic captions, choose Insert, Caption. In the Caption dialog box, choose AutoCaption. Select the type of object for which you want automatic captions, then choose Numbering.

4. In the Caption Numbering dialog box, select the Include Chapter Number option.

5. In the Chapter Starts with Style List box, select the lowest level of heading you want to include in your caption number. If you want only the chapter number, for example, select Heading 1 to get a caption such as Figure 1-3. If you want to include the chapter and first subheading number, however, select Heading 2 for a caption such as Figure 1.2-3.

6. In the Use Separator list, select the punctuation you want to separate the chapter number and the caption number. Options include a hyphen, a period, a colon, an em dash (a wide hyphen), and an en dash (a medium-wide hyphen).

7. Choose OK to return to the previous dialog box.

8. Choose OK to return to your document.

Formatting Captions

The Caption format style is the Normal style, with the addition of bold and a line space before and after the paragraph. You can reformat all your captions automatically by making changes to the Caption style. Alternatively, you can select the caption and apply manual formatting. Because most captions are a single line (and therefore, a single paragraph), you can apply paragraph formatting commands such as indentations and alignment, as well as text formatting commands such as italic or another font.

▶ **See** "Using Styles for Repetitive Formats," **p. 369**

Editing Captions

You can edit captions in several ways. You can change their labels or numbering styles, as described in the previous sections, "Changing Caption Labels" and "Changing Caption Numbering." You can format captions, as described in the previous section, "Formatting Captions." You can update captions, as described in the upcoming section, "Updating Captions."

You also can edit caption text. Editing a caption's text does not affect other captions of the same type. You can add text to the end of a caption called Figure 1, for example, and no other Figure captions are affected. You also can edit the field portion of a caption; that edit also does not affect other captions of the same type. To learn how to edit the field, see the section "Editing and Deleting Cross-References and Captions" later in this chapter.

Updating Captions

When you insert new captions using a label you previously have used in your document, Word includes the correct sequential caption number. Word renumbers existing captions when you insert a new caption between existing captions.

When you delete or move something a caption references, however, you must update it by selecting it and pressing F9. To update all the captions in your document at once, select the entire document and press F9.

Framing a Caption with Its Document Element

When you move an element for which you have inserted a caption, the caption does not move with the object. If you want the element and caption to move together, select them and add a text box to contain them as a single object. When an element and caption are both placed in a text box, you can use the mouse to drag them anywhere in your document.

To place a document element and its caption in a text box, follow these steps:

1. Select the element and its caption.
2. Choose Insert, Text Box, or click the Text Box button on the Drawing toolbar.

Alternatively, you can place the element in a text box and *then* insert its caption—the caption is included automatically inside the frame. See Chapter 26, "Inserting Text Boxes," for details on inserting, editing, and moving text boxes.

Part
VII

Ch
33

Editing and Deleting Cross-References and Captions

Cross-references and captions are fields; by default, you see in your document the result of the fields. You may see, for example, a cross-reference such as `Editing Cross-References` or a caption such as `Figure 3`. If you display fields, however, rather than field results, you see field codes, such as `{REF _Ref270669594\* MERGEFORMAT }` or `{ SEQ Figure \* ARABIC }`. Word uses fields so that it can update cross-references and captions if the information changes.

You can edit either the field result or the field code. Editing the field result is the same as editing text; however, the next time the field code is updated, the editing will be lost unless you unlock the results as described in Chapter 22, "Automating with Field Codes."

You also can edit the field code when it is displayed. You may want to edit the field code as a quick way of changing a reference or as a means of inserting a special formatting. Chapter 22 describes in detail editing field codes and adding formatting switches. Many cross-references and captions also include normal text preceding or following the field. Edit this text using Word's usual text-editing techniques; for details, see Chapter 5, "Editing a Document."

The key to editing a cross-reference or caption is in selecting and displaying the field code that creates the cross-reference or caption. To make selecting a field code easier, you can set viewing options to shade data from fields codes.

To shade any data from field codes, follow these steps:

1. Choose Tools, Options and select the View tab.

2. Select one of the following items from the Field Shading drop-down list:

Select this	To get this action
Never	Field codes and results are never shaded
Always	Field codes and results are always shaded
When Selected	Field codes and results are shaded only when they are selected or the insertion point is in the field code

3. Choose OK.

You can switch the entire document between field codes and results by pressing Alt+F9.

To edit or format a field result, move the insertion point within the field result. If the Field Shading option is on, the field results turn light gray (see Figure 33.12). Select the text you want to edit or format. Figure 33.13 shows selected text within a field result.

To delete a field code and its result, select across one field code marker or across the entire field result. The entire field result will turn darker (see Figure 33.14). Press the Delete key. It is easier to select and delete field codes if you display the field codes rather than field results.

TIP To select quickly the next field following the insertion point, press F11. To select the field prior to the insertion point, press Shift+F11.

To update the field, select it and press F9. To update a field, you either can highlight it by positioning the insertion point inside it, or you can select it by dragging across it.

FIG. 33.12

A field result appears with light shading when the insertion point is inside and Field Shading is turned on.

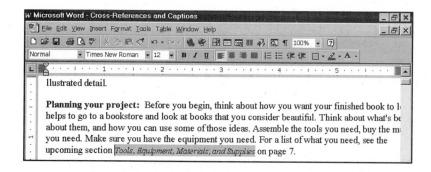

FIG. 33.13

This field result shows darker selected text that can be edited or formatted.

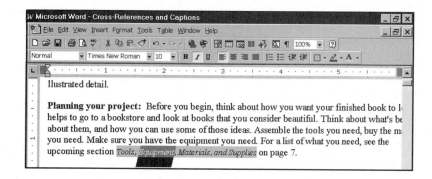

FIG. 33.14

Selecting the entire field result displays the entire result with dark shading. The field code can be deleted at this point.

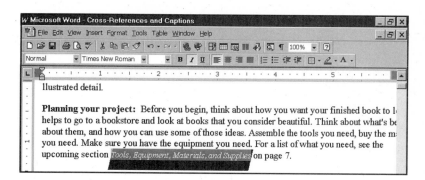

Part
VII
Ch
33

CHAPTER 34

Assembling Large Documents

You can work with any size document in Word 97, but several considerations dictate the most efficient approach to working with large documents. Large documents, as well as documents with many graphics, fields, bookmarks, and formatting, consume more memory and disk space. They can be slow to load, save, and work in, depending on how much memory you have and the speed of your computer.

Most of this chapter focuses on using master documents to work with large documents, because this is the most efficient and flexible way to manage large documents. However, you also learn how to break a large document into individual files and treat these files separately. You learn how to create tables of contents and indexes that span the information contained in these individual files.

Documents of 20 or fewer pages give the best performance in Word. If your documents are significantly larger than 20 pages, you can segment the documents into multiple files and rejoin them using the techniques described in this chapter. ■

Create a master document

Master documents integrate collections of smaller documents into a cohesive large document.

Work with subdocuments

Update subdocuments and pass on the updates to the master document.

Insert tables of contents, indexes, and cross-references in long documents

Your master document can have continuous page numbers, a common table of contents, common index, and headers and footers.

Understanding the Components of a Large Document

Although you can break a document up into smaller documents and work with and print these smaller files individually, there are many advantages to combining these smaller *subdocuments* into a *master document*, and using Word's powerful master document feature to organize and work with the large document. When you work in the Master Document view of a large document (see Figure 34.1), it's like working with an outline, so it is much easier to move around the document and to organize the document using the same techniques you use to organize an outline (see Chapter 21, "Organizing Content with an Outline"). There are also several tools in Master Document view that you can use to manage the subdocuments in a master document.

FIG. 34.1

You can use Master Document view to manage a large document.

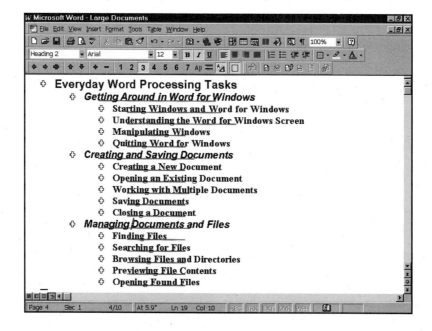

You can work with two views in the master document. Master Document view is similar to Outline view (refer to Figure 34.1), and enables you to organize your document using the same techniques you use to organize an outline with the buttons on the Outlining toolbar. Using the buttons on the Master Document toolbar, you can move and delete entire subdocuments, insert new subdocuments, combine subdocuments, and merge a sub-document so that it becomes part of the master document text. If you need to work with one of the subdocuments, you can quickly open it from the master document.

To view the entire document to edit and format it, you can switch to Normal view. In Normal view, you can work with the document just as if it were a single document. You can add a table of contents, index, and cross-references just as in any other document. You need to be in Normal view when you want to print the document. You can print in Master Document view if you want to obtain an outline of your document.

When you switch to Normal view for the master document, it's just like working on a single document, so you can use the standard procedures for adding page numbers, tables of contents, indexes, and cross-references, avoiding the complications of trying to accomplish these tasks using individual files. You can print the master document just as you would any file, so you don't have to open and print each individual file.

When necessary, you still can work with the individual subdocuments. For example, when you want each subdocument to have its own header and footer, you work with the documents individually. Also, different people can work on the individual subdocuments in a master document. Then you can open the master document to pull together all the subdocuments and make editing changes that affect the whole document—for example, adding a table of contents and an index—and print the entire document all at once.

Creating a Master Document

There are three ways to create a master document:

- Create a master document from scratch by entering an outline for your document, using one of the heading levels to indicate the beginning of each subdocument. You then create the subdocuments from the headings, using one of the buttons on the Master Document toolbar.
- Create a master document from an existing document.
- Combine several documents into a master document.

The three ways of creating a master document are discussed in the following sections.

Whatever method you use to create your master document, you must work in Master Document view and use the built-in heading styles (Heading 1–Heading 9) for the headings in your outline. You can use the promote and demote buttons on the Outlining toolbar to create your headings; Word automatically uses the heading styles. You can also apply the heading styles using the Style box on the Formatting toolbar.

Creating a Master Document from an Outlined Document

One way to create a Master Document is to first create a multi-level outline using Word's Outline feature. This can be an empty outline or a completed document that uses outline heading styles. Word can then turn that outline into a Master Document. All the outline headings at a level you specify become Word document files. You can then open these files and edit or fill them with normal Word content.

To create a new master document using an outline, follow these steps:

1. Open a new document.

2. Choose View, Master Document.

   When you switch to Master Document view, the Outlining and Master Document toolbars appear at the top of the screen (see Figure 34.2). These buttons are used to promote and demote outline headings and work with subdocuments. Table 34.1 summarizes the functions of the individual buttons on the Outlining and Master Document toolbars.

Outline toolbar   Master Document toolbar

FIG. 34.2
The Outlining and Master Document toolbars help you view and manage your long documents.

Table 34.1 Outline and Master Document Toolbar Functions

Button	Name	Function
	Promote	Promotes the heading (and its body text) by one level; promotes body text to the heading level of the preceding heading.
	Demote	Demotes the heading by one level; demotes body text to the heading level below the preceding heading.
	Demote to body text	Demotes a heading to body text and applies the Normal style.
	Move Up	Moves the selected paragraph(s) before the first visible paragraph that precedes the selected paragraph(s).
	Move down	Moves the selected paragraph(s) after the first visible paragraph that follows the selected paragraph(s).
	Expand	Expands the first heading level below the currently selected heading; repeated clicks expand through additional heading levels until body is expanded.
	Collapse	Collapses body text into heading, then lowest level headings into higher level headings.
	Display Heading	Displays all headings and text through the lowest level number you click.
	Display All	Displays all text if some is collapsed; displays only headings if all text is expanded.
	Show First Line Only	Toggles between showing all the body text in an outline and only the first line of text.
	Show Formatting	Toggles between showing normal character formatting in Outline view and Normal view.
	Master Document View	Toggles between showing Outline and Master Document view.
	Collapse Subdocuments	Displays only the Heading levels in the subdocuments.
	Create Subdocument	Creates subdocuments from selected outline items.
	Remove Subdocument	Removes the selected subdocument, leaving the text in the master document.

continues

Part **VII**

Ch **34**

Table 34.1   Continued

Button	Name	Function
	Insert Subdocument	Inserts the file selected in the Insert Subdocument dialog box into the master document.
	Merge Subdocument	Merges selected subdocuments into one subdocument.
	Split Subdocument	Splits the selected portion of a subdocument into another subdocument.
	Lock Document	Locks and unlocks the file for the selected subdocument.

3. Create an outline for the master document.

   You can use the buttons on the toolbar to promote and demote headings as you enter your outline. Decide on a heading level that will designate the beginning of all subdocuments. For example, you might use **Heading Level 2** to indicate the beginning of each subdocument.

4. Select the headings you want to create your subdocuments from.

   You can select as many headings as you want, but you must be sure that the first heading in the selection is the same level as the one you are using to indicate the beginning of subdocuments, as shown in Figure 34.3.

FIG. 34.3
The first heading level in your selection should be the level you want to convert to subdocuments.

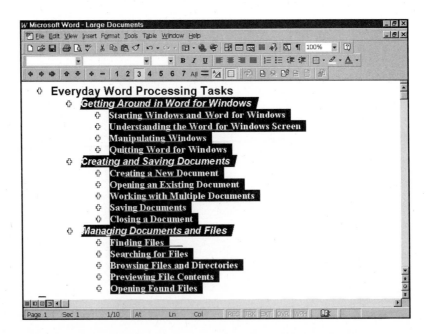

5. Click the Create Subdocument button on the Master Document toolbar.

   Word divides the master document into subdocuments, one subdocument for each heading level that you designate as the subdocument heading. Each subdocument is enclosed in a box, and a subdocument icon appears in the upper-left corner of the box, as shown in Figure 34.4.

6. Save the master document.

FIG. 34.4
Word creates a subdocument for each subdocument heading level.

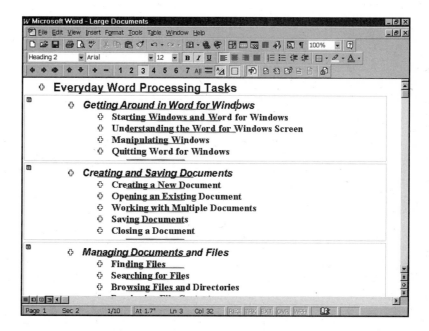

When you save the master document, Word automatically saves each of the subdocuments as a file. Word assigns a file name to each subdocument, using the first words in the first heading for the subdocument. For example, the file names for the subdocuments created from the outline shown in Figure 34.3 are Getting Around in Word for Windows.doc, Creating and Saving Documents.doc, and Managing Documents and Files.doc. Word uses numbers or other characters in the file name if the file names based on the headings conflict with other files in the folder.

Part VII
Ch 34

CAUTION

If you decide to rename a subdocument or save it in a different location on your hard disk, be sure to do it while you are in the master document; then save the master document again. First, open the subdocument from within the master document. To do this, double-click the subdocument icon in the upper-left corner of the box enclosing the subdocument. Then choose File, Save As to save the subdocument with a new name or in a new location. This prevents the links between the master document and the subdocuments from being broken.

TROUBLESHOOTING

I selected the headings that I wanted to convert to subdocuments and clicked the Create Subdocument button, but my subdocuments did not divide as I intended. The key to creating subdocuments from the headings in a master document is to make sure that when you select the headings that you want to create subdocuments from, you select all of the headings you want to convert to subdocuments. Also, the first heading in the selection must be assigned the heading level you want to use to begin all subdocuments.

For example, if the first heading in the selection is assigned Heading Level 2, all sections beginning with Heading Level 2 will be converted to subdocuments.

Creating a Master Document from an Existing Document

If you have already created a document, you can convert it to a master document. To do so, use the Outlining toolbar in Master Document view to set up headings in the document, and then create subdocuments from these headings, as described in the previous section.

To create a master document from an existing document, follow these steps:

1. Open the document you want to convert to a master document.

2. Choose <u>V</u>iew, <u>M</u>aster Document.

3. Use the buttons on the Outlining toolbar to assign heading levels to your document and to rearrange the headings, if necessary.

4. Complete steps 4–6 as outlined in "Creating a Master Document from an Outlined Document" previously in this chapter.

▶ **See** "Creating an Outline," **p. 679**

Building Your Master Document by Inserting Subdocuments

You can insert subdocuments into an existing master document. Use this method as a way of adding new documents at a specific location in your master document.

You also can insert subdocuments into a normal document. This changes the normal document into a master document. Use this method as a quick way of changing a normal document into a master document.

To insert an existing document into a normal or master document, follow these steps:

1. Open a new document or an existing master document.

2. Choose <u>V</u>iew, <u>M</u>aster Document.

3. Move the insertion point where you want to insert the document.

4. Click the Insert Subdocument button on the Master Document toolbar.

5. In the File <u>N</u>ame text box, type the name of the file you want to open, or select the folder you want to open from the Look <u>I</u>n list, and then select the file in the Insert Subdocument dialog box.

The file is inserted into the master document with its original file name. Word uses the formatting from the master's documents template if it is different from the subdocument's template. The original formatting is preserved in the subdocument file if you open it separately.

▶ **See** "Creating an Outline," **p. 679**

Working with the Master Document

Once you have set up your master document, you can use Master Document and Normal views to work with the document. In Master Document view, you can view the overall structure of the document, and reorganize the sections in the document. For example, it is very easy to reorder the subdocuments that make up the master document by using the mouse and the buttons on the Outlining toolbar. You should work in Master Document view when you need to make changes that affect the overall structure of the document. You can also open the individual subdocuments in Master Document view, because each subdocument appears as a hyperlink.

In Normal view, you can work with the document just as if it were a single document. You can format the document, add page numbers, tables of contents and other tables, indexes, and cross-references. When you switch to Normal view, each subdocument that makes up the master document is a *section* (see Chapter 13, "Formatting the Page Layout, Alignment, and Numbering"). You can apply section formatting to these sections. For example, you can set up different headers and footers in the individual sections. You also can click the hyperlink for a subdocument while in Normal view to open and edit the subdocument.

N O T E You can use the Master Document feature to make global changes, such as changing version numbers or acronyms, to a group of documents. Create a master document and open each of the documents as a subdocument. Display the master document in Normal view and make the global changes you want. Save the master document, close it, and delete it. Each subdocument is saved with the changes and has an extra section break at the end, which you can delete. ▨

Part

VII

Ch

34

Formatting the Master Document

Formatting a master document is no different than formatting a single document. You can create templates, styles, and AutoText for the master document and format all or any part of the master document. If a subdocument is based on a different template than the master document, the master document's template styles override the subdocument styles. If you open a subdocument file outside of the master document, the original template styles will still be in effect.

 TIP

To ensure consistency when you are writing large documents, read Chapter 6, "Using Templates and Wizards for Frequently Created Documents," and Chapter 11, "Using Styles for Repetitive Formats."

To insert headers and footers that are the same for the entire master document, set them up in the master document. These headers and footers are not inserted into the individual subdocuments, but only appear when viewed in the master document. If you want different headers and footers for the individual subdocuments, set them up in each subdocument. You can also modify the page numbers, margins, and other section-level formatting within subdocuments, and insert new section breaks within a subdocument. When you insert an existing file into a master document, any section formatting in that document is maintained. This helps if you already set up headers and footers in the individual documents you combine to create a master document and you want to maintain those headers and footers in the master document.

▶ **See** "Creating Headers and Footers," **p. 455**

 Another benefit of working in the master document is that you can move text and graphics among subdocuments without opening the individual subdocuments. You can even use the drag-and-drop technique for moving text and graphics from one subdocument to another. You need to be in Normal view of the master document to move text and graphics, and you need to expand the subdocuments using the Expand Subdocuments button on the Master Document toolbar. Click Collapse Subdocuments to collapse the subdocuments within the master document after you've finished editing.

▶ **See** "Moving, Copying, and Linking Text or Graphics," **p. 185**

Printing a Master Document

 Printing a master document is as simple as printing a single document. The ability to print an entire long document at once is one of the advantages that a master document has over working with individual files. To print the entire document, expand the subdocuments by clicking the Expand Subdocuments button, and then display it in Normal view. You can then choose File, Print to print the document.

To print an outline of your document, switch to Master Document view. You can then collapse or expand headings to display as much of the document as you want.

Sharing a Master Document

One advantage of using a master document to manage a long document is that several users can work together on the subdocuments of the master document at the same time. Word has a locking feature that enables anyone to open a master document. While locking is on, you can only edit the subdocuments which you created. However, you will be able to read the subdocuments created by others. Word uses the AUTHOR field in the summary information of a subdocument to determine the author of a subdocument.

Word allows you to lock or unlock a master document or a subdocument. If you want to provide absolute protection for a document against changes, use the techniques described in Chapter 3, "Creating and Saving Documents," to apply password protection to the document.

▶ **See** "Opening an Existing Document," **p. 85**

To lock or unlock a master document or a subdocument, follow these steps:

1. In Master Document view, expand the master document by clicking the Expand Subdocuments button on the Master Document toolbar.

2. To lock or unlock a master document, click anywhere in the master document.

   To lock or unlock a subdocument, click anywhere in the subdocument.

3. Click the Lock Document button on the Master Document toolbar.

   A padlock icon appears just below the subdocument icon when a subdocument is locked (see Figure 34.5). A master document, when it is locked, is marked as (Read-Only) in the title bar.

TROUBLESHOOTING

I am able to open a subdocument outside of the master document and then edit and save it, but whenever I open the same subdocument from within the master document, I am unable to edit and save it. The reason for this is that the subdocument has been locked in the master document. If you look just below the subdocument icon for the subdocument you are trying to work with, you will see a padlock symbol, which indicates that the subdocument is locked. When you open a locked subdocument, it is opened as a read-only document, and cannot be edited and saved with the same name. To unlock the subdocument, locate the insertion point anywhere in the subdocument and click the Unlock Subdocument button, the last button on the Master Document toolbar (refer to Figure 34.2).

Part
VII

Ch
34

FIG. 34.5
The padlock icon in a subdocument indicates that the subdocument is locked against changes.

Padlock icon ─

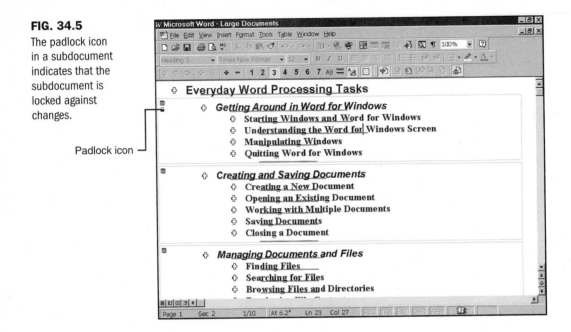

Working with Subdocuments Within the Master Document

You can work with subdocuments in the Master Document view of a master document. You can open a subdocument from within a master document if you need to edit the subdocument. You can also rearrange the order of subdocuments, and merge, split, or remove subdocuments.

Opening Subdocuments from Within a Master Document

You can quickly open a subdocument when you are in Master Document view. This is handy if you need to edit the subdocument. To open a subdocument, open the master document, switch to Master Document view, and double-click the subdocument icon for the subdocument you want to open. If you make any editing changes in the subdocument, be sure to save it. When you do, the changes are saved in both the subdocument and the master document.

Rearranging Subdocuments in a Master Document

When you work in a master document, it is easy to rearrange the order of the subdocuments in the master document by using the same methods you use to move the contents of an outline. You can move headings within a subdocument or move entire subdocuments.

To move a subdocument within a master document, follow these steps:

1. Switch to Master Document view and click the subdocument icon to select the entire subdocument.

2. Drag the subdocument to the new location.

   A gray line appears on-screen as you drag the selection. Drag the gray line to the point where you want to move the selection and release the mouse button.

You can also move individual headings within a subdocument by using the same techniques.

▶ **See** "Promoting and Demoting Headings," **p. 681**

Splitting, Merging, and Deleting Subdocuments

If a subdocument becomes larger than you would like, you can split it into subdocuments. Or, you can merge smaller subdocuments into one large subdocument.

To split a subdocument, follow these steps:

1. Open the master document and switch to Master Document view.

2. Click the Expand Subdocuments button if the subdocuments are not already expanded.

3. If necessary, create a heading at the point where you want to create the new subdocument.

   Apply the heading style used for the other subdocument headings to the new heading.

4. Select the heading.

 5. Click the Split Subdocument button on the Master Document toolbar.

6. Save the master document so that Word saves and names the new subdocument.

   Word uses the heading text as the file name for the new subdocument.

To merge two or more subdocuments, follow these steps:

1. Open the subdocument and switch to Master Document view.

2. If necessary, move the subdocuments you want to merge next to each other.

3. Select the entire contents of the subdocuments you want to merge.

4. Click the Merge Subdocument button on the Master Document toolbar.

Part

VII

Ch

34

5. Save the master document to save a new file for the merged subdocuments.

   Word uses the file name of the first subdocument to name the new combined file. You can delete the original subdocuments except, of course, for the first one.

   ▶ **See** "Promoting and Demoting Headings," **p. 681**

To remove a subdocument from a master document, follow these steps:

1. Open the master document and switch to Master Document view.

2. Expand the master document by clicking the Expand Subdocuments button on the Master Document toolbar.

3. If the subdocument you want to remove is locked, unlock it (see "Sharing a Document," earlier in this chapter).

4. Click the subdocument icon to select the subdocument you want to remove.

5. Press Delete to remove the subdocument and its contents from the master document. When you delete a subdocument, the subdocument file is still stored on the hard drive.

   Click the Remove Subdocument button on the Master Document toolbar to remove the subdocument and retain the text in the master document.

> **CAUTION**
>
> To delete a subdocument from a master document, do so while in Master Document view. If you simply delete the subdocument file from your hard disk, when you try to open the subdocument from within the master document, you receive an error message informing you that the specified file cannot be opened. Once you have deleted the subdocument from a master document, you can then safely delete the subdocument file from the hard disk.

Inserting Tables of Contents, Indexes, and Cross-References

When you work with a master document, one of the advantages is that you can use the same techniques you use in a single document to create tables of contents and other tables, indexes, and cross-references. To insert a table of contents or index into a master document, open the master document, expand the subdocuments by clicking the Expand Subdocuments button, and switch to Normal view. Then, use the normal methods for inserting the table of contents or index (see Chapter 31, "Creating Indexes and Tables of Contents"). You also must be working in Normal view of the master document to insert cross-references that make references across documents. When you update tables of contents, indexes, or cross-references, be sure to do so from within the master document to avoid error messages.

▶ **See** "Creating Cross-References," **p. 1029**

TROUBLESHOOTING

When I work on a subdocument containing cross-references, I get many error messages. The same is true of the subdocument that contains my table of contents and index. To work on cross-references and tables of contents and indexes, you must be in the master document. This is because cross-references, tables of contents, and indexes make references across documents. To replace the error messages in your subdocuments, open the master document, select the text containing the error messages, or position the insertion point anywhere in a table of contents or index, and press F9. The fields used to return this information will be updated.

Adding Page Numbers and Chapter Numbers to a Master Document

You will probably want to add page numbers to your master document that will appear in either the header or footer when you print the document. You can also add chapter numbers that will appear with the page numbers, for example, 1-2, 2-1, 3-1, designating both the chapter and page numbers for each page.

To add page numbering to a master document, follow these steps:

1. Open the master document and choose View, Normal.
2. Press Ctrl+A to select the entire document.
3. Choose Insert, Page Numbers.
4. Select the position for the page numbers from the Position drop-down list.
5. Select the alignment for the page numbers from the Alignment drop-down list.
6. Choose Format and select a format for the page numbers in Number Format drop-down list.
7. Choose OK twice to insert the page numbers.

You can also use include chapter numbers with the page numbers. To do so, you need to apply one of the built-in heading styles, for example, Heading 1, to the chapter titles. Also, because you will want the page numbers to start at 1 for each chapter, you need to manually set the starting page number for each of the subdocuments.

To include chapter numbers with the page numbers, follow these steps:

1. Open the master document and choose View, Normal.

   Each of the subdocuments appears as a section when you view the master document in Normal view.

2. Select the first section in the document.

3. If you have not already done so, apply one of the built-in heading styles to the chapter title (such as Heading 1).

4. Choose Format, Bullets and Numbering.

5. Select the Outline Numbered tab.

6. Select one of the chapter numbering styles.

   The chapter numbering styles are the ones that use Heading 1, Heading 2, and so on.

7. Choose OK.

8. Choose Insert, Page Numbers and then choose Format.

9. Select the Include Chapter Number option.

10. Select the heading style that corresponds to the style used for the chapter titles in the Chapter Starts with Style list.

11. Select a separator from the Use Separator list.

12. Set the starting page number to **1** in the Start At edit box.

13. Choose OK.

14. Select the next section and repeat steps 3–13.

   ▶ **See** "Inserting Page Numbers," **p. 464**

Simulating a Large Document from Individual Files

Another technique for assembling large documents is to print the smaller documents separately. For large documents that would overload memory if they were inserted or even linked into one large master document, this technique is preferable.

When you use this technique, you must set the starting numbers for pages, paragraphs, footnotes, and so on for each individual file to maintain sequential numbering across the larger document. You must also use {RD} (Referenced Document) field codes for creating tables of contents and indexes. The table of contents and index are created in a separate document, using {RD} field codes, one field code for each of the individual files that make up the document. You cannot use cross-references across files when you work with individual files, although you can use the new hyperlink feature to point the reader to references in other files.

Setting Starting Page Numbers

To set the starting numbers for the individual files, start with the first file in the series. Note the number of the last page and of any other sequentially numbered items, such as paragraphs, lines, footnotes, and items numbered using the {SEQ} fields (tables or figures, for example). Next, open the second file in the series and use the appropriate commands to set the starting numbers for each sequentially numbered item in that document. Follow this procedure for each of the individual files. To save time and to minimize the possibility that you have to repeat the process of setting starting numbers, carry out this procedure after all editing changes have been made.

To set the starting page numbers, follow these steps:

1. Choose Insert, Page Numbers.
2. Select the Format option.
3. Type or select the appropriate page number in the Start At text box (one higher than the number of the last page in the preceding file).
4. Choose OK twice.

To set the starting footnote numbers, follow these steps:

1. Choose Insert, Footnote.
2. Click the Options button.
3. Type or select the appropriate number in the Start At text box (one higher than the number of the last footnote in the preceding file).
4. Choose OK twice.

To set the starting line numbers, follow these steps:

1. Choose File, Page Setup.
2. Select the Layout tab.
3. Select the Line Numbers option.
4. Select the Add Line Numbering option.
5. Type or select the appropriate line number in the Start At text box (one higher than the number of the last line in the preceding file).

6. Select the Continuous option in the Numbering field.

7. Choose OK twice.

To set the starting number for paragraphs, follow these steps:

1. Select the group of paragraphs you want to renumber.

2. Choose Format, Bullets and Numbering.

3. Select the Numbered tab, select one of the numbering styles and click the Customize button.

4. Type the appropriate number in the Start At text box (one higher than the number of the last numbered paragraph in the preceding file).

5. Choose OK.

To set the starting numbers of items numbered using the {SEQ} field, follow these steps:

1. Choose Tools, Options and select the View tab.

2. Select the Field Codes option and choose OK.

3. Find the first {SEQ} field and type \r followed by the appropriate number (one higher than the last number in that sequence of items).

4. Repeat step 2 for each sequence in the document.

N O T E See Chapter 22, "Automating with Field Codes," for information on using the {SEQ} field code to create a sequentially numbered series of items. Also, you can learn how to insert chapter numbers using the {SEQ} code in "Inserting Chapter Numbers," later in this chapter. ▪

Creating Chapter Numbers for Individual Files

When you print the individual documents separately (not linking in a master document), you must manually insert chapter numbers if you want them to appear in your document. To do so, you add the chapter number to the header or footer, next to the page number code. The entry in the header or footer for Chapter 2, for example, might look like this:

```
2-{page}
```

If the order of the chapters changes, you must edit the chapter numbers that appear in the header or footer to maintain the proper sequencing.

You can also include chapter numbers with the page numbers by choosing Insert, Page Numbers. When you use this method, you must format your chapter titles with one of the built-in heading styles (such as Heading 1). See the section "Adding Page Numbers and Chapter Numbers to a Master Document" earlier in this chapter for the procedure on how to include chapter numbers with the page numbers using the Insert, Page Numbers command.

Printing Individual Files or Multiple Files

After you set the starting numbers for each of the files, you can print them individually. To print several documents with one command, choose File, Open and switch to the folder containing the files. Click the first file you want to print, hold down the Ctrl key, and select the remaining files you want to print. Next, right-click anywhere in the selection and choose Print from the shortcut menu.

Creating a Table of Contents

If you choose to assemble a large document from several smaller documents without using master documents, you must insert {RD} (Reference Document) fields to create indexes and tables of contents. These {RD} fields are inserted into a document separate from the individual documents. Insert one {RD} field for each separate file that makes up the larger document. You then choose Insert, Index and Tables to create the index and table of contents from the document containing the {RD} fields. This document then contains only the index and table of contents, not the text of the documents. You can print the table of contents and index separately and combine it with the larger document.

To create a separate index or table of contents, follow these steps:

1. Open a new file to contain the RD fields.
2. Press Ctrl+F9, the Insert Field shortcut key.
3. Type **rd** followed by a space and the name and path of the first file that makes up the document. If the files are all in the current directory, you do not need to include the path (**rd chapt1.doc**, for example). Use the full path name if the files are located in different directories. Use a double backslash where a single backslash normally is used in a path name.
4. Use the arrow keys to move outside the field and press Enter to start a new paragraph.
5. Repeat steps 2–4 for each of the files that makes up the document.
6. Position the insertion point where you want to locate the table of contents and choose Insert, Index and Tables.
7. Select the Table of Contents tab, select the format you want to use from the Formats list box, and choose OK.
8. Press Ctrl+Enter to separate the table of contents and index with a page break.

Part
VII

Ch
34

9. Position the insertion point where you want to locate the index, and choose Insert, Index and Tables.

10. Select the Index tab, select the format you want to use from the Formats list box and choose OK.

11. Choose Insert, Page Numbers to set the appropriate page numbers for the table of contents and index.

▶ **See** "Creating Tables of Contents," **p. 987**

To set separate starting page numbers for the table of contents and the index, you must insert a section break between them. Choose Insert, Break, select the Next Page option, and choose OK.

Figure 34.6 illustrates the field code view of a document set up to print the table of contents for a book.

FIG. 34.6

{RD} fields are used to create a table of contents.

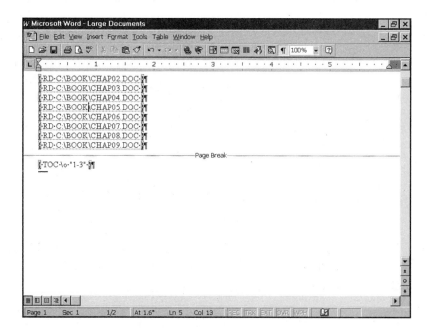

Using Word with Office and Networks

CHAPTER 35

Working with a Group of People

One of the fastest growing segments of the computer industry is networking. By connecting people's computers and giving them access to corporate data, companies are finding that people work more productively and accurately. In addition, they can complete projects much faster.

Because most projects involve groups of people working on the same or similar documents, it is important that you become familiar with how to use Word 97 and other Microsoft Office applications with groups of people. This chapter will show you that with the addition of electronic mail (or e-mail), you will find that you can quickly send Word documents to co-workers over a local network or to clients through a commercial online service. You can even fax a document from within Word. ■

Share binders that contain documents from different Microsoft Office applications

When you create reports based on different documents, use the Microsoft Binder to compile the documents into collated reports and to organize related documents.

Do group editing and revision on one document

Instead of using Word's shared document feature, you can work with group editing by tracking changes and comments.

E-mail and fax your Word documents

Use the File, Send To menu to e-mail and fax your Word documents without exiting Word.

Using Binders for Group Projects

Almost any project involving many people also involves many documents created by more than one application. When you are faced with projects that generate reports with many different documents, you should use the Microsoft Binder to compile the documents into collated reports and to organize related documents.

Microsoft Binder enables you to bind together documents from different Microsoft applications into a single large document. You can edit any document from within the binder so that you do not need to continually open and close different applications.

▶ **See** "Using Microsoft Office Binder to Group Documents," **p. 1102**

Sharing a Binder on a Network Using My Briefcase

If you are connected to a network, you can share a binder that you have created with other users on the network using My Briefcase. To share a binder using My Briefcase, follow these steps:

1. Move the binder file to a shared folder on your network.
2. Inform those users who will be working with the binder that they should copy the binder to their local My Briefcase.
3. Each user can now open the briefcase copy of the binder and work on it.
4. To update the briefcase, choose Briefcase, Update All.

   When the Update All command is issued, the changes in the user's copy of the binder are copied to the network copy, and any changes in the network copy of the binder are copied to the user's copy.

Editing and Revising as a Group

If you are working on a network, you can make your documents available to other users on the network so that they can review them. To make the document available to other users, simply put a copy of the document in a shared folder. However, to protect the document against permanent changes being made by other users, you must first prepare the document for review. You can protect the document so that other users cannot change the text but can add comments, called *annotations*. Annotations appear in a separate pane and are identified by the user's initials. Another option is to allow the user to make revisions, but the revisions are marked so that they are not incorporated into the document until you choose to do so. You can identify who made each revision and the time and date they were made. Word uses a different color to mark each user's revisions. For extra protection, you can attach a password to the document so that other users cannot unprotect the document and make changes that are not tracked.

To prepare a document for review by others, follow these steps:

1. Open the document you want to send out for review.
2. Choose Tools, Protect Document.
3. To allow tracked revisions to be made, select Tracked Changes.
4. To allow comments to be added to the document, but no changes to be made, select Comments.
5. To keep other users from turning off the protection you have selected, add a password.

    Be sure to remember the password, or you will not be able to unprotect the document.
6. Click OK.

▶ **See** "Using the Track Changes Feature," **p. 1010**

N O T E Use Word's highlighting feature to select text that you want to call to the attention of other users before you send out the document for review. You can also have each reviewer use a different color highlight to mark text they want to bring to your attention. You can use the Find command to locate any highlighted text in a document. ▪

▶ **See** "Highlighting Text," **p. 306**

Sending Faxes and Electronic Mail with WordMail

If you have a fax/modem and Office 97 installed, you can fax and e-mail your Word documents directly from your computer. Word comes with WordMail. In conjunction with Microsoft Exchange, you can fax and e-mail documents. WordMail is a built-in feature of Word for Windows 95. It enables Word to act as a fax and e-mail editor. Microsoft Exchange is a universal communications manager that is part of Windows 95. Microsoft Exchange takes care of both fax and e-mail transmissions. Together, WordMail and Microsoft Exchange make a powerful package.

The benefit of using WordMail as your e-mail editor is that you can use all the editing and formatting power of Word to improve the layout and appearance of your e-mail messages.

Part
VIII

Ch
35

You can, for example, format characters and paragraphs, create numbered lists, highlight important text using the Highlight tool in Word, and add borders and tables to your messages.

To use Microsoft Exchange you must install and configure Microsoft Exchange for use with your fax/modem and the e-mail systems to which your computer connects. Microsoft Exchange is an optional program that you had a chance to install when you installed Windows. If Microsoft Exchange is not available on your computer, you can rerun Windows 95 Setup and choose to install it. Microsoft Exchange includes a wizard that will guide you through its initial configuration. For additional help, please see Chapter 24, "Using Microsoft Exchange," in Que's *Special Edition Using Windows 95*.

Microsoft Exchange sends documents via fax or e-mail. It makes its choice on how to send your document depending upon which Microsoft Exchange Profile you have selected and which fax and communication numbers are available for the recipient.

Part of Exchange is a Personal Address Book. Within this Personal Address Book, you can store names, addresses, phone numbers, fax numbers, and different e-mail telephone and identification numbers.

Choosing to Use WordMail

If you decide to use WordMail as your e-mail editor, be aware that many of the formatting features in Word will not display in Microsoft Outlook or other e-mail editors. This means that the recipients of your e-mail messages must also use Word as their e-mail editor to display all the WordMail formatting—tables, borders, highlighting, and so on—in your messages.

N O T E Microsoft advises users that they should have at least 12 megabytes of memory to use WordMail as their e-mail editor. Also, if you are using Word to edit documents and you switch over to your e-mail system in which you are using WordMail, Word will run very slowly. Before you switch to WordMail, close all dialog boxes in Word. ▪

To choose WordMail as your e-mail editor, follow these steps:

1. Open the Start menu, click Programs, then Microsoft Outlook.
2. Choose Tools, Options to display the Options dialog box.
3. Select the E-mail tab.
4. If not checked, select the Use Microsoft Word as the E-mail Editor check box.
5. Click OK.

Using WordMail as your e-mail editor is no different from using Word to create documents. To learn how to send, read, reply to, and forward e-mail messages, see the online Help in Microsoft Exchange.

Choosing Your Microsoft Exchange Profile

Before sending a message, you will need to select the profile that you want to use for your Microsoft Exchange Mail system such as Microsoft Outlook or Microsoft Mail. The profile specifies whether a message will be sent via Microsoft Fax, Microsoft Mail, or another communication service. The profile also stores information required for each communication service. For example, a profile that includes fax includes the type of fax/modem used and your fax telephone number for use on the return line of the fax. If you specify Microsoft Mail, you need to specify the path to your post office, your name, and your password. You can define different profiles for your communications and give each profile a name.

If the profile you select has multiple communication methods available, Microsoft Exchange tries more than one communication services. It uses the different e-mail or fax addresses that are listed in the address book for an individual. If you want to restrict Exchange so that it only sends a fax, for example, then you should create a profile that has fax as the only available communication method. When using this profile, Exchange only looks at the fax numbers in the different address books.

> **CAUTION**
>
> You may want to specify different profiles for different types of communications. If Microsoft Exchange has trouble keeping your fax and e-mail messages separate, create a separate profile for each. When you want to send a fax, use the profile you have set up for only faxes. When you want to send an e-mail, use the profile that contains only e-mail information.

To specify your default Microsoft profile from Microsoft Outlook, follow these steps:

1. Start Microsoft Outlook.
2. If you do not have a default profile, the Choose Profile dialog box displays. From the Profile Name drop-down list box, select the profile you want to work with and click OK to access the main Outlook application window.

 TIP To define a new profile, choose New and follow the wizard that guides you through creating a new profile.

3. Choose <u>T</u>ools, <u>O</u>ptions to display the Options dialog box.
4. Select the General tab.

Part

VIII

Ch

35

5. Choose the Allows Use This Profile option button from the Startup Settings group box.

6. Select the desired default profile from the drop-down list box associated with the Allows Use This Profile option button. Select a profile that supports the communication service you need: electronic mail and/or fax.

7. Click OK.

From this point forward, you will not be prompted to choose a profile when sending a Word document through e-mail or fax.

Sending and Addressing Your Message

Once you have specified a Microsoft Exchange profile, you have far fewer dialog boxes to complete when sending a message. If you have previously selected a profile, follow these steps to send and address your Word document:

1. From Word, prepare the document that you want to send. Save it with the name you want it sent with.

2. Choose File, Send To, Mail Recipient.

   Your document appears in the Exchange document as an icon. This icon is your document embedded as an OLE object, as shown in Figure 35.1.

FIG. 35.1
Your Word document appears as an icon in the WordMail document. You can type and format additional information in the document.

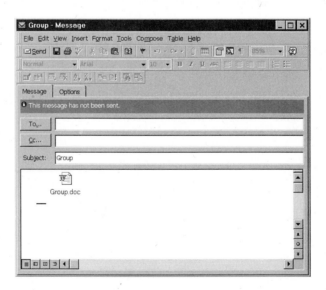

3. To address your document, click the To button in WordMail to display the Address Book dialog box shown in Figure 35.2.

FIG. 35.2

From the Address Book, you can select which address book you want to use, as well as who will receive a message and who will receive a copy.

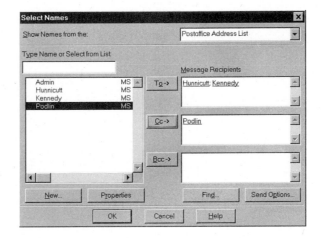

4. Choose an address book from the Show Names drop-down list.

   You may have different address books available from the Personal Address Book, Postoffice Address List, Microsoft Network, and so forth. Depending upon the transmission methods available in the profile you selected, Microsoft Exchange uses the appropriate fax or e-mail address and password from the address book.

5. To send an original document, click a name in the Type Name list then click the To button. To send a copy click the Cc button. Figure 35.3 shows a completed Address Book.

FIG. 35.3

You can add names to either list. To remove a name, right-click the name to access the shortcut menu and choose Cut.

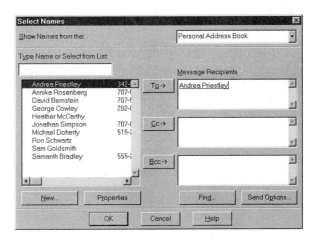

6. Choose OK to close the Address Book and return to WordMail. Figure 35.4 shows a document with To and Cc addressing as well as a subject and short note to accompany the document.

FIG. 35.4

You can type a subject line and include a note to go with your embedded Word document.

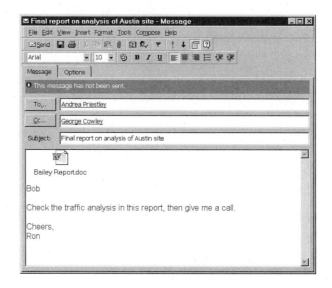

7. To send your e-mail message, choose File, Send or select the Send toolbar button.

Routing a Message

An alternative to sending a document from Word is to *route* the document. Routing a document from Word gives you more control over who gets the document and when they get it. When you route a document, you fill out a *routing slip* indicating who you want to receive the document and in what order. You may, for example, want a department head to receive and revise the document before it is sent on to a project manager and then to other personnel working on the project. If you want, you can choose to have everyone on the list receive the document at the same time. You can also request that the document be returned to you when everyone on the routing list has seen it.

To add or edit an existing routing slip that specifies who will see your document, and in what order they will see it, follow these steps:

1. Prepare your document and save it with the name you want it to have when sent.

2. Choose File, Send To, Routing Recipient. The Routing Slip dialog box appears, as shown in Figure 35.5.

FIG. 35.5

The routing slip specifies who sees your document and in what order they see it.

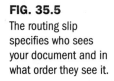
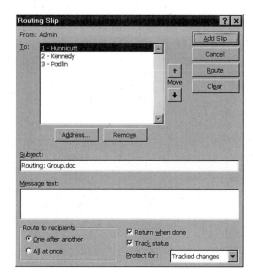

3. Click the Address button to display the Address Book dialog box.

4. Select the address book you want to use from the Show Names list. For each name you want on the routing list, click a name in the Type Name list, then click To. Choose OK when your recipient list is complete.

5. To move a name in the To: list up or down in the order in which it will be received, click the name, then click the up or down Move buttons.

6. If you want recipients to receive the document in the order shown, select the One After Another option. For everyone to receive the document simultaneously, select the All at Once option.

7. Choose Route to immediately send the document to the list of recipients. Choose Add Slip to attach this slip to the document so that it can be sent later.

If you chose to add the routing slip to your document, you can send it at a later time. To send a document that already has a routing slip attached, follow these steps:

1. Choose File, Send To, Next Routing Recipient to display the Send dialog box, shown in Figure 35.6.

FIG. 35.6

After routing slips have been attached, you can send the document to an individual on the routing slip.

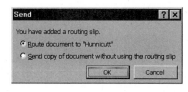

2. Choose OK to route the document.

N O T E   Sending and routing documents is a very efficient way to allow other users to review
your documents—adding comments and making revisions which you can then
incorporate into your document as you desire. You can use WordMail's revision and annotations
features in conjunction with e-mail to send out a document for review by other users, to collect
the revisions and annotations from each user, and then to get the document back to incorporate
these revisions and annotations. Word will automatically track these revisions and annotations. ■

Opening E-Mail

To open e-mail or faxes that you receive, minimize applications so that you can see your
desktop. Then follow these steps:

1. Double-click the Inbox or Outlook icon on the desktop.

2. New mail in the Inbox appears in bold type. Double-click new mail to read it.

3. If a document contains an icon for embedded data and your system has an application that can read that type of data, double-click the embedded icon. An application
   that can read the data opens and displays the icon's contents.

At this point you can work with the document as you would any other document, as long
as the document hasn't been protected with a password.   ●

CHAPTER 36

Using Word with Office Applications

One of the unique advantages of Windows applications is their capability to exchange and link information easily with other Windows applications. With Word 97, you also can import or link to files from many DOS applications, such as Lotus 1-2-3, AutoCAD, or dBASE. Through the use of Microsoft Query, you even can insert or link your Word documents to data found in an SQL server or mainframe. Figure 36.1 shows a letter with an embedded Microsoft Excel chart. ■

Copying and pasting data between applications

Use the Copy and Paste commands to transfer static copies of information from one application to another.

Embedding data into a Word document

Embed data into a Word document when you want the data to become part of the Word file, independent of the source document. You can edit the embedded object from within Word.

Linking data with Word documents

Link data from one application to another when you want the information in the destination document to automatically update when the source document changes.

Using the Microsoft Binder

Use the Office Binder to bring together documents from different Office 97 applications. Binder makes it easy to collate, edit, and print a project made up of different documents.

FIG. 36.1

Word documents can have data linked or embedded from other Windows applications like this chart from Microsoft Excel.

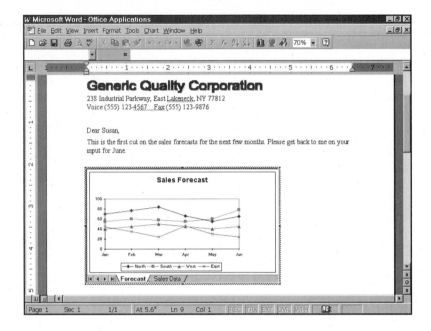

If you usually work with a single application, the value of linking, embedding, or pasting data may not be immediately apparent to you. After you begin to link, embed, or paste data, however, you will see how tasks involving multiple applications come together to produce a single integrated document. You can use Word with other applications, for example, to do the following:

- Create mail-merge data documents from a mailing list file kept in dBASE or Microsoft Excel, or from a network or mainframe file.

- Create sales projections, financial analyses, inventory reports, and investment analyses with worksheets and charts in Microsoft Excel or Lotus 1-2-3 for Windows, and link or embed these charts and tables into Word documents.

- Produce proposals and contracts that include designs from the major drafting programs.

- Produce advertising or marketing materials that include artwork created in different drawing and design applications.

Choosing to Paste, Link, or Embed Data

You can look at the various methods of exchanging data in many different ways: you can evaluate whether the source of the data is a file or an active application; you can evaluate whether you are exchanging text or graphic data; or you can evaluate which of the different procedures you can use.

N O T E This chapter includes references to source and destination documents. The *source* is the file on disk or document in an open application that supplies data. The *destination* is the document that receives the data.

Word provides the following primary methods for exchanging data:

- *Embedded Data.* The source data is encapsulated and inserted within the Word document. The data is contained within the Word document as an integral unit.

  Advantage: The data, such as a Microsoft Excel worksheet or chart, is stored within the Word document. You do not need to be concerned with broken links, renaming files, or sending linked files with the document, because it is all self-contained. Editing is done by simply double-clicking the embedded data, which then starts the source application and loads the data.

  Disadvantage: Do not use embedded data when you want to be able to change one source file and have many destination documents change. Each file containing embedded data must be updated individually. The original source and the embedded data are not linked. Word files containing embedded data can be very large.

- *Linking Data.* The source data is located in a source file on disk or in a Windows application.

  Advantage: The user can update the linked data when they open the Word document or while the document is open. Links may be dynamic, so that a change in one document is immediately reflected in another document. Changes to the source document are available to all linked documents, so updating multiple destination documents is easy.

  Disadvantage: The source data is updated by starting the source application and manually opening the source file and editing it. When you ship a Word document with links to other files, the other files and applications must be available.

- *Pasting Data.* The source data is converted to text or a graphic and inserted into Word.

Advantage: The source data takes up less storage than embedded data. There is no link—the information appears as a *snapshot*. The source application does not have to be available.

Disadvantage: The source data cannot be edited or updated; it must be re-created.

■ *Inserting or importing from a file.* The source data remains in a file on disk, separate from the Word document. Updating the Word document is done manually, or it can be automated through a macro. The source application does not need to be available to the user's computer, but a converter file that will convert the source file must be installed in Word.

Advantage: You do not need the source application because Word converts the file or graphic while inserting it. Changes to the source document may affect multiple destination documents.

Disadvantage: Changes to the data will be lost when you update the inserted file.

Use the following commands for exchanging data:

Command	Action
File, Open and Conversion	Use this command if the data is in a disk file, and you transfer large amounts of non-graphic data infrequently. Use this command to load large dBASE files, text files, or worksheets as a new Word document.
Insert, File	Use this command if the data is in a disk file and you need only portions of the file, or if you want to insert the file within an existing Word document. Data can be brought in unlinked or linked to the disk file (source). Updates from the source on disk can be controlled automatically or manually.
Insert, Picture	Use this command for a graphic in a disk file. You can bring in graphics unlinked or linked to the source file. Updates from the source on disk can be controlled automatically or manually. This is described in Chapter 25, "Inserting Pictures."
Insert, Object	Use this command to embed an object from another Windows application. Objects package all the data that you select and place it within the Word document. You do not need to be concerned with links to external files. You can edit data in objects.

Insert, Database	This command appears on the Database toolbar. Use this command to paste or link database information—like that used for mailing lists or product information—into your Word document. The database information can be from many different personal computer, mainframe, or network databases.
Edit, Paste	Use this command to paste data into a Word document that you may have copied from a running Windows application.
Edit, Paste Special without Linking	Data can be pasted in numerous different formats including as a picture, unformatted text, formatted text, or an embedded object. You must re-paste the data to update it.
Edit, Paste Special with Linking	Data can be pasted in numerous different formats. The formats include: picture, unformatted text, formatted text, or an embedded object. Data is linked to the source. When the source changes, you can update the data.

N O T E Before Word exchanges data with files or applications that use a data format other than Word or text, you must install the appropriate file converter. Before you can open dBASE files or insert ranges from a Microsoft Excel worksheet, for example, you must install the dBASE and Excel converter files. If you did not install the converter files when you installed Word 97, you can rerun the Word 97 or Office 97 installation program, and you can install them without completely reinstalling Word. You will need your original installation disks. ▪

ON THE WEB

For online support from Microsoft, visit the following World Wide Web site:

http://www.microsoft.com/support

You can also access Microsoft's extensive troubleshooting Knowledge Base at the following site:

http://www.microsoft.com/kb

For tutorials, tips, and add-ins for Microsoft Office applications, point your browser to:

http://www.ronperson.com

What You Need to Know About Data Formats

When you link data or embed an object, you have a choice of the form in which the data is stored. The data from the source can appear in the Word document in different forms such as tabbed text, a formatted table, a picture, or a bitmap, depending on the source application. Microsoft Excel data, for example, can appear in a number of forms. If you copy a range of Microsoft Excel cells and then choose Edit, Paste Special to paste them into a Word document, you see the following alternatives in the Data Type dialog box:

■ *Object*. The data is an embedded object with all data stored in the object inside the Word document. No link is maintained with the source document.

■ *Formatted Text (RTF)*. Text transfers with formats. Worksheets appear formatted as tables. You can edit or reformat data.

■ *Unformatted Text*. Text does not contain character or paragraph formatting. Worksheets appear as unformatted text with cells separated by tabs. You can edit or reformat data.

■ *Picture*. Pictures, text, database, or worksheet ranges appear as a picture. You can format them as pictures, but you cannot edit text in Word. Unlinking changes them to drawing objects.

■ *Bitmap*. Pictures, text, or worksheet ranges appear as a bitmapped picture. You can format them as pictures, but you cannot edit text in Word—resolution is poor.

■ *Picture (Enhanced Metafile)*. Pictures, text, database, or worksheet ranges appear as a picture using the Windows Enhanced Metafile format.

Exchanging Data Through Files

One of the easiest ways to bring large amounts of textual or numeric data into Word from another application is to use File, Open.

Chapter 3, "Creating and Saving Documents," describes how to change the Files of Type pull-down list to the All Files (*.*) option. This option lists all files so that you can see and open non-Word files. If you installed the appropriate file converter, Word will open and convert the file simultaneously.

Transferring Data with Copy and Paste

The simplest way to transfer small amounts of data or graphics from one application to another is to copy and paste in the same way that you move text or graphics within a document.

To copy from one Windows application to a Word document, follow these steps:

1. Select the text, cells, or graphic in the document that contains the original text or graphic.

2. Choose Edit, Copy or press Ctrl+C.

3. Click the Word button on the taskbar or press Alt+Tab until Word is selected, then release the keys.

   If the taskbar is not visible, press Ctrl+Esc.

4. Position the insertion point where you want the data to appear in the document.

5. Choose Edit, Paste.

Text is pasted into the document as formatted text; Excel worksheet cells or ranges paste in as a table; graphics paste in as a bitmapped picture. None of them are linked to their source document, but if you double-click a pasted picture, the appropriate drawing program on your computer will activate and load the picture.

Using Scraps to Transfer Data

When using Word with Windows 95, you will find a way to store and transfer data. You can use your mouse to select a part of a document and drag it to the desktop, where it becomes a *scrap*. A scrap is a file or portion of a file that you store on the desktop. You can use this scrap whenever and wherever you want, dragging it back into a document in the same application in which you created it or into a document in another application. You can use the scrap as many times as you want, and the scrap will remain on the desktop until you delete it. Scraps offer two major advantages over the Clipboard:

- You can store as many scraps as you want on the desktop, while the Clipboard can hold only one piece of information at a time.

- Scraps remain on the desktop even when you shut off your computer. Whatever is in the Clipboard disappears when you shut off your computer unless you make the effort to save each clipping to a file.

N O T E You can only use scraps with applications that support OLE.

To create a scrap, follow these steps:

1. Make sure that a part of the desktop is visible outside the window of the application you are working in.

2. Select the part of your document that you want to create a scrap from.

3. Drag the selection to the desktop with the right mouse button.

4. To create a scrap on the desktop and leave the selection in the original document, choose <u>C</u>reate Scrap Here from the shortcut menu.

   Or, to move the selection from the document to a scrap on the desktop, choose <u>M</u>ove Scrap Here.

The data you selected appears as a scrap on your desktop. To use the scrap in another document—which can be in the same application in which it originated or in another application—drag the scrap into the document and drop it where you want to insert it.

You can also drag scraps into a folder. You can, for example, create a new folder on your desktop for storing scraps and then drag scraps into this folder. If you work with a lot of scraps, folders can help you organize them. To create a folder on the desktop, right-click the desktop and choose Ne<u>w</u>, <u>F</u>older. Type a name for the folder and press Enter. Now you can drag and drop scraps into this folder. To use the scraps, double-click the folder to open a window showing its contents, and drag and drop scraps from the folder into your documents.

As with any icon, you can change the text that appears beneath the icon for a scrap. To change the text, click the icon once to select it and then a second time to edit the icon name. (Pause briefly before the second click or you will open the application for the scrap.) Type in a new name and press Enter.

To delete a scrap, right-click the scrap and choose <u>D</u>elete.

Dragging Data Between Applications

When working in Windows 95, you can use the mouse to copy information from one application to another—as long as both applications support OLE. With the mouse, transferring information becomes a simple drag-and-drop operation.

To copy information between applications with the mouse, follow these steps:

1. Select the part of the document that you want to copy to another application.

2. Drag the selection into the window for the receiving application and drop it where you want to insert the information.

   Or, if the window for the receiving application is not activated (visible), drag the selection onto the button for the receiving application in the taskbar, still holding onto the mouse button. When the application is activated, drop the selection where you want to insert it in the receiving application.

Embedding Data

When you need to include information from a Windows application in your Word document, and you want a copy of the information to go with the Word document, then you should use an *embedded object*. Embedded objects take the data from the source application and embed it into the Word document. If the recipient of the Word document wants to edit the embedded data, they can use their copy of the source application to make changes.

If you have worked with the WordArt or Microsoft Graph applications, you are familiar with embedded objects and how they work. These programs are shared applications that can be used within any Windows application that supports OLE. Other major applications with Object Linking and Embedding (OLE) capabilities can also embed their data into Word documents.

Consider the following advantages to embedding objects:

■ File management and the tracking of source documents is not a problem—the source data goes with the Word document.

■ Linked data is not destroyed when a source document cannot be found during an update.

■ Updating an embedded object is done in the source application. If the source application is OLE 1 compliant, then the source application starts and loads the data. If the source application is OLE compliant, you can edit the data without leaving the Word document.

Consider the following disadvantages to embedding objects:

■ The recipient must have the source application to edit the embedded object. However, you can convert the embedded object if the appropriate conversion filter has been installed.

■ The Word document becomes large, containing the Word document as well as all the embedded data.

Creating an Embedded Object

You can embed data in two ways. Both methods produce the same results. You can create completely new data and then embed it, all in the same action, or you can insert an existing file as an object. After you embed the data, it is referred to as an object.

Applications enable you to embed data work in two different ways. Applications using OLE 1 run and activate the source application you select and display a blank document in which you can create your embedded object. Applications that use OLE leave Word active on the screen. Word's menus and toolbars change to reflect the application you select. You are still, however, looking at the full Word document.

Figure 36.2 shows how Microsoft Graph appears when you insert a Microsoft Graph object. Because Microsoft Graph uses OLE, it enables you to work within the Word document. While a Microsoft Graph object is active in the Word document, Word's menus and toolbars change to those of Microsoft Graph.

FIG. 36.2

Some Windows applications enable you to create or edit an object while you remain in the Word document.

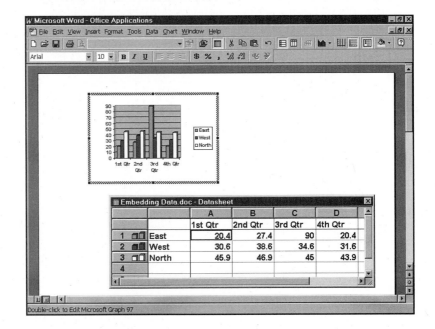

Creating a New Object   To create a new object and embed it, follow these steps:

1. Position the insertion point in the destination document where you want to insert the object.

2. Choose Insert, Object.

3. Select the Create New tab. The tab lists the types of objects you can embed (see Figure 36.3).

4. From the Object Type list, select the type of object you want to insert.

5. Select the Display as Icon check box if you want the embedded object to appear as an icon in the Word document. In most cases, you will not select this check box.

FIG. 36.3
From the <u>C</u>reate New tab of the Object dialog box, select the type of data you want to embed into your Word document. The Result box describes the type of object.

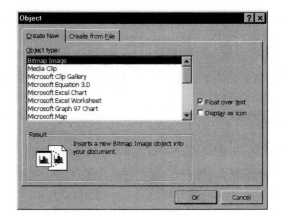

6. Select the Float Over <u>T</u>ext option if you want the object to be inserted in the drawing layer.

   Selecting this option enables you to position the object in front of or behind text and other objects using the commands on the Draw toolbar. If you don't select this option, the object is placed in the current paragraph and behaves like other text.

7. Click OK.

Create the data you want contained in the object. If a blank worksheet opens, for example, create the worksheet. If a blank drawing window appears, draw the object.

▶ **See** "Moving Drawings Below or Above the Text," **p. 919**

Embedding New Objects   To embed the new object after you have created it, use one of the following methods:

▪ If you are working in an OLE application—one where Word's menus have changed—click outside the object or use the method described in the application's manual or Help file to update the object and close the application.

▪ If you are working in an OLE 1 application—one where the application appears in a separate window—do one of the following:

   Choose <u>F</u>ile, <u>C</u>lose and Return to Document if you are editing a Word document embedded in a Word document.

   Or, choose <u>F</u>ile, E<u>x</u>it and respond with <u>Y</u>es if you want the destination document updated.

   Or, choose <u>F</u>ile, <u>U</u>pdate to update the embedded object but keep the application and object open.

An object appears in the Object Type list only if the application you use to create the object is registered with Windows and is capable of producing OLE objects.

Select the Display as Icon check box if you believe that the embedded data will take up too much room in the document. Data that appears as an icon displays an icon related to the application that created the data. When on-screen, the user can double-click the icon to read the actual data or see the graphic. Although the icon takes up less space on-screen, it still consumes the same amount of memory as a normally embedded object.

Embedding an Existing File or Object   To embed a file that already exists, follow these steps:

1. Position the insertion point in the destination document where you want to insert the object.

2. Choose Insert, Object.

3. Select the Create from File tab, as shown in Figure 36.4.

FIG. 36.4
From the Create from File tab of the Object dialog box, select the file you want to embed. The Result area describes the type of object.

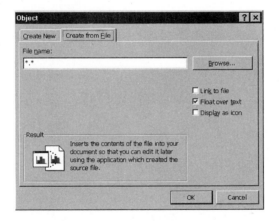

4. Click the Browse button to open the Browse dialog box.

5. Change to the drive and folder containing the file you want to insert. If you need to find the file, use the commands and text boxes at the bottom of the dialog box to search for the file.

6. Select the file from the File list box and click OK.

7. If you want to link the file to the document, select the Link to File option.

   If you do not select this option, there will be no link to the original file. If the data in the original file changes, it will not be updated in the worksheet.

8. Select the Display as Icon check box if you want the embedded file to appear as an icon on-screen and in print.

9. Select the Float Over <u>T</u>ext option if you want the object to be inserted in the drawing layer.

Selecting this option enables you to position the object in front of or behind text and other objects using the commands on the Draw toolbar. If you don't select this option, the object is placed in the current paragraph and behaves like other text.

10. Click OK.

The data you embed appears as a single object in the document. If you select the object, you will see it enclosed by white handles. You can edit that object at any time by double-clicking the object.

Embedding Part of a File   The preceding two methods required that you embed an entire file. The following method describes how to embed a portion of a file—for example, a range from an Excel worksheet. This example requires only as much memory as the range requires, so the Word document will be smaller.

To create an embedded object that is part of a file, follow these steps:

1. Position the insertion point in the destination document in which you want to insert the object.

2. Activate the application containing the data and select the portion of the data you want to embed. If you are using a Windows spreadsheet such as Excel, you select the cells you want to embed. If you are using a Windows database, such as Access, you select the data you want to embed.

3. Choose <u>E</u>dit, <u>C</u>opy or its equivalent in the application.

4. Switch to Word by clicking the Word button on the taskbar.

5. Choose <u>E</u>dit, Paste <u>S</u>pecial.

6. Select the object listed at the top of the <u>A</u>s list in the Paste Special dialog box.

7. Click OK.

The embedded data appears as a single object in your document. When it is not selected, it appears like either normal text or a graphic. When the object is selected, you can see the object surrounded by white handles. Double-click the object to edit it, using its source application.

Editing Embedded Objects

Embedded objects are easy to edit. With the mouse, simply double-click the embedded object. With the keyboard, select the object by moving the insertion point to one side of the object and pressing Shift+arrow key across the object. After you select the object, choose <u>E</u>dit, <u>O</u>bject. From the submenu, choose <u>E</u>dit. If the object's application is not open, it opens; if it is open, the application activates. The object then loads so that you can make changes.

To exit the object after you edit or format it, use the same procedures used to exit when you created the object:

- If Word's menus changed when you edited the object, click the Word document to return to Word and embed the object.
- If the object's application opened in a separate window, do one of the following:

  Choose <u>F</u>ile, <u>C</u>lose and Return to Document if you are editing a Word document embedded in a Word document.

  Or, choose <u>F</u>ile, E<u>x</u>it and then choose Return to close the application and update the embedded object.

  Or, choose <u>F</u>ile, <u>U</u>pdate to update the embedded object but keep the object's application and the object open.

Converting Embedded Objects

One problem you may face when exchanging files with others in your workgroup is receiving an embedded object you cannot open or edit. Suppose, for example, that you receive a Word document that contains an embedded Excel worksheet, but you do not have Excel. You can still work with this file, read the Excel worksheet, and even edit the worksheet.

> **N O T E** If you want to read or edit the embedded object, you do not need to have the application that was used to create the object installed on your computer, but you must have installed the converter required to convert that application's files. You can install these converters at any time by rerunning Setup and using your original Word or Office disks or CD-ROM.

To convert an embedded object into a different format, follow these steps:

1. Select the embedded object by clicking it or by moving the insertion point to one side, and then pressing Shift+arrow key. White handles appear around the object when it is selected.

2. Choose <u>E</u>dit, <u>O</u>bject.

3. Choose Con<u>v</u>ert from the submenu. The Convert dialog box appears.

4. Select the <u>C</u>onvert To option if you want to permanently convert the object to another format. Select the <u>A</u>ctivate As option if you want to temporarily convert the

object so that you can read or edit it. The object is stored back into the document in its original format.

5. Select the type of conversion you want from the Object Type list box.

6. Click OK.

If you must return the Word document to its original creator, but you need to read or edit the object for which you do not have an application, use the Activate As option in the Convert dialog box. This converts the object only while you are reading or editing it. After you close the object, it is converted back to its original format and stored back in the document. Using the Activate As option enables the original document creator to reopen the object using the original application that created it.

TROUBLESHOOTING

Double-clicking an embedded object opens a different application than I expected. Double-clicking an embedded object normally opens the application that created that object. If that application is not on your hard disk, but an application that can read that file is on your hard disk, the substitute application that is available will open.

My file contains an object for which the original application is not available. I need to edit the object. If the proper conversion files were installed in Word, you can convert the object from its current format into the format of an available application. You have a choice of leaving the object in its new converted format or only converting temporarily. To learn more about converting objects, refer to "Converting Embedded Objects" earlier in this chapter.

Linking Documents and Files

Linking data between applications enables one document to show the changes that occur in another document. This capability can be very useful in many business situations. For example, you may have an engineering proposal that is constructed from a standard Word template. The drawings within the template, however, are linked to graphics files and the cost estimates and schedules are linked to worksheet files. When you open the proposal in Word, or at any time, you can update the linked data so that the graphics, cost estimates, and schedules are always current.

There are two ways to link files. You can link the entire file by choosing Insert, File, or you can link data between Windows applications with Edit, Paste Special. Linking creates a communication channel between two open Windows applications. Data can be sent through this channel when information in the source changes, or when you manually request an update.

Linking Documents to Entire Files

If you need to include a graphic or portions of a file or worksheet in your Word document, you should become familiar with the methods for inserting files and importing graphics. Linking to files on disk has these advantages:

- The data resides in a disk file.

- All or part of a word processing, worksheet, or database file can be inserted and linked.

- Only a source file on disk is required. The source application need not be open or even on the system.

- The operator controls when the file or graphic data updates. This feature enables you to "freeze" the data in the destination document until you want an update.

- Files and graphics from DOS applications can be linked into Word documents.

Linking to files has the following disadvantages:

- Renaming or moving a source file can break the link. You then must edit the link so that the Word document can find it.

- Editing an inserted picture can break its link and change the graphic into an embedded object.

To link into your document, a file, or a portion of a file that is on disk and for which you have an installed converter, follow these steps:

1. Position the insertion point in the destination document at the place where you want the source data to appear.

2. Choose Insert, File. The Insert File dialog box opens (see Figure 36.5).

FIG. 36.5
Link a file or portion of a file into your document by choosing Insert, File.

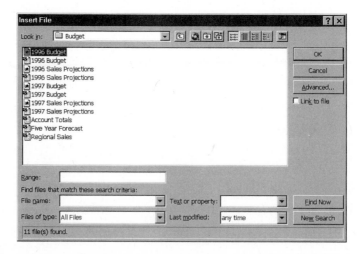

3. Change to the folder containing the source file. Select the file you want to insert from the File list box. If you do not see the file, select All Files (*.*) from the Files of Type list box.

4. To insert a portion of the file, type the name (for Microsoft Excel files), the bookmark (for Word files), or the range name (for 1-2-3 files) in the Range text box.

5. To link rather than insert the source document into the target document, select the Link to File check box.

6. Click OK.

If you are inserting a worksheet file and did not enter a range name, a dialog box appears from which you can select to insert the entire worksheet or select from the list of named ranges in the worksheet. When you later update the inserted worksheet, by selecting it and pressing F9, you again will have an opportunity to select the range to be updated.

N O T E   If you are inserting an Excel 5 or later version worksheet, you will also be given the opportunity to select a specific worksheet from the workbook you select in the Open Worksheet dialog box. Select the sheet you want to open, select the name or cell range in that sheet, and then click OK. ▩

If you insert a file without linking, data is entered as though it were typed. Worksheets are entered as Word tables.

If you select the Link to File check box, a link is created to the source document, using an INCLUDETEXT field code.

N O T E   Before you can choose Insert, File to insert data into a document, you have to save the source document to disk. ▩

Linking Documents to Part of a File

Edit, Paste Special is a useful command, primarily when you want to link two Windows applications and use features in a source application to update data or graphics in your Word document. You might use the command if you have a financial worksheet and charts in Microsoft Excel, for example, and the results and charts are part of an integrated Word report. You need to be able to work in Microsoft Excel and use its functions and its links to mainframe data. When the worksheets and charts change, however, the changes should pass immediately to the integrated report in Word, where you can print them.

Following are the advantages to using links created by Paste Special:

▩ You can link a single source document to many destination documents. Changes in the single source are available to all of the destination documents.

- The data resides in the source application's document. You can use the source application and all of its features to update the source document.

- The data or graphic is not embedded in the Word document (only the result is shown), so the document is much smaller than a document with embedded data.

- You can bring in all or part of a word processing, worksheet, or database file.

- Updates can be done automatically whenever the source data changes, or they can be done manually when you request them.

Following are some disadvantages to using links created by Paste Special:

- Renaming or moving a source file can disturb the link. You must edit the link so that the Word document can find the source file.

- The source application and file must be on disk and available to Word if you want to edit the data or graphic.

- Not all Windows applications can link data.

- Automatic updates can slow down computer response time.

Creating Links with the Copy and Paste Special Commands   Creating a link between Word and a Windows application is as easy as copying and pasting. When you give the Paste command, you create a link that updates automatically.

N O T E   If you copied data from a source application, but Edit, Paste Special does not enable
you to link, that source application may not be able to create linked data. ▪

To copy a range or a portion of a document and link it into the Word document, follow these steps:

1. Position the insertion point in the Word document where you want the linked data or graphic to appear.

2. Activate the source application and document, and make sure that the source has been saved.

3. Select the portion of the source document you want to link.

4. Choose Edit, Copy, or click the Copy button on the Standard toolbar.

5. Activate the Word document.

6. Choose Edit, Paste Special.

7. Select the Paste Link option.

8. From the As list, select the type of data format you want in the document.

9. Click OK.

TROUBLESHOOTING

When the link is updated, an error message appears that says `Error! Not a valid`
`Filename.` This error occurs when the link cannot find the source file that is supposed to contain
the source data, which could be caused by the source file being deleted, renamed, or moved to
another folder. First, choose Edit, Undo to restore the last linked data instead of displaying the
error message. Do not save the document to the original file name until you fix the problem.

You can use any of the following methods to resolve the problem of a lost link:

- Reconnect the link if you know where the original data file has moved or its new
  name. This is usually the best and easiest solution if you can still find the original
  file. Reconnecting a link is described in "Reconnecting Links When Names or Path
  Names Change" later in this chapter.

- Delete the linked data producing the error and re-create it with a new source. This
  is the best solution if you cannot find the original file and you need a link to a source
  file in another application.

- Lock a link so that the image of the last data is maintained and the field code that
  creates the link is kept for possible future use. This enables you to use the last
  image or text from the source data, while preserving the link field code in case you
  later find or re-create the source document. Locking a link is described in "Locking
  Links to Prevent an Update" later in this chapter.

- Freeze the text or image from the last link so that the text or data is like a normal
  unlinked graphic or text in the document. When you *freeze* linked data, you are
  undoing the link to the source document, but maintaining the text or graphic image
  in your Word document. The field code that maintained the link is deleted. To freeze
  linked data as it appears currently in the document, see "Converting Linked Data to
  Fixed Data" later in this chapter.

  ▶ **See** "Creating a Master Document," **p. 1047**

Managing Links

Keeping track of the many links found in a large or complex document can be a difficult
task. You can, however, use the Edit, Links command to make the job easier. When you
choose Edit, Links, the Links dialog box, shown in Figure 36.6, opens and displays a list of
all the links, their type, and how they update. From the buttons and check box, you can
update linked data, open linked files, lock links to prevent changes, cancel the link,
change a link between automatic and manual, or change the file names or directories
where the linked data is stored.

FIG. 36.6

The Links dialog box enables you to update, unlink, or protect links. If the source file moves or is renamed, you can relink to the source using the Links dialog box.

Passing Linked Documents to Other Computer Users

If you want to change the linked data in your document, you must have the source document the link is connected to as well as the application that created the data. When you give a document containing links to other users, make sure that you give them the source documents. They will need the source application if they want to make edits in the original data.

Reducing the Size of a Linked File

The linked data that appears in your Word document is actually a representation of the real data that exists in a source document. This image, however, still requires memory. If your document displays a link to a large graphics file, the representation of the graphics file alone can be very large.

You can reduce the size of a file containing links by not storing the graphic representation; instead, you store only the field codes that describe the links. When the document opens, these field codes reestablish the link to the source document and regenerate an image in your Word document.

The advantage to storing only the link is that you can significantly reduce your Word document file size if your document contains links to large graphics. The disadvantage to storing only the links is that documents with large files take longer to load as you re-create the images, and links that you cannot re-create will appear as rectangular place-holders on-screen.

To store a document as a reduced size file, follow these steps:

1. Choose Edit, Links.
2. Select the link you want stored as a link field without the graphic image.
3. Deselect the Save Picture in Document check box.
4. Click OK.

Opening the Source Document

In your Word document, you can edit linked data such as text or numbers just as though you typed them in the document. When you update the link, however, your changes disappear. To change linked data so that it remains, you need to edit the source document. The source application and source document must be open when you edit the link.

To open a source document that may be closed, follow these steps:

1. If you want to open a file specific to one link, select the linked data.

2. Choose Edit, Links to display the Links dialog box (refer to Figure 36.6).

3. From the Source File list, select the link you want to open. If you selected linked data in step 1, the link you want to open is already selected.

4. Choose the Open Source button. The source application opens.

5. Make your updates, edits, or formatting changes to the source document.

6. If you have made all the changes you want, save and then close the source document.

If the link is automatic, the Word document updates immediately. If the link is manual, you must update the linked data to see the change. Update linked data by selecting it and pressing F9.

> **CAUTION**
>
> When you rename or move a source file, make sure that the destination document is open; save the destination document after renaming or moving the source file. This step is recommended because the {LINK} field in the destination document stores the file and path name of the source file. You can see these names by selecting linked data and pressing Shift+F9. If you rename or move the source file while the destination document is closed, the {LINK} field will not be able to update itself to the new file or path name. If you accidentally lose a link, you can reconnect the link by using the technique described in "Reconnecting Links When Names or Path Names Change" later in this chapter.

N O T E To preserve manually applied formatting during an update to linked data, use the * mergeformat and * charformat field switches described in Chapter 22, "Automating with Field Codes." To preserve wide titles in a table, do not merge cells to give a title extra width in a cell. Instead, change individual cell widths to allow space for a wide title. ▦

Converting Linked Data to Fixed Data   To convert linked information to text or a graphic, select the linked information and then press Shift+Ctrl+F9 to unlink. The information changes—as if you had pasted it and not paste-linked it—into text, a picture, or a bitmap. You can also select the link, choose Edit, Links, choose the Break Link button, and then confirm with Yes.

Updating Links   To update individual links in a document so that the destination file receives new information, select the linked text or graphic, and then press F9. To update links selectively without scrolling through the document, choose Edit, Links. When the Links dialog box appears, select the links you want to update (use Ctrl+click to select multiple links), and then choose the Update Now button.

When you want to update all the links in an entire document, select the entire document by pressing Ctrl and clicking in the left boundary, or press Ctrl+5 (numeric pad). Then press the F9 key or choose Edit, Links and choose the Update Now button.

Changing Links Between Automatic and Manual   Choosing Edit, Paste Special creates an automatic link; pasted data normally updates immediately when the source information changes. This automatic updating process can slow your computer's operation if changes are frequent. If you do not need to see immediate changes, however, you can change an automatic link to a manual link.

To change between manually or automatically updated links, follow these steps:

1. Select the linked data or graphic.
2. Choose Edit, Links.
3. From the Update options at the bottom of the dialog box:

   Choose Manual to update a link by manually selecting it and pressing F9.

   Choose Automatic to automatically update a link when the source data changes.
4. Click OK.

To update a manual link, select the linked information and press F9. To prevent a link from updating, lock the link, as described later in the section "Locking Links to Prevent an Update."

Reconnecting Links When Names or Path Names Change   If a source's location, file name, or range name changes, you must update the field code that creates the link to reflect the new folder and file name. To update a linking field, choose Edit, Links, select the link you need to edit, and then choose the Change Source button to display the Change Source dialog box (see Figure 36.7). From this dialog box, you can select or type a new file name, path name, or item. (The item is a range name in a worksheet or bookmark in a Word document.)

If you are familiar with the operation and editing of field codes as described in Chapter 22, "Automating with Field Codes," you can display the field code for the link and edit the file name, path name, and item name directly. Remember that you need two backslashes to separate folders in a path name within a field code.

FIG. 36.7
You can reconnect source files to the destination even if you have moved or renamed the source file.

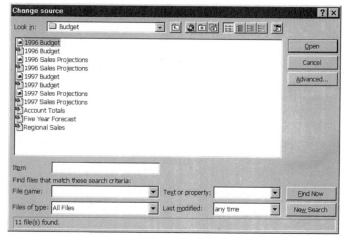

Locking Links to Prevent an Update You may want to prevent accidental updating of a link by locking the field. When the field is locked, its data will not change. The linking field code is preserved, however, so that at a later time you can unlock the field and update the linked data.

To lock a field, follow these steps:

1. Select the field you want to lock.

2. Choose Edit, Links, select the Locked check box, and click OK.

To unlock a locked field, follow these steps:

1. Select the field you want to lock.

2. Choose Edit, Links, deselect the Locked check box, and click OK.

▶ **See** "Updating, Unlinking, or Locking Fields," **p. 715**

Using Outlook with Word

Microsoft Office 97 includes a new and exciting application called Microsoft Outlook. Outlook is a productivity tool that helps you manage the resources on your desktop, as well as your e-mails, contacts, appointments, and tasks. You can schedule meetings and appointments with Outlook's group scheduling and even share resources (including files and folders) with other users. If you are connected to the Internet or an intranet, you can use Outlook to browse these resources. In short, Outlook helps you to pull together all your information, both personal and shared, making it much easier to manage and view this information.

It is not within the scope of this book to discuss how to use Microsoft Outlook. In this section, however, you learn some of the ways you can use Outlook with Word. To learn more about using Outlook, see the online help in Outlook.

Inserting Word Documents into a Message

You can share Word documents through e-mail by embedding a document, or portions of the document, directly in the e-mail message. When the recipients open the e-mail message, they can view the document, and if they have Microsoft Word on their computers, they can open and edit it.

To embed an entire Word document into a mail message, choose Insert, Object, as described in the section "Embedding an Existing File or Object" earlier in this chapter. When you use this method, the entire file is stored with the message and can be viewed and edited without affecting the original file.

To insert a portion of a document, follow the steps outlined in the section "Embedding Part of a File" in this chapter.

To insert a Word document into a mail message, follow these steps:

1. Open the Inbox and choose Compose, New Mail Message.
2. Address the message and fill in the Subject field.
3. Enter the text for the message in the text box and then locate the insertion point where you want to insert the Word document.
4. To insert an entire document, follow the steps in the section "Embedding an Existing File or Object" in this chapter.

   Or, to insert a portion of a workbook file, follow the steps in the section "Embedding Part of a File" in this chapter.
5. Send the message.

Figure 36.8 shows a mail message with a an Excel table embedded in it. If you double-click the embedded data, the workbook is opened in Excel.

Attaching a Word Document to a Task

Another way you can share your Word data with Outlook is to attach Word files to tasks in Outlook. By doing this, you can immediately access the Word documents associated with a particular task. When you open the task to begin working on it, you can double-click an icon representing the document associated with the task. The document opens in Word, ready for you to view and edit it.

FIG. 36.8

Share your Word documents by inserting them in your Outlook mail messages.

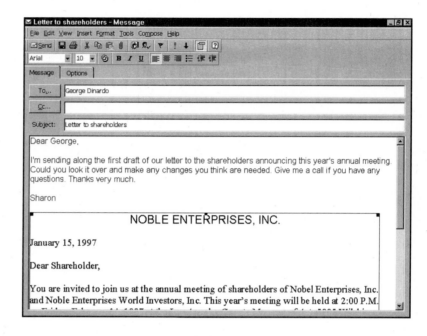

To attach a Word document to a task, follow these steps:

1. Activate the Task window and enter a new task or select an existing task in the task list.

2. Double-click the entry to open the task.

3. Click in the text box at the bottom of the window and choose Insert, Object.

4. Select Create from File.

5. Choose the Browse button to open the Browse dialog box.

6. Change to the drive and folder containing the file you want to insert. If you need to find the file, use the commands and text boxes at the bottom of the dialog box to search for the file (see Chapter 4, "Managing Documents and Files," for more information on finding files).

7. Select the Display as Icon option.

8. Choose OK.

An icon representing the file appears in the text box, as shown in Figure 36.9. When you double-click the icon, the workbook is opened in Word, where you can view and edit it as you normally would.

FIG. 36.9
Attaching an icon for a Word document to a task enables you to open the document directly from the Task window.

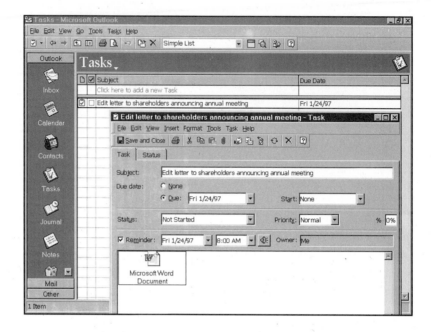

Using Microsoft Office Binder to Group Documents

One of the great advantages to working in Windows with Office 97 is the ability to create documents that use material from different applications. For example, a proposal to a client may contain material from Word, Excel, and Project. The proposal may begin with a letter of introduction, followed by answers to the bid request, and include documents containing project specifications, worksheets containing budget and resource items, charts showing costs and resource loading, as well as Gantt or Pert charts showing project management.

In the past, most people worked with each of these documents separately—storing, printing, and collating them as individual files. A few people tried linking or embedding everything into a Word document. The Binder enables you to work with the files involved in a project as though they are a single bound document. Within one window you can work with documents from many different Office 95 applications. As you switch between documents, the menus and toolbars change to reflect the application that created the document. You can easily switch between documents, insert new documents, print the entire project with contiguous page numbers, and store or e-mail the binder as a single file.

Creating a New Binder

You can start a new binder to group together documents from any Microsoft Office compatible applications, such as Word and Excel. Creating a new binder consists of opening a new, blank binder and adding documents from compatible applications to the binder. Each document you add becomes a *section* in the binder. You can also create a new binder based on one of the templates that comes with Binder.

To create a new binder, open the Start menu and choose Programs, Microsoft Binder. The Binder window opens with a blank binder, as shown in Figure 36.10. If the Binder window is already open, use its menu to choose File, New Binder. Click OK to open a new, blank binder.

FIG. 36.10

When you first open Microsoft Office Binder, you are presented with a new, blank binder to which you can add documents.

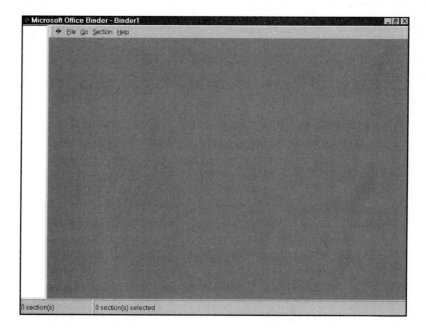

Opening an Existing Binder

TIP If you frequently use a binder template, create a shortcut to that template file. Double-clicking the shortcut will open a new binder containing that template. Binder templates are located in the Program Files\Microsoft Office\Templates\Binders folder.

To open a binder that already exists on your computer, follow these steps:

1. In the Binder window, choose <u>F</u>ile, <u>O</u>pen Binder.

2. Select the drive and folder containing the binder file in the Open Binder dialog box.

3. Select the binder file in the File list box.

4. Choose <u>O</u>pen.

 T I P   To open a file in the Open Binder dialog box, double-click the file in the list box. This selects the file and closes the dialog box in one step.

N O T E   Each time you open an existing or new binder, a new binder window opens. Unless you want to work on more than one binder at a time, you should close the binder you are working on before you open another binder; or you may end up with several binder windows open at the same time, using up your computer's memory unnecessarily.

Adding Documents to a Binder

Whether you are starting a new binder from scratch or working with an existing binder, the procedures for adding a new document to a binder are the same. You can add both new and existing documents to a binder. This gives you the flexibility to build your binder from new and old material. You can, for example, add an existing document from Microsoft Word, and then add a new document from Microsoft Excel. You can then work in the new worksheet from within the Binder.

N O T E   You can add a portion of a document into a binder by dragging the selected portion from the Office application into the left pane of the binder. Position the pointer in the left pane where you want the document and release the mouse button.

To add an existing document to a binder, follow these steps:

1. Select the document in either My Computer or Windows Explorer.

    If the left pane is not visible in the Binder window, click the double-headed arrow to the left of <u>F</u>ile on the menu bar.

2. Drag and drop the document on the left pane of the Binder window at the location in the binder where you want the document to be added.

An icon representing the document will appear in the left pane, and the document itself will appear in the right pane (see Figure 36.11). The document becomes a section in the binder. The menu bar and toolbar for the document's application will also appear, allowing you to work on the document from within the Binder (refer to Figure 36.10).

FIG. 36.11

When you add an existing document to a binder, an icon representing the document appears in the left pane of the Binder, and the document itself appears in the right pane.

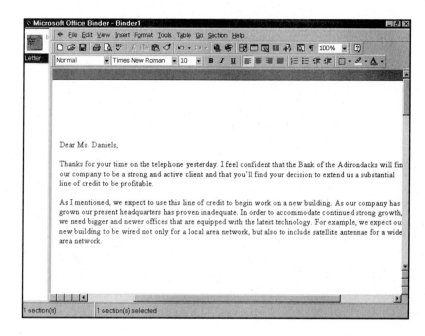

To add a new document to a binder, follow these steps:

1. Choose <u>S</u>ection, <u>A</u>dd to display the Add Section dialog box (see Figure 36.12).

FIG. 36.12

Select the type of document you want to add as a section to a binder in the Add Section dialog box.

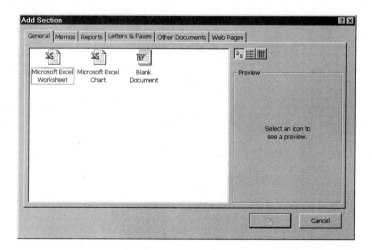

2. Select the type of document you want to add to your binder from the General tab or select one of the other tabs to see a list of templates, then select a template to base your new document on.

3. Choose OK.

The new, blank document appears as a section in the binder, and the menu and toolbars for the document's application appear (see Figure 36.13). An icon representing the document appears in the left pane of the Binder, with a section name assigned to it; for example, *Section 1*. The icon for a section indicates with which application the section's document is associated. You can work on the document from within the Binder.

FIG. 36.13

When you add a new document to a binder, a blank document is inserted as a section in the binder, and the menu and toolbars for the document's application appear.

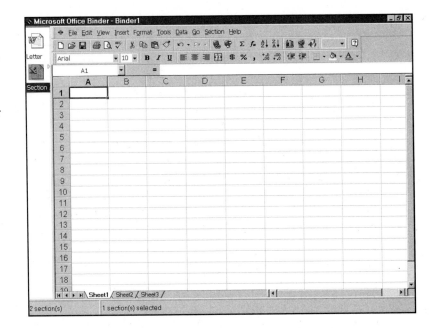

N O T E   To quickly add a new document after an existing document in a binder, select the existing document and click the right mouse button. Choose Add from the shortcut menu, select the type of document you want to add from the Add Section dialog box, and then click OK. ■

Selecting a Binder Document

When you want to work with, move, copy, or delete a document in a binder, you must select it first. You can even select multiple documents to carry out an action on more than one document at the same time.

To select documents, follow one of these steps:

■   To select a single document, click the document's button in the left pane of the Binder.

If the left pane is not displayed, click the double-headed arrow to the left of File in the menu bar.

■ To select two or more documents that appear consecutively in the left pane of the Binder, click the first document's icon, hold down the Shift key, and then click the last document's icon.

■ To select two or more documents that do not appear consecutively in the left pane, click the first document's icon and, while holding down the Ctrl key, click the icons for the other documents.

■ To select all the documents in a binder, choose Section, Select All.

After you have chosen the Select All command, you must choose Section, Unselect All to unselect the documents.

Moving a Binder Document

You can use the mouse or Section, Rearrange to reorder the documents in a binder. You can also move a document from one binder to another, or even from a binder to a folder in My Computer or Windows Explorer.

To move a document with the mouse, drag the icon for the document to where you want it in the left pane of the Binder. If the left pane is not visible, click the double-headed arrow to the left of File in the menu bar.

To move a document with a menu command, follow these steps:

1. Choose Section, Rearrange to display the Rearrange Sections dialog box (see Figure 36.14).

FIG. 36.14
Move sections around in a binder using the Rearrange Sections dialog box.

2. Select the section you want to move in the Reorder Sections list box.

3. Choose the Move Up or Move Down button to move the section to its new location.

4. Click OK.

To move a document from one binder to another, open both binders. Size and arrange the Binder windows so that the left panes in each window are visible. Select the document in the left pane of the source binder and drag and drop it to where you want it in the left pane of the destination binder.

If you want to move a document out of a binder into a folder, you can drag and drop it from the Binder window. To move the document, select it in the left pane and drag and drop it on the destination folder in My Computer or Windows Explorer with the right mouse button. When the shortcut menu appears, choose Move Scrap Here.

Copying a Binder Document

You can use the mouse or Section, Duplicate to make a copy of a document in a binder.

To copy a document with the mouse, follow these steps:

1. Select the document in the left pane of the Binder window.

   If the left pane is not visible, click the double-headed arrow to the left of File in the menu bar.

2. Drag and drop the document to where you want to insert a duplicate copy with the right-mouse button.

3. When the shortcut menu appears, choose Copy Here.

To copy a document with a menu command, follow these steps:

1. Select the document you want to duplicate in the left pane of the Binder window.

2. Choose Section, Duplicate to open the Duplicate Section dialog box.

3. Select the section after which you want the duplicate to be created in the list box.

4. Click OK.

 After you select the document you want to duplicate in the left pane of Binder, right-click the document and choose Duplicate to open the Duplicate Section dialog box.

To create a copy of a binder document in a My Computer or Windows Explorer folder, drag and drop the document from the left pane of the Binder window to the destination folder with the right mouse button. When the shortcut menu appears, choose Create Scrap Here.

Renaming a Binder Document

To rename a document in a binder, double-click the name under the document, type the new name, and then press Enter. Or select the document you want to rename, choose Section, Rename, type the new name, and then press Enter.

Deleting a Binder Document

To delete a document from a binder, right-click the document, click Delete, and then click OK when the confirmation dialog box appears. Or you can select the document and choose Section, Delete.

Hiding and Displaying Binder Documents

You can hide a document if you do not want it to appear in the binder for some reason, and do not want to delete it. To hide a document, select it and then choose Selection, Hide. To unhide a document, choose Section, Unhide, select the document in the Unhide Sections dialog box, and then click OK.

 TIP Double-click the name of the document you want to unhide in the Unhide Sections dialog box. This selects the file and closes the dialog box in one step.

Saving Binder Sections as Documents

You can save a section that you have added to a binder as a separate document. To save a binder section as a document, follow these steps:

1. Select the document in the left pane of the Binder window.

   If the left pane is not visible, click the double-headed arrow to the left of File in the menu bar.

2. Choose Section, Save As File to display the Save As dialog box.
3. Select the folder where you want to save the file.
4. Enter a name for the document in the File Name text box.
5. Click OK.

Unbinding a Binder into Separate Documents

You can unbind a binder so that its component parts are saved as separate files. When you unbind a binder, the original binder file remains intact.

To unbind a binder into its component documents, follow these steps:

1. Either in My Computer or Windows Explorer, locate the binder file on your hard disk.

2. Select the file and click the right mouse button.

3. Choose Unbind.

> **CAUTION**
>
> You cannot unbind documents if one of the documents in the binder is open.

The documents that make up the binder are saved as separate files in the same folder that the binder file is in.

Viewing a Document in its Application

If you want to view a document in a binder in its original application, select the document in the left pane of the Binder window and choose Section, View Outside. The original application will open along with the selected document. To return to the Binder, choose File, Close and Return To.

Printing and Collating from Multiple Applications

You can print all or selected sections of a binder using the File, Print Binder command. To print selected sections, select the sections you want to print using the methods outlined in "Selecting a Binder Document," earlier in the chapter.

To print a binder, follow these steps:

1. Choose File, Print Binder.

2. To print the entire binder, make sure that you have selected the All Visible Sections option. To print just the selected sections, select the Sections Selected in Left Pane option.

3. Specify the number of copies in the Number of Copies spinner box.

4. Select the Collate option if you want to collate multiple copies.

5. Select Consecutive in the Numbering Group if you want to number the pages in the binder consecutively from first to last page.

   Or, select Restart Each Section if you want page numbering to start at 1 for each section (document) in the binder.

6. Click OK.

To print a single document in a binder, select the document in the left pane of the Binder window. Choose Section, Print, select the desired options in the Print dialog box, and then click OK.

Using Binder Templates for Repetitive Documents

Templates are like blueprints that serve as the basis for creating a new binder. When you open a new binder based on a template, the basic parts of the template are already in place, saving you the trouble of creating the binder from scratch. When you save the binder, the original template on which the binder is based remains intact.

Using Binder's Built-In Templates Binder comes with two templates that you can use as a foundation for new binders that you create. These templates already contain sections for some of the typical binders that you may create for your business needs. After you open the template, you fill in your own information in each of the binder sections. The two templates that come with Binder are Proposal, and Marketing Plan and Report. Figure 36.15 shows the Proposal and Marketing Plan template. Notice that there are six sections in the binder, consisting of Microsoft Word, Excel, and PowerPoint documents.

FIG. 36.15

The Report template that comes with Microsoft Office Binder includes sections for a cover letter, executive letter, slide show, analysis, and data.

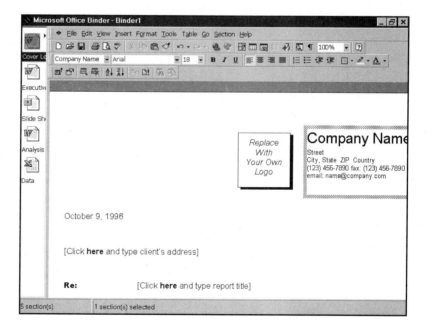

To start a new binder based on a Binder template, follow these steps:

1. Choose File, New Binder.
2. Select the Binders tab.
3. Click OK.

Now you can fill in your own information in each binder section and save the file by choosing File, Save Binder.

▶ **See** " Understanding Templates," **p. 93**

Creating a New Binder Template   If you have created a binder that you want to use as the basis of future binders, you can save the binder as a template. Before saving the binder as a template, you should delete any information that you do not want repeated in new binders based on the template.

To save a binder as a template, follow these steps:

1. Choose File, Save Binder As.
2. In the Save As dialog box, select the Program Files folder, then the Microsoft Office folder, then the Templates folder, and finally, the Binders folder.
3. Select Binder Templates from the Save As Type drop-down list.
4. Click OK.

When you want to start a new binder based on this template, select the template from the Binders tab of the New Binder dialog box.

▶ **See** "Working with Templates," **p. 198**

Customizing with Word

CHAPTER 37

Customizing and Optimizing Word Features

As you use Word 97, you might want to customize it to fit the way you work or to make trade-offs between increased performance and features. In Chapter 38, you will learn how to customize Word features such as menus, toolbars, and shortcut keys. But there are many other ways in which you can customize Word. This chapter contains suggestions and options to help you fine-tune Word and customize it for the way you work. ■

Improving the performance of Word

You can customize a number of settings in Word to improve speed and overall performance.

Starting Word or documents automatically

If you use Word as your primary application, you can use the Windows Startup folder to automatically run Word each time Windows starts.

Customizing the workspace and display

You can customize screen color and display elements in Word to make the environment more intuitive and easier to use.

Personalizing the mouse

You can make the mouse easier to handle by personalizing the speed at which it operates.

Get help from the Office Assistant

Both new and experienced users can benefit from the help offered by the Office Assistant.

Modifying Word for users with disabilities

With a few modifications to your Windows setup, you can make Word more accessible for users with limited hearing, vision, or movement.

> **N O T E**   To follow the examples in this chapter, it is assumed that Word for Windows has been
> installed in the C:\PROGRAM FILES\MICROSOFT OFFICE\WINWORD folder. If you have
> installed Word in a different folder, please substitute your Word folder's name in the following
> examples. ■

Customizing Commonly Used Features

Other chapters of this book discuss techniques for customizing many Word features. The
following list indicates some commonly customized features and the chapters in which
they are discussed:

If You Want to Customize	Refer to
Dictionary	Chapter 7, "Using Editing and Proofing Tools"
Document on startup	Chapter 6, "Using Templates and Wizards for Frequently Created Documents"
Documents that are frequently used	Chapter 6, "Using Templates and Wizards for Frequently Created Documents"
Font on startup (default font)	Chapter 9, "Formatting Characters and Changing Fonts"
Menus or commands	Chapter 38, "Customizing the Toolbar, Menus, and Shortcut Keys"
Page settings on startup	Chapter 13, "Formatting the Page Layout, Alignment, and Numbering;" Chapter 6, "Using Templates and Wizards for Frequently Created Documents"
Paragraph settings on startup	Chapter 10, "Formatting Lines and Paragraphs;" Chapter 6, "Using Templates and Wizards for Frequently Created Documents."

If You Want to Customize	Refer to
Procedures or commands	Chapter 39, "Introducing Visual Basic for Applications"
Screen display	Chapter 2, "Getting Started in Word"
Shortcut keys	Chapter 38, "Customizing the Toolbar, Menus, and Shortcut Keys"
Toolbars	Chapter 38, "Customizing the Toolbar, Menus, and Shortcut Keys"

Part
IX

Ch
37

 ON THE WEB

Additional information on customizing Word can be found at the following Microsoft Web site:

http://www.microsoft.com/msword

Improving the Performance of Word

Depending on the work that you do and the capability of your computer, Word may not perform as fast as DOS-based word processors. 80486 computers, minimum RAM memory, large graphics files, and long tables can make Word perform more slowly. You can make a number of trade-offs, however, to improve the speed of Word.

Modifying Word for Windows Settings

You can improve Word's performance by choosing certain options within Word. Significant performance improvements also can be made by increasing the memory available to Windows or by increasing the effective speed of your computer's hard disk.

To improve Word's performance from within Word, follow these steps:

1. Choose Tools, Options. The Options dialog box appears (see Figure 37.1).

FIG. 37.1

You can use the Options dialog box to customize many Word for Windows options.

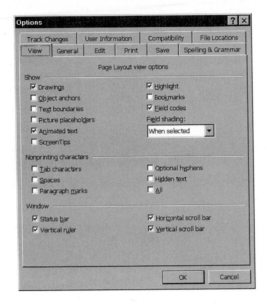

2. Select the tab listed in the first column of the following table; then select or clear the option or check box to make the performance trade-offs you want:

Tab	Option or Check Box	To Improve Performance; Trade-off
View	Picture Placeholders	Select for faster performance; pictures display as empty rectangles on-screen.
View	Animated Text	Clear for faster performance; text animation will not show on-screen.
Print	Draft Output	Select to print faster on dot-matrix printers; the document does not use the fonts shown on-screen. Some character formatting may be lost.
Print	Background Printing	Check to be able to continue working while document is printing; clear to print the document faster.
Save	Allow Fast Saves	Select to save more quickly by saving only the changes made to documents; files become larger

Tab	Option or Check Box	To Improve Performance; Trade-off
		and cannot be converted by other programs when saved with fast save.
Save	Embed TrueType Fonts	Clear to save more quickly; if you share your files with others who do not have TrueType fonts, they will not be able to view and print the file with the fonts used to create it.
Save	Embed Characters in Use Only	Select in conjunction with Embed TrueType Fonts to save more quickly and reduce document size; saves only the font styles actually used within the file. If you use 32 or fewer characters from a font, only those characters are embedded.
Save	Always Create Backup Copy	Clear to save more quickly; no duplicate copy (file extension BAK) is made during saves.
Save	Allow Background Saves	Select to allow continued editing while large files are saved to disk; editing commands and input may slow down slightly while Word performs a background save.
Save	Save AutoRecover Info Every	Clear to avoid being interrupted by timed saves to disk; no periodic saves are made unless you remember to make them yourself.
General	Background Repagination	Clear for better performance; page break markers and automatic page numbering aren't correct until you repaginate.

continues

continued

Tab	Option or Check Box	To Improve Performance; Trade-off
General	Provide Feedback with Animation	Clear for faster performance; on-screen animation for actions such as saving, printing, and repaginating is not displayed.
General	Update Automatic Links at Open	Clear to open files faster; linked data is not necessarily correct unless the individual link (or the entire document) is up-dated.
Spelling & Grammar	Check Spelling as You Type	Clear for faster performance; possible spelling errors are not automatically marked as you type.
Spelling & Grammar	Check Grammar as You Type	Clear for faster performance; possible grammar errors are not automatically marked as you type.

3. Choose OK.

You also can gain a few percentage points of performance by limiting the type or number of fonts you use. Use one or both of the following methods to improve performance by way of font selection:

■ *Do not use several different fonts within a single document.* This guideline is in keeping with a general rule of desktop publishing which suggests that no more than three fonts should be used in a document.

■ *Use TrueType fonts sparingly.* TrueType fonts slow computer and printer perfor-mance slightly. Instead, use the built-in fonts provided by the currently selected printer.

Printer fonts appear in the Font list of the Font dialog box (choose Format, Font) with a miniature printer to the left of their names.

Managing System Memory

Having more memory available can make Word run faster and enable you to work more efficiently in larger or more complex documents. You can get a significant improvement in performance by increasing your computer's memory to at least 16M for Windows 95. If you are running several applications at once, adding even more memory will improve performance.

You also can improve performance (although the gains are not as significant) by making the proper selections of Word features and using wise file and application management practices. The following tips also can help you improve performance:

- Exit all applications that are not being used while you are working in Word. Other applications also require memory.

- Close unneeded documents in Word or data files in other open Windows applications. Each document and application requires a portion of Windows' limited system resources memory.

- Close the Office Assistant if it is not being used, or customize the Office Assistant to reduce the resources it requires (see "Customizing the Office Assistant" later in this chapter).

- Use the disk defragmenting program that comes with Windows, to consolidate your hard disk so that information can be read and written more quickly. Start this program by opening the Start menu, then clicking Programs, Accessories, System Tools, and then Disk Defragmenter. Disk fragmentation occurs normally as you save and delete files. As time passes, files are saved in pieces scattered over the disk to make the best use of available space. Unfortunately, this process slows down read and write operations. Defragmenting reorganizes information on the disk so that each file is stored in a single contiguous location.

- Do not create large documents exceeding 30 to 50 pages in length. Instead, create smaller documents and link them together into a master document using the techniques described in Chapter 34, "Assembling Large Documents."

- Be sure to leave ample free space on the hard drive on which your Windows 95 virtual memory swap file is located. Windows 95 adjusts the size of the swap file dynamically, and you want to be sure there is plenty of room for this file to increase in size.

Starting Word or Documents on Startup

If you use Word as your primary Windows application, you might want it to run it each time you start Windows. You can do this by creating a shortcut for Word in the Windows Startup folder. This section explains how to do that, as well as how to create shortcuts on the desktop to start Word or load a specified document.

▶ **See** "Controlling Printing Options," **p. 274**
▶ **See** "Linking Documents and Files," **p. 1091**

Starting Word or Documents When Windows Starts

To start Word when Windows starts, you need to add Word to the Startup folder. You can do this by following these steps:

1. Open the Start menu, and click Settings, and then Taskbar. Choose the Start Menu Programs tab from the Taskbar Properties dialog box, as shown in Figure 37.2.

FIG. 37.2
Specify which programs or documents run on startup with the Start Menu Programs tab. You can also add programs to the Start menu.

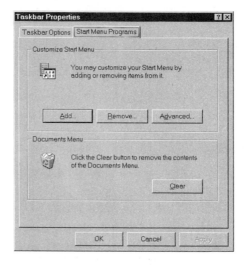

2. Click the Add button to display the Create Shortcut dialog box.

3. Click the Browse button to display the Browse dialog box. To start Word when Windows starts, open the folder containing Word and double-click the WINWORD.EXE file. This file is usually found in the C:\Program Files\Microsoft Office\Winword folder.

   If you want to start a document on startup, select All Files in the Files of Type list box. Open the folder to the document and double-click the document's file. The Browse dialog box will close; the file and path name of the selected file appears in the Command Line edit box.

4. Click the Next button to display the Select Program Folder dialog box.

5. Scroll down and select the Startup folder, which is a folder within the Programs folder, as shown in Figure 37.3.

6. Click the Next button to display the Select a Title for the Program dialog box.

7. Type the name you want to use to represent Word or the document. Click the Finish button to return to the Taskbar Properties dialog box.

8. Choose OK.

FIG. 37.3
Select the Startup folder if you want your document or application to start when Windows starts.

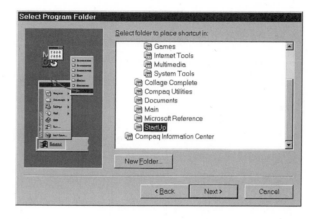

The next time you start Windows, the Word program or the document you selected will open automatically.

To stop a program or document from loading automatically, reopen the Start Menu Programs tab from the Taskbar Properties dialog box. Click the Remove button. Open the Startup folder in the Remove Shortcuts/Folders dialog box. Select the program or document you no longer want to startup and click the Remove button. Choose Close and OK.

Creating Desktop Shortcut Icons for Word or Documents

You can get quick access to Word or to a Word document from your desktop by adding a shortcut icon to your desktop for that file. Double-clicking a shortcut icon to Word will open Word. Double-clicking a shortcut icon to a Word document will open Word and load the document.

To create a shortcut icon to Word or a document, follow these steps:

1. Open My Computer or Windows Explorer.
2. Open the folder containing the application or document file for which you want to create a shortcut.
3. Drag the file to the desktop using the right mouse button. When you release the right mouse button, a shortcut menu displays.
4. Choose Create Shortcut(s) Here.

This will create a shortcut icon to the file you specified.

N O T E If you have too many shortcut icons on your desktop, you can create a shortcut folder in which to store them. Right-click on the desktop and choose New, Folder. Type a name for the folder and press Enter. You can drag and drop your shortcut icons into the folder. To use a shortcut, double-click the folder and then double-click the shortcut. ■

Delete shortcut icons by clicking them and then pressing the Delete key.

Customizing the Start Menu to Include Word or Documents

The contents of the Start menu can be customized. You can add a list of applications you use frequently, and then start those applications directly from the menu. By adding programs or documents to the Start menu you avoid having to display additional menus.

To quickly add Word to the highest level of the Start menu, drag Word's application file, WINWORD.EXE, from the Explorer or My Computer window and drop it on the Start button. WINWORD.EXE is usually located in the C:\PROGRAM FILES\MICROSOFT OFFICE\WINWORD folder.

To add Word or a document to the Start menu, follow these steps:

1. Right-click a gray area between buttons on the taskbar. Choose Properties.

   You can also open the Start menu and choose Settings, Taskbar.

2. Click the Start Menu Programs tab (refer to Figure 37.2).

3. Click the Add button to display the Create Shortcut dialog box.

4. Click the Browse button to display the Browse dialog box. This dialog box looks very similar to an Open File dialog box.

5. Find and click the file that starts the program or document file you want to add to the Start menu. Click the Open button once you have selected the file.

   To make a program easier to find you can limit the displayed files to program files by selecting Programs from the Files of Type list at the bottom of the dialog box. For example, if you wanted to start Word, you would open the PROGRAM FILES folder, open the MICROSOFT OFFICE folder, open the WINWORD folder, and then click WINWORD.EXE. Most program files use an EXE extension.

6. Click the Next button to display the Select Program Folder dialog box (refer to Figure 37.3).

7. Select the folder that corresponds to the location on the Start menu where you want the program to appear. Choose Next.

   For example, if you wanted the program you selected to appear at the top of the Start menu, you would select the Start Menu folder. If you wanted the program to appear as an item on the Programs menu, then you would select the Programs folder.

8. Type the name or words you want to appear on the Start menu in the edit box. Choose Finish.

N O T E When you install Microsoft Office, it automatically adds two items to the Start menu: New Office Document and Open Office Document. These menu items open a dialog box from which you can open either a new or existing Office document. This is another way to open Word, although it is not as direct as clicking a menu item for Word itself on the Start menu.

Microsoft Office also adds a shortcut for Word to the Programs folder, so you can open Word by clicking the Start button and choosing Programs, Microsoft Word. ▪

N O T E If you frequently copy files to the same folders, put shortcuts to those folders in the WINDOWS\SENDTO folder. The shortcuts to the folders will then show up on the Send To menu that appears when you right-click a file. ▪

To remove a program from the Start menu, you follow a similar process:

1. Display the Taskbar Properties dialog box as described earlier in this chapter.
2. Click the Start Menu Programs tab.
3. Click the Remove button to display the Remove Shortcuts/Folders dialog box.
4. Select the shortcut or folder you want to remove from the Start menu.
5. Click the Remove button to remove the file or folder.
6. Remove additional items or choose Close. Choose OK when you return to the Taskbar Properties dialog box.

Clearing the Documents List on the Start Menu

The Start menu contains a Documents list that shows a list of recently used documents. At times this list may become too long or you may want to clear the list so documents are easier to find. To clear the documents from the Documents menu, follow these steps:

1. Display the Taskbar Properties dialog box.
2. Select the Start Menu Programs tab.
3. Click the Clear button in the Documents Menu portion of the dialog box.
4. Choose OK.

Making Menus, Toolbars, and Shortcut Keys Globally Available

If you find that a template has menus, toolbars, and shortcut keys that you use frequently, you can make them available without using the Organizer to transfer them to the NORMAL.DOT template. (The Organizer is a feature described in Chapter 6, "Using Templates and Wizards for Frequently Created Documents.") Instead, copy the template file (DOT extension) containing these features into the \WINWORD\STARTUP directory. The template files are usually located in folders within the PROGRAM FILES\ MICROSOFT OFFICE\TEMPLATES folder.

Make sure you copy a template into the StartUp folder. If you move a template out of the Template folder, it will not appear in the New dialog box when you choose File, New. Be careful not to copy more templates into the StartUp folder than you really need, as it will increase the time it takes to start Word.

Customizing the Workspace and Display

If you work at your computer a lot, even small things like customizing screen colors or arranging screen elements can help you reduce stress. Refer to Chapter 38, "Customizing the Toolbar, Menus, and Shortcut Keys," for more information.

To change the display or your Word workspace, follow these steps:

1. Choose Tools, Options. The Options dialog box appears.
2. Select the tab listed in the first column of the following table. Then select or clear the associated option or check box depending on your display preferences:

Tab	Option or Check Box	To Change
General	Recently Used File List	The number of files shown under the File menu listed as having been recently opened
General	Measurement Units	The units used on the ruler (choice of inches, centimeters, points, or picas)

Tab	Option or Check Box	To Change
General	Provide Feedback With Sound	The status (on/off) of the audible sounds that provide feedback to indicate various actions or events
General	Provide Feedback With Animation	The status (on/off) of the animated cursors used to indicate actions such as printing and saving
General	Blue Background, White Text	To a white-on-blue screen, potentially reducing the eye strain caused by reading a black-on-white screen
View	Status Bar	Whether or not the status bar appears at the bottom of the screen
View	Horizontal Scroll Bar or Vertical Scroll Bar	Whether or not the horizontal or vertical scroll bars appear on-screen. Remove them if you use only the keyboard
View	Animated Text	The display (on/off) of text animation on the screen
View	ScreenTips	The display (on/off) of reviewers' comments when holding the mouse above a comment reference mark
View	Highlight	The display (on/off) of text highlights on the screen

Part
IX

Ch
37

continues

continued

Tab	Option or Check Box	To Change
View	<u>A</u>ll	The display (on/off) of nonprinting characters such as tabs, spaces, and paragraph marks
File Locations	<u>F</u>ile Types	The location of files used by Word. Select the file type and choose the Modify button. You can change the locations for Documents, ClipArt Pictures, User Templates, Workgroup Templates, User Options, AutoRecover Files, Tools, and StartUp

   3. Choose OK.

Customizing Mouse Settings

You can operate Word with different types of pointer movement devices. In the past most people have used the familiar desktop mouse. Some users prefer trackballs, while artists prefer graphics tablets. With Microsoft Office you can also use Microsoft's IntelliPoint mouse. The IntelliPoint mouse adds the additional features of scrolling, panning, and zooming to normal mouse movement. See "Scrolling, Panning and Zooming with IntelliPoint Mouse," in Chapter 5 to learn how to use the IntelliPoint mouse.

Customizing a Standard Mouse

You can customize the mouse to operate more slowly; you also can switch the button actions between left and right sides.

To customize the mouse, follow these steps:

   1. Start the <u>C</u>ontrol Panel found in the <u>S</u>ettings group on the Start menu.

   2. Double-click the Mouse icon. The Mouse Properties dialog box appears.

3. Change any of the following options:

Motion	Pointer Speed	The Speed of the on-screen pointer moves with respect to your movement of the hand-held mouse. Use the slow setting while learning.
Motion	Pointer Trail	Produces a shadowed trail of mouse pointers that makes the pointer easier to see on LCD panel displays (used in laptop computers).
Buttons	Double-Click Speed	The speed with which you must double-click for a double-click to be accepted. Use the slow setting while learning.
Buttons	Right-handed/ Left-handed Buttons	Swaps the active mouse button to the opposite side. Use for operating the mouse from the opposite hand.

Part

IX

Ch

37

4. Choose OK.

5. To close the Control Panel, click the X in the top-right corner.

Many newer mice have additional customizing options available (such as changing the size of the pointer or reversing the color of the pointer). These options, if available, appear in the Pointers tab of the Mouse Properties dialog box.

Customizing the IntelliPoint Mouse

The IntelliPoint Mouse from Microsoft gives you additional navigation capabilities over those of a normal mouse. Using the wheel between the left and right mouse buttons, you can scroll, zoom, and expand or collapse outlines. These advanced features of the IntelliPoint Mouse aren't available unless you install the IntelliPoint 2 drivers. These drivers have customizable features.

To customize the IntelliPoint Mouse, follow these steps:

1. Click Start, Settings, Control Panel to display the Control Panel window.

2. Double-click the Mouse application to display the Mouse Properties sheet shown in Figure 37.4. Select the Wheel tab.

3. Select Turn On The Wheel so the wheel can be used to scroll, pan, or zoom in or out of outlines. Click Settings to adjust scrolling speed.

FIG. 37.4
Control the wheel and
its button operation
from the Wheel tab.

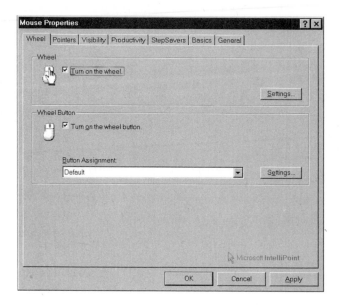

4. Select Turn On The Wheel Button so the wheel button can be used to pan across screens in the direction you drag the mouse. Click Settings to adjust panning speed.

5. Select an option from the Button Assignment list. The options are:

- *Default.* Holding down the wheel button as you drag pans the document in the direction of the drag.

- *Double-click.* Clicking the wheel button is the same as a double-click with a left or right button.

- *Help (F1).* Clicking the wheel button displays Help as though you pressed F1.

- *Switch to Shell.* Clicking the wheel button activates the Explorer.

- *Start.* Clicking the wheel button displays the Start menu.

6. Select other tabs to set other options specific to the IntelliPoint mouse. Other tabs and options are described in Table 37.1.

7. Choose OK.

Table 37.1   Options Specific to the IntelliPoint mouse

Options	Description
Visibility Tab	
Show Location of Pointer When You Press Ctrl Key	Helps you find the pointer by displaying an animated ring that encloses the pointer.

Options	Description
Visibility Tab	
Hide Pointer While Typing	Hides the pointer while you type so it isn't in your way.
Display Pointer Trails	Use on older laptops or overhead projections to help follow pointer movement.
Automatically Move Pointer to Opposite Edge	Wraps pointer around the screen edges. When it goes off one edge it appears on the other.
Productivity Tab	
Turn on the Odometer	Shows you how far you've "driven" your mouse.
Orientation	Teaches the software to compensate if you hold the mouse crooked.
Clicklock	Replaces holding down the mouse during long drags by just doing a long click to "lock."
Step Savers Tab	
Snap To	Automatically moves pointer to default button.
Focus	Activates a window or icon by moving the pointer over it as though you had clicked it.
ClickSaver	Do a single-click instead of a double-click.
SmartSpeed	Slows down the pointer as it nears an icon, control, or button.

Part
IX

Ch
37

Customizing the Office Assistant

The Office Assistant is an on-screen, interactive program that assists you when using any Microsoft Office application. Experienced users may make the assumption that the Office Assistant is only for new users; however, with a few modifications, even experienced users can benefit from this feature.

▶ **See** "Working with the Office Assistant," **p. 63**

> **CAUTION**
>
> Because the Office Assistant works across all Microsoft Office applications, customizations you make while in Word will also apply while working in other Office applications, such as Excel or PowerPoint.

Changing How the Office Assistant Operates

You can customize the Office Assistant to provide help that is suited to your level of experience.

 T I P   You can start the Office Assistant by clicking [icon] on the Standard Toolbar.

To customize the Office Assistant while working in Word, follow these steps:

1. If the Office Assistant is not already running, activate it by choosing Microsoft Word Help from the Help menu. The Office Assistant appears on-screen (see Figure 37.5).

FIG. 37.5

The Office Assistant can be customized by choosing the Options button.

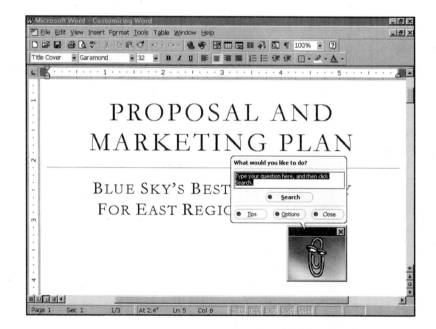

If the Office Assistant is already running, click the Office Assistant with the left mouse button to display the Office Assistant message box, as shown in Figure 37.5.

2. Choose Options to access the Office Assistant dialog box (see Figure 37.6).

3. Change any of the following options:

FIG. 37.6
You can customize the Office Assistant to provide only the help you need.

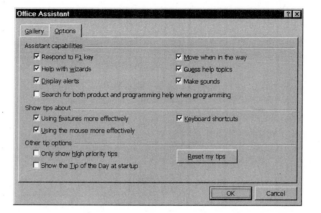

Respond to F1 Key	Select to display the Office Assistant (rather than the standard Help dialog box) when the F1 key is pressed. For more information about Help, see Chapter 2, "Getting Started in Word."
Help with Wizards	Select to have the Office Assistant provide instructions while using wizards. For more information about wizards, see Chapter 6, "Using Templates and Wizards for Frequently Created Documents."
Display Alerts	Select to have alerts displayed through the Office Assistant (when active) rather than through a standard dialog box.
Search for Both Product and Programming Help When Programming	Select to retrieve both product and programming help topics while working with Visual Basic for Applications (VBA); clear this option if you want to see only programming help topics while using VBA. For more information about VBA, see Chapter 39, "Introducing Visual Basic for Applications."

continues

continued

<u>M</u>ove When in the Way	Select to force the Office Assistant to automatically move when it is blocking dialog boxes or other screen elements; the Office Assistant will also shrink in size if it is not used within five minutes.
G<u>u</u>ess Help Topics	Select to display suggested Help topics based on your actions prior to asking for help.
Make <u>S</u>ounds	Select to hear sounds made by the Office Assistant.
Using <u>F</u>eatures More Effectively	Select to display tips about features you may not know and ideas on how to better utilize the features you do know.
<u>U</u>sing the Mouse More Effectively	Select to display tips about using the mouse more efficiently.
<u>K</u>eyboard Shortcuts	Select to display shortcut keys for the features you use.
Only Show <u>H</u>igh Priority Tips	Select to display only those tips that are important, such as tips about time-saving features.
Show the <u>T</u>ip of the Day at Startup	Select to display the Tip of the Day when Word or any other Office application starts.
<u>R</u>eset my Tips	Select to see tips you have already seen.

As you become more familiar with Word, you may want to change these settings so the Office Assistant continues to work efficiently with your increased skill-level.

Selecting an Assistant

You can use the Office Assistant Gallery to find an assistant that appeals to you. Each assistant has its own unique personality, from garish to subtle. If you find the Office Assistant annoying, try selecting a different assistant rather than turning off the Assistant feature.

To change the look of your assistant, follow these steps:

1. Make sure the Office Assistant is running (see the previous section for instructions).

2. Click the Office Assistant with the right mouse button and select <u>C</u>hoose Assistant from the shortcut menu. The Office Assistant dialog box appears with the <u>G</u>allery tab selected (see Figure 37.7).

FIG. 37.7
Use the Gallery to select any of nine assistants.

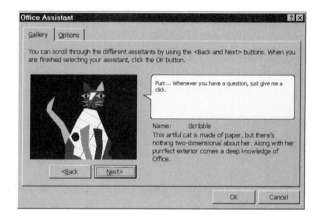

3. Use the <u>N</u>ext and <u>B</u>ack buttons to scroll through the different assistants.

4. When you find an assistant you like, choose OK.

 TIP You can sample the animation of an assistant by right-clicking the Office Assistant and choosing <u>A</u>nimate from the shortcut menu.

Customizing Word for the Hearing or Movement Impaired

Windows applications can be made more accessible for users with unique needs, whether those needs are for hearing, vision, or movement.

The hearing impaired can contact Microsoft Sales and Service on a text telephone at 800-892-5234. Technical support is available on a text telephone at 206-635-4948.

> **CAUTION**
>
> Accessibility options are not installed with a normal Windows installation. You can reinstall Windows from your original disk or CD-ROM and select the custom installation option that will enable you to select Accessibility options.

 ON THE WEB

A complete list of Microsoft products for users with disabilities can be found at the following Microsoft Website:

http://www.microsoft.com/windows/enable

Additional information and products for users with disabilities can be found at the following sites on the Word Wide Web:

http://www.adaptive-computer.com

http://www.frontiercomputing.on.ca

http://www.frontiercomputing.on.ca/sites.htm

Windows includes numerous options for people who find it difficult to use the keyboard, require larger fonts, or need visual cues and warnings rather than sounds. To access these options in Windows, follow these steps:

1. Click the Start button and choose Settings, Control Panel.
2. Double-click the Accessibility Options icon. The Accessibility Properties dialog box appears.
3. Make your selections and click OK.

The accessibility properties include the following tabs:

Tab	Description
Keyboard	Make the keyboard more tolerant and patient. Select Use StickyKeys if you need to press multiple keys simultaneously but are only able to press keys one at a time. Select Use FilterKeys to ignore short or repeated keystrokes. Select Use ToggleKeys to make a sound when you press Caps Lock, Num Lock, and Scroll Lock.
Sound	Provide visual warnings and captions for speech and sounds. Select Use SoundSentry to make Windows use a visual warning when a sound alert occurs. Select Use ShowSounds to display captions instead of speech or sounds.

Tab	Description
Display	Select colors and fonts for easy reading. Select Use High Contrast to use color and font combinations that produce greater screen contrast.
Mouse	Control the pointer with the numeric keypad. Select Use MouseKeys to use the numeric keypad and other keys in place of the mouse. The relationship of keys to mouse controls appears in the table that follows.
General	Turn off accessibility features, give notification, and add an alternative input device. Use Automatic Reset to set Windows so accessibility features remain on at all times, are turned off when Windows restarts, or are turned off after a period of inactivity. Notification tells users when a feature is turned on or off. The SerialKey device enables Windows to receive keyboard or mouse input from alternative input devices through a serial port.

Some of these accessibility features could be difficult for a disabled person to turn on or off through normal Windows procedures. To alleviate this problem, Windows includes special *hotkeys*. Pressing the keys or key combinations for the designated hotkey turns an accessibility feature on or off, or changes its settings. To turn on the hotkeys for an accessibility feature, click the Settings button in the location indicated in the table below and check the Use Shortcut option. The following table gives the hotkeys for different features:

Feature	Hotkey	Result
High-contrast mode	Left-Alt+Left-Shift+ Print Screen pressed simultaneously (select in the Display tab)	Alternates the screen through different text/background combinations
StickyKeys	Press the Shift key five consecutive times (select in the Sticky Keys group in the Keyboard tab)	Turned on or off

continues

continued

Feature	Hotkey	Result
FilterKeys	Hold down right Shift key for eight seconds (select in the FilterKeys group in the Keyboard tab)	Turned on or off
ToggleKeys	Hold down Num Lock key for five seconds (select in the Toggle Keys group in the Keyboard tab)	Turned on or off
MouseKeys	Press Left-Alt+Left-Shift+ Num Lock simultan- eously (select in the MouseKeys group in the Mouse tab)	Turned on or off

MouseKeys can be very useful for portable or laptop computer users and graphic artists, as well as for people unable to use a mouse. Graphic artists will find MouseKeys useful because it enables them to produce finer movements than those done with a mouse. Once MouseKeys is turned on, you can produce the same effects as a mouse by using these keys:

Action	Press this key(s)
Movement	Any number key except 5
Large moves	Hold down Ctrl as you press number keys
Single pixel moves	Hold down Shift as you press number keys
Single-click	5
Double-click	+
Begin drag	Insert (Ins)
Drop after drag	Delete (Del)

Customizing the Toolbar, Menus, and Shortcut Keys

Part of the power of Word 97 comes from its flexibility; you can change its shape to fit your work habits. You can create menus, toolbars, shortcut keys, and buttons that enable you to do things your way. You can add Word 97 commands that don't normally appear on the menu or toolbar. You can even assign macros that you create to commands, buttons, or shortcut keys. ■

Find and store customized features

Once you understand how Word stores and retrieves customizations, adding and modifying commands becomes a simple task.

Add, remove, and rearrange toolbar buttons

Drag-and-drop functionality makes it easy to modify the toolbars so they meet your word processing needs.

Assign Word's built-in commands or your macros to a toolbar button

Adding the commands and macros you use most often to toolbars makes them available with the click of the mouse.

Add or remove menus or commands

You can create and remove unwanted menus and commands from any of your templates; you can even customize the shortcut menus.

Create custom shortcut keys or custom toolbars

If you prefer to keep your hands on the keyboard, you can assign keyboard shortcuts to the commands you use most often.

CAUTION

Custom key assignments, menus, and toolbars combined with Word's easy-to-create macros enable you to build a word processor tailored to the work you do. This capability also holds a danger: you have the potential to modify the global menus and keyboard assignments so much that Word becomes difficult for other operators to use. For this reason, you probably should assign your menus, toolbar buttons, and key assignments to templates rather than assigning them globally.

Understanding Where and When Customizing Occurs

You have the ability to assign one of Word's built-in commands or one of your macros to a menu command, toolbar button, or shortcut key. However, unless you know a few rules about assigning commands and macros, you may cause conflicts. When conflicts occur, a command or macro other than the one you expect may run. When you assign a macro to a command, button, or shortcut key, it can be a global assignment or specific to a template or document.

ON THE WEB

Woody's Office Power Pack (WOPR) Web site offers free macros and other goodies for Word as well as hints on customizing your application. You can find it at

http://www.csn.net/wopr

For tutorials, tips, and add-ins for Microsoft Office applications point your browser to

http://www.ronperson.com

One of the most exciting new features of Word 97 is its capability to store macros and other customizations within your documents. In past versions, macros and customizations had to be stored in the template. This meant that if you shared documents with users who did not have the same templates, they were unable to benefit from your customization or macros. With Word 97, users will no longer need to have the same templates to access helpful macros and customizations that are stored in the document.

As an example, consider the need for a form that you might want to distribute via e-mail or from a Web site. Those using the form won't need to have the associated template to access any macros or toolbars associated with the document.

Global assignments—assignments that apply to *all* documents—can be stored in the NORMAL.DOT template or in a template residing in the /WINWORD/STARTUP folder. Template level assignments will apply only to documents based on the template in which the assignments are stored. For example, if you store an assignment into a letter template, then that assignment will only be available when you are working on a letter created with that template. Document level assignments will apply only to the document in which they were created.

Template and document level assignments will conflict with standard Word commands or global assignments of the same nature. Suppose, for example, you assign Ctrl+C to a Calculate macro in your Invoice template. Ctrl+C is the standard Word shortcut key for the Edit Copy command. If a document based on your Invoice template is open, Ctrl+C activates the Calculate macro rather than the Edit Copy command. To avoid confusion, Word follows a strict hierarchy—document assignments always take precedence over template assignments. Likewise, template assignments always take precedence over the global assignments stored in NORMAL.DOT. Assignments in the NORMAL.DOT file always take precedence over assignments in files in the STARTUP folder and assignments in the STARTUP folder always take precedence over standard Word commands. Here is an example of what happens each time you press Ctrl+N (the command to create a new file).

▶ **See** "Making Menus, Toolbars, and Shortcut Keys Globally Available," **p. 1126**

Word first looks at the document assignments to see if Ctrl+N exists. If not, it then looks at the template level assignments. If it doesn't find the assignment there, it looks into the NORMAL.DOT template. Next, Word looks through any templates in the STARTUP folder (if there is more than one template there, Word looks through them in alphabetical order). Finally, if it still hasn't found an assignment for Ctrl+N, it runs the standard Word command. If no command exists at all, then you will hear that familiar "beep" that indicates you are attempting an invalid action.

When you create custom menus, toolbars, or shortcut keys, always remember to open the document or a document that uses the template you want to change. Then, in the Customize dialog box, select either NORMAL.DOT or the specific template or document that should contain the new menu, toolbar, or shortcut key.

Customizing and Creating Toolbars

Word allows you to customize the existing toolbars and to create your own toolbars and toolbar buttons. Specifically, you can do the following:

- Change any of the supplied toolbars
- Design and edit your own toolbars
- Draw your own button images
- Assign a macro, command, font, AutoText entry, or style to a custom toolbar button

N O T E You must have a mouse to modify toolbars or create custom buttons. ■

Adding Buttons

Word offers more than 200 buttons, each with its own built-in commands, that you can add to any toolbar. Adding a button is as easy as dragging the button from a dialog box and dropping it at the desired location on the toolbar. The following example shows how you can add a button to a toolbar.

 T I P You can always return a predefined toolbar to its originally installed condition (see "Reorganizing Buttons" later in this chapter).

To add a new button to the toolbar, follow these steps:

1. If you want the button to appear only when documents that use a specific template are open, you must first open a document that uses that template.

2. Use the right mouse button to click any toolbar, and then choose Customize from the shortcut menu (or choose Tools, Customize). If the toolbar you want to customize is not displayed on-screen, select the Toolbars tab and then select the toolbar you want to modify by checking the box beside the toolbar name.

3. Select the Commands tab (see Figure 38.1).

FIG. 38.1

Add a button by dragging it from the Customize dialog box and dropping it on a toolbar.

4. Select a button category from the Categories list; your selection determines the items that appear in the Commands list (either buttons or lists of commands that do not have associated button images). If you choose All Commands in the Categories list box, the Commands list box displays a complete list of available Word commands.

N O T E If you choose Macros, Fonts, AutoText, or Styles from the Categories list box, corresponding lists appear, as described in "Assigning a Command or Macro to a Toolbar Button" later in this chapter. Chapter 39, "Introducing Visual Basic for Applications," discusses commands available in the Control Box category. Built-in Menus and New Menu are discussed in "Adding Commands to Menus" later in this chapter.

5. If you want this toolbar change to apply only to this document or to documents that use a specific template, select the template name or document name from the Save In list. (Remember that a document using the desired template must be open if you want to assign changes at the template level.) If you want the change to apply to all toolbars in all documents, select the Normal template.

6. Select the button you want by clicking it. Click Description to display a description of the selected button.

7. Drag the button from the dialog box and drop it onto the toolbar in the location where you want it to appear.

T I P You can customize the ScreenTips and image size for your toolbars by selecting the Options tab in the Customize dialog box, and then selecting or clearing the options you want to change. The option to Show Shortcut Keys In ScreenTips may be helpful when trying to memorize keyboard shortcuts.

8. You can customize the appearance of a button by right-clicking it on the toolbar and choosing the appropriate option from the shortcut menu:

Menu Option	Action
Reset	Resets the button image and text to its original format.
Delete	Removes the button from the toolbar; you can also drag a button from the toolbar to delete it.
Name	The text that will appear on the button if the option to display the button text is selected.
Copy Button Image	Copies the selected button image to the clipboard.

continues

continued

Paste Button Image	Pastes a copied button image onto the selected toolbar button; you can use Edit, Paste to paste a button image into a document.
Reset Button Image	Resets the button image to the default image; unlike the Reset command, this command resets the image only and not the text.
Edit Button Image	Opens the Button Editor and allows you to modify the image of the selected button; for further instructions, see "Drawing Your Own Button Images" later in this chapter.
Change Button Image	Allows you to select a button image from a predefined list.
Default Style	The button displays the image only and no text.
Text Only (Always)	The button displays only the button text; if you drag this button from the toolbar onto a menu, it will continue to display text only.
Text Only (in Menus)	The button displays the button image on toolbars, but will display only text if you drag the button onto a menu.
Image and Text	The button displays both the button image (if one exists) and text.
Begin a Group	Inserts a group divider on the toolbar when selected; removes a group divider when cleared.

9. Repeat steps 4 through 8 as necessary to add more buttons; when you are finished, choose Close to close the Customize dialog box.

T I P   If you are unsure of a button's function, select the button on the Commands tab of the Customize dialog box and choose the Description button.

If the toolbar becomes too crowded, the buttons will wrap to the next line. You can eliminate this crowding by removing buttons, rearranging buttons and groupings, or changing the width of drop-down list boxes (see the next section of this chapter for details). If you have many buttons you want to add, you might want to create your own custom toolbar, a process described in "Creating Your Own Toolbar" later in this chapter.

To move or copy buttons between toolbars, first display both toolbars and then open the Customize dialog box. To move the button, drag it from one toolbar to another. To copy the button, hold down the Ctrl key while you drag the button from one toolbar to another.

Reorganizing Buttons

If a toolbar gets crowded, you can remove buttons, reduce the size of drop-down list boxes, or reorganize the buttons.

To return a predefined toolbar to its originally installed condition, follow these steps:

1. Open a document that contains the toolbar you want to reset.

2. Use the right mouse button to click the toolbar, and then choose Customize from the shortcut menu. Select the Toolbars tab.

3. Select the toolbar you want to reset from the Toolbars list box, and then choose the Reset button. The Reset Toolbar dialog box appears.

4. In the Reset Toolbar dialog box, select the document or template in which you want the selected toolbar reset. If you want the reset to apply to all documents, select NORMAL.DOT.

5. Choose OK, and then choose Close to close the Customize dialog box.

6. When you close the document, you may be asked if you would like to save changes to the document or template. Choose Yes if you want to save your changes.

To change the width of a drop-down list box, such as the Style drop-down list box, follow these steps:

1. Use the right mouse button to click the toolbar, and then choose Customize from the shortcut menu.

2. While the Customize dialog box is on-screen, click a drop-down list box, such as Style, Font or Font Size, on the toolbar.

 TIP If the Customize dialog box is covering the drop-down list box you want to select, you can move the dialog box out of the way by clicking the dialog box title bar and dragging it to a different location on the screen—just as you can move virtually any Windows dialog box.

3. Move the mouse pointer to the right or left side of the drop-down list box. When the double arrow appears, click and drag the arrow left or right to resize the drop-down list box (see Figure 38.2).

4. Choose Close from the Customize dialog box.

If you want to remove a button from the toolbar, complete the following steps:

1. Use the right mouse button to click the toolbar, and then choose Customize from the shortcut menu. If the toolbar you want to customize is not displayed on-screen, select the Toolbars tab and then select the toolbar you want to modify by checking the box beside the toolbar name.

2. Select the Commands tab in the Customize dialog box, and then select the document or template you want to modify from the Save in drop-down list box.

3. While the Customize dialog box is on-screen, use the right mouse button to click the button you want to delete. The shortcut menu appears.

FIG. 38.2

When the Customize dialog box is open, you can click a drop-down list box and drag it to a new width.

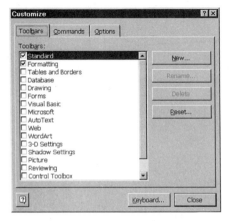

You also can delete a button while the Customize dialog box is open by using the left mouse button to drag it from the toolbar. As you drag the button from the toolbar, an X will appear beside the mouse pointer to indicate that the button will be deleted when the mouse is released.

4. Choose Delete from the shortcut menu.

To make a toolbar easier to view, you can move groups of buttons left or right or group them on the toolbar.

To reorganize a toolbar and move buttons to new locations, follow these steps:

You can visually group buttons on the toolbar while the Customize dialog box is open by right-clicking a toolbar button and selecting or clearing the Begin a Group option on the shortcut menu.

1. Use the right mouse button to click the toolbar, and then choose Customize from the shortcut menu.

2. Select the Commands tab in the Customize dialog box, and then select the document or template you want to modify from the Save in drop-down list box.

3. While the Customize dialog box is on-screen, drag a button to a new location. You can move the button to a new location on the same toolbar or you can drag it onto a different toolbar as long as that toolbar is visible on the screen. To make a toolbar visible on the screen, select the Toolbars tab in the Customize dialog box and select the toolbar you want to display.

4. An I-beam pointer appears as you drag the button you want to move along the toolbar. When the I-beam appears in the correct place, release the mouse. The button appears in the new location.

Creating Your Own Toolbar

If you need to add many new buttons, you might want to create your own toolbar. This technique is especially useful for creating a toolbar designed to work with documents that use a specific template. For example, you may want to create a custom toolbar to work with your Invoice template. Its tools and their arrangement may be designed specifically for invoicing.

You might also find it helpful to create a toolbar that contains commands you use often and that are not available on the existing toolbars. For example, you might add buttons to double space paragraphs, apply small caps, or insert the current date.

To create your own toolbar, follow these steps:

1. If you want this toolbar to appear with documents using a specific template, you must begin by opening a document that uses that template.

2. Use the right mouse button to click the toolbar, and then choose Customize from the shortcut menu.

3. Select the Toolbars tab in the Customize dialog box (see Figure 38.3).

4. Choose the New button to display the New Toolbar dialog box. The New Toolbar dialog box appears with the default toolbar name "Custom 1" (see Figure 38.4).

5. Type a more descriptive title for the toolbar in the Toolbar name edit box. The name can be up to 255 characters in length and can contain spaces and special characters such the asterisk (*) and ampersand (&).

 TIP You can rename a custom toolbar at any time by choosing the Rename button on the Toolbars tab in the Customize dialog box.

FIG. 38.3

Create a new toolbar by clicking the New button in the Customize dialog box.

6. From the Make Toolbar Available To list, choose the document or template with which the toolbar should appear. Select NORMAL.DOT if you want the toolbar to be available at all times.

FIG. 38.4

Type your new toolbar's name and select the template in which it should be stored.

7. Choose OK. The toolbar name appears at the bottom of the Toolbars list box in the Customize dialog box. Your new toolbar appears on top of the Customize dialog box; initially it is only large enough for one button.

N O T E Moving a newly created toolbar to the left or right side of the Customize dialog box will prevent the toolbar from becoming hidden beneath the dialog box. You can move the toolbar to the left or right side of the dialog box by dragging it with the left mouse button. If your toolbar should happen to disappear behind the Customize dialog box, don't worry. Simply clear the option for the new toolbar in the Toolbars list box on the Toolbars tab in the Customize dialog box. Once cleared, reselect the option and the toolbar will reappear. ▪

8. Click the Commands tab to display the available commands.

9. Drag the buttons you want from the Commands list box to the new toolbar. The toolbar will automatically expand as new buttons are added.

 If the new toolbar is blocking the list of commands, you can move it by using the left mouse button to drag the toolbar to a new location.

10. You can add Commands from any of the existing Categories. Choose Close when you are finished. The new toolbar contains the tools you added.

You can treat a custom toolbar like any other.

 Toolbars or menu bars that are attached to an edge of the program window are *docked*. You can move a docked toolbar or menu bar by dragging the move handle to a new location on-screen. If you move a toolbar or menu bar into the document window, it will change to a *floating toolbar*. To dock a floating toolbar or menu bar, drag the title bar of the floating toolbar or menu bar to any edge (top, bottom, or sides) of the program window.

 You can quickly float a docked toolbar by double-clicking the move handle. To quickly dock a floating toolbar, double-click the title bar and the toolbar will return to its last docked position.

To delete a custom toolbar, follow these steps:

1. Click the right mouse button while the pointer is positioned on the toolbar.
2. Choose Customize from the shortcut menu.
3. Select the Toolbars tab, and then select your custom toolbar from the Toolbars list box. Custom toolbars will appear at the bottom of the Toolbars list box.
4. Choose the Delete button. Respond with OK to confirm you want to delete it.
5. Choose Close to close the Customize dialog box.

Assigning a Command or Macro to a Toolbar Button

You provide yourself with fast access to frequently used Word commands by placing standard commands as buttons on the toolbar. But Word also enables you to accomplish some other useful goals by putting buttons of your own making onto the toolbar. With custom toolbar buttons you can do the following:

- Run Word commands that are not on menus or buttons
- Run your macros
- Change fonts and other formatting
- Insert AutoText
- Apply styles

You even get to select or draw an image for your custom buttons!

Take a moment to scan through the All Commands category on the Commands tab in the Customize dialog box. Many of these commands perform functions that would normally require the use of a menu or dialog box. Creating buttons for them can save you time.

▶ **See** "Creating an AutoText Entry," **p. 170**

▶ **See** "Changing Fonts," **p. 295**

▶ **See** "Creating Styles," **p. 393**

▶ **See** "Recording a Macro," **p. 1167**

To assign a command or macro to a button on the toolbar, follow these steps:

1. Right-click the toolbar and choose Customize. If the toolbar you want to customize is not displayed on-screen, select the Toolbars tab and select the toolbar you want to modify by checking the box beside the toolbar name.

2. Select the Commands tab, and then select either All Commands, Macros, Fonts, AutoText, or Styles from the Categories list.

3. Drag one of the commands, macros, fonts, AutoText names, or styles from the Commands list box onto your toolbar.

   If a button image exists for this command or style, a button with that image will appear on the toolbar. If a button image does not exist for the command you chose, the button will appear with a text label.

   The images shown next to commands in the Macros, Fonts, or Styles categories will not display on the toolbar when the command is added. Instead, they will appear as text. You can display or add a button image for these items as described in steps 4 and 5.

4. You can add a button image to the button (or change the existing button image) by right-clicking the button and choosing Change Button Image (see Figure 38.5). You can also draw your own button image as described in "Drawing Your Own Button Images," in the next part of this section.

5. To display only an image on the button, right-click the button and select the Default Style option on the shortcut menu (see Figure 38.5). Options are also available on the shortcut menu to display Text Only or an Image And Text. See "Adding Buttons" earlier in this chapter for details about each of these options.

6. Choose Close in the Customize dialog box.

Drawing Your Own Button Images

To draw a custom button image, follow these steps:

1. With the Customize dialog box on the screen, right-click the button you want to modify.

2. Choose Edit Button Image from the shortcut menu. The Button Editor appears on-screen with the selected image in the Picture box (see Figure 38.6).

3. If you want to draw a new image, choose the Clear button to clear the button image from the Picture box.

   Click a color and then click or drag in the Picture box to paint. Click the Erase color and then drag over the Picture to erase cells. Watch the Preview box to see what the tool looks like at its actual size. Click the Move buttons to reposition your drawing within the button.

4. Choose OK to accept the drawing and paste it onto the button.

5. Choose Close to close the Customize dialog box.

FIG. 38.5
Select one of many existing button images or create your own using the Button Editor.

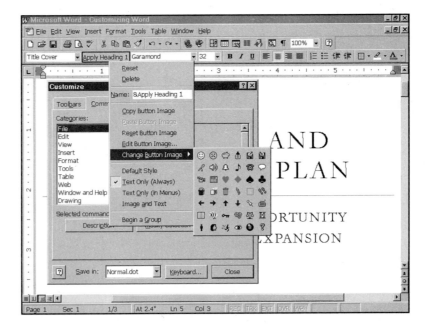

FIG. 38.6
Use the Button Editor to draw or modify a button image in the Picture box.

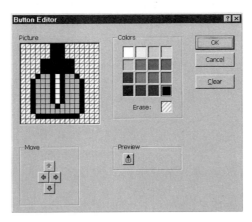

TROUBLESHOOTING

I'm wasting time reselecting and redrawing icons. What do I do? If you have buttons that you need occasionally and you don't want to reselect or redraw them every time you need them, create a toolbar used for storage. Drag copies of buttons you think you might need again onto this toolbar. If you need one of these buttons later, just display the storage toolbar you created. Then open the Customize dialog box and drag a copy of the needed button to an active toolbar. To drag a copy, press the Ctrl key while dragging.

Transferring Toolbars with the Organizer

At times, you will want to transfer a toolbar from one document or template to another. You or a coworker might create a template that has a toolbar you can use in another template. With Word's Organizer, it's easy to transfer toolbars between open templates.

To transfer toolbars between two open documents or templates, follow these steps:

1. Open a document or template containing the toolbar you want to copy.

N O T E   You will need to unprotect the templates if they are protected. You cannot transfer from or to a protected template. ▩

▶ **See** "Changing a Template," **p. 210**

2. Choose <u>T</u>ools, Templates and Add-<u>I</u>ns. The Templates and Add-Ins dialog box appears.

3. Choose the <u>O</u>rganizer button in the Templates and Add-Ins dialog box; the Organizer appears. Select the <u>T</u>oolbars tab (see Figure 38.7).

FIG. 38.7

Select a toolbar from any open template and copy it to any other open template.

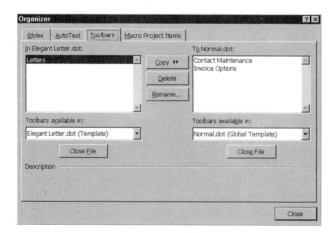

4. In the left side of the Organizer, select from the Toolbars Available In list the document or template containing the toolbar you want to copy.

5. In the right side of the Organizer, select from the Toolbars Available In list the document or template you want to receive a copy of the toolbar.

   If the document or toolbar is not listed there, choose the Close File button in the right side of the Organizer dialog box. The button face will change to read Open File. Choose the Open File button and select the document or template that you want to receive a copy of the toolbar.

6. In the left side of the Organizer, select from the In FileName list the toolbar you want copied.

7. Choose the Copy button. The toolbar is copied from the file on the left side to the file on the right side.

8. If you want to copy additional toolbars, return to step 4. If you are finished, choose the Close button. Be sure to save the files or templates when Word prompts you to do so or your changes will be lost.

Customizing the Menu

Word offers far more commands than you would ever want to put on the menu at a single time. But you might want to put the commands you use most often onto an existing or custom menu. In fact, you can add to the menu any macro, style, font, or AutoText that you want readily available. You can add these features to the menus associated with a specific document or template or to the global menus associated with the NORMAL.DOT template.

You can even customize the shortcut menus that appear when you click with the right mouse button!

N O T E The menu bar is a toolbar that contains menus rather than buttons. You can drag the menu bar to a new position on screen like a toolbar, but it cannot be hidden. You can customize the items that appear on the menu bar in the same manner as you customize a toolbar. ▪

  You can customize the animation of your menus (the way they appear to "drop down" when selected) by selecting a menu animation option on the Options tab in the Customize dialog box.

Adding Commands or Macros to Menus

You can add a command or macro to any built-in menu or new menu that you create. To make your menus easier to use, you can also add and remove separator lines between groups of commands, and you can place a new command anywhere on the menu. If you would like to customize a shortcut menu, please see "Customizing Shortcut Menus" later in this section.

To add a command to a menu, follow these steps:

1. Before you customize a menu, open the document or template in which you want to modify the menus.

2. Right-click the menu bar, and choose Customize. The Customize dialog box appears.

3. Select the Commands tab in the Customize dialog box.

4. Select the document or template you want to modify from the Save In list (select Normal for the global menu).

5. From the Categories list box, select the category that contains the command you want to add to the menu. If you select Macros in the Categories list, a list of macros in the selected template appears in the Commands list box.

6. Click the menu on the menu bar that you want to modify (see Figure 38.8). The menu will drop down.

FIG. 38.8
You can add to Word's menus any of hundreds of commands or your own macros, styles, and AutoText. Notice that when you select a menu to be modified, a black box appears around the menu name.

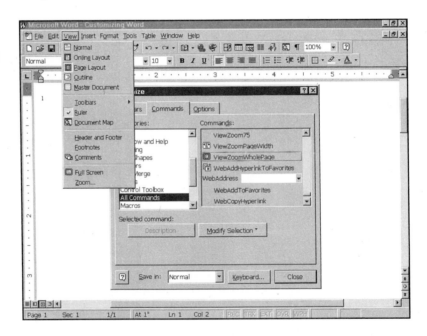

N O T E You may need to move the Customize dialog box to prevent the selected menu from covering the items in the Commands list box. You can move the dialog box by dragging the dialog box title bar with the left mouse button. ▪

7. Drag the command or macro you want to add from the Commands list box and drop it onto the menu in the desired location.

A horizontal I-beam appears on the menu as you move the mouse over it to indicate where the item will be added when the mouse button is released. The newly added item appears on the menu with a hotkey underlined.

8. You may need to review the selected hotkey. Often the underlined letter is already in use by another command on the menu. To fix this, right-click the menu item and reposition the ampersand (&) in the Name edit box on the shortcut menu. The letter following the ampersand is the letter that will appear underlined in the menu.

You can also change the name that appears on the menu for this command by changing the name in the Name edit box (see "Removing or Resetting Commands" later in this chapter for information on resetting command names and images).

Part

IX

Ch

38

N O T E If two or more items on a menu have matching hotkeys, Word will require the user to press the Enter key after typing the hotkey to verify that the correct menu item has been selected. Press the hotkey repeatedly to alternate between items. ▪

CAUTION

When changing hotkeys for menu items, it is often a good idea to change the hotkey for a newly added menu item rather than alter one of the existing menu commands. This will keep Word working consistently for users who use Word on more than one machine and will also ensure that the standard menu items match samples provided in manuals and the Online Help.

9. To start a new grouping, right-click (on the menu) the first item in the group and select Begin a Group from the shortcut menu. A separator line appears.

N O T E The "Begin a Group" command is a toggle. To remove a separator line, right-click the menu item immediately following the line and clear the Begin a Group option on the shortcut menu. ▪

10. If you want, make additional modifications to your menu items using the shortcut menu (see "Adding Buttons" earlier in this chapter for information on each of the commands found on the shortcut menu).

11. Return to step 4 to add more commands, or choose Close to close the Customize dialog box.

Removing or Resetting Commands

To remove a predefined or custom command from a menu, follow these steps:

1. Open a document or template with a menu containing the command you want to remove.

2. Right-click the menu bar, and choose Customize.

3. Select the Commands tab in the Customize dialog box.

4. Select the document or template you want to modify from the Save in drop-down list box (select Normal for the global menu).

5. Click the menu on the menu bar that you want to modify (refer to Figure 38.8).

6. Right-click the menu item you want to delete or reset.

   To reset the item to its original format, choose Reset from the shortcut menu.

   To delete the item from the menu, choose Delete from the shortcut menu.

7. If necessary, make additional changes to the menus, or choose Close if you are finished.

To restore menus to the original configuration provided by Word, follow these steps:

1. Open a document or template containing the menu you want to restore.

2. Right-click the menu bar, and choose Customize.

3. Select the Toolbars tab in the Customize dialog box.

4. Select Menu Bar in the Toolbars list box, and then choose the Reset button.

5. Choose the correct document or template from the Reset Toolbar dialog box, and then choose OK.

6. Choose Close to close the Customize dialog box.

Customizing Shortcut Menus

One of the most productive features in Word is the shortcut menu that appears when you right-click in a document or on the Word desktop. The options available on these menus vary depending on where you click. For example, if you click in a table, the shortcut menu contains table commands. You may find that some of these menus do not contain the commands you use most often. The good news is that you can easily add the commands you need!

To customize a shortcut menu, follow these steps:

1. Right-click the menu bar, and then choose Customize from the shortcut menu.

2. Select the Toolbars tab in the Customize dialog box.

3. Select Shortcut Menu from the Toolbars list box so it is displayed on-screen. You will see the Shortcut Menu toolbar with three drop-down menu options: Text, Table, and Drawing.

4. Left-click to select the option you would like to change.

   For example, if you want to modify what you see when you right-click a table cell, click the Table option and then click Table Cell; the commands available when you right-click a table cell are displayed (see Figure 38.9).

   ▶ **See** "Saving Time with Shortcut Menus," **p. 50**

FIG. 38.9
You can modify the options available on shortcut menus by selecting Shortcut Menu in the Toolbars list box.

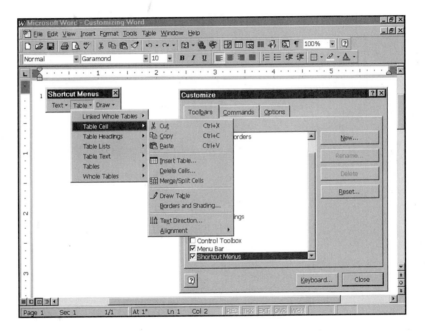

5. You can modify or remove items from the shortcut menu by right-clicking the menu option you want to change (see "Removing or Resetting Commands" earlier in this section).

   You can add commands by dragging them from the Customize dialog box and dropping them onto the shortcut menu (see "Adding Commands to Menus" earlier in this section).

T I P You can reset the shortcut menus back to their originally installed condition at any time (see "Reorganizing Buttons" earlier in this chapter).

6. Choose Close in the Customize dialog box when you have finished making changes.

Adding or Removing Menus

You can easily remove or add entire menus to simplify your documents or templates.

When you create templates designed for a specific type of work, you may want to remove menus that are not needed. In some cases, fewer menus means fewer training and support problems.

Likewise, you may find it helpful to add menus that contain commands specific to a document or template. For example, you might have a template such as an expense report that requires special commands or macros. You can add a Utilities menu that contains these items.

To add built-in or new menus, follow these steps:

1. Open the document or template that is to contain the added menu.

2. Right-click the menu bar, and choose Customize.

3. Select the Commands tab in the Customize dialog box.

4. Select the document or template you want to modify from the Save in drop-down list box (select Normal for the global menu).

5. To add a built-in menu, select Built-in Menus from the Categories list box. To create a new menu, select New Menu from the Categories list box.

6. Drag the desired menu from the Commands list box and drop it onto the menu bar in an appropriate location.

   If you selected the New Menu option under Categories, then you must drag the "New Menu" item from the Commands list box. If you want to rename the menu, right-click it on the menu bar and change the name in the Name edit box (see Figure 38.10).

7. Select the newly added menu on the menu bar. Add and remove menu items to customize the menu for your needs (see "Adding Commands to Menus" and "Removing or Resetting Commands" earlier in this chapter).

8. Return to step 4 to add more menus, or choose Close to close the Customize dialog box.

To remove a menu from the menu bar, follow these steps:

1. Open a document or template containing the menu you want to remove.

2. Right-click the menu bar, and choose Customize.

3. Select the Commands tab in the Customize dialog box.

4. Select the document or template you want to modify from the Save In drop-down list box (select Normal for the global menu).

5. Right-click the menu you want to delete, and then choose Delete from the shortcut menu.

FIG. 38.10
From the Customize dialog box, you can add and modify menus for your custom commands.

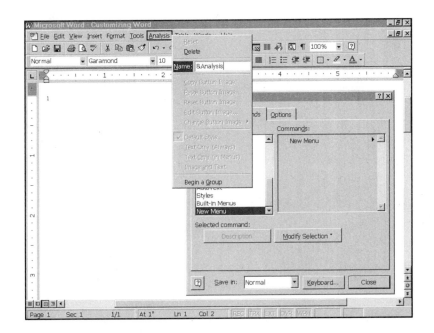

 You also can delete a menu by dragging it from the menu bar while the Customize dialog box is on-screen.

N O T E You may accidentally (or purposefully) delete the Tools menu or the Tools, Customize command. You are then faced with that sinking-in-the-pit-of-the-stomach feeling because you seem to have no way to reset the menu (it looks like you can't get to the Customize dialog box). But there is a way—simply right-click any menu or toolbar and choose Customize from the shortcut menu. You can then reset or add the desired menu items as mentioned in the sections above. ■

6. Choose Close to close the Customize dialog box.

Assigning Commands and Macros to Shortcut Keys

Shortcut keys enable you to perform routine operations quickly without moving from the keyboard to the mouse. You should consider assigning shortcut keys to frequently used menu options.

Word has many predefined shortcut keys already built into the program. Pressing Ctrl+B, for example, applies boldface to selected text. These key combinations are global; they work with all documents unless they have been deleted. Like custom menus and toolbars, shortcut keys follow the template hierarchy that was described at the beginning of this chapter.

▶ **See** "Inserting Frequently Used Material," **p. 169**

To assign key combinations to Word's predefined commands, your own macros, styles, fonts, or AutoText, follow these steps:

1. Open the document or template that will contain the keyboard shortcut.

2. Choose <u>C</u>ustomize from the <u>T</u>ools menu, and then choose the <u>K</u>eyboard button. The Customize Keyboard dialog box appears (see Figure 38.11).

FIG. 38.11

Assign shortcut keys to the commands and macros you use most to increase your work efficiency.

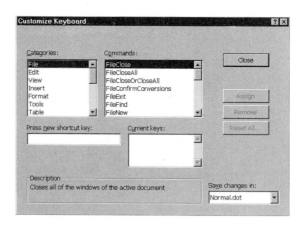

3. Select the document or template you want to contain the shortcut from the Sa<u>v</u>e Changes In drop-down list box.

4. Select from the <u>C</u>ategories list box, the category that contains the command to which you want to assign the shortcut key.

5. Select the desired command from the C<u>o</u>mmands list box.

Check the Current keys list box to see if the command you have selected has an existing shortcut key. It may already have one assigned.

N O T E If you have selected Macros, Fonts, AutoText, Styles, or Common Symbols from the Categories list box, the reference above the Commands list box will change to indicate the selected category. For example, if you select Macros from the Categories list box, Commands will change to read Macros.

6. Select the Press new shortcut key edit box, and then press the shortcut key combination you want. To enter a shortcut key combination, you must press a letter while holding down the Ctrl, Alt, or Shift key (Alt+Z, for example), or a combination of those keys (such as Ctrl+Alt+Q). Remove a key combination from the edit box by pressing the backspace key.

TIP You can create double-keystroke combinations, such as Alt+B,F, by pressing Alt+B, releasing them both, and then pressing F.

Part
IX

Ch
38

CAUTION

If the keystroke combination you press in step 6 has already been assigned, you will see the command to which it has been assigned underneath the edit box with the title Currently Assigned To: (on the left side of the dialog box). This message only appears while you are assigning a keystroke. Combinations that have not been assigned display as [unassigned].

7. Choose the Assign button.
8. Return to step 3 to continue making more shortcut key assignments or choose Close.

To return to the default keyboard assignments, display the Customize dialog box and choose the Keyboard button. Select the template or document containing the shortcut keys you want removed in the Save Changes In list; then choose the Reset All button. Choose Yes to confirm that you want to reset the key assignments for the selected template. Word restores the original shortcut keys for that template.

To remove a single shortcut key assignment, select in the Save Changes In list the document or template containing the shortcut key, and then select the command to be modified. The shortcut key will appear in the Current Keys list. Select the key in the Current Keys list and choose the Remove button. ●

CHAPTER 39

Introducing Visual Basic for Applications

For a number of years, Microsoft has hinted to the press and developers that their long-range strategy included a common application programming language used in all their applications. This language would be founded on BASIC, the most widely known computer language, and would provide power users and developers with a common application language (also known as macro language) between applications. This feature would reduce learning time and support costs. In addition, this language would provide the means for developers to develop systems that integrate multiple applications—enabling multiple applications to work together to solve business problems.

That long-awaited language is Visual Basic for Applications (VBA). Visual Basic for Applications is a subset of the highly successful Visual Basic language. It can also be considered a superset of the Visual Basic language because you will find in VBA, commands and objects not supported by Visual Basic. The first Microsoft products to include the language were Excel 5 and Project 4. A commonly asked question was, "When will Microsoft Word support Visual Basic for Applications?"

Create a procedure with the Macro Recorder

Microsoft Word's Macro Recorder is a great tool for automating commonly used tasks. After recording the task as a macro, you can use the macro over and over again.

Run a procedure

Running a procedure can be done in a variety of ways. You can use Tools, Macro, or you can assign a macro to a button.

Edit a procedure

You may want to make changes to your original recorded macro. Or you may want to correct a mistake. This is easily done by editing the recorded procedure.

Use data entry boxes

Using a Visual Basic function called InputBox, you can prompt a user for information and then use that information on your worksheet.

Display a message

The MsgBox function enables you to display messages to your user when they run a procedure you create. This allows you to display information such as the status of the procedure and let the user of the procedure know what is going on.

The answer is: now, with Microsoft Word 97. Visual Basic for Applications offers power users and developers the ability to use the most common Windows programming language, Visual Basic, and apply it to Word problems. It also enables users to more easily control other Microsoft applications. In Office 97, the Microsoft Office suite of applications uses Visual Basic for Applications.

If you are an experienced Word macro programmer, you may face the transition to Visual Basic for Applications with mixed feelings. You may have invested hundreds of hours in learning and developing with Word's previous WordBasic language. You may look forward to a more powerful, easier to use language shared between Microsoft applications, yet at the same time you hate to think of redeveloping applications and learning an entirely new language. Fortunately, a major feature of Word 97 is the easy migration of your WordBasic applications to Visual Basic for Applications. Microsoft Word automatically converts the WordBasic code found in templates created in previous versions of Word into Visual Basic.

T I P Always have a backup copy of any file containing WordBasic macros before opening it in Word 97 in case of any unforeseen problems.

If you are an experienced Excel Visual Basic for Applications developer, you will find the Microsoft Word Visual Basic environment familiar. When you are working with a Visual Basic macro, you use the Visual Basic Editor. The Visual Basic Editor exists outside of the Microsoft Word host application window. Even though the Visual Basic Editor does exist outside of the Word host application window, it is fully integrated with Word. This means when you develop a macro for Word, it is aware of which document or template to associate the macro with.

Some of the other new features to this release include:

- Support for ActiveX controls so you can extend the languages capabilities.
- The Project Explorer, which displays a list of components that makes up a project, such as modules.
- An improved object browser so you can easily see all the programmable objects in Word and other Office applications.
- Property windows which display properties and their settings for forms and ActiveX controls.

ON THE WEB

For online support from Microsoft, visit the following World Wide Web site:

http://www.microsoft.com/support

You can also access Microsoft's extensive troubleshooting KnowledgeBase at the following site:

http://www.microsoft.com/kb

For tutorials, tips, and add-ins for Microsoft Office applications point your browser to:

http://www.ronperson.com ■

Recording and Modifying VBA Modules

As an introduction to Visual Basic for Applications modules, you are going to let Word write the first module. Word's Macro Recorder records all your interactions with a document as a sequence of Visual Basic commands. These commands form a macro procedure that you can execute to replay your interactions. This capability is especially useful for formatting complex documents, because after you have recorded the formatting, you only have to replay the procedure to format another document.

Automating with Visual Basic for Applications

Visual Basic for Applications is a marriage between one of the most common programming languages and all the character formatting and text management power of the Word application. The language is not merely tacked onto Word, but has full access to all of Word's commands and structure. Because Word now supports Visual Basic for Applications, a programmer is not geared primarily toward task automation. A programmer can write an application that prompts a user for information and based on that information, the program performs different actions. A programmer can create an application that uses Word as the main host application, but with the use of OLE Automation, he or she can incorporate a variety of functionality from applications such as Excel and PowerPoint. Imagine being able to create an application that assists a user in the creation of a corporate quarterly report containing balance sheets and charts from Excel and also generates a slideshow based on the completed quarterly report in PowerPoint. This is just a small example of what you can do with Visual Basic for Applications.

To begin, you need to look at some terminology changes. In previous versions of Word the programming language is the WordBasic *macro language*, and a program is known as a *macro*.

Part
IX

Ch
39

The term *macro* generally refers to the capability to replay a sequence of keystrokes (or mouse clicks); however, the Word macro language extends far beyond that. With the switch from the Word macro language to Visual Basic for Applications, a macro is now called a *procedure*. This change brings the terminology more in line with modern programming practices.

A procedure is a block of Visual Basic statements that perform a specific function. Visual Basic statements are not usually executed alone, but rather as part of a procedure; thus a procedure is the smallest executable block of Visual Basic code. Procedures are generally short blocks of code with a straightforward purpose.

You can store one or more procedures together in a module. You can imagine a module as a specialized document containing paragraphs of VBA code called *procedures*. Storing procedures in modules is a convenient way to arrange and store them. Also, procedures in a module can share data with other procedures in the same module.

In the following sections, you familiarize yourself with Visual Basic for Applications by recording the creation of a series of paragraphs. This is obviously a simplistic example. The purpose of this demonstration is to show you what is recorded by the macro recorder, not to showcase the abilities of Visual Basic for Applications.

Starting the Recorder

Before starting the Macro Recorder, prepare a document by doing everything to it that you do not want included in the macro. This may include such things as opening a new document or scrolling to a specific location. Once you start the Macro Recorder, everything you do to Word is stored in a procedure.

To prepare the document and display the Record Macro dialog box, follow these steps:

1. Open a new document by choosing File, New and opening a new blank document from the General tab.

2. Choose Tools, Macro, Record New Macro to display the Record Macro dialog box shown in Figure 39.1.

The Record Macro dialog box shown in Figure 39.1 is where you set the options for the Macro Recorder. The Macro Name and Description fields are where you name your macro and add a description. Including a good, brief description here is important if you intend to keep this macro for more than a few days. If you do not use a good description, you probably will not remember what the macro does when you want to use it a year or so from now.

FIG. 39.1
The Record Macro dialog box enables you to set the name and other options for a new procedure.

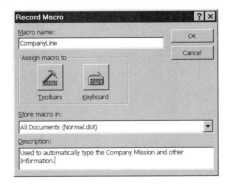

The Assign Macro To group has two choices: Toolbars and Keyboard. If you want to assign the macro to a toolbar button on a toolbar, select Toolbars. If you want to assign the macro to a keyboard shortcut such as Ctrl+9, select Keyboard. You can also run the macro by using the Tools, Macro, Macros command. The Store Macro In drop-down list box is where you specify a place to put this new macro. This list varies based on what templates and documents you have opened. Typical selections include All Documents, meaning the macro is saved with the NORMAL.DOT template; or the current document, meaning the macro is only available to the current document file.

Part
IX
Ch
39

To fill in the dialog box and start the Macro Recorder, follow these steps:

1. In the Macro Name box, type **CompanyLine**.

2. In the Description box, type **Used to automatically type the Company Mission and other Information**.

3. Leave the other fields at their default values, as shown in Figure 39.1, and click OK.

 The Stop Recording button appears as a floating toolbar, and the Macro Recorder now records what you do. It records all your keystrokes and mouse clicks until you click the Stop Recording button.

Recording a Macro

You now can create the macro by simply creating the document as you normally do. The macro we are creating is a very simple one that types headings and paragraphs for a standard company mission statement and some additional company information.

To create the document, follow these steps:

1. From the Style drop-down list choose Heading 1.

2. Type **Company Mission** and press Enter.

3. The style is now Normal. Type the following paragraph: **The mission of Acme Stores, Inc. is to provide the highest quality product at the lowest possible price. The customer should feel they are getting a high return for every dollar spent at Acme Stores. We hope to open our 1000th Acme store in the year 2000.**

4. Press Enter to start a new line.

5. From the Style drop-down list choose Heading 1.

6. Type **The Acme Team** and press Enter.

7. The style is now Normal. Type the following paragraph: **Our president, Howard Smith, started Acme Stores with the simple belief that he could do a better job than the retailer he was working for at the time. With an initial investment of $20,000 he opened his first store in 1986. With Howard's vision, Acme Stores has grown to 900+ in 1996.**

8. Press Enter to start a new line.

The document should now look like Figure 39.2.

FIG. 39.2
At this point, we have the completed document and are ready to turn off the Macro Recorder.

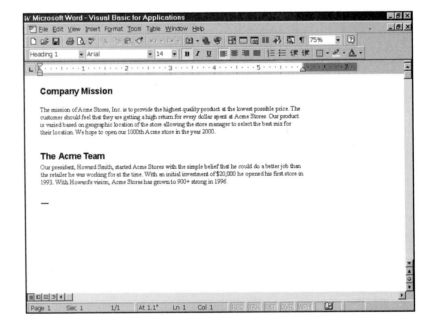

Stopping the Recorder

Stopping the recorder is easy; just click the Stop Recording button.

Examining the Procedure

To examine your newly created procedure, choose Tools, Macro, Macros. Select the macro from the list and choose Edit. Your procedure appears on-screen and looks like Figure 39.3.

FIG. 39.3
The Macro Recorder places the recorded commands in a module accessed through the Visual Basic Editor as shown here for the CompanyLine macro.

Project Explorer

Property Window

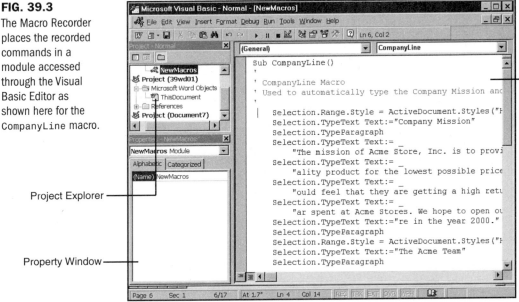

Code Window

The listing of the procedure is:

```
Sub CompanyLine()
'
' CompanyLine Macro
' Used to automatically type the Company Mission and other Information.
'
    Selection.Range.Style = ActiveDocument.Styles("Heading 1")
    Selection.TypeText Text:="Company Mission"
    Selection.TypeParagraph
    Selection.TypeText Text:= _
        "The mission of Acme Store, Inc. is to provide the highest qu"
    Selection.TypeText Text:= _
        "ality product for the lowest possible price. The customer sh"
    Selection.TypeText Text:= _
        "ould feel that they are getting a high return for every doll"
    Selection.TypeText Text:= _
        "ar spent at Acme Stores. We hope to open our 1000th Acme Sto"
    Selection.TypeText Text:="re in the year 2000."
    Selection.TypeParagraph
```

```
        Selection.Range.Style = ActiveDocument.Styles("Heading 1")
        Selection.TypeText Text:="The Acme Team"
        Selection.TypeParagraph
        Selection.TypeText Text:= _
            "Our president, Howard Smith, started Acme Stores with the si"
        Selection.TypeText Text:= _
            "mple belief that he could do a better job than the retailer "
        Selection.TypeText Text:= _
            "he was working for at the time. With an initial investment o"
        Selection.TypeText Text:= _
            "f $20,000 he opened his first store in 1986. With Howard's v"
        Selection.TypeText Text:= _
            "ision, Acme Stores has grown to 900+ strong in 1996."
        Selection.TypeParagraph
    End Sub
```

If you examine this listing and the steps you just took, you see that each step results in one or more lines of code inserted in the procedure.

The procedure text appears in three colors, with comments in green, keywords in blue, and everything else in black. Comments are explanatory text that documents the macro. Notice that the description you typed for the macro has been included as a comment. Keywords are words "owned" by the Visual Basic language. They are typically commands, predefined values, and so on.

Running the Procedure

To run this procedure, first open a new blank document. Next, choose Tools, Macro, Macros. The Macros dialog box shown in Figure 39.4 appears, showing all procedures to this document. In the dialog box, select the CompanyLine procedure and choose Run. Then the procedure runs, selecting styles and typing text. The completed document is identical to the one you created with the recorder running.

Understanding and Editing the Procedure

Now go back and take a closer look at the listing of the procedure by accessing the Visual Basic Editor by choosing Tools, Macro, Visual Basic Editor. Let's consider this procedure in a little more detail. Don't worry too much about the syntax of the statements yet. For now, get a feel for reading a Visual Basic procedure to gain a general understanding of what it does.

FIG. 39.4

The Macros dialog box enables you to select and execute procedures. The dialog box also provides an easy way to locate, edit, or delete procedures.

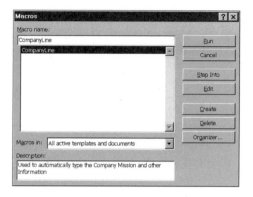

Procedure Headers and Footers

The first line is the procedure header, and the last line in the procedure is the procedure footer. These two lines in a procedure define the procedure's limits in Visual Basic.

```
Sub CompanyLine()
    .
    .
    .
End Sub
```

The first line of a procedure defines the procedure's name, type, and arguments. The type of a procedure is *Sub* or *Function*, and it determines whether the procedure returns a value. Function procedures perform a calculation and return a value. Sub procedures do not return a value. The *arguments* of a procedure are placed within parentheses and form a connection between values in this procedure and those in a procedure that calls this one. Our example macro procedure is a Sub procedure, its name is CompanyLine, and it has no arguments.

The procedure footer simply marks the end. When a procedure reaches the last line, the execution point in a program returns to the procedure that called it. If no procedure called it, control returns to the desktop.

Using Comments

The next four lines of the procedure, shown here, are comments:

```
'
' CompanyLine Macro
' Used to automatically type the Company Mission and other Information.
'
```

Part

IX

Ch

39

Notice that the comment line is the same text that you entered for the description when we recorded the macro. Any characters that follow a single quotation mark in a Visual Basic procedure are *comments*. Comments in a Visual Basic procedure are totally ignored when the procedure executes, so adding or deleting them has no effect on how a procedure runs. Comments, however, have a great effect on how understandable your procedures are. Use comments liberally in any procedures you plan to use more than once or twice. Although it seems easier to skip commenting your procedure, you will appreciate the effort in the future when you have to work with your procedure again. Comments can make it easier for you to quickly do corrections or changes.

Comments can comprise a whole line, as those above do. You also can place comments on the right, following any valid Visual Basic statement. Everything from the single quotation mark to the right end of the line is included in the comment.

Selecting a Style

The first thing you did when creating this procedure was to select a style from the Style drop-down list. The next line, shown here, does this:

```
Selection.Range.Style = ActiveDocument.Styles("Heading 1")
```

This line is a Visual Basic statement that sets the style for the current insertion point, identified as `Selection in the statement`. It tells Word to look in the current document template for the style, `ActiveDocument.Styles` for the style "Heading 1" and to select it.

Working with Text

The next line instructs Word to type text at the selection or insertion point:

```
Selection.TypeText Text:="Company Mission"
```

After typing the Company Mission line, press the Enter key to start a new line. This translates into the following Visual Basic statement:

```
Selection.TypeParagraph
```

After pressing Enter, type the first paragraph:

```
Selection.TypeText Text:= _
    "The mission of Acme Store, Inc. is to provide the highest qu"
Selection.TypeText Text:= _
    "ality product for the lowest possible price. The customer sh"
Selection.TypeText Text:= _
    "ould feel that they are getting a high return for every doll"
Selection.TypeText Text:= _
    "ar spent at Acme Stores. We hope to open our 1000th Acme Sto"
Selection.TypeText Text:="re in the year 2000."
```

Notice how the macro recorder broke the lines up into multiple statements. Also notice that when the paragraph was broken up, words are sometimes separated into two statements. For example, The word quality starts at the end of the first statement, "qu," and ends at the beginning of the next statement, "ality." Visual Basic and Microsoft Word do not bother trying to find logical line breaks. The breaks are determined by number of characters. All the lines, except the last one, contain 60 characters including spaces.

NOTE The last statement consists of a single long line broken into two shorter lines. The space and underscore (_) character at the end of the first line is the Visual Basic line-continuation mark. It is used to shorten long lines so that they fit on-screen and are easier to read. To break a line of code so it continues on the next line, type a space, then underscore, and then press the Enter key to move the insertion point to the next line so you can continue entering code. ■

The next line is a result of pressing the Enter key at the end of the paragraph:

```
Selection.TypeParagraph
```

After pressing the Enter key, you performed steps that were similar to previous steps. You selected a style, Heading 1, typed text, and pressed Enter:

```
Selection.Range.Style = ActiveDocument.Styles("Heading 1")
    Selection.TypeText Text:="The Acme Team"
    Selection.TypeParagraph
```

After the second heading, we typed another paragraph and pressed Enter to complete our macro:

```
Selection.TypeText Text:= _
    "Our president, Howard Smith, started Acme Stores with the si"
Selection.TypeText Text:= _
    "mple belief that he could do a better job than the retailer "
Selection.TypeText Text:= _
    "he was working for at the time. With an initial investment o"
Selection.TypeText Text:= _
    "f $20,000 he opened his first store in 1986. With Howard's v"
Selection.TypeText Text:= _
    "ision, Acme Stores has grown to 900+ strong in 1996."
Selection.TypeParagraph.
```

Communicating with a User

You may be thinking to yourself, "This macro doesn't seem very useful. I could have done it faster with a copy and paste." Well, you are probably right. The main point of the macro you created was to get you familiar with reading a Visual Basic for Application procedure. The other reason this particular example is used is to create a foundation to build on with additional Visual Basic for Application code.

Part
IX

Ch
39

When developing in Visual Basic, you typically record as much as you can and then add to it the additional features you cannot record. In a Visual Basic procedure, you are not limited to the simple playback of keystrokes. You can also, for example, communicate with users and prompt them for additional information so that you can customize the macro results.

Visual Basic gives you several easy ways to communicate with a user. Two of these ways are the InputBox function and the MsgBox function. The InputBox function enables you to prompt a user for input using a simple dialog interface. The MsgBox function enables you to display information to your user through a standard Windows message box.

Getting Data with a Data-Entry Box

Using Visual Basic, you can create dialog boxes to get new values and text from the user to customize the procedure to different situations. For example, you might want to prompt the user for their name so that you can insert it into a document. This is done with the InputBox function.

To add an input box to the CompanyLine procedure, follow these steps:

1. If you have the Module open, go to it. Otherwise, from Word, choose <u>T</u>ools, <u>M</u>acro, <u>M</u>acros. Select the macro and choose <u>E</u>dit.

2. Select all the text between the procedure header (Sub CompanyLine()) and the procedure footer (End Sub).

3. Choose <u>E</u>dit, <u>C</u>opy.

4. Choose <u>I</u>nsert, <u>P</u>rocedure.

FIG. 39.5

The Insert Procedure dialog box enables you to create a new procedure without recording a macro.

5. In the <u>N</u>ame text box, enter **CompanyLine2** and choose OK.

6. Choose <u>E</u>dit, <u>P</u>aste to paste a copy of the `CompanyLine` macro into the new module.

7. Move your insertion point to the end of the last line of the procedure before the `End Sub` statement.

8. Press Enter to add a new blank line.

9. Starting on this new blank line type the following. Be sure to include spacing as shown below:

```
Selection.TypeParagraph
Selection.TypeText Text:=InputBox("Please type your first and last name: ")
Selection.TypeText Text:=" is a proud member of the Acme team. "
Selection.TypeText Text:="As a member of the "
Selection.TypeText Text:=InputBox("Please type your department: ")
Selection.TypeText Text:=" group "
Selection.TypeText Text:=InputBox("Please type your first name: ")
Selection.TypeText Text:=" contributes enthusiasm and knowledge "
Selection.TypeText Text:="to our staff."
Selection.TypeParagraph
```

The `InputBox` function takes a prompt as an argument and causes a dialog box to display on-screen. When you type a value in the dialog box and choose OK, the function returns the value you typed to the program, which inserts it at the current insertion point. The completed macro is listed below with the additional lines in bold:

```
Sub CompanyLine()
    Selection.Range.Style = ActiveDocument.Styles("Heading 1")
    Selection.TypeText Text:="Company Mission"
    Selection.TypeParagraph
    Selection.TypeText Text:= _
        "The mission of Acme Store, Inc. is to provide the highest qu"
    Selection.TypeText Text:= _
        "ality product for the lowest possible price. The customer sh"
    Selection.TypeText Text:= _
        "ould feel that they are getting a high return for every doll"
    Selection.TypeText Text:= _
        "ar spent at Acme Stores. We hope to open our 1000th Acme Sto"
    Selection.TypeText Text:="re in the year 2000."
    Selection.TypeParagraph
    Selection.Range.Style = ActiveDocument.Styles("Heading 1")
    Selection.TypeText Text:="The Acme Team"
    Selection.TypeParagraph
    Selection.TypeText Text:= _
        "Our president, Howard Smith, started Acme Stores with the si"
    Selection.TypeText Text:= _
        "mple belief that he could do a better job than the retailer "
    Selection.TypeText Text:= _
        "he was working for at the time. With an initial investment o"
    Selection.TypeText Text:= _
        "f $20,000 he opened his first store in 1986. With Howard's v"
    Selection.TypeText Text:= _
        "ision, Acme Stores has grown to 900+ strong in 1996."
```

```
        Selection.TypeParagraph
        Selection.TypeParagraph
        Selection.TypeText Text:=InputBox("Please type your first and last name:")
        Selection.TypeText Text:=" is a proud member of the Acme team. "
        Selection.TypeText Text:="As a member of the "
        Selection.TypeText Text:=InputBox("Please type your department: ")
        Selection.TypeText Text:=" group "
        Selection.TypeText Text:=InputBox("Please type your first name: ")
        Selection.TypeText Text:=" contributes enthusiasm and knowledge "
        Selection.TypeText Text:="to our staff."
        Selection.TypeParagraph
    End Sub
```

Try this new procedure by opening a new blank document and then choosing Tools, Macro, Macros. In the Macro dialog box, select the CompanyLine2 macro and choose Run. The procedure types the standard text we had before and then prompts you for your first and last name using the input box shown in Figure 39.6. Your first and last name are inserted at the beginning of the new paragraph and more of the text of the document is typed. You are then prompted for your department by the input box shown in Figure 39.7. Also notice that you do not have to save the changes to your procedure. The Visual Basic Editor does this automatically for you.

Once you have typed the department in and pressed Enter, the text you typed is inserted into the paragraph. The last input box, shown in Figure 39.8, prompts you for your first name, inserts it, and completes the paragraph. The end result of this macro is shown in Figure 39.9. As you can see from the example, user input is useful whenever you want the user to be able to customize text.

FIG. 39.6

An input box is created with the InputBox function to input your first and last name.

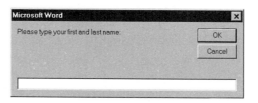

FIG. 39.7

The second input box requests your department.

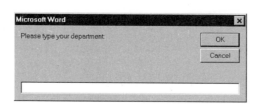

FIG. 39.8
The final use of the
`InputBox` function
is to request a first
name.

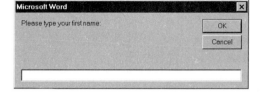

FIG. 39.9
The completed
document with the
inserted text you typed
in response to the
input boxes.

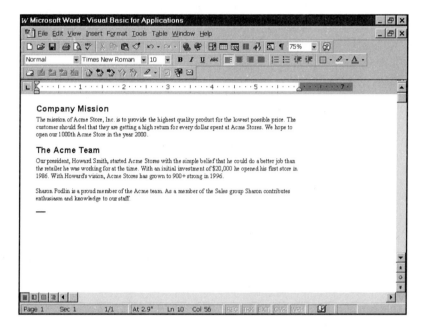

Every Visual Basic statement has a specific syntax. The syntax for any statement has several components. The Help system of the Visual Basic Editor contains the syntax for all Visual Basic for Applications statements. The first part of the syntax of a statement is the command itself so that you know how to spell it. After the command you'll see a list of arguments. Some of the arguments are required; others are optional. Optional arguments are contained within square brackets ([ ]). You can either use none of the optional arguments, some of them, or all of them. When using arguments, the order is important. Use the same order found in the syntax. Let's examine the syntax of the `InputBox` function:

```
InputBox(Prompt, [Title], [Default], [XPos], [YPos], [HelpFile], [Context])
```

The first item in the syntax listed above is the name of the function: `InputBox`. Even though InputBox is listed in mixed case with 'I' and 'B' capitalized, it is not required that you type it that way. When you have finished typing the function in a Visual Basic module and press Enter, the Visual Basic Editor automatically converts the capitalization for you.

The first word found in the argument list is Prompt. This is the text displayed in the dialog box. In our example, the prompt text was "Please type your department: ". Notice that the Prompt argument is not listed in square brackets. This is because it is required.

Following the Prompt argument are several optional arguments. The first is Title. The Title argument allows you to customize the title for the input dialog box. If you do not specify a value for the Title argument, your input box's title bar displays "Microsoft Word." If you want to have a different title such as "Team Information", change the second input box line as follows. Notice that when you type **InputBox** the syntax displays in a pop-up tip:

```
Selection.TypeText Text:=InputBox("Please type your department: ", "Team_
➥Information")
```

Another useful optional argument is Default. The value given for the Default argument automatically displays in the input area of the input box. If, for example, you know that most users of your macro are in the Sales group, use Sales for the Default argument. The user still has the option of typing in another value, but if they want to accept the default value, they just have to press Enter or choose the OK button, saving them time. If we continue to build on our previous InputBox statement and include a value for the Default argument, our statement will look like the following:

```
Selection.TypeText Text:=InputBox("Please type your department: ", "Team
Information", "Sales")
```

The XPos and YPos optional arguments are used to position the input box on the screen based on the X and Y position of the upper-left corner of the input box. The X and Y positions use a measurement called a *twip*. A twip is an extremely fine measurement equaling 1/1440th of an inch. The default is to display the input box in toward the middle of the screen. The HelpFile and Context optional arguments are used to build a custom help system.

What if you wanted to include a value for the Default argument but not for the Title argument? There are two ways to handle this situation. One way is to place the arguments in order by position. The following line of code demonstrates this:

```
Selection.TypeText Text:=InputBox("Please type your department: ",,"Sales")
```

Notice that there are two commas before the value for the Default argument. Even though you are not using the Title argument, you still have to create a placeholder for it. If you look at the original syntax statement for InputBox, you'll notice that there is a comma separating Prompt from Title and another separating Title and Default. We still have to use these commas even though we are not using the Title argument. As you can imagine, if you are working with a command that has several arguments and you only want to use the last argument, you have to type a lot of commas and hope you don't forget one. A way to get around this is to use named arguments. Every argument is given a name in the command's syntax. If you use the argument name, you don't have to worry about its position. Earlier we had the following code example:

```
Selection.TypeText Text:=InputBox("Please type your department: ", "Team
Information", "Sales")
```

In this example the `Title` argument is set to `"Team Information"` and the `Default` argument is set to `"Sales"`. You could rewrite this line as follows:

```
Selection.TypeText Text:=InputBox("Please type your department: ", _
Title:="Team Information", Default:="Sales")
```

Don't forget that named arguments also allow you to skip an unused argument. The following example demonstrates using a named argument to skip the `Title` argument:

```
Selection.TypeText Text:=InputBox("Please type your department: ",
Default:="Sales")
```

As you can see, this is much more readable. You instantly know what the values are being used for. Notice that the name of the argument is separated from its value by a colon and an equal sign. Remember that the position of named arguments does not matter. The following line accomplishes exactly the same as the previous example:

```
Selection.TypeText Text:=InputBox("Please type your department: ", _
Default:= "Sales", Title:= "Team Information")
```

Displaying a Message

In some instances, you may want to send a message to your user. You can use the `InputBox` function as shown in the previous section, but the input area might be confusing to another user. To simply send a message, use the `MsgBox` function, which works similarly to the `InputBox` function, but does not have an input area or Cancel button. By default, it has only an OK button for the user to acknowledge the message. The `MsgBox` function can perform more actions than just displaying a message. You also can use message boxes to display different types of built-in command buttons beyond the OK button. Examples of other buttons you can have on a message box are Cancel, Abort, Retry, Ignore, Yes, and No. Your programs can change actions depending upon which button a user clicks.

You can add a short message to the end of the current example to tell the user that the formatting has been completed. Using the procedure we used to create `CompanyLine2`, copy the previous listing to a new procedure and name it `CompanyLine3`. Add the bold text in the following listing to the procedure, select a blank worksheet, and run the procedure:

```
Sub CompanyLine()
    Selection.Range.Style = ActiveDocument.Styles("Heading 1")
    Selection.TypeText Text:="Company Mission"
```

```
        Selection.TypeParagraph
        Selection.TypeText Text:= _
            "The mission of Acme Store, Inc. is to provide the highest qu"
        Selection.TypeText Text:= _
            "ality product for the lowest possible price. The customer sh"
        Selection.TypeText Text:= _
            "ould feel that they are getting a high return for every doll"
        Selection.TypeText Text:= _
            "ar spent at Acme Stores. We hope to open our 1000th Acme Sto"
        Selection.TypeText Text:="re in the year 2000."
        Selection.TypeParagraph
        Selection.Range.Style = ActiveDocument.Styles("Heading 1")
        Selection.TypeText Text:="The Acme Team"
        Selection.TypeParagraph
        Selection.TypeText Text:= _
            "Our president, Howard Smith, started Acme Stores with the si"
        Selection.TypeText Text:= _
            "mple belief that he could do a better job than the retailer "
        Selection.TypeText Text:= _
            "he was working for at the time. With an initial investment o"
        Selection.TypeText Text:= _
            "f $20,000 he opened his first store in 1986. With Howard's v"
        Selection.TypeText Text:= _
            "ision, Acme Stores has grown to 900+ strong in 1996."
        Selection.TypeParagraph
        Selection.TypeParagraph
        Selection.TypeText Text:=InputBox("Please type your first and last name:_")
        Selection.TypeText Text:=" is a proud member of the Acme team. "
        Selection.TypeText Text:="As a member of the "
        Selection.TypeText Text:=InputBox("Please type your department: ")
        Selection.TypeText Text:=" group "
        Selection.TypeText Text:=InputBox("Please type your first name: ")
        Selection.TypeText Text:=" contributes enthusiasm and knowledge "
        Selection.TypeText Text:="to our staff."
        Selection.TypeParagraph
        MsgBox "The Standard Company Information is complete."
    End Sub
```

Because the last line of the macro is a message box, we know that the procedure is completed when the message box displays, as shown in Figure 39.10.

Testing User Input

What if you wanted to prompt the user for how many years they have been with the company and based on the number of years, have the procedure type different sentences? This can be done with an `If...Then` statement. The `If...Then` statement enables you to create a test, and based on the test, perform one action or set of actions if the result of the test was true, or another action or set of actions if the result was false. This type of test is referred to as *conditional logic*. It is called conditional logic because the logic, or which action to take, is based on which condition is met. The basic syntax for the `If...Then` statement is as follows:

```
If condition Then
    .
    .
    .
Else
    .
    .
    .
End If
```

FIG. 39.10
The `MsgBox` function creates a dialog box telling you that the macro has completed.

If you wanted to add a feature into our `CompanyLine3` procedure to test the amount of discount given, we could add an `If...Then` statement. The new procedure, which we'll name `CompanyLine4`, reads as follows:

```
Sub CompanyLine4()

Dim years

Selection.Range.Style = ActiveDocument.Styles("Heading 1")
Selection.TypeText Text:="Company Mission"
Selection.TypeParagraph
Selection.TypeText Text:= _
    "The mission of Acme Store, Inc. is to provide the highest qu"
Selection.TypeText Text:= _
    "ality product for the lowest possible price. The customer sh"
Selection.TypeText Text:= _
    "ould feel that they are getting a high return for every doll"
Selection.TypeText Text:= _
    "ar spent at Acme Stores. We hope to open our 1000th Acme Sto"
Selection.TypeText Text:="re in the year 2000."
Selection.TypeParagraph
Selection.Range.Style = ActiveDocument.Styles("Heading 1")
Selection.TypeText Text:="The Acme Team"
Selection.TypeParagraph
Selection.TypeText Text:= _
    "Our president, Howard Smith, started Acme Stores with the si"
Selection.TypeText Text:= _
    "mple belief that he could do a better job than the retailer "
Selection.TypeText Text:= _
    "he was working for at the time. With an initial investment o"
Selection.TypeText Text:= _
    "f $20,000 he opened his first store in 1986. With Howard's v"
Selection.TypeText Text:= _
    "ision, Acme Stores has grown to 900+ strong in 1996."
Selection.TypeParagraph
```

```
        Selection.TypeParagraph
        Selection.TypeText Text:=InputBox("Please type your first and last name:_")
        Selection.TypeText Text:=" is a proud member of the Acme team. "

        years = InputBox("How many years have you been with the company? ")
        If years =< 2 Then
            Selection.TypeText Text:="As a new member of the "
        Else
            Selection.TypeText Text:="As a long-term employee and member of the "
        End If

        Selection.TypeText Text:=InputBox("Please type your department: ")
        Selection.TypeText Text:=" group "
        Selection.TypeText Text:=InputBox("Please type your first name: ")
        Selection.TypeText Text:=" contributes enthusiasm and knowledge "
        Selection.TypeText Text:="to our staff."
        Selection.TypeParagraph
        MsgBox "The Standard Company Information is complete. "
    End Sub
```

The first line we added to this procedure was at the top of the procedure:

```
    Dim years
```

This line creates a *variable*. A variable is a temporary holding place for data. We need to place the input from the InputBox statement into a variable so that we can test it.

The indention of the If...Then statement is not required by Visual Basic but makes it easier to read. If you are typing this new procedure in, you do not have to type the comments, but you can see from the example that the indentions do make it easier for someone reading the procedure to know what is going on.

We first tested to see if the user had been with the company 2 years or less. If so, she is a new employee and the text inserted by the macro reflects that. If she has been with the company more than 2 years, she is a long-term employee. An example of the completed document is shown in Figure 39.11.

Getting In-Depth Help Online

You may have noticed that when you typed **MsgBox** and pressed the spacebar, the syntax for the MsgBox function displayed in a ScreenTip-style window. This is a new feature of Visual Basic for Applications and saves you from memorizing the syntax of the statement. The MsgBox function has an argument list beginning with the argument Prompt. The Prompt argument is displayed in a bold font denoting that it is a required argument. In our procedure, "The Standard Company Information is complete." was the value assigned to the Prompt argument. The other available arguments are displayed as a normal font and are enclosed in square brackets ([ ]).

FIG. 39.11

This is an example of a document created with the CompanyLine4 macro.

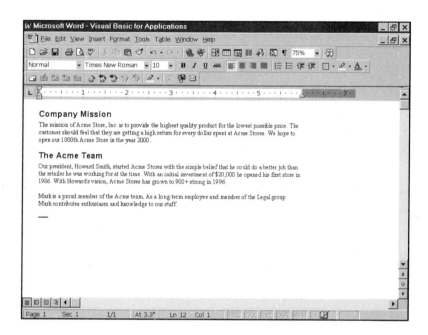

One of the best sources of technical information on Visual Basic is the Online Help. To get to the Help index for programming, choose Help, Contents and Index. If you want detailed help on the statement you are working with, place your cursor anywhere within the keyword and press F1. Help for that keyword automatically displays. ●

Services and Resources

This book attempts to be a complete user reference for Word 97. But, you may need answers to specific questions, and the information about Word continues to grow. This appendix includes some of the most valuable telephone numbers, information services, and Web sites relating to Word. In the following listings, you learn how you can browse Que books online, where to get technical support, how to order additional Microsoft products, how to get listings of local seminars and training companies, and how to get free software and updates. ■

Ordering Additional Que Books

The *Special Edition Using* series of books are the best-selling computer reference series in the world. Other books in this series with Ron Person as the lead author are:

- *Special Edition Using Word for Windows 95,* 07897-0084-0
- *Special Edition Using Word Version 6 for Windows,* 1-56529-469-6
- *Special Edition Using Microsoft Excel 97,* 0-7897-0960-0
- *Special Edition Using Excel for Windows 95,* 0-7897-0112-x
- *Special Edition Using Excel Version 5 for Windows,* 1-56529-459-9
- *Platinum Edition Using Windows 95,* 0-7897-0797-7
- *Special Edition Using Windows 95,* 1-56529-921-3
- *Special Edition Using Windows 3.11 Edition,* 1-56529-807-1

If you are interested in ordering additional copies of this book or other books in the *Special Edition Using* series, please check with your local bookstores. If your local bookstore is unable to supply you, please call

Macmillan Computer Publishing order line	Order books from Que, Sams, New Riders, and Hayden	800-428-5331
Macmillan Computer Publishing tech support	Problems with or errors in books. For software questions, please call the software vendor's support line.	317-581-3833

ON THE WEB

To preview sample chapters from Que books or to order books using the World Wide Web, point your Web browser to:

http://www.mcp.com/que

http://www.ronperson.com

To see all the books available through Macmillan Computer Publishing, the largest publisher of computer books in the world, point your Web browser to:

http://www.mcp.com

Technical Support for Microsoft Products

Standard technical support is available by telephone between 6 a.m. and 6 p.m., Pacific time. There is no charge for support for desktop applications, like those in Office, but the call is a toll call. Desktop application support has no time limit. Support for Windows operating system is limited to 90 days after your first support call.

Telephone Support Specialists

Listing of support telephone numbers for all Microsoft products	800-426-9400
Office for Windows	206-635-7056
Office for Macintosh	206-635-7055
Word for Windows	206-462-9673
Word for Macintosh	206-635-7200
Excel for Windows	206-635-7070
Excel for Macintosh	206-635-7080
Access for Windows	206-635-7050
PowerPoint	206-635-7145
Project	206-635-7155
Front Page	206-635-7088
Internet Explorer	206-635-7123
Windows 95	206-635-7000

Automated Fax Back Support

To get answers to frequently asked questions about Office and Windows products, you can request a free fax with questions and answers or technical white papers. This automated FastTips service is available seven days a week, 24 hours a day. It's best to order a fax of the FastTips map and catalog first. This will let you see a current listing of all the information you can request.

Desktop applications FastTips	Word, Microsoft Excel, PowerPoint, Access, Outlook, more	800-936-4100
Desktop operating systems FastTips	Windows 95, Windows 3.x	800-936-4200

World Wide Web Support and Software

Microsoft has a comprehensive support site on the World Wide Web. At the home page for this URL, you can select the product for which you need support from a list. Clicking the search button will then take you to detailed information on the product you selected. From this support site, you have access to newsgroups that contain conversations about products, questions, and answers from Microsoft support as well as from other readers. (If you are not using Internet Explorer version 3.0 or later, you will need to download the free newsgroup reader.) The support site also gives you access to device drivers, free sample files, frequently asked questions (FAQs), and the KnowledgeBase—Microsoft's database of technical support answers. To access the Microsoft Support site, point your Web browser to:

http://www.microsoft.com/support

The following table lists some of the most important Microsoft Word and Office product sites on the World Wide Web:

Topic	URL	Description
Support and Software		
Microsoft Home Page	**http://www.microsoft.com**	Home page
Microsoft Online Support	**http://www.microsoft.com/support**	Online answers to technical questions

Topic	URL	Description
Support and Software		
Ron Person & Co.	http://www.ronperson.com	Free software, training, tips on Office products
KnowledgeBase:	http://www.microsoft.com/kb	Troubleshooting database
Microsoft: Frequently Asked Questions	http://www.microsoft.com/support/default-faq.htm	Most frequently asked support questions
Technical newsgroups	http://www.microsoft.com/support/news	Microsoft technical newsgroups
Free drivers	http://www.microsoft.com/kb/softlib	Driver software
Free Microsoft software	http://www.microsoft.com/msdownload	Free software, add-ins, IE helpers
Support policy and phone numbers	http://www.microsoft.com/supportnet	Phone numbers and policy statements
Word		
Microsoft Word Home Page	http://www.microsoft.com/msword	Home page for Word information
Word free software	http://www.microsoft.com/msword/fs_wd.htm	Free add-ins, templates, wizards, converters
Word Viewer for Internet	http://www.microsoft.com/msword/fs_wd.htm	Word viewer for non-Word users
Office		
Microsoft Office Home Page	http://www.microsoft.com/msoffice	Home page for Office
PowerPoint Viewer for Internet	http://www.microsoft.com/msoffice/mspowerpoint/internet/viewer	PPT viewer for non-PPT users

continues

continued

Topic	URL	Description
Excel		
Microsoft Excel Home Page	**http://www.microsoft.com/msexcel**	Home page for Excel information
Excel Viewer for Internet	**http://www.microsoft.com/msexcel/ fs_xl.htm**	Viewer for non-Excel users
Excel Solver enhancements	**http://www.frontsys.com**	Solver developers, solver add-ins, and enhanced models
Excel-free software	**http://www.microsoft.com/msexcel/ fs_xl.htm**	Free upgrades, templates, wizards, and add-ins
Internet		
MS Internet Explorer home page	**http://www.microsoft.com/IE3**	Entry point to all of Microsoft's updates, s/w, support, and technical papers on Internet and intranet
Internet Explorer support	**http://www.microsoft.com/IESupport**	Questions and software enhancements
MS IE3 add-ins, helpers	**http://www.microsoft.com/IE3**	VRML, ActiveX, all the IE enhancements

If you do not have access to the Internet, you can download software and drivers from the following locations:

Microsoft Download Services (MSDL)	Microsoft's technical library of sample files, device drivers, patches, updates, and so on. Use Windows 95 Hyperterminal or any communication software to access.	206-936-MSDL (6735)

Compuserve	Go Microsoft
Prodigy	jump word: **Microsoft**
Genie	Microsoft Roundtable
America Online	keyword: **Microsoft**
The Microsoft Network	Computers and Software

Additional Technical Support

Technical Support Sales	For volume users, purchase 7X24 support, 800 access and subscriptions.	800-936-3500
Microsoft Wish Line	Request product changes and enhancements	206-936-WISH (936-9474)
Technet	CD-ROM subscription services with white papers and support database	800-344-2121
Microsoft Developer Network (MSDN)	CD-ROM subscription services for programmers	800-759-5474

Microsoft Product Information

The following phone numbers will help you get information about Microsoft products related to Word:

| Microsoft Customer Service | Product information and upgrades | 800-426-9400 |

Microsoft International Sales	International product information	206-936-8661
Microsoft Order Desk	Order supplemental, upgrade and replacement disks or manuals. (No product sales.)	800-360-7561
Microsoft Technical Sales Fax-Back	Request faxes of technical information about products	206-635-2222

Microsoft Training and Consultants

You can go to user-level or programmer-level classes through Microsoft certified training facilities. For programmer and systems engineer-level training, Microsoft also supports an online institute composed of independent training companies.

Microsoft Mindshare User Group Program	Learn about user groups (clubs) in your area	800-228-6738
User-level training	Authorized Training Centers (Solution Provider)	800-SOL-PROV (765-7768)
Programmer/systems engineer-level training	Authorized Technical Education Centers	800-SOL-PROV (765-7768) (Solution Provider)
Programmer and systems engineer online training	Microsoft Online Institute (MOLI)	800-449-9333; **http://moli. microsoft.com;** on MSN choose Edit, Goto, Other Location, **MOLI**

| Seminars | National seminars schedules and registrations | 800-550-4300; **http://www. microsoft.com /showcase** |
| Microsoft TV (MSTV) | Satellite telecasts of product use and support. Videos are available for purchase of previous broadcasts. | 800-597-3200 |

Index

Y-Z

QUE'S MICROSOFT® OFFICE 97 RESOURCE CENTER

For the most up-to-date information about all the Microsoft Office 97 products, visit Que's Web Resource Center at

http://www.mcp.com/que/msoffice

The web site extends the reach of this Que book by offering you a rich selection of supplementary content.

You'll find information about Que books as well as additional content about these new **Office 97 topics**:

- **Word**
- **Excel**
- **PowerPoint®**
- **Visual Basic® for Applications**
- **Access**
- **Outlook™**
- **FrontPage™**

Visit Que's web site regularly for a variety of new and updated Office 97 information.

Broaden Your Mind And Your Business With Que

The *Special Edition Using* series remains the most-often recommended product line for computer users who want detailed reference information. With thorough explanations, troubleshooting advice, and special expert tips, these books are the perfect all-in-one resource.

Special Edition Using Microsoft Excel 97
- ISBN: 0-7897-0960-0
- $34.99 USA
- Pub Date: 12/96

Special Edition Using Microsoft Office 97 Professional
- ISBN: 0-7897-0896-5
- $39.99 USA
- Pub Date: 12/96

Special Edition Using Windows 95
- ISBN: 1-56529-921-3
- $39.99 USA
- Pub Date: 8/95

For more information on these and other Que products, visit your local book retailer or call 1-800-772-0477.

que

Check out Que® Books on the World Wide Web
http://www.mcp.com/que

As the biggest software release in computer history, Windows 95 continues to redefine the computer industry. Click here for the latest info on our Windows 95 books

Make computing quick and easy with these products designed exclusively for new and casual users

Examine the latest releases in word processing, spreadsheets, operating systems, and suites

The Internet, The World Wide Web, CompuServe®, America Online®, Prodigy®—it's a world of ever-changing information. Don't get left behind!

Find out about new additions to our site, new bestsellers and hot topics

In-depth information on high-end topics: find the best reference books for databases, programming, networking, and client/server technologies

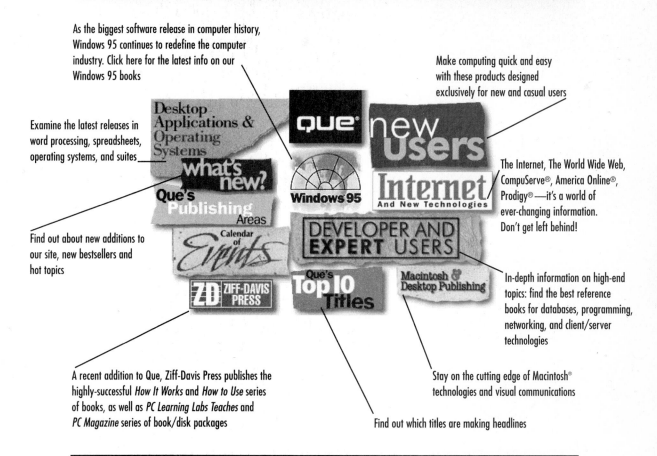

A recent addition to Que, Ziff-Davis Press publishes the highly-successful *How It Works* and *How to Use* series of books, as well as *PC Learning Labs Teaches* and *PC Magazine* series of book/disk packages

Stay on the cutting edge of Macintosh® technologies and visual communications

Find out which titles are making headlines

With 6 separate publishing groups, Que develops products for many specific market segments and areas of computer technology. Explore our Web Site and you'll find information on best-selling titles, newly published titles, upcoming products, authors, and much more.

- Stay informed on the latest industry trends and products available
- Visit our online bookstore for the latest information and editions
- Download software from Que's library of the best shareware and freeware

Complete and Return this Card
for a *FREE* Computer Book Catalog

Thank you for purchasing this book! You have purchased a superior computer book written expressly for your needs. To continue to provide the kind of up-to-date, pertinent coverage you've come to expect from us, we need to hear from you. Please take a minute to complete and return this self-addressed, postage-paid form. In return, we'll send you a free catalog of all our computer books on topics ranging from word processing to programming and the internet.

Mr. ☐　Mrs. ☐　Ms. ☐　Dr. ☐

Name (first) ☐☐☐☐☐☐☐☐☐☐☐☐　(M.I.) ☐　(last) ☐☐☐☐☐☐☐☐☐☐☐☐☐☐☐☐☐☐☐

Address ☐☐☐☐☐☐☐☐☐☐☐☐☐☐☐☐☐☐☐☐☐☐☐☐☐☐☐☐☐☐☐☐☐☐☐☐☐☐☐

City ☐☐☐☐☐☐☐☐☐☐☐☐☐☐☐☐☐☐　State ☐☐　Zip ☐☐☐☐☐ ☐☐☐☐

Phone ☐☐☐ ☐☐☐ ☐☐☐☐　Fax ☐☐☐ ☐☐☐ ☐☐☐☐

Company Name ☐☐☐☐☐☐☐☐☐☐☐☐☐☐☐☐☐☐☐☐☐☐☐☐☐☐☐☐☐☐☐☐☐☐

E-mail address ☐☐☐☐☐☐☐☐☐☐☐☐☐☐☐☐☐☐☐☐☐☐☐☐☐☐☐☐☐☐☐☐☐☐

1. Please check at least (3) influencing factors for purchasing this book.

Front or back cover information on book .... ☐
Special approach to the content .... ☐
Completeness of content .... ☐
Author's reputation .... ☐
Publisher's reputation .... ☐
Book cover design or layout .... ☐
Index or table of contents of book .... ☐
Price of book .... ☐
Special effects, graphics, illustrations .... ☐
Other (Please specify): _____ ☐

2. How did you first learn about this book?

Saw in Macmillan Computer Publishing catalog .... ☐
Recommended by store personnel .... ☐
Saw the book on bookshelf at store .... ☐
Recommended by a friend .... ☐
Received advertisement in the mail .... ☐
Saw an advertisement in: _____ ☐
Read book review in: _____ ☐
Other (Please specify): _____ ☐

3. How many computer books have you purchased in the last six months?

This book only .... ☐　　3 to 5 books .... ☐
2 books .... ☐　　More than 5 .... ☐

4. Where did you purchase this book?

Bookstore .... ☐
Computer Store .... ☐
Consumer Electronics Store .... ☐
Department Store .... ☐
Office Club .... ☐
Warehouse Club .... ☐
Mail Order .... ☐
Direct from Publisher .... ☐
Internet site .... ☐
Other (Please specify): _____ ☐

5. How long have you been using a computer?

☐ Less than 6 months　　☐ 6 months to a year
☐ 1 to 3 years　　　　　　☐ More than 3 years

6. What is your level of experience with personal computers and with the subject of this book?

	With PCs	With subject of book
New	☐	☐
Casual	☐	☐
Accomplished	☐	☐
Expert	☐	☐

Source Code ISBN: 0-7897-0962-7

7. Which of the following best describes your job title?

Administrative Assistant .... ☐
Coordinator .... ☐
Manager/Supervisor .... ☐
Director .... ☐
Vice President .... ☐
President/CEO/COO .... ☐
Lawyer/Doctor/Medical Professional .... ☐
Teacher/Educator/Trainer .... ☐
Engineer/Technician .... ☐
Consultant .... ☐
Not employed/Student/Retired .... ☐
Other (Please specify): _____ ☐

8. Which of the following best describes the area of the company your job title falls under?

Accounting .... ☐
Engineering .... ☐
Manufacturing .... ☐
Operations .... ☐
Marketing .... ☐
Sales .... ☐
Other (Please specify): _____ ☐

9. What is your age?

Under 20 .... ☐
21-29 .... ☐
30-39 .... ☐
40-49 .... ☐
50-59 .... ☐
60-over .... ☐

10. Are you:

Male .... ☐
Female .... ☐

11. Which computer publications do you read regularly? (Please list)

_____
_____
_____
_____
_____
_____
_____
_____
_____
_____

Comments: _____
_____
_____

Fold here and scotch-tape to mail.